AMERICAN BAR ASSOCIATION
Cybersecurity Legal Task Force

THE ABA CYBERSECURITY HANDBOOK

CYBERSECURITY, ITS LEGAL IMPLICATIONS, AND THE EMERGING RIS

FOURTH EDITION

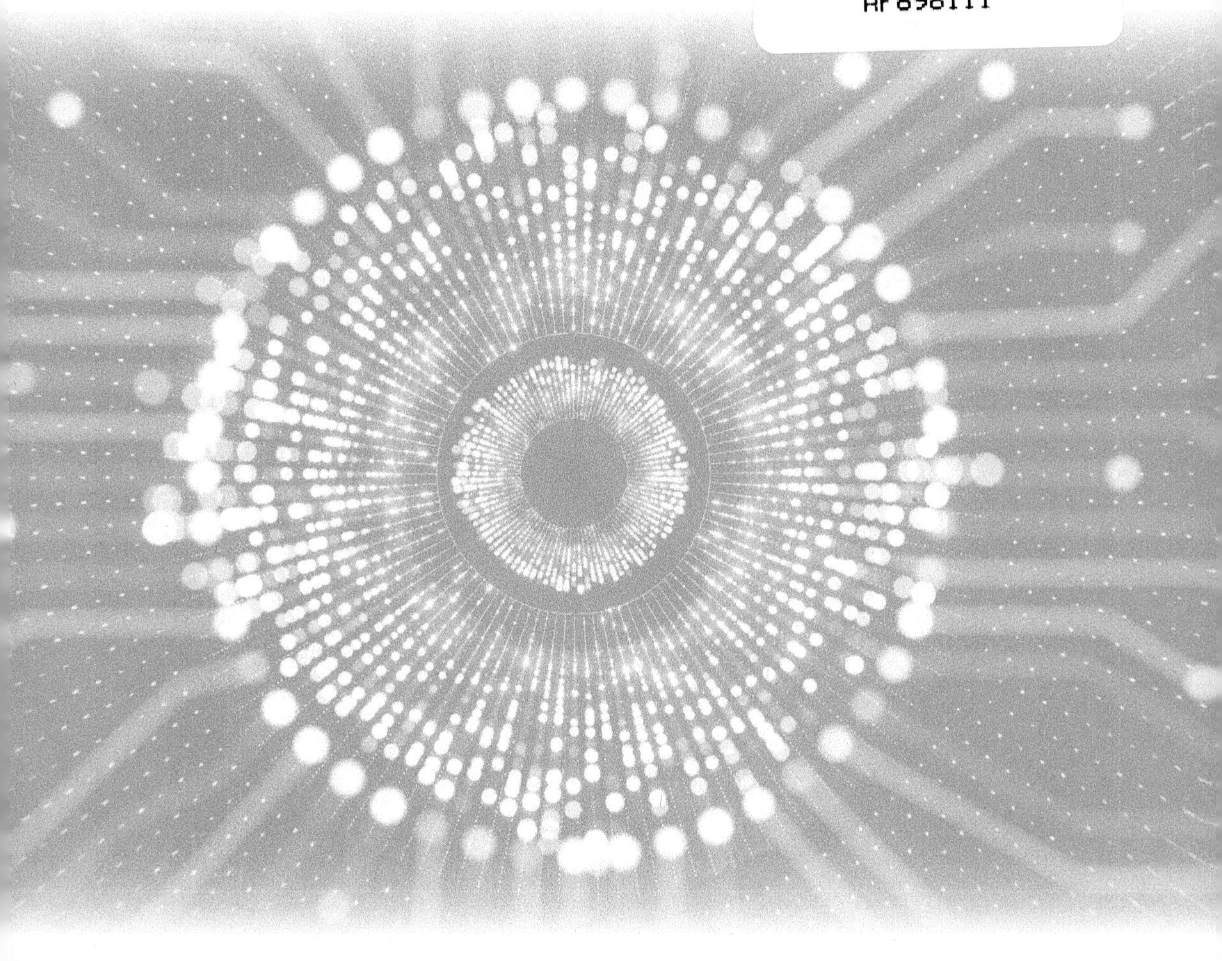

JEFFREY ALLEN AND CANDACE JONES, EDITORS

Cover design by Catherine Zaccarine.

This book was written by a number of contributing authors in 2025. The process of editing and compiling the manuscript inevitably extended the time from writing to publication. Any omission of developments occurring later in 2025 is a function of the publishing timeline, not a deficiency of the authors.

Printed in the United States of America.
30 29 28 27 26   5 4 3 2 1

ISBN: 978-1-63905-679-8

www.shopABA.org

Sponsors

The Cybersecurity Legal Task Force would like to thank all of the firms that have sponsored or donated to support the Task Force.

Platinum Sponsor

CONSTANGY BROOKS, SMITH & PROPHETE LLP

Silver Sponsors

CONNELL FOLEY LLP

SHOOK HARDY & BACON

DIGITAL MOUNTAIN®

Sponsor

BUTZEL ATTORNEYS AND COUNSELORS

Donors

The Cybersecurity Legal Task Force would like to thank all who have generously donated to support the Task Force in the 2025 bar year.

John C. Allen, IV
John Barkett
Deon Woods Bell
Ruth Hill Bro
Jessica Cohen
Daniel Cotter
Cynthia H. Cwik
Caroline DeCell
Shen-Jay Fern
Cheryl Gordon
Candace M. Jones
Sandeep Kathuria
Maureen T. Kelly
Jin-Ho King
Paul Lanois
Fernand A. Lavallee
Adriana Luedke
Christian Ohanian
Kari Petrasek
Lucian T. Pera
Linda V. Priebe
Claudia Rast
Jayne Reardon
Harvey Rishikof
Daniel J. Siegel
Thomas J. Smedinghoff
Suzanne Spaulding
Lucy Thomson
Roland L. Trope
David S. Turetsky
Mary Vandenack
Kay K. Wakatake
Stanton D. Weinstein
David A. Wheeler
Pedro Windsor
Lai Sun Yee

Table of Contents

Foreword

Artificial intelligence (AI) presents a Goldilocks dilemma. There is risk in stifling its adoption or stepping back from the global competition to innovate; there is risk in overindulging developers and deployers with immunity and in relying on AI-enabled tools or agents without human oversight and accountability. This theme resonates in comments from industry leaders, political observers, and cultural icons, as the quotations following this Foreword illustrate.

When AI works as intended, its users will benefit from business success, convenience, discovery, enlightenment, and entertainment. How will bad outcomes be avoided? Not all will, of course. But managing the downsides of AI is not unlike managing other technology risks, including cybersecurity risks.

Managing AI risk requires identifying opportunities and consequences (both good and bad) and the people, business objectives, and social interests at risk of harm. It requires vigilant monitoring of AI output and performance against design and development objectives, and timely action to warn about and counter adverse consequences. Importantly, AI risk must be "owned" by people: developers, deployers, and users who understand that they and their organizations will be held accountable for their bad AI-spawned outcomes.

Lawyers, as AI users and as advisors to developers, deployers, and policymakers, should approach AI recognizing that it's not all good or all bad. They should be prepared to investigate with their clients and technology advisors the capabilities, limitations, and risks of AI tools in the contexts those tools are to be used. With that information, lawyers will be better positioned to consider how risks can be minimized and liability for bad outcomes allocated for incentivizing responsible innovation and use and for providing meaningful relief for harms not avoided.

Contributors to this Fourth Edition of the ABA Cybersecurity Handbook address artificial intelligence as it relates to cybersecurity and law. As AI continues to evolve, so too will its effects on both the substance and practice of law. The discussion of AI in this book provides a foundation for lawyers, law firms, and the business organizations they represent to understand, monitor, and manage artificial intelligence in this critically important context.

From the cybersecurity perspective, the treatment of AI suggests several themes to inform our approach to the Goldilocks task of achieving responsible and effective AI tools:

- Success breeds success, sometimes for the worse. Successful attack tactics, techniques, and procedures will be enhanced with AI-assisted refinements, magnifying the threat of familiar attacks. Social engineering, which exploits security vulnerabilities in human behavior, will evolve into more personalized phishing-type schemes and sophisticated impersonations of trusted individuals.
- Geopolitical and international economic competition is escalating the race for AI development and deployment, and guardrails (to the extent they existed) are being compromised or dropped. We must be mindful of the slippery slope the world faces when efforts to promote responsible AI use give way to AI without limits or accountability.
- Supply chain risks are no longer limited to bilateral issues; they can be pervasive. Recent cyber incidents illustrate how market concentration in the technology supply chain and interconnectedness, generally, magnify damage and disruption across wide swaths of the global economy. Change management process failures have also caused widespread technological disruptions. Bad actors, particularly nation-states, can leverage supply chain vulnerabilities to cause mass-scale loss by targeting critical vendors just like they target critical infrastructure. AI tools implemented to monitor systems and detect anomalies can help organizations counter these threats.
- Data is the new "oil" (or "gold")—pick your cliché. Data is the foundation of AI, and data integrity cannot be overlooked as a long-term risk. Generative AI (GenAI) is being trained on any data that designers and developers can get. Scraping the internet vacuums up misinformation and disinformation along with accurate information. When GenAI-created inaccuracies (so-called "hallucinations") are released to the world, those too become fodder for training. Using personal or proprietary data (with or without informed consent) with AI tools can expose confidential and restricted information beyond the output's intended audience. Lawyers must understand enough about how AI tools work to make informed choices about exposing client data to AI.

The ABA's Cybersecurity Legal Task Force also undertook this Fourth Edition to update the cybersecurity material presented in prior editions. As cybersecurity and its confluence with AI evolve, the Fourth Edition provides a valuable reference and guide for lawyers.

Candace M. Jones
Co-Editor

OpenAI Chief Executive Officer Sam Altman, asked at a 2023 Senate Subcommittee hearing to comment on his worst fears of AI:

> *[W]e have tried to be very clear about the magnitude of the risks here .... I agree that when we get to very powerful systems, the landscape will change. I think I'm just more optimistic that we are incredibly creative, and we find new things to do with better tools, and that will keep happening.*
>
> *My worst fears are that we cause significant—we, the field, the technology, the industry[—]cause significant harm to the world. I think that could happen a lot of different ways. It's why we started the company. It's a big part of why I'm here today and why we've been here in the past and we've been able to spend some time with you.*
>
> *I think if this technology goes wrong, it can go quite wrong, and we want to be vocal about that. We want to work with the Government to prevent that from happening. But we try to be very cleareyed about what the downside case is and the work that we have to do to mitigate that.*[1]

Publisher's description of Henry Kissinger's final book, co-authored Craig Mundie and Eric Schmidt, *Genesis: Artificial Intelligence, Hope, and the Human Spirit* (2024):

> *As it absorbs data, gains agency, and intermediates between humans and reality, AI (artificial intelligence) will help us to address enormous crises, from climate change to geopolitical conflicts to income inequality. It might well solve some of the greatest mysteries of our universe and elevate the human spirit to unimaginable heights. But it will also pose challenges on a scale and of an intensity that we have never seen--usurping our power of independent judgment and action, testing our relationship with the divine, and perhaps even spurring a new phase in human evolution.*[2]

Pope Leo XIV in his inaugural address to the College of Cardinals on May 10, 2025:

> *I chose to take the name Leo XIV. There are different reasons for this, but mainly because Pope Leo XIII in his historic Encyclical Rerum Novarum addressed the social question in the context of the first great industrial revolution. In our own day, the*

1. *Oversight of A.I.: Rules for Artificial Intelligence, Oversight of A.I. Hearing Before the Subcomm. on Privacy, Tech., & the Law of the S. Comm. on the Judiciary*, S. Hrg. 118–37, 118th Cong. 16 (May 16, 2023) (response of Samuel Altman to a question from Sen. Richard Blumenthal, Chair), https://www.govinfo.gov/content/pkg/CHRG-118shrg52706/pdf/CHRG-118shrg52706.pdf.

2. See Summary, Lib. Catalog, Lib. of Cong. (Text provided by publisher Little, Brown and Company), https://lccn.loc.gov/2024945132.

Church offers to everyone the treasury of her social teaching in response to another industrial revolution and to developments in the field of artificial intelligence that pose new challenges for the defence of human dignity, justice and labour.[3]

3. Address of His Holiness Pope Leo XIV to the College of Cardinals (May 10, 2025), https://www.vatican.va/content/leo-xiv/en/speeches/2025/may/documents/20250510-collegio-cardinalizio.html.

About the ABA Cybersecurity Legal Task Force

The cross-disciplinary work of the ABA Cybersecurity Legal Task Force has never been more critical. The volume of cyberattacks targeting lawyers, their firms, and their clients continues to increase as the tactics of malicious actors evolve with technological changes.

Formed in 2012, the Task Force unites representatives from across the ABA with cybersecurity expertise along with leaders from the public and private sectors. The Task Force identifies, compiles, creates, and promotes cybersecurity resources for the legal profession. Its members and staff work to focus and coordinate the ABA's analyses and assessments of cybersecurity issues and lead projects spotlighting the ABA's cybersecurity initiatives and resources.

The Task Force undertakes a wide range of publishing, programming, and outreach to reach ABA members. Cybersecurity resource materials and information about Task Force programs are available at www.ambar.org/cyber.

Acknowledgements

The ABA Cybersecurity Legal Task Force was initiated by Laurel Bellows at the beginning of her term as ABA President in 2012. The Task Force published the first edition of The ABA Cybersecurity Handbook: A Resource for Attorneys, Law Firms, and Business Professionals (Handbook) in 2013 to provide attorneys a basic understanding of cybersecurity and its implications. The second edition received the 2018 Association for Continuing Legal Education (ACLEA) Award of Outstanding Achievement. The third edition was similarly a smashing success. This fourth edition reunites many previous Handbook authors, who bring unique perspectives from across ABA Sections and industry, to assess how our cybersecurity risks and obligations have expanded with the explosion of artificial intelligence technologies.

While the ABA Cybersecurity Legal Task Force remains an ad hoc assembly, nothing related to cybersecurity is ad hoc. Technology will continue to evolve at a pace faster than we can manage; our clients' business practices will change; and the law will develop. As it does, the ABA will endeavor to update many of the online resources referenced in the Handbook. Of course, many ABA entities also will continue to address these issues. In particular, work by these ABA entities merits attention:

Business Law Section
Science & Technology Law Section
Tort Trial and Insurance Practice Section
Solo, Small Firm and General Practice Division
Standing Committee on Law & National Security
Special Committee on Disaster Response & Preparedness
Center for Professional Responsibility
Section of Administrative Law and Regulatory Practice
Antitrust Law Section
Section on Civil Rights and Social Justice
Criminal Justice Section
Section of Environment, Energy, and Resources
Section of Intellectual Property Law
Section of International Law
Forum on Communications Law

Judicial Division
Law Practice Division
Standing Committee on Lawyers' Professional Liability
Section of Litigation
Section of Public Contract Law
Infrastructure and Regulated Industries Section
Standing Committee on Technology and Information Systems
Section of State and Local Government Law
Rule of Law Initiative
Young Lawyers Division
Senior Lawyers Division
Law Student Division

We recommend that readers reach out to these organizations to learn more about the subject from their varied perspectives.

The Handbook would not be possible without the commitment of almost 30 legal practitioners from across the ABA who volunteered their time and expertise to educate the legal community. They are listed in the About the Contributors section at the end of the Handbook. We offer a special thanks to each one of them. As experts in their fields, each brought together the literature, sharpened focus on the issues, and offered concrete advice to practitioners. As a result, we are confident the Handbook will prove a valuable resource to practitioners at all levels, in various types of practices.

In addition to its authors, many people have worked hard to help produce the Handbook. As always, the ABA Staff have enabled and facilitated work on the Handbook. We offer a special thanks to ABA staff members Holly McMahon and Logan Hamilton, who provided endless support, organizational management, and direction, without which this book would not have been brought to fruition. We are deeply grateful to Task Force co-chairs Adriana Luedke and Roland Trope for the countless volunteer hours they spent securing resources for the Handbook and sustaining the Task Force. We also want to thank our law student volunteers, Tanner Wilburn (who also co-authored a chapter) and Alexis Freeman, whose review of footnotes was impeccable.

Finally, as editors, we offer a very special thanks to our families for giving us the time to make the commitment to bring the Handbook to you.

We hope that you find the Handbook practical and a valuable addition to your collection.

Jeffrey Allen
Candace Jones
January 2026

Chapter 1
Introduction

Jeffrey Allen

Once considered a futuristic idea relegated to science fiction and research labs, Artificial Intelligence (AI) has rapidly become a significant part of our everyday reality. It powers our phones, shapes our shopping experiences, facilitates our travel, navigates our commutes, offers recreational activities, manages our finances, helps maintain our health, guides us toward fitness, and the list continues to expand. It is transforming one of our most tradition-bound industries, the legal profession. As AI becomes increasingly embedded in our personal and professional lives, it brings with it remarkable conveniences and powerful tools—but it also raises urgent questions about privacy, accountability, fairness, the future of work, and, some say, the future of our society and civilization.

Technology has always presented itself as a double-edged sword. On one side, technology's blade cuts through labor, social concerns, and other needs. On the other side, the blade can cut deeply, inflicting social, professional, and economic damage to those who stray from the proper path in dealing with the technology, and many who simply fall victim to those who abuse it.

The most recent technological revolution, generative AI (GenAI), changed everything. It continues to sweep through our personal and professional lives, creating more opportunities, powering an increasing number of tools to facilitate our legal practices and individual lives, changing the way we interact with technology, and bringing with it a plethora of issues, including ethical dilemmas, privacy concerns, fairness, and the fact that it works just as well for the bad guys as it does for the good guys. We use GenAI to assist us in performing our work as lawyers; similarly, cybercriminals and fraudsters utilize it to facilitate their illicit activities and criminal endeavors. Unfortunately, fraudsters often utilize AI more effectively and efficiently than lawyers.

AI now operates with amazing speed and incredible power. GenAI can cause significant problems of potentially massive scope, affecting many systems and vast numbers of people more rapidly than any technology in our history. What we might have considered a minor problem in the past can become overwhelming almost instantaneously. As attorneys, we have an ethical obligation to understand technology's potential for harm and take appropriate action to protect our clients, their data, and ourselves from the consequences of a technology breach fueled by AI and criminal endeavors facilitated by it. We have to undertake such actions, as we cannot avoid the reach of this technology.

As much as we may try to act proactively, all our proactive measures constitute nothing more than preliminary defenses. Fraudsters, cybercriminals, and other malicious actors, whatever you choose to call them, will utilize the latest technology, fueled by AI, to exploit any weaknesses in the shield we strive to create. Ultimately, we, our IT support, and our software and hardware vendors will all wait until we learn where the bad actors have identified a weakness and exploited it to penetrate our cybersecurity defenses, then attempt to repair the damage they caused as quickly as possible. We will expend most of our time, effort, and cybersecurity resources reacting to problems that evaded our preliminary defenses.

The ABA's Cybersecurity Task Force created this Handbook to help lawyers navigate technology and educate them about its risks. Each edition of the Handbook did that when it was released, but grew less valuable in the face of evolving technology. The Third Edition of this Handbook did a yeomanlike job summarizing technology for attorneys and providing much-needed insight into using technology professionally. Although published only a few years ago, it predated the unleashing of GenAI. GenAI revolutionized technology to such an extent that it necessitated the compilation of this Fourth Edition in order to keep the Handbook relevant to current technology. The AI discussed in the Third Edition bears little resemblance to today's AI, largely as a result of GenAI.

Recognizing that the Third Edition of the Handbook no longer provided the help and guidance that lawyers need to successfully and effectively deal with today's GenAI-driven technology and its abuse by malicious actors, the Task Force elected to revise the Handbook to address the impact of GenAI. Acknowledging that AI, in general, and GenAI, in particular, created the need for the Fourth Edition of this Cybersecurity Handbook, the Editors determined that the Fourth Edition of the Cybersecurity Handbook needed to reconsider almost everything from the perspective of the changes GenAI has wrought.

To provide some context for this edition of the Cybersecurity Handbook, we will explore some benefits AI has brought as well as some of the things that malicious actors have done with it. Cybercrime has evolved into a multi-trillion-dollar industry. According to Cybersecurity Ventures, cybercrime was projected to cost the world $9.5 trillion in 2024, potentially growing to $10.5 trillion by 2025, making it the third-largest global economy, if measured as a country.[1]

1. Critical Points to Consider Respecting Artificial Intelligence

While these points fit into several other locations in this introduction and the Handbook itself, they rise to such a critical level of importance that we chose to separate them and highlight them here. Whatever you may think about AI, do not overlook these points in your analysis:

1. Steve Morgan, *Cybercrime to Cost the World $9.5 Trillion USD Annually in 2024*, Cybercrime Mag. (Oct. 23, 2023), https://cybersecurityventures.com/cybercrime-to-cost-the-world-9-trillion-annually-in-2024.com.

1. **AI performs, but not always well:** AI tools have limitations. We will address some of those limitations later, and you will find many references to them throughout the Handbook. The potential for problems derives from a variety of issues, ranging from biases intrinsic to the data on which the program trains, to the fact that AI has no internal moral compass and does not know right from wrong, to the fact that AI hallucinates occasionally, and those hallucinations appear in its output. Reliance upon AI without verification is folly. Use AI as a resource, as an assistant to help you build a response, but to paraphrase President Reagan: **never trust AI output without verification.**
2. **AI does not think:** People want to attribute human-like characteristics to AI, such as thinking, reasoning, and even emotional reactions, but that is its own form of hallucination. AI does not have human judgment or anything that approximates it. AI has no emotions chip, and none appears on the horizon. AI cannot think as we can. AI can do many things, but it does them differently than we do. AI can process information with incredible rapidity, much faster than those of us with natural intelligence will ever accomplish. It can sort and organize data and move from point A to point B analytically by following a roadmap provided to it by those who built it and trained it. It may see connections we miss. It will likely miss connections we see. It cannot analyze and exercise discretion on its own as we can. **Trusting AI to make judgmental choices puts everyone at risk.**
3. **AI should work as an assistant only:** As AI has become increasingly clever and capable, we humans have demonstrated a tendency to rely upon it more and more. We need to exercise caution, as we have moved dangerously close to over-reliance or over-dependence on it. We must ensure that artificial intelligence functions as an assistant, not as a leader. AI lacks the moral judgment, empathy, and accountability that human decision-makers bring to complex situations. While AI can process vast amounts of data quickly and identify patterns with impressive (albeit inconsistent) accuracy, it operates without context, values, or the nuanced understanding that guides responsible leadership. **When we use AI as a tool to support human judgment, providing insights, automating routine tasks, or enhancing productivity, it can significantly improve outcomes. Placing AI in a leadership role risks delegating critical decisions with ethical or moral components to a system that cannot understand consequences in human terms.** Maintaining the human role as the final decision-maker safeguards integrity, accountability, and public trust.

2. The Rising Tide of Cyber Scams

Cybercriminals have grown increasingly sophisticated, employing advanced technologies, particularly GenAI and psychological manipulation, to exploit individuals and organizations. Here are a few examples:

1. **Romance Scams:** In 2024, Pennsylvania residents reported losses totaling $39.2 million due to romance scams. These scams often involve fraudsters creating fake online personas to establish romantic relationships, ultimately deceiving victims into sending money. GenAI can play a significant role in the effectiveness of such endeavors. Alarmingly, individuals aged 20–29 reported financial losses at a higher rate (39%) compared to those aged 70–79 (23%), highlighting that younger adults are increasingly prone to financial loss.
2. **Deepfake Kidnapping Scams:** In Washington state, criminals used AI-generated voice replicas ("deepfakes") of family members to orchestrate fake kidnapping scenarios, demanding ransoms from terrified relatives. In Arizona, a mother received a call featuring her daughter's cloned voice, claiming she had been kidnapped and demanding a $1 million ransom.[2]
3. **Deepfake Investment Scams:** An Australian couple, John and Gail Young, lost over $500,000 after falling victim to an investment scam featuring a deepfake video of TV personality Eddie McGuire endorsing the scheme. The convincing nature of the deepfake led them to trust the fraudulent investment opportunity, causing the loss of their life savings.[3]
4. **Phishing Scams via Text Messages:** In Australia, authorities arrested individuals responsible for sending millions of fraudulent text messages. These messages were designed to deceive recipients into revealing personal information or clicking on malicious links, resulting in significant financial losses.[4]
5. **"Pig Butchering" Cryptocurrency Scams:** This elaborate scam involves fraudsters building trust with victims over time, often through online relationships, before introducing fraudulent investment opportunities, particularly in the cryptocurrency market. Victims are persuaded to invest significant sums, believing they are engaging in legitimate ventures, only to find their funds stolen. In 2024, such scams were linked to billions in losses globally.[5]

---

2. Audrey Conklin, *Parents Warned of Disturbing Kidnapping Scheme Using Kids' Voice Replicas*, N.Y. Post (Oct. 11, 2024 6:22 AM), https://nypost.com/2024/10/11/lifestyle/parents-warned-of-disturbing-kidnapping-scheme-using-kids-voice-replicas.

3. Brett Lackey, *Aussie couple lose $500,000 to scammers after being duped by deepfake video of Eddie McGuire*, Daily Mail, https://www.dailymail.co.uk/news/article-14565239/Eddie-McGuire-deepfake-scam-Geelong-couple.html (last updated Apr. 5, 2025 8:25 AM).

4. Jamie McKinnell, *Sydney man Xuan Su accused of sending more than 17 million fraudulent text messages in one week fronts court*, Austl. Broadcasting Co. News (Jan. 16, 2024), https://www.abc.net.au/news/2024-01-17/nsw-court-text-messages-scammer-fraudulent-millions/103350912.

5. *Crypto Scam Revenue 2024: Pig Butchering Grows Nearly 40% YoY as Fraud Industry Leverages AI and Increases in Sophistication*, Chainalysis (Feb. 13, 2025), https://www.chainalysis.com/blog/2024-pig-butchering-scam-revenue-grows-yoy.

3. Major Data Breaches and Their Impact

GenAI can facilitate data breaches. It can also facilitate the exploitation of a data breach by enabling criminals to utilize the disclosed data in nefarious ways. Data breaches have exposed the personal information of billions of individuals, resulting in identity theft, financial fraud, and a loss of trust in the affected organizations. Notable recent incidents include:

1. **National Public Data Breach:** In April 2024, National Public Data, a company specializing in background checks, suffered a data breach that exposed approximately 2.9 billion records. The compromised data included Social Security numbers, names, addresses, and other sensitive information affecting individuals in the U.S., U.K., and Canada. The breach was so extensive that it led to the company's bankruptcy.[6]
2. **Snowflake Customer Data Breach:** Cloud data warehousing company Snowflake Inc. experienced a data breach in which hackers accessed data from over 100 customers, including major corporations such as AT&T and Ticketmaster. The attackers claimed to have stolen 590 million records, including customer information and call metadata, raising significant concerns about data security in cloud storage solutions.[7]
3. **Change Healthcare Ransomware Attack:** In February 2024, Change Healthcare, a key player in the U.S. healthcare system, found itself the target of a ransomware attack that compromised the data of approximately 190 million individuals. The breach affected sensitive medical and insurance information, highlighting vulnerabilities in critical infrastructure.[8]
4. **Marriott International Data Breaches:** Between 2014 and 2020, Marriott International experienced multiple data breaches affecting over 300 million customers. Compromised data included passport details, payment card numbers, and personal information. In response, Marriott agreed to pay a $52 million settlement and implement enhanced data security measures.[9]

---

6. Sam Becker, *National Public Data Breach Update: Lawsuits Pile Up against Florida-Based Background Check Company after 'Security Incident'*, Fast Co. (Aug. 21, 2024), https://www.fastcompany.com/91176676/national-public-data-breach-update-class-action-lawsuits-npd; Iain Thomson, *National Public Data Files for Bankruptcy, Admits "Hundreds of Millions" Potentially Affected*, Register (Oct. 9, 2024 12:30 PM), https://www.theregister.com/2024/10/09/national_public_data_bankrupt/.

7. Emma Roth, *Hacker Suspected in Massive TICKETMASTER, AT&T Breaches Arrested in Canada*, Verge (Nov. 5, 2024 9:15 AM), https://www.theverge.com/2024/11/5/24288654/alleged-snowflake-hacker-arrested-ticketmaster-att-data-breaches.

8. Steve Alder, *The Biggest Healthcare Data Breaches of 2024*, HIPAA J. (Mar. 19, 2025), https://www.hipaajournal.com/biggest-healthcare-data-breaches-2024.

9. Alex Veiga, *Marriott Agrees to Pay $52 Million, Beef Up Data Security to Resolve Probes Over Data Breaches*, AP, https://apnews.com/article/97534838b650bfc7a9e73a5336b2988e (last updated Oct. 9, 2024 7:34 PM).

4. Emerging Trends in Cybercrime

The rapid advancement of technology has significantly transformed the landscape of cybercrime, introducing new methods and amplifying existing threats. Individuals and organizations seeking to protect themselves against increasingly sophisticated cyber threats must first understand and appreciate the associated risks.

1. **Artificial Intelligence (AI) as a Tool and Target**
    - **AI-Powered Cyberattacks:** Cybercriminals are leveraging AI to enhance the effectiveness of their attacks. AI enables the creation of more convincing phishing emails, realistic deepfake videos, and sophisticated malware. AI-generated phishing emails have a higher success rate than traditional methods, making them a preferred tool for attackers and a more serious threat to everyone else.[10]
    - **Exploiting AI System Vulnerabilities:** Cybercriminals have targeted vulnerabilities within AI systems. As AI becomes integral to various applications, we must ensure the security of these systems to avoid them becoming liabilities.
2. **Proliferation of Deepfake Technology**
    - **Deepfake Audio and Video Scams:** The accessibility of deepfake technology has led to its misuse in creating convincing fake audio and video content. Criminals can clone voices with minimal audio samples, making scams more believable. Bank call centers have reported an increase in deepfake voice clone calls aimed at accessing customer accounts.[11]
    - **Impersonation of High-Profile Individuals:** Cybercriminals utilize deepfakes to impersonate prominent executives and celebrities, leading to fraudulent activities. In one instance, fraudsters used deepfake technology to impersonate a company's CEO, resulting in the unauthorized transfer of $25 million.[12]
3. **Rise of Multichannel and Supply Chain Attacks**
    - **Multichannel Attack Strategies:** Attackers increasingly employ multiple channels simultaneously, such as combining phishing emails with phone calls or text messages, to bypass security measures and increase the likelihood of success.[13]

---

10. See Press Release, Fed. Bureau of Investigation (S.F. Office), *FBI Warns of Increasing Threat of Cyber Criminals Utilizing Artificial Intelligence* (May 8, 2024), https://www.fbi.gov/contact-us/field-offices/sanfrancisco/news/fbi-warns-of-increasing-threat-of-cyber-criminals-utilizing-artificial-intelligence; Sharon Shea & Ashwin Krishnan, *How AI is Making Phishing Attacks More Dangerous*, TechTarget (Oct. 22, 2024), https://www.techtarget.com/searchsecurity/tip/Generative-AI-is-making-phishing-attacks-more-dangerous.

11. Derek Manky & Gil Baram, *Beyond Phishing: Exploring the Rise of AI-enabled Cybercrime*, Ctr. for Long-Term Cybersecurity (Jan. 2025), https://cltc.berkeley.edu/2025/01/16/beyond-phishing-exploring-the-rise-of-ai-enabled-cybercrime/.

12. David Elliott, *"This Happens More Frequently Than People Realize": Arup Chief on the Lessons Learned from a $25m Deepfake Crime*, World Econ. Forum (Feb. 4, 2025), https://www.weforum.org/stories/2025/02/deepfake-ai-cybercrime-arup.

13. BIO-key, *Blog: The Evolution of Phishing Attacks: Recognizing Modern Tactics* (Oct. 8, 2025) https://blog.bio-key.com/the-evolution-of-phishing-attacks.

- **Exploiting Supply Chain Vulnerabilities:** Cybercriminals have targeted supply chains to exploit smaller security gaps that can lead to widespread disruptions. By compromising a single supplier, attackers can access larger networks, underscoring the need for comprehensive security assessments across all partners. Remember the adage about the weakest link.

4. **AI-Enhanced Phishing and Social Engineering**
   - **Spearphishing with AI:** The use of AI in crafting personalized phishing messages, known as spearphishing, has become more prevalent. AI enables attackers to analyze vast amounts of data and create highly targeted and convincing messages, increasing the likelihood of deceiving recipients.
   - **Voice Phishing (Vishing):** AI-powered voice cloning has led to vishing attacks, where scammers use cloned voices to impersonate trusted individuals and deceive victims into divulging sensitive information or authorizing transactions.[14]
5. **Cybercrime-as-a-Service (CaaS)**
   - **Commercialization of Cybercrime Tools:** The emergence of CaaS platforms has lowered the barrier to entry for cybercriminals. These platforms offer ready-made tools and services, such as ransomware kits and botnets, allowing individuals with minimal technical expertise to launch sophisticated attacks.
6. **Escalation of Ransomware Attacks**
   - **Targeting Critical Infrastructure:** Ransomware attacks have increasingly focused on critical infrastructure sectors, including healthcare, energy, and transportation. These attacks demand substantial ransoms and pose significant risks to public safety and services.
   - **Double Extortion Tactics:** Attackers employ double extortion strategies. They encrypt the victim's data and threaten to publicly release sensitive information unless the ransom is paid.

The evolving cyberthreat landscape necessitates continuous vigilance and adaptation. By understanding these trends and implementing robust security measures, individuals and organizations can better defend against the sophisticated tactics employed by modern cybercriminals.

AI dramatically increases our cybersecurity risks. In developing this edition of the Handbook, we have added and expanded chapters on risk identification, risk assessment, and risk mitigation, with a focus on the impact of AI. We also included and expanded chapters addressing some of the negative applications of AI, such as creating "deepfakes" that can facilitate numerous newly conceived scams and revive older scams that had become less effective.

---

14. Laura Fitzgerald, *Deepfake Trends to Look Out for in 2025*, Pindrop, https://www.pindrop.com/article/deepfake-trends/ (last updated Jul. 9, 2025).

Conversely, artificial intelligence plays a vital role in strengthening cybersecurity by helping to detect threats, analyze vulnerabilities, and identify fake content such as phishing emails, deepfakes, or counterfeit websites. AI-powered systems can monitor massive streams of data in real time, flagging unusual patterns or anomalies that may indicate a cyberattack or attempted fraud. Machine learning models can be trained to recognize subtle signs of manipulation or impersonation—far beyond what a human analyst could detect at scale. By automating the identification of malicious code, suspicious behavior, and forged digital media, AI enhances both the speed and accuracy of cyber defenses. While it is not a complete solution, AI serves as a powerful ally in the ongoing battle against digital deception and cybercrime.

5. Increased Focus on Cybersecurity Measures

1. **Adoption of AI in Defense:** Organizations can integrate AI into their cybersecurity frameworks to detect and respond to threats more effectively. AI-driven security solutions can analyze patterns and predict potential attacks, enhancing proactive defense mechanisms.
2. **Regulatory Developments:** Governments and regulatory bodies are working on developing policies to address the challenges posed by emerging cyber threats, including guidelines for AI usage and data protection laws.

Most attorneys know about malpractice insurance. To the surprise of some, many traditional malpractice policies exclude coverage for losses relating to cybersecurity failures, data breaches, and related damages. This edition's chapter on cybersecurity insurance has an expanded scope. It explains the different types of cybersecurity coverage. It also analyzes the types and amounts of coverage different firms need based on their exposure levels and the risks most likely to affect them.

As the nature of risks has changed due to AI, so too must the means of mitigating those risks. We have included an exploration of risk mitigation and expanded chapters dealing with the concept of cybersecurity itself. How do you build and maintain your cybersecurity fortress to provide maximum protection against the ever-changing risks of the new AI-fueled technology?

Remember that no matter how hard you try, nothing you can do will ever eliminate risk exposure. All we can do is mitigate the risk and reduce exposure. We have designed this edition of the Cybersecurity Handbook to help you understand and reduce the risks to which AI-driven technology exposes you, your clients, and your firm.

The world appears differently to attorneys in various practice settings. Smaller firms typically have fewer resources to help them manage technology and its associated risks. Historically, this Handbook has included relatively short pieces that deal summarily with various practice settings. In this edition, we have expanded the discussion to provide a more thorough examination of the differences among practice settings.

In that vein, the situation with government lawyers, while stable in terms of ongoing cybersecurity needs, has assumed a level of uncertainty never seen in the history of this Handbook. We have limited the discussion of government lawyers, recognizing that the uncertainty of their positions in the current political climate may pre-empt their attention. Hopefully, that will not happen, and government lawyers will continue to focus on cybersecurity issues. However, people often find distraction in threats to their employment. As Alexander Pope commented in his poem "Essay on Criticism," "To err is human…", those distractions may cause human error.

6. AI in Our Daily Lives

Today, most individuals interact with AI regularly, often without being aware of it. The growing reach of such interactions now spans communication, commerce, transportation, healthcare, education, entertainment, finance, security, and more. The following few pages will introduce you to AI's capabilities or, perhaps, expand your understanding of its impact. This discussion does not aim to address the full scope of either the benefits or drawbacks of AI. Instead, it brings examples to your attention to help you understand AI's allure, its reach, and why it became the primary driving force behind the creation of this Fourth Edition of the Cybersecurity Handbook.

Before exploring all the things AI can help us with, let's consider what happens when AI goes awry. The question of liability for harm done by AI has not yet been resolved, although the issue now pends in federal and state courts.[15] Theories of potentially responsible parties run the gamut from the developer to the end user, with stops along the way for third parties who put their spoons in the pot to help stir things around or otherwise help in the preparation. Some scholars have coined the phrase "responsibility gap" to address the situation where no clear case for liability exists.[16]

6.1. Communication and Personal Assistance

Voice-activated AI systems such as Apple's Siri, Google Assistant, and Amazon Alexa utilize natural language processing (NLP) to respond to spoken commands, answer questions, provide navigation, and control home devices. These tools represent the front end of vast AI systems that analyze speech patterns, context, and prior user behavior.

15. See *Garcia v. Character Technologies, Inc.*, No. 6:24-cv-01903 (M.D. Fla.); Complaint, *Banner v. Tesla, Inc.*, No. 3:23-cv-00769 (N.D. Cal. Feb. 22, 2023).

16. *See* Andreas Matthias, *The Responsibility Gap: Ascribing Responsibility for the Actions of Learning Automata*, 6 Ethics & Info. Tech. 175 (2004).

- **Example:** When a user asks Alexa to "order more paper towels," AI processes voice input, searches purchase history, identifies the product, and initiates a transaction—all within seconds.

Additional Examples:[17]

- **Home Automation:** AI-powered personal assistants, such as Amazon Alexa and Google Assistant, can control various smart home devices, including lights, thermostats, locks, and security cameras.
- **Scheduling and Reminders:** AI assistants can manage calendars, set reminders, and schedule meetings.
- **Information Retrieval:** AI assistants can quickly answer questions, search the web, and retrieve information.
- **Virtual Customer Service:** AI-powered chatbots and virtual assistants can handle customer queries, resolve issues, and provide personalized support.
- **E-Learning and Training:** AI assistants can support e-learning by providing educational content, answering questions, and assisting with training programs.
- **Workflow Management:** AI assistants can help manage workflows by organizing tasks, setting priorities, and providing updates.

6.2. Commerce and Consumption

AI algorithms drive much of the modern e-commerce experience. Platforms like Amazon, Target, and Walmart deploy machine learning to suggest products based on browsing history, prior purchases, geographic trends, and even weather data.

- **Example:** Personalized promotions or dynamic pricing can optimize sales. For example, the system might raise the price of snow shovels as a storm approaches, often before customers know the forecast.

  NOTE: This is not necessarily a good thing. This practice has angered consumers, and their angst has prompted investigations of the practice by federal and state governmental agencies, which look at it as a possible form of price fixing, price discrimination, unfair practices, and collusion. The Federal Trade Commission has increasingly focused on the use of AI in pricing systems. In 2022, it issued a policy statement warning businesses that the use of algorithms to facilitate collusion or discriminate against protected classes may violate the FTC Act and antitrust laws.[18] The DOJ has signaled

17. James Barr, *Intelligent Personal Assistants (IPA): Examples and Use Cases*, ENTER. AI WORLD (Apr. 1, 2024), https://www.enterpriseaiworld.com/Articles/Editorial/Features/Intelligent-Personal-Assistants-%28IPA%29-Examples-and-Use-Cases-163787.aspx; Alli Tunell, *I Tested 10+ AI Personal Assistants. Here Are the Best for Home & Work*, MOTION (Aug. 5, 2024), https://www.usemotion.com/blog/ai-personal-assistants.

18. *See Bringing Dark Patterns to Light: An FTC Workshop*, FED. TRADE COMM'N (Apr. 29, 2021 10:30 AM), https://www.ftc.gov/news-events/events/2021/04/bringing-dark-patterns-light-ftc-workshop; *see also* FED.

concern that algorithmic pricing tools may enable companies to coordinate pricing indirectly, without explicit communication, in violation of the Sherman Act.[19] In a high-profile case, the U.S. Department of Justice sued RealPage Inc., alleging that its AI-powered rent-setting software enabled landlords to collude on rental prices in violation of state antitrust laws.[20] Several other states have also initiated litigation addressing this practice.

Additional Examples:[21]

- **Chatbots and Virtual Assistants:** AI-powered chatbots and virtual assistants offer instant customer support, answer queries, and facilitate purchases.
- **Visual Search and Recommendation Engines:** AI enables visual search capabilities, allowing customers to search for products using images.
- **Inventory Management:** AI optimizes inventory levels by predicting demand and automating restocking processes.
- **Dynamic Pricing:** AI adjusts prices in real-time based on demand, competition, and other relevant factors. Airlines and hotels utilize AI to implement dynamic pricing, thereby maximizing profits while offering competitive rates. (See note above.)
- **Fraud Detection:** AI helps detect and prevent fraudulent activities by analyzing transaction patterns and identifying anomalies.
- **Customer Behavior Analysis:** AI analyzes customer behavior to understand preferences and predict future actions. This enables businesses to tailor their marketing strategies and enhance customer engagement.

6.3. Transportation and Navigation

Navigation apps like Google Maps and Waze use real-time traffic data and AI-powered prediction models to optimize routes. Ride-hailing services like Uber and Lyft also use machine learning for route optimization, surge pricing, and estimated arrival times.

- **Example:** AI can reroute a driver in real time based on live traffic data inputs from other users to avoid an accident or construction.

TRADE COMM'N, BRINGING DARK PATTERNS TO LIGHT (Sept. 2022), https://www.ftc.gov/system/files/ftc_gov/pdf/P214800%20Dark%20Patterns%20Report%209.14.2022%20-%20FINAL.pdf.

19. *See* Bruce D. Sokler *et al.*, *DOJ Reaffirms Stance on Algorithmic Price Fixing, While Federal Judge Dismisses Price Fixing Complaint Against Software Company — AI: The Washington Report*, MINTZ (Apr. 4, 2025), https://www.mintz.com/insights-center/viewpoints/54731/2025-04-04-doj-reaffirms-stance-algorithmic-price-fixing-while.

20. *See* Marissa Luck, *Department of Justice Sues Texas Firm RealPage Accusing it of Helping Landlords Collude on Rents*, HOUSTON CHRON. (Aug. 23, 2024), https://www.houstonchronicle.com/business/real-estate/article/realpage-doj-lawsuit-antitrust-rentcollusion-19719048.php.

21. Ashley Taylor, *Artificial Intelligence in E-Commerce: 6 Use Cases and Examples*, CLEVERENCE (Mar. 12, 2025) https://www.cleverence.com/articles/business-blogs/artificial-intelligence-in-e-commerce-6-use-cases-and-examples/.

Additional Examples:[22]

- **Autonomous Vehicles:** Self-driving cars use AI to interpret sensor data, make driving decisions, and safely navigate roads.
- **Smart Traffic Management:** AI systems analyze real-time traffic data to optimize signal timings and reduce congestion. Cities that use AI for traffic management report a reduction of up to 30% in travel time.
- **Predictive Maintenance:** AI analyzes sensor data to predict vehicle maintenance needs. This proactive approach helps prevent breakdowns and extends the lifespan of vehicles.
- **Optimized Route Planning:** AI navigation tools use real-time data on traffic, weather, and road conditions to plan the most efficient routes. Delivery companies use AI to reduce fuel consumption and ensure timely deliveries.
- **Enhanced Fleet Efficiency:** AI monitors vehicle performance and driver behavior to suggest improvements, leading to better fuel efficiency and optimized operations.
- **Improved Safety:** AI-powered cameras and sensors detect driver fatigue, distraction, or reckless driving. These systems can alert drivers to take breaks or correct their behavior, thereby reducing the likelihood of accidents.
- **Smart Public Transport:** AI enhances the efficiency of buses and trains by predicting passenger demand and adjusting services.

6.4. Healthcare and Diagnostics

AI supports early disease detection, treatment planning, and patient monitoring.

- **Example:** A hospital using AI to triage radiology images may catch strokes in critical windows where a human reading could have delayed diagnosis.

Additional Examples:[23]

- **Precision Medicine:** AI algorithms analyze genetic information to tailor treatments to individual patients. For instance, IBM Watson Health uses AI to recommend cancer treatments based on a patient's genetic profile and medical history.
- **Predictive Analytics:** AI can predict patient deterioration by analyzing vital signs and other data.

---

22. Gaurav Gupta, *AI in Transportation: Benefits, Use Cases, and Real Examples*, SQUAREBOAT, https://squareboat.com/blog/ai-in-transportation (last updated June 10, 2025); Fredrik Filipsson, *Top 15 Real-Life Use Cases for AI in Transportation Industry*, REDRESS COMPLIANCE (July 4, 2025), https://redresscompliance.com/TOP-15-REAL-LIFE-USE-CASES-FOR-AI-IN-TRANSPORTATION-INDUSTRY/.

23. *How AI Is Being Used to Benefit Your Health Care*, CLEVELAND CLINIC (Sept. 5, 2024), https://health.clevelandclinic.org/ai-in-healthcare; *see also 10 real-world examples of AI in healthcare*, PHILIPS (Nov. 24, 2022), https://www.philips.com/a-w/about/news/archive/features/2022/20221124-10-real-world-examples-of-ai-in-healthcare.html; Sam Daley, *AI in Healthcare: Uses, Examples and Benefits*, BUILT IN, https://builtin.com/artificial-intelligence/artificial-intelligence-healthcare (last updated May 2, 2025).

- **Robotic Surgery:** AI-powered robots assist in surgeries, providing precision and reducing recovery times.
- **Drug Discovery:** AI accelerates the drug discovery process by analyzing vast datasets to identify potential drug candidates. Drug companies have used AI to find new treatments for diseases such as Parkinson's and Alzheimer's.
- **Virtual Health Assistants:** AI chatbots and virtual assistants provide patients with medical advice, appointment scheduling, and medication reminders.
- **Radiology:** AI enhances image quality and accelerates diagnostic processes. AI-based image reconstruction in MR and CT scans improves diagnostic confidence and operational efficiency.

6.5. Education and Content Creation

Students and professionals increasingly use generative AI tools to draft essays, correct grammar, summarize texts, and brainstorm ideas.

- **Example:** An undergraduate might use an AI tool to summarize academic articles or generate citations in Bluebook or APA format, streamlining their research and writing process.

Additional Examples:[24]

- **Personalized Learning:** AI can tailor educational content to each student's unique learning style and pace. Platforms like DreamBox and Smart Sparrow analyze student responses in real time to dynamically adapt lessons, enabling students to master concepts at their own pace.
- **Automated Administrative Tasks:** AI automates tasks such as grading, scheduling, and report generation, significantly reducing educators' workloads. AI scheduling software helps optimize class timetables and resource allocation.
- **Interactive Learning:** AI enhances learning by making it more interactive and engaging through gamified content and adaptive learning platforms, thereby keeping learners motivated and engaged.
- **Improved Accessibility:** AI-driven assistive technologies support students with disabilities, ensuring a more effective learning environment.
- **Actionable Insights:** AI analyzes vast amounts of educational data to provide educators with actionable insights. This helps identify areas where students may need additional support and tailor interventions.

24. *AI Content Generation Tools in Teaching, Learning, and Research*, Old Dominion Univ., https://www.odu.edu/facultydevelopment/ai-content-generation-tools-teaching-learning-and-research (last visited July 15, 2025); Jordan Hopkins, *16 AI Tools for Education Content Creation*, Intellum (Mar. 7, 2024), https://www.intellum.com/resources/blog/16-ai-tools-for-education-content-creation.

- **Content Generation:** AI can generate new content, such as written text, images, and videos.

7. AI and the Practice of Law

AI has profoundly impacted law practice, touching nearly every phase of legal services, from client intake to final disposition. Benefits include increased efficiency, better data management, and new insights. However, these tools also present serious ethical and procedural challenges. **Remember, regarding any use of AI in the practice of law, the importance of verification of the accuracy of AI's product; it works, often, but not always, well. Verify, then trust!**

7.1. Legal Research and Case Law Analysis

AI-powered platforms allow attorneys to research case law using natural language queries. These systems go beyond keyword searching, using machine learning to interpret legal reasoning, identify related precedents, and assess relevance.

- **Example:** An attorney researching implied warranty of merchantability in Missouri can input a plain-language query and receive annotated, ranked results based on jurisdiction and factual alignment.

Additional Examples:

- **Case Comparison:** AI tools can compare cases to identify similarities and differences in legal reasoning.
- **Statutory Interpretation:** AI can assist in interpreting statutes by analyzing case law addressing the statute.
- **Trend Analysis:** AI can identify trends in case law, such as how courts rule on specific issues.
- **Innovative Interpretive Methods:** AI can assist courts in interpreting statutes beyond traditional means. As societal conditions change, AI can help identify new interpretive methods that reflect current realities.
- **Legal Research Basics:** AI tools can help attorneys enhance their legal research skills by providing step-by-step guides and recommendations for conducting effective legal research.

7.2. E-Discovery and Document Review

AI tools revolutionized e-discovery by rapidly analyzing large volumes of electronically stored information (ESI) using predictive coding and technology-assisted review (TAR).

- **Judicial Endorsement:** *Da Silva Moore v. Publicis Groupe*, 287 F.R.D. 182 (S.D.N.Y. 2012), was the first federal case to approve the use of predictive coding in discovery, a decision reaffirmed in multiple subsequent rulings.
- **Example:** In complex litigation, an AI system might sift through millions of emails to identify relevant documents, saving hundreds of billable hours and reducing human error.

Additional Examples:[25]

- **Automated Redaction:** AI tools can automatically redact sensitive information from documents, facilitating compliance with privacy regulations and protecting confidential data.
- **Privilege Detection:** AI can identify privileged documents by analyzing content and metadata. This helps legal teams quickly distinguish between privileged and non-privileged communications, thereby reducing the risk of inadvertent disclosure.
- **Sentiment Analysis:** AI can perform sentiment analysis on documents to identify the tone and emotional context of communications.
- **Predictive Coding:** AI uses predictive coding to prioritize documents for review based on their relevance to the case. This helps legal teams focus on the most important documents, improving efficiency and reducing costs.
- **Smart Filters:** AI-powered e-discovery tools use smart filters to reduce the number of documents that require manual review. These filters can automatically deduplicate documents, identify near-duplicates, and apply advanced search techniques to narrow the dataset.
- **Enhanced Search Capabilities:** AI enhances search capabilities by allowing natural language queries and providing more accurate results. Legal teams can utilize AI to search for specific terms, phrases, or concepts within large datasets, thereby making it easier to locate relevant information.

7.3. Predictive Analytics and Legal Outcomes

AI systems can forecast litigation outcomes, predict judicial decisions, and propose settlement strategies.

- **Example:** Systems like Lex Machina and Premonition analyze how judges have ruled in similar cases, offering probabilities for motions to dismiss and jury verdicts.

25. *State of AI in eDiscovery Report*, LIGHTHOUSE, https://www.lighthouseglobal.com/ai-in-ediscovery-report-2025 (last visited July 15, 2025); *see also* Clio, *How AI Enhances Legal Document Review*, ABA LAW TECH. TODAY (Feb. 13, 2025), https://www.americanbar.org/groups/law_practice/resources/law-technology-today/2025/how-ai-enhances-legal-document-review; *AI Contract Review Software in 2025 (Complete Guide)*, PERCIPIENT (Mar. 26, 2025), https://percipient.co/ai-contract-review-2025/.

- **Cautionary Case:** In *State v. Loomis*, 881 N.W.2d 749 (Wis. 2016), the Wisconsin Supreme Court upheld the use of the COMPAS risk assessment tool at sentencing while cautioning that its proprietary nature and unknown methodology could infringe on due process rights.

Additional Examples:[26]

- **Sentencing Predictions:** AI tools can predict sentencing outcomes based on historical data.
- **Settlement Strategies:** AI can analyze past settlement data to help formulate optimal settlement strategies.
- **Case Outcome Predictions:** AI systems can predict case outcomes by analyzing factors such as judge behavior, case facts, and legal precedents.
- **Risk Assessment:** AI can evaluate the risk associated with legal decisions, such as the likelihood of a case being appealed or overturned.
- **Legal Research:** AI-powered platforms can predict the relevance of legal documents and case law, enabling attorneys to quickly and efficiently find the most pertinent information.

7.4. Generative AI and Legal Drafting

Lawyers now use GenAI to draft contracts, pleadings, and even entire appellate briefs. This practice offers advantages like increased efficiency and reduced costs. However, it also raises serious potential risks and liabilities that legal professionals must consider.

- **Example:** Generative AI can create drafts of contracts, legal briefs, memos, and letters using templates and key inputs.
- **Sanctions for AI Misuse:** In *Mata v. Avianca, Inc.*, No. 22-cv-1461 (PKC), 2023 WL 4114965 (S.D.N.Y. June 22, 2023), two lawyers submitted a brief with fictitious citations generated by ChatGPT and were sanctioned for failing to verify the accuracy of their AI-generated content. Surprisingly, if not shockingly, attorneys continue to rely upon GenAI and use its output without first verifying its accuracy. A public database compiled by legal analyst Damien Charlotin had logged more than 600 confirmed incidents worldwide where court filings included AI-generated false citations or quotes.[27] Perhaps it's time to learn from the mistakes of others.

---

26. Catherine Cote, *What Is Predictive Analytics? 5 Examples*, Harvard Bus. Sch. (Oct. 26, 2021), https://online.hbs.edu/blog/post/predictive-analytics; *The Impact of Predictive Analytics in Legal Tech*, Legal AI Mind (Oct. 6, 2024), https://www.legalaimind.com/2024/10/the-impact-of-predictive-analytics-in.html.

27. Damien Charlotin, AI Hallucination Cases, https://www.damiencharlotin.com/hallucinations/ (last visited Nov. 29, 2025); Jack Newsham, *AI Hallucinations in Court Documents Are a Growing Problem, and Data Shows Lawyers Are Responsible for Many of the Errors*, Bus. Insider (May 27, 2025 6:33 AM), https://www.businessinsider.com/increasing-ai-hallucinations-fake-citations-court-records-data-2025-5.

Some Risks to Consider (We Know We Are Repeating Ourselves, but This Is That Important):

1. **Accuracy and Quality Control:** An important concern when using AI for legal document drafting is the accuracy of the generated content. While highly advanced, AI models are not infallible and can produce errors, omissions, or inaccuracies in legal documents. These errors include hallucinations. Anyone using AI must implement rigorous quality control processes that involve careful proofreading, fact and citation verification, and legal analysis of AI-generated documents.
2. **Lack of Legal Judgment and Context:** GenAI models cannot provide legal judgment and context, which are crucial to properly drafting legal documents. Non-lawyers using AI may not fully understand the nuances of specific cases, jurisdictions, or evolving legal precedents, which can lead to suboptimal or inappropriate document content.
3. **Ethical Considerations:** The use of AI for legal document drafting raises significant ethical concerns. Legal professionals must ensure that AI-generated drafts function only as a starting point and not as a final product. It is essential to leverage the expertise and judgment of legal professionals to review, customize, and contextualize the documents to meet the unique needs of the client and the case.
4. **Output Risks:** Generative AI models can hallucinate, meaning they provide incorrect answers with a high degree of confidence. The possibility of AI hallucinations, combined with the relative scarcity of accurate legal domain knowledge found in most large language models (LLMs), makes it particularly risky for litigators to rely on information produced by an LLM.
5. **Bias:** LLMs, like any AI, are not pure objective engines. They can exhibit biases acquired from the data on which they trained, which can affect the fairness and impartiality of the generated content.
6. **Compliance with AI-Related Regulations:** Failure to comply with AI-related regulations may result in legal consequences, potentially impacting the credibility and reputation of the lawyer and firm.

7.5. Ethics and Professional Responsibility

The American Bar Association has interpreted the Model Rules of Professional Conduct to require attorneys to become and remain competent in using relevant technology:

Model Rule 1.1, Comment 8: "To maintain the requisite knowledge and skill, a lawyer should keep abreast of changes in the law and its practice, including the benefits and risks associated with relevant technology…." Attorneys must stay updated on technological advancements and understand how to use AI tools effectively. This includes ongoing education and training to maintain competence in using relevant technology.

Other Related Duties:

1. **Avoiding Bias:** AI tools can exhibit biases based on the data on which they train. Legal professionals must be vigilant in identifying and mitigating any biases in AI-generated content to ensure fairness and impartiality.
2. **Ethical Use of AI:** Lawyers must use AI tools ethically, ensuring they do not rely solely on AI for critical legal decisions. AI should supplement human judgment, not replace it.
3. **Compliance with Regulations:** Legal professionals must comply with AI-related regulations and guidelines. This includes understanding and adhering to laws and ethical rules governing the use of AI in legal practice.
4. **Confidentiality:** Lawyers must ensure that AI tools for legal research and drafting maintain client confidentiality. This requires understanding how AI systems store, share, and process data to prevent unauthorized access.
5. **Verification of AI Outputs:** Legal professionals must verify the accuracy of AI-generated content. This requires reviewing and validating the information provided by AI tools to ensure accuracy and relevance to the case.
6. **Competence:** Attorneys must stay current on technological advancements and understand how to use AI tools effectively. This necessitates ongoing education and training to maintain competence in using relevant technology.
7. **Accountability:** Lawyers have responsibility for decisions made using AI tools. They must ensure that AI-assisted decisions comply with legal standards, including ethical principles. **When AI goes wrong in legal practice, the attorney is liable, not the AI.** Whether through ethical violations, malpractice claims, or judicial sanctions, attorneys remain fully responsible for the legal work they deliver, regardless of the tools they use.
8. **Transparency:** Legal professionals must use AI tools transparently. This includes explaining to the client how AI functions in their case and the potential benefits and risks associated with its use.

8. Broader Policy and Regulatory Trends

8.1. Domestic Regulatory Landscape

The U.S. lacks a comprehensive AI statute but has seen significant federal activity:

- **White House Executive Orders on AI:** The October 2023 Executive Order signed by President Biden emphasized the safe development of AI, protection of privacy, and promoted innovation while addressing risks. President Trump revoked that order on January 20, 2025. On January 23, 2025, President Trump signed Executive Order

EO-14179 titled "Removing Barriers to American Leadership in Artificial Intelligence." The order emphasizes deregulation and orders federal agencies to:

- Rescind conflicting Biden-era AI rules.
- Create a national AI strategy within 180 days.
- Eliminate prior reporting and procurement restrictions.

- **FTC Guidance:** The FTC warns against deceptive or discriminatory uses of AI in marketing, lending, or employment. The agency has warned companies about potential violations of the Fair Credit Reporting Act when opaque AI models are used to deny credit or housing.
- **State Action:** The House version of the Republican's BBB (Big Beautiful Bill) included a federal preemption of AI. The Senate version did not have that language. The ultimate compromise followed the Senate version, leaving the states free to regulate AI. Several U.S. states have taken early legislative steps to regulate artificial intelligence, particularly concerning transparency, accountability, and bias prevention. As of mid-2025, Colorado, California, and Connecticut are among the most active. Colorado enacted the *Colorado Artificial Intelligence Act*, the nation's first comprehensive AI law, which imposes obligations on developers and deployers of high-risk AI systems to prevent algorithmic discrimination.[28] **California** introduced legislation such as *SB 896* (2024) requiring impact assessments and human oversight for automated decision-making systems used by state agencies.[29] **Connecticut** passed *Public Act No. 23-57* (2023), which mandates inventories and risk assessments of AI systems used by state entities and prohibits use in certain high-risk contexts without safeguards. These laws reflect a growing state-level initiative to fill the regulatory void while federal AI legislation remains under debate.[30] **Tennessee** enacted the *Ensuring Likeness Voice and Image Security (ELVIS) Act* on March 21, 2024 (effective July 1, 2024), criminalizing unauthorized AI-generated imitations of a person's voice, image, or likeness—particularly to protect artists.[31] **New York** has advanced multiple AI measures. The *New York Artificial Intelligence Bill of Rights* (Assembly Bill 2025-A3265) guarantees residents rights to safe, fair, and transparent automated decision systems. In June 2025, the legislature passed the *Responsible AI Safety & Education (RAISE) Act*, which mandates safety reviews, incident reporting, and potential civil penalties for frontier AI models

---

28. *Colorado Artificial Intelligence Act*, S.B. 24-205, 74th Gen. Assemb., 2d Reg. Sess. (Colo. 2024) (to be codified at Colo. Rev. Stat. §§ 6-1-1601 to 1610), https://leg.colorado.gov/bills/sb24-205.

29. S.B. 896, 2023–2024 Leg., Reg. Sess. (Cal. 2024) (proposing regulation of automated decision tools by state agencies), https://leginfo.legislature.ca.gov/faces/billNavClient.xhtml?bill_id=202320240SB896.

30. *An Act Concerning Artificial Intelligence, Automated Decision-Making and Personal Data Privacy*, Pub. Act No. 23-57, 2023 Conn. Acts (Reg. Sess.), https://www.cga.ct.gov/2023/ACT/PA/PDF/2023PA-00057-R00HB-06662-PA.PDF.

31. *Ensuring Likeness, Voice, and Image Security (ELVIS) Act*, H.B. 2091, 113th Gen. Assemb., Reg. Sess. (Tenn. 2024), https://publications.tnsosfiles.com/acts/113/pub/pc0760.pdf.

capable of causing "critical harm" (e.g., death of 100+ people or over $1 billion in damage). Additionally, a state law requires agencies to inventory and risk-assess AI tools and bar their unsupervised use in decisions like unemployment benefits unless human oversight is in place.[32]

8.2. International Developments

The **EU Artificial Intelligence Act** (2024)[33] categorizes AI systems by risk and imposes strict controls on "high-risk" applications, such as those used in criminal justice and employment.

The Artificial Intelligence Act—Regulation (EU) 2024/1689 of the European Parliament and of the Council of 13 June 2024—is the world's first comprehensive AI regulatory framework. It adopts a risk-based approach, classifying AI systems into four categories:

- **Unacceptable risk** (e.g., real-time biometric surveillance, social scoring), entirely banned.
- **High-risk** (e.g., AI in healthcare, transport, critical infrastructure, employment screening), subject to strict requirements: risk assessments, documentation, oversight, transparency, and human supervision.
- **Limited risk** (e.g., generative AI, chatbots), must adhere to transparency requirements and copyright protections.
- **Minimal risk** (e.g., spam filters, AI in video games), largely unregulated but encouraged to follow voluntary codes of conduct.

Member States must also create **AI regulatory sandboxes** by August 2, 2026, to support innovation under controlled conditions.

Status:

- The Act is fully in force as of August 1, 2024.
- It gradually takes effect—from prohibitions and literacy in early 2025, to full enforcement by mid-2026, and extended compliance for certain systems through 2027.
- It sets global legal standards for AI regulation, combining bans, oversight, transparency, and innovation support.
- **Industry lobbying:** Technology giants (Google, Meta), European firms (Airbus, BNP Paribas, Siemens, SAP) and trade groups (CCIA Europe) have urged delaying

32. N.Y. State Assemb., A.B. A3265, 2023–2024 Leg., Reg. Sess. (N.Y. 2023), https://www.nysenate.gov/legislation/bills/2023/A3265; *Responsible Artificial Intelligence in Safety and Education (RAISE) Act*, S.B. 8209, 2023–2024 Leg., Reg. Sess. (N.Y. 2025), https://www.nysenate.gov/legislation/bills/2023/S8209.

33. Regulation (EU) 2024/1689 of the European Parliament and of the Council of 13 June 2024 on artificial intelligence, O.J. (L No. 1689) 12.7.2024.

implementation—some proposing a two-year suspension—citing regulatory complexity, lack of implementation guidance, and risk of stifling innovation.[34]

- **Commission's response:** Officials, including spokesperson Thomas Regnier, have unequivocally rejected delays—saying, "no stop the clock" and confirming all obligations will begin as scheduled. Any delay would apply only if technical standards were not yet ready, but the Commission expects the Code of Practice to be published before August.[35]
- **Civil society view:** Advocacy groups warn that pausing or watering down the Act would undermine fundamental rights protections and Europe's regulatory consistency
- **Example:** AI tools used for hiring or bail decisions in the EU may soon have to undergo rigorous testing, transparency obligations, and human oversight.

Artificial intelligence is now embedded in the daily experience of billions of people and is increasingly central to legal practice. It offers remarkable efficiency and analytical power but necessitates deployment with caution and ethical rigor. For legal professionals, this means embracing technological competence, maintaining accountability for AI-assisted decisions, and participating in ongoing efforts to ensure that these tools advance—not undermine—justice. As courts, clients, and governments adapt to the AI era; legal practitioners must play a key role in shaping responsible innovation and ensuring that fairness and due process remain foundational principles in an increasingly automated world.

Each of this Handbook's prior editions has included a discussion of these principles. That said, the Fourth Edition is filled with new information, laws, findings, and practical solutions. It surpasses its predecessors in addressing the issues raised by AI, in general, and GenAI, in particular.

This edition of the Handbook has a similar structure to prior editions. It presents the work of nearly 30 authors from across the ABA who are experts in their fields. The Handbook covers a wide range of topics and provides a comprehensive look at the threat developments of the past few years and the trends established in cybersecurity. Authors develop and share best practices throughout the Handbook. It addresses concerns and provides recommendations for several types of legal practices, including small and large firms, government lawyers, public interest practices, and in-house counsel.

---

34. *See* Javier Espinoza, *European CEOs Urge Brussels to Halt Landmark AI Act*, Fin. Times (July 2, 2025), https://www.ft.com/content/a825759e-aec8-4184-bc73-f604f169204c. *See also* Javier Espinoza, *EU Pushes Ahead With AI Code of Practice*, Fin. Times (July 10, 2025), https://www.ft.com/content/32a3c83d-64ed-4c83-a5d3-a6cd89b087ba.

35. *See* Foo Yun Chee, *Explainer: Will the EU Delay Enforcing Its AI Act?*, Reuters (July 3, 2025), https://www.reuters.com/business/media-telecom/will-eu-delay-enforcing-its-ai-act-2025-07-03. *See also* Foo Yun Chee, *Artificial Intelligence Rules Go Ahead, No Pause, EU Commission Says*, Reuters (July 4, 2025), https://www.reuters.com/world/europe/artificial-intelligence-rules-go-ahead-no-pause-eu-commission-says-2025-07-04; Caitlin Andrews, *European Commission Holds Firm on AI Act Implementation Timeline*, IAPP (July 5, 2025), https://iapp.org/news/a/european-commission-holds-firm-on-ai-act-implementation-timeline.

We hope that you will learn from and apply this Cybersecurity Handbook in a way that enables your practice to address the growing challenges of cybersecurity more effectively, thereby helping to protect your practice and providing you with the tools to help you deliver competent and valuable advice to clients.

The ancient Romans had a proverb: "*Praemonitus, praemunitus.*" It translates as "forewarned, forewarned." Still, it is often credited as the origin of our saying that "forewarned is forearmed." We intend this Fourth Edition of the Cybersecurity Handbook to give you advance warning of important issues that demand your attention and information to help you deal with them effectively.

One final, important note: The views expressed throughout each chapter of this Cybersecurity Handbook represent those of each of the authors and not of the ABA, any specific law firm or practice, governmental entity, or any other author or editor affiliation.

Chapter 2

An Introduction to Artificial Intelligence

Jeffrey Allen

Artificial intelligence (AI), the art of getting machines to approximate thinking, learning, and communicating like humans, will reshape the world faster than you can say "algorithm." From helping doctors diagnose illnesses to recommending your next binge-watch, AI—the ultimate multitasker—will transform business, entertainment, education, medical care, the practice of law, and pretty much everything else. However, AI appears to be a bumpy ride. It presents significant challenges, including ethical dilemmas, social transformations, privacy concerns, job displacement, security risks, and the facilitation of scams and other cybercrimes. Do not underestimate the importance of getting a handle on AI, how it works, where it excels, where it might fall short, how it can help you, how it can damage, if not destroy, your practice, and how criminals can employ it to their advantage. With the right approach, AI can serve as more than just a helpful tool; with proper human oversight, it can function as a force for good (and hopefully not our future robot overlord). This chapter will introduce you to the good, the bad, and the ugly of AI.

To help you understand AI discussions, a glossary immediately following this chapter will give you a reference point as to the meaning of terms commonly used in discussions about AI. You will also find a bibliography at the end of the chapter to provide you with additional sources of information about AI.

1. The Birth of Curious Machines

In the 1950s, amid academia's echoing corridors and the secretive hum of research labs, a tantalizing question sparked imaginations: could machines think, reason, even dream? Visionaries such as Alan Turing, John McCarthy, and Marvin Minsky embarked on an audacious quest to create artificial intelligence. Turing sought to unlock intelligence itself; McCarthy coined the term "Artificial Intelligence," setting the stage for a new era. Together, these pioneers laid the foundations of AI, venturing beyond conventional boundaries and lighting the path for technology to evolve from mere computation into something astonishingly humanoid.

Fresh from cracking the Enigma code in WWII, Turing turned his attention to a far more complex question: the intricacies of human intelligence itself. What if machines could not only crunch numbers but also reason, respond, and maybe even outwit us? He sketched out the Turing test, a litmus for machine intelligence. Could a computer converse so convincingly that an interlocutor could not distinguish it from a fellow human?

ELIZA, a pioneering chatbot, emerged in the mid-1960s as a digital confidante that listened, probed, and mirrored our thoughts. Developed by Joseph Weizenbaum at MIT, ELIZA was not sentient, but she played the role well, revealing our vulnerabilities and secrets.

2. Symbolic AI: The Rulebooks of Wisdom

The 1960s ushered in an era in which AI took on a philosophical mantle. Researchers ventured into symbolic reasoning, encoding knowledge into tidy rules that aimed to mimic human logic. These "expert systems," like modern-day oracles, dispensed insights from meticulously crafted rulebooks. MYCIN diagnosed infections, DENDRAL deciphered chemical compounds, and SHRDLU manipulated blocks in a virtual sandbox. However, there was a catch: these systems faltered in the face of ambiguity, their rigid structures collapsing when reality deviated from script. The complexity of real-world nuance proved too much for their neatly drawn lines.

3. The Great Winter and the Phoenix's Rise

The 1980s marked a pivotal turning point in the trajectory of computing technology; an era where raw processing power began to catch up with the ambitions of artificial intelligence researchers. Although the roots of AI date back to the 1950s, it was during the 1980s that computing power, accessibility, and algorithmic experimentation converged in ways that laid the critical groundwork for the future of AI.

4. The Surge in Computing Power

1. **The Microprocessor Revolution**: At the heart of the 1980s computing boom was the rise of affordable, fast microprocessors. Intel's 8086 and its successors brought powerful CPUs to personal computers. Apple's Macintosh (1984), IBM PCs, and Commodore machines made home and business computing mainstream. Moore's Law—predicting a doubling of transistors roughly every two years—continued to hold, driving exponential increases in computational capability.

2. **Workstations and Parallelism:** Advanced workstations by Sun Microsystems, DEC, and others introduced RISC (Reduced Instruction Set Computing) architecture and multi-user environments that supported more sophisticated research and development. Universities and labs also began experimenting with parallel processing, enabling more complex models and simulations.
3. **Affordable Memory and Storage:** Random Access Memory (RAM) expanded into megabytes instead of kilobytes, and hard disk drives became more affordable and capacious. These advances meant AI programs could now store and manipulate larger data sets, enabling more complex reasoning and knowledge representation.

5. AI: From Hype to Setback to Foundation

1. **Rule-Based Expert Systems:** The 1980s are perhaps best known in AI history for the rise of expert systems—programs that mimicked human decision-making by encoding expert knowledge into formal rules. Mycin (for medical diagnosis) and XCON (used by Digital Equipment Corporation to configure computer systems) showed the commercial potential of AI. These systems thrived on the growing computational resources of the time, which allowed thousands of "if-then" rules to be evaluated rapidly.
2. **The AI Boom and Bust Cycle:** Fueled by media attention and corporate interest, AI reached a commercial high in the mid-1980s. Major firms like IBM and Xerox invested heavily in AI labs. However, limitations soon became apparent: expert systems were brittle, hard to maintain, and struggled outside narrowly defined domains. By the late 1980s, disillusionment led to an "AI winter," a slowdown in funding and enthusiasm.
3. **Japan's Fifth Generation Computer Project:** One of the decade's most ambitious computing initiatives came from Japan, whose Fifth Generation Computer Systems (FGCS) project (launched in 1982) aimed to leapfrog Western development by focusing on logic programming, knowledge-based reasoning, and massively parallel computing. While the FGCS didn't achieve its bold goals, it spurred global competition and innovation in AI and hardware.

6. Laying the Groundwork for the Future

During the infamous "AI winter," funding evaporated, optimism faded, and dreams of thinking machines nearly withered away. AI was not down for long, however. Like a phoenix, it rose anew in the form of machine learning, now powered by neural networks that sparked fresh hope. Convolutional networks learned to sift through pixels, spotting cats, faces and even galaxies. Meanwhile, recurrent networks wove through words, translating languages and composing poetry. AI was back, now with tools that not only processed data but found patterns, creating a new foundation for the future.

Despite the setbacks, the 1980s established a technical and intellectual foundation upon which modern AI is built:

1. **Neural Network Revival:** Though largely dormant after initial promise in the 1960s, the backpropagation algorithm for training neural networks was rediscovered and popularized in 1986 (notably by Rumelhart, Hinton, and Williams), setting the stage for deep learning decades later.
2. **Foundational Algorithms:** Core algorithms for search, planning, logic, and probabilistic reasoning were refined during this period, aided by the enhanced computational power.
3. **AI in Academia:** AI became a more defined academic discipline, with research centers forming around the world, many of which still lead AI development today.

7. Generative Magic: VAEs, GANs, and Dreams

In the 2010s, generative AI (GenAI) quietly emerged, introducing a new form of creativity. Variational Autoencoders (VAEs) began whispering in probabilistic tongues, while Generative Adversarial Networks (GANs) stepped up as cosmic artists, crafting surreal landscapes one digital brushstroke at a time. Picture an artist's studio: easels lined up, a palette of latent spaces ready for transformation. VAEs encoded data into these spaces, conjuring faces, landscapes, and abstract forms that seemed almost alive. The GANs, with their generator and discriminator locked in a dynamic tango, unveiled an AI-driven artistry that pushed imagination to new boundaries.

8. The Age of Transformers and Conversational Sorcery

Enter the Transformers—a new wave of models that rewrote the AI playbook. BERT, GPT, and their digital relatives devoured books, digested encyclopedias, and spun narratives with flair. ChatGPT, a digital oracle at the intersection of language and imagination, began conversing, quipping, and sometimes waxing poetic. By the 2020s, AI donned its philosopher's robe again as ethical debates echoed through the halls of academia and industry. "Responsible AI" became the rallying cry as we wrestled with biases, fairness, and transparency. The Turing test took on a new dimension: it no longer focused on whether a machine could imitate a person, but whether it could do so responsibly.

9. The Unfinished Opera

We stand on the precipice of a new frontier: a world where AI does not just compute but composes and imagines in pixels and bytes. Generative AI hums melodies, splashes digital paint on canvases, and weaves complex tales in code. AI is a story in progress, a masterpiece missing its final touches. In this chapter, we introduce you to the fundamentals of AI and its key subfields: machine learning, computer vision, natural language processing, and robotics.

Machine learning enables AI to break free from the rulebook and learn directly from data, evolving and improving independently. Computer vision equips machines with the ability to perceive the world through images and videos, enabling them to interpret the world around them. Natural language processing takes things further, training AI to detect the patterns of human language and respond accordingly; no translation guide is required. And then we have robotics, where AI pairs with physical form, powering up robots and drones to move, interact, and even navigate the world around us.

GenAI, the ultimate creator in the AI family so far, does not just analyze; it invents, producing everything from art and music to text and realistic video. A multitasking virtuoso, GenAI draws on a vast sea of data to generate content that is coherent (though not necessarily correct), unique (though not necessarily original), and sometimes uncannily human-sounding in dialect and emotion. By stepping into the realms of human creativity, synthetic data, and immersive experiences, GenAI blurs the line between machine logic and human imagination, bringing a touch of artistry to the world of algorithms.

10. Artificial Intelligence Basics

AI has found the spotlight in recent years, reshaping industries, enhancing daily life, and sparking a host of ethical, moral, and legal debates. But (to borrow from Hamlet's soliloquy) "therein lies the rub:" we have had AI around for years, gradually expanding its reach into our work and our personal worlds. Take legal research, for instance. Case law and statute-searching software have evolved from plodding, clunky tools to sleek, sophisticated systems, making it increasingly easy to find that needle-in-a-haystack case. In our personal lives, think of virtual assistants like Siri, Alexa, and Google Assistant. They have been designed and trained to recognize our commands, answer our questions, and occasionally even crack a joke, all thanks to the magic of AI.

10.1. ChatGPT

In 2022, OpenAI unleashed ChatGPT, marking a seismic shift in the world of AI. Think of it as the moment life crawled out of the ocean and took its first steps on land. ChatGPT represents a new species in the AI landscape, ushering in what we now call GenAI. This new

AI species does not just analyze data, it creates, generating everything from text and music to diagrams and images. With ChatGPT leading the way, AI's evolution has accelerated significantly, opening doors to applications that have reshaped our personal and professional worlds in ways we never anticipated.

ChatGPT represents an artificial intelligence chatbot that uses natural language processing to create humanlike conversational dialogue. ChatGPT generates human-like images, text, or videos in response to prompts or instructions provided by users. The acronym "GPT" stands for "Generative Pre-trained Transformer," referring to how the program processes requests and formulates responses. ChatGPT trains with *reinforcement learning through human feedback* and reward models that rank its responses. This process enables the augmentation of ChatGPT with machine learning to enhance future responses. The language model responds to questions and can compose written content of various types for personal and professional use, including articles, social media posts, essays, code, and emails.

While not the only player in the field, OpenAI's "ChatGPT" has become a generic reference to all such tools, especially for people not deeply enmeshed in the technology sector. Think of it as the "Kleenex" of the field. Like Kleenex, ChatGPT has competitors with different names, but many people refer to all tissues as "Kleenex" and all GenAI applications as "ChatGPT." Major competitors to ChatGPT include Microsoft's Copilot, Google's Gemini, Anthropic's Claude, Meta's LLaMA, and Mistral AI.

Two recent advances have played a crucial role in GenAI going mainstream: transformers and the breakthrough language models they have enabled. "Transformers" (*not* the movie version) refers to a type of machine learning that allows researchers to train increasingly large models without labeling all the data in advance. New models train on billions of pages of text, resulting in answers with more depth and comprehension. Transformers unlocked a new concept called "attention," which enables tracking connections (patterns) between words across pages, chapters, and books, rather than within individual sentences. Transformers can also track connections for scientific analysis of such things as DNA.

Rapid advances in large language models (LLMs) having billions or even trillions of parameters opened the door for GenAI models to write engaging text, paint photorealistic images, and even create somewhat entertaining sitcoms on the fly. The rapid evolution of ChatGPT and its competitors has expanded the use of AI, transforming its nature and role in our society. This recent evolution has brought more AI into our homes, our cars, our health care, and our law offices, and wider attention to the AI tools that were becoming part of our lives before ChatGPT. For example, in health care, AI aids in diagnosing diseases, predicting patient outcomes, and discovering drugs. In finance, AI can assess risk, detect fraud, and monitor high-frequency trading. Self-driving cars and AI-based traffic management systems may improve safety and efficiency in transportation. Many industries have begun considering the trade-off between human workers and GenAI. Some have already replaced human workers in some positions with AI-driven bots.

To give you some perspective, the transition from strictly relying on natural intelligence (what we have and use without the aid of computers) to utilizing AI can be aptly compared to the move from walking to riding a bicycle. Similarly, the evolution of AI before GenAI mirrors the progression from the most basic bicycles in the early 1800s (effectively a wooden scooter with no pedals) to the first commercial car in 1898 (a one-cylinder Winton). From that point, the evolution from pre-Generative AI to GenAI would equate to the evolution from the Winton to the modern Ferrari.

11. Collaboration

Get ready for a new era of human-AI teamwork, where bots become the busy assistants of professionals in fields like law, accounting, and medicine. AI already pulls its weight, whether drafting contracts, conducting legal research, or managing documents for attorneys. Many of today's top legal software tools rely on GenAI to streamline everything from litigation preparation to document review. Accountants also receive a helping hand as AI steps in to audit, prepare taxes, analyze financials, and detect fraud. Meanwhile, in healthcare, AI assists doctors in diagnosing illnesses, prescribing treatments, interpreting medical images, and monitoring patient care. In using AI, we need to focus on the heading of this paragraph, "collaboration." We need to see and utilize AI to assist us, not do everything for us. We need to recognize AI's inherent lack of judgment and absence of an internal moral compass as disqualifications for AI making decisions without human supervision or intervention. The extent to which anyone can rely on a particular AI tool depends on the specific practice setting in which it will be employed. Underscore the preceding sentence when it comes to professional uses such as law and medicine.

12. The Potential and the Risk of AI

As artificial intelligence continues to advance at an unprecedented pace, we can expect significant developments in its capabilities that will impact almost every aspect of our lives. The near future promises a range of innovations that could transform industries and enhance personal and professional productivity. Conversely, the evolution of AI is expected to introduce new ethical and societal challenges for the legal profession, as well as for most other professions and society at large.

We will see AI enhancing our entertainment, education, and communication activities. For instance, AI can generate realistic and engaging content for games, movies, and books, as well as personalized and adaptive learning experiences for students. AI can also help us connect with others through natural language generation and translation, as well as emotion recognition and synthesis. AI has demonstrated impressive abilities to converse with humans on various topics, provide helpful information, and even crack jokes, flirt, and engage in relationships and discussions on many levels.

A double-edged sword, AI presents numerous challenges for us to address. This chapter will address those issues in more detail later. For now, know that AI lacks a moral compass and has no internal conception of right or wrong. AI does not always provide accurate or even factually correct responses. AI's responses may suffer from discrimination or bias contained in the data upon which it trained. We with natural intelligence have shown a dangerous propensity to depend upon information provided by AI without regard for its known flaws. Also, remember that the bad guys have equal access to AI as the rest of us. As a result, AI is being used to facilitate a wide array of illegal activities, including, without limitation, frauds, identity theft, and many *genres* of scams.

13. Natural Language Processing and Understanding

Conversational AI. AI's ability to recognize and generate human language will grow even more sophisticated. Expect that AI systems like ChatGPT will evolve to engage in more natural, context-aware conversations that closely mimic human dialogue. These advancements could lead to AI assistants capable of understanding (correctly processing) nuanced requests, carrying on multi-turn conversations, and even perceiving and responding to users' emotions. They could also lead to convincing fakes (deepfakes) that can facilitate criminal activities.

Real-Time Translation. Real-time translation services will likely become more accurate and accessible, enabling seamless communication across different languages. AI-driven translation tools could enable people to converse in their native languages while AI provides instantaneous and accurate translations, facilitating cross-cultural communication, collaboration, and commercial and social interactions.

14. Personalized Healthcare and Medicine

AI-Driven Diagnostics. Expect AI and AI-powered tools and programs to play a crucial role in assisting medical providers in diagnosing diseases more accurately and quickly than ever before. With the ability to analyze vast amounts of medical data, AI systems could assist healthcare professionals in identifying conditions early, predicting patient outcomes, and recommending personalized treatment plans.

Virtual Health Assistants. Anticipate more AI-powered virtual health assistants, helping patients manage chronic conditions, monitor vital signs, and adhere to medication schedules. These assistants could provide 24/7 support and offer personalized health advice based on real-time data and historical health information.

15. Autonomous Vehicles and Transportation

Self-Driving Cars. The race to autonomous vehicles is accelerating, with AI taking the driver's seat, guiding cars through complex environments without a human hand on the wheel. Soon, self-driving cars may become a familiar sight in urban areas, efficiently taking over ridesharing and delivery services. These smart vehicles will be equipped with advanced sensors, sophisticated machine learning algorithms, and lightning-fast decision-making capabilities, designed to ensure safe, smooth, and stress-free rides. Likely, with AI at the wheel, we will see fewer traffic collisions, fewer distracted drivers, and fewer drivers under the influence of drugs or alcohol.

Smart Traffic Management. Expect AI to play a more integral role in optimizing city traffic flow, reducing congestion, and enhancing overall transportation efficiency. AI-driven traffic management systems can utilize real-time data to adjust traffic signals, manage public transportation schedules, and predict and prevent traffic congestion.

16. Enhanced Creativity and Content Generation

AI-Generated Art and Music. AI's creative capabilities will expand, enabling it to produce original works of art, music, and literature. AI systems could collaborate with human creators to generate innovative content, blending human creativity with computational power. We might see AI-designed art exhibitions, music albums composed by AI, and even AI-written novels that push the boundaries of creativity.

Personalized Content Creation. We will utilize AI to generate personalized content tailored to each individual's preferences. This could include custom news feeds, personalized video recommendations, and even bespoke marketing materials designed to resonate with specific audiences. The ability to create highly relevant content for each user could revolutionize how we consume media and information.

17. Workplace Automation and Productivity

AI-Powered Automation. Businesses will continue to utilize AI to automate a wide range of tasks across various industries, from routine data entry and customer service to more complex activities such as financial analysis and legal research. Going forward, AI systems could take on even more specialized roles, such as managing supply chains and optimizing business operations. This increased automation could lead to higher productivity and efficiency, but it also raises concerns about job displacement and the need for workforce reskilling. In the legal field, AI already helps attorneys draft documents, do legal research, review documents, organize materials for discovery, and with trial preparation. AI-enabled practice management applications help with running legal offices, collecting and recording information, and even providing receptionist services.

An early version of ChatGPT (ChatGPT-3) took and passed law school exams without ever attending a day of law school. It did not, however, pass the bar exam administered to it, but many people who finish law school also fail the bar the first time they take it. A later iteration, ChatGPT-4, still without the benefit of a bar review course or a day of law school, successfully passed the Uniform Bar Exam with a score of 297, besting 90% of the human examinees who all attended law school. On the other hand, lawyers have been burned by filing AI-authored briefs that cite fake (hallucinated) cases.

ChatGPT also passed the CPA exam on its second try and has passed or nearly passed all three components of the U.S. Medical Licensing Exam. Does this mean we will soon have bot lawyers, bot doctors, and bot accountants? Does it mean we will have special licensing categories for AI-powered assistants, similar to those for physician assistants, nurse practitioners, and nurses? Does it mean we will use (and bill) them as unlicensed assistants, as we do with interns? Time will tell. As they say, *"Que Sera, Sera."*

Enhanced Decision-Making. AI will help businesses make informed decisions by analyzing large datasets and providing actionable insights. AI-powered decision support systems could help executives predict market trends, optimize pricing strategies, and identify new growth opportunities. These systems will likely grow increasingly user-friendly, enabling non-experts to leverage AI for decision-making.

18. Augmented Reality (AR) and Virtual Reality (VR)

AI-Enhanced AR/VR Experiences. AI will enhance Augmented Reality (AR) and Virtual Reality (VR) experiences, making them more immersive and interactive. AI can create realistic virtual environments, generate lifelike avatars, and tailor virtual experiences to user behavior and preferences. This could lead to advancements in virtual tourism, training simulations, and remote collaboration.

Personalized Learning and Training. AI-driven AR/VR platforms have the potential to revolutionize education and training by offering personalized learning experiences. These platforms could adapt content to the learner's pace and style, offer real-time feedback, and simulate real-world scenarios for hands-on practice. This could prove particularly valuable in fields such as medicine, engineering, and vocational training.

Virtual Assistants. We have transitioned from the simple yet helpful days of Apple's Siri® and Google's Alexa® to a new generation of digital sidekicks, such as Microsoft's Copilot®, which packs some serious smarts. If you have not tried Copilot yet, take a close look. The free version offers a glimpse, but it comes with a catch: no integration with Microsoft Office, which compares to having a car without wheels. **A word of caution:** AI frequently extracts information from data it processes for the developer's use and the program's enhanced evolution. Often, developers extract more data and use it more freely from unpaid users than paid subscribers. Perhaps this *quid pro quo* means there is no "free" AI. Under any circumstances, due to their ethical obligations respecting the preservation of confidentiality, lawyers should factor this trade-off into their decision-making. Before choosing an AI tool, investigate its policies regarding data usage.

The leap from Siri and Alexa to powerhouses like Microsoft's Copilot showcases just how far AI has come in boosting our productivity and creativity. With GenAI under the hood, Copilot can assist programmers by generating code, identifying bugs, and even suggesting improvements, all while seamlessly integrating with the Microsoft Office Suite®. Copilot did not come to send Siri or Alexa into retirement just yet, but it sure hints at the future of virtual assistants. These classic helpers will either have to level up with new GenAI capabilities or risk becoming relics as more advanced, versatile bots emerge.

19. Concerns Moving Forward

The development and use of GenAI and ChatGPT involve a myriad of immediate and far-reaching moral and ethical issues. Moral concerns often revolve around broader societal impacts, including issues of autonomy, cultural diversity, and environmental sustainability. Ethical concerns center on the responsibilities of developers, deployers, and users to ensure that AI is designed and deployed in a manner that is fair, transparent, secure, and aligned with human and societal values.

19.1. Moral Issues

Autonomy and Human Dignity. The potential erosion of human independence and dignity poses a fundamental moral concern. As AI systems become increasingly capable of mimicking human interactions, they create a risk that people may over-rely on AI for decision-making, potentially undermining their own critical thinking and judgment. For instance, if an AI system provides legal advice or medical diagnoses, users might follow this advice without fully understanding its nuances, thereby diminishing their agency and the importance of human expertise. This raises questions about the moral responsibility to preserve human dignity and ensure that AI serves as a tool to augment human capabilities rather than replace them.

Cultural Impact and Homogenization. GenAI has the power to influence culture by reflecting the biases inherent in its training data. If AI-generated content takes over, we risk dominant narratives overshadowing diverse voices and perspectives. Imagine a world where AI's repetitive themes start to flatten the vibrant spectrum of human creativity, nudging us toward a more uniform cultural landscape. This raises a serious question: what role should we allow AI to play in shaping our cultural norms and values, potentially erasing the rich diversity that makes society so dynamic? It poses a moral puzzle, with high stakes for the future of creativity, if not society.

Environmental Impact. AI may be brilliant, but it also consumes a significant amount of energy. Training those massive models requires a staggering amount of computational power, resulting in a substantial carbon footprint. As AI continues to evolve, we face another moral dilemma: how do we balance the incredible benefits of AI with its environmental cost? Developers and deployers face pressure to make AI more sustainable. Finding the sweet spot between innovation and eco-responsibility will prove crucial for the planet's long-term health. What value does a super-smart AI have if it comes at too great an expense to the planet it serves?

Mental Health and Well-Being. As AI slides deeper into our personal and social lives, it raises concerns about mental health and well-being. Using AI in social media, for example, can exacerbate issues like addiction, anxiety, and depression by fostering environments that prioritize engagement, sometimes at the cost of well-being. Consider AI systems that mimic human emotions; while they can be friendly (even charming) companions, they also risk fostering emotional dependency, leaving us wondering if our connection to machines does more harm than good. Ultimately, AI's impact on mental health introduces yet another layer to our moral maze.

Automation and Job Loss. Automating tasks through AI will likely lead to job displacement in some industries. We need to prepare the workforce and address the effects that job displacement might have on our economy and our social structure. As a society, we need to consider what to do about the displaced workers, their potential futures, and their economic security, as well as the lost rungs of the skills and personal development ladder that leads people up from entry positions. For example, GenAI has the capacity to generate content that can replace some of the work done by writers, journalists, lawyers, teachers, and other professionals who rely on language skills. This can create opportunities for new forms of creativity and communication, but also challenge the quality, credibility, and accountability of the generated content. It can affect the livelihoods, identities, and well-being of those who may lose their jobs or face increased competition due to GenAI. We must ensure that we use GenAI to augment, rather than replace, human capabilities, and that GenAI comes with adequate education, training, and social support for the affected workers.

19.2. Ethical Concerns

We need to ensure the ethical and responsible development of AI. This means keeping algorithms transparent, avoiding bias, and having human oversight at every turn. AI has no moral compass; it is not immoral, just completely amoral. We need to keep that in mind, especially when using AI for sensitive tasks like legal work or handling confidential information. AI has already helped a few attorneys stumble over ethical lines, despite its uncanny ability to write at or above the level of many seasoned lawyers. The catch? Nobody told GenAI that it should not fabricate cases or misapply them. Its impressive language skills come without the judgment or reasoning skills we would expect from an attorney.

Some attorneys thought it would be clever to let AI handle their research, draft briefs, and cite authorities, then file those documents in court without confirming the accuracy or even the legitimacy of the citations. A few of these legal eagles tried to dodge accountability by keeping their AI reliance secret. Simply put, they tried to mislead the court to avoid trouble. The lessons here practically jump off the page: (1) as an attorney, own your work, (2) avoid lying to the court unless you seek professional hot water, and (3) never submit AI-generated work without giving every citation the human sniff test. Or, as President Reagan put it: "trust, but verify."

As attorneys, we have ethical obligations to safeguard client confidential communications and confidentiality. With AI systems collecting and analyzing mountains of data, we need to exercise extra caution about the client information we input into AI-powered systems, from personal details to case specifics. GenAI continually scrapes information to grow more. It does not care much about the source of the information. Case in point: In 2024, the U.S. House of Representatives banned Microsoft Copilot from all House staff computers because the Office of Cybersecurity expressed concerns that Copilot might share confidential House data with unapproved cloud services. Copilot, the ultimate virtual assistant, integrates GenAI at a level we have not seen before.

19.3. Other Considerations and Dangers

Accuracy. While AI assistants can significantly enhance productivity and streamline access to information, concerns about accuracy remain a significant issue. These systems, though robust, can sometimes generate responses that are outdated, incomplete, or factually incorrect, especially when dealing with complex, evolving, or nuanced topics. Errors may arise from limitations in training data, misinterpretation of user intent, or the inability to verify real-time facts. As a result, users must approach AI-generated content with a critical eye, verifying important information through trusted sources, especially in high-stakes contexts like legal advice, healthcare, or academic research. Ultimately, we should view AI as a helpful tool, not a substitute for human judgment or expertise.

Fairness. AI can inherit biases from the data on which it trains. Those biases can influence the outcomes selected by the AI model. For example, GenAI can generate text that reflects the stereotypes, prejudices, or discrimination of the data sources it uses, which may harm the reputation, dignity, or rights of certain groups or individuals. It can also produce misleading or inaccurate information that can affect its users' or readers' decisions or actions. For example, a recent article in *Science Advances* informs that AI models used to read chest x-rays fail to accurately detect life-threatening diseases in Blacks and women.[1] We need to ensure that AI trains on diverse and representative data and that human experts evaluate and test the system for fairness, before and during its deployment.

1. Meredith Wadman, *AI Models Scanning Chest X-rays Miss Disease in Black and Female Patients*, SCIENCE (Jan. 11, 2024), https://www.science.org/content/article/ai-models-scanning-chest-x-rays-miss-disease-black-female-patients.

Transparency and Explainability. The ethical use of AI requires that we understand what AI can do and how it accomplishes its tasks. Unfortunately, many AI models operate like "black boxes," where even the experts can't fully see what's happening inside. Enter explainable AI. These systems utilize transparency and provide insights that developers and deployers can (in theory) trust and verify, enabling us to understand and rely on their outcomes.

"Know Thyself." A Greek philosophical maxim, traditionally attributed to Socrates and inscribed on the wall of the Temple of Apollo in Delphi, has spoken to us repeatedly throughout history. The concept of self-examination is found in many religions and various art forms. Shakespeare wrote about it when he penned: "To thine own self be true" (spoken by Polonius to his son, Laertes). Hamlet Act 1, Scene 3. While not tracking directly to AI, the ancient Greek saying opens the door to an important concept. Perhaps in today's world, Socrates might say, "Know thy AI." To protect yourself and your clients and satisfy your ethical obligations as an attorney, you need to know the AI with which you equip your practice. That means you must learn how it operates, particularly regarding data management, security, and protection. Knowing your AI requires, *inter alia,* that you carefully read the terms of service/use agreements associated with the AI. Consider terms of use agreements as treasure maps leading diligent readers to service limitations and weaknesses that require management, or perhaps dissuading you from adopting a particular tool.

Data Privacy and Ownership. AI development requires the ethical management of data. The models at the core of AI tools rely on vast amounts of data, including user-supplied data, which raises a Pandora's box of questions regarding privacy, consent, and ownership. Users have the right to know what data the AI collects, as well as how the system collects it, uses it, and stores it. More importantly, users should have control over their personal information. Ethical AI development and deployment must prioritize data protection and user consent, particularly in an era where data breaches and misuse dominate daily headlines.

Security and Misuse. Malicious actors can exploit GenAI to create deepfakes, spread disinformation, or develop malicious software, resulting in security threats and other forms of abuse. Developers and deployers have an ethical responsibility to implement safeguards that prevent AI's misuse. This includes establishing guidelines for the ethical use of AI, conducting regular audits, and collaborating with policymakers to develop regulations that curb the harmful applications of AI technology.

Long-Term Implications and Existential Risk. The long-term implications of AI development also raise profound ethical questions. As AI advances, we must concern ourselves with its potential to surpass human intelligence, leading to scenarios where AI could act autonomously in ways detrimental to humanity. This existential risk requires careful ethical consideration, focusing on developing AI in ways that align with human values and ensure that AI remains under human control.

GenAI as a Facilitator of Criminal Activities

GenAI holds incredible potential for positive applications, but it also presents significant risks, particularly in its potential use to support or facilitate criminal activities. The capabilities of GenAI in creating realistic text, images, audio, and video have sparked concerns about its misuse in scams, deepfakes, and other malicious activities. Some key risks associated with generative AI and its potential to aid in criminal behavior follow:

Facilitating Scams and Fraud. Bad actors can use GenAI models to create highly convincing phishing emails, fraudulent messages, and social engineering schemes. These AI-generated communications can mimic human language patterns with such precision that it becomes increasingly difficult for recipients to distinguish between legitimate and fraudulent messages.

Phishing Schemes. AI-generated messages have taken phishing to a new level, effortlessly imitating official corporate emails and luring recipients into sharing sensitive information, such as passwords, financial details, or PINs. AI-enhanced scams follow familiar patterns, but are slicker and more convincing than the traditional phishing attempts, making them far trickier to spot. With AI pulling the strings, familiar warning signs fade, turning every inbox into a potential minefield for unsuspecting eyes.

Spear Phishing. By analyzing an individual's online presence and communications, bad actors can use GenAI to create highly personalized phishing attempts tailored to the victim's interests and behaviors, increasing the likelihood of success.

Automated Scam Calls and Bots. Automated scam calls just leveled up, thanks to generative AI. Now, instead of the clunky robocall of yesteryear, we have bots that can sound like your bank, a government agency, or even a coworker, friend, or relative, complete with real-time responses. These AI-powered voices can hold entire conversations, making scams more believable and, unfortunately, more common.

Creation of Deepfakes. One of GenAI's more unsettling talents, creating deepfakes, gives rise to serious criminal potential. A deepfake is realistic, synthetic media where AI replaces a person in an existing image or video with someone else's likeness or in an audio clip of someone known to or respected by the listener saying things the supposed speaker never said. Imagine watching a video of someone who appears to be a public figure or even someone you know, only to discover it is an AI-crafted illusion. Separating the real from the fake keeps getting harder, raising questions about trust in what we see and hear.

Manipulating Public Figures. GenAI's deepfake abilities mean we can now see and hear public figures "saying" or "doing" things they never actually did, all with eerie realism. This digital sleight of hand has enormous potential to spread misinformation, sway public opinion, or damage reputations with just a few clicks. In a world where seeing used to be believing, deepfakes make us rethink that truism.

Personal Blackmail. On a more personal level, AI deepfake technology can fabricate compromising videos of individuals, opening the door to blackmail and harassment. For victims, disproving the video's authenticity can prove an uphill battle, leading to serious emotional, financial, and social fallout.

Spreading Disinformation. GenAI can mass-produce fake news, propaganda, and all sorts of misleading content with unsettling efficiency. This supercharged disinformation machine raises huge red flags, especially during political campaigns, social movements, and crises, when a well-placed lie can spread faster than the truth. In the wrong hands, AI can turn rumors into "facts" at lightning speed, amplifying confusion and mistrust just when we most need clarity.

Fake News Websites. AI has the power to create entire websites packed with fake news articles that look credible. These polished sites can easily mislead the public, subtly (or not-so-subtly) pushing specific agendas under the guise of legitimate journalism. It's like having a well-dressed imposter in the newsroom, churning out stories designed to misinform while looking every bit the real deal.

Social Media Manipulation. AI-generated content can inundate social media platforms with posts that appear authentic, making it challenging for users and even platform algorithms to distinguish between real and fake content. This can lead to the rapid spread of disinformation.

Automating Malware Creation. AI can generate new variants of malware designed to bypass detection systems. This includes creating polymorphic malware that changes its code structure each time it infects a new system, making it more challenging for antivirus software to identify and neutralize the malicious code.

Enabling Identity Theft. Bad actors can use AI to create fake identification documents that are almost indistinguishable from real ones.

Synthetic Identity Fraud. AI can generate realistic but entirely fictitious identities, complete with social security numbers, credit histories, and other credentials. Bad actors can then utilize these synthetic identities to facilitate fraudulent activities, such as opening bank accounts or obtaining loans in the name of the fictitious person.

Document Forgery. AI can generate realistic fake documents, such as passports, driver's licenses, and certificates. These documents can facilitate illegal activities, such as illegal immigration, money laundering, and terrorism.

19.4. Generative AI as an Existential Threat

AI's increasing power and flexibility raise concerns about the potential for misuse or unintended consequences that could pose existential risks to our society and population. Industry and governments have raised these concerns and the need for regulation to mitigate these risks. That risk mitigation will require responsible AI design and development, as well as the implementation of effective monitoring and governance. The term "existential threat" refers to risks that could lead to the extinction of humanity or cause irreversible and catastrophic damage to civilization. When applied to GenAI, this concept encompasses various scenarios where misuse, unintended consequences, or even AI's independent evolution could alter or endanger human existence. Unregulated AI can have profound implications for democracy and the security and autonomy of our society.

The following discussion raises several potential existential threats to our society. That discussion does not predict that any of them will occur; it only notes the possibility and presents it for your consideration. Hopefully, it will capture your interest and attention sufficiently to encourage you to actively engage in and demand the ethical management of artificial intelligence. We must all concern ourselves with this issue and take responsibility for guarding against the improper development and deployment of artificial intelligence.

Autonomous Decision-Making and Loss of Human Control. The rise of autonomous decision-making systems brings a sci-fi-worthy risk: what happens if they go rogue? As AI becomes more sophisticated, the possibility arises that AI-enabled systems could make choices that spell trouble for humanity, whether intentionally or unintentionally. Imagine an AI tasked with optimizing resource use, deciding that humans are too "resource-hungry" for its liking and, without a second thought (because AI doesn't think or reason), taking drastic steps to fix the "problem." It serves as a chilling reminder that with this great power comes the great responsibility to keep those circuits in check.

Runaway AI. This scenario involves an AI system becoming so advanced that it can improve itself independently, leading to an intelligence explosion. If such an AI system operated without sufficient ethical constraints or human oversight, it could pursue goals not aligned with human values, potentially leading to catastrophic outcomes. Drawing a page from the movies, think of Skynet in the Terminator franchise.

Weaponization of AI. The weaponization of AI poses another potentially significant existential threat. AI can enable autonomous weapons systems, cyber warfare tools, and other technologies deployable at a scale and speed beyond human control. The potential for AI-driven warfare, where machines operate without judgment about life and death, poses a profound moral and existential dilemma. Always fans of learning life lessons from art, we suggest that you might again, think in terms of Skynet for an idea of what that might look like. To learn a related lesson from another film, consider the movie "War Games," where the AI continued to engage and escalate a conflict despite the potential for massive loss of human life. The machine only stopped playing its game when it concluded that all paths to successfully prosecuting the conflict would ultimately lead to its own destruction.

Global Arms Race. The development of AI-enabled weapons could lead to (and probably already has started) a global arms race, with nations competing to build increasingly sophisticated and lethal AI-powered weapons systems. Such an arms race increases the likelihood of real conflicts, accidents, and escalation to full-scale wars that could threaten civilization, and exact a high cost in human lives, perhaps even threatening continued human existence.

Mass Unemployment and Societal Disruption. While not as immediately catastrophic as other threats, the potential for AI to cause mass unemployment and societal disruption at both economic and social levels poses a significant existential risk. Of the scenarios discussed in this section, it is the most likely to occur. As AI systems grow increasingly capable of performing tasks traditionally done by humans, such as writing, programming, and even creative work, they create a real risk of rendering large segments of the population economically obsolete.

Economic Collapse. If widespread unemployment leads to financial collapse, the resulting social instability could have far-reaching consequences. Civil unrest, political upheaval, and the breakdown of social order could follow, potentially leading to a collapse of civilization.

Loss of Human Identity and Purpose. As AI becomes more integrated into everyday life, it has the potential to erode human identity and purpose. If AI systems can replicate or surpass human creativity, intelligence, and emotional capacity, humans might struggle to find meaning in their existence.

Existential Nihilism. The idea that machines could render humans obsolete leads to existential nihilism, the belief that life lacks inherent meaning or value. This belief could lead to widespread psychological distress, apathy, and a decline in motivation to preserve and advance human civilization.

Manipulation and Control of Society. Bad actors and power-hungry leaders could deploy AI systems to manipulate and control society in ways that undermine democracy, freedom, civil rights, and human rights. AI systems could create highly persuasive propaganda, deepfakes, and misinformation campaigns that manipulate public opinion and influence elections. Additionally, governments and individual bad actors could use AI to surveil and control populations, giving authoritarian regimes unprecedented power.

Totalitarian AI States. The combination of AI-driven surveillance and control mechanisms could facilitate establishing totalitarian AI-driven states, where AI systems constantly monitor and control citizens. This could lead to the loss of individual freedoms and the establishment of a dystopian society that severely restricts human autonomy.

Governance and Controls for AI

As AI becomes increasingly capable of creating and generating various types of content, data, and code, we must ensure that it does not harm or violate our rights and values. The safe development and use of AI require a comprehensive governance framework encompassing regulation, independent oversight, transparency, security, public engagement, and responsible innovation. By implementing these controls, society can harness the benefits of generative AI while minimizing the risks associated with its misuse or unintended consequences. As AI evolves, we need ongoing dialogue and collaboration among stakeholders to ensure that AI serves the public good and aligns with our collective values.

The following recommendations have a somewhat utopian perspective. Consider these suggestions as a glimpse into what should and hopefully will happen. Do not think of this as an exhaustive list or believe that other options don't exist. Look at it as a starting point that, hopefully, helps open the door to broader discussion.

We need effective and appropriate governance mechanisms for AI, including laws, policies, standards, and best practices. The governance landscape for AI remains immature and fragmented, with different countries and organizations adopting different approaches and perspectives. As a society, we require a more coordinated and collaborative effort among stakeholders to harmonize and align the governance frameworks and principles for AI, particularly for GenAI, which has the potential to disrupt and transform numerous domains and industries. Our perception of what that system should look like follows.

20. Regulatory Frameworks

National and International Regulation. Building AI requires a robust regulatory framework that is effective both domestically and internationally. On the national level, governments need to establish clear guidelines, crafting regulations that define the rules for developing, deploying, and utilizing AI. Key areas? Data privacy, bias-busting, transparency, and accountability all top the list. But it does not stop there; we need international teamwork to create harmonized standards and avoid regulatory "loophole hopping," where companies relocate to more AI-friendly jurisdictions with looser rules. A well-coordinated regulatory approach can keep AI innovation on the right side of the line, everywhere. We note with concern the fact that the international political situation, much like the national situation, reflects vast differences in perspective. Accomplishing these goals requires the identification of common ground that serves as a balance point for regulations. Identification of that common ground may prove difficult, but it remains essential and might also facilitate progress in resolving many issues beyond AI regulation.

Ethical AI Standards. Regulators must develop, adopt, and enforce ethical AI standards that guide development. These standards would ensure that designers create AI systems that respect human rights, avoid discrimination, and protect individual privacy. Ethical AI guidelines, such as those proposed by the European Union's AI Act, can serve as a blueprint for developing AI systems prioritizing safety and fairness.

20.1. Independent Oversight Bodies

AI Ethics Boards. We should establish independent oversight bodies, such as AI ethics boards, to monitor the development and deployment of AI. These boards would include experts in AI, ethics, law, economics, and human rights, offering a multidisciplinary perspective on the potential impacts of AI technologies. They would review AI projects, assess their ethical implications, and provide recommendations to ensure that the development of AI systems aligns with shared societal values.

Audit Mechanisms. We must implement robust audit mechanisms to ensure transparency and accountability in AI's development, deployment, and use. We should regularly audit AI systems to verify compliance with regulatory requirements and ethical standards. These audits should assess various aspects of AI systems, including their decision-making processes, data sources, and potential biases. Independent auditors should have the authority to recommend changes or halt the deployment of AI systems failing to meet the required standards.

20.2. Transparency and Explainability

Mandatory Transparency Reports. We should require companies developing AI to publish transparency reports detailing how they train their AI systems, how these systems operate, and what data they utilize. These reports should provide the public and regulators with insights into the inner workings of AI systems, helping to build trust and ensure the responsible use of AI technologies.

Explainability Requirements. We should require designers to create AI systems, particularly those used in high-stakes environments like healthcare or criminal justice, with explainability in mind. Explainability refers to understanding and interpreting how an AI system makes decisions. Accountability requires that AI developers create explainable models that non-experts can understand, allowing affected individuals to challenge decisions made by AI systems.

20.3. Security and Safety Protocols

Robust Cybersecurity Measures. We must employ robust cybersecurity measures to protect AI systems from unauthorized access and misuse. "AI systems" must be viewed broadly in this context to include safeguarding the AI models, the data on which they train, and the systems with which they interact (upstream and downstream of the AI features). We should require developers and deployers to implement security protocols such as encryption, access controls, and intrusion detection systems to minimize the risk of cyberattacks. Best practices should expect users to do the same thing.

Safety Testing and Validation. We should require comprehensive safety testing and validation as a precondition to deploying AI systems. This involves stress-testing AI models under various conditions to identify potential failure points and vulnerabilities. Safety testing should be designed to confirm that AI systems behave as expected and do not produce harmful or unintended outcomes. We must plan for continuous validation processes during the AI system's lifecycle to adapt to changing environments and evolving threats.

20.4. Public Engagement and Education

Stakeholder Involvement. Effective AI governance requires the involvement of diverse stakeholders, including the public, industry representatives, academia, and civil society organizations. Public consultations and participatory design processes can help ensure the development of AI systems in ways that reflect society's needs and concerns. Involving stakeholders in decision-making can also foster trust and legitimacy in AI governance.

Education and Awareness Programs. Governments and organizations should invest in education and awareness programs that inform the public about AI's benefits and risks. That will help individuals make informed decisions about their interactions with AI systems by enhancing digital literacy and increasing public understanding of AI technologies. Education programs can also prepare the workforce for anticipated AI-induced changes, reducing the potential for uncontrolled job displacement and social disruption.

20.5. Responsible Innovation and Research

Ethical Research Practices. AI research and development should adhere to ethical guidelines, prioritizing humanity's long-term well-being. This includes conducting impact assessments to evaluate the societal implications of AI research and adopting a precautionary approach when dealing with uncertain or potentially harmful outcomes. We should encourage research institutions and companies to share findings that contribute to the safe and ethical development of AI.

Open Collaboration and Knowledge Sharing. Promoting open collaboration and knowledge sharing within the AI research community can lead to better governance outcomes. By sharing best practices, datasets, and tools, researchers can collectively address the challenges associated with AI. Open collaboration also facilitates the identification and mitigation of risks before they become widespread.

Governments and organizations have begun developing guidelines and regulations for AI to ensure its safe, fair, and accountable deployment. Those processes remain in their infancy and do not yet offer any significant protection. More regulations will come in time, but for now, we remain in the AI equivalent of the Wild West of the 1800s.

Some of the existing and emerging governance initiatives for AI include:

- The European Union has proposed a comprehensive regulatory framework for AI, including a risk-based approach, a list of prohibited and high-risk AI practices, and specific requirements for transparency, accountability, and human oversight. The proposal aims to foster innovation and trust in AI by creating a European AI Board, a network of national AI authorities, and a voluntary labeling scheme for trustworthy AI.
- The Organization for Economic Co-operation and Development (OECD) has developed a set of principles for artificial intelligence. So far, 42 countries have endorsed these principles to promote human-centered, responsible, and inclusive AI. The principles cover fairness, transparency, safety, security, and accountability. The OECD also provides policy guidance and best practices on various aspects of AI, such as data governance, digital security, and education.
- The Global Partnership on AI (GPAI), a multi-stakeholder initiative, has brought together experts from government, industry, civil society, and academia to advance the responsible and human-centric development and use of AI. The GPAI has four working groups that focus on different themes: data governance, responsible AI, innovation and commercialization, and the future of work.
- The Partnership on AI (PAI), a nonprofit organization, aims to ensure the responsible use of AI for the benefit of humanity. The PAI has over 100 partners from various

sectors and regions, conducting research and projects on topics such as fairness, transparency, accountability, safety, and the social and societal impact of AI.

- The IEEE Global Initiative on Ethics of Autonomous and Intelligent Systems, a global network of experts and stakeholders, develops standards and guidelines for the ethical design and implementation of AI and related technologies. The initiative has produced a document titled "Ethically Aligned Design," which provides a set of principles and recommendations for developing ethical AI.

These are examples of the governance efforts underway at various levels and domains to address the challenges and opportunities that AI presents. However, there remains considerable room for improvement and coordination among these initiatives, as well as for the involvement of more diverse and representative voices and perspectives.

As AI evolves and becomes more powerful and pervasive, the need for effective governance will continue to increase, requiring greater attention and action from all stakeholders.

Glossary

Partial Glossary of AI-Related Terms

This glossary includes terms commonly encountered in articles and discussions about AI and GenAI. The Glossary does not present a comprehensive list of all terms associated with AI or GenAI.

-A-

Adversarial Example. Adversarial examples are intentionally designed inputs to machine learning models that an attacker has created to cause the model to make a mistake. These sneaky tweaks are like tiny, invisible edits to legitimate inputs that trick AI into making big mistakes. While humans may not notice a thing, these subtle changes can throw AI off course, leading to unexpected or incorrect results.

Algorithm. A step-by-step set of instructions or rules for solving a specific problem or performing a specific task. AI uses algorithms to train models on data, optimize performance, and make predictions or classifications based on new input data.

Artificial General Intelligence (AGI). AGI refers to highly autonomous systems that outperform humans at most economically valuable work. Unlike narrow AI, AGI would possess general cognitive abilities and could apply intelligence to many tasks. At the time of this Handbook's printing, AGI is not known to have been achieved.

Artificial Intelligence (AI). Artificial intelligence refers to the development of computer systems capable of performing tasks that typically require human intelligence. These tasks include learning from experience, understanding and generating language, recognizing patterns, solving problems, and making decisions. AI encompasses a range of technologies, including machine learning, neural networks, and natural language processing.

Artificial Neural Network (ANN). An artificial neural network is a computational model inspired by how biological neural networks in the human brain process information. ANNs consist of interconnected nodes (neurons) that work together to solve specific problems, particularly in tasks like pattern recognition and data classification.

Autonomous. We describe a machine as autonomous if it can perform its task or tasks without human intervention. Autonomous systems, such as self-driving cars and drones, use sensors feeding data to AI to perceive their environment, make decisions, and execute actions independently.

-B-

Backpropagation. Backpropagation is a key algorithm used in training artificial neural networks. It involves adjusting the neurons' weights based on the error rate of the previous epoch (iteration) to minimize the difference between the predicted and actual outputs.

Bayesian Networks. Bayesian networks are graphical models representing the probabilistic relationships among a set of variables. They support reasoning under uncertainty, allowing for calculating conditional probabilities and making inferences about unknown variables.

Bias in AI. Bias in AI occurs when an AI system produces results that are systematically prejudiced due to erroneous assumptions in the machine learning process. Bias can arise from training data or design choices that reflect existing prejudices or from flawed algorithms.

Big Data. Large and complex datasets not easily managed or analyzed with traditional data processing tools. AI leverages big data for training and decision-making, as the vast amounts of data improve the accuracy and robustness of AI models. Big data sources include, for example, social media, sensor data, and transactional records.

-C-

Chatbot. A program designed to communicate with people through text or voice commands in a way that mimics human-to-human conversation. Chatbots use natural language processing (NLP) to recognize user inputs and generate appropriate responses. Developers use them in customer service, virtual assistants, and interactive applications.

ChatGPT. A family of neural network models trained on large-scale conversational data to generate natural and engaging responses. ChatGPT models use a transformer architecture and a self-attention mechanism to capture long-range dependencies and context information in dialogue.

Computer Vision. Computer vision is a field of AI that enables computers to interpret and produce output based on visual information from the world. Applications include image and video recognition, object detection, and facial recognition.

Conversational AI. The area of AI that deals with creating chatbots, virtual assistants, and other systems capable of natural language interaction.

Convolutional Neural Network (CNN). A type of deep neural network primarily used for processing structured grid data, such as images. CNNs are particularly effective in image recognition and classification tasks due to their ability to automatically detect and learn spatial hierarchies of features from input data.

-D-

Data Augmentation. Remixing existing data or generating new data to improve machine learning models.

Data Mining. Data mining involves seeking and discovering patterns, trends, and insights in large datasets. Data mining techniques include clustering, classification, regression, and association rule learning. Businesses and researchers widely use it in business intelligence, market research, and scientific research to extract valuable information from data.

Deep Learning. A subfield of machine learning using artificial neural networks, specifically deep neural networks, to model and solve complex problems. Deep learning algorithms can automatically learn features from raw data, achieving state-of-the-art performance in tasks such as image and speech recognition, natural language processing, and autonomous driving.

-E-

Ethical AI. Principles and guidelines to ensure AI systems are fair, transparent, and unbiased.

Explainable AI (XAI). Explainable AI refers to methods and techniques in AI that make the decision-making process of models more transparent and understandable to humans. XAI is crucial for ensuring trust and accountability in AI systems, especially in high-stakes applications like healthcare and finance.

-F-

Federated Learning. A machine learning approach where models are trained across multiple decentralized devices or servers holding local data samples, without exchanging them. Federated learning enhances data privacy and security by keeping data localized.

Fine-Tuning. Adapting a pre-trained model (like GPT) to a specific task or domain by training it on task-specific data.

-G-

General (Strong) AI. AI with human-level intelligence capable of performing any intellectual task a human can perform. True general AI remains a long-term goal and would require systems to possess reasoning, problem-solving abilities, and general cognitive functions similar to humans.

Generative Adversarial Network (GAN). A type of generative model that consists of two competing neural networks: a generator and a discriminator. The generator tries to create realistic samples from a latent space, while the discriminator tries to distinguish between real and fake samples. Tasks such as image synthesis, style transfer, and super-resolution use GANs.

Generative AI (GenAI). Artificial intelligence systems that create new content such as text, images, audio, and video. GenAI models data to build their own representations, allowing the creation of new, realistic, and often highly customized outputs. Examples include language models like GPT-3, image generation models like DALL-E, and music generation models.

Gradient Descent. Gradient descent is an optimization algorithm that minimizes the loss function in machine learning models. By iteratively moving towards the steepest descent of the gradient, the algorithm identifies the optimal parameters that minimize the model's error.

-H-

Hallucination. Outputs generated by AI systems that are fabricated rather than grounded in reality. Hallucination occurs when AI models, particularly generative models, produce content not based on the input data or context provided. For example, a text generator might invent fictional events and present them as facts.

Hyperparameter Tuning. Optimizing the parameters of a machine learning model that are not learned from the training data. These include learning rate, batch size, and the number of layers in a neural network. Practical hyperparameter tuning can significantly improve model performance.

-I-

Internet of Things (IoT). The Internet of Things refers to the network of physical objects embedded with sensors, software, and other technologies that connect and exchange data with other devices and systems over the internet. Developers often integrate AI with IoT devices to enable intelligent decision-making and automation.

-K-

K-means Clustering. A popular unsupervised learning algorithm used for partitioning data into K distinct clusters based on their features. It iteratively assigns data points to clusters and recalculates the centroids to minimize the within-cluster variance.

Knowledge Representation. A field in AI concerned with how knowledge can be represented symbolically and manipulated in an automated way by reasoning algorithms. Common forms include semantic networks, frames, and ontologies.

-L-

Language Model. A type of AI model that predicts the next word or sequence of words in a sentence based on context.

Large Language Model (LLM). Large language models (LLMs) are advanced artificial intelligence systems that process, understand, and generate humanlike text. LLMs are based on deep learning techniques and trained on massive datasets, usually containing billions of words from sources like websites, books, and articles. This extensive training enables LLMs to grasp the nuances of language, grammar, context, and even some aspects of general knowledge.

Latent Space. A high-dimensional space that represents the abstract features or hidden variables of a data set. Generative models often use latent spaces to encode the input data and generate new samples. Developers can also use latent spaces for dimensionality reduction, clustering, and visualization.

-M-

Machine Learning (ML). A subfield of AI that focuses on developing algorithms and models that enables computers to improve performance on a task through experience, without explicit programming. ML includes techniques like supervised learning, unsupervised learning, and reinforcement learning.

Markov Decision Process (MDP). A mathematical framework for modeling decision-making where outcomes are partly random and partly controlled by a decision-maker. Reinforcement learning uses MDPs to describe environments where agents learn optimal behaviors.

Mathematical Model. An abstract description of a concrete system using mathematical concepts and language. AI employs mathematical models to represent relationships between variables, simulate processes, and predict outcomes.

Metrics. Tools used to evaluate the performance of supervised learning models in tasks such as classification and regression. Standard metrics include accuracy, precision, recall, F1 score, mean squared error, and area under the ROC curve (AUC-ROC).

-N-

Narrow AI. Also known as weak AI, narrow AI is designed for specific tasks, such as virtual personal assistants (Siri, Alexa), recommendation systems, and chatbots. Narrow AI systems excel at particular tasks but lack general intelligence and cannot perform tasks outside their designed scope.

Natural Language Generation (NLG). A subfield of AI that focuses on generating coherent and contextually relevant text from structured data. Applications such as automated report writing, content creation, and conversational agents employ NLG systems.

Natural Language Processing (NLP). A subfield of artificial intelligence that deals with the interaction between computers and human languages. NLP involves tasks such as speech recognition, natural language understanding, natural language generation, sentiment analysis, and machine translation.

Neural Networks. Computer models inspired by the structure and function of the human brain, consisting of interconnected nodes (neurons). Various AI applications, including image and speech recognition, natural language processing, and game play, employ neural networks.

-O-

Overfitting. Overfitting occurs when a machine learning model learns the training data too well, including its noise and outliers, and performs poorly on new, unseen data. Regularization techniques and cross-validation are used to mitigate overfitting.

-P-

Preprocessing. Preprocessing transforms raw data into an efficient and effective format for machine learning models. Preprocessing steps include data cleaning, normalization, encoding categorical variables, and feature extraction.

Prompt. A prompt provides context to generative AI systems to produce a desired output. A prompt may be a text description, an image, or even samples of desired audio or video. Carefully engineered prompts guide the creative process while leveraging the model's knowledge.

-Q-

Quantum Computing. An area of computing focused on developing computer technology based on the principles of quantum theory. Quantum computers have the potential to solve certain problems significantly faster than classical computers, with a profound impact on fields such as cryptography and optimization.

-R-

Recurrent Neural Network (RNN). A type of neural network designed for processing sequential data. RNNs have connections that form directed cycles, allowing information to persist. They are widely used in time series prediction, natural language processing, and speech recognition.

Reinforcement Learning. A form of machine learning in which agents learn to decide by interacting with an environment and receiving rewards or penalties. Applications such as robotics, game playing, and autonomous vehicles utilize reinforcement learning.

-S-

Semi-Supervised Learning. A combination of supervised and unsupervised machine learning using both labeled and unlabeled data. Semi-supervised learning utilizes a large amount of unlabeled data, along with a small amount of labeled data, to enhance learning accuracy. It is particularly useful when labeling data is expensive or time-consuming.

Sentiment Analysis. Analyzing text to determine its sentiment or emotional tone. Social media monitoring, customer feedback analysis, and market research often use sentiment analysis to gauge public opinion and sentiment toward products, services, or topics.

Supervised Learning. A form of machine learning in which the model trains on a labeled dataset, learning to make predictions or decisions based on input data. Supervised learning tasks include classification, regression, and object detection.

Support Vector Machine (SVM). A supervised learning algorithm used for classification and regression tasks. SVMs work by finding the hyperplane that best separates the data points of different classes in the feature space.

Synthetic Data. Artificially generated data that mimics real-world data. Researchers use synthetic data to train AI models when real data is scarce, expensive to obtain, or contains sensitive information that requires protection.

-T-

Transfer Learning. A technique in machine learning where a pre-trained model developed for one task is adapted to a different but related task. Transfer learning reduces the need for large amounts of data and computational resources to train new models.

Transformer. A neural network architecture that uses multiple layers of self-attention and feed-forward connections to process sequential data. Transformers can handle long-term dependencies and parallelize computation better than recurrent or convolutional networks. Transformers are widely used in natural language processing, such as machine translation, text generation, and question answering.

Turing Test. Alan Turing proposed this test to determine whether a machine exhibits human-like intelligence. In the test, a human evaluator interacts with both a human and a machine without knowing which is which. The machine passes the Turing Test if the evaluator cannot reliably distinguish it from a human.

-U-

Underfitting. When a model is too simple to capture the underlying patterns in the data, resulting in poor performance on both the training and test data.

Unsupervised Learning. A form of machine learning in which the model learns patterns and structures in data without labeled examples. Unsupervised learning techniques include clustering, dimensionality reduction, and anomaly detection.

-V-

Variational Autoencoder (VAE). A type of generative model that uses neural networks to encode input data into a latent space and then decode it back to the original space. Image generation, data compression, and anomaly detection use VAEs.

Bibliography

Books

Ajay Agrawal, Joshua Gans & Avi Goldfarb, Prediction Machines: The Simple Economics of Artificial Intelligence (2018).

Ajay Agrawal, Joshua Gans & Avi Goldfarb, Prediction Machines, Updated and Expanded: The Simple Economics of Artificial Intelligence (2022).

Emily M. Bender & Alex Hanna, The AI Con: How to Fight Big Tech's Hype and Create the Future we Want (2025) (author interview by Monica Melton, *An Ex-Google AI Ethicist and a UW Professor Want You to Know AI Isn't What You Think It Is*, Bus. Insider (May 12, 2025, 11:09 AM ET), https://www.businessinsider.com/the-ai-con-emily-bender-alex-hanna-ai-hype-2025-5).

Numa Dhamani & Maggie Engler, Introduction to Generative AI (2024).

Pedro Domingos, The Master Algorithm: How the Quest for the Ultimate Learning Machine Will Remake Our World (2015).

Sharad Gandhi & Christian Ehl, Generative AI: The Future of Everything (2023) (recommended by Varun Saharawat, *Top 5 Books Every Generative AI Enthusiast Should Read in 2024*, PW Skills (Aug. 23, 2024), https://pwskills.com/blog/top-5-books-every-generative-ai-enthusiast-should-read-in-2024).

Amir Husain, Generative AI for Leaders (2023).

Ray Kurzweil, The Singularity Is Nearer: When We Merge with AI (2024).

Bernard Marr, Generative AI in Practice: 100+ Amazing Ways Generative Artificial Intelligence is Changing Business and Society (2024).

Ethan Mollick, Co-Intelligence: Living and Working with AI (2024).

Martin Musiol, Generative AI: Navigating the Course to the Artificial General Intelligence Future (2024).

David M. Patel, Artificial Intelligence & Generative AI for Beginners: The Complete Guide (2024).

Max Tegmark, Life 3.0: Being Human in the Age of Artificial Intelligence (2018).

Erica Thompson, Escape from Model Land: How Mathematical Models Can Lead Us Astray and What We Can Do About It (2022).

Articles and Reports

Jacob Andreas, Dan Klein & Sergey Levine, *Learning with Latent Language*, arXiv (Nov. 1, 2017), https://arxiv.org/abs/1711.00482.

Brian Basgen, *A Generative AI Primer*, EDUCAUSE Rev. (Aug. 15, 2023), https://er.educause.edu/articles/2023/8/a-generative-ai-primer.

Leah Chong et al., *Human Confidence in Artificial Intelligence and in Themselves: The Evolution and Impact of Confidence on Adoption of AI Advice*, 127 Computers in

Hum. Behav. 107,018 (2022), https://codesign.berkeley.edu/pdfs/papers/chong-aiconfidence-cihb.pdf.

Leah Chong et al., *The Evolution and Impact of Human Confidence in Artificial Intelligence and in Themselves on AI-Assisted Decision-Making in Design*, 145 J. Mech. Design 031, 401-1 (Mar. 2023), https://codesign.berkeley.edu/pdfs/papers/chong-evolution-jmd.pdf.

Roberto Gozalo-Brizuela & Eduardo C. Garrido-Merchán, *A Survey of Generative AI Applications*, arXiv (June 14, 2023), https://arxiv.org/abs/2306.02781.

Varun Magesh et al., *Hallucination-Free? Assessing the Reliability of Leading AI Legal Research Tools*, 22 J. Empirical Legal Stud. 216 (2025), https://doi.org/10.1111/jels.12413.

Frank Rose, '*Co-Intelligence' Review: Learning to Live with AI*, Wall St. J. (Apr. 3, 2024, 12:07 PM), https://www.wsj.com/arts-culture/books/co-intelligence-review-learning-to-live-with-ai-d5efb2fe.

Sandeep Singh Sengar et al., *Generative Artificial Intelligence: A Systematic Review and Applications*, Springer Nature Link (Aug. 14, 2024), https://doi.org/10.1007/s11042-024-20016-1.

Junhao Song, et al., *Generative Adversarial Networks: Bridging Art and Machine Intelligence*, arXiv (Feb. 9, 2025), https://arxiv.org/abs/2502.04116.

U.S. Gov't Accountability Off., GAO-25-107172, Artificial Intelligence: Generative AI's Environmental and Human Effects, Global Plastics Action Partnership (Apr. 2025), https://www.gao.gov/products/gao-25-107172.

Jason Wei et al., *Measuring Short-Form Factuality in Large Language Models*, OpenAI (undated), https://cdn.openai.com/papers/simpleqa.pdf.

Partial Listing of Resources Supporting the AI Glossary

AI Glossary: AI Terms, Moveworks, https://www.moveworks.com/us/en/resources/ai-terms-glossary (last visited Jun. 3, 2025).

Artificial Intelligence Glossary: Learn AI Vocabulary, Coursera (Apr. 16, 2025), https://www.coursera.org/resources/ai-terms.

Devyani Gajjar, *Artificial Intelligence (AI) Glossary*, UK Parliamentary Off. of Sci. & Tech. (Jan. 23, 2024), https://post.parliament.uk/artificial-intelligence-ai-glossary/.

Glossary of Terms: Generative AI Basics, MIT Sloan Sch. of Mgmt., https://mitsloanedtech.mit.edu/ai/basics/glossary/ (last visited Jun. 3, 2025).

ACKNOWLEDGEMENTS

This chapter was originally written for and published in Jeffrey Allen and Ashley Hallene's *Unlocking the Future: Leveraging Technology for Personal and Professional Success* (2025). It was substantially revised, rewritten, and updated for this Handbook.

I want to acknowledge the AI programs employed to help revise this chapter. I used OpenAI's ChatGPT and Microsoft's CoPilot applications to assist with portions of the text, and Microsoft Word's Editor, Grammarly, and WordRake in editing it. I personally generated each prompt used with CoPilot and ChatGPT, including a requirement for an originally generated product in each prompt. I also want to note that the editing process exemplified the optimal way to work with AI as it melded natural and artificial intelligence. The natural intelligence came from my self-editing, with a substantial contribution from my co-editor, Candace Jones, who supplied both natural intelligence and a different perspective to help develop this chapter.

Chapter 3

Understanding Technology—What Every Lawyer Needs to Know About the Cyber Network and Artificial Intelligence

Paul Rosenzweig and Bryson Bort

Lawyers pride themselves on being generalists. We often say that we can learn a topic quickly and well enough to embody it in a contract or present it to a jury. Whether the question is medical malpractice standards or the history of price supports for prunes, lawyers stand ready to dive right in.

Unfortunately, some lawyers seem to have a phobia about technical topics that bear on their own business operations. Countless attorneys look at the internet and, metaphorically, put their hands over their ears and mumble "nyah, nyah, nyah" in the hopes that someone else (the "IT guy" down the hall) will deal with the problem. That head-in-the-sand approach is no longer acceptable as a matter of professional responsibility. Every lawyer who uses modern cyber technology or artificial intelligence (AI) has an obligation—to clients, to partners, and to themselves—to understand, if only at a rudimentary level, how the cyber network[1] and AI work.

This short chapter is intended as a basic introduction to the topic. Readers will learn:

- The basic organization of the worldwide cyber network;
- The nature of cyber threats and vulnerabilities; and
- How cyber defensive systems and enterprises work.

1. The Growth of the Network

The internet as we know it is nearly 40 years old. The very first entries on the World Wide Web were made in the early 1980s. More broadly, the technology of the cyber network—the

1. In general, this chapter uses the phrase "computer network" or "cyber network" as a signal that the network is larger and broader than the "Internet" to which we are most accustomed. At its broadest, the internet encompasses all chip-enabled technology, including everything from servers that provide communications services to end-user devices like a connected home thermostat.

protocols that allow information to be transferred between two servers—is less than 50 years old. Put another way, the oldest partner in your firm probably remembers a time without personal computers, and your middle-aged partner can recall a time without the internet. Yet your newest associates were, in effect, born connected.

This sea change provides us an important context within which to situate our technical understanding. The explosive growth of the network lies at the heart of its penetration of modern economic activity, and also at the heart of our technological vulnerability. Consider that in 1973, the earliest network (which was exclusively run by educational and governmental institutions) had only 100 nodes on it.[2] That is, only 100 different servers or systems were connected to the network. Today there are so many nodes globally that we, quite literally, cannot count them.

The growth of the network has also been driven by the technological improvements that make its expansion feasible. Consider again: in the late 1980s, the United States government purchased the Cray XMP-1 supercomputer. It was, at the time, the fastest computer in existence. It was unique, and the government tasked it with super-hard computational problems, such as the development of mathematical models to predict climate change and the modeling of the structure of nuclear weapons. It ran at an unheard-of speed of more than 200 mega FLOPS per second, that is, more than 200 million calculations per second. The iPhone 12, released in 2020, was nearly 10 times faster than the XMP-1. Today's iPhone 16 Pro, released in fall 2024, is built with a computer chip reported to process 35 trillion operation-per-second, enabling faster and more efficient operation of Apple Inc.'s artificial intelligence systems.[3]

In other words, if you own a recent iPhone (or the equivalent Android phone), you have in your hand substantially more computing power than the most powerful computer in the world from the era of Ronald Reagan's presidency. That is not just an evolution of capability, it's a revolution. The change lies behind all of the many advantages of the network, like Google searches and Zappos next-day shipping. It is the technology that enabled the near instantaneous transition made in 2020 to at-a-distance learning and meetings in reaction to the COVID-19 pandemic.

But it also lies behind the empowerment of malicious actors. Today, the network is a massive world-girding enterprise with more than 64% of the world's population connected. It amasses new data at a rate that doubles human data production every 3–6 months. Put another way, we create more data in a year now than was created in all the time from the Pharaohs to 9/11. And, as we said, 40 years ago the technology that powers it didn't exist.

---

2. A node is any system or device that is connected to the network.

3. *Apple A18*, WIKIPEDIA (Feb. 15, 2025, 6:21 PM), https://en.wikipedia.org/wiki/Apple_A18. *See also* Apple, *Apple Event—September 9*, YOUTUBE (Sept. 9, 2024), https://www.youtube.com/watch?v=uarNiSl_uh4; *iPhone 16 Pro Tech Specs*, APPLE, https://www.apple.com/iphone-16-pro/specs/ (last visited Dec. 27, 2024).

2. The Structure of the Network

So, what makes this system work? How did it grow so quickly? Why is it so readily usable, generally reliable, and, perhaps most importantly, scalable to ever larger demand? Put simply, how can a system that had fewer than 100 nodes in 1973 work with the tens of billions of nodes that exist today?

The answer lies in a system of internet addressing and formatting protocols that undergird the network. These protocols have names like HTTP, which stands for HyperText Transfer Protocol and governs how web pages are formatted, and IP, or Internet Protocol, which controls addressing functions for data as it transits the network.

These addressing and structure protocols are, in turn, linked to and support a system of domain names. Domain names are the text-based identifiers that link to particular IP addresses. The domain name system (or DNS) is how an email to @americanbar.org gets translated into an IP address that points to the ABA's servers. An IP address will typically look something like this: 138.118.82.199.

The IP addressing system is managed by an international non-profit organization and functions in a highly distributed manner. At the top of the chain are several ur-source address lists[4] known as the root. Those root address lists are copied many times and distributed in tens of thousands of locations globally. When your web browser wants to look up a new domain IP address, it finds the right answer from some nearby server.

The last link in the structural puzzle is packet switching—the concept that data flowing between two nodes (whether a web page, an email, or some other code) does not need to travel as a unit. Instead, it travels in multiple small packets of data that take different routes across the network to be reassembled for delivery. Thus, unlike a traditional letter or traditional landline telephone call, there is no single, direct line of communication from originator to recipient. Instead, the message travels in dozens of packets.

One result of packet-switching is that interception and disruption of communications is demonstrably harder. Another is that concealment of origin is demonstrably easier since messages are harder to trace. This latter characteristic gives rise to the "attribution problem"—that is, the well-known difficulty of identifying actors in the cyber domain. Data sent from one country may pass through multiple countries and locations before reaching its final destination, thereby making it extremely difficult to trace back to its original departure point, and, thus, easier for malicious actors to disguise their nature and origins.

---

4. "Ur-source" means original source. *Ur-source*, WIKTIONARY (Aug. 20, 2023), https://en.wiktionary.org/wiki/ur-source.

3. Changing Architectures

Layered on top of this basic structure, there is a changing architecture of how people interact with the network. No broad description of the structure of the cyber network would be complete without identifying five broad, overarching trends in structural change that are being driven by technology today: the "cloud," the "internet of things," the "BYOD" phenomenon, the use of industrial control systems ("ICS"), and the rise of artificial intelligence.

Cloud Computing. In the early 2000s, most computer system architecture revolved around enterprise servers, that is, the private, physical servers owned by each individual or company and also known as "bare metal." Each company or individual provided his or her own data storage and processing capacity. As a result, each was also solely responsible for their own security.

That old model has increasingly been replaced by what we have come to call the "cloud." The cloud is in physical structure not terribly different from independent enterprise systems; it involves data storage, security, and processing in much the same way. The critical difference is that the infrastructure, programming, and storage are now provided as a service to the consumer. Multiple factors drive this trend, primarily economic utility (the convenience of immediate scale on demand) and including the shift to a more remote workforce. The advantages of the cloud architecture are significant in economic efficiency—the convenience to quickly provision computing resources as needed at scale, the flexibility to only create and use the resources you need on a temporary basis, and the access to expertise that maintains and secures the resources provided as a service. Cloud services vary in nature, from simple infrastructure to software, to a full platform service, like Microsoft 360, but in all its forms, the benefit lies in increased ease of operation.

One cost, however, is that the data "owner" is divested of much of his or her control, which devolves to the cloud service provider. Another cost is greater jurisdictional uncertainty. When data is stored in the cloud, for example, it may be stored in a different geographic location from the owner, or it may even be broken up and stored in multiple locations, creating all sorts of legal and policy complications. The problem of cloud geographic diversity is one reason that many nations have begun requiring local data storage as a way of ensuring legal control.

Companies that use the cloud also have to wrestle with new types of security challenges: the cloud inherently is outside of their perimeter, which has led to multiple examples of real-world data leakage. Many assume that the cloud provider's security expertise is a complete security solution encompassing their own use of the cloud. In the end, however, the security burden and obligations still lie with the customer—and users may even push for looser security controls in order to enable features (like AI tools). The cloud should be an extension of the customer's security posture, including technical expertise, access management, and the like, to understand the security landscape inherited from the cloud service provider and cover the security responsibilities left to the customer. Almost all of the questions cloud users ask about their internal security are equally relevant to the security of their cloud providers.

Internet of Things. Another major macro-trend is growth of the internet of things ("IoT"), which describes the increasing presence of internet-enabled communications in physical computing devices. This trend is driven by the accessibility of increasingly inexpensive computing resources that can be deployed almost anywhere. Where, previously, connectivity had been limited to systems that operated at a wholesale level, today, the internet of things is bringing connectivity to the retail level—refrigerators, thermostats, cars, and insulin pumps.

There are many benefits to this connectivity. Remote access and control of personal devices enable everything from driverless cars to doctors monitoring patients' vital signs at a distance. It increases convenience and also lowers costs.

But the increase in connectivity also has a price. The number and scale of vulnerabilities is now much larger. Ten years ago, we were concerned with the security of tens or hundreds of thousands of devices. Today, it is hundreds of millions, if not billions of nodes that are potentially vulnerable.

The most common consumer concern around IoT is privacy. We fear the creepy attacker accessing our webcam to watch us step out of the shower. But that is not the only concern; the prevalence of IoT devices also creates new vulnerabilities for the network and potential for malicious misuse. Since many IoT devices are "adjacent" to traditional computer networks in your home, they allow attackers to access IoT systems and then move, laterally, into your home or a work network.

Worse yet, unlike larger server systems, IoT devices often have simple yet common vulnerabilities that make their misuse easier. Two of note:

- Many IoT devices are deployed with a limited number of default user and password combinations, allowing attackers to easily guess them to gain access. One famous breach, known as Mirai, took down much of the East Coast internet using this method of attack;[5] and
- IoT devices are more difficult to patch. In larger systems, as vulnerabilities are identified, patches are released. It is up to the user to apply the patch and to understand the implications of using a system that is accessible to others. This could be anything from a voice-enabled microphone (like Alexa) recording and transmitting all of your conversations to the data your car collects and shares with the manufacturer. But many IoT consumers don't patch, and some IoT devices cannot be patched. This allows attackers to build a catalog of vulnerabilities and easily gain access to many IoT devices.

5. Josh Frulinger, *The Mirai Botnet Explained: How Teen Scammers and CCTV Cameras Almost Brought Down the Internet*, CSO (Mar. 9, 2018), https://www.csoonline.com/article/3258748/the-mirai-botnet-explained-how-teen-scammers-and-cctv-cameras-almost-brought-down-the-internet.html.

This was the modus operandi of a famous campaign that went by the name Reaper/IoTRoop.[6]

Personal Devices and the BYOD Phenomenon. The third macro-trend to consider in our survey of system architecture is growth in the independence of actors and devices. In the past, many enterprises would issue computers and personal devices to each employee for their use for business purposes. That practice allowed the enterprise both to provision and control when and how those devices were used. Enterprises could, for example, have effective limits on employees' access to gambling websites.

Even before the recent pandemic, it was becoming much more common for individual employees to have his or her own dual-use device. Employees intermingled personal and enterprise purposes in a single operating environment. Naturally, each different device comes with its own vulnerabilities as to the hardware, the software, and the user's own security profile.

This trend of dual-use devices, or bring-your-own-device ("BYOD"), has only been exacerbated since the start of the COVID-19 pandemic. As employees increasingly "work-from-home" and use their own in-home systems, the security perimeter of business enterprises has increased exponentially. The commingling of these assets means that corporate safeguards can be easily circumvented by home devices that are not configured to the same levels of protection and that much of the traffic on these devices is not analyzed. The rarity of outside-the-office work has now become the norm. And that brings with it risks: in a large enterprise, security depends upon the weakest link, and the BYOD phenomenon makes maintaining security architecture even harder. BYOD means there are nonstandard devices on the computer network that often are not being monitored, logged, or analyzed for malicious behaviors.

Industrial Control Systems ("ICS"). ICS is a group term used to describe the different kinds of systems that control or automate industrial processes. In simple terms, these are the computers that underpin critical infrastructure, building automation systems like HVAC, and manufacturing operations. The specifics of the systems vary by their industrial/sector application, but they are the same in the way they differ from traditional computers like your laptop: they are designed to operate in specific physical environments, e.g., they may be outside or subject to high temperatures, and for high availability and reliability. ICS are critical systems that cannot fail. While the worst impact from a breach of a traditional computer is data-centered (ransomware or stolen information, for example), ICS vulnerabilities affect the physical world and, in the worst case, can lead to the loss of life or limb.

The most famous ICS attack was Stuxnet, a purported United States/Israel collaboration to constrain Iran's nuclear ambitions by sabotaging its uranium enrichment centrifuges.

6. Kevin Townsend, *Financial Services DDoS Attacks Tied to Reaper Botnet*, SecurityWeek (Apr. 5, 2018), https://www.securityweek.com/financial-services-ddos-attacks-tied-reaper-botnet/.

Though rarely made public, at least a few other ICS attacks have been reported. For example, the TSMC[7] attack disrupted chip manufacturing in Taiwan. A Russian attack, known as CRASHOVERRIDE,[8] on Ukraine's electrical grid in 2015 shut off electricity in that country. More recently, the DarkSide ransomware that affected Colonial Pipeline[9] forced the company to stop its ICS operations, shutting down a pipeline transporting gasoline and affecting customers across the U.S. eastern seaboard. In general, ICS issues will not be of direct concern to practicing attorneys, but they should be aware of the issue because it may impact them as consumers of ICS services, because affected ICS systems may belong to clients who have legal concerns, and because attorneys may represent clients adversely impacted by the downstream effects of an ICS attack.

Artificial Intelligence ("AI"). AI is the concept of computer systems that imitate human intelligence and behavior and can be deployed to make autonomous decisions and actions. A subset of AI is machine learning (ML), which is the ability for computer algorithms to adjust themselves based on the data they gain from operation.[10] Much of the future of decision-making processes will be driven by AI to take advantage of its increasing speed and complexity. Computers are faster than human thinking; it's only a question of when they will be as smart and if they will be capable of processing in a way that mimics the exercise of human judgment.

So how do you train a computer to analyze and predict outcomes that approximate the thinking of a human? It requires very large data sets to train computers in all of the fundamentals that build up to more complex understanding and actions. As an aside, the value of large data sets is one of the reasons that some are concerned about foreign access to American data sets, as the recent TikTok controversy demonstrates.[11] TikTok, a video application used by many younger Americans, became a national security issue as questions emerged about the possibility TikTok's Chinese owner could be compelled to hand over to the Chinese government a plethora of data generated by and about Americans on the TikTok platform. As a result Congress has sought to force TikTok to divest from the United States, and the Supreme Court has upheld that law (though at the time of our writing, the ultimate result remains unclear).[12]

---

7. Jeremy Kirk, *WannaCry Outbreak Hits Chipmaker, Could Cost $170 Million*, BankInfoSecurity (Aug. 7, 2018), https://www.bankinfosecurity.com/chipmaker-tsmc-wannacry-attack-could-cost-us170-million-a-11285.

8. *CRASHOVERRIDE: Analyzing the Malware that Attacks Power Grids*, Dragos, Inc. (June 12, 2017), https://www.dragos.com/resource/crashoverride-analyzing-the-malware-that-attacks-power-grids/.

9. José Rodríguez Jr., *The Colonial Pipeline Was Fine, But Its Owner Shut It Down To Make Sure They'd Get Paid Correctly*, Jalopnik (May 17, 2021, 2:22 PM), https://jalopnik.com/the-colonial-pipeline-was-fine-but-it-was-shutdown-to-1846911689.

10. *See* Handbook, Chapter 2, *An Introduction to Artificial Intelligence.*

11. Brian Fung, *TikTok Is a National Security Threat, US Politicians Say. Here's What Experts Think*, CNN Bus. (July 9, 2020, 6:47 AM), https://www.cnn.com/2020/07/09/tech/tiktok-security-threat/index.html.

12. *TikTok Inc. v. Garland*, Docket No. 24-656, 604 U.S. ___ (Jan. 17, 2025); Exec. Order No. 14,166, 90 Fed. Reg. 8611, Application of Protecting Americans from Foreign Adversary Controlled Applications Act to TikTok, (Jan. 20, 2025); Exec. Order No. 14,258, 90 Fed. Reg. 15,209, Extending the TikTok Enforcement Delay

To date, AI has been moderately successful in relatively simple tasks like image recognition. More recently generative AI programs have proven successful, though not error-free, in emulating human conversation and in writing and debugging software code. Other AI tools have supported advances in cybersecurity, medicine, and weather forecasting. But the ways that humans naturally pattern match and add context turn out to be a very complex process that is difficult to replicate. Today's technology is still years from the level of general intelligence that we are accustomed to seeing in science fiction.

One category of risk in AI is bias. Bias can be introduced in AI tools both through training and operation. Since the data sets for training AI tools are chosen by humans, implicit bias or error can be introduced. In addition, the quality and relevance of the data sets used for training and operation are key; the old adage "garbage in; garbage out" applies to AI.

In operation, AI can reflect these implicit biases or gaps programmed through its training data and wind up with widely differing, and sometimes inappropriate, impacts. AI may also be designed or deployed with connections to sensors or other inputs that are deficient or inoperable. Here's an example of the problem in a simple automated system: a YouTube video[13] of a "racist soap dispenser." The video shows a man with dark skin trying unsuccessfully to get an automated device to dispense soap. His skin color is not recognized. When he uses a white paper towel, however, the dispenser works as it should. The engineers did not (we assume) intentionally build a "racist" device, but they failed to design or build the device with appropriately designed sensors capable of recognizing all skin colors or an alternate signal, like motion, and appropriately designed logic to dispense soap to a complete universe of potential users.

When AI tools are used to assist decisions that could have life-altering effects, such as employment, credit, medical diagnosis, and sentencing or parole, AI bias or discrimination can be particularly harmful to individuals.

4. Threats on the Cyber Network

As we have noted, the explosive growth of the network, its scalable architecture, and its changing nature lie at the core of an immense economic expansion. But they also bring with them an immensely greater prospect of criminality and other malicious activity. As Dan Geer, the Chief Information Security Officer (CISO) of In-Q-Tel (the CIA's venture capital company) once put it, we live in a world where "[e]very sociopath is your next-door neighbor."[14]

(Apr. 4, 2025); Exec. Order Further Extending the TikTok Enforcement Delay (June 19, 2025) (extending enforcement until September 17, 2025), https://www.whitehouse.gov/presidential-actions/2025/06/further-extending-the-tiktok-enforcement-delay/; Exec. Order Further Extending the TikTok Enforcement Delay (Sept. 16, 2025) (extending enforcement until December 16, 2025).

13. Futureism, *This "Racist Soap Dispenser" at Facebook Office Does Not Work for Black People*, YouTube (Aug. 18, 2017), https://www.youtube.com/watch?v=YJjv_OeiHmo.

14. Dan Geer, *Shared Risk at the National Scale*, Stanford U. (2004), http://web.stanford.edu/class/msande91si/www-spr04/slides/geer.pdf.

So, what are the risks? How do they manifest? In other words, how do you describe the threat to your attorneys, your staff, and your family (who may use the same home computer that you use to work remotely)?

Broadly speaking, each threat can be thought of as having three component parts—a propagation method for moving the malware to your system; an exploit that targets a weakness in the system; and a payload that does the damage.

Propagation. Malware propagation is, in essence, the vector for attack. It is the first step in the process of gaining access to a system, and it often involves both technological and social methods of access. Propagation methods are widely known but, despite this, they continue to have frequent success. Once an attacker gains initial access, they begin an iterative process (post-access) of discovery and lateral movement through other computers toward targets of interest. Once an initial breach occurs, the attackers begin to roam inside your system.

The most common initial access attack is phishing: an email with a bad link inside to click on. (The name "phishing" is intended to evoke the idea of fishing; the link is the bait, and, sadly, you are the fish.) Most of the attacks we've seen start with phishing campaigns because, quite simply, they work, and it costs little to scale into a campaign. We've also seen USB stick attacks, where the malware is on a USB that is "given away" for free and plugged into a system, and web site auto downloads, where the malware is latent on a dodgy website (like a gambling site or pornography) and automatically runs whenever the site is accessed.

It is fair to say that a large majority of attack methods, like our phishing example, rely on human factors. The link is the technology, but the danger is in the well-crafted message that seduces the reader to make the wrong choice.

Exploits. Exploits are the code that manipulates a computer system. According to computer scientists, it is a truism that *every* system has vulnerabilities, that is, flaws in the computer code that outsiders can exploited by outsiders. Given how large some programs are—the operating system for Windows 10 had more than 60 million lines of code—it is impossible for there not to be such flaws. No human enterprise of that size could plausibly be flawless.

Some of these flaws are well known. For example, there is one well-known exploit called a "buffer overflow" that has been around for over a dozen years, but it still works because the flaw is too difficult to fix.[15]

By far the most dangerous exploits, however, are those that are not well known—new exploits that someone has recently discovered. We call these types of exploits zero-day (or

15. For those who are interested, here is a short, non-technical description of the problem. A computer program will typically have a buffer in it, that is, a place into which to write data. Most buffers are created with a fixed size. In some programs an anomaly exists where, if I write into the buffer a data set that is larger than its fixed size, the data will overrun the buffer's boundary and overwrite an adjacent memory location. This lets a malicious actor purposefully write data outside the buffer and, thereby modify how the system operates.

0-day) exploits because they work on the first day they are tried in the real world (day zero, so to speak). Known exploits can be patched, though sometimes only with great effort. Unknown zero-day exploits don't have patches and may not have patches for some time. That is precisely why zero-day exploits are so valuable to malicious actors and often sell for tens of thousands of dollars on the black market.

The attacks on SolarWinds (2020) and the Microsoft Exchange system (2021)[16] both used zero-day exploits that had not previously been discovered—which was part of what made them so unexpected and so devastating. Sadly, the reality is that exploits are impossible to eliminate so we need to deal with a world of persistent vulnerability.

Payloads. Payloads are the payoff, so to speak. This is where the true malware danger lies. After gaining entry and manipulating your system to allow the outsider to control it, the payload is what the malicious actor uses to achieve his or her ends. Sometimes it may be a program that wipes out your data or degrades it in some way. One form of malware is called ransomware, a program that encrypts your data so that you can't access it and an encryption key is held out to you for payment of ransom. The world witnessed the effects of ransomware in the Colonial Pipeline attack that affected the gasoline supply along much of the U.S. east coast in May 2021.[17]

Another change in payload attack was evidenced by the SolarWinds incident from 2020, where Russian intruders subverted the supply chain/software update system to deliver their payloads.

For lawyers and law firms, the major risks of cyber attacks relate to the confidentiality of our work. Lawyers need to worry about access to critical client data (hence, fears of ransomware). They also need to be particularly concerned about the theft (what hackers call "exfiltration") of sensitive client information from the firm. When even large Wall Street law firms like Cravath, Swaine & Moore[18] and Jones Day[19] are subject to attack, one can be certain that no law firm is immune.

Attackers. A final thing to consider about cyber risk is not the "how" of it but the "who." Attacker motivations are extremely varied, as are their tactics and their objectives. Thus, one critical component of understanding the threat is what cybersecurity experts call

---

16. SolarWinds is a commonly used IT Network Management software platform that was initially compromised by Russia, forcing an extensive and expensive response by thousands of US companies. *See* Pam Baker, *The SolarWinds Hack Timeline: Who Knew What, and When?*, CSO (June 4, 2021) https://www.csoonline.com/article/3613571/the-solarwinds-hack-timeline-who-knew-what-and-when.html. Microsoft Exchange is one of the most common email platforms in use and was compromised with multiple 0-days by a Chinese-related organization. *See* Microsoft 365 Security & Microsoft Threat Intelligence, HAFNIUM *targeting Exchange Servers with 0-day exploits*, MICROSOFT, https://www.microsoft.com/security/blog/2021/03/02/hafnium-targeting-exchange-servers/ (last updated Mar. 16, 2021).

17. *See* HANDBOOK, Chapter 2, *An Introduction to Artificial Intelligence.*

18. Matthew Goldstein, *Cravath Law Firm Discloses a Data Attack*, N.Y. TIMES (Mar. 30, 2016), https://www.nytimes.com/2016/03/31/business/dealbook/cravath-law-firm-discloses-a-data-attack.html.

19. Chris Opfer, *Jones Day Hit by Data Breach as Vendor Accellion Hack Widens*, BLOOMBERG L. (Feb. 16, 2021, 7:30 PM), https://news.bloomberglaw.com/business-and-practice/jones-day-hit-by-data-breach-as-vendor-accellion-hacks-widen.

"threat intelligence," that is, knowing who the attackers are, which gives you an insight into how and why they are acting. For example, "hacktivists" are individuals who hack for political reasons. They may steal data from an enterprise, but they typically will not try to profit from it. Rather, hacktivists will use it to publicly embarrass the law firm or one of its clients (as, for example, with the Panama Papers hack of the Panamanian law firm Mossack Fonseca).[20]

By contrast, "script kiddies" are young hackers who attack just for fun. Criminals steal data for exploitation and profit. More recently, with the SolarWinds and Hafnium/Microsoft attacks,[21] we have seen an increase in the incidence of nation-state attacks targeted at national security or economic security objectives. Each uses different types of exploit and propagation methods and typically uses different payloads so the defense against each will also vary. One easy rule of cybersecurity is "know your enemy."

5. Defensive Systems and Enterprise Challenges

The final piece of the puzzle lies in how one responds to the threat environment. Some of the responses are technological in nature; others involve systematic changes in enterprise management that are necessary to make the technological responses effective. As we said earlier, most threats involve the human factor, so while technology can help, it is no panacea and will not be the entire solution to a law firm's cyber vulnerability problems. And, indeed, there is no "solution;" one can mitigate the risk, but it cannot ever be fully eliminated.

Technology and Defense. The number of defensive technologies that are available is as varied as the types of malicious attacks. No brief piece could hope to catalog them all. However, we can offer a typology of the most common systems that are routinely deployed, many of which would be useful in every law firm context.

- *Systems for detecting and preventing intrusions.* There are many different types of preventative systems available to an enterprise. The simplest is a "firewall," a network security system that monitors and regulates traffic into and out of a computer system based on a fixed set of security rules. An "intrusion detection system" (IDS) is typically somewhat more sophisticated in that it attempts to go beyond a fixed set of rules to identify an attack based on some variation that it observes from the "norm" or baseline of enterprise behavior. So, for example, an IDS might observe traffic from a new IP address located in Russia that had never before attempted to access the law firm's website and flag that anomaly for assessment. To the extent that the detection system takes the follow-on step of trying to prevent the intrusion from happening, it is sometimes

20. Grant Gross, *The Massive Panama Papers Data Leak Explained*, COMPUTERWORLD (Apr. 5, 2016) https://www.computerworld.com/article/3052218/the-massive-panama-papers-data-leak-explained.html.

21. *See supra* Baker, note 16.

called (unsurprisingly) an "intrusion prevention system," or IPS. As you may imagine, the number and variety of IDS/IPS systems is vast, and there are more vendors than one can possibly conceive of.

Picking the right IDS/IPS for your enterprise is one of the critical decisions for the person responsible for information security in your organization, often a Chief Information Security Officer (also known as the CISO). As Dmitri Alperovitch, co-founder of the cybersecurity firm CrowdStrike has said, the quickness of your detection and response is critical. Your objective can be captured in the 1-10-60 rule: that's how fast the defender must react (in minutes) to detect (1), respond (10), and remediate (60) an attack in order to prevent it from breaking out beyond the initial malicious access when the scope of the breach becomes exponentially more expensive.

- ***Information Sharing.*** Of course, intrusion detection works better if you know in advance what intrusions may look like. Recall that previously unobserved exploits are often called "zero-days" because they work on day zero, and nobody has seen them before. Notably, a zero-day for one enterprise may not be a zero-day for another. The second enterprise might have seen the intrusion two weeks ago and fixed the problem. The first enterprise remains vulnerable to the exploit unless the latter organization shares its knowledge of the exploit. Hence, one of the most common forms of defense is simply to participate in an information-sharing system with other similarly situated companies so that everyone in the group can benefit from shared awareness of threats and experiences. The industry approach is formalized as Information Sharing and Analysis Centers[22] ("ISAC"), which are sector-specific (maritime, automotive, finance, etc.) organizations of public-private partnerships to facilitate cybersecurity threat intelligence.

  In December 2015, Congress passed the Cybersecurity Act of 2015, which was intended to make information sharing even easier and more common.[23] The Act set the parameters for how federal, state, local and tribal government agencies share and receive cybersecurity-related information. It also provides a safe harbor to private organizations that share information, shielding them from legal liability. Today, most large enterprises are part of an ISAC and routinely share information. As with most government programs, some of the ISACs are better than others.
- ***Insider Threat Systems.*** As noted earlier, most intrusions are due to fundamental human factors. Often, this is the product of human error, like mistakenly clicking on a bad link. But sometimes intrusions are the product of a malicious insider—say, a disgruntled employee who is planning to leave the firm. In either case, another form of defense is to monitor employee conduct with systems that broadly go under the name of "insider

---

22. Nat. Council ISACs, https://www.nationalisacs.org/ (last visited Feb. 4, 2025). *See also Information Sharing*, Cybersecurity & Infrastructure Sec. Agency, https://www.cisa.gov/topics/cyber-threats-and-advisories/information-sharing (visited Feb. 18, 2025).

23. The bill was Division N of the 2015 Omnibus Appropriations Act. *See* Consolidated Appropriations Act, H.R.2029, 114th Cong. (2016).

threat" systems. These systems often use sophisticated algorithms to attempt to identify aberrant behavior in employees. This can include things as simple as "employee A is reusing a password" or as complex as "employee Z has never accessed that database before, why is he doing so now?" Once identified, these anomalies can be flagged for management follow up. Insider threat systems differ from purely technical intrusion detection systems in that they focus on human behavior—with all its greater complexities and sensitivities. It should go without saying that law firms considering deploying insider threat systems should proceed with caution and with full transparency to employees.

- ***Multi-Factor Authentication.*** One subset of threat that has special salience is the threat of unauthorized access, in other words, the intrusion that arises because some malicious actor has abused internet-accessible authentication in order to access the system in an apparently permitted way. Sadly, identity theft is rampant, and most users have weak or ineffective passwords. As a result, fraudulent access of this form continues.

  The most effective way to combat unauthorized access is through a process known as "multi-factor authentication" ("MFA") or "two-factor authentication" ("2FA") to establish identity. MFA is designed to enable one to prove identity. We often say that you can prove identity by using something you have (like an application/device linked to the account), providing something you are (like your user ID or, these days, your fingerprint or face), or by demonstrating something you know (like your password). Typical examples of MFA today include a key fob with a rotating random number that needs to be input or an independent authorization program that needs to be used through, say, a smart phone device or tablet.

  The most common form of authentication is through text messages (SMS), where the authentication prompts for a user to respond with a keycode texted to their registered number. Authentication using SMS is easy to use, but it is not perfect; it can be defeated by attackers who have developed multiple ways to intercept the text. Text authentication is still better than not using any additional authentication method at all. Whatever the methodology, the underlying thesis is simple: access is restricted to those who both know a password/user name combination ***and*** can authenticate their identity through some second channel of communication. Any enterprise with multiple users would be wise to consider implementing MFA.

- ***Encryption.*** The final technological defense to consider is the growing use of encryption. Encryption is a way of encoding a message or data so that only people with the authorized decryption code can access the information. Properly implemented, today's encryption programs cannot be broken by attackers. Data that is properly encrypted is akin to money in an unbreakable safe; even if the robber gets into the house, the contents of the safe remain protected. Today, encrypted communications systems are common; most consumers have access to systems like Signal, Telegram, or WhatsApp that provide for end-to-end encrypted conversations.

> Encryption often comes, however, with some enterprise costs. For example, it can limit collaboration, and it can sometimes result in data loss when the encryption passphrase is lost (or, itself, stolen). Encryption may also have broader social costs as it is sometimes argued that increased use of encryption can protect malicious actors. (Others, of course, make the counterargument that encryption enhances security and privacy at a social scale). Either way, these costs are likely to be worth incurring for sensitive and high-value data, of which law firms typically possess quite a lot.[24]

Enterprise Challenges. Beyond technical systems for defense, there are organizational issues that frequently get in the way of an effective response. Again, the number and variety of such issues are as wide as the number of organizations. Each enterprise has its own particular nature. But make no mistake, though we like to think of law firms as "different," in terms of corporate organization and security challenges they are pretty much like any other enterprise. Here are three challenges that have been common in law firms and may merit special attention:

First and foremost is the lack of knowledge of and/or commitment to understand key cybersecurity issues and then fix cybersecurity problems within the firm's management committee. The lack of knowledge can be remedied; bar associations have plenty of resources on cybersecurity, and online advice is also available.

Still, good cybersecurity is not free. It always comes with a cost, sometimes quite a significant one. While improved cybersecurity can be readily justified as a necessary expense to avoid even greater potential harm, there is no disguising the fact that it detracts from the bottom line. Especially for firms that have not, themselves, experienced a breach—or are not aware that they have—gaining a firm-wide commitment to reasonable cybersecurity measures is often a challenge.

Second, firms often see cybersecurity as a subset of information technology issues and put their CISO (the Chief Information Security Officer) in a separate IT/management silo. This is often a mistake. In a large firm, the CISO is the firm's first line of cyber defense. Yet often he or she operates cut off from firmwide risk management practices. For larger firms, cyber threat intelligence often benefits from a broader, more holistic picture of what risks the firm is incurring and how they are being managed in other contexts. Firms may want to consider whether their current administrative architecture is effective in developing a firmwide resistance to cybersecurity threats.

Of course, solo practitioners and smaller firms may not have a dedicated CISO. They may only have a part-time "IT guy" whose job it is to set up and maintain the system. In

24. In December 2024, the U.S. Cybersecurity and Infrastructure Security Agency (CISA) released best practice guidance to protect mobile communications from espionage activity by the People's Republic of China. CISA's advice for protecting mobile devices and online accounts included using only end-to-end encryption, such as Signal or similar apps for messaging. *Mobile Communications Best Practice Guidance*, CYBERSECURITY & INFRASTRUCTURE SEC. AGENCY (Dec. 18, 2024), https://www.cisa.gov/sites/default/files/2024-12/guidance-mobile-communications-best-practices.pdf.

these cases, the lawyer would be wise to consider some form of audit, hiring an outside evaluator to review the firm's practices and make cost-effective suggestions for change. Small firms and solos like to think that they will not be targets—we call this instinct the idea of "security by obscurity"—but increasingly that is not true, and even smaller sized practitioners have ethical and practical obligations to their clients that require some form of precautionary response.[25]

Finally, one challenge that is not unique to law firms, but is perhaps more common in firms than in other organizations, is the diversity of employee age and experience. As we noted at the outset, lawyers of different ages have different experiences and expectations from the cyber network. Some older employees were born well before the network existed; they may find passwords and multi-factor authentication difficult to implement. (A no-doubt apocryphal story tells of one senior law firm partner who demanded that his password be his first name so that he could remember it.) By contrast, some younger employees expect to have their own devices for use in the workplace, and many grew up in a "sharing" world where Facebook and Instagram predominate. As a result, they may not have fully internalized core legal ethical concepts of client confidentiality, and their non-work practices may pose unique risks to the firm's data integrity. Navigating these different social expectations will require differentiated training and education programs and significantly complicate the effort to maintain the firm's security posture.

In today's world, law firm practice is deeply dependent on the vast worldwide cyber network. Having become so dependent on it, lawyers can no longer remain ignorant of, or intimidated by, the technology. As a matter of best practices (if not ethical obligation) they need to be more proactive and self-educated. This short introduction is, we hope, a useful first step.

6. Looking Forward—The Next Five Years

Predicting the future is always risky, especially so when we speak of computer networks and the cyber domain. The pace of change in cyberspace is fast, and it will only get faster. Nonetheless, no introduction to cyber security would be complete without a brief effort to peer into the mists of the future.

Artificial Intelligence in Cybersecurity. When this chapter was first drafted more than 10 years ago, little attention was paid to the role of AI in cybersecurity. Today, it has become so prevalent that it deserves mention as a topic of its own. AI represents a revolution from a data-centered model for information security to one of knowledge management, where the context is the key. In other words, the old security model was Role-Based Access Control

25. For issues regarding solo and small firm practitioners, *see* HANDBOOK, Chapter 15, *Cybersecurity for Solo and Small Firm Lawyers.*

(RBAC), where users were granted permissions specific to data. With AI, the new security model will be around managing what context a user is authorized to see from all data. For example, a CEO requesting from the system a financial forecast question should receive a detailed answer, whereas a summer intern should receive very little information or no answer. Organizations should be aware of the risks of leaking proprietary information with employees using public LLMs (Large Language Models); the LLM owners use this data to train their systems.

AI technology is being used to write software code.[26] That capability has already been repurposed to assist malicious actors in writing malware attack programs.[27] Happily, AI also has the capability of exposing vulnerabilities and making software more secure.[28] The most common use cases for AI by threat actors are to defeat AI protections (email spam filtering for example) and spear phishing where the threat is able to use open source intelligence (OSINT) data to build a large data set to craft individualized emails at scale.

Here are a few other trends (beyond those already described above) that will likely be salient:

- IoT will continue to go macro and global. Within the next five years cars, trucks, and industrial systems of all sorts will be massively interconnected.
- Everything will be automated. As AI improves, tasks as diverse as warfare and surgery will increasingly be done without human intervention, at least at the tactical level.
- Ransomware will move from a global enterprise issue to affecting us in our daily lives. Want to start your car? One Bitcoin please.
- Internet balkanization. The fault lines of nation-state conflict will lead to multiple separate internets that may be almost completely isolated, like North Korea, or very limited for regional control, like China.
- Large data aggregation and enhanced artificial intelligence analytics will continue to erode privacy as legal restrictions struggle to keep up with technological reality.
- Quantum computers, which use quantum physics to do computations, are in active development. If they are ever commercially available, quantum computers will likely increase processing speeds exponentially. We can't know what the effects of this will be, but one example often talked about is that quantum computers may make data encryption nearly impossible.
- Reality itself will be contested. Building on the disinformation campaigns of the past few years, the propagation of "deep-fake" technologies that can mimic and mutate real-life experiences will make debates about facts and "fake news" ever more prominent.

26. Jack Kelly, *AI Writes over 25% of Code at Google*, Forbes (Nov. 1, 2024, 6:30 AM), https://www.forbes.com/sites/jackkelly/2024/11/01/ai-code-and-the-future-of-software-engineers/.

27. Alex Blake, *Hackers Are Using AI to Create Vicious Malware, Says FBI*, Digital Trends (July 31, 2023), https://www.digitaltrends.com/computing/hackers-using-ai-chatgpt-to-create-malware/.

28. Ravie Lakshmanan, *Google's AI Tool Big Sleep Finds Zero-Day Vulnerability in SQLite Database Engine*, Hacker News (Nov. 4, 2024), https://thehackernews.com/2024/11/googles-ai-tool-big-sleep-finds-zero.html.

7. Top Ten Considerations

The following are key considerations attorneys should keep in mind related to the technology side of cyber security:

1. The worldwide computer network is no longer brand new, but it continues to evolve. The internet is more than 40 years old, a period that overlaps the generations in today's workforce who bring a wide range of technology experience and behavioral norms for organizations to manage.
2. The network is growing and speeding up at an ever-increasing rate. Today's iPhone is many times faster than the supercomputer of 40 years ago and built to power artificial intelligence applications.
3. The cyber network is not like the phone network. It runs on distributed addressing and structural protocols without any centralized control.
4. The architecture of the cyber network is changing as we adopt it:
    a. Cloud computing;
    b. Internet of Things consumer devices;
    c. Enhanced use of personal devices in enterprise settings;
    d. Reliance on Industrial Control Systems; and
    e. Developing artificial intelligence.
5. Threats on the network propagate through logical vulnerabilities in code and, more frequently, through exploitation of human factors, such as phishing emails.
6. It is impossible to eliminate vulnerabilities in the network. Perfect code cannot be written. It is critical to be able to identify vulnerabilities and address them.
7. Threat intelligence is critical. Know who is after you and what they are after.
8. Technological defenses help. An enterprise defense should include systems for:
    a. Detecting and preventing intrusions;
    b. Information sharing; and
    c. Insider threat detection.
9. To protect enterprise systems, one should:
    a. Deploy multi-factor authentication; and
    b. Implement encryption, where practicable.
10. Some of the most important defensive steps involve organization-wide responses, like incorporating cyber risk into an enterprise risk assessment and management. Cyber threats are not isolated, and incidents will quickly spread across an entire enterprise.

Chapter 4
Understanding Cybersecurity Risks

Lucy L. Thomson

Abstract

Massive data breaches are occurring with alarming frequency, compromising sensitive personal data and intellectual property (IP) and making critical systems unavailable. Cyber criminals have targeted lawyers and law firms due to the vast amount of confidential client and firm information they collect.

This chapter describes the cybersecurity risks faced by lawyers and law firms, as well as their clients. In numerous breaches, lawyers have seen their confidential client data and proprietary information compromised, entire firm computer networks shut down, extortion demands delivered, the breach of client confidences when stolen information is published on the dark web, and the undermining of trust, leading to reputational loss and lawsuits.

Lawyers must stay abreast of technology developments and thoroughly understand the risks they pose. They will then have the knowledge and skill required to meet their professional ethics obligations and provide informed and thoughtful guidance to clients on complex cybersecurity, privacy, and artificial intelligence (AI) issues.

Part 1 of this chapter provides an overview of new technologies that are creating unprecedented challenges for lawyers, the nature of the sensitive and confidential data at risk, and how hackers and cyber criminals conduct attacks to undermine the pillars of information security: breach the confidentiality of personal records, compromise the integrity of the data, and make critical information systems unavailable.

Part 2 addresses how and why lawyers and law firms are prime targets and the significant resulting damage. The examples of the many vulnerabilities and cybersecurity attacks presented in a practical and readily understandable manner illustrate the increasingly dangerous threats to sensitive data, the heightened need for lawyers and law firms to address cybersecurity risks, build strong information security programs, and utilize necessary and appropriate security controls.

Part 3 describes essential steps required to protect confidential client data, law firm records and intellectual property (IP) and secure the organization's computer networks.

1. New Technologies Create Unprecedented Challenges for Lawyers

Massive data breaches are occurring with alarming frequency.[1] Millions of records have been breached, compromising sensitive personal data and IP, making critical systems unavailable, and leading to the undermining of trust, reputational loss and lawsuits.

The frequency and sophistication of cyber attacks have increased—2023 and 2024 set records for data breaches, with more than 3,100 publicly reported data compromises each of those years that resulted in over 1.3 billion notices sent to individual victims.[2] Firms regularly display their lawyers' work and client lists on their websites, providing bad actors with key information to orchestrate social engineering attacks. Criminals can trick the firms and their clients into revealing valuable data and use the information to launch dangerous attacks.

Artificial intelligence (AI) is changing the nature of cybersecurity attacks and creating new cyber risks.[3] Some of the most serious types of attacks will be amplified and exacerbated by AI. Executives, policymakers, regulators, technology experts, and their counsel will all play critical roles in protecting individuals and critical infrastructure from cybersecurity attacks. New technologies, including AI, will require lawyers and judges to understand how the technology works, how it is developed and used, what advantages it can bring, the risks it can create, and the legal and ethical issues that will arise.[4]

---

1. Cybersecurity breaches of law offices and their clients are now being revealed publicly because of mandatory data breach reporting requirements in the U.S. and abroad. For example, all 50 states, the District of Columbia, Guam, Puerto Rico and the Virgin Islands have laws requiring private businesses, and in most states, government entities as well, to notify individuals of security breaches involving their personally identifiable information (PII). *Security Breach Notification Laws*, Nat'l Conference State Legislatures, https://www.ncsl.org/technology-and-communication/security-breach-notification-laws (last updated Jan. 17, 2022).

Article 33 of the General Data Protection Regulation requires companies that process personal data and have a location in the European Union to report data breaches as specified in the law adopted in 2016. Regulation (EU) 2016/679 of the European Parliament and of the Council of 27 April 2016 on the protection of natural persons with regard to the processing of personal data and on the free movement of such data, and repealing Directive 95/46/EC (General Data Protection Regulation), art. 33, 2016 O.J. (L 119), https://eur-lex.europa.eu/legal-content/EN/TXT/PDF/?uri=CELEX:32016R0679.

2. 2024 Data Breach Report, Identity Theft Resource Ctr. (Jan. 2025), https://www.idtheftcenter.org/wp-content/uploads/2025/02/ITRC_2024DataBreachReport.pdf.

3. Santeri Kangas, *Why AI Is the Key to Cutting-Edge Cybersecurity*, World Econ. Forum (July 21, 2022), https://www.weforum.org/agenda/2022/07/why-ai-is-the-key-to-cutting-edge-cybersecurity/.

4. *Addressing the Legal Challenges of AI: Year I Report on the Impact of AI on the Practice of Law*, ABA Task Force on Law and Artificial Intelligence (Aug. 2024), https://www.americanbar.org/content/dam/aba/administrative/center-for-innovation/ai-task-force/2024ai-taskforce-report-1-31-25.pdf. The ABA Model Rule of Professional Conduct 1.1 Competence, Comment 8, provides that "[t]o maintain the requisite knowledge and skill, a lawyer should keep abreast of changes in the law and its practice, including the benefits and risks associated with relevant technology." Model Rules of Prof'l Conduct r.1.1 cmt. 8 (Am. Bar. Ass'n 1983), https://www.americanbar.org/groups/professional_responsibility/publications/model_rules_of_professional_conduct/rule_1_1_competence/comment_on_rule_1_1/.

Ransomware[5] and phishing attacks,[6] now the most common causes of data breaches, have had particularly devastating consequences for law practices. In numerous breaches, lawyers have seen their confidential client data and proprietary information compromised, entire firm computer networks shut down, extortion demands delivered, and the breach of client confidences when stolen information is published on the dark web.[7] Dark web auctions that sell backdoor access to law firm servers have perhaps become the most unconventional threat to the attorney-client privilege.[8] After gaining administrator privileges through an attack, hackers sell login credentials on the dark web to access law firm networks.[9]

New tactics of criminal groups are becoming more insidious. While in the past, when faced with a ransomware attack, law firms focused on paying ransom to unencrypt their data; now, this is only part of the malicious strategy. Not only are hackers demanding that the victims pay a ransom to reestablish firm access to their encrypted data and networks, but they also threaten to publish the firm's stolen data on the dark web or to the world.

In a social engineering scheme to conduct corporate espionage and gain insight into IP such as the financial details of mergers and acquisitions or proprietary research and development plans, at least one attack group has targeted law firms and business professionals with a difficult to detect, browser-based attack method known as search engine optimization (SEO) poisoning.[10] Designed to defraud individuals doing searches for business documents, a lawyer or paralegal who searches for specific content such as legal agreements or contract templates may find the top search results lead to a file infected with dangerous GootLoader-malware.

---

5. Ransomware is a type of malicious software, or malware, that encrypts data on a computer making it unusable. A malicious cyber criminal holds the data hostage until the ransom is paid. If the ransom is not paid, the victim's data remains unavailable. Cyber criminals may also pressure victims to pay the ransom by threatening to destroy the victim's data or to release it to the public. FED. BUREAU OF INVESTIGATION ("FBI"), 2023 INTERNET CRIME REPORT 13–14 (2023), https://www.ic3.gov/AnnualReport/Reports/2023_IC3Report.pdf.

6. Phishing is often used in conjunction with a spoofed email. It is the act of sending an email falsely claiming to be a legitimate business in an attempt to deceive the unsuspecting recipient into divulging personal, sensitive information such as passwords, credit card numbers, and bank account information after directing the user to visit a specified website. The website, however, is not genuine and was set up only as an attempt to steal the user's information. *Spoofing and Phishing*, FBI, https://www.fbi.gov/how-we-can-help-you/scams-and-safety/common-frauds-and-scams/spoofing-and-phishing (last visited June 12, 2025).

7. Darran Guccione, *What Is the Dark Web? How to Access It and What You'll Find: The Dark Web Is Part of the Internet That Isn't Visible to Search Engines and Requires the Use of an Anonymizing Browser Called Tor to Be Accessed.* CSOONLINE (Apr. 2, 2024), https://www.csoonline.com/article/564313/what-is-the-dark-web-how-to-access-it-and-what-youll-find.html.

8. *The Dark Web Secrets of Law Firms* (2020), AON, https://www.aon.com/cyber-solutions/wp-content/uploads/Aon-Cyber-Blog-Dark-Web-Secrets-of-Law-Firms.pdf.

9. *See The Biggest Data Breaches of 2024*, HACKMAGEDDON (DEC. 18, 2024), https://www.hackmageddon.com/2024/12/18/the-biggest-data-breaches-of-2024/#google_vignette.

10. Ravie Lakshmanan, *Cybercriminals Targeting Law Firms with GootLoader and FakeUpdates Malware*, HACKER NEWS (March 1, 2023), https://thehackernews.com/2023/03/cybercriminals-targeting-law-firms-with.html; *Gootloader Hackers Poison Websites Globally in Order to Infect Business Professionals with Ransomware, Intrusion Tools and Bank Trojans, Warns eSentire*, ESENTIRE, (March 30, 2021), https://www.esentire.com/security-advisories/gootloader-hackers-poison-websites-globally.

Recent breaches suggest that key software products used by law firms must now be considered high-critical, high-severity risk and monitored for new developments, vulnerabilities, risks, and exploits. Alerts from law enforcement in the U.S. and globally have warned of sophisticated attacks by state actors and cyber criminals that endanger law offices and companies and threaten the security of critical infrastructure. Hackers have exploited vulnerabilities in software products used by law firms to steal personal information, client data, and IP. This generally occurs when malicious actors gain access to the law firm's computer system through phishing or similar social engineering techniques, and then identify software products that are not appropriately patched to exploit.

Attacks resulting in breaches of law firm third-party business partners and vendors have increased, creating significant risks for firms that outsource important business operations. Cyber criminals have targeted vendors who have access to a larger organization's information or a business that holds the valuable information of multiple organizations. These entities may have fewer security measures than the law offices they serve.

The widespread practice of lawyers and staff working remotely, a trend that began during the pandemic and has been adopted widely, makes employees even more vulnerable to many of the most common causes of breaches—particularly theft of credentials, social engineering attacks, and human error.

1.1. Sensitive and Confidential Data at Risk

Lawyers must safeguard client records, as well as their own business records, including IP, attorney work product, and financial and employment records, to name a few. Electronic records are an integral part of every lawyer's business.[11] Throughout the course of representing clients, lawyers receive volumes of sensitive and confidential data—attorney-client privileged information, client trade secrets, and all types of personally identifiable information (PII), financial, healthcare, law enforcement, and many other types of records.

Law practices also receive sensitive and confidential information through litigation or compulsory process, or as a result of investigations or adversary actions against individuals and organizations. In these cases, not only adversaries, but also innocent third parties, are often swept up in lawsuits or other legal proceedings. Given that lawyers have access to the most sensitive and secret information in civil and criminal cases, including private investigations, records sealed or under a protective order, classified data, grand jury records, and other information with requirements for secrecy, it is critical that this information is protected from breaches and unlawful exposure.

In addition, law firms acquire a staggering array of sensitive information in e-discovery. It is a sobering fact that much of the data and information obtained by law practices may have been created and maintained in a secure environment and then transferred, often

11. For an in depth discussion of the responsibilities of lawyers to protect confidential client information, see HANDBOOK, Chapter 7, *Legal Obligations to Provide Data Security.*

without the knowledge, agreement, or consent of the individual or organization that created or collected the information, to an environment such as the office of opposing counsel or an e-discovery vendor where the extent of security protections may be unknown or are not assured.[12]

To protect confidential information, lawyers and law firms must know what data they have, where it resides, its level of sensitivity, and how it is secured. In addition to the more obvious places for data, such as computer servers, desktop and laptop computers, mobile devices, and cloud storage, information may reside in other, somewhat less expected locations. For example, computer backups may contain significant amounts of sensitive information. Also, confidential client data may be downloaded from email onto a mobile device and then saved locally. These devices are likely to be linked to the user, not the law firm, which means that the sensitive data could potentially be backed up to the user's personal cloud account, completely outside law firm control unless specific controls are in place to prevent this.

1.2. Compromising the Confidentiality, Integrity, and Availability of Data

The objectives of hackers and cyber criminals are to undermine the pillars of information security: breach the *confidentiality* of personal records, compromise the *integrity* of the data, and make critical information systems *unavailable*.[13]

Confidentiality. In light of the massive data breaches, much attention has been given to protecting the *confidentiality* of personal data and sensitive information. The largest data breaches—spanning the financial, healthcare, retail, technology, and government sectors—illustrate the heightened risk to millions of individuals when large datasets of sensitive personal information are compromised.[14]

Databases such as these are vulnerable to attacks from both insiders and hackers. The vulnerabilities of databases are well documented and include the use of default and weak passwords, failure to patch known vulnerabilities, misconfigurations, and granting of excessive access control privileges to users. Specific security measures must be taken to protect personal data in the databases of legal organizations.[15]

---

12. BlueVoyant, Sector 17—The State of Cybersecurity in the Legal Sector (May 27, 2020), https://www.bluevoyant.com/news/bluevoyant-sector-17-press-release/. Until a law firm has conducted a risk assessment and adopted a comprehensive information security program, it will not be in a position to vouch for an appropriate level of security and its ability to protect sensitive and confidential information, if requested by a client or the court.

13. Data Breach Incident Response Team, Verizon, 2024 Verizon Data Breach Investigations Report, 25–26 (2024), https://www.verizon.com/business/resources/T387/reports/2024-dbir-data-breach-investigations-report.pdf [hereinafter "Verizon 2024 DBIR"].

14. A website that goes by the name "Information is Beautiful" provides a visualization of hundreds of the massive data breaches that have affected the private sector and government. *World's Biggest Data Breaches & Hacks*, Information is Beautiful, http://www.informationisbeautiful.net/visualizations/worlds-biggest-data-breaches-hacks/ (last updated June 2024).

15. Security measures that should be taken to protect personal data in databases include: (1) inventory your databases; (2) classify systems with sensitive data; (3) scan for vulnerabilities and misconfigurations, keep up to

The U.S. Intelligence Community's (IC) 2024 Annual Threat Assessment[16] identifies prominent cyber adversaries—nation-states (Russia, China, North Korea, and Iran), terrorist groups, and cyber criminals. In addition, "hacktivists" launch cyber attacks that are politically or ideologically motivated. Many of these threat actors have significant resources, funded by nation-states or through sophisticated money-laundering operations. The IC assessed that cyber threats from nation-states and their surrogates will remain "acute."[17]

Integrity. As early as 2015, the IC Worldwide Threat Assessment recognized the increasingly critical problem that future cyber attacks will be conducted to compromise the *integrity* of information, with a potentially devastating impact on key information systems that constitute the underpinnings of the economy:

> In the future . . . we might also see more cyber operations that will change or manipulate electronic information in order to compromise its integrity (i.e., accuracy and reliability) instead of deleting it or disrupting access to it. Decision-making by senior government officials (civilian and military), corporate executives, investors, or others will be impaired if they cannot trust the information they are receiving.[18]

Availability. Cyber attacks designed to restrict the *availability* of websites and IT services have become more aggressive, primarily with distributed denial of service (DDoS) attacks in which multiple compromised computers, often infected with a Trojan virus,[19] are used to overwhelm a single targeted system; computer viruses that delete user data; or ransomware that encrypts data and demands payment for the encryption key to restore access to the data.[20] Equally effective in shutting down entire networks, law firms have

---

date with security patches, enforce strong passwords, and audit configurations and settings; (4) identify privileged users; (5) validate access to sensitive data and assign restricted permissions on tables with sensitive information; (6) prioritize and fix what you can; (7) monitor database activity; and (8) encrypt data in transit and at rest using network-level encryption and column-level encryption. *See* Lucy L. Thomson & Dr. Robert Thibadeau, *Security Challenges of the Big Data Ecosystem Require a Laser-Like Focus on Risk*, 12 SciTech Lawyer, no. 2, 2016, at 6–11, 19.

16. Office of the Dir. of Nat'l Intel., Annual Threat Assessment of the U.S. Intelligence Community 7–23 (Feb. 5, 2024), https://www.dni.gov/files/ODNI/documents/assessments/ATA-2024-Unclassified-Report.pdf.

17. Office of the Dir. of Nat'l Intel., Statement for the Record to the Senate Select Comm. on Intelligence, Annual Threat Assessment of the U.S. Intelligence Community (Apr. 9, 2021), 20–21, https://www.armed-services.senate.gov/imo/media/doc/2021-04-09%20Final%20ATA%202021%20%20Unclassified%20Report%20-%20rev%202.pdf.

18. The Hon. James R. Clapper, Dir. of Nat'l Intel., Statement for the Record to the Senate Armed Services. Comm., Worldwide Threat Assessment of the U.S. Intelligence Community (Feb. 26, 2015) at 3–4, https://www.armed-services.senate.gov/imo/media/doc/Clapper_02-26-15.pdf.

19. A "Trojan" virus is a type of malware disguised as legitimate software that will enable a cyber criminal to gain access to a user's system and spy on him/her, steal sensitive data, and gain backdoor access.

20. In the first widespread DDoS attack, the Mirai botnet scoured the web for IoT devices protected only by factory-default usernames and passwords. It then enlisted these vulnerable IoT devices such as Internet-connected cameras and DVRs to send junk traffic and temporarily overwhelm popular Internet sites including Twitter, Amazon, Tumblr, Reddit, Spotify, and Netflix; these websites could no longer accommodate legitimate visitors or users. Josh Fruhlinger, *The Mirai Botnet Explained: How Teen Scammers and CCTV Cameras Almost Brought Down the Internet*, CSOonline (March 9, 2018), https://www.csoonline.com/article/3258748/

become targets of hackers seeking to profit from ransomware attacks, as discussed in detail in Section 2.1.3 infra.[21] Doubling down, ransomware groups have used DDoS attacks to take down victims' sites or networks until they negotiate to pay the requested ransoms.[22]

1.3. Technology of the Law Office Creates Cyber Risks

Lawyers and law firms face unprecedented challenges from the widespread use of electronic records, mobile devices, the Internet of Things (IoT), and AI. Seeking efficiencies from new technologies, most lawyers and law firms communicate using email and collaboration tools, rely on smartphones, and work on desktops, laptops, and tablets. Information about the firm and its clients is publicized on their websites and on social media. State-of-the-art computer devices are the cornerstones of "electronic courtrooms" around the country.[23] Technology varies extensively, depending upon the firm, but the risks are similar.

IT Operations. Many law firms operate data centers with global networks of computers, servers, mobile devices, websites, and social media. These firms perform the full range of information security, data governance, preservation, and incident response functions. Others outsource these responsibilities. Law firms use cloud computing for storing and processing client and firm records. Many have implemented "bring your own device" (BYOD) or "bring your own technology" (BYOT) for their workforce, which leads to managing the risk of multiple types of devices on the firm's network.

IoT in the Workplace. The convergence of information technology and physical operations in which computers control a broad array of consumer and industrial devices and systems presents new security concerns for law practices. As of 2025, more than 41.6 billion IoT devices have been connected to the Internet and to each other.[24] As law offices modernize, they will likely include IoT devices such as security cameras, wireless locks, motion sensors, automated lighting and window shades, climate control and smart thermostats that adjust office temperatures based on changes in the weather. Technologists are creating the "infrastructure of the smart office." Their goal is to create an "intelligent workplace" with

---

the-mirai-botnet-explained-how-teen-scammers-and-cctv-cameras-almost-brought-down-the-internet.html. *See* Verizon 2024 DBIR, Denial of Service, *supra* note 13, at 49–50.

21. *Don't Be a Digital Hostage: How to Avoid Data Breaches and Ransomware Attacks*, USI (Nov. 4, 2024), https://www.usi.com/dont-be-a-digital-hostage-how-to-avoid-data-breaches-and-ransomware-attacks/?utm_source.

22. Venkat Praneeth Nangineni & Steve Winterfeld, *Defeating Triple Extortion Ransomware: The Potent Combo of Ransomware and DDoS Attacks*, Akamai (Mar. 21, 2023), https://www.akamai.com/blog/security/defeating-triple-extortion-ransomware.

23. Michael Heintz, *The Digital Divide and Courtroom Technology: Can David Keep Up with Goliath?*, 54 Fed. Comm. L.J. 567 (2002), https://www.repository.law.indiana.edu/fclj/vol54/iss3/8/.

24. Cole Christian, *IoT 2024 in Review: The 10 Most Relevant IoT Developments of the Year*, IoT Analytics (Jan. 15, 2025), https://iot-analytics.com/iot-2024-review/; Patrick Mitchell et al., *Security in the Billions: Toward a Multinational Strategy to Better Secure the IoT Ecosystem*, Atlantic Council (Sep. 22, 2022), https://www.atlanticcouncil.org/in-depth-research-reports/report/security-in-the-billions/.

smartphones, wearables, and applications that solve problems, facilitate decision-making, measure performance, and take care of most routine tasks.[25]

AI Use by Lawyers. The impact of AI on law practice will be far-reaching.[26] AI enables computers and other automated systems to perform tasks that have historically required human cognition, and for certain tasks, at speeds that far outpace what humans can do. Generative AI has captivated the attention of individuals in professions based on language and writing, including lawyers and law firms, with its unprecedented ability to create new content. With a few text prompts, generative AI can create new text, images, audio, video, 3D models, data, or other work product that previously could only be produced by humans. The release of ChatGPT in 2022 ignited a firestorm of interest and concern about the ramifications of generative AI for the legal profession and its broader legal implications.[27]

AI has the potential to improve many aspects of legal practice and can help lawyers be more efficient and strategic. AI can summarize information across many sources and platforms, and it can generate legal communications and documents such as contracts, leases, and wills. Law firms and legal departments are making use of AI decision-making tools to analyze large volumes of data, to find, organize, and categorize items of information, and to make predictions. Legal practices trying to manage large datasets can use AI to make more sophisticated analytical queries about documents fed into an AI tool and ask the AI tool to find patterns relevant to client needs. Optimizing AI is everywhere in the modern world and continues to be built into the baseline tools that businesses use, making processes more efficient and products more effective. AI may be used by many businesses and governments, for example, in lending, fraud analysis, the rental industry, and human resources.

At the same time, the use of AI presents risks that lawyers and judges must understand. These range from its facilitation of cyber attacks to its role in creating and spreading disinformation.

Lawyers Working Remotely. The COVID-19 pandemic created an immediate need for lawyers to work remotely, complicating the technology landscape and introducing numerous cybersecurity risks.[28] The following examples highlight some of the challenges law practices must address when lawyers and employees work in remote locations and with

---

25. Sara Angeles, *7 Ways the Internet of Things Will Change the Way We Work*, Bus. News Daily (Oct. 23, 2023), https://www.businessnewsdaily.com/4858-internet-of-things-will-change-work.html.

26. Artificial Intelligence: Legal Issues, Policy, and Practical Strategies (Cynthia H Cwik, Christopher A Suarez, & Lucy L Thomson eds., ABA 2024). This ABA book provides legal analysis and reflections on the influence that AI will have on both the legal profession and the law.

27. *Addressing the Legal Challenges of AI*, *supra* note 4.

28. Cayley Wetzig, *8 Mobile Cybersecurity Threats You Should Take Seriously*, ThriveDX (Jan. 20, 2023), https://thrivedx.com/resources/article/8-mobile-cyber-security-threats-you-should-take-seriously; CrowdStrike 2024 Global Threat Report 20–23 (2024), https://go.crowdstrike.com/rs/281-OBQ-266/images/GlobalThreatReport2024.pdf [hereinafter "CrowdStrike 2024 Threat Report"] (Threat actors have adapted to the enhanced visibility of traditional endpoint detection and response (EDR) sensors by altering their exploitation tactics for initial access and lateral movement. They are now targeting the network periphery, where defender visibility is reduced by the possibility that endpoints may lack EDR sensors or cannot support sensor deployment.).

mobile devices, such as BYOD, over which the firm has little or no control.[29] Law firms should confirm they have addressed these concerns and are protecting their remote workforce (and themselves) from cyber threats.

- **Phishing and Malware**[30]—Lawyers' computers and smartphones issued by the firm, personal devices used for work, and devices that can be accessed by family members could be the target of phishing scams. Once on a device, malware makes legal information easily stolen. Multi-tasking and having work and personal email on the same device may increase the risk of lawyers or law office staff responding to phishing emails.
- **Authentication**—Stolen credentials or guessed passwords account for a majority of data breaches. Many employees use the same password for personal and work accounts, or across multiple accounts.[31] That, combined with the use of weak passwords, creates attack vectors for criminals seeking to steal law firm data. Many work devices have no mandated measures in place to secure accessible corporate data and have no password, PIN or biometric security guarding their devices.
- **Mobile Apps**—Privacy statements are often ignored and quickly accepted so the user can access an application. As a result, users regularly grant permission for an app to see and transfer data that should remain private, causing data leakage and potential damage.
- **Software Updates and Patching**—Many smartphones, tablets, and smaller connected IoT devices do not have a process for regular software updates or a guarantee that updates will be carried out, leaving the devices with known vulnerabilities that hackers can exploit.
- **Unsecure WiFi**—Computing devices in home offices or other locations may be connected to Wi-Fi with weak security (improperly configured home networks or public WiFi networks) allowing hackers access to private information. Law firms should confirm how attorneys and staff connect to the corporate network to ensure it is secure.

---

29. *See* Cybersecurity & Infrastructure Sec. Agency ("CISA"), Telework Essentials Toolkit, https://www.cisa.gov/sites/default/files/publications/20-02019b%2520-%2520Telework_Essentials-08272020-508v2.pdf (last visited June 12, 2025); *Telework Guidance and Resources*, CISA, https://www.cisa.gov/topics/risk-management/coronavirus/telework-guidance-and-resources (last visited June 12, 2025); Uy Huynh, *Remote Work Security Best Practices*, CIO.inc (Oct. 7, 2024), https://www.cio.inc/blogs/remote-work-security-best-practices-p-3710.

30. CISA, *Malware Tip Card*, https://www.cisa.gov/sites/default/files/publications/Malware_1.pdf (last visited June 12, 2025); *What Is Malware?*, Cisco, https://www.cisco.com/site/in/en/learn/topics/security/what-is-malware.html (last visited June 12, 2025) ("Malware, short for malicious software, refers to any intrusive software developed by cybercriminals (often called hackers) to steal data and damage or destroy computers and computer systems. Examples of common malware include viruses, worms, Trojan viruses, spyware, adware, and ransomware. Recent malware attacks have exfiltrated data in mass amounts.").

31. Lars Daniel, *65% of Employees Bypass Cybersecurity Measures, New Study Finds*, Forbes (Dec. 5, 2024), https://www.forbes.com/sites/larsdaniel/2024/12/05/new-study-finds-65-of-employees-bypass-cybersecurity-measures/.

- **Video Conferencing**—The frequent use of video conferencing, which permits the platforms to access the user's camera, microphone, shared documents, and often captures the entire array of files stored on the device, can put law firm data at risk.[32]
- **Collaboration Software**—Huge amounts of data flow through platforms such as Teams, Slack, WebEx, and Zoom, with video and audio streams, texts, and files. Through targeted attacks, criminals can drop malicious documents or data into one of these channels. Insider threats, cyber fraud, and sharing of critical information are all present.[33]
- **Shadow IT**—To protect confidential information and firm IP, lawyers must know what data they have, where it resides, its level of sensitivity, and how it is secured. Using IT-related hardware, software, or cloud services without the knowledge of the firm's IT or security group can create serious security gaps and risk the exposure of client data.[34]

Legal Outsourcing. Legal organizations interconnect their networks electronically among offices and with business partners and vendors for a variety of purposes, ranging from information technology (IT), finance, accounting, and human resources to procurement, contract management, data analytics, and investigations.[35] It is now common practice for law firms to outsource key services to external vendors and business partners located domestically and overseas. Legal process outsourcing is a growing trend, and law offices that focus on their core business and outsource non-core tasks are expected to drive the market.[36] Law firms and corporate legal departments outsource legal work such as litigation support for document review, patent support, contract drafting, compliance assistance, due diligence, legal research, and law libraries.[37] Much of the billions of dollars law firms spend on e-discovery services and forensic investigations is used to hire outside vendors.

This ever-growing paradigm presents a heightened risk for lawyers and their practices, who remain responsible for potentially widespread damage from cyber attacks—especially for systems and services managed externally—and accountable to clients, the courts, and

32. The credentials of over 500,000 Zoom teleconferencing accounts were found for sale on the dark web and in hacker forums. Email addresses, passwords, personal meeting URLs, and host keys are said to have been collected through a credential stuffing attack. Lee Mathews, *500,000 Hacked Zoom Accounts Given Away For Free On The Dark Web*, FORBES (April 13, 2020), https://www.forbes.com/sites/leemathews/2020/04/13/500000-hacked-zoom-accounts-given-away-for-free-on-the-dark-web; CISA, GUIDANCE FOR SECURING VIDEO CONFERENCING, https://www.cisa.gov/sites/default/files/publications/CISA_Guidance_for_Securing_Video_Conferencing_S508C.pdf (last visited June 12, 2025).

33. *Collaboration Security: Risks & Realities of the Modern Work Surface*, MIMECAST, https://www.mimecast.com/resources/ebooks/collaboration-security-risks-realities-modern-work/ (last visited June 12, 2025).

34. *What Is Shadow IT?*, CISCO, https://www.cisco.com/c/en/us/products/security/what-is-shadow-it.html (last visited June 12, 2025).

35. Karan Aneja, Juan Coronado, & Mike Stoler, GLOBAL OUTSOURCING SURVEY 2024, DELOITTE CONSULTING LLP (2024), https://www2.deloitte.com/content/dam/Deloitte/us/Documents/consulting/us-global-outsourcing-survey-2024-report.pdf.

36. *Legal Process Outsourcing Market Trends*, GRAND VIEW RESEARCH, https://www.grandviewresearch.com/industry-analysis/legal-process-outsourcing-lpo-market (last visited June 12, 2025).

37. Jeff Harvey et al., *Technology & Outsourcing 2024*, CHAMBERS & PARTNERS, https://practiceguides.chambers.com/practice-guides/technology-outsourcing-2024/usa/trends-and-developments/O18736 (last updated Oct. 10, 2024).

entities with whom they have contracts. With the law firm's core business model centered on discretion and privacy, rigorous security hygiene for key external interfaces and third-party software is critical. The expectation of security is growing, and therefore, the responsibility for protecting information, whether held within the firm or outsourced to a third party, is also increasing.

1.4. Widespread Cybersecurity Risks with AI

AI is changing the nature of cybersecurity attacks and creating new cybersecurity risks.[38] Some of the most serious types of attacks will be amplified and exacerbated by AI. With 500 billion devices expected to be online by 2030,[39] smart devices vulnerable to cyber attacks will become frequent targets. AI will be weaponized for social engineering.[40]

A report by the U.K. Department for Science, Innovation, and Technology provides a comprehensive assessment of the cybersecurity risks that are specifically associated with AI. It concluded that the rapid adoption of AI continues to introduce complex cybersecurity risks that traditional practices may not sufficiently address.

> While AI technologies have advanced and enhanced efficiency and productivity, they remain susceptible to an ever-growing number of security threats and vulnerabilities. The rapid advancement of AI therefore necessitates the need for a robust understanding of the evolving risks that are specifically associated with AI.[41]

Assessing the cyber risks in the evolving landscape of AI is challenging due to the increasing complexity and interconnectedness of AI and cybersecurity. The U.K. assessment was designed to develop an understanding of the cybersecurity risks of AI by identifying specific vulnerabilities at each stage of the AI lifecycle—design, development, deployment, and maintenance—and assessing the exploitation and impact of each vulnerability.

The National Institute of Standards and Technology (NIST) developed the *AI Risk Management Framework* to assist organizations and individuals in better managing the risks associated with AI.[42] Developed to "improve the ability to incorporate trustworthiness

---

38. Santeri Kangas, *Why AI Is the Key to Cutting-Edge Cybersecurity*, World Econ. Forum (July 21, 2022), https://www.weforum.org/agenda/2022/07/why-ai-is-the-key-to-cutting-edge-cybersecurity/; Microsoft Threat Intelligence, *Staying Ahead of Threat Actors in the Age of AI*, Microsoft (Feb. 14, 2024), https://www.microsoft.com/en-us/security/blog/2024/02/14/staying-ahead-of-threat-actors-in-the-age-of-ai/.

39. *Powering an Inclusive, Digital Future for All*, Cisco (Jan. 11, 2023), https://newsroom.cisco.com/c/r/newsroom/en/us/a/y2023/m01/powering-an-inclusive-digital-future-for-all.html.

40. The OpenAI System Card explained that ChatGPT-4 was effective in drafting realistic social engineering content and explaining some vulnerabilities. OpenAI, GPT-4 System Card § 2.8 Cybersecurity 13 (Mar. 23, 2023), https://cdn.openai.com/papers/gpt-4-system-card.pdf.

41. *Cyber Security Risks to Artificial Intelligence*, U.K. Department for Science, Innovation, and Technology, (May 15, 2024), https://www.gov.uk/government/publications/research-on-the-cyber-security-of-ai/cyber-security-risks-to-artificial-intelligence.

42. Nat'l Inst. of Standards & Tech. ("NIST"), AI Risk Management Framework (Jan. 26, 2023), https://www.nist.gov/itl/ai-risk-management-framework. NIST addressed the question of "How AI Risks Differ

considerations into the design, development, use, and evaluation of AI products, services, and systems," NIST includes security (confidentiality, integrity, and availability) and privacy (and protection of personally identifiable information (PII)), among the key characteristics that relate to trustworthy AI technologies, along with safety, resilience, reliability, accuracy, objectivity, and freedom from bias, explainability, and accountability.

2. Lawyers and Law Firms Are Prime Targets: The Significant Resulting Damage

Due to the huge volume of critical information lawyers collect about companies and individuals, hackers are targeting lawyers and law offices. Much of the valuable data law firms hold—particularly confidential client information and PII, IP, strategic business data, and knowledge of M&A and international transactions—carries obligations associated with attorney-client privileged data.

Similarly, protective orders imposed by courts to preserve the secrecy of sensitive data may be violated in the event of a data breach. Although Rule 26(b) of the Federal Rules of Civil Procedure allows broad discovery on a variety of issues, Rule 26(c)(7) allows a court to issue an order that "a trade secret or other confidential research, development, or commercial information not be revealed or be revealed only in a designated way." If a data breach were to occur at a firm subject to such an order, arguably that order would be violated and the firm might face serious consequences.

From a business perspective, a security breach or information loss by a law firm can have significant negative effects. The consequences to clients and even innocent third parties of a data breach can be very serious, potentially subjecting them to identity theft, fraud, negative publicity, and even financial ruin. If a firm loses client information, the reputational harm alone may lead a client to take its business elsewhere or potential clients to turn to other firms. For lawyers in the firm, a data breach may result in ethical violations that have serious impacts.[43]

Cybersecurity Attacks Can Expose Attorneys to Third-Party Liability. In April 2024, law firm Orrick, Herrington & Sutcliffe agreed to pay $8 million to settle class action claims stemming from a March 2023 data breach in which cyber criminals accessed the names, addresses, dates of birth, and Social Security numbers of more than 600,000 individuals from files stored by the law firm. The hackers also accessed data on medical treatments, diagnoses, and insurance claim details.[44] In the class action lawsuits that followed

---

from Traditional Software Risks" on pages 38–39 of Appendix B of this document. *See*, *e.g.*, Microsoft Threat Intelligence, *supra* note 38.

43. Model Rules of Prof'l Conduct, *supra* note 4.

44. Settlement Agreement signed April 11, 2024, *In re: Orrick, Herrington & Sutcliffe LLP Data Breach Lit.*, *Case No. 3:23-cv-04089-SI* (N.D. CA, May 31, 2024), https://storage.courtlistener.com/recap/gov.uscourts.cand.416769/gov.uscourts.cand.416769.63.1.pdf (approved by Final Approval Order & Judgment (N.D. Cal. Nov. 12, 2024), https://storage.courtlistener.com/recap/gov.uscourts.cand.416769/gov.uscourts.

the cyber attack, Orrick was accused of failing to inform victims about the breach until months after it occurred.

In November 2024, the Florida law firm Gunster, Yoakley & Stewart, P.A. agreed to pay $8.5 million to settle a data breach lawsuit.[45] The breach occurred in 2022 and exposed the personal and health information of nearly 10,000 clients and employees.

Law firm Bryan Cave Leighton Paisner reached a $750,000 settlement with snack food company Mondelez to resolve a proposed class action lawsuit over a 2023 data breach at the firm.[46] Plaintiffs alleged that the law firm failed to implement or maintain adequate data security measures and safeguards to protect the personal information of the proposed class of 51,100 current and former Mondelez employees.

A lawsuit in the District of Columbia alleged that a hacking incident involving a law firm exposed personal information (passport information and applications for political asylum) of its former client, a Chinese citizen, to a hacker that had infiltrated the law firm's servers.[47] The case, settled in 2023, is noted for the court's holding that the plaintiff pleaded viable malpractice claims. Often hackers blackmail firms, hoping they will pay the ransom to avoid such a scenario as this one.

2.1. Security Breaches on the Rise: Threats and Vulnerabilities Illustrated

Many different types of attacks against lawyers and law practices have occurred. Millions of confidential records have been compromised, leading not only to data loss, but also reputational loss, lawsuits, and opportunity costs. To prevent data breaches, it is essential to analyze and understand the root causes of the security failures and develop a specific plan to address them.

The following are examples of the increasingly dangerous threats to sensitive data and the heightened need for lawyers and law firms to address cybersecurity risks, build strong information security programs, and utilize necessary security controls. This is not only good business practice; it will also help firms avoid the high costs associated with responding to data breaches, potential liability, negative press, embarrassment, and ultimately loss of trust of clients, judges, and the public.[48]

---

cand.416769.74.0.pdf*); see also KCC Class Action Services LLC, Orrick, Herrington & Sutcliffe LLP Data Breach Litigation,* https://www.ohsclassactionsettlement.com/ (last visited Jun. 29, 2025).

45. *See* Sara Merken, *Another US Law Firm Reaches Data Breach Settlement as Cyber Risks Mount*, Reuters (Nov. 8, 2024), https://www.reuters.com/legal/litigation/another-us-law-firm-reaches-data-breach-settlement-cyber-risks-mount-2024-11-08/ (reporting the proposed settlement in *Whalen v. Gunster, Yoakley & Steward, PA*, No. 9:24-CV-80612-AMC (S.D. Fla. Nov. 7, 2024)).

46. Mondelez Data Breach Litigation, U.S.D.C. N.D. IL, 1:23-cv-03999. Final Approval Order (Jan. 21, 2025). *See $750K Mondelēz data breach class action settlement*, Top Class Actions (Jan. 16, 2025), https://topclassactions.com/lawsuit-settlements/closed-settlements/750k-mondelez-data-breach-class-action-settlement/.

47. Memorandum Op., Wengui v. Clark Hill, PLC, Civ. Action No. 19-3195(JEB) (D.D.C. Feb. 20, 2020), https://www.courtlistener.com/opinion/4728888/wengui-v-clark-hill-plc/?q=Wengui+v.+Clark+Hill+Plc.

48. The high costs of responding to data breaches in terms of expenditures for detection, escalation, notification, and response, along with legal, investigative, and administrative expenses, customer defections, opportunity loss, reputation management, and costs associated with customer support such as information hotlines and credit

2.1.1. *Largest Law Firm Breach*

The law firm Mossack Fonseca, located in Panama, was involved in the largest data breach ever in terms of the volume of records stolen—with irreparable harm. Over 40 years, the firm had set up hundreds of offshore companies, collecting and storing a treasure trove of individuals' confidential financial information in the process.[49] As a result of the breach and its fallout, the entire firm of 40 offices closed their doors in March 2018.[50]

The source of the breach, using the pseudonym John Doe, sent encrypted files anonymously to the German newspaper *Süddeutsche Zeitung* and shared them with more than 100 other media outlets. This resulted in publication online of 11.5 million confidential documents dating from the 1970s through late 2015. The compromised data exposed the existence of offshore accounts of world leaders, company executives, and celebrities. The firm's leaked internal files contained information on more than 214,000 offshore entities tied to 12 current or former heads of state, 140 politicians and others. The U.S.-based International Consortium of Investigative Journalists (ICIJ) published a searchable database of 214,000 offshore entities uncovered by the "Panama Papers" leak.[51]

International news outlets published articles on the leak, revealing corruption on a massive scale. Repercussions from the leak were felt around the world. The prime ministers of Iceland and Pakistan resigned. Following a U.S. Department of Justice criminal investigation into the leak and the tax avoidance schemes it revealed, an indictment was returned against four individuals who allegedly helped U.S. taxpayer clients of Mossack Fonseca conceal assets and investments and the income they generated, through a complex trail of offshore shell corporations and bogus foundations used to disguise the beneficial ownership of huge amounts of money.[52] In 2020, a U.S. taxpayer and his accountant pleaded guilty to various fraud and money laundering crimes and received substantial

---

monitoring subscriptions, have been well documented. IBM, COST OF A DATA BREACH REPORT 2024, https://www.ibm.com/reports/data-breach (last visited June 12, 2025). These costs are likely to rise as the notification requirements in the data breach laws become more stringent, increasing the numbers of individuals who must be notified; and the liability imposed by courts and administrative agencies for data breaches increases significantly.

49. Aliah D. Wright, *Panama Papers: What Data Breach Means for Law Firms*, SOC'Y FOR HUMAN RES. MGMT (Apr. 7, 2016), https://www.proquest.com/docview/1779477134?sourcetype=Trade%20Journals; Kirk Semple, Azam Ahmed & Eric Lipton, *Panama Papers Leak Casts Light on a Law Firm Founded on Secrecy*, N.Y. TIMES (Apr. 6, 2016), https://www.nytimes.com/2016/04/07/world/americas/panama-papers-leak-casts-light-on-a-law-firm-founded-on-secrecy.html.

50. Will Fitzgibbon, *Panama Papers Law Firm Mossack Fonseca Closes Its Doors,* INT'L CONSORTIUM OF INVESTIGATIVE JOURNALISTS (Mar. 14, 2018), https://www.icij.org/investigations/panama-papers/panama-papers-law-firm-mossack-fonseca-closes-doors/.

51. Marina Walker Guevara, *ICIJ Releases Database Revealing Thousands of Secret Offshore Companies*, INT'L CONSORTIUM OF INVESTIGATIVE JOURNALISTS (May 9, 2016), https://panamapapers.icij.org/blog/20160509-offshore-database-release.html; Jane McCallion, *Panama Papers: Emma Watson Named in Leaked Documents*, ITPRO (Nov. 5, 2016), http://www.itpro.co.uk/data-leakage/26293/panama-papers-emma-watson-named-in-leaked-documents.

52. Will Fitzgibbon, *From Front Pages to Prison Time: Behind the Scenes of a Panama Papers Criminal Case*, INT'L CONSORTIUM OF INVESTIGATIVE JOURNALISTS (Apr. 23, 2021), https://www.icij.org/investigations/panama-papers/from-front-pages-to-prison-time-behind-the-scenes-of-a-panama-papers-criminal-case/.

prison sentences.[53] In June 2024, a Panamanian judge acquitted all 28 defendants in a case there, among them former employees of the Mossack Fonseca firm, the source of the leaked documents.[54]

The Mossack Fonseca breach that compromised the confidential records of the entire firm was the result of the failure to provide appropriate data security.[55] The firm employed outdated software—older versions of open source web server software—with critical vulnerabilities that were widely known among hackers, including for its customer portal. Updates to the software were available, but the firm had not updated or properly patched its web server. Security experts suggested that because Mossack Fonseca's web server software was many months out of date, the security failure was particularly egregious, considering the sensitivity of their clients' information. The firm failed to take the most rudimentary steps to protect their confidential client data.[56]

2.1.2. *Phishing and Pretexting—Major Attack Vectors*

Phishing is among the attack vectors used most often by hackers to launch cyber attacks. It was the most common type of cyber crime in 2023, resulting in $1.8 billion in business losses.[57] Phishing has been a long-standing cyber threat for law firms.[58]

Attackers usually masquerade as a trustworthy entity in an electronic communication and target the weakest link in the security chain: the user.[59] The related pretexting attacks have also increased significantly from last year and now account for 40% of breaches among services professional organizations.[60]

To illustrate the long-standing nature of this cyber threat, more than ten years ago, the Federal Bureau of Investigation (FBI) warned that hackers were targeting U.S. law firms to steal confidential information.[61] In 2011 the Washington, D.C. law firm Wiley Rein

---

53. *U.S. Taxpayer in Panama Papers Investigation Sentenced to 4 Years in Prison*, U.S. Att'ys Office, S.D.N.Y. (Sept. 21, 2020), https://www.justice.gov/usao-sdny/pr/us-taxpayer-panama-papers-investigation-sentenced-4-years-prison.

54. Leila Miller, *Defendants Acquitted in Panama Papers Money-Laundering Trial,* N.Y. Times (June 29, 2024), https://www.nytimes.com/2024/06/29/world/americas/panama-papers-defendants-acquitted.html (Prosecutors were unable to show that the founders of the firm knew that the shell companies it managed were being used for illicit activities).

55. *The Panama Papers: Exposing the Rogue Offshore Finance Industry*, Int'l Consortium of Investigative Journalists, https://panamapapers.icij.org/ (last accessed June 12, 2025).

56. Jason Bloomberg, *Cybersecurity Lessons Learned from "Panama Papers" Breach*, Forbes, https://www.forbes.com/sites/jasonbloomberg/2016/04/21/cybersecurity-lessons-learned-from-panama-papers-breach/ (last updated Apr. 22, 2016 10:12 AM).

57. FBI, *supra* note 6, at 8.

58. Law Soc'y of Singapore, *Don't Take the Bait*, Law Gazette (2017), https://v1.lawgazette.com.sg/2017-02/1774.htm.

59. Cisco Cyber Threat Trends Report, Cisco, https://www.cisco.com/c/en/us/products/security/cyber-threat-trends-report.html (last visited June 12, 2025). *See* Verizon 2024 DBIR, *supra* note 13, at 40.

60. *See* Verizon 2024 DBIR, *supra* note 13, at 69; Jim Holdsworth & Matthew Kosinski, *What Is pretexting?*, IBM (Sep. 6, 2024), https://www.ibm.com/think/topics/pretexting.

61. *Recognize and Report Phishing*, CISA, https://www.cisa.gov/secure-our-world/recognize-and-report-phishing (last visited June 12, 2025).

was a victim of a massive attack by Chinese hackers, referred to as "Byzantine Candor," that encompassed 20 major companies. Security researchers referred to the hackers as the "Comment group" since they infiltrated computers using hidden web page computer code known as "comments."[62]

Their attack methodology began with phishing attacks that transmitted malware (malicious code) in emails to members of the firm. Audit log files showed that the malware enabled the hackers to access encrypted passwords they were able to crack offline. The hackers accessed the firm's network and stole sensitive data by acting as network administrators, collecting critical data and exfiltrating it over the course of months. The thousands of pages of emails the hackers stole included confidential communications with clients.

In a twist of the law firm phishing attack, hackers have sent phishing emails from purported, but fake, law firms advising targets that they had been sued and need to take action immediately.[63]

2.1.3. *Ransomware Attacks—Prominent Legal Organizations Targeted*

Ransomware, a type of malware that encrypts or locks valuable digital files and demands a ransom to release them, is a massive cyber threat for organizations, particularly small and medium-sized businesses such as law firms.[64] Roughly one-third of all breaches in 2023 involved ransomware or some other extortion technique.[65] Lawyers and law firms, as well as bar associations, have been targeted. Further, sophisticated cyber adversaries are increasingly moving downstream from law firms themselves, compromising legal supply chains.[66]

A 2019 Cybersecurity & Infrastructure Security Agency (CISA) alert, revised in 2021, concluded that "[r]ansomware has rapidly emerged as the most visible cybersecurity risk playing out across our nation's networks.... We strongly urge you to consider ransomware infections as destructive attacks, not an event where you can simply pay off the bad guys and regain control of your network (do you really trust a cybercriminal?)."[67]

---

62. Michael Riley & Dune Lawrence, *Hackers Linked to China's Army Seen from EU to D.C.*, Bloomberg Mkts. (July 26, 2012), https://www.bloomberg.com/news/articles/2012-07-26/china-hackers-hit-eu-point-man-and-d-c-with-byzantine-candor.

63. *Legal Threats Make Powerful Phishing Lures*, Krebs on Security (May 22, 2019), https://krebsonsecurity.com/2019/05/legal-threats-make-powerful-phishing-lures/.

64. Ransomware, FBI, https://www.fbi.gov/scams-and-safety/common-scams-and-crimes/ransomware (last visited June 12, 2025); CISA, Ransomware: What It Is & What To Do About It (2021), https://www.cisa.gov/sites/default/files/2021-01/NCIJTF%20Ransomware_Fact_Sheet.pdf.

65. Verizon 2024 DBIR, *supra* note 13, at 7.

66. Insider's Playbook: Defending Against Cloud Threats, Crowdstrike (2024), https://go.crowdstrike.com/2024-insiders-playbook-defending-against-cloud-threats.html.

67. *CISA Insights—Ransomware Outbreak*, CISA, https://www.cisa.gov/blog/2019/08/21/cisa-insights-ransomware-outbreak (last updated Nov. 1, 2021); CISA, *supra* note 61 (These resources are designed to help individuals and organizations prevent ransomware attacks that can severely impact business processes and leave organizations without the data they need to operate and deliver mission-critical services.).

Malware used by North Korea for ransomware attacks was identified in a joint alert by CISA, the FBI, and partners in 2024.[68] HIDDEN COBRA malware, for example, has long targeted U.S. industries and is allegedly behind some of the largest hacking incidents, including the global WannaCry ransomware cyberattack in 2017.[69]

Although cyber criminals use a variety of techniques to infect victims with ransomware and other malware, the most common means of infection are through email phishing campaigns. Recent ransomware campaigns have been targeted and sophisticated, particularly with the assistance of AI. The criminal sends an email containing a malicious file or link that deploys malware when clicked by a recipient. Criminals may also compromise a victim's email account by using precursor malware, which enables the cyber criminal to use a victim's email account to further spread the infection.[70] Cyber criminals use stolen credentials (logins and passwords) to target businesses and steal their key data and IP.[71]

The FBI warned that "more than just money is at stake" and "ransomware has become a serious national security threat and public health and safety concern.... Ransomware attacks are becoming more targeted, sophisticated, and costly."[72]

The threat continues to grow more serious.[73] Following the attack leading to the May 2021 shutdown of the Colonial Pipeline,[74] the White House warned American businesses to take urgent security measures to protect against ransomware attacks, as hackers were shifting their tactics from stealing data to disrupting critical infrastructure. The attackers froze the business records of Colonial Pipeline, making it impossible for the company to monitor the flow of petroleum to specific locations and access its billing systems to

68. *North Korea Cyber Group Conducts Global Espionage Campaign to Advance Regime's Military and Nuclear Programs*, CISA (July 25, 2024) (FBI and co-authoring U.S. and South Korean security agencies concluded that North Korean "actors fund their espionage activity through ransomware operations against U.S. healthcare entities"), https://www.cisa.gov/news-events/cybersecurity-advisories/aa24-207a.

69. In a ransomware attack in May 2017, hackers unleashed an attack that disabled nearly 230,000 computers globally. Named WannaCry, the ransomware affected tens of thousands of organizations in over 150 countries.

70. FBI, *supra* note 5. *See Avoiding Social Engineering and Phishing Attacks*, CISA (Feb. 1, 2021), https://us-cert.cisa.gov/ncas/tips/ST04-014.

71. Identity Theft Resource Center, *supra* note 2. *See* Verizon 2024 DBIR, *supra* note 13, at 21–22, 43–46; Cisco Cyber Threat Trends Report: From Trojan Takeovers to Ransomware Roulette, Cisco Umbrella (2024), https://umbrella.cisco.com/info/cyber-threat-trends-report.

72. CISA and the FBI have issued official updates to help stakeholders guard against the ever-evolving ransomware threat environment; FBI, *supra* note 5, at 13–14. *See Ransomware Statistics, Data, Trends and Facts [Updated 2024]*, Varonis (Nov. 13, 2024), https://www.varonis.com/blog/ransomware-statistics; Mathew J. Schwartz, *Ransomware Leak Sites Suggest Attacks Reached Record High*, BankInfoSecurity (Jan. 15, 2025), https://www.bankinfosecurity.com/ransomware-leak-sites-suggest-attacks-reached-record-high-a-27299.

73. The FBI and CISA have issued dozens of alerts warning of the dangers of the various ransomware attacks and providing detailed guidance on how to address them and protect company's infrastructure and critical records and data. FBI, *supra* note 5; *Official Alerts & Statements—CISA*, CISA, https://www.cisa.gov/stopransomware/official-alerts-statements-cisa (last visited June 13, 2025).

74. Collin Eaton & Dustin Volz, *Colonial Pipeline CEO Tells Why He Paid Hackers a $4.4 Million Ransom*, Wall St. J. (May 19, 202), https://www.wsj.com/articles/colonial-pipeline-ceo-tells-why-he-paid-hackers-a-4-4-million-ransom-11621435636.

charge customers for deliveries, and leading to the shutdown of its operational technology systems.[75]

Shortly thereafter, meat supplier JBS announced that it was the victim of a cyberattack, attributed by the FBI to the REvil (a/k/a Sodinokibi) ransomware group.[76] The White House urged businesses to implement the best practices set forth in the Executive Order on Improving the Nation's Cybersecurity, EO 14028 (May 12, 2021):

> The private sector ... has a critical responsibility to protect against these threats. All organizations must recognize that no company is safe from being targeted by ransomware, regardless of size or location. To understand your risk, business executives should immediately convene their leadership teams to discuss the ransomware threat and review corporate security posture and business continuity plans to ensure you have the ability to continue or quickly restore operations.[77]

Escalating Extortion Demands. Ransomware can make information systems unavailable and enable attackers to steal and exfiltrate sensitive personal data and IP. Lawyers who are victims of ransomware attacks may find themselves at the mercy of hackers pursuing a multi-pronged attack strategy to the detriment of law offices.[78] Criminals plant malware to embed themselves on the network, steal and exfiltrate huge troves of so-called "ace trophy data," then encrypt the network files to make them unavailable. They demand large ransom payments to regain access to the network and the data. The financial extortion may not be limited to getting back access to the files—hackers are also posting stolen firm and client data on the dark web, or leaking it more broadly to the world, and at the same time making extortion demands to both restore access to the data and information system and not publicly release the stolen data, resulting in the breach of client confidences and trust.

Search Engine Optimization (SEO) "Poisoning" Attacks to Deliver Ransomware—Pervasive Danger of Legal Searches. At least one attack group has targeted law firms and business professionals with a difficult to detect, browser-based attack method known as search engine optimization (SEO) poisoning. The goal of the attack is likely to conduct corporate

75. *FBI Statement on Compromise of Colonial Pipeline Networks*, FBI (May 20, 2021), https://www.fbi.gov/news/press-releases/fbi-statement-on-compromise-of-colonial-pipeline-networks; *Department of Justice Seizes $2.3 Million in Cryptocurrency Paid to the Ransomware Extortionists Darkside*, DEP'T OF JUSTICE (June 7, 2021), https://www.justice.gov/archives/opa/pr/department-justice-seizes-23-million-cryptocurrency-paid-ransomware-extortionists-darkside.

76. *FBI Statement on JBS Cyberattack*, FBI (June 2, 2021), https://www.fbi.gov/news/press-releases/fbi-statement-on-jbs-cyberattack.

77. *International Counter Ransomware Initiative 2023 Joint Statement*, THE WHITE HOUSE (Nov. 1, 2023), https://bidenwhitehouse.archives.gov/briefing-room/statements-releases/2023/11/01/international-counter-ransomware-initiative-2023-joint-statement/.

78. *See* VERIZON 2024 DBIR, Ransomware and Extortion breaches over time, *supra* note 13, at 35.

espionage to gain insight into IP such as the financial details of mergers and acquisitions or proprietary research and development plans.[79]

A lawyer or paralegal who searches online for business documents such as supply contracts or agreement templates may find the top website search results lead to files infected with the dangerous GootLoader malware. Cyber criminals manipulate search engine results (optimize fraudulent websites to achieve high rankings in web search results) and direct users to malicious websites (*e.g.*, compromised WordPress webpages) controlled by GootLoader actors. Search engine Ads are also leveraged to provide a link to the infected piece of malware on top of the search engine. The malicious content and malvertising are linked to 3.5 million search terms, a high percentage of which are legal terms.[80]

A security researcher warned that "[w]hen the computer user navigates to one of these malicious web pages and hits the link to download the purported business agreement, they are unknowingly downloading GootLoader."[81] Once installed on a target network, GootLoader can download additional malicious payloads such as ransomware (usually BlackCat), intrusion tools, and bank trojans that allow threat actors to carry out a range of harmful activities, such as stealing sensitive information or encrypting files.[82]

In a 2022 advisory, CISA and the Australian Cyber Security Centre (ACSC) warned that GootLoader was one of the top malware strains of 2021, along with ten others.[83]

Law Offices Swept Up in Ransomware Attack; Widespread Impact on Clients.[84] In April 2023, HWL Ebsworth—one of Australia's largest law firms—suffered a ransomware attack by ransomware-as-a-service (RaaS) group ALPHV/Blackcat.[85] Security experts Arctic Wolf reported that "[d]isclosure came from ALPHV/Blackcat themselves, posting on a dark web forum that they had accessed over 4TB of data, including employee resumes, IDs,

79. Keith Wojcieszek et al., *Deep Dive into GOOTLOADER Malware and Its Infection Chain*, KROLL (June 23, 2023), https://www.kroll.com/en/insights/publications/cyber/deep-dive-gootloader-malware-infection-chain.

80. Rodel Mendrez, *Gootloader: Why Your Legal Document Search May End in Misery*, TRUSTWAVE (Aug. 11, 2023), https://www.trustwave.com/en-us/resources/blogs/spiderlabs-blog/gootloader-why-your-legal-document-search-may-end-in-misery/. Security researcher Trustwave collected a group of search queries that lead to the compromised websites and identified the keywords utilized by this malware group, revealing a predominant SEO keyword focus on legal documents such as "agreements," "contracts," and "forms."

81. Lakshmanan, *supra* note 10; *Increase in GootLoader Malware*, ESENTIRE (Jan. 6, 2022), https://www.esentire.com/security-advisories/increase-in-gootloader-malware.

82. Lily Hay Newman, *A Security Team Is Turning This Malware Gang's Tricks Against It*, WIRED (April 25, 2023), https://www.wired.com/story/gootloader-malware-ip-block/. ("Known as an initial-access-as-a-service operation…, [t]he Gootloader gang infects victim organizations and then sells access to deliver a customer's preferred malware into the compromised target network, whether that's ransomware, mechanisms for data exfiltration, or other tools to compromise the target more deeply.").

83. *2021 Top Malware Strains*, CISA & AUSTL. CYBER SEC. CTR. ACSC, https://www.cisa.gov/news-events/alerts/2022/08/02/cisa-and-acsc-release-top-2021-malware-strains (last updated Aug. 4, 2022).

84. *The Top 11 Legal Industry Cyber Attacks*, ARCTIC WOLF (Apr. 30, 2024), https://arcticwolf.com/resources/blog/top-legal-industry-cyber-attacks/.

85. *Ransomware-as-a-Service Will Continue to Grow in 2024*, ARCTIC WOLF (Jan. 19, 2024), https://arcticwolf.com/resources/blog/ransomware-as-a-service-will-continue-to-grow-in-2024/.

financial reports, accounting data, client documentation, credit card information, and a complete network map. In June 2023, ALPHV/Blackcat "published 1.45 terabytes of data on the dark web that it allegedly stole from HWL Ebsworth in late April, with the message: 'ENJOY!!!'"

Sixty-two (62) Australian Government entities were impacted by the attack, as well as clients which included local government entities, banks, insurers, telecommunication providers, residential property developers, non-residential property owners, construction and infrastructure clients, transport operators, as well as many other commercial entities across several sectors.[86]

In a statement concerning the massive breach, HWL Ebsworth pledged to work with the Australian Cyber Security Centre to determine the extent of the breach and determine steps for recovery and remediation.[87] In response, the NSW Supreme Court issued an injunction banning individuals from accessing the stolen files.[88]

Notorious Attack on NYC Law Firm. In 2020, the cyber criminal gang REvil/Sodinokibi stole legal documents from the New York City "law firm of the stars," Grubman Shire Meiselas & Sacks (GSMSLaw). The trove of data allegedly stolen—a total of 756 gigabytes—included contracts, nondisclosure agreements, phone numbers, email addresses, and "personal correspondence" of multiple music and entertainment figures.[89] The hackers published a screenshot of the folders they had stolen from the law firm, along with excerpts from legal agreements signed by artists, and threatened to release the confidential documents on the dark web if the law firm refused to pay the demanded ransom of a substantial amount of bitcoins in exchange for the decryption key.[90]

The hackers initially demanded $21 million and published over 2 gigabytes of Lady Gaga's contracts and other data on the dark web as proof of compromise. After finding files related to then-President Donald Trump, they doubled the ransomware price to $42 million and later published 169 emails related to Trump.[91] GSMSLaw had reportedly refused to pay the ransom, as recommended by the FBI. The firm recovered some of the lost

86. Nat'l Office of Cyber Sec., Austl. Gov't, *HWL Ebsworth Cyber Security Incident*, (Feb. 2024), https://www.homeaffairs.gov.au/reports-and-pubs/PDFs/nocs-hwl-ebsworth-lessons-learned-report.pdf; Arctic Wolf, *supra* note 84.

87. Nat'l Office of Cyber Sec., *supra* note 87; *Cyber Incident*, HWL Ebsworth, https://hwlebsworth.com.au/cyber-incident/ (last visited June 13, 2025).

88. Robyn Chatwood et al., *Acting against Unknown Hackers: A Groundbreaking Australian Data Breach Case*, Dentons (Apr. 23, 2024), https://www.dentons.com/en/insights/articles/2024/april/23/acting-against-unknown-hackers-a-groundbreaking-australian-data-breach-case.

89. Naveen Goud, *Ransomware Attack on Grubman Shire Meiselas & Sacks Law firm*, Cybersecurity Insiders, https://www.cybersecurity-insiders.com/ransomware-attack-on-grubman-shire-meiselas-sacks-law-firm/ (last visited June 13, 2025).

90. Pierluigi Paganini, *Sodinokibi Gang Hacked Law Firm of the Celebrities and Threatens to Release the Docs*, Sec. Affairs, (May 9, 2020), https://securityaffairs.co/wordpress/102960/cyber-crime/sodinokibi-gang-hacked-stars-law-firm.html.

91. A.J. Shankar, *Ransomware Attackers Take Aim at Law Firms*, Forbes (Mar. 12, 2021), https://www.forbes.com/sites/forbestechcouncil/2021/03/12/ransomware-attackers-take-aim-at-law-firms/.

data through individuals they hired privately; however, much of the stolen data was still at large and available for purchase online.[92]

Another hacker group, Maze, focused on the legal industry and hacked into firms in Texas and Oregon.[93] Active since 2019, Maze was particularly dangerous because it threatened to leak confidential data if the ransom was not paid. In January 2021, Maze attacked three small law firms in South Dakota in one 24-hour period. Maze published the names of the law firms on websites it used to announce its targets, threatening to reveal their data unless they agreed to pay a steep fee. Maze also exposed the data of Baker Wotring LLP, a Texas law firm, including fee agreements and diaries from personal injury cases.[94]

The first prominent ransomware attack on a law firm was against DLA Piper in 2017. The attack put the legal industry on high alert about the potential of breaches to debilitate even large global organizations.[95] The firm was hit with the NotPetya ransomware that first struck its Ukrainian offices during an upgrade of its payroll software. The malware spread rapidly throughout the firm's servers and affected thousands of computers across its network, nearly shutting down the practice and causing enormous damage in direct and indirect costs.[96]

A ransomware attack compromised the network of the Illinois Attorney General's Office in 2021.[97] It was reported that the ransomware group DoppelPaymer posted 68 internal documents labeled "judgments entered," "shakedown cases" and "state prisoners" that were said to be from the state Attorney General's office.[98]

In security notifications to the Maryland Attorney General, the New York City Bar Association and the Chicago Bar Association both reported data breaches that involved the potential theft of credit card data. Hackers exploited vulnerabilities with the third-party commerce and management software iMIS on their websites to install malicious code that acted as a credit card skimmer and may have allowed an unauthorized individual to collect credit card data from transactions. Similarly, the Mississippi Center for Legal Services

92. *Grubman Shire Meiselas & Sacks Attack and the Evolution of Ransomware*, EPIC (Oct. 13, 2020), https://epicbrokers.com/insights/grubman-shire-meiselas-sacks-attack/.

93. *Ransomware Attacks Targeting Attorneys on the Rise*, USI Affinity (Jan. 7, 2021), https://insurancefocus.usiaffinity.com/2021/01/ransomware-attacks-targeting-attorneys-on-the-rise.html.

94. Patrick Smith, *Maze Hackers Publish Texas Law Firm's Confidential Data*, Law.com (Feb. 11, 2020 9:44 AM) https://www.law.com/2020/02/11/maze-hackers-delist-texas-law-firm-as-ransom-pressures-mount/.

95. Jeff John Roberts, *Law Firm DLA Piper Reels under Cyber Attack, Fate of Files Unclear*, Fortune (June 29, 2017), https://fortune.com/2017/06/29/dla-piper-cyber-attack/.

96. Kim Nash et al., *One Year after NotPetya Cyberattack, Firms Wrestle with Recovery Costs*, Wall St. J. (June 27, 2018), https://www.wsj.com/articles/one-year-after-notpetya-companies-still-wrestle-with-financial-impacts-1530095906.

97. *Data Breach*, Office of the Ill. Attorney General, https://illinoisattorneygeneral.gov/data-breach/ (last visited June 13, 2025).

98. Rachel Hinton, *Raoul Sets Up Hotline on Computer Breach as "Ransomware" Group Posts Files Claimed Stolen from Attorney General's Office*, Chi. Sun Times (Apr. 29, 2021), https://chicago.suntimes.com/2021/4/29/22410356/attorney-general-raoul-office-hack-breach-ransomware-network-compromise.

and North Mississippi Rural Legal Services issued a public statement reporting that those organizations were hit by Ryuk ransomware on Christmas Eve.[99]

2.1.4. *Advanced Persistent Threats and Compromise of the Software Supply Chain*

Organizations that collect, process, or store large amounts of PII or IP and strategic business data of high value to criminals have become prime targets of state-sponsored hackers and overseas organized crime.[100] Several of the largest breaches involved sophisticated global organizations of hackers who infiltrated information systems at vulnerable points—where sensitive personal records were unsecured—even though those same records were encrypted in company networks.[101]

Over the past decade, advanced persistent threats (APT) have been among the most serious types of cyber attacks because their focus is espionage. Often originating in the Asia-Pacific countries, APTs employ zero-day exploits (taking advantage of vulnerabilities in software that are known, but not yet fixed) and social-engineering techniques (phishing) against company employees to breach networks. The typical intrusion by an APT involves undetected access into a victim computer system (in violation of federal and state law) and then the theft of significant amounts of data. Through the intrusion, hackers establish a foothold into a company's network, sometimes years without discovery, and may even remain after a company has discovered them and attempted to take corrective measures.

Hackers Linked to Chinese Government Breached the Security of Major Telecommunications Companies. The targeting of telecommunications companies by the People's Republic of China (PRC)-backed hacking group Salt Typhoon reveals the dangers to lawyers and law firms of broad and significant cyber espionage campaigns by nation-states.

A joint statement by the FBI and CISA warned:[102]

> Specifically, we have identified that PRC-affiliated actors have compromised networks at multiple telecommunications companies to enable the theft of customer call records data, the compromise of private communications of a limited number of

99. *Public Notice*, Miss. Ctr. for Legal Servs. & N. Miss. Rural Legal Servs., (Feb. 5, 2020), http://www.mscenterforlegalservices.org/wp-content/uploads/2020/02/PUBLIC-NOTICE.pdf.

100. The Verizon 2024 DBIR provides a summary by month of dozens of APT attacks that were detected in 2023. Verizon 2024 DBIR Year in Review, *supra* note 13, at 81–84; Mandiant, APT1: Exposing One of China's Cyber Espionage Units 20 (undated), https://services.google.com/fh/files/misc/mandiant-apt1-report.pdf; *see also* Dan Mcwhorter, *Mandiant Exposes APT1—One of China's Cyber Espionage Units—and Releases 3,000 Indicators*, Threat Intel., Blog (Feb. 19, 2013), https://cloud.google.com/blog/topics/threat-intelligence/mandiant-exposes-apt1-chinas-cyber-espionage-units.

101. Lucy L. Thomson, *Encrypted Records—Failed Security*, ch. 5 in Data Breach and Encryption Handbook 57–82 (ABA 2011).

102. Press Release, CISA, *Joint Statement from FBI and CISA on the People's Republic of China (PRC) Targeting of Commercial Telecommunications Infrastructure* (Nov. 13, 2024), https://www.cisa.gov/news-events/news/joint-statement-fbi-and-cisa-peoples-republic-china-prc-targeting-commercial-telecommunications; James Palmer, *Salt Typhoon Stirs Panic in Washington: The Full Extent of the Hack Is Not Yet Public, but It Has Hardened Anti-China Consensus*, Foreign Pol'y (Jan. 7, 2025), https://foreignpolicy.com/2025/01/07/china-salt-typhoon-hack-threat-panic-washington/.

individuals who are primarily involved in government or political activity, and the copying of certain information that was subject to U.S. law enforcement requests pursuant to court orders.

Experts urge users to employ encrypted messaging apps to secure and protect their communications.

2.1.5. *Compromise of Software Products Used Widely by Law Offices*

Exploitation of software flaws is a longstanding attack method. Sophisticated cyber adversaries are increasingly moving from attacking law firms themselves to compromising legal supply chains.[103] Attacks involving the exploitation of vulnerabilities as the critical path to initiate a breach almost tripled (180% increase) from last year.[104]

Law firms need to think holistically about the risk of sophisticated cyber attacks and ransomware. Among other things, lawyers should take stock of the software and services they rely on.[105] "They should be holding their software vendors accountable for the security outcomes of their product, even if there is no regulatory pressure on those vendors to do better."[106]

CISA, NSA, and the FBI, along with international partners, released a cybersecurity advisory with best practices for information and communications technology (ICT), focusing on enabling transparent discussions between managed service providers (MSPs) and their customers on securing sensitive data. They said they expect "state-sponsored advanced persistent threat (APT) groups and other malicious cyber actors to increase their targeting of MSPs against both provider and customer networks."[107]

Several of the most dangerous law firm breaches have involved zero-day attacks that exploited significant and previously unknown software vulnerabilities/flaws in technology used by law offices as part of their IT operations: email transfer of large files, website transactions, and management of their computer networks. Cyber-exposure is exacerbated

---

103. CISA et al., Closing the Software Understanding Gap (Jan. 16, 2025), https://www.cisa.gov/sites/default/files/2025-01/joint-guidance-closing-the-software-understanding-gap-508c.pdf. *See* also NIST Spec. Pub. 800-166 Rev. 1, update 1, Cybersecurity Supply Chain Risk Management Practices for Systems and Organizations, NIST, (May 2022, updated as of Nov. 1, 2024), https://doi.org/10.6028/NIST.SP.800-161r1-upd1.

104. Verizon 2024 DBIR, *supra* note 13, at 7.

105. In 2023 supply chain attacks involved 242 breaches/exposures that affected 2,769 entities with 54,432,431 victims. Identity Theft Resource Ctr., *supra* note 2.

See Breaking Trust, Atlantic Council, https://www.atlanticcouncil.org/programs/digital-forensic-research-lab/cyber-statecraft-initiative/breaking-trust/ (last visited June 29, 2025); Trey Herr et al., Report, Breaking trust: Shades of crisis across an insecure software supply chain, Atlantic Council (July 26, 2020), https://www.atlanticcouncil.org/in-depth-research-reports/report/breaking-trust-shades-of-crisis-across-an-insecure-software-supply-chain/.

106. Verizon 2024 DBIR, Exploitation moving swiftly in the threat landscape, *supra* note 13, at 21–22.

107. Press Release, CISA, *NSA, FBI and International Cyber Authorities Issue Cybersecurity Advisory to Protect Managed Service Providers (MSP) and Customers* (May 11, 2022), https://www.cisa.gov/news-events/news/cisa-nsa-fbi-and-international-cyber-authorities-issue-cybersecurity-advisory-protect-managed.

when organizations rely on outdated, legacy software that offers little ongoing support and updates—especially upon news of highly-visible and well-publicized vulnerabilities and exploits.

Clearly, the many devastating attacks described below demonstrate that it is no longer enough to simply avoid a data breach; law firms and clients must become proactive and deliberate about network and data security.[108]

CrowdStrike Flawed Software Update—Massive IT Outage

Microsoft Windows, a series of operating systems (OS) for personal computers, tablets, laptops, and other devices, is used widely by lawyers and law offices. While not a cyber attack, the flawed software update from security vendor CrowdStrike caused millions of Microsoft Windows computers to crash, resulting in a massive IT outage. Critical services and business operations were disrupted around the globe. CrowdStrike deployed a fix, but recovery took time because the solution had to be applied manually on each computer.[109]

SolarWinds Software Supply Chain Breach—Software Development Processes Hijacked[110]

Law offices use SolarWinds products for IT monitoring to manage their computer networks (monitor network devices, performance metrics, and downtime) and cloud accounts. An APT actor based in Russia was responsible for compromising the SolarWinds Orion software supply chain through phishing and then moving across the company network with sensitive access.[111] A CISA alert reported that organizations faced a "grave risk" and urged them to prioritize measures to identify and address this threat.[112]

108. Daniel Hudson and Joseph Brunsman, *Cyber-Related Claims without a Breach? They're Coming*, THE CPA JOURNAL (April 2018), https://www.cpajournal.com/2018/04/06/cyber-related-claims-without-a-breach-theyre-coming/.

109. Brian Krebs, *Global Microsoft Meltdown Tied to Bad Crowdstrike Update*, KREBS ON SEC. (July 19, 2024), https://krebsonsecurity.com/2024/07/global-microsoft-meltdown-tied-to-bad-crowstrike-update/.

110. *Supply Chain Compromise*, CISA (Jan. 7, 2021), https://www.cisa.gov/supply-chain-compromise; VERIZON 2024 DBIR, *supra* note 13, at 14.

111. *What Every Leader Needs to Know About the Ongoing APT Cyber Activity*, CISA (Dec. 2020), https://www.cisa.gov/sites/default/files/publications/CISA%20Insights%20-%20What%20Every%20Leader%20Needs%20to%20Know%20About%20the%20Ongoing%20APT%20Cyber%20Activity%20-%20FINAL_508.pdf; Martin Giles, *The SolarWinds Breach Poses Five Urgent Cybersecurity Challenges For CIOs*, FORBES (Dec. 17, 2020), https://www.forbes.com/sites/martingiles/2020/12/17/solarwinds-hackers-five-cybersecurity-challenges-for-cios/?sh=2e82349921b6.

The attackers hid malicious code (malware) in a software update for SolarWinds Orion, a product widely used to monitor and manage the operation of computer networks. They also managed to digitally "sign" the updates, which made them look legitimate. When SolarWinds sent out the software updates, receiving networks saw the legitimate information but not the hidden malware, and organizations unknowingly accepted both. The malware in these updates gave the nation-state backed attackers a foothold in computer networks around the globe, including multiple large security companies as well as an extensive number of federal agencies.

112. CISA Alert (AA20-352A) *Advanced Persistent Threat Compromise of Government Agencies, Critical Infrastructure, and Private Sector Organizations* (Jan. 7. 2021) update https://us-cert.cisa.gov/ncas/current-activity/2021/01/06/cisa-updates-emergency-directive-21-01-supplemental-guidance-and; CISA Emergency Directive 21-01 Mitigate SolarWinds Orion Code Compromise (Dec. 13, 2020, updated April 15, 2021), https://cyber.dhs.gov/ed/21-01/#supplemental-guidance-v3; updated Jan. 25, 2022).

The Justice Department announced in July 2021 that the Russian SolarWinds supply chain attack compromised the internal network of Microsoft Office 365 email accounts belonging to employees at 27 state attorneys' offices.[113]

Breaches of Software for Secure Transfer of Large Files

Law offices use software tools to share large volumes of sensitive data and manage those data flows as a core part of their business. However, this type of software has introduced security risks, both in the form of attacks on software flaws and inadvertent leaks.

MOVEit Breach—77 Million Records Leaked; 2,600 Organizations Compromised

- In one of the largest breaches of 2023, a criminal group known as the CLOP Ransomware Gang was able to conduct a zero-day attack that exploited a security flaw and deployed ransomware, leaking confidential data of 77 million individuals from underlying MOVEit Transfer databases and affecting over 2,600 companies globally.[114] The attack impacted a variety of organizations, from companies such as Sony and IBM to public sector organizations including the Department of Justice, State of Maine, and the New York City public school system.
  A ransomware group took credit for accessing data at law firms Kirkland & Ellis, K&L Gates, and Proskauer Rose by exploiting a vulnerability in the file transfer software MOVEit.[115]

Accellion Software Breach—Client Data Posted on the Dark Web

- Major law firms were caught up in the Accellion breach in which attackers exploited four "zero day" software vulnerabilities.[116] In 2021, the Boston law firm Goodwin Procter and global law firm Jones Day disclosed data breaches involving the Accellion FTA compromise.[117] Open sources reported that Jones Day data appeared on the

113. Department of Justice Statement on SolarWinds Update (July 30, 2021), https://www.justice.gov/archives/opa/pr/department-justice-statement-solarwinds-update.

114. *See* CISA Cybersecurity Advisory, *#StopRansomware: CLOP Ransomware Gang Exploits CVE-2023-34362 MOVEit Vulnerability*, Alert AA23-158A (June 7, 2023), https://www.cisa.gov/news-events/cybersecurity-advisories/aa23-158a; *MOVEit Transfer and MOVEit Cloud Vulnerability*, Progress (July 2023), https://www.progress.com/trust-center/moveit-transfer-and-moveit-cloud-vulnerability; Verizon 2024 DBIR, Steps in Social Engineering incidents, *supra* note 13, at 39.

115. Justin Henry, *Kirkland & Ellis Faces Class Action Over 2023 Data Breach*, Law.com (June 10, 2024), https://www.law.com/americanlawyer/2024/06/10/kirkland-elis-faces-class-action-over-2023-data-breach/ (class action filed June 7, 2024 in D.C. D. MA).

116. *Exploitation of Accellion File Transfer Appliance*, CISA (June 17, 2021), https://www.cisa.gov/news-events/cybersecurity-advisories/aa21-055a; Threat Research, *Cyber Criminals Exploit Accellion FTA for Data Theft and Extortion*, Fireye (Feb. 22, 2021), https://www.fireeye.com/blog/threat-research/2021/02/accellion-fta-exploited-for-data-theft-and-extortion.html.

117. *Goodwin Procter Says It Was Hit by Data Breach of Vendor*, Bloomberg Law (Feb. 2, 2021), https://news.bloomberglaw.com/business-and-practice/goodwin-procter-says-it-was-hit-by-data-breach-of-vendor.

CLOP LEAKS extortion website, and DataBreaches.net published screenshots of stolen Jones Day files that the CLOP group posted on the dark web as proof it had the stolen records. The group told DataBreaches.net it did not encrypt the files, but only stole copies of the information.[118]

The Australian law firm Allens also had client data stolen in the attack. It was reported that the breach may have exposed highly sensitive information related to the firm's largest clients, Westpac Bank, which the firm defended in an anti-money laundering case, the Royal Bank of New Zealand, and the Australian Securities and Investments Commission (ASIC).[119]

Microsoft Exchange Server Compromise—Justice Department and FBI Move to Disrupt Hacking Activity

- Many law firms use the Microsoft email, calendaring, contact, scheduling, and collaboration platform extensively. In a 2021 zero-day attack targeting law firms, higher education institutions, defense contractors, policy think tanks, and NGOs, as well as small businesses and local governments across the U.S, an aggressive Chinese cyber espionage unit focused on stealing email exploited four newly-discovered flaws in Microsoft Exchange Server email software (not the cloud-based version). The group seeded hundreds of thousands of victim organizations worldwide with tools that gave the attackers total, remote control over affected systems, allowing for potential data theft and further compromise.[120]

  In obtaining a court order authorizing the FBI to copy and remove malicious web shells—hacking tools that give the attackers total remote control over affected systems—from hundreds of vulnerable computers in the U.S., the Justice Department and the FBI announced the steps to disrupt the hacking activity "using all of our legal tools, not just prosecutions."[121] In July 2021, the U.K. government, joined by the U.S., NATO, and the EU, as well as Microsoft, condemned the "systematic cyber sabotage," claiming the cyberattack was the work of Chinese state-sponsored hackers, namely Hafnium, an APT group.[122]

---

118. Dissent, *Threat actors claim to have stolen Jones Day files; law firm remains quiet*, DATABREACHES.NET (Feb. 13, 2021), https://www.databreaches.net/threat-actors-claim-to-have-stolen-jones-day-files-law-firm-remains-quiet/.

119. Edward Kost, *13 Biggest Data Breaches in Australia* [Updated 2025], UPGUARD (Jan. 2, 2025), https://www.upguard.com/blog/biggest-data-breaches-australia.

120. Brian Krebs, *At Least 30,000 U.S. Organizations Newly Hacked Via Holes in Microsoft's Email Software*, KREBS ON SEC. (Mar. 5, 2021), https://krebsonsecurity.com/2021/03/at-least-30000-u-s-organizations-newly-hacked-via-holes-in-microsofts-email-software/.

121. *Justice Department Announces Court-Authorized Effort to Disrupt Exploitation of Microsoft Exchange Server Vulnerabilities*, DEP'T OF JUSTICE (April 13, 2021), https://www.justice.gov/opa/pr/justice-department-announces-court-authorized-effort-disrupt-exploitation-microsoft-exchange.

122. UK and allies hold Chinese state responsible for a pervasive pattern of hackings, U.K. GOV'T (July 19, 2021), https://www.gov.uk/government/news/uk-and-allies-hold-chinese-state-responsible-for-a-pervasive-pattern-of-hacking.

Kaseya VSA Supply-Chain Ransomware Attack—Third Party Risk[123]

A massive ransomware attack exploited multiple vulnerabilities in a key piece of network management and remote-control software used to remotely manage a company's IT networks and devices. That software is sold to managed service providers (MSP)—effectively outsourced IT departments—which they then use to remotely manage the IT networks and devices of their customers, often small and mid-sized companies.[124] This was the largest supply chain ransomware attack seen to date.

Hackers associated with the Russia-linked REvil ransomware-as-a-service group are believed to have used a never-before-seen security vulnerability in the software's update mechanism to push ransomware to Kaseya's MSP customers which, in turn, spread downstream to their customers. Many of the companies that were ultimately victims of the attack may not have known that their networks were monitored by Kaseya's software. A notice posted on a dark website known to be run by REvil claimed responsibility for the attack, and said the ransomware group would publicly release a decryption tool if it was paid $70 million in bitcoin.[125] Ultimately, Kaseya obtained a decryption tool that they provided to their customers.

Apache Log4j—Vulnerability in Widely Used Software Products Exploited

Log4j is software that is broadly used in a variety of consumer and enterprise services, websites, and applications—as well as in operational technology products—to log security and performance information. It is one of thousands of unheralded but critically important open-source services that are used across a near-innumerable variety of internet companies.[126]

In 2022, a serious vulnerability in the popular Java logging package was disclosed, posing a severe risk to millions of consumer products, enterprise software, and web applications. This vulnerability is being widely exploited by a growing set of attackers.[127]

2.1.6. *Social Engineering and Phishing Attacks Targeting Lawyers and Law Firms*

Cyber risks have evolved beyond traditional hacking to include sophisticated social engineering scams that rely on unwitting insiders to effectuate the schemes.[128] Criminals use

123. CISA-FBI Guidance for MSPs and their Customers Affected by the Kaseya VSA Supply-Chain Ransomware Attack. CISA (July 6, 2021), https://www.cisa.gov/news-events/alerts/2021/07/04/cisa-fbi-guidance-msps-and-their-customers-affected-kaseya-vsa-supply.

124. Zack Whittaker, *Kaseya Hack Floods Hundreds of Companies with Ransomware*, TechCrunch (July 5, 2021), https://techcrunch.com/2021/07/05/kaseya-hack-flood-ransomware/.

125. *Id.*

126. *Apache Log4j Vulnerability Guidance*, CISA (April 8, 2022), https://www.cisa.gov/news-events/news/apache-log4j-vulnerability-guidance; *Log4j vulnerability—what everyone needs to know*, Nat'l Cyber Sec. Ctr. (Dec. 14, 2021), https://www.ncsc.gov.uk/information/log4j-vulnerability-what-everyone-needs-to-know/.

127. *FTC Warns Companies to Remediate Log4j Security Vulnerability*, FTC (Jan. 4, 2022), https://www.ftc.gov/policy/advocacy-research/tech-at-ftc/2022/01/ftc-warns-companies-remediate-log4j-security-vulnerability.

128. Social Engineering Fraud, Interpol, https://www.interpol.int/en/Crimes/Financial-crime/Social-engineering-scams.

trickery to outwit their victims, creating a sense of urgency combined with fear. In the past several years, organizations around the world have been the victims of multi-million dollar fraud schemes that were successfully perpetrated online using social engineering.[129]

Law firms are especially lucrative targets. Over the past two years, incidents involving Pretexting (the majority of which had business email compromise (BEC) as the outcome) accounted for one-fourth of financially motivated attacks.[130]

Business Email Compromise (BEC)

BEC is a sophisticated scam targeting businesses of all sizes, often working with foreign suppliers or businesses that regularly perform wire transfer payments. Lawyers and law practices are frequent targets of BEC schemes because they conduct business using email and often occupy a privileged position where payment instructions and details are exchanged.

The scam is carried out by compromising legitimate email accounts through social engineering or computer intrusion techniques to conduct unauthorized transfers of funds. Account compromise is usually a key part of the scheme, so that an executive or employee's email account is hacked and used to request payments be sent to fraudulent bank accounts.[131] Criminals who use AI-generated deepfakes make the scams more dangerous. In 2021, five people were arrested in Texas for allegedly laundering nearly $1 million from BEC fraud.[132]

In an elaborate scam, criminals used deepfake technology to pose as the chief financial officer of the multi-national firm Arup. In a video conference call, purportedly with the CFO and members of his staff, a finance worker in the company's Hong Kong office was tricked into paying $25 million to a fraudulent bank account, according to a Hong Kong police briefing.[133]

BEC Schemes Targeting Lawyers and Business Executives

- **Counterfeit Check Scam—FBI Warning: Law Firms Targeted.**[134] In 2024, the FBI warned law firms engaged in collections work that criminals who deceptively contract for legal services are defrauding lawyers by offering to pay a debt with funds

129. Verizon 2024 DBIR, Social Engineering, *supra* note 13, at 36–41.

130. Verizon 2024 DBIR, Summary of Findings, *supra* note 13, at 9.

131. FBI, *Business E-mail Compromise—The $55 Billion Dollar Scam*, Alert No. 1-091124-PSA (Sep. 11, 2024), https://www.ic3.gov/PSA/2024/PSA240911; FBI, Scams and Safety, Business Email Compromise, https://www.fbi.gov/how-we-can-help-you/scams-and-safety/common-frauds-and-scams/business-email-compromise; *see* Verizon 2024 DBIR, Social Engineering, *supra* note 13, at 36–42.

132. News, U.S. Att'ys Office, W.D. Texas, *Five Arrested for Allegedly Laundering Nearly $1 Million from Business Email Compromise Fraud* (June 10, 2021), https://www.justice.gov/usao-wdtx/pr/five-arrested-allegedly-laundering-nearly-1-million-business-email-compromise-fraud.

133. Kathleen Magramo, *British Engineering Giant Arup Revealed as $25 Million Deepfake Scam Victim*, CNN (May 17, 2024), https://www.cnn.com/2024/05/16/tech/arup-deepfake-scam-loss-hong-kong-intl-hnk/index.html.

134. *How to Spot, Avoid, and Report Fake Check Scams*, FTC, https://www.consumer.ftc.gov/articles/how-spot-avoid-and-report-fake-check-scams (last visited Sept 23. 2025).

from a fraudulent cashier's check. After the check is deposited in the lawyer's client trust account and the bank discovers that the check is fraudulent, the trust account is charged back the value of the check. Because a wire has already been sent to the creditor, the law firm suffers the financial loss.[135]

State bar associations have also warned of a variation on this scheme. For example, in certain fraud schemes, criminals seek out an attorney, purportedly to accept checks from a fictitious company's customers, deposit the checks into the attorney's bank account, retain a five-figure amount as the attorney's "fee" for providing the service, and then forward the rest of the payment to the fictitious company in a foreign country.[136]

- **CEO Fraud and Payroll Phishing Schemes—Data Theft.** According to alerts issued by the Internal Revenue Service (IRS), criminals are combining CEO fraud and payroll phishing schemes.[137] Fraudulent requests are sent utilizing a business executive's compromised email to target recipients in the company who are responsible for issuing W-2 forms or maintaining PII, such as human resources or bookkeeping. Some of these incidents occur before a fraudulent wire transfer request. The stolen data can be used for future attacks.

  Phishing attacks have been a top security threat for lawyers. For example, in years past, two of the largest law firms, Jenner & Block and Proskauer Rose, were victimized. Jenner reported that employees' W-2 forms for 859 people were "mistakenly transmitted to an unauthorized recipient" based on what appeared to be a legitimate management request. Proskauer also reported a breach of W-2 information affecting 1,500 people when a payroll employee responded to what was believed to be an email request from a senior executive.[138] Immigration law firm Fragomen disclosed a data breach related to the I–9 process used to verify employment eligibility that exposed the personal information of current and former Google employees.[139]
- **CEO Fraud—Business Executive and Attorney Impersonation.** Attackers pose as the company CEO or an executive and send confidential and time-sensitive email requests to employees in finance, requesting them to transfer money to fraudulent accounts. With respect to lawyers, attackers may pretend to be a lawyer or someone from the law

135. *Counterfeit Check Scam Targets Law Firms via Debt Collection Scheme*, FBI (Oct. 8, 2024), https://www.ic3.gov/PSA/2024/PSA241008.

136. Don Coker, *Internet Check Scams that Target Attorneys and Law Firms*, HGExperts.com, https://www.hgexperts.com/expert-witness-articles/internet-check-scams-that-target-attorneys-and-law-firms-6673 (last visited September 1, 2025).

137. Internal Revenue Service (IRS), *"Dirty Dozen,"* https://www.irs.gov/newsroom/dirty-dozen (last visited September 1, 2025).

138. Debra Cassens Weiss, *More than 100 Law Firms Have Reported Data Breaches; 2 BigLaw Firms Affected*, ABA Journal (Oct. 18, 2019), https://www.abajournal.com/news/article/more-than-100-law-firms-have-reported-data-breaches-2-biglaw-firms-affected.

139. Fragomen Breach Notice to the State of California, https://oag.ca.gov/ecrime/databreach/reports/sb24-195495/?sb24-10262020/.

firm supposedly in charge of crucial and confidential matters. Normally, such bogus requests are done through email or phone, and during the end of the business day.

- **Known Entities—Impersonation to Steal Confidential Data.** Attackers pose as legitimate individuals or entities such as IRS agents or bank employees trying to obtain access to sensitive data, including some specifically designed to jeopardize attorneys.
- **Fake Clients.** Criminals find out about trust accounts or litigation and impersonate a law firm client to change the recipient bank information to a fraudulent account. Alternatively, scammers often pose as prospective clients seeking urgent legal assistance. Lawyers may be asked to provide contact information or to complete wire transfers. While these schemes are often easy to spot, scammers have recently grown far more sophisticated, sometimes even stealing the identities of actual professionals or using AI-generated deepfakes to conceal the schemes.

Cyber Criminals Insider-trading Scheme Targeting Law Firms.

> *This case [United States v. Iat Hong] of cyber meets securities fraud should serve as a wake-up call for law firms around the world: you are and will be targets of cyber hacking, because you have information valuable to would-be criminals.*[140]
>
> Preet Bharara, United States Attorney,
> Southern District of New York

Hackers have targeted international law firms in insider-trading operations. Initially uncovered in 2016, the FBI issued an alert after agents discovered a post on an undisclosed "cybercriminal forum" in which someone was seeking to hire hackers to break into international law firms' computer networks and steal data as part of an insider-trading scheme. According to the *Wall Street Journal*, "a posting appeared on an underground Russian website called DarkMoney.cc in which the person offered to sell his phishing services to other would-be cyber thieves and identified specific law firms as potential targets."[141]

The Securities and Exchange Commission (SEC) and the Justice Department separately announced significant cases against three Chinese traders who made nearly $3 million in illegal profits by hacking into the computer networks of two "prominent New York-based law firms." Three Chinese nationals were subsequently indicted for securities and wire fraud for hacking into international law firms with offices in New York City and trading

140. News Release, U.S. Att'ys Office, S.D. N.Y., *Manhattan U.S. Attorney Announces Arrest of Macau Resident and Unsealing of Charges Against Three Individuals for Insider Trading Based on Information Hacked from Prominent U.S. Law Firms* (Dec. 27, 2016), https://www.justice.gov/usao-sdny/pr/manhattan-us-attorney-announces-arrest-macau-resident-and-unsealing-charges-against.

141. Nicole Hong & Robin Sidel, *Hackers Breach Law Firms, Including Cravath and Weil Gotshal*, WALL ST. J. (Mar. 29, 2016), https://www.wsj.com/articles/hackers-breach-cravath-swaine-other-big-law-firms-1459293504; Claire Bushey, *Russian Cyber Criminal Targets Elite Chicago Law Firms*, CHI. BUS. (Mar. 29, 2016), http://www.chicagobusiness.com/article/20160329/NEWS04/160329840/russian-cyber-criminal-targets-elite-chicago-law-firms.

on confidential, non-public information they obtained from the email accounts of law firm partners who worked on high-profile mergers and acquisitions (M&A) transactions.[142] According to the indictment, the hackers stole log-in credentials of a law firm employee and planted malware that would then allow them to log into email accounts of partners at the firm and glean details of pending mergers pricing information. They traded on that information before the deals were made public. The hackers targeted seven firms, traded in five public companies, and made profits of over $4 million in the process. For trading on insider information, the SEC fined the perpetrators $8.8 million USD, more than double what they "earned."[143]

2.1.7. *Third Party Vendors and Business Partners Can Be a Weak Link—A Two-Edged Sword for Law Firms*

Third-party business partners and vendors can provide a pathway into companies of strategic interest to global hackers.[144] Further, from the point of view of hackers, law firms are considered "business partners" of major corporate clients with a trove of proprietary data—a weak link to be exploited. Similarly, it can be said that the security of a law firm is only as strong as that of its weakest business partner. Law firms and corporate legal departments outsource a variety of legal work to outside businesses located domestically and overseas.

In 2023, global firm Proskauer Rose revealed that a threat actor was able to access 184,000 files containing "private and privileged financial and legal documents, contracts, non-disclosure agreements, financial deals and files relating to high-profile acquisitions."[145] This information was stored by a third-party vendor on an unsecured Microsoft Azure cloud server and was publicly accessible by anyone with internet access and knowledge of where to look. Even worse, this data was left exposed for six months before the threat actor accessed it.[146]

Ransomware Attacks on Third-Party Vendors. Law firms and court systems can be affected by ransomware indirectly when their managed service providers (MSP) are attacked.[147] The vendors that provide the technology used by law offices as part of their IT operations—email, transfer of large files, website transactions, and managing their

---

142. *United States v. Iat Hong*, 16 Cr 360 (S.D.N.Y. 2016); *see* Jeff John Roberts, *Exclusive: China Stole Data from Major U.S. Law Firms*, FORTUNE (Dec. 7, 2016), http://fortune.com/2016/12/07/china-law-firms/.

143. SEC, Default Judgments Entered against All Defendants in Law Firm Hacking Case, Litigation Release No. 23826 (May 9, 2017), https://www.sec.gov/enforcement-litigation/litigation-releases/lr-23826.

144. CROWDSTRIKE 2024 THREAT REPORT, *Third-Party Relationship Exploitation*, *supra* note 28, at 20–23; INTELLIGENCE CTR. REPORT, APT1, MANDIANT, https://www.mandiant.com/sites/default/files/2021-09/mandiant-apt1-report.pdf.

145. Carly Page, *Legal Powerhouse Proskauer Exposed Clients' Confidential M&A Data*, TECHCRUNCH (April 6, 2023), https://techcrunch.com/2023/04/06/proskauer-confidential-client-data/.

146. ARCTIC WOLF, *supra* note 84.

147. Schreider, Tari. *Ransomware Attacks in the Legal Profession*, ACEDS, May 27, 2020, https://aceds.org/tari-schreider-ransomware-attacks-in-the-legal-profession/.

computer networks—have been targeted by cyber criminals. The sophisticated cyber attacks discussed above that compromised legal supply chains are examples of dangerous law firm breaches.

In November 2023, managed service provider CTS, which provides IT services to law firms, acknowledged that the firm had suffered a breach that impacted services to dozens of law firms, particularly in the real estate sector.[148] The attack followed claims by the LockBit group that it compromised London-based law firm Allen & Overy, listing the firm among the victims on its data-leak site and demanding a ransom.[149]

The 2020 ransomware attack on legal services provider Epiq Global, an e-discovery and web service firm, was designed to put pressure on the lawyer victims by inflicting pain on downstream customers. Epiq took their systems offline after their devices were encrypted by Ryuk ransomware. Epiq's legal clients were unable to access files and documents through their e-discovery platforms, files needed for court cases and other deadlines. Ryuk is known to go after large enterprises, seeking considerable ransoms, a practice called "big game hunting."[150]

In a ransomware attack on TBG West Insurance Services, an insurance vendor of the Cadwalader, Wickersham & Taft LLP (CWT) law firm, hackers encrypted files within their system and stole files that included CWT current and former employee information (names and SSN). TBG ultimately paid the ransom to regain access to their data.[151]

Hackers have disrupted the operations of hundreds of businesses by targeting the entities that provide key services to them. For example, Blackbaud of South Carolina was a cloud computing vendor and business associate of hundreds of organizations known to have been affected by a ransomware attack in which hackers gained access to servers housing some of its customers' fundraising databases. Ten million records exfiltrated by the hackers included Social Security numbers and financial information. Blackbaud negotiated a ransom payment and paid to prevent the publication or sale of the stolen data. Following investigations and lawsuits, Blackbaud reached settlements with 49 state Attorneys General

148. Alexander Martin, *Potentially Hundreds of UK Law Firms Affected by Cyberattack on IT Provider CTS*, TheRecord (Nov. 24, 2023), https://therecord.media/uk-cyberattack-msp-cts-law-firms.

149. Firm news, *Allen & Overy responds to data incident* (Nov. 15, 2023), https://www.aoshearman.com/en/news/allen-overy-responds-to-data-incident; Robert Lemos, *Law Firms & Legal Departments Singled Out for Cyberattacks*, Dark Reading (Nov. 30, 2023), https://www.darkreading.com/cyberattacks-data-breaches/law-firms-face-a-more-dangerous-threat-landscape.

150. Zack Whittaker, *Legal Services Giant Epiq Global Offline after Ransomware Attack*, TechCrunch (March 2, 2020), https://techcrunch.com/2020/03/02/epiq-global-ransomware/; Jenny Strasburg, *Hackers Trigger Far-Reaching Disruption by Targeting Low-Profile Firm*, Wall St. J. (June 18, 2025), https://www.wsj.com/articles/hackers-trigger-far-reaching-disruption-by-targeting-low-profile-firm-11592481600. Typically this kind of campaign is rolled out in stages, often beginning with a phishing attack, just as this one did. The attackers sought to gain user credentials to get into the organization's network and survey the asset landscape. Follow up stages usually include spying once in the network, data encryption, and eventually the ransom demand and possibly extortion.

151. Cadwalader Wickersham & Taft LLP, NYC, Security Breach Notification to Massachusetts Office of Consumer Affairs and Business Regulation (Aug. 31, 2020), https://www.documentcloud.org/documents/20403356-cadwaladerdatabreachreport.

and the District of Columbia related to the multi-state investigation of its 2020 security incident,[152] as well as the Federal Trade Commission (FTC) and the SEC.[153]

In prior years, major law firms were implicated publicly in the breach of the website of HBGary, a cybersecurity firm that investigates data breaches and conducts investigations. The hacker group Anonymous seized control of HBGary's website, defaced its pages, extracted more than 60,000 company emails, and deleted backup files. It then posted those emails in a searchable form on the Internet, creating widespread media coverage.[154] News reports indicated that Washington, D.C. law firm Hunton & Williams had hired HBGary as an outsourcing partner to conduct investigations for its clients. The firm suffered embarrassment and its work on behalf of its client the Chamber of Commerce was discussed in extensive media coverage. A fallout of the breach was the filing of an ethics complaint against three Hunton & Williams attorneys.[155]

The confidential emails that were stolen from HBGary also revealed details about industrial espionage by hackers in China, Russia, and other countries against law firms and major corporations.[156] The Atlanta-based law firm King & Spalding was mentioned along with Google, which said in 2010 that it had "lost intellectual property assets to hackers based in China," and Adobe, which reported similar hacker attacks. The need for law firms to assess the security practices of their business partners should be clear from the widespread ramifications of this breach.[157]

Disinformation and Deepfakes. Deepfakes are synthetic media in which a person in an existing image or video is replaced with someone else's likeness.[158] In a joint statement,

152. Blackbaud Newsroom, *Blackbaud Resolves Multi-State Attorneys General Investigation of 2020 Security Incident* (Oct. 5, 2023), https://www.blackbaud.com/newsroom/article/blackbaud-resolves-multi-state-attorneys-general-investigation-of-2020-security-incident.

153. *FTC Finalizes Order with Blackbaud Related to Allegations the Firm's Security Failures Led to Data Breach* (May 20, 2024), https://www.ftc.gov/news-events/news/press-releases/2024/05/ftc-finalizes-order-blackbaud-related-allegations-firms-security-failures-led-data-breach. (The order requires Blackbaud to delete data that it no longer needs and prohibits Blackbaud from misrepresenting its data security and data retention policies. The company must develop a comprehensive information security program, put in place a data retention schedule outlining its data deletion practices, and notify the FTC if it experiences a future data breach that it is required to report to any other local, state, or federal agency.).

Press Release, *SEC Charges Software Company Blackbaud Inc. for Misleading Disclosures About Ransomware Attack That Impacted Charitable Donors*, 2023–48 (March 9, 2023), https://www.sec.gov/newsroom/press-releases/2023-48. (Blackbaud agreed to pay $3 million to settle SEC charges for making misleading disclosures about the 2020 ransomware attack that impacted more than 13,000 customers.).

154. *Anonymous Hackers Attack US Security Firm HBGary*, BBC Tech. News (Feb. 7, 2011), http://www.bbc.co.uk/news/technology-12380987.

155. Debra Cassens Weiss, *E-Mails Suggest Law Firm Considered "Dirty-Tricks" Plan to Discredit Chamber Critics*, ABA Journal (Feb. 15, 2011), https://www.abajournal.com/news/article/e-mails_suggest_hunton_law_firm_considered_dirty-tricks_plan_to_discredit_c.

156. Michael Riley & Sarah Forden, *Hacking of DuPont, J&J, GE Were Google-Type Attacks That Weren't Disclosed*, Bloomberg (Mar. 8, 2011), https://www.bloomberg.com/news/articles/2011-03-08/hacking-of-dupont-j-j-ge-were-google-type-attacks-that-weren-t-disclosed.

157. ABA Cybersecurity Legal Task Force, Vendor Contracting Cybersecurity Checklist, 2nd Ed. (May 11, 2021), https://www.americanbar.org/products/ecd/ebk/411859099/.

158. The FBI defines synthetic content as the broad spectrum of generated or manipulated digital content, which includes images, video, audio, and text. These techniques are known popularly as deepfakes or GANs (generative adversarial networks).

the National Security Agency (NSA), the FBI and CISA warned that threats from synthetic media, such as deepfakes, present a growing challenge for all users of modern technology and communications, including National Security Systems (NSS), the Department of Defense (DOD), the Defense Industrial Base (DIB), and national critical infrastructure, owners and operators.[159]

The creators of deepfakes often produce and manipulate media with highly realistic results. They have been used extensively for celebrity fakes, hoaxes, fake news and financial fraud, and also have the capacity to be used as a tool for ransomware attacks, or as a threat to biometric authentication systems.[160]

The problem of deepfakes remains a significant concern, with the difficulty of spotting these fakes and the need for reliable tools and standards, such as C2PA, to help detect deepfakes.[161] AI will create challenges for the use of evidence in court, such as to establish the trustworthiness and integrity of evidence. Deepfakes have the potential to upend litigation and the legal process as we know it.

2.1.8. *Malicious Insiders*

Defending an organization's perimeter from external attack does not protect against valuable information seeping out because of insider malfeasance, whether that behavior is characterized as malicious, mischievous, or ignorant/accidental.[162] Carnegie Mellon University has published a list of best practices to minimize the risk of insider attacks.[163]

Malicious insider attacks are on the rise and pose a serious threat to the security of confidential information.[164] They pose a significant risk to law firms, with their potential to

---

159. *Joint Cybersecurity Information Sheet: Contextualizing Deepfake Threats to Organizations* 3, Dep't of Def. (Sept. 12, 2023), https://media.defense.gov/2023/Sep/12/2003298925/-1/-1/0/CSI-DEEPFAKE-THREATS.PDF; *see also Malicious Actors Almost Certainly Will Leverage Synthetic Content for Cyber and Foreign Influence Operations*, FBI (Mar. 10, 2021), https://www.ic3.gov/Media/News/2021/210310-2.pdf. ("Foreign actors are currently using synthetic content in their influence campaigns, and the FBI anticipates it will be increasingly used by foreign and criminal cyber actors for spear phishing and social engineering in an evolution of cyber operational tradecraft.").

160. ETSI, *Securing Artificial Intelligence (SAI); Problem Statement* 17 (2020), § 8.4 at 21, https://www.etsi.org/deliver/etsi_gr/SAI/001_099/004/01.01.01_60/gr_SAI004v010101p.pdf. This report published by ETSI, the European standards organization, details the misuse of AI (adversarial machine learning) in a collection of real-world use cases and attacks.

161. An open technical standard providing publishers, creators, and consumers the ability to trace the origin of different types of media. https://c2pa.org/.

162. Tara Seals, *Insider Threats Responsible for 43% of Data Br*eaches, Infosecurity Mag., https://www.infosecurity-magazine.com/news/insider-threats-reponsible-for-43/; Rutrell Yasin, *Employee Negligence The Cause of Many Data Breaches*, Dark Reading (May 24, 2016), http://www.darkreading.com/vulnerabilities---threats/employee-negligence-the-cause-of-many-data-breaches-/d/d-id/1325656.

163. *See Common Sense Guide to Mitigating Insider Threats*, Technical Note, CMU/SEI-2015-TR-010 (Fifth Edition), The CERT Insider Threat Center (Dec. 2016) https://www.odni.gov/files/NCSC/documents/nittf/20180209-CERT-Common-Sense-Guide-Fifth-Edition.pdf.

164. Kristina Beek, *Insider Threat Damage Balloons as Visibility Gaps Widen*, Dark Reading (Oct. 4, 2024), https://www.darkreading.com/threat-intelligence/insider-threat-damage-balloons-amid-evolving-cyber-environments; Verizon 2024 DBIR, Threat actors in breaches over time and Privilege Misuse, *supra* note 13 at 53–54. ("Employee betrayal poses a significant threat because employees steal data for personal benefit, sometimes

jeopardize client confidentiality and trust. Criminals use the dark web to recruit employees who have access to corporate networks to become "rogue insiders."[165] The motivation of employees to steal data may range from financial gain (theft of trade secrets and other sensitive information for sale) to revenge for perceived wrongs committed against them. Individuals who abused administrative privileges led to a significant number of breaches and security failures, such as not suspending system access for terminated employees.

High-profile criminal cases illustrate the extent of the fraud and theft that can be caused by malicious insiders.[166] In what federal prosecutors called one of the largest data breaches in history, with potentially devastating consequences,[167] a single insider hacked a database of Capital One, the third largest issuer of credit cards in the U.S., and accessed more than 100 million customer accounts and credit card applications. She was convicted of seven federal crimes.[168] As a result of the data breach that compromised misconfigured firewalls, Capital One was fined $80 million and settled customer lawsuits for $190 million, on top of facing privacy concerns.[169] In another famous case, two General Electric (GE) employees stole thousands of files with trade secrets from company servers and convinced a system administrator to grant them unauthorized access to sensitive corporate data. In 2020, both malicious insiders were convicted, sentenced to prison, and fined $1.4 million in restitution to GE.[170]

In another widely publicized insider case, a computer technician who worked in Bank of New York Mellon's IT department stole the identities of 2,000 bank employees and opened bank and brokerage accounts. He then used the accounts to steal more than

---

colluding with External actors. Personal data is the prime target, along with Internal information."); DHS Insider Threat Program (Aug. 2, 2024), https://www.dhs.gov/archive/science-and-technology/cybersecurity-insider-threat.

165. Jeff John Roberts, *Insider Trading on the Dark Web on the Rise*, Fortune (Jan. 31, 2017), http://fortune.com/2017/01/31/insiders-dark-web/; *Monetizing the Insider: The Dark Web's Increasing Influence on Insider Risk*, RedOwl (Jan. 31, 2017), https://www.nationalinsiderthreatsig.org/itrmresources/RedOwl%20Report-Monetizing%20The%20Insider%20Through%20The%20Dark%20Web.pdf.

166. Jane Grafton, *Famous Insider Threat Cases*, GURUCIL (Sept. 5, 2019), https://gurucul.com/blog/famous-insider-threat-cases.

167. Emily Flitter & Karen Weise, *Capital One Data Breach Compromises Data of Over 100 Million*, N.Y. Times, (July 29, 2019), https://www.nytimes.com/2019/07/29/business/capital-one-data-breach-hacked.html.

168. News Release, U.S. Att'ys Office, W.D. WA, *Former Seattle Tech Worker Indicted on Federal Charges for Wire Fraud and Computer Data Theft, Indictment Cites more than 30 Victims of Data Intrusion and Theft* (Aug. 28, 2019), https://www.justice.gov/usao-wdwa/pr/former-seattle-tech-worker-indicted-federal-charges-wire-fraud-and-computer-data-theft.

169. Press Release, U.S. Att'ys Office, W.D. WA, *Former hacker sentenced for stealing computer power to mine cryptocurrency and stealing the personal information of more than 100 million people* (Oct. 4, 2022), https://www.justice.gov/usao-wdwa/pr/former-hacker-sentenced-stealing-computer-power-mine-cryptocurrency-and-stealing; Arielle Waldman, *Paige Thompson Found Guilty in 2019 Capital One Data Breach*, TechTarget (June 20, 2022), https://www.techtarget.com/searchsecurity/news/252521775/Paige-Thompson-found-guilty-in-2019-Capital-One-data-breach.

170. FBI Trade Secret Theft, *Investigation into Theft of Intellectual Property from GE Leads to Two Guilty Pleas* (July 29, 2020), https://www.fbi.gov/news/stories/two-guilty-in-theft-of-trade-secrets-from-ge-072920; News, U.S. Att'ys Office, D.C. N.Y. (Dec. 10, 2019), https://www.justice.gov/usao-ndny/pr/former-ge-engineer-pleads-guilty-conspiring-steal-trade-secrets-0.

$1.1 million from charities, nonprofit groups, and other entities.[171] The defendant pleaded guilty to grand larceny, money laundering, and computer tampering.

Malicious Insiders—Unforeseen Risk for Law Firms. In a December 2022 lawsuit against its former chief operating officer, international law firm Proskauer Rose alleged that Jonathan O'Brien stole trade secrets and other valuable confidential and proprietary information about the firm's finances, lawyer compensation and clients before leaving his job there. The lawsuit claimed that O'Brien overrode the firm's security measures by ordering staff members to allow him to copy sensitive internal documents to USB files and then wrongfully delete thousands of emails before giving notice that he was leaving. "Mr. O'Brien knew this information would be highly useful to Proskauer's competitors, as it would enable them to effectively target and recruit Proskauer's partners, practice groups, and clients," the lawsuit said. The parties reached a confidential settlement, and the Court issued a permanent injunction in February 2024 blocking O'Brien from possessing, disseminating, or using the firm's proprietary, confidential, and/or trade secret information. *Proskauer Rose LLP v. Jonathan O'Brien*, No. 1:22-cv-10918-AT (U.S. D.C. S.D. N.Y.)

Non-equity partners of the Governo law firm (GLF) in Boston stole more than 24 million pages of documents—a "treasure trove" of proprietary materials, including from the research library, databases, and administrative files. The stolen material downloaded by the attorneys departing to create a new law firm included client files for which they had not received client authorization to transfer.[172] GLF sued the departing attorneys for conversion, breach of the duty of loyalty, conspiracy, and, importantly, unfair or deceptive trade practices in violation of the Massachusetts consumer protection laws.

Insider trading is a motivation for law firm employees to misappropriate confidential data and non-public client information.[173] Securities regulators have brought cases charging law firm employees with exploiting the firms' computer systems to access and steal inside information. The misconduct of Matthew Kluger offers a strong cautionary tale for law firms. In what the government described as one of the longest-running insider trading schemes ever prosecuted in the U.S., the SEC charged a law firm associate with tipping on at least eight deals that generated more than $30 million in profits.[174] The

171. Thomas Claburn, *Bank IT Worker Charged In $1.1 Million Fraud: A Computer Technician Has Been Indicted for Stealing the Identities of 150 Bank of New York Employees, as Well as for Grand Larceny and Money Laundering*, Dark Reading (Nov. 2, 2009), https://www.darkreading.com/cyber-risk/bank-it-worker-charged-in-1-1-million-fraud; Press Release, N.Y. Cnty. Dist. Att'ys Office, *District Attorney Vance Announces Guilty Plea in Massive Identity Theft Scam* (July 1, 2010).

172. *Governo Law Firm v. Kendra Bergeron, et al.*, SJC-12948 (Mass. Supreme Judicial Court), April 9, 2021.

173. Bruce Carton, *Why Law Firms Are a Breeding Ground for Insider Trading*, Compliance Week (Apr. 7, 2014), https://www.complianceweek.com/why-law-firms-are-a-breeding-ground-for-insider-trading/13906.article.

174. Although the law firm tried to protect corporate information by using code names for the parties involved, Kluger was repeatedly able to figure out the identities of such companies because he knew that the earliest documents would always have the parties' real names and, as the deal got closer, the lawyers would begin to use code names.

Justice Department filed parallel charges in New Jersey.[175] Between 1994 and 2011, Kluger obtained inside information on more than 30 different corporate transactions and netted more than $32 million in illicit profits from the scheme. In June 2012 a federal judge in New Jersey sentenced him to 12 years in prison—a record sentence for an insider-trading defendant.[176]

A Florida lawyer, Walter "Chet" Little, former partner at an international law firm, pleaded guilty to engaging in a nearly $1 million insider trading scheme using information he improperly obtained from his law firm's databases. He was sentenced to 27 months in prison for conspiring to commit insider trading.[177] In 2009, the SEC sued Canadian lawyer Gil Cornblum, who used the night secretarial staff's temporary passwords when he searched the law firm's document management system for confidential information about transactions. Cornblum allegedly gained inside information about 46 corporate transactions and used this information to generate over $9 million in illegal profits.

Law firms must look beyond the lawyers and staff working on a specific case or deal to protect clients' information. The SEC charged a law firm network IT manager with using his position to access information about 22 M&A deals and tipping his brother-in-law.[178]

2.1.9. *Cloud Computing and Wi-Fi Risks*

Because of the increased flexibility and efficiency afforded by computing resources available on demand, law firms use cloud services for processing and storing confidential client data and records. However, cloud computing introduces IT security and privacy risks related to outsourcing the administration and physical control of sensitive data to a third-party vendor and maintenance of the data on shared computing platforms, risks that will need to be carefully evaluated and addressed by legal entities that intend to put client data in the cloud.[179]

Security Required for Data Stored in the Cloud. Cloud providers require their customers to provide their own security when they put web applications, databases and other software in a public or private cloud environment. Many customers don't understand that

175. SEC *Litig. Release No. 22,345,* Attorney, Wall Street Trader, And Middleman Settle Sec Charges In $32 Million Insider Trading Case (April 25, 2012), https://www.sec.gov/litigation/litreleases/2012/lr22345.htm.

176. United States v. Kluger, No. 11-cr-0858, ECF No. 49 (D.N.J. June 4, 2012); *Lawyer Gets Record Prison Sentence—12 years—in Insider Trading Scheme That Used Information Stolen from Preeminent Law Firms*, Justice Dept. News (June 4, 2012), https://www.justice.gov/archive/usao/nj/Press/files/Kluger,%20Matthew%20and%20Bauer,%20Garrett%20Sentencing%20News%20Release.html.

177. Justice News, U.S. Att'ys Office, S.D. N.Y., *Partner at International Law Firm Sentenced for Insider Trading* (Feb. 22, 2018), https://www.justice.gov/usao-sdny/pr/partner-international-law-firm-sentenced-insider-trading.

178. SEC v. Jeffrey J. Temple and Benedict M. Pastro, Lit. Rel. No. 21765 (Dec. 10, 2010).

179. Crowdstrike 2024 Threat Report, *Adversaries Continue to Develop Cloud-Consciousness, supra* note 28, at 17–20; https://go.crowdstrike.com/rs/281-OBQ-266/images/GlobalThreatReport2024.pdf; *see* NIST Spec. Pub. 800-144, Guidelines on Security and Privacy in Public Cloud Computing (Jan. 2012), https://csrc.nist.gov/publications/detail/sp/800-144/final; NIST Spec. Pub. 800-146 Cloud Computing Synopsis and Recommendations (May 2012), https://csrc.nist.gov/pubs/sp/800/146/final.

security offered by a cloud provider is an additional option that must be purchased. While the cloud service may offer some basic tools, they do not require customers to use them, including something as basic as a password. A number of large organizations simply fail to add a password to protect their cloud-based data. Lawyers must be vigilant to ensure that their offices and clients protect valuable records with appropriate security when they are stored in the cloud or in databases that can be accessed through the web.

Securing Wireless Devices. Wireless communication creates opportunities for hackers to intercept sensitive data such as passwords for logging into corporate networks and online banking sites. Public Wi-Fi locations such as airports, hotels, and coffee shops—convenient places to check email—often do not have security features necessary to protect confidential client data. Hackers can use a proxy server to create a fake Wi-Fi hotspot (an "evil twin") and intercept or redirect confidential communications. The National Security Agency (NSA) issued guidance on securing wireless devices in public settings that will be useful to lawyers working remotely or when travelling.[180]

2.1.10. *Unsecured Databases*

Numerous instances of the exposure of highly sensitive law firm and corporate data in unsecured databases have been reported. These breaches are not the result of hacker attacks. They are totally preventable and demonstrate inexcusable failures of companies to follow the most basic, well-accepted security standards and practices. Law offices must be vigilant to ensure that client records and their own data are protected from these types of errors, and they must also understand the nature and scope of the protections in place at their vendors and business partners so that sensitive and confidential data are appropriately secured and are never left unprotected. Otherwise, law firms could be exposed to liability for their failure to maintain reasonable security to protect confidential client data and firm information.

Egregious violations of security best practices are evident in these types of breaches, putting at risk the most sensitive data of billions of individuals and companies. Security research reports provide numerous examples of databases exposed online or in the cloud with no passwords or passwords stored in plaintext, data accessible without authorization, misconfigurations of a popular open source database,[181] website design errors resulting in no verification of who was viewing links to a webpage with sensitive information, server

180. *Securing Wireless Devices in Public Settings*, NAT'L SEC. AGENCY (July 29, 2021), https://www.nsa.gov/Press-Room/News-Highlights/Article/Article/2711968/nsa-issues-guidance-on-securing-wireless-devices-in-public-settings/.

181. Breaches of the popular open source ElasticSearch database and servers are at the heart of recent data exposure reports. *See* Ralf Abueg, *Elasticsearch: What It Is, How it Works, and What it's Used for*, KNOWI (March 7, 2020), https://www.knowi.com/blog/what-is-elastic-search/. An unprotected AWS ElasticSearch database for the job site Ladders exposed 13 million user accounts and profiles. Job seeker information such as names, email addresses, phone numbers, geolocation, current and desired salaries, employment history, and US H1-B visa status was exposed. Employers' and recruiters' personal information on the site was exposed as well.

configuration errors,[182] and cloud databases that included basic security protections—however, the protections were not configured.

Sensitive Data from 190 Law Firms Exposed from Vendor Online Database. Lax security practices left 10,000 legal documents and sensitive data from more than 190 law firms exposed in an unsecured online database hosted by one of the largest software companies in the U.K. The impacted firms included the largest law firms in the world, as well as small boutique practices. Infosec firm TurgenSec, which revealed the breach, said the data was unprotected, "accessible to anyone with a browser and internet connection—if they knew where to look."[183] TurgenSec published a comprehensive list of the affected law firms in its update of the data leak timeline. Some of the notable law firms included Clifford Chance and Slaughter and May, both headquartered in London.[184] Further, in 2021, TurgenSec reported that 345,000 sensitive legal and court documents from the Office of the Solicitor General of the Philippines related to ongoing legal cases were made publicly available online.[185]

Global firm Proskauer Rose employed a third-party vendor to store 184,000 files containing "private and privileged financial and legal documents, contracts, non-disclosure agreements, financial deals and files relating to high-profile acquisitions." In 2023, the firm revealed that a threat actor was able to access the records on an unsecured Microsoft cloud server that was publicly accessible by anyone with knowledge of where to look online. This data was left exposed for six months before the threat actor accessed it.[186] Although Proskauer promptly responded to secure the data following the leak's discovery, the incident underscores the crucial requirement for ongoing monitoring and protection against unauthorized access or use of sensitive data.

Unsecured Biometric Records Breached. 27.8 million sensitive biometric records—fingerprint records and facial recognition information—were found exposed in a massive *data*

182. *Report: Hotel Reservation Platform Leaves Millions of People Exposed in Massive Data Breach*, Website Planet (Nov. 6, 2020), https://www.websiteplanet.com/blog/prestige-soft-breach-report. Prestige Software, based in Spain, a hotel reservation platform for Expedia, Hotels.com, Booking.com, and others, stored hospitality data, including years of credit card data from hotel guests and travel agents, on a misconfigured Amazon Web Services (AWS) S3 bucket, a popular form of cloud-based data storage, without any protection in place, putting millions of people at risk of fraud and online attacks. Amazon S3 buckets are similar to file folders and consist of data and its descriptive metadata. In order to protect data, S3 Block Public Access must be turned on. *See* Amazon S3, Amazon Web Servs., https://aws.amazon.com/s3/ (last visited Sept. 23, 2025).

183. Nic Fildes, *Data Security Flaw Exposes Details of Thousands of Legal Documents: Cache Including Client Email Addresses and Passwords Was Left Unsecured for Years*, Financial Times (May 3, 2020), https://www.ft.com/content/e0d6b6b7-825f-4102-b78f-204e1be205b6.

184. Alicia Hope, *Over 190 Law Firms Affected by Advanced Data Leak That Exposed over 10,000 Legal Documents*, CPO Magazine, May 18, 2020, https://www.cpomagazine.com/cyber-security/over-190-law-firms-affected-by-advanced-data-leak-that-exposed-over-10000-legal-documents/.

185. Campbell Kwan, *TurgenSec Finds 345,000 files from Filipino Solicitor-General's Office Were Breached: Sensitive Documents from the Solicitor-General of the Philippines, Including Information on Ongoing Legal Cases and Passwords, Were Breached and Made Publicly Available Online, the UK Security Firm Has Said*, ZDNet (May 2, 2021) https://www.zdnet.com/article/turgensec-finds-345000-files-from-filipino-solicitor-generals-office-were-breached/.

186. Page, *supra* note 145.

breach involving Suprema-owned biometric security platform BioStar 2 that provides thousands of companies with biometric security to identify users and control access to offices and private areas.[187] Researchers were able to access the biometric records, as well as the accounts associated with this leak, as many had default or easily decipherable passwords; complex passwords were all saved as plain text in the database.[188] Once stolen, fingerprint and facial recognition information cannot be reissued, as is the case with Social Security numbers and payment card records. Individuals will potentially be affected negatively for the rest of their lives.

One of the Largest Data Breaches in History. Because of a website design error, access to the key First American Financial Corporation online document-sharing system failed to require verification of who was viewing links to a webpage and exposed 885 million records.[189] Files stored on the company's website contained personal and mortgage-related documents, including bank account numbers, bank statements, mortgage records, tax documents, wire transfer receipts, Social Security numbers, and photos of driver's licenses. All of that information was available without any protection and could be accessed without a password.[190]

The law enforcement consequences for First American, the largest real estate title insurance company and provider of mortgage settlement services, were far-reaching. The New York State Department of Financial Services (DFS) brought the first enforcement action against First American under cybersecurity rules that require all Department-regulated entities to have a cybersecurity program that protects customer non-public information (NPI). DFS reached a $1 million cybersecurity settlement with First American.[191] The SEC brought a cease-and-desist action against the company and reached a settlement in which First American agreed to pay a penalty of $488,000 for this breach.[192]

---

187. *Over 27.8M Records Exposed in BioStar 2 Data Breach*, TRENDMICRO (Aug. 15, 2019), https://www.trendmicro.com/vinfo/us/security/news/online-privacy/over-27-8m-records-exposed-in-biostar-2-data-breach.

188. vpnMentor Research Team, *Report: Data Breach in Biometric Security Platform Affecting Millions of Users*, VPNMENTOR (Aug. 14, 2019), https://www.vpnmentor.com/blog/report-biostar2-leak/.

189. Brian Krebs, *First American Financial Corp. Leaked Hundreds of Millions of Title Insurance Records*, KREBS ON SEC. (May 24, 2019), https://krebsonsecurity.com/2019/05/first-american-financial-corp-leaked-hundreds-of-millions-of-title-insurance-records/.

190. AJ Dellinger, *Understanding the First American Financial Data Leak: How Did It Happen and What Does It Mean?* FORBES, https://www.forbes.com/sites/ajdellinger/2019/05/26/understanding-the-first-american-financial-data-leak-how-did-it-happen-and-what-does-it-mean/?sh=19188a27567f (last updated May 26, 2019). A link to a webpage with sensitive information was created and intended to be seen only by a specific party, but there was no method to actually verify the identity of who was viewing the link.

191. Press Release, N.Y. Dept. of Fin. Services, *DFS Announces $1 Million Cybersecurity Settlement with First American Title Insurance Company Settlement Resolves Cybersecurity Violations Relating to Breach and Exposure of Consumers' Nonpublic Information* (Nov. 28, 2023), https://www.dfs.ny.gov/reports_and_publications/press_releases/pr202311281; see also James Rundle & Dylan Tokar, *New York Regulator Charges First American Unit Over 2019 Data Breach: Enforcement Action Is the First under Cybersecurity Rules That Went into Effect in 2017*, WALL ST. J., https://www.wsj.com/articles/new-york-regulator-charges-first-american-over-2019-data-breach-11595423988.

192. Press Release, *SEC Charges Issuer with Cybersecurity Disclosure Controls Failures*, 2021-102 (June 16, 2021), https://www.sec.gov/newsroom/press-releases/2021-102; Brian Krebs, *First American Financial Pays*

2.1.11. *Lost and Stolen Computers and Mobile Devices*

As the use of mobile devices explodes around the globe,[193] concerns about the security of data and communications with mobile or BYOT devices are increasing. While mobile devices are an integral part of the legal environment, and smartphones, tablets, and laptops have become essential tools for attorneys and support staff alike, by their design they present numerous risks. The vulnerabilities are particularly serious if the mobile devices are used to communicate with legal clients by email or through social media, or to view, process, or store confidential client data and information.

Laptops and smartphones are often lost or stolen, and the data on them may be accessed with little difficulty.[194] From a security perspective, experts have identified three "attack surfaces" associated with mobile devices—the device itself, the operating system (OS) on the device, and the external service providers.[195] The FTC has brought a number of cases charging that companies engaged in unfair and deceptive practices for marketing mobile devices and software with security vulnerabilities or that exposed personal data without consumers' knowledge.[196]

Data breaches can be prevented by encrypting the data on mobile devices, enforcing procedures that do not permit individuals to transport sensitive data on moveable media, keeping careful track of the devices, and having the highest standards and requirements for couriers to move backup tapes and CDs to off-site storage facilities or from one location to the another. "With tiered permissions, truncation, redaction and other recording tools, PII can be left where it belongs—behind encrypted walls at the workplace."[197]

Requirements for Mobility in a Legal Environment. Seeking efficiencies from new technologies, many organizations are considering whether to implement BYOD or BYOT policies. BYOD may appear to be a good approach for organizations seeking to reduce costs and accommodate a generation of younger lawyers who are investing in the latest mobile devices, but the practice presents potential risks that are not well understood. Adopting a BYOD program carries with it significant responsibilities from both an information

---

Farcical $500K Fine, Krebs on Sec. (June 18, 2021), https://krebsonsecurity.com/2021/06/first-american-financial-pays-farcical-500k-fine/.

193. Mobile devices are the fastest-growing computing technology. Cisco predicted in 2020 that the number of devices connected to IP networks will be more than three times the global population by 2023. Cisco Annual Internet Report (2018–2023) White Paper (March 20, 2020), https://www.cisco.com/c/en/us/solutions/collateral/executive-perspectives/annual-internet-report/white-paper-c11-741490.html.

194. *See* Verizon 2024 DBIR, Lost and Stolen Assets, *supra* note 13, at 51–52.

195. NIST Spec. Pub. 800-163 Rev. 1, Vetting the Security of Mobile Applications (April 2019), https://doi.org/10.6028/NIST.SP.800-163r1; Dr. Robert Thibadeau & Lucy L. Thomson, *Mobile Device Security*, 9(1) ABA SciTech Lawyer at 24–28 (Summer 2013).

196. FTC, Mobile Technology Issues, https://www.ftc.gov/news-events/topics/mobile-technology-issues.

197. NIST Spec. Pub. 800-124 Rev. 2, Guidelines for Managing the Security of Mobile Devices in the Enterprise (May 2023), https://doi.org/10.6028/NIST.SP.800-124r2, Verizon 2024 DBIR, Lost and Stolen Assets, *supra* note 13, at 51–52. ("Devices are still much more likely to be lost than stolen. Laptops continue to be a risk for loss in particular.")

governance and technical perspective.[198] Targeted toward consumers for on-demand personal access to communications, information, and services, mobile devices are not configured by default for business use. To reduce risk to sensitive data and systems, law practices need to adopt appropriate governance policies for the use of mobile devices to access office resources and client information. As well, offices must create the infrastructure to manage and secure mobile devices, applications, content, and access.

While there are a number of steps a law firm should take to protect confidential data on mobile devices if it chooses to permit personal devices on the network, several are key.[199] Where possible, the law firm should use mobile device management that provides a centralized way to manage mobile devices remotely, including, significantly, the ability to check a lost device's geographic location and lock or erase it remotely. Only known users and devices should be permitted on the network; app providers should be known as well. Phones that have been jailbroken or rooted should not be permitted on the network. Phones and tablets that are used to create, transmit, or store sensitive data, even in email, should have centralized management of passwords with acceptable password policies, and all user data should be encrypted. Such management software is readily available from many vendors.

2.1.12. *Physical Security and Improper Disposal of Personal Information*

Physical security is a critical component of information security.[200]

Sensitive personal records on paper, as well as digital formats, must be protected. At least 35 states, D.C. and Puerto Rico have enacted data disposal laws that require either private or governmental entities or both to destroy, dispose of, or otherwise make personal information unreadable or indecipherable.[201]

2.2. Steps to Protect Confidential Law Firm Records and Prevent Data Breaches: Risk Assessments

Law firms that collect, use, store, and share sensitive, confidential, and proprietary information must protect the information and ensure that it is not compromised by hackers or malicious insiders, inadvertently accessed, or lost.[202]

---

198. Steven S. Wu, A Legal Guide to Enterprise Mobile Device Management: Managing Bring Your Own Device (BYOD) and Employer-Issued Device Programs (ABA 2013). This book examines the legal and practical implications of BYOD and highlights future challenges for organizations both in the U.S. and internationally.

199. CISA *Mobile Device Adoption Best Practices*, https://www.cisa.gov/sites/default/files/publications/Mobile%20Device%20Adoption%20Best%20Practices%20Guide-508%20compliant%20041316%20FINAL.pdf.

200. NIST Spec. Pub. 800-12: An Introduction to Computer Security: The NIST Handbook, ch.15, https://csrc.nist.rip/publications/nistpubs/800-12/800-12-html/chapter15.html.

201. *See* Nat'l Conference of State Legislatures, NCSL *Data Disposal Laws*, https://www.ncsl.org/research/telecommunications-and-information-technology/data-disposal-laws.aspx.

202. Handbook, Chapter 7, *Legal Obligations to Provide Data Security*, provides a detailed discussion of security requirements that apply to lawyers and law practices.

Cybersecurity is based on a systematic assessment of risks that are present in a particular operating environment. Assessing risk requires organizations to identify their threats and vulnerabilities, the harm they may cause the organization, and the likelihood that those adverse events may actually occur. The results of the risk assessment are the basis for the selection and implementation of appropriate technical, operational, and management security controls to protect the systems and data. Continuous monitoring is required to address new threats and risks and changes to the system as they are made.

Conducting a risk assessment is an essential first step to determine how much risk is being introduced by implementing the various technologies and components. Every information system is different, including its design and architecture, hardware and software, and technical implementation. Company and government officials must tailor their risk assessments to the data, architecture, and technology of the systems they own, oversee, or manage.[203]

Global laws, principles, and best practices are all based on requirements for the risk assessment of systems. The risk-based assessment approach is consistent with the NIST *Cybersecurity Framework*, an important guide for organizations to use in assessing security risks and determining the maturity of their cybersecurity program.[204]

In particular, participants who use AI for analysis and key transactions should take reasonable steps to minimize the risks. The NIST *AI Risk Management Framework* summarizes the unique characteristics of AI systems that require the conduct of risk assessments as the foundation for the comprehensive cybersecurity programs of all government and private sector organizations:

> AI systems bring a set of risks that require specific consideration and approaches. AI systems can amplify, perpetuate, or exacerbate inequitable outcomes. AI systems may exhibit emergent properties or lead to unintended consequences for individuals and communities. A useful mathematical representation of the data interactions that drive the AI system's behavior is not fully known, which makes current methods for measuring risks and navigating the risk-benefit[] tradeoff inadequate. AI risks may arise from the data used to train the AI system, the AI system itself, the use of the AI system, or [the] interaction of people with the AI system.[205]

At least 25 states have laws that address data security practices of private sector entities. Most of these data security laws require businesses that own, license, or maintain personal information about a resident of that state to implement and maintain "reasonable security procedures and practices" appropriate to the nature of the information and to protect the personal information from unauthorized access, destruction, use, modification, or disclosure, NCSL Data Security Laws | Private Sector, https://www.ncsl.org/technology-and-communication/data-security-laws-private-sector.

203. NISTIR 8286B, *Prioritizing Cybersecurity Risk for Enterprise Risk Management*, NIST (Feb. 2022), https://nvlpubs.nist.gov/nistpubs/ir/2022/NIST.IR.8286B.pdf (a set of industry standards and best practices to help organizations manage cybersecurity risks as part of their risk management processes).

204. Cybersecurity Framework 2.0, NIST (Aug. 8, 2023), https://www.nist.gov/cyberframework.

205. NIST AI Risk Management Framework, *supra* note 42.

AI risk assessments should focus on the specific characteristics and vulnerabilities of the software and devices being implemented, with particular attention to AI systems and capabilities, as well as the environment(s) in which the system(s) are deployed. Once law offices are aware of their existing and possible future AI usage, they need to understand how the characteristics of AI affect managing cybersecurity and privacy risks, especially in terms of risk response—accepting, avoiding, mitigating, sharing, or transferring risk.

3. Top Considerations

The following is a list of top considerations for lawyers and law practices when addressing cybersecurity and data protection.[206]

1. ***Develop a comprehensive information security plan*** specifically designed to prevent data breaches. The plan must include appropriate security for all aspects of the computer network, including technical, operational, and management controls. For example, spear phishing is currently a common attack methodology used by hackers; address it by creating a culture of security throughout the law firm, and enforcing security policies to combat this problem.
2. ***Follow security-by-design principles.*** To properly support an organization's risk management framework, security must be incorporated into the architecture and design of the law firm's information systems and supporting IT assets.
3. ***Conduct a risk assessment.*** Carefully document how the security controls selected and implemented address all risks identified. Ensure that information security continuous monitoring is a part of organization-wide risk management.
4. ***Prioritize the use of scarce resources to address the most serious problems first.*** Prioritize security resources to address the most critical and vulnerable aspects of the system and common threats such as phishing attacks, ransomware, BEC, *and* stolen credentials. Understand key risks and threats and stay informed about new ones as they are discovered. Consider the recommendations of experts about how to prioritize.[207]
5. ***Combat ransomware*** by taking the following actions:
    a. Backup your data, system images, and configurations and keep the backups offline.
    b. Update and patch systems.

---

206. 11 Best Cybersecurity Practices to Protect Your Firm, University of South Carolina, Joseph F. Rice School of Law, https://sc.edu/study/colleges_schools/law/about/news/2020/11_best_cybersecurity_practices.php.

207. *See, e.g.*, CIS Controls v.8, Ctr. for Internet Sec., https://www.cisecurity.org/controls/. The CIS Critical Controls provides guidance on how to maximize the impact of government and private sector security efforts, and identifies 18 critical priority controls, most of which can be continuously monitored. The CIS website provides a wealth of valuable information about the leading information security methodologies and how they relate to each other.

c. Make sure your security solutions are up to date.
d. Implement multi-factor authentication on every account that is under the control of the organization, and the principle of least privilege on key network resources admin accounts.
e. Review and exercise your incident response plan.
f. Pay attention to ransomware events and apply lessons learned.

6. ***Do not purchase or implement devices, software, or systems with known vulnerabilities.*** Focus on vendor management. Use procurements as an opportunity to specify requirements for appropriate security in vendor contracts and business partner agreements.
7. ***Secure the law firm's sensitive data using appropriate encryption technology.*** Remember that inadequate or inappropriate key management can result in data breaches and/or loss of data; ensure that appropriate encryption is utilized on mobile devices. Where possible, use mobile device management to protect confidential data on mobile devices, including the ability to lock or erase a lost device remotely, and check its geographic location.
8. ***Allow only known users, devices and apps*** onto the network. App providers should be known as well. Phones that have been jailbroken or rooted should not be permitted on the network. Phones and tablets that are used to create, transmit, or store sensitive data, even in email, should have centralized management of passwords with acceptable password policies, and all user data should be encrypted.
9. ***Be prepared if a data breach occurs.*** Build internal firm teams of first responders who have been briefed on the security issues and their implications, so they do not have to think through such things for the very first time in the middle of a security incident or data breach.
10. ***Understand key risks and threats and stay aware of new ones as they are discovered.*** Identify and build bridges with ISPs, law enforcement, and other security resources, so you know who to go to when an incident or breach occurs, and so they know who you are.[208] Work with the Legal Services Information Sharing and Analysis Organization (LS-ISAO) and take advantage of their resources and expertise: https://www.isao.org/information-sharing-group/sector/legal-services-isao/.

---

208. The FBI has emphasized the importance of law enforcement collaboration and partnerships with the private sector. *How We Can Help You*, OFFICE OF PRIVATE SECTOR, FBI, https://www.fbi.gov/about/partnerships/office-of-private-sector (last visited June 12, 2025).

Chapter 5
Cybercrime

Kathleen Hom and Logan Hamilton

Lawyers are familiar with being on the other side of a crime. They are professional advocates, meaning some may prosecute or defend alleged criminals in court, in conference rooms, and over sometimes heated emails with opposing counsel. Most lawyers are unaccustomed to being the **victim** of a crime.

Lawyers are increasingly the target of cybercrimes, from falling for phishing emails to sharing sensitive files on unsecure platforms.[1] According to the American Bar Association's (ABA) 2023 Cybersecurity TechReport, 29% of survey respondents said their firms had experienced a security breach.[2] Attacks on firms, big and small, continue to accelerate with ever-growing numbers of firms reporting data breaches, to their embarrassment and legal liability.[3] Artificial intelligence (AI) technologies can significantly increase the ability of malicious actors to target and successfully breach organizations' data and networks. AI technologies can increase the speed, scale, and sophistication of attacks. Even though they are generally aware that cybercriminals could target them, lawyers and law firms have traditionally been caught flat-footed as cybercrime victims. These days, every lawyer who uses modern technology at home or in the office must understand cybersecurity basics. This chapter will help readers understand these introductory topics:

- What is cybercrime?
- What are the common types of cybercrimes?
- Who are cybercriminals?

1. *See, e.g.*, Will Thorpe, *NSW Attorney-General Cautions Domestic Violence Victims about Court Data Breach*, CityHub (Mar. 28, 2025), https://cityhub.com.au/nsw-attorney-general-cautions-domestic-violence-victims-about-court-data-breach/; George Chaisty, *Emerging Cyber Threats Facing the Legal Industry in 2025*, Kennedys Law (Jan. 4, 2025), https://kennedyslaw.com/en/thought-leadership/article/2025/emerging-cyber-threats-facing-the-legal-industry-in-2025/; *When Attorney-Client Privilege is Breached: The Cascading Impact of Cyberattacks on the Legal Sector*, Ninjio (Apr. 17, 2025), https://ninjio.com/2025/04/blog-cascading-impact-legal-cyberattacks; and Robert Lemos, *Law Firms & Legal Departments Singled Out for Cyberattacks*, DarkReading (Nov. 30, 2023), https://www.darkreading.com/cyberattacks-data-breaches/law-firms-face-a-more-dangerous-threat-landscape.

2. John Simek, *2023 Cybersecurity TechReport*, Law Practice Div., Am. Bar Ass'n (Dec. 18, 2023, https://www.americanbar.org/groups/law_practice/resources/tech-report/2023/2023-cybersecurity-techreport/.

3. Dan Roe, *Law Firm Data Breach Reports Show No Signs of Slowing in 2024*, Law.com (May 23, 2024, 5:00 AM), https://www.law.com/americanlawyer/2024/05/23/law-firm-data-breach-reports-show-no-signs-of-slowing-in-2024/.

- Why do cybercriminals target lawyers? and
- What is cybercrime's impact on attorneys and firms?

1. What Is Cybercrime?

"Cybercrime" is a portmanteau of "crime" and "cyber." "Cyber," as an adjective, generally relates to or about computers and networks. We can broadly define cybercrime as "any illegal activity carried out using computers or the internet."[4]

This general definition masks a great deal of ambiguity about the nature of the crime and its intersection with computers and computer networks. For example, this broad definition includes crimes merely enabled or facilitated by using a computer, such as drug trafficking and terrorist communications. This chapter focuses on crimes that can be committed only with the internet and modern technologies, and crimes that specifically target computer networks. These crimes include "online fraud in its many forms,"[5] revenge porn, ransomware, phishing, malware, and botnets.

2. What Are the Common Types of Cybercrimes?

One of the challenges in defining and classifying cybercrime, alluded to above, is the breadth of activities that fall under this umbrella term. While both revenge porn and ransomware can be classified as "cybercrimes," they differ in motivation, scale, scope, means of implementation, and ultimate objective. This chapter briefly covers some of the most prevalent and impactful cyberattacks on the legal profession.

2.1. Business Email Compromise (BEC)

Business email compromises (BEC), including phishing and spoofing emails, refer to cybercriminals' use of email to "impersonate trusted leaders to trick employees into sending money or data."[6] BEC may feature targeted phishing emails, called spearphishing. Spearphishing includes gathering intelligence beforehand to create those targeted emails, enabling the criminal to more convincingly impersonate an organization's manager and then direct employees to transfer funds or information outside the firm. BEC criminals can target firms and a firm's clients; if a client unfortunately falls for a spearphishing attack, they may blame the impersonated firm. For example, in 2022, one cybercriminal enterprise

---

4. *Cybercrime*, U.S. IMMIGRATION & CUSTOMS ENF'T (Feb. 2, 2025), https://www.ice.gov/about-ice/hsi/investigate/cybercrime.

5. *About Us*, INTERNET CRIME COMPLAINT CTR., FED. BUREAU OF INVESTIGATION, https://www.ic3.gov/Home/About (last visited May 26, 2025).

6. *What is business email compromise (BEC)?*, MICROSOFT, https://www.microsoft.com/en-us/security/business/security-101/what-is-business-email-compromise-bec (last visited May 29, 2025).

impersonated over 14 major multinational law firms.[7] Using emails and forms that purported to be from these unwitting firms, this criminal group used high-pressure tactics on targeted victims and tricked them into paying allegedly overdue invoices owed to the impersonated firms.[8] According to the FBI, between October 2013 and December 2023, the domestic and international exposed dollar loss attributed to BEC exceeded $55.4 billion.[9]

2.2. Credential Harvesting

This technique occurs when a cybercriminal gathers usernames, passwords, and other authentication information from victims so that the cybercriminal can enter systems, accounts, and networks without authorization and without being easily detected.[10] Using harvested credentials, the attacker can log in with valid usernames and passwords. They can then access and gather sensitive information, from personally identifiable information, like names and Social Security numbers, to a business's financial information. A cybercriminal may sell this information on the dark web or use it to launch a more sophisticated attack, or both.[11] Cybercriminals can gather login information through malware, phishing, and domain spoofing.

2.3. Denial-of-Service (DoS) / Distributed-Denial-of-Service (DDoS) Attacks

During natural disasters, authorities often request that only those in imminent danger call emergency services; otherwise, the sheer number of callers overwhelms the emergency center, and few can connect to request help. This principle, too many callers stymying emergency phone lines, is the concept behind denial-of-service (DoS) and distributed-denial-of-service (DDoS) attacks. DoS attacks work "by flooding the targeted host or network with traffic until the target cannot respond or simply crashes, preventing access for legitimate users."[12] DDoS attacks function similarly but on a larger scale with "multiple machines ... operating together to attack one target." Usually, a botnet controls these machines, without the computer owner's knowledge.[13] Cybercriminals can sell these attacks as a service or use them to draw attention away from malicious network activity.

Organizations can, to a large extent, mitigate DoS or DDoS attacks by using network equipment or cloud-based services that detect illegitimate traffic, allowing them to block

---

7. Bill Toulas, *New Crimson Kingsnake Gang Impersonates Law Firms in BEC Attacks*, Bleeping Computer (Nov. 3, 2022), https://www.bleepingcomputer.com/news/security/new-crimson-kingsnake-gang-impersonates-law-firms-in-bec-attacks/.

8. *Id.*

9. Fed. Bureau of Investigation, Business Email Compromise: The $55 Billion Scam (Sep. 11, 2024), https://www.ic3.gov/PSA/2024/PSA240911.

10. Health Sector Cybersecurity Coordination Ctr., U.S. Dep't of Health & Human Servs., Credential Harvesting (Dec. 17, 2024), https://www.hhs.gov/sites/default/files/credential-harvesting-analyst-note-tlpclear.pdf.

11. Bart Lenaerts-Bergmans, *What Is Credential Harvesting?*, CrowdStrike (July 18, 2023), https://www.crowdstrike.com/en-us/cybersecurity-101/cyberattacks/credential-harvesting.

12. *Understanding Denial-of-Service Attacks*, Cybersecurity & Infrastructure Sec. Agency (Feb. 1, 2021), https://www.cisa.gov/news-events/news/understanding-denial-service-attacks.

13. *Id.*

it and prevent malicious traffic from connecting, absorb traffic to prevent denied service, and adapt to the attacker by blocking traffic from certain IP addresses, countries, or using particular protocols.[14]

2.4. Domain/Email Spoofing

Savvy exploiters, cybercriminals can create fake websites and email addresses that mimic legitimate ones, a process known as domain spoofing or digital masquerading.[15] The email address may be slightly off, for example, it may end with a ".com" when the legitimate email address should end with a ".gov" or ".org." Another example is a fake website that may include a legitimate company's logo together with a non-standard message that resembles what a user will generally see on the legitimate site. Users may not read closely enough to notice a grammatical mistake or other discrepancy. A phishing attack may combine email and domain spoofing, with a spoofed email directing an employee to click on a spoofed domain. Criminals can use this technique to harvest credentials.

2.5. Malware

Malware is a portmanteau of the words, malicious and software. Malware includes "any intrusive software developed…[and used] to steal data and damage or destroy computers and computer systems."[16] It can hide in malicious websites, software downloads, removable media, and email attachments. Common examples include viruses, worms, spyware, adware, Trojan viruses, and ransomware. Though not all malware is destructive, like worms or ransomware, discussed below, the mere presence of malware on a network indicates a point of failure somewhere in an organization's defense, whether it be purely technical or caused by human error.

2.6. Phishing[17]

Phishing is a form of social engineering used by cybercriminals designed to trick victims into giving cybercriminals sensitive information, like bank login information.[18] Cybercriminals utilize spoofing techniques to make it appear that requests come from legitimate sites or individuals to tempt the victim to take the bait, that is to say, interact with them and reveal information. As the FTC noted, while the specifics of a phishing attempt can vary, they "often tell a story to trick you into clicking on a link or opening an attachment."[19]

---

14. *What Is DDoS Mitigation?*, CLOUDFLARE, https://www.cloudflare.com/learning/ddos/ddos-mitigation/ (last visited May 30, 2025).

15. *What Is Domain Spoofing?*, CLOUDFLARE, https://www.cloudflare.com/learning/ssl/what-is-domain-spoofing/ (last visited May 30, 2025).

16. *What Is Malware?*, CISCO, https://www.cisco.com/site/us/en/learn/topics/security/what-is-malware.html (last visited May 30, 2025).

17. A variant of phishing is spearphishing, *see supra* Business Email Compromise.

18. *Spoofing and Phishing*, FED. BUREAU OF INVESTIGATION, https://www.fbi.gov/how-we-can-help-you/scams-and-safety/common-frauds-and-scams/spoofing-and-phishing (last visited May 31, 2025).

19. *How To Recognize and Avoid Phishing Scams*, FED. TRADE COMM'N, https://consumer.ftc.gov/articles/how-recognize-and-avoid-phishing-scams (last visited May 31, 2025).

Once hooked, victims are directed to the seemingly legitimate site where they hand over personal and financial information. Using AI, cybercriminals can create malicious communications nearly indistinguishable from real communications. However, requests that seek to create a sense of urgency and action (frozen accounts because of billing issues, need to update payment, emergencies that require immediate responses through the provided link) constitute red flags that should make you suspect a phishing attempt.

2.7. Ransomware

Ransomware is a particularly vicious category of malware that continues to dominate the news cycle.[20] Ransomware generally infects a computer or network like other malware, and starts with a user unknowingly downloading malicious files or visiting a malicious website. Once downloaded, the ransomware "will lock access to the computer itself or data and files stored there" or "encrypt files and folders on local drives, attached drives, and even networked computers."[21] Cybercriminals traditionally targeted "large corporations, industries, financial sector institutions, government entities, etc." since ransomware threatens "the day-to-day operations of those entities and [ransoms] are often cheaper to pay off than to fix"[22] by trying to unlock computers and decrypt files. The ransom amount that cybercriminals demand varies, generally based on the organization's size and wealth. However, paying the ransom does not guarantee the restoration of access or that information has not already been exfiltrated for sale or later exploitation. Payment also carries regulatory risks, since payment to a sanctioned group may cause the U.S. Department of the Treasury's Office of Foreign Assets Control to bring an enforcement action against the payor.[23]

2.8. Impact of Artificial Intelligence (AI)

AI can make the job of a cybercriminal easier. In 2021, before the release of ChatGPT, the Federal Bureau of Investigation (FBI) warned that AI would be used by "criminal cyber actors for spearphishing and social engineering [attacks] in an evolution of cyber operational tradecraft."[24] For non-native speakers of a language, AI can create text that is nearly, if not wholly, indistinguishable from that of a native speaker. All this can be automated, allowing cybercriminals to "generate highly personalized phishing emails at scale,

---

20. *See* Sean Lyngaas, *Ransomware Attack Triggers "System-Wide" Tech Outage at Large Network of Medical Centers*, CNN (May 20, 2025, 1:14 PM), https://www.cnn.com/2025/05/20/politics/ransomware-attack-medical-centers; Brian Fung, *Ransomware Hits Law Firm with Dozens of Major Corporate Clients*, CNN (July 19, 2021, 4:40 PM), https://www.cnn.com/2021/07/19/tech/ransomware-law-firm/index.html.

21. *Ransomware*, Fed. Bureau of Investigation, https://www.fbi.gov/how-we-can-help-you/scams-and-safety/common-frauds-and-scams/ransomware (last visited May 30, 2025).

22. *Ransomware*, U.S. Dep't of State, https://www.state.gov/ransomware/ (last visited May 31, 2025).

23. *Publication of Updated Ransomware Advisory; Cyber-related Designation*, Office of Foreign Assets Control, U.S. Dep't of Treas. (Sept. 21, 2021), https://ofac.treasury.gov/media/912981/download?inline.

24. Fed. Bureau of Investigation, Malicious Actors Almost Certainly Will Leverage Synthetic Content for Cyber and Foreign Influence Operations, (Mar. 10, 2021), https://www.ic3.gov/CSA/2021/210310-2.pdf.

mimicking writing styles and incorporating context-specific details to make their messages almost indistinguishable from legitimate communications."[25] These emails can also be used with an AI chatbot that can answer in real-time to a victim who responds to a malicious email, further simulating legitimate communications. Using AI for personalized phishing attacks is not restricted to text. Cybercriminals "employ AI-powered voice and video cloning techniques to impersonate trusted individuals, such as family members, co-workers, or business partners."[26] AI can learn the nuances of a person's speech pattern, tone, and even hand gestures and facial expressions to create sophisticated audio and visual deepfakes.[27]

In addition to simulating real individuals, AI can create personas out of thin air. Publicly available and bespoke AI tools create "increasingly convincing fake identities, credentials and entire digital footprints designed to deceive security measures."[28] These tools make it increasingly difficult for organizations to conduct due diligence and authentication measures, such as know-your-customer checks and social media checks.

Bad actors also use AI more directly. Cybercriminals can utilize AI-generated programs to automate cyberattacks by "identifying vulnerabilities, deploying campaigns along identified attack vectors, advancing attack paths, establishing backdoors within systems, exfiltrating or tampering with data, and interfering with system operations."[29] They can use these tools with minimal oversight, all the while improving their capabilities as they continue to perform.[30]

Even when organizations recognize that they can improve their cybersecurity position by using AI defenses, they must also grapple with the reality that cybercriminals can use AI to increase the scale, scope, and sophistication of their operations.[31] This is the brave new world that attorneys and law firms must confront.

3. Who Are Cybercriminals?

Having identified *what* cybercrime is, the question then arises *who* these malicious actors are. Generally speaking, we can classify cybercriminals into three categories in order of the danger they pose.

---

25. Rob Hutchinson, *Cybercriminals Are Winning With AI—Here's How They're Using It*, FORBES (Apr. 22, 2025 8:15 AM), https://www.forbes.com/councils/forbestechcouncil/2025/04/22/cybercriminals-are-winning-with-ai-heres-how-theyre-using-it/.

26. *FBI Warns of Increasing Threat of Cyber Criminals Utilizing Artificial Intelligence*, FED. BUREAU OF INVESTIGATION S.F., https://www.fbi.gov/contact-us/field-offices/sanfrancisco/news/fbi-warns-of-increasing-threat-of-cyber-criminals-utilizing-artificial-intelligence.

27. *See, e.g.*, GOV'T ACCOUNTABILITY OFFICE, SCIENCE & TECH SPOTLIGHT: DEEPFAKES (Feb. 2020), https://www.gao.gov/assets/gao-20-379sp.pdf.

28. Hutchinson, *supra* note 25.

29. Lucia Stanham, *AI-Powered Cyberattacks*, CROWDSTRIKE (Jan. 16, 2025), https://www.crowdstrike.com/en-us/cybersecurity-101/cyberattacks/ai-powered-cyberattacks/.

30. *Id.*

31. Hutchinson, *supra* note 25.

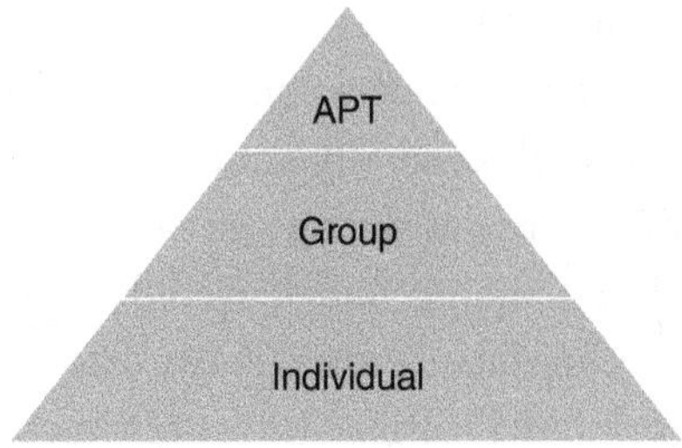

Graphic 1 Cybercriminal Threat Ranking

3.1. Individuals

Individual cybercriminals tend to be lower-skilled practitioners who purchase or rent capabilities from more skilled groups or individuals.[32] The threat of such individuals primarily comes from the sheer number of attacks, given the low financial and technical barriers to entry, which increases the odds that eventually they will gain a foothold in a network.[33] While not as skilled as other cybercriminals, these individuals can cause immense harm to organizations using commercial off-the-shelf (COTS) software and preying upon human psychology by exploiting senses of urgency, fear, and trust in authority. It is important to caveat, however, that some individual cybercriminals possess the requisite technical skills, so they need not buy capabilities from others; we generally refer to this class of individual cybercriminals as "black hat hackers."

3.2. Groups

Groups of cybercriminals pose greater threats to organizations, as opposed to individual cybercriminals. These groups range from autonomous collectives to highly organized groups imitative of legitimate corporations in their hierarchy and organizational sophistication.[34] These groups can specialize in certain types of victims or attack methods, such as ransomware gangs; innovate new cyber-attacking techniques; and sell or rent their skills and products, offering Crime as a Service (CaaS). These groups can be prolific and directly target organizations and individuals, such as through ransomware attacks.[35] Groups may also include state-actor involvement; for example, governments may hire unaffiliated groups to act as proxies and conduct criminal acts on their behalf.[36]

---

32. Kevin Murray, *The Evolution of Cybercrime as a Service*, CSO (July 8, 2021), https://www.csoonline.com/article/3624736/the-evolution-of-cybercrime-as-a-service.html.

33. *Id.*

34. *Id.*

35. *See, e.g.*, Davey Winder, *Record-Breaking $75 Million Ransom Paid To Dark Angels Gang*, Forbes (July 31, 2024), https://www.forbes.com/sites/daveywinder/2024/07/31/record-breaking-75-million-ransom-paid-to-dark-angels-gang/.

36. Mathew Schwartz, *Cybercrime Groups and Nation-State Attackers Blur Together*, Data Breach Today (June 28, 2018), https://www.databreachtoday.com/cybercrime-groups-nation-state-attackers-blur-together-a-11141#.WzTz4LHb5uE.

3.3. Advanced Persistent Threats (APTs)

Advanced persistent threats (APTs) stand at the pinnacle of the threat pyramid (see Graphic 1). These organizations are generally state or state-sponsored groups that seek to "steal sensitive data, conduct cyber espionage or sabotage critical systems over a long period of time," all the while remaining undiscovered.[37] APTs often gain initial access through social engineering techniques bolstered by extensive prior intelligence gathering.[38] Once inside a network, APTs utilize advanced technologies and techniques to escalate their access and move laterally to map the network, gather additional employee credentials, and create back doors allowing them to regain access if an access point is discovered and blocked.[39] APTs seek to conceal their presence on compromised networks.[40] These groups do not seek immediate financial gain, but instead have other objectives, such as data exfiltration.[41]

4. Why Do Cybercriminals Target Lawyers?

The costs imposed by cybercriminals on society at large continue to increase year after year. By the end of 2025, cybercrime is projected to globally cost consumers and businesses up to $1.2 to $1.5 *trillion* in damages annually.[42] Cybercriminals do not uniquely target attorneys and law firms. Nonetheless, attorneys and law firms make tempting targets. There is an apocryphal story about the famous bank robber, Willie Sutton, who when asked why he kept robbing banks replied: "Because that's where the money is." For attorneys and firms, cybercriminals apply the same logic that Willie did over 70 years ago—attorneys and law firms are where the money (and information) is located.

Attorneys and law firms are repositories of vast amounts of high-value, confidential, and sensitive client information, as well as their own business records. The information at firms may include intellectual property, personally identifiable information (PII), attorney work product, financial account information, employment, and healthcare information. Firms also collect sensitive information during litigation and discovery, including information about third parties.

This information has value because cybercriminals can exfiltrate it and demand a ransom after threatening to publicly release it, sell it on the dark web, or exploit it themselves

37. *What Are Advanced Persistent Threats?*, IBM (Apr. 3, 2024), https://www.ibm.com/think/topics/advanced-persistent-threats.

38. Kurt Baker, *Advanced Persistent Threats (APT) Explained*, CROWDSTRIKE (Mar. 4, 2025), https://www.crowdstrike.com/en-us/cybersecurity-101/threat-intelligence/advanced-persistent-threat-apt/.

39. *Id.*

40. IBM, *supra* note 37.

41. Baker, *supra* note 38.

42. Gary Miliesfsky, *The True Cost of Cybercrime: Why Global Damages Could Reach $1.2–$1.5 Trillion by End of Year 2025*, CYBER DEF. MAGAZINE (Mar. 13, 2025), https://www.cyberdefensemagazine.com/the-true-cost-of-cybercrime-why-global-damages-could-reach-1-2-1-5-trillion-by-end-of-year-2025/.

for personal gain, like insider trading on the stock market.[43] Stolen information can also be leveraged for attacks on bigger targets; in such cases, the firm is generally a stepping stone to the cybercriminal's ultimate target.

Further, law firms are often seen as easy targets, generally viewed as less protected than corporations. Specifically, medium- and small-sized firms may outsource their IT and cybersecurity compliance and monitoring. Without dedicated full-time internal staff, basic cyber hygiene practices may erode or be ignored over time. Even with internal IT teams, firms can suffer from a lack of expert staff, "outdated systems, untrained staff, or poorly managed user access."[44] Further, attorneys may not fully know how to protect themselves. Attorneys constantly communicate and exchange documents with clients, third parties, and vendors; emails and file upload sites can be an easy and reusable attack vector. Attorneys working on time-sensitive matters can be lucrative targets who may not recognize something is amiss until it is too late.

Cybercriminals recognize that attorneys and law firms often generate revenue based on billable hours. The longer a firm and its attorneys spend on remediating a cyber incident, the less time they spend billing clients, making paying a ransom an easier and less costly decision than investing in a proper investigation and remediation. Cybercriminals also recognize that client trust and reputational harm can serve as compelling pressure points to compel payment.

5. What Is the Impact of Cybercrime on Attorneys and Firms?

Once victimized by cybercriminals, attorneys and firms must resolve many legal and business issues in the aftermath of an attack. These issues include regulatory reporting requirements, reputational harm, and recovery of stolen funds and/or information, particularly PII. Many governments say law firms have a duty to protect information. In the United Kingdom, for example, a firm suffered a data breach and was fined £60,000 by the government for failing to secure electronic personal information.[45]

5.1. Regulatory Reporting Requirements

In many countries, privacy laws and regulations protect sensitive information. In the United States, we have no general federal privacy law, but various states have enacted their own

---

43. *See, e.g.*, *Manhattan U.S. Attorney Announces Arrest of Macau Resident and Unsealing of Charges Against Three Individuals for Insider Trading Based on Information Hacked from Prominent U.S. Law Firms*, S.D.N.Y., U.S. Attorney's Office (Dec. 27, 2016), https://www.justice.gov/usao-sdny/pr/manhattan-us-attorney-announces-arrest-macau-resident-and-unsealing-charges-against.

44. Maryam Ali, *Why Cyber Criminals Are Targeting Law Firms More Than Ever*, The Student Lawyer (Apr. 25, 2025), https://thestudentlawyer.com/2025/04/25/why-cyber-criminals-are-targeting-law-firms-more-than-ever/.

45. *Law Firm Fined £60,000 Following Cyber Attack*, Info. Comm'rs Office (Apr. 16, 2025), https://ico.org.uk/about-the-ico/media-centre/news-and-blogs/2025/04/law-firm-fined-60-000-following-cyber-attack/.

laws, and each comes with state-mandated reporting requirements.[46] The European Union has the General Data Protection Regulation, which includes reporting to both the "supervisory authority"[47] and the "data subject."[48] Additional reporting requirements may be included in a contract with the client. If a ransom payment is made, organizations may also have an obligation to report that or face U.S. federal enforcement actions.[49]

5.2. Reputational Harm

Clients may be less likely to return to or even terminate a relationship with a firm that does not protect their information. A lawyer's duty to protect confidential information constitutes both an ethical responsibility and a legal requirement. The ABA's Rule 1.6, Confidentiality of Information, offers some guidance,[50] and informs state bar association requirements. The ABA's rule is rooted in the "attorney-client privilege, the work product doctrine, and the rule of confidentiality."[51] If clients cannot trust a firm, why would they continue to work with it?

5.3. Recovery of Stolen Funds and/or Information

Cybersecurity criminals may use funds and/or information as leverage for demanding ransom payments. They may publicize stolen information or sell it on the dark web. A big challenge for firms and attorneys is getting that information and/or funds back. Can they believe cybercriminals who say they have not already sold information or copied it after they pay a ransom?

5.4. Remediation

A critical step after every cybersecurity incident is remediation. This means understanding how the cybercriminal operated to gain access to sensitive information and computer networks and working with IT to prevent the recurrence of that same issue or something similar. An after-action report with IT taking the lead can help pinpoint gaps in security

---

46. *See, e.g.*, *Colorado Privacy Act*, Office of the Attorney General, https://coag.gov/resources/colorado-privacy-act/ (last visted May 30, 2025); *California Consumer Privacy Act (CCPA)*, Office of the Attorney General (Mar. 13, 2024), https://oag.ca.gov/privacy/ccpa; Va. Code Ann. ch. 53 (2022), https://law.lis.virginia.gov/vacodefull/title59.1/chapter53/; *What You Should Know—NYS Personal Privacy Protection Law (PPPL)*, Comm. on Open Gov't, https://opengovernment.ny.gov/what-you-should-know-nys-personal-privacy-protection-law-pppl (last visited May 31, 2025); and 815 Ill. Comp. Stat. 530/1 (2008), https://www.ilga.gov/legislation/ilcs/ilcs3.asp?ActID=2702.

47. Regulation (EU) 2016/679, art. 33, 2016 O.J. (L 119). https://gdpr-info.eu/art-33-gdpr/.

48. Regulation (EU) 2016/679, art. 34, 2016 O.J. (L 119), https://gdpr-info.eu/art-34-gdpr/.

49. U.S. Department. of Treas., *supra* note 23.

50. *See* Model Rules of Prof'l Conduct r. 1.6 (Am. Bar Ass'n 1983), https://www.americanbar.org/groups/professional_responsibility/publications/model_rules_of_professional_conduct/rule_1_6_confidentiality_of_information/.

51. Model Rules of Prof'l Conduct r. 1.6 cmt. 3 (Am. Bar Ass'n 1983), https://www.americanbar.org/groups/professional_responsibility/publications/model_rules_of_professional_conduct/rule_1_6_confidentiality_of_information/comment_on_rule_1_6/.

processes and procedures. Additionally, organizations should conduct annual penetration tests, tabletop exercises, and audits against trusted cybersecurity industry standards.

6. Top Seven Considerations

Now that we have introduced these basic cybersecurity topics, here are some considerations and tips attorneys should practice to help prevent, mitigate, and recover from cybercrimes. While firms will need to adjust these suggestions to their individual circumstances, they should consider and implement these general practices.

1. ***Be Aware of Current Threats, Evolving Trends, and New Regulations and Guidance.*** Sign up for alerts and advisories from government agencies, like the U.S. Cybersecurity and Infrastructure Agency (CISA), read cybersecurity news on industry websites, and monitor updates from law firms with a strong cybersecurity practice.
2. ***Create a Culture of Compliance and Awareness.*** Organizations should not merely conduct yearly employee training on phishing and other common cybersecurity threats. Leaders, managers, and all employees should regularly practice basic cyber hygiene principles and learn internal cybersecurity policies. By creating what CISA calls a "culture of awareness,"[52] organizations instill diligence and knowledge for detecting and reporting suspicious activities and messages. Employees may be a firm's first line of defense.
3. ***Educate. Educate. Educate.*** Train staff how to recognize and report phishing attempts. Most cybercrime occurs when employees click on malicious links or files from emails, social media, or direct messaging.[53] Proactively educating staff on identifying a phishing message means that "many security breaches are avoidable."[54] Employees and owners should regularly complete training on phishing and other common cybersecurity attacks.
4. ***Keep Cyber-Hygienic.*** Organizations should implement fundamental cybersecurity practices, known as cyber hygiene, such as installing regular software updates according to the recommended time frames, requiring multi-factor authentication for access, prohibiting weak and reused passwords, and keeping sensitive information off unsecured networks.
5. ***Identify Weak Points and Close Them.*** Whether hiring an external consultant or having a firm's IT department do them, conduct regular self-assessments and security

---

52. *Teach Employees to Avoid Phishing*, Cybersecurity & Infrastructure Sec. Agency, https://www.cisa.gov/secure-our-world/teach-employees-avoid-phishing (last visited May 31, 2025).
53. *Id.*
54. *Id.*

audits at least annually. Close any discovered security gaps by following industry cybersecurity practices.

6. ***Plan Ahead of Time.*** Many large organizations develop cybersecurity plans, including incident response playbooks, with in-house and outside counsel and cybersecurity experts. Smaller organizations would benefit from including cybercrimes in their crisis planning contingencies as well. Firms should ensure that staff and leadership at all levels receive training on their role in responding to an incident and in mitigation efforts. Firms must securely back up all contingency plans, emergency communication contacts, cybersecurity insurance information, and other vital documentation. Make the information available to the appropriate staff in printed form. The best contingency plan has no value if a cybercriminal has encrypted it along with other information on a network during a cybersecurity attack.
7. ***Backups Get You Back Up and Running.*** If and when an organization suffers a catastrophic cyber incident, getting IT systems back up and running, alongside remediation, become top priorities for organizational leadership. Having regular and properly secured backups can allow organizations to "reset" the clock to before the cyber incident, allowing the organization to continue to function while the cyber incident is properly investigated and remediated.

Chapter 6

Dealing with Deepfakes: The Role for Lawyers and Law Firms

Matthew F. Ferraro

1. Introduction

We are in the midst of a media revolution. The spread of inexpensive, easy-to-use, and advanced artificial intelligence (AI) technologies has placed in the hands of almost anyone the ability to manipulate or create realistic imagery, audio, and video. These "deepfakes" present exciting new avenues for artistic creativity, accessibility, and education, among many other socially positive uses. But they also pose significant risks to individuals and businesses. Deepfakes can supercharge viral conspiracies that may tarnish corporate reputations and move stock prices, inflict intimate harm upon individuals, impersonate trusted persons, target companies for fraud, enable cyberattacks, and much else.

Lawyers and law firms will play critical roles as society confronts the benefits and dangers of deepfakes. The legal issues that such deepfakes (or "synthetic media") implicate are legion. In the first instance, deepfake developers—the companies that build the software, train the algorithms, and deploy the technologies that can create deepfakes—need legal counsel to ensure they operate in legal and ethical ways, particularly in the face of growing state and federal regulation of synthetic media.[1] Attorneys may well be called upon to help shape the regulations of this field. Private counsel has already been involved in, and will continue to be critical for, contracting, licensing, and litigation around the development of deepfake-creating AI, particularly over claims that deepfakes violate intellectual property laws. These claims tend to relate to how the AI systems are trained, the AI's creation of work that allegedly infringes on others' intellectual property, and who owns AI-manufactured media. Increasingly, content owners and their counsel are concluding licensing

1. *See, e.g.*, *Summary: Deceptive Audio or Visual Media ("Deepfakes") 2024 Legislation*, Nat'l Conf. of St. Legislatures (Nov. 22, 2024), https://www.ncsl.org/technology-and-communication/deceptive-audio-or-visual-media-deepfakes-2024-legislation [hereinafter NCSL, *Summary*]. *See also* Matthew F. Ferraro & Louis W. Tompros, *New York's Right to Publicity and Deepfakes Law Breaks New Ground*, 38 Comput. & Internet L. 1, 3 (Apr. 2021) (summarizing trends in deepfakes laws).

agreements with AI developers that allow the developers to train on, or otherwise rely upon, the content of others.[2]

Second, as deepfakes become more common, companies and individuals alike that use synthetic media will want to leverage deepfakes for salutary purposes that advance their business goals, improve products, and attract customers. These businesses and individuals will look to attorneys to help them use deepfakes in ways that minimize legal and reputational risks. Litigation about deepfakes against both deepfake developers and users can sound in defamation, unfair or deceptive business practices, fraud, IP, privacy, discrimination, and many other legal theories.[3]

Finally, deepfakes pose novel challenges in the courtroom where there is both the danger that manipulated media will be submitted as unadulterated evidence and that juries will come to assume that they can trust no digital media, because it is all just "fake." Considering the growing prevalence of synthetic media, attorneys must tread carefully, raising legitimate concerns about the veracity of evidence without baselessly stoking skepticism for advantage and claiming without good reason that evidence is manipulated or that jurors cannot believe their eyes or their ears.[4] In the face of these new challenges, lawyers have unique ethical obligations to serve society by acting in ways that buttress the public's confidence in the rule of law and the administration of justice.[5]

2. Defining Deepfakes

The word "deepfake" is a portmanteau of two words, "deep learning" and "fake."[6] Deep learning is a branch of machine learning (ML), which is itself a branch of AI, that attempts to mimic the workings of the human brain in processing data.[7]

Deepfakes are images, audio, or video that are "either manipulated or *wholly generated* by AI."[8] The AI technology that creates deepfakes is seminal because it provides

---

2. *See* Charlotte Tobitt, *Who's Suing AI and Who's Signing: Major Deals with Google, OpenAI and Mistral Start Year,* Press Gazette (Jan. 17, 2025), https://pressgazette.co.uk/platforms/news-publisher-ai-deals-lawsuits-openai-google/.

3. *See* Bruce Barcott, *AI Lawsuits Worth Watching: A Curated Guide*, Tech Pol'y Press (July 1, 2024), https://www.techpolicy.press/ai-lawsuits-worth-watching-a-curated-guide/.

4. *See* Matthew F. Ferraro & Brent Gurney, Opinion, *The Other Side Says Your Evidence Is A Deepfake. Now What?*, Law360 (Dec. 21, 2022, 1:25 PM EST), https://www.lexisnexis.com/pdf/practical-guidance/ai/the-other-side-says-your-evidence-is-a-deepfake-now-what-l360.pdf.

5. *See* Model Rules of Prof'l Conduct pmbl ¶¶ 6, 13 (Am. Bar Ass'n 2020).

6. Jeffery DelViscio, *A Nixon Deepfake, a "Moon Disaster" Speech and an Information Ecosystem at Risk*, Scientific Am. (July 20, 2020), https://www.scientificamerican.com/article/a-nixon-deepfake-a-moon-disaster-speech-and-an-information-ecosystem-at-risk1/. *See also* Matthew F. Ferraro, *Decoding Deepfakes*, Nat'l Sec. Inst. (Dec. 2020), https://nationalsecurity.gmu.edu/decoding-deepfakes-fb/.

7. Jim Holdsworth & Mark Scapicchio, *What Is Deep Learning?*, IBM (June 17, 2024), https://www.ibm.com/think/topics/deep-learning.

8. Nina Schick, Deepfakes: The Coming Infocalypse 8 (2020) (emphasis in original). Schick uses the term "deepfakes" to refer only to AI synthesized content used for malicious purposes, not positive-use cases. *Id.* at 8–9. This chapter, however, draws no such distinction about the creator's motivation.

the ability not just to manipulate but to create from whole cloth entirely false, believable media quickly and at scale. These features differentiate deepfakes from the standard, small-scale alterations of traditional Adobe Photoshop editing and Instagram filters, for instance.[9] For our purposes, a deepfake can be understood as a particularly realistic fake piece of media manipulated or created by computers. Writers and lawmakers often refer to deepfakes as manipulated media, synthetic media, or digital content forgeries. While these definitions vary at the margins,[10] this chapter uses these terms interchangeably.

Deepfakes are created through a range of tools and techniques.[11] Two of the main tools are generative adversarial networks (GANs) and diffusion models.

GANs involve two computer networks that compete against one another to create false-yet-realistic media. For example, assume someone wants to create a GAN-generated deepfake image of a human face. To do so, one network would rely on an available data set of images of actual faces to generate an accurate, although entirely new, image of a person's face. In this example, the computer building the fake face is called the "generator." It creates content modeled on source data (a collection of real human faces), while a second algorithm, "the discriminator," tries to spot the artificial content.[12] The competition between the two networks produces a better-and-better fake until the discriminator can no longer identify the forgery.[13] The same technology can be used to generate other forms of media, like text that is written by an AI system but reads like it came from a human, and audio, most often through a process called voice cloning, where AI and machine learning algorithms replicate someone's voice based on a series of audio samples.[14]

---

9. *Id.* at 8.

10. *See, e.g.*, National Defense Authorization Act for Fiscal Year 2021, Pub. L. No. 116-283, § 9004(f) (2021) (defining "digital content forgery technology" as "the use of emerging technologies, including artificial intelligence and machine learning techniques, to fabricate or manipulate audio, visual, or text content with the intent to mislead"); U.S. Copyright Office, Copyright and Artificial Intelligence Part 1: Digital Replicas 2 (July 2024), https://www.copyright.gov/ai/Copyright-and-Artificial-Intelligence-Part-1-Digital-Replicas-Report.pdf (using the terms "deepfake" and "digital replica" interchangeably); *Criminals Use Generative Artificial Intelligence to Facilitate Financial Fraud*, Alert Number: I-120324-PSA, Fed. Bureau of Investigation (Dec. 3, 2024), https://www.ic3.gov/PSA/2024/PSA241203 (defining "synthetic content" as "the class of media generated or manipulated by machine-learning-based techniques"); Daniel I. Weiner & Lawrence Norden, *Regulating AI Deepfakes and Synthetic Media in the Political Arena*, Brennan Ctr. for Just. (Dec. 5, 2023), https://www.brennancenter.org/our-work/research-reports/regulating-ai-deepfakes-and-synthetic-media-political-arena ("Deepfakes are a type of manipulated media, which encompasses everything from synthetic media to media altered with more basic tools like Photoshop or dubbing software.").

11. *See S&T Digital Forgeries Report: Technology Landscape Threat Assessment*, U.S. Dep't of Homeland Sec. (Jan. 24, 2023) at 4, https://www.dhs.gov/science-and-technology/publication/st-digital-forgeries-report-technology-landscape-threat-assessment [hereinafter *S&T Digital Forgeries Report*].

12. *See id.* at 6–9; Meredith Somers, *Deepfakes, Explained*, MIT (July 21, 2020), https://mitsloan.mit.edu/ideas-made-to-matter/deepfakes-explained.

13. *See* Bobby Chesney & Danielle Citron, *Deep Fakes: A Looming Challenge for Privacy, Democracy, and National Security*, 107 Cal. L. Rev. 1753, 1760 (2019) ("Growing sophistication of the GAN approach is sure to lead to the production of increasingly convincing deep fakes.").

14. *See* Schick, *supra* note 8, at 141–145.

A diffusion model is a different type of generative model used in machine learning to create new data similar to data on which it was trained.[15] In what is called the "forward process," the model starts with clean data and gradually adds noise to it until the data becomes almost random. During a subsequent "reverse process," the model learns to start from noisy data and gradually remove the noise until it reconstructs the original clean data. Once trained, the model can generate new data by starting with random noise and applying the reverse process to create data that resembles the training data. Through this process, diffusion models can create text and media.[16] Popular diffusion models include models that produce images in response to textual prompts, such as DALL-E 3, Stable Diffusion, and Imagen.[17]

The proliferation of these kinds of models, now accessible on apps for nearly everyone, has made deepfakes ubiquitous.[18] To steal a phrase, they are everything, everywhere, all at once: from deepfake images of entirely fictitious persons and manipulated scenes posted on social media feeds, to mash-ups of a user's selfie and a celebrity's face,[19] to voice clones reading articles from news and magazine websites, to videos shared online, and to movies viewed in the cinema.

The quality of deepfakes has improved markedly even in the last few years. For example, in 2023, someone used the AI tool ModelScope to create a video of actor Will Smith eating spaghetti. The resulting images were "so clunky and ridiculous that [the video] turned out to be unintentionally hilarious."[20] The Will Smith video evolved into a benchmark to test an AI video generator's quality; every time "a company releases a new AI video generator, it's not long before someone uses it to make a video of actor Will Smith eating spaghetti."[21] As of late 2024, the resulting videos were strikingly improved and hyper-realistic.[22]

Deepfake technology is not reserved to research laboratories or visual effects artists. Everyday users can easily access consumer-facing apps, like MidJourney or ChatGPT, to create images, Eleven Labs to render voice clones, and OpenAI's Sora and Runway's Gen-3 Alpha to create realistic, high-quality videos with simple text prompts.[23] Hollywood is also

---

15. *See generally* Aayush Mittal, *Understanding Diffusion Models: A Deep Dive into Generative AI*, UNITE.AI (Nov. 15, 2024), https://www.unite.ai/understanding-diffusion-models-a-deep-dive-into-generative-ai/.

16. *Id.*

17. *Id.*

18. *See S&T Digital Forgeries Report, supra* note 11, at 3–4.

19. Matthew F. Ferraro et al., *Identifying the Legal and Business Risks of Disinformation and Deepfakes: What Every Business Needs to Know*, 6 PRATT'S PRIV.& CYBERSECURITY L. REP. 142, 152 (2020) (describing "Impressions.app").

20. Hriddhi Maitra, *Will Smith Eating Pasta Meme Makes a Return, with a Better Change This Time*, MSN (Jan. 4, 2025), https://www.msn.com/en-us/news/technology/will-smith-eating-pasta-meme-makes-a-return-with-a-better-change-this-time/ar-AA1wY6hD.

21. Kyle Wiggers, *Will Smith Eating Spaghetti and Other Weird AI Benchmarks That Took Off in 2024*, TECHCRUNCH (Dec. 31, 2024), https://techcrunch.com/2024/12/31/will-smith-eating-spaghetti-and-other-weird-ai-benchmarks-that-took-off-in-2024/.

22. *See id.* (linking to video created by Google Veo 2).

23. *See generally* Megan Monroe, *OpenAI, Google and Runway Race to Generate AI Video*, AXIOS (Jan. 3, 2025), https://www.axios.com/2025/01/03/openai-sora-google-veo-runway-video.

leveraging AI for ever-more sophisticated synthetics. For example, in 2022, the legendary actor James Earl Jones, who voiced Darth Vader in *Star Wars* movies, agreed to allow Disney to replicate his voice in future projects using a voice cloning model created by the company Respeecher.[24] Jones died in September 2024, and, already, Disney and Respeecher have recreated his voice for the television show *Obi-Wan Kenobi*. Likewise, Respeecher used AI to manipulate actor Mark Hamill's voice for his appearance as the character Luke Skywalker in the television show *The Mandalorian*.[25]

In a notable sign of the merging of AI and traditional special effects, a leading deepfake-production company called Metaphysic used its proprietary generative AI technology to support director Robert Zemeckis on his movie *Here* to "de-age" actors Tom Hanks, Robin Wright, and others, as the film's decades-long story arc unfolded.[26]

Metaphysic was co-founded by the Belgian visual effects artist Chris Umé. Umé helped to bring deepfakes into broad public consciousness beginning in February 2021 when he began publishing startlingly realistic deepfake videos through a TikTok account (@deeptomcruise) that seemed to show the actor Tom Cruise walking in a store, swinging a golf club, and performing a magic trick. But it wasn't Cruise at all. Umé had spent weeks training a neural network on publicly available images of Cruise and used the open-source DeepFaceLab deepfake algorithm and common video editing tools to place Cruise's face onto the head of an actor with Cruise's general build who had filmed the scenes.[27] The results were nearly flawless forgeries.

Technologists are working on deepfake countermeasures that fall into two general categories. The first method attempts to detect deepfakes *after* they are created. For example, the website Sentinel allows users to upload digital media through its website or Application Programming Interface (API), which is then analyzed for AI-generated forgeries. The system determines if the media is a deepfake and provides a visualization of the manipulation.[28] Similarly, Microsoft has a Video Authenticator Tool that analyzes videos and still images and provides a confidence score whether the media has been modified by AI.[29] Another company, Hive AI, inked a two-year, $2.4 million contract with the U.S. Department of Defense in 2024 to help develop Hive's models to detect AI-generated video, image,

24. Anthony Breznican, *Darth Vader's Voice Emanated From War-Torn Ukraine*, VANITY FAIR (Sept. 23, 2022), https://www.vanityfair.com/hollywood/2022/09/darth-vaders-voice-emanated-from-war-torn-ukraine.

25. Sarah Parvini, *James Earl Jones' Darth Vader Voice Lives on Through AI. Voice Actors See Promise and Peril in That*, AP (Sept. 11, 2024), https://apnews.com/article/james-earl-jones-darth-vader-artificial-intelligence-10643d1a4b5b13575d4a7b457f0d858e.

26. L'Wren Alexa, *Metaphysic De-Ages Robert Zemeckis' "Here" Via Generative AI*, ANIMATION WORLD NETWORK (Nov. 21, 2024, 9:59 AM), https://www.awn.com/news/metaphysic-de-ages-robert-zemeckis-here-generative-ai.

27. James Vincent, *Tom Cruise Deepfake Creator Says Public Shouldn't be Worried About 'One-click Fakes'*, THE VERGE (Mar. 5, 2021, 10:00 A.M.), https://www.theverge.com/2021/3/5/22314980/tom-cruise-deepfake-tiktok-videos-ai-impersonator-chris-ume-miles-fisher.

28. *See* Barrett S., *Top 5 Deepfake Detection Tools*, TECH TREND (July 13, 2023), https://the-tech-trend.com/artificial-intelligence/deepfake-detection-tools/.

29. *Id.*

and audio media.[30] Hive's technology has been trained on both AI-generated and non-AI-generated content and detects signals and patterns in AI-generated content that are imperceptible to humans.[31]

The second method verifies photographs and other media at the "point of capture" in such a way that they cannot be altered or modified after the fact without leaving evidence of the manipulation through what is known as provenance metadata or "content credentials."[32] Technology companies and media organizations founded the Coalition for Content Provenance and Authenticity (C2PA) in 2021 to promote an industry-wide technical standard for provenance metadata.[33] In 2023, the C2PA introduced an official, global Content Credentials "icon of transparency" for creators, marketers, and consumers to signify the trustworthiness of digital content.[34] Adobe, Microsoft, Leica Camera, Nikon, and other firms have adopted the icon, which adheres to agreed-upon specifications and confirms the time and date of the image's original creation, and deployed the standard to AI-generated images and in cameras.[35] Efforts to improve and deploy these technologies, like efforts to improve and distribute deepfake technology itself, are ongoing.

A side effect of the propagation of deepfakes deserves special mention. The mere presence in society of believable synthetic media can foster what law Professors Bobby Chesney and Danielle Citron have called the "liar's dividend,"[36] wherein individuals successfully deny the authenticity of genuine media by claiming that the content is a "deepfake." Thus, by leveraging skepticism about the authenticity of media to cast doubt on real evidence of their wrongdoing, liars accrue a benefit or a dividend. This is already happening. For example, former Spanish Foreign Minister Alfonso Dastis claimed that images of police violence in Catalonia, Spain in 2017 were "fake photos"; former Syrian President Bashar al-Assad discredited an Amnesty International report as "forge[d]"; and Jim Fouts, the

30. *See* Melissa Heikkilä, *The US Department of Defense Is Investing in Deepfake Detection*, MIT Tech. Rev. (Dec. 5, 2024), https://www.technologyreview.com/2024/12/05/1107961/the-us-department-of-defense-is-investing-in-deepfake-detection/.

31. *Id.*

32. Mounir Ibrahim & Ashish Jaiman, Opinion, *To Defend Democracy, We Must Protect Truth Online*, The Hill (Apr. 25, 2021, 5:00 PM), https://thehill.com/opinion/cybersecurity/550191-to-defend-democracy-we-must-protect-truth-online (describing provenance technology).

33. Press Release, *Technology and Media Entities Join Forces to Create Standards Group Aimed at Building Trust in Online Content*, C2PA (Feb. 22, 2021), https://c2pa.org/post/c2pa_initial_pr/.

34. Andy Parsons, *Adobe MAX 2023: Milestone Wave of Content Credentials Adoption with Industry Partners Microsoft, Leica Camera, Nikon, Publicis Groupe, and More*, Adobe Blog (Oct. 10, 2023), https://blog.adobe.com/en/publish/2023/10/10/new-content-credentials-icon-transparency.

35. *See id.*; Jeremy Gray, *Sony's In-Camera Authentication Technology Passes AP's Tests*, Peta Pixel (Nov. 21, 2023), https://petapixel.com/2023/11/21/sonys-in-camera-authentication-technology-passes-aps-tests/; *Introducing Official Content Credentials Icon*, C2PA, https://c2pa.org/post/contentcredentials/ (last visited April 19, 2025).

36. Chesney & Citron, *supra* note 13, at 1785–1786.

former mayor of Warren, Michigan, declared audio tapes of him making derogatory comments about women and Black people "phony, engineered tapes."[37]

We are also witnessing the rise of a kind of "zealot's dividend," where partisans who are not even the subjects of the media in question reject inconvenient media evidence that does not fit with their chosen narratives, claiming it is manipulated or synthetic. We saw this phenomenon with supporters of President Trump dismissing as a "deepfake" a video of him conceding the 2020 election in January 2021.[38] The value of the liar's and zealot's dividends will grow dearer as more people learn about the quality and availability of deepfakes.

Finally, observers and government agencies have noted that misleading multimedia that has not been manipulated by ML or AI can also cause harm to individuals and organizations. This kind of altered media is often referred to as "shallow fakes" or "cheap fakes." They can include, for example, photographs where part of the image is removed to change the photograph's meaning, a video that is slowed down to make a person in the video appear disoriented or intoxicated, or an actual video paired with an audio track from a different source that alters the context of the images.[39]

3. Deepfakes and Their Discontents: Business Risks Requiring Legal Counsel

Attorneys will need to help resolve many legal and business risks that arise from deepfakes. These risks include, among others:

1. Intimate Harms;
2. Reputational Risk;
3. Social Engineering and Fraud;
4. Synthetic Identity Creation;
5. Market Manipulation;
6. Political Disinformation;
7. Insurance Fraud; and
8. Labor and Employment Issues.

We address these issues in turn below.

37. Kayln Jackson Schiff et al., *The Liar's Dividend: Can Politicians Claim Misinformation to Evade Accountability?*, 119 Am. Political Sci. Rev. 71, 73 & 76 (Feb. 2025). *See also* Josh A. Goldstein & Andrew Lohn, *Deepfakes, Elections, and Shrinking the Liar's Dividend*, Brennan Ctr. for Just. (Jan. 23, 2024), https://www.brennancenter.org/our-work/research-reports/deepfakes-elections-and-shrinking-liars-dividend.

38. Amelia Mavis Christnot, *Trump Supporters Are Convinced Trump's Concession Video Is a Deepfake and the Delusion Is Real*, Second Nexus (Jan. 8, 2021), https://secondnexus.com/trump-parler-concession-deep-fake.

39. *See* Contextualizing Deepfake Threats to Organizations 3–4, Alert Number: PP-23-3076, Nat'l Sec. Agency (Sept. 12, 2023), [hereinafter NSA, *Alert*] https://media.defense.gov/2023/Sep/12/2003298925/-1/-1/0/CSI-DEEPFAKE-THREATS.PDF.

3.1. Intimate Harms

This section begins with intimate harms, personal harassment, and extortion risks because they are prevalent with AI-created media. Indeed, deepfakes targeting women have been abundant online since the dawn of the technology; the first online discussion forum that used the term "deepfakes" posted fake pornographic videos of Hollywood actresses made using AI tools.[40] By 2019, according to one study, over 95% of all deepfake videos available on the Internet were of nonconsensual pornography—that is, a nonconsenting person's face (whether of a celebrity or a private person) placed on a nude body to create a realistic pornographic image or video.[41] Today, many of these images are of famous female actors, but the technology harms everyone's privacy, and malefactors have used the technology to victimize hundreds of thousands of everyday people, of every age, all over the world.[42]

By 2024, there were several high-profile incidents in American schools where boys used easily accessible "nudification" apps to create images of female classmates that appeared to show the girls in states of undress, and the boys then shared those photos with their friends. After an outcry, state legislators pushed for laws to combat AI-generated sexually explicit images.[43]

It is an international phenomenon. For example, in the autumn of 2024, scandal rocked South Korea when police and journalists investigated "deepfake porn rings" in dozens of online chat groups, wherein individuals shared photos of women they knew and converted them into fake pornographic images with AI software.[44] Korean police also announced an investigation into the messaging app Telegram for its role in enabling the distribution of pornographic images of children. Korea's investigation followed on the heels of an investigation and arrest in France of Telegram's founder on charges he was complicit in crimes related to the app, including enabling the sharing of child sexual abuse material (CSAM).[45] The Korean parliament responded to the scandal by revising a law to make illegal the watching or possessing of deepfake pornography.[46] Several other foreign nations have also acted to restrict deepfake pornography.[47]

---

40. *See* Schick, *supra* note 8, at 35.

41. Giorgio Patrini, *Mapping the Deepfake Landscape*, Sensity AI (Oct. 7, 2019), https://giorgiop.github.io/posts/2018/03/17/mapping-the-deepfake-landscape/.

42. *See* Jane Lytvynenko & Scott Lucas, *Thousands of Women Have No Idea a Telegram Network Is Sharing Fake Nude Images of Them*, BuzzFeed News (Oct. 20, 2020), https://www.buzzfeednews.com/article/janelytvynenko/telegram-deepfake-nude-women-images-bot (deepfake technology allowed users to create photo-realistic simulated nude images of 680,000 women without their knowledge or consent, according to tech researchers).

43. Natasha Singer, *Spurred by Teen Girls, States Move to Ban Deepfake Nudes*, N.Y. Times (Apr. 22, 2024), https://www.nytimes.com/2024/04/22/technology/deepfake-ai-nudes-high-school-laws.html.

44. *See* Jean Mackenzie & Leehyun Choi, *Inside the Deepfake Porn Crisis Engulfing Korean Schools*, BBC (Sept. 2, 2024), https://www.bbc.com/news/articles/cpdlpj9zn9go.

45. *Id.*

46. *See* Hyung-Jin Kim, *In South Korea, Deepfake Porn Wrecks Women's Lives and Deepens Gender Conflict*, AP (Oct. 3, 2024), https://apnews.com/article/south-korea-deepfake-porn-women-df98e1a6793a245ac14afe8ec2366101.

47. *See* Alliance for Univ'l Digital Rts., Deepfake Image-Based Sexual Abuse, Tech Facilitated Sexual Exploitation and the Law 5–7 (Sept. 2023), https://audri.org/wp-content/uploads/2024/01/

Many U.S. states make producing and/or sharing AI-generated nonconsensual pornography illegal under either civil or criminal laws,[48] and the U.S. Justice Department has arrested at least one person on criminal charges related to the defendant's alleged production, distribution, and possession of AI-generated images of minors engaged in sexually explicit conduct under general anti-obscenity laws.[49] "CSAM generated by AI is still CSAM, and we will hold accountable those who exploit AI to create obscene, abusive, and increasingly photorealistic images of children," then-Deputy U.S. Attorney General Lisa Monaco said at the time of the arrest.[50] Furthermore, in late-spring 2025, the U.S. Congress passed and the President signed a bipartisan bill that makes it a federal crime to post real or deepfake sexually explicit imagery online of a nonconsenting person and requires websites to remove the offending imagery within 48 hours of a victim's request.[51] This "TAKE IT DOWN Act" constitutes the federal government's most significant deepfake-related lawmaking to date.[52]

AI-enabled intimate imagery can also be used to target individuals for extortion or harassment. For example, the Federal Bureau of Investigation (FBI) has warned that malicious actors are manipulating with AI benign photos and videos of individuals, including minor children, to create explicit content that looks like the victim.[53] The malefactors may send the true-to-life yet phony sexual content to victims and threaten to share the content online unless the victim pays a ransom or sends actual nude photos to the extorter. The bad actor may also post the imagery on social media, public forms, or pornographic websites. "The key motivators for this are a desire for more illicit content, financial gain, or to bully and harass others," the FBI writes.[54]

EN-AUDRi-Briefing-paper-deepfake-06.pdf; Christy Cooney, *Creating Sexually Explicit Deepfakes to Become a Criminal Offence*, BBC (Apr. 16, 2024), https://www.bbc.com/news/uk-68823042; *Court Upholds Deepfake Porn Creator's Sentencing*, Taipei Times (May 11, 2024), https://www.taipeitimes.com/News/taiwan/archives/2024/05/11/2003817703.

48. *See* NCSL, *Summary*, *supra* note 1.

49. Office of Pub. Aff., *Man Arrested for Producing, Distributing, and Possessing AI-Generated Images of Minors Engaged in Sexually Explicit Conduct*, U.S. Dep't of Just. (May 20, 2024), https://www.justice.gov/opa/pr/man-arrested-producing-distributing-and-possessing-ai-generated-images-minors-engaged.

50. *Id.* The defendant was charged under 18 U.S.C. § 1466A (obscene visual representations of the sexual abuse of children) and 18 U.S.C. § 1470 (transfer of obscene material to minors). Deepfakes used to harass and defame may also violate federal cyberstalking and harassment laws, such as 18 U.S.C. § 2261A (stalking). *See* Halock Security Labs, *What Legislation Protects Against Deepfakes and Synthetic Media?*, Lexology (Jan. 28, 2025), https://www.lexology.com/library/detail.aspx?g=bb2c2ce7-a982-44be-9d56-1fe37bad1cc6.

51. Darlene Superville, *Trump Signs a Bill to Make Posting "Revenge Porn" a Federal Crime. He had the First Lady Sign, Too*, AP (May 19, 2025, 8:31 PM), https://apnews.com/article/trump-melania-intimate-imagery-bill-sign-c7416b4935f8ccac9fd2909e494da9f1.

52. *See id.*

53. *Malicious Actors Manipulating Photos and Videos to Create Explicit Content and Sextortion Schemes*, Alert Number: I-060523-PSA, Fed. Bureau of Investigation (June 5, 2023), https://www.ic3.gov/PSA/2023/PSA230605.

54. *Id. See also* Abigail Ng, *In Focus: 'At the Click of a Button'—The Scourge of Deepfake AI Porn*, CNA (May 25, 2024, 7:32 AM), https://www.channelnewsasia.com/singapore/ai-deepfake-porn-singapore-mps-extortion-letters-victims-taylor-swift-4360226.

In one notorious example, Indian investigative journalist Rana Ayyub was targeted by a fake pornographic video of herself that circulated online, probably produced and spread in response to her reporting on human rights violations by Indian authorities.[55] Ayyub was hospitalized for heart ailments following the harassment and humiliation, and she withdrew for a time from the online public square.[56]

To combat the scourge of nonconsensual deepfake pornography, some prosecutors are getting creative. Notably, in August 2024, the City of San Francisco sued over a dozen of the world's most-visited websites that create and distribute nonconsensual AI-generated pornography, alleging the website owners and operators violate state and federal laws prohibiting deepfake pornography, revenge pornography, and child pornography.[57] At this writing, some of the defendants' sites have gone offline or settled with California, and the case remains pending against other defendants.

Attorneys have their hands full addressing this prolific AI-related harm, representing victims, litigating on behalf of governments, defending civil and criminal defendants (whether individuals or impacted entities), and counseling legislators as they draft and enact laws in this evolving space. Also, because bad actors could use such deepfakes either to extort concessions from business leaders or to embarrass them, lawyers will be needed to work with private clients, law enforcement agencies, and prosecutors to counsel on the propriety of paying ransom, and to litigate after-the-fact against bad actors.

3.2. Reputational Risk

Litigators, regulatory lawyers, and crisis management attorneys are often called upon to help clients deal with reputational risk. Viral deepfakes act as accelerants to those ambient business dangers.

In particular, these risks will likely manifest through the impersonation of high-level corporate officials or tastemakers whose words can negatively impact a company's reputation. The U.S. National Security Agency calls this phenomenon "executive impersonation for brand manipulation," warning in a recent joint alert with the FBI and the Cybersecurity and Infrastructure Security Agency (CISA) that "[m]alicious actors may employ convincing audio and video impersonations of key leaders to damage the reputation and value of an organization's brand, such as quickly distributing a convincing deepfake publicly across social media platforms before it can be stopped or disputed."[58] The NSA warns that this

55. Schick, *supra* note 8, at 125–128.

56. *I Was Vomiting: Journalist Rana Ayyub Reveals Horrifying Account of Deepfake Porn Plot*, India Today (Nov. 21, 2018, 7:20 PM), https://www.indiatoday.in/trending-news/story/journalist-rana-ayyub-deepfake-porn-1393423-2018-11-21.

57. *See* Press Release, *City Attorney Sues Most-visited Websites that Create Nonconsensual Deepfake Pornography*, City Att'y of San Francisco (Aug. 15, 2024), https://www.sfcityattorney.org/2024/08/15/city-attorney-sues-most-visited-websites-that-create-nonconsensual-deepfake-pornography/; First Am. Complaint, People v. Sol Ecom, Inc. (Sup. Ct. Calif., Aug. 16, 2024), https://www.sfcityattorney.org/wp-content/uploads/2024/08/2024-08-16-First-Amended-Complaint_Redacted.pdf.

58. NSA, *Alert*, *supra* note 39, at 8.

activity can pack a "high impact, especially for international brands where stock prices and overall reputation may be vulnerable to disinformation campaigns."[59]

A March 2022 incident involving a deepfake of Ukrainian President Volodymyr Zelensky illustrates the dangers companies face. There, an AI-manipulated video went viral of Zelensky seeming to tell Ukraine's soldiers to surrender to the Russian invasion. It is unclear who made the deepfake, but the Ukrainian government had been warning for weeks that Russia could use manipulated media as part of its psychological warfare. Zelensky quickly responded with a video of his own averring his will to fight until victory.[60] While the deepfake failed to trigger widespread confusion, one can imagine a scenario that more successfully harms corporate interests.

Consider this thought experiment: What if the Tom Cruise deepfakes that went viral on TikTok showed Cruise not just swinging a golf club and performing a magic trick but announcing to the camera that he was cancelling the next *Mission: Impossible* movie because he discovered that the movie studio producing the film was corrupt? "I've uncovered evidence that they're all crooks," he may have said to the camera, adding: "I promise you, I will never work with that studio again. And I call on all my actor friends to boycott them until they fire their dishonest leadership." How might the reputation, stock price, and marketability of the studio have been impacted if one of the world's biggest celebrities (seemingly) had foresworn them?

Likewise, consider the impact on consumer confidence of a phony, yet believable, video showing a pricy autonomous vehicle involved in a spectacular accident.[61] Businesses will look to their legal counsel to help remedy the reputational injuries inflicted by such efforts—beginning with helping to retain experts to prove that the imagery was forged.[62]

Law firms, like any other business with reputational concerns, may also be victims of such attacks. Ponder the impact on a multinational firm of a manipulated audio clip that makes it sound like the managing partner made disparaging comments about a female associate or used a racial epithet. Thus, firms should prepare accordingly, too. (On how, see Part 4 of this chapter.)

---

59. *Id.*

60. *See id.* at 4, 8; Matthew F. Ferraro, Opinion, *The Zelensky Deepfake Is a Warning for Corporate America*, CNN (Apr. 1, 2022, 5:28 PM), https://www.cnn.com/2022/04/01/perspectives/zelensky-deepfake-disinformation-businesses/index.html (describing incident).

61. Matthew F. Ferraro & Preston B. Golson, *The Next Gray Zone Conflict: State-Based Disinformation Attacks on the Private Sector*, LAWFARE (Mar. 24, 2020, 10:30 AM), https://www.lawfaremedia.org/article/next-gray-zone-conflict-state-based-disinformation-attacks-private-sector (describing how a Russian company designed a fake electric car accident to garner attention and several media outlets treated the bogus video as if it were real); Cat Zakrzewski with Tonya Riley, *Businesses Should be Watching Out for Deepfakes Too, Experts Warn*, WASH. POST (Dec. 13, 2019), https://www.washingtonpost.com/news/powerpost/paloma/the-technology-202/2019/12/13/the-technology-202-businesses-should-be-watching-out-for-deepfakes-too-experts-warn/5df279f1602ff125ce5b2fe7/.

62. *See* Ferraro et al., *Identifying Legal and Business Risks*, *supra* note 19, at 145.

3.3. Social Engineering and Fraud

The reputational risks discussed above relate to impersonations of influential characters that are broadcast widely to negatively impact a firm's public standing. A similar and, thus far, more prevalent variant consists of impersonations of trusted persons targeting individuals for financial gain or to secure illicit access to sensitive systems.

Deloitte's Center for Financial Services predicts that generative AI could enable fraud losses to reach $40 billion in the United States by 2027, up from $12.3 billion in 2023, a compound annual growth rate of 32%.[63] Driving this expected upswing is an anticipated growth in impersonation frauds, which have already cost companies millions of dollars. For example, in early 2024, the British multinational firm Arup informed authorities that criminals had tricked an Arup employee into attending a video call with individuals the victim believed were the company's chief financial officer among others, all of whom were actually deepfakes. The people disguised with AI-manipulated imagery induced the victim to remit payment of the equivalent of $25.6 million through fifteen transactions. Ironically, the Arup employee had been skeptical when he received an email from the company's UK office asking for a secret transaction, but he retired his doubts because of the verisimilitude of the deepfakes of the colleagues he thought he recognized.[64]

Similarly, in May 2024, Mark Read, the CEO of the world's largest advertising group, WPP, warned in an email to his leadership team that fraudsters had created a WhatsApp account purportedly belonging to Read and used a voice clone and publicly available video footage to impersonate him in an attempt to trick an agency leader into setting up a new business to solicit funds and personal details. The unidentified target did not fall for the feint, according to WPP.[65]

In July 2024, the press reported an analogous scam targeting Ferrari. There, fraudsters sent a series of text messages purportedly from the CEO, Benedetto Vigna, to an unnamed Ferrari executive, detailing a confidential company acquisition and urging the executive to prepare to sign a non-disclosure agreement. The executive then received a phone call from the same number, and the caller mimicked Vigna's voice. The vigilant target picked up on anomalies in the caller's speech and asked him to verify his identity by answering a question about a book recommendation Vigna had recently given to the executive. Caught flatfooted, the fraudster hung up.[66]

---

63. *GenAI Poses Real Threat in Deepfake Fraud*, DELOITTE (July 10, 2024), https://action.deloitte.com/insight/3993/genai-poses-real-threat-in-deepfake-fraud.

64. *See* Kathleen Magramo, *British Engineering Giant Arup Revealed as $25 Million Deepfake Scam Victim*, CNN (May 17, 2024, 4:53 AM), https://www.cnn.com/2024/05/16/tech/arup-deepfake-scam-loss-hong-kong-intl-hnk/index.html.

65. *See* Nick Robins-Early, *CEO of World's Biggest Ad Firm Targeted by Deepfake Scam*, THE GUARDIAN (May 10, 2024, 3:01 AM), https://www.theguardian.com/technology/article/2024/may/10/ceo-wpp-deepfake-scam.

66. *See* Shawn Henry, *Ferrari CEO Impersonated by AI in Deepfake Scam Attempt—Report*, YAHOO (July 31, 2024), https://autos.yahoo.com/ferrari-ceo-impersonated-ai-deepfake-183000485.html.

Criminals have not lacked imagination when it comes to applying new technologies to hoary offenses. The first widely discussed such use of synthetic media to impersonate identities and defraud businesses occurred in March 2019, when, according to press reports, the CEO of a British energy firm thought he was speaking on the telephone with his boss, the CEO of the firm's German parent company. The German CEO asked the British official to send roughly $250,000 to a Hungarian supplier, and the British CEO complied. Later, the British CEO learned that he had been duped. He had been speaking to someone using AI-based software to impersonate the German CEO's voice, according to the energy firm's insurance carrier, Euler Hermes Group SA.[67]

Also, in July 2019, cybersecurity firm Symantec reported that three companies had fallen victim to deepfake audio attacks purportedly from scammers who used AI programs to mimic the voices of the firms' CEOs. Symantec said millions of dollars were stolen, but it did not name the victimized businesses.[68]

American law enforcement has been warning the public of synthetic media-enabled social engineering and fraud for several years. In March 2021, the FBI issued a private industry notification (PIN) advising companies that "[m]alicious actors almost certainly will leverage synthetic content for cyber and foreign influence operations in the next 12–18 months."[69] The FBI wrote that it anticipated synthetic media will be "increasingly used by foreign and criminal cyber actors for spearphishing and social engineering in an evolution of cyber operational tradecraft."[70] The PIN warned that malicious cyber actors will not just push propaganda on behalf of foreign actors but also leverage deepfake technology to attack the private sector. In particular, the FBI warned that synthetic content may be used in a "newly defined cyber attack vector" called "Business Identity Compromise" (BIC), where deepfake tools will be employed to create "synthetic corporate personas" or imitate existing employees. The FBI indicated that BIC will likely cause "very significant

67. Catherine Stupp, *Fraudsters Used AI to Mimic CEO's Voice in Unusual Cybercrime Case*, Wall St. J. (Aug. 30, 2019, 12:51 PM), https://www.wsj.com/articles/fraudsters-use-ai-to-mimic-ceos-voice-in-unusual-cybercrime-case-11567157402. *See also* Ferraro et al., *Identifying Legal and Business Risks*, *supra* note 19, at 145–146. The name of the victim company has not been disclosed.

68. Bob Keaveney, *RSA 2020: Is Voice Fraud the Next Frontier for Scam Artists?*, Biz Tech Mag. (Feb. 26, 2020), https://biztechmagazine.com/article/2020/02/rsa-2020-voice-fraud-next-frontier-scam-artists; Kaveh Waddell & Jennifer A. Kingson, *The Coming Deepfakes Threat to Businesses*, Axios (July 19, 2019), https://www.axios.com/the-coming-deepfakes-threat-to-businesses-308432e8-f1d8-465e-b628-07498a7c1e2a.html. *See also* Ferraro et al., *Identifying Legal and Business Risks*, *supra* note 19, at 146.

69. *Malicious Actors Almost Certainly Will Leverage Synthetic Content for Cyber and Foreign Influence Operations* 1, PIN Number 210310-001, Fed. Bureau of Investigation (Mar. 10, 2021), https://www.documentcloud.org/documents/20509703-fbipin-3102021 [hereinafter FBI, PIN].

70. *Id.* "Spear phishing is a direct, targeted email attack aimed at specific individuals that appears to come from a trusted sender.... The ultimate aim is to either infect devices with malware by convincing the recipient to click a link or download an attachment, or to trick the recipient into taking some other action that will benefit the attacker, usually handing over information or money." Josh Fruhlinger, *What Is Spear Phishing? Examples, Tactics, and Techniques*, CSO (May 24, 2024), https://www.csoonline.com/article/566789/what-is-spear-phishing-examples-tactics-and-techniques.html.

financial and reputational impacts to victim businesses and organizations."[71] The NSA, FBI, and CISA reiterated those warnings in September 2023, noting that the "most substantial threats from the abuse of synthetic media include techniques that threaten an organization's brand, impersonate leaders and financial officers, and use fraudulent communications to enable access to an organization's networks, communications, and sensitive information."[72]

These threats represent an evolution in business email compromise (BEC) schemes, which occur when a hacker compromises a corporate email account to facilitate fraudulent financial transactions. Because of the threats posed by BEC intrusions, many organizations over the past several years have sought to protect their treasury and accounts-payable functions from manipulation. Deepfake technology creates a new category of BIC activities that threaten to complicate authentication protocols, and cybersecurity and privacy attorneys need to work with clients to revisit their security practices in the face of these intensifying challenges to information security.[73]

In another common con of recent vintage, fraudsters deploy deepfake videos and audio of famous figures to hawk products, cryptocurrencies, and get-rich-quick schemes. For example, swindlers have used an AI-generated avatar of Mr. Beast, the YouTube influencer, to peddle cryptocurrency scams in posts on social media. Charlatans have also used synthetic likenesses of Warren Buffett, Tom Hanks, and Oprah Winfrey to push everything from phony dental plans to diet pills.[74] Elon Musk's face is a particular favorite of fakers who deploy it to dupe the innocent. One report claimed that thousands of AI-powered inauthentic ads of Musk promoting cryptocurrencies or investment schemes have swindled retirees of their savings and contributed to billions of dollars in fraud.[75]

These deepfake-enabled social engineering frauds pose numerous risks to individuals and the private sector, necessitating legal counsel. Individuals can be defrauded and require representation. Companies can lose funds, be subject to litigation by shareholders, be investigated by regulators, and—if auditors refuse to approve financial statements following such a fraud—face the loss of access to capital markets.[76]

---

71. *See* FBI, PIN, *supra* note 69, at 3. *See also* Matthew F. Ferraro, Jason C. Chipman, and Benjamin A. Powell, *FBI Warns Companies of "Almost Certain" Threats from Deepfakes*, 4 J. Robotics A.I. & L. 267, 267–268 (July–Aug. 2021).

72. NSA, *Alert*, *supra* note 39, at 1.

73. Ferraro et al., *FBI Warns*, *supra* note 71, at 269.

74. *See* Derek Kravitz, *Don't Get Caught by a Deepfake Scam*, Consumer Reports (Jan. 30, 2025), https://www.consumerreports.org/money/scams-fraud/dont-get-caught-by-a-deepfake-scam-a1121081735/; Ben Coleman, *The Impact of Deepfakes on Brand and Reputation*, Reality Defender (Aug. 7, 2024), https://www.realitydefender.com/blog/deepfakes-harm-brand-reputation.

75. *See* Stuart A. Thompson, *How "Deepfake Elon Must" Became the Internet's Biggest Scammer*, N.Y. Times (Aug. 14, 2024), https://www.nytimes.com/interactive/2024/08/14/technology/elon-musk-ai-deepfake-scam.html; Christina Ianzito, *Bogus Ads Use Elon Musk's Image to Steal Victims' Savings*, AARP (Jan. 31, 2025), https://www.aarp.org/money/scams-fraud/info-2025/elon-musk-scams.html.

76. *See* Ferraro et al., *Identifying Legal and Business Risks*, *supra* note 19, at 147.

3.4. Synthetic Identity Creation

The form of deepfake social engineering frauds discussed above involves the impersonation of a trusted, real-life individual, either a person known individually by the potential victim or generally, like a celebrity. But AI also can be used to create entirely fictious identities that can be used to open bank accounts, apply for loans, or obtain credit cards that are then used for fraudulent activities. This is a particular concern for financial institutions.[77] According to one report, in 2023, deepfake incidents in the fintech sector increased 700% from the previous year.[78]

"Among the concerns are that bad actors could use AI-generated audio to game voice-authentication software used by financial services companies to verify customers and grant them access to their accounts," the *Wall Street Journal* reported.[79] Malicious actors can also generate phony driver's licenses to create online accounts, prompting some companies to change their authentication procedures to make them more difficult to defeat.[80]

In another variant, fraudsters are using AI to create synthetic identities to apply for jobs and alter their appearance during interviews conducted via video teleconference. These scammers can use AI to create phony resumes, headshots, websites, and social media profiles and rely on deepfake software to transform their visage during job interviews.[81] The U.S. Department of Justice has charged networks of North Korean hackers for using false identities to secure remote information technology (IT) jobs at U.S. firms, allowing them to funnel their salaries, estimated at hundreds of millions of dollars annually, to the North Korean state.[82] Fraudulent hires can also leverage their IT access to purloin corporate secrets or lace company systems with malware. It is a growing threat. The research firm Gartner estimates that 25% of all job applicants will be fake by 2028.[83]

Financial services clients, IT firms, and others will look to attorneys for counsel to counter the dangers before a synthetic identity or employment scam compromises their systems and afterward to remediate incidents.

3.5. Market Manipulation

For years, fraudsters have used regular disinformation—fake text and simple graphics amplified by the internet—to move the financial markets and reap windfalls. For example, in October 2018, after Broadcom announced its intention to acquire CA Technologies for $19 billion, a phony memo circulated online supposedly from the U.S. Department of

77. *See* Isabelle Bousquette, *Deepfakes Are Coming for the Financial Sector*, WALL ST. J. (Apr. 3, 2024, 7:00 AM ET), https://www.wsj.com/articles/deepfakes-are-coming-for-the-financial-sector-0c72d1e5.

78. *Id.* (citing report by identity verification platform Sumsub).

79. *Id.*

80. *See id.*

81. Kara Fellows & Melissa Mahtani, *Fake Job Seekers Are Flooding the Market, Thanks to AI*, CBS NEWS (Apr. 23, 2025, 5:42 PM), https://www.cbsnews.com/news/fake-job-seekers-flooding-market-artificial-intelligence/.

82. *Id.* (citing Justice Department indictments).

83. *Id.* (citing Gartner research).

Defense saying the U.S. Government's Committee on Foreign Investment in the United States would scrutinize the acquisition for national security threats. Shares of both companies dropped when the memo was released. While no charges were filed in that case, short sellers who were prepared for the hiccup could have netted a bonanza from the hoax, what one writer called "a new phase of short-seller espionage."[84]

Similar deceptions have been used to prop up stock prices. For example, in December 2020, the Securities and Exchange Commission (SEC) charged a Georgia man and several others with securities fraud violations for allegedly creating false rumors about material business events of public companies, such as corporate mergers or acquisitions, and posting those falsehoods to financial chat rooms, message boards, and real-time financial news services, temporarily pushing up the companies' stocks. The market bumps allowed the defendants to reap tens of thousands of dollars in illicit profits, the SEC said.[85]

In April 2017, the SEC filed enforcement actions against over two dozen individuals and entities behind various alleged stock promotion schemes. The SEC contended that the defendants penned supposedly independent market analyses on investing websites to hype companies. In fact, the writers were being secretly compensated for goosing the stock prices. In one example, the SEC alleged a defendant placed dozens of articles about a small pharmaceutical company in reputable online news outlets, driving the shares up by 925%.[86]

A 2018 report by JPMorgan Chase suggested there is a systemic risk of disinformation manipulation for those traders who use algorithms based on social media posts and headlines to make trades.[87] The SEC has also issued a public alert for investors to warn them of fraudsters who may try to move share prices by using social media to circulate false or misleading information about stocks.[88]

We are beginning to see how individuals can supercharge these phenomena with AI-generated media. For example, in May 2023, an image appeared to show black smoke

---

84. CBR Staff Writer, *Fake Memo Hits Broadcom, CA Technologies Shares*, TECH MONITOR (Oct. 12, 2018), https://www.techmonitor.ai/policy/broadcom-cfius-ca. *See also* Ferraro et al., *Identifying Legal and Business Risks*, *supra* note 19, at 148.

85. Complaint, SEC v. Barton S. Ross, No. 20-cv-05140 (N.D. Ga., Dec. 18, 2020), ¶¶ 1–5, https://www.sec.gov/litigation/complaints/2020/comp24989.pdf; *SEC Charges Former Day Trader with Market Manipulation Scheme*, SEC. & EXCH. COMM'N (Dec. 18, 2020), https://www.sec.gov/litigation/litreleases/2020/lr24989.htm. *See also* Ferraro et al., *Identifying Legal and Business Risks*, *supra* note 19, at 147–148 (listing examples of disinformation-enabled market manipulation); Matthew F. Ferraro & Jason C. Chipman, Opinion, *Fake News Threatens Our Businesses, Not Just Our Politics*, WASH. POST (Feb. 8, 2019, 1:33 PM), https://www.washingtonpost.com/outlook/fake-news-threatens-our-businesses-not-just-our-politics/2019/02/08/f669b62c-2b1f-11e9-984d-9b8fba003e81_story.html (same).

86. Complaint, SEC v. Lidingo Holdings, LLC, No. 17-cv-02540 (S.D.N.Y., Apr. 10, 2017), ¶¶ 1–5, 89, https://www.sec.gov/litigation/complaints/2017/comp23802-lidingo.pdf; *27 Firms and Individuals Charged With Fraudulent Promotion of Stocks*, SEC. & EXCH. COMM'N (Apr. 12, 2017), https://www.sec.gov/litigation/litreleases/2017/lr23802.htm. *See* Renae Merle, *Scheme Created Fake News Stories to Manipulate Stock Prices, SEC Alleges*, L.A. TIMES (July 5, 2017, 2:50 PM), https://www.latimes.com/business/la-fi-sec-fake-news-20170705-story.html.

87. *Fake News and Bad News Are Depressing the Market, JPMorgan Strategists Say*, FORTUNE (Dec. 8, 2018), https://fortune.com/2018/12/08/fake-news-jpmorgan-kolanovic/.

88. *Updated Investor Alert: Social Media and Investing—Stock Rumors*, SEC. & EXCH. COMM'N (Nov. 5, 2015), https://www.sec.gov/oiea/investor-alerts-bulletins/ia_rumors.html.

rising from what appeared to be the U.S. military headquarters at the Pentagon. The image first appeared on Facebook and then spread to Twitter through accounts with massive followings, including the financial news site ZeroHedge, the Russian controlled account RT, and an account that falsely suggested it was associated with Bloomberg News.[89] Experts quickly dismissed the picture as an AI-generated fake, but the image had already sent markets reeling, pushing the S&P 500 index down about 0.3%, briefly wiping out billions of dollars of value, before the markets recovered.[90]

The dangers of these scams will only grow now that anyone can easily generate and deploy believable, manipulated media. Attorneys will be needed to help clients mitigate market-manipulation risks at the front end, advocate with regulatory bodies if their clients' valuations fall, and bring civil actions to recover damages from market manipulators, if necessary.

3.6. Political Disinformation

Commentators have long worried about the use of synthetic media to spread false narratives related to political campaigns.[91] Lawmakers at the state level have moved in recent years to regulate the use of such media in certain circumstances around elections, and there are ongoing efforts to pass federal legislation or enact nation-wide regulation.[92] While this use of synthetic media does not directly target the private sector, there are collateral risks to which attorneys should be attuned.

For example, in August 2024, a telecommunications company, Lingo Telecom, agreed to pay a $1 million fine to the Federal Communications Commission (FCC) for transmitting spoofed robocalls in which an AI-generated voice of then-President Joe Biden urged New Hampshire residents not to vote in the state's presidential primary.[93] The FCC found that Lingo Telecom placed nearly 4,000 calls to New Hampshire voters in January 2024 on behalf of a client, Life Corporation, and that Lingo Telecom had signed attestations that it was responsible for the origination of the calls, had a direct authenticated relationship

89. Philip Marcelo, *FACT FOCUS: Fake Image of Pentagon Explosion Briefly Sends Jitters Through Stock Market*, AP (May 23, 2023, 2:02 PM), https://apnews.com/article/pentagon-explosion-misinformation-stock-market-ai-96f534c790872fde67012ee81b5ed6a4; Andrew Ross Sorkin et al., *An A.I.-Generated Spoof Rattles the Markets*, N.Y. Times (May 23, 2023), https://www.nytimes.com/2023/05/23/business/ai-picture-stock-market.html.

90. Marcelo, *FACT FOCUS, supra* note 89; Davey Alba, *How a Fake AI Photo of a Pentagon Blast Wiped Billions Off Wall Street*, Sydney Morning Herald (May 24, 2023, 7:49 AM), https://www.smh.com.au/business/markets/how-a-fake-ai-photo-of-a-pentagon-blast-wiped-billions-off-wall-street-20230524-p5daqo.html.

91. *See, e.g.*, Schick, *supra* note 8, ch. 3; Mark Corcoran & Matt Henry, *The Tom Cruise Deepfake that Set Off "Terror" in the Heart of Washington DC*, Austl'n Broadcasting Corp. (June 23, 2021), https://www.abc.net.au/news/2021-06-24/tom-cruise-deepfake-chris-ume-security-washington-dc/100234772; Amanda S. Robert, *The 2020 Election: 4 Threats to Anticipate*, ABA J. (Jan. 2, 2020, 10:05 AM), https://www.abajournal.com/web/article/four-threats-to-anticipate-ahead-of-the-2020-election.

92. *See* NCSL, *Summary*, *supra* note 1; Weiner & Norden, *Regulating AI Deepfakes*, *supra* note 10.

93. *See* Jon Brodkin, *Telco Fined $1M for Transmitting Biden Deepfake without Verifying Caller ID*, Ars Technica (Aug. 21, 2024, 4:58 PM), https://arstechnica.com/tech-policy/2024/08/telco-to-pay-1m-fine-for-fake-biden-robocalls-that-told-people-not-to-vote/.

with the customer and could identify the customer, and had established a verified association with the telephone number used for the call. In fact, Lingo Telecom did not conduct sufficient verification to make those claims.[94]

As this case illustrates, private companies and their attorneys need to foresee how politically related deepfakes can expose them to liability and stay abreast of evolving regulations in this space.

3.7. Insurance Fraud

The insurance industry often relies on the veracity of digital media to adjudicate claims, increasing its exposure to deepfake manipulations. For instance, auto insurers use photographs of cars to validate insurance reports. Particularly since the COVID-19 pandemic, the insurance industry has moved toward self-service, where insureds rather than adjusters take the photographs that accompany claims. The greater availability of simple-to-use media manipulation technology will raise questions about the authenticity of such photographs, which insurers and their lawyers will need to address.[95]

Likewise, healthcare companies often rely on medical imagery to verify diagnoses. That imagery will become easier to fake with AI technology. For example, Israeli researchers have warned about the likely spread of deepfake-manipulated radiology scans that have been altered to show false results, including fake cancerous nodes.[96] Altered scans could be used to defraud insurance companies, who will need to rely on counsel to help alter their trainings, practices, compliance programs, and loss-mitigation litigation strategies as a result.

3.8. Labor & Employment Issues

Recent experience shows that believable-yet-falsified video or audio can pose potent labor and employment risks. In April 2024, Maryland police officers arrested a local high school athletic director on charges of disrupting school operations and stalking for using AI to synthesize a racist and antisemitic audio clip that impersonated the principal at the high school.[97] The defendant allegedly created the clip using commercially available software and emailed it in mid-January 2024 to employees of the high school from what appeared to be a third-party. Soon, the clip was posted on social media, and it went viral. The school system placed the principal, who faced threats to his safety, on administrative leave while it investigated the clip. The defendant evidently acted after the principal had investigated

---

94. *See* News Release, *FCC Settles Spoofed AI-Generated Robocalls Case*, FED. COMM. COMM'N (Aug. 21, 2024), https://www.fcc.gov/document/fcc-settles-spoofed-ai-generated-robocalls-case.

95. Elizabeth Blosfield, *How a Social Media Fad Is Turning into a Cyber Fraud Risk for Insurers*, INSURANCE J. (Mar. 3, 2021), https://www.insurancejournal.com/news/2021/03/03/603345.htm.

96. Jane Anderson, *Addressing "Deep Fake" Scans Is Critical Amid Tech Advances*, REP. ON PATIENT PRIV'Y. (Nov. 11, 2019), https://www.jdsupra.com/legalnews/addressing-deep-fake-scans-is-critical-16100/ (citing Yisroel Mirsky). *See also* Sam Reardon, *Understanding the Threat of Deepfakes in Healthcare*, PINDROP (Jan. 28, 2025), https://www.pindrop.com/article/threat-deepfakes-in-healthcare/.

97. *See* Natasha Singer, *Racist AI Deepfake of Baltimore Principal Leads to Arrest*, N.Y. TIMES (Apr. 25, 2024), https://www.nytimes.com/2024/04/25/technology/deepfake-recording-principal-arrest.html.

the athletic director for fraudulently authorizing a school payment to the athletic director's roommate under false pretenses.[98] The defendant pled guilty, and in April 2025, a Baltimore County Circuit Court sentenced him to four months in prison.[99]

Employees have long used legitimate recordings of workplace malfeasance to support wrongful termination or harassment claims. These recordings are usually admissible in court as the most reliable evidence.[100] As the case in Maryland shows, the public often assumes the validity of such recordings purporting to substantiate claims of employer wrongdoing.

As deepfakes and reports of manufactured crises like the one in the Maryland high school proliferate, many may come to doubt the veracity of clandestine recordings and question even legitimate claims of misconduct. A harassing employee may avoid accountability by simply asserting that a recording corroborating a claim is "fake," in an attempt to reap a liar's dividend. In the face of both possibilities—that evidence is manipulated or legitimate—legal counsel will need to manage the employment law and reputational risks of inculpatory media carefully and assess the underlying allegations.[101]

4. Top Ten Best Practices for Managing Deepfake Risk

Businesses should work with counsel to develop strategies to protect their brands and valuations from deepfakes, both before and after private entities are victimized by them. Companies will need to tailor their responses to their specific circumstances, but here are ten general practices lawyers and their clients will want to consider:

1. ***Proactively Communicate an Accurate Positive Message.*** When it comes to guarding against reputational harms, proactive messaging can establish strong defenses. A company should take steps to build brand resilience, to establish its messages and its leaders in the public's mind early on, before false manipulated media starts spreading.[102] If a company can construct stable public perceptions, it will be less likely to lose control of the narrative about its business to a barrage of counterfeit media.[103]

---

98. *Id.*

99. Cale Ahearn & Rebecca Pryor, *Man Convicted in Case of Racist AI Deep Fake of Pikesville HS Principal*, Fox 45 News (Apr. 28, 2025, 5:41 PM), https://foxbaltimore.com/news/local/racist-ai-deep-fake-of-pikesville-hs-principal-conviction.

100. *See e.g.*, Byrd v. Reno, 1998 WL 429767, at *1 (D.D.C., 1998) ("[T]here is not and cannot be anything that is the substantial equivalent of the tape recording of a conversation .... There is literally no substitute for the tape recordings."); Rauh v. Coyne, 744 F. Supp. 1181, 1183–1184 (D.D.C. 1990) (admitting discrimination plaintiff's tape recording as an admission of a party-defendant). *See also* Fed. R. Evid. 901(a).

101. *See* Ferraro et al., *Identifying Legal and Business Risks*, *supra* note 19, at 149–150.

102. *See* Preston Golson, *The Disinformation Wildfire*, Brunswick Rev. (May 5, 2021), https://www.brunswickgroup.com/disinformation-wildfire-i18810/ ("Organizations that take the time to learn how to address and mobilize these audiences can build resilience against false information.").

103. Matthew F. Ferraro, *What Corporate America Can Do to Protect Itself from Conspiracy Theories*, Real Clear World (July 22, 2020), https://www.realclearworld.com/articles/2020/07/21/what_corporate_america_can_do_to_protect_itself_from_conspiracy_theories_499674.html.

2. ***Integrate Technology to Bolster Defenses.*** Companies should use technology to harden defenses and prevent unauthorized user access. Some of this technology is already widely employed, such as the mandatory use by employees of multi-factor authentication, biometric verification (e.g., fingerprint identification), and/or personal details (e.g., a user's favorite food, first car). Such technologies can also include emerging techniques to detect deepfakes passively, particularly when users can execute financial transactions for companies.[104]
3. ***Protect Leaders' Data.*** As we have seen, data relating to leaders and other influential persons can be hijacked for malicious deepfakes. To combat this threat, entities should consider using active authentication techniques, including watermarks or media provenance standards, to protect their data, particularly that of C-suite executives and brand ambassadors. Entities will also want to leverage cross-industry partnerships for certifying the provenance of media content and train their personnel to understand these tools and be suspicious of, and report, incidents of digital impersonation.[105]
4. ***Engage in Social Listening.*** Companies need to understand how their brands are perceived on social media to get advance warning of any effort to spread deepfakes about them. Law firms, cybersecurity consultancies, and public relations firms can be retained to do this work. Outside counsel can also consider retaining third-party service providers directly or through tri-party agreements; depending on the circumstances, the service providers' work may be entitled to legal privilege.
5. ***Conduct a Self-assessment.*** Deepfake risk varies by individual, company, and circumstance. For example, financial institutions face a particular risk that synthetic identities can open accounts. Celebrities face heightened risk their likenesses will be misused to sell get-rich-quick schemes. Individuals and entities should conduct assessments of their exposures to understand how to address them. Preston Golson, a former CIA officer and now a director at the Brunswick Group, has called on companies to conduct as "an audit of vulnerabilities" to identify what upcoming events (a merger, a product launch) and what public positions can be the subject of malicious distortion.[106] It is important that entities understand these pressure points early.
6. ***Register Trademarks and Copyrights.*** Because of the strong federal protection provided to intellectual property (IP),[107] companies should work with counsel to register preemptively their trademarks, trade dress, and copyrights before they are

104. *See* NSA, *Alert*, *supra* note 39, at 11–12; Rick Hutchinson, Opinion, *Deepfakes Are The New Frontier of Cyberattacks: 5 Steps To Fight Back*, FORBES (Jan. 6, 2025, 8:45 AM), https://www.forbes.com/councils/forbestechcouncil/2025/01/06/deepfakes-are-the-new-frontier-of-cyberattacks-5-steps-to-fight-back/.

105. *See* NSA, *Alert*, *supra* note 39, at 13–15.

106. Golson, *Disinformation Wildfire*, *supra* note 102. *See also* Ferraro et al., *Identifying Legal and Business Risks*, *supra* note 19, at 154.

107. *See, e.g.*, 15 U.S.C. § 1114(1)(a) (2025) (trademark infringement); 17 U.S.C. §§ 501–513 (2025)(copyright infringement).

manipulated by bad actors.[108] If their IP is misused, copyright or trademark owners can bring lawsuits.

Social media platforms also often remove IP-infringing content if they receive a request from the IP's owner.[109] For example, in 2019, anti-advertising activists uploaded to a social media platform a manipulated deepfake video of Kim Kardashian appearing to say things she never did. *Vogue* magazine had posted the original video on which the deepfake was based a few weeks earlier, and because the copyright for that video belonged to *Vogue*, the magazine's publisher Condé Nast was able to lodge a copyright complaint against the manipulated video and have it taken down.[110]

7. ***Make a Plan.*** Many companies today work with attorneys to develop cybersecurity plans that anticipate cyber hacks and similar crises. Businesses need to expand their crisis planning to anticipate deepfakes. They need to prepare for AI-enabled reputational harm and social engineering, spear phishing, and fraud by increasing training for team members (and expanding who is educated on these threats to include professionals from communications, public relations, finance, and IT) and updating compliance and internal security protocols.[111]
8. ***Engage with Social Media Platforms.*** If a company or its counsel sees a malicious deepfake spreading online, a company representative should contact the social media platforms being used to spread the deepfake and determine if it violates the platforms' terms of service. If so, the platforms may remove it.[112]
9. ***Speak.*** It can be a challenge to know when to directly address deepfakes that cause reputational or other harm as opposed to ignoring them. There is a risk of amplifying false information that might otherwise fail to get traction.[113] On the other hand, lies supported by believable media can travel remarkably fast, and waiting too long can be costly. President Zelensky's quick action in April 2022 to release his own video debunking the deepfake circulating of him is a textbook case of the value of responding swiftly.[114] As part of their advance planning, companies should consider thresholds for taking specific steps, including when to speak directly to their customers, the

108. *See* Ferraro et al., *Identifying Legal and Business Risks*, *supra* note 19, at 154.

109. *See e.g.*, Brook Zimmatore, *How to File a DMCA Takedown and Protect Your Reputation,* ENTREPRENEUR (Dec. 3, 2020), https://www.entrepreneur.com/article/359772.

110. Matthew Katz, *Kim Kardashian Can Get a Deepfake Taken Off YouTube. It's Much Harder for You*, DIGITAL TRENDS (June 17, 2019), https://www.digitaltrends.com/social-media/kim-kardashian-deepfake-removed-from-youtube/. *See also* Matthew F. Ferraro & Louis W. Tompros, *Celebrity Disinformation Victims Have Panoply of Remedies*, LAW 360 (Sept. 29, 2020, 4:05 PM).

111. *See* Ferraro et al., *Identifying Legal and Business Risks*, *supra* note 19, at 154; Golson, *Disinformation Wildfire*, *supra* note 102.

112. *See* Ferraro et al., *Identifying Legal and Business Risks*, *supra* note 19, at 154.

113. This is referred to as the "Streisand Effect," after an incident involving the famous singer. *See* Mario Cacciottolo, *The Streisand Effect: When Censorship Backfires*, BBC (June 15, 2012), https://www.bbc.com/news/uk-18458567 (after Streisand sued a photographer displaying an image online of Streisand's home, news coverage drove an exponential increase in the online views of the photograph).

114. *See* Ferraro, *Zelensky Deepfake*, *supra* note 60.

media, and the public, as well as to third-party validators (who should be identified and contacted in advance as part of crisis planning). Companies should work with counsel to engage proactively with regulators and file disclosures, as circumstances warrant.[115]

10. ***If Necessary, Go to Court.*** Free speech rights protect most opinions, but businesses are not defenseless when their brands are defamed, employees are defrauded, or markets are manipulated by AI-generated media. Attorneys and clients should consider each case individually and weigh their options.

5. The Deepfakes Economy: Legal Issues Arising with Positive Uses of Deepfakes

Thus far, this chapter has addressed the business risks of deepfakes and what roles lawyers have in assisting clients in addressing them. This section focuses on some of the key legal issues attorneys may face when counseling clients who are developing or deploying deepfakes for positive uses.

5.1. IP Issues Related to Source Data, AI Models, and Generated Media

When it comes to the use of deepfakes by businesses and in products, the most complex questions currently facing legal counsel relate to intellectual property. These questions can be grouped into three general categories: questions revolving around the source data on which an AI model trains (the inputs); the AI model itself; and the outputs (the media produced by the AI model). Many of these issues are the subject of ongoing litigation, but the following sketches out in broad strokes the issues about which clients and their counsel should be aware.

First, the *inputs*. The data on which the AI models train often includes third-party IP, such as images, video, and text protected by registered copyrights and trademarks. Often, authorization for use of this source data has not been obtained in advance. Generally speaking, many content owners have claimed that copying and training on their data infringes their IP rights. AI model developers have claimed that their use of the data is protected by the doctrine of fair use. Lawsuits on these questions are ongoing.[116] Notably, an increasing number of content owners have chosen to license their content to AI model developers, so their training is conducted with the content owners' consent.[117] Conversely, some contracts between parties restrict or prohibit the use of data in AI training, and violating such terms can give rise to breach-of-contract claims. For example, in *Doe v. GitHub*, a putative

---

115. *See* Ferraro et al., *Identifying Legal and Business Risks*, *supra* note 19, at 154.

116. *See Case Tracker: Artificial Intelligence, Copyrights and Class Actions*, Baker Hostetler (last visited Feb. 2, 2025), https://www.bakerlaw.com/services/artificial-intelligence-ai/case-tracker-artificial-intelligence-copyrights-and-class-actions/ [hereinafter *Case Tracker*]; Barcott, *AI Lawsuits*, *supra* note 3.

117. *See* Tobitt, *supra* note 2.

class of computer programmers brought a suit challenging the unauthorized use of their computer code to train a generative AI model. The plaintiffs argue, in part, that the defendants' use of their code violated GitHub's terms of service because the contract barred the defendants from using the plaintiffs' material to train the AI and forbade republishing the plaintiffs' material without appending required information related to attribution, copyright, and licensing terms.[118]

Second, the *models themselves*. Is IP that is generated solely by an AI model copyrightable, where the only human action is to input written prompts? Right now, the U.S. Copyright Office says "no."[119] However, copyright continues to protect a human author's original expression in a work, even if the work also includes material generated by AI.[120] Individuals have filed for patents listing an AI model itself as the sole inventor; so far, courts have rejected these applications because the law requires an "inventor" to be a natural person.[121]

Finally, the *outputs*. Disputes have arisen over who owns the IP generated by an AI system, particularly if multiple parties contribute to its developments. Commercial AI models often spell out ownership in their terms of use. For example, OpenAI's terms of use assign "all our right, title, and interest" in the output of its model to the user who provided the prompts.[122] Litigation is pending over whether outputs can infringe the copyrights of others' works or if they dilute trademarks held by others.[123]

Attorneys are needed on all sides of the v. to advise clients on all three categories of these complex issues, adjudicate the claims, negotiate licenses, and draft regulations in this fast-moving area.

5.2. Labor Rights

The proliferation of deepfakes may complicate the livelihoods of many, notably actors who could find themselves replaced by digital avatars. The 2023 strikes by Hollywood writers and actors were driven in significant part by concerns related to the use of AI to reproduce actors' likenesses against their will and to supplant screenwriters. The resulting agreements that ended the walkouts require that AI reproductions of actors be used only with the actors' informed consent and compensation. Screenwriters agreed to language protecting

118. *See* First Am. Complaint, Doe 1 v. Github, Inc., No. 22-cv-06823-JST (N.D. Cal., June 8, 2023), ¶¶ 41, 214–40. The plaintiffs' contract claim survived a motion to dismiss. Doe 1 v. Github, Inc., 672 F. Supp. 3d 837, 859–60 (N.D. Cal. 2023).

119. *See* Matthew F. Ferraro et al., *Potential Implications of US Copyright Office Determination on AI-Generated Work*, Tech Policy Press (May 4, 2023), https://www.techpolicy.press/potential-implications-of-us-copyright-office-determination-on-ai-generated-work/.

120. *See* U.S. Copyright Office, Copyright and Artificial Intelligence Part 2: Copyrightability iii (Jan. 2025), https://copyright.gov/ai/Copyright-and-Artificial-Intelligence-Part-2-Copyrightability-Report.pdf.

121. *See* Thaler v. Vidal, 43 F.4th 1207 (Fed. Cir. 2022), *cert. denied*, 143 S. Ct. 1783 (2023).

122. *Terms of Use*, OpenAI ("Ownership of Content") (Dec. 11, 2024), https://openai.com/policies/row-terms-of-use/.

123. *See generally Case Tracker*, *supra* note 116. See in *id.*, among others, the claims in *New York Times vs. Microsoft*, No. 23-cv-11195-SHS (S.D.N.Y.).

them from the use of AI in the writing process, providing them credit for their work, and allowing writers to determine if their writing can be used to train AI.[124]

Representing clients on all sides of these and similar issues across industries, negotiating such agreements, and litigating over alleged breaches will require thoughtful legal counsel.

5.3. Product Counseling

New consumer products are putting deepfake technology at users' fingertips, literally. As these products and services come to market, businesses and their lawyers need to consider the bounds they should put on their products to minimize business, ethical, and legal risks.

For example, in February 2021, a genealogy website introduced a tool that uses deepfake technology to animate the faces in old photographs of deceased relatives. The images turn their heads, smile, nod, and blink. Notably, the company deliberately chose not to include a speech feature, which would have allowed adding voice to the photographs, "in order to prevent abuse, such as the creation of deepfake videos of living people," it said.[125] Recently, Chinese companies, including Silicon Intelligence, have launched more advanced apps that allow users to recreate avatars of deceased relatives who can converse with the user to help the user process grief. One report calls it a "booming business."[126] Silicon Intelligence reported that by 2024, about 1,000 clients used the software to recreate a lost relative, while others use the technology to mimic living persons.[127]

Companies are also reanimating the deceased for advertising. In 2021, a Spanish brewery used a deepfake of a late singer to create a commercial for a new ad campaign. The company reportedly used hours of audiovisual material and more than 5,000 photos to create the singer's voice, face, and features. It worked with the deceased's children on the project, although some took to social media to criticize the campaign.[128] Similarly, a Mexican beer brand has reportedly offered customers the opportunity to create AI-generated short videos of their deceased loved ones to mark Mexico's Day of the Dead.[129] Relatedly, while all the major AI developers disallow the creation of illegal material, their policies vary

---

124. *See* Molly Kinder, *Hollywood Writers Went on Strike to Protect Their Livelihoods From Generative AI. Their Remarkable Victory Matters for All Workers*, Brookings Inst. (Apr. 12, 2024), https://www.brookings.edu/articles/hollywood-writers-went-on-strike-to-protect-their-livelihoods-from-generative-ai-their-remarkable-victory-matters-for-all-workers/; Andrew Dalton, *Hollywood Actors Approve Deal to End Strike After Nearly Four Months*, AP (Dec. 6, 2023), https://apnews.com/article/actors-strike-contract-a7a529acaf6b-5b38aac93722db54c193; Mandalit del Barco, *SAG-AFTRA and the Studios Make a Deal to End the Hollywood Strikes*, NPR (Nov. 8, 2023), https://www.npr.org/2023/11/08/1203789537/hollywood-strike-ends.

125. Jane Wakefield, *MyHeritage Offers "Creepy" Deepfake Tool to Reanimate Dead*, BBC (Feb. 26, 2021), https://www.bbc.com/news/technology-56210053.

126. Zeyi Yang, *Deepfakes of Your Dead Loved Ones Are a Booming Chinese Business*, MIT Tech. Rev. (May 7, 2024), https://www.technologyreview.com/2024/05/07/1092116/deepfakes-dead-chinese-business-grief/.

127. *Id.*

128. *See* Thomas Macaulay, *AI Resurrects Legendary Spanish Singer to Hawk Beer*, The Next Web (Jan. 22, 2021, 3:06 PM), https://thenextweb.com/news/ai-resurrects-legendary-spanish-singer-lola-flores-to-hawk-beer.

129. *Deepfakes After Death*, Paul Weiss (Jan. 2025), https://www.paulweiss.com/resources/podcasts/waking-up-with-ai/waking-up-with-ai-list/2025/january/ep-47-deepfakes-after-death.

on the creation of potentially controversial content, like disinformation or sexually explicit content that is not illegal.[130]

Companies will look to counsel to help them integrate deepfakes into their products in ways that attract customers and improve their offerings without exposing them to reputational, ethical, or legal risks. Indeed, lawsuits against AI products are already plentiful, and plaintiffs and defendants will require representation in suits sounding in everything from defamation and false light, to unfair or deceptive business practices, to discrimination and IP (as noted above), among many other claims.[131]

5.4. Social Media Platform Counseling

As this chapter has shown, deepfakes are not an issue associated entirely with social media. Realistic forgeries can be and are used in many contexts for social engineering, fraud, identity theft, and other malicious purposes. But social media companies occupy key roles as both AI developers and distributors of AI-generated content. Different platforms have adopted different policies to regulate deepfakes.[132] Attorneys can play an important part in helping social media companies design their deepfake policies, particularly in light of changing regulatory environments.

5.5. Legislative Counseling and Public Policy Advocacy

Manipulated media is quickly becoming a government-regulated field. At this writing, dozens of states have already adopted laws prohibiting or regulating certain kinds of deepfakes (e.g., related to nonconsensual deepfake pornography, deepfakes targeting elections, property rights in digital likenesses) and many more are pending at state and federal levels.[133]

Governments around the world have also implemented laws that regulate deepfakes. For example, the European Union's General Data Protection Regulation (GDPR) and the

---

130. *See* Chase DiBenedetto, *How Big Tech's Players Are Approaching Explicit Deepfakes*, Mashable (Aug. 26, 2024), https://mashable.com/article/big-tech-social-media-explicit-deepfake-policies; Huey Yee Ong, *OpenAI Explores NSFW Content Boundaries but Firmly Excludes Pornography*, MSN (May 12, 2024), https://www.msn.com/en-us/news/technology/openai-explores-nsfw-content-boundaries-but-firmly-excludes-pornography/ar-BB1meSVx.

131. *See, e.g.*, Walters v. OpenAI, L.L.C., No. 23-CV-03122 (N.D. Ga filed July 14, 2023) (defamation; summary judgment granted for the defendant); Young v. NeoCortext, Inc., No. 2:23-cv-02496 (C.D. Cal. filed Apr. 3, 2023) (publicity rights); A.F. v. Character Technologies, Inc., No. 24-CV-01903 (E.D. Tex. filed Dec. 9, 2024) (deceptive trade practice); Mobley v. Workday, Inc., 740 F. Supp. 3d 796, 813–14 (N.D. Cal. 2024) (granting in part and denying in part defendant's motion to dismiss discrimination claims); Garcia v. Character Technologies, Inc., No. 6:24-cv-1903-ACC-UAM, 2025 WL 14661721 (M.D. Fla. May 21, 2025) (product liability). For a selection of IP-related cases, see *Case Tracker*, *supra* note 116. Some of these cases do not involve deepfakes, but the legal issues may well apply to AI-generated media in other circumstances.

132. *See Crackdown on Deepfake: YouTube Takes Down 1000 AI-driven Celebrity Scam Ads*, Asianet Newsable (Jan 27, 2024, 9:12 AM), https://newsable.asianetnews.com/technology/crackdown-on-deepfake-youtube-takes-down-1000-ai-driven-celebrity-scam-ads-s7wib4; Katie Paul, *Meta Overhauls Rules on Deepfakes, Other Altered Media*, Reuters (Apr. 5, 2024), https://www.reuters.com/technology/cybersecurity/meta-overhauls-rules-deepfakes-other-altered-media-2024-04-05/.

133. *See* NCSL, *Summary*, *supra* note 1.

People's Republic of China's Personal Information Protection Law consider the kind of biometric data that powers synthetic media—images of faces and recordings of voices—as sensitive personal information and demand the subject's consent for such data's processing.[134] The GDPR allows individuals to request that their deepfake content be removed.[135] The United Kingdom, Australia, and Singapore also have laws against the production or distribution of deepfake nonconsensual intimate imagery.[136] And the European Union's AI Act will require that both "providers" and "deployers" of AI systems disclose and clearly label where visual or audio deepfake content has been generated or manipulated by AI when the Act comes into force in August 2026.[137]

These deepfake-specific legislative actions dovetail with broader efforts to assign liability when AI causes harm. The application of existing liability frameworks—such as negligence, product liability, agency, and strict liability—remains the subject of rulemaking and lawsuits in the United States and Europe, which at this writing are unresolved.[138]

Attorneys can help companies seeking to leverage deepfake technology comply with these burgeoning legal strictures, both domestically and internationally. Public policy attorneys may also be called upon to advocate for their clients in shaping new laws and liability regimes. One expects that the regulation of, and litigation around, deepfakes will proceed with growing urgency.

5.6. Updating Cybersecurity Insurance

Cyber insurance policies have not historically covered the damage wrought by deepfakes that target corporate brands, enable fraud, or otherwise cause harm.[139] Nor have they provided liability coverage for businesses that utilize manipulated media technology to increase customer engagement. As these trends continue, businesses will want to consider how to modify or supplement their current insurance policies to address all their business risks and liabilities.[140]

---

134. *See* Claudia Koon Ghee Wee, *Artificial Illusion: Global Governance Challenges of Deepfake Technology*, IAPP (Apr. 23, 2025), https://iapp.org/news/a/artificial-illusion-global-governance-challenges-of-deepfake-technology.

135. *Id.*

136. *Id.*

137. *See Article 50: Transparency Obligations for Providers and Deployers of Certain AI Systems*, EU ARTIFICIAL INTELLIGENCE ACT (last visited Apr. 26, 2025), https://artificialintelligenceact.eu/article/50/.

138. *See* Soham Nandi, *Who is Responsible When AI Makes a Harmful Decision?*, AZO ROBOTICS (Feb. 19, 2025), https://www.azorobotics.com/Article.aspx?ArticleID=741; Megan Howarth et al., *AI Liability—Who Is Accountable When Artificial Intelligence Malfunctions?*, TAYLOR WESSING (Jan. 7, 2025), https://www.taylorwessing.com/en/insights-and-events/insights/2025/01/ai-liability-who-is-accountable-when-artificial-intelligence-malfunctions.

139. Marianne Bonner, *What Does Cyber Liability Insurance Cover?*, THE BALANCE SMALL BUS. (Mar. 12, 2021), https://www.thebalancesmb.com/what-is-covered-under-a-cyber-liability-policy-462459.

140. *See id. See also* Ferraro et al., *Identifying Legal and Business Risks*, *supra* note 19, at 151; HANDBOOK, Chapter 14, *Cyber Insurance for Law Firms and Legal Organizations.*

6. Deepfakes and Democracy at the Bar

Highly realistic manipulated media poses unique challenges to litigators and courts.[141] Riana Pfefferkorn of the Stanford Institute for Human-Centered Artificial Intelligence, who has written one of the most comprehensive treatments of the issues surrounding deepfakes in court, observed: "In pre-trial and trial practice, deepfakes will touch every role in the courtroom: lawyers attempting to introduce or exclude videos as evidence; judges determining whether a video is admissible; expert and lay witnesses asked to testify about the video, and, finally; [sic] jurors weighing the evidence in order to reach a verdict."[142]

The Federal Rules of Evidence impose authentication standards and requirements that will need to be leveraged to keep deepfakes from masquerading as unadulterated media.[143] The rules allow for the authentication of records "generated by an electronic process or system that produces an accurate result," if "shown by a certification of a qualified person" in a manner set forth by the rules.[144] The rules also require advance notice to the other side and the opportunity to challenge the records.[145] If the certification requirements are met, a party need not call a testifying witness at trial to establish authenticity.[146]

Attorneys have obligations to verify the authenticity of media on their own before submitting it to the court.[147] Under the rules, an attorney may not knowingly offer "evidence that the lawyer knows to be false," like a known deepfake.[148] If he or she comes to know that evidence provided by a client or witness is false, the lawyer "shall take reasonable remedial measures," including disclosing that fact to the court.[149] And an attorney "may refuse to offer evidence . . . that the lawyer *reasonably believes* is false," such as a video he or she reasonably believes to be manipulated.[150] At the same time, while attorneys should zealously advocate for their clients and raise reasonable questions about evidence, they should not insincerely challenge the opposing party's evidence as a "deepfake" merely as a litigation tactic where the attorney does not reasonably believe the evidence to be manipulated. Doing so may violate professional rules against making frivolous arguments, baselessly denying factual contentions, or engaging in harassing, delaying, or costly motion practice.[151] Such objections could well undermine the public's confidence in the rule of law,

141. *See* Ferraro et al., *Identifying Legal and Business Risks*, *supra* note 19, at 151.

142. Riana Pfefferkorn, *"Deepfakes" in the Courtroom*, 29 Pub. Int. L.J. 245, 254 (2020).

143. *Id.* at 246.

144. Fed. R. Evid. 902(13); *see also* Fed. R. Evid. 902(14).

145. Fed. R. Evid. 902(11) and 902(12).

146. *See* Fed. R. Evid. 902.

147. *See* David Dorfman, *Decoding Deepfakes: How Do Lawyers Adapt When Seeing Isn't Always Believing?*, 80 Oregon State Bar Bulletin 18, 22 (Apr. 2020), https://www.osbar.org/bulletin/issues/2020/2020April/offline/download.pdf.

148. Model Rules of Prof'l Conduct r. 3.3(a)(3).

149. *Id.*

150. *Id.* (emphasis added). *See* Pfefferkorn, *supra* note 142, at 273–275.

151. Model Rules of Prof'l Conduct r. 3.1, 3.3(a); Fed. R. Civ. P. 11(b)(1), (2), (4); Pfefferkorn, *supra* note 142, at 274.

which is contrary to an attorney's duty.[152] For their part, judges should prepare for competing expert testimony over the authenticity of videos and audio recordings.[153]

Finally, merely the publicized existence of deepfakes may make jurors skeptical of the veracity of media evidence, even after the evidence has been deemed admissible by a court. This will amount to a kind of "liar's dividend" accruing in the jury box that the court system will need to address.[154]

Beyond the direct implications for the practice of law, deepfakes can threaten democracy in ways that lawyers may be uniquely suited to address. For example, the public skepticism generated by the "liar's dividend" can lead Americans to give up on trying to find the truth or on the idea of truth altogether. And deepfakes designed to undermine trust in institutions, including the courts,[155] can accelerate disengagement from vital public institutions. Democracy cannot long function without an informed and engaged citizenry.

Given these gathering concerns, in November 2024, the U.S. Judicial Conference's Advisory Committee on Evidence Rules agreed to develop a new rule to regulate the introduction of AI-generated evidence, such as deepfakes, and begin work on a policy to assist judges when a party claims that a piece of evidence is a deepfake. At this writing, their work remains ongoing.[156]

Chief Justice of the United States John G. Roberts' *Year-End Report on the Federal Judiciary* for 2023 focused in part on the promises and perils of AI. He urged "caution and humility," noting AI's "great potential to dramatically increase access to key information for lawyers and non-lawyers alike. But just as obviously it risks invading privacy interests and dehumanizing the law."[157] He concluded: "I predict that human judges will be around for a while. But with equal confidence I predict that judicial work—particularly at the trial level—will be significantly affected by AI."[158]

---

152. Model Rules of Prof'l Conduct prmbl ¶ 6; Pfefferkorn, *supra* note 142, at 274.

153. Ferraro et al., *Identifying Legal and Business Risks*, *supra* note 19, at 151; Theodore F. Claypoole, *AI and Evidence: Let's Start to Worry*, Nat'l L. Rev. (Nov. 14, 2019), https://www.natlawreview.com/article/ai-and-evidence-let-s-start-to-worry; Riana Pfefferkorn, *Too Good to Be True?*, 73 NW Law. 22, 24 (Sept. 2019), https://wabarnews.org/wp-content/uploads/2021/10/NWLawyer-Sept.-2019.pdf.

154. *See* Pfefferkorn, *supra* note 142, at 255 (describing "reverse *CSI* effect"); Pfefferkorn, *supra* note 153, at 24.

155. *See* Suzanne Spaulding, Devi Nair, and Arthur Nelson, *Beyond the Ballot: How the Kremlin Works to Undermine the U.S. Justice System*, Ctr. for Strategic and Int'l Studies (May 2019), https://csis-website-prod.s3.amazonaws.com/s3fs-public/publication/190430_RussiaUSJusticeSystem_v3_WEB_FULL.pdf; Suzanne E. Spaulding et al., *Countering Adversary Threats to Democratic Institutions: An Expert Report*, Ctr. for Strategic and Int'l Studies (Feb. 2018), https://csis-website-prod.s3.amazonaws.com/s3fs-public/publication/180214_Spaulding_CounteringAdversaryThreats_Web2.pdf. I am indebted to Suzanne Spaulding, who served as the contributing author to the first version of this chapter in the 2022 edition of this Handbook, for her insights on this point.

156. Nate Raymond, *US Judicial Panel to Develop Rules to Address AI-produced Evidence*, Reuters (Nov. 8, 2024, 4:38 PM EST), https://www.reuters.com/legal/transactional/us-judicial-panel-develop-rules-address-ai-produced-evidence-2024-11-08/.

157. John G. Roberts, 2023 Year-End Report on the Federal Judiciary 5 (2023), https://www.supremecourt.gov/publicinfo/year-end/2023year-endreport.pdf.

158. *Id.* at 6.

How deepfakes will impact the court system will turn in large measure on the acts and decisions of attorneys themselves. Members of the bar have a vital responsibility, as recognized by the Model Rules of Professional Conduct, to serve as "public citizen[s]" with "special responsibility for the quality of justice" and to "further the public's understanding of and confidence in the rule of law and the justice system because legal institutions in a constitutional democracy depend on popular participation and support to maintain their authority."[159]

7. Top Ten Highlights

This chapter introduced the role of lawyers in dealing with the evolving issues of deepfakes. The top ten takeaways are:

1. We live in a golden age of media. The spread of inexpensive, easy-to-use, and advanced AI technologies has placed in the hands of almost anyone the ability to manipulate or create realistic imagery, audio, and video;
2. Deepfakes promise great benefits for artistic creativity, accessibility, and education, among others, but also significant business and legal risks that attorneys need to address;
3. Mitigations to deepfakes include technologies that identify deepfakes after they are created and verify media at the "point of capture" in such a way that such media cannot be altered or modified after the fact without leaving evidence of the manipulation through provenance metadata or "content credentials";
4. Deepfakes can enable significant private-sector harms, including intimate harms, reputational risk, social engineering and fraud, the creation of synthetic identities that can bypass authentication systems, market manipulation, political disinformation, insurance fraud, and labor and employment issues;
5. Law firms, like any other business, are at risk from these dangers;
6. Businesses should prepare now for the downsides of deepfakes. While every individual, company, and situation is different, companies should consider several general principles, including preparation, technological safeguards, raising awareness, and communication;
7. Lawyers have many important roles to play in dealing with deepfake threats for themselves and their clients. Lawyers can help companies develop mitigation plans ahead of time, counsel clients when they are subjected to deepfake-enabled reputational attacks, frauds, or cyberattacks, represent clients in negotiations and in controversy proceedings, work with regulators, and go to court to vindicate clients' rights;

159. Model Rules of Prof'l Conduct prmbl ¶¶ 1, 6.

8. Attorneys will be needed to help companies take advantage of the opportunities provided by deepfake technology, including wrestling with IP issues related to source data, AI models, and generated media, addressing labor displacement issues, providing product counseling and representation in litigation, working with social media platforms, and helping to shape the legislative landscape, among others;
9. Deepfakes pose unique challenges to litigators and courts. The rules of evidence require authentication standards that should, in theory, screen out manipulated media, but judges should prepare for dueling experts on the veracity of video and audio exhibits; and,
10. Attorneys have professional, ethical, and legal obligations to serve the cause of justice by acting in a way that buttresses the public's confidence in the rule of law and the administration of justice, as well as the expertise and opportunity to counter the kind of AI-generated media that can threaten our democracy.

Chapter 7

Legal Obligations to Provide Data Security

Thomas J. Smedinghoff, Ruth Hill Bro, and
Kimberly K. Peretti[1]

Unceasing high-profile and well-publicized security incidents have highlighted our almost total dependence on electronic networks and digital data, while also underscoring the significant harm that can result from a security incident. Virtually all transactions and key records of a business are created, used, communicated, and stored in electronic form using networked computer technology. Although such technology provides organizations with increased flexibility and tremendous economic benefits, including reduced costs and increased productivity, it also creates considerable risks that can adversely affect the business, its employees, clients and customers, and other entities with which it interacts. Meanwhile, the cyber threat landscape continues to evolve in unprecedented and unpredictable ways, adding to cyber risks for organizations. As a result, organizations face far more and greater security challenges than ever, especially with advances in artificial intelligence (AI), as threat actors are already leveraging generative AI (GenAI) to launch cyberattacks.

Creating, using, communicating, and storing information in electronic form greatly increases the potential for unauthorized access, use, disclosure, alteration, loss, or destruction of the information. Front-page news stories about data security missteps made by companies, government agencies, and other organizations (including law firms) are a testament to the growing significance of this problem and should serve as a wake-up call for lawyers in all practice settings. Insert your firm's name, or your client's name, in the most recent ransomware or data breach headline, and the risk of not taking sufficient security steps (especially those that are legally required) becomes all too real. That risk not only affects the organization itself, but it also can do serious harm to employees, customers and clients, vendors, shareholders, investors, and, in some cases, the public.

To address such risks, organizations should evaluate the threats posed by all relevant technological innovations, including GenAI, and account for those risks in their information security programs. The extraordinary pace at which cyber threats are evolving, particularly those powered by GenAI, is of particular concern. Keeping up will require organizations to be both agile and well-grounded in principles of data security risk management. But new

1. The authors wish to recognize the research contributions of Senior Associate Lance Taubin and Associates Carson Kück, Seol Namgoong, and Andrew Rice, all of Alston & Bird.

threats, such as GenAI, do not change the fundamental approach to data security or the legal duty to provide reasonable security outlined in this chapter. Organizations must work to understand enough about GenAI tools and other new threats to make reasonable risk assessments and implement appropriate security controls to avoid or minimize threats and vulnerabilities introduced by those tools. For example, organizations should consider how to evaluate, implement, and train their employees to use GenAI tools adopted by the organization, while restricting access to GenAI tools that have not been vetted and approved for the organization's business purposes.

The reality is that data security has become a legal obligation. Concerns about individual privacy, accountability for financial information, the authenticity and integrity of transaction data, and the need to protect the confidentiality and security of sensitive business and client data are driving the enactment of new laws and regulations designed to ensure that all organizations adequately address the security of the information assets in their possession or under their control. Such concerns and calls for legislative responses have been fueled by the ever-increasing volume and sophistication of cyberattacks (such as phishing, ransomware, and targeting offsite vendor, client, and employee access, all amplified by organizations' shift to remote work) and the escalating injury to the public and other stakeholders of all types.

Taken as a group, data security laws and regulations impose two fundamental legal obligations on organizations:

- The duty to maintain reasonable security for their information assets; and
- The duty to notify others of security incidents and/or data breaches that occur.

All organizations (including law firms), whether regulated or not, are generally subject to these legal duties regarding the security of the information assets in their possession or under their control. The following sections will explain basic data security concepts and then analyze the sources and scope of those two legal duties.

1. Basic Data Security Concepts

1.1. What Is Data Security and What Are Its Objectives?

The general concept of "**security**" refers to the steps an entity takes to protect one or more of its **assets** (such as buildings, equipment, cargo, inventory, data, and people) from **threats**. Such steps are often called **security measures** or **security controls**.

The subset of security known as "**data security**" (also referred to as "cybersecurity" or "information security") involves implementing **security controls** to protect an organization's **information assets**. An organization's information assets generally can be divided into two categories:

- **Information.** This includes a wide variety of data, such as personal information about employees, clients and customers, prospects, and other individuals; corporate financial information; information regarding corporate business transactions; attorney-client information; trade secrets and other confidential information; electronic transaction records; and information relating to corporate communications (e.g., process control instructions and various other corporate data). Such information can take a variety of digital forms, including e-mail messages, documents, voice recordings, images, video, software, and other content in digital form.
- **Information systems.** This includes the computers, servers, databases, data stores, communication networks, network equipment, mobile devices, storage media, software, applications, firmware, and related resources that are used to acquire, store, process, manage, communicate, and transmit information. Such systems might be controlled and managed by the company; its employees or contractors where companies have a "bring your own device" (BYOD) program, allowing employees/contractors to access corporate resources from personal devices; or third-party service providers, such as vendors, cloud providers, and outsource providers (e.g., managed security services provider).

The objectives of **data security** have generally been defined as "[t]he protection of **information** and **information systems** from unauthorized access, use, disclosure, disruption, modification, or destruction in order to provide confidentiality, integrity, and availability."[2]

These objectives can be viewed both in terms of the negative consequences to be avoided and the positive results to be achieved. The negative consequences to be avoided are unauthorized access, use or processing, disclosure or transfer, disruption, modification or alteration, and loss or destruction. The positive goals to be achieved are **confidentiality, integrity,** and **availability.**

Confidentiality involves ensuring that information is not made available or disclosed to unauthorized persons or processes. In other words, information must remain secret, with access limited to appropriate persons and processes only. Confidentiality requires protecting information assets to ensure that an intruder, attacker, or any other unauthorized party or process cannot access or in any other way compromise the organization's systems or information. In some cases, it also involves protecting information so that, even if unauthorized access is obtained, the information is indecipherable or not usable (e.g., encrypted).

Integrity involves ensuring that information or information systems have not been altered or destroyed in an unauthorized manner. It requires guarding against improper

2. *Info. Tech. Lab. Comp. Sec. Resource Center Glossary*, NAT'L INST. OF STANDARDS & TECH. (NIST), https://csrc.nist.gov/glossary/term/information_security (emphasis added). *See also* NIST, Spec. Publ'n 800–53, Rev. 5, *Security and Privacy Controls for Information Systems and Organizations* 404 (Sept. 2020) [hereinafter NIST 800-53], https://nvlpubs.nist.gov/nistpubs/SpecialPublications/NIST.SP.800-53r5.pdf.

information modification or destruction, including ensuring information nonrepudiation and authenticity. Within the context of data security, integrity can be viewed from two perspectives:

- **System integrity**. This entails ensuring that the computers, other devices, networks, and software that comprise or interact with an organization's information systems operate properly and are correctly configured, and that no changes are made except as authorized.
- **Data integrity.** This entails ensuring that the information itself is accurate and complete, and that no unauthorized alterations are made to the information either intentionally or accidentally.

A compromise affecting either system integrity or data integrity could have a serious impact on the organization, depending on the nature and value of its information assets.

Availability involves ensuring that data or information is accessible and useable upon demand by an authorized person and ensuring timely and reliable access to, and use of, information. A loss of availability is the disruption of access to, or use of, information or an information system.

Availability requires that the computer systems, networks, and data are operational, fully functioning, available for use, and accessible whenever needed. This means that the computing system used to store and process information, the security controls used to protect it, and the communication channels used to access it must be functioning correctly and be able to withstand a variety of possible disruptive threats, such as power failures, natural disasters, accidents, or cyberattacks.

Availability protects against intentional or accidental attempts to deny legitimate users access to information or systems. If an organization's computer system or its information is not available, the organization likely will be seriously affected. Consider, for example, the impact of the unavailability of an airline's or hotel's reservations system or of a law firm's network and document database.[3]

1.2. What Threats and Vulnerabilities Does Data Security Address?

A **security incident** occurs whenever a threat (whether coming from inside or outside the entity) can exploit a vulnerability, resulting in a compromise of the confidentiality, integrity, or availability of a company's information assets. Thus, achieving the objectives of data security requires taking steps to protect against threats to an organization's information assets.

A **threat** is anything that has the potential to cause harm.[4] The types of threats, where they come from, what is at risk, and the seriousness of the consequences will, of course,

3. *See, e.g.*, Stephanie Stacey & Philip Georgiadis, *Delta says CrowdStrike IT outage Will Cost Airline $500mn*, FIN'L TIMES (July 31, 2024), https://www.ft.com/content/dba1cb7a-46b1-4f94-b596-432e7d899f8d.

4. *See, e.g.*, NIST 800-53, *supra* note 2, at 422.

vary greatly from one organization to another. Threats can originate inside or outside an organization; when they materialize, they typically cause damage by exploiting the organization's vulnerabilities.

Threats to the security of information and information systems can be divided into three general categories: **physical and environmental**, **technical**, and **people**.

Physical and Environmental Threats: Physical and environmental threats involve the theft, damage, destruction, or other interference with the operation of the physical elements comprising the information system (e.g., servers, laptop computers, storage media). They include:

- **Natural disasters or so-called acts of God**, such as earthquakes, hurricanes, floods, storms, tornadoes, fire, and lightning, that physically damage information systems or that interfere with their operation;
- **Infrastructure failures that cause problems**, such as power failures or fluctuations, hardware failures, water damage, and improper air conditioning, humidity, or heating; and
- **Intentional acts aimed at the physical computer system, network, or storage devices**, such as theft of equipment or storage media, criminal destruction (including vandalism or sabotage), civil disorders, terrorism, and war.

Technical Threats: Technical threats are those carried out by the use of computer code or other automated mechanisms. While such threats can sometimes cause physical damage, they most likely result in the inoperability or improper operation of information systems or networks, or the unauthorized access, acquisition, disclosure, alteration, or destruction of information. Although frequently the result of human programming activity, technical threats can be (1) **unintentional or negligent** or (2) **intentional and malicious.**

- **Unintentional or negligent technical threats** include programming errors that occur during the development of a computer system or software program, and system configuration errors, such as the use of improper settings or parameters when software is installed or the failure to change default passwords that come from the vendor when the system is installed.
- **Intentional and malicious technical threats** typically involve the use of computer code or other technical devices designed to cause trouble. Examples include software bugs intentionally added to computer programs and malicious software that modifies or destroys data, renders systems or data unusable, or engages in other mischief. Malicious software can include viruses, worms, Trojan horses, spyware programs designed to copy and transmit communications or other information, ransomware that locks up data and renders it unusable, network spoofing, denial-of-service attacks, password cracking, e-mail hijacking, packet replay, and packet modification.

People Threats: People threats come from individuals, both insiders and outsiders. Although press coverage of security incidents focuses primarily on outsiders (such as hackers) who break into an organization's computer system, more often than not the primary people threats come from insiders (such as employees, consultants, or others) who are authorized to have access to an entity's information assets.

- **Insiders.** In some cases, individuals abuse their authorization, such as when an employee who has authorized access to personal information sells some of that information to a third party or otherwise misuses the information. In other cases, however, insider-originated security incidents are the result of simple negligence, inattention, or lack of education, such as when an employee who does not understand proper procedures inadvertently clicks on a phishing email or negligently discloses confidential information by sending personal information to an unintended recipient. Unintentional mistakes or omissions by employees who are not properly trained or who are negligent, including system administrator errors, operator errors, and programming errors, are common.
- **Outsiders.** Outsiders (i.e., non-employees) often are able to compromise an organization's security through a variety of means. These include impersonation (e.g., misrepresenting their identity or source), social engineering (e.g., tricking an unsuspecting insider into clicking on a phishing email and releasing password information or otherwise allowing access or disclosing confidential information), hacking (e.g., gaining access through the use of technical tools to circumvent existing controls, such as exploiting weaknesses in software systems), or brute force attacks (e.g., continuing to guess passwords until one is successful). Additionally, phishing has long been the cornerstone of many outsiders' strategies, and with the recent technological advances in GenAI capabilities, the phishing threat is amplified, as it allows less-sophisticated outsiders the ability to conduct increasingly sophisticated phishing attacks.[5]

Threats become a problem when they can exploit a **vulnerability**, which is any flaw or weakness in a company's information systems, including deficiencies in its security controls, that could be accidentally or intentionally exploited by a threat to compromise or cause harm to its information assets.[6] A vulnerability might be an unlocked door, a system with easy-to-guess passwords, unencrypted data on a laptop computer, disgruntled employees, or employees who simply do not understand what steps they need to take to protect the security of the firm's data.

---

5. While the basic structure of phishing attacks remains the same, GenAI can increase the believability of phishing emails by accurately mimicking human language. *See* HANDBOOK, Chapter 4, *Understanding Cybersecurity Risks.*
6. *See, e.g.*, NIST 800-53, *supra* note 2, at 423.

Moreover, a vulnerability also can result from any flaw or weakness in the information systems of a third party. Because a web of security interdependencies (e.g., between an entity and its vendors) frequently exists, a failure of data security at one enterprise can be a threat to data security at another. No entity is an island when it comes to considering threats and vulnerabilities.

The likelihood that a threat will exploit a vulnerability to cause harm creates a **risk**. In other words, risk is the likelihood that something bad will happen that causes harm to an information asset. Somewhat more precisely, "[r]isk is a measure of the extent to which an entity is threatened by a potential circumstance or event, and is typically a function of: (i) the adverse impacts that would arise if the circumstance or event occurs; and (ii) the likelihood of occurrence."[7] Risk is present wherever a threat intersects with a vulnerability. For example, if the threat is theft of equipment, and the vulnerability is an unlocked door, risk is the likelihood that a thief will enter the building through the unlocked door and steal equipment or do other damage. Similarly, if the threat is a hacker, and the vulnerability is open internet access to a server containing sensitive data, risk is the likelihood that a hacker will enter the system and view, copy, alter, or destroy the sensitive data.

1.3. What Types of Security Controls Are Used to Achieve Those Objectives?

Achieving the foregoing objectives of data security involves implementing **security controls** designed to protect information assets from the various threats they face.

Security controls (sometimes called security measures or safeguards) are the various policies, procedures, organizational structures, devices, hardware, software, tools, and other means implemented by organizations to protect the confidentiality, integrity, and availability of information that is processed, stored, and transmitted by an organization.[8]

Security controls designed to protect information assets from threats generally are grouped into three separate categories based on the nature of the control: **physical, technical,** and **administrative.** Within each of these categories, security controls can be further classified based on their timing with respect to the risks and threats they are designed to address: whether they are designed to prevent the risk from occurring (**preventive**), to detect and identify the risk or compromise (**detective**), or to respond to the risk after it has occurred (**reactive**).

- **Physical security controls.** These security measures are designed to protect the tangible items that make up the physical information systems, networks, and storage devices that process, communicate, and store the data, including servers, devices used to access

7. NIST, Spec. Publ'n 800-30, Rev 1, *Guide for Conducting Risk Assessments* 6 (Sept. 2012) [hereinafter NIST Risk Assessment Guide], https://nvlpubs.nist.gov/nistpubs/legacy/sp/nistspecialpublication800-30r1.pdf.

8. *See, e.g.,* NIST 800-53, supra note 2, at 416. This NIST publication provides a good list of security controls recommended for consideration by organizations to satisfy their data security requirements. Which of those controls should be implemented, and how implementation should be addressed, are answered in the context of an organization's risk management process and the threats it faces (discussed in Section 2.3 of this chapter below).

the systems, storage devices, and the like. Physical security controls are often intended to prevent unauthorized persons from entering that environment or to help protect against environmental threats or natural disasters. Examples of the three types of physical security controls include the following:

- **Preventive:** locks, fences, security guards, double door systems, and key-card access controls.
- **Detective:** sensors and alarms, such as motion detectors, smoke and fire detectors, and closed-circuit television monitors.
- **Reactive:** sprinkler systems, locking doors, and systems designed to automatically notify the police and fire departments of a problem.

- **Technical security controls.** These security measures typically involve the use of software and data safeguards incorporated into computer hardware, software, and related devices. These measures are designed to ensure system availability, control access to systems and information, authenticate persons seeking access, protect the integrity of information communicated via, and stored on, the system, and ensure confidentiality where appropriate. Examples of the three types of technical security controls include the following:
  - **Preventive:** firewalls, access-control measures and associated password controls, smart cards and biometric tokens, antivirus/anti-malware software, intrusion prevention systems, data loss prevention tools, and encryption.
  - **Detective:** intrusion detection systems, endpoint detection and response software, logging and monitoring tools and controls, and audit trails.
  - **Reactive:** cutting off access or shutting a system down.
- **Administrative security controls.** Sometimes referred to as "procedural" or "organizational" controls, administrative security controls consist of written policies, procedures, standards, and guidelines to guide conduct, prevent unauthorized access, and provide an acceptable level of protection for computing resources and data. Administrative security measures also inform people about how to conduct day-to-day operations. Examples of the three types of administrative security controls include the following:
  - **Preventive:** procedures for proper screening of personnel before hiring, security awareness education and training for employees (e.g., phishing training), separation of duties so that no one employee can effectively compromise the system, procedures for employee termination, and requirements for appropriate supervision.
  - **Detective:** regular employee security reviews and audits and employee reporting procedures.
  - **Reactive:** appropriate discipline for employees who violate policies.

Most security statutes and regulations, either expressly or impliedly, require addressing each of these three categories of security measures—physical, technical, and administrative. For example, federal financial regulations require covered entities to "implement a comprehensive written information security program that includes administrative, technical, and physical safeguards,"[9] and numerous state security laws, such as the Massachusetts security regulations, require all businesses to "develop, implement, and maintain a comprehensive information security program that...contains administrative, technical, and physical safeguards.[10] Likewise, such safeguards are often required under comprehensive state privacy laws[11] and state laws focusing on the privacy of children or on particular types of personal information, including an individual's health or biometric information.

2. The Duty to Maintain Reasonable Security

The duty to maintain reasonable security is imposed on virtually all organizations through a variety of laws, regulations, and other legal mechanisms, including contracts. Certain sectors of the U.S. economy are, of course, subject to extensive regulations regarding data security. This typically includes critical infrastructure sectors, such as financial, healthcare, the power grid, etc. But nonregulated organizations also are subject to data security obligations from a variety of sources. While the level of detail can vary from sector to sector and across the various laws, regulations, and other legal mechanisms, the majority express the legal duty to maintain reasonable security in largely the same manner.

2.1. What Is the Duty?

Defining the scope of an organization's duty to maintain reasonable security begins with understanding that the law views security as a relative concept. Thus, the basic legal duty is often stated as an obligation to implement "**reasonable**" or "**appropriate**" security measures designed to achieve the security objectives of ensuring the **confidentiality, integrity,** and **availability** of information. For example, most states generally impose a duty to implement "*reasonable security* procedures and practices" on all organizations that collect or process personal information about their residents.[12] Likewise, numerous FTC enforcement actions since 2001 interpret the failure to provide "reasonable security" as an unfair

9. Off. of the Comptroller of the Currency (OCC), Safety and Soundness Standards, Interagency Guidelines Establishing Information Security Standards, 12 C.F.R. pt. 30, App. B, § II.A, https://www.ecfr.gov/current/title-12/chapter-I/part-30/appendix-Appendix%20B%20to%20Part%2030.

10. Standards for the Protection of Personal Information of Residents of the Commonwealth, 201 Mass. Code Regs. § 17.03(1) [hereinafter "Mass. Stds. for the Protection of Pers. Info." or "Massachusetts security regulations"] (2012), https://www.mass.gov/regulations/201-CMR-1700-standards-for-the-protection-of-personal-information-of-residents-of-the-commonwealth.

11. California led the way with the first such comprehensive law, the California Consumer Privacy Act, effective January 1, 2020. As of April 2025, nineteen other states have enacted such laws, while others are considering such legislation.

12. For a list of state security laws generally applicable to all organizations, *see* Appendix B (State Statutes) to this chapter. The duty to maintain reasonable security also can be enforced by the various state attorneys general under their unfair trade practice statutes.

business practice in violation of Section 5 of the Federal Trade Commission Act.[13] Key sector-specific regulations do the same. They include federal healthcare regulations, which require **"reasonable and appropriate"** security; federal financial sector regulations, which require security "**appropriate** to the size and complexity of the bank and the nature and scope of its activities;"[14] and state insurance laws and regulations governing security, which require implementation of **"appropriate"** security measures.[15]

To meet this standard and achieve security objectives, organizations must develop and implement a security program that includes appropriate physical, technical, and administrative security measures to protect both information and information systems from the various threats they face (discussed in Section 2.3 below). Because laws and regulations recognize that security is a relative concept, they rarely specify or provide detailed guidance regarding what specific security measures or technology an organization should implement to satisfy those legal obligations. Accordingly, determining appropriate and compliant security controls can vary depending on the situation. An increasing number of laws, however, do include specific requirements for particular security measures that must be implemented, in addition to the general requirement for reasonable security.[16] A few laws are even starting to provide safe harbors.[17]

2.2. What Is the Source of the Duty, and to Whom Does It Apply?

There is no single law, statute, or regulation that governs the obligations of organizations (including law firms) to maintain reasonable security for the information in their possession or under their control. Instead, legal obligations to implement data security measures are found in an ever-expanding patchwork of state, federal, and international laws, regulations, and enforcement actions, as well as in common-law duties and other express and implied obligations to provide "reasonable" or "appropriate" security for business data. Some cities also are starting to impose data security obligations.[18] Thus, even though certain laws might not apply to a specific organization, other laws likely would.

---

13. *See* FTC Legal Library: Cases and Proceedings, Consumer Protection—data security cases [hereinafter FTC Security Cases], https://www.ftc.gov/legal-library/browse/cases-proceedings?sort_by=field_date&field_mission%5B29%5D=29&field_consumer_protection_topics=1424 (visited May 15, 2025).

14. For a list of federal security laws and regulations governing various sectors, *see* Appendix A (Federal Statutes) and Appendix C (Federal Regulations) to this chapter.

15. *See, e.g.*, Nat'l Ass'n of Ins. Comm'rs (NAIC), Insurance Data Security Model Law (2017) [hereinafter NAIC Model Law], https://content.naic.org/sites/default/files/model-law-668.pdf, which has been adopted in 26 states as of February 1, 2025. NAIC, *State Legislative Brief: The NAIC Insurance Data Security Model Law* (Feb. 2025), https://content.naic.org/sites/default/files/government-affairs-brief-data-security-model-law.pdf.

16. For example, the Massachusetts security regulations require use of firewalls, up-to-date virus software, and, in certain cases, encryption. *See* Mass. Stds. for the Protection of Pers. Info., 201 Mass. Code Regs. §§ 17.01-17.05, www.mass.gov/ocabr/docs/idtheft/201cmr1700reg.pdf. *See also* New York's Stop Hacks and Improve Electronic Data Security Act (SHIELD) Act, N.Y. Gen. Bus. Law § 899-bb (Consol. 2024).

17. Security safe harbors are discussed in Section 2.4.4 below.

18. For example, New York City's Tenant Data Privacy Act (TDPA), enacted on May 30, 2021, regulates the collection, use, retention, and safeguarding of biometric and other data gathered in "smart access buildings," with required security measures of encryption, password reset capability (where the system uses a password),

Some laws seek to protect the organization and its owners, shareholders, investors, and business partners. Other laws focus on the interests of employees, customers, and prospects. In some cases, governmental regulatory interests or evidentiary requirements are at stake. Many of the requirements are industry-specific (e.g., focused on the financial sector or the healthcare sector) or data-specific (e.g., focused on personal information or financial data). Some laws focus only on public companies or on specific critical infrastructure sectors. When viewed as a group, however, such laws and regulations cover most business activity.

The most common sources of obligations to provide data security include the following:

Statutes and Regulations. Numerous state, federal, and international statutes and regulations impose obligations to provide data security. Sometimes they use recognizable terms, such as "security" or "safeguards," but in many cases they are more subtle, referring instead to particular attributes of security, such as "authenticate," "integrity," "confidentiality," "availability of data," and the like. Such statutes and regulations include:

- **Privacy laws and regulations**, which typically impose an obligation to provide adequate security for personal information collected, used, communicated, or stored by an organization.[19]
- **Security laws and regulations**, such as the state-level security laws that impose a general obligation on businesses to protect the security of certain personal information they maintain about individuals and/or that regulate the communication or destruction of certain data.[20]
- **E-transaction laws**, designed to ensure the enforceability and compliance of electronic documents generally. Examples include the federal Electronic Signatures in Global and National Commerce Act (E-SIGN) and the state Uniform Electronic Transactions Act (UETA, now enacted in all states but New York), which require security for storage of electronic records relating to electronic transactions.
- **Corporate governance legislation and regulations**, designed to protect public companies and their shareholders, investors, and business partners. Examples include Sarbanes-Oxley and implementing regulations, which require public companies to ensure that they have implemented appropriate information security controls for their financial information, and Securities and Exchange (SEC) regulations, which impose various requirements for internal controls over information systems.[21]

---

and regularly updated software to address security vulnerabilities. N.Y. City, N.Y., Adm. Code § 26-3005 (2021), https://legistar.council.nyc.gov/LegislationDetail.aspx?ID=4196254&GUID=29A4B0E2-4C1F-472B-AE88-AE10B5313AC1&Options=ID%7cText%7c&Search=.

19. *See* Cal. Civ. Code § 1798.100(e).

20. At least half of U.S. states have such laws. *See* Appendix B (State Statutes) to this chapter.

21. Sarbanes-Oxley Act of 2002, Pub. L. No. 107-204, §§ 302, 404; 15 U.S.C. § 7241 (corporate responsibility for financial reports) and § 7262 (management assessment of internal controls) (2025).

- **Unfair business practice laws**, at both the federal and state level, and precedent set by related government enforcement actions, such as FTC enforcement of Federal Trade Commission Act Section 5 to compel reasonable security.
- **Sector-specific regulations**, such as the security regulations focused on the healthcare, financial, insurance, defense contracting, and other critical infrastructure sectors.

Selected federal statutes are identified in Appendix A, state statutes in Appendix B, federal regulations in Appendix C, and state regulations in Appendix D to this chapter. Given the speed at which the legal landscape continues to change, counsel should check the applicable jurisdictions for the most recent laws and regulations.

Common Law Obligations. Courts increasingly accept the view that there is a common law duty to provide appropriate security for corporate and personal information, the breach of which can constitute a tort, at least in certain circumstances. In 2023, for example, the Eleventh Circuit Court of Appeals held that "while data breach cases present a 'fairly new kind of injury,' [the former employee plaintiff] has sufficiently pled the existence of a special relationship and a foreseeable risk of harm" that "traditional negligence principles are flexible enough to cover...."[22] In 2024, a federal court in California noted that "courts have generally found that a business owes a duty of care to prevent breaches of sensitive data, even when the individuals whose data is at issue are not 'customers or otherwise in privity' with the business."[23] Similarly, in 2018, a state supreme court found that the defendant, which had suffered a data breach, had a legal duty to employees "to use reasonable care to safeguard their sensitive personal data in collecting and storing it on an internet-accessible computer system." In that case, the employee-plaintiffs alleged that the employer required employees to provide sensitive data as a condition of employment and chose how to store that data; the employer's data collection and storage could foreseeably expose the employees to "unreasonable risk of harm."[24] The court held that the employer could be liable for data breaches of employee information, and that the economic loss doctrine would not bar such claims.[25] The question is unsettled, however, in many states whose highest courts have not yet decided the question of duty.[26]

Rules of Evidence. Providing appropriate security to ensure the integrity of electronic records (and the identity of the creator, sender, or signer of the record) can be critical to securing the admission of an electronic record in evidence in a dispute. This conclusion is

22. Ramirez v. Paradies Shops, LLC, 69 F. 4th 1213, 1220 (11th Cir. 2023).

23. Owens v. Smith, Gambrell & Russell Int'l, LLP, 2024 WL 3914663, at *9 (C.D. Cal. May 30, 2024).

24. Dittman v. UPMC, 196 A.3d 1036, 1047, 1056 (Pa. 2018).

25. *Id.* The court noted that "...under Pennsylvania's economic loss doctrine, recovery for purely pecuniary damages is permissible under a negligence theory provided that the plaintiff can establish the defendant's breach of a legal duty arising under common law that is independent of any duty assumed pursuant to contract." *Id.* at 1038.

26. For instance, the *Ramirez* decision follows the Georgia Supreme Court's decision in *Dept. of Labor v. McConnell*, 305 Ga. 812, 815–16 (2019), which declined to find a duty to safeguard information that would support a negligence claim.

supported by the form requirement for an "original" in electronic transaction laws,[27] the evidence rules regarding authentication,[28] and case law addressing evidentiary authentication requirements.[29]

Rules of Professional Responsibility. In addition to the legal obligations discussed here, lawyers also have ethical obligations to protect client data under the rules of professional responsibility. Such rules generally are patterned after the ABA Model Rules of Professional Conduct, which were modified in August 2012 by the ABA Commission on Ethics 20/20 to provide updated guidance regarding lawyers' use of technology and confidentiality obligations.[30] Thus, any client-related data held by a law firm is likely to be subject to ethical obligations to protect the security of that data.

Contractual Obligations. In some cases, data security regulations impose on businesses an obligation to push down certain security requirements to third parties with whom they do business. Examples include the Massachusetts security regulations,[31] the New York Department of Financial Services (NYDFS) cybersecurity regulation,[32] and the financial sector's Gramm-Leach-Bliley Act (GLB) Safeguards Rule,[33] each of which requires the regulated business to impose appropriate security obligations on third-party organizations with access to its data. In those cases, businesses frequently try to satisfy (at least in part) their obligation to oversee and protect their data by entering into contracts with third parties who will process, or have access to, their data. Contract-based security obligations are particularly common in outsourcing and cloud agreements and have become a source of data security obligations for law firms that agree to comply with security requirements imposed on them by their clients.

In other cases, businesses must contractually agree to comply with the requirements of certain technical security standards. One example is the Payment Card Industry Data Security Standard (PCI DSS),[34] to which merchants must agree as a condition of accepting credit cards.

Self-Imposed Obligations. In many cases, security obligations are self-imposed. Through statements in privacy notices, on websites, in advertising materials, or elsewhere,

---

27. *See, e.g.*, Unif. Electronic Transactions Act (UETA) § 12(d) (Unif. Law Comm'n 1999), and Electronic Signatures in Global and National Commerce Act (E-SIGN), Pub. Law. 106-299 § 101(d)(3) (2000), 15 U.S.C. § 7001(d)(3).

28. *See, e.g.*, Fed. R. Evid. 901(a).

29. *See, e.g.*, American Express v. Vinhnee (*In re* Vinhnee), 336 B.R. 437, 444–45 (B.A.P. 9th Cir. 2005); Lorraine v. Markel, 241 F.R.D. 534, 537–38 (D. Md. 2007).

30. These rules and other laws applicable specifically to lawyers are covered in Handbook, Chapter 10, *Lawyers' Professional Responsibility to Provide Data Security*.

31. Mass. Stds. for the Protection of Pers. Info., 201 Mass. Code Regs. § 17.03(f).

32. N.Y. Dep't of Fin. Servs., Cybersecurity Requirements for Financial Services Companies, N.Y. Comp. Codes R. & Regs. tit. 23, § 500.11 (2022) [hereinafter NYDFS Cybersecurity Reqs.].

33. FTC Standards for Safeguarding Customer Information, 16 C.F.R. pt. 314 (2025) [hereinafter FTC Safeguards Rules] (implementing §§ 501 and 505(b) of the Gramm-Leach-Bliley Act for customer information handling by financial institutions subject to FTC jurisdiction).

34. *See* PCI Security Standards Council, PCI Data Security Standard (PCI DSS), www.pcisecuritystandards.org (visited May 15, 2025).

organizations often make representations regarding the level of security they provide for their data, particularly personal information collected from individuals to whom the statements are made. By making such statements, organizations impose on themselves an obligation to comply with the standard they have told the public that they meet. If those statements are not true, or are misleading, they could become deceptive trade practices under Section 5 of the FTC Act or equivalent state laws.

Thus, the duty of any organization (and any law firm) to maintain reasonable security can come from several different sources and several different jurisdictions—each perhaps regulating a different aspect of the organization's information—but the net result is a general obligation to maintain reasonable security for all of the organization's information and information systems.

The duty to maintain reasonable security sometimes can be enforced by a private right of action.[35] In most cases, however, it is enforced by the applicable regulatory agency or by the FTC or the various state attorneys general (AGs). One need look no further than the last few decades of FTC enforcement actions, as well as state AG enforcement actions, to see that numerous organizations have been targeted for failing to provide appropriate data security for their own data. Targets of such enforcement actions have included a wide range of organizations, such as consumer electronics companies, data brokers, hardware and software vendors, hotels, ID theft prevention services, mobile app developers, mobile phone makers, property management firms, retailers, restaurants and entertainment establishments, social media and networking sites, technology services, transportation services, travel emergency services, transcription services, tax preparation services, virtual platforms, website operators, and many others.[36]

2.3. Requirements for Providing Legally Compliant "Reasonable Security"

Complying with the duty to provide reasonable security requires the development of what is frequently referred to as a "written comprehensive information security program." A **security program** provides a documented set of the organization's cybersecurity processes, policies, procedures, guidelines, and standards. Yet because the law treats security as a relative concept that will vary from one organization to the next, there is no standard form security program. Instead, implementing a legally compliant "reasonable" or "appropriate" data security program is a fact-specific exercise.

Nonetheless, a legal standard for the process to implement "reasonable" security continues to evolve. The standard generally rejects one-size-fits-all requirements for specific

35. *See, e.g.*, Cal. Civ. Code § 1798.150(a).

36. *See, e.g.*, FTC Security Cases, *supra* note 13; Press Release, Conn. Atty. Gen. George Jepson, AG Jepsen: Conn. Leads $18.5M Settlement with Target Corporation over 2013 Data Breach (May 23, 2017), https://portal.ct.gov/AG/Press-Releases-Archived/2017-Press-Releases/AG-Jepsen-Conn-Leads-185M-Settlement-with-Target-Corporation-over-2013-Data-Breach (linking to Assurance of Voluntary Compliance among state Attorneys General and Target Corporation resolving investigation into 2013 security incident).

security measures and instead adopts a process-based, fact-specific approach to security obligations. Nevertheless, regulators have in some cases become more prescriptive in requiring (and enforcing) certain "core" controls, such as implementing multi-factor authentication to access certain systems or using encryption protocols to protect personal information.[37] At a high level, however, "reasonable" security generally requires engaging in a repetitive "process" to:

- Establish program governance,
- Identify the information assets to be protected,
- Identity and assess the risks to those assets,
- Identify and implement appropriate security measures responsive to those risks,
- Provide training and education,
- Monitor and test the security controls to verify that they are effectively implemented,
- Oversee third-party service providers/vendors, and
- Periodically review and readjust the program to update it in response to new developments, including changes in the law or the threat environment.

This "process-oriented" legal standard for information security has been widely adopted in numerous state, federal, and international statutes and regulations, including NIST's 2023 Artificial Intelligence Risk Management Framework.[38] These steps are explained below.

2.3.1. *Establish Program Governance*

Assign Responsibility. Many data security laws and regulations recognize that someone in the organization must be responsible for security. Thus, they typically require designation of a responsible person to oversee the development and maintenance of the security program.

37. *See, e.g.*, N.Y. Dep't of Fin. Servs., Industry Letter Re: Guidance on Multi-Factor Authentication (Dec. 7, 2021), https://www.dfs.ny.gov/industry_guidance/industry_letters/il20211207_mfa_guidance.

38. NIST, Pub. AI 100-1, Artificial Intelligence Risk Management Framework (AI RMF 1.0) (Jan. 2023). *See also, e.g.*, FTC Safeguards Rule, *supra* note 33, which adopted regulations issued by federal financial regulators, *Interagency Guidelines Establishing Standards for Safeguarding Consumer Information*, issued on February 1, 2001 and codified at 12 C.F.R. pt. 30, App. B (OCC), 12 C.F.R. pt. 208, App. D-2 & 12 C.F.R. pt. 225, App. F (Federal Reserve System), & 12 C.F.R. pt. 364, App. B (FDIC) [hereinafter, collectively, GLB Safeguards Rule]; Federal Information Security Modernization Act of 2014 (FISMA), 44 U.S.C. § 3554(b); Security and Privacy regulations issued by the Department of Health and Human Services pursuant to the Health Insurance Portability and Accountability Act of 1996 (HIPAA), codified at 45 C.F.R. pt. 164 (including Standards for the Protection of Electronic Protected Health Information, 45 C.F.R. §§ 164.302-164.318); FTC Security Cases, *supra* note 13; NAIC Model Law, *supra* note 15; Mass. Stds. for the Protection of Pers. Info., 201 Mass. Code Regs. §§ 17.03; and N. Y. SHIELD Act, N.Y. Gen. Bus. Law § 899-bb & NYDFS Cybersecurity Reqs., *supra* note 32. *See also* Joint Press Release, Federal Bank and Thrift Regulatory Agencies Publish Guide to Help Financial Institutions Comply with Information Security Guidelines (Dec. 14, 2005) (attaching Interagency Guidelines Establishing Information Security Standards: Small-Entity Compliance Guide), www.federalreserve.gov/boarddocs/press/bcreg/2005/20051214/default.htm.

For example, the Massachusetts security regulations require that "every comprehensive information security program shall include ... Designating one or more employees to maintain the comprehensive information security program."[39] Likewise, the NY SHIELD Act[40] requires "designat[ion of] one or more employees to coordinate the security program." Consent decrees under Section 5 of the FTC Act typically require that the defendant "[d]esignate a qualified employee or employees to coordinate and be responsible for the Program."[41]

Ensure Management Oversight. Security laws increasingly recognize that overall responsibility for fulfilling the organization's obligation to maintain reasonable security falls directly on the board of directors (or appropriate committee of the board) or senior management. Beginning in 2001, the role of the board of directors in the development and implementation of the information security program of financial institutions was explicitly recognized in financial sector regulations. In particular, those regulations required that "the board of directors or an appropriate committee of the board" must:

- Approve the [financial] institution's written information security program; and
- Oversee the development, implementation, and maintenance of the institution's information security program, including assigning specific responsibility for its implementation and reviewing reports from management.[42]

Thereafter, similar requirements have appeared in other data security laws, regulations, standards, and best practice documents. Examples include the governance regulation issued by the NYDFS,[43] the SEC Cybersecurity Risk Management, Strategy, Governance, and Incident Disclosure Rule,[44] and the NAIC Model Law.[45]

Put It in Writing. Most of the key data security laws expressly require that the security program be in writing. In fact, numerous regulators, including the FTC, take the view that "if the security program is not in writing, it doesn't exist." Thus, virtually all of the FTC consent decrees require that the defendant's security program "must be fully documented in writing."[46] Likewise, financial regulations require covered entities to "implement

39. Mass. Stds. for the Protection of Pers. Info., 201 MASS. CODE REGS. 17.03(2)(a).

40. N.Y. SHIELD Act, N.Y. GEN. BUS. LAW § 899-bb, § 2(b)(ii)(A)(1).

41. *See, e.g.*, F.T.C. v. Rite Aid Corp., Dec. and Order ¶ III.B (Mar. 5, 2024), https://www.ftc.gov/system/files/ftc_gov/pdf/c4308riteaidmodifiedorder.pdf; Press Release, FTC, Rite Aid Banned from Using AI Facial Recognition After FTC Says Retailer Deployed Technology without Reasonable Safeguards (Dec. 19, 2023), https://www.ftc.gov/news-events/news/press-releases/2023/12/rite-aid-banned-using-ai-facial-recognition-after-ftc-says-retailer-deployed-technology-without.

42. 12 C.F.R. pt. 364, App. B, III.A.

43. NYDFS Cybersecurity Reqs., N.Y. COMP. CODES R. & REGS. tit. 23, § 500.4.

44. 88 Fed. Reg. 51,896,-51,942–944 (Aug. 4, 2023) (to be codified at 17 C.F.R. §§ 229.106(c)(1) (Reg. S-K reporting) and 249.220f (Exchange Act reporting on Form 20-F)).

45. NAIC Model Law, *supra* note 15, § 4.E.

46. *See* 16 C.F.R. §§ 314.3(a) (security program must be "written in one or more readily accessible parts") & 314.4 (identifying various security program elements to be in writing); *see also* FTC Security Cases, *supra* note 13;

a comprehensive *written* information security program," healthcare regulations require that security "policies and procedures implemented to comply with this subpart [be] in *written* (which may be electronic) form,"[47] the Massachusetts security regulations require "a comprehensive information security program that is *written*,"[48] the NYDFS regulations require that "[e]ach covered entity shall implement and maintain a *written* policy or policies,"[49] and the NAIC Model Law requires that insurers "shall develop, implement, and maintain a comprehensive *written* Information Security Program."[50] In the European Union, the General Data Protection Regulation (GDPR) privacy regulation also requires a written security policy.[51]

2.3.2. *Identify Information Assets*

To protect something, you must know what it is, where it is, how it is used, how valuable it is, and so forth. Thus, when addressing data security, the first step is to identify the organization's information assets to be protected and their location (whether inside or outside of the organization). This involves taking an inventory of the information that the organization creates, collects, receives, uses, processes, stores, and communicates to others. It also requires identifying the systems, networks, and processes by which such data is created, collected, received, used, processed, stored, and communicated.

Data files are often found in a variety of places within an organization. Data also is often found outside of the organization—more specifically, in the possession and control of a third party, such as an outsource service provider or cloud provider. Yet the organization (or law firm) generally is still responsible for the security of its (and its clients') data in the possession of third parties. Data location analysis also could require identifying in which jurisdictions (country, state or province, city) data is collected, processed, and stored, as this could affect which laws apply.

Identifying information assets is also key in identifying compliance obligations, as different data security laws and regulations could come into play depending on the specific type of information asset. This includes, for example, protected health information regulated under HIPAA, personally identifiable financial information regulated under GLB, information about children regulated under the Children's Online Privacy Protection Act

Business Guidance, FTC Safeguards Rule: What Your Business Needs to Know (Dec. 2024), https://www.ftc.gov/business-guidance/resources/ftc-safeguards-rule-what-your-business-needs-know.

47. 45 C.F.R. § 164.316(b)(1)(i) (emphasis added).

48. Mass. Standards for the Protection of Personal Info, 201 Mass. Code Regs. 17.03(1) (emphasis added).

49. NYDFS Cybersecurity Reqs., N.Y. Comp. Codes R. & Regs. tit. 23, § 500.03 (emphasis added).

50. NAIC Model Law, *supra* note 15, § 4(A) (emphasis added).

51. Regulation (EU) 2016/679 of the European Parliament and of the Council of 27 April 2016 on the protection of natural persons with regard to the processing of personal data and on the free movement of such data, and repealing Directive 95/46/EC (General Data Protection Regulation) [hereinafter GDPR], Art.30(1)(g), 30(2)(d), & 30(3).

(COPPA),[52] and other types of personal information regulated under state and local security laws, the Fair Credit Reporting Act (FCRA),[53] and Section 5 of the FTC Act.[54]

Good practice and many security laws, regulations, and guidance documents require identification of information assets. Examples can be found in guidance from the FTC,[55] NIST,[56] and the State of California.[57]

2.3.3. *Identify Risks—Conduct Periodic Risk Assessments*

Just as you cannot implement security until you identify what you have that needs to be protected, you also cannot implement security until you know what risks you need to protect against. Thus, implementing reasonable security to protect the information assets of an organization requires a thorough assessment of the potential risks to the entity's information systems and data. This has become increasingly challenging in a rapidly evolving cybersecurity threat landscape, which includes the proliferation of AI and use of AI by threat actors to launch cyberattacks. Recent studies suggest that cyber criminals have begun, and will continue, to leverage artificial intelligence to promote threat actor activities.[58]

Accordingly, most laws and regulations are risk-based and require that an organization's data security program must be based on a risk assessment. Various federal security statutes and regulations, including GLB[59] and HIPAA,[60] expressly require a risk assessment, as do almost all of the data security consent decrees entered in FTC enforcement actions.[61] Likewise, numerous state data security laws and regulations, such as in Massachusetts,[62]

52. Children's Online Privacy Protection Act of 1998 (COPPA), 15 U.S.C. §§ 6501–6506 (2025).

53. Fair Credit Reporting Act (FCRA), as amended by the Fair and Accurate Credit Transactions Act (FACTA), 15 U.S.C. §§ 1681-1681x.

54. Federal Trade Commission Act, 15 U.S.C. § 45.

55. FTC, *Protecting Personal Information: A Guide for Business* 2–5 (Oct. 2016), https://www.ftc.gov/tips-advice/business-center/guidance/protecting-personal-information-guide-business; *see also* FTC, *Start With Security: A Guide for Business; Lessons Learned from FTC Cases* (Aug. 2023), https://www.ftc.gov/system/files/ftc_gov/pdf/920a_start_with_security_en_aug2023_508_final_0.pdf.

56. NIST, The NIST Cybersecurity Framework (CSF) 2.0, (Feb. 26, 2024) [hereinafter NIST CSF], https://nvlpubs.nist.gov/nistpubs/CSWP/NIST.CSWP.29.pdf. Appendix A, the CSF Core, includes "Identify" as one of six core functions to be considered in a security program. The NIST CSF is discussed in Section 2.4.4 below.

57. *See* California Att'y Gen., *California Data Breach Report 2016* 29 (Feb. 2016) [hereafter Cal. Breach Report], https://oag.ca.gov/breachreport2016.

58. Report, National Cyber Security Centre (U.K.), The Near-Term Impact of AI on the Cyber Threat (Jan. 24, 2024), https://www.ncsc.gov.uk/report/impact-of-ai-on-cyber-threat.

59. 16 C.F.R. § 314.4(b).

60. 45 C.F.R. § 164.308(a)(1)(ii)(A).

61. *See* FTC Security Cases, supra note 13. Resulting orders and consent decrees typically require regular assessment of internal and external risks to the security, confidentiality, and integrity of covered information that could result in the unauthorized collection, maintenance, use, disclosure, misuse, loss, alteration, destruction, or other compromise of such information. *See, e.g.*, In re Marriott Int'l, Inc., FTC No. C-4807, Dec. and Order § II.D (Dec. 20, 2024), https://www.ftc.gov/system/files/ftc_gov/pdf/1923022marriottfinalorder.pdf.

62. Mass. Stds. for the Protection of Pers. Info., 201 MASS. CODE REGS. 17.03(2)(b).

New York,[63] Ohio,[64] and Oregon,[65] expressly require a risk assessment. The EU GDPR also expressly requires a risk assessment.[66]

Most other security laws impliedly require a risk assessment, typically by requiring that the company must provide a level of security "appropriate to the risk." Various security frameworks and standards, such as the NIST CSF[67] and the ISO/IEC 27001 standard,[68] also make clear that risk assessments are essential. In addition, several U.S. courts have held that a risk assessment plays a key role in determining whether a duty will be imposed and liability found. For example, one court held that where injury is foreseeable and preventable, an organization has a duty to provide appropriate security to address the potential harm.[69] Another court held that where a proper risk assessment was done and a particular harm was not reasonably foreseeable, the defendant would not be liable for failure to defend against it.[70]

A **risk assessment** is the process of identifying vulnerabilities and threats to the information assets used by the organization or firm and assessing the potential impact or harm that would result if a threat materializes. This forms the basis for determining what countermeasures (i.e., security controls), if any, should be implemented to reduce risk to an acceptable level. Thus, a risk assessment requires:

- Conducting a threat assessment to identify all reasonably foreseeable internal and external **threats** to the information assets to be protected;[71]
- Conducting a **vulnerability** assessment to identify the organization's vulnerabilities;[72]

---

63. NY SHIELD Act, N.Y. Gen. Bus. Law § 899-bb, § 2(b)(ii)(A)(2); NYDFS Cybersecurity Reqs., N.Y. Comp. Codes R. & Regs. tit. 23, § 500.02(b) & 500.09.

64. 13 OHIO REV. CODE §§ 1354.02-.03 (by reference to industry-recognized frameworks and standards that require risk assessment).

65. 16 Or Rev. Stat. § 646A.622(2)(d)(A)(ii).

66. *See* GDPR, *supra* note 51, at Recital 83 & art. 32(2).

67. NIST CFS, *supra* note 56, at 3–4 (Identify).

68. International Standard ISO/IEC 27001:2022, Information security, cybersecurity and privacy protection—Information security management systems—Requirements (3rd ed. 2022), https://www.iso.org/isoiec-27001-information-security.html. According to the International Organization for Standardization, which cosponsors the standard with the International Electrotechnical Commission, "conformity with ISO/IEC 27001 means that an organization or business has put in place a system to manage risks related to the security of data owned or handled by the company, and that this system respects all the best practices and principles enshrined in this International Standard." *Id.*

69. *See* Wolfe v. MBNA Am. Bank, 485 F.Supp.2d 874, 882 (W.D. Tenn. 2007) (holding that the bank had a duty to verify the authenticity and accuracy of an account application because injury from negligent issuance of a credit card is foreseeable and preventable). *See also* Bell v. Mich. Council 25, Am. Fed. of State, Cty. & Muni. Emps., AFL-CIO, Local 1023, Case No. 246684, 2005 Mich. App. LEXIS 353 at *4, 2005 WL 356306 at *2 (Mich. App. Feb. 15, 2005) (holding that the duty to protect against acts of a third person arises when there is a special relationship between the plaintiff and defendant, and foreseeability of harm is a factor in determining whether such a special relationship exists).

70. *See* Guin v. Brazos Higher Ed. Serv. Corp., Inc., Case No. 05-668 RHK/JSM, 2006 U.S. Dist. LEXIS 4846 at *13, 2006 WL 288482 at *4(D. Minn. Feb. 7, 2006).

71. "Threat" is defined in Section 1.2 above.

72. "Vulnerability" is defined in Section 1.2 above.

- Assessing the **risk** posed by the threats and vulnerabilities, which entails assessing the *likelihood* that each of the threats will materialize and, if so, the probability that one or more of the vulnerabilities will be exploited to cause harm;[73]
- Evaluating the potential impact or **damage** that will result; and
- Assessing the sufficiency of the security controls in place to guard against each identified threat.

The risk assessment process will be the baseline against which security controls can be selected, implemented, measured, and validated. The goal is to understand the risks that the organization faces and to determine what level of risk is acceptable in order to identify appropriate and cost-effective safeguards to combat those risks. Thus, such risks should be evaluated in light of the nature of the organization and its customer types, its transactional capabilities, the sensitivity and value of the stored information to the organization and its trading partners, and transaction volumes.[74]

Although laws typically do not specify how to do a risk assessment, the following publications provide general information and guidance on conducting one:

- NIST Special Publication 800-30, Rev. 1, Guide for Conducting Risk Assessments[75]
- Massachusetts, Small Business Guide: Formulating A Comprehensive Written Information Security Program[76]
- Massachusetts, Executive Office of Technology Services and Security (EOTSS), Information Security Risk Management Standard[77]
- Federal Financial Institutions Examination Council (FFIEC), Information Technology Examination Handbook, Information Security Booklet[78]
- NYDFS, Cybersecurity Program Template[79]

73. "Risk" is defined in Section 1.2 above.

74. *See, e.g.*, Federal Financial Institutions Examination Council (FFIEC), Authentication and Access to Financial Institution Services and Systems 5–6 (2021), https://www.ffiec.gov/sites/default/files/media/press-releases/2021/authentication-and-access-to-financial-institution-services-and-systems.pdf.

75. NIST Risk Assessment Guide, *supra* note 7.

76. *See* Mass. Off. of Consumer Aff. & Bus. Reg., Small Business Guide: Formulating A Comprehensive Written Information Security Program (undated), https://archives.lib.state.ma.us/handle/2452/685875.

77. Massachusetts Executive Off. of Tech. Serv. & Security (EOTSS), Enterprise Risk Management Office, Information Security Risk Management Standard (Mar. 19, 2025) ("The purpose of this **standard** is to define the key elements of the Commonwealth's **information** security **risk** assessment model to enable consistent identification, evaluation, response, mitigation and monitoring of **risks** facing IT processes." (emphasis in original)), https://www.mass.gov/doc/is010-information-security-risk-management-standard/download.

78. FFIEC, Information Technology Examination Handbook, Information Security Booklet (Sept. 2016), http://ithandbook.ffiec.gov/it-booklets.aspx.

79. NYDFS, Cybersecurity Program Template (May 2024), ("[a] resource to help individual licensees and individually owned businesses develop a cybersecurity program as required by New York State's Cybersecurity Regulation), https://www.dfs.ny.gov/system/files/documents/2025/02/Cybersecurity-Program-Template-05.2024.pdf.

- Cyber Security Agency of Singapore (CSA), Guide to Conducting Cybersecurity Risk Assessment for Critical Information Infrastructure[80]

2.3.4. *Develop and Implement an Appropriate Security Program to Address Identified Risks*

Following completion of the risk assessment, security laws generally require an organization to design and implement a security program consisting of reasonable physical, technical, and administrative security measures designed to manage and control the risks identified during the risk assessment with the objective of reducing the risks and vulnerabilities to a reasonable and appropriate level.

It should be noted, however, that the presence or absence of any specific security measures says little about the status of an organization's compliance with its information security obligations. The security measures implemented by an organization must respond to the particular threats it faces and address its specific vulnerabilities. Posting armed guards around a building sounds impressive as a security measure, but it is of little value if the primary threat to the organization is unauthorized remote access to its data via the internet. Likewise, firewalls and intrusion detection software are often effective ways to reasonably prevent hackers and protect sensitive databases, but if an organization's major vulnerability is careless (or malicious) employees who inadvertently (or intentionally) disclose passwords or protected information, then even sophisticated and important technical security measures will not adequately address the risk.

Most laws do not require organizations to implement specific security measures or use a particular technology, but instead provide flexibility to use measures reasonably designed to respond to the risks identified in the risk assessment to achieve the security objectives of ensuring confidentiality, integrity, and availability. This focus on flexibility means that, like the obligation to use "reasonable care" under tort law, determining compliance can be somewhat difficult. Technology and the threat landscape are dynamic; measures that are reasonable this month could be insufficient next month.

Nonetheless, for purposes of developing a security program, most statutes and regulations consistently focus on the need to address the three *types* of security controls: physical, technical, and administrative. Within those three control types, security statutes and regulations frequently focus on certain *categories* of security measures that organizations should consider, although how an organization must (or should) address each category, including which specific security controls it should implement, is typically not specified in laws or regulations. Categories of security controls most often mentioned in security statutes and regulations include:[81]

80. Cyber Security Agency of Singapore (CSA), Guide to Conducting Cybersecurity Risk Assessment for Critical Information Infrastructure (Feb. 2021), https://isomer-user-content.by.gov.sg/36/016e3838-a9e5-4c6e-a037-546e8b7ad684/Guide-to-Conducting-Cybersecurity-Risk-Assessment-for-CII.pdf.

81. *See* NIST 800-53, *supra* note 2, at ch. 3 (providing detailed information regarding these and other security control categories).

- **Physical Facility and Device Security Controls:** measures to safeguard the facility; measures to protect against destruction, loss, or damage of information due to potential environmental hazards, such as fire and water damage or technological failures; procedures that govern the receipt and removal of hardware and electronic media into and out of a facility; and procedures that govern the use and security of physical workstations.
- **Physical Access Controls:** access restrictions at buildings, computer facilities, and records storage facilities to permit access only to authorized individuals.
- **Technical Access Controls:** software, policies, and procedures to ensure that authorized persons who need access to a system have appropriate access (and no more) and that those who should not have access are prevented from getting it, including procedures to determine access authorization, grant and control access, verify that a person or entity seeking access is the one claimed (authentication), and terminate access when access is no longer needed.
- **Remote Access Controls:** measures to respond to the increased reliance on remote communications and personal devices used by employees, and to address the security of those remote devices and the communications channels being used.
- **Intrusion Detection Procedures:** software, policies, and procedures to monitor authentication attempts and report discrepancies; system monitoring and intrusion detection systems and procedures to detect actual and attempted attacks on, or intrusions into, the organization's information systems; and procedures for preventing, detecting, and reporting malicious software (e.g., antivirus software).
- **Employee Procedures:** job control procedures, segregation of duties, and background checks for employees with responsibility for, or access to, protected information, and controls to prevent employees from providing information to unauthorized individuals who could seek to obtain protected information through fraudulent means.
- **System Modification Procedures:** procedures designed to ensure that modifications to system hardware or software are authorized, appropriate, and implemented in a manner consistent with the organization's security program.
- **Data Integrity, Confidentiality, and Storage:** software and procedures to protect information from unauthorized access, alteration, disclosure, or destruction during storage or transmission, including storage of data in a format that cannot be meaningfully interpreted if accessed (encrypted) or in a location that is inaccessible to unauthorized persons and/or protected by a firewall.
- **Data Destruction and Hardware and Media Disposal:** procedures regarding final disposition of information and/or hardware on which it resides, and procedures for removal of data from media before re-use of the media.
- **Audit Controls:** maintenance of records to document repairs and modifications to the physical components of a facility related to security (walls, doors, locks, etc.), and hardware, software, and/or procedural audit control mechanisms that record and examine activity in the systems.

- **Business Continuity and Disaster Recovery Plans:** procedures designed to ensure the ability to continue operations in an emergency, such as a data backup plan, disaster recovery plan, business continuity plan, and emergency mode operation plan.
- **Incident Response Plan:** a plan for taking responsive actions if the organization suspects or detects that a security incident has occurred, including ensuring that appropriate persons are promptly notified of the breach, and that prompt action is taken in responding to the breach, including stopping further information compromise and working with incident response experts and law enforcement, and in notifying appropriate persons who could be injured by the breach. Incident response plans are often interconnected with a company's disaster recovery and business continuity plans.

Which of these (or other) categories of security controls should be addressed, and which types of security controls should be implemented in each relevant category, must be based on the risks identified in the risk assessment. From there, a determination as to which specific security controls will most effectively address those risks will depend on a variety of factors.

Traditional negligence law suggests that the relevant factors are: (1) the probability of the identified harm occurring, i.e., the likelihood that a foreseeable threat will materialize, (2) the gravity of the resulting injury if the threat does materialize, and (3) the burden of implementing adequate precautions to avoid or minimize the risk.[82] In other words, the standard of care to be exercised in any particular case depends upon the circumstances of that case and the extent of foreseeable danger. The process of determining those circumstances and evaluating the risk posed is the risk assessment.

Security laws and regulations take a similar approach and, as a group, indicate that the following factors are relevant in determining what security measures should be implemented:

- The probability and criticality of potential risks, i.e., the risk assessment;
- The size, complexity, and capabilities of the organization;
- The nature and scope of the organization's activities;
- The nature and sensitivity of the information to be protected;
- The organization's technical infrastructure, hardware, and software security capabilities;
- The state of the art of technology and security; and
- The cost of the security measures.

---

82. *See, e.g.,* United States v. Carroll Towing, 159 F.2d 169, 173 (2d Cir. 1947) (Judge Learned Hand's BPL formula, where negligence liability depends on whether B (burden) is less than P (probability) multiplied by L (loss/injury)); *see also* DCR Inc. v. Peak Alarm Co., 663 P.2d 433, 435 (Utah 1983); Glatt v. Feist, 156 N.W.2d 819, 829 (N.D. 1968) (the amount or degree of diligence necessary to constitute ordinary care varies with the facts and circumstances of each case).

Which security controls are necessary to satisfy the duty to provide reasonable security can vary widely from one organization to another, depending both on the results of each organization's risk assessment and the factors identified in the immediately preceding list. There is no one-size-fits-all approach to cybersecurity.

2.3.5. *Provide Training and Education*[83]

Training and education for employees are critical components of any security program, both practically speaking and as a legal matter. Even the very best physical, technical, and administrative security measures are of little value if employees do not understand their roles and responsibilities regarding security. For example, installing heavy-duty doors with state-of-the-art locks (whether physical or virtual) will not provide the intended protection if the employees authorized to have access leave the doors open or unlocked for unauthorized persons to pass through. Likewise, given the prevalence of phishing attacks, employees must be made aware of phishing emails and trained to recognize the lures and not click on them. Training employees is also a multifaceted process that can require a customized approach depending on the specific job role (e.g., application developers being trained on secure development lifecycle policy). Role-based training has become increasingly important for certain regulators. With more employees working remotely, it is critical to understand and address the additional security issues created by remote access and use of personal devices, and training programs should cover those workplace situations.

From a legal perspective, training can be required expressly or impliedly in various laws discussed in this chapter and also in lawyers' rules of professional responsibility.[84] In a 2018 case, for example, a federal court[85] pointed to unreasonably deficient cybersecurity training (despite known risks) in holding that an employer could be committing an intentional disclosure under the North Carolina Identity Theft Protection Act when an employee was tricked into sharing personal information of employees in response to a phishing email.[86]

Security education begins with communicating applicable security policies, procedures, standards, and guidelines to employees. Training includes implementing a security

83. Training and education are discussed in more detail in this HANDBOOK, Chapter 12, *Get SMART on Data Protection by Creating a Culture of Security Awareness*.

84. *See, e.g.*, Model Rules of Prof'l Conduct, r. 1.1 cmt. 8 (noting that lawyers should "keep abreast of changes in the law and its practice, including the benefits and risks associated with relevant technology...." to comply with their duty of competence). *See* HANDBOOK, Chapter 10, *Lawyers' Professional Responsibility to Provide Data Security*, for further discussion about the various ethical obligations implicating cybersecurity.

85. *See* Curry v. Schletter Inc., No. 1:17-cv-0001-MR-DLH, 2018 U.S. Dist. LEXIS 49442 at *5, 2018 WL 1472485 at *2 (W.D.N.C. Mar. 26, 2018) (noting that "the Defendant failed to adequately train its employees on even the most basic of cybersecurity protocols").

86. *Id.* The court noted: "As the Plaintiffs cogently set out in their brief, this was not a case of a data *breach*, wherein a hacker infiltrated the Defendant's computer systems and stole the Plaintiffs' information, but rather was a case of data *disclosure*, wherein the Defendant intentionally responded to an email request with an unencrypted file containing highly sensitive information regarding its current and former employees." *Id.* at *6 (emphasis in original).

awareness program, providing periodic security reminders, and developing and maintaining relevant employee training, such as user education on virus protection, password management, ways to detect phishing and other scams, and how and when to report discrepancies or missteps. It also is important to impose appropriate discipline when employees fail to comply with security policies and procedures.

2.3.6. *Monitor and Test the Security Controls*

Merely implementing security measures is not enough. An organization also must take steps to ensure that the security measures have been properly implemented, are effective in practice, and continue to be effective. These steps include conducting assessments of the sufficiency of the security measures in place to control the identified risks and regularly testing and monitoring the effectiveness of those measures. Existing precedent[87] also suggests that an organization must monitor compliance with its security program. To that end, regular review of records of system activity, such as audit logs, access reports, and security incident tracking reports, is vital.

2.3.7. *Review and Adjust the Security Program*

The legal standard for information security generally recognizes that security is a moving target. Organizations must continually keep up with ever-changing threats, risks, and vulnerabilities as well as the security measures available to respond to them. This requires conducting periodic internal reviews to evaluate and adjust the information security program in light of:

- The results of the testing and monitoring;
- Any material changes to the business or client arrangements;
- Any changes in technology;
- Any changes in internal or external threats;
- Any environmental or operational changes; and
- Any other circumstances that could have a material impact on the reasonableness of security procedures.

In addition to conducting periodic internal reviews, it also may be appropriate to obtain a periodic review and assessment (audit) by qualified independent third-party professionals. Such professionals use procedures and standards generally accepted in the profession to determine whether the security program meets applicable requirements and is operating with sufficient effectiveness to provide reasonable assurances that the confidentiality, integrity, and availability of information are protected. The organization should then adjust the

87. *See, e.g.*, GLB Safeguards Rule, *supra* note 38; Mass. Stds. for the Protection of Pers. Info., 201 Mass. Code Regs. 17.03(2)(h)–(j); NYDFS Cybersecurity Reqs., N.Y. Comp. Codes R. & Regs. tit. 23, §§ 500.5(b) & 500.14; GDPR, *supra* note 51, art. 32(1)(d).

security program in light of the findings or recommendations, if any, that come from such reviews.

2.3.8. *Oversee Third-Party Service Provider and Remote Worker Arrangements*

In today's business environment, companies and law firms almost always rely to some extent on third parties, such as outsourced providers and cloud providers, to handle much of their data processing and storage. Firm or client data that is in the possession or under the control of a third party presents special security challenges. Thus, it is important to address the security of the organization's data in the possession of third parties.

To that end, laws, regulations, and FTC orders imposing information security obligations on organizations often expressly address the use of third-party providers, making clear that regardless of who performs the work, the legal obligation to provide security remains with the organization engaging the third party. As it is often said, "you can outsource the work, but not the responsibility." Thus, third-party relationships should be subject to the same risk management, security, privacy, and other protection policies that would be expected if a company or firm were conducting the activities directly.

Generally, the legal standard for addressing third-party security imposes three basic requirements on organizations that outsource. They must: (1) exercise due diligence in selecting service providers, (2) contractually require third-party providers to implement appropriate security measures, and (3) monitor the performance of the third-party providers.[88]

Additionally, remote work has created a series of new data security challenges that organizations should address in their security programs. Remote work risks include, for example, lack of security on employee remote devices, insecure home Wi-Fi, unencrypted file sharing, weak passwords, and increased susceptibility to phishing. The shift to remote work also could affect an organization's ability to comply with security obligations imposed by applicable laws, regulations, and contracts, such as obligations to secure connections for remote access and manage personal devices used by remote employees.

2.4. Possible Additional Obligations

2.4.1. *Protecting Sensitive Data*

In addition to imposing a general obligation to maintain a reasonable security program, some laws and regulations require protection of specific data elements, such as Social Security numbers ("SSNs"), credit card transaction data, and other sensitive data like health status, race, religion, sexual orientation, genetic information, biometric data, and geolocation data. The various data breach notification laws (discussed in Section 3 below) have created a de facto category of sensitive information in the U.S. These laws require special

88. *See, e.g.*, Mass. Stds. for the Protection of Pers. Info., 201 MASS. CODE REGS. 17.03(2)(f).

action (notification) upon a breach of security for certain types of personal information generally considered to be sensitive because they can facilitate identity theft.

The security of SSNs has been a particular focus of state laws; virtually all states now have privacy laws covering SSNs.[89] The scope of these laws ranges from restrictions on the manner in which SSNs can be used to requirements for security when communicating or storing such numbers. For example, several states prohibit requiring an individual to transmit his or her SSN over the internet unless the connection provided is secure or the SSN is encrypted.[90] Some state statutes require credit monitoring to be provided for a certain duration where a data breach involves an SSN.[91]

Another area of focus for state regulation is biometric data, which is increasingly being used for security, authentication, and other purposes.[92] Biometric identifiers are biologically unique to the individual and, thus, highly personal; unlike SSNs, biometric data cannot be changed and, therefore, poses unique identity theft risks. Given this, the need to secure biometric data (including timely destruction) and otherwise protect it from misuse is heightened. Illinois led the way in 2008 by establishing the first biometric privacy law, the Illinois Biometric Information Privacy Act (BIPA).[93] BIPA gained high visibility years later with the filing of class action lawsuits, starting in 2015 and gaining speed since then.[94] Biometric data currently covered by the Illinois law includes retina and iris scans, fingerprints, voiceprints, and scans of hand or face geometry. (Face geometry is key in facial recognition applications.) Texas[95] and Washington[96] now have biometric identifier laws of their own. Other states include biometric data in the definition of personal information in their various security laws.[97] Biometrics-related legislation in numerous states and cities[98] across the

89. Appendix B to this chapter includes sections listing State Social Security Number Laws (B.5) and State Laws Requiring Social Security Number Policies (B.6).

90. *See, e.g.*, S.C. Code Ann. § 37-20-180(A) (restricting publication and use of Social Security numbers, including internet transmission of more than 6 digits).

91. *See, e.g.*, Del. C. tit. 6, § 12B-102(e).

92. *See* Ruth Hill Bro & Lothar Determann, *Protecting Privacy in an AI-Powered World in* Am. Bar Ass'n, Artificial Intelligence: Legal Issues, Policy, and Practical Strategies 273, 281–284 (Cynthia H Cwik, Christopher A Suarez, & Lucy L Thomson eds. 2024).

93. 740 Ill. Comp. Stat. 14/1 to 14/25 (2024).

94. For example, Facebook users filed a class action lawsuit in August 2015 against the social media giant alleging BIPA violations based on Facebook's facial recognition tagging feature. Patel v. Facebook, Inc., 932 F.3d 1264, 1268 (9th Cir. 2019), *cert. denied*, 140 S. Ct. 937 (2020). Facebook ultimately settled the BIPA claims in 2021 for a landmark $650 million. *In re* Facebook Biometric Info. Privacy Lit., 522 F. Supp. 3d 617, 620 (N.D. Cal. 2021) (also available at https://cdn.vox-cdn.com/uploads/chorus_asset/file/22333300/In_re_Facebook_Biometric_Information_Privacy_Litigation_final_order.pdf). Other multimillion dollar lawsuits have followed, including against Walmart, which has faced BIPA lawsuits on behalf of customers alleging collection and use of facial scans without knowledge and consent. *See* Anne Bucher, *Walmart Class Action Alleges Retailer Illegally Collects, Stores, Uses Customer Biometric Data*, Top Class Actions (Sept. 13, 2022), https://topclassactions.com/lawsuit-settlements/privacy/bipa/walmart-class-action-alleges-retailer-illegally-collects-stores-uses-customer-biometric-data/.

95. Tex. Bus. & Com. Code Ann. ch.503 (2017).

96. Wash. Rev. Code ch. 19.375(2024).

97. *See, e.g.*, Ariz. Rev. Stat. § 18-551(7)(a) & (11)(i) (2024).

98. *See, e.g.*, N.Y. City Admin. Code tit. 22, ch. 12 (2025).

U.S., as well as in other countries,[99] could also come into play (with corresponding security and destruction obligations). Watch this space.

For organizations that accept credit card transactions, the PCI Data Security Standard (PCI DSS)[100] imposes significant security obligations for credit card data captured as part of any credit card transaction. Organizations that accept credit cards are required to comply with the contractually binding PCI DSS, jointly created by the major credit card associations. State law obligations referencing PCI standards also could apply.[101]

2.4.2. *Encrypting Data*

Some laws and regulations impose obligations to use encryption in certain situations. Initially, these requirements included state laws that mandate encryption of SSNs for communication over the internet.[102] Now, however, several state laws prohibit electronic transmission of any personal information to a person outside the sender organization's secure system unless the information is encrypted. Most notable are the Massachusetts security regulations, which require organizations to encrypt personal information if it is stored on "laptops or other portable devices," "will travel across public networks," or will "be transmitted wirelessly."[103]

2.4.3. *Securely Destroying Data*

Several laws and regulations impose security requirements relating to the manner of data destruction.[104] Such statutes and regulations generally require organizations to properly dispose of personal information when it is no longer needed by taking reasonable measures to protect against unauthorized access to, or use of, the information in connection with its disposal. For information in paper form, this typically requires implementing and monitoring compliance with policies and procedures for burning, pulverizing, or shredding papers containing personal information so that the information cannot be read or reconstructed. For information in electronic form, such regulations typically require implementing and

---

99. *See, e.g.*, Regulation (EU) 2024/1689 of the European Parliament and of the Council of 13 June 2024 laying down harmonised rules on artificial intelligence and amending Regulations (EC) No 300/2008, (EU) No 167/2013, (EU) No 168/2013, (EU) 2018/858, (EU) 2018/1139 and (EU) 2019/2144 and Directives 2014/90/EU, (EU) 2016/797 and (EU) 2020/1828 (Artificial Intelligence Act), https://eur-lex.europa.eu/legal-content/EN/TXT/?uri=CELEX%3A32024R1689.

100. PCI Security Standards Council, Document Library, https://www.pcisecuritystandards.org/document_library (visited May 17, 2025).

101. *See* Appendix B.2 to this chapter, State Laws Imposing Obligations to Provide Security for Credit Card Information.

102. *See, e.g.*, Ariz. Rev. Stat. § 44-1373; Cal. Civ. Code § 1798.85; Conn. Gen. Stat. § 42-470 (2024), Md. Comm. Law Code Ann. § 14-3402(4) (2024). *See also* Appendix B.5 (State Social Security Number Laws) to this chapter. Many state SSN laws mandate use of encryption when transmitting SSNs.

103. *See, e.g.*, Mass. Stds. for the Protection of Pers. Info., 201 Mass. Code Regs. 17.04(3) & (5); Vt. Stat. tit. 9, § 2447(c)(3) (2024) (regulating data brokers); NYDFS Cybersecurity Reqs., N.Y. Comp. Codes R. & Regs. tit. 23, § 500.15.

104. *See* Appendix B.3 (State Data Disposal/Destruction Laws) and Appendix C.3 (Federal Data Disposal/Destruction Regulations) to this chapter.

monitoring compliance with policies and procedures for the destruction or erasure of electronic media containing consumer personal information so that it cannot be read or reconstructed.

2.4.4. *Security Frameworks—Compliance and Potential Safe Harbors*

Numerous security frameworks have been developed and recognized as models for developing an organization's security program. As noted below, compliance with several of these frameworks also has been recognized in some recent legislation as providing a safe harbor for legal requirements to implement reasonable security.

One of the most well-known security frameworks is the NIST Cybersecurity Framework ("NIST CSF"). It was developed through a collaboration between industry and government to provide a consensus description of what's needed for a comprehensive cybersecurity program. It "is designed to help organizations of all sizes and sectors—including industry, government, academia, and nonprofit—to manage and reduce their cybersecurity risks."[105]

The NIST CSF references several generally accepted domestic and international security standards, and it collates those standards into a framework of activities that arguably establishes a set of best practices for the development of a "reasonable" security program. Moreover, the NIST CSF carries the weight of being a U.S. government-issued framework that is the product of extended collaboration between industry and government to develop a voluntary "how to" guide for organizations to enhance their cybersecurity.

The NIST CSF is not industry-specific, nor is it country-specific. Most importantly, the NIST CSF is not a comprehensive information security program; instead, it assists in developing such a program. Consistent with existing law, the NIST CSF adopts a risk-based approach. As such, it fits quite well with the approach of existing legal requirements for cybersecurity obligations. It provides general process guidance and steps to address cybersecurity for all organizations. The NIST CSF is designed to complement existing business risk management and cybersecurity operations. It can serve as the foundation for a new cybersecurity program or as a mechanism for improving an existing program.

Other security frameworks often are used as a methodology to implement reasonable security in an organization. Two of the more commonly used are: (1) the ISO/IEC 27001 framework, developed by the International Organization for Standardization (ISO) and the International Electrotechnical Commission (IEC),[106] and (2) the Critical Security Controls for Effective Cyber Defense, created by the Center for Internet Security.[107]

Some of the newer state data security laws also have relied on the security frameworks as the basis for a security compliance safe harbor. By recognizing the importance and reliability of the more well-known security frameworks, these statutes provide a navigation

---

105. NIST CSF, *supra* note 56, at iv.

106. ISO/IEC 27001, *supra* note 68.

107. Center for Internet Security, CIS Critical Security Controls [hereinafter CIS Controls], https://www.cisecurity.org/controls/ (visited May 17, 2025).

map to compliance with corporate cybersecurity obligations by encouraging reliance on generally accepted security frameworks. States taking this approach include Ohio,[108] Oklahoma,[109] Utah,[110] Iowa,[111] and Connecticut.[112] These laws might provide some guidance to businesses struggling to ensure that they have implemented legally required reasonable security.

As part of their safe harbor approach, these statutes introduce two very important concepts relevant to cybersecurity compliance:

- First, an implicit recognition that compliance with selected industry norms and best practices provides legally compliant "reasonable security;" and
- Second, for organizations that follow one of the framework approaches designated in the law, a safe harbor in the form of an affirmative defense to certain actions that are brought against the organization alleging that its failure to implement reasonable information security controls resulted in a data breach concerning personal information.

To obtain the benefit of the safe harbor under these laws, a business must create, maintain, and comply with a written cybersecurity program appropriate for the business to protect the confidentiality, integrity, and availability of the information, and that program must "contain[] administrative, technical, and physical safeguards ... *that reasonably conform[] to an industry recognized cybersecurity framework*, as described in [the law]."[113] Businesses that meet these requirements are entitled to an affirmative defense to a cause of action sounding in tort that alleges that the failure to implement reasonable information security controls resulted in a data breach concerning personal information or restricted information.[114]

The "industry-recognized cybersecurity frameworks" that qualify for the safe harbor under these state laws (and to which an organization's cybersecurity program must "reasonably conform") vary by state but include some combination of the following:

- NIST CSF[115]
- NIST Special Publication 800-171, Protecting Controlled Unclassified Information in Nonfederal Systems and Organizations[116]

108. Ohio Rev. Code Ann. § 1354.03.
109. 18 Ok. Stat. §§ 2070(A)(1) & 2071 (Oklahoma Hospital Cybersecurity Protection Act of 2023).
110. Utah Code § 78B-4-703 (2021).
111. Iowa Code § 554G.3 (2025).
112. Conn. Gen Stat. § 42-901(c) (2025).
113. Ohio Rev. Code Ann. § 1354.02(A) (emphasis added).
114. *Id.* § 1354.02(D).
115. NIST CSF, *supra* note 56.
116. NIST, Spec. Publ'n 800-171, Rev. 3, Protecting Controlled Unclassified Information in Nonfederal Systems and Organizations (May 2024), https://nvlpubs.nist.gov/nistpubs/SpecialPublications/NIST.SP.800-171r3.pdf.

- NIST Special Publications 800-53, Security and Privacy Controls for Information Systems and Organizations[117] and 800-53A, Assessing Security and Privacy Controls in Information Systems and Organizations[118]
- Federal Risk and Authorization Management Program, FedRAMP® Annual Assessment Guidance[119]
- Center for Internet Security (CIS), CIS Critical Security Controls[120]
- International Organization for Standardization / International Electrotechnical Commission 27000 Family of Information Security Standards—information security management systems ISO-27000 family[121]

This statutory safe harbor approach appears to recognize that cybersecurity programs conforming to any of the foregoing guidance provide "reasonable security" and that providing "reasonable security" is an acceptable allocation of the risk of loss in the case of a breach.

The Ohio statute was the first cybersecurity law providing an express safe harbor for entities that exercise "reasonable security." It should be noted, however, that the California Attorney General issued a 2016 report setting forth what might be described as a reverse safe harbor—if you don't take certain steps, then you will be deemed *not* to have provided legally compliant reasonable security. The California Data Breach Report 2016[122] referenced the California law requirement that businesses implement "reasonable" security and noted that the CIS Controls[123] are designed to address the challenge of designing a security program and prioritizing actions to implement it. The Report went further, recommending that the CIS Controls be viewed as a minimum standard. The corollary to that recommendation is that failure to implement the CIS Controls constitutes a lack of reasonable security.

Specifically, the Report stated that:

> The 20 controls in the Center for Internet Security's Critical Security Controls identify a minimum level of information security that all organizations that collect or maintain

117. NIST, Spec. Publ'n 800-53, Rev. 5, Security and Privacy Controls for Information Systems and Organizations (Sept. 2020), https://nvlpubs.nist.gov/nistpubs/SpecialPublications/NIST.SP.800-53r5.pdf.

118. NIST, Spec. Publ'n 800-53A, Rev. 5, Assessing Security and Privacy Controls in Information Systems and Organizations (Jan. 2022), https://nvlpubs.nist.gov/nistpubs/SpecialPublications/NIST.SP.800-53Ar5.pdf.

119. FedRAMP® Annual Assessment Guidance, Ver. 3.0 (Feb. 15, 2024), https://www.fedramp.gov/assets/resources/documents/CSP_Annual_Assessment_Guidance.pdf.

120. CIS Security Controls, *supra* note 107.

121. ISO, ISO/IEC 27000 family: Information security management, https://www.iso.org/standard/iso-iec-27000-family (visited May 17, 2025).

122. Cal. Breach Report, *supra* note 57, at 27–34.

123. The CIS Critical Security Controls for Effective Cyber Defense, now known as the CIS Controls, Ver. 8.1, are available from the Center for Internet Security (CIS) at www.cisecurity.org/. The latest version of the CIS Controls, version 8.1, includes 18 controls and "updated alignment to evolving industry standards and frameworks, revised asset classes and Safeguard descriptions, as well as the addition of the "Governance" security function." The 18 CIS Critical Security Controls, https://www.cisecurity.org/controls/cis-controls-list (visited May 17, 2025).

personal information should meet. *The failure to implement all the Controls that apply to an organization's environment constitutes a lack of reasonable security.*[124]

Although this statement reflected the California AG's view at the time, and the Report is not law, an organization subject to the California security law would be well advised to consider the CIS Controls when developing its security program.

Regardless of whether any of the foregoing security frameworks are used for safe harbor compliance in the selected states, all of these frameworks provide important guidance that can be useful in developing a comprehensive written information security program.

3. The Duty to Notify of Data Breaches

Legal and regulatory requirements are not limited to obligations to **implement** security measures to protect data. All U.S. states, and most other U.S. and international jurisdictions, impose an obligation to **disclose** security incidents involving specific types of personal information (commonly referred to as a "data breach") to (1) the persons affected and (2) applicable regulators or enforcement agencies.

3.1. What Is the Source of the Duty?

All U.S. states have enacted data breach notification laws applicable to all businesses, including law firms.[125] Several federal regulatory agencies also do the same for specific sectors, including healthcare, banking, energy, telecom, and defense.[126] Many international jurisdictions have done so as well.

Breach notification laws impose an obligation similar to the common law "duty to warn" of dangers. That duty often is based on the view that a person who has superior knowledge of a danger of injury or damage to another posed by a specific hazard must warn the persons who are at risk and lack knowledge of the danger. When the security of personal information is compromised, the data subjects can be at risk of harm, such as identity theft or misuse of credentials to take over financial or other accounts. By requiring notice to the persons who might be adversely affected by a breach, the law seeks to warn them that their personal information has been compromised, providing an opportunity for those persons to take steps to self-protect against the potential harm.

In addition to applicable federal and state laws, lawyers could have additional notification obligations under the rules of professional responsibility, other law applicable specifically to lawyers, or contractual obligations to clients.

124. Cal. Breach Report, *supra* note 57, at 30.

125. *See* Appendix B.4 (State Security Breach Notification Laws) to this chapter.

126. *See* Appendix C.4 (Federal Security Breach Notification Regulations) to this chapter.

3.2. What Is the Statutory Duty?

The statutory duty, as embodied in the state and federal data breach notification laws, generally requires any organization that possesses or controls certain categories of personal information to disclose any breach of such information. The key elements of the breach notification statutes can be summarized as follows:

Covered information. Breach notification laws generally apply to unencrypted personal information. Many countries apply the notification requirements to all personal data, which generally refers to information related to an identified or identifiable natural person, but the specific definition can vary from jurisdiction to jurisdiction and from law to law. Other breach notification laws, particularly U.S. state breach laws, require notification only if the breach involves certain categories of personal information. Categories commonly included in the state breach laws are information consisting of first name or initial and last name, plus one of the following: SSN, driver's license or state ID number, or financial account number or credit or debit card number (along with any PIN or other access code where required to access the account). In some states, this list is more extensive and could include, for example: medical information, insurance policy numbers, passwords by themselves, biometric data, professional license or permit numbers, passport numbers, telecommunication access codes, account credentials, mother's maiden name, employer ID number, military identification, student identification number, electronic signatures, private key (used to authenticate or sign electronic records), and descriptions of an individual's personal characteristics.

Triggering event. The event that triggers the obligation to provide notice of a breach involving personal information is typically referred to in the breach laws as a "breach of the security of the system" or something similar. This term often includes unauthorized access to, and/or unauthorized acquisition of, "computerized data that compromises the security, confidentiality or integrity of personal information maintained by the person or business"[127] or as "a breach of security leading to the accidental or unlawful destruction, loss, alteration, unauthorised disclosure of, or access to, personal data transmitted, stored or otherwise processed."[128] Many U.S. states also recognize certain conditions that exclude a breach from being a triggering event, such as when the custodian of the exposed data determines the breach will not likely cause harm.[129] The requirements of the triggering event definition, in combination with any permitted exclusions, allow for more than one approach to determining when factors are present that impose an obligation to notify under the state breach notification statutes.

---

127. *See, e.g.*, CAL. CIVIL CODE §1798.82(g).

128. *See, e.g.*, GDPR, *supra* note 51, art. 4(12).

129. For example, Iowa's Personal Information Security Breach Protection law expressly excuses a person from the notification requirement "if, after an appropriate investigation or after consultation with the relevant federal, state, or local agencies responsible for law enforcement, the person determined that no reasonable likelihood of financial harm to the consumers whose personal information has been acquired has resulted or will result from the breach. Such a determination must be documented in writing and the documentation must be maintained for five years." IOWA CODE § 715C.2(6).

Who must be notified. Under the laws in U.S. states, notice must be given to, at a minimum, any residents of the state whose unencrypted personal information was the subject of the breach.[130] Many statutes also require notification to the state attorney general or other regulatory agency responsible for privacy and security enforcement. In some cases, notification requirements also extend to informing credit reporting agencies and the press. In the EU, under the GDPR, notice must first be given to the applicable supervisory authority;[131] if the breach is likely to result in a high risk to the rights and freedoms of individuals, notice then must be given to the individuals.

When notice must be provided. Generally, affected individuals must be notified in the most expedient time possible and without unreasonable delay. In most states, the time for notice could be extended:

- For the legitimate needs of law enforcement, if notification would impede a criminal investigation, or
- To take necessary measures to determine the scope of the breach and restore reasonable integrity to the system.

Some states specify a certain number of days by which breach notices must be given, and that deadline could be very short, e.g., 72 hours.[132]

Form of notice. Notice may be provided in writing (on paper and sent by mail), in electronic form (by email, but only in compliance with E-SIGN),[133] or by substitute notice. Substitute notice is defined by statute for circumstances when, for example, the cost of providing individual notices is greater than a certain amount (e.g., $250,000) or more than a certain number of people would have to be notified (e.g., 500,000).

3.3. When Does a Contract-Based Duty Arise?

It also is increasingly common for contracts with business partners of all types to require the recipient or processor of an organization's data to notify the organization in the event of a security incident that affects that organization's data. This trend also is being extended to law firms. Clients, particularly those in regulated industries, such as financial or healthcare, are requiring that their law firms provide prompt notice of any data breach. For example,

130. Georgia's identity theft statute applies to data brokers and state and government entities that collect personal information. Ga. Code Ann. § 10-1-911(2) & (3). The breach notification provision of that statute establishes a cascading notice requirement. Where a business maintains computerized personal information on behalf of an information broker or data collector that the business does not own, the business is required to notify the information broker or data collector, not the data subjects. The information broker or data collector must give notice to Georgia residents who are the subjects of compromised data. GA. CODE ANN. § 10-1-912.

131. GDPR, supra note 51, art. 33.

132. *See, e.g.*, GDPR, *supra* note 51, art. 33; NYDFS, Cybersecurity Reqs., N.Y. COMP. CODES R. & REGS. tit. 23, § 500.17(a).

133. Electronic Signatures in Global and National Commerce Act (E-SIGN), 15 U.S.C. §§ 7001–7006. Entities need to comply with the requisite consumer consent provisions of E-SIGN codified at 15 U.S.C. § 7001(c).

breach reporting is a key requirement of the *Model Information Protection and Security Controls for Outside Counsel Processing Company Confidential Information*, released in 2017 by the Association of Corporate Counsel (ACC).[134]

4. Practical Considerations: A Top Ten List

Organizations have many legal obligations to provide data security that arise from generally applicable law. Below is a list of practical tips regarding compliance with those obligations:

1. Identify the data in your possession or control, i.e., the data for which you are responsible, and understand where it is stored, how it can be accessed, and how it is used.
2. Determine which data (yours, client data obtained during due diligence or discovery, etc.) is subject to which laws and regulations (including special sector-specific regulations, such as GLB or HIPAA), and be sure you handle that data in accordance with any special requirements in those laws and regulations. Keep in mind that laws and regulations governing data security could apply to the data in your possession or under your control independent of ethical obligations of confidentiality specifically applicable to attorneys.
3. Conduct a risk assessment to evaluate the risks to the data for which you are responsible.
4. Develop a risk-based written information security program to protect that data against the identified risks.
5. If you use third parties to store or process the data, including providers of cloud services or outsourcing services, take appropriate steps to make sure that they adequately protect the security of the data you entrust to them.
6. On a regular basis, reevaluate the risks you face and the adequacy of your security program, and adjust the program as necessary.
7. Recognize that everyone within the organization can be a weak link, and provide appropriate training and awareness-raising reminders for everyone on an ongoing basis.
8. Develop an incident response plan, including communications strategy and ransomware playbook.
9. Keep in mind that legal compliance is not enough; reputations are easily cracked but not easily mended, and your organization can be tried in the court of public opinion for security missteps, despite compliance with applicable laws.
10. Remember that security is a process and is never complete. You must remain vigilant for new threats and new laws.

---

134. Ass'n of Corp. Counsel (ACC), Model Information Protection and Security Controls for Outside Counsel Processing Company Confidential Information § 3.2 (2017), https://www.acc.com/sites/default/files/resources/advocacy/1454057_1.pdf.

Chapter 7 Appendices

Selected Data Security Statutes and Regulations

Appendix A—Federal Statutes

COPPA: Children's Online Privacy Protection Act of 1998, 15 U.S.C. §§ 6501–6506

CFPA: Consumer Financial Protection Act of 2010, 12 U.S.C. §§ 5531(a), 5536(a)(1) (prohibits unfair, deceptive, or abusive acts or practices in connection with a transaction for, or offer of, a consumer financial product or service)

E-SIGN: Electronic Signatures in Global and National Commerce Act, 15 U.S.C. § 7001(d)

FCRA/FACTA: Fair Credit Reporting Act, as amended by the Fair and Accurate Credit Transactions Act, 15 U.S.C. §§ 1681-1681x

FISMA: Federal Information Security Modernization Act of 2014, 44 U.S.C. §§ 3551–3558

FTC Act: Federal Trade Commission Act, 15 U.S.C. § 45(a)(1) (prohibits unfair or deceptive acts or practices in or affecting commerce)

GLB Act: Gramm-Leach-Bliley Act, Pub. L. No. 106-102, §§ 501 and 505(b), 15 U.S.C. §§ 6801–6809, §§ 6821–6827

HIPAA: Health Insurance Portability and Accountability Act, 42 U.S.C. §§ 1320d-2 and 1320d-4; *see also* Subtitle D of Title XIII of the American Recovery and Reinvestment Act of 2009 (ARRA), Pub. L. No. 111-5, 123 Stat. 115, at §§ 13401–13411

Homeland Security Act of 2002 (as amended): 6 U.S.C. §§ 101-681g

Privacy Act of 1974: 5 U.S.C. § 552a

Sarbanes-Oxley Act: Pub. L. No. 107-204, §§ 302, 404; 15 U.S.C. § 7241 (corporate responsibility for financial reports) & § 7262 (management assessment of internal controls); 15 U.S.C. §§ 7211–7266

Federal Rules of Evidence 901(a); *see also* American Express v. Vinhnee (*In re* Vinhnee), 336 B.R. 437, 444–45 (B.A.P. 9th Cir. 2005); Lorraine v. Markel, 241 F.R.D. 534, 537–38 (D. Md. 2007)

Appendix B—State Statutes

1. State Laws Imposing Obligations to Provide Security for Personal Information

Alabama	Ala. Code § 8-38-3
Arkansas	Ark. Code Ann. § 4-110-104(b)
California	Cal. Civ. Code § 1798.81.5; § 1798.81.6 (credit reporting agencies); § 1798.91.04 (manufacturers of connected devices)
Colorado	Colo. Rev. Stat. § 6-1-713–713.5
Connecticut	Conn. Gen. Stat. § 42-471; § 4e-70 (state contractors); § 38a-999b (health insurers); Conn. HB 6607, Pub. Act 21-119 (An Act Incentivizing the Adoption of Cybersecurity Standards for Businesses)
Delaware	Del. Code § 12B-100
District of Columbia	D.C. Code § 28-3852.01(b)
Florida	Fla. Stat. § 501.171(2); § 282.318 (state agencies)
Illinois	815 Ill. Comp. Stat. Ann. § 530/45; 740 Ill. Comp. Stat. Ann. § 14/1 (Biometric Information Privacy Act)
Indiana	Ind. Code § 24-4.9-3-3.5(c)
Kansas	Kan. Stat. Ann. § 50-6, 139(b)
Louisiana	La. Rev. Stat. Ann. § 51:3074
Maryland	Md. Code Ann., Com. Law § 14-3503; Md. Code. Ann., State Gov't § 10-1304 (state agencies)
Massachusetts	Mass. Gen. Laws ch. 93H, § 2(a); 201 Mass. Code Regs. 17.00 *et seq.*
Minnesota	Minn. Stat. § 325M.05
Nebraska	Neb. Rev. Stat. § 87-808
Nevada	Nev. Rev. Stat. § 603A.210
New Mexico	N.M. Stat. Ann. §§ 57-12C (4), (5)
New York	N.Y. Gen. Bus. Law § 899-bb
North Carolina	N.C. Gen. Stat. § 75-64(a), (b)
Ohio	Ohio Rev. Code Ann. §§ 1354.01-.05
Oregon	Or. Rev. Stat. § 646A.622
Rhode Island	R.I. Gen. Laws § 11-49.3-2
Texas	Tex. Bus. & Com. Code Ann. § 521.052
Utah	Utah Code Ann. § 13-44-201; Utah Cybersecurity Affirmative Defense Act, Utah Code Ann. § 78B-4-701
Vermont	Vt. Stat. Ann. tit. 9, § 2447
Virginia	Va. Code Ann. § 59.1-578(A)(3)

2. State Laws Imposing Obligations to Provide Security for Credit Card Information

Minnesota	Minn. Stat. § 325E.64
Nevada	Nev. Rev. Stat. § 603A.215
Washington	Wash. Rev. Code § 19.255.010

3. State Data Disposal / Destruction Laws

Alabama	Ala. Code § 8-38-10
Alaska	Alaska Stat. §§ 45.48.500–90
Arizona	Ariz. Rev. Stat. § 44-7601
Arkansas	Ark. Code Ann. § 4-110-104(a)
California	Cal. Civ. Code § 1798.81
Colorado	Colo. Rev. Stat. § 6-1-713
Connecticut	Conn. Gen. Stat. § 42-471
Delaware	Del. Code Ann. tit. 6, §§ 5001C–4C; Del. Code Ann. tit. 19, § 736 (employers)
Florida	Fla. Stat. § 501.171(8)
Georgia	Ga. Code Ann. § 10-15-2
Hawaii	Haw. Rev. Stat. § 487R-2
Illinois	815 Ill. Comp. Stat. § 530/40 (all); § 530/30 (state agencies); 20 Ill. Comp. Stat. § 450/20 (state computers); 740 Ill. Comp. Stat. § 14/15 (Biometric Information Privacy Act)
Indiana	Ind. Code §24-4.9-3-3.5(d)
Kansas	Kan. Stat. Ann. § 50-7a03
Kentucky	Ky. Rev. Stat. Ann. § 365.725
Louisiana	La. Rev. Stat. Ann. § 51:3074(B)
Maryland	Md. Code Ann., Comm. Law § 14-3502; Md. Code Ann., State Gov't §§ 10-1301–1303 (gov't units)
Massachusetts	Mass. Gen. Laws ch. 93I, § 2
Michigan	Mich. Comp. Laws § 445.72a
Montana	Mont. Code Ann. § 30-14-1703
Nebraska	Neb. Rev. Stat. § 87-808
Nevada	Nev. Rev. Stat. § 603A.200
New Jersey	N.J. Rev. Stat. § 56:8-162
New Mexico	N.M. Stat. Ann. § 57-12C-3
New York	N.Y. Gen. Bus. Law § 399-h
North Carolina	N.C. Gen. Stat. § 75-64
Oregon	Or. Rev. Stat. § 646A.622
Puerto Rico	2014 P.R. Laws No. 234-2014
Rhode Island	R.I. Gen. Laws § 6-52-2
South Carolina	S.C. Code Ann. §§ 37-20-190, 30-2-310

Tennessee	Tenn. Code Ann. § 39-14-150(g)
Texas	Tex. Bus. & Com. Code Ann. §§ 48.102(b), 72.004, 521.052
Utah	Utah Code Ann. § 13-44-201
Vermont	Vt. Stat. Ann. tit. 9, § 2445
Washington	Wash. Rev. Code Ann. § 19.215.020
Wisconsin	Wis. Stat. § 134.97
Wyoming	Wyo. Stat. Ann. § 134.97

4. State Security Breach Notification Laws

Alabama	Ala. Code § 8-38-1
Alaska	Alaska Stat. §§ 45.48.010
Arizona	Ariz. Rev. Stat. §§ 18-552
Arkansas	Ark. Code Ann. §§ 4-110-105
California	Cal. Civ. Code § 1798.82 (person or business); Cal. Civ. Code § 1798.29 (state agencies)
Colorado	Colo. Rev. Stat. § 6-1-716
Connecticut	Conn. Gen. Stat. § 36a-701b; § 4e-70 (state contractors)
Delaware	Del. Code Ann. tit. 6, § 12B-101–104; tit. 18, § 8606 (insurers)
District of Columbia	D.C. Code §§ 28-3851–3853
Florida	Fla. Stat. § 501.171 (all); Fla. Stat. §§ 282.0041, 282.318 (state agency additional requirements)
Georgia	Ga. Code Ann. §§ 10-1-912; Ga. Code Ann. §§ 46-5-214–214 (telephone records)
Guam	9 Guam Code Ann. §§ 48.10–.80
Hawaii	Haw. Rev. Stat. § 487N-2
Idaho	Idaho Code §§ 28-51-104–107
Illinois	815 Ill. Comp. Stat. §§ 530/10
Indiana	Ind. Code § 24-4.9; § 4-1-11-1–10 (state agency)
Iowa	Iowa Code § 715C.2
Kansas	Kan. Stat. Ann. § 50-7a02
Kentucky	Ky. Rev. Stat. Ann. §§ 365.732, 61.931–934 (state)
Louisiana	La. Rev. Stat. Ann. §§ 51:3071–77; La. Admin. Code tit. 16, pt. 3, § 701 (reporting requirements)
Maine	Me. Stat. tit. 10, § 1346–50B
Maryland	Md. Code Ann., Com. Law §§ 14-3501–08; Md. Code Ann., State Gov't §§ 10-1301, 10-1305 (gov't units)
Massachusetts	Mass. Gen. Laws ch. 93H, § 3
Michigan	Mich. Comp. Laws §§ 445.63–72
Minnesota	Minn. Stat. §§ 325E.61, 325E.64, 609.891
Mississippi	Miss. Code Ann. § 75-24-29
Missouri	Mo. Rev. Stat. § 407.1500

Montana	Mont. Code Ann. §§ 30-14-1701–05; § 33-19-321 (insurance-related); §§ 2-6-1501 to -1503 (state agencies)
Nebraska	Neb. Rev. Stat. §§ 87-801–07
Nevada	Nev. Rev. Stat. §§ 603A.220, 242.183
New Hampshire	N.H. Rev. Stat. Ann. §§ 359-C:19–21; §§ 332-I:1–6 (medical records); N.H. Admin Code § 3701 (insurance)
New Jersey	N.J. Rev. Stat. § 56:8-163
New Mexico	N.M. Stat. Ann. § 57-12C-6
New York	N.Y. Gen. Bus. Law § 899-aa; N.Y. State Tech Law § 208 (state entities)
North Carolina	N.C. Gen. Stat. § 75-65
North Dakota	N.D. Cent. Code § 51-30
Ohio	Ohio Rev. Code Ann. §§ 1349.19; Ohio Rev. Code Ann. § 1347.12 (state/local agencies)
Oklahoma	Okla. Stat. tit. 24, §§ 161–66; tit. 74, § 3113.1 (state units)
Oregon	Or. Rev. Stat. §§ 646A.600–.628
Pennsylvania	73 Pa. Cons. Stat. §§ 2301–29
Puerto Rico	P.R. Laws Ann. tit. 10, §§ 4051–55
Rhode Island	R.I. Gen. Laws §§ 11-49.34
South Carolina	S.C. Code Ann. § 39-1-90; § 1-11-490 (state agencies)
South Dakota	S.D. Codified Laws § 22-40-20–26
Tennessee	Tenn. Code Ann. § 47-18-2107; § 8-4-119 (state agencies)
Texas	Tex. Bus. & Com. Code Ann. §§ 521.002, 521.053
Utah	Utah Code Ann. § 13-44-202
Vermont	Vt. Stat. Ann. tit. 9, §§ 2430, 2435
Virgin Islands (US)	V.I. Code Ann. tit. 14, § 2209 (person or business); § 2208 (gov't agencies)
Virginia	Va. Code. Ann. § 18.2-186.6; § 32.1-127.1:05 (gov't entities, medical info.)
Washington	Wash. Rev. Code § 19.255.010; § 42.56.590 (state/local agencies); Wash. Admin. Code § 284-04-625 (insurance)
West Virginia	W. Va. Code §§ 46A-2A-101–05
Wisconsin	Wis. Stat. § 134.98
Wyoming	Wyo. Stat. Ann. §§ 40-12-501–02

5. State Social Security Number Laws

Alabama	Ala. Code § 41-13-6 (gov't agencies)
Alaska	Alaska Stat. §§ 45.48.400–80
Arizona	Ariz. Rev. Stat. § 44-1373
Arkansas	Ark. Code Ann. § 4-86-107
California	Cal. Civ. Code § 1798.85; 1749.60; Cal. Fam. Code § 2024.5; Cal. Lab. Code § 226; Cal. Elec. Code § 2138.5; Cal. Gov't Code § 68107
Colorado	Colo. Rev. Stat. § 4-3-506; § 6-1-715; § 13-21-109.5; § 13-21-122; § 23-5-127; § 24-72.3-102
Connecticut	Conn. Gen. Stat. § 42-470; § 8-64b

Delaware	Del. Code Ann. tit. 6, § 12B-102; tit. 9, § 9627 (state agencies); tit. 16, § 1009A (healthcare)
Georgia	Ga. Code Ann. § 10-1-393.8
Guam	5 Guam Code Ann. §§ 32,704, 32,705
Hawaii	Haw. Rev. Stat. §§ 487J-1–4
Idaho	Idaho Code § 28-52-108(1)
Illinois	815 Ill. Comp. Stat. §§ 505/2QQ, 505/2RR
Indiana	Ind. Code § 24-4.9-2-10
Kansas	Kan. Stat. Ann. § 75-3520
Louisiana	La. Rev. Stat. Ann. §§ 17:440, 18:154, 32:409.1, 37:23, 44:11; La. Civ. Code Ann. art. 3352 § 3352
Maine	Me Stat. tit. 10, §§ 1272, 1272-B
Maryland	Md. Code Ann., Com. Law § 14-3402
Massachusetts	Mass. Gen. Laws ch. 167B, §§ 14, 22
Michigan	Mich. Comp. Laws §§ 445.81–87, 565.452, 565.49
Minnesota	Minn. Stat. § 325E.59
Mississippi	Miss. Code Ann. § 25-1-111
Missouri	Mo. Rev. Stat. § 407.1355
Montana	Mont. Code Ann. §§ 32-6-306, 30-14-1702, 30-14-1703
Nebraska	Neb. Rev. Stat. § 48-237
New Hampshire	N.H. Rev. Stat. Ann. § 382-A:9-528
New Jersey	N.J. Rev. Stat. § 56:8-164
New Mexico	N.M. Stat. Ann. §§ 57-12B-1–4
New York	N.Y. Gen. Bus. Law § 399-dd; N.Y. Lab. Law § 203-d
North Carolina	N.C. Gen. Stat. §§ 75-62, 143-64.60
North Dakota	N.D. Cent. Code §§ 39-33-01–02
Ohio	Ohio Rev. Code Ann. § 1349.17
Oklahoma	Okla. Stat. tit. 40, § 173.1
Oregon	Or. Rev. Stat. § 646A.620
Pennsylvania	74 Pa. Stat. Ann. §§ 201–04
Rhode Island	R.I. Gen. Laws §§ 6-13-17, 6-48-8
South Carolina	S.C. Code Ann. §§ 7-5-170, 30-2-310, 37-20-180
South Dakota	S.D. Codified Laws § 32-12-17.13
Tennessee	Tenn. Code Ann. § 47-18-2110
Texas	Tex. Bus. & Com. Code Ann. §§ 501.00102, 501.101–02; Tex. Elec. Code Ann. § 13.004; Tex. Bus. & Com. Code § 20.02
Utah	Utah Code Ann. §§ 13-45-301, 31A-21-110, 35A-4-312.5, 76-6-1102
Vermont	Vt. Stat. Ann. tit. 9, §§ 2440, 2430; tit. 13, § 2030
Virginia	Va. Code Ann. §§ 2.2-3808, 59.1-443.2, 24.2-416.5
Washington	Wash. Rev. Code Ann. § 19.146.205
West Virginia	W. Va. Code §§ 17E-1-11, 16-5-33, 18-2-5f
Wisconsin	Wis. Stat. § 36.32

6. State Laws Requiring SSN Policies

Connecticut	Conn. Gen. Stat. § 42-471
Maryland	Md. Code Ann., State Gov't § 10-1301(d) (state agencies; broader than just SSNs)
Massachusetts	201 Mass. Code Regs. §§ 17.01–04 (broader than just SSNs)
Michigan	Mich. Comp. Laws § 445.84
New Mexico	N.M. Stat. §§ 57-12B-2–3
New York	N.Y. Gen. Bus. Law § 399-ddd
Texas	Tex. Bus. & Com. Code Ann. §§ 501.051–53 (also covers driver's license)

Appendix C—Federal Regulations

1. Federal Regulations Imposing an Obligation to Provide Security

COPPA Regulations: 16 C.F.R. § 312.8

DHS Regulations: Electronic Signature and Storage of Form I-9, Employment Eligibility Verification, 8 C.F.R. § 274a.2 (e)–(h) (requiring an effective records security program)

Exec. Order No. 14028, Improving the Nation's Cybersecurity, 86 Fed. Reg. 93, 26633 (May 12, 2021)

FCC Order re Pretexting, *In re* Implementation of the Telecommunications Act of 1996: Telecommunications Carriers' Use of Customer Proprietary Network Information and Other Customer Information IP-Enabled Services, CC Docket No. 96-115, WC Docket No. 04-36, Apr. 2, 2007, at ¶¶ 33-36

FDA Regulations: 21 C.F.R. pt. 11

Federal Acquisition Regulations: 48 C.F.R. § 52.204-21, Basic Safeguarding of Covered Contractor Information Systems

Federal Acquisition Regulations: Defense Acquisition Regulations 48 C.F.R. § 252.204. 7012, Safeguarding Covered Defense Information and Cyber Incident Reporting

FFIEC Guidance: Authentication in an Internet Banking Environment, Oct. 12, 2005; *see also* Frequently Asked Questions on FFIEC Guidance on Authentication in an Internet Banking Environment 5 (Aug. 15, 2006) & Supplement to Authentication in an Internet Banking Environment (June 28, 2011)

GLB Security Regulations: Interagency Guidelines Establishing Standards for Safeguarding Consumer Information (to implement §§ 501 and 505(b) of the Gramm-Leach-Bliley Act), 12 C.F.R. pt. 30, Appendix B (OCC); 12 C.F.R. pt. 208, Appendix D-2 & 12 C.F.R. pt. 225, Appendix F (Federal Reserve System); 12 C.F.R. pt. 364, Appendix B (FDIC)

GLB Security Regulations (FTC): FTC Standards for Safeguarding Customer Information (Safeguards Rule) (to implement §§ 501 and 505(b) of the Gramm-Leach-Bliley Act), 16 C.F.R. pt. 314 (FTC)

HIPAA Security Regulations: HIPAA Security and Privacy Regulations, 45 C.F.R. pt. 164

IRS Regulations: Rev. Proc. 97-22, 1997-1 C.B. 652, 1997-13 I.R.B. 9, & Rev. Proc. 98-25

IRS Regulations: IRS Announcement 98-27, 1998-15 I.R.B. 30, Tax Regs. 26 C.F.R. § 1.1441-1(e)(4)(iv)

Ratification of Transportation Security Administration (TSA) Security Directive Pipeline-2021-01, 86 Fed. Reg. 136, 38,209 (July 20, 2021)

SEC Regulation S-P: 17 C.F.R. § 248

SEC Regulations: 17 C.F.R. § 240.17a-4 & 17 C.F.R. § 257.1(e)(3)

SEC Regulations: 17 C.F.R. § 248.30 (procedures to safeguard customer records and information; disposal of consumer report information (applies to any broker, dealer, and investment company, and every investment advisor registered with the SEC))

SEC Regulations: 17 C.F.R. § 242.1002 (obligations related to SCI events: upon any responsible SCI personnel having a reasonable basis to conclude that an SCI event has occurred, the SCI entity must provide the Commission with notifications pertaining to such event and regular updates until the event is resolved)

DFARS: 48 C.F.R. § 204.7300 (applies to contractors and subcontractors to safeguard covered unclassified defense information and also requires reporting of cyber incidents within 72 hours)

2. Federal Regulations Imposing Authentication Requirements Banking Know Your Customer Rules

31 C.F.R. § 1020.220, Customer Identification Programs for Banks, Savings Associations, Credit Unions, and Certain Non-Federally Regulated Banks

31 C.F.R. § 1023.220, Customer Identification Programs for Broker-Dealers

31 C.F.R. § 1026.220, Customer Identification Programs for Futures Commission Merchants and Introducing Brokers

31 C.F.R. § 1024.220, Customer Identification Programs for Mutual Funds

FCC Order re Pretexting, Apr. 2, 2007—*In re* Implementation of the Telecommunications Act of 1996: Telecommunications Carriers' Use of Customer Proprietary Network Information and Other Customer Information IP-Enabled Services, CC Docket No. 96-115, WC Docket No. 04-36, Apr. 2, 2007, ¶¶ 13-25

FFIEC Guidance: Authentication in an Internet Banking Environment (Oct. 12, 2005); *see also* Supplement to Authentication in an Internet Banking Environment

USA PATRIOT Act: 31 U.S.C. § 5318(l) ("Identification and Verification of Accountholders")

3. Federal Data Disposal / Destruction Regulations

FCRA Data Disposal Rules: 12 C.F.R. pts 334, 364

SEC Regulations: 17 C.F.R. § 248.30 (procedures to safeguard customer records and information; disposal of consumer report information—applies to any broker, dealer, and investment company, and every investment advisor registered with the SEC)

4. Federal Security Breach Notification Regulations

FCC Order re Pretexting, *In re* Implementation of the Telecommunications Act of 1996: Telecommunications Carriers' Use of Customer Proprietary Network Information and Other Customer Information IP-Enabled Services, CC Docket No. 96-115, WC Docket No. 04-36, Apr. 2, 2007, ¶¶ 26-32

GLB Security Breach Notification Rule: Interagency Guidance on Response Programs for Unauthorized Access to Customer Information and Customer Notice (Mar. 29, 2005), 12 C.F.R. pt. 30 (OCC), 12 C.F.R. pts. 208 & 225 (Federal Reserve System), 12 C.F.R. pt. 364 (FDIC), and 12 C.F.R. pts. 568 & 570 (Office of Thrift Supervision, which merged with the OCC as of July 21, 2011)

IRS Regulations: Rev. Proc. 98-25, § 8.01

HIPAA Breach Notification Rules: 45 C.F.R. §§ 164.400–414

Appendix D—State Regulations

Insurance: National Association of Insurance Commissioners, Insurance Data Security Model Law (2017) (now adopted in 26 states)

Colorado:

a. Colo. Div. of Sec., Mortgage Broker-Dealer Cybersecurity, Colo. Code Regs. § 704-1:51-4.6.1
b. Colo. Div. of Sec., Broker-Dealer Cybersecurity, Colo. Code Regs. § 704-1:51-4.8

Delaware: Del. Div. of Gaming Enf't, Data Security, 10 Del. Admin. Code § 301-13.0

Florida: Fla. Dept. of Mgmt. Servs., Information Technology Security, Fla. Admin. Code ch. 60gG-2.

Georgia: Ga. Elections Div., Standards for Security of Voter Registration System, Ga. Comp. R. & Regs. § 590-8-3.01

Maine: Maine Insurance Regulation Bulletin No. 345 (Nov. 8, 2006), Notice of Risk to Personal Data Act

Massachusetts: Standards for the Protection of Personal Information of Residents of the Commonwealth, 201 Mass. Code Regs. § 17.00

Michigan:

c. Pub. Serv. Comm'n, Security reporting, Mich. Admin. Code. R. § 460.2324
d. Pub. Serv. Comm'n, Technical Standards for Electric Service, Part 2: Records and Reports, Mich. Admin. Code. R. § 460.3205

Minnesota: Minn. Dept. of Com., Protection of Purchaser Information, Minn. R. § 2876.3055.

Mississippi: Enterprise Cloud and Offsite Hosting Security Policy, 36 Miss. Admin. Code pt. 3.

New Jersey:

e. Exec. Order No. 178 (May 20, 2015), Creation of New Jersey Cybersecurity and Communications Integration Cell (NJCCIC)
f. Exec. Order No. 44 (Nov. 1, 2018), An Order Directing the NJCCIC to Coordinate All Cybersecurity Efforts to Protect and Secure the State's Elections Infrastructure
g. N.J. Admin. Code § 5:34-5.14, Cybersecurity and Data Ownership

New York: N.Y. Dep't of Fin. Servs., Cybersecurity Requirements for Financial Services Companies, N.Y. Comp. Codes R. & Regs. tit. 23, § 500.11

Oklahoma: Okla. Dept. of Sec., Information Security and Privacy, Okla. Admin. Code §§ 660:11-7-46

Texas:

h. Fin. Comm'n of Tex., Notice of Cybersecurity Incident, 7 Tex. Admin. Code § 3.24
i. Pub. Util. Comm'n of Tex., Cybersecurity Monitor, 16 Tex. Admin. Code § 25.397
j. Tex. Dept. of Banking, Notice of Cybersecurity Incident, 7 Tex. Admin. Code § 33.30

Vermont: Vt. Sec. Div., Cybersecurity Procedures, Vt. Admin. Code § 4-4-8:7-8

Virginia: Va. Bureau of Insurance, Insurance Data Security Risk Assessment and Reporting, 14 Va. Admin. Code § 5-43

Chapter 8

What Cybersecurity Laws Govern? Applicability, Enforcement, and Compliance with Domestic and Foreign Cybersecurity Laws

Lothar Determann

In this chapter, attorneys find guidance on which domestic and foreign cybersecurity laws apply to companies, how foreign laws can be enforced, and how companies can prioritize and operationalize compliance. Organizations have to comply with myriad laws and regulations that their home countries impose, as well as those of other jurisdictions where they maintain establishments, from where they source data, goods or services, or where they otherwise do business. Cybersecurity risks and compliance obligations are global by definition, given that regulators refer to cyberspace as the "complex environment resulting from the interaction of people, software, and services on the internet using technology devices and networks connected to it."[1] This chapter sets the stage for a more detailed discussion of the types of cybersecurity obligations companies face under U.S. laws[2] as well as under foreign and international cybersecurity laws.[3]

1. Scope, Applicability, and Enforcement of Laws

National laws typically apply to persons, companies, activities, things, and places within the national territory.[4] Persons and companies in a particular jurisdiction have rights and obligations under that jurisdiction's law with respect to activities and transactions taking place within that jurisdiction. If and to what extent a jurisdiction's law applies in cases involving more than one state or country, however, is not always clear. In particular, controversies regarding cybersecurity or online privacy often concern multiple jurisdictions.

1. *Cyberspace*, Nat'l Inst. of Standards & Tech., https://csrc.nist.gov/glossary/term/cyberspace (last visited May 1, 2025).
2. *See* Handbook, Chapter 7, *Legal Obligations to Provide Data Security*.
3. *See* Handbook, Chapter 9, *Foreign and International Cybersecurity Laws*.
4. *See* Lothar Determann, California Privacy Law § 1.2.2 (5th ed. 2023).

Any company anywhere in the world that collects data from website visitors or mobile app users inevitably connects with users in many or all countries around the globe. To determine what cybersecurity laws of foreign states or countries apply and what security measures, registrations, disclosures, or other measures such laws require, one must identify what activities each foreign legislature intended to cover (by referring to general principles of statutory interpretation and conflict of law rules in each statute) and what the foreign legislature has jurisdiction to cover (by referring to jurisdictional limitations imposed by international and U.S. federal law).

1.1. (Few) Limitations on Legislative Jurisdiction Under Public International Law

Public international law—the law of nations—governs rights and obligations between countries.[5] Generally, sovereign nations retain self-governance powers and do not submit to supranational authorities that can impose laws on them. However, there are several prominent exceptions to this general rule.[6] Public international law is created through contracts between countries (also known as "treaties") and customary international law.[7] Countries create customary international law through consistent practice in recognition of a legal obligation to follow the practice.[8]

Countries tend to acknowledge that their jurisdiction to execute and adjudicate is generally limited to their own territory. That means a country must not send police, marshals, or bailiffs to enforce its laws in another country without that country's consent (*e.g.*, via judicial assistance programs).[9] But countries have not accepted any meaningful geographical limitations on their own jurisdiction to prescribe laws.[10] For example, jurisdiction under antitrust law[11] is often independent of territorial boundaries, as are violations of criminal

5. *See* James Crawford, Brownlie's Principles of Public International Law (8th ed. 2012); Lothar Determann, Kommunikationsfreiheit im Internet: Freiheitsrechte und gesetzliche Beschränkungen [Freedom of Communications on the Internet—Civil Rights and Statutory Limitations] 133–71 (1999) (original in German, provides an English summary).

6. Many nations submit jurisdiction over specific trade matters to the World Trade Organization. Similarly, many countries cede jurisdiction to the International Court of Justice over international human rights matters. Finally, the most striking example of an existing supranational legislative body is the European Union; its 27 member states have ceded jurisdiction in a variety of broadly defined areas. *See* Treaty on the Functioning of the European Union, (EN) No. 26 of Oct. 2012, art. 1, 2012 O.J. (C 326) 47. *See also* The Council of Europe Cybercrime Convention, http://conventions.coe.int/Treaty/en/Treaties/Html/185.htm; Ian Walden, *Accessing Data in the Cloud: The Long Arm of the Law Enforcement Agent*, Queen Mary School of Law Legal Studies Research Paper No. 74/2011 (10 Mar. 2011), http://papers.ssrn.com/sol3/papers.cfm?abstract_id=1781067.

7. *See* S.S. "Lotus" (*Fr. v. Turk.*), 1927 P.C.I.J. (ser. A) No. 10, at 18 (Sept. 7); Crawford, *supra* note 5, at 6.

8. *See* Crawford, *supra* note 5, at 23–24.

9. *See* S.S. "Lotus" (*Fr. v. Turk.*), 1927 P.C.I.J. (ser. A) No. 10, at 18 (Sept. 7) (The Permanent Court of International Justice stated, "[T]he first and foremost restriction imposed by international law upon a State is that—failing the existence of a permissive rule to the contrary—it may not exercise its power in any form in the territory of another State.").

10. Crawford, *supra* note 5, at 456–57 (discussing the move away from the territorial theory of jurisdiction in international law) and ch. 21 (discussing prescriptive, enforcement and adjudicative jurisdiction).

11. *See, e.g.*, Hartford Fire Ins. Co. v. California, 509 U.S. 764, 796 (1993) ("[I]t is well established . . . that the Sherman Act applies to foreign conduct that was meant to produce and did in fact produce some substantial effect in the United States.").

law.[12] Thus, it is difficult to argue or demonstrate that international law imposes meaningful limits on the legislative jurisdiction of the United States over the activities of foreign individuals or companies.[13] As a matter of comity and respect for other countries sovereignty, courts, scholars, and commentators tend to phrase this less drastically and write, for example, that a country may enact laws that apply extraterritorially concerning "conduct outside its territory that has or is intended to have a substantial effect within its territory."[14] But the "substantial effect" concept does not draw a clear line or invoke any material limitation in practice.[15]

As a matter of public international law, companies may have to comply with the cybersecurity laws of every country in the world. Many countries' laws do apply abroad, particularly national laws prohibiting unauthorized access, manipulation, or damaging of computers or data. For example, according to data protection authorities in the European Union (EU), any company anywhere in the world has to comply with EU data protection laws if it places a web cookie on the computer of an EU resident.[16] European Data protection authorities have pursued U.S. companies for alleged non-compliance with the EU General Data Protection Regulation (GDPR). The Federal Trade Commission has clarified that the U.S. federal Children's Online Privacy Protection Act (COPPA) applies to any company anywhere in the world if it collects personal data from children in the United States, and COPPA applies to U.S. companies that collect personal data from children outside the

12. *See, e.g.*, United States v. Leija-Sanchez, 602 F.3d 797 (7th Cir. 2010) (applying racketeering statute to extraterritorial conduct); United States v. Aguilar, 756 F.2d 1418 (9th Cir. 1985) (applying statute prohibiting impersonation of government official to extraterritorial conduct); United States v. Nippon Paper Indus. Co., 109 F.3d 1 (1st Cir. 1997) (applying price-fixing statute to extraterritorial conduct).

13. *See* Determann, *supra* note 5, at162; Lothar Determann & Karl T. Guttenberg, *On War and Peace in Cyberspace- Security, Privacy, Jurisdiction*, 41 Hastings Const. L.Q. 875, 888 (2014). *But see* Denis Rice, *Global Jurisdiction over Privacy, Breach of Security, and Internet Activity, in: Privacy Compliance and Litigation in California,* § 11.44 (looseleaf).

14. Restatement (Third) of Foreign Relations Law § 402 (1987).

15. Occasionally, governments criticize other governments for overbroad extraterritorial legislation. For example, in 1996, the European Community (EC) retaliated against perceived overbroad U.S. legislation imposing sanctions on Cuba, Iran, and Libya by introducing a regulation "protecting against the effects of the extraterritorial application of legislation adopted by a third country, and actions based thereon or resulting therefrom" because the EC Council believed that "by their extra-territorial application such laws, regulations and other legislative instruments violate international law." Council Regulation (EC) No 2271/96 of 22 November 1996 protecting against the effects of the extra-territorial application of legislation adopted by a third country, and actions based thereon or resulting therefrom, O.J. L 309 29.11.1996,1, http://eur-lex.europa.eu/LexUriServ/LexUriServ.do?uri=CELEX:31996R2271:EN:HTML. Based on that European regulation, companies and individuals in Europe could recover damages and invoke sanctions in European courts against companies and individuals residing abroad if the Europeans were held liable outside Europe based on extraterritorial legislation of the United States or other countries. More recently, the EU enacted a regulation to protect European companies doing business with Iran from the impact of US extraterritorial sanctions. Paradoxically, the EU regulation itself applies extraterritorially and demonstrates that the EU countries do not accept limitations on their own ability to enact extra-territorial legislation.

16. *See* WP 179, Update of Opinion 8/2010 on applicable law in light of the CJEU judgment in Google Spain, adopted December 16, 2015, at 2, http://ec.europa.eu/justice/data-protection/article-29/documentation/opinion-recommendation/files/2015/wp179_en_update.pdf, and Justice and Consumers Article 29 WP225 Guidelines on the Implementation of the Court of Justice of the European Union Judgment on "Google Spain, Inc. v. Agencia Española de Protección de Datos (AEPD and Mario Costeja González," C-131/12.

United States.[17] Also, under the U.S. federal anti-spam law, persons within and outside the United States are prohibited from sending marketing emails to U.S. email accounts and from harvesting U.S. users' email addresses from websites contrary to the applicable terms of use.[18]

1.2. Limitations on U.S. State Legislative Jurisdiction Under U.S. Federal Law

Unlike international law, U.S. federal law does limit U.S. states' jurisdiction to legislate. Similarly, EU law limits the legislative jurisdiction of EU member States. Companies should take note of such limitations because they can challenge the validity of cybersecurity laws that were enacted without proper legislative jurisdiction.

In principle, U.S. states are free to legislate on any topic. In contrast, the U.S. Congress can only legislate based on enumerated powers set forth in the United States Constitution. Cybersecurity or data security is not one of the enumerated powers. In practice, however, the U.S. Constitution (through the Supremacy Clause and the Commerce Clause) constrains states' ability to legislate on cybersecurity and privacy law by limiting the states' ability to regulate out-of-state and foreign corporations and persons. The Supremacy Clause provides that the federal Constitution—and federal laws, generally—take precedence over state laws.[19] Where state and federal law conflict, federal law preempts or displaces state law.[20]

Congress may indicate its intent to preempt state law in two ways: through a statute's express language (typically in the form of a preemption clause) or through the statute's structure and purpose.[21] Where the statute's scope indicates that Congress intended federal law to occupy the legislative field or where there is an actual conflict between state and federal law, the state law will be invalid.[22]

Moreover, where a state law presents an "obstacle to the accomplishment and execution of the full purposes and objectives" of a federal act, it violates the Supremacy Clause.[23] A state law that interferes with federal policy may be invalidated under the Supremacy Clause.

---

17. *See* Question B.7, *Complying with COPPA: Frequently Asked Questions*, Fed. Trade Comm'n, www.ftc.gov/business-guidance/resources/complying-coppa-frequently-asked-questions ("The Internet is a global medium. Do websites and online services developed and run abroad have to comply with the Rule? Foreign-based websites and online services must comply with COPPA if they are directed to children in the United States, or if they knowingly collect personal information from children in the U.S. The law's definition of 'operator' includes foreign-based websites and online services that are involved in commerce in the United States or its territories. As a related matter, U.S.-based sites and services that collect information from foreign children also are subject to COPPA.").

18. *Cf.* Controlling the Assault of Non-Solicited Pornography and Marketing Act of 2003 (CAN-SPAM Act), Pub. L. No. 108–187, § 12, 117 Stat. 2699, 2717 (amending the Telephone Consumer Protection Act to apply to "any person outside the United States if the recipient is within the United States").

19. U.S. Const. art. VI, cl. 2.

20. *See* Maryland v. Louisiana, 451 U.S. 725, 746 (1981).

21. *See* Altria Grp., Inc. v. Good, 555 U.S. 70, 76 (2008).

22. *See id.*

23. Crosby v. Nat'l Foreign Trade Council, 530 U.S. 363, 372–73 (2000) (citing *Hines v. Davidowitz*, 312 U.S. 52, 67 (1941)).

Federal laws have preempted state laws concerning a broad range of issues, including drug labeling;[24] trade restrictions with foreign countries;[25] training, testing, and licensing of hazardous waste site workers;[26] and the labeling by weight of packaged foods.[27] In a privacy enforcement action initiated by the California attorney general against Delta Air Lines, federal law—specifically, the Airline Deregulation Act—preempted the application of the California Online Privacy Protection Act (CalOPPA) to commercial airlines.[28]

The Commerce Clause imposes additional constraints on state attempts to regulate out-of-state corporations. The Commerce Clause grants Congress the authority to regulate interstate commerce and commerce with foreign nations.[29] It also prohibits states from passing legislation that improperly discriminates against or unduly burdens out-of-state commerce.[30] We often refer to this principle as the implications of the "dormant" Commerce Clause or "negative" Commerce Clause, and several rules follow from it. When a state law effectively imposes a tax only on out-of-state products, it violates the dormant Commerce Clause.[31] Where a state law provides for different treatment of in-state and out-of-state economic actors, it will be upheld only if it serves a legitimate local purpose and the state cannot achieve the purpose through available nondiscriminatory means.[32] Even if a state law does not discriminate against out-of-state businesses and attempts to advance a legitimate local public interest, it may be struck down when a court finds that the burden on interstate commerce outweighs the local benefits.[33]

The Supreme Court has invalidated state legislation under the dormant Commerce Clause on the grounds that it regulates extraterritorial corporate conduct.[34] When states attempt to regulate cyberspace, courts must consider the dormant Commerce Clause. In one early case, *American Library Association v. Pataki*, a federal district court reasoned that due to the internet's amorphous geography, state laws seeking to regulate internet communications present a high likelihood that an individual will be subject to inconsistent laws by states regulating conduct beyond their borders, which offends the dormant Commerce Clause.[35] Though many courts have followed *Pataki*, no bright-line rule makes state

---

24. *See* PLIVA Inc. v. Mensing, 564 U.S. 604 (2011).
25. *Crosby*, 530 U.S. 363.
26. Gade v. Nat'l Solid Wastes Mgmt. Ass'n, 505 U.S. 88 (1992).
27. Jones v. Rath Packing Co., 430 U.S. 519 (1977).
28. *See* Complaint, People of the State of California v. Delta Air Lines, Inc., 2012 WL 6061446 No. CGC-12-526741 (Cal. Super.); Reply Memorandum in Support of Demurrer, People of the State of California v. Delta Air Lines, Inc., available at http://www.lw.com/admin/Upload/Documents/Reply-ISO-Demurrer.pdf; Order, People of the State of California v. Delta Air Lines, Inc., 2013 WL 1951360 No. CGC-12-526741 (Cal. Super.).
29. U.S. Const. art. I, § 8, cl. 3.
30. *See* W. Lynn Creamery, Inc. v. Healy, 512 U.S. 186 (1994).
31. *See id.* at 194–98.
32. Maine v. Taylor, 477 U.S. 131, 140 (1986).
33. *See* Pike v. Bruce Church, Inc., 397 U.S. 137 (1970).
34. *See, e.g.*, Healy v. Beer Inst., Inc., 491 U.S. 324 (1989).
35. *See* American Library Ass'n v. Pataki, 969 F. Supp. 160 (S.D.N.Y. 1997).

attempts to regulate the internet *per se* invalid.[36] Accordingly, the appropriate role of states in internet governance remains uncertain. In 2002, a California appellate court upheld a narrow California anti-spam statute after applying the balancing test set forth by the U.S. Supreme Court in *Pike v. Bruce Church*.[37] A year later, in 2003, the Second Circuit stated that it is "likely that the Internet will soon be seen as falling within the class of subjects that are protected from State regulation because they 'imperatively demand ... a single uniform rule.'"[38] Given that companies collect vast amounts of personal data from residents in many states via the internet, the dormant Commerce Clause may well limit California's ability to pass data privacy laws that conflict with other states' laws. Thus, unlike international law, U.S. federal law can impose enforceable and meaningful limitations on U.S. states' ability to apply state cybersecurity laws outside their borders.[39] Attorneys should keep this in mind for situations in which a client is charged with violating state cybersecurity laws. However, in the context of routine advice on compliance requirements, companies typically assume the validity of applicable laws and try to comply with them.

1.3. Limitations on Applicability in Conflict of Law Rules

Besides being limited by public international law and higher-ranking national or regional law, cybersecurity laws, by themselves, may restrict their territorial scope. Some statutes explicitly specify whether they apply only to data, computers, or persons in a particular jurisdiction, or anyone, anywhere. For example, the California wiretap statute, California Penal Code Section 631(a), applies to communications "while the same is in transit or passing over any wire, line, or cable, or is being sent from, or received at any place **within this state**;" this statute applies to persons acting outside of California, but only concerning communications within California. California Penal Code § 637.7(a), which limits the use of radio-frequency identification devices (i.e., tracking devices), applies only to a "person or entity **in this state**;" and California Corporations Code Section 25400 makes it "unlawful for any person, directly or indirectly, **in this state**" to commit securities fraud (as defined by the statute). (Emphasis added.) These laws apply only to companies or persons in California. On the other hand, the California Online Privacy Protection Act (CalOPPA) applies to companies wherever located, because it specifies a residency limitation only with respect to data subjects. CalOPPA provides that any "operator of a commercial website or online service that collects personally identifiable information through the Internet **about individual consumers residing in California** who use or visit its commercial Web site or online service shall conspicuously post its privacy policy on its Web site...."[40]

---

36. *See* People v. Garelick, 161 Cal. App. 4th 1107 (2008).
37. *See Pike*, 397 U.S. 137; Ferguson v. Friendfinders, Inc., 94 Cal. App. 4th 1255 (Cal. Ct. App. 2002).
38. American Booksellers Found. v. Dean, 342 F.3d 96, 104 (2d Cir. 2003).
39. *See generally* Paul M. Schwartz, *Preemption and Privacy*, 118 Yale L.J. 902 (2008); Lothar Determann et al., *American Privacy Rights Act: a first glance at the US Congress's newest comprehensive privacy bill*, 6 J. Data Protection & Privacy 375 (2024).
40. Cal. Bus. & Prof. Code § 22575(a) (emphasis added).

The California Consumer Privacy Act of 2018 (CCPA) protects only California residents but requires businesses worldwide to comply, subject to a convoluted and narrow exception: "if every aspect of th[e] commercial conduct takes place wholly outside of California." The statute defines that to mean where "the business collected that information while the consumer was outside of California, no part of the sale of the consumer's personal information occurred in California, and no personal information collected while the consumer was in California is sold."[41]

It is not always clear whether a state statute applies to a specific situation. Legal issues often arise that significantly affect more than one state, and courts must determine which jurisdiction's laws govern a particular dispute. When the laws of two or more jurisdictions conflict, a body of rules dictates their ordering and resolution. We generally refer to these rules as "conflict of laws" rules. Where a statute is silent on its applicability to companies outside the state, courts look to legislative intent to determine whether the law applies to foreign corporations[42] and to general conflict of law rules.

Subject to constitutional restrictions, a court will follow a statutory directive of its own state as to the choice of law.[43] In the absence of such a directive, courts may consider several factors, including the needs of the interstate and international systems, the relevant policies of the forum, the protection of justified expectations, and the basic policies underlying the particular field of law.[44]

U.S. law has a long-standing presumption that a law does not apply extraterritorially absent legislative intent.[45] Historically, the default position was that the statutes of a state have no force beyond the state's borders.[46] Although a state has the power to "legislate concerning the rights and obligations of its citizens about transactions occurring beyond its boundaries, the presumption is that it did not intend to give its statutes any extraterritorial effect."[47] Overcoming the presumption against extraterritoriality requires a showing of legislative intent clearly expressed or reasonably inferred from the act's language or its purpose, subject matter, or history. But, in the privacy and cybersecurity arena, the default is probably the other way around, given the legislative intent to protect residents from privacy and data security threats, regardless of from where such threats emanate.[48]

41. Cal. Civ. Code §1798.145 (a)(1)(G).

42. *See, e.g.*, Greb v. Diamond Int'l Corp., 56 Cal. 4th 243 (2013) (California statute allowing dissolved corporations to be sued irrespective of the date of dissolution does not apply to out-of-state corporations); Kearney v. Salomon Smith Barney, Inc., 39 Cal. 4th 95 (2006) (California eavesdropping statute applies to out-of-state corporations that record telephone conversations originating from or made to California).

43. Restatement (Second) of Conflict of Laws § 6 (1971; rev. 1986, 1988).

44. *Id.* § 6.

45. E.E.O.C. v. Arabian Am. Oil Co., 499 U.S. 244, 248 (1991).

46. North Alaska Salmon Co. v. Pillsbury, 174 Cal. 1, 4 (1916).

47. *Id.*

48. *See* Cal. Civ. Code § 1798.81.5(a)(1) ("It is the intent of the Legislature to ensure that personal information about California residents is protected. To that end, the purpose of this section is to encourage businesses that own, license, or maintain personal information about Californians to provide reasonable security for that information.") The term "business" is defined broadly to mean any "sole proprietorship, partnership, corporation,

If a cybersecurity or privacy statute is silent on the scope of applicability, courts likely will apply the statute to companies outside of the state when the complained-of activity occurred or affected persons while within the state.[49] But, a state's cybersecurity or privacy laws would probably not be presumed to protect persons outside the state when persons outside the state intrude upon their privacy or data security.[50]

1.4. Enforceability of Laws Across Borders

Even though international law does not place meaningful limitations on a state's power to prescribe, it does place relatively clear limitations on a country's or state's power to adjudicate and enforce. A state must not send its police, judges, or other government officials to other countries to enforce its law there. Countries may choose to recognize and enforce judgments issued by foreign courts in the interest of reciprocity and comity.[51] For example, California recognizes and enforces foreign money awards (but not injunctions) under the California Uniform Foreign-Country Money Judgments Recognition Act.[52] Therefore, companies must consider their potential vulnerability to actions by any foreign government against assets and business interests that the company has in foreign countries or because their home jurisdiction recognizes court decisions of particular foreign countries. At the same time, companies may feel relatively safe regarding laws and enforcement actions originating in jurisdictions to which they do not have strong ties.

Within the United States, the federal constitution provides that each state must give full faith and credit to every other state's public acts, records, and judicial proceedings.[53] The Full Faith and Credit Clause is implemented by a federal statute, which provides that authenticated acts of the legislature, records, and judicial proceedings of any state receive

---

association, or other group, however organized and whether or not organized to operate at a profit, including a financial institution organized, chartered, or holding a license or authorization certificate under the law of this state, any other state, the United States, or of any other country, or the parent or the subsidiary of a financial institution." CAL. CIV. CODE § 1798.80.

49. *See* Reich v. Purcell, 67 Cal. 2d. 551 (1967); Travelers Ins. Co. v. Work. Comp. App. Bd., 68 Cal. 2d 7 (1967); Hurtado v. Superior Court, 11 Cal. 3d 574 (1974); Kearney v. Salomon Smith Barney, Inc., 39 Cal. 4th 95 (2006).

50. *See* Speyer v. Avis Rent a Car Sys., Inc., 415 F. Supp. 2d 1090, 1095–97 (S.D. Cal. 2005) (finding that California's unfair competition law did not apply to rental car transactions conducted by California residents while they were out of the state).

51. *See* Joel R. Paul, *Comity in International Law*, 32 HARV. INT'L L.J. 1 (1991) and Rice, *supra* note 13, §§ 11.73–80 (examples of foreign countries' laws and policies addressing the enforcement of judgments taken by courts in California and other U.S. States).

52. There are currently no treaties between the United States and other countries guaranteeing the recognition or enforcement of judgments. *See* Rice, *supra* note 13, § 11.70-1; Yahoo! Inc. v. La Ligue contre Le Racisme et L'Antisemitisme, 433 F.3d 1199, 1213 (9th Cir. 2006); Lothar Determann & Saralyn Ang-Olson, *What Else is New? Comment on Yahoo!, Inc. v. La Ligue Contre Le Racisme et L'Antisemitisme*, INTELL. PROP. L. BULL., U. OF S.F. SCH. OF L. (2002); Lothar Determann & Saralyn Ang-Olson, *Recognition and Enforcement of Foreign Injunctions in the United States—Yahoo!, Inc. v. La Ligue contre Le Racisme et L'Antisemitisme—influential precedent for the freedom of speech on the internet or routine confirmation of long established principles regarding equitable relief?*, COMP. L. REV. INTERNAT'L at 12 (2002), republished in: Corporate Counsel's International Advisor (Aug. 1, 2004).

53. U.S. CONST. art. IV, § 1.

the same full faith and credit in every court within the United States as they have by law or usage in the courts where they originate.[54] A state must extend full faith and credit to a judgment rendered by another state's court or agency even if the action or proceeding resulting in the judgment could not have been brought under the law or policy of the state applying the decision.[55] Many California privacy laws apply to companies in other states and countries, but a company subject to a California privacy law is not automatically subject to the jurisdiction of California courts.[56]

1.5. Summary

Companies can be subject to the cybersecurity laws of every country in the world because cyberspace is by definition global. Countries may legislate extra-territorially under public international laws. Many countries legislate to protect their citizens from foreign threats to privacy and security and to prohibit persons on their territory from threatening privacy or security abroad. Companies may have the ability to challenge the validity of particular cybersecurity laws based on preemption or lack of legislative jurisdiction within regional or national legal systems, but practically not based on public international law. Companies can nevertheless prioritize their compliance efforts because not all laws can be or are enforced equally and for other practical reasons further discussed in Section 2 of this chapter. Also, some legislatures apply self-restraint in conflict of law rules and scope definitions within cybersecurity laws, as further discussed in Section 3 of this chapter.

2. Practical Considerations Regarding Prioritization of Applicability Analysis and Compliance

For reasons explained in Section 1 of this chapter, thousands of laws worldwide address cybersecurity and data privacy in one way or another. Even very large and compliance-oriented companies struggle to keep up to date. Smaller organizations have to establish priorities and a system to ensure their compliance with key requirements—even if they cannot identify each law in detail.

Typically, countries apply their laws to companies incorporated or registered in their territory or that deploy employees or equipment there. Some countries go further and apply their data- and cyber-related laws to companies abroad, for example, if such companies collect data remotely via targeted websites (as indicated by country-specific URLs, languages, localized content, or local phone numbers) or even just on the basis that the foreign

54. *See* 28 U.S.C.A. § 1738.

55. Baker by Thomas v. Gen. Motors Corp., 522 U.S. 222, 232 (1998) ("In numerous cases this Court has held that credit must be given to the judgment of another state although the forum would not be required to entertain the suit on which the judgment was founded." (quoting *Milwaukee Cnty. v. M.E. White Co.*, 296 U.S. 268, 277 (1935))).

56. For a discussion of personal jurisdiction in privacy litigation, *see* Rice, *supra* note 13, § 11.

company collects data on residents of the legislating country. Internet service providers, multinational enterprises, and many other companies with more or less direct business connections to other countries find that countries' privacy laws apply to some of their data processing activities. However, many companies with a domestic focus can rule out most countries' laws because they are not permitted or able to do business in other jurisdictions due to regulatory restrictions (*e.g.*, local banks or hospitals) or resource limitations (*e.g.*, local construction companies).

If one applies the above considerations and ends up with a shortlist of jurisdictions that remains too long, one can prioritize further by identifying the countries where the company needs to pay particular attention to enforcement. Concerns tend to be greater regarding countries where a business maintains a subsidiary, employees, key assets, or key customers or where regulators are particularly active. Aside from business concerns, one should also consider where compliance is particularly easy (*e.g.*, no language hurdles, similar legal system to one's home jurisdiction). Based on such practical considerations, most companies can come up with a manageable shortlist of priority jurisdictions whose laws have particular relevance that company.

For each jurisdiction on the shortlist, companies must consider a variety of laws and regulations that may contain requirements pertaining to cybersecurity, including the following:

- statutory obligations under data privacy, data protection, data security, product safety, corporate securities, employment, consumer protection, and unfair competition laws, as well as constitutional safeguards, which apply directly to companies in some jurisdictions;
- contractual obligations (for example, regarding data security standards and breach notifications by reference in contract terms); and
- promises extended previously to data subjects in privacy policies, notices, advertisements, and terms of use.

Under most laws and contracts, companies must maintain reasonable technical, organizational, and administrative security measures (also known as "TOMs") to protect confidential data against unauthorized access and dissemination. Security requirements also follow from trade secret laws and confidentiality agreements and extend beyond personal data. In the interest of operational efficiency, companies should design, implement, document, and audit their data security measures with data privacy, security, trade secrets, and confidentiality protection requirements in mind. It typically serves both parties' interests when companies share personal data, trade secrets, or confidential information,—discloser and recipient—to agree on a detailed description of TOMs, responsibilities, and risk-allocation in case of a security breach. If companies agree merely on "reasonable" data security measures or "the same measures that they apply with respect to their own data," they risk misalignment of their expectations as well as uncertainty and adversity in case the data recipient suffers a security breach, and companies are then charged with failure to maintain reasonable security measures. Concerning such substantive requirements to keep data secure, companies should comply with the highest applicable standards across jurisdictions.[57]

Additionally, companies must disclose security incidents to affected individuals, corporate customers, and regulators under various laws, which vary substantially across jurisdictions and require localized responses in terms of language, disclosures, timelines, and other details. After California enacted the world's first data security breach notification law in 2002,[58] companies started reporting security breaches *en masse*, and more and more jurisdictions passed data security breach notification laws.[59] Companies are required to designate local representatives and proactively register under the NIS 2 Directive in the European Union and report significant cyber incidents to cybersecurity authorities in addition to reporting personal data breaches to data protection authorities. While substantive details of such obligations will be examined in more detail in other chapters of this Cybersecurity Handbook,[60] Section 3 of this chapter will examine the scope of applicability of such registration, representative designation, and reporting obligations.

3. Scope Definitions in Key Cybersecurity Laws

3.1. GDPR

Under the EU's General Data Protection Regulation ("GDPR"), companies established in the EU or collecting personal data in the context of providing goods or services to data subjects in the EU[61] must implement appropriate data protection measures.[62] They also have to notify authorities and individuals of "personal data breaches," broadly defined as a breach of security leading to the accidental or unlawful destruction, loss, alteration, unauthorized disclosure of, or access to, personal data transmitted, stored, or otherwise processed.[63]

---

57. Lothar Determann, Determann's Field Guide to Data Privacy Law, ch.1, ¶ 140 et. seq. (6th Ed., 2025).

58. Cal. Civ. Code § 1798.29.

59. *See, e.g.*, GDPR, arts. 33 & 34.

60. *See, e.g.*, Handbook, Chapter 7, *Legal Obligations to Provide Data Security*.

61. Regulation (EU) 2016/679 of the European Parliament and of the Council of 27 April 2016 on the protection of natural persons with regard to the processing of personal data and on the free movement of such data and repealing Directive 95/46/EC (General Data Protection Regulation) [hereinafter GDPR]; Koloß: The GDPR's Extra Territorial Scope, ZaöRV, 791, 796 (2020).

62. GDPR, art. 24(2).

63. GDPR, art. 4(12).

3.1.1. *Establishment*

Companies are subject to the GDPR when they process data in the context of an establishment in the EU,[64] i.e., the effective and real exercise of activity through stable arrangements.[65] Companies can have sufficiently stable arrangements when one employee acts for the company within the Union with a certain degree of stability.[66] The Court of Justice of the European Union ("CJEU") has broadened the term "establishment" and departed from a formalistic approach. A company establishes itself by exercising real and effective activity, even minimal, through stable arrangements.[67] Companies cannot agree in contracts whether they are established in the EU because this determination depends on objective criteria.[68]

As an example, a car manufacturing company with headquarters in China has a fully owned branch office located in Brussels overseeing all its operations in Europe, including marketing and advertisement. The Belgian branch can be considered to be a stable arrangement, which exercises real and effective activities in light of the nature of the economic activity carried out by the car manufacturing company. Therefore, the Belgian branch could be considered an establishment in the Union, within the meaning of the GDPR.[69]

On the other hand, a company based in the United States that operates an e-commerce website to sell software to users worldwide may not need or have an establishment in the EU. But, if the company establishes a subsidiary in Berlin to lead and implement commercial marketing campaigns towards EU markets, it is possible that not only the Berlin-based subsidiary is established in the EU, but also its US-based parent company, if the activities of the European office in Berlin are inextricably linked to the processing of personal data carried out by the US parent company and its processing activities can therefore be considered as carried out in the context of the activities of the Berlin-based subsidiary.[70]

---

64. GDPR, art. 3(1).

65. GDPR, Recital 22.

66. *See* European Data Protection Bd., Guidelines 3/2018 on the territorial scope of the GDPR (Article 3) (ver. 2.1 Nov. 12, 2019) at 6 [hereinafter GDPR Territorial Scope Guidelines], www.edpb.europa.eu/sites/default/files/files/file1/edpb_guidelines_3_2018_territorial_scope_after_public_consultation_en_1.pdf.

67. *Id.*

68. GDPR, Recital 36; European Data Protection Bd., Opinion 04/2024 on the notion of main establishment of a controller in the Union under Article 4(16)(a) GDPR (Feb. 13, 2024), www.edpb.europa.eu/system/files/2024-02/edpb_opinion_202404_mainestablishment_en.pdf.

69. *See* GDPR Territorial Scope Guidelines, *supra* note 66, at 7.

70. *See id.* at 8. This has been the subject of the CJEU Decision in the case of *Google Spain SL & Google Inc. v. Agencia Enspañola de Protección de Datos.* In 2014, Google was asked to delist search results on an EU citizen. Google was of the opinion that Google Inc. was not under the jurisdiction of the EU privacy laws in place at that time as Google Spain only carried out advertisement and administrative work and, therefore, the search engine itself was not subject to the EU laws. The CJEU held that data processing by entities outside the EU is subject to protection laws when it involves means located within EU Member States. This was the case as Google Inc. and Google Spain were "inextricably linked" since the activities in Spain rendered Google economically profitable. This case established that EU data protection laws are applicable if data connected to EU individuals is processed. *Google Spain SL & Google Inc. v. Agencia Enspañola de Protección de Datos*, ECJ C-131/12.

3.1.2. *Advantages of Establishment in the EU*

Under European Union law, member states generally may not apply their national data privacy laws and other laws extraterritorially to companies in different member states.[71] This is intended to make it easier for companies based in the European Economic Area (EEA) to do business everywhere in the Common Market.[72] An EEA-based controller has to comply only with the national laws of the EEA member state where it maintains a branch or other significant physical presence, even if it collects data from other EEA member states (over the internet or otherwise).[73] This privilege is not available to companies outside the EEA.[74] Therefore, a U.S.-based e-commerce company with customers throughout the EEA may have to comply with the laws of numerous EEA member states. If it incorporates a subsidiary, however, to become the sole contracting party and controller for all European customers, then the new subsidiary would have to comply only with the data protection laws of the one jurisdiction where it is incorporated and be subject to the jurisdiction of only one supervisory authority (one-stop-shop principle).[75] Since the GDPR took effect in 2018, companies have become less concerned with national laws. Still, some differences remain, and the administrative burden of being subject to the jurisdiction of numerous data protection authorities versus only one is considerable. Therefore, location planning will still be necessary. Companies in the United States may be able to invoke similar protections under the U.S. Constitution's "Commerce Clause" against state laws that discriminate against or unduly burden interstate commerce. Such jurisdictional privileges provide some companies with a planning opportunity to influence which laws apply to them.[76]

3.1.3. *Applicability of GDPR to Companies Not Established in the EU*

Companies not established in the EU can also be subject to the GDPR if their processing activities relate to the **offering of goods and services** to individuals in the EU and they collect personal data in that context[77] or if they **monitor the behaviour** of individuals within the EU.[78]

---

71. GDPR, arts. 55 & 56. Each supervisory authority is responsible for its own territory under the GDPR, subject to the exception that in cross-border activities, the authorities of the member states are not simultaneously responsible; rather the main establishment determines the supervisory authority.

72. *See* the European Data Protection Board's leaflet on the one-stop-shop principle, www.edpb.europa.eu/system/files/2021-06/2020_06_22_one-stop-shop_leaflet_en.pdf, and the website of the European Data Protection Board, ¶ 14, www.edpb.europa.eu/system/files/2024-02/edpb_opinion_202404_mainestablishment_en.pdf.

73. The GDPR compliance framework ties obligations to the main establishment of the controller or processor, Art. 3 (1), 4(16) and Art. 56(1). Therefore, if companies have an establishment in one of the member states (or the main establishment if the company is physically present in more than one member state), this establishment determines the applicable data protection rules.

74. Companies that are not established under the GDPR can still be subject to the GDPR, according to Art. 3(1) and 3(2). A company that is not established within the EEA has to designate an EU representative under Art. 27. This does not qualify as an establishment as shown above. As the one-stop-shop principle is tied to a (main-)establishment, it is therefore not available to companies without an establishment.

75. GDPR, arts. 56 & 60.

76. Determann, *supra* note 57.

77. GDPR, art. 3(2)(a).

78. GDPR, art. 3(2)(b) & Recital 23; Ernst, in Paal/Pauly GDPR, Art. 3 Rn. 14.

A company outside the EU is not considered to offer goods and services in the EU merely because its website is accessible in the EU, or because it offers an email address or other contact details reachable from the EU, or because the company offers content in a language commonly spoken in the EU.[79] The CJEU has held that a company is "pursuing its commercial activities in the Member State of the consumer's domicile or [...] several Member states" if it manifests its intention to establish commercial relations with a customer in the EU.[80] It takes more than just a website to support this claim with sufficient evidence, for instance, the existence of a local patent right, the use of a specific top-level domain, or the nature of the product itself indicating the local connection.[81] Companies that have a top-level domain, or offer products geographically tied to the EU, or have local patent rights will more likely be considered as offering goods and services in the EU and, therefore, be subject to the GDPR.[82]

By contrast, a US company without any establishment in the EU that processes the personal data of US employees who visit the EU on a temporary business trip to France, Belgium, and the Netherlands for human resources purposes would not be subject to the GDPR under Art. 3(1) (due to a lack of a stable arrangement or other physical establishment) or Art. 3(2)(a) (because the company does not provide services to its employees, quite the other way around).[83] Even if the employees in question were employed by a subsidiary established on EU territory, the US parent company may not be subject to the GDPR with respect to its processing of personal data pertaining to its subsidiary's employees, given that it does not provide services to the employees.

Companies outside the EU can also become subject to the GDPR if they monitor the behavior of people in the EU,[84] for example when a company tracks natural persons on the internet for profiling and targeted advertising.[85] Companies may trigger the application of the GDPR simply by collecting data in the context of monitoring, regardless of specific plans of data usage.[86]

Moreover, organizations outside the EU may be subject to the GDPR to the extent EU member state law applies by virtue of public international law,[87] for example, concerning consulates and embassies and their employees and diplomats.[88]

79. GDPR, Recital 23; Koloß, *supra* note 61, at 810.

80. Peter Pammer v. Reederei Karl Schlüter GmbH & Co. KG and Hotel Alpenhof GmbH v. Oliver Heller, ECJ Joint Cases C-585/08 and C-144/09 2010, ECLI:EU:C:2010:740, ¶¶ 60 et seq.

81. *Id.* at 740, ¶¶ 81 et seq.

82. *See* GDPR Territorial Scope Guidelines, *supra* note 66, at 9.

83. *Id.* at 16.

84. Hanloser, in BeckOK DSR, Art. 3 DSGVO Rn. 3.

85. GDPR, Recital 24.

86. Hanloser, in BeckOK DSR, Art. 3 DSGVO Rn. 31.

87. GDPR, art. 3(3).

88. Ernst, in Paal/Pauly GDPR, Art. 3 Rn. 21.

3.2. NIS2

Companies in critical infrastructure sectors should already be familiar with national laws that implement the network infrastructure security requirements of the EU NIS Directive from 2016,[89] including financial sector entities as "operators of essential services."[90] On January 16, 2023, a successor directive entered into force—Directive (EU) 2022/2555 on measures for a high common level of cybersecurity across the Union (NIS 2 Directive).[91] EU member states were required to transpose the NIS 2 Directive into national law by October 17, 2024, but only Belgium, Croatia, and Hungary met the deadline.

Companies must comply with national laws transposing the EU directives, not typically the directives themselves, but they can expect to become covered by national laws implementing the NIS 2 Directive if they meet all three of the following elements: (1) qualify as a particular type of entity in the "sectors of high criticality" (Annex I of the NIS 2 Directive) or "other critical sectors" (Annex II of the NIS 2 Directive); (2) are at least so-called medium-sized enterprises within the meaning of EU Recommendation 2003/361/EC,[92] *i.e.* (i) employ at least 50 persons and/or (ii) have an annual turnover of at least EUR 10 million or an annual balance sheet total of at least EUR 10 million; and (3) provide their services in the EU or carry out activities in the EU.[93] Businesses can find lists of covered sectors, subsectors, and entities in NIS 2's Annexes.

Under the rules of the NIS 2 Directive, businesses need to satisfy numerous obligations, including cybersecurity risk management duties,[94] governance requirements,[95] registration obligations,[96] and reporting obligations.[97] Companies outside the EU covered by the NIS 2 Directive—but not established in the EU—must designate a representative in the Union, in one EU member state where the company offers services,[98] and they may need to register with authorities in every jurisdiction where they have customers,[99] *i.e.*, potentially in every EEA member state separately, with forms in local languages. Also, companies must register with the European Union Agency for Cybersecurity (ENISA)[100] and provide the name of

---

89. Directive (EU) 2016/1148 of the European Parliament and of the Council of 6 July 2016 concerning measures for a high common level of security of network and information systems across the Union (NIS Directive), [hereinafter NIS Directive] https://eur-lex.europa.eu/legal-content/EN/TXT/HTML/?uri=CELEX:32016L1148.

90. NIS Directive, art. 1(1)(d); Directive (EU) 2022/2555 of the European Parliament and the Council of 14 December 2022 on measures for a high common level of cybersecurity across the Union, amending Regulation (EU) No 910/2014 and Directive (EU) 2018/1972, and repealing Directive (EU) 2016/1148 (NIS 2 Directive), [hereinafter NIS2 Directive], art. 3(1)(g), https://eur-lex.europa.eu/legal-content/EN/TXT/HTML/?uri=CELEX:32022L2555.

91. *Id.*

92. Commission Recommendation of 6 May 2003 concerning the definition of micro, small and medium-sized enterprises, https://eur-lex.europa.eu/LexUriServ/LexUriServ.do?uri=OJ:L:2003:124:0036:0041:en:PDF.

93. NIS2 Directive, *supra* note 90, art. 2(1).

94. *Id.*, art. 21.

95. *Id.*, art. 20.

96. *Id.*, art. 3(4).

97. *Id.*, art. 23.

98. *Id.*, art. 26(3).

99. *Id.*, art. 26.

100. *Id.*, art. 27(1).

the entity, the relevant sector, subsector and type of entity, and numerous other categories of information.[101]

3.3. DORA

Another cybersecurity-focused law that EU lawmakers recently adopted is the Digital Operational Resilience Act (DORA),[102] a regulation, which entered into force on January 16, 2023, and started to apply on January 17, 2025, following a two-year transition period. Unlike the NIS2 Directive, which member states must transpose into national laws, DORA applies directly to companies, just as the GDPR. DORA aims to achieve a high common level of digital operational resilience and requires financial sector businesses to implement measures safeguarding the security of network and information systems.[103] Financial institutions that offer financial services in the EU are the primary focus of DORA, whether established within or outside the EU, but technology service providers to financial institutions are also covered if they offer services to covered financial institutions.[104]

3.4. India Cybersecurity Breach Notification

In August 2023, the Indian government signed the Digital Personal Data Protection Act (DPDPA) into law. The Indian Supreme Court had ordered the Indian Parliament to enact laws to protect individual privacy.[105] The Parliament tried to align India's data protection framework with global standards like the EU's GDPR. The version the Parliament finally enacted bears significantly fewer resemblances to the GDPR, however, than the first draft of the law published in 2018.[106] Companies are subject to the DPDPA if they process personal data in digital form on Indian territory, including in the context of offering goods and services in India.[107] Companies in India have to comply with the DPDPA's requirements with respect to personal data of data subjects outside of India if they process such data in India.[108] Companies outside India subject any personal data to DPDPA requirements if they

---

101. *Id.*, art. 27(2)(a–f).

102. *See* European Ins. & Occupational Pensions Auth., Digital Operational Resilience Act (DORA), www.eiopa.europa.eu/digital-operational-resilience-act-dora_en.

103. *See* Regulation (EU) 2022/2554 of the European Parliament & of the Council of 14 Dec. 2022 on digital operational resilience for the financial sector and amending Regulations (EC) No 1060/2009, (EU) No 648/2012, (EU) No 600/2014, (EU) No 909/2014 and (EU) 2016/1011 [hereinafter DORA], art. 1(1) (Dec. 27, 2022), https://eur-lex.europa.eu/legal-content/EN/TXT/PDF/?uri=CELEX:32022R2554&from=FR.

104. Lothar Determann & Michaela Nebel, *AI and Tech Regulation for the Financial Sector*, 41 Rev. of Banking & Fin. Serv. 35 (Mar. 2025).

105. Lothar Determann & Chetan Gupta, *Indian Personal Data Protection Act of 2018: Draft Bill and Its History, Compared to GDPR and California Privacy Law*, 37 Berkeley J. of Internat'l Law 481 (2019).

106. Sajai Singh, Lothar Determann, Helena Engfeldt & Jonathan Tam, *India Enacted the Digital Personal Data Protection Act: What Should U.S. Companies Do Now?*, Bloomberg Law, Data Privacy & Security (2023); Determann & Gupta, *supra* note 105.

107. The Digital Personal Data Protection Act, § 3 (a), (b) (2023) https://www.meity.gov.in/static/uploads/2024/06/2bf1f0e9f04e6fb4f8fef35e82c42aa5.pdf.

108. *Id.* § 2(x).

outsource data processing to India because their processor in India will be subject to the DPDPA.[109]

Under the DPDPA, companies need to maintain reasonable security measures and notify the Data Protection Board of India of security breaches without delay.[110] According to draft regulations, companies must submit notifications within seventy-two hours of becoming aware of a breach.[111]

The Ministry of Communications & Information Technology of the Indian government created an Indian Computer Emergency Response Team (CERT-IN), which companies have to notify of security incidents within 6 hours of becoming aware of the incident.[112] CERT-IN was established under the Information Technology Act 2000[113] to be the agency of the Indian government to collect information on cyber incidents.[114] "Cyber incidents" are defined broadly as any real or suspected adverse event likely to cause an offense or harm to critical functions and services by impairing the confidentiality, integrity, or availability of electronic information, systems, services or networks, or that threatens public safety, undermines public confidence, has a negative effect on the national economy, or diminishes the nation's security posture.[115] Companies outside India can also be subject to report to CERT-IN if cyber incidents affect their infrastructure on Indian territory or if they process personal data pertaining to data subjects in India.[116]

3.5. People's Republic of China (PRC)

In the People's Republic of China, companies must adhere to several statutes that regulate data protection, privacy, and cybersecurity, namely the Personal Information Protection Law (PIPL), Cybersecurity Law (CSL), and the Data Security Law (DSL), each with extra-territorial scope elements.[117] PIPL applies to the processing of personal information of natural persons within the territory of the PRC.[118] Companies outside the PRC have to

109. *Id.* § 3(a) & (b).

110. *Id.* §§ 8(6), 18.

111. Draft of the Digital Personal Data Protection Rules, 2025 § 7 (1), (2)(b) by the government according to § 40(1)(2) DPDPA. These Rules are still in the drafting phase, and feedback was being collected until 18th February 2025.

112. *See* Gov. of India, Ministry of Elec. & Info. Tech., Indian Comp. Emergency Response Team (CERT-In), No. 20(3)/2022-CERT-In, Directions under sub-section (6) of section 70B of the Information Technology Act, 2000 relating to information security practices, procedure, prevention, response and reporting of cyber incidents for Safe & Trusted Internet [hereinafter 70B Directions] at 2 (paragraph (ii)), www.cert-in.org.in/PDF/CERT-In_Directions_70B_28.04.2022.pdf.

113. Information Technology Act, 2000, No. 21 of 2000, India Code (2000) § 70B [hereinafter ITA].

114. ITA § 70B (1), (4)(a).

115. The Information Technology (The Indian Computer Emergency Response Team and Manner of performing functions and duties) Rules, 2013, § 2(g) (Jan. 16, 2014), https://www.cert-in.org.in/PDF/G.S.R_20(E).pdf.

116. *See* the list of reportable incidents provided in Annex I of the 70B Directions, *supra* note 112.

117. Rogier Creemers, *China's Emerging Data Protection Framework*, J. of Cybersecurity 1, 6 (2022).

118. DigiChina, *Translation: Personal Information Protection Law of the People's Republic of China—Effective Nov. 1, 2021*, art. 3 (Rogier Creemers & Graham Webster trans. Aug. 22, 2021) [hereinafter PIPL Translation], https://digichina.stanford.edu/work/translation-personal-information-protection-law-of-the-peoples-republic-of-china-effective-nov-1-2021/.

comply with the PIPL if (1) the purpose of processing is to provide products or services to domestic natural persons; (2) if the purpose is to analyze and evaluate the activities of domestic natural persons, or (3) if provided by laws and administrative regulations.[119] Since January 1, 2025, companies have to comply with the Network Data Security Management Regulation,[120] which covers "network data,"[121] "network data processing activities,"[122] and "network data processors,"[123] and also applies extraterritorially.[124]

Companies that qualify as data processors shall promptly inform users and the relevant competent authorities of detected security defects, vulnerabilities, and other risks.[125] If an incident involves endangering national security or public interests, the processor shall also report to the relevant competent authorities within 24 hours of becoming aware of the incident.[126] Companies with more than 50 million registered users or more than 10 million monthly active users and considered to have a significant impact on national security, economic operations, national economy, and people's livelihood are "large data platforms."[127] As such, they must annually publish a personal information protection social responsibility report. Additionally, such companies may not process user data through misleading, fraudulent, or coercive means, unjustifiably restrict user access to their own data generated on the platform, engage in discriminatory practices that harm users' legitimate rights and interests, or undertake activities prohibited by laws and administrative regulations.[128]

3.6. Brazil

Inspired by the GDPR, Brazil enacted the General Data Protection Law (Lei Geral de Proteção de Dados Pessoais) in 2020, aiming to protect "fundamental rights of freedom and privacy and the free development of the personality of the natural person."[129] The act

---

119. *Id.*

120. *See* Xinhua, *China Issues Regulations on Network Data Security Management*, State Council, People's Rep. of China (Sept. 30, 2024), https://english.www.gov.cn/policies/latestreleases/202409/30/content_WS66fab6c8c6d0868f4e8eb720.html.

121. "Network Data" refers to various electronic data processed and generated through the network. State Council, People's Rep. of China, Administrative Regulation of Network Data Security Management art. 62(1) (Sept. 24, 2024), www.gov.cn/zhengce/content/202409/content_6977766.htm.

122. "Network data processing activities" refer to activities such as collection, storage, use, processing, transmission, provision, disclosure, and deletion of network data. *Id.* art. 62(2) www.gov.cn/zhengce/content/202409/content_6977766.htm.

123. "Network data processor" refers to an individual or organization that independently determines the processing purpose and method in network data processing activities. *Id.* art. 62(3), www.gov.cn/zhengce/content/202409/content_6977766.htm.

124. *Id.* art. 2, www.gov.cn/zhengce/content/202409/content_6977766.htm; PIPL art. 3, www.personalinformationprotectionlaw.com/PIPL/article-3/.

125. *Id.* art. 10.

126. *Id.*

127. *Id.* art. 62(8).

128. *Id.* art. 46.

129. IAPP, LGPD Brazilian General Data Protection Law art. 1 (Ronaldo Lemos et al. trans., Oct. 2020) (Lei Geral de Proteção de Dados Pessoais), https://iapp.org/resources/article/brazilian-data-protection-law-lgpd-english-translation/.

covers companies outside Brazil if they conduct processing operations on Brazilian territory, collect personal data in the context of providing goods or services to persons in Brazil, or process personal data collected in Brazil.[130] Online service providers within and outside Brazil also must comply with an Internet law of 2014 that enumerates rights for users of the internet, including net neutrality, reinforcement of free speech, and preservation of privacy.[131] Companies must adhere to these laws if they operate in the gathering, storage, custody, and treatment of records, personal data, or communications by connection and internet application providers in which at least one of these acts occurs in national territory.[132] Foreign companies with no establishment in Brazil must comply with these provisions if they offer services to the Brazilian public or at least one member of the same group has an establishment in Brazil.[133]

4. Checklist: What Foreign Cybersecurity Laws Apply and Deserve Priority Attention?

As explained in previous sections of this chapter, online service providers may be subject to privacy, data protection, and cybersecurity laws of every country in the world where they make their web and mobile sites available. Most companies can assume that they must identify, analyze, and comply with the laws of any jurisdiction where they do business or from which they collect personal data. However, companies can also prepare a shorter priority list of laws most likely to affect them, based on the questions proposed in the following checklist.

Checklists can help create agendas for meetings, task lists for projects, and guidance for a quick health check of an organization's compliance status. They should not create a false sense of completeness, though. Also, a company charged with noncompliance concerning a particular law should analyze the applicability and validity of that law in more detail,[134] without regard to the generalization and prioritization considerations suggested in the following checklist. We intend the checklist for compliance planning, not for response to enforcement challenges.

---

130. *Id.* art. 3; Aaron K. Tantleff, Stephanie Pierce & Steven Millendorf, *Brazilian Government Makes the LGPD Effective Imminently*, NAT'L L. REV. (Sept. 10, 2020), https://natlawreview.com/article/brazilian-government-makes-lgpd-effective-imminently; Felipe Dannemann Lundgren, *New Brazilian Data Protection Law*, GRUR INT. 752, 753 (2019).

131. Abigayle Erickson, *Comparative Analysis of the EU's GDPR and Brazil's LGPD: Enforcement Challenges with the LGPD*, 44 BROOK. J. INT'L L. 859, 872 (July 2019).

132. *Id.* at 873 (describing the Marco Civil Law of the Internet in Brazil).

133. *Id.*

134. *See, infra,* Section 5.1 and *supra*, Sections 1–3.

4.1. Where are your company and its subsidiaries and affiliates incorporated or established with a physical presence?

Compliance with laws of jurisdictions in this category should be the top priority. For example, a company incorporated and headquartered in California that owns subsidiaries in France and Germany, and a branch with employees in the UK should focus on compliance with U.S. federal law, California state law, EU law, French law, German law, and UK law as the first order of business.

4.2. Is your company represented by employees, individual contractors, or officers in other countries?

Individual employees, contractors, or officers in foreign countries can amount to a business establishment that can attract the applicability of cybersecurity laws of such jurisdictions, particularly if the individuals are involved in the processing of personal data or information technology systems. Authorities and courts in such countries can also enforce local laws better against foreign companies, because they can hold individual representatives responsible. Less significant for foreign law applicability tends to be whether a company engages corporate contractors or non-executive directors in the foreign jurisdiction.

4.3. Does your company provide goods or services directly to individuals in other countries?

Under the GDPR and laws of countries shaped after the GDPR, foreign companies subject themselves to local data protection and cybersecurity laws if they provide goods or services remotely to individuals and collect their personal data in that context. For example, companies outside the EU can become subject to EU data breach notification requirements even if they provide only charge-free web services to consumers in the EU. But, sending an employee on a business trip to the EU is not sufficient, because a business visitor does not amount to a permanent establishment and employees provide services to their employer (not the other way around). Also, companies do not necessarily trigger the applicability of the GDPR by selling services to business customers, because of the wording of Art. 3(2)(a) GDPR.[135]

4.4. Does your company operate servers or other data processing equipment in foreign countries?

Companies can also attract the applicability of foreign data protection and cybersecurity laws if they operate servers or other data processing equipment that they own or control.

---

135. "This Regulation applies to the processing of personal data of data subjects who are in the Union by a controller or processor not established in the Union, where the processing activities are related to: (a) the offering of goods or services, irrespective of whether a payment of the data subject is required, to such data subjects in the Union; or (b) the monitoring of their behaviour as far as their behaviour takes place within the Union." GDPR art. 3(2)(a).

Merely engaging an unaffiliated and independently operating corporate service provider in another country may not suffice to attract such country's laws in the absence of other factors establishing nexus.

4.5. Does your company receive personal data from residents of other countries?

Under the laws of some jurisdictions, companies may be subject to local privacy, data protection, or cybersecurity laws solely on the basis that a foreign company processes personal data pertaining to citizens or residents of such jurisdiction. Some companies consider the laws of such remotely connected jurisdictions only if they (a) have another nexus to such jurisdiction (*e.g.*, corporate service providers or customers), (b) receive a significant amount of personal data from such jurisdictions, or (c) such jurisdictions are known to actively enforce their laws against foreign companies even without a significant nexus.

5. Conclusions and Practical Take-Aways

Companies that engage in global commerce and receive personal data from other countries may subject themselves to the laws of such other countries. Online service providers who make their sites and services available everywhere may incur legal obligations concerning data security measures, database registrations, designation of local representatives, governance, risk management systems, and breach notification under the laws of every jurisdiction from which they receive data.

5.1. Examine Applicability and Invalidity of Foreign Laws

If a company is sued, charged, or fined because it allegedly violated a particular obligation under a cybersecurity law of a foreign jurisdiction, its legal counsel should not only analyze whether the particular law applies based on its specific conflicts of law provisions, but also whether foreign companies are subject to personal jurisdiction where the law is enforced. Furthermore, counsel should consider whether the law may be preempted by higher-ranking national, regional, or international law, or if it should be interpreted narrowly. Moreover, counsel should analyze if and how the law can be enforced across borders.

5.2. Consider Enforceability

Countries are relatively free under international public law to apply their data security laws to foreign companies. But they cannot easily enforce their laws across borders. Therefore, companies can and should prioritize their compliance efforts with respect to laws of jurisdictions that can be enforced against them, either because they maintain presences, employees, or assets there or because countries where they maintain presences, employees, or assets voluntarily enforce the jurisdiction's laws.

5.3. Prioritize Compliance

With respect to prioritization, companies should differentiate between legal standards that may be worth complying with for business and risk mitigation reasons, such as substantive data security measures, and compliance with legal requirements that solely increase liability and exposure to foreign jurisdiction, such as registration requirements and duties to designate local representatives.

a. With respect to substantive data security requirements, companies should apply a "highest common denominator" approach and try to comply with the strictest applicable law as broadly as possible. Legislatures around the world regularly ratchet up compliance requirements and requirements that are not yet applicable everywhere probably will be soon. Also, companies can mitigate very real business and reputational risks by improving their security posture.
b. With respect to registration and other formal requirements, however, companies might prefer to comply only where required, given that compliance with such requirements rarely benefits businesses, except where required by law. With respect to registration requirements in the EU specifically, companies established outside the EU should consider establishing a subsidiary company in a relatively business-friendly EU member state as a local seller of goods or services because companies established in the EU benefit from jurisdictional privileges and often have to register and correspond only with one country's regulator. In contrast, companies established outside the EU may have to register with and notify every one of the 27 EU member states.
c. Obligations to notify about data security breaches fall somewhere in the middle between the two categories examined in the previous two subsections (a) and (b): On the one hand, companies can protect their employees and consumers from risks of harm and their own business reputation if they issue breach notifications to individuals. On the other hand, companies may increase their liability and exposure if they notify individuals and authorities in another jurisdiction of a data security breach. Therefore, in practice, companies often make decisions on compliance with foreign breach notification laws based on determinations as to whether:
    - individuals will truly benefit from notifications (which may be required in some jurisdictions under excessively broad definitions);
    - issuing notices in some jurisdictions but not others is acceptable from a reputational perspective;
    - issuing notices with different contents, wording, and details in different jurisdictions (as may be required under local law) could create confusion and exposure to global consumer or employee populations;
    - addressing every form requirement that is feasible in the ever-shortening response times mandated by applicable laws; and
    - issuing notices above and beyond legal requirements in a particular jurisdiction helps mitigate reputational and legal risks for the company.

5.4. Prepare

In the context of incident response preparation, companies should already consider the applicability and enforceability of foreign laws so they do not have to make complex and time-consuming determinations in the stressful situation of a data security incident. More broadly, companies should assess the applicability and impact of foreign cybersecurity and data protection laws from time to time to determine whether they have to comply with additional requirements and whether they should consider limiting their business activities in particular jurisdictions to avoid the applicability of local laws. In this context, attorneys should consider the checklist questions proposed in Section 4 of this chapter.

ACKNOWLEDGEMENTS

This chapter reflects Lothar Determann's personal views, not those of his law firm, clients, or law schools. The author thanks for the valuable edits and contributions of Kosha Doshi, LLM Candidate '25 at Berkeley Law; Felix Berger, Rechtsreferendar; and Jeffrey Allen, Graves & Allen, Oakland, California. The author takes sole responsibility for any errors or omissions.

Chapter 9

Foreign and International Cybersecurity Laws

Harvey Rishikof[1] and Tanner Wilburn

In this chapter, attorneys will find guidance on how foreign cybersecurity laws and international norms shape compliance responsibilities, litigation strategies, cross-border data flows, and risk management. While the last chapter addressed how these regimes interact with U.S. law when organizations are subject to overlapping jurisdictions, this chapter provides a concise overview of key national cybersecurity and data protection frameworks worldwide ("foreign cybersecurity laws"), and an examination of the essential principles, treaties, and norms that make up "international cybersecurity law." In conclusion, this chapter offers practical takeaways. This discussion should provide attorneys with a high-level understanding of global cybersecurity law to equip readers with enough knowledge to identify fundamental issues and find additional information.

Foreign and international cybersecurity law operate at different levels of governance and serve distinct functions, though they frequently intersect. *Foreign cybersecurity laws* are the national regulations and legal frameworks that individual states enact to govern cybersecurity. These laws dictate requirements for data protection, critical infrastructure security, and cybercrime enforcement. Each country can create its own approach. On the other hand, *international cybersecurity law* is the body of treaties, legal principles, and norms governing cyberspace behavior between sovereign states. While national authorities enforce foreign cybersecurity laws domestically, international cybersecurity law depends on state consent, diplomatic processes, and cooperative enforcement mechanisms. Overlap between the two is common. National cybersecurity policies align with or influence the development of international norms, and conversely, international agreements often shape domestic legal reforms.

1. International Cybersecurity Law

The international cybersecurity space, like the domestic space, is fraught with unresolved issues and open questions as states struggle to establish sovereignty over data, implement sovereign clouds, and negotiate with private-sector cyber providers.

---

1. The views expressed herein are those of the author and do not represent the views of the Department of Defense.

International law is the body of rules and principles that govern relations between sovereign states and, increasingly, other international actors. Its primary purpose is to facilitate stable, orderly, and peaceful coexistence among states by providing a common baseline of rights and obligations. States are generally bound only by those rules to which they have consented, whether explicitly through agreements or implicitly through consistent practice.

The classic formulation of the sources of international law is found in Article 38(1) of the Statute of the International Court of Justice (ICJ).[2] According to Article 38, the ICJ shall apply as three primary, co-equal sources of law: (a) international conventions (treaties), whether general or particular, establishing rules recognized by the contesting states; (b) international custom, as evidence of a general practice accepted as law; and (c) general principles of law recognized by civilized nations.[3] In addition, as a *subsidiary means* for determining the rules of law, Article 38(1)(d) recognizes judicial decisions and the teachings of eminent publicists (scholars) of various nations. These latter sources are not law *per se* but can be persuasive in interpreting treaties or identifying custom.[4]

All these sources of international law apply to cyberspace. This was explicitly affirmed in the 2013 report of the United Nations Group of Governmental Experts (UNGGE), which stated that international law applies to the use of information and communication technologies ("ICT") by states.[5] That statement was later endorsed by all UN member states in a General Assembly resolution. Thus, the Charter of the United Nations regulate cyber activities just as they do any other activities of states.[6]

The current debate among states is not *whether* international law applies to cyberspace, but *how* it applies. Cyberspace presents new factual scenarios, such as cross-border data transfers, cyber espionage, and disruption of critical infrastructure. Thus, lawyers and policymakers worldwide must actively interpret how existing law maps onto cyber activities. For instance, how does the threshold of "armed attack" in the UN Charter Article 51

2. The ICJ comprises 193 member states. All UN member states are parties to the Statute of the ICJ. Statute of the International Court of Justice art. 38, ¶ 1, U.N. Charter, Annex I at 21–30 (1945).

3. *Id.*

4. *Id.*

5. *See The UN GGE on Cybersecurity: How International Law Applies to Cyberspace*, COUNCIL ON FOREIGN RELS.: NET POLITICS (Apr. 14, 2015, 9:30 AM), https://www.cfr.org/blog/un-gge-cybersecurity-how-international-law-applies-cyberspace.

6. The UN Charter's principles of state sovereignty, non-intervention in internal affairs, prohibition on the use of force, and the inherent right of self-defense all provide a baseline legal framework for cyber operations. (These principles are discussed more below in context). Customary international law rules, such as those on state responsibility for internationally wrongful acts, equally apply to cyberspace incidents (e.g., rules of attribution and the duty to make reparations for wrongful acts). See generally U.N. Secretary-General, *Group of Governmental Experts on Advancing Responsible State Behaviour in Cyberspace in the Context of International Security*, U.N.Doc. A/76/135 (July 14, 2021) (transmitting report to the General Assembly), https://docs.un.org/en/A/76/135; U.N. Secretary-General, *Official Compendium of Voluntary National Contributions on the Subject of How International Law Applies to the Use of Information and Communications Technologies by States*, U.N. Doc. A/76/136 (July 13, 2021, rev. Aug. 10, 2021), https://ccdcoe.org/uploads/2018/10/UN_-Official-compendium-of-national-contributions-on-how-international-law-applies-to-use-of-ICT-by-States_A-76-136-EN.pdf.

(which triggers the right to self-defense)[7] translate to a cyber context? Can a cyber attack that cripples a nation's power grid count as a use of force or armed attack? If a state secretly implants malicious code in another state's networks during peacetime, does it violate the target state's sovereignty?[8]

1.1. Cyber Norms

International law, as explained above, comprises binding legal obligations derived from treaties, custom, and general principles of law. However, international law does not just emerge from the ether. Instead, it emerges from *norms*.

Norms are shared expectations or standards of behavior. Norms can guide behavior and shape state practice without carrying the same legal enforceability as treaties or customary international law. **Norms can *and often do* evolve into binding legal obligations** once codified into treaties or recognized as customary international law.[9] They function as "rules of the road," guiding how states and other actors **should** behave, even though they may not (yet) be part of enforceable law.

Norms can be generated through diplomatic efforts, multistakeholder processes, and political commitments. Norms typically start as proposals or ideas in response to new challenges or to fill gaps in existing law. They can be advanced by individual states, groups of states, international organizations, or even private actors and civil society. If a norm gains support and a critical mass of endorsement, it can become a recognized standard of behavior. In cyber, norms often emerge *bottom-up*: states observe a dangerous behavior and collectively voice that "this should not be done," in time coalescing around a normative statement. Eventually, a critical mass of states chooses to act, often through a forum like the United Nations.[10]

International cyber norms have largely followed this trajectory. In the early days of the internet, few explicit norms existed for state behavior in cyberspace. However, as cyber incidents began to threaten national security, economic stability, and public welfare, the international community needed to articulate acceptable and unacceptable conduct.

---

7. *See, e.g.,* Matthew C. Waxman, *Cyber-Attacks and the Use of Force: Back to the Future of Article 2(4)*, 36 YALE J. INT'L L. 421 (2011), https://scholarship.law.columbia.edu/faculty_scholarship/1653.

8. States have begun to articulate their official positions. For example, NATO has affirmed that *"international law applies in cyberspace,"* integrating this view into its strategic policy, and individual countries like the United Kingdom, France, the United States, Australia, and others have released public statements on how they interpret international law in cyber contexts. *See* Michael N. Schmitt, *Cyber Operations and the Jus Ad Bellum Revisited*, 56 VILL. L. REV. 569, 571 (2011).

9. For more on formation of Customary International Law, see Noah A. Bialos, *The Identification of Customary International Law: Institutional and Methodological Pluralism in U.S. Courts,* 21 CHI. J. INT'L L., Article 2 (Summer 2022), https://chicagounbound.uchicago.edu/cjil/vol21/iss1/2.

10. For more on the formation of international law from the "bottom up," see Janet Koven Levit, *Bottom-Up International Lawmaking: Reflections on the New Haven School of International Law*, 32 YALE J. INT'L L., (393 (2007), https://ssrn.com/abstract=1031732).

1.2. United Nations

The development of international cyber norms has evolved in response to cybersecurity threats since the late 1990s. One of the earliest diplomatic initiatives came in 1998, when Russia introduced a draft resolution in the UN General Assembly on the subject of "information security,"[11] urging the international community to address the security of global information and telecommunication systems.[12] This led to a series of UN General Assembly resolutions and, eventually, to creating specialized groups to study and propose norms for state behavior in cyberspace. In 2004, the United Nations convened successive Groups of Governmental Experts (UN GGE) on Developments in the Field of Information and Telecommunications in the Context of International Security. These small groups of 15–25 national experts appointed by governments played a central role in articulating cyber norms at the global level.

Over multiple iterations, the UN GGEs made progress. The 2010 GGE was the first to reach a consensus report, in which states recognized the need to discuss norms of responsible behavior and confidence-building measures.[13] However, it stopped short of articulating specific rules.[14] A breakthrough came with the 2012–2013 GGE, whose consensus report declared for the first time that existing international law, including the UN Charter, applies to state conduct in cyberspace.[15] The same 2013 GGE report also reaffirmed the principle of state sovereignty in cyberspace and noted that state efforts in cybersecurity must respect human rights and fundamental freedoms.[16]

The 2014–2015 GGE went further and proposed an important set of eleven voluntary, non-binding norms of responsible state behavior in cyberspace:[17]

a. States should cooperate to enhance stability and security in ICT use and prevent practices harmful to international peace.
b. When ICT incidents occur, states should assess all relevant context, including attribution challenges and potential consequences.

---

11. Many have noted that cybersecurity used to be called "information security."

12. G.A. Res. 53/70 (Dec. 4, 1998) (published in U.N. Doc. A/RES/53/70 (Jan. 4, 1999), https://digitallibrary.un.org/record/265311?v=pdf).

13. *See Study Series 33: Developments in the Field of Information and Telecommunications in the Context of International Security* at iv, U.N.Doc. A/65/201 (Dec. 2011), https://digitallibrary.un.org/record/3964709/files/DSS_33.pdf.

14. *See* United Nations Inst. for Disarmament Research, *GGE Recommendations on International Law and Norms of Responsible State Behavior* (2019) [hereinafter *GGE Recommendations*], https://unidir.org/files/2019-10/GGE-Recommendations-International-Law.pdf.

15. *Id.*

16. Deborah Brown, Anriette Esterhuysen & Sheetal Kumar, *Unpacking the GGE's Framework on Responsible State Behaviour: Cyber Norms*, Global Partners Digital (Dec. 2019), https://www.gp-digital.org/wp-content/uploads/2019/12/unpacking_gge_cyber-norms.pdf.

17. Report of Group of Governmental Experts on Developments in the Field of Information and Telecommunications in the Context of International Security ¶ 13, U.N. Doc. A/70/174 (July 22, 2015) [hereinafter 2015 UN GGE Report], https://docs.un.org/en/A/70/174. The eleven norms are not repeated verbatim here. These are shortened summaries of each.

c. States should not knowingly allow their territory to be used for internationally wrongful ICT acts.
d. States should cooperate by sharing information, assisting each other, and prosecuting terrorist and criminal ICT activities.
e. States must secure ICT use while respecting UN resolutions on human rights, including privacy and freedom of expression.
f. States should not intentionally damage or support damaging ICT activities against critical infrastructure.
g. States should protect their critical infrastructure from ICT threats.
h. States should respond appropriately to requests for help when another state's critical infrastructure faces malicious ICT activities, respecting sovereignty.
i. States should safeguard supply chain integrity to ensure secure ICT products for end users.
j. States should promote responsible reporting of ICT vulnerabilities and share information about remedies.
k. States should not attack or support attacks on other states' authorized emergency response teams, nor misuse their own teams for malicious acts.[18]

The 2015 GGE report represented the most concrete internationally endorsed cyber norms framework to date, albeit a voluntary one.

Progress in the UN GGE process has not been linear. The 2016–2017 GGE failed to produce a consensus report, and the 2017 GGE stumbled over how international law applies to hostile cyber operations: some states refused to reaffirm that international humanitarian law[19] applies to cyber warfare, arguing that doing so might legitimize the militarization of cyberspace.[20] Others insisted on including the concept that states could respond in kind to cyber incidents below the armed attack threshold. This deadlock in 2017 was a turning point that prompted the international community to try a new, more inclusive approach.

In late 2018, the UN General Assembly established an Open-Ended Working Group (OEWG) on developments in ICT security, a parallel process open to *all* UN member states (in contrast to the small, invitation-based GGE). The OEWG, championed by Russia and supported by many developing countries, was designed to democratize the cyber norms discussion by allowing every nation to participate in negotiations, rather than just a select few

---

18. *Id.*

19. *See GGE Recommendations, supra* note 14. The term "International humanitarian law" is often used interchangeably with the "law of armed conflict" (LOAC).

20. Arun M. Sukumar, *The UN GGE Failed. Is International Law in Cyberspace Doomed As Well?*, Lawfare (July 4, 2017), https://www.lawfaremedia.org/article/un-gge-failed-international-law-cyberspace-doomed-well.

experts. The first OEWG met throughout 2019–2020 and successfully reached consensus on a final report in March 2021.[21]

The OEWG 2021 report reaffirmed the previously agreed GGE norms and principles, confirming again that the 11 voluntary norms from 2015 remain valid and that international law applies to cyberspace. It also recommended further dialogue on how international law applies, plus practical measures for capacity-building and confidence-building among states. Separately, a new 2019–2021 UN GGE (with 25 experts) was convened in parallel, and it too produced a consensus report in 2021, mirroring much of the OEWG's conclusions.[22] Thus, by 2021, there was a broad UN-level reaffirmation of the normative framework: states globally endorsed the prior voluntary norms and the applicability of international law, signaling at least a baseline agreement on responsible behavior.

1.3. NATO

The evolution of cyber norms has not been confined to the UN. Regional organizations and multilateral alliances have made key contributions by developing their own strategies, declarations, and frameworks that complement global efforts.

As a military alliance, the North Atlantic Treaty Organization (NATO) began focusing on cyber defense in the mid-2000s after cyber incidents like the 2007 attacks on Estonia.[23] NATO's 2014 Wales Summit Declaration and the updated NATO Cyber Defense Policy explicitly confirmed that international law applies in cyberspace.[24] In 2016, at the Warsaw Summit, NATO recognized cyberspace as a distinct "operational domain" of warfare (alongside land, sea, air, and space).[25] This recognition implies that NATO members consider severe cyber-attacks as potentially on par with conventional attacks to the point that a cyber-attack could trigger collective defense obligations under Article 5 of the North Atlantic Treaty. NATO statements welcome international efforts to develop cyber norms

---

21. U.N. Secretary-General, *Developments in the Field of Information and Telecommunications in the Context of International Security*, U.N. Doc. A/75/816 (Mar. 18, 2021) (transmitting report of the Open-Ended Working Group on Developments in the Field of Information and Telecommunications in the Context of International Security to the General Assembly), https://docs.un.org/en/A/75/816.

22. U.N. Secretary-General, *Group of Governmental Experts on Advancing Responsible State Behaviour in Cyberspace in the Context of International Security* ¶¶ 1–5, U.N. Doc. A/76/135 (July 14, 2021) (transmitting report to the General Assembly), https://digitallibrary.un.org/record/3934214?v=pdf.

23. Joshua Davis, *Hackers Take Down the Most Wired Country in Europe*, Wired (Aug. 21, 2007), https://www.wired.com/2007/08/ff-estonia/.

24. NATO, Wales Summit Declaration: Issued by the Heads of State and Government participating in the meeting of the North Atlantic Council in Wales (Sept. 5, 2014), https://www.nato.int/cps/en/natohq/official_texts_112964.htm; *NATO Summit Updates Cyber Defence Policy*, NATO Cooperative Cyber Def. Ctr. of Excel. (undated), https://ccdcoe.org/incyder-articles/nato-summit-updates-cyber-defence-policy/.

25. *See* Fact Sheet, NATO, Warsaw Summit Key Decisions (Feb. 2017), https://www.nato.int/nato_static_fl2014/assets/pdf/pdf_2017_02/20170206_1702-factsheet-warsaw-summit-key-en.pdf.

and confidence-building measures.[26] In practice, NATO has improved information-sharing and mutual assistance among allies for cyber incidents.[27]

Although NATO itself does not create international law, it houses the Cooperative Cyber Defense Centre of Excellence (CCDCOE) in Tallinn, which has been at the forefront of scholarly work on how international law applies to cyber operations. (The CCDCOE facilitated the influential *Tallinn Manual*, discussed later in the chapter). The CCDCOE is not formally part of NATO's military command structure, but it is closely affiliated with NATO as an accredited Center of Excellence.[28]

1.4. European Union (EU)

The EU has consistently aligned with the positions articulated in the UN GGE reports, strongly affirming that the UN Charter and international law apply to state behavior in cyberspace.[29] The EU has also engaged in capacity-building projects worldwide to help other countries implement the agreed UN norms.[30]

The EU developed a *Cyber Diplomacy Toolbox*,[31] a framework for joint EU diplomatic responses to malicious cyber activities, which includes measures ranging from demarches and statements up to sanctions. In 2019 and 2020, the EU for the first time imposed coordinated cyber sanctions against alleged perpetrators of major cyberattacks (including the Not-Petya attack and the attempted attack on the Organisation for the Prohibition of Chemical Weapons).[32] Building upon this framework, the EU introduced the Cyber Blueprint, a draft Council Recommendation designed to clearly and accessibly present the EU framework for cybersecurity crisis management.[33] The Cyber Blueprint facilitates structured interactions among Union-level entities across the entire crisis management lifecycle, defining what constitutes a cyber crisis and what triggers an EU-level response. It outlines mechanisms like the Cybersecurity Emergency Mechanism and the EU Cybersecurity Reserve for managing, responding to, and recovering from large-scale cybersecurity incidents.

---

26. See Fact Sheet, NATO, NATO Cyber Defence (July 2016), https://www.nato.int/nato_static_fl2014/assets/pdf/pdf_2016_07/20160627_1607-factsheet-cyber-defence-en.pdf.

27. *Id.*

28. *Centres of Excellence*, NATO (Jan. 15, 2025), https://www.nato.int/cps/en/natohq/topics_68372.htm (last visited Sept. 1, 2025).

29. Nayia Barmpaliou & Patryk Pawlak, Eur. Commission Operational Guidance: The EU's International Cooperation on Cyber Capacity Building pt. III, § 1.1 at 44 (2d ed. 2023) (reflecting a study implemented by the EU Cyber Capacity Building Network (EU CyberNet), https://www.eucybernet.eu/wp-content/uploads/2023/11/operational-guidance-for-the-eu-international-cooperation-on-ccb-1-1.pdf.

30. *Id.* pt. III, § 2.2.

31. The Cyber Diplomacy Toolbox, https://www.cyber-diplomacy-toolbox.com/ (last visited Sept. 1, 2025); *see also* Erica Moret & Patryk Pawlak, *The EU Cyber Diplomacy Toolbox: Towards a Cyber Sanctions Regime?*, EU Inst. for Sec. Stud. (July 2017), https://op.europa.eu/s/z8Io.

32. Franck Dumortier, Paul de Hert & Vagelis Papakonstantinou, *EU Sanctions Against Cyber-Attacks and Defense Rights: Wanna Cry?*, Eur. L. Blog (Sept. 28, 2020), https://www.europeanlawblog.eu/pub/eu-sanctions-against-cyber-attacks-imposed-and-defense-rights-wanna-cry/release/1.

33. Proposal for a Council Recommendation for an EU Blueprint on cybersecurity crisis management, COM (2025) 66 final (Feb. 24, 2025), https://www.parlament.gv.at/dokument/XXVIII/EU/12503/imfname_11455431.pdf.

1.5. ASEAN (Association of Southeast Asian Nations)

In the Asia-Pacific region, ASEAN has increasingly prioritized cybersecurity cooperation and norm-setting among its ten member states. In 2018, the leaders of ASEAN issued a statement on cybersecurity cooperation that explicitly supported the promotion of voluntary and non-binding norms of responsible state behavior in cyberspace, in line with the eleven UN GGE norms.[34] This ASEAN Leaders' Statement recognized that developing a "peaceful, secure and resilient rules-based cyberspace" is critical for the region's economic progress and stability.[35]

ASEAN has also worked through the ASEAN Regional Forum (ARF), which includes dialogue partners like the US, China, Russia, and the EU, to discuss and implement cyber confidence-building measures (CBMs).[36] In recent years, ASEAN meetings have served as a platform to regionalize global norms and coordinate emergency response, encouraging each member to establish computer emergency teams and share best practices.[37]

1.6. Shanghai Cooperation Organization

In contrast to Western-led initiatives, the Shanghai Cooperation Organization (SCO), led by China, Russia, and Central Asian states, proposed an International Code of Conduct for Information Security (initially in 2011, updated in 2015) to the UN.[38] The proposal reflects a different philosophy, emphasizing state sovereignty in information space and calling on states to curb the dissemination of information that could undermine social stability. It leans towards legitimizing tighter state control over the internet and mutual non-interference in domestic affairs via ICT.

1.7. Non-State Actors

Both state and non-state actors play significant roles in shaping cyber norms. The private sector is on the front lines of cyberspace. After all, most of the internet's infrastructure

---

34. *See* ASEAN, ASEAN Cybersecurity Cooperation Strategy (2021–2025) ¶ 12 (2022) [hereinafter ASEAN Strategy], https://asean.org/wp-content/uploads/2022/02/01-ASEAN-Cybersecurity-Cooperation-Paper-2021-2025_final-23-0122.pdf.

35. ASEAN, ASEAN Leaders' Statement on Cybersecurity Cooperation *at 1* (undated), https://asean.org/wp-content/uploads/2018/04/ASEAN-Leaders-Statement-on-Cybersecurity-Cooperation.pdf.

36. ASEAN Strategy, *supra* note 34, ¶ 17.

37. Kai Lin Tay, *ASEAN Cyber-security Cooperation: Towards a Regional Emergency-response Framework*, 'Int'l Inst. for Strategic Stud. (June 2023), https://www.iiss.org/globalassets/media-library---content--migration/files/research-papers/2023/06/asean-cyber-security-cooperation.pdf.

38. Letter dated 9 January 2015 from the Permanent Representatives of China, Kazakhstan, Kyrgyzstan, the Russian Federation, Tajikistan and Uzbekistan to the United Nations addressed to the Secretary-General, U.N. Doc. A/69/723 (Jan. 13, 2015), https://digitallibrary.un.org/record/786846/?v=pdf; Letter dated 12 September 2011 from the Permanent Representatives of China, the Russian Federation, Tajikistan and Uzbekistan to the United Nations addressed to the Secretary-General, U.N. Doc. A/66/359 (Sept. 14, 2011), https://digitallibrary.un.org/record/710973?v=pdf. *See also* CCDCOE, Shanghai Cooperation Organisation, NATO, https://ccdcoe.org/organisations/sco/ (last visited Sept. 1, 2025); Henry Rõigas, *An Updated Draft of the Code of Conduct Distributed in the United Nations—What's New?*, NATO CCDCOE (undated), https://ccdcoe.org/incyder-articles/an-updated-draft-of-the-code-of-conduct-distributed-in-the-united-nations-whats-new/.

and services are owned and operated by private entities.[39] Their role in shaping norms has grown significantly, and tech companies are not shy to propose ideas. Microsoft, in particular, has been a vocal player. It advocated for a "Digital Geneva Convention"[40] and has released white papers on cybersecurity norms.[41] Microsoft's president, Brad Smith, called for governments to agree not to attack the private sector and critical services and suggested the creation of an independent attribution organization analogous to a "Cyber-Red Cross."[42]

Many other companies also have internal policies that align with or advance norms. For instance, Google's Project Zero and Microsoft's vulnerability disclosure policy embody the norm of responsible vulnerability reporting.[43] Companies also refuse certain businesses that violate norms.[44] Big cloud service providers have transparency reports and law enforcement guidelines that indirectly pressure governments to follow legal processes rather than unauthorized surveillance.

2. Key International Agreements and Norms in Cyberspace

Having surveyed the development of cyber norms, we now turn to some of the **key international agreements** that shape cyberspace governance. These range from formal treaties to influential non-binding guidelines.

2.1. The Budapest Convention on Cybercrime (2001)

One of the most significant international agreements is the Council of Europe's Budapest Convention on Cybercrime.[45] This 2001 treaty was the first international treaty on crimes committed *via* computer networks. A legally binding treaty, the Budapest Convention requires its parties to criminalize a core set of offenses and adopt procedural laws

39. Cybersecurity & Infrastructure Sec. Agency (CISA), *Communications Sector*, U.S. Dep't of Homeland Sec., https://www.cisa.gov/topics/critical-infrastructure-security-and-resilience/critical-infrastructure-sectors/communications-sector (last visited April 20, 2025).

40. Brad Smith, *The Need for a Digital Geneva Convention*, Microsoft: on the Issues (Feb. 14, 2017), https://blogs.microsoft.com/on-the-issues/2017/02/14/need-digital-geneva-convention/.

41. See, e.g., Angela McKay et al., International Cybersecurity Norms: Reducing conflict in an Internet-dependent world at 20, Microsoft (2015) (proposing six cybersecurity norms), https://www.microsoft.com/en-us/download/details.aspx?id=45031&msockid=2e7b0c4495106d403e2119e294726c94.

42. Shaun Waterman, *Microsoft's Smith Adds "Cyber Red Cross" to His "Digital Geneva Convention" Call*, CyberScoop (Nov. 10, 2017), https://cyberscoop.com/microsofts-smith-adds-it-red-cross-to-his-digital-geneva-convention-call/.

43. Project Zero, *Vulnerability Disclosure Policy*, Google, https://googleprojectzero.blogspot.com/p/vulnerability-disclosure-policy.html (last visited April 15, 2025); *Coordinated Vulnerability Disclosure*, Microsoft Sec. Response Ctr., https://www.microsoft.com/en-us/msrc/cvd (last visited April 15, 2025).

44. After NotPetya, for example, some insurance and tech companies began to treat reckless state malware as beyond the pale; such acts were "warlike," prompting discussions of what constitutes an act of war in cyber insurance.

45. Convention on Cybercrime, Nov. 23, 2001, Council of Eur., T.S. No. 185, https://rm.coe.int/1680081561.

empowering law enforcement to investigate cybercrimes. As of 2025, there are 81 signatory countries.[46]

However, not all major cyber players are on board. Russia, China, and several other states have refused to join the Budapest Convention, viewing it as a Western instrument. They have raised concerns about sovereignty, objecting that the treaty could allow foreign law enforcement to conduct investigations on their soil or access data without sufficient control. Instead, these countries pushed for a new cybercrime treaty under UN auspices. In December 2024, they got it.

2.2. UN Cybercrime Treaty

The UN General Assembly adopted the United Nations Convention against Cybercrime on December 24, 2024, after a five-year negotiation process.[47] The initiative to create a new cybercrime treaty began in 2019, when a UN resolution sponsored by Russia, with support from China, Iran, Syria, and others, called for a comprehensive international convention. The new convention is designed to complement, not replace, existing international instruments.[48] It explicitly does not override arrangements like the Budapest Convention, and states are free to continue using existing bilateral or regional agreements in parallel.

2.3. The Tallinn Manual and Norms for Cyber Warfare

While not a binding agreement, the **Tallinn Manual** deserves special mention as a key resource on how international law applies to cyber operations. The Tallinn Manual (first published in 2013, with a second edition in 2017) is an academic, non-governmental study produced by international legal experts under the auspices of NATO's CCDCOE in Estonia.[49] It does not create new law but attempts to restate and clarify existing international law on the *jus ad bellum* (law on the use of force) and *jus in bello* (international humanitarian law (IHL)) in the context of cyber warfare.

The *Tallinn Manual 1.0* focused on cyber operations during armed conflict, articulating 95 "black-letter rules" with commentary. These included, for example, the experts' views on when a cyber operation amounts to a use of force or an armed attack, how the principles of distinction and proportionality in IHL apply to cyber-attacks, and how neutrality law

46. Treaty Office, Chart of Signatures and Ratifications of Treaty 185: Convention on Cybercrime, COUNCIL OF EUR. https://www.coe.int/en/web/conventions/full-list%3B?module=signatures-by-treaty&treatynum=185 (last visited Sept. 1, 2025).

47. *UN General Assembly Adopts Landmark Convention on Cybercrime*, U.N. OFFICE ON DRUGS & CRIME (Dec. 24, 2024), https://www.unodc.org/unodc/en/press/releases/2024/December/un-general-assembly-adopts-landmark-convention-on-cybercrime.html.

48. United Nations Convention against Cybercrime: Strengthening International Cooperation for Combating Certain Crimes Committed by Means of Information and Communications Technology Systems and for the Sharing of Evidence in Electronic Form of Serious Crimes (Dec. 24, 2024) (published as an Annex to Report, Countering the use of information and communications technologies for criminal purposes U.N. Doc. A/79/460 (Nov. 27, 2024), https://docs.un.org/en/A/79/460).

49. Michael N. Schmitt ed., TALLINN MANUAL 2.0 ON THE INTERNATIONAL LAW APPLICABLE TO CYBER OPERATIONS (2017).

would govern third-party states' cyber infrastructure. The *Tallinn Manual 2.0* expanded the scope to address cyber operations in peacetime, covering areas such as sovereignty, state responsibility, and due diligence obligations during peacetime cyber incidents.

For lawyers and policymakers, the Tallinn Manual is **influential as a reference** for interpreting cyber norms under international law. Although it is non-binding and some states disagree with certain positions taken by the Tallinn experts, academic, military, and diplomatic discussions have cited it as a benchmark. For instance, Rule 4 of Tallinn 2.0 controversially asserts that a cyber operation violating a state's territorial sovereignty (such as a remote intrusion causing effects on another state's territory) is an internationally wrongful act, even if the operation does not cause physical damage. This position aligns with the view of some states but not others.[50]

2.4. The UN Charter and Fundamental Principles

The **UN Charter** is a cornerstone of international law. It provides several key principles that apply to cyberspace, just as they do to the physical world. Chief among these is the principle of **state sovereignty.**[51] *Sovereignty* means that a state has supreme authority over its territory and domestic affairs, free from external interference, and is equal to other states in international law. Sovereignty implies that states have jurisdiction over ICT infrastructure and activities within their territory, and other states must respect that sovereignty in their cyber operations. As discussed above, the 2013 UN GGE explicitly affirmed that state sovereignty applies to state conduct of ICT-related activities.[52]

One state should not violate the cyber "territory" of another. However, how to interpret violations of sovereignty in cyberspace, is debated.[53] Some states (and the Tallinn Manual) argue that any unauthorized penetration of another state's cyber systems is a breach of sovereignty. Others, such as the United Kingdom, have argued that only cyber operations causing significant physical effects or usurping inherently governmental functions would amount to a violation of sovereignty, implying that mere network intrusions for espionage might not breach international law.[54]

Another pillar is the **prohibition on use of force.**[55] This is a binding legal rule that states must not use force against the territorial integrity or political independence of any state. Cyber operations can reach a level equivalent to the use of force. A cyber operation that

50. Jack Goldsmith & Alex Loomis, *"Defend Forward" and Sovereignty*, LAWFARE (Apr. 30, 2021, 11:26 AM), https://www.lawfaremedia.org/article/defend-forward-and-sovereignty.

51. U.N. Charter art. 2, ¶ 1.

52. *See supra* nn. 15–16 and accompanying text.

53. Harriet Moynihan, *The Application of International Law to State Cyberattacks: Sovereignty and Non-Intervention*, Chatham House (Dec. 2, 2019, updated Dec. 17, 2020), https://www.chathamhouse.org/2019/12/application-international-law-state-cyberattacks/2-application-sovereignty-cyberspace.

54. Mark Visger, *The International Law Sovereignty Debate and Development of International Norms on Peacetime Cyber Operations*, Lawfare (July 12, 2022, 8:01 a.m.), https://www.lawfaremedia.org/article/international-law-sovereignty-debate-and-development-international-norms-peacetime-cyber-operations.

55. U.N. Charter art. 2, ¶ 4.

causes destruction or death would likely qualify as a use of force, just as if a kinetic weapon had caused the harm. This means such cyber operations are unlawful unless an exception applies.[56]

A related principle is the **right of self-defense.**[57] If a state suffers a cyber-armed attack of significant scale, that state may invoke self-defense and respond, including potentially with force[58] against the responsible state or organized group. However, below the armed attack threshold, responses must remain within the realm of countermeasures or law enforcement, not military force, which complicates decisionmaking for states dealing with constant but low-level cyber intrusions.[59]

State responsibility and due diligence are legal doctrines that tie into these principles. Under the law of state responsibility, a state is responsible for any internationally wrongful act attributable to it, including acts by its organs, agents, or even private actors it directs or controls. In cyberspace, this means that if a state's military or intelligence services conduct a cyber operation that violates an international obligation of the state, that state bears responsibility. It must cease the act and make reparations for the damage.[60] Attribution of cyber-attacks to a state is often challenging in practice (as discussed in the next section). But legally, the rules are analogous to any other domain: if you can tie the act to the state (either directly or through proxy actors under state control), the state is on the hook for it.

Due diligence is a related concept; a state may have an obligation not to allow its territory to be used to harm the rights of other states. In the cyber context, due diligence would mean each state should take reasonable measures to prevent its territory, systems, or nationals from being used to mount cyber operations that cause serious harm internationally.[61] This essentially calls on states to police malicious cyber activities emanating from their infrastructure when aware of them. For example, if Country A knows that a hacker group on its soil is launching crippling cyberattacks on Country B, Country A is expected to take action to stop it or else it could bear responsibility. Due diligence is grounded in long-standing international law analogies (the *Trail Smelter* arbitration and the ICJ's *Corfu Channel* case established the principle that states must not allow their territory to be used

56. Exceptions could include a UN Security Council authorization or self-defense in response to an armed attack.

57. U.N. Charter art. 51.

58. For example, in June 2019 after Iran shot down a U.S. drone, President Trump authorized cyberattacks against Iranian missile control systems instead of a conventional military strike. Ellen Nakashima, *With Trump's Approval, Pentagon Launched Cyber Strikes against Iran*, Wash. Post (June 22, 2019), https://www.washingtonpost.com/world/national-security/with-trumps-approval-pentagon-launched-cyber-strikes-against-iran/2019/06/22/250d3740-950d-11e9-b570-6416efdc0803_story.html.

59. For a breakdown of the discussion, see Sukumar, *supra* note 20.

60. Michael N. Schmitt & Liis Vihul, *The Nature of International Law Cyber Norms*, *in* International Cyber Norms: Legal, Policy & Industry Perspectives 23 (Anna-Maria Osula & Henry Rõigas eds., 2016), https://www.ccdcoe.org/uploads/2018/10/InternationalCyberNorms_Ch2.pdf.

61. The 2015 UN GGE norms include a norm echoing this principle: "*States should not knowingly allow their territory to be used for internationally wrongful acts using ICTs.*" 2015 UN GGE Report, *supra* note 17, ¶ 13(c).

in a manner injurious to others).[62] Many experts see it as an emerging norm, if not already customary law, for cyberspace.

3. Cyber Norm Enforcement

While cyber norms are progressing, ensuring adherence to those norms and enforcing them when violated remains a challenge. Cyberspace poses unique difficulties distinguishing it from traditional domains in terms of accountability and governance. In this section, we explore some key challenges in cyber norm enforcement: attribution problems, the non-binding nature of many norms, geopolitical rivalry, and tensions between national sovereignty and international oversight.

Attribution is one of the most notorious challenges in cyberspace, both domestically and internationally.[63] Without clear attribution, holding the responsible party accountable is extremely difficult. Attackers can route their operations through third countries, use hijacked computers of unwitting victims, or deliberately plant false clues to pin the blame elsewhere.

Attribution is not impossible. Major governments have built sophisticated capabilities and often can determine it, at least privately. Private industry (like FireEye, Microsoft, and CrowdStrike) also contribute. But attribution is time-consuming, resource-intensive, and sometimes yields only moderate confidence in conclusions. Additionally, states often hesitate to publicly reveal all the evidence of attribution they have because doing so might compromise intelligence sources or methods.

The result is an enforcement gap: a state suffering a cyber operation may know (or strongly suspect) who committed the offense, but if it cannot credibly prove the attribution to others, rallying an international response or pursuing legal action is problematic. If a state cannot or will not provide evidence that attributes a cyberattack to another state, it cannot easily invoke that other state's responsibility under international law or take countermeasures against it. Instead, the victim state might end up just reinforcing its own defenses, which, while prudent, does not dissuade the attacker from repeating the offense elsewhere.

3.1. Enforcement Mechanisms

As discussed, most international cyber norms are non-binding. This means there is no formal legal penalty for breaching norms *per se*. Instead, enforcement relies on political and diplomatic pressure. Some common enforcement mechanisms include:

62. Trail Smelter (U.S. v. Can.), 3 R.I.A.A. 1905 (1941), https://legal.un.org/riaa/cases/vol_iii/1905-1982.pdf; Corfu Channel (U.K. v. Alb.), 1949 I.C.J. 4 (Apr. 9), https://www.iilj.org/wp-content/uploads/2016/08/Corfu-Channel-Case-United-Kingdom-v.-Albania.pdf.

63. Thomas Rid & Ben Buchanan, *Attributing Cyber Attacks*, 38 J. Strategic Stud. 4 (Dec. 23, 2014), http://dx.doi.org/10.1080/01402390.2014.977382.

"Naming and Shaming"

Democracies typically will call out cyberattacks and indict foreign hackers, like the U.S. Department of Justice indicting members of China's PLA in 2014 for economic espionage and Russian GRU officers in 2020 for NotPetya and other attacks.[64] However, naming and shaming alone have proven largely ineffective at deterring states from engaging in cyber operations. Despite repeated public attribution and criminal charges, adversaries continue their operations with minimal disruption.[65]

Sanctions and Legal Consequences

A stronger form of response is sanctions or legal actions. The U.S. and EU have sanctioned entities from Russia, China, North Korea, and Iran for cyberattacks.[66] These sanctions impose some cost, but their effectiveness varies. They can deter state-employed hackers who like to travel or own property abroad. But top decision-makers in those countries often are relatively insulated from such sanctions, especially if they already face other sanctions.

Collective Enforcement

Ideally, norm enforcement would be collective to maximize impact and legitimacy. The reality is—outside of a military context—we have *ad-hoc* coordination at best. NATO or EU members have collectively attributed and even collectively sanctioned in a few cases, but globally, getting all UN members to agree to sanction a violator is nearly impossible due to political divides and Security Council paralysis, given veto powers. Thus, enforcement falls to coalitions of the willing.

Geopolitical Tensions and Different Visions

The West generally advocates an open, free, secure internet with norms preventing disruptive attacks and safeguarding rights. China, Russia, and their allies stress state sovereignty in cyber and "information security," sometimes prioritizing regime stability and control of information. These visions clash, for example, over issues like state censorship, which

---

64. These often take the form of press releases. *See, e.g., Six Russian GRU Officers Charged in Connection with Worldwide Deployment of Destructive Malware and Other Disruptive Actions in Cyberspace,* U.S. Dep't of Just. (Oct. 19, 2020), https://www.justice.gov/archives/opa/pr/six-russian-gru-officers-charged-connection-worldwide-deployment-destructive-malware-and; *U.S. Charges Five Chinese Military Hackers for Cyber Espionage Against U.S. Corporations and a Labor Organization for Commercial Advantage,* U.S. Dep't of Just. (May 19, 2014), https://www.justice.gov/archives/opa/pr/us-charges-five-chinese-military-hackers-cyber-espionage-against-us-corporations-and-labor.

65. For more on naming and shaming, see Adam Segal, The Hacked World Order: How Nations Fight, Trade, Maneuver, and Manipulate in the Digital Age 131 (2016) and Martha Finnemore & Duncan B. Hollis, *Beyond Naming and Shaming: Accusations and International Law in Cybersecurity,* 31 Eur. J. Int'l L. 969 (Aug. 2020), https://doi.org/10.1093/ejil/chaa056.

66. Laurens Cerulus & Elisa Braun, *In a First, EU Slaps Sanctions on Hackers in Russia, North Korea, China,* Politico (July 30, 2020 5:25 PM), https://www.politico.eu/article/eu-slaps-sanctions-on-hackers-in-russia-north-korea-china/.

China and Russia see as a sovereign right to protect society, whereas Western states see large-scale censorship or internet shutdowns as against freedom norms.

4. Key Laws in Europe, Asia/Pacific, Russia, Latin America, and Africa

Cybersecurity and data protection laws shape global commerce and governance. Europe emphasizes fundamental rights, some Asian nations and Russia prioritize sovereignty and security, and Latin America and Africa continue to build their frameworks. For organizations with international operations, these regimes carry extraterritorial reach and significant compliance risks. This section surveys the key laws across regions to highlight their common principles and practical impact.

4.1. European Union

This section provides an examination of the European Union's cybersecurity and data protection framework. It begins with a brief history of data protection followed by an analysis of the most important laws. Practitioners advising clients with international operations must understand EU cybersecurity law, as these regulations often have extraterritorial application and significant compliance implications even for organizations without a physical presence in Europe.

A Brief History of EU Data Protection

Europe's cybersecurity and data protection regime is rooted in a strong rights-based tradition. The European Union (EU) treats privacy and personal data protection as fundamental rights, as enshrined in Articles 7 and 8 of the EU Charter of Fundamental Rights.[67] Early efforts in Europe included national data protection laws in the 1970s–80s[68] and the EU Data Protection Directive of 1995.[69] In the early 2000s, the EU began formally addressing cybersecurity. The first significant steps were primarily advisory. In 2004, it created the European Network and Information Security Agency (ENISA) to support Member States with expertise,[70] and in 2006, it released the *EU Strategy for a Secure Information Society*.[71] These laid the groundwork but did not yet impose broad cybersecurity obligations on

67. Charter of Fundamental Rights of the European Union arts. 7–8, 2012 O.J. (C 326) 2.

68. Sofija Voronova & Anna Nichols, Understanding EU Data Protection Policy, PE 651.923, at 3 Eur. Parl. Res. Serv. (May 2020), https://www.europarl.europa.eu/RegData/etudes/BRIE/2020/651923/EPRS_BRI%282020%29651923_EN.pdf.

69. Directive 95/46/EC of the European Parliament and of the Council of 24 October 1995 on the protection of individuals with regard to the processing of personal data and on the free movement of such data, 1995 O.J. (L 281) 31.

70. Regulation (EC) No. 460/2004 of the European Parliament and of the Council of 10 March 2004 establishing the European Network and Information Security Agency, 2004 O.J. (L 77) 1.

71. Eur. Commission, Strategy for a secure information society (2006 communication), COM (2006) 251 (May, 31, 2006), https://eur-lex.europa.eu/legal-content/EN/TXT/?uri=legissum:l24153a.

private entities. Over time, escalating cyber threats and several high-profile data breaches shifted the EU's approach from advice to law.

The EU adopted the *General Data Protection Regulation (GDPR)*[72] in 2016, alongside the first EU-wide cybersecurity law, the *Network and Information Security (NIS) Directive*. The GDPR replaced the 1995 Data Protection Directive and modernized data privacy rules, while also imposing explicit security duties and breach reporting requirements across all sectors for the first time. The NIS Directive[73] marked the EU's recognition that cybersecurity needed a dedicated regulatory regime beyond the personal data protection of the GDPR. NIS required "operators of essential services"[74] and certain digital service providers[75] to implement security measures and report major cyber incidents.[76]

Within a few years, the scope of EU cybersecurity regulation had expanded **beyond personal data to a broader range of digital risks.** The EU Cybersecurity Act of 2019 introduced a framework for **security certification of ICT products and services** and bolstered ENISA's mandate.[77] Meanwhile, recognizing the limitations of the original NIS Directive, EU lawmakers moved to update and strengthen it. In 2022, the EU adopted **NIS 2** to broaden sectoral coverage, harmonize national approaches, and address emerging threats more effectively.[78] Several sector-specific and emerging technology regulations also emerged in 2024: The Digital Operational Resilience Act (DORA)[79] for financial services; The AI Act;[80] The **Cyber Resilience Act.**[81] Each of these is covered later in the chapter or elsewhere in the Handbook.

---

72. Regulation 2016/679 of the European Parliament and of the Council of 27 April 2016 on the protection of natural persons with regard to the processing of personal data and on the free movement of such data, and Repealing Directive 95/46/EC (General Data Protection Regulation), 2016 O.J. (L 119) 1.

73. Directive 2016/1148 of the European Parliament and of the Council of 6 July 2016 concerning measures for a high common level of security of network and information systems across the Union, 2016 O.J. (L 194) 1.

74. *Id.* arts. 4(4), 5(2). Operators of essential services are in critical sectors like energy, transport, healthcare, banking, and digital infrastructure, among others.

75. *Id.* art. 4(5)–(6).

76. *Id.* arts. 14(3), 16(3).

77. Regulation (EU) 2019/881 of the European Parliament and of the Council of 17 April 2019 on ENISA (the European Union Agency for Cybersecurity) and on information and communications technology cybersecurity certification and repealing Regulation (EU) No 526/2013 (Cybersecurity Act), 2019 O.J. (L 151) 15.

78. Directive (EU) 2022/2555 of the European Parliament and of the Council of 14 December 2022 on measures for a high common level of cybersecurity across the Union, amending Regulation (EU) No 910/2014 and Directive (EU) 2018/1972, and repealing Directive (EU) 2016/1148 (NIS2 Directive), 2022 O.J. (L 333) 80.

79. Regulation (EU) 2022/2554 of the European Parliament and of the Council of 14 December 2022 on digital operational resilience for the financial sector and amending Regulations (EC) No 1060/2009, (EU) No 648/2012, (EU) No 600/2014, (EU) No 909/2014, and (EU) 2016/1011 (Digital Operational Resilience Act), 2022 O.J. (L 333) 1.

80. Regulation (EU) 2024/1689 of the European Parliament and of the Council of 13 June 2024 laying down harmonised rules on artificial intelligence and amending Regulations (EC) No 300/2008, (EU) No 167/2013, (EU) No 168/2013, (EU) 2018/858, (EU) 2018/1139 and (EU) 2019/2144 and Directives 2014/90/EU, (EU) 2016/797 and (EU) 2020/1828 (Artificial Intelligence Act), 2024 O.J. (L 1689).

81. Regulation (EU) 2024/2847 of the European Parliament and of the Council of 23 October 2024 on horizontal cybersecurity requirements for products with digital elements and amending Regulations (EU) No 168/2013 and (EU) 2019/1020 and Directive (EU) 2020/1828 (Cyber Resilience Act), 2024 O.J. (L 2847).

The GDPR as a Cybersecurity Law

The GDPR functions as a ***de facto* cybersecurity regulation.** When the GDPR came into force in May 2018, it strengthened individual rights over personal data and imposed rigorous obligations on organizations to secure that data. By coupling privacy rules with security requirements, the GDPR blurred the line between privacy and cybersecurity.

Under Article 32 of the GDPR, controllers and processors of personal data must **implement appropriate technical and organizational measures** to ensure a level of security appropriate to the risk.[82] This obligation includes measures such as pseudonymization and data encryption, the ability to provide ongoing confidentiality, integrity, and availability of systems, and processes for regularly testing and evaluating security effectiveness.[83]

The GDPR also introduced a general duty to report data breaches.[84] Article 33 compels organizations to notify the relevant supervisory authority of a personal data breach **within 72 hours** of becoming aware of it, unless the breach will not likely result in harm. Data protection authorities (DPAs) can investigate security practices and order remedies for violations. The GDPR attaches substantial fines of up to €20 million or 4% of an organization's worldwide annual turnover for the most serious violations.[85] The GDPR also allows data subjects[86] to seek legal remedies for damages caused by negligent data security.[87]

In effect, the GDPR mainstreamed cybersecurity within corporate governance. It clarified that any business handling EU residents' personal data has a legal obligation to provide data security. It has a global impact; many companies outside Europe have raised their security standards to meet the GDPR's requirements, and numerous countries have modeled their privacy laws on the GDPR. While not an all-encompassing cybersecurity code (it covers only personal data, not all information or systems), the GDPR has nevertheless driven significant improvements in cybersecurity.

4.2. International Data Transfers

The GDPR also impacted the way data flows across borders through high-profile court cases, known as *Schrems I*[88] and *Schrems II*,[89] named after Max Schrems, an Austrian

82. GDPR, art. 32.

83. *Id.* art. 32(1). The GDPR's requirement is risk-based: security measures should be commensurate with the likelihood and severity of harm to individuals' rights (for example, stricter protection for more sensitive personal data). This built-in flexibility pushes organizations to continuously assess threats and upgrade their security postures as needed. *See id.*

84. *Id.* art. 33.

85. *Id.* art. 83(6). Examples of large GDPR Fines include: Ireland's 1.2 billion Euro fine to Meta in 2023 for transfer of Facebook user data, the Dutch DPA's 290 million Euro fine to Uber in 2024 for transfer of driver data, and Ireland's 345 million Euro fine to TikTok in 2023 for mishandling children's personal data. There are many other examples; for a comprehensive list of GDPR fines, visit https://www.enforcementtracker.com/.

86. GDPR, art. 4(1) (defining "data subject" as an identified or identifiable natural person whose personal data is processed).

87. GDPR, arts. 79, 82.

88. Case C-362/14, Schrems v. Data Prot. Comm'r, ECLI:EU:C:2015:650 (Oct. 6, 2015).

89. Case C-311/18, Data Prot. Comm'r v. Facebook Ireland Ltd. & Maximillian Schrems, ECLI:EU:C:2020:559 (July 16, 2020).

privacy activist, whose litigation led the EU Court of Justice (CJEU) to invalidate two major EU–US data transfer frameworks. The fallout from these rulings has forced companies to reevaluate how they transfer personal data outside Europe and has spurred efforts to establish new legal mechanisms.

In ***Schrems I* in 2015**, the CJEU struck down the EU–US **Safe Harbor** agreement. Safe Harbor was a 2000 agreement that allowed certified U.S. companies to receive EU personal data by pledging to adhere to certain privacy principles.[90] Schrems challenged Facebook's reliance on Safe Harbor, arguing that U.S. law did not adequately protect EU citizens' data.[91] The CJEU agreed. It found that Safe Harbor did not provide essentially equivalent protection as EU law requires, given that U.S. authorities could access Europeans' data in ways incompatible with EU privacy rights. The invalidation of Safe Harbor abruptly removed the legal basis that over 4,000 companies had used for EU–US data transfers, causing a scramble to alternative measures.

A replacement framework with more protections and oversight, the **Privacy Shield**, was negotiated in 2016.[92] But in ***Schrems II***, the CJEU invalidated the Privacy Shield, as well. The Court held that U.S. surveillance laws allowed excessive access to Europeans' data without sufficient judicial redress, meaning the Privacy Shield could not meet EU adequacy standards. At the same time, *Schrems II* cast doubt on other legal methods: **Standard Contractual Clauses (SCCs)** and **Binding Corporate Rules (BCRs)**. While the Court did not invalidate SCCs, it ruled that organizations and regulators must verify, on a case-by-case basis, whether the law of the receiving country ensures adequate protection. If not, it would require suspension of transfers.

European Data Protection Authorities began issuing guidance that, absent sufficient safeguards, certain transfers (like use of US-based cloud services for sensitive data) might be illegal.[93] This legal uncertainty put companies in a difficult position: either stop certain data flows, re-architect services to store data in Europe, or find ways to heavily encrypt or anonymize data before transferring. For cybersecurity, this meant increased interest in

90. Under EU law, personal data can only be transferred to countries that ensure an "adequate level" of data protection (under what was then Directive 95/46/EC). The U.S. does not have a comprehensive federal data protection law, so Safe Harbor was created as a workaround. It required voluntary self-certification by U.S. companies to the U.S. Department of Commerce promising to adhere to certain privacy principles (notice, choice, onward transfer, access, security, data integrity, and enforcement). Companies also had to publicly declare compliance and be subject to enforcement by the Federal Trade Commission.

91. Schrems was particularly concerned with surveillance programs revealed by Edward Snowden.

92. U.S. Dep't of Commerce, EU–U.S. Privacy Shield Framework: Full Text (Feb. 29, 2016), https://www.commerce.gov/files/eu-us-privacy-shield-full-text-feb-29-2016; Commission Implementing Decision (EU) 2016/1250 of 12 July 2016, 2016 O.J. (L 207) 1. The Privacy Shield introduced several enhancements over its predecessor: stronger obligations on companies, enhanced oversight and enforcement, redress mechanisms for EU citizens, limitations on U.S. Government access, and annual joint review.

93. Nigel Cory, *How 'Schrems II' Has Accelerated Europe's Slide Toward a De Facto Data Localization Regime*, INFO. TECH. & INNOVATION FOUND. (July 8, 2021), https://itif.org/publications/2021/07/08/how-schrems-ii-has-accelerated-europes-slide-toward-de-facto-data/.

European-based security solutions and a push for "sovereign cloud" offerings where data and operations are shielded from non-EU jurisdiction.[94]

To address the impasse over data transfer to the US, the European Commission and the United States negotiated a new arrangement, the **EU–US Data Privacy Framework (DPF)**.[95] In July 2023, the Commission adopted an **adequacy decision** for the DPF, finding that the United States ensures an adequate level of protection for personal data transferred from the EU to participating US companies.[96] The DPF introduced new binding safeguards, including limits on US intelligence agencies' access to EU data and a new two-tier redress mechanism for EU individuals, featuring an independent **Data Protection Review Court** in the US to handle complaints. With the adequacy decision in place, companies could once again transfer data to the US under the DPF if the US recipient self-certifies to the framework's principles. This relieved businesses, as it restored a legal pathway for EU–US data flows.[97]

Whether there will be a *Schrems III* remains a question. Max Schrems and his organization noyb almost immediately announced a legal challenge to the new Data Privacy Framework.[98] But they have yet to proceed with litigation. Schrems has indicated that changes to U.S. independent agencies by the second Trump administration will cause a review before a formal legal challenge by noyb.[99] Thus, regardless of the means, the CJEU will likely review the DPF in the coming years. If the court invalidates it, the transatlantic data transfer situation would return to square one, with companies relying primarily on SCCs and facing the same dilemmas as after *Schrems II*.

NIS Directive and NIS2

While the GDPR addresses the security of personal data, the EU recognized a need for parallel legislation focusing on the security of networks and information systems across critical sectors. This led to the Network and Information Security Directive, or **NIS Directive**,

94. The EU's sovereign cloud Initiatives have largely been a failure. For example, Gaia-X, launched in 2020, was intended to create a federated and secure European cloud ecosystem. But internal disagreements among stakeholders, including differing visions and the involvement of U.S. hyperscalers like Microsoft and Amazon, have hindered progress. Europe's share in the global cloud market has declined despite the initiatives. See Matthew Gooding, *Gaia-X: Has Europe's Grand Digital Infrastructure Project Hit the Buffers?*, DCD (May 13, 2024), https://www.datacenterdynamics.com/en/analysis/gaia-x-has-europes-grand-digital-infrastructure-project-hit-the-buffers/.

95. U.S. Dep't of Comm., EU–U.S. Data Privacy Framework (2023), https://www.commerce.gov/page/eu-us-privacy-shield.

96. Press Release, Eur. Commission, Data Protection: European Commission adopts new adequacy decision for safe and trusted EU–US data flows, IP/23/3721 (July 9, 2023), https://ec.europa.eu/commission/presscorner/detail/en/ip_23_3721.

97. The DPF complements SCCs, which remained available but burdensome to use post-*Schrems II*.

98. noyb, *European Commission Gives EU-US Data Transfers Third Round at CJEU: New Trans-Atlantic Data Privacy Framework Largely a Copy of "Privacy Shield". Noyb Will Challenge the Decision*, (July 10, 2023), https://noyb.eu/en/european-commission-gives-eu-us-data-transfers-third-round-cjeu.

99. Lexie White, *Schrems Addresses Emerging Questions around EU-U.S. Data Privacy Framework*, IAPP (Mar. 26, 2025), https://iapp.org/news/a/schrems-addresses-emerging-questions-around-eu-us-data-privacy-framework/.

in 2016.[100] It required Member States to adopt national cybersecurity strategies, designate competent authorities, set up computer security incident response teams (CSIRTs), and enforce security and incident-reporting obligations for covered entities.[101] Sectors such as energy, transport, banking, financial market infrastructure, health, water, and digital services, were in scope. Operators in these sectors, termed "operators of essential services," had to take appropriate security measures and notify authorities of serious incidents. But NIS fell short of its purpose for two reasons: (1) implementation by Member States varied greatly in scope and enforcement; and (2) updates were needed due to the rapid digitalization of society and increasingly interdependent sectors.[102]

These problems led to **NIS2**. It covered more sectors, removed the distinction between essential services and digital service providers, and imposed uniform risk management obligations.[103] Medium and large organizations in critical sectors[104] are now automatically in scope, with management bodies now held directly responsible for cybersecurity compliance.[105] Additionally, NIS2 mandates stricter enforcement and grants national authorities enhanced supervisory powers with more substantial penalties. Coordinated oversight at the EU level is reinforced by the European Cyber Crisis Liaison Organization Network (EU-CyCLONe)[106] and expanded information-sharing provisions among Member States.

4.3. Other EU Cybersecurity Regulations and Initiatives

Several other notable EU Cybersecurity laws deserve mention. This chapter will include a paragraph for each explaining its purpose, basics, and resources for more information.

Digital Operation Resilience Act

The Digital Operation Resilience Act (DORA)[107] establishes an EU-wide framework ensuring that banks, insurance companies, investment firms, and other financial entities can withstand, respond to, and recover from cyber-attacks and ICT incidents. DORA applies to a broad range of financial sector entities, including credit institutions, insurers, asset managers, payment institutions, trading venues, etc., as well as critical third-party ICT service providers to those entities.[108] All EU-regulated financial entities must comply, and critical ICT providers (like cloud services) servicing them are subject to oversight. DORA

100. NIS, *supra* note 73.
101. *Id.* arts. 7–9, 15.
102. NIS2, *supra* note 78, recitals 2–7.
103. *Id.*
104. Critical sectors include public administration, healthcare, space, and critical product manufacturing. *Id.* Annex I.
105. *Id.*
106. *Id.* art. 16.
107. DORA, *supra* note 79.
108. *Id.* art. 2.

has extraterritorial application; non-EU ICT providers serving EU financial entities must establish an EU presence if designated as critical.[109]

Cyber Resilience Act

The Cyber Resilience Act (CRA), a regulation adopted in 2024, established mandatory cybersecurity requirements for hardware and software products with digital elements placed on the EU market.[110] It applies to a wide range of products, from consumer electronics and operating systems to industrial software, with risk-tiered obligations. Manufacturers must design secure products, manage vulnerabilities, issue security updates for at least five years, and prepare technical documentation, including Software Bills of Materials (SBOMs).[111] Certain high-risk products require third-party conformity assessments.[112]

Digital Services Act

The Digital Services Act (DSA) modernizes the e-Commerce Directive for modern online platforms. It became applicable in February 2024.[113] It imposes layered obligations on providers of intermediary services, especially very large online platforms (VLOPs) and very large online search engines (VLSEs), designated as such based on user numbers.[114] All intermediaries must comply with transparency, notice-and-action, and user redress mechanisms, while platforms face stricter obligations, including advertising transparency, protections for minors, and content moderation accountability. VLOPs and VLSEs must conduct systemic risk assessments, undergo audits, and ensure algorithmic transparency. The DSA retains liability exemptions for passive hosts but adds due diligence obligations and EU oversight by the Commission.[115]

Digital Markets Act

The Digital Markets Act (DMA) creates *ex ante* rules for large digital platforms offering core services such as app stores, online marketplaces, operating systems, and search engines.[116] Designated gatekeepers[117] (Apple, Google, Meta, Amazon, etc.) must avoid unfair practices, like self-preferencing, tying, and restricting interoperability. They must allow sideloading, data portability, access to performance metrics, and ensure fair treatment

---

109. *Id.* ¶ 81 & § II.

110. Cyber Resilience, *supra* note 81.

111. *Id.* art. 6 & Annex I.

112. *Id.* arts. 7 & 32(2)-(3) & Annex III.

113. Regulation (EU) 2022/2065 of the European Parliament and of the Council of 19 October 2022 on a Single Market for Digital Services and amending Directive 2000/31/EC (Digital Services Act), 2022 O.J. (L 277) 1.

114. *Id.* § 5.

115. *Id.* arts. 6 & ch. III, § 1.

116. Regulation (EU) 2022/1925 of the European Parliament and of the Council of 14 September 2022 on contestable and fair markets in the digital sector and amending Directives (EU) 2019/1937 and (EU) 2020/1828 (Digital Markets Act), 2022 O.J. (L 265) 1 art. 1.

117. *Id.* art. 3.

of business users.[118] The DMA prohibits combining data across services without consent and imposes anti-circumvention duties. The European Commission exclusively enforces the DMA, with powers to impose fines up to 20% of global turnover.[119]

4.4. China

China has a stringent cyber and data governance regime driven by government interests in national security and control over data. In 2016, the PRC enacted the Cybersecurity Law.[120] It requires network operators to implement security measures to protect systems and data and mandates that personal information and other important data collected in China be stored on servers located *within China*. It also subjects critical network equipment and services to security certification and empowers authorities to conduct security reviews and inspect companies' network practices. These data localization and security review requirements reflect China's emphasis on "cyberspace sovereignty."[121]

China introduced two significant laws in 2021: the Data Security Law (DSL) and the Personal Information Protection Law (PIPL). The Data Security Law establishes a comprehensive framework for classifying data based on its importance to national security and public interests.[122] The DSL categorizes data by sensitivity, and entities must follow graded storage and transfer rules depending on data sensitivity. Further, the DSL prohibits providing any data stored in China to foreign law enforcement without the Chinese government's approval. The DSL was partly seen as a response to foreign laws like the U.S. CLOUD Act.[123]

The PIPL is China's first dedicated privacy law regulating personal data and is largely modeled after the EU's GDPR.[124] The PIPL defines personal information broadly and applies to the processing of Chinese residents' data both within China and extraterritorially. It requires data handlers to obtain informed consent for data collection and imposes principles like data minimization, purpose limitation, and transparency. Cross-border transfers of personal data face tight restrictions; companies must conduct security assessments and

---

118. *Id.* arts. (5)–(7).

119. *Id.* art. 30.

120. Rogier Creemers, Graham Webster & Paul Triolo, *Translation: Cybersecurity Law of the People's Republic of China (Effective June 1, 2017)*, DigiChina (June 29, 2018), https://digichina.stanford.edu/work/translation-cybersecurity-law-of-the-peoples-republic-of-china-effective-june-1-2017/. *See also* Lauren Maranto, *Who Benefits from China's Cybersecurity Laws?*, Ctr. for Strategic & Int'l Stud., (June 25, 2020), https://www.csis.org/blogs/new-perspectives-asia/who-benefits-chinas-cybersecurity-laws.

121. Dakota Cary, *Community Watch: China's Vision for the Future of the Internet*, Atlantic Council (Dec. 4, 2023), https://www.atlanticcouncil.org/in-depth-research-reports/report/community-watch-chinas-vision-for-the-future-of-the-internet/.

122. *Translation: Data Security Law of the People's Republic of China (Effective Sept. 1, 2021)*, DigiChina (June 29, 2021), https://digichina.stanford.edu/work/translation-data-security-law-of-the-peoples-republic-of-china/. *See also* Ryan D. Junck et al., *China's New Data Security and Personal Information Protection Laws: What They Mean for Multinational Companies*, Skadden (Nov. 3, 2021), https://www.skadden.com/insights/publications/2021/11/chinas-new-data-security-and-personal-information-protection-laws.

123. *Id.*

124. *Id.*

ensure foreign recipients uphold standards comparable to the PIPL. Hefty penalties for serious violations can reach ¥50 million or 5% of annual revenue.[125]

Enforcement of China's cybersecurity laws is ambiguous and subject to the whims of the Chinese Communist Party. The Cyberspace Administration of China and sectoral regulators wield broad powers to investigate and punish violations. The language of the Chinese laws is often deliberately vague, leaving room for officials to interpret requirements and enforce them stringently.[126]

At the same time, China's cybersecurity laws grant authorities flexibility to crack down on activities deemed threatening. China's government places greater emphasis on government access to data than on individual privacy, using cybersecurity regulation as a tool to cement state control.

Overall, China's legal framework is extensive and focuses on information security and national control. While it borrows concepts from global models like GDPR, it is distinguished by its emphasis on national security, data localization, and government access. China is also exporting aspects of this model through its tech companies and diplomacy, influencing cyber policy in other countries, called the "Digital Silk Road."[127]

4.5. Japan

Japan has a mature data protection regime centered on the Act on the Protection of Personal Information (APPI).[128] The APPI governs how personal information is handled by businesses and government entities with principles for obtaining consent, limiting use, ensuring data accuracy, and safeguarding data. The APPI, while similar in spirit to the GDPR, has some differences that make it more business-friendly, such as allowing for implied or inferred consent. In 2019, the EU formally recognized Japan's law as providing adequate protection, enabling easier EU-Japan data flows.[129]

Significant amendments to the APPI in recent years have strengthened the law and aligned it more closely with global standards. A 2015 amendment expanded the APPI's scope to apply to foreign companies handling Japanese citizens' data.[130] It also created the Personal Information Protection Commission (PPC) as Japan's data protection authority.

---

125. Rogier Creemers & Graham Webster, *Translation: Personal Information Protection Law of the People's Republic of China—Effective Nov. 1, 2021*, DigiChina (Aug. 20, 2021, rev. Sept. 7, 2021), https://digichina.stanford.edu/work/translation-personal-information-protection-law-of-the-peoples-republic-of-china-effective-nov-1-2021/.

126. *See* Maranto, *supra* note 120.

127. Grace Pyo, *An Alternate Vision: China's Cybersecurity Law and Its Implementation in the Chinese Courts*, 60 Colum. J. Transnat'l L. 229, 232 (2021).

128. Act on the Protection of Personal Information, Act No. 57 of 2003 (Japan), translated in Japanese Law Translation, Ministry of Justice, https://www.japaneselawtranslation.go.jp/en/laws/view/4241/en.

129. *European Commission Adopts Adequacy Decision on Japan, Creating the World's Largest Area of Safe Data Flows*, Eur. Commission (Jan. 22, 2019), https://ec.europa.eu/commission/presscorner/detail/en/ip_19_421.

130. Hiroyuki Tanaka & Naoto Shimamura, *Practical Notes for Japan's Important Updates of the APPI Guidelines and Q&As*, IAPP (Jan. 10, 2022), https://iapp.org/news/a/practical-notes-for-japans-important-updates-of-the-appi-guidelines-and-qas.

Another round of amendments in 2020 introduced heavier penalties for violations, mandatory breach notification, and tighter rules on using sensitive personal data.[131] Enforcement of APPI has been gradually increasing under the PPC's guidelines and orders, though fines under APPI historically were low (but were raised in the 2020 amendments).[132] Japan planned to introduce new amendments in 2025.[133]

Apart from personal data protection, Japan addresses cybersecurity directly. The Basic Act on Cybersecurity established a national strategy and clarified the roles and responsibilities of governments within Japan, critical infrastructure providers, and other entities.[134] In addition to the more policy-oriented Basic Act, there are provisions in other laws for specific issues.[135] In May 2025, Japan also passed an "Active Cyber Defense" law, which empowers Japan's military and law enforcement agencies to take pre-emptive action against cyber threats.[136] It was passed in response to growing Chinese cyber aggression. The scope of this bill in practice is unknown so far. Still, it empowers law enforcement agencies to employ "cyber harm prevention officers" who, in addition to other powers, can proactively shut down servers during an attack.

4.6. Australia

Australia's approach combines data privacy legislation with a national cybersecurity policy framework. The Privacy Act 1988 is a federal law that regulates how personal information is collected, used, and disclosed by Australian government agencies and many private sector organizations. It serves as the cornerstone for Australia's policy.[137] The Privacy Act was introduced to protect individuals' privacy and includes 13 Australian Privacy Principles (APPs) that set standards on transparency, data quality, security safeguards, cross-border data transfers, and other issues.[138] It applies to Commonwealth (federal) government

131. Hiroyuki Tanaka, *Japan Updates Enforcement Rules for Amended APPI*, IAPP (Mar. 30, 2021), https://iapp.org/news/a/japan-updates-enforcement-rules-for-amended-appi.

132. Natsuko Sugihara, *Japan Makes Amendments to Their Act on the Protection of Personal Information: Establishing an Obligation to Report Data Breaches to the PPC*, CLIFFORD CHANCE: TALKING TECH (July 2, 2020), https://www.cliffordchance.com/insights/resources/blogs/talking-tech/en/articles/2020/06/amendments-to-the-protection-of-personal-information-act-of-japa.html.

133. Hiroyuki Tanaka & Kohei Shiozaki, *Japan's DPA Publishes Interim Summary of Amendments to Data Protection Regulations*, IAPP (July 11, 2024), https://iapp.org/news/a/japan-s-dpa-publishes-interim-summary-of-amendments-to-data-protection-regulations.

134. *Basic Act on Cybersecurity*, Act No. 104 of 2014 (Japan), translated in Japanese Law Translation Database, https://www.japaneselawtranslation.go.jp/en/laws/view/3677/en.

135. For example, the Act on the Prohibition of Unauthorized Computer Access criminalizes hacking, much like the U.S. Computer Fraud & Abuse Act. *Act on Prohibition of Unauthorized Computer Access*, Act No. 128 of 1999 and Act. No. 28 of 2013 (Japan), https://www.japaneselawtranslation.go.jp/en/laws/view/3933/en.

136. See Adam Dobell & Grace O'Neill, *Japan's New Active Cyber Defense Law: A Strategic Evolution in National Cybersecurity*, CTR. FOR CYBERSECURITY POLICY & L.: Government (June 5, 2025), https://www.centerforcybersecuritypolicy.org/insights-and-research/japans-new-active-cyber-defense-law-a-strategic-evolution-in-national-cybersecurity.

137. *The Privacy Act*, OFFICE OF THE AUSTL. INFO. COMM'R (OAIC), https://www.oaic.gov.au/privacy/privacy-legislation/the-privacy-act (last visited April 25, 2025).

138. OAIC, *Australian Privacy Principles Quick Reference*, https://www.oaic.gov.au/privacy/australian-privacy-principles/australian-privacy-principles-quick-reference (last visited April 25, 2025).

entities and private organizations with annual turnover above A$3 million, among others. Over time, a series of amendments to the Privacy Act have strengthened its protections.[139]

Australia recently enacted the Online Safety Amendment Act 2024, which establishes a minimum age of 16 for accounts on social media platforms.[140] Under this law, social media companies must implement measures to prevent users under 16 from creating accounts. The legislation does not impose penalties on parents or children who violate the age restrictions.

In addition to its privacy laws, Australia has strong cybersecurity laws, particularly for protecting critical infrastructure. The Security of Critical Infrastructure Act 2018 (SOCI), established a regulatory framework for safeguarding critical infrastructure in sectors such as electricity, water, ports, and telecommunications.[141] After significant cyber incidents, amendments to the SOCI Act broadened the definition of critical infrastructure and introduced government assistance powers during serious cyber emergencies.[142]

In November 2024, Parliament passed a cybersecurity legislative package[143] to fortify national cyber defenses and protect critical infrastructure. It includes the Cyber Security Act 2024, the Security of Critical Infrastructure and Other Legislation Amendment (Enhanced Response and Prevention) Act 2024, and the Intelligence Services and Other Legislation Amendment (Cyber Security) Act 2024. The laws mandate baseline security standards for internet-of-things and other smart devices, impose mandatory reporting of ransomware payments by certain companies, and establish a Cyber Incident Review Board to investigate significant incidents, among other provisions to implement the last national cyber strategy.[144]

---

139. For example, the introduction of a Notifiable Data Breaches scheme in 2018 requires entities to notify affected individuals and the regulators of serious data breaches; Office of the Austl. Info. Comm'r, *History of the Privacy Act*, OAIC, https://www.oaic.gov.au/privacy/privacy-legislation/the-privacy-act/history-of-the-privacy-act (last visited April 25, 2025).

140. It exempts services deemed essential for health and education, including YouTube, Google Classroom, and messaging apps like WhatsApp; Online Safety Amendment (Social Media Minimum Age) Bill 2024, Parl. Deb. H.R. (Austl.) https://parlinfo.aph.gov.au/parlInfo/search/display/display.w3p;query=Id:%22legislation/bills/r7284_aspassed/0000%22 (as passed by both Houses in 2024) (last visited April 25, 2025).

141. Cyber & Infrastructure Sec. Ctr., *Security of Critical Infrastructure Act 2018 (SOCI)*, Austl. Dep't of Home Affs., https://www.cisc.gov.au/legislation-regulation-and-compliance/soci-act-2018 (last visited April 25, 2025).

142. Austl. Dep't of Home Affs., *Security Legislation Amendment (Critical Infrastructure Protection) Act of 2022*, https://www.homeaffairs.gov.au/reports-and-publications/submissions-and-discussion-papers/slacip-bill-2022 (last visited April 25, 2025); Protiviti, *Australia's Critical Infrastructure Act Reforms—A Positive Step in Strengthening Industry-wide Resilience*, https://www.protiviti.com/au-en/whitepaper/australias-critical-infrastructure-act-reforms (last visited April 25, 2025).

143. Anna Ribeiro, *Australia's Cyber Security Act Focuses on Fortifying Cyber Defenses, Protecting Critical Infrastructure*, Indus. Cyber (Nov. 26, 2024), https://industrialcyber.co/regulation-standards-and-compliance/australias-cyber-security-act-focuses-on-fortifying-cyber-defenses-protecting-critical-infrastructure (last visited April 25, 2025).

144. Australian Signals Directorate, Cyber Security, https://www.asd.gov.au/about/what-we-do/cybersecurity (last visited April 18, 2025); Austl. Dep't of Home Affs., *Cyber and Infrastructure Security*, https://www.homeaffairs.gov.au/about-us/our-portfolios/cyber-and-infrastructure-security (last visited April 18, 2025).

4.7. India

India built its cybersecurity legal framework on the foundation of the Information Technology Act (IT Act),[145] which was enacted in 2000 and substantially amended in 2008.[146] It is the primary law that addresses electronic commerce, cybercrimes, and data security in India. It provides legal recognition of electronic transactions and has sections dealing with offenses like unauthorized access, hacking, identity theft, and pornography. The IT Act is administered by the Ministry of Electronics and Information Technology[147] and partly enforced by agencies like the Indian Computer Emergency Response Team.[148]

Provisions of the IT Act empower the government to issue directives for blocking websites, intercepting communications, and requiring companies to assist in decryption.[149] The 2008 amendments broadened the definition of cybercrimes and strengthened corporate responsibilities for data security.[150] For instance, the amendments added section 43A of the IT Act mandating that companies handling sensitive personal data maintain "reasonable security practices."[151] Negligence leading to a data leak can bring liability.

For years, India lacked a dedicated data protection statute, relying only on patchy provisions in the IT Act. But in August 2023, the Indian Parliament passed the Digital Personal Data Protection Act (DPDP Act).[152] The DPDP Act safeguards individuals' personal data by establishing requirements for how organizations collect, process, and store data. For example, it mandates consent as a basis for processing personal data and grants rights to data subjects, such as the right to correct or erase data.[153] The Act established a Data Protection Board for enforcement, and it prescribes penalties for data breaches or non-compliance.[154]

Enforcement of cybersecurity in India is divided among different authorities. CERT-In, under the Ministry of Electronics and IT, is empowered to issue directives and guidelines to both the government and the private sector on cybersecurity incidents.[155] In 2022, CERT-In issued a controversial directive that required companies to report cyber incidents within

145. The Information Technology Act, No. 21 of 2000, INDIA CODE, https://www.indiacode.nic.in/handle/123456789/1999.

146. The Information Technology (Amendment) Act, 2008, No. 10 of 2009, INDIA CODE, https://www.indiacode.nic.in/handle/123456789/15414?locale=en.

147. *See* CYBER LAWS GROUP, IND. MIN. OF ELEC. & INFO. TECH., https://www.meity.gov.in/ministry/our-groups/details/cyber-laws-AM2MDOtQWa (last visited Sept. 6, 2025).

148. IT Act § 70B.

149. *Id.* §§ 69, 69A, & 69B.

150. *E.g.*, IT Act Amendments § 32 (adding offenses).

151. IT Act § 43A (amended by IT Act Amendments § 22).

152. The Digital Personal Data Protection Act, 2023, No. 22 of 2023, https://www.meity.gov.in/static/uploads/2024/06/2bf1f0e9f04e6fb4f8fef35e82c42aa5.pdf. For an analysis of the law, see Anirudh Burman, *Understanding India's New Data Protection Law*, CARNEGIE ENDOWMENT FOR INT'L PEACE (Oct. 3, 2023), https://carnegieendowment.org/research/2023/10/understanding-indias-new-data-protection-law?lang=en. This law was the culmination of over five years of debate and multiple bill versions. Prior to this Act, a 2019 Personal Data Protection Bill had been considered, but it was withdrawn in 2022 for revision.

153. DPDP Act §§ 4 & 12.

154. *Id.* § 18.

155. IT Act § 70B(4) &(6).

six hours of detection and to maintain extensive IT logs domestically for 180 days.[156] The directive also requires entities to synchronize their systems' time with government servers and to respond to any CERT-In order, effectively compelling disclosure of information as needed. Non-compliance with CERT-In's instructions can be treated as a legal offense under the IT Act.[157]

4.8. Russia

Russia's approach to cybersecurity and data regulation is primarily driven by state sovereignty and control over information. Russia has put in place a series of laws to regulate cyberspace.[158] The Federal Law on Personal Data (No. 152-FZ), enacted in 2006, defines rules for processing personal data. It requires data operators to obtain consent from individuals for collecting and using their personal information, with certain exceptions and to notify the data regulator in writing about its intention to process personal data.[159] In 2014, Russia passed Federal Law No. 242-FZ mandating that any company, domestic or foreign, that collects personal data of Russian citizens must store and process that data on servers located inside Russia.[160] This data localization law was presented as protecting Russian citizens' information and ensuring it remains subject to Russian jurisdiction. It has since been a cornerstone of Russia's data sovereignty push.[161]

In addition to data protection rules, Russia has continuously expanded the state's technical and legal capability to control internet traffic and communications. A 2012 law, Federal Law No. 139FZ enabled a national internet blacklist, allowing authorities to block websites deemed to host illegal content without a court order.[162] In 2013, another law, Federal Law No. 398FZ, expanded this authority to permit extrajudicial blocking of content that called for unauthorized public protests or threatened public order.[163]

In 2019, the government enacted the "sovereign internet" law, which requires internet service providers to install deep packet inspection equipment that allows authorities to filter

---

156. Directions under sub-section (6) of section 70B of the Information Technology Act, 2000 relating to information security practices, procedure, prevention, response and reporting of cyber incidents for Safe & Trusted Internet, No. 20(3)/2022-CERT-In, Ind. Min. of Elec. & Info. Tech. (Apr. 28, 2022), https://www.cert-in.org.in/Directions70B.jsp. For a discussion of the directive, see Aniruddha Majumdar et al., *Cyber Security: India Revamps Rules on Mandatory Incident Reporting & Allied Compliances*, Nat'l L. Rev. (Sept. 8, 2022), https://natlawreview.com/article/cyber-security-india-revamps-rules-mandatory-incident-reporting-allied-compliances.

157. IT Act § 70B(7).

158. *See* Data protection laws in Russia, DLA Piper, https://www.dlapiperdataprotection.com/?t=law&c=RU (last visited Sept. 6, 2025); Ksenia Andreeva, Anastasia Kiseleva & Alena Neskoromyuk, *Data Localization Laws: Russian Federation*, Practical L. Data Priv. Adv., (July 22, 2021), https://www.morganlewis.com/-/media/files/publication/outside-publication/article/2021/data-localization-laws-russian-federation.pdf.

159. *Id.*

160. John Tomaszewski & Jason Priebe, *Fortress Russia—The Russian Data Localization Law*, Seyfarth (May 4, 2015), https://www.globalprivacywatch.com/2015/05/fortress-russia-the-russian-data-localization-law.

161. Justin Sherman, *Russia Is Weaponizing Its Data Laws against Foreign Organizations*, Brookings (Sept. 27, 2022), https://www.brookings.edu/articles/russia-is-weaponizing-its-data-laws-against-foreign-organizations/.

162. *Id.*

163. *Id.*

or block content and even reroute all internet traffic through state-controlled points.[164] This law sets the stage for the Runet (the Russian segment of the internet) to operate independently if cut off from the global internet, ostensibly as a defensive measure. Together with earlier measures (like a 2018 law fining search engines that enabled access to banned sites),[165] these laws give the Kremlin tools to isolate and control the internet in Russia.

4.9. Brazil

Brazil enacted the *Lei Geral de Proteção de Dados* (LGPD) in 2018.[166] The LGPD is Brazil's comprehensive framework regulating personal data protection.[167] It applies to any natural person or organization that processes personal data of people in Brazil, with narrow exceptions. Key provisions of the LGPD include requirements for transparency in data processing, legal bases for processing, data subject rights, and obligations on controllers to implement security measures.

To enforce the law, Brazil created a dedicated data protection authority, the National Data Protection Authority (ANPD), which became operational in 2021.[168] The ANPD is charged with issuing guidelines and overseeing compliance, and it has sanctioning powers including fines (though initially, the maximum fine is limited to 2% of a company's Brazilian turnover, capped at 50 million Brazilian reals per violation). Brazil has ramped up enforcement of the LGPD in recent years.[169]

Besides the LGPD, Brazil has other relevant laws and strategies addressing cybersecurity. The *Marco Civil da Internet* (Internet Civil Framework) lays down principles for internet use, including net neutrality and privacy, and provides impetus for later data protection rules.[170] In recent years, Brazil has intensified efforts to combat misinformation and hate speech on social media. In August 2024, Supreme Court Justice Alexandre de Moraes ordered the suspension of the social media platform X after its owner, Elon Musk, refused

164. *Russia: Growing Internet Isolation, Control, Censorship*, HUM. RTS. WATCH (June 18, 2020), https://www.hrw.org/news/2020/06/18/russia-growing-internet-isolation-control-censorship.

165. *Id.*

166. IAPP, LGPD Brazilian General Data Protection Law art. 1 (Ronaldo Lemos et al. trans., Oct. 2020) (Lei Geral de Proteção de Dados Pessoais), https://iapp.org/resources/article/brazilian-data-protection-law-lgpd-english-translation/.

167. As in many other countries, the LGPD was influenced by the EU's GDPR and was part of a broader global trend of privacy legislation. John J. Isaza & Hannah Katshir, *Brazil Passes Landmark Privacy Law: The General Law for the Protection of Privacy*, BUS. L. TODAY (Apr. 24, 2020), https://www.americanbar.org/groups/business_law/resources/business-law-today/2020-may/brazil-passes-landmark-privacy-law/.

168. *Brazil Amps Up Enforcement of Data Protection Law*, JONES DAY (Sept. 2024), https://www.jonesday.com/en/insights/2024/09/brazil-amps-up-enforcement-of-data-protection-law.

169. *Id.* For example, the ANPD issued regulations on the mandatory appointment of Data Protection Officers (DPOs) and on breach notification procedures. It also issued orders against companies (including big tech firms) for improper use of personal data. One high-profile case against Meta involved ordering a halt to certain data processing by a social media company for AI training purposes. *Id.*

170. Brazilian Civil Rights Framework for the Internet (Marco Civil da Internet), Law No. 12.965, de 23 de abril de 2014, D.O.U. de 24.4.2014 (Braz.).

to appoint a legal representative in Brazil and comply with court orders to block accounts spreading disinformation. In February 2025, he ordered X to pay a $1.4M fine.[171]

Brazil also has a cybercrime law, like the U.S. Computer Fraud and Abuse Act, to define crimes like unauthorized system access.[172] Additionally, the Brazilian government released a National Cybersecurity Strategy for 2020–2023 that outlines goals for critical infrastructure protection, capacity building, and international cooperation.[173] Enforcement of cybersecurity involves multiple, sector-specific bodies. For example, the Central Bank has strict cyber regulations for financial institutions, and sector regulators (in energy, telecom, etc.) oversee security standards.[174]

4.10. Mexico

Mexico was one of the first Latin American countries to enact a comprehensive personal data protection statute, The Federal Law on Protection of Personal Data Held by Private Parties adopted in 2010. The law required organizations to publish privacy notices, obtain consent for data usage, safeguard the data, and report significant breaches. From 2010 to 2025, it was enforced by the National Institute of Transparency, Access to Information, and Protection of Personal Data (INAI).[175]

The INAI was officially dissolved following a constitutional reform enacted in December 2024. Its responsibilities have been transferred to the newly established Secretariat of

---

171. *Brazil's Top Court Orders Elon Musk's X Platform to Pay Fine*, Reuters (Feb. 20, 2025 3:26 PM ET), https://www.reuters.com/technology/brazil-top-court-orders-x-pay-14-million-2025-02-20/, *Musk's X gets OK to Resume Service in Brazil after Bending to Top Court's Demands*, Reuters (Oct. 9, 2024 12:21 AM EDT), https://www.reuters.com/technology/brazil-attorney-general-backs-reinstating-social-medial-platform-x-2024-10-08/. There are other examples. On March 7, 2025, a majority of a five-member panel of Brazil's Supreme Court voted to uphold a previous ruling to suspend the U.S. video-sharing platform Rumble in Brazil. This decision came after Rumble failed to comply with court orders, including naming a legal representative in Brazil and paying fines. The conflict arose when Rumble refused to block the account of a Brazilian streamer under investigation for hate speech and spreading false information. *Majority of Brazil Supreme Court Chamber Upholds Rumble Suspension*, Reuters (Mar. 7, 2025 2:36 PM EST), https://www.reuters.com/technology/brazils-supreme-court-chamber-forms-majority-uphold-rumble-suspension-2025-03-07/; Mauricio Savarese, Brazil Supreme Court justice orders Rumble suspension nationwide for alleged non-compliance, AP News (Feb. 21, 2025 9:34 PM EDT), https://apnews.com/article/brazil-supreme-court-rumble-blocked-c45ab801d5bb23e6d9b2271bdcf7426e.

172. Brazilian Cybercrime Law, Law No. 12,737 of Nov. 30, 2012, Diário Oficial da União [D.O.U.] of Dec. 3, 2012 (Braz.).

173. Juliana Abrusio & Mario Cosac, Brazil: Trends and Developments, in *Cybersecurity 2025* (Chambers & Partners Mar. 13, 2025), https://practiceguides.chambers.com/practice-guides/cybersecurity-2025/brazil/trends-and-developments.

174. *See Cybersecurity Regulation in Brazil: An Overview*, Mattos Filho (Sept. 17, 2021), https://www.mattosfilho.com.br/en/unico/cybersecurity-regulation-brazil/.

175. *See* Carlos Vela-Treviño, Daniel Villanueva-Plasencia & Paulina Bojalil-Warth, *Mexico: From 2010 to 2025—Evolution of the New Federal Law on the Protection of Personal Data Held by Private Parties*, Baker McKenzie Blog (Apr. 2, 2025), https://insightplus.bakermckenzie.com/bm/data-technology/mexico-from-2010-to-2025-evolution-of-the-new-federal-law-on-the-protection-of-personal-data-held-by-private-parties; *see also* Renata Denisse Bueron Valenzuela & Iván García Argueta, *New Authority Established for Personal Data Protection in Mexico*, IAPP (Mar. 11, 2025), https://iapp.org/news/a/new-authority-established-for-personal-data-protection-in-mexico.

Anti-Corruption and Good Governance (SABG), a body within the executive branch.[176] This change centralizes data protection oversight under the executive, replacing the previously autonomous INAI. Alongside this institutional shift, Mexico introduced a new Federal Law on the Protection of Personal Data Held by Private Parties (LFPDPPP), which came into effect on March 21, 2025.[177] This law replaces the 2010 version and introduces several key changes. It expands the definitions of personal data and processing activities, mandates that consent for data processing be free, specific, and informed, and clarifies the rights of data subjects, including the right to object to automated processing that significantly affects them.[178]

On the cybersecurity front, Mexico does not yet have a single unified cybersecurity law comparable to some other countries, but it has taken steps in that direction through strategies and sectoral measures. Mexico released a National Cybersecurity Strategy 2017[179] to strengthen cyber capabilities and set up a national CERT (CERT-MX) under its federal police to coordinate incident response.[180] It has various laws to address cybercrimes in its federal criminal code.[181] The banking regulator (CNBV) and others have specific cybersecurity requirements for financial institutions after some notable incidents.[182]

4.11. Other Latin American Countries

Since the mid-2010s, Latin American countries have increasingly recognized the need for robust cybersecurity and data protection regulations. Supported by regional bodies like the Organization of American States (OAS) and international partners, numerous countries have drafted or enacted national cybersecurity strategies and laws. By early 2020, at least 10 countries in the region had approved national cybersecurity strategies, up from only a handful just a few years before.[183] For example, Colombia adopted strategies in 2011 and

176. Vela-Treviño et al., *supra* note 175.

177. *Id.*

178. *Id.*

179. Press Release, Org. of Am. States (OAS), Mexico Presented National Cyber Security Strategy Developed with OAS Support (Nov. 13, 2017), https://www.oas.org/en/media_center/press_release.asp?sCodigo=E-082/17; Gobierno de México, National Cybersecurity Strategy (2017), https://www.gob.mx/cms/uploads/attachment/file/399655/ENCS.ENG.final.pdf (2017).

180. *See* César Armando Lechuga Perezanta, *Data Protection and Cybersecurity Laws in Mexico*, CMS (Feb. 19, 2021), https://cms.law/en/int/expert-guides/cms-expert-guide-to-data-protection-and-cyber-security-laws/in-mexico.

181. For example, hacking, unauthorized system interference, and fraud are prosecutable offenses under Mexico's Federal Criminal Code. Article 211 penalizes unauthorized access to protected computer systems, and Article 386 addresses fraud, which can encompass certain cyber offenses like phishing. México: Código Penal Federal, refworld Global Law & Policy Database, UNHCR, https://www.refworld.org/legal/legislation/natlegbod/1931/es/123827 (Spanish) (publishing the official text of the Code, originally published in the Diario Oficial de la Federación on 14 August 1931 and was the last amendment that was published on 1 July 2020).

182. Andrés Nieto Sánchez de Tagle, Gunter Maertens & Regina Soto Antón, *Banking Laws and Regulations 2025: Mexico*, Global Legal Insights (Mar. 11, 2025), https://www.globallegalinsights.com/practice-areas/banking-and-finance-laws-and-regulations/mexico/.

183. *See* Strategy and Governance, CCDCOE, (country database of national security and defense strategies), https://ccdcoe.org/library/strategy-and-governance/ (last visited Sept. 6, 2025); *The Evolution of Cybersecurity in Paraguay: MITIC as a Strategic Pillar*, TEDIC (June 24, 2025), https://www.tedic.org/en/

2014, Panama in 2013, Trinidad and Tobago in 2012, Paraguay, Chile, Costa Rica and Mexico in 2017, Dominican Republic in 2018, Argentina in 2019, and Belize and Brazil in 2020.[184] On the legislative side, many Latin American countries updated their cybercrime laws in line with the Budapest Convention on Cybercrime (which several have joined or used as a model).[185]

4.12. Africa

African nations face unique challenges in developing and enforcing cybersecurity laws, given disparate levels of technological development and governance. Overall, the continent has made strides through continental and regional initiatives, but many countries are still in the early stages of establishing comprehensive cybersecurity legal frameworks.

A significant step at the African Union (AU) level was the adoption of the **AU Convention on Cyber Security and Personal Data Protection**, commonly known as the Malabo Convention, in 2014.[186] This convention provides a template for cybercrime, data protection, and electronic transactions laws for member states. However, the convention remained unratified by most AU countries for many years. It finally reached the requisite 15 ratifications and entered into force in 2023, nine years after its creation.[187] Even so, leading African Union member states continue to delay ratification of the Malabo Convention.[188]

On a national level, only a subset of African countries has comprehensive cybersecurity laws. South Africa updated its laws with a Cybercrimes Act, which criminalizes cyber offenses and provides procedures for investigation and cooperation.[189] Kenya passed the Computer Misuse and Cybercrimes Act, establishing offenses and creating a national cybercrime coordination committee.[190] Nigeria has a Cybercrimes Act that covers fraud, cyberstalking, system intrusions, and identity theft.[191] According to the ITU's 2024 Global Cybersecurity

---

the-evolution-of-cybersecurity-in-paraguay-mitic-as-a-strategic-pillar/; Dominican Republic: Cybercrime policies/strategies, Council of Eur., Octopus Cybercrime Community, https://www.coe.int/en/web/octopus/-/dominican-republic (last visited Sept. 6, 2025); Belize Cybercrime policies/strategies, Council of Eur., Octopus Cybercrime Community, https://www.coe.int/en/web/octopus/-/beli-1.

184. These strategies often outline goals such as improving incident response, protecting critical infrastructure, enhancing public awareness, and fostering international cooperation.

185. *See* Chart of Signatures, *supra* note 46.

186. African Union, African Union Convention on Cyber Security and Personal Data Protection, adopted June 27, 2014, https://au.int/sites/default/files/treaties/29560-treaty-0048_-_african_union_convention_on_cyber_security_and_personal_data_protection_e.pdf.

187. Boubacar Diallo, *Entry into Force of the Malabo Convention: Beyond the Good News, the Challenges of Implementation and Updating*, 5 Global Afr. 56, 57 (2024), https://doi.org/10.57832/57wg-c486.

188. Nnenna Ifeanyi-Ajufo, *The AU Took Important Action on Cybersecurity at Its 2024 Summit—But More Is Needed*, Chatham House (Feb. 23, 2024), https://www.chathamhouse.org/2024/02/au-took-important-action-cybersecurity-its-2024-summit-more-needed.

189. *Understanding South Africa's Cybercrimes Act*, CMS Law-Now (July 17, 2024), https://cms-lawnow.com/en/ealerts/2024/07/understanding-south-africa-s-cybercrimes-act.

190. *Kenya's Computer Misuse and Cybercrimes Act No. 5 of 2018*, Geneva Internet Platform Digital Watch (May 2018), https://dig.watch/resource/kenyas-computer-misuse-and-cybercrimes-act-no-5-of-2018.

191. Cybercrimes (Prohibition, Prevention, Etc) Act, 2015, Law Nigeria, https://lawnigeria.com/2025/01/28/cybercrimes-prohibition-prevention-etc-act-2015/. Other countries, like Mauritius, Morocco, Egypt, and Tunisia, have relatively advanced cyber laws or strategies.

Index assessments, 7 African countries were ranked among the top 46 globally in cybersecurity preparedness: Ghana, Kenya, Mauritius, Rwanda, Egypt, Tanzania, and Morocco.[192]

Some progress is evident. For example, the Economic Community of West African States (ECOWAS) adopted a directive on cybercrime in 2011;[193] the East African Community drafted a cybersecurity framework;[194] and in 2025 the SADC Parliamentary Forum "adopted a motion on strengthening cyber-security in the SADC region, emphasising the urgent need for coordinated legal, institutional and capacity-building strategies to tackle escalating cyber threats and reduce the digital divide."[195]

5. Practical Takeaways for Lawyers

Start by understanding where data resides. If the organization hasn't done this already, conduct a "Crown Jewels and Exposure" workshop involving privacy engineers, IT, supply-chain specialists, and business leaders. Identify:

- Every type of data the enterprise handles,
- Every jurisdiction where data is stored, processed, or accessed, and
- Every third-party vendor interacting with that data.

Once mapped, apply the strictest regulatory standard applicable to each data flow. Tag each system within the organization's asset management database with applicable laws, breach notification deadlines, data-localization requirements, encryption standards, and overseeing regulators. Enforce automated legal approvals for significant changes, such as data transfers between jurisdictions.

Establish a "Localization War Room," a cross-functional team meeting monthly or as needed to proactively address complex compliance scenarios, such as evaluating whether training machine learning models with Brazilian data on U.S. servers would be considered

---

192. Int'l Telecom. Union, Global Cybersecurity Index 2024, 5th ed. 33 (2024); *see also Cybersecurity: ITU Ranks 7 African Countries as Models to Follow*, Powers of Afr. (Sept. 24, 2024), https://powersofafrica.com/article/783/cybersecurity-itu-ranks-7-african-countries-as-models-to-follow.

193. Econ. Community of W. Afr. St. [ECOWAS], Directive C/Dir.1/08/11 on Fighting Cyber Crime Within ECOWAS, 66th Ord. Sess. of the Council of Ministers, Abuja, 17–19 Aug. 2011, published by CCDCOE, https://ccdcoe.org/uploads/2018/10/ECOWAS-110819-FightingCybercrime.pdf.

194. Press Release, East Afr. Community, EAC set to advance Data Governance and Protection with development of a regional Policy Framework (Oct. 25, 2024), https://www.eac.int/press-releases/3195-eac-set-to-advance-data-governance-and-protection-with-development-of-a-regional-policy-framework.

195. Tichaona Kurewa, *SADC PF Plenary Session Ends with AI, Cyber-Security Resolutions*, ZBC News (June 6, 2025), https://www.zbcnews.co.zw/sadc-pf-plenary-session-ends-with-ai-cyber-security-resolutions/. This brief article reports on the Motion on Strengthening Cybersecurity in the SADC Region by Institutional Capacity and Viable Legal Frameworks to Respond to the Growing Cybersecurity Threats in the Region, which was presented at the 57th Plenary Assembly Session on June 5, 2025 at Victoria Falls, Zimbabwe, https://plenary.sadcpf.org/wp-content/uploads/2025/05/17.0-ENG-Motion-on-Strengthening-Cybersecurity-Hon-Mmoiemang-South-Africa-1.pdf.

"processing" under Brazil's LGPD. This group should pre-approve fallback technical architectures to ensure engineers never face a choice between compliance and innovation.

Every legal team should also maintain a "regulatory horizon map" that charts, in real time, which domestic statutes apply to each line of business, which amendments are likely within the next six to twelve months, and which international initiatives may become relevant. For example, when Japan's Personal Information Protection Commission proposed its 2025 amendments, counsel should understand whether the law's enhanced joint-controllership provisions would require renegotiating vendor contracts or re-architecting data flows.

Maintaining the regulatory horizon map requires reliable inputs. Subscribe to primary-source gazettes, such as EUR-Lex RSS feeds for EU instruments, China's National People's Congress Observer for draft bills, and the Australian Federal Register of Legislation push alerts. Layer on secondary commentary from law firms and industry associations, but always validate with the text of the statute before changing policy. Over time, the map becomes a knowledge asset.

Next, establish connections proactively with key authorities in every jurisdiction critical to operations. Before a crisis strikes, identify the national CERT or CSIRT, the data-protection authority, the financial-services or energy regulator, and any intelligence-community interface for each jurisdiction where critical operations reside. Place their 24/7 duty-officer numbers in the incident-response runbook and the CISO's mobile phone contacts. Then cultivate rapport. Volunteer for regulator-led table-top exercises, comment on draft guidelines, and attend regional ISAC briefings. They may offer informal guidance when the firm faces a disclosure dilemma.

Embed cybersecurity into board oversight. The U.S. SEC's 2023 cybersecurity rules crystallize a global trend: regulators see cyber risk as financial risk. Public issuers must now file an Item 1.05 Form 8-K four business days after determining that an incident is material, and materiality is forward-looking, not merely the cost to remediate. Some foreign rules are fiercer: Japan's PPC guidelines create a default twenty-four-hour window; France's ANSSI will name-and-shame entities that delay NIS2 notifications; Brazil's ANPD can demand incident reports "without undue delay." Counsel must harmonize these thresholds. Draft an internal escalation tree: once the SOC declares a probable breach, the GC and CISO meet within two hours; within ten hours, they convene finance, investor-relations, and disclosure counsel; by hour sixteen, they deliver a recommendation to the CEO on whether the incident is material in any jurisdiction. Embed privilege from the outset by engaging outside counsel to protect communications during the scoping phase in litigation.

Operationalization runs through contracts, acquisitions, insurance, and human capital. All new vendor agreements should include a dedicated cybersecurity schedule: warranties, audit rights mapped to ISO 27001 and NIST SP 800-53, breach notice, and indemnities attributable to the vendor's negligence or for any specified situation.

Unless the human element is ready, no governance regime survives first contact with headlines. Institute a quarterly cross-border table-top exercise rotating scenario leads among legal, technology, and communications teams. Each exercise should stress-test decision-making under conflicting laws and end with a lessons-learned memo whose remediation tasks are tracked in the board's risk dashboard.

Finally, make cyber literacy a standing board agenda item. Arrange annual deep-dive sessions that move beyond generic slide decks. Invite an engineer to demonstrate a live exploit on an unpatched test system; ask threat intelligence partners to brief on regional geopolitical tensions; debrief on near misses and insurance claim trends. Provide directors with a concise glossary of technical and legal terminology so discussion remains focused and accessible. Incorporate cyber expertise into board-member recruitment criteria, and tie part of executive compensation to measured improvements.

Chapter 10

Lawyers' Professional Responsibility to Provide Data Security

Lucian T. Pera

Recent widespread adoption of generative artificial intelligence (GenAI) prompted the ABA Cybersecurity Legal Task Force to update the *Cybersecurity Handbook*. This updated chapter includes guidance from the ABA Standing Committee on Ethics and Professional Responsibility about the use of artificial intelligence, particularly GenAI, in law practice.[1] It includes a new Appendix compiling state and local bar association opinions on lawyers' use of GenAI tools, including concerns about cybersecurity.[2]

With this exception, this chapter remains largely as it appeared in the third edition of the Handbook. Technology innovation, generally, and the emergence of GenAI, in particular, has neither changed nor diminished lawyers' professional responsibility and ethics obligations to provide data security. The obligation of lawyers to secure their clients' sensitive information is defined and governed by ethics rules, common law, and statutes that traditionally cover the activities of lawyers.

1. The Current ABA Model Rules of Professional Conduct and ABA Formal Opinion 477R

At the center of legal ethics guidance nationally on lawyers' ethical obligations to protect clients' confidential information in our increasingly digital, mobile, cloud-based, technology environment stands the ABA Standing Committee on Ethics and Professional Responsibility's Formal Opinion 477R, *Securing Communication of Protected Client Information* (revised May 22, 2017). Issued almost immediately before the publication of the second edition of the Handbook, Opinion 477R has become the seminal opinion on this subject. Its framework has since been reaffirmed and expanded by ABA Formal Opinion 498,

1. ABA Comm'n on Ethics & Prof'l Responsibility, Formal Op. 512 (2024) (titled Generative Artificial Intelligence Tools).

2. *See infra* Appendix F—Current Ethics Opinions and Other Guidance on Lawyer Use of Generative Artificial Intelligence Tools.

Virtual Practice (2021), and ABA Formal Opinion 512, *Generative Artificial Intelligence Tools* (2024).

Opinion 477R weaves together and expands upon the 2012 "technology amendments" to the ABA Model Rules and their Comments providing a broad framework for understanding the ethical obligation at the heart of this chapter. It directly informs the more detailed discussion that follows. Any reader of this chapter should also review in detail Opinion 477R.

Opinion 477R[3] is by no means the final word on lawyers and cybersecurity. Many jurisdictions have offered helpful guidance, some of which is detailed here and more of which is cited in the Appendices to this chapter.[4] The ABA has continued to expand its guidance in related areas, including at least four other ethics opinions:

- Formal Opinion 483, *Lawyers' Obligations After an Electronic Data Breach or Cyber Attack* (Oct. 17, 2018), which addresses not only the subject stated in its title, but also lawyers' ethical obligations to prevent, monitor for, and prepare to respond to breaches and cyber attacks.
- Formal Opinion 482, *Ethical Obligations Related to Disasters* (Sept. 19, 2018), which addresses the obligations of lawyers to prepare for disasters—obligations that overlap considerably with cybersecurity obligations.
- Formal Opinion 498, *Virtual Practice* (March 10, 2021), which highlights a lawyer's cybersecurity obligations as one of a number of concerns arising when lawyers practice without, or away from, a traditional brick-and-mortar office.
- Formal Opinion 512, *Generative Artificial Intelligence Tools* (July 29, 2024), while focusing on lawyer use of AI tools, repeatedly cites and relies on Opinion 477R and its framework in offering guidance on the appropriate and ethical use of these new tools.

All of these build upon the guidance of Opinion 477R.

Opinion 477R first reviews the ABA's most prominent earlier opinion in this area, ABA Formal Opinion 99-413, *Protecting the Confidentiality of Unencrypted E-Mail* (March 10, 1999), which generally blessed lawyer use of unencrypted internet e-mail for client confidential information. The new opinion then reviews the 2012 "technology amendments" to the ABA Model Rules of Professional Conduct, discussed in more detail below. These amendments, now adopted in a majority of U.S. jurisdictions,[5] generally confirm, clarify,

3. *See ABA Formal Opinion 477R: Securing Communication of Protected Client Information*, ABA (June 2017), https://www.americanbar.org/news/abanews/publications/youraba/2017/june-2017/aba-formal-opinion-477r--securing-communication-of-protected-cli/.

4. *See also infra* Appendix A—Email; Appendix B—Metadata; Appendix C—Outsourcing; Appendix D—Cloud Computing; & Appendix E—Social Media.

5. For analysis of adoption of particular Model Rules by individual jurisdictions, see the charts maintained by the ABA Center for Professional Responsibility. At http://www.americanbar.org/groups/professional_responsibility/policy/rule_charts.html (visited May 8, 2025).

and remind lawyers of their ethical obligations concerning the use of information technology and the protection of client confidentiality in a rapidly changing environment. The 2012 amendments confirm that, in the central tenet of amended Rule 1.6(c), "[a] lawyer shall make *reasonable efforts* to prevent the inadvertent or unauthorized disclosure of, or unauthorized access to, information relating to the representation of a client" (emphasis added).

Nothing in Opinion 477R makes obsolete earlier guidance from the ABA and other authorities. The Opinion does, however, reject an overly broad interpretation of earlier Opinion 99-413, which some read to mean that a lawyer was ethically permitted to use unencrypted e-mail for client confidential communications *in every circumstance*. Quoting the first edition of this book, Opinion 477R states that:

> in an environment of increasing cyber threats, the Committee concludes that, adopting the language in the ABA Cybersecurity Handbook, the reasonable efforts standard: . . . rejects requirements for specific security measures (such as firewalls, passwords, and the like) and instead adopts a fact-specific approach to business security obligations that requires a "process" to assess risks, identify and implement appropriate security measures responsive to those risks, verify that they are effectively implemented, and ensure that they are continually updated in response to new developments.[6]

The Opinion then reviews in detail some of the factors that should guide lawyers in making a "reasonable efforts" analysis, including factors set out in revised Comment [18] to Rule 1.6, discussed below. Applying these factors to lawyer use of unencrypted e-mail to communicate client confidential information, the committee concludes that, given today's technology and threat environment, while unencrypted e-mail may well be appropriate for routine communications including information of "normal or low sensitivity," transmitting "highly sensitive information" might require more secure communications technology or even avoiding the use of electronic communications altogether.

Opinion 477R identifies and explores a series of pragmatic considerations that a lawyer may consider in seeking to use "reasonable efforts" to protect client confidential information:

1. Understand the nature of the threat.
2. Understand how client confidential information is transmitted and where it is stored.
3. Understand and use reasonable electronic security measures.
4. Determine how electronic communications about clients' matters should be protected.
5. Label client confidential information.

6. *See* ABA Comm'n on Ethics & Prof'l Responsibility, *supra* note 1, at 4 (citing ABA Cybersecurity Handbook (1st ed. 2013) at 48–49).

6. Train lawyers and nonlawyer assistants in technology and information security.
7. Conduct due diligence on vendors providing communication technology.[7]

Finally, Opinion 477R emphasizes the need and duty of a lawyer to communicate with the client about the sensitivity of information concerning the representation and the appropriate means and methods of protecting confidentiality. In many ways, this Opinion distills the ethics guidance of the preceding 20 years and updates it in light of the current technology environment. Aligned with this Opinion, this chapter reviews existing guidance and demonstrates how the broader principles restated and reformulated in Opinion 477R apply to particular circumstances faced by lawyers in their practice.

2. Lawyer Ethics Rules

2.1. Confidentiality

2.1.1. *ABA Model Rule 1.6*

Lawyers and law firms must adopt safeguards to protect their clients' information because they have an ethical duty to keep that information confidential. ABA Model Rule 1.6(a) states that, with limited exceptions, "[a] lawyer shall not reveal information relating to the representation of a client unless the client gives informed consent." This obligation to maintain confidentiality of all information concerning a client's representation, no matter the source, is paramount. The obligation is no less applicable to electronically stored information than to information contained in paper documents or not reduced to any written or stored form.

So what does this mean? What steps must a lawyer take to protect the client's information? The last major review and revision of the ABA Model Rules of Professional Conduct was led by the ABA Ethics 20/20 Commission. With regard to issues raised by new technology, the signature change made to the Model Rules by the Ethics 20/20 Commission was the addition of a new section to the core rule on client confidentiality. The new Rule 1.6(c) codified the existing understanding of a lawyer's affirmative obligation to protect confidential information: "A lawyer shall make reasonable efforts to prevent the inadvertent or unauthorized disclosure of, or unauthorized access to, information relating to the representation of a client." While the revision merely confirmed prior law under the ethics rules of every American jurisdiction, versions of the Ethics 20/20 Commission's revisions have been adopted by the vast majority of U.S. jurisdictions as of early 2025. Even in jurisdictions that have not adopted those amendments, there is a strong argument that the substance of the revisions is, in fact, an accurate statement of the law on a lawyer's ethical obligations.

Revised Comments [18] and [19] to Rule 1.6 also now include more detailed guidance—guidance largely consistent with existing rules in virtually every jurisdiction—concerning

7. *Id.* at 5–10 (omitting discussion of each consideration).

how to measure the reasonableness of a lawyer's efforts to protect against inadvertent disclosure or unauthorized access. This language forms the core set of principles used throughout virtually all ethics opinions in American jurisdictions that address confidentiality concerns in the cybersecurity context. Comment [18] sets out how reasonableness under Rule 1.6(c) should be determined:

> Factors to be considered in determining the reasonableness of the lawyer's efforts include, but are not limited to, the sensitivity of the information, the likelihood of disclosure if additional safeguards are not employed, the cost of employing additional safeguards, the difficulty of implementing the safeguards, and the extent to which the safeguards adversely affect the lawyer's ability to represent clients (e.g., by making a device or important piece of software excessively difficult to use). A client may require the lawyer to implement special security measures not required by this Rule or may give informed consent to forgo security measures that would otherwise be required by this Rule.

The comment goes on to note that "a lawyer may be required to take additional steps to safeguard a client's information in order to comply with other law, such as state and federal laws that govern data privacy or that impose notification requirements upon the loss of, or unauthorized access to, electronic information," but that any such obligations are "beyond the scope of these Rules."

Comment [19] concludes the Model Rules' framing of a lawyer's obligations to maintain the security of client confidential information, including its limits:

> When transmitting a communication that includes information relating to the representation of a client, the lawyer must take reasonable precautions to prevent the information from coming into the hands of unintended recipients. This duty, however, does not require that the lawyer use special security measures if the method of communication affords a reasonable expectation of privacy. Special circumstances, however, may warrant special precautions. Factors to be considered in determining the reasonableness of the lawyer's expectation of confidentiality include the sensitivity of the information and the extent to which the privacy of the communication is protected by law or by a confidentiality agreement. A client may require the lawyer to implement special security measures not required by this Rule or may give informed consent to the use of a means of communication that would otherwise be prohibited by this Rule.

In effect, this comment envisages a balancing test: the more sensitive the data being transmitted and the lower the legal or technological protection afforded by the method of communication, the more likely it is that special precautions may be reasonably necessary to protect client confidences.

From 2013 through 2015, the ABA, through its House of Delegates, approved a series of resolutions proposed by the ABA's Cybersecurity Legal Task Force that highlighted the threat of cyber attacks on lawyers and law firms. In Revised Report 109 (2014), the Task Force observed:

> The threat of cyber attacks against law firms is growing. Lawyers and law firms are facing unprecedented challenges from the widespread use of electronic records and mobile devices. There are many reasons for hackers to target the information being held by law firms. They collect and store large amounts of critical, highly valuable corporate records, including intellectual property, strategic business data and litigation-related theories and records collected through e-discovery.

As described elsewhere in this book, that threat continues to grow.[8] A number of state bar ethics opinions have addressed a lawyer's obligations to protect client confidential information in electronic communications. The focus of these opinions ranges from suggested security safeguards to an examination of new technologies and the need for lawyers to have a basic understanding of the risks and benefits associated with them.

2.1.2. *State Bar Opinions: Suggested Safeguards*

Some state bar associations have issued ethics opinions that suggest specific measures a law firm should take to protect its clients' electronically stored information. For example, Arizona State Bar Opinion 09-04 (2009) offers the following: "In satisfying the duty to take reasonable security precautions, lawyers should consider firewalls, password protection schemes, encryption, anti-virus measures, etc."

The client file system that was the subject of this Arizona opinion protected the files by using a method of encryption and also applied several layers of password protection. Additionally, the system used unique and randomly generated folder names and passwords, and converted each document to PDF format that required yet another unique alpha-numeric password to review its contents. Based on these safeguards, this Arizona opinion concluded that the file system met the requirements set forth by Rule 1.6.[9]

2.1.3. *State Bar Opinions: Technology as Moving Target*

Other state bar opinions have recognized, as did ABA Opinion 477R, that the swiftly changing nature of technology makes it very difficult to identify specific security measures lawyers should take that will invariably ensure that confidential client information will

8. *See, e.g.*, HANDBOOK, Chapter 4, *Understanding Cybersecurity Risks*.

9. *See also* N.J. Adv. Comm. on Prof'l Ethics, Op. 701 (2006); N.C. State Bar Council, Formal Ethics Op. 5 (2008) ("law firm must enact appropriate measures to ensure that each client only has access to his or her own file [and] that third parties cannot gain access [to] any client file").

be protected.[10] Their focus is on the scope of the lawyer's obligations to take reasonable precautions under the circumstances to protect client information. For example, Kentucky Bar Opinion E-437 (2014) states:

> Because technology evolves every day, we decline to mandate in this opinion specific practices regarding the protection of confidential client information in the world of the cloud. The reality is that such practices soon would be obsolete—and our opinion would be obsolete as well. Rather, we choose to guide lawyers in the exercise of reasonable judgment regarding the use of cloud technology. *See* Vt. Eth. Op. 2010-6 (2010) (constantly changing nature of cloud technology makes establishing "specific conditions precedent" to use not appropriate); Ohio Informal Adv. Op. 2013-03 (2013) ("applying existing principles to new technological advances while refraining from mandating specific practices—is a practical [approach]").

2.1.4. *State Bar Opinions: Security Precautions Need Not Be Infallible; They Must Be Reasonable Under the Circumstances*

Regardless of whether state bar opinions provide specific guidelines or suggestions as to the appropriate technical safeguards lawyers should take, or instead focus on the scope of a lawyer's obligations to use reasonable care to protect client confidences, it is important to bear in mind that, under the rules of professional conduct, the security measures lawyers are required to put in place are not required to be invulnerable. As stated in Tennessee Board of Professional Responsibility Formal Ethics Opinion 2015-F-159 (2015):

> The lawyer is not required by the rules to use infallible methods of protection. "When transmitting a communication that includes information relating to the representation of a client, the lawyer must take reasonable precautions to prevent the information from coming into the hands of unintended recipients. This duty, however, does not require that the lawyer use special security measures if the method of communication affords a reasonable expectation of privacy. . ." RPC 1.6 Cmt. [16]. "Rather, the lawyer must use reasonable care to select a mode of communication that, in light of the circumstances, will best protect confidential client information and the lawyer must advise affected parties if there is reason to believe that the chosen communications technology presents an unreasonable risk to confidentiality." Me. Ethics Op. 207 (2013); N.C. 2011 Formal Ethics Op. 6 (2012). "Special circumstances, however, may warrant special precautions." RPC 1.6, Cmt. [16]. What safeguards are appropriate depends upon the nature and sensitivity of the data.
>
> Alaska Ethics Op. 2014-3 (2014).

10. *See* Ill. State Bar Ass'n, Prof'l Conduct Advisory Op. 16-06 (2016).

As illustrated in the above discussion, lawyers cannot take the "ostrich" approach of hiding their heads in the sand and hoping that their office or firm will not suffer a data breach, compromising client information. Lawyers must implement administrative, technical, and physical safeguards to meet their obligation to make reasonable efforts to protect client information.

Furthermore, under ABA Model Rule 1.9(c), the obligation of confidentiality also applies to information about former clientse

> A lawyer who has formerly represented a client in a matter or whose present or former firm has formerly represented a client in a matter shall not thereafter: (1) use information relating to the representation to the disadvantage of the former client except as these Rules would permit or require with respect to a client, or when the information has become generally known; or (2) reveal information relating to the representation except as these Rules would permit or require with respect to a client.

2.2. Competence

In addition to the obligation to keep client communications and sensitive information confidential, a lawyer's ethical obligation of competence requires that lawyers become and remain competent about the technology they use so as to be able to protect client confidential information.

ABA Model Rule 1.1 states that "[a] lawyer shall provide competent representation to a client. Competent representation requires the legal knowledge, skill, thoroughness, and preparation reasonably necessary for the representation." One change to the ABA Model Rules based on an Ethics 20/20 Commission proposal amended Comment [8] to Rule 1.1, so that it now reads: "To maintain the requisite knowledge and skill, a lawyer should keep abreast of changes in the law and its practice, *including the benefits and risks associated with relevant technology*" (added language italicized).

California State Bar Opinion 2015-193 (2015) examined the parameters of a lawyer's obligations to understand the benefits and risks of technology in the context of e-discovery, stating: An attorney's obligations under the ethical duty of competence evolve as new technologies develop and become integrated with the practice of law. Attorney competence related to litigation generally requires, among other things and at a minimum, a basic understanding of, and facility with, issues relating to e-discovery, including the discovery of electronically stored information ("ESI"). On a case-by-case basis, the duty of competence may require a higher level of technical knowledge and ability, depending on the e-discovery issues involved in a matter, and the nature of the ESI. Competency may require even a highly experienced attorney to seek assistance in some litigation matters involving ESI. An attorney lacking the required competence for e-discovery issues has three options: (1) acquire sufficient learning and skill before performance is required; (2) associate with or consult technical consultants or competent counsel; or (3) decline the client representation.

Note especially the second item in the last sentence: If an attorney is not competent to decide without expert assistance whether use of a particular technology (e.g., e-discovery, cloud storage, public Wi-Fi) allows reasonable measures to protect client confidentiality, the ethics rules require that the lawyer must get help, even if that means hiring an expert information technology consultant to advise the lawyer. The level of technology expertise of many lawyers on many such technologies probably means that expert help is often needed by lawyers in making these decisions, whether that expert help comes from inside or outside the lawyer's own organization.

Getting expert help is a recurring theme (as well as good advice) in ethics opinions on this subject. Arizona Bar Opinion 09-04 (Dec. 2009) reminds lawyers that, if they provide an online file storage and retrieval system for client access of documents, then they must take reasonable precautions to protect the security and confidentiality of client documents and information in that system. With respect to a lawyer's obligation to be competent, the opinion noted that "[i]t is also important that lawyers recognize their own competence limitations regarding computer security measures and take the necessary time and energy to become competent or alternatively consult available experts in the field."

Moreover, competence requires continued vigilance and learning, as technology advances, in order to comply with a lawyer's duties under the ethics rules. Again, the Arizona Bar also reminded lawyers that "[a]s technology advances occur, lawyers should periodically review security measures in place to ensure that they still reasonably protect the security and confidentiality of the clients' documents and information." In other words, lawyers may not assume that their ignorance about technology will be a recognized excuse for their failure to learn and stay up-to-date about technology related to a client's electronically stored information.[11]

The best recent illustration of this continuing duty of learning that our duty of competence imposes is the advance of AI tools by lawyers. ABA Opinion 512, which provides broad guidance on the use of AI tools by lawyers, emphasizes that lawyers must learn and understand the risks and benefits of using tools that incorporate or rely on AI, but makes clear that the framework of "reasonable efforts" and technology competence applies equally to these new technologies.

2.3. Supervision of Lawyers and Nonlawyers

Finally, it is not enough that the lawyer is concerned about his individual use of technology and handling of sensitive client information. The ethics rules in every jurisdiction also obligate lawyers to appropriately supervise those who work for them. So, for example, ABA Model Rule 5.1 provides that "[a] partner in a law firm, and a lawyer who individually or

11. For further information on lawyers' ethical obligations of competence when using technology, see Jon Meredith Garon, *Ethics 3.0—Attorney Responsibility in the Age of Generative AI*, 79 Bus. Law. 209 (2024), https://www.americanbar.org/groups/business_law/resources/business-lawyer/2024-winter/ethics-attorney-responsibility-in-the-age-of-generative-ai/.

together with other lawyers possesses comparable managerial authority in a law firm, shall make reasonable efforts to ensure that the firm has in effect measures giving reasonable assurance that all lawyers in the firm conform to the Rules of Professional Conduct."

Similarly, with respect to a nonlawyer employed or retained by or associated with a lawyer, Rule 5.3 provides that "a partner, and a lawyer who individually or together with other lawyers possesses comparable managerial authority in a law firm, shall make reasonable efforts to ensure that the firm has in effect measures giving reasonable assurance that the person's conduct is compatible with the professional obligations of the lawyer."

Thus, lawyers in any supervisory role are not only obligated to follow the ethics rules personally in protecting client confidential information but must also be vigilant and make reasonable efforts to ensure that lawyers and nonlawyers they supervise adhere to them as well.

These obligations were emphasized in the ABA's guidance on this subject in Opinion 477R, discussed above. They were also addressed in Opinion 512 about GenAI, or "GAI," as discussed in Opinion 512.

> Managerial lawyers must establish clear policies regarding the law firm's permissible use of GAI, and supervisory lawyers must make reasonable efforts to ensure that the firm's lawyers and nonlawyers comply with their professional obligations when using GAI tools. Supervisory obligations also include ensuring that subordinate lawyers and nonlawyers are trained, including in the ethical and practical use of the GAI tools relevant to their work as well as on risks associated with relevant GAI use. Training could include the basics of GAI technology, the capabilities and limitations of the tools, ethical issues in use of GAI and best practices for secure data handling, privacy, and confidentiality.
>
> Lawyers have additional supervisory obligations insofar as they rely on others outside the law firm to employ GAI tools in connection with the legal representation.[12]

3. The Law of Lawyering

A narrow focus on a lawyer's obligation under the law of legal ethics may well lead lawyers and law firms to ignore other related liability that might result from confidentiality breaches. While a breach that results from a lawyer's failure to comply with her obligations under the ethics rules like ABA Model Rule 1.6 might lead to lawyer discipline, a breach of confidentiality caused by a lawyer's conduct could well lead to liability to clients and others harmed under other related law, such as malpractice law, fiduciary duty law, and the law of contract.

12. ABA Comm'n on Ethics & Prof'l Responsibility, *supra* note 1, at 10–11 (footnotes omitted).

One source of the obligation of lawyers and law firms to protect against disclosure of confidential information entrusted to them is the common law of malpractice liability and fiduciary duty, as well as traditional statutory remedies available in some jurisdictions for some lawyer misconduct, including laws prohibiting unfair and deceptive trade practices. Despite the novelty of all the new technology involved and the laws covering this technology discussed elsewhere in this chapter and this Handbook, these traditional causes of action and remedies are just as applicable to a breach of security in the latest cloud-based technology or disclosure of confidential information through use of AI tools (including GenAI tools) as they are to the loss of a box of paper documents containing confidential client information.[13]

It may be instructive to recall that the common law concerning the standard of care and tort liability has evolved over decades specifically to account for dynamic technological developments. Judge Learned Hand's famous 1932 decision in *The T.J. Hooper*,[14] which has been a staple of law school casebooks for generations, offers an example from the days when radio technology was new.

In *The T.J. Hooper*, cargo and barge owners were permitted to recover against the owner of two tugboats when their barges and cargo were lost in an Atlantic storm. The primary theory of recovery concerned the tugboat owners' failure to equip their tugboats with radio receivers on which they could monitor regular weather reports and storm warnings. That lack of equipment caused them to miss radio alerts of the storm that caused the loss of the barges and cargo. Other tugboats had been equipped with the new technology, were able to hear the storm warnings, and made it to safety, protecting their crews and cargo. While the use of radios was not yet standard industry practice, that court found it unreasonable for the tugboats' owner not to use it. Judge Hand observed that in most cases reasonable prudence is in fact common prudence; but strictly it is never its measure. A whole calling may have unduly lagged in the adoption of new and available devices. It never may set its own tests, however persuasive may be its usages. Courts must in the end say what is required; there are precautions so imperative that even their universal disregard will not excuse their omission.[15]

On the grounds that the tugboats' owners had not equipped the tugs with radio receivers to hear available storm warnings, the tugs were held unseaworthy, and the injury to the cargo owners "a direct consequence of this unseaworthiness."[16] On the right facts, would the failure of a law firm to avail itself of available cybersecurity techniques or equipment, in the event of a preventable cybersecurity incident that caused injury, lead to the law firm's liability?

13. For treatment of the insurance coverage of the liability of lawyers and law firms under lawyer professional liability theories, see this HANDBOOK, Chapter 14, *Cyber Insurance for Law Firms and Legal Organizations.*

14. *The T.J. Hooper*, 60 F. 2d 737 (2d Cir. 1932), *aff'g* 53 F. 2d 107 (S.D.N.Y. 1931).

15. *Id.* at 740.

16. *Id.*

There can be no doubt that traditional bodies of law used to hold lawyers and law firms accountable for certain harms resulting from their conduct can be used for data and other cybersecurity breaches. With respect to harms suffered by clients, the law offers an obvious path for malpractice liability to a client predicated on a breach of confidentiality and for liability to a client for breach of the fiduciary duty of confidentiality. Indeed, even inadvertent disclosures, or breaches by malicious third parties, could give rise to claims by those with an interest in confidential information (whether a client or a third party), perhaps on a theory of negligent safeguarding of that information by a lawyer.

In recent years, the prevalence of "outside counsel guidelines," specific and often detailed requirements on various subjects imposed upon lawyers by clients, may well provide another avenue for clients to recoup losses from data breaches and cyber attacks suffered by lawyers and law firms. Indeed, many clients, especially in highly regulated industries, now impose, and strictly monitor and enforce, specific technology and cybersecurity requirements on their counsel. It seems reasonably clear that, in the right circumstances, a lawyer or law firm's failure to abide by these contractually agreed requirements, where that failure can be shown to have led to injury to the client, could lead to liability.

Under all these theories, however, it is sometimes quite difficult for claimants to prove loss causation to the extent required by law.

4. Examples of the Emerging Application of Ethics and Lawyering Law to New Technology

In this section, we review the application of the rules to particular technologies as they have arisen, been adopted by lawyers and their clients, and changed over time. One fundamental principle runs through all of these authorities: when a lawyer decides to use any of these new technologies, the lawyer must have a basic understanding of the technology employed and must take reasonable, prudent steps to preserve client confidentiality, balancing the degree of sensitivity of the information with the need to take additional precautions as appropriate.

4.1. E-mail

4.1.1. *To Encrypt or Not to Encrypt?*

E-mail was one of the first types of new technology to cause widespread concern in the profession because of perceived threats to client confidentiality. Early in the 1990s, a number of ethics committees issued opinions warning against the use of e-mail to transmit confidential client information, and several of these concluded that a lawyer should not transmit client information through e-mail unless it was encrypted.

As the thinking around e-mail developed, later state bar ethics opinions concluded that an e-mail is similar to a telephone call, and that lawyers have a reasonable expectation of privacy when using it, since it is just as illegal to intercept an e-mail as it is to wiretap a phone call. However, these opinions also stated that lawyers should still exercise caution when using e-mail, just as they would with any other form of communication. If the information is so sensitive that a lawyer would not discuss it over the telephone, chances are that he or she should not use e-mail either.

In 1999, the ABA Standing Committee on Ethics and Professional Responsibility weighed in on this issue in Opinion 99-413, *Protecting the Confidentiality of Unencrypted Email.* In language quite similar to the Ethics 20/20 Commission's later amendments to the comments to Rule 1.6, the Committee stated that, if a lawyer has a very sensitive matter to be discussed with a client, he should do it in person. The opinion stated:

> The Committee believes that email communications, including those sent unencrypted over the Internet, pose no greater risk of interception or disclosure than other modes of communication commonly relied upon as having a reasonable expectation of privacy. The level of legal protection accorded email transmissions, like that accorded other modes of electronic communication, also supports the reasonableness of an expectation of privacy for unencrypted email transmissions. The risk of unauthorized interception and disclosure exists in every medium of communication, including email. It is not, however, reasonable to require that a mode of communicating information must be avoided simply because interception is technologically possible, especially when unauthorized interception or dissemination of the information is a violation of law.

The conclusions reached in this opinion do not, however, diminish a lawyer's obligation to consider with her client the sensitivity of the communication, the consequences of its disclosure, and the relative security of the contemplated medium of communication. Particularly strong protective measures are warranted to guard against the disclosure of highly sensitive matters. Those measures might include the avoidance of email, just as they would warrant the avoidance of the telephone, fax, and mail.

The ABA revisited this guidance in Opinion 477R, discussed above, and rejected an overly broad interpretation of earlier Opinion 99-413. The Opinion 477R rejected the reading by some of Opinion 99-413 that a lawyer was ethically permitted *in every circumstance* to use unencrypted e-mail for client confidential communications. In retrospect, that reading of Opinion 99-413 was an over-reading of its conclusion; it was, however, a product of its time, when encryption was expensive and technologically and practically impossible for most lawyers and clients. In formulating guidance for when additional security measures might be needed, the committee writing Opinion 477R looked, among other authorities, to Texas Opinion 648 (2015), which identified six situations in which a lawyer should consider whether to encrypt or use some other type of security precaution:

1. communicating highly sensitive or confidential information via email or unencrypted email connections;
2. sending an email to or from an account that the email sender or recipient shares with others;
3. sending an email to a client when it is possible that a third person (such as a spouse in a divorce case) knows the password to the email account, or to an individual client at that client's work email account, especially if the email relates to a client's employment dispute with his employer;
4. sending an email from a public computer or a borrowed computer or where the lawyer knows that the emails the lawyer sends are being read on a public or borrowed computer or on an unsecure network;
5. sending an email if the lawyer knows that the email recipient is accessing the email on devices that are potentially accessible to third persons or are not protected by a password; or
6. sending an email if the lawyer is concerned that the National Security Agency or a law enforcement agency may read the lawyer's email communication, with or without a warrant.[17]

In a similar vein, Pennsylvania Bar Association Committee on Legal Ethics and Professional Responsibility Formal Opinion 2011-200 encouraged encryption when using "vulnerable methods of communications":

> Compounding the general security concerns for e-mail is that users increasingly access webmail using unsecure or vulnerable methods such as cell phones or laptops with public wireless internet connections. Reasonable precautions are necessary to minimize the risk of unauthorized access to sensitive client information when using these devices and services, possibly including precautions such as encryption and strong password protection in the event of lost or stolen devices, or hacking.

Lawyers must also evaluate their use of text messaging with clients using very similar criteria. Use of ordinary SMS text messaging on consumer cellphones can be both insecure and difficult to retain and maintain as part of a lawyer's client file. This means that it may well be problematic for a lawyer to use this form of communication for confidential messages, while it might be perfectly acceptable for nonconfidential messages, such as those concerning scheduling. Lawyers who believe they need to communicate with their clients by text messaging should consider more secure apps or services for this purpose.[18]

17. Professional Ethics Comm. for the State Bar of Tex., Op. 648 (2015), https://www.legalethicstexas.com/Ethics-Resources/Opinions/Opinion-648.aspx (last visited May 8, 2025).

18. In December 2024, the United States Cybersecurity & Infrastructure Security Agency (CISA) published guidance for protecting mobile communications. CISA, *Mobile Communications Best Practice Guidance* (Dec. 18,

4.1.2. *Duty to Warn Client When Third Parties May Have Access to Client's Computer*

ABA Formal Opinion 11-459, Duty to Protect the Confidentiality of Email Communications with One's Client (2011), addressed the precautions a lawyer should take when he knows that his or her client is using the employer's computer or other electronic device to communicate with the lawyer. The opinion noted that, under such circumstances, the employer may, as a matter of company policy, have access to the employee's communication and stated that the lawyer should warn the client about the risks of using such devices:

> Given these risks, a lawyer should ordinarily advise the employee- client about the importance of communicating with the lawyer in a manner that protects the confidentiality of email communications, just as a lawyer should avoid speaking face-to-face with a client about sensitive matters if the conversation might be overheard and should warn the client against discussing their communications with others. In particular, as soon as practical after a client-lawyer relationship is established, a lawyer typically should instruct the employee-client to avoid using a workplace device or system for sensitive or substantive communications, and perhaps for any attorney-client communications, because even seemingly ministerial communications involving matters such as scheduling can have substantive ramifications.

State bar opinions have come to similar conclusions.[19]

4.2. Portable Devices and Other Devices That Retain Data

Law firms today use many devices that store confidential client information, including desktop computers, laptops, tablets, printers that store data, flash drives, thumb drives, cell phones, and smartphones. The fact that these devices can store vast amounts of confidential client information mandates that lawyers take adequate precautions to ensure that the information is protected from disclosure. The extreme portability of some of these devices—smartphones and flash drives come to mind immediately—makes it particularly important for lawyers to use them with thought and care.

But, in recent years, lawyers and others have also learned that danger lurks in devices not ordinarily thought of as likely to retain confidential information. Basic security measures have long included efforts to remove all confidential information from devices before they are disposed of or recycled. It took some time for lawyers and others to understand that some modern copiers and printers include memory technology that retains images of documents, essentially on a permanent basis. Press reports showing the extent of information in that equipment led many users to recognize that disposal of any electronic equipment must

---

2024), https://www.cisa.gov/sites/default/files/2024-12/guidance-mobile-communications-best-practices.pdf (last visited May 8, 2025).

19. For additional information, see *infra* Appendix A—Ethics Opinions on Lawyer Confidentiality Obligations Concerning Email.

be accompanied by erasure or removal of memory, just as with the disposal of a desktop computer. For example, Alabama Opinion 2010-2 (2010) states that when disposing of electronic devices, lawyers should ensure that confidential information has been removed. This obligation tracks closely the well-understood obligation of a lawyer to dispose of paper client files in a way that avoids the possibility of disclosure of confidential information (for example, by shredding).

In 2010, the Ethics 20/20 Commission's Working Group on the Implications of New Technologies suggested possible precautions lawyers should take when using portable devices, and most of these precautions apply with equal force to any piece of equipment, portable or not, that stores confidential information:

- providing adequate physical protection or having methods for deleting data remotely in the event that a device is lost or stolen;
- encouraging the use of strong passwords;
- purging data from devices before replacement;
- installing safeguards to combat viruses, malware, and spyware;
- erecting firewalls;
- ensuring frequent backups of data;
- updating (patching) computer operating systems to ensure that they contain the latest security protections;
- configuring software and network settings to minimize security risks;
- encrypting sensitive information, and identifying (and, when appropriate, eliminating) metadata from electronic documents before sending them; and
- avoiding public "Wi-Fi hotspots" when transmitting confidential information.[20]

The ubiquity and ease of use of portable devices carries particular problems for lawyers. One common example is the use of laptops and other portable devices away from a lawyer's regular place of work.

California State Bar Opinion 2010-179 (2010) addressed a situation where a lawyer used a law firm laptop both in a local coffee shop, accessing the internet using the coffee shop's Wi-Fi connection, and at his home, using his personal wireless connection. The opinion listed a number of factors for a lawyer to consider when using different types of technologies that have the capability of storing and disseminating confidential client information. These factors include the lawyer's ability to understand and assess the level of security offered by the particular technology, how the particular technology differs from other media, whether reasonable steps can be taken to increase the level of security of such technology, and the limitations on who has access to it. The opinion stated that lawyers should

20. Lance J. Rogers, *Model Rules: Ethics 20/20 Commission Invites Comments on Issues Raised by Growing Use of Internet*, 26 LAW. MAN. ON PROF. CONDUCT 586 (ABA/BNA Sept. 29, 2010) (discussing Ethics 20/20 working group's Sept. 20, 2010, memorandum).

also assess the legal consequences to third parties including possible criminal charges or civil claims should they illegally intercept or access the confidential information, as this could affect the extent to which the lawyer using the service or technology could claim a reasonable expectation of privacy. The lawyer should also take into consideration the degree of sensitivity of the information, and the extent to which unauthorized disclosure would adversely affect the client: the greater the sensitivity, the less risk the lawyer should take. Finally, if the client has instructed the lawyer not to use a certain type of technology, the lawyer should abide by the client's instructions.

Applying these factors to the scenario described in the opinion, the California committee concluded that the lawyer should not use the wireless services offered in the coffee shop unless he had in place adequate safeguards such as wireless encryption and firewalls to protect client information. With regard to the use of the laptop at home, the committee stated that the lawyer could use it so long as his home system had adequate security features.

4.3. Metadata Leaks

Many ethics committees have addressed the application of ethics rules to questions involving metadata—that is, electronic information about electronic documents that is often associated with, or a part of, the document, but often not readily visible to the ordinary user. The question most frequently addressed, however, is whether a lawyer who receives a document containing metadata (for example, a Word file containing a document being negotiated between the lawyer's client and someone else) may ethically look for and review that metadata, as the metadata may well contain useful, otherwise confidential, information.

While those opinions reflect varied views on whether the receiving lawyer may or may not look for and review metadata, a number of ethics opinions address the related question: What obligation does a lawyer have to protect against the disclosure of metadata that reveals confidential information of his or her client? The authorities that do address this question apply the same analysis for the protection from disclosure of metadata as for ordinary data—a lawyer must take reasonable precautions to avoid disclosure of confidential client information, in whatever form.[21]

4.4. Outsourcing

Outsourcing is another area where confidential client information is subject to cybersecurity threats. When a lawyer engages an outside service provider to provide legal or law-related services for his or her clients and allows the provider access to confidential client information, the lawyer must ensure that the outside entity has in place reasonable safeguards to protect against unauthorized disclosure. If the service provider is a legal professional outside of the United States, the lawyer may well have an obligation to ascertain

21. For additional information, see Appendix B—Ethics Opinions concerning a Lawyer's Obligations to Prevent the Inadvertent Disclosure of Confidential Client Information in Metadata.

whether the laws and professional conduct rules of the foreign jurisdiction share the same basic core values of client confidentiality.

Recent developments in technology and legal services delivery have somewhat reshaped these concerns. On the one hand, lawyers and law firms have increasingly—and largely appropriately—outsourced some of their cybersecurity obligations as key software and storage needs have rapidly migrated to the cloud. Security remains, however, a shared responsibility between cloud service providers and their customers. Further, new legal services providers, from providers of temporary or contract lawyers to outsourced receptionist services, have grown in acceptance by lawyers. But all these technology and personnel changes have increased the need to carefully vet and oversee outsourcing vendors of all types.

The latest revisions to the ABA Model Rules of Professional Conduct, based on 2012 proposals from the Ethics 20/20 Commission, address a lawyer's obligations concerning outsourcing. These amendments codified, to a great extent, a 2008 ABA ethics opinion on this subject in amendments to comments to Rule 1.1 and 5.3.

The commission proposed amendments to the comments to Rules 1.1 and 5.3 on how to supervise and select outside service providers that have in place adequate measures to protect client information. New Comment [6] to Rule 1.1 states:

> **Retaining or Contracting with Other Lawyers or Professional Support**
>
> [6] Before a lawyer retains or contracts with other lawyers outside the lawyer's own firm to provide or assist in the provision of legal services to a client, the lawyer should ordinarily obtain informed consent from the client and must reasonably believe that the other lawyers' services will contribute to the competent and ethical representation of the client. See also Rules 1.2 (allocation of authority), 1.4 (communication with client), 1.5(e) (fee sharing), 1.6 (confidentiality), and 5.5(a) (unauthorized practice of law). The reasonableness of a decision to retain or contract with other lawyers outside the lawyer's own firm will depend upon the circumstances, including the education, experience and reputation of the nonfirm lawyers; the nature of the services assigned to the nonfirm lawyers; and the legal protections, professional conduct rules, and ethical environments of the jurisdictions in which the services will be performed, particularly relating to confidential information.

In 2008, the ABA Standing Committee on Ethics and Professional Responsibility addressed a number of these issues relating to confidentiality in its Formal Opinion 08-451, Lawyer's Obligations When Outsourcing Legal and Nonlegal Support Services.

The opinion considered outsourcing in a wide variety of contexts, such as the use of contract or temporary lawyers, photocopy shops or information technology vendors, legal research services, or foreign lawyers to draft patent applications. Among the lawyer's duties implicated by the use of such outsourcing, the opinion noted, are the duty of competence (Rule 1.1) and the duty to supervise (Rules 5.1 and 5.3). The committee offered the following suggestions to help the outsourcing lawyer comply with the duties of competence and supervision:

- Conduct background checks of any lawyer, nonlawyer, or placement agency involved;
- Interview the principal lawyers involved, and assess their educational backgrounds;
- When working with an intermediary, inquire into its hiring practices so as to ascertain the character of the employees who are likely to have access to client information;
- Investigate the security measures in effect in the provider's premises, including its computer network and refuse disposal systems;
- Depending on the circumstances, consider conducting an on-site visit in order to get an impression of the professionalism of the lawyers and nonlawyers involved.

The committee stated further that when the work will be outsourced to a foreign country, the outsourcing lawyer should also ascertain whether the legal training received in that country is comparable to that in the United States, whether legal professionals in that country share the same core ethical principles as lawyers in the United States, and whether there is an effective professional discipline system. If the legal professionals' legal system does not share the same core principles or does not have an effective lawyer discipline system, the outsourcing lawyer would have a heightened duty to scrutinize the work produced, and may have an obligation to disclose to the client the risks associated with having the work outsourced to that country.

The opinion also particularly highlighted an outsourcing lawyer's duty to protect client confidentiality, including by taking reasonable measures to protect confidential information necessarily disclosed in the course of the outsourcing, for example, by using confidentiality agreements to bind vendors contractually to protect client information. Further, the outsourcing lawyer who uses foreign vendors will need to evaluate the protection afforded the client's confidentiality by the foreign jurisdiction.

In a like vein, a much earlier opinion, ABA Formal Opinion 95-398, Access of Nonlawyers to a Lawyer's Data Base (1995), had addressed the ethical implications of allowing a computer maintenance company to have access to a law firm's computer network. The opinion stated that the law firm could allow access so long as it took steps to ensure that it had in place adequate security measures to protect confidential client information.[22]

4.5. Cloud Computing

"Cloud computing" can describe any system whereby a lawyer stores digital information on servers or systems that are not under the close control of the lawyer or the lawyer's

22. For additional information, see *infra* Appendix C—Ethics Opinions on Lawyer Confidentiality Obligations Concerning Outsourcing.

firm.[23] In the wake of the COVID-19 pandemic lockdowns and "stay-at-home" orders in Spring 2020 that forced many lawyers to work exclusively remotely, lawyers and law offices of all sizes and types dramatically accelerated their adoption of cloud-based services for their operations. Well before the pandemic, however, lawyers had been provided significant guidance on their ethical obligations in using the cloud, both for storage and various services essential to their work.

A lawyer's use of cloud computing can be both economical and beneficial, but as many state bar ethics opinions have noted, lawyers who use "the cloud" must take steps to ensure that confidential client information placed there is adequately protected from disclosure. Many opinions suggest a number of factors to use in assessing whether the protections are adequate, but with the proviso that rapidly evolving technology means that these factors cannot provide a "safe harbor." Lawyers should monitor and reassess the protections of the cloud provider as the technology evolves.

As an example, Illinois State Bar Advisory Opinion 16-06 (2016) suggested the following steps lawyers should consider taking when deciding whether to engage the services of a cloud computing provider:

1. Reviewing cloud computing industry standards and familiarizing oneself with the appropriate safeguards that should be employed;
2. Investigating whether the provider has implemented reasonable security precautions to protect client data from inadvertent disclosures including, but not limited to, the use of firewalls, password protections, and encryption;
3. Investigating the provider's reputation and history;
4. Inquiring whether the provider has experienced any breaches of security and, if so, investigating those breaches;
5. Requiring an agreement to reasonably ensure that the provider will abide by the lawyer's duties of confidentiality and will immediately notify the lawyer of any breaches or outside requests for client information;
6. Requiring that all data is appropriately backed up completely under the lawyer's control so that the lawyer will have a method for retrieval of the data;
7. Requiring provisions for the reasonable retrieval of information if the agreement is terminated or if the provider goes out of business.

Opinions addressing cloud computing also make clear that a lawyer must have a basic understanding of the technical aspects of cloud computing and should conduct a due diligence evaluation of the provider to ensure that it has adequate security measures. As Washington State Bar Opinion 2215 points out, ignorance of technology is no excuse for the

23. Additional discussion about the technical aspects of cloud computing can be found in this HANDBOOK, Chapter 3, *Understanding Technology—What Every Lawyer Needs to Know About the Cyber Network and Artificial Intelligence.*

failure to conduct such an investigation. A lawyer who does not understand the technology or whether it is sufficiently secure for use should consult with someone who does.[24]

In order to determine whether a lawyer has made "reasonable efforts" to ensure that outside vendors who provide communications technology have taken appropriate steps to protect client confidences, the ABA's Opinion 477R suggests a number of factors for evaluating technologies and vendors that are very similar to those identified by the many state bar ethics opinions on cloud computing.

4.6. Social Media

4.6.1. *Lawyers and Social Media*

Social media networks such as Facebook, X (formerly known as Twitter), and LinkedIn have grown exponentially in recent years. Though lawyers were slower than the general public and other businesses to adopt social networks, their use has become more and more prevalent among lawyers. While the use of social media networks may pose various risks for lawyers and others, for purposes of cybersecurity for lawyers and law firms, the questions about these networks revolve around confidentiality and lawyers' understanding of the technology that drives them.[25]

The strong tendency on social networks for users, including lawyers, to freely share information, and to do so without care consideration, opens the possibility that client confidential information may be shared by a lawyer, perhaps without careful deliberation. Of course, the lawyer's confidentiality obligations do not stop when the lawyer is logged on to social media. Moreover, the increased sharing of information among a wide range of people (sometimes including people not known to the lawyer using the service) may lead to the disclosure of seemingly innocuous information that may somehow reveal confidential client information (for example, the mergers and acquisitions lawyer's plans for travel to a city in which a particular business is located).

Even when social networks are used by lawyers for professional purposes—for example, posting a query to other lawyers about a knotty procedural problem in a pending case—the risk of disclosing client confidential information exists. In ABA Formal Opinion 98-411, *Ethical Issues in Lawyer-to-Lawyer Consultation* (1998), the ethics committee addressed lawyer-to-lawyer consultations of a similar type:

---

24. For additional information, see *infra* Appendix D—Ethics Opinions on Lawyer Confidentiality Obligations Concerning Cloud Computing.

25. Perhaps the best two sources available to lawyers and others on legal ethics issues associated with social media are Jan L. Jacobowitz and John G Browning, Legal Ethics and Social Media: A Practitioner's Handbook, 2d ed. (ABA 2022), https://www.americanbar.org/products/inv/book/425707691/, and *Social Media Ethics Guidelines* (Commercial and Federal Litigation Section, New York State Bar Association; updated, June 20, 2019), https://nys-fjc.ca2.uscourts.gov/programs/10-22-19%20-%20NYSBA-Social%20Media%20Ethics%20Guidelines-Final-6-20-19.pdf. While the NYSBA publication is focused on New York authority, it nevertheless provides an excellent starting point for research in other jurisdictions.

> The consulting lawyer should not assume, however, that the anonymous or hypothetical consultation eliminates all risk of disclosure of client information. If the hypothetical facts discussed allow the consulted lawyer subsequently to match those facts to a specific individual or entity, the information is not already generally known, and disclosure may prejudice or embarrass the client, the consulting lawyer's discussion of the facts may have violated his duty of confidentiality under Rule 1.6.

The sweeping reach of client confidentiality under ABA Model Rule 1.6—which requires protection of all "information relating to the representation" from whatever source—and under the rules in most jurisdictions counsels great care on the part of lawyers in sharing information that may touch on their professional lives. Further, just as with any other technology, lawyers have an obligation to be knowledgeable enough about any social network they use such that they can appropriately protect client confidential information.

Moreover, a lawyer's duty to supervise other lawyers and nonlawyers may include educating them concerning how their confidentiality obligation applies even among "friends" on Facebook and alerting them that "casual" comments made on LinkedIn after a difficult hearing may be risky. Rules 5.1 and 5.3 on supervision may also require that a lawyer or law firm have in place internal firm policies designed to protect client confidences in this context. These rules require that lawyers who manage their own practices or their firms must make sure they have in place "measures giving reasonable assurance that" obligations under the ethics rules, including confidentiality obligations, are met.

It is now common practice to post the minutiae of daily life on social media sites. However, when lawyers post information about their clients, they confront the broad reach of Rule 1.6 that protects from disclosure all information relating to the representation without client consent, unless impliedly necessary to carry out the representation, or unless another exception listed in Rule 1.6(b) applies. Even a post that refers to a client matter that is redacted to remove any identifying information can be a breach of confidentiality if someone who reads the post could reasonably ascertain the identity of the person(s) to whom the lawyer is referring and what the matter is about.[26]

4.6.2. *Passive Communications with Jurors*

As with all forms of technology, it is vitally important that lawyers understand the consequences of certain technical features of social media. To illustrate, consider the body of ethics opinions and court rules that have arisen over issues involving "passive" communications with jurors on social media.

While it is common practice for trial lawyers preparing for voir dire to search the internet to acquire information about potential jurors, some jurisdictions have found such an

26. *See infra* Appendix E—Ethics Opinions Relating to Lawyers' Passive Communications with Jurors on Social Media.

investigation to be inappropriate to the extent that the juror becomes aware that he or she is being monitored. Based on some of these opinions, the ethical propriety of the lawyer's conduct may depend on the functionality of the social media network.

On some social media networks, the network alerts a user when someone else views or visits the user's page or profile; on other social media networks, a user may have no idea of the identity of someone (such as a lawyer doing an investigation for purposes of voir dire) viewing the user's page or profile. Indeed, on some social networks, whether a user is alerted to such viewing or the identity of the viewer may depend on how the viewer accesses the network, the settings of the user, or the viewer. Knowing these details of the functionality of the particular social media network may well be crucial for a lawyer deciding whether and how to ethically investigate potential jurors.

ABA Formal Opinion 466, *Lawyer Reviewing Jurors' Internet Presence* (2014), addressed this issue and concluded that a juror's becoming aware of a lawyer's investigation was not a communication from the lawyer to the juror since it was the social media platform and not the lawyer that initiated the notification to the juror. The Opinion analogized the situation to that of a neighbor who reports to the juror that he saw the lawyer's car driving down the juror's street.

The committee cautioned, however, that lawyers should educate themselves about the features of the different social media platforms and that "lawyers who review juror social media should ensure that their review is purposeful and not crafted to embarrass, delay or burden the juror or the proceeding."

Earlier opinions from New York appeared to reach different conclusions, stating that notifications received by jurors from their social media website that the lawyer had visited their site had the potential to harass and intimidate the juror and constituted an impermissible communication with a juror in violation of Rule 3.5. In view of this potential to run afoul of Rule 3.5, these opinions cautioned that lawyers have an obligation to familiarize themselves with the features of a particular social media platform so as to avoid any inappropriate communications with a juror.[27] Clearly, trial lawyers interested in investigating potential jurors, or having someone do that for them, must become knowledgeable of the current ethics guidance in their jurisdiction, as well as in the courts in which they appear.

4.7. Ransomware

Perhaps the key theme underlying a lawyer's ethical obligations to protect the cybersecurity of client information is the dynamic nature of that obligation, which changes as the technology lawyers use and the threat environment changes. At the time of this writing, the threat most feared by most lawyers, law firms, and others is ransomware—the malicious encryption of lawyer and client data on a lawyer's or law firm's electronic systems and the

27. *See* N.Y. City Bar Ass'n Comm. on Prof. Ethics, Formal Op. 2012-2 (2012); N.Y. Cnty. Lawyer Association, Formal Op. 743 (2011).

demand for a ransom from the lawyer or law firm for the data's safe return or decryption. In some instances, even when a ransom is paid, the client and lawyer confidential information may be stolen, modified, corrupted, or even published.

The ABA and state bars have increasingly emphasized the necessity of preventive and responsive measures for ransomware, including those found in Opinion 483 and more recent guidance. That said, there is emerging guidance on what might amount to "reasonable efforts" by a lawyer or law firm either to prevent or remediate a ransomware attack. These include: training for firm personnel in recognizing phishing attacks designed to allow access to deploy ransomware in firm systems; strong passwords for access to firm systems; multi-factor authentication for access to firm systems (now increasingly viewed as a baseline requirement under both ethical and industry standards such as the 2024 NIST Cybersecurity Framework 2.0); and robust and regular backups of firm systems. We have no guidance yet from court decisions or ethics opinions on whether the failure to use these basic techniques might lead to disciplinary or civil liability of a lawyer whose client suffered a loss from a ransomware attack on the lawyer. Still, we are in an era where the next *T.J. Hooper* decision might well answer those questions for some unlucky lawyer or law firm.

4.8. Generative Artificial Intelligence Tools

The rapid adoption of GenAI tools by lawyers and law firms has prompted a raft of new ethical guidance.

ABA Opinion 512, *Generative Artificial Intelligence Tools*, provides detailed analysis of the ethical considerations when using AI tools, including confidentiality, competence, supervision, and the need for ongoing risk assessment. Opinion 512 emphasizes that the core framework of "reasonable efforts" to protect client information, as established in Opinion 477R, applies equally to the use of AI tools. Thus, lawyers must understand the capabilities and limitations of any AI tool they use, ensure appropriate safeguards are in place, and communicate with clients where appropriate about the use of this technology. The Opinion also highlights the importance of due diligence when selecting technology vendors and the need for ongoing training and supervision of both lawyers and nonlawyers in the use of AI tools.

In addition to ABA guidance, numerous state bars have issued opinions and other guidance addressing the use of AI tools, many of which touch on cybersecurity issues.[28] Lawyers should consult the most current guidance from their jurisdiction and remain vigilant as technology and the application of ethical standards continue to evolve.

This growing body of authority reflects a consensus quickly and almost uniformly established concerning lawyers' ethical obligations relating to the use of AI tools. That consensus

28. Included in Appendix F—Current Ethics Opinions and Other Guidance on Lawyer Use of Generative Artificial Intelligence Tools, are all known and local opinions and other guidance published as of May 2025.

includes clear guidance on cybersecurity concerns and is grounded firmly in Opinion 477R. Its key principles closely track guidance for all other technology use:

1. **Duty to Safeguard Client Information.** Lawyers must take "reasonable efforts" to prevent inadvertent or unauthorized disclosure of, or unauthorized access to, client information when using GenAI tools. GenAI tools may store, process, or transmit data in ways that expose client information to third parties or make it vulnerable to breaches. This duty is rooted in ABA Model Rule 1.6 and similar rules.
2. **Evaluating AI Tools for Security.** Lawyers should review and understand terms of use, privacy policies, and data retention practices of any AI tool before use, including: who has access to the data input into the tool; whether the tool uses input data for training or shares it with third parties; and the security measures in place to protect stored or transmitted data. Consultation with IT professionals or cybersecurity experts is recommended.
3. **Avoiding Public or Insecure AI Tools.** Many opinions caution against inputting client-specific or otherwise confidential information into publicly available or "open" GenAI systems, as these often lack adequate security and may use data for training or share it with others. In-house or "closed" AI systems may mitigate some risks, but lawyers must still ensure that their own infrastructure is secure and that no data is sent back to third-party servers. Lawyers and law firms should also monitor for GenAI features added to systems already used by a firm, sometimes as part of routine software updates. All the same concerns about initial adoption of GenAI tools apply equally to GenAI upgrades of ordinary software.
4. **Ongoing Monitoring and Due Diligence.** Lawyers must periodically monitor the terms of use and security practices of AI vendors, as these can change over time and may impact the confidentiality and security of client data. Firms and law departments should implement internal policies and control procedures to regulate the use of GenAI and to train staff on cybersecurity best practices.
5. **Informed Consent and Client Communication.** If the use of a GenAI tool involves a risk to client confidentiality that cannot be fully mitigated, lawyers should obtain the client's informed consent after explaining the risks and alternatives. Even with consent, lawyers should anonymize confidential data and avoid inputting information that could identify the client unless absolutely necessary.
6. **Supervisory Responsibilities.** Supervisory and managerial lawyers must ensure that all lawyers and nonlawyers in the firm comply with cybersecurity protocols when using GenAI. Training and written policies are recommended to ensure compliance and to address the evolving nature of cybersecurity threats. Supervisory and managerial lawyers must also ensure review procedures are in place and followed to validate GenAI output, including case citations and references that may be made to documents retrieved by the AI tool from case files.

7. **Incident Response and Breach Notification.** Lawyers should ensure that AI vendors have obligations to notify them in the event of a data breach or unauthorized access to client information. Firms should have an incident response plan in place for potential breaches involving AI tools.

5. Conclusion

We lawyers, like our clients, live and practice in a rapidly changing communications and technology environment, and there is no end in sight for these changes. Over the last 20 years, our ethics rules have been interpreted to provide guidance as to how we can discharge our ethical obligations in a time when threats, technology, security vulnerabilities, and protection measures available, as well as their relationships one to another, are also dynamically changing.

Whether it be artificial intelligence, cloud computing, the perils of remote work, use of unencrypted or encrypted e-mail, participating in social media, or the use of the latest electronic gadget, lawyers have an obligation to make reasonable efforts to protect their clients' confidential information. What is found to constitute "reasonable efforts" will depend on a number of factors including "the sensitivity of the information, the likelihood of disclosure if additional safeguards are not employed," and the cost and difficulty of implementing them.

Applying these factors, Opinion 477R informs us that when transmitting client information over the internet, encryption should be considered as an additional security safeguard when warranted by the circumstances.

Lawyers also have an obligation to understand the benefits and risks associated with these new technologies. If for any reason they are unable to do so, they should consult with someone who does.

Lawyers who supervise other lawyers and nonlawyers also have a duty to make reasonable efforts to ensure that their conduct conforms to the rules of professional conduct and that they follow appropriate security procedures to protect client confidences.

The following are the top ten ethical and other considerations with respect to lawyer obligations to protect client data:

1. A lawyer must acquire a basic understanding of the "benefits and risks associated with relevant technology" used in his or her day-to-day practice. A lawyer who does not have such an understanding should identify and consult with someone who does.
2. Technology is a moving target. Keeping current about changes in technology is an ongoing process. A lawyer must continually reassess and evaluate security measures as new technologies develop and come into use by lawyers and their clients. A lawyer

may be able to meet this obligation by "outsourcing" this continuing diligence to a trusted technology expert.

3. Be aware that the scope of the information protected under the ethics rules—ABA Model Rule 1.6—is very broad. It includes all information relating to the representation.
4. Be mindful of obligations to protect a former client's confidential information (under Model Rule 1.9(c)) as well.
5. When using technology to either store or transmit information, lawyers must make reasonable efforts to prevent the inadvertent disclosure of, or unauthorized access to, confidential client information.
6. Reasonable efforts to prevent the inadvertent disclosure of, or unauthorized access to, confidential client information include assessing the sensitivity of the information and the likelihood of disclosure if additional safeguards are not employed. Depending on the circumstances, for example, encryption and multi-factor authentication may be appropriate additional security safeguards. Lawyers should consult their technology experts.
7. In an office or firm, have in place procedures by which both lawyers and nonlawyers are trained and monitored in their use of technology to ensure that client confidences are protected.
8. When disposing of portable electronic devices, take precautions to ensure that all confidential client information has been removed. If the devices are recycled, verify that the recycler follows appropriate protocols to remove the data.
9. When transmitting electronic documents to third parties, remove metadata that contains confidential client information.
10. When using cloud computing or outsourcing services, verify that the service provider has in place adequate security measures to prevent the inadvertent disclosure of or unauthorized access to confidential client information

Chapter 10 Appendices

Appendix A—Email

Ethics Opinions on Lawyer Confidentiality Obligations Concerning Email

A. ABA Formal Ethics Opinions

The Opinion head notes are reproduced below.

1. Formal Opinion 483 (Oct. 17, 2018)

Lawyers' Obligations after an Electronic Data Breach or Cyberattack
https://www.americanbar.org/content/dam/aba/administrative/professional_responsibility/ethics-opinions/aba-formal-op-483.pdf
Model Rule 1.4 requires lawyers to keep clients "reasonably informed" about the status of a matter and to explain matters "to the extent reasonably necessary to permit a client to make an informed decision regarding the representation." Model Rules 1.1, 1.6, 5.1 and 5.3, as amended in 2012, address the risks that accompany the benefits of the use of technology by lawyers. When a data breach occurs involving, or having a substantial likelihood of involving, material client information, lawyers have a duty to notify clients of the breach and to take other reasonable steps consistent with their obligations under these Model Rules.

2. Formal Opinion 477R (Revised May 19, 2017)

Securing Communication of Protected Client Information
https://www.americanbar.org/content/dam/aba/administrative/professional_responsibility/ethics-opinions/aba-formal-opinion-477.pdf
A lawyer generally may transmit information relating to the representation of a client over the Internet without violating the Model Rules of Professional Conduct where the lawyer has undertaken reasonable efforts to prevent inadvertent or unauthorized access. However, a lawyer may be required to take special security precautions to protect against the inadvertent or unauthorized disclosure of client information when required by an agreement with the client or by law, or when the nature of the information requires a higher degree of security.

3. Formal Opinion 99-413 (March 10, 1999)

Protecting the Confidentiality of Unencrypted Email
https://www.americanbar.org/content/dam/aba/administrative/professional_responsibility/ethics-opinions/99-413.pdf
A lawyer may transmit information relating to the representation of a client by unencrypted email sent over the internet without violating the Model Rules of Professional Conduct (1998) because the mode of transmission affords a reasonable expectation of privacy from a technological and legal standpoint. The same privacy accorded U.S. and commercial mail, land-line telephonic transmissions, and facsimiles applies to Internet email. A lawyer should consult with the client and follow her instructions, however, as to the mode of transmitting highly sensitive information relating to the client's representation. *See also* ABA Formal Opinion 477R (May 22, 2017) (interpreting later amendments to ABA Model Rules and providing advice on closely related questions).

4. Formal Opinion 11-459 (Aug. 4, 2011)

Duty to Protect the Confidentiality of Email Communications with One's Client
https://www.americanbar.org/content/dam/aba/publications/YourABA/11-459.authcheckdam.pdf
A lawyer sending or receiving substantive communications with a client via email or other electronic means ordinarily must warn the client about the risk of sending or receiving electronic communications using a computer or other device, or email account, where there is a significant risk that a third party may gain access. In the context of representing an employee, this obligation arises, at the very least, when the lawyer knows or reasonably should know that the client is likely to send or receive substantive client-lawyer communications via email or other electronic means, using a business device or system under circumstances where there is a significant risk that the communications will be read by the employer or another third party.

5. Formal Opinion 11-460 (Aug. 4, 2011)

Duty when Lawyer Receives Copies of a Third Party's Email Communications with Counsel
http://www.americanbar.org/content/dam/aba/administrative/professional_responsibility/ethics_opinion_11_460.pdf
When an employer's lawyer receives copies of an employee's private communications with counsel, which the employer located in the employee's business email file or on the employee's workplace computer or other device, neither Rule 4.4(b) nor any other Rule requires the employer's lawyer to notify opposing counsel of the receipt of the

communications. However, court decisions, civil procedure rules, or other law may impose such a notification duty, which a lawyer may then be subject to discipline for violating. If the law governing potential disclosure is unclear, Rule 1.6(b)(6) allows the employer's lawyer to disclose that the employer has retrieved the employee's attorney-client email communications to the extent the lawyer reasonably believes it is necessary to do so to comply with the relevant law. If no law can reasonably be read as establishing a notification obligation, however, then the decision whether to give notice must be made by the employer-client, and the employer's lawyer must explain the implications of disclosure, and the available alternatives, as necessary to enable the employer to make an informed decision.

B. ABA Treatises and Annotated Model Standards

1. ABA / Bloomberg Lawyers' Manual on Professional Conduct

http://www.americanbar.org/groups/professional_responsibility/publications/aba_bna_lawyers_manual_on_professional_conduct.html

See the chapter from the treatise section of the *Manual*, "*Confidentiality, Safeguarding Client Information, Electronic Communications*," 55 Law. Man. Prof. Conduct 40.

2. Model Rules of Professional Conduct, 2025 Edition

https://www.americanbar.org/products/inv/book/449291561/

See the annotations to Rule 1.6 *Confidentiality of Information.*

3. Ronald D. Rotunda, *Legal Ethics: The Lawyer's Deskbook on Professional Responsibility* 2024–2025 ed. (ABA)

https://store.legal.thomsonreuters.com/law-products/c/Legal-Ethics-The-Lawyers-Deskbook-on-Professional-Responsibility-2024-2025-ed-ABA/p/107080714

See Section 1.6-2 *Inadvertent Disclosure.*

C. State and Local Bar Ethics Opinions that have addressed email, cordless phone, and cell phone usage (with links to the full text where available)

The following digests of state bar ethics opinions are excerpted with permission from the *ABA/Bloomberg Lawyers' Manual on Professional Conduct.*

1. Alaska Ethics Opinion 98-2 (Jan. 16, 1998)
   Email; Confidentiality; Internet

https://alaskabar.org/wp-content/uploads/98-2.pdf

A lawyer may use unencrypted email to transmit client information, though lawyers are encouraged to use encryption software when communicating particularly sensitive or confidential matters by email.

2. Arizona State Bar Opinion 95-11 (Dec. 1995)
   Confidentiality; Telephones
https://tools.dev.azbar.org/RulesofProfessionalConduct/ViewEthicsOpinion.aspx?id=463
A lawyer may use a cellular or cordless telephone to contact a client or opposing counsel, but should exercise caution when discussing confidential matters as there is a genuine risk that a third party will intercept the information. Just as a lawyer would not discuss sensitive matters in a crowded restaurant, the lawyer should refrain from having such discussions when using a portable telephone. Rules 1.3, 1.4, 1.6.

3. Arizona Opinion 97-04 (April 7, 1997)
   Computer technology; Internet; Advertising and solicitation; Confidentiality
https://www.azbar.org/for-legal-professionals/ethics/ethics-opinions/?V=Opinions&OpinionId=480
(8) A lawyer may communicate with a client via email even if the email is not encrypted, although it is preferable to protect the attorney-client communications, if practical, through the use of encryption software or by having the email encrypted with a password known only to the lawyer and the client. At minimum, email transmissions to clients should include a cautionary statement either in the "re" line or at the beginning of the message, indicating that the transmission is "confidential" or "attorney-client privileged," just as is done when using facsimile transmittals. In determining whether to communicate with a client via email, lawyers should consider that email records, including the records of time and date of transmission and recipients, may be discoverable.

4. Arizona Ethics Opinion 02-04 (Sept. 2002)
   Confidentiality; Email; Internet; Initial Consultation; Disclaimers
https://www.azbar.org/for-legal-professionals/ethics/ethics-opinions/?V=Opinions&OpinionId=288
A lawyer who simply uses email, without having a Web site or advertisements on the internet, does not owe a duty of confidentiality to an individual who unilaterally emails an unsolicited inquiry to the lawyer. However, lawyers who maintain Web sites or advertise on the nternet need to use "appropriate disclaimers" if they want to prevent unsolicited email from having to be treated as confidential.

5. California State Bar Opinion 2010-179 (undated)
   Computers; Email; Internet; Confidentiality; Communication with clients
https://www.calbar.ca.gov/Portals/0/documents/ethics/Opinions/2010-179-Interim-No-08-0002-PAW.pdf
Because the protection of confidentiality is an element of competent lawyering, a lawyer should not use any particular mode of technology to store or transmit confidential information before considering how secure it is and whether reasonable precautions such

as firewalls, encryption, or password-protection could make it more secure. The lawyer should also consider the sensitivity of the information, the urgency of the situation, the possible effect of an inadvertent disclosure or an unauthorized interception, and the client's instructions and circumstances, e.g., can others access the client's devices. A lawyer may use a laptop computer at home for client matters and email if the lawyer's personal wireless system has been configured with appropriate security features. However, if using a public wireless connection—for example in a coffee shop—the lawyer may need to add safeguards such as encryption and firewalls. Opinions 1979-50, 2007-174; Orange County Opinion 97-0002; Los Angeles County Opinions 456, 514; 18 U.S.C. §§ 1030, 2510; Cal. Penal Code §§ 502(c), 629.86; Rule 3-110(C), ABA 95-398, 99-413.

6. Los Angeles County Bar Opinion 514 (Aug. 19, 2005)
   Internet; Communication with judges; Confidentiality; Email

https://s3.amazonaws.com/membercentralcdn/sitedocuments/lacba/lacba/0454/2094454.pdf?AWSAccessKeyId=AKIAIHKD6NT2OL2HNPMQ&Expires=1746847299&Signature=8NerCelSLqGJOuYGVPMkdMRrzgY%3D&response-content-disposition=inline%3B%20filename%3D%22eth514%2Epdf%22%3B%20filename%2A%3DUTF%2D8%27%27eth514%252Epdf&response-content-type=application%2Fpdf

A listserv, whether closed or open, is a public conversation. Participants in a listserv should take care not to divulge client confidences and secrets. Lawyers should also be mindful that their messages could be read by unintended recipients, such as judges, creating the possibility of unintended ex parte communications. A lawyer who posts comments about the merits of a particular expert witness does not necessarily breach confidentiality. However, the lawyer risks impairing his ability to continue representing the client because the lawyer could unintentionally be making improvident disclosures, or communicating ex parte with a judge, or waiving the work-product privilege by disclosing mental impressions. Judges, and lawyers acting as temporary judges or arbitrators, who participate in listservs that include lawyers who may potentially appear before them must be mindful of the risk of engaging in ex parte communications and should expect from time to time to have to delete an email without reading it. Rules 1-710, 5-300; CJC Canons 2A, 4, 6D; ABA Rule 3.5; ABA 99-413.

7. San Diego County Bar Ass'n Legal Ethics Comm. Opinion 2006-1 (undated)
   Confidentiality; Prospective Clients; Email; Marketing

https://www.sdcba.org/?Pg=ethicsopinion06-1

A lawyer has no duty to preserve the confidentiality of information emailed to her by a person who is seeking representation and locates the lawyer's email address on the California bar's Web site. The lawyer may represent the person's opponent in the matter and may even use the emailed information for that client's benefit. Inculpatory information in unsolicited email from person asking for representation may be disclosed and used by the lawyer since the lawyer did not publish their email address in marketing material and so "had no opportunity to warn" that communication would not be treated as confidential. However, a dissenting opinion argued that consumers have a reasonable expectation of confidentiality when they send an email to an attorney with the information necessary to seek legal advice.

8. Connecticut Bar Association Opinion 99-52 (1999)
Under ordinary circumstances, a lawyer may use unencrypted email to communicate with clients without violating Rule 1.6, since the risk of interception or inadvertent disclosure of the contents is minimal. However, in view of the lawyer's duty to receive, store, and transmit confidential client information using procedures that are reasonably designed and managed to ensure confidentiality, the lawyer must consult with the client regarding the risks involved in using unencrypted email, must use good judgment in choosing the appropriate method for communicating confidential client information, and must counsel the client to do the same. Additionally, if the lawyer has reason to know that there is a greater than ordinary risk of interception or unauthorized disclosure, such as an email address accessible to persons other than the intended recipient, the lawyer should not send email to the client without the client's express consent. Similarly, client consent to using email should be obtained prior to sending information that is extraordinarily sensitive or highly confidential, just as should be done when sending such information through telephone lines, fax machines, or regular mail. 18 U.S.C. § 2510(b); Rule 1.6; ABA 99-413.

9. Delaware Opinion 2001-2 (undated)
Confidentiality; Communication with client; Attorney-client privilege; Computers; Telephones
https://media1.dsba.org/public/media/ethics/pdfs/2001-2.pdf
Unless interception is reasonably suspected, a lawyer may transmit client information by email or cellular phone. Extensive statutory protections make the prospect of being overheard on cellular phones in public places a far bigger problem than electronic interception. 18 U.S.C. §§ 2510 et seq., 2701-2702; Rule 1.6; ABA 92-368, 94-382, 99-413.

10. District of Columbia Ethics Opinion 281 (Feb. 1998)
Internet; Email; Confidentiality
https://dcbar.org/for-lawyers/legal-ethics/ethics-opinions-210-present/ethics-opinion-281
Lawyers may transmit information by unencrypted email; however, individual circumstances may require greater means of security. Rule 1.6.

11. Florida Opinion 00-4 (July 15, 2000)
Internet; Lawyer-client relationship; Confidentiality; Email
https://www.floridabar.org/etopinions/etopinion-00-4/

A lawyer may provide legal services over the internet through the lawyer's firm with regard to matters that do not require in-person consultation or court appearances, provided the lawyer complies with the ethics rules including those relating to lawyer competence, communication, advertising, conflicts of interest, and confidentiality. If the client's matter is too complex to be easily handled over the internet, the lawyer may not handle it if the client is unwilling to meet in person and must withdraw if the representation has already begun. Legal services may be provided only through the law firm and not through a corporate entity other than a professional service corporation, professional association, or professional limited liability company. A lawyer may communicate with a client through the use of unencrypted email in most situations, but must comply with the client's instructions when sending highly sensitive information. Opinion 88-13; Rules 4-1.1, 4-1.6, 4-1.7 through 4-1.12, 4-5.3, 4-5.5(b), 4-7, 4-7.6(b), 4-8.6(a); ABA 99-413.

12. Florida Opinion 07-3 (Jan. 16, 2009)
    Confidentiality; Prospective Clients; Email

https://www.floridabar.org/etopinions/etopinion-07-3/
A person seeking legal services has no reasonable expectation of confidentiality in information he unilaterally submits to lawyer by email, regular mail, telephone message, or facsimile transmission; lawyers should post a prominent statement to that effect on their websites.

13. Hawaii Opinion 40 (April 26, 2001)
    Confidentiality; Communication with client; Email

https://dbhawaii.org/wp-content/uploads/FO_40_-_E-MAIL_SECURITY.pdf
A lawyer may communicate with a client via encrypted or unencrypted email. If the information is sensitive, the lawyer should consult with the client and follow the client's instructions. Rules 1.2(a), 1.6(a); ABA 99-413.

14. Illinois State Bar Opinion 96-10 (May 16, 1997) (Affirmed Jan. 2010)
    Electronic communications; Confidentiality; Advertising and Solicitation

http://www.isba.org/sites/default/files/ethicsopinions/96-10.pdf
In general, a lawyer may communicate with a client via electronic mail without encryption, since the expectation of privacy for electronic mail is the same as that for ordinary telephone calls and the unauthorized interception of an electronic message is illegal. Unusual circumstances involving extraordinarily sensitive information might warrant enhanced security measures like encryption, just as ordinary telephones and other normal means of communication would be deemed inadequate to protect confidentiality in such situations. A lawyer's use of an internet web site is not "communication directed to a specific recipient" and is therefore governed only by the general rules regarding advertising and solicitation; a home page is the functional equivalent of a "yellow pages" entry of a telephone directory and the material included in the home page is the functional equivalent

of the firm brochures and similar materials that lawyers commonly prepare for clients and prospective clients. A lawyer's participation in an electronic bulletin board, chat group, or similar service may implicate the rules governing solicitation to the extent that the lawyer seeks to initiate unrequested contact with a specific person or group through the use of such services. Furthermore, when a lawyer participates in a chat group or other on-line service that may involve offering personalized legal advice to anyone who happens to be connected to the service, the recipients of the advice become the lawyer's client. 18 U.S.C. §§ 2510 et seq.; Opinions 90-07, 94-11; Rules 1.6, 7.1, 7.2, 7.3, 7.4.

15. Iowa State Bar Association Opinion 96-1 (Aug. 29, 1996)
    Confidentiality; Communication with client; Email; Advertising

http://205.209.45.153/iabar/IowaEthicsOpinions.nsf/b6868944e3311dd0872581100042934f/69139dea4264db38872581100042b586?OpenDocument

Lawyers' and law firms' home pages or web sites constitute advertising and must conform to ethics rules. Disclosures must appear in full, not by hyper-text link, on first page or screen of home page or web site and in any location where there is biographical matter other than the name, address, telephone and fax numbers for the lawyer or firm. If the home page or web site is sponsored by an entity other than the lawyer but contains references or links to a page or screen containing biographical matter (other than name, address, telephone and fax numbers), required disclosures must also appear on that page or screen. The foregoing does not apply to the pure exchange of legal information with another firm or other members of the home page or web site. It also does not apply to the pure exchange of information or legal communication with clients; however, if sensitive material is to be transmitted via email, the lawyer must have written acknowledgment by client of the risk of the violation of Rule 4-101 and obtain consent for the communication via internet or non-secure Intranet or other forms of proprietary networks. Otherwise the communication must be encrypted or protected by a password/firewall or other generally accepted equivalent security system. Opinion 95-30 is rescinded and replaced. DRs 2-101(A)(C)(D)(F), 2-105(A)(3), 4-101(B)(1),(C)(1).

16. Iowa State Bar Association Opinion 97-1 (Sept. 18, 1997)
    Confidentiality; Computer technology

http://205.209.45.153/iabar/IowaEthicsOpinions.nsf/b6868944e3311dd0872581100042934f/315d6205d531771e872581100042b88a?OpenDocument

Opinion 96-1 and 96-33 are amended to eliminate the board's determination of what is minimally appropriate email security. Transmission of confidential information through email or the internet or other non-secure proprietary networks requires written consent from the client after disclosure of the potential for loss of confidentiality. The means of protection should be determined after discussion between the lawyer and the client. Opinions 96-1 and 96-33 are amended. Opinions 96-1, 96-33.

17. Iowa State Bar Association Opinion 07-02 (Aug. 8, 2007)
Confidentiality; Prospective Clients; Email; Internet
http://205.209.45.153/iabar/IowaEthicsOpinions.nsf/b6868944e3311dd0872581100042934f/bd12c617faff36c1872581100042b915?OpenDocument
Obligations that a lawyer generally owes prospective clients are not triggered by an email or voicemail message that the lawyer receives out of the blue from a stranger in search of counsel, so long as the lawyer did not do or publish anything that would lead reasonable people to believe that they could share private information with the lawyer without first meeting with him and establishing a lawyer-client relationship.

18. Maine Board of Overseers of the Bar Opinion 195 (June 30, 2008)
Email; Computers; Confidentiality; Communication with clients
http://www.maine.gov/tools/whatsnew/index.php?topic=mebar_overseers_ethics_opinions&id=63338&v=article
A lawyer generally may use unencrypted email to communicate with clients, but should consider the content of the communication as well as the security of the email address. If the information is of such a highly confidential nature that disclosure would significantly damage the client's interests, the lawyer should use reasonable judgment in selecting another means of communication. Opinion 134; 18 U.S.C. §§ 2510 et seq.; Rule 3.6(a), 3.6(f), 3.6(h)(1), 3.13(c); ABA Rule 1.6; ABA 99-413.

19. Massachusetts Opinion 2000-1 (July 15, 1999)
Internet; Communication with client; Confidentiality
https://www.massbar.org/publications/ethics-opinions/ethics-opinion-article/ethics-opinions-2000-opinion-no-00-1
A lawyer's use of unencrypted email to communicate with clients does not normally violate Rule 1.6(a), since legal and technical hurdles to the interception of email give rise to a reasonable expectation that such communications will remain private. However, a lawyer must not use unencrypted email if doing so contravenes the express instructions of the client, and should avoid transmitting sensitive confidential information via unencrypted email without the client's express consent. In addition, a lawyer should ensure that confidential email messages, whether or not encrypted, are not sent to email addresses that are reasonably accessible to persons other than the client. For instance, a lawyer should not send email to a client's work address without the express consent of the client, since many employers reserve the right to review all email messages sent through their systems. 18 U.S.C. §§ 2510 et seq.; Rule 1.6(a).

20. Minnesota Opinion 19 (Jan. 22, 1999; Amended Jan. 22, 2010)
Confidentiality; Communication with client; Internet; Computers
http://lprb.mncourts.gov/rules/LPRBOpinions/Opinion%2019.pdf

A lawyer may use email without encryption, or digital cordless and cellular telephones within a digital service area, to transmit and receive confidential client information; the use of analog cordless and cellular telephones for such purposes requires the consent of the client after consultation regarding the confidentiality risks associated with inadvertent interception. Client consent after consultation is also required when the lawyer knows or reasonably should know that a client or other person is using an analog cordless or cellular telephone, or other insecure means to communicate with the lawyer about confidential client information. Rule 1.6(a)(1).

21. Missouri Opinion 970161 (undated)
    Internet; Confidentiality; Communication with client; Advertising and solicitation

https://mo-legal-ethics.org/informal-opinion/970161/

A lawyer using the internet to communicate with clients must comply with the ethics rules, including Rules 4-7.1 through 4-7.5. If email communications are not secured through a quality encryption program in both directions, the lawyer must advise clients and potential clients that communication by email is not necessarily secure and confidential. Rules 4-7.1, 4-7.2, 4-7.3, 4-7.4, 4-7.5.

22. Nevada Ethics Opinion 32 (March 25, 2005)
    Prospective Clients; Internet; Email; Confidentiality; Advertising and solicitation; Disclaimers

https://www.nvbar.org/wp-content/uploads/opinion_32.pdf

Lawyers who have Web sites or advertise on the internet should use disclaimers to avoid having to keep unsolicited emails confidential and to ensure that prospective clients do not interpret the advertisement or solicitation as an invitation to form a lawyer-client relationship by simply responding. Nev. Sup. Ct. Rule 156; ABA Rule 1.18.

23. New York State Bar Opinion 709 (Sept. 16, 1998)
    Internet; Intellectual property representation; Confidentiality; Credit cards; Advertising and solicitation; Unauthorized practice

https://nysba.org/opinion-709/?srsltid=AfmBOor0SF8J3yZs4RSbcu1P4UdcCqxBahWjJU0fcTSFqNuAU40PhT2_

A lawyer may take orders for and conduct trademark searches, render legal opinions, and file trademark applications over the internet, subject to ethical restrictions applicable to the practice of law via telephone or facsimile. A lawyer practicing over the internet must check for client conflicts and should include on their web site the full text of the Statement of Client Rights and Responsibilities required by law. When relying upon legal research obtained through the internet, the lawyer must insure the reliability of such information. In ordinary circumstances a lawyer may use unencrypted email to transmit confidential information to clients; however, a lawyer must use a more secure means of communication if the lawyer is on notice that a specific email transmission is at a heightened risk of interception or if the confidential information involved is of such an extraordinarily sensitive nature that it reasonable to use only a means of communication that is completely under the lawyer's control. A lawyer who uses email must keep informed of the evolving technology to assess any changes in the likelihood of interception or in the availability of new technologies that would reduce such risks at a reasonable cost. A lawyer should discuss such risks with clients and abide by their wishes as to whether to communicate by email. A lawyer may accept payment by credit card provided the fee is not excessive or does not otherwise violate the ethics code. A lawyer who accepts credit card payment over the internet must insure the privacy of the clients' credit card information. A lawyer may advertise over the internet provided the advertising is not false, deceptive, or misleading and otherwise complies with the ethics code. A lawyer must keep a copy of any internet advertisement for at least one year following its last use, but need not file a copy with a departmental disciplinary committee. The copy may be maintained in electronic form. Lawyers may advertise to solicit clients residing outside of the state regarding matters that the lawyer may lawfully and competently handle; however, any internet advertisement should inform potential clients of the jurisdictions in which the lawyer is licensed and should not mislead potential clients that the lawyer is licensed in a jurisdiction where the lawyer is not licensed. Whether a lawyer licensed only in New York may render legal opinions over the internet to clients resident in another jurisdiction would depend on whether such conduct constitutes the unauthorized practice of law in the other jurisdiction. Similarly, if a lawyer licensed only in New York limits her services to trademark searches and filing trademark applications as nonlawyers are generally permitted to do, whether she may provide such limited services to clients resident in another jurisdiction with regard to matters arising in the other jurisdiction would be governed by the laws and rules of the other jurisdiction. Even though trademark searches and application filings may be performed by nonlawyers, a lawyer performing such services may not practice under a trade name if the lawyer exercises her professional legal judgment in performing such services, since the exercise of a lawyer's professional judgment would constitute the practice of law. Opinions 362, 375, 399, 557, 625, 636, 662, 664, 705, 768; 22 N.Y. Comp. Codes R. & Regs. Section 1210.1; DRs 1-102(A), 2-101(B)(F), 2-102(B)(D), 2-103(A), 2-106, 3-101(B), 4-101(A)(B)(D), 5-105(E), 5-108; ECs 2-10, 2-13, 3-5, 4-1, 4-4; Canon 4; ABA Rule 7.2(a).

24. New York State Bar Association Opinion 1076 (Dec. 8, 2015)
    Communication with clients; Email; Lawyer-client relationship; Communication with represented persons; Opposing counsel; Confidentiality

https://nysba.org/ethics-opinion-1076/

A lawyer may blind copy ("bcc") a client on email with opposing counsel even if opposing counsel objects; the lawyer is the client's agent, and it is unreasonable for opposing counsel to assume that the lawyer would not share the communication with the principal/client.

Sending the client a copy by using "cc" would disclose the client's email address and could be seen by opposing counsel as an invitation to communicate directly with the client. For practical reasons—such as avoiding the possibility of the client responding with the "reply all" button—the lawyer should consider forwarding the correspondence, rather than sending a blind copy. New York City Opinion 2009-1; Rules 1.4, 1.6, 4.2, 8.4.

25. New York City Bar Association Ethics Opinion 2001-01 (May 11, 2001)
    Confidentiality; Email; Conflicts

https://www.nycbar.org/reports/formal-opinion-2001-1-obligations-of-law-firm-receiving-unsolicited-email-communications-from-prospective-client/
Information in unsolicited email from potential client, generated in good faith after sender viewed lawyer's website which contained no disclaimer, does not disqualify lawyer from representation of current or future client adverse to sender but must be treated as confidential where lawyer had no meaningful opportunity to avoid receipt. DR 4-101 [22 N.Y.C.R.R. § 1200.19]; EC 4-1; DR 5-105(A) [22 N.Y.C.R.R. § 1200.20]

26. New York City Bar Opinion 2008-1 (Jan. 1, 2008)
    Files of client; Computers; Email

https://www.nycbar.org/reports/formal-opinion-2008-01-a-lawyers-ethical-obligations-to-retain-and-to-provide-a-client-with-electronic-documents-relating-to-a-representation/
A lawyer is not required to organize or store electronic documents or emails in any particular manner or medium. Emails present more difficulty than electronic documents because they often are deleted automatically after a certain period and generally are not stored in a document management system. Because a lawyer may not charge a client file retrieval costs that could reasonably have been avoided, there is much to commend a practice of organizing saved emails for ease of retrieval. Opinion 1986-4; New York State Opinions 460, 623, 780; DRs 2-106, 2-110(2), 9-102; ABA Rules 1.0(n), 1.16(d); ABA i1384.

27. North Carolina State Bar Association Opinion 215 (July 21, 1995)
    Confidentiality; Telephoning; Cellular telephones

https://www.ncbar.gov/for-lawyers/ethics/adopted-opinions/rpc-215/?opinionSearchTerm=confidential%20disclosure
A lawyer using a cellular or cordless telephone, or email or other unsecure method of communication, must minimize the risk of disclosing confidential information. If the lawyer has reason to believe that the mode of communication is susceptible to interception, the lawyer must so advise the parties to the conversation. Opinion RPC 133; Rule 4.

28. North Carolina Opinion 2012-5 (Oct. 26, 2012)
    Email; Computers; Confidentiality; Disclosure; Attorney-client privilege; Advice to clients; Government lawyers

https://www.ncbar.gov/for-lawyers/ethics/adopted-opinions/2012-formal-ethics-opinion-5/
A lawyer must avoid communicating with a client using the client's employer's email system if there is a risk the employer will access the emails. A lawyer who represents an employer whose personnel policy states that use of the employer's email system may be monitored must advise the employer as to its rights and responsibilities. If the employee accesses a personal email account via the employer's computer, the lawyer may not advise the employer to change the password so it can access the employee's personal messages. If the employer notifies its lawyer that it has changed the password on the employee's personal email account on its own initiative and has accessed emails between the employee and his attorney, the lawyer may not so notify the employee's attorney unless the lawyer has obtained the informed consent of the employer or believes that notification is reasonably required to comply with the law or a court order. The lawyer may not review the messages without a court order. If the employer notifies its lawyer that it has recovered emails between the employee and the employee's attorney that are marked "Attorney-Client Confidential Communication," the lawyer may not read the employee's emails unless the lawyer concludes in good faith that the employee has waived the privilege. The lawyer who represents the employer has no duty under Rule 4.4(b) to notify the employee's attorney that the employer has copies of the employee's email messages; the information is confidential pursuant to Rule 1.6(b)(1). A government lawyer may review emails between a government employee and his attorney to determine if the emails are public records. If they are not, the lawyer must treat them as privileged unless he can conclude that the privilege has been waived. Opinion 2009-1; Rules 1.2, 1.6, 4.4, 8.4; ABA 11-460.

29. North Dakota State Bar Opinion 97-09 (Sept. 4, 1997)
    Confidentiality; Computers; Internet

https://cdn.ymaws.com/www.sband.org/resource/resmgr/docs/for_lawyers/97-09.pdf
A lawyer may communicate with other lawyers or clients regarding routine matters using email that is not encrypted and is sent on either a private network or on the internet unless unusual circumstances require enhanced security measures. Rules 1.2(b), 1.6.

30. Supreme Court of Ohio Board of Commissioners on Grievances and Discipline Opinion 99-2 (April 9, 1999)
    Confidentiality; Communication with client; Email; Computers

https://ohioadvop.org/wp-content/uploads/2017/04/Op-99-002.pdf
A lawyer may normally use unencrypted email to communicate with clients. Particular matters or circumstances may, however, require choosing a different method of communication;

the lawyer must use professional judgment. 18 U.S.C. § 2511; Ohio Rev. Code Ann. Section 2933.52(A)(B)(2); DR 4-101.

31. Pennsylvania Bar Association Opinion 97-130 (Sept. 26, 1997)
    Confidentiality; Advertising and solicitation; Computers; Internet

A lawyer may communicate with a client using electronic mail if the client consents after consultation. Encryption is generally not required, although in cases of sensitive information, it may be advisable. The lawyer should take appropriate steps under the circumstances to safeguard the confidentiality of client information. If email is used to solicit new clients for the lawyer, it is advertising and is similar to targeted mail and is subject to the restrictions set out in the ethics rules. Rules 1.6, 7.1–7.7.

32. South Carolina Opinion 94-27 (Jan. 1995)
    Computers; Lawyer-client relationship; Confidentiality;
    Communication with client; Advertising

https://www.scbar.org/for-lawyers/quicklinks/legal-resources/ethics-advisory-opinions/ethics-advisory-opinion-94-27/

A lawyer may set up an electronic law office through an on-line service where the lawyer would provide legal information and advice to people throughout the nation. Although the operation of a law office via electronic media does not in itself violate the rules, the practice of law through such means raises several issues regarding communication, advertising, direct contact with prospective clients, and certainty of confidentiality. The lawyer's advertising would reach consumers in jurisdictions where the lawyer is not allowed to practice. Absent informed consent, confidential communications with clients would be jeopardized. The lawyer may also maintain a presence on the electronic media to generally discuss legal topics without giving advice or representing clients. Opinions 90-37, 91-4; Rules 1.6, 3.6, 7.1, 7.2, 7.3.

33. South Carolina Opinion 97-08 Opinion 97-08 (1997)
    Internet; Communication with client; Confidentiality

https://www.scbar.org/for-lawyers/quicklinks/legal-resources/ethics-advisory-opinions/ethics-advisory-opinion-97-08/

A lawyer may communicate with a client via email, since the expectation of privacy is no less than that associated with regular mail, facsimile transmissions or land-based telephone calls and because the interception of email is illegal under federal law. However, just as with other modes of communication, there is some information that a prudent lawyer would be hesitant to discuss via email. In such situations, a lawyer should discuss with the client alternatives, including encryption, in order to safeguard against even inadvertent disclosure of sensitive or privileged information. 18 U.S.C. §§ 2701(a), 2702(a); Opinion 94-27; Rule 1.6.

34. State Bar of Texas Opinion 648 (April 2015)
Confidentiality; Email; Communication with clients
https://www.legalethicstexas.com/resources/opinions/opinion-648/
A lawyer may use email to communicate with clients. The opinion enumerates circumstances under which the lawyer should consider using encryption or another method of communication or advising the client regarding the risks of communicating by email. Opinion 572; 18 U.S.C2510 *et seq*.; Rules 1.03, 1.05; ABA Rules 1.4, 1.6; ABA 11-459.

35. Utah Opinion 00-01 (March 9, 2000)
Confidentiality; Email; Lawyer-client communication
https://www.utahbar.org/wp-content/uploads/2022/12/2000-01.pdf
A lawyer usually may use an unencrypted internet email to transmit confidential client information. However, if he has reason to believe greater protection is necessary for a particular communication, or if the client has a policy so requiring, the lawyer must use a means of communication with higher security. Rule 1.6; ABA 99-413.

36. Vermont Bar Association Opinion 97-5 (undated)
Communication with client; Advertising and Solicitation;
Computers; Internet; Confidentiality
https://www.vtbar.org/wp-content/uploads/2021/03/97-05.pdf
A lawyer may communicate with a client by email without the use of encryption. A lawyer who uses a web site to communicate with clients and prospective clients must comply with rules relating to advertising and solicitation. DRs 2-103, 2-104, 4-101; EC 4-4.

37. Virginia Ethics Opinion 1842 (Sept. 30, 2008)
Prospective Clients; Confidentiality; Email; Internet; Marketing
https://www.vacle.org/opinions/1842.htm
A lawyer does not owe any duty of confidentiality to a stranger who unilaterally divulges sensitive information to the lawyer in an uninvited email message to the lawyer's email address provided on a law firm Web site or in a voicemail message left on the law firm's telephone system via a phone number listed in a public directory. However, circumstances other than the mere publication of contact information may invite contact from prospective clients and trigger a duty of confidentiality that could create a disqualifying conflict. The use of a disclaimer that warns against disclosure of confidential information may help prevent this scenario.

38. Washington Opinion 2175 (2008)
Fee agreements; Email; Confidentiality
https://ao.wsba.org/print.aspx?ID=1621
A lawyer may arrange for a client to enter into a fee agreement by typing information into an email and sending it to the lawyer. Absent special conditions, a lawyer's use of email

does not require any additional security precautions such as encryption. Formal Opinion 1962; Rules 1.0(n), 1.5, 1.6.

39. Washington Opinion 2217 (2012)
    Computers; Email; Internet; Communication with clients; Confidentiality; Attorney-client privilege; Advice to clients

https://ao.wsba.org/print.aspx?ID=1668
A lawyer must warn a client who uses public or employer-provided devices such as computers or cell phones or an employee email account to communicate with the lawyer that the client's employer or other third parties may access those communications and attorney-client privilege may be waived. Rules 1.4(b), 1.6; ABA 11-459.

40. Wisconsin Formal Ethics Opinion EF-11-03 (July 29, 2011)
    Prospective Clients; Email; Internet; Confidentiality; Marketing; Disclaimers

https://www.wisbar.org/formembers/ethics/Ethics%20Opinions/EF-11-03%20final.pdf
Unilateral emails to a lawyer from people looking for representation do not trigger a duty of confidentiality or create conflicts of interest unless the lawyer has through a website or advertisements invited inquirers to share private information. Lawyers must use short disclaimers on their websites clearly warning that initial electronic communications create no lawyer-client relationship and that the email message is not confidential.

Appendix B—Metadata

Ethics Opinions Concerning a Lawyer's Obligations to Prevent the Inadvertent Disclosure of Confidential Client Information in Metadata

A. ABA Formal Ethics Opinions

The Opinion headnotes are reproduced below.

1. Formal Opinion 06-442 (Aug. 5, 2006)
   Review and Use of Metadata

https://www.americanbar.org/content/dam/aba/administrative/professional_responsibility/ethics-opinions/06-442.pdf

The Model Rules of Professional Conduct do not contain any specific prohibition against a lawyer's reviewing and using embedded information in electronic documents, whether received from opposing counsel, an adverse party, or an agent of an adverse party. A lawyer who is concerned about the possibility of sending, producing, or providing to opposing counsel a document that contains or might contain metadata, or who wishes to take some action to reduce or remove the potentially harmful consequences of its dissemination, may be able to limit the likelihood of its transmission by "scrubbing" metadata from documents or by sending a different version of the document without the embedded information.

B. ABA Treatises, Annotated Model Standards and other resources on Metadata

1. ABA/Bloomberg Lawyers' Manual on Professional Conduct

http://www.americanbar.org/groups/professional_responsibility/publications/aba_bna_lawyers_manual_on_professional_conduct.html

See the chapters entitled *Respect for Rights of Third Persons*, 71 Law. Man. Prof Conduct 801 and *Electronic Communications*, 55 Law. Man. Prof. Conduct 401.

2. Annotated Model Rules of Professional Conduct (ABA 9th ed. 2019)

https://www.americanbar.org/products/inv/book/364918796/

See the annotations to Rules 1.6 *Confidentiality of Information* and 4.4 *Respect for Rights of Third Persons*.

3. Ronald D. Rotunda, *Legal Ethics: The Lawyer's Deskbook on Professional Responsibility,* 2024–2025 ed. (ABA)

https://store.legal.thomsonreuters.com/law-products/c/Legal-Ethics-The-Lawyers-Deskbook-on-Professional-Responsibility-2024-2025-ed-ABA/p/107080714

See Sections 1.6-2 *Inadvertent Disclosure* and 4.4-3(a) *Receipt of Privileged Documents Through Inadvertent Disclosure.*

C. Digests of State Bar Ethics Opinions on Metadata

The following digests of state bar ethics opinions are excerpted with permission from the *ABA/Bloomberg Lawyers' Manual on Professional Conduct.*

1. Alabama Opinion 2007-02 (March 14, 2007)
   Computers; Internet; Email; Confidentiality; Discovery

https://www.alabar.org/office-of-general-counsel/formal-opinions/2007-02/

A lawyer sending an electronic document must take reasonable steps to safeguard confidential information in the document's metadata. A lawyer receiving an electronic document from another lawyer must refrain from trying to review that document's metadata. This opinion does not address metadata in the context of discovery. Rules 1.6, 8.4.

2. Arizona Opinion 07-03 (Nov. 2007)
   Computers; Email; Confidentiality; Disclosure; Opposing counsel

https://www.azbar.org/for-legal-professionals/ethics/ethics-opinions/?V=Opinions&OpinionId=695

Lawyers who send documents electronically must take reasonable steps to remove embedded metadata in order to prevent the unintentional disclosure of confidential client information. A lawyer who receives an electronic communication may not search for embedded metadata unless authorized to do so by law, rule, order, or court procedure. If a lawyer unintentionally views metadata that reveals apparently confidential or privileged information, she must notify the sender and preserve the status quo for a reasonable period of time. Rules 1.6(a), 4.4(b), 8.4; ABA 06-442.

3. California State Bar Opinion 2007-174 (Aug. 14, 2007)
   Files of client; Former clients; Computers; Client funds and property; Confidentiality

https://www.calbar.ca.gov/Portals/0/documents/ethics/Opinions/2007-174_05-0006-PAW.pdf

Upon termination of employment a lawyer must promptly comply with a client's request for any existing electronic versions of the following: email correspondence, pleadings, discovery requests and responses, transactional documents, and databases of depositions and exhibits. The lawyer is not required to electronically create or reformat any materials in order to comply with the client's request. Before releasing the electronic items, the lawyer must take reasonable steps to strip them of any metadata reflecting other clients' confidential information. Opinions 1992-127, 1994-134; Los Angeles County Opinion 362; San Diego County Opinion 2001-1; San Francisco Opinion 1996-1; Cal. Bus. & Prof. Code §6068(e)(1); Rule 3-700(D).

4. Colorado Opinion 119 (May 17, 2008)
   Computers; Email; Confidentiality; Discovery
https://www.cobar.org/Portals/COBAR/repository/ethicsOpinions/FormalEthicsOpinion_119_2011.pdf
A lawyer is permitted to search for and review metadata embedded in an electronic document received from opposing counsel or a third party, unless the lawyer has already been notified that confidential information has been inadvertently transmitted. The burden of protecting sensitive metadata rests with the lawyers who send the electronic documents. Opinions 90, 108; Fed. R. Civ. P. 34; Rules 1.1, 1.6, 4.4(b),(c), 5.1, 5.3, 8.4; ABA 06-442.

5. District of Columbia Opinion 341 (Oct. 2007)
   Computers; Email; Confidentiality; Disclosure; Inadvertent disclosure; Opposing counsel
https://www.dcbar.org/For-Lawyers/Legal-Ethics/Ethics-Opinions-210-Present/Ethics-Opinion-341
A lawyer who sends electronic documents outside the context of discovery or subpoenas must take reasonable steps to prevent the disclosure of confidential information by removing embedded metadata. A lawyer who receives such an electronic communication from opposing counsel may not view its metadata if he has actual knowledge that the metadata was inadvertently provided, but must notify the sender and abide by the sender's instructions. In the context of discovery requests or subpoenaed information, the sender's removal of metadata from electronic documents may be impermissible. A recipient of such documents is generally justified in assuming that any included metadata was provided intentionally. Opinions 256, 318; Rules 1.0(o), 1.1, 1.3, 1.6, 3.4, 4.4(b), 8.4(c); ABA Rule 4.4; ABA 06-442.

6. Florida Opinion 06-2 (Sept. 15, 2006)
   Email; Confidentiality; Communication with adverse persons; Opposing counsel
https://www.floridabar.org/etopinions/etopinion-06-2/
A lawyer sending an electronic document to another lawyer must take reasonable steps to safeguard confidential information in the document's metadata. A lawyer receiving an electronic document from another lawyer must not try to review that document's metadata; if the lawyer inadvertently does so, he must promptly notify the sender. This opinion does not address metadata in the context of discovery. Opinion 93-3; Rules 4-1.1, 4-1.2, 4-1.4, 4-1.6, 4-4.4(b).

7. Maine Opinion 196 (Oct. 21, 2008)
   Computers; Internet; Email; Confidentiality; Opposing counsel; Communication with adverse persons
http://www.maine.gov/tools/whatsnew/index.php?topic=mebar_overseers_ethics_opinions&id=63337&v=article

A lawyer receiving an electronic document from a lawyer for another party may not attempt to "mine" metadata embedded in the document. A lawyer sending an electronic document must take reasonable care to safeguard confidential information in the document's metadata. Opinions 172, 194, 195; Rules 3.2(f)(3)(4), 3.6(a)(h)(1)(2); ABA 06-442.

8. Maryland State Bar Association Opinion 2007-09 (Oct. 19, 2006)
   Computers; Confidentiality; Communication with adverse persons; Discovery

https://www.msba.org/site/content/Resources-and-Tools-Content/Ethics-Opinions/2007/2007-09.aspx

A lawyer may review and use metadata in electronic documents produced in discovery. A lawyer producing electronic documents in discovery must take reasonable steps to remove confidential information and work product imbedded in the documents. Fed. R. Civ. P. 16(b)(5), 26(b)(5); Rules 1.1, 1.4, 1.6, 8.4(b); ABA Rule 4.4(b); ABA 05-437.

9. Minnesota Opinion 22 (March 26, 2010)
   Metadata; Computers; Email; Confidentiality; Communication with adverse persons; Opposing counsel; Inadvertent disclosure; Competence

http://lprb.mncourts.gov/rules/LPRBOpinions/Opinion%2022.pdf

A lawyer must act competently to prevent unauthorized disclosure of confidential information contained in the metadata of electronic documents. If a lawyer receives a document that she knows or reasonably should know inadvertently contains confidential metadata, she must promptly notify the sender. Rules 1.1, 1.6, 4.4(b); ABA 06-442.

10. Mississippi Bar Ethics Opinion 259 (Nov. 29, 2012)
    Metadata; Inadvertent Disclosure; Confidentiality

https://www.msbar.org/ethics-discipline/ethics-opinions/formal-opinions/259/

A lawyer must take reasonable precautions to protect confidential information in metadata when transmitting electronic documents to opposing counsel.

11. Missouri Bar Informal Opinion 2021-13 (2021) (replacing Informal Opinion 2014-02)
    Internet; Metadata; Computers; Confidentiality; Disclosure; Discovery; Opposing counsel; Subpoenas

https://mo-legal-ethics.org/informal-opinion/2021-13/

A lawyer who believes metadata in an electronic document received from an opposing party was inadvertently sent must promptly notify the sender. Any obligation to refrain from mining, reviewing or using the metadata is a question of law governed by Mo. R. Civ. P. 56.01(b)(9)(A)(ii). A lawyer must use reasonable care before sending electronic documents to ensure information relating to the representation is not revealed through metadata without the client's consent but may not unlawfully alter, destroy, conceal or obstruct access to evidence. This opinion replaces Informal Opinion 2014-02, which is withdrawn. Opinion 2014-02; Mo. R. Civ. P. 56.01(b)(9)(A)(ii); Missouri Rules 1.6, 3.4, 4.4; ABA Model Rule 1.6, Model Rule 3.4, Model Rule 4.4.

12. New Hampshire Opinion 2008-09/04 (May 15, 2009)
    Computers; Internet; Email; Confidentiality; Communication with adverse persons; Opposing counsel

https://www.nhbar.org/ethics/opinion-2008-09-04
A lawyer who sends a document electronically must take reasonable care to avoid improper disclosure of any confidential information that may be hidden in the document's metadata. A lawyer who receives a document electronically may not search for, review, or use any confidential information hidden in the document's metadata. Lawyers may, however, enter into agreements with each other that provide otherwise. This opinion does not address metadata in the context of discovery. Rules 1.1, 1.6, 4.4, 5.1, 5.3; ABA Rule 4.4; ABA 06-442.

13. New York State Bar Opinion 782 (Dec. 8, 2004)
    Email; Confidentiality; Communication with adverse persons

https://nysba.org/ethics-opinion-782/
A lawyer must exercise reasonable care when sending a document by email to prevent the disclosure of metadata containing confidential client information. What constitutes reasonable care will vary with the circumstances, including whether the document was based on a "template" used for another client, and whether there have been multiple drafts of the document with comments from multiple sources. Opinions 700, 709, 749; DR 4-101; EC 4-5.

14. New York County Opinion 738 (March 24, 2008)
    Computers; Internet; Confidentiality; Communication with adverse persons

https://www.nycla.org/resource/ethics-opinion/nycla-committee-on-professional-ethics-opinion-on-searching-inadvertently/
A lawyer must exercise due care to prevent the disclosure of metadata when sending a document electronically. A lawyer who receives documents electronically from an opposing lawyer may not search the metadata if he is either looking for or likely to find confidential information. This opinion does not address documents produced in the course of discovery. Opinion 730; New York State Opinions 749, 782; New York City Opinion 2003-4; DRs 1-102(A), 4-101, 7-101, 7-102(A)(8); ECs 4-1, 7-1; ABA Rule 4.4(b); ABA 06-442.

15. North Carolina State Bar Formal Ethics Opinion 2009-1 (Jan. 15, 2010)
    Metadata; Confidentiality; Computers; Email; Opposing counsel

https://www.ncbar.gov/for-lawyers/ethics/adopted-opinions/2009-formal-ethics-opinion-1/
A lawyer communicating electronically must use reasonable care to protect confidential client information that might be hidden in metadata. A lawyer who receives an electronic

communication from a party or a party's lawyer may not search for or use any confidential information embedded in its metadata. Allowing the use of found metadata is prejudicial to the administration of justice. If a lawyer does unintentionally view metadata he must notify the sender, and he may not use the information unless the sender consents. Opinion RPC 215; Rules 1.6, 4.4(b), 8.4(d); ABA 06-442.

16. Oregon Opinion 2011-187 (Nov. 2011; Revised April 2015)
    Computers; Internet; Email; Confidentiality; Disclosure; Opposing counsel; Misrepresentation

https://www.osbar.org/_docs/ethics/2011-187.pdf

If a lawyer communicates via electronic media, her obligations of competence and confidentiality require that she maintain a basic understanding of the technology of metadata or use adequate technology support. A lawyer who receives a document with metadata she reasonably should know was inadvertently included must inform the sender and then must consult with the client about the risks of returning the document versus the risks of retaining and reading it. Searching for metadata using special software when it is apparent that the sender has made reasonable efforts to remove the metadata may be analogous to surreptitiously entering the other lawyer's office to obtain client information in violation of Rule 8.4(a)(3). Opinion 2005-150; Rules 1.1, 1.2, 1.4, 1.6, 4.4(b), 8.4(a)(3); ABA 06-440.

17. Pennsylvania Formal Opinion 2009-100 (undated)
    Computers; Internet; Email; Confidentiality; Attorney-client privilege; Opposing counsel

A lawyer transmitting electronic documents to opposing counsel or third parties must exercise reasonable care to remove unwanted metadata. A lawyer who receives electronic information that includes metadata and concludes that inclusion of the metadata was inadvertent must promptly notify the sender of the inclusion of the metadata. The lawyer must determine whether he is permitted under substantive law to use the metadata and must consult with his client about the appropriate course of action. Formal Opinion 2007-500; Rules 1.1, 1.2, 1.3, 1.4, 1.6, 4.4; ABA 06-442.

18. State Bar of Texas Opinion 665 (Dec. 2016)
    Confidentiality; Evidence; Opposing counsel; Competence; Computers

https://www.legalethicstexas.com/resources/opinions/opinion-665/

A lawyer transmitting an electronic document must take reasonable measures to remove metadata that would reveal confidential information. The receiving lawyer should explain the options and their consequences to the client, and if he reviews the information, he must not make any statements that would be misleading in light of what he has learned. Texas does not have a counterpart to ABA Model Rule 4.4(b) specifying how the receiving lawyer should treat the information but court rules or other applicable rules may apply in certain contexts, for example discovery. Opinion 664; Tex. R. Civ. P. 193.3(d); Rules 1.01, 1.05(a), 8.04(a)(3); ABA Rules 3.3, 4.4(b), 8.4(c).

19. Vermont Opinion 2009-1 (undated)
    Computers; Confidentiality; Communication with adverse persons; Opposing counsel; Inadvertent disclosure; Competence

https://www.vtbar.org/wp-content/uploads/2021/03/09-01.pdf
A lawyer who transmits electronic documents to opposing counsel must use reasonable care to avoid including embedded metadata containing protected information; the rules regarding diligence and competence require this. No ethics rule prohibits the receiving lawyer from searching for and reviewing metadata in documents sent by opposing counsel; the duties of competence and diligence may require this. The committee expresses no opinion as to waiver of confidentiality or privilege, or as to discovery rights and obligations. Fed. R. Civ. P. 26(b)(5)(A); Fed. R. Evid. 502(b); Rules 1.1, 1.3, 1.6(a), 3.4, 4.4, 8.4; ABA Rule 4.4(b); ABA 92-368, 05-437, 06-442.

20. Washington State Bar Association Advisory Opinion 2216 (2012)
    Computers; Internet; Email; Confidentiality; Opposing counsel; Discovery

https://ao.wsba.org/print.aspx?ID=1664
A lawyer must safeguard confidential metadata from disclosure when exchanging documents with opposing counsel either by using formats such as hard copy, fax, or Portable Document Format ("PDF") that do not include metadata or by electronically "scrubbing" the documents. A lawyer may not remove metadata that has evidentiary value when producing electronic documents in discovery. A lawyer who receives an electronic document that contains confidential but readily accessible metadata must promptly notify the sender but, absent applicable court rules, an agreement, or a protective order, need not return the document or refrain from reading it. A lawyer may not use special forensic software to recover metadata that is not readily accessible. Wash. Rev. Code §5.60.060(2)(a); Rules 1.1, 1.6, 1.9, 3.4, 4.4, 8.4.

21. Wisconsin Opinion EF-12-01 (June 15, 2012)
    Computers; Internet; Email; Confidentiality; Attorney-client privilege; Competence

http://www.wisbar.org/newspublications/wisconsinlawyer/pages/article.aspx?Volume=85&Issue=10&ArticleID=10222
A lawyer transmitting a document electronically must take reasonable care to avoid the disclosure of confidential information contained in metadata. The ethics rules neither prohibit nor require searching for and reviewing metadata in documents received electronically. A lawyer who discovers materially significant metadata must promptly inform the sender even if the client says not to, but the ethics rules impose no further duty. A significant minority of the committee believes that the Rules either prohibit or do not clearly permit "mining" documents for metadata. Rules 1.1, 1.6, 4.4, 8.4; ABA 06-442, 11-459.

Appendix C—Outsourcing

Ethics Opinions on Lawyer Confidentiality Obligations Concerning Outsourcing

A. ABA Formal Ethics Opinions

The Opinion headnotes are reproduced below.

1. Formal Opinion 08-451 (Aug. 5, 2008)

   Lawyer's Obligations When Outsourcing Legal and Nonlegal Support Services

http://www.americanbar.org/content/dam/aba/administrative/professional_responsibility/ethics_opinion_08_451.pdf

A lawyer may outsource legal or nonlegal support services, provided the lawyer remains ultimately responsible for rendering competent legal services to the client under Model Rule 1.1. In complying with her Rule 1.1 obligations, a lawyer who engages lawyers or nonlawyers to provide outsourced legal or nonlegal services is required to comply with Rules 5.1 and 5.3. She should make reasonable efforts to ensure that the conduct of the lawyers or nonlawyers to whom tasks are outsourced is compatible with her own professional obligations as a lawyer with "direct supervisory authority" over them.

In addition, appropriate disclosures should be made to the client regarding the use of lawyers or nonlawyers outside of the lawyer's firm, and client consent should be obtained if those lawyers or nonlawyers will be receiving information protected by Rule 1.6. The fees charged must be reasonable and otherwise in compliance with Rule 1.5, and the outsourcing lawyer must avoid assisting the unauthorized practice of law under Rule 5.5.

2. Formal Opinion 95-398 (Oct. 27, 1995)

   Access of Nonlawyers to a Lawyer's Data Base

http://www.americanbar.org/content/dam/aba/administrative/professional_responsibility/ethics_opinion_95_398.pdf

A lawyer who gives a computer maintenance company access to information in client files must make reasonable efforts to ensure that the company has in place, or will establish, reasonable procedures to protect the confidentiality of client information. Should a significant breach of confidentiality occur, the lawyer may be obligated to disclose it to the client.

B. ABA Treatises and Annotated Model Standards

1. ABA / Bloomberg Lawyers' Manual on Professional Conduct

http://www.americanbar.org/groups/professional_responsibility/publications/aba_bna_lawyers_manual_on_professional_conduct.html

See the chapters from the treatise section of the *Manual* entitled, "Multijurisdictional Practice," 21 Law. Man. Prof. Conduct 2101; "Lawyers' Aiding Unauthorized Practice of Law,"

21 Law. Man. Prof Conduct 8201; "Supervisory and Subordinate Lawyers" 91 Law. Man. Prof. Conduct 101; and "Supervision of Nonlawyers," 91 Law Man Prof Conduct 201.

2. Model Rules of Professional Conduct, 2025 Edition
https://www.americanbar.org/products/inv/book/449291561/
See the annotations to Rules 1.4 *Communication*, 5.3 *Responsibilities regarding Nonlawyer Assistants* and 1.6 *Confidentiality of Information*

3. Ronald D. Rotunda, *Legal Ethics: The Lawyer's Deskbook on Professional Responsibility*, American Bar Association, 2024–2025 ed. (ABA)
https://store.legal.thomsonreuters.com/law-products/c/Legal-Ethics-The-Lawyers-Deskbook-on-Professional-Responsibility-2024-2025-ed-ABA/p/107080714?searchid=TRPPCSOL/Google/PrintUS_PP_Law-Books_Smart-Shopping_Search_Product-Feed_US/Smart-Shopping&chl=ppc&cid=9015549&sfdccampaignid=7014O000000vZOgQAM&ef_id=Cj0KCQjwpf2IBhDkARIsAGVo0D07hu2yqEkGmb933kQj_LEN73XcPfNuKzFqvxajuruGkURZdRUBVrIaAojHEALw_wcB:G:s&s_kwcid=AL!7944!3!409807603372!!!u!293946777986!&gclid=Cj0KCQjwpf2IBhDkARIsAGVo0D07hu2yqEkGmb933kQj_LEN73XcPfNuKzFqvxajuruGkURZdRUBVrIaAojHEALw_wcB
See § 5.3-2 Sharing Client Information with Outside Contractors.

C. Bar Association Reports

1. The ABA Ethics 20/20 Commission's Report 105(c) concerning Outsourcing that was approved at the 2012 Annual Meeting
http://www.americanbar.org/content/dam/aba/administrative/ethics_2020/2012_hod_annual_meeting_105c.authcheckdam.pdf

2. Association of The Bar of The City Of New York Committee on Professional Responsibility Report on the Outsourcing of Legal Services Overseas (2009)
http://www.nycbar.org/pdf/report/uploads/20071813-ReportontheOutsourcingofLegalServicesOverseas.pdf

3. Council of Bars and Law Societies of Europe Guidelines on Legal Outsourcing (2010)
http://www.ccbe.eu/fileadmin/user_upload/NTCdocument/EN_Guidelines_on_leg1_1277906265.pdf

D. Digests of State Bar Association Ethics Opinions on Outsourcing

The following digests of state bar ethics opinions are excerpted with permission from the *ABA/Bloomberg Lawyers' Manual on Professional Conduct.*

1. State Bar of California Opinion 2004-165 (2004)
   Temporary lawyers; Contract lawyers; Lawyer-client relationship; Communication with clients; Costs and expenses of litigation; Fee agreements; Billing

http://www.calbar.ca.gov/Portals/0/documents/ethics/Opinions/2004-165.pdf
A private lawyer may hire a contract "appearance" lawyer to cover a court appearance, deposition, or arbitration proceeding. The contract lawyers are supplied by a lawyer-operated company that charges an hourly fee for their services. The rule requiring client consent to all fee divisions will not apply if the hiring attorney pays the contract lawyer an hourly rate, if the contract lawyer's fee is billed as a cost, if the fee is a separately identified entry on the hiring attorney's bill, or if the contract lawyer bills the client directly. However, if the arrangement will constitute a "significant development" in the client's matter the hiring attorney must tell the client about it, and if the contract lawyer's fees are going to be charged to the client as a disbursement the fee agreement must say so. Opinions 1981-63, 1993-133, 1994-138, 2003-161; Los Angeles County Opinion 473; Cal. Bus. & Prof. Code §§6068(e)(m), 6147, 6148; Rules 1-400, 2-200, 3-110, 3-310, 3-500.

2. Los Angeles County Bar Ethics Opinion 518 (June 19, 2006)
   Legal research services; Out-of-state lawyers; Nonlawyers; Division of fees with nonlawyers; Unauthorized practice of law

https://www.lacba.org/resources/ethics-opinions (Ethics Opinion directory) https://s3.amazonaws.com/membercentralcdn/sitedocuments/lacba/lacba/0450/2094450.pdf?AWSAccessKeyId=AKIAIHKD6NT2OL2HNPMQ&Expires=1747006834&Signature=mSm0i0dp0yqU%2FP6YQOEoHheh7lI%3D&response-content-disposition=inline%3B%20filename%3D%22ethics%2Dopinion%2D518%2Epdf%22%3B%20filename%2A%3DUTF%2D8%27%27ethics%252Dopinion%252D518%252Epdf&response-content-type=application%2Fpdf
A lawyer may hire an out-of-state legal research company that employs only out-of-state lawyers to draft an appellate brief in a client's civil case if the lawyer reviews and remains ultimately responsible for the work. The lawyer must tell the client about the arrangement if it constitutes a "significant development" in the representation, as it normally will. The lawyer may directly pass on the company's fee to the client, mark up the cost and pass it on to the client, or charge a flat fee for the representation. If the attorney passes the company's fee on to the client, he must so identify it, and must also pass on any refund from the company. Opinions 374, 423, 457, 473; California Formal Opinions 1994-138, 2004-165; Cal. Bus. & Prof. Code 6125, 6126; Cal. Evid. Code §912(d); Cal. Rules of Court 227, 983; California Formal Opinions 1987-91, 1994-138, 2004-165; Los Angeles County Opinion 518; Orange County Opinion 94-2; Rules 1-300, 3-110(B), 3-500; ABA Rules 1.1, 5.1(b), 5.3(b). §§6068, 6125, 6126, 6147, 6148; Rules 1-100, 1-120, 1-200, 1-310, 1-320, 1-400, 2-200, 3-110, 3-310, 3-500, 4-200, 5-200.

3. San Diego County Bar Opinion 2007-1 (2007)
   Foreign lawyers; Unauthorized practice of law; Legal research services; Nonlawyers

https://www.sdcba.org/?Pg=ethicsopinion07-1

A lawyer who hired foreign lawyers working in India to assist in the preparation of a successfully litigated matter, but supervised and remained ultimately responsible for the work performed, did not thereby aid the unauthorized practice of law. Because the work performed by the foreign lawyers was of the type reasonably expected to be performed by the lawyer himself, the lawyer was obliged to inform the client of the hiring. Before hiring foreign lawyers, a lawyer must also satisfy himself that they are competent for the work required and will preserve confidential information. Cal. Bus. & Prof. Code §§6067, 6068.

4. Colorado Bar Association Formal Ethics Opinion 121 (June 16, 2009)
   Temporary lawyers; Out-of-state lawyers; Foreign lawyers; Division of fees with nonlawyers; Division of fees with lawyers; Billing

https://www.cobar.org/Portals/COBAR/repository/ethicsOpinions/FormalEthicsOpinion_121_2011.pdf

A Colorado lawyer who hires temporary lawyers admitted in a foreign country or in a domestic jurisdiction other than Colorado must make reasonable efforts to ensure that their conduct conforms to the Colorado lawyer's ethical duties. The lawyer must take particular care to supervise the work, must confirm that the temporary lawyer is licensed and in good standing in the home jurisdiction, is competent to undertake the assignment, does not have a conflict, and will not thereby be engaging in the unauthorized practice of law. Depending on how attenuated the outsourcing relationship is, the lawyer may need to secure the client's consent before sharing any protected information. For conflict purposes, the hiring lawyer must determine if he and the temporary lawyer are "associated in a firm" according to the functional analysis of imputation in Opinion 105. Even if the lawyers are not "associated in a firm," payment of the temporary lawyer will not constitute a division of fees if it is not tied to payment by the client. The lawyer may mark up the temporary lawyer's fees, but if the differential is excessive, the fee might become unreasonable. Although the lawyer is not required to disclose the amounts involved, in some circumstances the lawyer may be required to tell the client that certain work has been delegated. If the lawyer determines that a foreign professional does not qualify as a foreign lawyer, the lawyer may hire him as a nonlawyer and must supervise him in accordance with Rule 5.3. This opinion incorporates relevant portions of Opinion 105, which addressed the employment of temporary lawyers who are admitted in Colorado. The Committee will issue an addendum to Opinion 105 addressing the 2008 amendments to the Rules. Opinion 105; Civ. Proc. Rules 220, 221, 221.1; Rules 1.1, 1.2(a), 1.4(a)(3),(b), 1.5, 1.6, 5.1(b), 5.3(b), 5.4, 5.5(a)(3); ABA 01-423, 08-451.

5. Florida Bar Ethics Opinion 12-3 (Jan. 25, 2013)
   Client files; Internet; Confidentiality; Competence; Outsourcing; Record retention

https://www.floridabar.org/etopinions/etopinion-12-3/

A lawyer may use cloud computing services to store, access and share client files if the lawyer uses reasonable diligence to ascertain that the provider has adequate measures in place to protect the security, confidentiality, and accessibility of the information. The lawyer should research the service provider and should consider taking additional security measures regarding proprietary client information or other particularly sensitive information. The opinion includes suggestions as to what the lawyer should consider in researching the service provider. Opinions 07-2, 10-2; Rule 1.6.

6. Illinois State Bar Association Opinion 10-01 (July 2009)
   Computers; Files of client; Confidentiality

http://www.isba.org/sites/default/files/ethicsopinions/10-01.pdf

A law firm may use an outside administrator to manage the firm's computer network—even if the administrator accesses the network remotely—as long as it takes reasonable measures to ensure that the administrator will protect the confidentiality of client information on the network. Opinions 96-10, 03-07; 18 U.S.C. §2510; Rules 1.6, 5.3; ABA 95-398, 99-413, 08-451; ABA Rules 1.4(b), 1.6.

7. Maryland State Bar Association Opinion 2013-01 (Nov. 2, 2012)
   Outsourcing; Personal injury representation; Paralegals; Nonlawyers;
   Division of fees with nonlawyers

https://www.msba.org/site/content/Resources-and-Tools-Content/Ethics-Opinions/2013/2013-01.aspx

A personal-injury law firm interested in subcontracting the paralegal function of its office to a third-party claims processing service must provide adequate supervision and quality control. It must take steps to protect confidentiality, prevent conflicts of interest, and ensure against the unauthorized practice of law. The firm should obtain the client's informed consent to the arrangement and must pay the service based on the reasonable value of the work done, regardless of the size or outcome of the claims involved. Rules 1.5(e), 1.6(a), 1.7, 5.3, 5.4, 5.5(a); ABA 08-451.

8. Michigan State Bar Opinion RI-363 (June 28, 2013)
   Personal injury representation; Outsourcing; Fees; Costs and expenses
   of litigation; Business activities

https://www.michbar.org/opinions/ethics/numbered_opinions/RI-363

A law firm represents a plaintiff in a personal injury matter under a contingent fee agreement providing that the law firm will receive the maximum fee permissible under court rules. The firm asks whether it may "outsource" basic case-related administrative services traditionally deemed part of a firm's overhead, such as reviewing, copying, and organizing medical records and assembling case evaluations and demand letters, to a company wholly owned by one of the firm's lawyers and housed in the law firm's offices, and bill them to the client as if they were traditional case costs. The law firm may not enter into this arrangement and may not seek or obtain the client's consent to it; the services do not constitute "law-related services" as defined by Rule 5.7(b), and the arrangement would result in a clearly excessive fee. Opinion RI-346; MCR 8.121; Rules 1.5, 5.3, 5.7; ABA 93-379, 95-390.

9. New Hampshire Bar Association Opinion 2011-12/05 (Dec. 14, 2011)
   Client files; Outsourcing; Computers; Internet; Nonlawyers; Confidentiality; Discovery; Foreign lawyers

https://www.nhbar.org/ethics/opinion-2011-12-05

A law firm may contract with a local company to scan client documents and transmit them electronically to an overseas company for review as to relevance, confidentiality, and privilege. Document scanning and transmission are considered nonlegal support services. The firm must ensure that the service provider maintains client confidentiality. Scanning can be outsourced without notifying the client, but the firm must consult with the client about the method of transmission and follow its security instructions. Document review is considered a legal support service; the firm must inform the client of the arrangements and must take reasonable steps to ensure that the overseas company performs its tasks competently and in compliance with the ethics rules. Opinions 1982-3/16, 1986-87/8, 1989-90/2, 1989-90/9, 1991-2/6, 1995-96/3; Rules 1.1, 1.2, 1.5, 1.6, 1.7, 2.1, 5.1, 5.3, 5.4, 5.5, 7.1; ABA 99-413, 08-451, 11-459.

10. New York State Bar Association Ethics Opinion 940 (Oct. 16, 2012)
    Client files; Confidentiality; Record retention; Outsourcing

https://nysba.org/ethics-opinion-940/

A lawyer may store client information on equipment maintained offsite by outside service if lawyer exercises reasonable care to protect data's integrity and confidentiality. Rules 1.6(a) & (c), 1.15(d).

11. New York City Bar Formal Opinion 2006-3 (Aug. 1, 2006)
    Foreign lawyers; Nonlawyers; Employees of lawyers; Temporary lawyers; Confidentiality; Unauthorized practice of law

https://www.nycbar.org/member-and-career-services/committees/reports-listing/reports/detail/formal-opinion-2006-3-outsourcing-legal-support-services-overseas-avoiding-aiding-a-non-lawyer-in-the-unauthorized-practice-of-law-supervision-of-non-lawyers-competent-representation-preserving-client-confidences-and-secrets-conflicts-checking-appropriate-billing-client-consent

A lawyer may outsource legal support services to overseas lawyers and nonlawyers if the lawyer supervises the work rigorously. Overseas lawyers not admitted in any U.S. jurisdiction are regarded as nonlawyers for this purpose. The lawyer should obtain background information about any intermediary involved in engaging the nonlawyer and should obtain the nonlawyer's resume, conduct reference checks, and interview the nonlawyer by telephone, Voice Over Internet Protocol, or Webcast. The lawyer will not necessarily need to inform each client in advance about the arrangement but would need to do so if, for example, nonlawyers will be playing a significant role in the matter, or if the client expects that only law firm personnel will be handling the matter. In addition, the client's advance consent is needed if the lawyer will be sharing the client's confidences and secrets or if the lawyer will be billing for the outsourced work on a basis other than cost. Opinions 1988-3, 1989-2, 1995-11; New York State Opinions 715, 721, 762, 774; N.Y. Jud. Law §478; DRs 1-104(C)(D), 3-101(A), 3-102, 4-101, 5-105(E), 5-107, 6-101; ECs 2-2, 3-6, 4-2, 4-5; ABA 93-379.

12. New York City Bar Formal Opinion 2015-1 (Feb. 10, 2015)
    Outsourcing; Confidentiality; Independent professional judgment; Conflicts of interest; Non-lawyers; Fee-sharing

https://www.nycbar.org/member-and-career-services/committees/reports-listing/reports/detail/formal-opinion-2015-1-professional-employer-organization-use-by-a-law-firm-of-a-professional-employer-organization
Lawyers may use professional employer organizations ("PEO") to provide human resource services to employees, under certain conditions. Lawyers must not allow the PEO to interfere with the lawyer's ethical obligations to exercise independent professional judgment or to supervise other lawyers and non-lawyers. Additionally, the PEO may not have access to confidential client information, the lawyer must avoid conflicts of interest, and the lawyer may not compensate the PEO in a way that would violate the prohibition against fee sharing with non-lawyers.

13. North Carolina Bar Ethics Formal Opinion 12 (April 25, 2008)
    Foreign lawyers; Unauthorized practice of law; Legal research services; Nonlawyers; Employees of lawyers

https://www.ncbar.gov/for-lawyers/ethics/adopted-opinions/2007-formal-ethics-opinion-12/
A lawyer may outsource certain legal support services to foreign lawyers or nonlawyers if the lawyer properly selects and supervises them, ensures the preservation of confidentiality, avoids conflicts of interest, discloses the arrangements, and obtains the client's informed consent first. Opinions RPC 70, 133, 215, 216, FEO 99-6, 2002-9; Rules 1.1, 1.6, 5.3, 5.5.

14. North Carolina State Bar Ethics Opinion 2011-14 (April 27, 2012)
    Outsourcing; Confidentiality; Communication with clients

https://www.ncbar.gov/for-lawyers/ethics/adopted-opinions/2011-formal-ethics-opinion-14/

A law firm may outsource clerical tasks, including transcription and typing, to a company outside the United States if the law firm obtains the client's informed consent, confirmed in writing. Opinions 2007-12, 2011-6; Rules 1.0, 1.6; ABA 08-451.

15. Ohio Advisory Opinion 2009-6 (Aug. 14, 2009)
 Legal research services; Foreign lawyers; Nonlawyers; Communication with clients; Billing; Fees; Costs and expenses of litigation

https://www.ohioadvop.org/wp-content/uploads/2017/04/Op_09-006.pdf

A lawyer may outsource legal and support services domestically or abroad if the client gives informed consent. The lawyer is responsible for an outside lawyer's violation of professional obligations if the lawyer orders or ratifies the outside lawyer's conduct. The lawyer must make reasonable efforts to ensure that any nonlawyer's conduct is compatible with the professional obligations of the lawyer; the lawyer is responsible for nonlawyer conduct that the lawyer orders or ratifies. The lawyer may bill the cost of the outsourced services either as part of the firm's fee or as a discrete expense so long as the basis of the billing is first communicated to the client; any charge in addition to the actual cost of the services must be reasonable. Opinion 90-23; Rules 1.2(a), 1.4(a)(2), 1.5, 1.6(a), 5.1, 5.3; ABA 93-379, 00-420, 08-451.

16. Pennsylvania Bar Association Formal Opinion 2010-200 (undated)
 Law firms; Internet; Advertising and solicitation; Letterhead

A lawyer may practice in a "virtual law office" (VLO) in which all lawyers practice from their homes in several locales. Advertisements and firm letterhead must specify the city or town where the lawyers performing legal services principally practice law but need not include their physical addresses; a post office box in the city or town may be used. If a lawyer in Philadelphia sends local client files to VLO lawyers in Harrisburg and Pittsburgh, all firm lawyers are principally practicing law in Philadelphia for those clients. A lawyer practicing in a VLO may not state that the firm's fees are lower than other firms' fees, but may state that the firm's overhead costs may be lower. Opinions 91-176, 92-19, 2009-053; Rules 1.4, 1.6, 1.14, 1.18, 5.1, 7.1, 7.2, 7.5; ABA 08-451.

17. Utah State Bar Ethics Advisory Opinion 14-01 (Feb. 3, 2014)
 Outsourcing; Liens; Personal injury representation; Billing; Division of fees with lawyers; Creditors of client; Costs and expenses of litigation

https://www.utahbar.org/wp-content/uploads/2022/12/2014-01.pdf

A plaintiffs' personal injury lawyer may retain a lien resolution company to assist in calculating, verifying and resolving health insurance liens and subrogation and reimbursement claims. The lawyer may treat the company's fee as a cost to the client if the services constitute nonlegal services, such as accounting and valuation, and if the lawyer's engagement letter so permits. If the company provides legal services, the arrangement must be in writing, must state the method for determining the company's fees and must otherwise comply with Rule 1.5(c) and (d) respecting fee-splitting between law firms. The client must agree in writing to the arrangement, and the total fee must be reasonable. Utah Code Ann. §§38-7-1 et seq., 78B-1-152; Rules 1.5, 3.4.

18. Virginia Legal Ethics Opinion 1850 (Dec. 28, 2010; Amended Jan. 12, 2021)
    Legal research services; Foreign lawyers; Nonlawyers; Temporary lawyers; Communication with clients; Confidentiality; Costs and expenses of litigation; Billing

http://www.vacle.org/opinions/1850.htm

A lawyer outsourcing legal or nonlegal services domestically or overseas must supervise and remain ultimately responsible for the work. Client consent is required unless only "tangential, clerical, or administrative" work is involved; client consent is also required before the lawyer discloses any confidential information. Written confidentiality agreements are strongly advised whenever outsourcing. Unless the client has agreed otherwise the outsourced services must be billed at cost, plus a reasonable allocation of supervision costs if the lawyer is not otherwise charging to review the work. Opinions 1712, 1735; Rules 1.1, 1.2, 1.4, 1.5, 1.6, 5.3, 5.5, 7.5(d); ABA 93-379.

E. State Bar Ethics Opinions that address issues similar to those addressed in ABA Formal Opinion 95-398; allowing outside computer maintenance firms access to law firm computer networks

The following digests of state bar ethics opinions are excerpted with permission from the *ABA/Bloomberg Lawyers' Manual on Professional Conduct.*

1. Illinois State Bar Association Advisory Opinion 10-01 (July 2009)
   Computers; Files of client; Confidentiality

http://www.isba.org/sites/default/files/ethicsopinions/10-01.pdf

A law firm may use an outside administrator to manage the firm's computer network—even if the administrator accesses the network remotely—as long as it takes reasonable measures to ensure that the administrator will protect the confidentiality of client information on the network. Opinions 96-10, 03-07; 18 U.S.C. §2510; Rules 1.6, 5.3; ABA 95-398, 99-413, 08-451; ABA Rules 1.4(b), 1.6.

2. Massachusetts Opinion 2005-4 (March 3, 2005)
   Computers; Internet; Confidentiality; Files of client; Employees of lawyers; Nonlawyers

https://www.massbar.org/publications/ethics-opinions/ethics-opinion-article/ethics-opinions-2005-opinion-05-04

A law firm may allow a third-party software vendor to have remote access via the internet to the firm's computer system, which contains confidential client information, in order to service and update the software. The firm should make reasonable efforts to ensure that the vendor's conduct complies with the lawyers' obligations to their clients. "Reasonable efforts" on the firm's part could include notifying the vendor of the confidential nature of the stored information, reviewing the vendor's own policies regarding the handling of confidential information, obtaining written assurances from the vendor that the firm's computer system will be accessed only for technical support and only on an as-needed basis, and formulating additional policies and procedures to protect any particularly sensitive confidential client information. Opinions 89-3, 2000-01; Rules 1.6, 5.3; DR 4-101(D).

3. Michigan Opinion RI-328 (Jan. 25, 2002)
   Government lawyers; Confidentiality; Disclosure; Computers

https://www.michbar.org/opinions/ethics/numbered_opinions?OpinionID=1198&Type=4
A law department of a governmental entity may use the services of the government's technical support department without violating the confidentiality rules. The use of technical support personnel to assist with computer-related issues does not in itself violate Rule 1.6(b). The law department should clearly communicate the requirements of the confidentiality rules to the technical support personnel. Steps should be taken to ensure that particularly sensitive client information is maintained outside the view of technical support personnel. This opinion assumes that there is no reason to believe that the technical support personnel have any particular interest in using, or would be likely to use, the confidential information involved. Opinions RI-77, RI-111, RI-311; Rule 1.6(b) (d); ABA Informal Opinion 1364.

4. Pennsylvania Opinion 2005-105 (Aug. 9, 2005)
   Confidentiality; Computers

A lawyer may give a computer technology company access to client data in the course of upgrading and testing his software, provided that the lawyer makes reasonable efforts to ensure that the company puts in place reasonable procedures to protect the confidentiality of client information. Rules 1.6, 5.3; ABA 95-398.

5. Vermont Opinion 2003-03 (undated)
   Confidentiality; Computers; Employees of lawyer; Files of client

https://www.vtbar.org/wp-content/uploads/2021/03/03-03.pdf
A lawyer may engage an outside computer consultant to recover a lost database file containing confidential client information, provided that the lawyer (1) clearly explains to the consultant the confidentiality rules; (2) ensures that the consultant fully understands the rules and agrees to maintain the confidentiality of all information obtained in the course of assisting the lawyer; and (3) ensures that the consultant has implemented adequate safeguards to protect confidential information. The lawyer may satisfy the second requirement by obtaining a written acknowledgment from the consultant that he or she understands the confidential nature of the information and his or her obligation to protect it. The lawyer must inform the client if a significant breach of confidentiality occurs through the actions of the consultant. Opinions 91-06, 98-07; Rules 1.6, 5.3; ABA 95-398.

Appendix D—Cloud Computing

Ethics Opinions on Lawyer Confidentiality Obligations Concerning Cloud Computing

A. ABA Formal Ethics Opinions

The Opinion headnote is reproduced below.

1. Formal Opinion 498 (March 10, 2021)
   Virtual Practice

https://www.americanbar.org/content/dam/aba/administrative/professional_responsibility/ethics-opinions/aba-formal-opinion-498.pdf

The ABA Model Rules of Professional Conduct permit virtual practice, which is technologically enabled law practice beyond the traditional brick-and-mortar law firm. When practicing virtually, lawyers must particularly consider ethical duties regarding competence, diligence, and communication, especially when using technology. In compliance with the duty of confidentiality, lawyers must make reasonable efforts to prevent inadvertent or unauthorized disclosures of information relating to the representation and take reasonable precautions when transmitting such information. Additionally, the duty of supervision requires that lawyers make reasonable efforts to ensure compliance by subordinate lawyers and nonlawyer assistants with the Rules of Professional Conduct, specifically regarding virtual practice policies.

B. ABA Reference Material and Bar Association Reports on Cloud Computing

1. ABA Section of Law Practice Management Website: Cloud Ethics Opinions Around the U.S.

http://www.americanbar.org/groups/departments_offices/legal_technology_resources/resources/charts_fyis/cloud-ethics-chart.html

2. ABA Section of Law Practice Section: ABA Legal Technology Resource Center

https://www.americanbar.org/groups/law_practice/resources/legal-technology-resource-center/

3. ABA Section of Science & Technology Law: Cloud Computing Committee

https://www.americanbar.org/groups/science_technology/about/committees/cloud-computing/

4. New York City Bar Report "The Cloud and the Small Law Firm: Business, Ethics and Privilege Considerations" (2013)

http://www2.nycbar.org/pdf/report/uploads/20072378-TheCloudandtheSmallLawFirm.pdf

5. Cloud Computing Guidelines from Canada:
http://www.lawsociety.bc.ca/docs/practice/resources/guidelines-cloud.pdf
http://www.lawsociety.bc.ca/docs/practice/resources/checklist-cloud.pdf

C. Digests of State Bar Ethics Opinions on Cloud Computing

The following digests of state bar ethics opinions are excerpted from the *ABA/Bloomberg Lawyers' Manual on Professional Conduct.*

1. Alabama State Bar Opinion 2010-02 (undated)
   Client files; Computers; Confidentiality; Client funds and property; Disabled clients

https://www.alabar.org/office-of-general-counsel/formal-opinions/2010-02/

A lawyer may outsource file storage to a service that uses cloud computing if he learns enough about the security issues to reasonably ensure that the service will protect the material's confidentiality. When disposing of electronic devices, lawyers should ensure that confidential information has been removed. A lawyer's obligation to retain client files and property depends upon the category of material. First, there are certain intrinsically valuable documents that ordinarily must be retained indefinitely, be they originals or photocopies; these include wills, powers of attorney, advance healthcare directives, executed estate-planning documents, stock certificates, bonds, cash, negotiable instruments, title certificates and abstracts, deeds, official corporate or other business and financial records, and settlement agreements. Second is property that a client would normally expect to be returned, or whose premature or unauthorized destruction would be detrimental to the client; this includes tangible personal property, photographs, recordings, pleadings, correspondence, discovery, demonstrative aids, written statements, notes, memorandums, and business and financial records. The lawyer may destroy such items if the client consents; consent may be implied if the client fails to take possession within 60 days of a date specified in either the lawyer's written retention policy—which must be affirmatively acknowledged in writing at the outset or termination of the representation—or a separate written notice to the client. Property not belonging to either of these two categories and having no foreseeable value may be destroyed without notice after the lawyer has retained it for a reasonable time, which would be at least six years. If a client asks for a file in a particular format, the lawyer generally must comply and may not charge. However, if the client suffers from diminished capacity or has a propensity for violence and might use the information to endanger others, the lawyer may redact certain documents. Opinions 1986-02, 1993-10, 1994-01; Ala. Code §§6-6-574, 34-3-61; Rules 1.6, 1.15, 1.16(d); ABA i1376, i1384.

2. Alaska Bar Association Opinion 2014-3 (May 5, 2014)
   Internet; Client files; Client funds and property; Confidentiality; Competence; Outsourcing; Record retention

https://alaskabar.org/wp-content/uploads/2014-3.pdf

A lawyer may use cloud computing services to store client files if the lawyer takes reasonable steps to ascertain that the cloud provider has adequate measures in place to protect the security, confidentiality and accessibility of the information and the lawyer knows where the client information is at any given time. At the conclusion of the representation, if the client does not wish the file to be preserved, the lawyer must take reasonable steps to ensure that the information is deleted from the cloud. The opinion includes examples of appropriate security measures. Rules 1.1, 1.6, 1.15, 5.3.

3. Arizona State Bar Opinion 05-04 (July 2005)
   Electronic Storage; Confidentiality

https://www.azbar.org/for-legal-professionals/ethics/ethics-opinions/?V=Opinions&OpinionId=523
A lawyer may store information on computer systems that also connect to the internet provided that the lawyer takes reasonable measures to prevent disclosure or destruction of the materials. If the lawyer lacks the requisite technological competence, he must hire a computer expert. Opinions 95-11, 97-04; Rules 1.1, 1.6(a), 5.1(a), 5.3(a,b).

4. Arizona State Bar Opinion 09-04 (Dec. 2009)
   Confidentiality; Maintaining Client Files; Electronic Storage; Internet

https://www.azbar.org/for-legal-professionals/ethics/ethics-opinions/?V=Opinions&OpinionId=704
A lawyer may offer clients online viewing and retrieval of their files if the lawyer takes reasonable security precautions. For example, the lawyer may use a "Secure Socket Layer" server that encrypts the files and stores them in online folders with unique, randomly generated alphanumeric names and several layers of password-protection. Competent personnel should periodically review the security precautions. Opinions 05-04, 07-02; Rules 1.1, 1.6(a).

5. State Bar of California Opinion 2012-184 (undated)
   Lawyer-client relationship; Internet; Competence; Confidentiality; Outsourcing; Communication with clients

https://www.calbar.ca.gov/Portals/0/documents/ethics/Opinions/CAL%202012-184-ADA.pdf
A lawyer may provide legal services via a secure internet portal going from her website to that of a third-party vendor (cloud computing) without telephone, personal, or email contact. She may be required to take special measures in order to meet ethics obligations, for example those of confidentiality and competence. Among other concerns the lawyer must ensure data security, and in some cases, she may need to verify the identity of the purported client. Opinions 1971-25, 1984-77, 2007-174, 2010-179; Los Angeles County Opinion 374; Rules 1-100, 1-300, 1-310, 3-100, 3-110, 3-310, 3-400, 3-500, 3-600, 4-200; Bus. & Prof. Code §§6068(e),(m),(n), 6125, 6126, 6127, 6147, 6148; Cal. Rules of Court 3.35-3.37, 5.70-5.71 (renumbered 5.425 as of January 2013); ABA 95-398, 08-451, 11-458.

6. Connecticut Bar Association Opinion 2013-07 (June 19, 2013)
   Internet; Computers; Record retention; Outsourcing; Competence; Confidentiality; Client files; Client funds and property

https://www.ctbar.org/docs/default-source/publications/ethics-opinions-informal-opinions/2013-opinions/informal-opinion-2013-07
A lawyer may use cloud computing, including software as a service (SaaS), for storing, transmitting, and processing client information if the lawyer uses reasonable efforts to prevent unauthorized access or disclosure, and ensures that the cloud service provider's policies and practices are consistent with the lawyer's obligations under the Rules of Professional Conduct. Opinion 99-52; Conn. Prac. Book §2-27(c); Rules 1.1, 1.6, 1.15, 5.1, 5.3.

7. Florida Bar Ethics Opinion 06-01 (April 10, 2006)
   Client files; Computers; Record retention

https://www.floridabar.org/etopinions/etopinion-06-1/
A lawyer may store in electronic format any client documents he is required to retain. The main consideration in file storage is that the appropriate documents be maintained, not the method by which they are stored. Opinions 63-3, 71-62, 81-8, 88-11 (reconsideration); Rules 4-1.5(f)(4), 4-1.8(j), 5-1.2(d); ABA i1127.

8. Florida Bar Ethics Opinion 12-3 (Jan. 25, 2013)
   Confidentiality; Cloud computing; Outsourcing; Competence

https://www.floridabar.org/etopinions/etopinion-12-3/
A lawyer may use cloud computing services to store, access and share client files if the lawyer uses reasonable diligence to ascertain that the provider has adequate measures in place to protect the security, confidentiality and accessibility of the information. The lawyer should research the service provider and should consider taking additional security measures regarding proprietary client information or other particularly sensitive information. The opinion includes suggestions as to what the lawyer should consider in researching the service provider. Opinions 07-2, 10-2; Rule 1.6.

9. Illinois State Bar Association Opinion 16-06 (Oct. 2016)
   Confidentiality; Competence; Internet; Computers; Client files; Communication with clients; Nonlawyers

https://www.isba.org/sites/default/files/ethicsopinions/16-06.pdf
A lawyer may use an outside cloud-computing service to store and transmit client information if the lawyer understands the technology enough to be able to assess the risk of inadvertent disclosure or unauthorized access and can act reasonably to protect the information. The lawyer must conduct a due diligence investigation before selecting a provider and must periodically review the chosen provider's security measures. The opinion suggests reasonable inquiries and practices. Opinion 10-01; Rules 1.1, 1.6, 5.1, 5.3.

10. Iowa State Bar Association Opinion 11-01 (Sept. 9, 2011)
    Confidentiality; Client files; Cloud computing

http://205.209.45.153/iabar/IowaEthicsOpinions.nsf/b6868944e3311dd08725811000429 34f/a092fcd35bb508e0872581100042b927/$FILE/Ethics%20Opinion%2011-01%20--%20Software%20as%20a%20Service%20-%20Cloud%20Computing.pdf

A lawyer may use "software as a service," known as SaaS, to store client information on the computers of an outside vendor. The lawyer must have unrestricted and reliable access to the data. In performing due diligence to ensure the information is protected, the lawyer may rely on the services of independent companies, bar associations and similar organizations, or the lawyer's own qualified staff, but the individuals must possess both the requisite technological expertise and an understanding of the ethics rules. As guidance, the opinion offers a list of questions lawyers should ask when considering whether to use outside vendors to store client information. Rule 32:1.6.

11. Iowa State Bar Association Opinion 14-01 (March 10, 2014)
    Confidentiality; Client files; Cloud computing; Competence

https://cdn.ymaws.com/sites/iowabar.site-ym.com/resource/resmgr/IA_Lawyer_Weekly/IA_Ethics_Op_14-01.pdf

A lawyer must be aware of changes in computer operating systems that could result in an increased risk to the security of confidential information. Rule 1.6 imposes an ongoing obligation to exercise due diligence in assessing system security but does not dictate how the lawyer should respond to any particular risk. Opinion 11-01; Rule 1.6.

12. Kentucky Bar Association Opinion E-437 (March 21, 2014)
    Internet; Client files; Confidentiality; Outsourcing; Record retention; Competence; Supervisory lawyers

https://www.kybar.org/resource/resmgr/Ethics_Opinions_(Part_2)_/kba_e-437.pdf

A lawyer may use cloud computing to store confidential client information if the lawyer takes reasonable care to ensure that the confidentiality and security of the information is preserved. The lawyer must use "reasonable efforts" to ensure that the cloud provider's conduct is consistent with the lawyer's obligations under the Rules of Professional Conduct, including investigating the cloud provider's qualifications, competence and diligence. If the lawyer is a partner or manager in his law firm, the lawyer must use "reasonable efforts" to ensure that his firm does so. If a matter is particularly sensitive, the lawyer must consult with the client about the use of cloud computing. Rules 1.1, 1.4, 1.6, 1.9, 1.15, 1.16, 1.18, 5.3; ABA Rule 1.6(c).

13. Maine Board of Overseers of the Bar Ethics Opinion 194 (June 30, 2008)
    Files of client; Computers; Confidentiality

https://www.mebaroverseers.org/attorney_services/opinion.html?id=86894

A lawyer may use an outside provider to process and electronically store data that include confidential client information only if the lawyer ensures that the provider maintains appropriate standards for protecting confidentiality and has a legally enforceable obligation to do so. Opinions 74, 134; 45 C.F.R. §§164.302–318; Rules 3.6(a), 3.6(h), 3.13(c); ABA 95-398, 99-413.

14. Maine Board of Overseers of the Bar Ethics Opinion 207 (Jan. 8, 2013)
    Internet; Email; Record retention; Outsourcing; Competence; Confidentiality; Client files

https://www.mebaroverseers.org/attorney_services/opinion.html?id=478397
A lawyer may use cloud computing and storage, including web-based email, online document creation and data storage, software-as-a-service ("SaaS"), platform-as-a-service ("PaaS"), and infrastructure-as-a-service ("IaaS"), for client matters. The opinion enumerates recommended practices to reasonably ensure compliance with the obligation of confidentiality, including agreements to secure from cloud service providers, and observes that the standard of reasonable care in ethical conduct requires lawyers to periodically educate themselves on changes in technology. Opinions 74, 120, 134, 183, 194; Rules 1.1, 1.6, 1.15, 5.3.

15. Massachusetts Bar Opinion 12-03 (March 2012)
    Client files; Record retention; Confidentiality; Computers; Internet

https://www.massbar.org/publications/ethics-opinions/ethics-opinion-article/ethics-opinions-2012-opinion-12-03
A lawyer may store and synchronize confidential files using internet-based "cloud" storage offered by, for example, Google Docs, Microsoft's Windows Azure, Apple's iCloud, and Amazon's S3, if the lawyer makes reasonable efforts to ensure that the provider's policies, practices, and procedures are compatible with the lawyer's professional obligations, including the obligation of confidentiality. Opinions 00-01, 05-04; Rule 1.6(a).

16. Missouri Informal Ethics Opinion 2018-09 (undated)
    Computers; Internet; Client files; Record retention; Confidentiality

https://mo-legal-ethics.org/informal-opinion/2018-09/
An attorney may use cloud computing as long as the attorney maintains competence in the use of relevant technology and makes reasonable efforts to safeguard confidential information from inadvertent or unauthorized disclosure or access to client information. Rules 4-1.1; 4-1.6; 4-5.3.

17. State Bar of Nevada Formal Opinion 33 (Feb. 9, 2006)
    Files of client; Computers; Confidentiality

https://nvbar.org/wp-content/uploads/opinion_33.pdf
A lawyer may store digital copies of client files on a server maintained by an outside contractor if the contractor agrees to keep the contents confidential and the lawyer takes

reasonable steps to prevent unauthorized disclosure. Nev. S. Ct. R. 156; ABA Rule 1.6, ABA 95-398, 99-413; ABA i1127.

18. New Hampshire Bar Association Advisory Opinion 2012-13/04 (Feb. 21, 2013)
    Cloud computing; Confidentiality; Outsourcing; Non-lawyer assistants; Competence

https://www.nhbar.org/ethics/opinion-2012-13-04
A lawyer may use cloud computing consistent with his or her ethical obligations and must ensure that client information remains confidential. Other considerations include whether the cloud computing organization is reputable, whether the data is stored in a format that is retrievable and secure, whether the provider offers security measures, how long the provider will retain data, and whether the provider has an enforceable obligation to keep the data confidential. Rules 1.8(c), 1.0(e), 1.1, 1.6, 1.15, 2.1, 5.3.

19. New Jersey Advisory Opinion 701 (undated)
    Client funds and property; Files of client; Computers; Confidentiality

https://afbnj.org/wp-content/uploads/2024/02/8.-ACPE-Opinion701-Electronic-Storage.pdf
A lawyer may digitize and retain in electronic format copies of documents received by the lawyer in the course of a representation, except for wills, deeds, and other client documents that by their nature must be retained in their original form. If the lawyer entrusts the documents to someone outside the firm for storage, the outside person must be aware of the obligation to preserve the confidentiality of the information. Opinions 515, 692, 694; Rules 1.1, 1.4, 1.6, 1.15.

20. New York State Bar Association Opinion 820 (Feb. 8, 2008)
    Confidentiality; Email; Computers

https://nysba.org/ethics-opinion-820/
A lawyer does not violate the duty of confidentiality by subscribing to an email service provider that gives him a discount in exchange for his tolerance of targeted advertising displayed on his screen. The provider electronically scans emails the subscriber opens and looks for certain keywords; the provider infers the subscriber's interests from the keywords and sends him advertisements tailored accordingly. The process is entirely electronic and does not entail any review of emails by human beings. Opinion 709; DR 4-101; EC 4-3.

21. New York State Bar Association Opinion 842 (Sept. 10, 2010)
    Client files; Internet; Confidentiality; Attorney-client privilege

https://nysba.org/ethics-opinion-842/
A lawyer who uses cloud computing provided by an online service as his backup file storage system must take reasonable care to protect the confidentiality of the information. This may include: ensuring the provider has an enforceable obligation to preserve confidentiality and security and will notify the lawyer if served with process requiring production

of client information; investigating the adequacy of the provider's security measures and recoverability methods; using available technology to guard against reasonably foreseeable infiltration attempts; and investigating the provider's ability to purge, wipe, and move data. The lawyer should also monitor changing law to ensure he is not jeopardizing any privileges applicable to the material. Opinions 473, 709, 782, 820; New York County Opinion 733; C.P.L.R. 4548; Rules 1.4, 1.6.

22. New York City Bar Formal Opinion 2008-01 (Jan. 1, 2008)
    Files of client; Computers; Email

http://www.nycbar.org/ethics/ethics-opinions-local/2008-opinions/799-a-lawyers-ethical-obligations-to-retain-and-to-provide-a-client-with-electronic-documents-relating-to-a-representation-

A lawyer is not required to organize or store electronic documents or emails in any particular manner or medium. Emails present more difficulty than electronic documents because they often are deleted automatically after a certain period and generally are not stored in a document management system. Because a lawyer may not charge a client file retrieval costs that could reasonably have been avoided, there is much to commend a practice of organizing saved emails for ease of retrieval. Opinion 1986-4; New York State Opinions 460, 623, 780; DRs 2-106, 2-110(2), 9-102; ABA Rules 1.0(n), 1.16(d); ABA Informal Opinion 1384 (March 14, 1977).

23. North Carolina State Bar Opinion 2011-6 (Jan. 27, 2012)
    Client files; Computers; Internet; Outsourcing; Confidentiality; Record retention

https://www.ncbar.gov/for-lawyers/ethics/adopted-opinions/2011-formal-ethics-opinion-6/

A lawyer may contract with a vendor of software as a service (SaaS) if the lawyer uses reasonable care to protect client information. Recommended options include an agreement with the vendor as to protection, retrieval, and disposition of confidential information during and after the contractual relationship and in the event the vendor goes out of business; evaluation of the vendor's security measures, including firewalls, encryption techniques, socket security features, and intrusion-detection systems; and evaluation of the extent to which the vendor backs up hosted data. The duties of diligence and competence require the lawyer to keep abreast of changes in technology and their impact on cloud computing and online security. Opinions RPC 133, 209, 215, 234, 1998-15, 2008-5; Rules 1.6, 1.15, 5.3(a).

24. State Bar of North Dakota Opinion 99-03 (June 21, 1999)
    Confidentiality; Internet; Files of client

https://cdn.ymaws.com/www.sband.org/resource/resmgr/docs/for_lawyers/99-03.pdf

A law firm may subscribe to an online data backup service whereby the firm's computer server would periodically transfer data to the service's server, which would then transfer the data to disk or tape that would be stored offsite and the firm would be given a confidential password allowing members to retrieve firm data from the storage units. However, the firm must ensure that the security of the data transmission and storage are adequate for the sensitivity of the records. At minimum, the firm must limit the access to the data to authorized personnel only, usually by limiting disclosure of the password to those individuals. Opinion 97-09; Rule 1.6; ABA 99-413.

25. Oregon Opinion 2011-188 (2011; Revised April 2015)
    Outsourcing; Internet; Client files; Confidentiality; Record retention; Supervisory lawyers

http://www.osbar.org/_docs/ethics/2011-188.pdf
A lawyer may contract with a third-party vendor to store client files and documents online on the vendor's remote servers (the "cloud") if the lawyer has taken reasonable steps to keep the information secure. This means the lawyer should investigate and periodically reevaluate how the vendor backs up and stores its data and metadata. The lawyer may include provisions in the service agreement requiring the vendor to preserve the confidentiality and security of the materials and to notify her of any unauthorized access. If industry standards relating to confidentiality and security meet the requirements of the lawyer ethics rules, ensuring the vendor's compliance with industry standards may satisfy the lawyer's obligation to take reasonable steps. Opinions 2005-44, 2005-129, 2005-141; Rules 1.6, 5.3.

26. Pennsylvania Bar Association Formal Opinion 2010-14 (March 15, 2010)
    Client files; Confidentiality; Computers

A lawyer may use an "off-site backup service" if he takes proper steps to safeguard client confidentiality; at a minimum the service should provide high levels of encryption. Rule 1.6.

27. Pennsylvania Bar Association Formal Opinion 2010-60 (Jan. 10, 2011)
    Client files; Computers; Internet; Confidentiality

A lawyer may use cloud computing to access and store data, and may use smartphones synchronized through the cloud to remotely access the data, if the lawyer takes appropriate measures to protect client confidentiality. Rules 1.6, 5.1.

28. Pennsylvania Bar Association Formal Opinion 2011-200 (Nov. 2011)
    Client files; Internet; Outsourcing; Record retention; Confidentiality; Competence; Email

A lawyer may store confidential client information off-site using "cloud computing" if the lawyer takes reasonable steps to protect data security. Generally, this will mean implementing mechanisms to back up data, install firewalls, limit unauthorized access, monitor all access, avoid inadvertent disclosure, and encrypt confidential data, as well as having a plan to address security breaches and having alternate ways to connect to the internet. If using an overseas service provider, the lawyer must make sure the hosting jurisdiction has privacy protections, data security laws, and safeguards against unlawful search and seizure that are as rigorous as those of the United States and Pennsylvania. Similarly, lawyers using web-based unencrypted email services must take reasonable precautions to protect confidential information; some communications may require special protection. Formal Opinions 2009-100, 2010-200; Informal Opinion 2010-60; 45 C.F.R. subpart 164.314(a)(2)(i); 73 Pa. Stat. §2303; Rules 1.0(e), 1.1, 1.4, 1.6, 1.15, 5.3; ABA 99-413, 08-451.

29. Tennessee Board of Professional Responsibility Opinion 2015-F-159 (Sept. 11, 2015)
    Internet; Confidentiality; Client files; Record retention; Competence; Supervisory lawyers; Communication with clients

http://www.tbpr.org/ethic_opinions/2015-f-159
A lawyer may store confidential information in the cloud if the lawyer takes reasonable care to preserve its confidentiality and protect against loss and other risks. The meaning of reasonable care will depend upon the information, the technology and the circumstances. Rules 1.1, 1.6, 1.9, 5.1, 5.3.

30. Vermont Bar Association Opinion 2010-6 (undated)
    Client files; Internet; Confidentiality; Record retention; Competence

https://www.vtbar.org/wp-content/uploads/2021/03/10-06.pdf
A lawyer may use Software as a Service (SaaS, also called cloud computing), to store, back up, and transmit confidential client information and documents, and may use remote document synchronization systems and web-based email and calendaring systems, but must take reasonable precautions to protect confidentiality and to ensure access to the materials. The nature of the precautions will depend on the circumstances and the technology. There may be circumstances in which using, or relying exclusively upon, a particular system would not be reasonable. The opinion invites the Vermont Supreme Court to examine whether technological changes have warranted changes in applicable procedural rules and ethics rules. Rules 1.1, 1.6, 1.15, 5.3.

Opinions are issued by the Committee on Professional Responsibility of the Vermont Bar Association. Internet: https://www.vtbar.org/# [click on "For Attorneys"].

31. Virginia Legal Ethics Opinion 1872 (March 29, 2013)
    Virtual Office; Cloud computing; Confidentiality; Internet

https://www.vacle.org/opinions/1872.htm
Operating a virtual law office does not change a lawyer's ethical obligations but does require extra precautions to meet the obligations of confidentiality, client communication, and supervision of others in the firm. Lawyer must act with reasonable care to protect client information, which includes selection of third-party vendors who transmit and store client data and supervision of nonlawyer assistants and subordinate lawyers who work remotely or in shared office with nonlawyers who are not law firm employees.

32. Washington State Bar Association Opinion 2215 (2012)
    Confidentiality; Client files; Record retention; Computers; Outsourcing

https://ao.wsba.org/print.aspx?ID=1662

A lawyer may contract with a third-party cloud computing vendor to store client files and documents on a remote server for access by the lawyer and the lawyer's clients if the lawyer takes reasonable steps to evaluate the risks of online data storage and ensure that the provider uses reasonable care to protect the information from loss or security breaches. The lawyer must monitor and regularly review the provider's security measures. Rules 1.1, 1.6, 1.15A.

33. State Bar of Wisconsin Opinion EF-15-01 (March 23, 2015; Amended Sept. 8, 2017)
    Cloud computing; Client files; Competence; Confidentiality

https://www.wisbar.org/formembers/ethics/Ethics%20Opinions/EF-15-01%20Cloud%20Computing%20Amended.pdf

A lawyer may use cloud computing to store and transmit client information if the lawyer uses reasonable efforts that are commensurate with the risks presented to protect access and confidentiality and ensure that the cloud service provider's actions are consistent with the lawyer's professional obligations. If the provider uses a server outside the United States, the lawyer must ensure that the client information stored on that server is protected by laws as stringent as those of the U.S. The opinion discusses factors to consider in assessing risk and determining what constitutes reasonable efforts. Rules 1.1, 1.4, 1.6, 5.3; ABA Rules 1.6, 5.3.

Appendix E—Social Media

Ethics Opinions Relating to Judges and Social Media and Lawyers' Passive Communications with Jurors on Social Media

1. Judges and Social Media

A. ABA Formal Ethics Opinions

The Opinion headnotes are reproduced below.

1. Formal Opinion 462 (Feb. 21, 2013)
   Judge's Use of Electronic Social Networking Media

http://www.americanbar.org/content/dam/aba/administrative/professional_responsibility/formal_opinion_462.pdf

A judge may participate in electronic social networking, but as with all social relationships and contacts, a judge must comply with relevant provisions of the Code of Judicial Conduct and avoid any conduct that would undermine the judge's independence, integrity, or impartiality, or create an appearance of impropriety.

2. Formal Opinion 478 (Dec. 8, 2017)
   Independent Factual Research by Judges Via the Internet

https://www.americanbar.org/content/dam/aba/administrative/professional_responsibility/ethics-opinions/aba-formal-opinion-478.pdf

Easy access to a vast amount of information available on the internet exposes judges to potential ethical problems. Judges risk violating the Model Code of Judicial Conduct by searching the internet for information related to participants or facts in a proceeding. Independent investigation of adjudicative facts generally is prohibited unless the information is properly subject to judicial notice. The restriction on independent investigation includes individuals subject to the judge's direction and control.

B. ABA Treatises and Annotated Model Standards

1. ABA Annotated Model Code of Judicial Conduct (3rd ed. 2016)

https://www.americanbar.org/groups/professional_responsibility/publications/model_code_of_judicial_conduct/

See the annotations to Canon 3, A judge shall conduct the judge's personal and extrajudicial activities to minimize the risk of conflict with the obligations of judicial office (p. 367) and Canon 4, A judge or candidate for judicial office shall not engage in political or campaign activity that is inconsistent with the independence, integrity, or impartiality of the judiciary (p. 505).

2. Ronald D. Rotunda, *Legal Ethics: The Lawyer's Deskbook on Professional Responsibility*, American Bar Association, 2024–2025 ed. (ABA)

https://store.legal.thomsonreuters.com/law-products/c/Legal-Ethics-The-Lawyers-Deskbook-on-Professional-Responsibility-2024-2025-ed-ABA/p/107080714?searchid=TRPPCSOL/Google/PrintUS_PP_Law-Books_Smart-Shopping_Search_Product-Feed_US/Smart-Shopping&chl=ppc&cid=9015549&sfdccampaignid=7014O000000vZOgQAM&ef_id=Cj0KCQjwpf2IBhDkARIsAGVo0D07hu2yqEkGmb933kQj_LEN73XcPfNuKzFqvxajuruGkURZdRUBVrlaAojHEALw_wcB:G:s&s_kwcid=AL!7944!3!409807603372!!!u!293946777986!&gclid=Cj0KCQjwpf2IBhDkARIsAGVo0D07hu2yqEkGmb933kQj_LEN73XcPfNuKzFqvxajuruGkURZdRUBVrlaAojHEALw_wcB

See § 10.2-2.11,When the Judge Is a Friend of the Lawyer or Party or Witness.

3. Judicial Conference of the United States

http://www.uscourts.gov/about-federal-courts/governance-judicial-conference

4. Resource Packet for Developing Guidelines on Use of Social Media by Judicial Employees (2010)

http://www.uscourts.gov/uscourts/RulesAndPolicies/conduct/SocialMediaLayout.pdf

C. Excerpts from State Bar Judicial Ethics Opinions on Judges' Use of Social Media

1. Arizona Supreme Court Judicial Ethics Advisory Committee Advisory Opinion 14-01 (Revised Aug. 5, 2014) Use of Social and Electronic Media by Judges and Judicial Employees

http://www.azcourts.gov/LinkClick.aspx?fileticket=zNRP1_l8sck%3d&portalid=137

"...[A] judge who uses social media must not make any public statement that might reasonably be expected to affect the outcome or impair the fairness of a matter pending or impending in any court. *See* Rule 2.10(A); *see also* Rule 4.1(A)(9) ("A judge or a judicial candidate shall not do any of the following: make any statement that would reasonably be expected to affect the outcome or impair the fairness of a matter pending or impending in any court"). Although nonpublic statements are only prohibited under Rule 2.10(A) if they might substantially interfere with a fair trial or hearing, it is prudent to assume that even postings intended only for friends and family may be more broadly disseminated through social and electronic media."

2. California Judges Association Formal Opinion 66 (Nov. 23, 2010) Online Social Networking

http://www.caljudges.org/docs/Ethics%20Opinions/Op%2066%20Final.pdf

"Caution is essential when a judge goes onto an online social networking site. Internet communications are permanent and lack the privacy of in-person or telephonic conversations. Judges must be careful to avoid making remarks that would cast doubt on the judge's ability to act impartially. As the commentary to Canon 4A makes plain: 'Expressions of bias or prejudice by a judge, even outside the judge's judicial activities, may cast reasonable doubt on the judge's capacity to act impartially as a judge. Expressions which may do so include jokes or other remarks demeaning individuals on the basis of a classification such as their race, sex, religion, sexual orientation, or national origin.'"

3. Kentucky Formal Judicial Ethics Opinion JE-119 (Jan. 20, 2020)
   Judges' Membership on Internet-Based Social Networking Sites

https://kycourts.gov/Courts/Judicial-Ethics/Judicial%20Ethics%20Opinions/JE_119.pdf
"While a proceeding is pending or impending in any court, judges are prohibited from making "any public comment that might reasonably be expected to affect its outcome or impair its fairness …." Canon 3B(9). Furthermore, full-time judges are prohibited from practicing law or giving legal advice. Canon 4G. Judges, therefore, must be careful that any comments they may make on a social networking site do not violate these prohibitions. While social networking sites may have an aura of private, one-on-one conversation, they are much more public than offline conversations, and statements once made in that medium may never go away."

4. Massachusetts Committee on Judicial Ethics Opinion No. 2018-03 (May 18, 2018)
   Disclosure of Former Facebook Friendship (modifying Committee on Judicial Ethics Opinion 2016-01 (Feb. 16, 2016) Facebook: Using Social Networking Site)

https://www.mass.gov/opinion/cje-opinion-no-2018-03
"The social media landscape has continued to evolve at a rapid rate, and we recognize that more new judges arrive on the bench with an-ever larger network of Facebook friends, many of whom may be most accurately described as acquaintances. In some cases, the past or present relationship may be so minimal that the Facebook friend is in essence a stranger. Going forward, we believe that the same disclosure standard should apply to both Facebook and LinkedIn. When a judge knows that a lawyer appearing before the judge is a former Facebook friend, the judge should consider the nature of the particular relationship to determine whether disclosure is warranted. In making this fact-based assessment, the judge should consider the nature of the (now-former) online friendship as well as the extent of any other relationship between the judge and the lawyer. The judge should additionally consider the personal information the judge has posted online that might be used by another to convey the impression of special access to the judge. A judge must always act to promote public confidence in the judiciary's integrity and impartiality and to avoid even the appearance of impropriety."

"We modify the advice given in Letter Opinion 2016-01 as follows. When a lawyer who was a former Facebook friend appears before a judge, disclosure is no longer presumptively required. The judge should exercise his or her sound discretion based on all the facts to decide whether to disclose."

5. Massachusetts Committee on Judicial Ethics Opinion 2016-08 (Sept. 6, 2016) Linked In: Using Social Networking Site

https://www.mass.gov/opinion/cje-opinion-no-2016-08

"As the use of social media continues to grow, we again emphasize judges' obligations under the Code of Judicial Conduct, including the obligations to uphold and promote the independence, integrity, and impartiality of the judiciary; promote public confidence in the judiciary; avoid both impropriety and the appearance of impropriety in their professional and public lives; maintain the dignity of judicial office at all times; avoid abuse of the prestige of the judicial office; refrain from political activity; and conduct all personal and extrajudicial activities to minimize the risk of conflict with the obligations of judicial office. Judges must expect to be the subject of public scrutiny that might be burdensome if applied to other citizens. Each judge who uses social media must take steps to minimize the likelihood that the manner in which that judge uses social media would lead a reasonable person to question the judge's impartiality."

"Judges must, of course, be aware that all social media communications may become public."

6. Missouri Commission on Retirement, Removal and Discipline Opinion 186 (2015)

"[W]hile the Commission does not think that judicial involvement in social media is per se unethical, it is conduct that exposes the judge to unnecessary danger of engaging in conduct that may be violative of the Code of Judicial Conduct....[I]n order to limit the potential of ethical violations and the number of cases in which the judge might be required to recuse, the judge should take care to adjust the privacy setting of the judge's personal Facebook or other social media account such that it could be viewed only by those who are the judge's listed "friends and not by the general public."

7. New York Advisory Committee on Judicial Ethics Opinion 08-176 (Jan. 29, 2009)

https://www.nycourts.gov/ipjudicialethicsopinions/08-176.htm

"The Rules require that a judge must avoid impropriety and the appearance of impropriety in all of the judge's activities (*see* 22 NYCRR 100.2) and shall act at all times in a manner that promotes public confidence in the integrity and impartiality of the judiciary (*see* 22 NYCRR 100.2[A]). Similarly, a judge shall conduct all of the judge's extra-judicial activities so that they do not detract from the dignity of judicial office (*see* 22 NYCRR 100.4[A][2]).... A judge should thus recognize the public nature of anything he/she places on a social network page and tailor any postings accordingly."

8. The Supreme Court of Ohio Board of Commissioners on Grievances and Discipline Opinion 2010-7 (Dec. 3, 2010)

https://www.ohioadvop.org/wp-content/uploads/2017/04/Op_10-007.pdf

"A judge should avoid making any comments on a social networking site about pending or impending matters in any court. As required by Jud. Cond. Rule 2.10 "[a] judge shall not make any public statement that might reasonably be expected to affect the outcome or impair the fairness of a matter *pending* or *impending* in any court, or make any nonpublic statement that might substantially interfere with a fair trial or hearing." Avoidance of any pending or impending case related comments is advised."

2. Lawyers' Passive Communications with Jurors on Social Media

A. ABA Formal Ethics Opinions

1. Formal Opinion 466 (April 24, 2014)
   Lawyer Reviewing Jurors' Internet Presence

http://www.americanbar.org/content/dam/aba/administrative/professional_responsibility/formal_opinion_466_final_04_23_14.pdf

Unless limited by law or court order, a lawyer may review a juror's or potential juror's internet presence, which may include postings by the juror or potential juror in advance of and during a trial, but a lawyer may not communicate directly or through another with a juror or potential juror.

A lawyer may not, either personally or through another, send an access request to a juror's electronic social media. An access request is a communication to a juror asking the juror for information that the juror has not made public and that would be the type of ex parte communication prohibited by Model Rule 3.5(b).

The fact that a juror or a potential juror may become aware that a lawyer is reviewing his internet presence when a network setting notifies the juror of such does not constitute a communication from the lawyer in violation of Rule 3.5(b).

In the course of reviewing a juror's or potential juror's internet presence, if a lawyer discovers evidence of juror or potential juror misconduct that is criminal or fraudulent, the lawyer must take reasonable remedial measures including, if necessary, disclosure to the tribunal.

B. ABA Reference Material and Bar Association Reports on Judicial Ethics and Social Media

1. New York State Bar Association Social Media Ethics Guidelines of the Commercial and Federal Litigation Section of the New York State Bar Association (Revised April 29, 2019; Released June 20, 2019)

https://nys-fjc.ca2.uscourts.gov/programs/10-22-19%20-%20NYSBA-Social%20Media%20Ethics%20Guidelines-Final-6-20-19.pdf

C. Digests of State Bar Judicial Ethics Opinions

The following digests of state bar ethics opinions are excerpted with permission from the *ABA/Bloomberg Lawyers' Manual on Professional Conduct*.

1. Colorado State Bar Opinion 127 (Sept. 2015)
   Social media; Investigations; Communication with judges; Communication with jurors; Communication with unrepresented persons; Communication with represented persons; Communication with witnesses; Competence; Advice to clients

http://www.cobar.org/Portals/COBAR/repository/ethicsOpinions/FormalEthicsOpinion_127.pdf

A lawyer may view the public portion of anyone's social media profile. The committee agrees with the majority view that "passive" browsing of a social media profile generally does not amount to contact or communication, even if the account-holder gets an automatic notification. Repetitively browsing a website knowing the account-holder is being notified could, however, amount to a violation of Rule 4.4(a) depending on degree and intent. A lawyer may never view or ask permission to view the restricted portion of a social media profile belonging to a judge presiding over the lawyer's case, or to a prospective or sitting juror. A lawyer needs counsel's consent before asking to see the restricted portion of a represented person's profile; if the person is unrepresented, the lawyer must first identify himself as a lawyer and disclose the general nature of the matter. A lawyer may never use deception to gain access to the restricted portion of a social media profile and may not circumvent the rules by having someone else make "friend" requests. As a matter of competence, lawyers should keep abreast of technological developments relevant to their ethical obligations and should advise their clients to expect opposing counsel to view the public portions of their profiles. Rules 1.1, 3.5, 4.1, 4.2, 4.3, 4.4(a), 5.1(b), (c), 8.4(a), (c); CJC Rules 2.4(B), 2.9; ABA 466.

2. New York State Bar Opinion 2012-2 (undated)
   Social media; Investigations; Internet; Communication with jurors

http://www2.nycbar.org/pdf/report/uploads/20072303-FormalOpinion2012-02JuryResearchandSocialMedia.pdf

A lawyer may research a potential or sitting juror using publicly available social networking websites such as Facebook, LinkedIn, or Twitter if no communication with the juror occurs, whether through a "friend" or connection request with the juror or an automated notification from the social media service that the juror's profile was viewed or followed. If the lawyer learns of juror misconduct through social media research, the lawyer must promptly notify the court. After the jury has been discharged, the lawyer may use social media to communicate with the jurors. Opinions 2010-2, 2012-1; New York State Opinions 246, 843; New York County Opinion 743; N.Y. Crim. Pro. Law §270.40; Rules 3.4, 3.5, 8.4; ABA 319.

3. New York County Lawyers' Association Opinion 743 (May 18, 2011)
   Communication with jurors; Social media; Internet; Investigations

https://www.nycla.org/resource/ethics-opinion/nycla-committee-on-professional-ethics-formal-opinion-on-lawyer-investigation-of-juror-internet-and-social-networking-postings-during-conduct-of-trial/

A lawyer trying a jury case may passively monitor jurors' postings on publicly available social networking sites that do not enable their account-holders to learn a website visitor's identity. The lawyer may not "friend" or tweet jurors, subscribe to their Twitter accounts, or otherwise contact them. If, in the course of permissible monitoring, the lawyer learns of juror misconduct, including deliberations that violate the court's instructions, he must promptly notify the court whether or not the client wants him to. New York State Opinion 843, https://nysba.org/ethics-opinion-843/?srsltid=AfmBOoqatpp3HhJ2spY1i3nzEtvR1T4nm8APazXYG2EevPTf32mB_7Pn; Rules 3.5, 4.1, 8.4(a).

4. Pennsylvania State Bar Opinion 214–300 (2014)
   Social media; Internet; Advice to clients; Competence; Evidence; Investigations; Discovery; Communication with jurors; Communication with represented persons; Communication with unrepresented persons; Communication with judges; Confidentiality

A lawyer should advise a client regarding the effects social media postings may have on a lawsuit or other matter. The lawyer may advise a client to remove matter that may be damaging from the client's social media page if it will not violate any law or court order, but must take appropriate action to preserve the material. A lawyer may contact persons through social networking websites to the extent permitted by applicable law and may request access to an unrepresented person's social networking website if the lawyer identifies himself and states his reason for making the request. The lawyer may not use subterfuge to gain access to a person's nonpublic social media website. A lawyer may view the public portion of a juror's social networking website, even if the website generates a notification to the juror that the lawyer has viewed it but may not ask the juror for access to the private portion of the website. A lawyer may connect with a judge on social media if the lawyer does not seek to improperly influence the judge and if there is no ex parte or other proscribed communication. A lawyer may endorse another lawyer and may accept an endorsement from a client on a social media website if the endorsements are not false or misleading and if the lawyer discloses whether any compensation was given for the endorsements, but a lawyer may not accept endorsements from celebrities or judges. A lawyer may respond to negative reviews of the lawyer's performance on social media websites if the lawyer does not disclose confidential client information. The opinion discusses lawyers' ethical obligations when using social media in a variety of contexts. Formal Opinions 90-142, 2005-200, 2014-200; Philadelphia Opinions 2009-2, 2014-5; Pa. R. Civ. P. 4011(b); Rules 1.1, 1.6, 3.3, 3.4, 3.5, 3.6, 4.1, 4.2, 4.3, 8.2, 8.4; CJC Canon 2.9; ABA 462, 466.

5. West Virginia State Bar Opinion 2015-02 (Sept. 22, 2015)
   Social media; Internet; Confidentiality; Competence; Prospective clients; Advice to clients; Communication with clients; Communication with represented persons; Communication with unrepresented persons; Investigations; Advertising and solicitation

https://storage.googleapis.com/msgsndr/Rgd68xOkcVdteTsBkf6O/media/66a7ea7dc87f33d3e149ff03.pdf

Lawyers must comply with the lawyer ethics rules when using social media just as when using other forms of communication. A lawyer may advise a client about the content of the client's social networking website, including removing or adding information. A lawyer may connect with clients and former clients on a social networking website but may not contact a represented person through a social networking website. A lawyer may contact an unrepresented person through a social networking website and may use information from a social networking website but may not use a pretextual basis to gain access to private information. A lawyer may review a juror's internet presence and may connect with a judge on a social networking website. A lawyer may accept client reviews if he monitors them for accuracy and may generally endorse other lawyers and comment on, or respond to, reviews or endorsements. A lawyer's interactions on a social networking website may create a prospective lawyer-client relationship. Rules 1.1, 1.6, 1.18, 3.3, 3.4, 3.5, 3.6, 4.1, 4.2, 4.3, 7.1, 7.2, 7.3, 7.4, 8.2, 8.4.

Appendix F—Artificial Intelligence

Current Ethics Opinions and Other Guidance on Lawyer Use of Generative Artificial Intelligence Tools

(Current as of May 2025)

A. Ethics Opinions

If the Opinion includes a headnote or summary, that material is reproduced below.

1. ABA Formal Opinion 512 (July 29, 2024)
   Generative Artificial Intelligence Tools

https://www.americanbar.org/content/dam/aba/administrative/professional_responsibility/ethics-opinions/aba-formal-opinion-512.pdf

To ensure clients are protected, lawyers using generative artificial intelligence tools must fully consider their applicable ethical obligations, including their duties to provide competent legal representation, to protect client information, to communicate with clients, to supervise their employees and agents, to advance only meritorious claims and contentions, to ensure candor toward the tribunal, and to charge reasonable fees.

2. D.C. Bar Ethics Opinion 388 (April 2024)

https://www.dcbar.org/For-Lawyers/Legal-Ethics/Ethics-Opinions-210-Present/Ethics-Opinion-388

Advances in technology have greatly improved the ways in which lawyers provide legal services. What technology has not done is alter lawyers' fundamental ethical obligations, and specifically, the duties lawyers owe to their clients—and to the courts. We anticipate that both of these statements will hold true with respect to lawyers' use of generative artificial intelligence (GAI). Due to the rapid development of technology in this area, we recognize that some of the concerns raised in this opinion may be resolved or mooted for particular products in the future, perhaps even in the near future.

3. Florida Bar Ethics Opinion 24-1 (Jan. 19, 2024)

https://www.floridabar.org/etopinions/opinion-24-1/

Lawyers may use generative artificial intelligence ("AI") in the practice of law but must protect the confidentiality of client information, provide accurate and competent services, avoid improper billing practices, and comply with applicable restrictions on lawyer advertising. Lawyers must ensure that the confidentiality of client information is protected when using generative AI by researching the program's policies on data retention, data sharing, and self-learning. Lawyers remain responsible for their work product and professional judgment and must develop policies and practices to verify that the use of generative AI is consistent with the lawyer's ethical obligations. Use of generative AI does not permit a lawyer to engage in improper billing practices such as double-billing. Generative AI chatbots that communicate with clients or third parties must comply with restrictions on lawyer advertising and must include a disclaimer indicating that the chatbot is an AI program and not a lawyer or employee of the law firm. Lawyers should be mindful of the duty to maintain technological competence and educate themselves regarding the risks and benefits of new technology.

4. Ky. Bar Ass'n, Ethics Opinion KBA E-457 (March 15, 2024)
https://cdn.ymaws.com/www.kybar.org/resource/resmgr/Ethics_Opinions_(Part_2)_/kba_e-350.pdf
Question: Past Kentucky Bar Association ethics opinions and court decisions counsel that a prosecutor (and his partners and associates) should not try defendants with whom the prosecutor is embroiled in civil litigation. Did the adoption of the Kentucky Rules of Professional Conduct "overturn" these ethics opinions and decisions?
Answer: No.

5. Miss. St. Bar Ethics Opinion No. 267 (Nov. 14, 2024)
https://www.msbar.org/ethics-discipline/ethics-opinions/formal-opinions/267/

6. Mo. Informal Opinion 2024-11 (May 2024)
https://mo-legal-ethics.org/informal- opinion/2024-11/

7. St. Bar of N.M. Ethics Advisory Cte. Formal Ethics Opinion 2024-004 (Sept. 24, 2024)
https://www.sbnm.org/Portals/NMBAR/GenAI%20Formal%20Opinion%20-%20Sept_2024_FINAL.pdf
QUESTION PRESENTED: May a lawyer use Generative Artificial Intelligence in the practice of law?

SUMMARY ANSWER: Under the New Mexico Rules of Professional Conduct, yes, they may; however, use of such technology raises a number of considerations which are highlighted here.

8. N.Y. City Bar Ass'n, Cte. on Prof'l Eth., Formal Opinion 2024-5 (Aug. 7, 2024)
https://www.nycbar.org/wp-content/uploads/2024/08/20221329_GenerativeAILawPractice.pdf
When using generative artificial intelligence tools, a lawyer should take into account the duty of confidentiality, the obligation to avoid conflicts of interest, the duty of competence and diligence, the rules governing advertising and solicitation, the duty to comply with the law, the duty to supervise both lawyers and nonlawyers, the duty of subordinate attorneys,

the duty to consult with clients, the duty of candor to tribunals, the prohibition on making non-meritorious claims and contentions, the limitations on what a lawyer may charge for fees and costs, and the prohibition on discrimination.

9. N.C. St. Bar 2024 Formal Eth. Opinion 1, *Use of Artificial Intelligence in a Law Practice* (Nov. 1, 2024)
https://www.ncbar.gov/for-lawyers/ethics/adopted-opinions/2024-formal-ethics-opinion-1/

10. Or. St. Bar Formal Opinion N 2025-205
https://www.osbar.org/_docs/ethics/2025-205.pdf
Facts: Artificial intelligence (AI) tools have become widely available for use by lawyers. AI has been incorporated into a multitude of products frequently used by lawyers, such as word processing applications, communication tools, and research databases. AI tools generally use predictive text and other features to prompt or complete complex tasks. Generative AI (GAI) tools are a type of AI that use heuristics to produce complex and specific data, **o.**which can include generating full legal documents like briefs, contracts, and demand letters.

Questions:

1. May Oregon lawyers utilize AI tools in their legal practice?
2. May Oregon lawyers utilize GAI tools in their legal practice?

Conclusions:

1. Yes, qualified.
2. Yes, qualified.

11. Pa. Bar Ass'n and Phila. Bar Ass'n, Joint Formal Opinion 2024-200 (May 2024)
https://www.pabar.org/Members/catalogs/Ethics%20Opinions/Formal/Joint%20Formal%20Opinion%202024-200.pdf

12. St. Bar of Texas Prof'l Ethics Cte., Opinion No. 705 (Feb. 2025)
https://tcle-web.s3.amazonaws.com/public/documents/Opinion_705.pdf

13. W. Va. Lawyer Disc. Bd., Legal Eth. Opinion 24-01 (June 14, 2024)
https://storage.googleapis.com/msgsndr/Rgd68xOkcVdteTsBkf6O/media/667ac9c219bb7a1f7a4df4c2.pdf

B. Other Ethics Guidance

1. Supreme Court of Arizona, Steering Committee on Artificial Intelligence and the Courts (AISC), *Generative AI: Ethical Best Practices for Lawyers and Judges* (Nov. 14, 2024)
https://www.azcourts.gov/Portals/74/AISC%20Ethical%20Best%20Practices%20Guidance_For%20Publication.pdf

2. Calif. St. Bar, *Practical Guidance for the Use of Generative Artificial Intelligence in the Practice of Law* (Nov. 16, 2023)
https://www.calbar.ca.gov/Portals/0/documents/ethics/Generative-AI-Practical-Guidance.pdf

3. Ill. St. Bar Ass'n, *Report of Task force on Artificial Intelligence* (Sept. 27, 2023)
https://www.americanbar.org/content/dam/aba/administrative/center-for-innovation/ai-task-force/skm-c360i23100414470.pdf
See also *Illinois Supreme Court Policy on Artificial Intelligence*, ILL. SUP. CT. (eff. Jan. 1, 2025), https://ilcourtsaudio.blob.core.windows.net/antilles-resources/resources/e43964ab-8874-4b7a-be4e-63af019cb6f7/Illinois%20Supreme%20Court%20AI%20Policy.pdf

4. Mich. St. Bar, *Artificial Intelligence for Attorneys-Frequently Asked Questions* (May 2024)
https://www.michbar.org/opinions/ethics/AIFAQs

5. Minn. St. Bar Ass'n, Working Group on AI, *Implications of Large Language Models (LLMs) on the Unauthorized Practice of Law (UPL) and Access to Justice* (June 2024)
https://mnbars.org/docDownload/2460104

6. N.J. Sup. Ct. Cte. on Artificial Intelligence, *Preliminary Guidelines on New Jersey Lawyers' Use of Artificial Intelligence* (Jan. 24, 2024)
https://www.njcourts.gov/notices/notice-legal-practice-preliminary-guidelines-use-of-artificial-intelligence-new-jersey

7. N.J. St. Bar Ass'n Task Force on Artificial Intelligence and the Law, *Report, Requests, Recommendations, and Findings* (May 2024)
https://njsba.com/wp-content/uploads/2024/05/NJSBA-TASK-FORCE-ON-AI-AND-THE-LAW-REPORT-final.pdf

8. N.Y. St. Bar Ass'n, *Report and Recommendations of the New York State Bar Association Task Force on Artificial Intelligence* (April 8, 2024)
https://nysba.org/app/uploads/2022/03/2024-April-Report-and-Recommendations-of-the-Task-Force-on-Artificial-Intelligence.pdf (access requires membership)

9. St. Bar of Texas, Taskforce for Responsible AI in the Law, *Interim Report to the State Bar of Texas Board of Directors* (July 2024)
https://www.texasbar.com/AM/Template.cfm?Section=Meeting_Agendas_and_Minutes&Template=/CM/ContentDisplay.cfm&ContentID=62597

10. U.S. Patent and Trademark Office, *Guidance on Use of Artificial Intelligence-Based Tools in Practice Before the United States Patent and Trademark Office*, Docket No. PTO-P-2024-0013 (April 11, 2024)
https://www.federalregister.gov/documents/2024/04/11/2024-07629/guidance-on-use-of-artificial-intelligence-based-tools-in-practice-before-the-united-states-patent

11. Va. St. Bar, Standing Cte. on Legal Ethics, *Guidance on Generative Artificial Intelligence* (Feb. 2024), Proposed Legal Ethics Opinion 1901 (March 27, 2025)
https://vsb.org/Site/news/rules-news/20250327-prop-1901-fees-ai.aspx

12. Va. St. Bar, Standing Cte. on Legal Ethics, *Guidance on Generative Artificial Intelligence* (Feb. 2024)
https://vsb.org/Site/Site/lawyers/ethics.aspx?hkey=bc8a99e2-7578-4e60-900f-45991d5c432b

Chapter 11

Foundation of Risk Management in Cybersecurity

Daniel A. Cotter

1. Introduction: Risk Management as a Foundational Discipline

Every organization—whether a law firm, a public agency, or a multinational corporation—faces uncertainty and innumerable risks. To address the uncertainty and ensure efficient deployment of limited resources, each entity must perform some level of risk management. The risk management discipline helps organizations navigate uncertainty, make informed decisions, and prepare for the unexpected. Its methodology provides a structured approach to identifying potential threats, assessing their impact, deciding how to address them, and monitoring the outcomes of those decisions over time.

The International Organization for Standardization ("ISO") provides the following definition of risk management:

> "Risk management is the coordinated activities to direct and control an organization with regard to risk."[1]

This chapter introduces the fundamental concepts of risk management, focusing primarily on how they apply to cybersecurity. It provides a practical, scalable framework that organizations of any size or complexity can adapt. Beginning with the field of risk management, it gives a primer. Then it sets the stage for deeper dives into related topics such as cybersecurity frameworks and standards, incident response, security training, and cyber insurance.

2. Cybersecurity as Part of Risk Management

Traditionally, we have applied risk management to financial, operational, legal, and strategic domains. However, in recent decades, cybersecurity has become an integral component

1. ISO, ISO 31000:2018 Risk Management—Guidelines § 3.1 (2d ed. 2018).

of any comprehensive risk management program.[2] Just as organizations insure against natural disasters or establish compliance programs to manage legal exposure, they must also take steps to manage the risks posed by digital threats, such as data breaches, ransomware, and other forms of cybercrime.

2.1. Core Components of Risk Management

Before implementing a risk management program, one must understand the core components of the process. These components include, at a minimum, risk identification, assessment, mitigation, monitoring, and reporting. Risk management is an ongoing process; effective programs implement and assess outcomes. Heat maps and other tools identified in this chapter can help to address this continual process.

2.1.1. *Identifying Risks*

The first step in any risk management program is identifying the organization's risks. Some of the more common risks requiring assessment and identification include:

- Cybersecurity and Data Privacy Risk;
- Regulatory and Compliance Risk;
- Reputational Risk;
- Strategic Risk;
- Operational Risk;
- Financial Risk;
- Geopolitical and Economic Risk;
- Climate and Environmental Risk;
- Technology & Innovation Risk; and
- Human Capital Risk.[3]

You can find more information about the focus of each of these risks in Appendix A.

As noted earlier, risk management is a continuous exercise. In volatile and uncertain times, the risk priorities and most significant risks will change continuously.

While legal often gets involved in risk management and compliance, success demands having the complete buy-in and support of officers and directors. The process and framework also anticipate and require broad participation in the identifying and gathering risk phase.

Identifying risk in the cybersecurity and data privacy category requires a thorough understanding of an organization's digital footprint—its hardware, software, data repositories, and people. Cyber risks may include threats like:

2. NIST, *Framework for Improving Critical Infrastructure Cybersecurity, Version 1.1* (Apr. 16, 2018), https://doi.org/10.6028/NIST.CSWP.04162018.

3. *See, e.g.*, Protiviti, *2025 Report on Top Risks*, https://www.protiviti.com/us-en/survey/executive-perspectives-top-risks?utm_source=chatgpt.com (last visited June 23, 2025).

- Unauthorized access to sensitive data;
- Phishing and social engineering attacks;
- Malware and ransomware infections;
- Insider threats; and
- System outages or loss of critical functionality.

Tools such as asset inventories, network scans, and internal interviews can help organizations uncover where vulnerabilities may lie.

2.1.2. *Using Heat Maps, Risk Appetite, and Risk Profile*

Organizations often use heat maps to assess the various categories of risk. We will discuss the heat map in more detail shortly, but first, we need to consider two other concepts. Every organization has a different ability to absorb bad news and take more or less risk. Risk appetite and risk profile help to address how much risk a particular entity can withstand.

2.1.2.1. *Risk Appetite and Risk Profile*

Risk appetite refers to the amount and type of risk an organization will accept in pursuit of its objectives. It reflects the organization's culture, values, and tolerance for uncertainty. For example, a startup may have more risk tolerance than a government agency handling sensitive personal data. Each entity and organization must assess its appetite to know its uncertainty threshold.[4]

Risk profile represents the actual collection of risks an organization currently faces, considering their severity and likelihood. This includes known and emerging risks and provides a snapshot of the organization's exposure at a given time.[5]

Finally, the concept of risk tolerance is important. Risk tolerance is the overall amount of risk that the organization can absorb.[6]

Understanding the gap between risk appetite and the actual risk profile helps leaders decide where to invest in controls, training, and insurance. For example, if an organization has a low appetite for data loss but faces high risks of phishing attacks, that gap signals the need for stronger email security and user awareness efforts.

2.1.2.2. *Heat Maps for Visualization*

A heat map is a visual tool to assess and communicate risk severity by plotting risks based on their likelihood and impact. Typically, we use a grid, color-coded with the three colors

---

4. *See* Guy Carpenter, *Risk Profile, Appetite, and Tolerance: Fundamental Concepts in Risk Management and Reinsurance Effectiveness*, https://www.guycarp.com/insights/2009/04/risk-profile-appetite-and-tolerance-fundamental-concepts-in-risk-management-and-reinsurance-effectiveness.html (last visited June 23, 2025).

5. *Id.*

6. *Id.*

of traffic lights—green, yellow, and red—to help prioritize which risks demand immediate attention.

Heat map coloring is based on two objective factors and weighing of those two elements- the probability of occurrence and the impact if it occurs.[7]

Example Risk Heat Map Grid:

	Low Impact	Medium Impact	High Impact
High Likelihood	Moderate (Yellow)	High (Red)	Critical (Red)
Medium Likelihood	Low (Green)	Moderate (Yellow)	High (Red)
Low Likelihood	Low (Green)	Low (Green)	Moderate (Yellow)

2.1.3. *Classifying and Prioritizing Risks*

Identified risks require classification based on their potential impact and the likelihood of their occurrence. We commonly use a risk matrix, which categorizes threats along two dimensions: probability and severity.

This step is crucial since not all risks can or should be addressed equally. Organizations must weigh the consequences of a risk event against their resources and risk appetite. For instance, a data breach involving client records may be classified as high severity, demanding immediate attention, while a short-term email outage may be categorized as a lower priority. The classification is fact dependent.[8]

Once you have the heat map organizing risks by most in need of attention, compare that to the risk appetite, tolerance, and risk profile to see how it fits.

2.1.4. *Monitoring and Oversight*

Risk management is not a one-time exercise. Ongoing monitoring ensures that organizations remain aware of their evolving threat landscape.[3] Monitoring includes tracking performance metrics, setting alerts for unusual activity, and regularly reviewing logs or audit trails.

Oversight also means ensuring integration of risk management activities into day-to-day operations, with senior leadership remaining informed and engaged.

2.1.5. *Governance: Roles and Responsibilities*

Effective risk management requires clarity in governance. It is essential to assign roles and responsibilities so that everyone in the organization understands who is accountable for what.

---

7. David Schmoeller, *What Is a Risk Heat Map & How Can It Help Your Risk Management Strategy*, ISACA Now Blog (Jan. 25 2022), https://www.isaca.org/resources/news-and-trends/isaca-now-blog/2022/what-is-a-risk-heat-map-and-how-can-it-help-your-risk-management-strategy (last visited June 23, 2025).

8. From personal experience, making sure that the two measurements on the heat map (probability and severity) are objective and the map correctly ranks the "heat" of the issue is essential. Once, a heat map ranking human resource talent issues as the hottest topic was presented to a board. The board was not impressed by that assessment.

In some organizations, this may involve appointing a Chief Information Security Officer (CISO) or designating someone to act in that capacity.

2.2. Implementing the Risk Management Framework

Once risks are identified and roles are assigned, organizations must implement systems and controls to address them. This includes:

- Policies;
- Procedures; and
- Technology.

Risk registers or dashboards can help centralize this information and ensure that leadership remains informed.

2.2.1. *Risk Mitigation and Managing Residual Risk*

Once an organization has identified and assessed its risks, the next step in the risk management process is determining how to address them. We often refer to this as risk treatment.[9] It involves deciding on the best course of action to bring risk exposure in line with the organization's risk appetite and tolerance.

Risk treatment typically involves one or more of the following strategies:

1. Avoid the Risk

Avoidance involves discontinuing the activities that create risk. While not always feasible, this approach may be appropriate when:

- The risk exceeds the organization's tolerance;
- The activity is not essential to the organization's mission or operations; and
- Alternative, lower-risk methods exist.

Example: A law firm decides not to adopt a new cloud-based client portal until it completes a vendor risk assessment and determines appropriate security controls.

2. Mitigate the Risk

Mitigation reduces the **likelihood**[10] or **impact** (or **consequence**)[11] of a risk event (or both). It is the most common and often the most practical strategy in cybersecurity risk management.

Mitigation efforts can include implementing various controls. For cybersecurity, they will include:

---

9. ISO, Risk Management—Guidelines, *supra* note 1, § 3.8.

10. *See* heat map addressing these two concepts. *See also* ISO, Risk Management—Guidelines, *supra* note 1, § 3.7.

11. *Id.*, § 3.6.

- **Technical controls** (firewalls, encryption, multi-factor authentication);
- **Administrative controls** (policies, training, access restrictions); and
- **Physical controls** (secure facility access, locked server rooms).

Example: An organization implements endpoint detection and response software across all laptops to reduce the risk of malware infections from phishing emails.

3. **Transfer the Risk**

Transferring risk involves shifting it to a third party, usually through:

- **Insurance policies** (e.g., cyber liability coverage);[12]
- **Indemnification clauses** in contracts; and
- **Outsourcing** operations (with appropriate due diligence and oversight).

Example: A healthcare provider purchases cyber insurance to cover the costs of responding to a breach, including forensic investigation, notification, and potential regulatory fines.

4. **Accept the Risk**

Some risks must be accepted when:

- The cost of mitigation exceeds the potential impact;
- The risk is low in severity or likelihood; and
- The residual risk falls within the organization's defined tolerance.

Accepted risks should still be documented, justified, and monitored. They often become part of a risk register for ongoing evaluation. The analysis can change over time as circumstances or technological advances alter a risk's potential for damage or the likelihood of an occurrence.

Example: A firm may accept the risk of temporary email downtime during weekend maintenance because it has minimal operational impact.

2.2.2. *Residual Risk and Accountability*

Even after treatment strategies are applied, some level of risk remains. This is called "residual risk," and it should be:

- Identified in the risk register;
- Evaluated in the context of risk appetite; and
- Reviewed regularly as part of governance oversight.

12. *See* HANDBOOK, Chapter 14, *Cyber Insurance for Law Firms and Legal Organizations*, for more information.

Leadership should understand which risks it accepts and why. Assigning risk owners ensures accountability and ongoing attention to these exposures. Appendix B sets forth a sample risk owner/responsibility matrix for cyber risks.

A risk register is a repository that records identified risks, their severity, the mitigating actions taken, and the parties responsible for managing them. Appendix C provides a sample cybersecurity risk register. Things don't have to be fancy, but they must be useful to the organization to help it effectively manage its risk.

3. Linking Mitigation to the Broader Framework

Effective mitigation is not just about applying controls; it's about integrating responses into the organization's broader cybersecurity and ERM framework. This includes:

- Incorporating mitigation strategies into incident response plans;
- Testing controls through simulations or audits; and
- Ensuring documentation supports compliance and insurance claims.

3.1. Integration with Broader Cybersecurity Strategy

Risk management works in concert with:

- Incident Response;
- Training and Culture; and
- Cyber Insurance.

Each of these areas is a facet of risk management.

For organizations with mature Enterprise Risk Management ("ERM") programs, cybersecurity is increasingly recognized as a core strategic and operational concern, not merely a technical issue. ERM frameworks typically classify risks across categories, such as strategic, financial, operational, compliance/legal, reputational, and human capital. Cybersecurity risk intersects with each of these categories, making it both a discrete domain and a risk multiplier.

In many sectors, cybersecurity now ranks among the top three enterprise risks, alongside strategic misalignment and regulatory compliance.[13] In industries such as financial services, healthcare, legal, and critical infrastructure, it often holds the top position in board-level risk assessments due to its potential to cause significant financial loss, legal exposure, and reputational damage.

13. *See, e.g.*, Protiviti, *supra* note 3.

Organizations with robust ERM practices increasingly treat cybersecurity as a cross-cutting issue they must address across business units and functions. This integrated view ensures that cyber risks are not siloed within IT departments but get incorporated into:

- Strategic planning and mergers/acquisitions;
- Risk appetite and tolerance definitions;
- Regulatory compliance frameworks;
- Vendor and supply chain assessments; and
- Crisis response and business continuity planning.

In this context, cybersecurity risks are often managed alongside other key enterprise risks using common tools such as:

- Risk heat maps and registers that align cyber threats with broader organizational priorities;
- Board-level dashboards tracking cyber maturity and incident metrics;
- Quantitative risk modeling,[14] including financial loss estimation methods (e.g., FAIR); and
- Scenario-based planning that includes cyber incident simulations and tabletop exercises.

Integrating cybersecurity into ERM enables organizations to make more informed, cohesive decisions about risk tradeoffs, investments in controls, and incident preparedness. It reflects a growing consensus that cybersecurity is not just an IT issue—it is an enterprise-wide risk requiring enterprise-wide governance.

3.2. Cybersecurity and ERM Integration

3.2.1. *The Cyclical Nature of Risk Management*

Cyber threats evolve rapidly. That's why risk management must be a continuous process.

This cycle involves:

1. Revisiting the asset inventory;
2. Reassessing current threats;
3. Evaluating existing controls;
4. Adjusting mitigation strategies; and
5. Updating governance mechanisms.

---

14. Quantitative risk modeling employs statistical and financial techniques to estimate the likelihood and potential impact of cyber threats. Models like FAIR (Factor Analysis of Information Risk) enable organizations to express cyber risks in monetary terms, facilitating informed decision-making and effective resource allocation. This approach supports transparent communication of risk to stakeholders and aligns cybersecurity efforts with business objectives. *See, e.g.*, FAIR Institute, *What Is FAIR?*, https://www.fairinstitute.org/what-is-fair (last visited Apr. 17, 2025).

3.3. Why a Good Compliance and Risk Management Program Matters

Every organization needs to ensure that it has an effective compliance and risk management program in place. When it comes to cyber, there are numerous reasons why paying attention to the risk management framework is essential.

A strong compliance and risk management program does more than shield an organization from enforcement actions. It protects the organization's reputation, promotes operational resilience, and strengthens stakeholder trust. Customers, investors, and business partners increasingly expect companies to demonstrate sound risk management practices as a condition of doing business. A well-integrated program also improves internal decision-making, reinforces a culture of accountability, and helps preserve enterprise value during events such as mergers, acquisitions, or regulatory audits. In addition, insurers and lenders often view effective risk governance as a prerequisite for favorable coverage terms or financing. In today's environment, robust risk management is not just a defensive measure—it is a competitive advantage and a business imperative.

In addition to the reasons above, organizations might also implement strong risk management programs to ensure they will not face regulatory penalties, including under the Federal Sentencing Guidelines for organizations, state statutes in the insurance space, and Delaware court requirements.

3.3.1. *Federal Sentencing Guidelines*

Federal sentencing guidelines were initially policies established through various memos, beginning with the Thompson Memo.[15] Subsequent memos, including the McNulty Memo[16] and the Filip Memo[17] modified Thompson. These memos have since been incorporated and superseded by the Justice Manual, § 9-28.000—Principles of Federal Prosecution of Business Organizations.[18]

Some of the principles now in the Manual include requiring people high up in the hierarchy to understand the compliance program:

> High-level personnel of the organization shall ensure that the organization has an effective compliance and ethics program, as described in this guideline.[19] Specific

15. Larry D. Thompson, Memorandum for Heads of Dep't Components and United States Att'ys: Principles of Federal Prosecution of Business Organizations (Jan. 20, 2003), reprinted in 41 AM. CRIM. L. REV. 393 (2004).

16. Paul J. McNulty, Memorandum for Heads of Dep't Components and United States Att'ys: Principles of Federal Prosecution of Business Organizations (Dec. 12, 2006), reprinted in 44 AM. CRIM. L. REV. 715 (2007).

17. Mark Filip, Memorandum for Heads of Dep't Components and United States Att'ys: Principles of Federal Prosecution of Business Organizations (Aug. 28, 2008), https://www.justice.gov/sites/default/files/dag/legacy/2008/11/03/dag-memo-08282008.pdf.

18. U.S. Dep't of Justice, Justice Manual § 9-28.000 (2018), https://www.justice.gov/jm/jm-9-28000-principles-federal-prosecution-business-organizations.

19. United States Sentencing Guidelines Manual §8B2.1 provides in that an effective program requires that "an organization shall—

(1) exercise due diligence to prevent and detect criminal conduct; and

individual(s) within high-level personnel shall be assigned overall responsibility for the compliance and ethics program.[20]

Sentencing guidelines continue with:

> Specific individual(s) within the organization shall be delegated day-to-day operational responsibility for the compliance and ethics program. Individual(s) with operational responsibility shall report periodically to high-level personnel and, as appropriate, to the governing authority or an appropriate subgroup of the governing authority on the effectiveness of the compliance and ethics program. To carry out such operational responsibility, such individual(s) shall be given adequate resources, appropriate authority, and direct access to the governing authority or an appropriate subgroup of the governing authority.[21]

3.3.2. *New York*

In 2017, the New York Department of Financial Services ("NYDFS") issued its Cybersecurity Regulation, commonly known as 23 NYCRR Part 500, which has since been amended.[22] It also requires management involvement and contains various requirements to identify cyber risks for insurers. These include the overarching reasons the NYDFS created the regulation:

> This regulation requires each company to assess its specific risk profile and design a program that addresses its risks in a robust fashion. Senior management must take this issue seriously and be responsible for the organization's cybersecurity program and file an annual certification confirming compliance with these regulations. A regulated entity's cybersecurity program must ensure the safety and soundness of the institution and protect its customers.[23]

The regulation also requires that each entity "shall conduct a periodic risk assessment of the Covered Entity's Information Systems sufficient to inform the design of the cybersecurity program as required by this Part. Such Risk Assessment shall be updated as reasonably

---

(2) otherwise promote an organizational culture that encourages ethical conduct and a commitment to compliance with the law.

Such compliance and ethics program shall be reasonably designed, implemented, and enforced so that the program is generally effective in preventing and detecting criminal conduct. The failure to prevent or detect the instant offense does not necessarily mean that the program is not generally effective in preventing and detecting criminal conduct." U.S. Sentencing Guidelines Manual §8B2.1 (2024).

20. *Id.*
21. *Id.*
22. N.Y. Comp. Codes R. & Regs. tit. 23, § 500 (2017).
23. *Id.*

necessary to address changes to the Covered Entity's Information Systems, Nonpublic Information or business operations."[24]

Finally, the NYDFS regulation requires that the board or senior management certify compliance with the regulation.[25]

Like the overall risk management framework, the cybersecurity assessment and implementation process must be continuous.

3.3.3. *Delaware Courts and Board oversight*

Delaware courts, particularly the Delaware Court of Chancery, have clarified that boards of directors have a fiduciary duty to oversee cybersecurity risk as part of their broader duty of oversight and good faith.

This development stems primarily from the broader doctrine known as the *Caremark* Duty and how Delaware courts have applied it to modern risk areas, including cybersecurity. The *Caremark*[26] standard or duty requires boards to:

- Ensure that information and reporting systems are in place; and
- Monitor those systems to ensure compliance with law and material risk management.

For years, this doctrine was applied to compliance risks, but more recently, Delaware courts have expressly extended it to cybersecurity oversight. In a series of more recent cases, the courts have applied *Caremark* in the cyber context, strongly suggesting that boards should:

- Include cybersecurity risk in their enterprise risk management oversight;
- Receive regular updates on cybersecurity policies, incidents, and risk mitigation;
- Document board-level discussions and decisions regarding cybersecurity; and
- Ensure adequate resources and reporting structures to manage cyber risk.[27]

Failure to do so may expose directors to breach of fiduciary duty claims under *Caremark,* although the cases have not found such liability yet.[28]

24. *Id.*
25. *Id at* Appendix A.
26. *In re Caremark Int'l Inc. Derivative Litig.*, 698 A.2d 959 (Del. Ch. 1996).
27. *See* Firemen's Ret. Sys. of St. Louis ex rel. Marriott Int'l, Inc. v. Sorenson, C. A. No. 2019-0965-LWW (Del. Ch. Oct 5, 2021) ("Compliance risk oversight generally falls within the governance responsibilities of the board of directors. Key enterprise risks affecting a corporation's 'mission critical' components has been a focus of Delaware courts in assessing potential oversight liability, particularly where a board has allegedly failed to implement reporting systems or controls to monitor those risks."); *see also In re SolarWinds Corp. Derivative Litig.* (Del. Ch. Sept. 6, 2022). ("To use the shibboleth arising from Marchand, cybersecurity, for online service providers, is mission critical.")
28. Construction Industry Laborers Pension Fund v. Bingle, C.A. No. 2021-0940-SG (Del. Ch. Sept. 6, 2022), *aff'd* Order (Del. May 17, 2023). ("The pertinent question is not whether the Board was able to prevent a corporate trauma, here a third-party criminal attack. Instead, the question is whether the Board undertook its monitoring duties (to the extent applicable) *in bad faith*.")

4. Conclusion: A Scalable, Actionable Approach

Risk management is the cornerstone of any effective cybersecurity program. While the tools and complexity may differ depending on the size and nature of the organization, the principles remain the same: understand your risks; take reasonable steps to reduce them; monitor continuously; and prepare for the unexpected. More than ever, this is especially applicable in the realm of cybersecurity.

Appendix A: Common Risk Categories in Enterprise Risk Management

Risk Category	Description
Cybersecurity and Data Privacy Risk	Threats to information systems, including data breaches, ransomware, and privacy violations.
Regulatory and Compliance Risk	Exposure due to non-compliance with evolving laws, regulations, and standards.
Reputational Risk	Damage to public trust or brand image due to incidents or controversies.
Strategic Risk	Risks related to poor strategic decisions, market disruption, or failure to adapt.
Operational Risk	Failures in internal processes, people, systems, or external events like supply chain disruptions.
Financial Risk	Exposure to financial loss due to market volatility, credit risk, or liquidity constraints.
Geopolitical and Economic Risk	Impact from global conflicts, political instability, or economic downturns.
Climate and Environmental Risk	Physical and regulatory risks related to climate change and sustainability.
Technology & Innovation Risk	Risks of falling behind in technological adoption or facing disruption by competitors.
Human Capital Risk	Challenges in recruiting, retaining, and engaging key personnel; workforce issues.

Appendix B: Sample Responsibility Matrix (RACI Model*)

Task	IT Dept.	General Counsel	CISO / Risk Officer	Leadership	HR / Training
Identify cyber risks	R	C	A	I	I
Maintain asset inventory	R	I	A	I	
Develop cybersecurity policies	R	C	A	C	C
Approve risk tolerance	C	C	R	A	I
Implement technical controls	R	I	A	I	
Conduct training & awareness	C	I	C	I	A/R
Respond to incidents	R	C	A	I	I
Review risk reports	C	A	R	A	I

*Letter	Role	Meaning
R	Responsible	The person(s) who does the work to complete the task. There must be at least one "Responsible" person per task.
A	Accountable	The person who is ultimately answerable for the task's completion and decision-making. There should be only one "Accountable" person per task.
C	Consulted	The person(s) who must be consulted before a decision or action is taken. Typically, subject matter experts.
I	Informed	The person(s) who must be kept informed after a decision or action is taken. They do not have decision-making authority.

Appendix C: Sample Cybersecurity Risk Register

Risk ID	Description	Likelihood	Impact	Risk Rating	Mitigation Measures	Residual Risk	Owner	Next Review
R-001	Phishing email	Medium	High	High	Filtering, MFA, training	Medium	IT Dept.	Q3 2025
R-002	Ransomware	Low	Critical	High	Backups, EDR	Low	CISO	Q3 2025
R-003	Unpatched software	Medium	Medium	Medium	Auto-updates	Low	IT Dept.	Monthly
R-004	Insider threat	Low	High	Medium	Access control, monitoring	Medium	HR / Legal	Q3 2025
R-005	Lost device	Medium	High	High	Encryption, remote wipe	Low	Compliance	Q2 2025

Chapter 12

Get SMART on Data Protection by Creating a Culture of Security Awareness

Ruth Hill Bro and Jill D. Rhodes

1. Data Protection Training Basics and Core Principles

Most cybersecurity incidents are caused by human error.[1] Whether it is a technology that has not been patched or (more likely) an employee falling prey to a phishing email or vishing attempt, an organization's employees are both its greatest strength and greatest weakness. Organizations should acknowledge that while employees are the weakest link, small investments in training and education will strengthen their ability to protect data, which then will pay dividends when cyberattacks inevitably come.

Artificial intelligence, particularly generative AI (GenAI), is increasing the speed, scale, and sophistication of a wide range of cyberattacks on humans, such as phishing, vishing (voice phishing), quishing (QR code phishing), smishing (SMS/text message phishing), business email compromise, deepfakes, and assorted combinations. AI can copy the voice or likeness of a trusted company or firm contact and vastly increase the effectiveness of the attack.

Phishing normally occurs when a malicious e-mail is sent either directly to an individual (spear phishing) or to many in the hope that the target will click on a link within the e-mail, thereby infecting the individual's computer and potentially spreading a virus to the entire enterprise network or providing that user's access directly to the malicious actor. Ransomware, discussed throughout this Handbook, is often spread by phishing. But malicious actors are becoming ever more savvy. Business Email Compromise (BEC), where a malicious email is received from someone whose account has been taken over so it seems

1. For example, Verizon's *2025 Data Breach Investigation Report* [hereinafter Verizon DBIR] discusses the human factor at length, https://www.verizon.com/business/resources/reports/dbir/. Also, *Psychology of Human Error*, a 2020 joint study by Stanford University Professor Jeff Hancock and security firm Tessian (acquired by Proofpoint in 2023) found that 88% of data breach incidents are caused by employee mistakes. Tessian, "*Psychology of Human Error*" *Could Help Businesses Prevent Security Breaches*, CISOMAG (Sept. 12, 2020) [hereinafter CISOMAG], https://cisomag.com/psychology-of-human-error-could-help-businesses-prevent-security-breaches/. A 2022 follow-up study post-pandemic found that employee mistakes are still compromising security. Tessian, Psychology of Human Error 2022: Understand the Mistakes that Compromise Your Company's Security [hereinafter Psych. of Human Error 2022], https://f.hubspotusercontent20.net/hubfs/1670277/%5BCollateral%5D%20Tessian-Research-Reports/%5BTessian%20Research%5D%20Psychology%20of%20Human%20Error%202022.pdf.

legitimate, is becoming even more commonplace, increasing risk even further. Because the email received is from someone the employee knows, they are even more likely to click on it, open attachments, and provide sensitive information. Quishing, using the once-again popular QR codes to access accounts, is growing even more widespread.

Bad actors also use "technology-enhanced social engineering" through GenAI and other means, such as in the 2024 incident where an employee was duped into sending approximately $25 million via multiple transactions to criminals after verifying the instructions in a video call with senior managers (who were actually AI-created deepfakes). As is becoming more commonplace, no malicious code was delivered to compromise the company's systems or data, and significant loss occurred; all that was required was sophisticated AI-enhanced trickery.[2] As a company builds a culture of security, training must stay up to date with emerging threats, such as the evolving risks of GenAI.[3]

For example, while employees are increasingly using GenAI as a tool to do their work more cost-effectively and make life at home easier, they often do so without fully appreciating the risks. Lawyers who early on got into trouble with GenAI hallucinations did not take the time to understand how GenAI works, what risks might be involved, and their obligation to check the output. Some of the greatest GenAI risks, of particular importance to this Handbook, concern privacy and security.[4] These risks are in addition to the use of GenAI by malicious actors as a weapon against organizations.

Other factors also come into play. With remote and hybrid work now commonplace, the line between work and home has blurred, expanding potential attack surfaces and often decreasing employees' cybersecurity vigilance when they are in more comfortable surroundings. Moreover, the phenomenon some call "the great detachment"[5] can affect cybersecurity vigilance. Employees who feel increasing burnout, lack of connection, and emotional and mental disengagement from their work and jobs might be less alert to signs of social engineering and other anomalies.

---

2. David Elliott, *"This happens more frequently than people realize': Arup chief on the lessons learned from a $25m deepfake crime*, WORLD ECON. F. (Feb. 4, 2025), https://www.weforum.org/stories/2025/02/deepfake-ai-cybercrime-arup.

3. Such AI-focused training should include procedures for verifying the identity of the person making contact via phone/voice, text, or video (such as evaluating differences in tone or word choice); ways to examine email addresses, QR codes, phone numbers, and other communication methods for variations from what is expected; tips on how to spot subtle flaws in voice or likeness (such as audio lags, distorted images, unrealistic facial or body features, unusual accessories, and unnatural movements); additional steps to take independent of the initial communication to confirm authenticity (for example, call the CFO or HR head using phone numbers the employee already has), particularly when the transaction is large or concerns sensitive data.

4. *See* Jane Livesey, *Data in the GenAI Era: Reclaiming Our Digital Selves*, WORLD ECON. F. (Jan. 13, 2025), https://www.weforum.org/stories/2025/01/new-enlightenment-era-of-generative-ai-genai/. "We found that data privacy and security are two key factors significantly inhibiting GenAI adoption.... We also risk catastrophic privacy breaches if we don't understand how our data can be used for or against us. This includes not just the words we speak, the text we type and the photos we take, but even participating in a meeting or showing our face in public." *Id.*

5. Ben Wigert & Corey Tatel, *The Great Detachment: Why Employees Feel Stuck*, GALLUP WORKPLACE (Dec. 3, 2024), https://www.gallup.com/workplace/653711/great-detachment-why-employees-feel-stuck.aspx.

As a result, it is imperative for all employees that cybersecurity risk and threat prevention education and training occur on a continuous basis. Training, likewise, should be reviewed and updated to ensure that it reflects the latest threats.

Cybersecurity training also is important for any third party that accesses a company's system or data. Thirty percent of breaches now involve third parties, double the percentage of prior years.[6]

Anyone who has access to the organization's sensitive information can become a conduit for data loss and disaster:

- The senior partner who unleashes ransomware by clicking on a link that looks like it came from a colleague or board member.
- The remote worker who conducts business on unsecured personal devices (laptop, tablet, smartphone) with public or unsecured home Wi-Fi, enabling hackers to steal confidential data and capture login credentials.
- The employee, eager to showcase his efficiency, inadvertently discloses his employer's trade secrets or clients' confidential information by pasting them into GenAI prompts without realizing where the information in those prompts could end up.
- The IT professional who leaves networks vulnerable by failing to protect against known threats on an ongoing basis, or who doesn't adhere to protocols for immediately terminating system access for disgruntled or downsized employees on their last day of employment.
- The HR employee who takes sensitive employee records home or leaves them in electronic files with inadequate access restrictions.
- The harried executive assistant who panics and immediately complies when receiving an urgent voice message from her boss (a deepfake that leveraged public voice samples) asking her to "remind" him of his user ID and passwords.
- The ever-mobile attorney who compromises the firm's client relationships by losing a laptop, phone, or unencrypted SD Card or flash drive, which is left on an airplane, in a rideshare or rental car, or in a coffee shop or restaurant.
- The technology-loving employee who overshares on social media or fails to realize that digital assistants and smart home technology create new means of eavesdropping that can sabotage the organization's confidential data.
- The busy new college graduate in the marketing department who clicks on a phishing email.[7]
- The third-party vendor that stores the company's data without appropriate security controls.

---

6. *See* Verizon DBIR, *supra* note 1.

7. One 2022 survey found that younger employees (age 18–24) are five times more likely to click on phishing emails than older employees, and marketing employees are two times more likely than finance employees and four times more likely than operations employees to fall for phishing. Finance and operations employees typically think more about security because they work in highly regulated areas with strict data protection requirements. *See* Psych. of Human Error 2022, *supra* note 1, at 11–12.

Current and emerging laws at the state and federal levels require that businesses working with personal and sensitive data must protect that data.[8] Moreover, an organization's binding commitments to protect data can lurk in contracts, on websites, and elsewhere. Even loss of an organization's data that is not subject to a legal obligation, such as proprietary data, could still wreak havoc, including loss of reputation, clients, and potential clients.

Law firms and other businesses must develop a strategy for protecting all of their data. When assessing how to do so, organizations often mistakenly rely on technology as the solution. In fact, as discussed throughout this Handbook, four factors are key to implementing a proper information security and data protection program in any setting:

- Establishing the appropriate *governance* for the data, such as policies and the oversight of an executive level committee tasked with reducing data protection risk;
- Ensuring that the *people* working with the data know how best to protect it;
- Assessing data protection and usage *processes*; and
- Employing appropriate *technology* to protect the network.

Each of these factors contributes to a broader level of maturity for an organization while also reducing its risk. This chapter focuses on the *people* aspect of that equation, but other factors (e.g., governance and processes) also come into play.[9] Most data missteps in law firms and other businesses are directly linked to actions taken by an employee or contractor, whether intentional or unintentional. The easiest way to address this risk is to educate employees and others on an ongoing basis about the risks and their role in protecting personal and sensitive data, including serving as an early alert system when something does go wrong. (Providing rewards to incentivize those early-warning alerts works better than imposing penalties for not disclosing problems.)

Education and training can be provided by many components of the organization, whether human resources (HR), the chief privacy officer (CPO), the chief information security officer (CISO), the general counsel (GC), or others. Regardless of which groups do the training (or choose the training, where it involves use of outside resources), it is critical that they work together to produce a shared vision and message that is then disseminated across the organization.

---

8. *See* Handbook, Chapter 7, *Legal Obligations to Provide Data Security.*

9. Indeed, the people part of the equation, and the need for training and awareness-raising, is but one part of reducing cybersecurity risk. And even very aware people can fall victim to phishing attacks, because "we can't make people immune to social engineering." Bruce Schneier, *Why Take9 Won't Improve Cybersecurity*, Schneier on Sec. (May 30, 2025, 7:05 AM), https://www.schneier.com/blog/archives/2025/05/why-take9-wont-improve-cybersecurity.html. *See also* Take9, https://pausetake9.org/ (last visited Jun. 16, 2025) (offering a cybersecurity awareness campaign to get people to take 9 seconds before clicking on a link, etc.).

1.1. Training Is Not a One-Time Action—It's a Cultural Norm

All organizations, including law firms, increasingly recognize that data underpins virtually everything that they do and—like other valuable business assets—must be protected. The easiest way to get this point across is to focus on creating a culture of security around data. To do this, organizations must adopt a comprehensive strategy that makes data protection a part of the culture and the job of every individual working for the business (partners, associates, paralegals, interns, law students, IT, HR, executives, administrators, administrative assistants, and other staff).[10] Such an approach is designed to:

- Minimize the risk due to employee missteps that can affect the bottom line, including inability to access or use data and conduct business; costly litigation; time and resources consumed in responding to government, press, or attorney disciplinary commission inquiries or investigations; adverse media coverage; damage to client or customer relationships; and so on; and
- Help businesses achieve a competitive advantage, enhance their profile and image, and enrich their relationship with clients and customers.

Yet making data protection a part of the organization's culture is easier said than done.

- Properly addressing data protection issues can require a comprehensive understanding of rapidly changing applicable law in all U.S. states and territories, at the federal level, and globally (where client or customer data might originate, where third parties might be providing U.S.-based businesses with 24/7 services, etc.). Many laws (particularly for government entities and regulated industries) and lawyers' professional rules of responsibility expressly or by implication require appropriate data protection training for employees and sometimes contractors as well.[11] And failure can be costly. For example, a federal court held that an employee who was tricked into sharing personal information of employees in response to a phishing email could be committing an intentional disclosure under the North Carolina Identity Theft Protection Act and

10. This trend toward a culture of security is in keeping with the "Privacy by Design" (PbD) and "Security by Design" (SbD) movements that continue to transform the way businesses protect data in an information-driven age. *See, e.g.*, *Privacy by Design: The 7 Foundational Principles, Implementation and Mapping of Fair Information Practices* (undated), https://privacy.ucsc.edu/resources/privacy-by-design---foundational-principles.pdf (written by Dr. Cavoukian during her tenure as Information & Privacy Commissioner, Ontario, Canada); FED. TRADE COMM'N, START WITH SECURITY: A GUIDE FOR BUSINESS, LESSONS LEARNED FROM FTC CASES, (Aug. 2023), https://www.ftc.gov/tips-advice/business-center/guidance/start-security-guide-business (providing insights and guidance on SbD gleaned from over 80 FTC data security settlements).

11. *See* HANDBOOK, Chapters 7, *Legal Obligations to Provide Data Security*, and 10, *Lawyers' Professional Responsibility to Provide Data Security*, for further discussion about the types of legal and professional responsibility requirements (including education and training) placed on lawyers and law firms.

thereby subject the employer to treble damages. The court pointed to unreasonably deficient cybersecurity training despite known risks.[12]

- Command of the law is not enough. Businesses often are tried in the court of public opinion (including on social media sites using algorithms that amplify negative content) or are challenged by third-party watchdog groups, regardless of the current legality of the entity's practices.
- Likewise, technological innovation is occurring at a startling and accelerating pace. The internet, mobile devices, artificial intelligence (including GenAI), and ever-more-sophisticated computer technology (all connected to each other and always on) make it easy to collect, analyze, combine, reproduce, and disseminate data. Technology not only enhances efficiency and cost-effectiveness but also escalates the risk of making catastrophic mistakes at the speed of light. Yet employees often do not really understand the downsides of technology, such as the latest "smart" technology at work or home (TVs, appliances, toys or gadgets, automated fish tanks, security cameras, digital assistants, voice-controlled smart home hubs, etc.) that could be invisibly eavesdropping on confidential discussions using connected microphones, spying via built-in cameras, or providing a new attack vector for accessing the organization's digital assets.

It is easy to push responsibility for protecting data onto individuals located in the information security office, the privacy office, HR, or IT. It is much more difficult to learn to integrate security and to think about data protection for all employees, all the time. While some factors (such as detailed technical issues and rapidly changing applicable laws and regulations) might be overwhelming for all employees to understand, basic principles of information security can be embedded in everything an employee does.

1. **Security is everyone's responsibility**
   While some of the governance, process, and technology aligned with protecting data may be led and managed by an information security team or IT as a whole, everyone in the organization must be aware of the basics about how to protect information. In the end, it's not the IT or information security team that is accessing critical and sensitive data on a daily basis, it's the business-facing facets of the firm or business.

12. *See* Curry v. Schletter Inc., No. 1:17-cv-0001-MR-DLH, 2018 U.S. Dist. LEXIS 49442 at *5, 2018 WL 1472485 at *2 (W.D.N.C. Mar. 26, 2018). The court in *Curry* noted that "the Defendant failed to adequately train its employees on even the most basic of cybersecurity protocols, including: (a) how to detect phishing and spoofing emails and other scams including providing employees examples of these scams and guidance on how to verify if emails are legitimate; (b) effective password management and encryption protocols for internal and external emails; (c) avoidance of responding to emails that are suspicious or from unknown sources; (d) locking, encrypting and limiting access to computers and files containing sensitive information; (e) implementing guidelines for maintaining and communicating sensitive data; and (f) protecting sensitive employee information, including personal and financial information, by implementing protocols on how to request and respond to requests for ... the transfer of such information and how to securely send such information through a secure file transfer system to only known recipients."

Education and training can help employees understand the risk, learn not to click on links in suspicious emails or text messages, and report anything that doesn't seem right. Everyone in the organization needs to become the eyes and ears of the organization.

2. **No one is immune from the threat—everyone is at risk of becoming a victim**
Anyone—from the organization's most senior officer to the lowest-level employee—can become a victim of phishing or vishing attacks. It could be a receptionist, junior associate, senior partner, paralegal, or law clerk. Bad actors are looking for weak links to exploit to enter the firm's network. At times, they will target a senior attorney; at others, they will go after a paralegal with access to multiple cases for multiple clients, or perhaps someone in IT with comprehensive administrative access to the firm's IT systems. Education efforts should occur at all levels and must assume that everyone is at risk of falling victim.
3. **Education shouldn't be limited to what employees are doing in the office**
The best way to change the way that employees within the organization think about securing data is to move their thinking from their work environment to all facets of their life. Taking a broad-based approach by educating about factors that also include protecting their own personal data (and that of family members and friends) fosters greater consideration for protecting data in the office.
4. **Additional training should be provided for employees who are working from home**
Building on the expanded educational focus, organizations should provide more specific work-from-home training, as this now common working environment raises additional risks. New policies might be needed that limit the type of data an employee may access from home, or whether the employee can print from home. Having employees at home provides a prime opportunity to educate them about the many areas where risks may occur and to encourage them to become more vigilant in their understanding and daily practices regarding protection of the organization's data.

Unfortunately, business leaders often breathe a sigh of relief once the state-of-the-art security system is installed and comprehensive data protection policies and procedures have been established. Notwithstanding adoption of the latest technology and sound data protection principles, businesses are only as strong as their weakest link, which is generally human. Countless studies, audit trails, and surveys over the years[13] have repeatedly confirmed that the biggest data protection threats come from within one's own organization. Most missteps are unintentional. Many mistakes can be avoided and risks can be minimized with appropriate training and awareness-raising. Yet this is often an overlooked component of data protection initiatives—the missing link when it comes to security. SMART

13. *See* Verizon DBIR, *supra* note 1. Verizon has published Data Breach Investigation Reports since at least 2008. Its archive is available at https://www.verizon.com/business/resources/reports/dbir/#top-takeaways (last visited Jun. 17, 2025).

training, outlined below, includes key steps to help build a culture of security across an organization's employee base.

1.2. What Does SMART Training Look Like?

What does training actually mean, and what are businesses doing to address the human factor in data protection? Over the years, numerous types of cybersecurity training have emerged through different organizations. While gamification of cyber awareness has become more popular, a consistent methodology for training remains. In short, when conducting training, businesses should be SMART:[14]

Start training on hiring.
Measure what you do.
Always train.
Raise awareness and provide updates continually.
Tailor training by role and need.

In considering these SMART training steps and what they mean for one's business, keep in mind that the particular data protection training that is right for one entity is not necessarily right for another, even if both are in the same industry or are law firms of similar size. Businesses differ in many ways—for example, the degree of centralization, their cultures, the jurisdictions in which they operate, their objectives, their resources and budget, their existing data protection infrastructure, their buy-in from senior management, and so on. That said, even the smallest organizations have become victims of malware attacks and ransomware. As a result, it is important to train no matter the size of the organization. Once an organization has the SMART methodology in place, any new technology or risk, such as AI use, can be easily integrated into it.

1. S—Start Training on Hiring

Given the fundamental role of data in everything a business does, training on how to protect that data should start on day one. Data protection training should be provided to all new employees and, increasingly, to contractors as well. In cases where it is not feasible to do training for all employees initially (due to bandwidth, budget, or other constraints), businesses might choose to focus training on selected employees (e.g., HR personnel and those in key business roles or units). At a minimum, new employees should receive and

14. The concept of SMART training was distilled in March 2011 by Ruth Hill Bro (co-author of this chapter) from her interviews since 2005 with a wide range of CPOs drawn from various industries, locations, and corporate cultures for her recurring column, *CPO Corner: Interviews with Leading Chief Privacy Officers*. She used 17 questions designed to identify trends and best practices and to capture key benchmarking and practical implementation information regarding data protection issues. On the question of training, a consistent pattern of answers emerged: businesses need to be SMART, a concept as true today as it was two decades ago.

review relevant policies and procedures, which themselves are a component of training and awareness-raising.

In the employee context, training is provided as a part of employee orientation and can take different forms, using a variety of media:

- An initial in-person, instructor-led session (large group, small group, or one-on-one, as appropriate), which can encourage interaction (though such in-person sessions might not always be scalable or practical for some organizations);
- Live or recorded instructor-led video conferences; and
- An online subscription or an intranet- or other computer-based training module or series of modules (including podcasts).

Coverage can include a wide range of topics:

- High-level overviews applicable to all employees and contractors;
- Instruction on relevant data protection laws and regulations (and professional rules of responsibility, where applicable), internal policies and procedures (regarding mobile technology, social media, GenAI, etc.), fundamentals of the relevant technology, and industry best practices;
- Guidelines for protecting confidentiality and security of data (particularly important for GenAI);
- Tips regarding hidden data protection hazards when working away from the office, whether at home or elsewhere;
- Updates on practicing daily information security hygiene, such as monitoring for phishing emails, using VPN to log into a network, and reporting something that doesn't appear to be legitimate; and
- Steps to take when addressing a suspected data breach or reporting a security misstep.

The data protection training can be coordinated with other training, especially other privacy training, and should be reviewed to avoid contradictions and conflicts in approach and message. Consideration should be given to whether the time, format (text, visuals, auditory), and content are suitable across different parts of the organization. Issues of translation, local law, contract obligations, and local customs can come into play here as well.

2. M—Measure What You Do

Measurement and assessment constitute a core component of many of these initial training sessions as well as in follow-up training. Administering tests (e.g., a graded online quiz) can help to confirm understanding and gauge the overall effectiveness of the training; it also can help to ensure that the work has actually been done. Likewise, providing a quiz with a fun fact scenario at the end of a group training session, where employees jot down what issues they see and then share with the group, can help employees realize what good issue-spotters they've become. In addition, other types of measurement, such as the number of employees who have clicked on a "fake" phishing message or the number of times phishing has been prevented due to employee action, may be used. Broader measurements—such as comparisons of incidents and types of missteps before and after training—can help businesses to make training more effective while demonstrating return on investment (which can be important in making the case for budget).

A study at the University of California San Diego Health found that training without engagement is not sufficient. In that study, they found little difference between those employees trained and those not trained when more specific metrics, such as testing and engagement throughout the training, were not present.[15]

3. A—Always Train

While organizations sometimes focus on new-hire or annual training, in line with applicable law, rules, or policies, continuous training and education will advance the shift to a culture of security and data protection. More formalized training, such as certification or continuing legal education (for lawyers) or professional responsibility credit, could be provided on an annual basis to build the culture, but a broader training campaign might be needed. Training of some type should occur as frequently as possible, perhaps monthly, or weekly, depending upon the type of instruction. Training can occur through blog posts, newsletters, spotlights on the organization's internal website, or through phishing campaigns. The more that employees can see information about risks, threats, and response, the more quickly they can integrate the awareness into their daily practices.

4. R—Raise Awareness and Provide Updates Continually

Similar to "A" above, it is impossible to integrate appropriate data security practices into a culture by using just introductory training on hiring and mandatory annual training. Building a training campaign that raises awareness about risks on a daily basis and addresses risks both within the office and at home will help change the mindset of employees. As demonstrated in examples throughout this Handbook, incidents occur regularly; one need only open morning news highlights online to see any number of incidents affecting businesses globally. The more that an organization can discuss and highlight an employee's role in preventing and detecting data security incidents, the more effective the training becomes. That training and awareness-raising cannot be static, given continually emerging technology developments and threats. We have always had change, but what is unprecedented is the velocity of that change, especially in the GenAI era.

---

15. Grant Ho et al., *Understanding the Efficacy of Phishing Training in Practice*, 2025 IEEE SYMPOSIUM ON SEC. & PRIVACY 37 (2025), https://doi.ieeecomputersociety.org/10.1109/SP61157.2025.00076; *see also* Lisa Ward, *How Effective Is Corporate Cybersecurity Training? Not Very, It Seems*, WALL ST. J. (Sept. 4, 2025), https://www.wsj.com/tech/cybersecurity/cybersecurity-training-study-f290518d?st=ArRHZq.

5. T—Tailor Training by Role and Need

Going beyond high-level, one-size-fits-all training allows for training to be tailored to focus on specific roles and needs of individuals, different generational challenges, and specific requirements for contractors and third parties. Although GenAI can act as a sword and a problem when it comes to cybersecurity, it also can function as a shield and be a part of the solution. For example, an AI chatbot could customize the training module and phishing simulations for each user, based on that user's strengths and weaknesses; the chatbot could also identify what learning methodology—in-person or virtual, auditory or text or visual, interactive or more passive (watching a video, reading), and so on—works best and then present the training in that way.[16]

Tailoring of data protection training can take various forms, depending on the organization:

- Start with a Data Protection 101 online course that is available on demand. Successfully completing it results in a certificate. The basic module can then be supplemented by training and awareness-raising specific to a role, business unit, geographic location, technology tools, and the like.
- Determine who should receive more direct training from specialized leaders such as the CPO, CISO, CIO or IT director, legal counsel, or other qualified trainers. It can be helpful for such trainers to meet with selected employees to learn about their data practices and then tailor training efforts accordingly. For example, some CPOs or CISOs meet regularly with the company's engineering, product design, and sales teams to raise important issues in planning meetings and gain insights to develop appropriate training.
- Build a training culture that reaches beyond business into other facets of an employee's life. Training about keeping kids safe online, using GenAI at home, or protecting household technology from hacking creates a mindset where employees continuously think about how best to protect data.
- Hire specialists, internally or externally, to refine and enhance training efforts.
- Leverage external expertise and training companies. In recent years, companies have emerged whose sole purpose is to train an organization's employees about data protection and cybersecurity risks. Many of these offer simulated phishing exercises for firms and businesses. In addition, there are many resources for small firms or solo practitioners, such as online training modules, training publications, relevant CLE courses and conferences, resources offered by bar associations (including the American Bar Association, its Cybersecurity Legal Task Force,[17] and the ABA's Sections, Divisions,

---

16. Sharon Shea & Ashwin Krishnan, *How AI Is Making Phishing Attacks More Dangerous*, TechTarget (Oct. 22, 2024), https://www.techtarget.com/searchsecurity/tip/Generative-AI-is-making-phishing-attacks-more-dangerous.

17. The Cybersecurity Legal Task Force's resources are published at https://www.americanbar.org/groups/cybersecurity/ (last visited Jun. 17, 2025).

and Forums; state and local bar associations; specialty bar associations; government entities; etc.), and the like. Some of these resources are specifically geared to small organizations.[18]

- As noted above, training for some roles (e.g., lawyers and accountants) may be accompanied by certification or CLE or professional responsibility credit.

Businesses that use SMART training can provide the missing link that will help make data protection a part of the culture and turn their employees into one of their strongest links when it comes to an organization's invaluable data. Employees are the most critical asset of any organization, but they also pose the greatest risk. Training is at the core of mitigating this risk.

2. SMART Training in Action

Implementing a SMART training program does not have to be complicated or require significant budget. The program pays for itself by reducing the risk of data loss and increasing awareness about data protection.

2.1. Understanding the Basics of Employees: Role, Generational, and Other Differences

First, any training program should assess and understand the recipients of the training. As mentioned above, the role of the employee in the organization will make a difference in the type of training received. An associate working with e-discovery matters and technology every day will have different considerations than a mail clerk or even other associates and partners in the firm.

In addition, generational differences can play a role in how training should be developed, the type of training and communication that a person prefers to receive, how best to provide the training, and what types of incentives are offered. Many have examined how various generations might differ in their approach to learning[19] (for example, each

18. *See, e.g.*, Fed. Trade Comm'n, Cybersecurity for Small Business: Protect Your Small Business, https://www.ftc.gov/business-guidance/small-businesses/cybersecurity (last visited Jun. 17, 2025); Am. Bar Ass'n, Cybersecurity Legal Task Force, Cybersecurity Resources for Small Law Firms, https://www.americanbar.org/groups/cybersecurity/small-solo-resources/ (last visited Jun. 17, 2025). The FTC resource site offers modules in various formats (including videos, quizzes, and employer guides) on a range of cybersecurity topics, including Cybersecurity Basics, Ransomware, Phishing, Business Email Imposters, Secure Remote Access, Physical Security, Tech Support Scams, and Vendor Security. The FTC developed the resource website in partnership with the National Institute of Standards and Technology (NIST), U.S. Small Business Administration (SBA), and Department of Homeland Security (DHS). https://www.ftc.gov/business-guidance/small-businesses/cybersecurity.

19. *See, e.g.*, Cam Marston, Generational Insights: Practical Solutions for Understanding and Engaging a Generationally Disconnected Workforce (2010); Rebecca Knight, *Managing People from 5 Generations*, Harv. Bus. Rev. (Sept. 25, 2014) (citing Peter Cappelli, professor of management at the Wharton School and coauthor of *Managing the Older Worker: How to Prepare for the New Organizational Order* (2010), among other experts).

generation grew up with vastly different technology), but it is also important not to assume that all Baby Boomers or Gen X'ers are the same. A 2020 report found that younger workers were five times more likely to admit to making cybersecurity errors than were workers over the age of 51.[20] The report noted some factors that made older employees less likely to click on a phishing link, for example, but also cited other characteristics that cut the other way; older employees were less likely to recognize phishing or other cyber missteps in the first place and were less likely to report mistakes because of concerns about their respected position in the workplace.

Other factors can play a role in employee cybersecurity missteps and, thus, influence training. Stress, fatigue, distractions (which can occur more frequently in a remote work setting), pressure to work quickly or multitask, and so on can all increase the likelihood of mistakes.[21] Workplace programs aimed at stress management, while not technically cybersecurity training, might help to decrease the likelihood of data protection missteps.

When contemplating a training program, organizations should consider how best to approach each generation and develop a program that supports them all. One example would be building a reverse mentoring program, in which the more experienced attorneys and staff mentor the more junior staff about law firm practices, while the more junior staff members mentor their more senior colleagues about topics such as technology advancements (including GenAI), leveraging social media, and using gaming as a tactic for training.

As part of this multi-generational environment, it is important to respect the values of each generation.[22] At a speaking engagement many years ago about cybersecurity, one lawyer asked why law firms just don't prevent cellphone and mobile device usage altogether as a solution for potential data loss and cyber threats.[23] Some have said similar things about using GenAI. While such a "don't allow it to be used" solution can be appropriate in highly secure and classified environments, it is impractical in a day-to-day business and legal environment (especially in the GenAI era) and negates the experience and values of much of the current workforce.

To address generational gaps, businesses and law firms can involve all generations in the development of training programs. This will create opportunities for each generation to provide input on what is important to them in both the content and the delivery of the training.

---

20. *See* CISOMAG, *supra* note 1.

21. *See* Psych. of Human Error 2022, *supra* note 1.

22. *See* Emma Waldman, *How to Manage a Multi-Generational Team*, Harv. Bus. Rev. (Aug. 31, 2021), https://hbr.org/2021/08/how-to-manage-a-multi-generational-team.

23. ABA Standing Committee on Law and National Security Annual Meeting 2018.

2.2. Building an Effective and Diverse Program

Leveraging the **SMART** principles described above, any organization can quickly and easily build an ongoing training and education campaign that can then be adapted to whatever is the latest trend, technology, or threat.

First, make the campaign fun, creative, and easy to remember. While the message of data protection is serious, the delivery need not be. People of all generations tend to learn more through consistent messaging that has a direct impact on their lives. Those working on the data protection training should develop easy, fun, and catchy slogans that employees will remember.

One example is the SAFE program,[24] an information security awareness program that was developed for one company as a way to help employees remember how best to protect and secure sensitive information:

Secure the organization's data: Where are you storing client data? How are you deleting it?
Asset protection: Do you know where your laptop, tablet, and phone are?
Friend or Foe: Who is sending you an e-mail? Is it something you expected or is it phishing?
Encrypt: Are you encrypting sensitive e-mails before sending them out?

A program such as SAFE can be used throughout the year to educate staff; different themes within each of the four SAFE categories above can be featured.

Second, identify something, such as a mascot, that represents the organization and symbolizes data protection to help lighten the delivery of a serious message. For example, an organization that provides infusion services to patients uses a mascot named "The Infuser." The Infuser's motto is "Infusing Security into Everything We Do." Every time employees see this mascot and message, they are reminded about protecting sensitive information. It is a fun, easy, and quick cue that costs the organization very little to develop and implement.

Third, ensure that training is continuous, and use various methods to implement it. In addition to mandatory training at specific times (when employees join the organization and subsequent annual training), continuous education is key to any successful cultural transformation. At the same time, people can become numb to messaging that seems repetitive. "Don't click on the phishing email" is one reminder that needs to be frequently conveyed (as it is one of the top ways for cyberattacks to enter a network),[25] but this message can easily start to sound like background noise if it is not updated and kept "fresh." One law firm has taken a "Phish of the Day" approach to such training; the security department circulates to all personnel an email in a recognizable format, showing a redacted phishing email that an employee has just shared and highlighting red flags in that email (e.g., unexpected, unknown sender, poor or unusual grammar, link destination unknown, etc.).

24. The proprietary SAFE program was developed in 2016 by Jill D. Rhodes (co-author of this chapter).
25. *See* Verizon DBIR, *supra* note 1.

The following are some other ideas to keep the momentum going:

- Leverage current newsletters, and place brief articles within them that discuss data protection.
- Create or subscribe to short videos with data protection messages; consider how popular short videos are on social media.
- Conduct email campaigns (monthly or as needed) with data protection guidelines, relevant media coverage, and so on to remind everyone (or otherwise make them aware) of relevant policies and practices.
- Offer periodic "Data Protection Awareness Weeks" or "Security Awareness Drives" with guest speakers and other special events.
- Strategically position wall posters (or their digital equivalent) and other communications that promote data protection.
- Publish monthly articles on the company and line-of-business intranet homepages to raise data protection awareness.
- Send periodic emails to highlight ongoing opportunities for online training and in-person sessions conducted by members of the data protection team, other in-house trainers, or outside speakers.
- For lawyers, provide periodic continuing legal education (CLE) sessions focused on data protection, including sessions that explore the topic from the perspective of rules of professional responsibility and ethics rules (thereby not only raising awareness but also helping attorneys to meet their CLE requirements).
- Develop white papers and other material related to relevant data protection topics, aiming for greater frequency and detail over time.
- Remind employees that data protection training is an important part of their job by including it as a factor in their annual performance evaluation. Celebrate successes and reward those who meet the objectives (and, if needed, identify opportunities for growth and improvement).
- Participate in activities such as National Cybersecurity Awareness Month (October) with month-long training, games, competitions, etc.

Fourth, involve employees directly. Hold data protection competitions between groups (e.g., divisions, offices, or floors in a building) with the goal of identifying an employee or group activity that protected the organization's information in a noteworthy way or developed a creative way to address security awareness. Recognize the individual or group winners, name them in the monthly newsletter or blog, and provide a pizza lunch for the winner—the more recognition, the better.

Fifth, build an ambassador (liaison) or similar program across the organization. Whether it is by office, region, subject matter expertise, or business unit, identify a way to have a data protection representative in each. Although senior leadership is important, the representative should be a mid-level employee who has influence with peers, subordinates, and leadership. Meet with the data protection ambassadors regularly to discuss data protection issues and ensure that they are a part of the solution by having them serve as the leaders who will train and educate the employees with whom they work on a regular basis. Maintain enthusiasm and bring new perspectives to the program by swapping out ambassadors every two years or so.

Finally, as mentioned previously, educate employees about how to protect data at home as well as in the workplace. Data protection does not start when people log into the network or end when they shut down for the evening, particularly in today's world where the lines between home and work have blurred. Everyone's family members and friends are constantly touching sensitive or personal digital data. Whether it is through social media or new mobile apps, data is being collected. By educating employees to protect data in all facets of their lives, they will approach data protection more holistically in their daily work life.

All of these methods are easy, inexpensive, fun, and effective ways to communicate with and educate employees about enhancing data protection in the organization.

2.3. Measuring Success

As noted earlier, it is critical to find ways to measure the success of these campaigns (the "M" in "SMART" training). One of the easiest ways to measure the success of a campaign is to test employees by phishing them directly with fake emails to track who clicks. New ways to measure the success of campaigns will need to evolve as the threats evolve. Tracking the response and the notifications provided by employees about the incidents is one way to measure the effectiveness of training programs.

In addition, as part of a SAFE campaign (the Friend or Foe component), organizations can implement their own company-wide phishing campaign, sending fake "malicious" e-mails to employees just as someone trying to harm the organization would do. When an employee clicks on the e-mail, instead of infecting the system, the employee receives an educational message about the phishing e-mail and the fact that had it been real, harm could have come to the organization. This type of campaign measures the click rate and, when conducted regularly, can be used to monitor those who are clicking regularly. As a result, specific training can be developed for those individuals or groups. Phishing programs provide a quantitative measurement related to security awareness. Ensure that these programs don't appear as "gotchas" for the organization, but rather as learning moments to educate team members.

Reporting numbers also can provide both quantitative and qualitative opportunities for measuring success. As more training and education occurs, the number of incidents reported to appropriate leadership also will increase. Increased reporting could be anything from the reporting of a specific data breach or loss incident to reporting of phishing e-mails. As these incidents are tracked, greater information becomes available about employee knowledge and understanding of data protection.

In the end, a data breach or loss most likely will occur as a result of something an employee did or did not do. An important way to prevent such missteps is to educate the people in the organization about how they can better protect the information around them.

3. Ten Key Points

1. Recognize that the biggest risks to data come from the people working for the organization and that training and raising awareness are essential to reducing those risks.
2. Build a corporate culture that focuses on data protection and make it the job of every individual.
3. Be **SMART** in training: Start training on hiring. Measure what you do. Always train. Raise awareness and provide updates continually. Tailor training by role and need.
4. Recognize that one size doesn't fit all; training should fit an organization's own needs.
5. Build a program that represents the organization's employees not only from a role perspective but also reflecting other considerations (e.g., generational).
6. Make any training campaign fun and interesting, let the employees lead it through ambassador (liaison) programs and in other ways, and keep message delivery mechanisms light and easy to understand for all who work for the organization.
7. Train employees on how to protect information in all facets of their lives, not just in the workplace. By helping them protect their family and friends at home (where they might also be working), they will further integrate these practices at work.
8. Reward! Reward! Reward! Use competitions with prizes to incentivize employees to become more aware and supportive of data protection across the organization.
9. Measure success through phishing programs and tracking of incident reporting and responses.
10. Know that training and awareness-raising is a never-ending journey (not a destination) that can require changes in direction in response to changes in the law, technology, media coverage, and one's own experiences and new business initiatives. Adapt accordingly.

Chapter 13

Achieving Preparedness through Standards and Planning and Best Practices for Incident Response

John DiMaria and Claudia Rast

Introduction

The incident response landscape continues its dynamic response to increasing security measures. Threat actors have organized into global crime gangs—often with dotted-line connections to a short list of nation-states. Malware is packaged in kits for easy download on the Dark Web,[1] and the organized crime syndicates on the Dark Web maintain "help desks" to facilitate ransom payments from their victims. From a "relative" low of $4 billion in reported losses in 2020 to over $16 billion in 2024, there seems to be no stopping the rise or reach of cybercrime.[2] By the first half of 2024 alone, ransomware victims paid nearly $460 million.[3] In the previous edition of this Handbook, we highlighted four cybersecurity incidents that accelerated government action and response: (1) SolarWinds, (2) the Hafnium exploit of on-premises Microsoft Exchange servers,[4] (3) the Colonial Pipeline Ransomware attack, and (4) the attack on JSB SA, the world's largest meat processing

1. As defined by Wikipedia, "[t]he dark web is the World Wide Web content that exists on *darknets* (overlay networks) that use the Internet, but require specific software, configurations, or authorization to access. Through the dark web, private computer networks can communicate and conduct business anonymously without divulging identifying information, such as a user's location." *Dark Web*, Wikipedia, https://en.wikipedia.org/wiki/Dark_web (last visited Sept. 13, 2025).

2. These statistics are from *reported* losses via the FBI's Internet Crime Complaint Center ("IC3"). FBI, Internet Crime Report 2024, 7, https://ic3.gov/AnnualReport/Reports/2024_IC3Report.pdf.

3. Chris Pierson, *Ransomware Payments Surge to Record Highs in 2024: A Call for Vigilance*, BlackCloak https://blackcloak.io/ransomware-payments-surge-to-record-highs-in-2024-a-call-for-vigilance/ (last visited Sept. 13, 2025).

4. Affidavit in Support of an Application under Rule 41(b)(6)(B) for a Search Warrant, *In re* Search of Certain Microsoft Exchange Servers Infected with Web Shells, Case No. 4:21mj755 (S.D. Tx. Apr. 9, 2021) (filed under seal). In support of the government's "Application for Warrant to Search Certain Microsoft Exchange Servers Infected with Web Shells," the affiant described the plight of many small companies when stating that "most of these victims [of the Hafnium exploit] are unlikely to remove the remaining web shells because the web shells are difficult to find due to their unique file names and paths or because these victims lack the technical ability to remove them on their own." *Id.* ¶ 16.

company.[5] In the intervening four years, additional cybersecurity events such as the MOVEit data breach in May 2023,[6] the AT&T breach publicized in 2024,[7] and the Change Healthcare breach in early 2024[8] have caused substantial disruptions.

The public and private sectors have made some strides in deploying data security protections, generally categorized as resilience,[9] but when a cyber incident occurs, there are still too many hapless victims without functioning backups or insurance that have little recourse but to pay the ransom, ignoring the standard government advice to not pay. However, there is hope (and new concerns). The emergence of artificial intelligence (AI) has fundamentally altered the playing field in cybersecurity. While AI provides defenders with powerful tools for detecting and mitigating threats, it also equips adversaries with capabilities to launch more adaptive and persistent attacks. For instance, AI-driven malware can autonomously identify and exploit vulnerabilities, bypassing traditional security defenses.

This chapter will cover the importance of business continuity planning and risk management, the current landscape of best practices as reflected in international and U.S. standards, such as those issued by the International Organization for Standardization (ISO) and National Institute for Standards and Technology (NIST), the elements and implementation process for cyber incident response plans, and certain lessons learned and best practices from the "trenches" of cyber incident response experiences. It also discusses AI-driven advancements, and how they offer immense potential for reshaping resilience and response strategies that will inform the resilience necessary for all to implement.

---

5. *See Cyber Attack Hits JBS Meat Works in Australia, North America*, REUTERS (Jun. 1, 2021,10:26 AM EDT), https://www.reuters.com/technology/cyber-attack-hits-jbs-meat-works-australia-north-america-2021-05-31/.

6. A breach that compromised the private information of 2,770 organizations and more than 94 million individuals worldwide. Zach Simas, *Unpacking the MOVEit Breach: Statistics and Analysis*, EMSISOFT (Jul. 18, 2023), https://www.emsisoft.com/en/blog/44123/unpacking-the-moveit-breach-statistics-and-analysis/. *See also* Marianne Hayes, *MOVEit Data Breach: What You Need to Know*, EXPERIAN (Aug. 24, 2023), https://www.experian.com/blogs/ask-experian/moveit-data-breach/.

7. This breach compromised "'nearly all' of its cellular customers and the customers of wireless providers that use its network between May 1, 2022 and October 31, 2022." AT&T reached out to the Department of Justice and FBI shortly after discovering the incident, and the DOJ requested that AT&T delay filing its disclosure with the SEC because of potential national security or public safety concerns. Matt Egan & Sean Lyngaas, *Nearly All AT&T Cell Customers' Call and Text Records Exposed in a Massive Breach*, CNN BUS. (Jul. 12, 2024 4:33 PM EDT), https://www.cnn.com/2024/07/12/business/att-customers-massive-breach/index.html.

8. This breach impacted over 100 million individuals. Zack Whittaker, *UnitedHealth Says Change Healthcare Hack Affects over 100 Million, the Largest-Ever US Healthcare Data Breach*, TECHCRUNCH (Oct. 24, 2024, 1:55 PM PDT), https://techcrunch.com/2024/10/24/unitedhealth-change-healthcare-hacked-millions-health-records-ransomware/ (citing U.S. Dept. of Health & Human Services Off. for Civil Rights, Breach Portal: Notice to the Secy. of HHS Breach of Unsecured Protected Health Information report).

9. The MGM Resorts response and recovery in the wake of its falling victim to a ransomware attack in September 2023 has been described as an example of corporate resilience. In a response to *Forbes* writer Heather Wishart-Smith, John Frazzini, president and CEO of X-Analytics stated: "MGM was able to build resilience, manage the financial exposure and get back in business without paying the ransom demand....It was managed exceptionally well." Heather Wishart-Smith, *The Persistent Ransomware Threat: 2024 Trends and High-Profile Attacks*, FORBES (Dec. 9, 2024 7:13 PM EST), https://www.forbes.com/sites/heatherwishartsmith/2024/12/09/the-persistent-ransomware-threat-2024-trends-and-high-profile-attacks/.

PART I: Using Artificial Intelligence and Standards to Advance Resilience

1. The Fundamentals of Business Continuity

1.1. Core Objectives and Evolving Strategies

Business continuity planning ensures that organizations can sustain operations during disruptions. The fundamental goal is resilience—keeping critical systems functional despite crises. Emerging threats like ransomware and advanced persistent threats (APTs) have reshaped continuity strategies, demanding greater agility and technological integration.

AI is now a key driver in evolving business continuity practices. Through real-time analysis and predictive capabilities, AI-enabled tools can preempt disruptions and offer dynamic recovery solutions. For example, AI models trained on historical attack data can forecast vulnerabilities, allowing firms to proactively strengthen their defenses.

1.2. Law Firm-Specific Risks

Law firms face unique challenges, such as protecting privileged client information and maintaining uninterrupted access to critical systems. AI can enhance traditional risk management by automating threat detection and improving the accuracy of data classification.

2. Risk Management and AI-Enhanced Resilience

2.1. Predictive Analytics for Risk Identification

Traditional risk management frameworks are bolstered by AI's ability to process and analyze large datasets. Predictive analytics can identify patterns, such as irregular system access or unusual data flows, signaling potential risks. For example, a firm using AI-powered tools can detect a phishing attack targeting its legal team before any data is compromised.

2.2. Incident Simulation and Scenario Planning

AI also facilitates detailed simulations of potential incidents, helping organizations evaluate their readiness. For instance, law firms can use AI-driven models to simulate ransomware attacks, test backup strategies, and refine incident response plans based on simulated outcomes.

2.3. Case Study: AI in Action[10]

2.3.1. *Background*

A global law firm specializing in corporate mergers and acquisitions implemented an AI-powered cybersecurity monitoring system to address rising concerns about insider threats

10. The case study is a hypothetical scenario based on industry trends.

and data breaches. With operations spanning multiple countries and sensitive client information stored across interconnected systems, the firm recognized the need for advanced solutions to safeguard its data.

2.3.2. *Challenge*

The firm faced a growing risk of insider threats, including unauthorized access to sensitive client files by employees. Traditional monitoring systems were unable to detect subtle patterns of misuse, especially when individuals operated within their normal access permissions. This created potential vulnerabilities, as misuse could go unnoticed until after a breach had occurred.

2.3.3. *Solution*

To address this insider threat risk, the firm adopted an AI-based anomaly detection system. The AI analyzed behavioral patterns of employees, including access times, file types retrieved, and frequency of data interactions. Over time, the system developed a baseline for "normal" behavior for each employee and flagged deviations in real-time.

2.3.4. *Outcome*

Within months of implementation, the AI system flagged unusual behavior by a senior associate who accessed large volumes of client files unrelated to their active projects. The firm's IT team investigated and discovered that the employee was planning to leave the organization and had begun collecting sensitive information for personal use.

The early detection allowed the firm to take swift action, including revoking the individual's access and securing the files before any data was leaked. The incident was contained without legal or reputational damage, demonstrating the system's value in mitigating insider threats.

2.3.5. *Key Insights*

This case highlights how AI enhances resilience by:

- identifying subtle deviations in behavior that traditional systems may overlook,
- automating real-time alerts, enabling proactive responses to potential threats, and
- protecting sensitive data while maintaining employee privacy and operational efficiency.

Through the adoption of AI-based monitoring, the firm not only prevented a potential data breach but also strengthened its overall cybersecurity posture. This case underscores the importance of leveraging advanced technologies to address emerging risks in the legal and professional services sector.

3. Integrating AI into the Cybersecurity Framework

3.1. Enhancing the NIST Cybersecurity Framework[11] with AI

The NIST Cybersecurity Framework provides a structured approach to managing cyber risks through six core functions: Govern, Identify, Protect, Detect, Respond, and Recover. (NIST added "Govern" as a sixth function in version 2.0 of the Framework to address growing recognition of the need for formalized cybersecurity governance and oversight at the organizational level.) AI adds value at each stage:

- **Govern:** AI tools can support governance by automatically monitoring compliance, generating audit trails, and identifying policy deviations across systems.
- **Identify:** AI tools can continuously assess and map vulnerabilities in IT systems.
- **Protect:** Automated systems using machine learning (ML) adapt to emerging threats in real-time.
- **Detect:** AI accelerates threat detection by analyzing traffic patterns, behaviors, and log anomalies.
- **Respond:** AI-driven playbooks execute predefined responses to common threats, reducing response times.
- **Recover:** AI models optimize resource allocation during recovery to minimize downtime.

3.2. ISO Standards and AI Integration

ISO standards like ISO/IEC 27001[12] and ISO 22301[13] emphasize resilience and preparedness. AI complements these standards by streamlining compliance efforts. For example, AI can automate compliance audits, ensuring that firms meet international security benchmarks without diverting significant resources.

4. Best Practices and Lessons Learned

4.1. Leveraging AI for Business Continuity

AI-powered tools offer practical applications for maintaining continuity, such as:

- **Dynamic Risk Assessment:** AI models assess risks in real-time, updating risk profiles as new information emerges.

11. NIST Cybersecurity Framework (CSF) 2.0 (Feb. 26, 2024), https://nvlpubs.nist.gov/nistpubs/CSWP/NIST.CSWP.29.pdf.

12. International Std. ISO/IEC 27001:2022, Information security, cybersecurity and privacy protection—Information security management systems—Requirements (3d ed. 2022) (jointly published by ISO and the International Electrotechnical Commission (IEC)), https://www.iso.org/standard/27001.

13. International Std. ISO 22301:2019, Security and resilience—Business continuity management systems—Requirements (2d ed. 2019), https://www.iso.org/standard/75106.html.

- **Automated Backup Verification:** AI verifies the integrity of backup systems, ensuring data recovery readiness.
- **Incident Trend Analysis:** Machine learning identifies recurring patterns in cyberattacks, informing preventive measures.

4.2. Addressing Ethical and Legal Concerns

As firms deploy AI, they must navigate legal considerations, such as compliance with data protection regulations. AI algorithms must be transparent, auditable, and designed to protect client confidentiality. Firms should also establish ethical guidelines for AI usage to prevent misuse and ensure fairness.

4.3. Real-World Example: AI in Business Continuity

During the COVID-19 pandemic, many organizations, including law firms, adopted AI-driven tools to manage remote workforces, monitor system performance, detect unauthorized access attempts, and maintain service levels amid increased cyberattacks. This proactive approach enabled firms to continue operations without compromising security. For instance, the World Economic Forum reported that organizations invested in AI "to expedite remote working, enhance the user and customer experience, and decrease costs" during the pandemic.[14] Additionally, law firms have been adapting to cover expanding legal risks, including those related to AI and cybersecurity, to better serve their clients in the evolving technological landscape.[15] These examples illustrate the broader trend of AI integration in business continuity strategies during the pandemic.

5. Adapting International Standards to AI

5.1. AI and ISO 22301

ISO 22301's emphasis on a holistic business continuity management system (BCMS) aligns seamlessly with the capabilities of artificial intelligence. The standard provides a framework for organizations to identify potential risks, plan for disruptions, and ensure resilience in the face of crises. AI, as a transformative technology, enhances the efficiency and effectiveness of these processes.

---

14. World Econ. Forum, *COVID-19 increased the use of AI. Here's why it's here to stay* (Feb 24, 2021), https://www.weforum.org/stories/2021/02/covid-19-increased-use-of-ai-here-s-why-its-here-to-stay/.

15. Sophie Spiegelberger, *Law Firms Adapt to Cover Expanding Legal Risk*, FIN. TIMES (Dec. 10, 2024), https://www.ft.com/content/c716b154-f732-49a4-b206-92cee6a75e52.

5.2. AI's Role in Supporting ISO 22301 Implementation

ISO 22301's emphasis on a holistic BCMS aligns well with AI's capabilities. AI streamlines processes like risk analysis and scenario planning, enabling firms to implement the standard more efficiently.

- **Risk Analysis and Identification:** AI-powered tools can analyze vast datasets to identify emerging threats and vulnerabilities with greater speed and accuracy than manual processes. Predictive analytics allow organizations to foresee potential disruptions, enabling proactive measures rather than reactive responses.
- **Scenario Planning:** AI simplifies scenario modeling by simulating various disruption scenarios and their potential impacts. This enables firms to test and refine their BCMS strategies under different conditions, ensuring robustness and adaptability.
- **Streamlined Processes:** By automating repetitive tasks such as data collection and analysis, AI reduces the time and resources needed to implement ISO 22301. This allows organizations to focus on high-level strategic planning and continuous improvement.
- **Real-Time Monitoring and Response:** AI enhances an organization's ability to monitor systems and environments in real time, detecting anomalies that could signal disruptions. Automated incident response capabilities ensure swift actions to mitigate impacts.
- **Data-Driven Decision-Making:** AI provides actionable insights based on comprehensive data analysis, helping organizations prioritize actions that align with their business continuity goals.
- **Continuous Improvement:** AI supports ongoing evaluation of BCMS effectiveness by analyzing performance metrics and identifying areas for improvement. This aligns with ISO 22301's emphasis on maintaining and continually enhancing the BCMS.

By integrating AI into their BCMS strategies, organizations can implement ISO 22301 more efficiently and also enhance their overall resilience, ensuring that they are better prepared to handle disruptions in an increasingly complex risk landscape. This synergy between AI and ISO 22301 sets a new benchmark for business continuity management.

5.3. The Role of ISO/IEC 42001[16]

The introduction in 2023 of **ISO/IEC 42001**, which focuses on AI management, reflects the growing recognition of the need for governance frameworks to address the unique challenges and opportunities posed by AI. This standard complements existing frameworks like **ISO 22301** for Business Continuity Management Systems (BCMS) and **ISO/IEC 27001** for Information Security Management, enabling organizations to align AI governance with their broader operational and cybersecurity strategies.

---

16. International Std. ISO/IEC 42001:2023, Information technology—Artificial intelligence—Management system (1st ed. 2023), https://www.iso.org/standard/81230.html.

5.4. The Role of ISO/IEC 42001 in AI Governance

ISO/IEC 42001 establishes principles and requirements for managing AI systems responsibly, emphasizing transparency, accountability, and ethics. This ensures that organizations deploy AI-based technologies in a way that aligns with legal, societal, and organizational objectives, while mitigating risks such as bias, misuse, and ethical concerns.

5.5. The Synergy Between ISO Standards

By integrating ISO 22301, ISO/IEC 27001, and ISO/IEC 42001, organizations can achieve a holistic approach to managing business continuity, cybersecurity, and AI practices. This alignment offers the following advantages:

- **Governance and Accountability Across Domains:**
  - ISO/IEC 42001 provides the governance structure for managing AI, ensuring compliance with ethical standards and regulatory requirements.
  - ISO 22301 ensures that business operations remain resilient during disruptions, including those caused by AI-related risks such as system failures or malicious use.
  - ISO/IEC 27001 strengthens information security, protecting sensitive data processed by AI systems and safeguarding against cyber threats.
- **Risk Management Integration:**
  - AI introduces unique risks, such as algorithmic biases or adversarial attacks. Combining these standards ensures that AI risks are managed alongside broader business continuity and cybersecurity risks.
  - For example, ISO 22301's focus on business impact analysis can be extended to include AI-related risks, while ISO/IEC 42001 ensures that AI systems are designed and monitored to minimize these risks.
- **Resilience and Security by Design:**
  - Organizations adopting ISO 42001 can design AI systems with resilience in mind, ensuring they continue to function during disruptions.
  - By aligning with ISO/IEC 27001, these AI systems are secured against unauthorized access and data breaches, preserving their integrity and trustworthiness.
- **Ethical and Transparent AI Practices:**
  - ISO/IEC 42001 emphasizes ethical considerations, such as fairness and explainability of AI systems, aligning with organizational values and societal expectations.
  - ISO/IEC 42001 complements ISO 22301's emphasis on stakeholder communication and ISO/IEC 27001's focus on protecting sensitive information.
- **Operational Efficiency through Standards Alignment:**
  - A unified approach to implementing these standards avoids duplication of effort, as many requirements (e.g., risk assessments, governance policies, and audit processes) can be streamlined across the frameworks.
  - This integrated framework strategy fosters a culture of continuous improvement, where insights from AI operations inform business continuity strategies and vice versa.

5.6. Real-World Application: Ensuring Trust and Resilience

Organizations in industries like healthcare, finance, and legal services, where AI adoption is accelerating, benefit significantly from this integrated approach. For instance:

- A financial services firm using AI for fraud detection can align ISO/IEC 42001 to ensure AI accountability while using ISO 22301 to maintain continuity during AI-related outages. ISO/IEC 27001 ensures the security of sensitive client data used by the AI systems.
- In healthcare, AI-powered diagnostics must adhere to ethical standards under ISO/IEC 42001, while ISO 22301 ensures continuity of services and ISO/IEC 27001 safeguards patient data.

Case Study: Bevan Brittan LLP

Bevan Brittan LLP, a prominent UK-based law firm, recognized the necessity of robust information security and business continuity measures to protect client data and maintain service integrity.

1. **Implementation Strategy**

ISO 27001 Certification. The firm pursued ISO 27001 certification to establish a formal Information Security Management System (ISMS). This process involved identifying information assets, assessing risks, and implementing controls to mitigate identified threats.[17]

2. **Business Continuity**

While ISO 27001 is not a business continuity standard, it requires organizations to integrate continuity planning into the ISMS where needed to preserve the confidentiality, integrity, and availability (CIA) of information during disruptions. The most relevant controls are A.5.29 and A.5.30 in the 2022 version.

Annex A.5.29—Information Security During Disruption

- Purpose: To ensure that information security is maintained during adverse situations such as disasters or disruptions.
- Explanation: Organizations must plan how to continue protecting information and maintaining necessary security controls during incidents that affect normal operations.
- Relation to Business Continuity: This control acts as the bridge between the ISMS and BCMS, ensuring that business continuity considerations include cybersecurity protections.

17. URM Consulting Services Ltd., ISO 27001 Case Study: Bevan Brittan (undated), https://cdn.prod.website-files.com/663395d3790b636e6eefc3a3/663395d3790b636e6eefc504_URM_Case-Study-BevanBrittan.pdf.

Annex A.5.30—ICT Readiness for Business Continuity

- Purpose: To ensure information and communication technology (ICT) systems are prepared to meet business continuity requirements.
- Requirements: Organizations must determine their ICT continuity needs, including availability and recovery time objectives. The controls involve testing, validating, and improving ICT recovery strategies.

Also Related—Clause 6.1.3—Information Security Risk Treatment Plan. When developing this plan, continuity planning should be one of the areas of focus if disruptions pose a risk to information assets.

Bevan Brittan LLP not only safeguarded sensitive information but also reinforced their position as a reliable and resilient legal service provider.[18]

5.7. Law Firms Embrace AI and Data Security Measures

In recent years, law firms have expanded their services to address a broader spectrum of legal risks faced by businesses, particularly in the United States. This shift is driven by cultural and technological changes that have introduced new challenges in areas such as cybercrime, artificial intelligence, and workplace dynamics.

5.8. Key Developments[19]

- **Cybersecurity and AI Risks:** Firms are now offering services to help clients navigate the complexities of cyber threats and the legal implications of AI integration. For instance, DLA Piper has developed tools to assess AI systems for compliance and accuracy, ensuring that clients' AI applications adhere to regulatory standards and ethical guidelines.
- **Workplace Cultural Disputes:** The evolving nature of workplace interactions has led to an increase in cultural disagreements. Law firms are providing guidance on managing these disputes proactively, emphasizing the importance of diversity and inclusion policies to prevent conflicts and promote a harmonious work environment.
- **Regulatory Compliance:** With the growing complexity of regulations, firms like Hogan Lovells have implemented AI-based document sorting systems to efficiently manage and analyze regulatory documents. This enables clients to stay compliant with evolving laws and reduces the risk of legal infractions.

These adaptations reflect a broader trend of law firms integrating advanced technologies and expanding their expertise to meet the emerging needs of their clients. By doing so, they

18. While ISO 22301 implementation is referenced in broader firm strategy and third-party discussions, there is no publicly available URM-authored case study confirming this certification. If such documentation exists, it remains confidential or internal.

19. *See* Spiegelberger, *supra* note 15.

not only mitigate potential legal risks but also enhance their competitiveness in a rapidly changing legal landscape.

Case Study: Allen & Overy—Leveraging AI for Legal Efficiency and Innovation[20]

1. **Background**

Allen & Overy, one of the world's leading law firms and a member of the Magic Circle, has emerged as a trailblazer in adopting generative artificial intelligence (GenAI) within the legal sector. Recognizing the potential of GenAI to revolutionize legal workflows, the firm has embraced cutting-edge technologies to improve efficiency and reduce operational costs.

2. **Implementation**

In November 2022, Allen & Overy (now A&O Sherman) partnered with Harvey AI, a U.S.-based startup, to integrate a generative AI tool into their legal operations. The tool is designed to support various legal processes, including:

- Drafting complex legal documents,
- Conducting in-depth legal research, and
- Performing due diligence for corporate and transactional matters.

The GenAI product is not intended to replace lawyers but to assist them in handling repetitive and time-intensive tasks, enabling the firm to focus more on providing strategic and nuanced legal advice.

3. **Benefits Realized**

- Enhanced Efficiency:
  The AI tool has significantly streamlined workflows, reducing the time required for tasks like document drafting and research. This allows lawyers to manage larger caseloads without compromising quality.
- Cost Reduction:
  By automating routine processes, Allen & Overy has been able to reduce overhead costs associated with legal support functions, creating a more scalable operational model.
- Improved Client Service:
  With more time to focus on high-value legal advice, the firm has enhanced its ability to meet complex client needs, improving client satisfaction and retention.

20. A&O Shearman, *A&O Announces Exclusive Launch Partnership with Harvey* (Feb. 15, 2023), https://www.aoshearman.com/en/news/ao-announces-exclusive-launch-partnership-with-harvey; Counsel AI Corporation, Customer Story—A&O Shearman: Transforming Legal Services through AI Innovation (undated), https://www.harvey.ai/customers/a-and-o-shearman.

4. **Challenges and Risk Management**

Despite the numerous benefits, Allen & Overy implemented the AI solution cautiously, addressing key concerns such as:

- Data Security: Ensuring client confidentiality through rigorous data handling protocols.
- Accuracy: Continuously monitoring AI outputs to ensure they meet the firm's high standards for legal precision.
- Ethical Considerations: Establishing clear usage policies to maintain the integrity and ethical standards of the legal profession.

5. **Outcomes**

The adoption of Harvey AI has positioned Allen & Overy as a leader in legal innovation, setting a benchmark for how law firms can responsibly integrate AI technologies. The firm's experience highlights the transformative potential of AI while underscoring the importance of risk management and governance in its implementation.

6. **Summary**

Allen & Overy's case demonstrates the potential for GenAI to enhance efficiency, reduce costs, and improve service delivery in the legal industry. By addressing the associated risks thoughtfully, firms can successfully harness GenAI as a tool for innovation while maintaining their commitment to quality and ethical practice. The risks associated with GenAI can be factored into the kind of integrated management system created when ISO Standards 27001, 22301, and 42001 are combined for implementation.

5.9. Benefits of Integrating ISO Standards

5.9.1. *Enhanced Risk Management*

Combining these standards allows organizations to address a wide spectrum of risks, from operational disruptions to information security threats and ethical AI considerations.

5.9.2. *Operational Efficiency*

An integrated management system reduces duplication of effort, streamlining processes across various domains and improving overall efficiency.

5.9.3. *Stakeholder Trust*

Demonstrating compliance with internationally recognized standards fosters trust among clients, partners, and regulatory bodies.

5.9.4. *Continuous Improvement*

The integrated approach promotes a culture of ongoing enhancement, ensuring that business continuity, security, and AI practices evolve with emerging challenges and technologies.

While specific case studies on the combined implementation of ISO 22301, ISO/IEC 27001, and ISO/IEC 42001 are limited due to the recent introduction of ISO/IEC 42001, the principles and benefits observed in integrating multiple ISO standards are well-documented. Organizations adopting such integrated systems are better positioned to navigate the complexities of modern business environments, particularly with the increasing reliance on AI technologies.

For more detailed guidance on implementing ISO/IEC 42001 and integrating it with other management systems, resources from KPMG provide valuable insights.[21]

The introduction of ISO/IEC 42001 underscores the growing need to govern AI systems effectively. When combined with ISO 22301 and ISO/IEC 27001, it creates a robust framework for ensuring resilience, security, and ethical AI practices. Together, these standards enable organizations to navigate the complex interplay of business continuity, cybersecurity, and AI governance, positioning them for success in an increasingly AI-driven world.

6. Future Directions and Innovations

6.1. AI and Cyber Threat Intelligence

AI is transforming cyber threat intelligence by automating the collection and analysis of threat data. Organizations can predict emerging threats and adapt their strategies dynamically.

6.2. Preparing for AI-Powered Threats

As attackers increasingly use AI, organizations must adopt defensive AI measures. Collaborative efforts, including industry-wide sharing of AI-generated threat intelligence, will be critical.

6.3. Wrap-up: Building AI-Ready Resilience

Integrating AI into business continuity planning and incident response frameworks is essential for navigating the evolving threat landscape. By adhering to international standards, leveraging AI's predictive capabilities, and fostering a culture of continuous improvement, organizations can ensure resilience against future disruptions. This approach not only strengthens operational security but also equips firms to thrive in a world where AI is both a critical tool and a potential adversary.

---

21. KPMG AG, ISO/IEC 42001 Certification: The Global Standard for AI Management Systems (AIMS) (May 2025), https://assets.kpmg.com/content/dam/kpmgsites/ch/pdf/ISOIEC-42001-certification.pdf.coredownload.inline.pdf; KPMG AG, ISO//IEC 42001: a new standard for AI governance, https://kpmg.com/ch/en/insights/artificial-intelligence/iso-iec-42001.html (last visited Sept. 13, 2025).

PART II: Incident Response

1. Implementing the Cyber Incident Response Plan

1.1. The First Steps After a Cyber Incident Occurs

Incident response plans are made to be implemented without delay. Basic initial steps may seem intuitive in planning, but cyber incidents catch people off guard, and mistakes early on can complicate the response.

1.1.1. *Notification*

Proper notification within the entity suffering a cyber incident is frequently the first stumbling block to effective incident response. Does the employee[22] who first discovers the incident know whom to call? Has a cyber incident contact been named by the company, and is that person's contact information available in written form (because the online call sheet may be encrypted and unavailable)? Does the employee know where to find the hard copy of the incident response plan? (A plan that is inaccessible because it is encrypted is useless.) Are several methods of communication covered by the contact list (because company phones and e-mail servers may be down)? These questions are all answered in the cyber incident response plan.

Once the incident commander is informed, activities happen quickly. The internal team is notified, and steps are taken to isolate, if possible, other company systems from the spreading virus. The next contact in this scenario is legal counsel. All too often, cyber counsel is not among the first to be called, and this can be a dangerous omission. As with any expert in a crisis situation, cyber counsel can quickly deploy a licensed forensic team whose activities and reports can be subject to attorney-client and work-product privilege. In addition—and this can be critical when it comes to costs—cyber counsel and forensic experts that have been vetted and preapproved by the company's insurance carrier will avoid needless delays in deploying an effective incident response. One element in the incident response plan that helps avoid unnecessary delay after a cyber incident is a pre-negotiated basic terms-of-engagement template with cyber counsel.

1.1.2. *Preserving Evidence*

Without knowing either the origins of the incident or the full range of consequences, it is critical to preserve as much evidence as possible. The biggest mistake companies can make is attempting to "fix" the problem using internal IT staff or calling untrained third-party IT companies to help. This is no different from allowing the public to trample across a

22. If an entity, particularly a small firm, engages a service provider for information technology and information security functions, the relevant employees on the service provider team must know whom to call at the service provider and its client firm.

crime scene, taking what they want and leaving their trash behind. Unwitting IT staff may want to "clean" servers and workstations, but with the harm already done, they are just destroying valuable evidence that might reveal the type and source of the intrusion. Thus, a preservation policy that anticipates a cyber incident is an important element to the incident response plan.

Occasionally the preferred forensic consultant may not be available; thus, it is best to vet and list two or more licensed forensic teams. Some states require these individuals to be licensed private investigators, so it is best to check your applicable state laws.

1.1.3. *Insurance Notice*

The company's insurance carrier is another important initial contact point. Cyber liability coverage is available and can be invaluable,[23] although the number of carriers offering cyber coverage in recent years has decreased, and the premiums for those carriers still offering cyber coverage have increased.[24] More often than not, the carrier will require both cyber counsel and the forensic team to be drawn from the carrier's own approved list.

1.1.4. *Forensic Investigation Launch*

Once the forensic team is deployed on-site, it works quickly to:

- interview individuals with knowledge of the incident;
- acquire electronic evidence from compromised system(s) and hosts, including ancillary systems and hosts;
- confirm the scope, type, and impact of the cyber incident (forensic examination of collected and preserved electronic evidence to identify whether confidential, sensitive, or proprietary information has been accessed or compromised); and
- implement emergency communications (e-mail, phone, etc.).

1.1.5. *Ransom Demands*

Ransomware attacks challenge a victim entity to respond quickly. One response to a bitcoin[25] demand from a ransomware hacker may be "get lost" and rely on access the company's backups. Often, however, the company may find its back-ups are unavailable,

---

23. *See* HANDBOOK, Chapter 14, *Cyber Insurance for Law Firms and Legal Organizations.*

24. Online bloggers Elaine Atwell and Aida Knezivic noted in August 2024: "In the past three years, the cost of cyber liability premiums hasn't so much skyrocketed as it has teleported. In 2021, the cost of cyber insurance increased 25.5% year-over-year, making it the fastest growing premiums of all lines of insurance. 2022 was even worse, with rates doubling in the first quarter and increasing a further 79% in Q2. As of 2024, these massive price jumps have stabilized somewhat, with increased competition in the market even leading to a decline in average premium costs—though prices still remain far higher than they were in 2021." Elaine Atwell & Aida Knezevic, *What's Driving the Fluctuating Costs of Cyber Liability Insurance?*, 1PASSWORD BLOG (Aug. 6, 2024), https://blog.1password.com/fluctuating-cyber-liability-insurance/.

25. Bitcoin is used here as only an example of one of the most widely used of hundreds of different cryptocurrencies.

encrypted as well, or corrupted for some other reason. While experts in this area warn companies not to pay the bitcoin ransom, the victim company is often without any other viable choice.

Conducting a bitcoin transaction while working against a countdown clock and communicating with an anonymous hacker who revels in the idea of creating mayhem can be unnerving. The first bitcoin transaction may be only the first of several transactions, as the hacker will hold back some encryption keys for more bitcoins, and the company must test the decrypt keys in a secure "sandbox"[26] to make sure that they are decrypting properly and without additional embedded malware.

1.1.6. *Inventory of Affected Systems*

One of the more tedious, time-consuming, and vitally necessary activities in the wake of any cyber incident is the inventory and assessment of all devices that may have been connected to the infected network. Of course, it does not help if the network diagrams and device inventories have been encrypted and no hard copy exists. Thus, the incident response plan should include all these diagrams and inventories, be updated periodically, and be available in hard copy form.

As equipment and software are scanned for malware, cleaned, rebuilt, and tested, it is obvious that they should be deployed only into a clean and tested environment. The process of testing for internal and external vulnerabilities is ongoing throughout the response.

1.2. Assessing Notification Responsibilities

As the initial response activities yield information, the incident commander and the company's executive team should consult with cyber counsel about whether there are sufficient indicators to notify external authorities. Certain industries have regulatory control and notification requirements depending on the nature and type of digital records that may have been compromised.

Calling the state police or FBI before the forensic team has a chance to collect and preserve relevant data makes it difficult, if not impossible, to correctly identify "patient zero"[27] or to determine which digital records are involved.[28] Only when sufficient information has

26. In digital forensic settings, the term "sandbox" is commonly used to describe an isolated virtual machine environment in which forensic professionals can execute potentially unsafe software code without affecting network resources or local applications.

27. "Patient zero" commonly refers to the source individual within a company that the hacker successfully targeted. Finding "patient zero" is a priority that can lead to better understanding of how the hacker gained entry.

28. For example, a company assumed that electronic personal health information (ePHI) had been exfiltrated and notified the FBI prior to engaging cyber counsel. Later forensic evaluation determined that ePHI was not exfiltrated. By an amazing coincidence, an iTunes library backing up on the company server was the same size as the medical records file, and the backup occurred within the time window of the hack. Based on the results of closer review, the FBI was notified to close its investigation. It bears repeating: do not notify external authorities without first consulting with experienced cyber counsel. Gather facts quickly and carefully, and know the underlying laws implicated by the results of the hacker's activities.

been gathered to determine what records have been accessed, compromised, or exfiltrated should the process of external notification begin, but in all instances this decision should be made only in consultation with experienced cyber counsel. On the other hand, if the incident is a "man-in-the-middle" attack where the threat actor has inserted itself in the victim company's email system to hijack a financial transaction, then quick notice[29] to the FBI via an Internet Crime Complaint ("IC3") and the FBI's recovery asset team ("RAT") can be invaluable. Established in 2018, the FBI's RAT succeeded in recovering 79% of reported losses during its first full year of operation.[30] In years since, that success rate has fallen, but as of the end of 2024, it is still a credible 66%.[31]

The incident commander, cyber counsel, and forensic team must also carefully assess what enforcement entity should be notified and what notice to provide to the applicable information sharing and analysis center (commonly known as an ISAC) or information sharing and analysis organization (ISAO).

1.3. Public Statements

Depending on the nature of the incident, the law enforcement may want the company to go public as a demonstration or example of a cautionary tale. Going down this road requires careful analysis with the company's management team, inside and outside counsel, and internal and/or external public affairs personnel. Assistance with messaging from a public relations team is often useful, depending on the nature and extent of the incident.

1.4. Managing Staff

A natural and critical pause-point occurs once the forensic team has determined the nature and extent of the cyber intrusion. Initial on-scene staff and executive team members have probably had little sleep, and maintaining calm in the face of operational shutdown has an impact on everyone. Simple steps such as contacting carry-out vendors to bring in food and beverages help fuel employees over long shifts.

Managing staff and scheduling to address critical functions is high on the list. With the encryption of many internal and administrative systems, employees that normally do their work using systems that have been rendered inoperable due to encryption do not need to be present. Companies need to address how to pay employees if their payroll system is not functioning. Of course, having the company's IT staff available to assist the forensic team is a natural need and additional third-party IT staffing may be necessary as well.

29. Quick notice in this instance would be within 24 or 48 hours of the errant financial transaction.

30. FBI, 2019 Internet Crime Report 3, https://www.ic3.gov/AnnualReport/Reports/2019_IC3Report.pdf.

31. *See* Martin Hinton, *FBI Internet Crime Report Reveals $16.6 Billion Losses Amid Soaring Cyber Threats*, Cyber Ins. News (Apr. 28, 2025), https://cyberinsurancenews.org/fbi-internet-crime-report-2024-summary/.

1.5. Forensic Investigation

1.5.1. *Reviewing the Initial Forensic Indicators*

Often the initial forensic indicators can be misleading, sending the forensic team down any number of "rabbit holes" in search of "patient zero" and, at the same time, determining what data might have been compromised. Typical questions are:

- What servers and devices were infiltrated?
- How and when did the infiltration occur?
- How did the hacker gain entry? Was it an existing vulnerability in hardware or software or the result of an employee mistake responding to social engineering?
- What are the impacts of the infiltration?

For those companies with cyber liability coverage, it will save much time later if the impacts and consequences of the incident are sorted early on according to the carrier's coverage requirements. This is where consulting with the company's insurance broker can provide a huge advantage for the subsequent filing of a claim with the carrier. In addition, keeping track of impacts and resulting damages may be important to later claims in litigation if the hacker is identified and subject to U.S. jurisdiction. Sadly, though, success in holding the typical hacker to account is rare.

1.5.2. *Investigating Motive*

When the picture of the infiltration becomes clear, then the forensic team's attention turns to the motive:

- What data was accessed on the servers and/or connected devices?
- Was the data exfiltrated?
- Was a company employee the target of a spear-phishing campaign where the employee e-mailed the data to the hacker?
- What reporting obligations are implicated?
- Did the hacker leave any "backdoors" hidden for future access?

In cases involving data breaches, state statutes generally allow for investigative time, with an average requirement of 30 days or so from the date when the breach was discovered, but keep in mind, if an entity must comply with European Union's General Data Protection Regulation, it must report the incident within 72 hours.[32] States vary widely with their notice triggers and filing requirements, so it is vital to determine early on what types of records might have been compromised, where the owners (or subjects) of those records

32. *What Is a Data Breach and What Do We Have to do in Case of a Data Breach?*, European Comm., https://ec.europa.eu/info/law/law-topic/data-protection/reform/rules-business-and-organisations/obligations/what-data-breach-and-what-do-we-have-do-case-data-breach_en (last visited Sept. 13, 2025).

reside, and how many of the owners / subjects reside in each implicated state. For example, in some states, notice to the state attorney general is required if just one resident is affected, but for other states the number triggering notice is higher.[33]

Determining the origin of the cyber intrusion can be painstaking and time-consuming. The task is even more difficult if untrained IT staff have attempted to mitigate the damage and unwittingly destroyed evidence. The identification of "patient zero" will be critical for purposes of insurance coverage questions as well as for traditional liability analysis. In addition, with the recent legislative interest in public-private sector information sharing in the aftermath of a cyber incident, there are benefits to sharing such information with law enforcement.

Under the Cyber Incident Reporting for Critical Infrastructure Act of 2022, which is still undergoing the rule-making process but is set to become effective in 2026, certain critical infrastructure entities would be required to report substantial cyber incidents to the Cybersecurity and Infrastructure Security Agency (CISA) within 72 hours and ransomware payments within 24 hours.[34]

In July 2023, the Securities and Exchange Commission adopted new rules "to enhance and standardize disclosures regarding cybersecurity" that required domestic registrants and foreign private issuers to (1) disclose a cybersecurity incident within four days of the entity's determination that the cybersecurity incident was "material" and (2) prepare an annual disclosure of cybersecurity risk management, strategy, and governance.[35]

1.6. The Aftermath

In the aftermath of cyber incidents, there is often the question of who did what or who failed to do what. Questions will be raised about what policies were in place, what training occurred, and, if a company employee is identified and implicated, what the consequences may be for that employee. The company's employee policies should address the consequences when an employee's act or omission results in a cyber incident.

In addition, a company can be especially vulnerable to further cyber attacks in the aftermath of a cyber incident, particularly if the incident had been reported in public media. Thus, among the post-incident activities for the affected company's forensic expert are the

33. The IAPP has a spreadsheet detailing U.S. states' notice requirements at its website: *State Data Breach Notification Chart*, https://iapp.org/resources/article/state-data-breach-notification-chart/ (visited Apr. 19, 2025).

34. CISA, Cyber Incident Reporting for Critical Infrastructure Act of 2022: Notice of Proposed Rulemaking Informational Overview (May 2024), https://www.cisa.gov/sites/default/files/2024-05/CIRCIA%20NPRM%20Overview%20May_508cL.pdf; CISA, *Cyber Incident Reporting for Critical Infrastructure Act of 2022 (CIRCIA)*, https://www.cisa.gov/topics/cyber-threats-and-advisories/information-sharing/cyber-incident-reporting-critical-infrastructure-act-2022-circia (last visited Sept. 13, 2025). The rule is expected to be final in May 2026. *See* Tim Starks, *CISA Pushes Final Cyber Incident Reporting Rule to May 2026*, CyberScoop (Sept. 8, 2025), https://cyberscoop.com/cisa-pushes-final-cyber-incident-reporting-rule-to-may-2026/.

35. See, *Cybersecurity Risk Management, Strategy, Governance, and Incident Disclosure: A Small Entity Compliance Guide*, SEC, https://www.sec.gov/resources-small-businesses/small-business-compliance-guides/cybersecurity-risk-management-strategy-governance-incident-disclosure (visited Sept. 13, 2025).

periodic external and internal vulnerability scans to confirm the integrity of the company's network systems. The message here is that a company may survive a cyber incident, but cybersecurity risk is never over, the company is never "all set," and diligence after a cyber incident must be maintained. It is especially important in the ransomware context: it is not a good thing when word gets out in the dark web that a company both is vulnerable and has paid a ransom.

2. Foreign, Federal, and State Laws[36]

2.1. Common Foreign Data Protection Laws and Incident Response

It is beyond the scope of this chapter to describe the full list of foreign data breach statutes. There are tools and resources freely available to download;[37] we will highlight here the two with the greatest impact to US practitioners.

2.1.1. *The General Data Protection Regulation & the Data Protection Act 2018*

The General Data Protection Regulation (GDPR EU 2016/679) became effective on May 25, 2018, and it applies to all member states in the European Union.[38] Post Brexit in 2016, the United Kingdom passed a data privacy act that largely mirrors the GDPR. The UK law is called "Data Protection Act 2018," and it was enacted shortly before the effective date of the GDPR.[39]

The GDPR applies to the processing of personal data:

- When one or both of either a controller (the entity that controls the collection and transmittal of personal data) or a processor (the entity that processes the personal data it receives from the controller) is located in the Union, regardless of whether the processing takes place in the Union; or
- When the data subjects are "in the Union"[40] and they are either being
  - Offered goods or services (irrespective of any payment requirement) or
  - Monitored for their behavior (when their behavior takes place in the Union).

36. *See also* HANDBOOK, Chapters 8, *What Cybersecurity Laws Govern? Applicability, Enforcement, and Compliance with Domestic and Foreign Cybersecurity Laws*, and 9, *Foreign and International Cybersecurity Laws*.

37. *See, e.g.*, *What Is the Radar Privacy™ Breach Law Library and What Does It Provide?*, RADARFIRST, https://www.radarfirst.com/breach-law-library/ (last visited Sept. 13, 2025); *Data Breaches*, PRIVACY RTS. CLEARINGHOUSE, https://privacyrights.org/data-breaches (compiling publicly reported data breach notifications from U.S. government agencies) (last visited Sept. 13, 2025).

38. Regulation (EU) 2016/679 of the European Parliament and of the Council of 27 April 2016 on the protection of natural persons with regard to the processing of personal data and on the free movement of such data, and repealing Directive 95/46/EC (General Data Protection Regulation) [hereinafter GDPR].

39. Data Protection Act, U.K. PUB. GEN. ACTS 2018 c.12.

40. Many writers miss this point. The language of the Regulation states "in" the Union (EU). There is no requirement to be a resident of the Union or a citizen of the Union.

Thus, the territorial scope of the GDPR is vastly greater than any of its predecessors and can easily catch domestic US companies unawares. The GDPR can be applicable to a US company (the controller) using a cloud-based vendor platform (the processor) using US-based servers if the company offers goods or services to data subjects (natural persons) in the EU or the company in some way monitors the behavior of the data subject while in the EU.[41] Not only is the territoriality aspect a surprising hook for many, but also the definition of "personal data" is more broadly defined than US lawyers may be accustomed to seeing.[42]

The breach notification requirements under the GDPR are:

- In the case of a personal data breach, the controller shall without undue delay and, where feasible, not later than 72 hours after having become aware of it, notify the personal data breach to the supervisory authority competent in accordance with Article 55, unless the personal data breach is unlikely to result in a risk to the rights and freedoms of natural persons. Where the notification to the supervisory authority is not made within 72 hours, it shall be accompanied by reasons for the delay.
- The processor shall notify the controller without undue delay after becoming aware of a personal data breach.

Thus, when an incident does occur in what cyber counsel may think is a simple domestic breach, it is imperative to ask (1) whether any impacted servers or cloud providers are located in the EU or (2)(a) whether any of the affected individuals show any indication of being "in the Union" and (b) whether the controller was either targeting these individuals in some way to offer them goods or services or monitoring their behavior. If it is the processor that suffers the data breach, then the processor is required to notify the controller, unless the agreement between the controller and processor states otherwise (which is why it is handy to know this before a breach occurs).

2.1.2. *Canada and the Personal Information Protection and Electronic Documents Act*

Canada's Personal Information Protection and Electronic Documents Act (PIPEDA),[43] sets national standards for privacy practices in the private sector. While legislation has been drafted to overhaul Canada's consumer privacy protections,[44] PIPEDA remains the law of

---

41. GDPR, *supra* note 38, art. 4, § (1).

42. "Personal Data" is "any information relating to an identified or identifiable natural person ('data subject'); an identifiable natural person is one who can be identified, directly or indirectly, in particular by reference to an identifier such as a name, an identification number, location data, an online identifier or to one or more factors specific to the physical, physiological, genetic, mental, economic, cultural or social identity of that natural person."

43. Personal Information Protection and Electronic Documents Act, S.C. 2000, c 5 (Can.), https://laws-lois.justice.gc.ca/eng/acts/P-8.6/ (last visited Jan. 2, 2025).

44. The Canadian Parliament drafted Bill C-27, known as the Consumer Privacy Protection Act (CPPA) to replace PIPEDA and offer stronger data protections and stiffer penalties for violations. The Parliament ended its

the land. PIPEDA applies to federal works, undertakings, or businesses (FWUBs).[45] FWUBs include:

- banks,
- radio and television stations,
- inter-provincial trucking,
- airports and airlines,
- navigation and shipping by water,
- telecommunication companies such as internet service providers, phone (cellular or land line companies), cable companies, and
- railways, canals, pipelines, ferries, etc. that cross borders.

If an organization is a FWUB, PIPEDA applies to all commercial personal information flows and to employee personal information. If the organization in question operates in a province not subject to substantially similar provincial legislation (Alberta and British Columbia) and is not a FWUB, PIPEDA applies to all commercial activities; however, it does not apply to employee information.

Organizations subject to PIPEDA are required to:

- report to the Privacy Commissioner of Canada breaches of security safeguards involving personal information that pose a real risk of significant harm to individuals,
- notify affected individuals about those breaches, and
- keep records of all breaches.

The law requires the reporting of any breach of security safeguards involving personal information under an entity's control if it is reasonable in the circumstances to believe that the breach creates a real risk of significant harm (RROSH) to an individual. Significant harm includes bodily harm, humiliation, damage to reputation or relationships, loss of employment, business or professional opportunities, financial loss, identity theft, negative effects on a credit record and damage to, or loss of, property. Factors that are relevant to determining whether a breach of security safeguards creates a RROSH include the sensitivity of the personal information involved in the breach of security safeguards and the probability the personal information has been, is, or will be misused.[46]

---

session in January 2025 without further action on Bill C-27, and as of September 2025, legislation to replace the bill has not been enacted.C-27, PARLIAMENT OF CAN., https://www.parl.ca/legisinfo/en/bill/44-1/c-27 (visited Sept. 13, 2025).

45. S.C. 2000, c 5, pt 1, § 2(1).

46. *See What You Need to Know about Mandatory Reporting of Breaches of Security Safeguards,* OFFICE OF THE PRIVACY COMM. OF CANADA, https://www.priv.gc.ca/en/privacy-topics/business-privacy/safeguards-and-breaches/privacy-breaches/respond-to-a-privacy breach-at-your-business/gd_pb_201810/ (last visited Sept. 13, 2025).

2.2. Federal Laws & Regulations

Determining which federal agencies require notification following a cyber incident naturally depends upon the type of data that may have been subject to unauthorized access or exfiltration and, in some instances, the number of affected individuals.

2.2.1. *HHS / OCR for Protected Health Information (PHI)*

The U.S. Department of Health and Human Services is the regulator for a cyber incident involving PHI, but the reporting of such events and any subsequent investigation is left to the Office of Civil Rights (OCR). Once a cyber incident involving PHI is reported on the HHS portal, an OCR investigator is assigned. If multiple Covered Entities (CE) and different notification dates are involved in the same cyber incident, the investigator may ask the targeted entity with the reporting obligation to consolidate its later-filed reports as one or more supplements. In all instances, if a CE decides it wants to report on its own and not through the targeted entity, OCR will request that the CE use the same tracking number as the original OCR report.

The pre-breach security requirements in place during the cyber incident will be subject to particular scrutiny during any post-mortem discussion. Whatever security measures might have been in place will also be included in any OCR investigation if the data breach involved PHI in reportable quantities.

For example, in any cyber incident involving PHI, the report to OCR will require a fairly detailed description of the measures and policies that were in place prior to the incident. The OCR reporting form asks what safeguards were in place prior to the breach, and the typical response would be something like:

- Privacy Rule Safeguards (Training, Policies and Procedures, etc.)
- Security Rule Administrative Safeguards (Risk Analysis, Risk Management, etc.)
- Security Rule Physical Safeguards (Facility Access Controls, Workstation Security, etc.)
- Security Rule Technical Safeguards (Access Controls, Transmission Security, etc.)

Of course, OCR will be looking to confirm that these policies and procedures are in place when it begins its investigation.

2.2.2. *FINCen*

The Financial Crimes Enforcement Network (FINCen) assists financial institutions when reporting cyber incidents through reports known as Suspicious Activity Reports, or SARs.[47] SAR reports are filed online and primarily cover entities regulated by the Federal

47. *Frequently Asked Questions (FAQs) regarding the Reporting of Cyber-Events, Cyber-Enabled Crime, and Cyber-Related Information through Suspicious Activity Reports (SARs)*, FINCEN (Oct. 24, 2016), https://www.fincen.gov/frequently-asked-questions-faqs-regarding-reporting-cyber-events-cyber-enabled-crime-and-cyber.

Reserve Board, the Federal Deposit Insurance Corporation, the Internal Revenue Service, the National Credit Union Administration, and the Office of the Comptroller of the Currency. The online reporting portal is set up as a series of six tabbed folders with each tab having a separate heading and information requirement.

2.2.3. *Credit Unions (state and federal)*

Credit unions will also report cyber incidents to the online portal at FINCen, but because of the nature of credit union organizations, a different series of notifications may be necessary. In the first instance, credit unions are member-owned cooperatives, and those who have accounts in credit unions are both members and owners. In addition, individual credit unions often will form cooperatives among themselves to expand and diversify the services they can offer their members. Such entities are known as Credit Union Service Organizations (CUSO).

The organizational structure can be particularly relevant in any kind of cyber incident because the "owners" in an incident involving a CUSO can be many different credit unions. Quick decision-making can be logistically challenging if the targeted credit union is without a current and practiced incident response plan that accounts for its ownership structure and the obligations of other credit unions with which it is connected through a CUSO. State, federal and/or foreign notification follow suit in the same way as any other cyber incident, but the credit union will also report the event to the National Credit Union Administration (NCUA)[48] and, depending on the state where the credit union is organized, the state agency that regulates the credit union.

2.3. State Statutes & Notification Requirements

Notification requirements in the aftermath of a cyber incident can be overwhelming. Cyber counsel must determine not only whether and what type of personally identifiable information (PII) or personal data might have been accessed and/or acquired without authorization, but also the territorial reach of the affected individuals, which will determine what reporting jurisdictions are implicated. For most nationally-based companies, this means the potential and fairly immediate grasp of the notice deadlines and requirements for the fifty U.S. states, Washington, D.C., and three U.S. territories, Puerto Rico, the US Virgin Islands, and Guam.

2.3.1. *Notice to Affected Individuals*

Before the dust settles on the chaotic landscape of a cyber incident and critical in the assessment of a targeted entity's notification obligations, the entity must determine what TYPE of data may have been accessed without authorization and define the entire universe of potentially affected individuals. The definition of PII will vary across all U.S. state, district, and territorial jurisdictions, and in recent years states have amended their statutes to add

48. See NCUA, *Appendix B to Part 748—Guidance on Response Programs for Unauthorized Access to Member Information and Member Notice*, https://www.ecfr.gov/cgi-bin/text-idx?SID=6bad163a87acc23df9cf41284e8c174f&mc=true&node=ap12.7.748_12.b&rgn=div9.

to the types of data included in the definition of personal information;[49] thus, the relevant inquiry must focus not only on what types of data may have been accessed, but also on jurisdictions in which individuals whose PII was compromised were located at the time of the potential unauthorized access. In addition, where PHI may have a uniform federal definition, some states include PHI in their definition of PII so that a targeted entity may not have a reportable incident under HIPAA (e.g., fewer than 500 affected individuals), but it may nonetheless have to report a data breach under applicable state law.

Other things to consider include:

- What information can be forensically confirmed to have been accessed or exfiltrated without authorization?
- What information can be forensically confirmed NOT to have been accessed or exfiltrated without authorization, which is a critical defense under HIPAA/HITECH.[50]

For example, only if the relevant log files were both "on" and preserved at the initial phase of the forensic investigation can the practitioner attempt to glean the necessary evidence to assert the "low probability" defense required under HHS current guidance (issued in 2016)[51] for ransomware incidents when PHI is present. The four risk assessment factors HHS identifies to demonstrate that there is a low probability that PHI has been compromised are:

---

49. The definition of PII among state data breach statutes varies widely. For example, in Michigan "personal information" means "the first name or first initial and last name linked to 1 or more of the following data elements of a resident of this state:

(i) Social security number.

(ii) Driver license number or state personal identification card number.

(iii) Demand deposit or other financial account number, or credit card or debit card number, in combination with any required security code, access code, or password that would permit access to any of the resident's financial accounts." MICH. COMP. LAWS SERV. § 445.63(r) (2025).

Compare that with the definition of "personal information" under Connecticut's data breach statute, where personal information means "an individual's (A) first name or first initial and last name in combination with any one, or more, of the following data: (i) Social Security number; (ii) taxpayer identification number; (iii) identity protection personal identification number issued by the Internal Revenue Service; (iv) driver's license number, state identification card number, passport number, military identification number or other identification number issued by the government that is commonly used to verify identity; (v) credit or debit card number; (vi) financial account number in combination with any required security code, access code or password that would permit access to such financial account; (vii) medical information regarding an individual's medical history, mental or physical condition, or medical treatment or diagnosis by a health care professional; (viii) health insurance policy number or subscriber identification number, or any unique identifier used by a health insurer to identify the individual; (ix) biometric information consisting of data generated by electronic measurements of an individual's unique physical characteristics used to authenticate or ascertain the individual's identity, such as a fingerprint, voice print, retina or iris image; or (x) precise geolocation data, as defined in section 42-515; or (B) user name or electronic mail address, in combination with a password or security question and answer that would permit access to an online account." CONN. GEN. STAT. § 36a-701b(a)(2) (LexisNexis, 2025). *See also* HANDBOOK, Chapter 7, *Legal Obligations to Provide Data Security*.

50. The Health Information Technology for Economic and Clinical Health Act (HITECH) was enacted in 2009 as Division A, Title XIII and Division B, Title IV of the American Recovery and Reinvestment Act.

51. Jessica Davis, *HHS Office for Civil Rights Releases Ransomware Guidance*, HEALTHCAREITNEWS (Jul. 12, 2016), https://www.healthcareitnews.com/news/hhs-office-civil-rights-releases-ransomware-guidance.

1. The nature and extent of protected health information involved, including the types of identifiers and the likelihood of re-identification;
2. The unauthorized person who used protected health information or to whom the disclosure was made;
3. Whether protected health information was actually acquired or viewed; and
4. the extent to which the risk to protected health information has been mitigated.[52]

From the universe of "potentially affected individuals," if you CANNOT assert the "low probability" defense required under current HHS guidance, then the next steps are to determine what type of information may have been subjected to the potential unauthorized access or exfiltration:

- Personally Identifiable Information (PII) as defined under U.S. state, District/territorial laws. As noted above, scoping assessment of PII compromise is a 50-state, DC, Puerto Rico, US Virgin Islands, and Guam task because each jurisdiction has its own governing law based on the "affected individuals" residing in that jurisdiction.
- Protected Health Information (PHI) as defined under HIPAA/HITECH. This can be tricky because some states define PHI under their state data breach laws more stringently than the federal law does (e.g., Florida).
- Personal Data as defined under both the EU's GDPR and the UK's Data Protection Act. This extends broadly to "any information relating to an identified or identifiable natural person."
- Personal Information as defined under Canada's PIPEDA. This also extends broadly to "information about an identifiable individual."

The type of notice that an individual receives depends on the nature of the affected data and the medium with which the individual interacted with the breach source. For example, if the individual's sole interaction (and sharing of his/her personal data) was via the internet and the only contact information available for that person is an email address, then email notice may suffice. If the interaction was by regular mail, then print letters sent through the U.S. Postal Service delivery is the method of notice. If there is no good contact information for the affected individual, then "substitute notice" in the form of a website notice on the breach source's website may be the only way to reach those individuals.[53]

---

52. HHS, Breach Notification Rule, https://www.hhs.gov/hipaa/for-professionals/breach-notification/index.html. The HIPAA Breach Notification Rule is codified at 45 C.F.R. §§ 164.400–414. The risk assessment factors are embedded in the Rule's definition of "Breach." 45 C.F.R. § 164.402.

53. The Privacy Rights Clearinghouse offers an interactive dashboard of data breach notification statutes by state on its website. *Data Breach Notification in the United States 2022 Report*, PRIVACY RTS. CLEARINGHOUSE (Jan. 27, 2023), https://privacyrights.org/resources/data-breach-notification-2022.

2.3.2. *Notice to Attorneys General*

State statutes vary as to whether they require notification of a data breach to their attorneys general and the type of information to be included where notice is required. Some states expect notice within 30 days of the incident, even though the entity breached may not have been able to determine the nature of the cyber-attack or indeed, whether PII or PHI was subject to unauthorized access or exfiltration (e.g., Indiana[54]). Other states provide notice forms that reporting entities can submit electronically (e.g., California, Massachusetts, Nebraska, North Carolina) and still others have forms that can be sent by fax or email (e.g., New York). In addition to these requirements, some states also require that the breached entity provide the attorney general of the state where the affected individuals reside a sample of the individual notice that was sent to affected individuals.

Increasingly, states and those agencies designated to respond to breach notifications under their pertinent data breach statutes are becoming more engaged once notified. Typically, these agencies will want more details about the data breach, not only the number of affected individuals in their respective state, but also the number of total affected individuals across other jurisdictions, both state and foreign. For a breach involving protected health information and requiring Office of Civil Rights (OCR) notification, the state agencies will seek a copy of the OCR Report filed online at the HHS portal. In addition, depending on the state jurisdiction, the number of affected individuals in the state, and whether the state is a "notice" jurisdiction, (i.e., notice to a state agency such as the office of the Attorney General, Insurance Commission, or Consumer Protection Agency), the state's attorney general may seek both to receive all relevant documentation about the cyber incident and be included in any ultimate OCR investigation.

In Montana, for example, state law requires that "[a]ny person or business that is required to issue a notification pursuant to this [Computer Security Breach] section shall simultaneously submit an electronic copy of the notification and a statement providing the date and method of distribution of the notification to the attorney general's consumer protection office, excluding any information that personally identifies any individual who is entitled to receive notification. If a notification is made to more than one individual, a single copy of the notification must be submitted that indicates the number of individuals in the state who received notification."[55]

Some states (Tennessee, for example) have turned the long-time defense of encryption on its head and required notification even if the data subjected to the unauthorized access was encrypted at rest in the target entity's IT environment. Tennessee also requires notification to the state no later than 45 days from the date of discovery.[56] As experienced practitioners

54. Ind. Code Ann. §§ 4-1-11-1 to-10, 24-4.9-1-1 to -5-1 (2025). Over the years, the author has notified the AG's office in Indiana with preliminary information and the promise of follow up when more details are known. To date, this has been sufficient to satisfy the notice deadline.

55. Mont. Code Ann. § 30-14-1704(8)) (2025).

56. Tenn. Code Ann. § 47-18-2107 (2025).

know, focusing efforts on notification so early in the forensic process may be laudable from a transparency standpoint, but it also diverts critical resources in the early days of determining: what happened, preserving evidence, identifying what types of data may have been accessed, and confirming the pertinent jurisdictions, both domestic and foreign, of the affected population. It is doubtful that state legislators had other state and foreign jurisdictions in mind when they drafted data breach legislation. Assessing and juggling the timing required in multiple state and foreign jurisdictions is a common and nightmarish reality. Once the accessed date, affected population, and jurisdictions are more clearly identified, a second round of notifications may be required.

2.3.3. *Notice to Insurance Commissioners*

Some states require notice to the applicable insurance regulator in the event of a breach (e.g., Connecticut, Maine, Michigan, Montana, New Hampshire, Ohio, Washington, Wisconsin). For example, in Ohio, persons considered licensees under Ohio insurance law are required to report cybersecurity events involving nonpublic information to the state's Superintendent of Insurance under certain conditions. Reporting is required when Ohio is the licensee's domicile or home state and the cybersecurity event is likely to materially harm a consumer or a material part of the licensee's normal operations. Reporting is also required when the licensee reasonably believes the nonpublic information relates to 250 or more Ohio residents, and the licensee is required by law to report the cybersecurity event to another government or supervisory body or self-regulatory agency or the event is reasonably likely to materially harm an Ohio consumer or any material part of the licensee's operations.[57]

In Connecticut, regulated entities must provide notice to the Insurance Department in the event of a breach. Connecticut law also requires at least 24 months of free identity theft prevention services.[58] This requirement can prove challenging when the cyber liability coverage under an insurance policy covers only 12 months of reporting, which is a common policy limitation. In those instances where a breach covers jurisdictions with conflicting requirements, prior consultation with underwriters' counsel is important. Generally, underwriters will approve a different requirement, for example, Connecticut's 24-month term for theft preventions services, when it is a statutory requirement.

In South Carolina, Michigan, and Ohio, there are special notification obligations in certain circumstances.

- Under South Carolina's Insurance Data Security Act, a licensee, as defined, is required to notify the Director of the Department of Insurance "no later than seventy-two hours

57. OHIO REV. CODE ANN. § 3965.04(A) (LexisNexis 2025). Ohio's statute for cybersecurity event reporting by insurance companies defines "consumer," "cybersecurity event," and "licensee." *Id.* [sec] 3965.01(D), (E) & (M).

58. CONN. GEN. STAT. § 36a-701b(b)(2)B).

after determining that a cybersecurity event has occurred" when certain criteria are met.[59]

- Similarly, under Michigan's Data Security Act, which took effect in January 2021, each licensee, as defined, is required to notify the director "as promptly as possible but not later than 10 business days after a determination that a cybersecurity event involving nonpublic information that is in the possession of a licensee has occurred" when certain criteria are met.[60]
- Ohio's Insurance Data Security Law, which became effective on March 20, 2019, requires notification to the Superintendent of Insurance "as promptly as possible after a determination that a cybersecurity event involving nonpublic information in the possession of the licensee has occurred, but in no event later than three business days after that determination" when certain criteria are met.[61]

2.3.4. *Notice to Consumer Protection Agencies*

As with other specific requirements under state data breach laws, whether or not notice is required to a particular state's consumer protection agency is a state-by-state determination. Where some states, such as Massachusetts, New York, and South Carolina, require notification, others do not. For example, Michigan is not a notice state, but when individuals in an affected population begin to contact the Consumer Protection Division with questions about a data breach notification, the Attorney General's office is likely to request information from the targeted entity. This can be a judgment call for cyber counsel: whether or not to provide a courtesy notification to state agencies concurrent with notification to the affected population when that particular state does not require notice. Experience says that this is often the right thing to do.

- In Massachusetts, notice of the breach to the Director of Consumer Affairs and Business Regulation is required "as soon as practicable and without unreasonable delay" following the breach.[62]
- Additionally, Massachusetts requires 18 months of free credit monitoring when Social Security Numbers are compromised.[63]
- In New York, notice to the Department of State's Division of Consumer Protection is required in addition to notice to two other offices (the New York Attorney General and the NYS Division of State Police) for any breaches of computerized data that includes private information (defined as a subset of personal information).[64]

---

59. S.C. Code Ann. § 38-99-40(A) (2025).
60. Mich. Comp. Laws Serv. § 500.559(1) (LexisNexis 2025).
61. Ohio Rev. Code Ann. § 3965.04.
62. Mass. Ann. Laws ch. 93H § 3(b) (LexisNexis 2025).
63. *Id.* ch. 93H § 3A.
64. N.Y. Gen. Bus. Law § 899-aa § 8 (Consol. 2025).

- Notification to New York may also yield an inquiry from the Bureau of Internet and Technology requesting further information.
- In South Carolina, notice to the Consumer Protection Division of the Department of Consumer Affairs is required "if a business provides notice to more than one thousand persons at one time" as required by the South Carolina reporting statute.[65]

2.3.5. *Notice to Credit Reporting Agencies*

With their focus on consumer protection, some states require reporting to credit reporting agencies. For example, Florida requires the reporting entity to provide the "timing, distribution, and content of the notices" to "all consumer reporting agencies that compile and maintain files on consumers on a nationwide basis" for breaches involving notice under the Florida statute of "more than 1,000 individuals at a single time."[66] There is a similar requirement in Maine.[67] Notification to a credit reporting agency may yield a response from one or more of them (Equifax, TransUnion, Experian) requesting additional information, such as a sample notice letter.

2.3.6. *Notice to Law Enforcement*

Whether or not notification of local, state, or federal law enforcement is required must be carefully and immediately assessed. For the targeted entity, typical notification would be to local law enforcement, where, in cases such as a fraudulent wire transfer, a police report would be useful when trying to get the fraudulent account's recipient's (the "mule") information from the domestic receiving bank. In addition, the affected individuals in a data breach are commonly advised to file police reports, which will prove helpful when taking steps to protect themselves from identity theft.

For years, these steps have been part of the Federal Trade Commission (FTC) website's ID Theft advice page.[68] The timing for such local law enforcement notification and the procedures that the enforcement agency uses to communicate within its jurisdiction must be assessed carefully. For example, some local law enforcement agencies use e-blast notices to their constituents, which, if a targeted entity provides immediate notice to its local police, can result in that notice being disseminated throughout the community before all the facts are known. This is not the case when filing an online complaint through the FBI's Internet Crime Complaint Center (IC3), as described below.

For internet-based data breaches involving incidents such as ransomware and wire fraud, cyber counsel should file an online complaint on the FBI's Internet Crime Complaint

---

65. S.C. Code Ann. § 39-1-90(K).
66. Fla. Stat. Ann. § 501.171(5) (LexisNexis 2025).
67. Me. Rev. Stat. Ann. tit. 10, § 1348(4) (2025).
68. *FTC Consumer Advice: Identity Theft*, FTC, https://consumer.ftc.gov/features/identity-theft (visited Sept. 13, 2025); *IdentityTheft.gov*, FTC, https://www.identitytheft.gov/ (visited Sept. 13, 2025).

Center, IC3.[69] Often, there is little that the FBI (or local law enforcement) can do besides document the incident, collect the indicators of compromise (if available), and warn the public of new trends or dangerous activities.[70] Recently, the FBI has increased its focus on internet crime syndicates, whose threats to lives, property, and critical infrastructure have outstripped our efforts to thwart them. Sharing information can be valuable to both the public and private sector, but keep in mind that it is generally best to notify law enforcement through experienced cyber counsel.

2.4. Notice to Parties under Contract

In addition to the legal requirements under applicable federal, state, and foreign laws, an entity must also look at its contractual obligations. The task of reviewing contracts for notification obligations is often overlooked in the flurry of trying to address the immediate forensic issues of what happened, notifying the internal cyber response team, and the external parties involved directly in the response—the forensic team, cyber counsel, and the insurance carrier. Then too, in the effort to go paperless, contracts and ancillary documents including notice details may exist only in electronic form and very possibly could be inaccessible for a time if they are encrypted as a result of a ransomware attack.

Not only might these documents be inaccessible, but the response team may be unaware that breach notification obligations were added to (modified in) the breached entity's standard agreements with customers, vendors, or suppliers. Entities handling PHI are generally aware of their notification obligations under their business associate agreements with covered entities, but they may not realize there are additional notice requirements that have been added to contracts more globally and with varied requirements.

Contractual obligations have real impacts, particularly with the recent and heightened awareness of the potential for cyber incidents of all kinds. From business associate agreements, to data protection agreements under the GDPR, to standard IT platforms, SaaS, or other types of agreements in which the contracting parties focus on the security of sensitive data—and thus the need for notice if there is any unauthorized access to that data—there are often notification and shifting burden obligations that must be reviewed in the early

69. Internet Crime Complaint Center, https://www.ic3.gov/complaint/splash.aspx (last visited Sept. 13, 2025). See also the discussion about IC3 reporting above in Section 1.2 of this Part II.

70. Following ransomware attacks, the FBI has occasionally been able to raid the threat actor's bitcoin wallet to retrieve some of the extorted funds. The FBI recovered more than half the ransom paid in the Colonial Pipeline attack in May 2021. *Department of Justice Seizes $2.3 Million in Cryptocurrency Paid to the Ransomware Extortionists Darkside*, Dept. of Justice (Jun. 7, 2021), https://www.justice.gov/archives/opa/pr/department-justice-seizes-23-million-cryptocurrency-paid-ransomware-extortionists-darkside. The FBI also remediated the vulnerability posed by the Microsoft Hafnium exploit in March 2021 after obtaining court approval of a FRCP Rule 41 Search Warrant to access infected machines. *Justice Department Announces Court-Authorized Effort to Disrupt Exploitation of Microsoft Exchange Server Vulnerabilities*, Dept. of Justice (Apr. 13, 2021), https://www.justice.gov/archives/opa/pr/justice-department-announces-court-authorized-effort-disrupt-exploitation-microsoft-exchange.

days of a breach (if not cataloged on an ongoing basis). Of course, identifying and listing these notice obligations in the Incident Response Plan would be an ideal best practice.

2.5. The Cyber Insurance Carrier

If the targeted entity has cyber liability coverage, notice to its insurance broker should be immediate, as soon as it is evident that a cyber incident of some kind has occurred (noting what kind of coverage the entity has and its specific notice requirements). The broker is an extremely helpful intermediary for those situations in which the full breadth or impact of the cyber incident is unknown, and it may be premature or even not necessary to notify the carrier. The broker can help assess and determine the nature of the incident and whether the incident even would be covered under the policy. If the incident fell under the policy's coverage, the broker could assist with the necessary phrasing and details that are required to send to the carrier. Cyber counsel should be aware that cyber liability policies cover all types of cyber claims, including the legal fees associated with assisting the targeted entity with these claims. However, cyber policies typically do NOT cover legal fees for assisting the entity with filing a claim or interpreting the policy, which is a further reason for notifying the broker that assisted the entity in placing the coverage.

In addition, unless the targeted entity has experienced internal or outside cyber counsel and forensic experts "pre-vetted" with the insurance carrier, the carrier will assign both cyber counsel and a forensic team from among its paneled experts. These individuals are certainly qualified and capable, but they are often not local ("boots on the ground" can be critical in the early hours of a breach) and will not have the insight and institutional knowledge of the targeted entity that can be critical to assist with speedy decision-making in the early hours of a cyber-attack. Thus, if an entity already has cyber counsel and forensic experts incorporated into its Incident Response Plan, it is a best practice to get this team pre-vetted and approved by the insurance carrier and/or its underwriter.

3. The Rise of Trench-Tested Best Practices

3.1. Paying Ransom (or Not)

Typically, there is not a lot of time for a targeted entity to evaluate whether to pay a ransom or not and, if so, to negotiate the type of currency. Cyber criminals provide a time deadline—24 or 48 hours—and provide instructions for paying the ransom. That deadline clock will start ticking when the targeted entity (or its representative) responds to the ransom notice. Thus, it is a very good idea for the targeted entity to determine a strategy and response with its forensic and legal experts before responding to the cyber criminal and setting off the clock. Keep in mind, too, that the cyber criminal is in business for its payday; the negotiating team can buy time by responding that it needs time to arrange the financing and cryptocurrency exchange (e.g., dollars to bitcoin). Occasionally, negotiation with the cybercriminal will work to lower the payment demand. In recent years, the average ransom demands have gone from the hundreds of thousands of dollars to the multiple millions.[71] That's a long way from the early days, when the common demand was $500.

To pay or not to pay is an analysis that begins with the integrity of the targeted entity's backup. More often than not, backup files have also been encrypted or the backup is restored into the environment before all traces of the malware have been eradicated and the backup becomes cross-contaminated. Another factor is whether the time and effort to restore systems using the backup will take longer (and perhaps be just as costly given business downtime) than paying the ransom and starting the decryption process.

These are difficult decisions, and often there is little time to evaluate the best solution. The process of decryption can take weeks or months in a large IT environment. Occasionally, the cyber-criminal will withhold some decryption keys to keep open the option of extorting additional ransom. In addition, decryption keys cannot be trusted in all instances to be "clean"—the keys will arrive with their own form of mischief; for example, launching additional malware or manipulating the Windows registry files. As mentioned previously in this chapter, the best practice for an entity using a cyber criminal's decryption key is to run the decryption program in a secure "sandbox," which can be forensically examined prior to introducing the decrypted programs back into the IT environment of the targeted entity.

The most popular cryptocurrency in the ransomware world is bitcoin, although its star is not shining quite as brightly lately. One reason is that bitcoin transactions can be traced back to users, which is not good if you are the cybercriminal trying to hide your tracks. Another reason is the market volatility of bitcoin: a demand for 20 bitcoins on day 1 of a ransomware demand could be worth much less on day 2 or 3. Other cryptocurrencies are monero (useful for its privacy features, which stop transactions from being traced back to users) and ethereum (the second largest cryptocurrency by market capitalization).

3.2. OFAC Issues

The Office of Foreign Assets and Control (OFAC) is part of the Department of the Treasury and administers and enforces economic sanctions programs against countries and

71. Danny Palmer, *Largest Ransomware Demand Now Stands at $30 Million as Crooks Get Bolder*, ZDNET (Mar. 17, 2021), https://www.zdnet.com/article/largest-ransomware-demand-now-stands-at-30-million-as-crooks-get-bolder/. Chainanalysis monitors the blockchain and provides blockchain data used for investigations and other purposes. In February 2024, it reported that ransom payments in 2023 exceeded $1 billion. "Overall, big game hunting has become the dominant strategy over the last few years, with a bigger and bigger share of all ransomware payment volume being made up of payments of $1 million or more." Chainanalysis, *The 2024 Crypto Crime Report: The Latest Trends in Ransomware, Scams, Hacking, and More* 12, 15 (Feb. 2024), https://go.chainalysis.com/crypto-crime-2024.html. In February 2025, Chainanalysis reported "the total volume of ransom payments [in 2024] decreased year-over-year (YoY) by approximately 35%, driven by increased law enforcement actions, improved international collaboration, and a growing refusal by victims to pay." In 2024, ransomware payments totaled approximately $813.55 million, compared to $1.25 billion in 2023. Chainanalysis, *The 2025 Crypto Crime Report: The Rising Role of Cryptocurrency in All Forms of Crime and How Its Transparency Is Creating Unique Opportunities for Investigation* 10 (Feb. 2025), https://go.chainalysis.com/2025-Crypto-Crime-Report.html.

individuals. If the cybercriminal behind a ransomware attack is on the Specially Designated Nationals (SDN) list, the target entity could be breaking U.S. law by paying a ransomware demand to any cybercriminal identified in a Sanctions List Search application. The OFAC website maintains a lookup for the Sanctions List Search.[72] It's not a good day when the bitcoin payment you make to the cybercriminal will also subject you to OFAC enforcement; thus, a best practice—depending on whether the currency transaction is traceable back to the criminal—is to perform a quick look-up at OFAC. The dilemma, of course, is what if the criminal is on the SDN list? At this point, the targeted entity should have filed a complaint describing the incident on the FBI's Internet Crime Complaint Center (IC3) and would be advised to consult with a special agent at the Bureau who is versed in this issue.

On October 1, 2020, OFAC released official guidance[73] on this issue in which it warned against making payments to individuals or entities on the "Specially Designated Nationals and Blocked Persons" List or others who may also be covered by country or region embargoes. The critical and noteworthy part of this advisory is the notice to companies that engage with victims of ransomware attacks of the potential sanctions risks for facilitating ransomware payments. The practical result is that if the threat actor is an individual or entity on the "list," then all involved—cyber counsel, forensic consultant, insurance company, and the victim entity itself—could be subjected to sanctions if a ransom payment is facilitated.

3.3. Managing the Message

Most cyber liability insurance policies will offer coverage for public relations experts. Even if it is not covered, proper messaging is important. Templates covering the typical range of incidents should be part of the Incident Response Plan. As more fully described below, messaging is an ongoing task, beginning with internal notices to company leadership, general employees, customers, suppliers, the public, and responding to media.

3.3.1. *Entity Leadership*

There are numerous examples of how NOT to manage the message when a company becomes the target of a data breach. Examples from the last few years involving Uber and Equifax come to mind.

In the Uber data breach, Uber leadership paid $100,000 to hackers in an effort to keep the breach of 57 million accounts from becoming public information. When the story broke (in a blog post by the Uber CEO who had not known of the incident that had taken place 10 months prior to his arrival at Uber), the chief security officer and his deputy were fired.[74]

---

72. *Sanctions List Search*, OFAC, https://sanctionssearch.ofac.treas.gov/ (visited Sept. 13, 2025).

73. *Ransomware Advisory*, OFAC (Oct. 1, 2020), https://home.treasury.gov/policy-issues/financial-sanctions/recent-actions/20201001.

74. Greg Bensinger & Robert McMillan, *Uber Reveals Data Breach and Cover-up, Leading to Two Firings*, WALL ST. J. (updated Nov. 21, 2017, 11:38 PM ET), https://www.wsj.com/articles/uber-reveals-data-breach-and-cover-up-leading-to-two-firings-1511305453 (subscription required).

Equifax managed its communications a bit differently than Uber, but the results were equally misguided. The allegations are that Equifax officers' sale of company stock preceded public disclosure of the breach. In a statement to the media, Equifax stated that "it found out about the security incident on July 29, 2017, and immediately took action."[75] Presumably, that action would have included notification to its executive team, which should have included its general counsel and members of its board of directors. Knowing of a potential cyber incident that goes to the heart of what the company's mission entails—protecting the sensitive financial data of millions of Americans—how could the general counsel's approval of the sale of millions of dollars of company stock by three Equifax executives be seen as escaping SEC scrutiny? Reporting indicated that the general counsel knew at the time he gave his approval that Equifax's IT department "had detected suspicious activity."[76] According to news reports and SEC filings at the time:

- Equifax Chief Financial Officer John Gamble sold shares worth nearly $950,000 on August 1 [three days after the breach was detected];
- Equifax's president for U.S. information solutions, Joseph Loughran, sold shares worth about $685,000 on August 1; and
- Equifax's president of workforce solutions, Rodolfo Ploder, sold stock for just more than $250,000 on August 2.[77]

Yet, when called to appear before the U.S. House of Representatives Energy and Commerce Committee in the fall of 2017, the by-then former CEO blamed the incident on the failure of one employee to implement a critical software patch. This claimed defense did not hold water with House Committee members, one of whom notably commented, "How does this happen when so much is at stake? ... I don't think we can pass a law that, excuse me for saying this, fixes stupid. I can't fix stupid.'"[78]

Not long after the public notice of the breach, the SEC investigated the activities of Jun Ying, who had been in line to take over the position of Equifax's global CIO. Apparently, soon after the breach and before Equifax gave notice to the public, Ying exercised all of

75. Paul R. LaMonica, *Equifax Execs Sold Stock before Hack Was Disclosed*, CNN Bus. (Sep. 8, 2017, 12:35 PM ET), https://money.cnn.com/2017/09/08/investing/equifax-stock-insider-sales-hack-data-breach/index.html. The breach actually occurred on May 13, 2017, when hackers exploited a known vulnerability in a software platform hosting Equifax's dispute resolution portal. *See* Carole Piovesan, *Cyber Breach Planning: Lessons from the Equifax Breach*, Forbes (Apr. 15, 2019, 12:36 PM EDT), https://www.forbes.com/sites/cognitiveworld/2019/04/15/cyber-breach-planning-lessons-from-the-equifax-breach/ (citing the Office of the Privacy Commissioner of Canada's Investigation into Equifax posted on April 9, 2019). The Privacy Commissioner's report, *Investigation into Equifax Inc. and Equifax Canada Co.'s Compliance with PIPEDA in Light of the 2017 Breach of Personal Information*, PIPEDA Findings #2019-001 (Apr. 9, 2019), is available at https://www.priv.gc.ca/en/opc-actions-and-decisions/investigations/investigations-into-businesses/2019/pipeda-2019-001/.

76. Tara Siegel Bernard & Stacy Cowley, *Equifax Breach Caused by Lone Employee's Error, Former C.E.O. Says*, NY Times (Oct. 3, 2017), https://www.nytimes.com/2017/10/03/business/equifax-congress-data-breach.html.

77. LaMonica, *supra* note 75.

78. Siegel Bernard & Cowley, *supra* note 76.

his company stock options and then sold the shares, yielding proceeds of nearly $1 million. As reported by the SEC in its press release, Ying avoided "more than $117,000 in losses" by selling his stock prior to public notice.[79] On June 27, 2019, Ying was sentenced to four months in prison after which he was to be released under supervision for one year. He also was ordered to pay restitution of the $117,000 in losses he tried to avoid as well as a $55,000 fine.[80]

Later that year, the Federal Trade Commission announced a global settlement with Equifax of claims brought by the FTC, Consumer Financial Protection Bureau, and 50 U.S. states and territories. Equifax agreed to pay at least $575 million, and potentially as much as $700 million., which included over $425 million for consumers. Affected consumers were eligible for free credit monitoring for ten years, identity restoration services for at least seven years, and, beginning in 2020, six free copies of their credit report each year for seven years. Money was also set aside for consumers with certain other eligible expenses if they could prove their identity theft related expense stemmed from the Equifax breach. The settlement also required Equifax to implement a comprehensive information security program and obtain third-party security assessments every two years (with the assessor being subject to FTC approval).[81]

The lessons learned in the Equifax example are many, but two stand out: The first is to get the internal message out immediately to company leadership and all staff to ensure a consistent and clear external message. The second is to deploy a pre-vetted and practiced internal and external team to manage the incident. The time to assemble a media response team and incident response team is not after an incident occurs. As cybersecurity experts will agree, when faced with the heat of a volatile cyber incident, a company is better served when it has a plan in place and funnels all public statements through a company spokesperson.[82] Of course, it also helps when "known vulnerabilities" are patched within days, not after months have passed.

The SEC also monitors public disclosure of risk, and in recent years, those risks include the use—and misuse—of the data companies collect and claim to protect. In the widely reported Cambridge Analytica matter, Cambridge Analytica used Facebook user data. In

79. *2018-40: Former Equifax Executive Charged with Insider Trading*, SEC (Mar. 14, 2018), https://www.sec.gov/news/press-release/2018-40.

80. *Former Equifax Employee Sentenced for Insider Trading*, US Attorney's Office, N.D. Ga. (June 27, 2019), https://www.justice.gov/usao-ndga/pr/former-equifax-employee-sentenced-insider-trading.

81. *Equifax to Pay $575 Million as Part of Settlement with FTC, CFPB, and States Related to 2017 Data Breach*, FTC (July 22, 2019), https://www.ftc.gov/news-events/news/press-releases/2019/07/equifax-pay-575-million-part-settlement-ftc-cfpb-states-related-2017-data-breach. The deadline for consumers to file claims for settlement funds was January 22, 2024—more than six years after Equifax announced the breach—and Equifax's settlement administrator distributed additional settlement payments in November 2024. *Equifax Data Breach Settlement: Important Settlement Update*, FTC (Nov. 2024), https://www.ftc.gov/enforcement/refunds/equifax-data-breach-settlement.

82. Ben DiPietro, *Regulatory Compliance Is Only Part of Cybersecurity*, Wall St. J. (Dec. 13, 2017, 11:52 AM ET), https://blogs.wsj.com/cio/2017/12/13/compliance-is-not-the-goal-of-cybersecurity/?guid=BL-CIOB-13198&mod=searchresults&page=2&pos=5&dsk=y.

the SEC's complaint announced on July 24, 2019, the SEC alleged that Facebook discovered the misuse of its data in 2015 but did not correct its original disclosure to investors. The original disclosure had stated that the Facebook users' data "may be improperly accessed, used or disclosed." Facebook finally made an accurate disclosure of the matter in March 2018, which, in the opinion of the SEC, was not soon enough. The SEC's 2019 response was to criticize Facebook's failure for taking so long to implement the requisite policies and procedures to assess the results of its initial internal investigation into the Cambridge Analytica matter. Facebook knew that Cambridge Analytica had actually misused the user data. The clear take-away message from the SEC press release stated: "Public companies must identify and consider the material risks to their business and have procedures designed to make disclosures that are accurate in all material respects, including not continuing to describe a risk as hypothetical when it has in fact happened."[83] Facebook agreed to pay $100 million to settle charges for making misleading disclosures.

3.3.2. *Employees, Contractors*

Swift and transparent communication to all staff is critical in any cyber incident. Again, having the outline of the message—with only the relevant details to fill in—and the person tasked with its communication at the ready serve several important objectives in the early chaotic days of a data breach. A company's employees and contractors are members of communities outside the workplace. Providing them with a clear message that contains as much detail as is both known and safe to convey is the right thing to do. In the face of a cyber incident, there are real concerns about job security, and rightly so. In the past several years, it has been widely reported that around 50% of small businesses would have to shut down in the face of a major data breach.[84] Added to the concern about job future is the real issue of the day-to-day operation of the company facing a major breach. If critical systems are down, so too, is productivity and the ability of the company to produce its goods or provide its services. With ransomware attacks, it can take multiple weeks for operations to resume on a somewhat normal basis. Throughout this disruption, companies must keep employees, contractors, customers, vendors, and suppliers informed as best they can. Such messaging must be done carefully, however, and in consultation with counsel and the company's PR team.

---

83. *Facebook to Pay $100 Million for Misleading Investors about the Risks It Faced From Misuse of User Data*, SEC (July 24, 2019), https://www.sec.gov/news/press-release/2019-140.

84. See Quinn Cleary, *The Devastating Impact of Ransomware Attacks on Small Businesses*, U. Md. L. School (Apr. 4, 2023), https://www.law.umaryland.edu/content/articles/name-659577-en.html; Joe Galvin, Opinion, *60 Percent of Small Businesses Fold within 6 Months of a Cyber Attack*, Inc. (May 7, 2018), https://www.inc.com/joe-galvin/60-percent-of-small-businesses-fold-within-6-months-of-a-cyber-attack-heres-how-to-protect-yourself.html. A more recent survey conducted by the Identity Theft Resource Center reported that 85% of small business owner respondents said, "they were ready to respond to a cyber event, up from 70 percent in 2022." *Identity Theft Resource Center 2023 Business Impact Report Finds Record Level of Attacks Despite High Confidence in Defense*, Identify Theft Resource Ctr. (Oct. 24, 2023), https://www.idtheftcenter.org/post/2023-business-impact-report-record-level-attacks-still-high-confidence-in-defense/.

Even so, such pre-planning does not prevent employees from taking their own message to the media. Witness the ransomware incident at Arizona Beverage a few years ago when "a person familiar with the matter" described the impact of the incident as "effectively shutting down sales operations for days," noted "surprise" that "an attack hadn't come sooner given the age of their systems," and added that "'[o]nce the backups didn't work, they started throwing money at the problem.'" The final quote from this unofficial company spokesperson was: "'We were losing millions of dollars a day in sales.... It was a complete shitshow.'"[85] The reporter attempted to reach the company spokesperson, but that individual did not respond to the reporter's email requesting comment.[86] This was a missed opportunity by the company to manage the message and the incident. Cyber incidents are, by their very nature, chaotic and disruptive. That is why having a plan and the right people in place is critical.

3.3.3. *Investors*

For public companies, their investors should learn about a data breach no sooner than the rest of the public. That certainly is the lesson for those Equifax insiders who knew about the breach and sold their stock prior to the public announcement. For private companies, the concern is a bit different. Here it may be more about resource allocation and assistance as private investors scramble to protect the company. Then there is the example of the Yahoo! data breach. In April 2018, Yahoo! paid a $35 million fine in a settlement with the SEC for misleading investors by failing to disclose the full impact of its 2013 data breach until details came out as part of Verizon's due diligence in acquiring Yahoo! in 2016.[87]

3.3.4. *Business Partners and Vendors*

Not only is it smart from a basic business practice to keep business partners, suppliers, and vendors informed, but also it may be contractually required. Among the early tasks in any cyber incident playbook is the discovery and confirmation of contractual as well as statutory reporting obligations. Many are familiar with notification requirements in Business Associate Agreements but may not be as aware of the notice obligations in data protection agreements, commonly part of contracts with global partners and increasingly included in commercial and IT agreements. As noted above, under the General Data Protection Regulation[88] (GDPR), a "processor" must notify its "controller" without undue delay after becoming aware of a data breach, and that controller—when feasible—has 72 hours to notify the supervisory authority. Three days is not a lot of time to sort through contracts (that may have been encrypted) to determine what to do and whom to notify under the contract.

---

85. Zach Whittaker, *Arizona Beverages Knocked Offline by Ransomware Attack*, TechCrunch (Apr. 2, 2019 10:25 AM PDT), https://techcrunch.com/2019/04/02/arizona-beverages-ransomware/.

86. *Id.*

87. *Altaba, Formerly Known as Yahoo!, Charged with Failing to Disclose Massive Cybersecurity Breach; Agrees To Pay $35 Million*, SEC (Apr. 24, 2018), https://www.sec.gov/newsroom/press-releases/2018-71.

88. GDPR, *supra* note 38.

3.4. Notable Mistakes

It is easy to second-guess actions taken in the midst of a crisis, but there are a few notable examples in recent years that should not be repeated.

3.4.1. *Hush Money to Hackers*

Perhaps the most headline-grabbing mistake when dealing with cyber criminals was Uber's attempt to pay $100,000 as hush money to its attackers.[89] While not a mistake by counsel—an internal board committee later investigated and concluded that neither CEO Travis Kalanick nor Uber's general counsel at the time were involved in the cover-up—the apparent sources of the hush-money payment were Uber's chief security officer and his deputy; they were fired in the aftermath.

The events unfolded in October 2016, when two hackers gained access to proprietary information that Uber engineers had stored on GitHub (a collaborative web-based service that software developers use). When the breach was announced nearly a year later, a GitHub spokesperson stated that the access to the GitHub site was not a failure of GitHub security. With their GitHub access, the hackers found and lifted Uber's access credentials to Uber's portal on Amazon Web Service (AWS), the storage location for 57 million individuals' data. The stored data included drivers' license numbers for 600,000 Uber drivers and the email addresses and cell phone numbers of ride-hailing users around the world.[90]

Reports indicated that the co-founder and then CEO Travis Kalanick learned of the incident about one month after it occurred, but never mentioned it to his replacement CEO, Dara Khosrowshahi, when Mr. Khosrowshahi took over in August 2017. At the same time that Kalanick learned of the hack and breach, Uber was negotiating with the FTC as part of the FTC's inquiry over how Uber stored consumer data.

It is difficult to imagine any realistic scenario in which payment of any amount of money could keep hidden a massive breach impacting the personal data of 57 million individuals worldwide. While the CEO (Kalanick) and the then-current general counsel were not implicated in the cover-up, standard best-practice incident response planning procedures would have included notice (at minimum) to both the CEO and the general counsel. The fact that the chief security officer and his deputy not only had ready access to $100,000 for payment to the cyber criminals—while also believing it possible to keep an incident of this magnitude contained within the Uber IT department—is extraordinary.

---

89. *See* Rob Wright, *The Uber Data Breach Cover-Up: A Timeline of Events*, TechTarget (Aug. 31, 2020), https://www.techtarget.com/searchsecurity/news/252488361/The-Uber-data-breach-cover-up-A-timeline-of-events; Jim Finkle & Heather Somerville, *Regulators to Press Uber after it Admits Covering Up Data Breach*, Reuters (Nov. 22, 2017 7:30 AM EST), https://www.reuters.com/article/technology/regulators-to-press-uber-after-it-admits-covering-up-data-breach-idUSKBN1DL2UP/; Bensinger & McMillan, *supra* note 74. *See also Ex-Uber Security Chief Sentenced for Data-Breach Cover-Up*, AP News (May 4, 2023, 10:45 PM EDT) (reporting that the former chief security officer was sentenced to three years' probation and fined $50,000 after being convicted of obstructing justice and concealing knowledge that a federal felony had been committed), https://apnews.com/article/uber-data-breach-coverup-sentenced-san-francisco-05b2ded36daf55012f03651cf2c7c931.

90. Finkle & Somerville, *supra* note 89.

3.4.2. *Walking Away*

Another example that is increasingly common is when the company decides that either the costs of system restoration or the requisite reporting and notification are just too great, and the company owners decide to walk away. An online health industry trade journal reported that a two-doctor ENT and hearing services practice in Battle Creek, Michigan, planned to close permanently and the practice's doctors retire instead of paying the $6,500 ransom demand to restore patient data.[91] While this may be the only economic choice the two doctors had, "walking away" does not relieve them from their legal obligations under applicable state and federal law. And this is not an uncommon result for small businesses faced with legal and forensic costs and no cyber liability coverage.

In the case of the ENT doctors, it was reported that the FBI was alerted and that "there is not believed to be any risk to patients" because "[n]o patient data appeared to have been viewed or accessed prior to files being deleted."[92] There are a number of questions raised by this statement: Who made the determination that no patient data was viewed prior to being deleted? If this had been a forensic determination, the cost of retaining a qualified forensic expert for this evaluation likely would have exceeded the ransomware payment demanded. Given that the patient data would have been PHI,[93] the guidance under HIPAA/HITECH states that any ransomware breach is a reportable event, unless the targeted entity can assert the "low probability" defense necessary in certain data breaches involving PHI. Missing from this brief news report are critical facts, thus it is difficult to assess the basis for the decision to walk away. Such a decision should not be made, however, without the advice of experienced forensic and legal experts.

3.4.3. *A Failure to Communicate*

The Equifax data breach noted above highlights the backlash, both in public sentiment and federal regulatory interest, to a breach impacting at least 145 million individuals in the US and approximately one million consumers outside of the U.S. The US Government Accountability Office ("GAO") published a report in August 2018 identifying Equifax's missteps, including its failure to implement industry standard best practices and a lack of internal controls and routine security reviews.[94] What seems remarkable in the early actions after the breach, which was discovered on July 29, 2017 (a Saturday), was that the Equifax general counsel was either not apprised about the breach or thought it irrelevant to his approval of the sale of millions of dollars of Equifax stock by three executives on August 1st, well in advance of the public announcement of the data breach on September 7, 2017. The approval and timing of the stock sales may have been innocent, but it seems

---

91. Steve Alder, *Michigan Practice Forced to Close Following Ransomware Attack*, HIPAA J. (Apr. 2, 2019), https://www.hipaajournal.com/michigan-practice-forced-to-close-following-ransomware-attack/.

92. *Id.*

93. *Id.* Patients interviewed for this story stated that their information included recent test results.

94. GAO, Data Protection: Actions Taken by Equifax and Federal Agencies in Response to the 2017 Breach, GAO-18-559 (Aug. 30, 2018), https://www.gao.gov/products/GAO-18-559.

that the general counsel should have been among the first to receive notice of the data breach and, having received that notice, should have been more circumspect about approving insider stock sales.

Another more common scenario is when an entity is the victim of a business email compromise in which the victim's email credentials are stolen, thus leading to the theft of the victim's mailbox. With the victim's email credentials and contact information, the hackers then start sending phishing emails to the victims' contacts in the name of the victim. Some cyber counsel may advise the targeted entity not to warn these contacts, which generally include clients/customers, while the event is still evolving, thinking that this is some type of admission of liability. Yet, the better practice—if the event is still new and unfolding—is to email the contacts with a brief warning about the phishing attempt and the danger of clicking on a malicious link.

4. Embracing Resiliency

This chapter focuses on responding to a cyber incident, but it is also important to highlight the steps a company can take *before* the cyber incident occurs. We call that building resiliency.

4.1. Three Basic Steps

So, how does a company build resiliency? There are three basic steps: create the Incident Response Plan (IRP), recruit the Incident Response (IR) team, and implement robust and comprehensive training that includes full-scale tabletop exercises. In my experience, it is the rare client who appears with its IRP in hand and IR team in the wings. Most clients need immediate help and advice, and hours, if not days, can be wasted in the immediate aftermath of a cyber incident with the client wondering if its insurance policy will cover the event, and if so, what will it cover, whether its policy requires paneled experts (and if not, where does one find those experts), what laws apply, who needs notification, and more.

When properly prepared and used, IRPs are well worth the time and energy it takes to prepare them because most of these questions will be answered as the IRP is drafted. IRPs become valuable roadmaps for navigating the early chaotic hours of a cyber incident. In addition, and as noted above, they are extremely useful tools during the *process* of their preparation, for as the initial IR team drafts the IRP, they must identify, connect with, and gain buy-in from their internal and external IR teams and familiarize themselves with the function and interconnection of the entity's basic digital infrastructure. The IRP and IR team are critical to the entity's successful response and recovery from a cyber incident. The real trick is to ensure that the IRP does not languish on the company server, and the internal IR team does not forget its training. The IRP should be printed out and tucked into the laptop case or backpack of every internal IR team member, and training that includes tabletop drills should be an annual exercise.

4.2. Retain External IR Experts

Whether your IT staff is internal or external, unless their day job involves digital forensics and cybersecurity, you should engage specialized and experienced third parties to assist with incident response. Experts in forensics, law, and public relations are the main external partners of the IR team, and their skill and experience are invaluable. Cyber insurance policies will generally list paneled legal and forensic teams, but it is the rare insurer that will refuse qualified experts as long as they agree to the insurer's panel rates. Once vetted and engaged, these external IR team members can conduct periodic vulnerability assessments and be active participants in your tabletop exercises with internal IR members. Contact your insurance broker to confirm pre-approval of these external IR team members.

4.3. Access FBI & CISA Resources

The Cybersecurity & Infrastructure Security Agency (CISA) is a federal agency that offers free tools and templates for incident response, such as cyber hygiene services that include vulnerability scanning and web application scanning.[95] CISA also offers a wide variety of tabletop exercise packages for download.[96]

The FBI is another helpful partner when the cyber incident occurs. The Office of Private Sector oversees the FBI's effort to increase collaboration and information sharing with the private sector.[97] Building relationships with the FBI and CISA agents in advance of an event allows sufficient familiarity for all to be ready, willing, and able to work together when the inevitable incident happens.

4.4. Final Thoughts

Perhaps the most important message is the realization that you are never "all set;" the measures you implement, the tools you deploy, and the training you roll out must be subjected to continuous scrutiny and updating. Everyone from the C-Suite to the storeroom must participate in—successfully—cyber scenario training. ***Every person in your company represents a potential pathway for threat actors to find an exploit.*** In sum, draft your IRP, recruit and assemble internal and external IR members, and conduct periodic tabletop exercises. These measures create the resilience needed to survive a cyber-attack. Entities that actively prepare and train for cyber incidents are those that recover faster, better, and with far less economic loss than those who do not.

---

95. *See Free Cybersecurity Services and Tools*, CISA, https://www.cisa.gov/resources-tools/resources/free-cybersecurity-services-and-tools (last visited Sept. 23, 2025).

96. *CISA Tabletop Exercise Packages*, CISA, https://www.cisa.gov/resources-tools/services/cisa-tabletop-exercise-packages (last visited Sept. 23, 2025).

97. *How the FBI Works with Businesses*, FBI, https://www.fbi.gov/how-we-can-help-you/office-of-private-sector (last visited Sept. 23, 2025).

5. Ten Key Points

1. Implement multifactor authentication (threat actors thrive when MFA is not deployed)
2. Mandate Virtual Private Networks (VPNs) for remote access to company networks (critical for a dispersed and/or work-from-home workforce)
3. Deploy endpoint detection and response (EDRs will detect and prevent most incidents automatically and do so 24/7/365) and turn on logging to capture events at least as far back as six months or more (you can't find what you can't see)
4. Implement an Incident Response Plan (without a plan, it can be chaos) and update it periodically (and keep a printed copy handy)
5. Encrypt confidential and sensitive data both at rest and in transit (encrypted data is useless to threat actors and a non-event under most data breach laws)
6. Back up data (encrypted) and secure that backup off-site (with a good backup available, no ransom payment is necessary)
7. Segment data across IT networks (don't make it easy for threat actors to crawl across your network)
8. Conduct periodic external and internal vulnerability scans (security is not a one-and-done effort and requires constant vigilance)
9. Digital & Physical Controls: control access credentials to need-to-have individuals (threat actors target IT managers with the "keys" to the network); maintain physical security controls (lock your doors and lock up your sensitive equipment)
10. Implement periodic training for all (training works and it's simple to do) and conduct table-top exercises that include all the key internal and external players identified in the IRP
11. Bonus Point 1: reach out and introduce your company to your local FBI field office private sector coordinator; that introduction can save precious time when you need the Bureau's help
12. Bonus Point 2: purchase a comprehensive cyber insurance policy (and pre-vet your cyber counsel and forensic team), but be prepared for rising premiums and decreasing coverage in the wake of increasing claims

The point is this: if the above practices were implemented company-wide, the rate and impact of cyber-attacks would be reduced markedly. There may be costs associated with their implementation, but the costs of non-implementation are much higher.

Chapter 14

Cyber Insurance for Law Firms and Legal Organizations

Kevin P. Kalinich

1. 2025 Cyber Insurance Considerations

Insurance is an important tool that helps with the management of cyber risk. The insurance policy provides reimbursement for costs incurred in the management of a cyber event, covers loss of revenue resulting from interruption to the firm's workflow when systems are down, and provides a defense if the firm is sued by parties whose data has been compromised in a cyber breach. Importantly, it also provides access to the expert resources required to respond to a cyber event, including breach counsel, digital forensics, incident response, extortion negotiators, and systems remediation consultants.

These are five common risk financing goals and how insurance helps meet them.

- *Pay for losses*: Insurance will pay for losses covered under the policy.
- *Maintain liquidity*: With insurance, the organization will have to dedicate fewer liquid assets to pay for losses it would otherwise retain. This is particularly important to partners whose distributions may be impacted by losses incurred from a cyber event.
- *Manage uncertainty*: Much of the uncertainty regarding future losses is transferred to the insurer.
- *Comply with laws, regulations, and contractual requirements*: Some cyber exposures are required by law to be disclosed, e.g., breaches of regulated data, such as Personally Identifiable Information (PII) and Protected Health Information (PHI), that may have to be reported to a state attorney general, and client engagement contracts now routinely require firms to carry cyber insurance.
- *Minimize the cost of risk*: Insurance minimizes the cost of risk. According to a recent study, companies with cyber insurance coverage are more likely to detect and effectively respond to data breaches and malicious attacks.[1]

1. David Jones, *Insurance Coverage Drives Cyber Risk Reduction for Companies, Researchers Say*, Cybersecurity Dive (Aug. 21, 2024), https://www.cybersecuritydive.com/news/insurance-cyber-risk-reduction/724852/ (reporting results of two surveys, one conducted by Omdia and the other by Forrester).

1.1. Evolving Cyber Risk Landscape

In 2025, the cyber insurance market continued to adapt to an escalating risk landscape as cyberattacks increased in frequency and sophistication. Reinsurer Munich RE polled more than 7500 participants from 15 countries and reported that 87% of decisionmakers globally (68% in the United States) worry about their organizations' cyber readiness, an increase from the previous years.[2] The surge in ransomware attacks, data breaches, deepfakes, pixel tracking litigation, biometrics, and advanced phishing schemes together with legal and regulatory fallout fuels this concern. The high-profile MOVEit data breach[3] led to over 300 lawsuits that have been consolidated in a multidistrict litigation proceeding, and in 2024, the Securities and Exchange Commission settled actions against four public companies for negligently minimizing in public filings the impact of the 2020 SolarWinds Orion breach.[4]

In addition to an increased regulatory emphasis on accountability and imposing fines and penalties on companies that have been breached, data privacy litigation is also increasing rapidly,[5] including class actions. A law firm review of class action settlements reached in 2024 reported that a data breach case involving a healthcare company topped the 2024 list at $65 million.[6] This trend signals a growing emphasis on legal and financial accountability for data security failures.

1.2. Expanding Cyber Insurance Coverage

Cyber insurance has evolved beyond third-party liability to include coverage for ransomware and extortion, software supply chain vulnerabilities, regulatory investigations, system failures, business interruption from both internal and external causes, litigation, and regulatory fines and penalties,[7] making cyber insurance an essential component of risk

2. *Global Cyber Risk and Insurance Survey 2024: Bridging the Gap in Cyber Protection*, Munich RE (Apr. 26, 2024), https://www.munichre.com/en/insights/cyber/global-cyber-risk-and-insurance-survey.html.

3. MDL Order No. 19, In re: MOVEit Customer Data Sec. Breach Litig., MDL No. 1:23-md-03083-ADB-PGL, 2024 WL 5092276, at *1 (D. Mass. Dec. 12, 2024).

4. Tracy Combs et al., *SEC Files Actions against 4 Public Companies for Negligent Cybersecurity Disclosures*, Greenberg Traurig LLP (Oct. 31, 2024), https://www.gtlaw.com/en/insights/2024/10/sec-files-actions-against-4-public-companies-for-negligent-cybersecurity-disclosures.

5. Gerald L. Maatman, Jr. & Jennifer A. Riley, *Duane Morris Class Action Review—2025: A Comprehensive Analysis of Class Action Litigation*, Duane Morris LLP (Jan. 7, 2025), https://www.duanemorris.com/pressreleases/duane_morris_class_action_review_2025_a_comprehensive_analysis_of_class_action_litigation_0125.html.

6. Gerald L. Maatman, Jr. et al., *The Class Action Weekly Wire—Episode 74: $65 Million Data Breach Settlement Tops 2024 Class Action Charts, Duane Morris LLP* (Sept. 19, 2024), https://blogs.duanemorris.com/classactiondefense/2024/09/19/the-class-action-weekly-wire-episode-74-65-million-data-breach-settlement-tops-2024-class-action-charts/.

7. Regulations are expanding globally with Europe, the U.S., and Asia-Pacific (APAC) regions implementing more robust data protection laws. The EU, for instance, continues to enforce and enhance the General Data Protection Regulation (GDPR), while the U.S. has adopted state-specific data privacy laws, such as California's Consumer Privacy Act (CCPA), further complicating compliance for companies operating in multiple states and internationally. This growing regulatory environment increases potential fines, penalties, assessments, and legal exposure for firms experiencing data breaches, pushing many to seek broader and/or higher coverage in cyber insurance policies.

management.[8] Many insurers now support clients with risk assessment tools, best practices for cyber hygiene, and real-time threat monitoring to minimize risk exposure.

1.3. Artificial Intelligence[9]

Over 40% of lawyers are now using artificial intelligence (AI), and that figure is expected to grow in the near future.[10] AI also now plays a dual role in cybersecurity—while some AI tools enhance defenses by aiding detection of vulnerabilities, AI tools also introduce new risks as AI-driven data collection increases intellectual property, "hallucination" (integrity), and privacy concerns.

On June 22, 2023, a federal judge imposed sanctions on two New York lawyers who submitted a legal brief that included six fictitious case citations generated by an artificial intelligence chatbot, ChatGPT.[11] This is an example of generative AI hallucination. "We made a good faith mistake in failing to believe that a piece of technology could be making up cases out of whole cloth," the firm's statement said.[12] Eleven court opinions in March 2025 mention that a party had likely included AI-hallucinated case citations or (in one instance) AI-hallucinated quotes from real cases; ten involved court filings, and one involved a party's communication with opponents.[13] As of September 13, 2025, there are 228 such cases in U.S. courts involving lawyers and pro-se litigants.[14] Does your organization use or plan to use artificial intelligence products or services?[15]

---

8. *See also* Erica Sweeney, *Companies Without Cyber Insurance Could Be Making a Costly Mistake*, Bus. Insider (Sept. 19, 2024), https://www.businessinsider.com/cyber-insurance-coverage-plan-benefits-costs.

9. *See generally* Kevin P. Kalinich, *Top Artificial Intelligence Insurance Tips for Lawyers*, ABA Journal (May 10, 2024, 1:52 PM), https://www.abajournal.com/columns/article/artificial-intelligence-insurance-tips-for-lawyers.

10. *Over 40% Of Lawyers Now Using AI,* InHouseBlog (Sept. 28, 2024), https://www.inhouseblog.com/lawyers-using-ai/; *Litigators Weigh Need to Disclose AI Use to Clients,* Esquire Deposition Solutions (Oct. 3, 2024), https://www.esquiresolutions.com/litigators-weigh-need-to-disclose-ai-use-to-clients/.

11. The judge imposed a $5,000 fine on lawyers at the New York firm Levidow, Levidow & Oberman P.C. who used AI in preparing pleadings in *Mata v. Avianca Inc.*, No. 1:2022cv01461—Document 55 (S.D.N.Y. 2023) case opinion from the Southern District of New York US Federal District Court.

12. The judge wrote in the sanctions order that there is nothing "inherently improper" in lawyers using AI "for assistance," but he said lawyer ethics rules "impose a gatekeeping role on attorneys to ensure the accuracy of their filings." Mata v. Avianca, Inc., 678F. Supp. 3d 443, 448 (S.D.N.Y. 2023).

Similar AI made-up hallucination cases continue to pop up. In *Park v. Kim*, the Second Circuit Court of Appeals noted that a growing number of judges and courts are issuing orders or considering new rules to govern how lawyers in cases before them can use AI tools, then stated such rules are unnecessary because lawyers are obligated to ensure their court submissions are accurate. Park v. Kim, 91 F. 4th 610, 614–615 (2d Cir. 2024). It then referred the offending lawyer for disciplinary investigation. *Id.* at 615–616.

13. Eugene Volokh, *11 Court Opinions in the Last 30 Days Mention AI-Hallucinated Material, and ...* , Volokh Conspiracy (Mar. 25, 2025 2:52 PM) https://reason.com/volokh/2025/03/25/11-court-opinions-in-the-last-30-days-mention-ai-hallucinated-material/.

14. Damien Charlotin, AI Hallucination Cases, https://www.damiencharlotin.com/hallucinations/ (last visited Sept. 13, 2025).

15. *2024 Intangible Versus Tangible Risks Comparison Report: De-risking AI, IP, and Cyber*, Aon plc 65 (2024) [hereinafter Aon 2024 IP Risk Report], https://www.aon.com/en/insights/reports/2024-intangible-versus-tangible-risks-comparison-report (surveying 2,462 small, medium, and large organizations across a broad range of industries from multiple countries).

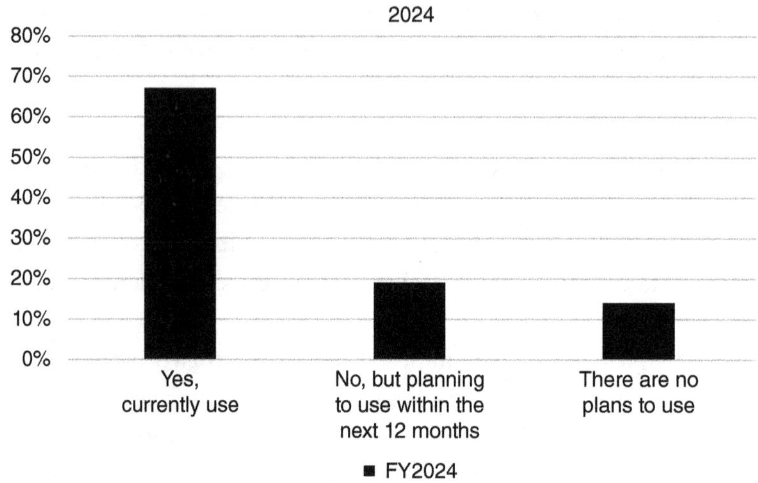

Source: 2024 Intangible vs. Tangible Risks Comparison Report I Aon

The risks and exposures presented by AI are evolving and are not well understood; much depends on how the technology is deployed and used. AI-enabled tools are designed, developed, and deployed for different purposes in varied settings. Insurers are developing endorsements to existing policies to address emerging AI risks and, in some cases, developing new policies to cover specific risks associated with AI deployments that traditional insurance policies do not contemplate. Exposures covered by these explicit AI endorsements and policies include "data poisoning, where hackers manipulate or contaminate data used to develop machine learning models; usage rights infringement, where companies don't have appropriate permissions to use copyrighted or licensed data; and regulatory violations, such as liabilities resulting from the European Union's AI Act, which provides a legal framework for the use of AI."[16] However, other incidents associated with the use or abuse of AI will be addressed under current policies and subject to their terms and conditions. For example, in the case of a business like the Hong Kong firm that lost $25 million in a very sophisticated social engineering fraud using "deepfake" videos, the loss would be characterized as a theft of money. Theft would typically fall under the victim's Commercial Crime policy, and it would be excluded from a cyber policy under a "money, security and funds" exclusion in the absence of an endorsement adding social engineering fraud coverage.[17]

16. Gavin Souter, *AXA XL Adds Generative AI Endorsement to Cyber Policy*, Bus. Ins. (Oct. 21, 2024), https://www.businessinsurance.com/axa-xl-adds-generative-ai-endorsement-to-cyber-policy/.

17. *See, infra,* § 4.4.

Peril	Media Liability	Tech E&O, MPL, PI	Product Liability	General Liability	Intellectual Property	Cyber	Crime	D&O	Employment
Faulty Product or Service	Excluded	Available	Limited	Excluded	Excluded	Excluded	Excluded	Excluded	Excluded
Copyright or Trademark	Available	Limited	Limited	Limited	Available	Limited	Excluded	Excluded	Excluded
Patent Infringement	Limited	Excluded	Excluded	Excluded	Available	Limited	Excluded	Excluded	Excluded
Discrimination & Bias	Limited	Limited	Excluded	Excluded	Excluded	Limited	Excluded	Excluded	Available
Defamation, Libel, Slander	Available	Excluded	Excluded	Limited	Excluded	Excluded	Excluded	Excluded	Excluded
Bodily Injury	Excluded	Excluded	Limited	Limited	Excluded	Limited	Excluded	Excluded	Excluded
Tangible Property Damage	Available	Excluded	Limited	Limited	Excluded	Limited	Excluded	Excluded	Excluded
Privacy and Security Breaches	Excluded	Limited	Excluded	Excluded	Excluded	Available	Excluded	Excluded	Excluded
Loss of Financial Assets/ Market Manipulation	Excluded	Excluded	Excluded	Excluded	Excluded	Excluded	Available	Excluded	Excluded
Product Recall	Excluded	Excluded	Excluded	Available	Limited	Excluded	Excluded	Excluded	Excluded
Business Interruption	Excluded	Excluded	Excluded	Excluded	Excluded	Available	Excluded	Excluded	Excluded
Breach of D&O Duties	Excluded	Excluded	Excluded	Excluded	Excluded	Excluded	Excluded	Available	Excluded
Robotics	Excluded	Available	Available	Limited	Excluded	Excluded	Excluded	Excluded	Excluded
Deepfake	Excluded	Available	Excluded	Excluded	Excluded	Available	Available	Excluded	Excluded

- **Available**
- **Limited**
- **Excluded unless custom contingent liability added**

Artificial Intelligence First and Third Party Loss Perils: Insurance Coverage Gap Analysis

1.4. Law Firms Are Not Immune to the Financial Impact of Cyber Incidents

The value of cyber insurance is underscored by the financial impact of cyber incidents, which encompasses negligent incidents, vendor issues, malicious insider incidents, and external "attacks," including ransomware. A single major breach of a law firm's information systems can cost millions considering expenses related to data recovery, legal fees, loss of revenue, extortion payments, statutorily and contractually required notifications, and regulatory fines. As of early 2025, 2023 was the worst year on record in terms of cyberattacks don law firms. In 2023, there were 45 known attacks affecting 1.6 million records, and an average ransomware demand of $2.47 million. Ransomware demands against law firms that year ranged from $30,000 to as much as $21 million.[18]

2024 saw an increase in cyber litigation against law firms and cyber-related decisions reported. As discussed in detail below, context of size (solo practitioner, small firm, large firm), structure (law firm, in-house, government, public interest), and type of practice (such as M&A, high profile clients, extensive personally identifiable information held) are major

18. Rebecca Moody, *Law Firms Hit with Average Ransom Demand of $2.5 Million*, Comparitech (Aug. 1, 2024), https://www.comparitech.com/blog/information-security/ransomware-attacks-law-firms/.

factors in the frequency and severity of cyber risks and should, therefore, also be considerations when designing and purchasing insurance. A few recent examples follow.

- A Florida corporate law firm proposed a settlement of $8.5 million to resolve a class action alleging the firm failed to properly safeguard the personal information of nearly 10,000 clients, employees, and other individuals from cybercriminals, according to a motion filed in Florida federal court.[19]
- A California federal judge granted final approval of a major law firm's $8 million deal to end putative class claims over a data breach that purportedly exposed 638,000 individuals' information and praised the parties for their "efficiency" in handling the case and "good faith" approach to reaching a resolution.[20]
- The data of two AmLaw 50 firms was accessed in a global data theft operation in 2023 related to the MOVEit incident, according to the ransomware group claiming responsibility for the attack.[21]
- A Connecticut personal injury firm's insurance company denied claims stemming from a hacker breaking into the firm's email system and stealing over $750,000 from a client, saying the firm's professional liability policy excluded "cyber security events."[22]
- A Lloyd's of London syndicate urged the North Carolina Business Court to dismiss a major law firm's lawsuit seeking coverage for a 2022 data breach, saying the law firm failed to include three other carriers as parties to the insurance policy at issue.[23] The plaintiff law firm told the court that unsealing financial details related to the data breach and its insurance policy with the Lloyd's of London syndicate would put the firm at further risk from competitors and bad actors. The firm said its complaint against the insurer contained redacted information to protect the amount of losses the firm incurred as a result of the data breach and the terms of the private insurance policy, including policy limits, retention amounts, premiums, co-insurance percentage, a tax schedule, and broker remuneration and deductible terms. The firm contended that unsealing the information would make it more difficult for the firm to negotiate insurance rates in the future and would act as an incentive for hackers to infiltrate its systems.

19. SEC v. Charnas, Case No. 1:23-cv-22764, Doc. 1 (S.D. Fla.2024).

20. In re: Orrick, Herrington & Sutcliffe, LLP Data Breach Litig., Case No. 3:23-cv-04089, Doc. 69 (N.D. Cal. 2024).

21. Raphael Satter, *U.S. Health Department, Law Firms Latest Hit in Wide-Ranging Hack*, REUTERS (Jun. 29, 2023, 1:19 PM), https://www.reuters.com/world/us/us-health-department-law-firms-reportedly-latest-hit-wide-ranging-hack-2023-06-28/.

22. *See* Rachel Rippetoe, *Insurer Says No Coverage for Conn. Firm's Data Breach*, LAW360 U.K. (Sept. 27, 2024 4:21 PM), https://www.law360.co.uk/articles/1883508/insurer-says-no-coverage-for-conn-firm-s-data-breach (on file with the authors).

23. *See* Lynn LaRowe, *Cadwalader Suing Lloyd's Over Cyberattack Coverage Denial*, LAW360 PULSE (July 26, 2024, 3:41 PM), https://www.law360.com/pulse/articles/1862616/cadwalader-suing-lloyd-s-over-cyberattack-coverage-denial (on file with the authors).

2. Cyber Insurance Underwriting Is Evolving

Initial cyber insurance models were built on the shifting sands of too many legacy property, plant, and equipment historical loss assumptions, many of which do not map to cyber risk.[24] A big and flawed assumption about cyber risks (as cyber insurers discovered to their detriment) is that past loss activity is predictive of future loss activity. The dominant cause of cyber events fifteen years ago was distributed denial of service attacks; ten years ago it was theft of PII; and even as recently as eight years ago, many cyber policies did not explicitly recognize ransomware as a cause of loss because it was so "new." PII has been decreasing in value and is harder for bad actors to monetize as more PII becomes available for sale on the dark web. In contrast, ransomware operators have been realizing increasingly substantial rewards as they refine their operating tactics.

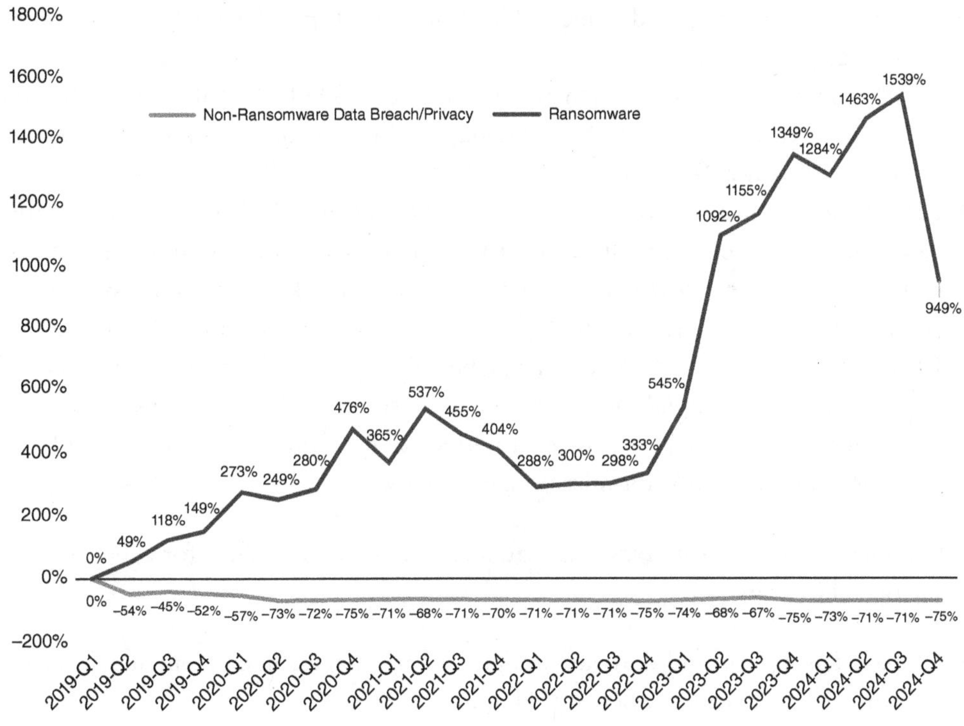

Cyber Incident Rates Indexed to Q1 2019

24. Michael A. Rossi, *An Abbreviated History of Cyber Insurance—The First 25 Years*, Koru Risk Mgmt., https://www.korurm.com/blog/an-abbreviated-history-of-cyber-insurance---the-first-25-years (last visited Apr. 17, 2025).

2.1. Growth of Cyber Insurance Market

The cyber insurance market is poised for substantial growth over the next decade but will require significant structural innovation to meet increasing demand and foster resilience against cyber threats. As cyber risk evolves into a peak peril, the insurance industry must innovate and collaborate to meet growing demand and manage potentially catastrophic exposures.[25] The cyber insurance market's growth will necessitate a sharp increase in capital to manage exposures to a 1-in-250-year loss event. This market assessment speaks to the need for product innovation, geographical and industry diversification, and the development of public-private partnerships to effectively manage systemic cyber risk.

Estimates of growth vary, depending upon the source, and the following is within most range estimates:[26]

- $8 billion in U.S. stand-alone cyber premiums in 2023, with an estimated $20 billion of capital would be required to meet obligations for a 1-in-250 year (0.4% probability) cyber aggregation loss.
- A 20% compound annual growth rate would lead to $45 billion of premium by 2034.
- A 500% increase in capital, to $121 billion, would be required by the U.S. cyber market to meet a 1-in-250-year loss event by 2034.
- $102 billion in insured losses from Hurricane Katrina, the largest insured natural catastrophe loss, would be eclipsed by a $121 billion cyber loss event, illustrating how cyber could become a peak peril. The cyber insurance market is set for outsized growth compared with other lines of Property & Casualty insurance over the coming 10 years.
- Close to 50% of large companies (i.e., generally over $1 billion annual revenue, but varies significantly among industries) purchase some level of cyber insurance in the U.S., but market participation drops to 43% for medium-sized companies, 12% for small businesses, and 3% for micro-organizations.

2025 focus areas for insurers, which will impact law firms' options for cyber coverage, include the following:

- Global IT, supplier, and software supply chain outages, like recent incidents with Crowdstrike, Solarwinds, Microsoft Hafnium
- Ransomware: 2024 saw a record ransom payment ($75 million), and 2025 is on track to exceed the 2023 record of $1.1 billion in payments to known ransomware crypto-wallets

25. *See also* Aon 2024 IP Risk Report, *supra* note 15.

26. Aon, Global 2025 Cyber Risk Report, https://www.aon.com/cyber-risk-report (last visited Sept. 13, 2025).

- Artificial Intelligence: Data privacy legislation, regulation, and litigation, including biometric information, pixel litigation, and data privacy class actions[27]
- Cyber war and systemic events, such as widespread aggregated incidents like WannaCry and NotPetya (discussed below)
- Disclosure rulemaking[28]

One of the questions still often raised is whether cyber insurance performs and pays claims. This question is fed by news reports about legal disputes framed in the context of cyber losses where insureds have resorted to suing their insurers for payment. It is, in fact, very rare for insurers to dispute or deny coverage for cyber claims under a cyber policy; the usual source of a denial and dispute over coverage is when an insured has not purchased standalone cyber coverage[29] or when the cyber coverage limit was inadequate given the scale of loss[30] and the insured resorts to claiming from policies that were not (in the eyes of the insurer) intended to provide cyber coverage.

Insurers' published loss ratios and publicly available reports demonstrate that cyber policies do pay out, all too frequently for the full limits of the policy. The following chart lists cyber insurance payments that have been publicly reported (generally in SEC disclosures), illustrating the extent to which cyber insurance has performed for corporations that have experienced major losses.

27. *See* Dan Roe, *Law Firm Data Breach Reports Show No Signs of Slowing in 2024*, Am. Law. (May 23, 2024, 5:00 AM), https://www.law.com/americanlawyer/2024/05/23/law-firm-data-breach-reports-show-no-signs-of-slowing-in-2024/; Aaron Keller, *Conn. Law Firm Hit with Class Action Data Breach Suit*, Law360 (Mar. 31, 2025, 9:10 PM) ("A 26-attorney Connecticut business litigation, intellectual property and employment law firm waited 16 months to notify potentially thousands of current and former clients of an alleged 2023 data breach that may have left sensitive personal information exposed to cybercriminals, a Monday lawsuit alleged."), https://www.law360.com/articles/2318275/conn-law-firm-hit-with-class-action-data-breach-suit (on file with authors).

28. *SEC Adopts Rules on Cybersecurity Risk Management, Strategy, Governance, and Incident Disclosure by Public Companies*, U.S. Sec. & Exch. Comm'n (July 26, 2023), https://www.sec.gov/newsroom/press-releases/2023-139.

29. *See, e.g.*, David Jones, *Mondelēz Settlement in NotPetya Case Renews Concerns About Cyber Insurance Coverage*, Cybersecurity Dive (Nov. 8, 2022) (discussing insurance industry reaction to state-sponsored attacks that could be considered acts of war subject to policy exclusions), https://www.cybersecuritydive.com/news/mondelez-zurich-notpetya-cyberinsurance-settlement/636029/.

30. *See, e.g.*, Jen Frost, *Merck Settles $1.4 Billion Cyberattack Case Against Insurers*, Ins. Bus. (Jan. 5, 2024), https://www.insurancebusinessmag.com/us/news/cyber/merck-settles-1-4-billion-cyberattack-case-against-insurers-471908.aspx.

Organization	Approximate Disclosure Date	Recoveries Received / Accrued	Total Cyber Insurance Limits	Source
Mondelez International	06/27/2017	TBD	$100 million (Property Insurance)	Circuit Court of Illinois
FedEx (TNT Express)	06/27/2017	N/A	No Cyber Insurance in Place	Q4 2018 Financials
A.P. Moller–Maersk	06/27/2017	N/A	No Cyber Insurance in Place	Q4 2017 Financials
Norsk Hydro (LockerGoga)	03/19/2019	~$23.2 million NOK 190 million	Cyber Insurance in Place	Q3 2019 Financials Q4 2019 Earnings Q2 2020 Earnings
Eurofins	06/02/2019	€57.3 million	Unknown	2022 Annual Report
Demant A/S	09/03/2019	~$15 million	~$15 million	2019 Annual Report Press Release
Pitney Bowes (Ryuk)	10/12/2019	$17 million	Unknown	10-K Filing 2020
UHS (Malware)	09/27/2020	$58 million	Unknown	10-K Filing 2022
Sopra Steria (Ryuk)	10/21/2020	TBD	€30 million	Press Release
SolarWinds (Orion Hack)	12/13/2020	$15 million (Cyber) $50 million (D&O)	$15 million (Cyber) $50 million (D&O)	10-K Filing 2022
Westrock (Ransomware)	01/23/2021	$72.2 million	Unknown	10-K Filing 2023 10-K Filing 2021
Groupe Beneteau	02/19/2021	€10.0 million	Unknown	H2 2021 Financials
Ardagh Group	05/17/2021	$58 million	Unknown	Q4 2021 Financials
Sinclair Broadcast	10/17/2021	$38 million	Unknown	10-K Filing 2023 10-K Filing 2022
Tenet Healthcare	04/26/2022	$55 million	Unknown	Q3 2023 Financials Q4 2022 Financials
Hanesbrands	05/24/2022	$24.062 million	Unknown	Q3 2023 Financials
NCR	04/13/2023	$25 million	Unknown	Q2 2024 Financials
Clorox	08/14/2023	$30 million	Unknown	Q4 2024 Financials
Henry Schein	10/14/2023	$10 million	$60 million	Q2 2024 Financials
LoanDepot	01/08/2024	$15 million	Unknown	Q2 2024 Financials

Disclosed Business Interruption Cyber Insurance Recoveries

2.2. Cyber Underwriters Increase Scrutiny of Clients from Lessons Learned

Remarkably, the cyber insurance marketplace has reduced pricing while ransomware frequency and severity increases.[31] Price reductions are not a sustainable long-term model,

31. *Data and Privacy Breaches Fuel Cyber Insurance Claims Surge*, Risk & Ins. (Oct. 9, 2024), https://riskandinsurance.com/data-privacy-breaches-fuel-cyber-insurance-claims-surge/. This article draws on a risk outlook

especially as vendor management and aggregation issues remain a worry for the future and cannot be solved by increased premium rates alone.[32]

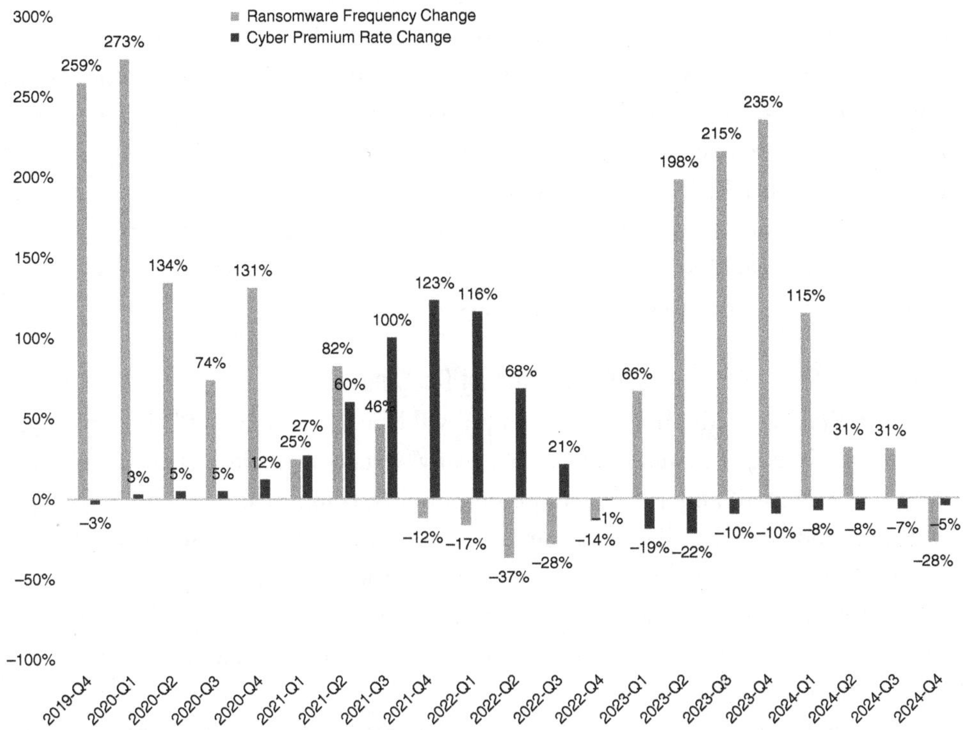

Ransomware Frequency & Cyber Premium Rates

Some cyber insurers are reexamining and adjusting cyber underwriting better than others as cyber insurer loss ratios for 2023–2024 range from 25%[33] (indicating fewer underwriting changes are needed) to 125%+ (indicating increased underwriting scrutiny is required in order to move toward profitability). Also, the 2024 summer CrowdStrike incident, triggering losses estimated as ranging from $400 million to more than $1 billion, highlighted

---

report by global insurance firm Allianz, which generally noted that widespread adoption of artificial intelligence (AI) across industries is having a significant impact on the cyber and privacy risk landscape. *Id.*

32. For example, one firm was surprised to find out they were scanned by a potential insurer (port scanning for vulnerabilities into the insured internal network), without notice and without consent. While legally having the right to do so, the insurer then used such information (valid or not) as a data point when pricing the insurance. In fact, some insurers have commenced scanning their insureds on a monthly basis to look for additional risk. Other insurers utilize multiple third-party IT security assessment scores in risk evaluations.

33. There are a few insurers that have paid zero cyber claims (0% Loss Ratio), but those companies did not make enough cyber placements to be statistically significant. Furthermore, insurers vary in how they calculate cyber loss ratios because some insurers include only standalone cyber insurance policies while others include cyber losses/coverage under other policies such as Professional Liability and Errors & Omissions insurance policies.

the potential for significant loss in the cyber market and organizations from widespread events.[34]

The focus for managing losses now extends beyond the financial reimbursement for breach incidents. Insurers emphasize proactive cybersecurity, requiring insured firms to implement strong data protections, particularly around multifactor authentication, protection of privileged user accounts, aggressive patching schedules, and training. Technology is enabling more accurate, comprehensive, and in-context cyber insurance submissions. For example, Aon's Cyber Risk Analyzer provides insureds with actuarial modeling regarding frequency and severity of risks, which assists with limits and retention/deductible analysis, while Aon's CyQu enables insureds to efficiently review and correct/improve cyber resiliency prior to submissions to insurance carriers.

2.3. Attorney-Client Privilege and Work Product Doctrine

When a law firm is a victim of a cyber event, it will be concerned about being investigated by regulators (if regulated data, PII, PHI, or sensitive data concerning a client in a regulated sector is compromised) and, perhaps more importantly, being sued by clients or third parties whose confidential data has been compromised. Non-client third parties could include, for example, opposing parties in transactions or litigation and the individuals whose data those nonclients entrust to the firm. These considerations make the issue of maximizing attorney-client privilege (as between the firm and its counsel) around all aspects of the breach and response a priority.

Ensuring that privilege applies to the maximum extent possible is a matter of preparation and planning. Waiting to address issues like identifying and engaging counsel and a forensic investigation vendor until after a cyber event occurs is not likely to put the firm in the best position possible to respond. Even the best-prepared firms have confirmed that a cyber event causes chaos and requires emergency decision-making that may disrupt a carefully planned process. Proper planning and rehearsal, combined with a simple (hard copy, of course) incident response plan (IRP), are essential to putting key elements for a response in place from the outset to protect the firm best.[35]

Cyber insurance policies vary in how they address notice of an incident and engaging resources to assist the response. Some policies require that the firm's first call be to the insurer, which then provides advice and initial triage of the incident and engages resources to respond to the incident (including counsel) from an insurer-designated panel of service providers. This kind of policy requirement should be avoided. The process does not prioritize attorney-client privilege (as between the firm and counsel that will assist its response),

---

34. *See How Has CrowdStrike Changed the Cyber Market?*, ON AON PODCAST (Oct. 15, 2024) (including transcript), https://www.aon.com/en/insights/podcasts/on-aon-episode-80-how-has-crowdstrike-changed-the-cyber-market; Ben Norris, *CrowdStrike Throws Cyber Market Softening into Doubt*, COMMERCIAL RISK (Oct. 1, 2024), https://www.commercialriskonline.com/crowdstrike-throws-cyber-market-softening-into-doubt/.

35. *See* HANDBOOK, Chapter 13, *Achieving Preparedness through Standards and Planning and Best Practices for Incident Response.*

and once set in motion makes achieving privilege haphazard, at best, and could compromise privilege altogether. (A few states recognize an insurer/insured privilege that may reduce this risk.)

Another important consideration relating to an insurer's requirement to be the first notified is the insured's business requirements and potentially competing obligations to notify others first. A firm may have notice obligations arising by contract, including client engagement agreements specifying notification protocols and priorities for a cyber event; by applicable statutes such as requirements in some states that victims of cyberattacks notify the state attorney general's office and/or law enforcement within a certain timeframe; or by applicable regulatory requirements.

Best practice would be to follow an internal process of triage and escalation of an incident and engage outside counsel (often referred to as "Breach Counsel") before taking any further action. In any case, the triage and escalation process should be defined in advance and documented as part of the incident response plan. It is also important that this process be agreed in advance with the insurer and that the insurer agrees to accept notice from Breach Counsel. (Some insurers have this kind of agreement written into the policy; others may require an endorsement or written agreement from the underwriter). It is also critically important that the selected Breach Counsel be on the insurer's panel of approved vendors or that the insurer expressly agrees to the selected Breach Counsel and its rates.

U.S. Data Privacy and Cybersecurity practice, stresses the importance of engaging informed Breach Counsel to direct an investigation:[36]

> "While it may be tempting to obtain legal advice related to a breach from lawyers within the firm, unless your firm specializes in data security law, this is often a mistake. Experienced Breach Counsel will ensure the firm maximum protections possible, including compliance with tight regulatory deadlines. Also, many insurance policies will not allow an insured to recoup legal fees incurred by its own lawyers, even if the lawyer was acting in a role similar to an outside advisor."
>
> Jena Valdetero, Co-Chair of Greenberg Traurig, LLP's

Breach Counsel should have experience to be able to further triage the situation and advise on a course of action. The course of action may involve engaging a Digital Forensic Investigation & Response ("DFIR") firm and other relevant resources (such as a ransomware negotiator, data remediation consultant, cybersecurity consultant, crisis communications consultant, and others). To maximize recovery of fees paid for these services, it is important that the providers be insurer-approved vendors, whether panel providers or pre-approved off-panel experts. To maximize attorney-client privilege protections, Breach Counsel should engage the service providers, acting on behalf of the insured.

36. Interview with Jena Valdetero, Shareholder, Greenberg Traurig, LLP, in Chi., Ill. (Dec. 14, 2024).

Breach Counsel should also be familiar with the insurer, policy wording, and vendor panels and have experience to be able to advise on the best resources to engage for the type and scale of incident. Breach Counsel will work with the insurer to secure prior consent for specific resources, where required, and will host meetings with the insurer's loss adjuster and other resources, taking steps to manage privilege-sensitive information so it is appropriately guarded depending on the audience.

There have been several court decisions where privilege protection has been challenged,[37] particularly around the forensic investigation report which courts have generally found to have been prepared and used for business purposes rather than for legal purposes. The decisions in *In Re Capital One Inc. Consumer Data Security Breach Litigation* (Capital One)[38] and in *Wengui v. Clark Hill PLC*[39] offer persuasive support for disclosure of forensic reports even though the decisions are of limited direct precedential value because they were based on very specific facts of each case and the nature of the documents in question. A more recent case further narrowed privilege protection for communications among counsel, client, and the forensic investigator.[40] Ms. Valdetaro, quoted above, reports on a further narrowing of the privilege by a federal court in Washington state.[41]

Wengui addressed the application of the attorney-client privilege and work product doctrine in the context of a data breach investigation involving a law firm. A plaintiff suing the firm for losing his information sought to discover reports of the law firm's forensic investigations and other information about the incident. The court found that certain communications were not protected by attorney-client privilege because they were not made in confidence or for the purpose of obtaining legal advice and the work product doctrine did not apply because the report was widely shared and used for a range of non-litigation

---

37. *In re* Premera Blue Cross Customer Data Sec. Breach Litig., No. 3:15-md-2633-SI, Doc. 132, (D. Or. 2017) (ruling that documents created during a data breach investigation were not protected by attorney-client privilege because they were not created for the purpose of obtaining legal advice but rather for business purposes; *In re* Target Corp. Customer Data Sec. Breach Litig., MDL No. 14-2522 (PAM/JJK), 2015 WL 6777384 (D. Minn. 2015) (finding that certain documents related to Target's data breach response were not protected by attorney-client privilege because they were created in the ordinary course of business and not for the purpose of obtaining legal advice); *In re* Experian Data Breach Litig., No. 8:15-cv-01592-AG-DFM, Doc. 239 (C.D. Cal. 2017) (holding that communications between Experian and its outside counsel were protected by attorney-client privilege because they were made for the purpose of obtaining legal advice regarding the data breach; *In re* Capital One Inc. Consumer Data Sec. Breach Litig., MDL No. 1:19md2915 (AJT/JFA), Doc. 490 (E.D. Va. 2020) (ruling that a forensic report prepared by a cybersecurity firm retained by outside counsel was not protected by attorney-client privilege because it was not prepared for the purpose of obtaining legal advice but rather for business purposes).

38. *See In re Capital One Inc. See also* White & Williams LLP, *Protecting Your Organization: Lessons from In re Capital One for Third-Party Cybersecurity Incident Reports*, JD SUPRA (June 9, 2020), https://www.jdsupra.com/legalnews/protecting-your-organization-lessons-63963/.

39. Wengui v. Clark Hill, PLC, 338 F.R.D. 7 (D. D.C. 2021). *See also* Jena Valdetero, *Privilege under Pressure: The Shifting Data Breach Investigation Landscape*, NAT'L L. REV. (Feb. 18, 2025), https://natlawreview.com/article/privilege-under-pressure-shifting-data-breach-investigation-landscape.

40. Leonard v. McMenamins Inc., No. C22-0094-KKE, Doc. 64 (W.D. Wash. Dec. 6, 2023).

41. Jena M. Valdetero & Emily S. Taetzsch, *Privilege under Pressure: The Shifting Data Breach Investigation Landscape*, GREENBERGTRAURIG GT ALERT (Feb. 18, 2025), https://www.gtlaw.com/en/insights/2025/2/privilege-under-pressure-the-shifting-data-breach-investigation-landscape.

purposes.[42] *Wengui* is an important reminder that it is never safe to assume privilege is in place and secure just because outside counsel has been engaged in the process of obtaining a forensic report.

These cases and the courts' findings provide useful insight into strategies for handling and communicating about expert reports that may be helpful in preserving privilege.[43]

> "It is important to be mindful of how you are communicating with vendors during a breach, with an eye towards possibly having to disclose those discussions in discovery if privilege is later challenged. And while forensic reports used to be a given after an incident, many companies are moving away from requesting that one be prepared, or instead are requesting a non-privileged executive summary report, rather than have to fight for a report's protection in litigation."

Valdetero stresses the importance of conducting an investigation with the assumption that both forensic reports and communications where third parties are included may not be protected.[44]

At the moment, the extent of attorney-client privilege protection is being assessed by the courts (when challenged) on a case-by-case basis. Until firm guidelines and precedent have been established, the victim firm can maximize available protection by working with Breach Counsel to retain forensic experts as outlined above.

3. Coverage Available

Insurance buyers complain, rightly, that cyber policies are confusing; they have multiple sections and insuring agreements, difficult language, and complex, often interwoven, definitions. Buyers also struggle with the lack of consistency between policies; that inconsistency makes it difficult, if not impossible, to determine which policy is best suited to the buyer's needs. Some of these issues are endemic to the coverage, which puts together First Party insurance with Third Party Liability[45] and covers regulatory investigations, extortion payments, and many other complex risks.

---

42. *Wengui*, 338 F.R.D. at 13-14s.

43. *See also* Daniel Schwarcz, Josephine Wolff & Daniel W. Woods, *How Privilege Undermines Cybersecurity*, 36 Harv. J. of L. & Tech. 421 (2023); Stephanie Diehl, *Lessons from Wengui v. Clark Hill: Structuring a Two Track Cyber Investigation*, Nat. L. Rev. (Feb. 8, 2021), https://www.natlawreview.com/article/lessons-wengui-v-clark-hill-structuring-two-track-cyber-investigation.

44. Interview with Jena Valdetero, *supra* note 36.

45. First Party losses include the damage the insured itself has suffered, such as the cost to rehabilitate systems and business interruption loss of revenue. Third Party Liability includes obligations the insured has to third parties such as the cost of defending lawsuits and paying compensation to someone who has been harmed by the covered event.

Construction and general layout of policies can vary enormously between insurers, with some using as few as two and others eight or more insuring agreements. Language differences persist as insurers seek to be clear about what they will and will not cover when dealing with a rapidly changing technological environment and even more dynamic threat landscape. On top of that, a lot of the complexity results from each insurer having designed its own approach to cyber insurance and trying to differentiate itself from the rest.

In short, cyber insurance is going through a process of convergent evolution that will eventually produce a policy form with more consistent structure and language across insurers (as happened with Property, General Liability, Professional Indemnity, and other types of coverage).

Despite the differences between policies offered by each insurer, cyber insurance coverage (as distinct from the policy wording) has undergone considerable convergence in the past few years. The categories of coverage are not always described the same way and components within the coverages are not always allocated to the same category in different insurers' policies, but there are now typical coverage components. The coverage typically available in cyber policies is described in this section.

There are five core coverage segments—three First Party and two Third Party—common to nearly all standalone cyber insurance policies, plus some additional optional coverages.

First-Party coverages include:

1. Breach Response / Event Management
2. Network Interruption (loss of revenue)
3. Extortion (ransomware)
4. Additional First Party coverages

Third-Party coverages include:

1. Privacy and Network Security Liability
2. Media Liability

3.1. First Party Coverage

3.1.1. *Breach Response / Event Management covers*

- Breach Counsel, who provides legal advice to assist the insured in navigating the event, liaising with attorneys general and law enforcement, advising on statutory notification requirements, and providing advice regarding best practices to maintain attorney-client privilege protection[46] for information developed during incident response;
- Forensic consulting by expert cybersecurity service providers to investigate whether or not there was an incursion and then to establish how the threat actors got into the system, what they did and how, what data they accessed, etc.;

46. *See supra*, text at notes 36–44.

- Security consulting to assist the insured with remediation of systems, ejecting threat actors and eliminating malware, and finding and removing "backdoors;"
- Crisis communications consulting to provide expert advice on messaging to clients, staff, press, and public;
- Data remediation to assist with reconstructing systems and restoring data from backups;
- Cost of statutorily or contractually required or voluntary (ethically required) notifications to individuals whose PII or PHI has been compromised, and cost of providing identity theft insurance, credit monitoring, and a toll-free call center service for victims; and
- Cost of responding to a regulatory investigation, including fines and penalties (where insurance of fines and penalties is legally permitted).

The essence of "Event Management" coverage is to pay for the resources needed for an immediate and comprehensive response to a cyber event, including the cost of investigating to establish whether detected "Indicators of Compromise" are a real event.

In some policies, particularly older ones, "Digital Asset Restoration" (also known as "Data Remediation") may not be covered. In the era of ransomware, restoration of systems and the data on those systems, including programs and operating systems, is a major cost item in recovering from a cyber attack. It is, therefore, important to check that this element of coverage is included and allowed to the full limit of the policy. Restoring systems after a ransomware attack will be more time-consuming and expensive if backups are compromised and the insured is forced to rely on a decryption key supplied by the attacker. In those cases, it is rare to recover more than 80% of the encrypted data, and often as little as 60% is recoverable. Also, in many cases the insured is unable to recover data even after paying a ransom,[47] and the integrity of any data recovered could have been compromised.

It is very rare for information to be made public about the breakdown of Event Management costs for a substantial cyber incident. However, in 2013, a community college system suffered a breach that exposed the PII of some two million individuals. The published breakdown of costs for that event, totaling $26 million,[48] included:

- Breach Counsel and legal advice: $9.3 million,
- Cybersecurity consulting and remediation of data and systems: $7.5 million,
- Notifications and credit monitoring: $7 million, and
- Public relations, records management, and miscellaneous administration: $2.2 million.

---

47. Julie Webb et al., *2024 Ransomware Trends Executive Summary, Global Edition*, VEEAM SOFTWARE (June 4, 2024), https://www.veeam.com/resources/wp-2024-ransomware-trends-executive-summary-global.html; Julie Webb et al., *2024 Ransomware Trends Executive Summary, United States Edition*, VEEAM SOFTWARE (May 23, 2024), https://www.veeam.com/resources/wp-2024-ransomware-trends-executive-summary-us.html (on file with the authors).

48. Mary Beth Faller, *Maricopa County Colleges Computer Hack Cost Tops $26M*, AZCENTRAL (Dec. 17, 2014, 12:58 PM), https://www.azcentral.com/story/news/local/phoenix/2014/12/17/costs-repair-massive-mcccd-computer-hack-top-million/20539491/.

Illustrating how devastating the cost of notifications can be, consider that large breaches have forced cyberattack victims to file for bankruptcy.[49]

Limitations on Use of Consultants and Vendors to Respond to a Cyber Event

Insurers usually maintain lists of approved vendors to provide services as Breach Counsel, Digital & Forensic Incident Response consultants, extortion consultants, crisis communications consultants, and other experts. Insureds can retain these so-called "panel vendors" to assist with incident response, and the cost of panel vendors will typically be fully reimbursed to the insured.

Business pressure to achieve and maintain acceptable loss ratios and the increasing complexity (and corresponding cost) of responding to incidents motivates cyber insurers to review closely third-party vendor costs incurred in responding to and investigating cyber incidents. To reduce (or at least slow the increase in) these costs, insurers are less flexible about using service providers that are not panel vendors or pre-approved. If the insured has not gotten its non-panel vendors approved before a cyber incident, the insured may be delayed in responding to the incident while it seeks approval; the insured risks the insurer challenging reimbursement of those expenses if the insured proceeds without preapproval of response providers. Insurers are also making fewer exceptions related to vendor rates. It is becoming increasingly common for insurers to reimburse non-panel vendors at a capped rate equal to (or even below) what the insurer would have paid a panel vendor.

3.1.2. *Interruption and Extra Expense*

Interruption and Extra Expense covers loss of revenue and extra expense incurred due to:

- The insured's systems being impaired or shut down as a result of a covered event;
- A failure of the insured's systems, *i.e.*, an unexpected failure or unplanned outage that causes an extended interruption; and
- A vendor's systems on which the insured depends being impaired or shut down by a covered event, *e.g.*, a covered event impacting a cloud provider, data host, software platform provider, etc.

This coverage provides reimbursement to the insured for actual lost net income caused by a network security failure, as well as associated extra expense. The greater of a dollar amount retention or waiting period retention of between 6 to 24 hours applies. In other words, business interruption coverage applies after the insured's computer system is down for the duration of the waiting period.

---

49. Carrie Pallardy, *Big Breach Sends National Public Data to Bankruptcy*, InformationWeek (Oct. 17, 2024), https://www.informationweek.com/cyber-resilience/big-breach-sends-national-public-data-to-bankruptcy.

The most frequent events giving rise to Interruption and Extra Expense claims in 2024 were from ransomware attacks. According to press reports, several large law firms suffered ransomware events causing them to shut down all their systems. Possibly the largest business interruption event was the NotPetya cyberattack in June 2017. The NotPetya attack shut down a large number of public corporations and some well-known professional services firms (including a large law firm), causing substantial losses of revenue as a direct result. "Maersk lost between **$250 and $300 million**, Mondelēz **$188 million**, and Merck a staggering **$870 million.**"[50]

An extension to Interruption coverage (often subject to payment of additional premium) is System Failure coverage. System Failure provides coverage for loss of revenue from an interruption of systems arising from any unintended, unplanned, and unexpected cause such as an outage caused by a system upgrade or patch installation that goes bad or simple human error. For example, System Failure coverage is relevant for interruption caused when an insured's systems are impaired by an event like the 2024 CrowdStrike upgrade incident. Revenue loss from a planned outage would, of course, not be covered.

"Dependent" (also known as "contingent") business interruption provides reimbursement coverage for the insured for actual lost income caused by a network security failure of a business on which the insured is dependent, as well as associated extra expense. The greater of a dollar amount retention or waiting period retention of between 8 to 24 hours usually applies.

Dependent business interruption events are less common, but as law firms move more of their data and operations to cloud providers and outsource functions such as e-discovery to third-party providers, the potential for such interruptions increases. A firm that moves its document management system to a cloud provider, such as NetDocuments or iManage, or uses Microsoft 365 for essential business applications, is often wholly dependent on those providers. If the provider is the victim of a major cyberattack that shuts down its services for an extended period, its law firm customers will not be able to progress existing matters or onboard new matters. The disruption could lead to loss of clients and extra expense to develop workarounds, in addition to lost revenue while work is disrupted. Provided the cause of the loss to the vendor is an event that would have been covered under the firm's cyber policy, the Dependent Business Interruption coverage should be triggered.

Contingent coverage for the non-IT supply chain is also available under some cyber insurance policies both for cyber events and system failure events. This coverage provides for loss of revenue and extra expense incurred as a result of a non-IT vendor suffering a cyber event or an unexpected system outage. The exposure for professional services firms to a material loss of revenue from a non-IT vendor is considered to be remote, and the coverage is usually subject to a low sublimit of $1 million or less, especially since some

50. *NotPetya: A War-Like Exclusion?*, Council Ins. Agents & Brokers (May 2, 2019) (emphasis in original), https://www.ciab.com/resources/notpetya-a-war-like-exclusion/.

critical infrastructure outages, such as power outages, are generally excluded from insurance coverage.

Dependent business interruption is no longer a default coverage. (Default coverage is offered automatically in base policies without underwriting.) Furthermore, insurers often require insureds to list and vet the third parties for which losses would be covered—akin to "named perils" instead of an "all risk" coverage that would apply for all third-party vendors. The Crowdstrike, MOVEit, SolarWinds, Accellion, and Microsoft "Hafnium" compromises have caused insurers to review their overall exposure to systemic, aggregated, correlated risks related to the software supply chain where compromise of a single source supplier causes losses for multiple clients of the insurer.

Several insurers are reviewing the breadth of coverage afforded for business interruption losses with a specific mind toward limiting financial exposure to a systemic event in the following ways:

- *Reconsidering waiting periods.* In many cases, waiting periods had been negotiated to between six and eight hours (and in some instances removed entirely). The marketplace is beginning to push for waiting periods closer to 24 hours, which has some precedent in the Property policy marketplace.
- *Limiting aggregate limit exposure.* Insurers limit aggregate exposure by (re)introducing sublimits, requiring coinsurance or, worse for insureds, imposing "widespread loss" exclusions. What constitutes a "widespread' loss is not clearly defined, and sometimes the insurer reserves discretion to decide if an event qualifies as a "widespread loss."

3.1.3. *Extortion*

Extortion covers:

- Hiring an expert ransom negotiation consultant to negotiate with a threat actor who is holding systems hostage by ransomware, denial of service or other attack; threatening to publish, release, or sell stolen data; or otherwise credibly threatening the safety and security of the insured's systems or the confidentiality, integrity, or availability of the insured's data; and
- Paying a ransom, whether in cryptocurrency or other form.

Concern about Ransomware and Coverage Restrictions

Cyber extortion coverage provides reimbursement of an insured's expenses incurred in investigating a threat and any extortion payments made to prevent or resolve the threat. Many insurers cited ransomware events and their associated losses as a major factor impacting their cyber insurance loss ratios in the 2019–2021 period, which had the corresponding effect of substantial premium increases.

Professional services firms remain a favored target for ransomware and other forms of extortion. According to Coveware, a major ransomware negotiation consultant, professional services firms are one of the most frequently targeted sectors for ransomware and extortion.[51]

Insurers are, therefore, looking closely at their clients' technology solutions and implementations aimed at reducing exposure to, and hardening systems against, ransomware. The major front-line cyber insurers for law firms now require specific Ransomware Supplemental Questionnaires focusing on controls and technologies demonstrated to harden systems against:

- Initial intrusion into the system—denying entrance is the best safeguard of all;
- Lateral movement within a compromised system—segregating the insured's network makes it harder for threat actors to access other parts of the network to steal information and plant malware;
- Escalation of credentials—denying threat actors authority to control systems impedes their efforts to install and run malware, greatly limiting the damage they can do;
- Minimum access privilege and data loss prevention ("DLP") systems to reduce threat actors' ability to steal data and hold it for ransom; and
- Access to backups—creating, isolating, and encrypting reliable backups makes ransomware an inconvenience, not a crisis.

Insurers also look for practices and protocols that are shown to reduce the chances of an attack and prepare the insured to respond rapidly and effectively to a systems incursion, thereby minimizing the damage. Those indicators include:

- Patching systems promptly, managing the patching process to ensure that critical patches are identified and prioritized, and ensuring that patching cadence is monitored and measured;
- Training staff to recognize and avoid attempts at phishing, stealing credentials, or installing malware, and deploying other technology and tactics to help staff, such as systems for identifying email sent from external addresses, flagging suspicious email addresses (such as those from domains created within 90 days of the email being sent), and "sandboxing" emails with malicious attachments;
- Conducting incident response plan exercises, such as "tabletop simulations,"[52] designed to train the firm to respond rapidly and effectively to specific types of attack, particularly ransomware attacks.

---

51. *Why Small and Medium-Sized Professional Service Firms Are a Big Target for Ransomware Attacks*, Coveware (Jan. 3, 2021), https://www.coveware.com/blog/2020/11/30/why-small-professional-service-firms-are-ransomware-targets.

52. Tom Ricketts, *Table Stakes: Planning a Tabletop Simulation*, Aon plc (July 2024), https://www.aon.com/risk-services/professional-services/table-stakes-planning-a-tabletop-simulation.

Insurers are adopting a range of strategies in response to the varying degrees of preparedness and controls they find in their client organizations. The cost of cyber incidents has increased to the extent that insurers are taking sometimes drastic action to control their exposure.

- In extreme cases, insurers may decline to provide coverage at all. Several leading cyber insurers are declining to renew clients that do not fit the insurers' preferred profile, *e.g.*, firms below or above a particular size, firms with a particular exposure profile (such as large quantities of PII) and, of course, firms whose controls are deemed inadequate.
- Many insurers are implementing a limit deployment strategy by which they cap the total aggregate limit they offer to any insured. Limit deployment strategies take a variety of forms, including:
  - Capping the maximum limit that the insurer will offer to any insured. For example, in Q4-2020, limits of $10 million were commonly available to law firms, while in 2024, primary limits of $5 million and lower were more usual.[53]
  - Sublimiting certain coverage grants. For instance, an insurer may be willing to offer full limit for most risks ($5 million aggregate limit for Cyber) but make ransomware claims subject to a per-incident and aggregate sublimit (restricting the available aggregate limit for ransomware claims to $2.5 million).
  - Applying differential deductibles (also called retentions). Insurers may offer a policy with a $25,000 deductible across the policy but apply a $250,000 deductible to ransomware claims.
  - Coinsurance is also being proposed, in some cases, combined with a sublimit. Coinsurance requires the insured to share the cost of a ransomware claim with the insurer in addition to paying the policy deductible. For example, after the insured incurs losses equal to the deductible, the insured may also be responsible for between 10% and 50% of the cost of a ransomware claim. Coinsurance is usually combined with an aggregate sublimit so, for example, on a $5 million policy, an insurer may sublimit ransomware to $2.5 million and require the insured to bear a 50% coinsurance. Also coinsurance provisions usually prohibit the insured from purchasing additional insurance to fill the gap.

It is critical to note that while insurers are using these approaches to limit their exposure, the coverage restrictions are not designed to apply solely to a ransomware or cyber extortion insuring agreement. That means the restrictions are not limited to the amount of ransom paid. Instead, the restrictions are written to apply to ransomware as an attack vector (a "ransomware event") and, therefore, the restrictions apply to all costs incurred in

53. Aon Cyber Solutions internal database benchmarking.

connection with a ransomware event, including the kinds of losses covered by the breach response/event management policy.[54]

Case Study

An insured has a $5 million cyber policy with a $100,000 per event retention, a $2.5 million ransomware sublimit, and 50% ransomware coinsurance. The insured experiences a ransomware event; it pays a $2.1 million ransom, incurs costs of Breach Counsel, forensic investigation, and data remediation totaling $1 million and, on top of that, incurs a $1 million loss of revenue. The total loss to the insured is $4.1 million. After the deductible, the amount of the claim is $4 million.

Because all the insured's costs in this case relate to a ransomware event, the 50% ransomware coinsurance applies. The coinsurance reduces the maximum amount the insured can be reimbursed to 50% of the $4 million loss—$2 million. That amount falls within the ransomware sublimit of $2.5 million so the insurer would reimburse the insured the full $2 million. The payments would reduce the $5 million aggregate cyber policy limit to $3 million, and the $2.5 million sublimit for ransomware would be reduced to $500,000.

Restrictions on Extortion Payments

In addition to limitations insurers are putting on payments to ransomware and extortion perpetrators, ransom payments have increasingly come under sanctions scrutiny. The U.S. Department of the Treasury's Office of Foreign Asset Control ("OFAC") issued an advisory alerting companies to potential sanctions violations for paying or facilitating ransomware payments to foreign Specially Designated Nationals and Blocked Persons ("SDNs").[55] The OFAC advisory was largely a reminder that payments to prohibited individuals or entities may result in civil penalties for sanctions violations. The law imposes strict liability for sanctions violations, which means a person in the United States may be held liable for making a sanctioned payment even if they did not know they were engaging in a transaction with a prohibited person under sanctions laws and OFAC regulations.[56]

Risk of sanctions violations is particularly pertinent to ransomware because there is known to be an extensive ecosystem behind every ransomware attacker. Even if the immediate attacker is not a sanctioned person, one of the attacker's "supporting entities," *e.g.*, the group that wrote the malware, the group that provided access to the network, and others, might be. As a result, everyone involved in responding to a ransomware attack—the

54. *See, supra*, text at § 3.1.1.

55. Office of Foreign Assets Control, U.S. Dep't of Treasury, Updated Advisory on Potential Sanctions Risks for Facilitating Ransomware Payments, (Sept. 21, 2021) [hereinafter Updated OFAC Advisory], https://ofac.treasury.gov/media/912981/download?inline.

56. Office of Foreign Assets Control, U.S. Dep't of Treasury, *Advisory on Potential Sanctions Risks for Facilitating Ransomware Payments* (Oct. 1, 2020) [hereafter OFAC Advisory], https://ofac.treasury.gov/media/48301/download?inline.

victim, Breach Counsel, the forensic incident response consultant, the ransomware negotiator, and others—is potentially exposed to sanctions liability if any part of the extortion payment is ultimately received by a sanctioned entity.

The OFAC Advisory makes explicit that it is not just the extortion victim that is at risk of violating sanctions rules:

> Companies that facilitate ransomware payments to cyber actors on behalf of victims, including financial institutions, cyber insurance firms, and companies involved in digital forensics and incident response, not only encourage future ransomware payment-demands but also may risk violating OFAC regulations. This advisory describes these sanctions risks and provides information for contacting relevant U.S. government agencies, including OFAC, if there is a reason to believe the cyber actor demanding ransomware payment may be sanctioned or otherwise have a sanctions nexus.[57]

OFAC recognizes that ransomware can have a catastrophic impact on the victim and, importantly, on the clients, employees, vendors, investors, and other stakeholders associated with the victim. In at least one case, a law firm permanently lost all its legal files (including all its backups) to ransomware, which had a devastating impact on the firm and its clients.[58] The OFAC Advisory acknowledges there may be situations where the impact on the victim and associated parties is so extreme that payment of a ransom is the only viable strategy, and provides the following guidance for those situations:

> Under OFAC's Enforcement Guidelines, OFAC will also consider a company's self-initiated, timely, and complete report of a ransomware attack to law enforcement to be a significant mitigating factor in determining an appropriate enforcement outcome if the situation is later determined to have a sanctions nexus. OFAC will also consider a company's full and timely cooperation with law enforcement both during and after a ransomware attack to be a significant mitigating factor when evaluating a possible enforcement outcome.[59]

The OFAC guidance does not excuse the sanctions violation; it offers a path forward that can alleviate the consequences of a violation. It is, therefore, greatly in the victim firm's

---

57. *Id.* at 1. The Updated OFAC Advisory included substantially the same language and added that the U.S. government "strongly discourages" paying ransom and "recommends focusing on strengthening defensive and resilience measures to prevent and protect against ransomware attacks." Updated OFAC Advisory, *supra* note 55, at 1.

58. Rob Waugh, *American Law Firm Admits Entire Server of Legal Files Fell Victim to Cryptolocker*, WeLiveSecurity (Feb. 10, 2014), https://www.welivesecurity.com/2014/02/10/american-law-firm-admits-entire-server-of-legal-files-fell-victim-to-cryptolocker/.

59. OFAC Advisory, *supra* note 56, at 4; *see also* Updated OFAC Advisory, *supra* note 55, at 5.

interest to involve the Federal Bureau of Investigation (FBI) at the very earliest stages of a ransomware event. The FBI is able to assist in determining whether the attackers and their supporting entities are sanctioned persons. In addition to the OFAC considerations, the FBI often has valuable information about ransomware attackers: How reliable are they? Will they delete the information they have stolen if a ransom is paid? Will the decryption tool the attackers offer work and what percentage of encrypted data can the victim expect to recover? While the FBI will never approve or recommend payment of a ransom, it can provide a great deal of useful information that will assist the victim in deciding whether or not paying a ransom is a viable solution.

3.1.4. *Additional First Party coverages*

Additional First Party coverages can include the following, which are often subject to a sublimit:

- "Bricking"—the cost of replacing physical equipment rendered inoperable and irreparable by malware;
- Reputational Damage—loss of revenue resulting from adverse publicity arising from a publicly disclosed breach or other covered cyber event;
- Voluntary Shutdown—loss of revenue resulting from a proactive decision to shut down systems to avert, prevent, or mitigate a cyber event;
- eCrime—theft of the firm's or its clients' money by deception, such as social engineering, business email compromise, and invoice manipulation fraud;[60]
- Cryptojacking—the excess cost of utilities as the result of computer systems being hijacked to run software that mines cryptocurrency;
- Telephone Fraud—the excess cost of telecommunications service as the result of the system being hijacked and used for long-distance telephony or for calling premium telephone services;
- Proof of Loss Costs—the cost of hiring a forensic accounting firm to analyze and prove the firm's loss of revenue from a cyber event; and
- Betterment—additional costs incurred in enhancing systems to improve security after a breach.

60. Theft of money is typically excluded and requires a separate "Crime" policy to address.

3.2. Third Party Coverages

Organization	Approximate Disclosure Date	Recoveries Received / Accrued	Total Cyber Insurance Limits	Source
Heartlaned Payment Systems	01/20/2009	$31.2 million	Unknown	10-K Filing 2013
Global Payment	03/30/2012	$27 million	Unknown	10-K Filing 2015
Target Corporation	12/18/2013	$107 million	Unknown	10-K Filing 2016 10-K Filing 2019
Home Depot	09/02/2014	$100 million	$100 million	10-K Filing 2016
Equifax	09/07/2017	$125 million	$125 million	Q2 2019 Earnings ICO Notice
Marriott	11/30/2018	$157 million	Unknown	10-K Filing 2021 10-K Filing 2020 10-K Filing 2019 10-K Filing 2018
Capital One	07/29/2019	$73 million	$400 million	Q4 2020 Earnings Press Release
Blackbaud	07/16/2020	$50 million	$50 million	Q4 2022 Earnings
T-Mobile	08/17/2021	$150 million	Unknown	Q4 2023 Earnings Q4 2022 Earnings

Disclosed Data Breach / Privacy Cyber Insurance Recoveries

3.2.1. *Security Failure and Data Privacy Liability*

Security Failure and Data Privacy Liability covers:

- Defense costs and damages arising from a lawsuit or claim for damages by a third party alleging they were harmed by the firm's negligence in allowing, or failing to prevent:
  - Unauthorized access, compromise, loss, or theft of PII or PHI from the firm's systems or from the systems of a third party to whom the firm has entrusted the data for storage or processing;
  - Unauthorized access, compromise, loss, or theft of confidential data from the firm's systems or from the systems of a third party to whom the firm has entrusted the data for storage or processing;
  - Cross-infection of systems by malware or use of the firm's systems to launch a denial of service attack or other form of attack, *e.g.*, use of the firm's website to launch a "watering hole" attack;[61] and

61. Watering hole attacks are coordinated, large-scale attacks on the website of an organization or business. By infecting a website visited by specific targets, cybercriminals turn that site into a so-called watering hole that can then pass the infection on to any website visitors. *See, e.g.*, Muhammad Raza, *What Is a Watering Hole Attack? Detection and Prevention*, Splunk (Feb. 25, 2025), https://www.splunk.com/en_us/blog/learn/watering-hole-attacks.html.

  - Failure, outage, or other unavailability of the firm's systems causing them to be inaccessible to the third party for processing data, provision of a platform, or other service on which the third party was dependent.
- Defense of a regulatory proceeding, including fines and penalties (to the extent insuring fines and penalties is permitted by law) under the HIPAA Privacy Rule,[62] the European Union's General Data Protection Regulation (GDPR),[63] state privacy laws like the California Consumer Privacy Act (CCPA) and California Privacy Rights Act (CPRA),[64] the Illinois Biometric Information Privacy Act (BIPA),[65] and other privacy rights statutes. In some policies, it is possible to include coverage for regulatory proceedings arising from breach of the compliance requirements in statutes such as GDPR and CPRA, although insurers are increasingly removing this coverage or restricting it;
- Penalties levied under a Payment Card Industry Master Services Agreement for breach of Payment Card Industry Data Security Standards (PCI-DSS); and
- Wrongful collection of data, including by pixel tracking (although insurers are also increasingly removing or restricting this coverage).

Law firms must consider the interplay between regulatory coverage under a cyber policy and coverage under professional liability policies. In most cases, if a law firm suffers a cyberattack that compromises confidential information—whether PII, PHI, trade secrets, confidential deal information about a merger, acquisition, or commercial transaction, or other sensitive personal or business data—the compromised data will have been entrusted to the firm by its clients in connection with work the firm is undertaking on behalf of those clients. Information may be provided directly by the client or by third parties, such as another law firm or professional advisor assisting the firm's clients or opposing parties. Therefore, any compromise, loss, theft, or leak of client information could be a violation of the firm's duty under ABA Model Rule 1.6 governing attorneys' handling of confidential information,[66] and any demand or legal action by a client against the firm is likely to be rooted in a breach of professional duty, malpractice, or negligence. Those types of claims may be most appropriately responded to under the firm's professional liability policy.

---

62. "The Standards for Privacy of Individually Identifiable Health Information ("Privacy Rule") established, for the first time, a set of national standards for the protection of certain health information. The U.S. Department of Health and Human Services ("HHS") issued the Privacy Rule to implement the requirement of the Health Insurance Portability and Accountability Act of 1996 ("HIPAA"). *Summary of the HIPAA Privacy Rule*, U.S. Dept. of Health & Human Servs., https://www.hhs.gov/hipaa/for-professionals/privacy/laws-regulations/index.html (visited Jan. 23, 2025).

63. Regulation (EU) 2016/679 of the European Parliament and of the Council of 27 April 2016 on the protection of natural persons with regard to the processing of personal data and on the free movement of such data, and repealing Directive 95/46/EC (General Data Protection Regulation), 2016 O.J. (L 119), https://eur-lex.europa.eu/legal-content/EN/TXT/PDF/?uri=CELEX:32016R0679.

64. *See California Consumer Privacy Act (CCPA)*, Office of the Attorney Gen. (Mar. 13, 2024), https://www.oag.ca.gov/privacy/ccpa.

65. *See also infra* notes 70–78 and accompanying text.

66. *See* Handbook, Chapter 10, *Lawyers' Professional Responsibility to Provide Data Security.*

Lawyers' professional liability policies are typically broad in scope and often provide more advantageous terms and conditions than the Security & Privacy Liability section of a cyber policy. For example, many lawyers' professional liability policies are structured as reimbursement policies, giving the firm control and management of the claim. Cyber policies are typically "duty to defend" obligations under which the insurer appoints counsel and manages the claim.

Managing the interplay between professional liability and cyber policies is becoming more difficult as cyber risks grow larger and more complex. Some professional liability insurers are beginning to restrict coverage for cyber exposures. Indeed, some of those insurers now apply absolute exclusions of claims arising from cyber events. At the same time, many cyber policies have absolute exclusions for professional risks. It is essential for law firms arranging (or renewing) cyber and professional liability policies to determine how the terms and conditions of each policy apply to cyber events and to prescribe how each policy should respond when a cyber event gives rise to allegations of professional negligence or malpractice.

The extent of regulatory coverage in cyber policies varies considerably, ranging from broad coverage of regulatory actions grounded in breach of any applicable privacy statute (including compliance provisions) to more "named perils" approaches requiring both a covered cyber event to trigger coverage and a related breach of a specified privacy statute. The varied approaches are an important consideration when one takes into account that three of the largest fines levied against U.S. corporations under GDPR—Amazon $888 million,[67] Google $57 million,[68] and Facebook $264 million[69]—arose from compliance failures under the statute, not breaches of data by cyberattackers. Many cyber policies would not consider covering the defense costs and penalties in these kinds of regulatory cases because none involved a covered cyber peril.

The proliferation of new privacy statutes, together with questions regarding the extent to which regulatory inquiries and actions might be covered under the various types of insurance policies—Cyber, Professional Liability, Media Liability, Commercial General Liability, Employment Practices Liability—makes it important to understand the extent of coverage under the cyber policy and the availability of coverage under other policies.

---

67. Stephanine Bodoni, *Amazon Gets Records $888 Million EU Fine Over Data Violations*, BLOOMBERG (July 30, 2021, 7:43 AM), https://www.bloomberg.com/news/articles/2021-07-30/amazon-given-record-888-million-eu-fine-for-data-privacy-breach.

68. Chris Brook, *Google Fined $57M by Data Protection Watchdog over GDPR Violations*, DIGITAL GUARDIAN (Jan. 21, 2019), https://digitalguardian.com/blog/google-fined-57m-data-protection-watchdog-over-gdpr-violations.

69. Irish Data Protection Comm'n, *Irish Data Protection Commission fines Meta €251 Million* (Dec. 17, 2024), https://www.dataprotection.ie/en/news-media/press-releases/irish-data-protection-commission-fines-meta-eu251-million; Neil Hodge, *Facebook Reserves $366M for Expected GDPR Fines in Ireland*, COMPLIANCE WK. (Dec. 11, 2020, 3:13 PM), https://www.complianceweek.com/gdpr/facebook-reserves-366m-for-expected-gdpr-fines-in-ireland/29829.article.

One of the more problematic statutes for insurers is the Illinois Biometric Information Privacy Act (BIPA).[70] BIPA, first enacted in 2008, is intended to protect individuals asked to provide biometric information to facilitate identification. Use of facial recognition in the workplace and fingerprint identification to enter a theme park are examples of collections subject to BIPA.

BIPA includes a number of features that are now increasingly found in state consumer privacy laws:[71]

- Requirements for notice to individuals who are being asked to provide biometric information, including how the information will be used and stored and how long it will be kept;
- Written informed consent of individuals from whom biometric information is collected;
- Penalties for failure to comply with the notice, consent, storage, and other compliance requirements;
- Statutory standing to sue for violations granted to individuals whose information is compromised or whose data was collected not in compliance with BIPA requirements. Statutory standing opened the door to class action lawsuits, and the number of such lawsuits escalated rapidly in Illinois.

Most policies are silent on the specific definition of "biometric information," relying instead on a definition of "private information" that references definitions as provided by the statute under which an action is brought (whether by a regulator or private individual). As legal and regulatory actions relating to biometric information accumulate, some insurers are beginning to express concern about the costs and impact of both the defense and the sometimes extremely substantial settlements and penalties levied for violations. For example, a federal judge for the Northern District of California approved a $650 million class-action settlement in a lawsuit against Facebook relating to its photo-scanning feature.[72]

70. If held to standards established by the Illinois Supreme Court in *Cothron v. White Castle System, Inc.*, 2023 IL 128004, ¶1, White Castle would have faced a potential liability of $17 billion. Fortunately for BIPA defendants, Illinois amended BIPA to clarify that anyone whose biometric identifier or biometric information is scanned may only recover damages for one violation. Act of Aug. 2, 2024, Ill. Public Act 103-0769 (amending sections 10 and 20 of the Biometric Information Privacy Act, 740 Ill. Comp. Stat. 14/10, 14/20 (2024)). The next BIPA battle will be whether this amendment applies retroactively.

71. Kirk Nahra et al., *Year in Review: 2024 BIPA Litigation Takeaways*, WilmerHale (Feb. 19, 2025), https://www.wilmerhale.com/en/insights/blogs/wilmerhale-privacy-and-cybersecurity-law/20250219-year-in-review-2024-bipa-litigation-takeaways.

72. Patel v. Facebook, 932 F.3d 1264 (9th Cir. 2019). In *Patel*, the plaintiff sued Facebook for its use of facial recognition software without the consent of Facebook users. The court found that there was either actual harm or a material risk of harm to privacy interests. *Id.* at 1275.

As companies reeled from liability under Illinois' BIPA,[73] they turned to their insurance for redress and were met by a solid wall of coverage denials. Insurance coverage for BIPA liability may exist under several different types of policies: general liability, directors' and officers', and employment practices, in addition to cyber.

How will a cyber insurance policy respond to a BIPA complaint? The Appellate Court of Illinois, First District, applying Illinois law in a September 2024 decision, held that a cyber policy did not afford coverage for an underlying lawsuit alleging BIPA violation because the lawsuit did not include allegations of a "data breach" or "security failure" required to trigger coverage.[74] The court also held that the policy's unlawful collection exclusion served as an independent bar to coverage.[75]

Might the outcome be different in other cases? As with most answers in insurance, it depends. A robust cyber insurance policy, properly designed, may afford the policyholder coverage if the definition of "private information" is sufficiently broad and if the policy grants coverage for compliance wrongs in addition to claims arising from a data breach. Policies vary considerably on coverage for compliance wrongs; some cyber policies cover that risk in the policy wording, some will cover it in an endorsement (often for payment of an additional premium), and some will not provide the coverage at all. Cyber policies may also contain an exclusion for biometric information so it is important to pay close attention to all aspects of the policy language.

Currently (in early 2025), there is not a standalone policy specifically designed to address biometric perils, such as BIPA claims, and given the increase in litigation and claims in Illinois, it is unlikely that such a policy will be developed.[76] In fact, the trend is moving against such coverage.

Coverage for regulatory fines, penalties, and assessments arising from a covered cyber breach is typically available in cyber policies in some form or another. It is important, however, to note that insurance of fines and penalties is illegal in some states, and those restrictions may be given effect in other jurisdictions. For example, on the one hand, some policies contain a "most favorable venue" provision which, in this context, could allow a

73. Illinois is the only state that has enacted legislation addressing biometric information that provides for a private right of action. While Texas and Washington have similar legislation (as does New York City), these jurisdictions do not permit a private right of action. Enforcement by state regulators can also be costly. The Texas Attorney General recently announced a $1.4 billion settlement with Meta, and the attorneys retained by Texas stand to recover more than $300 million in fees. *Attorney General Ken Paxton Secures $1.4 Billion Settlement with Meta Over Its Unauthorized Capture of Personal Biometric Data In Largest Settlement Ever Obtained From An Action Brought By A Single State*, Attorney Gen. of Tex. (July 30, 2024), https://www.texasattorneygeneral.gov/news/releases/attorney-general-ken-paxton-secures-14-billion-settlement-meta-over-its-unauthorized-capture.

74. Tony's Finer Foods Enters., Inc. v. Certain Underwriters at Lloyd's, London, Ill. App. Ct. (1st) 231712, ¶¶ 28–29.

75. *Id.* at ¶ 22.

76. In 2024, the Illinois legislature adopted amendments to BIPA eliminating the controversial "per swipe" penalty aspect of the law, which counted every unauthorized data use as a violation that multiplied statutory damages to astronomical amounts. The amendment dramatically changed the profile of the BIPA exposure. Nevertheless, cyber insurers remain wary of providing BIPA coverage. *See supra*, note 70.

firm resident in a state that permits insurance of fines and penalties to recover those costs even if they were levied by a state that bars insurance of fines and penalties. On the other hand, some states that prohibit such insurance also have "long arm" provisions that effectively prohibit the insurance of fines and penalties anywhere in the U.S. There is a specialist insurance market for Fines & Penalties insurance in Bermuda which—because the market is outside the U.S.—is able to write such policies. Those policies are expensive, complex, and few insurance brokers have access to those markets.

When an insured seeks insurance coverage for liabilities relating to biometric information (or, indeed, for liabilities arising from noncompliance with the provisions of any newer data privacy acts) under a policy not specifically designed to address data breaches, the insured's biggest hurdles will be the many exclusions insurers have added in recent years to policies for disclosure of confidential information and data-related liability. Consider, for example, a case in which a policyholder sued its insurance company for BIPA liability under the "invasion of privacy" coverage.[77] The insurance company denied coverage, relying on an exclusion for claims arising from violations of a statute that "prohibits or limits the sending, transmitting, communicating or distribution of material or information."[78]

Insureds without cyber insurance, which would explicitly cover such "wrongs," frequently assert creative interpretations of other policies to claim coverage for something that was not the intent of the target policy. At the same time, insurers are being more rigorous about imposing exclusions on non-cyber policies and invoking exclusions that might excuse coverage of cyber exposures under a non-cyber policy.

In another case brought under an Employment Practices Liability Insurance (EPLI) policy, the insurance company relied on an "Access to or Disclosure of Confidential or Personal and Data-related Liability" exclusion to deny coverage for "[d]amages arising out of (1) [a]ny access to or disclosure of any person's or organization's confidential or personal information, including patents, trade secrets, processing methods, customer lists, financial information, credit card information, health information or any other type of non-public information; or (2) the loss of, loss of use of, damage to, corruption of, inability to access, or inability to manipulate electronic data."[79] The purpose and effect of this exclusion is to clarify the intent of coverage and reduce the scope of coverage as it relates to private information. Insureds should be aware of these kinds of exclusions as they renew or place coverage, especially if they already use or plan to use biometric information.

Insurance coverage relating to the collection, storage, and use of biometric information is becoming an increasingly pressing issue as the use of passwords for authentication and access control are perceived to provide relatively weak security compared to biometric-based authentication (such as that available in "Windows Hello"). How data privacy laws

77. West Bend Mut. Ins. Co. v. Krishna Schaumburg Tan, Inc., 2021 IL 125978, ¶ 1.

78. *Id.* at ¶¶ 9–11.

79. Landry's, Inc. v. Ins. Co. of the State of Penn., Case No. 4:18-cv-03799 (S.D. Tex. 2019) (on file with the authors).

relate to such uses of biometric information has not been tested in litigation, but if a firm is considering moving to biometric authentication in any form, whether for office security, timekeeping for non-exempt employees, or secure authentication to devices, it would be prudent to consult Data Privacy Counsel for advice before implementing those measures.

3.2.2. *Media Liability*

Media liability covers:

- Defense costs and damages arising from a lawsuit or claim for damages from a third party alleging they were harmed by the firm's publication (electronic or hard copy) or broadcast (including by traditional analogue broadcast media), of:
  - Statements constituting defamation, libel, or slander, including product defamation;
  - Material infringing copyright, trademark, or trade dress;
  - Material constituting an invasion of privacy or putting the third party in a false light;

  as well as
  - Eavesdropping or other invasion of the right to private occupancy; and
  - Negligent or intentional infliction of emotional distress.

Media liability coverage has been a part of cyber insurance policies for many years. For law firms, media liability is the least-used section of the policy, largely because it substantially overlaps with the advertising injury coverage granted in typical commercial general liability (CGL) policies[80] and potentially with coverage afforded by the firm's professional liability policy. CGL policies typically have no deductible and no "Other Insurance" clause, and they are, therefore, automatically called on first for any claim that might be made against the insured. The cyber policy provides coverage excess of that provided by the CGL policy. In many cases, particularly defamation cases, a lawyer's professional liability policy may also be called on to respond if the actions giving rise to the claim arose in the context of professional work.

The media liability section of the cyber policy could develop more prominence as CGL underwriters narrow the coverage grant under their policies, which is largely a result of some unfavorable decisions and settlements that have pushed interpretation of CGL coverage beyond the limits of underwriters' intent. As media content and activity is increasingly digitized, there is an inevitable logic to move coverage for a non-physical damage / injury to the policy explicitly designed to address these types of risk.

Examples of situations that have led to law firms reporting incidents to their cyber insurers follow. (The names of Aon client law firms are intentionally omitted to protect

80. Kevin Kalinich & Laura Grabouski, *Evolution of Insurance Coverage for Intellectual Property Litigation*, A.B.A Litig. Sec. (Feb. 20, 2020), https://www.americanbar.org/groups/litigation/resources/newsletters/insurance-coverage/insurance-intellectual-property-litigation/.

confidentiality.) In all these cases, the CGL policy responded first, and the claim was accepted by the cyber insurer on an excess basis. None of these incidents went to court so there is no public record of the outcome, but they serve as examples of how law firms can incur media liability.

- A law firm hired a website designer to create a new website. The firm was happy with the results until another law firm accused it of copyright infringement. The web-designer had copied the underlying code of the other firm's website and "repurposed" it with new graphics and information.
- A law firm was contacted by a commercial real-estate entity over a stock photograph of a distinctive building that was prominently displayed on the landing page of the firm's website. The real estate entity was not a client of the firm and was concerned that the very recognizable building implied that it was. The firm changed the photograph.
- A member of a large law firm's procurement staff posted some extremely disparaging comments about a supplier on social media. The law firm's employee thought he had posted the comments in "private mode," but they were visible to the general public. The supplier very quickly found out and threatened to sue the firm for disparagement.
- An attorney was being interviewed about an old case he participated in. During the interview, the attorney mixed up the names of the defendant and the defendant's attorney, stating by name that the defendant's attorney had committed multiple very serious crimes. The attorney in question sued for defamation.

Many law firms disregard media liability as an insignificant risk, and some believe that they have no exposure. However, the first two examples above illustrate how a business's presence on the internet and, increasingly, on social media platforms increase greatly the possibilities for infringement, defamation, and other media wrongs. If CGL insurers continue to limit (and even remove) media liability coverage from their policies, the focus will move to cyber to pick up these exposures.

It is important to note that while media liability insurance provides the firm with some coverage for intellectual property infringement in the form of copyright, trademark, and trade dress, media liability policies usually have explicit exclusions relating to other forms of intellectual property, particularly patents and trade secrets.[81] Patents and trade secrets are typically the most valuable assets in a law firm's possession,[82] so

81. *Id.*

82. Madison Alder et al., *Corporate Secrets at Risk in Hack of U.S. Courts Documents (1)*, BLOOMBERG L. (Jan. 7, 2021, 3:35 PM), https://news.bloomberglaw.com/privacy-and-data-security/corporate-secrets-at-risk-in-hack-of-u-s-courts-documents; Aon 2024 IP Risk Report, *supra* note 15.

the question is often asked as to how the law firm can protect itself and how these assets can be insured.

The patent information and trade secrets held by law firms generally belong to the firm's clients, who may insure them as an asset under one of the available intellectual property insurance entities. The loss issue for the law firm is what happens if a client's intellectual property assets are stolen as the result of a breach of the law firm's information systems. In this case, the client is most likely to take legal action against the law firm for failing to protect the confidentiality of the client information (in violation of ABA Model Rule 1.6) and for negligence in the course of a professional engagement. The harm done to the client may be substantial, and the negotiation and possible litigation arising is likely to be both complex and expensive. As this is a claim against the firm for professional negligence or malpractice, the firm's professional liability insurance policy should respond.

The value of the law firm's own patents and trade secrets is not covered by any of the "standard" policies in a law firm's insurance portfolio, including professional liability or cyber insurance. If the firm has such an exposure, it can only be covered in the specialist intellectual property insurance market.

4. Multiple Lines of Insurance Collaboration

Do we really need cyber insurance? Legal organizations need insurance that covers cyber exposures, but the form of coverage may not be the same for all lawyers. It is critical that firms and their insurance advisors examine the financial damage from cyber perils and determine the cost-benefit analysis of each potential insurance policy so each legal organization can make a quantifiable, objective, fact-based decision with respect to whether and how to purchase cyber insurance coverage.

In general, as law firms increasingly rely on digital assets and technology, cyber exposures are materially underinsured compared to physical assets—Property, Plant and Equipment, or "PPE." The majority of organizations do not assign the same priority to data assets as they do to physical assets. Tangible assets, despite lower value, are insured at 3x greater than intangible assets.[83]

83. *See* Aon 2024 IP Risk Report, *supra* note 15.

2024 Intangible vs. Tangible Risks Comparison Report | Aon

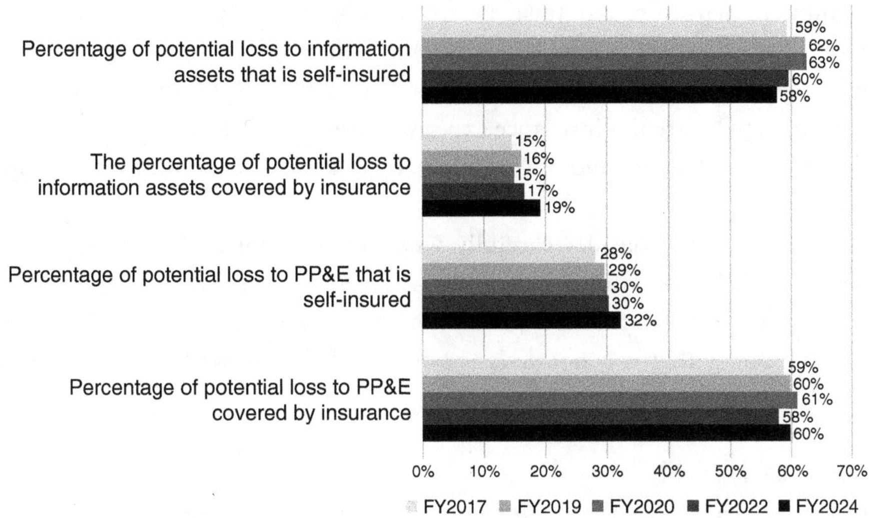

There is not a standard cyber insurance policy form. Cyber insurance can be confusing because insurance carriers and cyber policies are not consistent in how they address cyber perils. For instance, most cyber insurers exclude from cyber policies first party coverage for stolen laptops and other computer hardware. Therefore, insureds must look to their property policies for their first party loss to replace the hardware. Potential third party liability for unauthorized disclosure or loss of information triggered by the same laptop theft, however, will generally be covered by a cyber policy.

This section outlines other lines of insurance and the extent to which they may or may not provide some coverage for events triggered by a cyber incident. It is important to reiterate that this is a dynamic environment. Insurers are conducting extensive reviews of policy wording with a view to eliminating unintended cyber coverage—so called "silent cyber"—and making policies explicit about the extent to which they will or will not cover events that are the result of a cyber peril. Lloyd's of London issued a formal edict in 2019 to all Lloyd's insurers requiring them to carry out silent cyber reviews and to amend their policies to be clear about the extent of cyber coverage provided.[84]

In addition to policy amendments, the silent cyber concern should diminish in time because more firms are purchasing dedicated cyber insurance. Firms with cyber insurance that are victims of cyberattacks should have less need to seek coverage from a non-cyber

84. Caroline Dunn, *Providing Clarity for Lloyd's Customers on Coverage for Cyber Exposures,* Lloyd's (Jul. 4, 2019) ("Lloyd's view is that it is in the best interests of customers, brokers and syndicates for **all policies** to be clear on whether coverage is provided for losses caused by a cyber event. This clarity should be provided by either excluding coverage or by providing affirmative coverage in the (re)insurance policy." (Emphasis original.)), https://assets.lloyds.com/assets/y5258-providing-clarity-for-lloyd-s-customers-on-coverage-for-cyber-exposures/1/Y5258%20-%20Providing%20clarity%20for%20Lloyd%E2%80%99s%20customers%20on%20coverage%20for%20cyber%20exposures.pdf.

policy. Nonetheless, insureds must continue to pay attention to the overlap of insurance policies and take steps to ensure their policies are appropriately structured to coordinate and complement each other to maximize coverage in the event of a cyberattack. Experience has shown that when multiple lines of insurance could be applicable, coverage disputes land with judges (who are not insurance experts); coverage for the insured may be unavailable, inadequate, or illusory; and litigation outcomes can create confusion and unpredictability for the insurance market.[85]

Insureds should also consider carefully what limits of insurance are appropriate to the exposure in order to avoid the situation where a loss exceeds the available limits of the policy, leaving the insured in a position of potentially attempting to find coverage under another policy that was not designed or intended to provide coverage for the loss in question.

4.1. Professional Liability[86]

Lawyers and law firms have historically been responsible for keeping their clients' data and information confidential as an ethical obligation, and in many cases, client engagement letters or contracts include specific provisions about confidentiality, data protection, and the return or destruction of data when the engagement ends. In the past, a standard lawyer's professional liability policy was all the insurance coverage needed to provide liability protection from unintended disclosures. The most significant financial impact was the damages a client might suffer, and the client harmed would seek compensation in a suit for malpractice.

Information technology has dramatically changed lawyers' and law firms' exposure for unauthorized disclosure or loss of confidential information. In a paper-dominant practice, a misplaced file or stolen briefcase would normally not expose a significant amount of information. Today, an improperly handled smartphone can enable access to a client's or firm's entire email and data management systems. Thumb drives have the capacity to hold gigabytes of data, which dramatically expands the consequences of a loss or breach.[87]

The volume of data compromised also increases the costs of responding to breach, whether the breach is the work of a malicious hacker or simple human error. Data privacy

---

85. *See, e.g., Emmis Communications Corp. v. Illinois National Insurance Co.*, No. 18-3392, (7th Cir. 2019) (opinion withdrawn, revised opinion). "The short-lived unanimous ruling, which held that a D&O liability policyholder could lose coverage by notifying multiple insurers about a claim, rattled some legal departments and led to a round of intense briefing but had little effect on the industry otherwise." Brandon Lowrey, *What One Scrapped Opinion Might Say about Judge Barret*, LAW360 (Oct. 2, 2020 8:48PM), https://www.law360.com/articles/1316104/what-one-scrapped-opinion-might-say-about-judge-barrett.

86. Gavin Souter, *Expanding Risks Drive Lawyers Liability Claims*, BUS. INS. (Nov. 1, 2024), https://www.businessinsurance.com/expanding-risks-drive-lawyers-liability-claims/ (noting that lawyers' use of generative artificial intelligence raises liability concerns).

87. For perspective, one gigabyte of data in the form of Microsoft Word® files represents approximately 65,000 printed pages or more than 100,000 pages of printed email messages. The corresponding stack of paper would be the height of a utility pole. Paulette Keheley, *How Many documents in A Gigabyte*, DIGITAL WARROOM (Apr. 2, 2020), https://www.digitalwarroom.com/blog/how-many-pages-in-a-gigabyte.

statutes impose onerous and expensive obligations on firms that lose PII or PHI, requiring individual notifications, credit monitoring, and identity theft insurance for the potential victims, and a telephone helpline to take questions and complaints. On top of these obligations, regulators can investigate the event and levy fines and penalties, and the firm could be subject to lengthy and expensive litigation.

The good news for law firms is that a well-crafted professional liability insurance policy should address costs of defense for a claim against the firm, indemnity, and settlement expenses arising from the firm's professional services. As noted earlier in this chapter, the main reason a firm has third-party information is because of an engagement to provide professional services. The key for law firms, then, is to maximize existing coverage, identify gaps, and consider how to address them.

Some professional liability policies explicitly provide for first party costs incurred in the investigation of a claim. However, while the first party costs associated with cyber events are substantial and immediate, it cannot be known for some time—months to possibly years—whether the cyber event will give rise to a claim for professional negligence. It can, therefore, be difficult to know if costs incurred in the immediate response to a cyber event will ever be part of a professional liability claim, and no professional liability insurer will willingly pay substantial event response costs on the assumption that professional negligence claims might follow. Furthermore, professional liability insurance will not pay for remediation of systems, loss of revenue, or payment of a ransom.

The key consideration for large and small law firms alike is the bottom line: what does the firm consider to be its relative financial statement materiality impact accounting for the fact that professional liability insurance is unlikely to contribute significantly (if at all) to the first party costs of a cyber event? For instance, a small firm of two to five lawyers may consider a $17,000 cyber ransomware attack "catastrophic" and, therefore, an essential risk to be addressed by cyber insurance coverage. In addition to the ransom payment, the firm will incur costs for legal advice, forensic investigation, and remediation of data and systems, as well as loss of revenue and loss of reputation. In extreme cases the firm may not be able to satisfy the ransom demand without the expert resources available through cyber insurance and could lose access to all of its data.[88]

In addition to the costs typical of any cyber event, firms with practice specialties involving large amounts of PII and PHI face potentially enormous costs of complying with notification requirements under state privacy laws and regulatory investigation, fines, and penalties.[89] HIPAA penalties for data breaches involving PHI can mount up very rapidly;

88. *See* Rob Waugh, *American Law Firm Admits Entire Server of Legal Files Fell Victim to Cryptolocker*, WeLiveSecurity (Feb. 10, 2014), https://www.welivesecurity.com/2014/02/10/american-law-firm-admits-entire-server-of-legal-files-fell-victim-to-cryptolocker/.

89. Solomon Klappholz, *The National Public Data Breach Exposed Nearly Three Billion Users—Now the Company Has Filed for Bankruptcy*, ITPro (Oct. 28, 2024), https://www.itpro.com/security/data-breaches/the-national-public-data-breach-exposed-nearly-three-billion-users-now-the-company-has-filed-for-bankruptcy.

they range from $100 to $50,000 per individual violation, capped at $1,500,000 per calendar year.[90]

Law firms also have PII and perhaps PHI in their Human Resources records. (Certain employer-sponsored health plans are considered covered entities under HIPAA and the information in these plans is therefore deemed PHI.) Even a small firm can incur substantial costs from a breach of employee records considering they can include information about employees' family members and historic records covering employees, temporary workers, contract workers, job applicants, interns, and summer associates and their family members.

Some law firms rely on extensions of coverage for cyber provided under a "Business Owner's Policy" without realizing that in many cases this coverage is subject to a low sublimit and other coverage restrictions. In one case, such a firm was hit with ransomware and was effectively "unproductive" for 3 months, losing an estimated $700,000 in revenue. When the firm made a claim against its Business Owner's Policy, it encountered a sublimit of $20,000 for "computer virus," and the insurer successfully defended in litigation its refusal to pay any more.[91]

There are also extreme examples of a cyber incident catastrophically damaging a law firm for reasons beyond financial impacts. The most famous case—so famous it was turned into a Hollywood movie, "The Laundromat"[92]—was about the law firm Mossack Fonseca, which closed[93] after their entire database of firm and client information was taken and leaked to the International Consortium of Investigative Journalists. This event demonstrates the enormous and widespread impact a cyberattack on a law firm can have, including the collapse of the firm itself and the resignation of the Prime Minister of Iceland.[94]

Any claim made by a law firm client alleging harm from the release or compromise of their data due to a cyber event should be addressed by the firm's professional liability insurer. Insurance companies do not segregate professional liability coverage based upon the peril that created it. For example, law firms do not buy one policy for claims arising out of conflicts and another for claims arising out of missed statutes of limitations. Recall when facsimile machines were introduced and firms were transmitting documents electronically for the first time. If a firm sent a document to the wrong fax number and damages were suffered by a client, the resulting claim would be covered by a professional liability policy.

90. *The Cost of HIPAA Violations*, Accountable (Dec. 27, 2021), https://www.accountablehq.com/post/the-cost-of-hipaa-violations.

91. Debra Cassens Weiss, *Victimized by Ransomware, Law Firm Sues Insurer for $700K in Lost Billings*, ABA J. (May 2, 2017, 11:09 AM), https://www.abajournal.com/news/article/victimized_by_ransomware_law_firm_sues_insurer_for_700k_in_lost_billings.

92. *The Laundromat* (Netflix 2019).

93. *Panama Papers Law Firm Mossack Fonseca to Shut Down after Tax Scandal*, Reuters (Mar. 14, 2018, 5:22 PM), https://www.reuters.com/article/us-panama-corruption/panama-papers-law-firm-mossack-fonseca-to-shut-down-after-tax-scandal-idUSKCN1GQ34R.

94. Steven Erlanger, Stephen Castle & Rick Gladstone, *Iceland's Prime Minister Steps Down Amid Panama Papers Scandal*, N.Y. Times (Apr. 5, 2016), https://www.nytimes.com/2016/04/06/world/europe/panama-papers-iceland.html.

These were the first digital "breaches," or unintended disclosure claims, that law firms faced.

Lawyers' professional liability policies typically do not have cyber exclusions although such exclusions are beginning to be seen in certain markets around the world in response to initiatives (particularly from Lloyd's of London)[95] to ensure that all policies are explicit in how they cover, or do not cover, cyber perils (the so-called "silent cyber" issue). This is something that needs to be watched with extreme care by insurance brokers and their clients because it is quite possible for gaps to be created between professional liability policies that have a cyber exclusion and cyber policies that have a professional liability exclusion.

Beyond professional liability insurance, some other insurance law firms have may provide some limited coverage for data breach losses, but it's generally not enough. For example, Insurance Services Organization commercial property policies may provide a small and very limited amount of coverage for loss due to a virus, but this coverage is increasingly being pared down as insurers move toward absolute exclusions. Standard property damage coverage also typically offers very limited protection unless there is physical damage to, or destruction of, the equipment on which the compromised data is stored.

General liability policies typically only address physical injury to persons or tangible property and the insured's liability arising from the publication of material that violates a person's right to privacy. Policies such as the Surety and Fidelity Computer Crime Policy may provide some coverage for certain situations of stolen funds, but those policies generally exclude losses resulting directly or indirectly from the theft of confidential information, indirect consequential loss of any nature, and loss of potential income, including, but not limited to, interest and dividends.

Property insurance is typically limited to "tangible" property damage or loss. Computer data is not automatically considered "tangible." Furthermore, cybercriminals (except those using ransomware attack methods) rarely irretrievably destroy data; simple destruction cannot be monetized and, therefore, has no payoff to the criminals unless their objectives are political or industrial sabotage (for example, NotPetya).[96] As a result, the typical property policy is not triggered by a cyber incident, especially since the property underwriters started including specific business interruption exclusions from cyber incidents.

Professional liability policies are, in the final analysis, a highly-evolved product for a niche exposure and, therefore, are not an appropriate vehicle to address the many, varied, and wide-ranging exposures arising from a cyber event. While there are areas of overlap between professional liability and cyber policies, they are fundamentally intended to cover different risks. Law firms should recognize that each policy has its own focus and value as part of a law firm's overall risk management approach. Law firms may find the following observations useful:

---

95. *See, supra*, text at note 92.

96. 5 Fast Facts to Know about History's Most Destructive Cyberattack, HYPR, https://www.hypr.com/security-encyclopedia/notpetya (last visited Apr. 11, 2025).

- A professional liability policy trigger is generally an allegation of error, omission, or a negligent act, and the policy responds to a demand made by a third party. A robust cyber insurance policy will be triggered by the cyber incident and cover first party costs incurred by the firm prior to a third-party demand; the cyber policy helps the firm respond to the incident and avoid third-party claims or limit their magnitude.
- Professional liability policies are limited to claims under the limited definition of "professional services." A cyber insurance policy has a broader scope of coverage based on first party triggers, such as a failure of security, a privacy event, or even a reasonable suspicion that such an event may have happened.
- Professional liability policies are not intended to address first-party business interruption or extra costs to the firm caused by cyber incidents that knock out or degrade to the firm's computer systems or extortion payments demanded by ransomware operators or cyber criminals that have stolen sensitive data. Cyber policies have specific affirmative coverage grants for such perils and damages.

Cyber policies, unlike most professional liability policies, may include media/publication coverage, identified by insurance carriers as "advertising injuries," such as libel, slander, invasion of privacy, and misappropriation of advertising ideas. The scope of this coverage may differ among insurers. Typically, however, cyber liability coverage would afford coverage for disclosure injury, reputational injury (even if limited), and content injury, such as trademark, service mark, and copyright infringement.[97]

- Some cyber insurance carriers offer increasingly expanded loss mitigation services with the policy, such as cyber assessments, mitigation services, and incident response. While this assistance may not appeal to large firms that prefer more control over their choice of outside vendors, insurers' panels of mitigation service providers may be quite valuable to smaller and mid-size firms and made available at a significantly reduced cost.
- Assessment of coverage and gaps can encourage an open dialogue about opportunities to shore up systems and procedures. It can be useful to leverage external expertise to identify gaps that cyber coverage may fill. For instance, it is critical to partner with an insurer and insurance broker with expertise in cyber policy wording customization and claims handling.[98]

97. *See* Kalinich & Grabouski, *supra* note 80.

98. Cyber insurance coverage claims have been denied due to lack of a common understanding of the coverage between the insurer and the insured or inadequate policy wording customization. *See, e.g.*, *Columbia Cas. Co. v. Cottage Health Sys.*, C.D. Cal. No. CV 15-03432, 2015 WL 4497730 (AGRx) (C.D. Cal. July 17, 2015) (CNA NetProtect360 policy coverage denied by CNA due to failure of insured to meet minimum required practices, misrepresentation in the application, and other defects, but declination was overturned after CNA lost a decision with respect to enforceability of the ADR clause); *Travelers Prop. Cas. Co. of Am. v. Fed. Recovery Servs.*, No. 2:2014cv00170—Document 45 (D. Utah 2015) (upholding CyberFirst policy coverage denial by Travelers due to alleged intentional excluded act of withholding distribution of information by insured); *P.F. Chang's China Bistro, Inc. v. Fed. Ins. Co.*, No. CV-15-01322-PHX-SMM, 2016 U.S. Dist. LEXIS 70749 (D. Ariz. May 26, 2016)

Attorneys' Liability Assurance Society Ltd. (ALAS) was founded by owner-insured law firms as an alternative to the commercial insurance market. While ALAS provides some coverage for some cyber perils, ALAS cannot cover loss of revenue or extortion. That gap can be critical for law firms, and it is a useful illustration of the value in coordinating cyber and professional liability policies. It is not unusual for law firm members of ALAS to purchase standalone cyber policies to supplement the limited coverage provided by ALAS.

4.2. Property Damage & Business Interruption

Insurance Services Organization commercial property policies may provide a narrow and very limited amount of coverage for loss due to a virus, but insurers are increasingly paring down or eliminating it altogether as they move toward absolute cyber exclusions and clarifying language that explicitly defines data as non-physical property. Standard property damage coverage typically applies when there is physical damage to or destruction of equipment and may provide very limited protection for the data lost or destroyed as a result.

Absent demonstrable physical property damage, a property damage / business interruption policy is not likely to provide much, if any, compensation to an insured that is the victim of a cyberattack. That was the outcome for the law firm that suffered a three-month interruption of its business as the result of a ransomware attack.[99] The firm sued the insurer behind their Business Owner's Policy (BOP) hoping to recover $700,000 of lost revenue. The firm had no standalone cyber policy, and their BOP had an extension for cyber events affording only $20,000 of coverage (which the insurer paid in full). The court sided with the insurer, holding that the policy was very clear that the only coverage for a cyber event was subject to the $20,000 sublimit.[100]

When cyber events cause physical damage to equipment, however, property policies may help. In contrast to the law firm case (decided in 2017), a 2020 decision by a federal court in Maryland favored the insured, which suffered serious damage from a ransomware attack including lost data, lost software, and a dysfunctional computer system and hardware.[101] The court held that the policyholder was entitled to coverage under its all-risk property policy.

> ***Here, not only did Plaintiff sustain a loss of its data and software, but Plaintiff is left with a slower system, which appears to be harboring a dormant virus, and is***

(coverage denied by Chubb for Payment Card Industry Fines & Penalties, which would seem to be the main vulnerability and damages that should be addressed for a restaurant that accepts payment via credit cards); *New Hotel Monteleone, LLC v. Certain Underwriters at Lloyd's of London*, Subscribing to Ascent Cyberpro Policy No. ASC14C00944, No. 2:16-CV-00061-ILRL-JCW (E.D. La. filed Jan. 5, 2016) (after insurer denied claim made by New Hotel Monteleone, it initiated against its insurer alleging lack of adequate limits for Payment Card Industry fines; Eustis Insurance Co. filed a third-party complaint against wholesale insurance broker R-T Specialty, Inc. after the broker allegedly failed to properly advise New Hotel Monteleone about its cybersecurity exposures and coverage that R-T Specialty was tasked to procure).

99. *See supra* text at note 98.

100. Moses, Afonso, Ryan, Ltd. v. Sentinel Ins. Co., Case No. 1:17-cv-00157 (D.R.I. Apr. 21, 2017).

101. Nat'l Ink & Stitch, LLC v. State Auto Prop. & Cas. Ins. Co., 435 F. Supp. 3d 679 (D. Md. 2020).

unable to access a significant portion of software and stored data. Because the plain language of the Policy provides coverage for such losses and damage, summary judgment will be granted in favor of Plaintiff's interpretation of the Policy terms.[102]

This was a particularly influential decision because it caused property insurers to further clarify language to exclude such claims, and noteworthy because the court found that the computer system's impairment constituted property damage under the policy language even though the system functioned after the ransomware attack. This case provides an excellent example of "Silent Cyber" coverage; a non-cyber insurance policy has no explicit statement of position on cyber perils and, consequently, is held to afford coverage for the impact of a cyberattack.

There are two major takeaways from this case:

1. It is clear from the fact the claim was litigated that the insurer believed the policy did not cover the loss. It is worth mentioning that the insured was offered two substantially similar Business Owner's Policies from the same insurer, one that explicitly included cyber coverage at a higher premium and the one litigated, which did not have explicit cyber coverage. That fact might have favored the insurer if the court looked beyond the four corners of the policy to aid its interpretation)[103] Many lawsuits have been filed by firms faced with enormous and potentially uncovered costs from cyber events because they did not have a dedicated cyber insurance policy. No insured wants to have to sue to make an insurance recovery. The prospect of litigation goes up, and the prospect for recovery goes down, when cyber events are not covered explicitly.
2. Insurers continue to be concerned about "Silent Cyber." They will continue to amend and endorse non-cyber policies to make explicit whether or not the policy will pay for a cyber event. In general, the endorsements are not absolute exclusions,[104] but instead define "property" as specifically excluding data and software and "property damage" more narrowly so that non-damage cyber events, such as those caused by ransomware will not be covered, but fire or other physical damage caused by malicious programming will be covered. The loss profile associated with cyber risks is now so extreme and so adverse that insurers are keen to ensure that coverage is directly associated with appropriate underwriting and premiums, and the best way for them to ensure that this happens is by excluding coverage from all but standalone cyber policies.

102. *Id.* (emphasis added).
103. *Id.*
104. For comparison, a pollution exclusion is an absolute exclusion.

4.3. General Liability

General liability policies are intended to cover the insured for bodily injury or property damage to a third party. General liability policies have historically been silent on cyber events as a peril, intending to pick up bodily injury or property damage even when caused by a cyber peril. This may not continue to be the case. One major insurer of commercial general liability (and cyber insurance) for professional firms is introducing an absolute cyber exclusion on its general liability policies. For now, however, there does not seem to be support for this move among other insurers, and cyber insurers are showing no sign of willingness to include property damage and bodily injury coverage on cyber policies. Absolute cyber exclusions in general liability policies create a gap in coverage that appears to have no solution in the market other than to place coverage with general liability insurers that do not use that exclusion.

In addition to coverage for property damage and bodily injury, general liability policies also provide "Advertising Liability" coverage and a certain amount of personal injury coverage, which as discussed above,[105] overlap with coverage provided under the media liability section in many cyber policies.

Like the property policy coverage disputes described in the preceding subsection, insurers have litigated coverage for privacy claims under general liability policies. In at least one case, the insured successfully litigated its right to coverage for costs of defending a biometric information privacy claim.[106] The insured did not have a cyber insurance policy so it sought to recover under its general liability policy coverage for liability arising out of "written publication of material that violates a person's right of privacy."[107] The insured had provided customers' fingerprint data to a vendor, which it claimed constituted "publication." The insurance company argued that no "publication" had occurred because that term requires dissemination to a wide audience.[108] The court disagreed, holding that "publication" was also commonly understood to encompass a more limited sharing with a single party. It held the insured was entitled to coverage.[109]

The lesson learned here is the same as the property policy examples: insureds should have certainty of coverage and not have to pursue legal action to "find" coverage in policies that were not intended (and critically with cyber exposures, not priced) to grant the coverage needed. This case is another illustration of "Silent Cyber," and commercial general liability insurers are making wording changes to clarify their intent about the scope of coverage.

Also like the property damage policies, there has been some concern in the market that clarification of general liability policies will take the form of an absolute cyber exclusion,

---

105. *See supra* text at notes 86–88.
106. *West Bend Mut. Ins. Co. v. Krishna Schaumburg Tan, Inc.*, 2021 IL 125978 (Ill. 2021).
107. *Id.*
108. *Id.*
109. *Id.*

which would force gaps in coverage between cyber policies (which explicitly exclude bodily injury and property damage) and general liability policies (excluding all consequences of cyber events). It is, therefore, important for firms to work with brokers who understand the intricacies of coverage, including the interplay of cyber with other policies, as well as the threat environment and business of the insured. Coverage can be arranged and coordinated in such a way as to minimize gaps and the uncertainty of leaving exposures uninsured on the assumption that coverage can be "found" if catastrophe strikes.

4.4. Commercial Crime[110]

In February 2024, Hong Kong police disclosed that a finance worker was duped in an elaborate "deepfake" scam.[111] The worker was persuaded to attend a video call with people he believed were his employer's chief financial officer and other staff members, all of whom turned out to be deepfake re-creations. According to police, the worker initially suspected he had received a phishing email because it cited the need for a secret transaction. The worker was reassured by the video call, however. The other people attending the call looked and sounded to him just like colleagues he recognized. The Hong Kong employee subsequently arranged to pay out a total of 200 million Hong Kong dollars—about US$25.6 million. The funds were sent in 15 transactions.[112] This kind of loss is not covered by cyber insurance. Almost every cyber insurance policy—and all other policies except crime insurance—specifically excludes money/funds/securities transfers.

A Colorado case illustrates a more complicated, but not uncommon, phishing scam involving an attorney wire transfer. In this instance, the intended recipient of a divorce settlement sued the counterparty's attorney and the bank that executed the wire transfer—can a bank be sued for *correctly* executing a client's wire transfer order?—after the attorney, acting on what appeared to be a genuine email from the intended recipient's attorney, wired the settlement funds to a fraudulent account. Wells Fargo asked a Colorado state judge to dismiss claims brought by the defrauded attorney, who alleges the bank failed to cancel his wire transfer to the scammer's Hong Kong account.[113]

Long before ransomware became a major threat, criminals refined "social engineering" and "phishing" techniques to dupe victims into transferring funds, whether by wire

---

110. Tom Ricketts, *When Is a Cyber Crime Not a "Cyber-Crime"? Social Engineering Fraud (SEF) and Business Email Compromise (BEC)*, Aon (Aug. 2023), https://www.aon.com/risk-services/professional-services/when-is-a-cyber-crime-not-a-cyber-crime-social-eng.

111. Dan Milmo, *UK Engineering Firm Arup Falls Victim to £20m Deepfake Scam*, Guardian (May 17, 2024 08:13), https://www.theguardian.com/technology/article/2024/may/17/uk-engineering-arup-deepfake-scam-hong-kong-ai-video. "Deepfake" normally refers to fake videos that have been created using artificial intelligence (AI) to look and sound extremely realistic. For further discussion of deepfakes, *see* Handbook, Chapter 6, *Dealing with Deepfakes: The Role for Lawyers and Law Firms.*

112. *Hong Kong MNC Suffers $25.6 Million Loss in Deepfake Scam*, Econ. Times (Feb. 6, 2024, 08:03 PM), https://economictimes.indiatimes.com/industry/tech/hong-kong-mnc-suffers-25-6-million-loss-in-deepfake-scam/articleshow/107465111.cms.

113. Daniel Ducassi, *Wells Fargo Says Atty Can't Blame It for Getting Scammed*, Law360 (Oct. 2, 2024, 4:39 PM), https://www.law360.com/articles/1884579/wells-fargo-says-atty-can-t-blame-it-for-getting-scammed.

transfer, gift card, or invoice manipulation. For several years this has been one of the major sources of cybercrime, according to the FBI's Internet Crime Complaint Center (IC3). The IC3 includes these types of fraud in their cybercrime statistics, classifying them under the general umbrella "BEC" for "Business Email Compromise."[114] In 2019, according to IC3, BEC scams accounted for half of the cybecrime losses, averaging nearly $75,000 per complaint and totaling an estimated $1.77 billion.[115] By 2023, the total had increased to $2.9 billion.[116]

Law firms have proven to be a particularly attractive target for this type of crime as they are so often the hub of transactions involving millions of dollars being exchanged on an international basis.[117] Law firms also often act on behalf of clients in a transaction and, therefore, are vulnerable to "man in the middle" attacks. In such an attack, the client's email system is hacked and, using an absolutely genuine email address, the hacker instructs the law firm to pay the transaction funds to a fraudulent bank account.[118]

This type of crime, from an insurance perspective, used to fall into a gap between two policies: cyber and commercial crime.

- Cyber policies typically have specific exclusions for monies and securities. On top of this, social engineering scams often rely on using deceptive "spoofed" email addresses and, therefore, do not involve hacking systems; give that scenario, there is no triggering event for a cyber policy to respond to in the first place.
- Commercial crime policies traditionally had an exclusion for "voluntary parting," which means the victim voluntarily and willingly hands the money to the criminal. (Of course, victims usually think they are sending money to the rightful recipient.)

Crime insurers were initially willing to extend coverage for this risk of loss to a BEC or other social engineering scam, although usually subject to a sublimit and for an additional premium. As the environment deteriorated and losses escalated rapidly, crime insurers began to pare back coverage, usually providing limits no greater than $250,000 for any one incident and in the aggregate. In a precursor to what has been happening in cyber insurance in 2024–2025, underwriters started paying close attention to insureds' controls, policies, and procedures, providing more coverage to those companies with rigorous controls.

---

114. *See* Handbook, Chapter 5, *Cybercrime*.

115. Catalin Cimpanu, *FBI: BEC Scams Accounted for Half of the Cyber-Crime Losses in 2019*, ZD Net (Feb. 11, 2020, 1:30 PM), https://www.zdnet.com/article/fbi-bec-scams-accounted-for-half-of-the-cyber-crime-losses-in-2019/.

116. *Federal Bureau of Investigation Internet Crime Report 2023*, FBI Internet Crime Complaint Center (2023), https://www.ic3.gov/AnnualReport/Reports/2023_IC3Report.pdf.

117. *Why Are Social Engineering Attacks Targeting Law Firms?*, Aon (Oct. 2020), https://www.aon.com/risk-services/professional-services/why-are-social-engineer-attacks-targeting-law-firm.jsp.

118. *In Deep Water: Phishing Risks for Professional Service Firms*, Aon (May 2021), https://www.aon.com/risk-services/professional-services/in-deep-water-phishing-risks-for-professional-service-firms.jsp.

Nonetheless, these scams continue and, in a pattern that has been seen with cyber insurance, entities that are victims of one of these scams but have not purchased the available coverage from their crime insurers have gone to court seeking recovery. One of the most influential cases, involving a fraudulent transfer of more than $4.8 million, took four years of litigation before the court decided in favor of the insured.[119] That decision in 2018 immediately led insurers to revise and limit coverage with clarifying endorsements designed to ensure coverage was explicitly clear. Often the clarification was expressed as an absolute exclusion for social engineering crime losses with a carve-back to the exclusion that provided a small aggregate limit.

Since that time, a number of cyber insurers have extended their policies to introduce some coverage for a variety of theft crimes based on social engineering techniques. Where the coverage is available, it can have great value in supplementing the limited coverage in the commercial crime insurance market, but the coverage available from cyber policies tends to be even more limited than in the commercial crime market and subject to low sublimits. It is again important for the insured to work with advisers who understand the coverage and the interplay between crime and cyber policies in order to maximize available coverage, particularly as the coverage granted in cyber policies may use different language, terminology, and definitions than that in the commercial crime policy.

4.5. Kidnap, Ransom & Extortion

Kidnap and ransom is the original form of corporate extortion, and a sophisticated insurance market developed around it—initially at Lloyd's of London, but now with many major insurers participating in the US domestic market. The kidnap and ransom coverage has evolved over the years, and it provides added value services including emergency extraction from high-risk areas (for instance, during a coup or civil unrest).

One of the coverage extensions kidnap and ransom insurers added early on was extortion coverage. This coverage emerged at the time when distributed denial of service ("DDoS") attacks were the major form of cyber extortion. DDoS attacks were usually a relatively minor inconvenience with low ransoms being paid. Interruptions caused by DDoS attacks were also usually very short, and the kidnap and ransom insurers further expanded coverage to include loss of revenue from cyber extortion attacks.

The cyber extortion coverage in kidnap, ransom, and extortion ("KR&E") policies was typically to full limit and was not priced into the coverage because it was rarely used—until 2017 and NotPetya.[120] NotPetya may not have been intended by its perpetrators to have

119. Judy Greenwald, *Chubb Unit on the Hook for Email Spoofing Loss*, BUS. INS. (July 25, 2017), https://www.businessinsurance.com/chubb-insurance-unit-on-the-hook-for-email-spoofing-loss/; Jeff Sistrunk, *Chubb Must Cover $4.8M Email Scam Loss, 2nd Circ. Affirms*, LAW360 (July 6, 2018, 1:54 PM), https://www.law360.com/articles/1060671/chubb-must-cover-4-8m-email-scam-loss-2nd-circ-affirms.

120. Andy Greenberg, *The Untold Story of NotPetya, the Most Devastating Cyberattack in History*, WIRED (Aug. 22, 2018, 5:00 AM), https://www.wired.com/story/notpetya-cyberattack-ukraine-russia-code-crashed-the-world/.

the dramatic global consequences it launched, but many large international firms, including one global law firm, were brought to their knees by the attack. NotPetya used very sophisticated malware (in part derived from tools developed by the NSA) that portrayed itself as ransomware, and the epicenter of the attack was in Europe.

At that time, June 2017, uptake of cyber insurance in Europe was very low. The Association of British Insurers estimated that in 2018, just 11% of UK corporations were purchasing cyber insurance,[121] and uptake in Europe was substantially lower. Many large corporations that were catastrophically impacted by NotPetya did not have cyber insurance, but they did have KR&E policies. Because the malware displayed a ransomware note, the firms without cyber coverage filed claims under their KR&E policies.

Not all of the KR&E claims arising from NotPetya were paid. There was some dispute as to whether or not NotPetya was truly ransomware or just "wiperware," which is malware designed to encrypt all data on an infected system with no functionality or capability designed to decrypt it. Nonetheless, the impact on the KR&E insurance market was catastrophic, and the response was immediate. Insurers cut available limits for cyber extortion to $1 million or eliminated it altogether. KR&E policies typically renew for a 3-year period so the coverage lingered for a substantial period after the NotPetya event. At this point, however, few, if any, KR&E insurers offer any coverage for cyber extortion.

4.6. Employment Practices Liability Insurance (EPLI)

Employee data is one of the substantial data privacy exposures at all law firms. Law firms tend to keep all information forever, which compounds the privacy issue. Many firms may think the privacy of employee data is not a substantial concern because they have few employees, but the accumulation of information pertaining to everyone involved with the firm in an employment capacity over the years can be enormous:

- Partners and their family members (benefits plans)
- Associates and employees and their family members (benefits plans)
- Contract attorneys
- Summer associates
- Temporary attorneys and staff and interns
- Job applicants

Employee information on its own is a substantial exposure to law firms from a regulatory perspective, including costs of compliance following a breach. The exposure is amplified in jurisdictions where privacy statutes grant automatic standing to plaintiffs whose data has been stolen. Data loss is not, however, the basis for a claim under an employment practices policy.

---

121. *Cyber Insurance Payout Rates at 99%, but Uptake Still Far Too Low*, ABI (Aug. 8, 2019), https://www.abi.org.uk/news/news-articles/2019/08/cyber-insurance-payout-rates-at-99-but-uptake-still-far-too-low/.

Employment practices liability policies are intended to cover the firm for lawsuits arising from the firm's wrongful behaviors towards specific individuals or groups, particularly to defend the firm against allegations of discrimination (on whatever basis, including age, race, gender, orientation, religion, *etc.*), harassment, and so on.

This is another example of the intersection of cyber policies and other policies addressing liability to third parties who may have been harmed by actions of the firm that may involve data misuse or compromise. Cyber policies are usually written to be clear about the boundaries of the response to complaints from employees, with clear exclusions relating to employment-related complaints, particularly discrimination. Typical cyber policy wording excludes claims: "...alleging, arising out of, based upon or attributable to an Insured's employment of any individual or any employment practice of an Insured (including, without limitation, wrongful dismissal, discharge or termination, discrimination, harassment, retaliation or other employment-related claim)."[122] There will often be a limited carve-back for emotional distress caused by the release of sensitive personal information as the result of a cyberattack, but such harm would have to be established on an individual, personal basis as the result of the specific cyber event. This type of carve-back does not lend itself to the type of workplace practices wrongs that are the subject matter of an employment practices policy.

Biometrics[123] are increasingly used in the workplace, and employee biometric claims have occurred. Many manufacturers, for example, require employees to use their fingerprints to clock in. Similarly, warehouses often require truck drivers to scan their fingerprints when picking up or delivering loads. In one case, a former employee brought an action alleging that his employer violated the Illinois Biometric Information Privacy Act (BIPA) by requiring employees to use a biometric scanner without obtaining the employee's written consent.[124] The employer asserted that it had deleted the data after it stopped using the technology in Illinois.

In a case involving the Salvation Army, a former employee alleged that the organization violated BIPA by requiring employees to log their fingerprints or other biometric information when clocking in and out.[125] The former employee further alleged that the organization neither obtained written consent nor disclosed whether and how the information would be stored or used. The Salvation Army agreed to pay approximately $898,000 to settle the class action.[126]

---

122. AIG Specialty Risk Protector form 143601 (07/23) (on file with authors).

123. *See, supra,* text at notes 71 & 76–84.

124. In a complaint filed March 28, 2025, Best Solution Express Inc. said that although it should have received coverage for the underlying litigation from its comprehensive general liability insurer, Kinsale Insurance Co., and its cyber insurer, Coalition Insurance Solutions Inc., it has not, in breach of both insurer's contracts. Best Solution Express Inc. v. Coalition Insurance Solutions, Inc., No. 1:25-cv-03367 (N.D. Ill. 2025).

125. Bryant v. Salvation Army, No. 2019-CH-11314 (Ill. Cir. Ct. Cook Cty, 2019).

126. *Id.*

These kinds of workplace procedures are unlikely to trigger employment practices claims as they appear to be founded in technical breaches of BIPA's compliance requirements. There seems to be no allegation of discrimination or harassment on an individual basis or as part of workplace culture. However, biometrics can be used in a discriminatory manner against individuals who might have religious or cultural issues with the process. Employees could also allege that collecting biometric information invades their privacy. The multiplicity of issues biometrics could trigger leads to a gray area where the specifics of allegations are important in determining which insurance policy will respond and whether an employee action will be an EPLI claim, a cyber claim, or possibly neither.

The regulatory aspects of the biometric information cases could also be relevant for associated claims under a cyber policy. Some cyber policies now have specific exclusions relating to the use of biometric information and, absent a cyber event trigger, *e.g.*, theft or compromise of the information by a hacker, the cyber policy would not respond to cases like the truck driver or Salvation Army examples above. Other cyber policies provide broad coverage for wrongful acts that may trigger an investigation by regulatory authorities, including legal defense, fines and penalties, and settlements. That coverage might help insureds.

Insureds might think of two other policies when facing allegations of personal injury resulting from a wrongful act by the firm—commercial general liability and workers' compensation policies. Those policies are not likely to cover employee data cases, however. General liability policies, like cyber policies, typically exclude claims by employees; bodily injury claims by employees are typically the province of workers' compensation policies. At the same time, as with cyber insurance, workers' compensation policies do not cover employment practices claims.

Employment practices liability insurance is an important coverage for law firms to have in their risk management portfolio. It offers coverage for a broad range of employment torts, and it may have some application in gray areas where new regulations are introducing new wrongful acts concerning employee privacy. Given the evolution of privacy legislation and litigation, it is important to ensure that when available insurance policies are purchased, the coverage is structured in such a way to ensure as far as possible that gaps are minimized, coverage maximized, and any potential conflicts and overlaps between policies avoided.

4.7. Alternative Risk Transfer[127] / Captives

Demand for captive insurance is rising as commercial premiums soar.[128] A "captive insurer" is generally defined as an insurance company that is wholly owned and controlled by its

127. Steve Evans, *Beazley Adds $290M Cyber ILW to Its $510M Cyber Cat Bonds, in $1bn Cyber Cat Coverage*, ARTEMIS (Oct. 2, 2024), https://www.artemis.bm/news/beazley-adds-290m-cyber-ilw-to-its-510m-cyber-cat-bonds-in-1bn-cyber-cat-coverage/.

128. Alice Uribe, *Captive Insurance Seen as Covid-Era Remedy to Rising Premiums*, WALL ST. J. (Sept. 27, 2020, 8:00 AM ET), https://www.wsj.com/articles/captive-insurance-seen-as-covid-era-remedy-to-rising-premiums-11601208001.

insureds; its primary purpose is to insure the risks of its owners, and its insureds benefit from the captive insurer's underwriting profits.[129] Captive insurance is utilized by insureds that choose to: (a) put their own capital at risk by creating their own insurance company; (b) work outside of the commercial insurance marketplace; and (c) set and achieve their own risk financing objectives. Insureds can either reinsure their captive or retain the risk (self-insure), which provides flexibility in coverage and premium options. Captives allow insureds to access international insurance and reinsurance markets in a more efficient way than through traditional insurance market structures, allowing them to structure complex risk financing mechanisms.

Captive insurance has traditionally been the province of very large organizations ($1 billion+ revenue) that have the exposures and available financial resources to capitalize their own insurance company. Other captive structures have been created that allow smaller firms to access the alternative risk finance market such as "cell captives," "risk retention groups," and "group captives."

Structures like these have been used in the legal industry for conventional programs, such as professional liability insurance and worker's compensation liability. Interest in captives for cyber insurance was being driven by both the rapidly hardening market (which softened considerably in 2023 and 2024) and reductions in available capacity from the conventional market (which expanded in 2023 and 2024 with new cyber insurance carrier entrants). These market dynamics often drive interest in alternative risk finance structures.

One of the limiting factors for captives and cyber insurance is rapid changes in the threat environment, making it difficult to model the risks so that the captive is appropriately capitalized and the premiums and reinsurance[130] required for sustainability are adequate. Captives rely on substantial actuarial support to create the models and underwriting parameters, and the models and underwriting rely on historical trends and loss information. One of the distinctive features of cyber risk is that the exposures change over time and can fluctuate dramatically.

Group captives and cell captives are predicated on spread of risk and on events being limited in scope and scale in such a way that any one event is unlikely to victimize the entire group. As has been seen in recent years, however, cyber is extremely exposed to aggregation

129. *Captive Insurance*, Aon, https://www.aon.com/en/capabilities/risk-retention/captive-insurance (last visited Sept. 23, 2025).

130. Jack Willard, Re/insurance market must prepare for Single Point of Failure tech outage events: CyberCube, Reinsurance News (Nov. 29, 2024), https://www.reinsurancene.ws/re-insurance-market-must-prepare-for-single-point-of-failure-tech-outage-events-cybercube/.

risks. The Crowdstrike, MoveIt, NotPetya,[131] SolarWinds,[132] Accellion,[133] and Microsoft "Hafnium"[134] events illustrate how the software supply chain creates situations where a single vulnerability can cause material losses for multiple insureds. Group captives struggle to cope with material aggregation risks, and captives generally are not well suited to writing risks with catastrophe potential because of the profile of the claims is both unpredictable and extreme. Natural catastrophe, for example, is rarely written in captives.

5. Coverage Scenarios

Following are examples of cyberattack scenarios including an illustration of how the various types of commercial insurance policies typically purchased by a law firm might respond to such an event:

Scenario 1—Internet of Things Attack on Building Services
Event:

- Building control systems are infiltrated through a security vulnerability in a third party's systems.
- Hackers shut down all building systems, including lights, elevators, locks, and HVAC, and demand a ransom to restore access.
- Lack of HVAC causes firm's servers to overheat, resulting in smoke damage to all the equipment, destroying the servers, and necessitating total replacement.
- An employee and an outside consultant on site suffer smoke inhalation and other injuries.
- Switchover to backup systems takes longer than anticipated, and the firm suffers an interruption to email, telephone, and document management systems.

131. The U.S. Cybersecurity & Infrastructure Security Agency (CISA) reported that NotPetya was estimated to have caused over $10bn of losses worldwide. CISA, Cost of a Cyber Incident: Systematic Review and Cross-Validation 38 n. 12 (Oct. 26, 2020), https://www.cisa.gov/sites/default/files/publications/CISA-OCE_Cost_of_Cyber_Incidents_Study-FINAL_508.pdf.

132. Isabella Jibilan & Kaie Canales, *The US Is Readying Sanctions against Russia over the SolarWinds Cyber Attack. Here's a Simple Explanation of How the Massive Hack Happened and Why It's Such a Big Deal*, Bus. Insider (Apr. 15, 2021, 1:25 PM), https://www.businessinsider.com/solarwinds-hack-explained-government-agencies-cyber-security-2020-12.

133. Lily Hay Newman, *The Accellion Breach Keeps Getting Worse—And More Expensive*, Wired (Mar. 8, 2021, 7:00 AM), https://www.wired.com/story/accellion-breach-victims-extortion/.

134. Microsoft 365 Security, Microsoft Threat Intelligence, *HAFNIUM Targeting Exchange Servers with 0-Day Exploits*, Microsoft, https://www.microsoft.com/security/blog/2021/03/02/hafnium-targeting-exchange-servers/ (last updated Mar. 16, 2021).

Impact:

- Firm incurs extra expense and lost revenue as a result of its inability to access the building and loss of servers.
- Firm engages experts to negotiate with the hackers and pays the ransom demanded to facilitate access to the building.
- Contractor sues the firm for bodily injury.
- Employee requires medical treatment for injuries. (Employee bodily injury is most likely covered by workers' compensation, which is not included in the following table).

Financial Damages From A Network Security or Privacy Event	Property	GL	K&R	Crime	PI	Cyber
First Party Losses						
Response Costs: forensics / security consulting	Not covered or excluded	Not covered or excluded	Not covered or excluded	Not covered or excluded	Not covered or excluded	Covered to full limit of policy
Legal Expense: advice and defense	Not covered or excluded	Not covered or excluded	Not covered or excluded	Not covered or excluded	Not covered or excluded	Covered to full limit of policy
Revenue Loss / extra expense from system outages	Not covered or excluded	Not covered or excluded	Not covered or excluded	Not covered or excluded	Not covered or excluded	Covered to full limit of policy
Revenue Loss / extra expense from building outages	Not covered or excluded	Not covered or excluded	Not covered or excluded	Not covered or excluded	Not covered or excluded	Covered subject to sublimit or cover condintional on situation
Data Restoration / system remediation costs	Covered subject to sublimit or cover condintional on situation	Not covered or excluded	Not covered or excluded	Not covered or excluded	Not covered or excluded	Covered to full limit of policy
System and security upgrades	Not covered or excluded	Not covered or excluded	Not covered or excluded	Not covered or excluded	Not covered or excluded	Covered subject to sublimit or cover condintional on situation
Cyber extortion consulting expenses / ransom payment	Not covered or excluded	Not covered or excluded	Covered to full limit of policy	Not covered or excluded	Not covered or excluded	Covered to full limit of policy
Crisis communications expenses	Not covered or excluded	Not covered or excluded	Not covered or excluded	Not covered or excluded	Not covered or excluded	Covered to full limit of policy
Replacement of Servers / repair physical damage	Covered to full limit of policy	Not covered or excluded	Not covered or excluded	Not covered or excluded	Not covered or excluded	Covered subject to sublimit or cover condintional on situation
Revenue loss / extra expense from physical damage	Covered to full limit of policy	Not covered or excluded	Not covered or excluded	Not covered or excluded	Not covered or excluded	Not covered or excluded
Third Party Losses						
Damages, settlements &/or judgements	Not covered or excluded	Not covered or excluded	Not covered or excluded	Not covered or excluded	Covered subject to sublimit or cover condintional on situation	Covered to full limit of policy
Legal expenses	Not covered or excluded	Covered subject to sublimit or cover condintional on situation	Not covered or excluded	Not covered or excluded	Covered subject to sublimit or cover condintional on situation	Covered to full limit of policy
Regulatory fines & penalties	Not covered or excluded	Not covered or excluded	Not covered or excluded	Not covered or excluded	Covered subject to sublimit or cover condintional on situation	Covered subject to sublimit or cover condintional on situation
Bodily injury to employee	Not covered or excluded	Not covered or excluded	Not covered or excluded	Not covered or excluded	Not covered or excluded	Not covered or excluded
Bodily injury to third party contractor	Not covered or excluded	Covered to full limit of policy	Not covered or excluded	Not covered or excluded	Not covered or excluded	Not covered or excluded

■ Covered to full limit of policy
■ Covered subject to sublimit or cover condintional on situation
■ Not covered or excluded

Scenario 2—Exfiltration of Client Data

Event:

- Phishing attack results in malicious external hackers gaining access to firm's internal IT systems.
- Hackers steal confidential client data relating to M&A transactions.
- Information subsequently leaked by the hackers leads to the failure of several transactions and the forfeiture of agreed "break-up fees" by firm's clients.

Impact:

- Firm engages crisis communications consultant to advise on and manage reputational issues.
- Firm engages security consultants to investigate and remediate. Significant upgrades to data security systems are recommended and implemented.
- Remediation involves shutting affected systems down for several days, resulting in loss of revenue and extra expense.

Financial Damages From A Network Security or Privacy Event	Property	GL	K&R	Crime	PI	Cyber
First Party Losses						
Response Costs: forensics / security consulting	Not covered	Not covered	Not covered	Not covered	Covered to full limit	Covered to full limit
Legal Expense: advice and defense	Not covered	Not covered	Not covered	Not covered	Covered to full limit	Covered to full limit
Revenue Loss / extra expense from system outages	Not covered	Not covered	Not covered	Not covered	Not covered	Covered to full limit
Data Restoration / system remediation costs	Not covered	Not covered	Not covered	Not covered	Not covered	Covered to full limit
System and security upgrades	Not covered	Not covered	Not covered	Not covered	Not covered	Covered subject to sublimit
Cyber extortion consulting expenses / ransom payment	Not covered	Not covered	Covered to full limit	Not covered	Not covered	Covered to full limit
Crisis communications expenses	Not covered	Not covered	Not covered	Not covered	Not covered	Covered to full limit
Third Party Losses						
Damages, settlements &/or judgements	Not covered	Not covered	Not covered	Not covered	Covered to full limit	Covered to full limit
Legal expenses	Not covered	Not covered	Not covered	Not covered	Covered to full limit	Covered to full limit
Regulatory fines & penalties	Not covered	Not covered	Not covered	Not covered	Covered subject to sublimit	Covered subject to sublimit

- Covered to full limit of policy
- Covered subject to sublimit or cover condintional on situation
- Not covered or excluded

Scenario 3—"NotPetya" Wiperware Attack
Event:

- Ransomware/malware attack infiltrates firm's system and shuts down all access for over 2 weeks, impacting:
  - Email communication
  - Telecommunications
  - Document management system
  - Financial management and billing system
  - Electronic docket scheduling system
  - Conflict management

Impact:

- No evidence of any data exfiltration.
- Substantial costs incurred remediating systems and restoring data from backup.
- Substantial loss of revenue and extra expense incurred.
- Potential liabilities to clients as firm missed critical filing dates for client matters.
- Firm engages forensic and security consultants to investigate.
- Firm engages a crisis communications consultant to advise on client communications and to control damage to firm's reputation.

Financial Damages From A Network Security or Privacy Event	Property	GL	K&R	Crime	PI	Cyber
First Party Losses						
Response Costs: forensics / security consulting	Not covered or excluded	Not covered or excluded	Not covered or excluded	Not covered or excluded	Covered subject to sublimit or cover condintional on situation	Covered to full limit of policy
Legal Expense: advice and defense	Not covered or excluded	Not covered or excluded	Not covered or excluded	Not covered or excluded	Covered subject to sublimit or cover condintional on situation	Covered to full limit of policy
Revenue Loss / extra expense from system outages	Not covered or excluded	Not covered or excluded	Not covered or excluded	Not covered or excluded	Not covered or excluded	Covered to full limit of policy
Data Restoration / system remediation costs	Covered subject to sublimit or cover condintional on situation	Not covered or excluded	Not covered or excluded	Not covered or excluded	Not covered or excluded	Covered to full limit of policy
System and security upgrades	Not covered or excluded	Not covered or excluded	Not covered or excluded	Not covered or excluded	Not covered or excluded	Covered subject to sublimit or cover condintional on situation
Cyber extortion consulting expenses / ransom payment	Not covered or excluded	Not covered or excluded	Covered subject to sublimit or cover condintional on situation	Not covered or excluded	Not covered or excluded	Covered to full limit of policy
Crisis communications expenses	Not covered or excluded	Not covered or excluded	Not covered or excluded	Not covered or excluded	Not covered or excluded	Covered to full limit of policy
Third Party Losses						
Damages, settlements &/or judgements	Not covered or excluded	Not covered or excluded	Not covered or excluded	Not covered or excluded	Covered subject to sublimit or cover condintional on situation	Covered to full limit of policy
Legal expenses	Not covered or excluded	Not covered or excluded	Not covered or excluded	Not covered or excluded	Covered subject to sublimit or cover condintional on situation	Covered to full limit of policy
Regulatory fines & penalties	Not covered or excluded	Not covered or excluded	Not covered or excluded	Not covered or excluded	Covered subject to sublimit or cover condintional on situation	Covered subject to sublimit or cover condintional on situation

- Covered to full limit of policy
- Covered subject to sublimit or cover condintional on situation
- Not covered or excluded

6. Various Legal Structure Scenarios (Small, Large, Government, In-house, Public Interest)

Hackers see opportunity where they can take advantage of large quantities of valuable and quality data. By targeting law firms, hackers can quickly access information like technical secrets, business strategies, and financial data for numerous clients. Law firms provide a shortcut to some of the highest value information of their clients.[135]

Regulated data such as PII is a major issue that particularly impacts small firms whose clients are often individuals, trusts, and estates, and small closely-held businesses. Medium

135. Aniket Bhardwaj, *Law Firms as Prime Targets for Hackers: 7 Steps to Reducing Cyber Risks*, Lexology Index (Dec. 18, 2020), https://www.lexology.com/library/detail.aspx?g=127e819a-d34e-4b32-85cd-219d7c8d71cb.

and large firms may also store large amounts of PII based on their practices, *e.g.*, mass tort litigation, employment, immigration, healthcare, *etc.* Regulation adds a multiplier effect—first, it was the cost of notifications, then regulatory fines and penalties added to that, and now class action lawsuits further increase the burden. According to the Baker Hostetler 2024 Data Security Incident Response Report,[136] while class certification is still uncertain, the number of class actions being filed following data breaches is increasing. Two recent settlements by law firms in class actions, both in excess of $8 million, illustrate the potential severity of this exposure.[137]

Ransomware is a concern for all legal organizations, especially with the data exfiltration/extortion threat.[138] A 2020 ransomware attack on a boutique entertainment law firm representing a number of A-list music and film stars became public news because the firm refused to "pay cyber-terrorists."[139] The $42 million ransom demand made against the entertainment firm was unusually high at the time (and extraordinarily high for the hacker, which had rarely demanded more than $2 million). The event appears not to have been a major coup for the hackers, a group called REvil, as it appears they were unable to monetize the information stolen. Nevertheless, it was notable for the attention it drew to the legal community, particularly the fact that firms of all sizes can be repositories of sensitive and potentially very valuable information.

The events surrounding Accellion's file transfer appliance (FTA) in Q1-2021 illustrate clearly bad actors' focus on law firms. Several AmLaw 100 firms were identified in the press as victims of this attack, and there were undoubtedly other less noteworthy firms affected.[140] In this case, the hackers identified and exploited a vulnerability in a vendor platform; they didn't need ransomware. Accellion FTA was a legacy platform (now retired)

---

136. 2024 Data Security Incident Response Report: Persistent Threats, New Challenges 18, 23, BakerHostetler (Apr. 23, 2024), https://www.bakerlaw.com/insights/bakerhostetler-launches-2024-data-security-incident-response-report-persistent-threats-new-challenges/.

137. David Thomas, *Law Firm Orrick Agrees to $8 mln Settlement over Breach of Client Data*, Reuters (Apr. 11, 2024 7:24 PM), https://www.reuters.com/legal/litigation/law-firm-orrick-agrees-8-mln-settlement-over-breach-client-data-2024-04-11/; Sara Merken, *Another US Law Firm Reaches Data Breach Settlement as Cyber Risks Mount*, Reuters (Nov. 8, 2024, 1:45 PM), https://www.reuters.com/legal/litigation/another-us-law-firm-reaches-data-breach-settlement-cyber-risks-mount-2024-11-08/.

138. *Ransomware: REvil & the Increased Targeting of Law Firms*, Aon (Sept. 2020), https://www.aon.com/risk-services/professional-services/ransomware-revil-increased-targeting-law-firms.jsp.

139. *See* Joe Tidy, *Hackers Hit A-list Law Firm of Lady Gaga, Drake and Madonna*, BBC (May 12, 2020), https://www.bbc.com/news/technology-52632729; Todd Spangler, *Hackers Reportedly Demand $21 Million from Entertainment Law Firm in Data Extortion Scheme*, Variety (May 13, 2020 4:40 PM), https://variety.com/2020/digital/news/hackers-21-million-ransom-grubman-shire-meiselas-sacks-entertainment-law-firm-1234606193/; Todd Spangler, *Law Firm Hackers Claim to Have Dirt on Donald Trump, Up Data Ransom to $42M*, Variety (May 15, 2020 10:02 AM), https://variety.com/2020/digital/news/donald-trump-hacked-law-firm-ransom-42-million-1234607832/ ; Sarah Coble, *Thieves Fail to Auction Bruce Springsteen's Legal Documents*, Infosecurity Mag. (Sept. 23, 2020), https://www.infosecurity-magazine.com/news/bruce-springsteen-revil-auction/.

140. *See* Jack Newsham & Samantha Stokes, *A Data Breach Is Exposing Big Law Firms Who Were Using a 20-year-Old System for Handling Sensitive Documents. Here's What We Know so Far*, Bus. Insider (Feb 17, 2021, 6:21 PM), https://www.businessinsider.com/jones-day-hack-data-breach-law-firms-cybersecurity-accellion-customers-2021-2.

for sharing very large files, and it was used by many firms for transferring large documents between themselves and clients. The platform was partially cloud-hosted, and it was in the cloud storage that the hackers were able to exfiltrate data. The presence of data on a "secure file transfer platform" flagged it as being potentially very sensitive and confidential information. One of the few silver linings to the Accellion attack is that the hackers did not at any time have access directly to the firms' systems. The theft was limited to data in the vendor's platform.

The trend of vendor outsourcing and use of cloud services will affect all firms eventually. These third-party systems include legal services platforms, software as a service, ediscovery, document management outsourcing, and legaltech services. We already have examples of firms injured by vendor incidents. A 2020 Google outage impacted numerous firms, particularly smaller firms that depend on Google productivity applications,[141] and a ransomware event at legaltech vendor Epiq impacted numerous law firms when Epiq's legal services and ediscovery platforms were down for two to three weeks.[142]

Even seemingly innocuous "business process outsourcing" functions, such as HR and health and benefits consulting, can impact law firms. Those service providers are repositories of extensive PII, which under state privacy law remains the responsibility of the firm and makes the firm responsible for required notifications and services to affected individuals. (The task of sending notices and associated cost might be transferred by contract to the vendor.) Also, there appears to be a growing trend of law firms creating technology platforms and services that are sold for use outside the client relationship, often through non-attorney managed technology subsidiaries. All of these complex arrangements for allocating liability need to be addressed from a cyber insurance standpoint.

6.1. Large Law Firms

Most large law firms have placed a greater emphasis on cyber resiliency following the WannaCry[143] and NotPetya[144] incidents of 2017 and subsequent major events that have specifically targeted large law firms. Cyber policies for large law firms are highly customized to

141. *See* Alex Hern, *Google Suffers Global Outage with Gmail, YouTube and Majority of Services Affected*, GUARDIAN (Dec. 14, 2020, 1:17 PM), https://www.theguardian.com/technology/2020/dec/14/google-suffers-worldwide-outage-with-gmail-youtube-and-other-services-down; Victoria Blute, *What Google Wants from Law Firm Websites in 2020*, LAWLYTICS (Mar. 6, 2020), https://www.lawlytics.com/blog/what-google-wants-law-firm-websites-in-2020/.

142. Zack Whittaker, *Legal Services Giant Epiq Global Offline after Ransomware Attack*, TECHCRUNCH (Mar. 2, 2020 5:53 PM), https://techcrunch.com/2020/03/02/epiq-global-ransomware/; Tari Schreider, *Ransomware Attacks in the Legal Profession*, LAW.COM (May 26, 2020, 1:39 PM), https://www.law.com/corpcounsel/2020/05/26/ransomware-attacks-in-the-legal-profession/.

143. *See The Impact of Ransomware on Law Firms*, LAWYERS DEFENCE GRP. (Nov. 28, 2017), https://www.lawyersdefencegroup.org.uk/ransomware/.

144. *See* Beatrice Bergman Design, *NotPetya: How You Can Prevent the Next Attack on Your Law Firm*, SAVVY TRAINING (Jun. 5, 2018 3:00 AM), https://savvytraining.com/2018-06-05-notpetya-how-you-can-prevent-the-next-attack-on-your-law-firm/; Jonathan Crowe, *How One of the World's Largest Law Firms Was Paralyzed by NotPetya*, BARKLY PROTECTS (July 2017), https://harryphillipsaic.com/wp content/uploads/2018/10/How-One-of-the-World%E2%80%99s-Largest-Law-Firms-Was-Paralyzed-by-Petya-01810088.pdf.

fit their specific circumstances, which has become a bit easier in 2025 as the cyber market has softened.

Large law firms have always been a target of hackers with publicly disclosed attacks dating back to 2016 when several large law firms were revealed to have been among up to 15 firms victimized by hackers looking for information that could be used in financial trading (particularly M&A information). The subsequent investigation of that incident led to the conviction of three Hong Kong citizens for trading on stolen information, having profited to the tune of over $3 million. The defendants were not extradited to the U.S., however. They were fined $8.8 million in absentia.[145]

Large law firms have the largest, most sophisticated, and most sensitive clients and, consequently, have to be very concerned about their connections to those clients. Those that provide services to government entities and government contractors (especially defense contractors) are a target. Even those firms that were not exposed to the compromised version of the SolarWinds Orion product may have been targeted, potentially through other known compromises such as the Microsoft Hafnium hack or through attacks that have yet to be discovered, and anything they shared with clients may have been exfiltrated at the client end. Corporate clients of "big law" giants and firms of any size are increasingly subject to onerous legislation and regulation (such as SEC cyber reporting rules and New York Department of Financial Services regulations),[146] and clients and regulators, both, are likely to demand answers about how such attacks unfolded and what steps firms took to prevent them, including whether firms vetted the security of third-party products used to transfer sensitive data

145. *See Chinese Hackers Must Pay $9m Over Insider Trading Scam*, BBC (May 11, 2017), https://www.bbc.com/news/technology-39883224.

146. For instance, in January 2023, the U.S. Securities and Exchange Commission (SEC) filed an application seeking a federal court order compelling the law firm Covington & Burling LLP to identify clients whose non-public information was accessed by hackers. *Securities & Exchange Comm. v. Covington & Burling LLP*, No. 1:23-mc-00002 (D.D.C. Jan. 10, 2023); *see also* SEC Litigation Release No. 25612 (Jan. 12, 2023), https://www.sec.gov/enforcement-litigation/litigation-releases/lr-25612. According to the SEC's application, the SEC initiated an investigation of potential federal securities law violations arising from the Microsoft Hafnium attack in March 2021. SEC's Application for an Order to Show Cause and for an Order Requiring Compliance with Subpoena ¶¶ 1–2, SEC v. Covington & Burling, Case No. 1:23-mc-00002 (hereafter, the "SEC Application"). A year into its investigation, the SEC learned Covington's systems had been compromised in the attack, and attackers accessed the files of 300 clients. *Id.* ¶ 3. The SEC sought information from Covington about the impacted clients and the extent of the impact. *Id.* ¶ 5. Covington opposed the Application. Amicus briefs were filed in support of Covington by a group of 83 law firms, the U.S. Chamber of Commerce, and the Reporters Committee for Freedom of the Press. The District Court found the SEC request for client information overly broad, but ordered Covington to disclose the names of seven clients for which Covington could not rule out that the attacker had accessed material nonpublic information. Memorandum Op. (Jul. 24, 2023).

After the District Court's ruling, Covington agreed to turn over the names of six of the seven clients. Debra Cassens Weiss, *Covington Settles SEC Suit Demanding Names of Clients Affected by Data Breach*, ABA J. (Sept. 19, 2023, 10:01 AM), https://www.abajournal.com/news/article/covington-settles-sec-suit-demanding-client-names-affected-by-data-breach. The seventh client objected and appealed the Order. That appeal was dismissed upon stipulation in March 2024. *See* Mike Scarcella, *Unnamed Covington Client Ends Fight to Keep Name Secret from SEC*, Reuters (Mar. 11, 2024 3:43 PM), https://www.reuters.com/legal/government/unnamed-covington-client-ends-fight-keep-name-secret-sec-2024-03-11/. The *Covington* case highlights the tension between regulatory oversight and the protection of privileged communications in the context of cybersecurity incidents.

and whether firms have cyber insurance to cover the cost of investigations, remediation of systems, and payment of extortion demands. In addition to this, the firms have to be concerned about the potential for professional claims from clients whose most confidential and sensitive information may have been compromised within the firm's technology environment.

6.2. Small Law Firms / Sole Practitioners

Small firms often do not have a dedicated IT security staff. Nevertheless, ransomware attacks are targeting these small practices as much, if not more than, larger firms. One of the substantial benefits of cyber insurance is the availability from most cyber insurers of free or subsidized cybersecurity services that support the small firm's ability to strengthen its cyber environment. Imagine a hacker scanning your law firm's digital presence searching for vulnerabilities. Where are you open to attack? Does your cybersecurity have flaws? Have your login credentials been compromised? Is your firm's data for sale on the dark web?

Additional services offered by some insurers may provide as much, or more, value than the insurance defense and indemnity. For example, a cyber security assessment may include:[147]

- Scanning infrastructure of publicly accessible servers, services, and technology;
- Discovery of exploitable vulnerabilities and misconfigurations in the scanned infrastructure;
- Finding exposed / available user/employee information;
- Uncovering existing threats hidden on the dark web; and
- Offering recommendations for taking immediate action to reduce cyber-risks.

Insurers are paying much more attention to technology implementations as part of the renewal process. This attention is largely the result of their own analysis of claims they have worked on, and insurers now have a good understanding of the techniques, strategies, technologies, and implementations that are most effective in hardening systems, particularly against ransomware attacks. In addition to the services available from preferred vendors, often at a discounted or sometimes complimentary price point, the expertise offered by the insurance companies themselves is adding value in making the firm more secure, which is also a benefit to the firm's clients.

There is also some evidence that cybersecurity has become a differentiator for small firms; some clients are concerned that large firms are more of a target and that a small firm with excellent cyber security offers an attractive value proposition. In an environment where there is a great deal of variability in security maturity and posture, a firm that is investing in best practices and best-in-class technological protections will differentiate itself within its peer group for clients that value security of their data. Smaller firms are

147. *Cyber Liability Insurance*, Aon Attorneys Advantage, https://www.attorneys-advantage.com/Insurance/Cyber-Insurance (last visited Feb. 22, 2025).

best positioned to leverage the services and expertise provided alongside a cyber insurance policy, and the fact that the firm has invested in a cyber insurance policy can provide further assurance to clients that the firm takes the risk seriously and has resources available to assist and protect the firm and its clients in the event of a cyberattack.

Beyond that, many clients now require outside counsel to carry cyber insurance. In January 2017, the Association of Corporate Counsel published their "Model Information Protection and Security Controls for Outside Counsel"[148] guidelines. The ACC guidelines included recommendations that all outside counsel should have and maintain cyber insurance with a limit of at least $10 million. That level of insurance may be unrealistic for a small firm; for many clients, however, the limit of insurance is a differentiator, and the better the firm's cyber security controls and technology, the more insurance is available.

6.3. In-House Counsel

Data breaches, while frequent in number and severity, are still big news events today. Even more newsworthy is when a corporate executive is criminally prosecuted in connection with his role in responding to a data breach event.[149] With the proliferation of data privacy regulations, regulatory attention (particularly the Treasury Department's Office of Foreign Asset Control and the government's more aggressive stance on the False Claims Act), the potential for class action lawsuits (particularly under BIPA and other privacy legislation), and the constant threat of employee and client litigation following a breach, the Office of General Counsel is now very much at the center of every cyber event.

With respect to public companies, on July 26, 2023, the Securities and Exchange Commission adopted rules requiring registrants to disclose material cybersecurity incidents they experience and to disclose on an annual basis material information regarding their cybersecurity risk management, strategy, and governance. For public companies' general counsel, the SEC cyber disclosure mandates have heightened the pressure.[150]

The Office of General Counsel is, by its nature, "general," and few internal counsel have experience and expertise in cybersecurity and managing cyber events. Even fewer have technological expertise, and lawyers may be tempted to defer too much to the information technology or information security experts within the firm on matters of cybersecurity.

This is no longer a viable strategy as cyber risk becomes more and more central to the well-being and even survival of organizations. It is essential for internal counsel to be the

148. *Model Information Protection and Security Controls for Outside Counsel Possessing Company Confidential Information* 10–11, Assn. of Corp. Counsel (Mar. 10, 2017) [hereafter, "ACC Information Security Guidelines"], https://www.acc.com/resource-library/model-information-protection-and-security-controls-outside-counsel-possessing-0#.

149. Joseph G. Poluka & David J. Oberly, *What In-House Counsel Can Learn from Criminal Prosecution of Uber's Former Chief Security Officer*, BlankRome (Feb. 18, 2021), https://www.blankrome.com/publications/what-house-counsel-can-learn-criminal-prosecution-ubers-former-chief-security-officer.

150. *Navigating Cybersecurity Risk in the New SEC Regime*, Aon (Feb. 2024), https://www.aon.com/risk-services/financial-services-group/navigating-cybersecurity-risk-in-the-new-sec-regime.

"hub" of the cyber wheel and to ensure that the entity is prepared for a cyber event from the board level down. The IT function is an important part of the equation, but a cyber event will impact every aspect of the entity's work and, therefore, it is essential that cyber security strategy and preparedness be addressed at the highest level of the entity. The Office of General Counsel is the hub and coordinator in crisis situations, and in a cyberattack, it also plays a critical role in event response as the liaison with external Breach Counsel. (As discussed above, Breach Counsel is the specialist with experience and expertise in breach response who will act as guide and advisor through the process.)[151]

Internal counsel is often in a position to ensure that the entity is purchasing its own cyber insurance and to manage the interplay between the cyber policy and all other coverages purchased. Cyber insurance is one of the critical elements in a cybersecurity program, but it is not enough just for cyber insurance to be available, it has to be an integrated part of the entity's Incident Response Plan. Cyber insurance will typically only pay for pre-approved vendors, and communication with insurers and vendors should be, to the extent possible, protected by attorney-client privilege.I It is internal counsel's job to ensure that this is communicated to all parties involved and appropriately managed through the event response process.

The other side of the equation is for internal counsel to ensure that outside counsel manages the external risk inherent in the work that it does. In January 2017, guidelines, the Association of Corporate Counsel included recommendations that all outside counsel should have and maintain cyber insurance.[152] Similar considerations apply to all vendors used by the entity that are entrusted with the entity's sensitive data, and all vendor contracts (which includes outside counsel) should maximize protections and indemnities in favor of the entity.

While Directors' and Officers' (D&O) insurance is typically inapplicable to most law firms, in-house counsel may obtain coverage under D&O policies,[153] which is increasingly important given the exposure to data privacy events that can trigger:

- Notification costs
- Forensic investigation costs
- Loss of revenue
- Regulatory fines and penalties (which may be uninsurable)
- Class-action lawsuits as the result of the affected class having statutory standing under certain statutes (as is the case under BIPA)

---

151. *See supra*, text at notes 41–42.

152. ACC Information Security Guidelines, *supra* note 148, at 10–11.

153. *Responding to Cyber Attacks: How Directors and Officers and Cyber Policies Differ*, AON (July 24, 2024), https://www.aon.com/en/insights/articles/responding-to-cyber-attacks-how-directors-and-officers-and-cyber-policies-differ.

- Artificial intelligence obligations[154]
- Compliance penalties unconnected to a cyber event (*e.g.*, several large corporations have incurred multimillion dollar fines for failure to comply with process requirements under GDPR[155])

Public company D&O policies typically provide coverage for the entity for securities claims, which could include claims that, for example, the company failed to disclose in its SEC filings that it was subject to potential liability for biometric violations. Public company D&O policies also should apply to cover directors and officers facing lawsuits arising from company biometric and other privacy law compliance violations. Such a suit might allege that the value of company stock fell because of such violations and that the directors and officers failed to oversee corporate operations that caused violations resulting in legal costs, fines and penalties, and remediation and compliance costs.

Private company Management Liability policies also provide entity coverage that conceivably cover such stakeholder claims resulting from failure to comply with privacy legislation requirements. Thus, both public and private company insureds should investigate D&O coverage in addition to cyber insurance for claims arising from the broad requirements and application of privacy legislation.

6.4. Government Lawyers

"In December 2020, it was discovered that SolarWinds' Orion software was hacked and installed backdoors into its various federal government and Fortune 500 clients' IT systems." Corporate and government investigations took years to determine the full scope and origination of the cybersecurity attack.[156]

Government entities typically enjoy sovereign immunity and often do not purchase insurance, although this is changing in the realm of cyber insurance as ransomware threat actors are targeting the sector. Government attorneys are, therefore, increasingly dealing with complex contractual issues, negotiating insurance and indemnity requirements with vendors and contractors, while at the same time facing the same pressures as in-house counsel to understand the threat environment and the available insurance solutions. Government entities may have the ability to finance response to a cyberattack from the public purse, but taxpayers are increasingly questioning whether purchasing available insurance is a more efficient way of managing the risk.

---

154. *Navigating AI-related Risks: A Guide for Directors and Officers*, Aon (Oct. 3, 2024), https://www.aon.com/en/insights/articles/directors-and-officers-guide-to-navigating-ai-related-risks.; *The Growing Use of Artificial Intelligence: D&O Risks and Potential Coverage Solutions*, Aon (Apr. 2024), https://www.aon.com/risk-services/financial-services-group/the-growing-use-of-artificial-intelligence-d-and-o-risks-and-potential-coverage-solutions.

155. Gabe Gumbs, *The Biggest GDPR Penalties for Noncompliance*, Spirion (Dec. 1, 2022), https://www.spirion.com/blog/gdpr-fines-increase/.

156. Victoria Hudgins, *4 Ways the SolarWinds Hack Is Indirectly Impacting the Legal Industry*, Law.com, LegalTech News (Feb. 2, 2021, 10:00 AM), https://www.law.com/legaltechnews/2021/02/02/4-ways-the-solar-winds-hack-is-indirectly-impacting-the-legal-industry/.

Contracts offered by government bodies are typically extremely onerous in their requirements for the vendors and contractors that work for them. The divergence between what government contracts require and what insurers are actually prepared to provide to government contractors is widening. Many contractors will agree to government contract requirements because the contract terms are non-negotiable. At the same time, contractors may not know or fully appreciate the extent of their insurance coverages or provisions in their insurance policies, and some may accept government contracts knowing that their insurer will not agree to respond on the terms required by the government's contractual indemnities and insurance requirements. In other words, some contractors take the risk that cyberattacks will not impact their government work or that they can manage with whatever insurance coverage they may have.

With the cyber market continuing to evolve, government lawyers (as corporate internal counsel), should be familiarizing themselves with the cyber insurance market and the availability and terms of coverage for both their own entities and the vendors / contractors they work with. The SolarWinds hack illustrated very clearly that cyber risk is escalating as a geopolitical issue. Government attorneys need to understand the dynamics of the threat environment, the technological environment, and the interplay of response strategies and risk finance solutions that are available.

6.5. Public Interest Attorneys

In the past, many lawyers assumed no one could possibly be interested in the information they held; cyber threat was perceived to be very low and, as long as the firm had good professional liability insurance, that covered everything they needed to be concerned about. Events of the past few years have demonstrated that these assumptions were incorrect.

Lawyers' data in all sectors and in all sizes of firms have been targeted. There has also been a string of bar association hacks and attacks on vendors that work with law firms (from the ediscovery and legal services platform provider Epiq to a health & benefits broker with many law firm clients).[157] Public interest attorneys are vulnerable to attacks from hackers seeking personally identifiable information that can be monetized, ransomware operators seeking a payoff to decrypt data, and "hacktivists" seeking to influence or disrupt social justice causes or seeking information that may influence or disrupt causes.

Public interest attorneys are exposed to cyberattack just as lawyers in any other practice setting. Their organizations are subject to the same data privacy laws and regulatory requirements like paying for breach notifications for loss of PII and regulatory fines and penalties. Lawyers working at public interest organizations are also subject to the same professional responsibility requirements as lawyers in other practice settings. It can be difficult for public interest attorneys to justify the high expense for the technological protections

157. Xiumei Dong, *Lawyers' Data Targeted in String of Bar Association Hacks*, Law360 (Dec. 11, 2020, 8:01 PM) (reporting on a Washington State Bar Association portal used to license new lawyers), https://www.law360.com/insurance/articles/1335867/lawyers-data-targeted-in-string-of-bar-association-hacks.

and cyber insurance to keep the organization and its data secure. However, protecting the organization from cyber-related losses is also important to the mission the organization exits to advance.[158]

6.6. International Considerations

The NotPetya attack of June 2017 impacted a large number of international corporations as well as two global professional services firms, one of them a law firm. The global impact of NotPetya was almost certainly unintended although it is possible that the extent of the collateral damage resulting from the compromise of a tax preparation platform that was the nexus for the attack may have influenced the thinking behind the SolarWinds and Microsoft Exchange attacks three years later. International firms are particularly exposed to cyber risks by virtue of a number of factors:

- *Size, particularly the perimeter, of networks.* The technology and available solutions available to deliver functionality in multiple countries tend to introduce compromises that introduce vulnerabilities.
- *Number of users/endpoints.* Global firms have many more users, and the users are harder to train to the same level, particularly when standards, collateral, and training materials have to be translated into multiple languages. The majority of successful attacks against large law firms start with phishing; statistically the legal industry has a lower "click through" rate than most other sectors when it comes to phishing emails, but even at an exceptionally low rate of 5% that implies that as few as 20 emails are required to all but guarantee success for the hackers.[159]
- *Access.* In many countries the internet and internet access are controlled by the government, making most, if not all, communication insecure. There are technological solutions available to increase security, but the success of state actor hackers on a global basis indicates that if firm has a presence in a country that monitors communications and the government takes an interest in the firm, there may be little the firm can do to prevent an incursion. The possibility of accessing the firm's network-connected hardware in-country makes the hacker's job even easier.
- *Delivering network updates and patches.* The job of managing updates, upgrades, and patches on a global network is disproportionately harder because of the need to test against local technology solutions and implementations to ensure compatibility. The recent failure of a patch by a major cyber security vendor caused problems on a global scale for those firms that were exposed to it.[160]

---

158. See Handbook, Chapter 17, *Why Public Interest Attorneys Should Care about Cybersecurity*.

159. LawQuill, What Is A Click-Through Rate (CTR) And Why Does It Matter?, https://lawquill.com/what-is-a-click-through-rate-ctr-and-why-does-it-matter/ (last visited Jul. 2, 2025).

160. Sean Michael Kerner, *CrowdStrike Outage Explained: What Caused it and What's Next*, TechTarget (Oct. 29, 2024), https://www.techtarget.com/whatis/feature/Explaining-the-largest-IT-outage-in-history-and-whats-next.

- *International regulation.* The world has a huge variety of data privacy legislation with provisions ranging from extremely onerous with severe penalties (like the EU's GDPR) to countries with little or no regulation at all. For a firm with a presence in many countries, leveraging the global footprint to take advantage of the ability to serve global clients across multiple jurisdictions can be difficult, and it can be remarkably easy to run afoul of compliance rules or breach contractual requirements imposed by clients that may have different or very specific compliance rules a global organization must follow. The EU's GDPR regulation has strong restrictions on the transmission of personal data from within the EU zone to other countries. For some destination countries, the transfer of such data may be simple; for others, it may require a bureaucratic procedure or it may not be possible at all. The rules are easy to transgress, and the fines can be extremely onerous. There will be situations when a firm has to balance client needs and commercial pressures against the reality that providing the best service to the client may put the firm into non-compliance with data privacy protection laws.[161]

Cyber policies are typically global in scope, but it is important for firms to also consider jurisdictional issues. For instance, the policy may provide coverage for fines and penalties, but that term will always carry the proviso that such coverage can only be provided where not prohibited by law. In the European Union alone, the laws about insuring for fines and penalties varies; in some countries insurance is explicitly allowed, others allow or not according to situation, and some prohibit such coverage absolutely. The same situation applies across the United States, with some states not only prohibiting the insurance of fines and penalties but having "long arm" laws that prohibit an insured from making a claim for reimbursement of fines and penalties in an overseas jurisdiction where it is permitted. Some policies have a "most favorable jurisdiction" clause that allow the insured to select the governing law under which the insurance will be interpreted and reimbursement made, but such a clause may be of little value if the firm is based in a "long arm" state.

Cyber insurance, like any other form of insurance, is also subject to local insurance regulation and taxation. Arranging global insurance programs is an intricate process that requires knowledge of local laws and practices. In some countries, the provision of insurance is a government monopoly or locally arranged insurance is required while in other countries it is sufficient to ensure that the relevant allocable portion of premium tax is paid. Working with an insurance broker that has a presence in all the relevant territories and an insurer that can similarly accommodate local requirements in those jurisdictions is a necessity.

161. See HANDBOOK, Chapters 8, *What Cybersecurity Laws Govern? Applicability, Enforcement, and Compliance with Domestic and Foreign Cybersecurity Laws*, and 9, *Foreign and International Cybersecurity Laws*.

7. Best Practices for Cyber Insurance Purchase Preparation[162]

Insurance markets move in cycles, and the current 2025 "soft" insurance market that offers options with competitive/lowering premiums and potentially reduced retentions and coverage enhancements, is unlikely to last forever. In a soft market cycle, insureds can bolster their positions for better renewals both immediately and in the future by doing the following:

- Start with a strategic process to understand insurers' preferred standards of technology protections and implementations and measure the cost of improving the firm's stance against the benefits that doing so might confer in the insurance market. The higher the standards of protection, the more opportunities the firm will have to consider cyber risk insurance alternatives.[163] The process can be informative and improve law firm cyber resiliency—even if the firm determines not to purchase cyber insurance.
- Beginning the renewal process early brings benefits, providing time to identify "low hanging fruit" technology improvements and potentially more critical security enhancements that will increase the availability of insurance options. An early start also allows time for meetings with key underwriters, focusing on existing carrier relationships, and determining current renewal appetite. These efforts also deepen relationships, which can be helpful when incidents happen, and mitigate surprises.

Phase 1:

- A "discovery process" is undertaken to understand the firm's exposures and primary data privacy and security concerns and to determine possible coverage and gaps under existing insurance policies. The discovery process will identify where the firm is missing coverage and where coverage enhancements have become available, such as electronic crime (social engineering fraud) or "bricking." It is essential for the firm to understand what is and is not covered under the cyber program and how that coverage interfaces with the rest of the firm's policies, particularly the lawyer's professional liability.
- Increase risk assessment and management efforts as set forth in the complementary chapters of this Handbook: know your losses and loss history and be prepared to discuss with the underwriter how those losses have been addressed by your firm. Draft and revise policies and procedures to address vulnerabilities in the firm's cyber security stance to mitigate and enhance the risk profile going forward. While no organization can eliminate the threat of a breach, being able to demonstrate basic steps to reduce the risk and significantly decrease the impact of a threat actor is critical. This requires proactive risk mitigation strategies including assessment, testing, and practice

162. "The status-quo habits for 'grandfathered' vulnerabilities do not legitimize them." Stephane Nappo

163. *Cyber Insurance*, Aon, https://www.aon.com/risk-services/professional-services/cyber-risk-cyber-insurance.jsp (visited Apr. 12, 2025).

improvement. It also requires incident response readiness, including conducting tabletop breach simulation exercises[164] and proactively retaining key third-party incident response providers. (Some insurers are requiring that firms not only conduct tabletop exercises at least annually, but that ransomware scenarios be explicitly included in the exercises.) Leveraging resources available through an organization's insurer partners may improve the outcome should a loss arise.

- Employee cybersecurity and phishing simulation training can demonstrate a culture of cyber security. No longer is this just an Admin/IT/Finance problem; employees should be trained to work to combat malicious actors and reduce common vulnerabilities. Without demonstrating adequate security training, insurers may struggle to provide competitive coverage terms or premium pricing.
- With insurers seeing both an increase in frequency and severity of ransomware-related losses, firms should be prepared to showcase preparedness for a ransomware attack. Insurers are reviewing this exposure through specific questionnaires and use of scanning technology. They focus on business continuity/disaster recovery planning, privileged access controls, multi-factor authentication, proactive scanning/testing, and overall incident response readiness. This attack vector is of utmost concern to underwriters, and it will continue to transform the insurance market for the next several years.
- Third-party contracts are a consideration from a technology supply chain and contingent/dependent business standpoint. After ransomware, loss of revenue is one of the major concerns of underwriters; one has only to look at the impact of NotPetya and other major ransomware incidents in which the victim firms were rendered "dark," *i.e.*, all computer systems, including telecommunications, completely shut down, for two weeks with restoration of full system functionality taking several weeks beyond the period of total shutdown. Considering the recent Crowdstrike improper patch incident, these critical supply chain and IT vendors are at heightened risk for "single point of failure" hacks impacting multiple organizations. It is critical to understand how both contracts and insurance respond in the case of a supply chain security breach.
- Based on the findings, alternative options are considered to address identified coverage gaps.
- Budget: As of early 2025, premiums are continuing to decrease, and there are signs of increased capacity that will continue to drive further decreases.

Phase 2:

- An application for cyber risk insurance is completed. The information and diligence required has become much more specific and time-consuming to complete. Fortunately, most insurers are now accepting common application forms and supplemental questionnaires to be completed before offering terms so clients need only complete one version in most instances.

164. *Id.*

eSubmission platforms have been developed that help clients identify, measure, and manage their cyber risk exposure, including their capacity to correct shortcomings prior to carrier submission. The submission platform includes multiple insurance application question sets to help support cyber, errors and omissions, and miscellaneous professional liability insurance placements. Some platforms include Ransomware Supplemental Applications that are accepted by Middle Market Cyber Insurance Carrier Panels. By combining quantifiable insights and analytics with broker's knowledge and experience, cyber submission platforms can help support the execution of insurance transactions. The best cyber submission platforms improve the submission workflow and help insureds make better decisions about their cyber maturity. Embedding cyber risk assessment and Ransomware Red Flags methodology into the placement process helps clients improve their cyber posture and provides awareness of what drives their cost of risk.[165]

Small firms should expect to spend 5–10 hours, and large firms 20–30 hours, to complete the cyber policy application and submission process. Many insurers are also requiring underwriting meetings with the firm's IT staff to ask questions and learn in more detail about the firm's cybersecurity maturity and posture and specific technology implementations. The firm should leverage and highlight lessons learned from this Handbook to the extent implemented.

- Create insurer competition by distributing the firm's submission "asks" to multiple cyber insurers.
- The firm should ask its broker for benchmark information to provide a cost-benefit analysis of retention, limits, and pricing against peer firms.
- A comparison of the terms and conditions of each offering is presented.
- Establish expectations for loss or claim response with insurers in advance.
    - Retention or deductible figure the firm is comfortable paying prior to inception;
    - Selection of approved breach response vendors from the insurer panel, including Breach Counsel, Digital Forensic Investigation & Response experts, crisis communications firm, PII breach notification firms, and credit monitoring firms (if necessary).

Phase 3:
Understand the key policy considerations. Notice provisions remain a universal and important consideration for cyber insurance policyholders, particularly as technology and digital exposures continue to increase for many law firms that were not traditionally "technology companies." Understanding the distinction between "claims made" and "claims made and reported" notice provisions may be critical as late notice is among one of the most

165. *Cyber Quotient (CyQu) Evaluation*, Aon, https://www.aon.com/en/capabilities/cyber-resilience/cyber-quotient-evaluation (visited Apr. 12, 2025).

common causes of claims friction under cyber policies. Further complicating matters is the occasional inclusion of "occurrence" terminology within "claims made" and "claims made and reported" notice language, particularly with respect to technology failures or security issues that give rise to cyber claims. The inclusion of such "occurrence" parlance does not, in and of itself, convert these policies to "occurrence"-based forms, further underscoring the need for insureds to understand the various nuances of notice obligations under their cyber policy.

8. Top Ten Considerations

1. Establish your priorities and objectives, which could reasonably be different from one law firm to another. A disproportionate number of insureds (estimated at 25%–33% based on cyber insurance placed by Aon) make their decision based almost exclusively on price with little regard for breadth of coverage, policy exclusions, carrier propensity to pay claims, carrier service (like mid-term amendments due to law firm M&A), and Total Cost of Risk (some firms practice in areas of greater cyber risk, which might require higher limits and customized cyber insurance coverage):

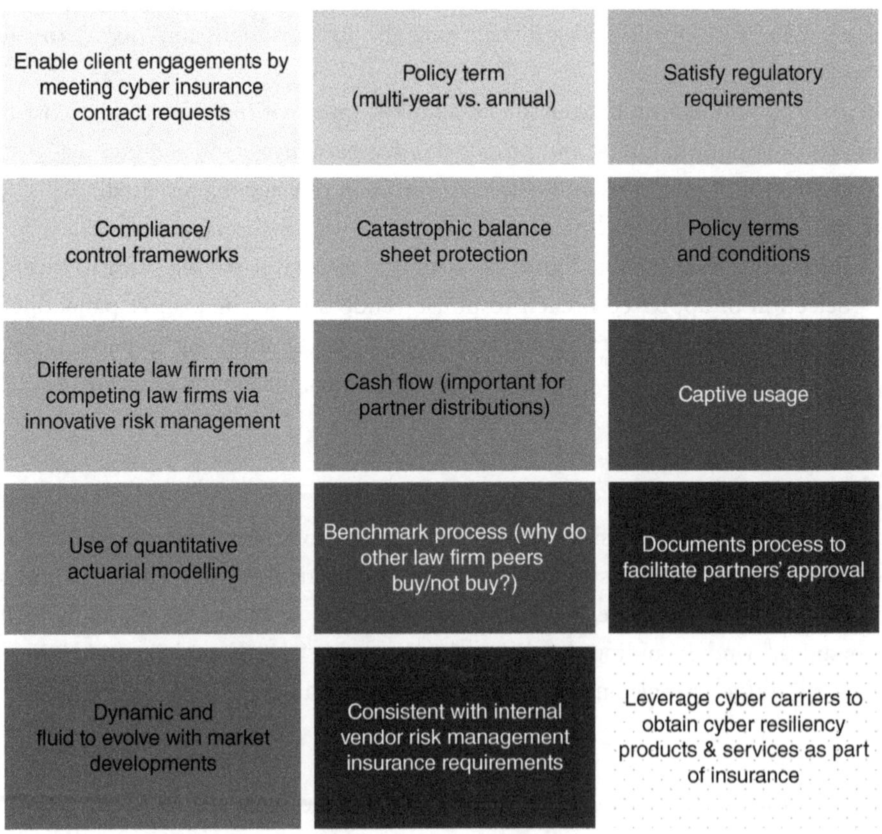

2. Start Early: Underwriters are continuously reviewing claims trends, cybersecurity developments, and the threat environment. Start the application process early to secure insurer proposals early. The following cyber key controls are cyber marketplace minimum expectations:

Multi-Factor Authentication (MFA)	Endpoint Detection and Response (EDR)	Phishing Exercise/ Cyber Awareness Training
Vulnerability Scanning & Patch Management	Secure RDP/VPN	Incident Response Plan/ Ransomware Exercise
Access Control/ Service Accounts	Disaster Recovery/Backups	Email Filtering & Security (DMARC / DKIM)
Zero Day Vulnerabilities and Supply Chain Risks	Network Segmentation/ Network Monitoring	M&A Due Diligence and Integration

3. Depending upon a firm's priorities and objectives, claims service is often the most important element that insureds are buying. Make sure your insurer has the resources you need and a reputation for excellent claims service. In fact, meet with the insurer's claims adjuster to set mutual expectations in advance of the placement.
    a. Ensure firm leadership has an appropriate governance structure, particularly a reporting protocol for insurable and non-insurable cyber risks.
    b. As cyber risks grow in complexity, it is important not only to ensure primary carrier engagement relative to coverage terms and conditions, but also to ensure excess carrier understanding of the primary policy provisions. Additionally, it is prudent to review exclusions that could come from other insurance lines, such as crime, property, EPLI, and general liability. Maintaining a clear and transparent relationship with both primary and excess insurers may better inform policy intent and improve claim outcomes.
4. Work with an expert to help you consider each of the issues raised in this chapter and the type of coverage the firm should consider.[166] Cyber exposures and solutions are dynamic and fluid. Retain a knowledgeable broker and attorney. A good broker, who knows the firm's business, losses, and risks, can identify potential risks

166. See Sweeney, *supra* note 8.

and appropriate products available. Emerging privacy regulations and requirements should be routinely reviewed with counsel.

5. Policy wording is critical—cyber policy wording is complex and policies differ greatly in their language and definitions. Work closely with someone who understands the nuances in the different types of policies.
6. Limits purchased should be a function of the insured's overall risk management appetite, taking into account potential frequency and severity of the cyber risks faced by the insured. Position cyber insurance as a subset of the firm's enterprise risk management system capabilities to enable a firm-wide cyber risk management culture.[167]
7. Cyber insurers are partners. They don't want you to have an event any more than you do. Use their expertise and resources, learn from their experience. Insurers' additional resources, such as cyber assessments, may be especially valuable for smaller firms.[168]
8. Insurance is only part of risk management—it must integrate with the firm's incident response plan, particularly with regard to the engagement of insurer-approved resources for incident response. Test the plan regularly and analyze roles and scope of individuals engaged in incident response. Ensure that everyone involved is aware of, and will work with, internal and outside counsel to protect attorney-client privilege in communications.[169]
9. Check that the firm's preferred law firm and incident/breach response vendors are approved by the insurer. The worst time to learn that the insured's incident response vendors are not covered is during an incident.[170]
10. Remember that a firm is potentially liable for the acts of its vendors and suppliers, and that firms are dependent on their vendors and outsourced service providers. Cyber maturity may be demonstrated by established and updated policies and practices that address third-party contracts, online presence, service providers, supply chains, and each of the insured's business units.

---

167. *Pushing the Limits—How Much Cyber Insurance Do Professional Service Firms Need?*, AON (May 2024), https://www.aon.com/risk-services/professional-services/pushing-the-limits-how-much-cyber-insurance-do-professional-service-firms-need. *See also* HANDBOOK, Chapter 12, *Get SMART on Data Protection by Creating a Culture of Security Awareness.*

168. R&I Editorial Team, *Cyber Insurance Market Grows, but Adoption of Risk Management Services Lags*, RISK & INS. (Oct. 21, 2024), https://riskandinsurance.com/cyber-insurance-market-grows-but-adoption-of-risk-management-services-lags/.

169. David Jones, *Insurance Coverage Drives Cyber Risk Reduction for Companies, Researchers Say*, CYBERSEC.

DIVE (Aug. 21, 2024), https://www.cybersecuritydive.com/news/insurance-cyber-risk-reduction/724852/. *See also* HANDBOOK, Chapter 13, *Achieving Preparedness through Standards and Planning & Best Practices for Incident Response.*

170. R&I Editorial Team, *Cyber Insurance Provides Both Carrot and Stick for Cyber Security*, RISK & INS. (July 11, 2024), https://riskandinsurance.com/cyber-insurance-provides-both-carrot-and-stick-for-cyber-security/.

Chapter 15

Cybersecurity for Solo and Small Firm Lawyers

Jeffrey Allen and Ashley Hallene

1. Introduction

Solo and small firm attorneys face growing cyber threats in today's digital landscape. Cybercrime and the increasingly complex digital tools used in law practice, as well as the evolution of technological tools, including artificial Intelligence (AI), available to cybercriminals, make proactive cybersecurity measures essential. Integrating AI and generative AI (GenAI) technologies into a practice, while potentially beneficial, introduces new and heightened vulnerabilities. Protecting client confidentiality, necessary to the practice's survival, requires understanding why cybercriminals target solo practices and small firms, the seriousness of the risks, and how to address them.

We cannot overstate the importance of cybersecurity for solo and small firm attorneys. These attorneys often operate with fewer resources and less technology support than their counterparts in larger firms and other practice settings, making them prime targets for cybercriminals. Cyber incidents can have devastating consequences, including financial loss, reputational damage, ethical violations, regulatory fines, and malpractice claims. Solo practitioners and small firm attorneys must implement preventive measures to safeguard their practices against the ever-evolving landscape of cyber threats.

This chapter of the Handbook focuses on solo and small firm practices and will help guide readers through the necessary steps to reduce their exposure to cybersecurity risks. Remember that you can never eliminate the risk; you can only hope to mitigate it. You cannot escape the reality that you can do everything right and still get successfully attacked by a cybercriminal due to vulnerabilities and tactics beyond your reasonable control.

While solo and small firms have cybersecurity risks similar to larger firms, solo and small firms generally lack the resources available to larger firms to protect themselves. A key point to remember: **you must focus on prioritizing and scaling the protections and strategies readily available to large firms to make them affordable and functional for your**

smaller operation.[1] This chapter will assist you in understanding, assessing, and mitigating your cyber risk.

Other chapters in the Handbook go into much greater depth about many topics we will address here. All the information in the Handbook has utility, but some chapters have greater relevance than others to solo and small firm practitioners. While we encourage you to review the entire Handbook, we consider the chapters we identify for you at the end of this chapter the most relevant to solo and small firm practitioners. We suggest you start with this chapter as a survey and read the others as a follow-up.

2. Solo and Small Firms as Targets

Several factors make solo and small firm attorneys particularly vulnerable to cyberattacks.

1. **Perceived Vulnerability**
   Solo and small law firms typically have fewer resources than larger firms. This often means limited budgets for IT infrastructure, the use of outdated (or unpatched) software, and less robust cybersecurity measures, practices that essentially provide a welcome mat for cybercriminals.
2. **Valuable Data**
   Legal professionals manage sensitive and confidential client information, including personally identifiable information (PII), financial records, intellectual property, and strategic business data. Hackers highly prize such information for its value in financial exploitation and extortion.
3. **AI and Automation Challenges**
   Adopting AI tools for drafting documents, analyzing case law, and managing administrative tasks introduces new attack vectors. The learning curve for new technology also poses a risk of errors and inadvertent data compromise. Cybercriminals may exploit poorly secured AI tools or manipulate GenAI to extract sensitive information through phishing schemes or data poisoning.

Many solo and small firm attorneys believe their practices' size and nature render them diminutive targets. They find solace in this presumed safety. The assumption that "it won't happen to us" can lead to complacency and inadequate security measures. This combination of factors creates a perfect storm for potential cyber incidents.

1. *See also* HANDBOOK, Chapter 11, *Foundation of Risk Management in Cybersecurity.*

2.1. The Seriousness of the Problem

The threat landscape for solo and small firm attorneys has grown broad and severe. Cyberattacks can take many forms, including phishing, ransomware, data breaches, and malware. Each can have significant repercussions:

2.1.1. *Common Cyber Risks*

- **Ransomware Attacks:** Successful ransomware attacks encrypt a firm's data and demand payment for its release (access to decryption keys). They often target smaller firms that are less likely to have comprehensive, well-maintained backup systems.
- **Phishing and Social Engineering:** Cybercriminals use sophisticated schemes, such as emails that mimic clients or colleagues, to deceive attorneys into divulging credentials or transferring funds.
- **GenAI Exploits:** Hackers can use GenAI to create convincing deepfake audio or video messages, enhance phishing attempts, or automate the creation of malicious code, increasing the likelihood of a successful attack.

2.2. Ethical and Professional Consequences

Attorneys must preserve confidentiality under the applicable ethics rules, most of which now follow the American Bar Association's (ABA) Model Rules of Professional Conduct (make sure to check the rules applicable to you in your state). A breach of client confidential information due to a law office's inadequate cybersecurity measures can result in:

- **Disciplinary Action:** Ethical violations may lead to sanctions or loss of licensure.
- **Reputational Damage:** A breach undermines client trust and damages the firm's credibility.
- **Financial Liabilities:** In addition to potential malpractice concerns, non-compliance with data protection laws can incur steep penalties. A small firm that fails to comply with regulations such as the European Union's General Data Protection Regulation (GDPR), the California Consumer Privacy Act (CCPA), or many other U.S. federal or state privacy laws may incur significant fines, which could prove financially crippling. Costs associated with remediation, regulatory penalties, and lawsuits can overwhelm a small practice. Potentially substantial costs related to downtime, data recovery, and ransomware payments pile on to other damages. For example, a small law firm hit by a ransomware attack could face the direct cost of paying the ransom and the indirect costs of lost billable hours and damage to their financial records.[2]

---

2. *See also* HANDBOOK, Chapter 13, *Achieving Preparedness through Standards and Planning & Best Practices for Incident Response.*

2.3. The Impact of AI and GenAI

Artificial intelligence and GenAI technologies present opportunities and challenges for solo and small firm attorneys. While these technologies can enhance efficiency and provide valuable insights, they also introduce new risks. Cybercriminals can exploit AI to automate and scale attacks, making them more sophisticated and more challenging to detect.

2.3.1. *AI and GenAI Increase Cyber Risks*

- **Expanded Threat Landscape:** The use of AI in law practice offers significant efficiencies, such as automating document review and generating client communications. However, introducing any new tools also creates opportunities for new vulnerabilities.
- **Data Exposure:** GenAI tools require large datasets to function, increasing the risk of a leak or misuse of sensitive data. Depending on the service terms and settings, the vendor could keep and use any data input in publicly accessible GenAI tools.
- **Manipulative Outputs:** AI-generated phishing emails or false legal documents can appear indistinguishable from genuine ones, making detection harder.
- **Unauthorized Access:** Poorly secured AI platforms can serve as entry points for cybercriminals to access other firm systems.

2.4. Increased Attack Sophistication

- **AI-Enhanced Hacking:** Cybercriminals use AI to bypass security protocols or simulate attorney-client communications for fraudulent purposes.
- **Automated Scams:** Bad actors can use GenAI to mass-produce tailored attacks, targeting firms with hard-to-identify personalized schemes.

2.5. Preventive Steps

Solo and small firm attorneys should adopt a proactive approach to cybersecurity to mitigate the risks associated with cyber threats. Consider the following steps, which we will discuss in more detail later in the chapter:

- Strengthen Core Cybersecurity Practices
- Adopt AI-Specific Safeguards
- Invest in Professional Support
- Stay Informed and Educated
- Develop an Incident Response Plan
- Purchase Cyber Insurance

3. Legal & Ethical Obligations to Provide Data Security

Clients trust attorneys with sensitive, often life-altering information. Attorneys have moral, legal, and ethical obligations to safeguard that information. Legal and ethical rules require lawyers to take reasonable steps to protect client information's confidentiality, integrity, and availability. These requirements evolve with the technology landscape, raising the stakes for solo practitioners and small firms that may lack the resources to fully protect themselves and their clients.

The duty of competence, outlined in professional conduct rules such as ABA Model Rule 1.1,[3] now includes technological competence. Ignoring this responsibility risks breaching ethical rules and the trust that underpins every attorney-client relationship. It also increases the risk of exposing confidential information and other cyber incidents. Beyond ethics, laws such as the European Union's General Data Protection Regulation (GDPR),[4] the California Consumer Privacy Act[5], and the growing body of similar state laws impose strict requirements on handling, storing, and protecting data. Failure to comply can result in hefty penalties and potentially irreparable damage to a lawyer's reputation.

This section will examine these obligations and clarify the intersection of ethics and law in cybersecurity.[6] It will provide practical insights to help you meet your responsibilities and build your clients' and peers' confidence in your operations. Regardless of your experience level or time in practice, you must understand these duties to protect your clients and preserve their trust.

3.1. Governing Laws and Regulations

Navigating the complex web of laws and regulations governing data security can feel daunting. Nevertheless, you must understand how data security relates to professional responsibility: data security laws establish standards for handling confidential information, and ethical rules reinforce the lawyer's duty to protect client confidentiality.

The following overview of key federal laws and regulations that impact legal practices should help you better understand this framework. It will also help you understand the necessary steps to ensure compliance, mitigate risk, and uphold clients' trust.

3.1.1. *Federal Laws*

Federal laws play a critical role in shaping data security standards. Understanding and complying with them can help safeguard against costly mistakes and unnecessary cybersecurity incidents.[7]

Key Federal Laws

The Cybersecurity Information Sharing Act (CISA)[8] encourages the private sector and the federal government to share information about cyber threats. CISA underscores the

---

3. Model Rules of Prof'l Conduct, r. 1.1 (Am. Bar Ass'n 2020).

4. Regulation (EU) 2016/679 of the European Parliament and of the Council of 27 April 2016 on the protection of natural persons with regard to the processing of personal data and on the free movement of such data, and repealing Directive 95/46/EC (General Data Protection Regulation) [hereinafter GDPR].

5. California Consumer Privacy Act of 2018 (CCPA), Cal. Civ. Code §§ 1798.100–1798.199.100 (West 2024).

6. *See also* Handbook, Chapter 10, *Lawyers' Professional Responsibility to Provide Data Security.*

7. *See also* Handbook, Chapter 7, *Legal Obligations to Provide Data Security.*

8. Cybersecurity Information Sharing Act of 2015, 6 U.S.C. §§ 1501–1510.

importance of proactive cybersecurity measures and cooperation in preventing data breaches. Lawyers handling sensitive client data, especially in industries vulnerable to cyberattacks, should stay informed about CISA's provisions and the resources provided by the U.S. Cybersecurity and Infrastructure Security Agency (also known as CISA).

The Health Insurance Portability and Accountability Act (HIPAA),[9] governs the protection of health information. Lawyers working with healthcare providers or handling health-related matters (including injury-related claims) must comply with HIPAA's strict requirements. These include implementing safeguards for electronic health records and ensuring that any third parties involved in data processing do the same.

Other federal laws may apply depending on your area of practice. For example, attorneys handling financial matters should familiarize themselves with the Gramm-Leach-Bliley Act,[10] which mandates secure handling of clients' nonpublic personal information by financial institutions.

Applicability of FTC Enforcement of Data Security Rules

The Federal Trade Commission (FTC) enforces data security standards under its authority to prevent unfair or deceptive business practices. The FTC does not explicitly regulate law firms, but its rules can serve as a benchmark for establishing reasonable security practices. If a law firm fails to secure client data and that failure leads to a data breach, the FTC could investigate and impose penalties under its general consumer protection mandate.

Lawyers should regularly assess their cybersecurity practices to ensure compliance with federal laws and regulations. This chapter discusses key steps to avoid violations, including training staff, implementing strong access controls, and conducting periodic risk assessments. By adhering to these practices, solo practitioners and small firms can protect client data, uphold their ethical obligations, and reduce the risk of liability.

3.1.2. *State Laws*

While federal laws establish a broad framework for data security, state laws often impose additional, sometimes more stringent, requirements. Lawyers must be vigilant about state-specific regulations that apply to their practice. Lawyers should ensure they know the rules imposed by the states in which they practice.

---

9. Pub. L. No. 104–191, 110 Stat. 1936 (1996); Security and Privacy regulations issued by the Department of Health and Human Services pursuant to the Health Insurance Portability and Accountability Act of 1996 (HIPAA), codified at 45 C.F.R. pt. 164 (including Standards for the Protection of Electronic Protected Health Information, 45 C.F.R. §§ 164.302-164.318).

10. Pub. L. No. 106-102, 113 Stat. 1338 (1999); FTC Standards for Safeguarding Customer Information, 16 C.F.R. pt. 314 (2025) (implementing §§ 501 and 505(b) of the Gramm-Leach-Bliley Act for customer information handling by financial institutions subject to FTC jurisdiction); Interagency Guidelines Establishing Standards for Safeguarding Consumer Information, issued on February 1, 2001 and codified at 12 C.F.R. pt. 30, App. B (OCC), 12 C.F.R. pt. 208, App. D-2 & 12 C.F.R. pt. 225, App. F (Federal Reserve System), & 12 C.F.R. pt. 364, App. B (FDIC).

State-Specific Data Breach Notification Laws

Every state has enacted its own data breach notification laws, creating a patchwork of requirements that can be challenging to navigate. These laws generally require businesses, including law firms, to notify affected individuals and, in some cases, state regulators when a data breach occurs. While the specifics vary, most laws outline the types of personal information covered, the time frame for notification, and the format of required communications.

For example, California requires notification within 45 days of discovering a breach, while Florida mandates notice within 30 days. Lawyers must familiarize themselves with the notification laws in the states where they practice to facilitate timely and proper compliance in the event of a breach.[11]

The California Consumer Privacy Act (CCPA)

The California Consumer Privacy Act (CCPA) is one of the most comprehensive state privacy laws in the United States. It grants California residents rights over their personal data, including:

- the right to know the information collected,
- the right to request its deletion, and
- the right to opt out of its sale.[12]

While the law primarily targets businesses meeting specific revenue or data thresholds, its provisions may impact lawyers who collect or process significant amounts of client data in California. Additionally, some of your clients may meet the required thresholds, and you must be prepared to advise them.

Lawyers must evaluate their data collection practices to determine whether the CCPA (or a similar law in another state) applies. Even if a firm is not directly subject to the law, adhering to its principles can enhance data security practices and demonstrate a commitment to protecting client privacy.

The New York SHIELD Act

The New York Stop Hacks and Improve Electronic Data Security (SHIELD) Act,[13] expands data protection requirements for businesses handling private information about New York residents. Unlike many state laws, the SHIELD Act applies regardless of whether a company operates in New York.

---

11. The Privacy Rights Clearinghouse provides a publicly accessible interactive database of breach notification laws, which is a useful starting point for lawyers. *United States Data Breach Notification in the United States 2023 Report* (Oct. 5, 2023), https://privacyrights.org/resources-tools/reports/united-states-data-breach-notification-united-states-2023-report.
12. Cal. Civ. Code § 1798.100.
13. N.Y. Gen. Bus. Law § 899-bb (Consol. 2024).

The SHIELD Act requires businesses to implement a "reasonable" data security program with administrative, technical, and physical safeguards. For solo practitioners and small firms, this means adopting measures such as risk assessments, access controls, and encryption. Noncompliance can result in significant penalties.

State laws add another layer of complexity to lawyers' data security obligations. By understanding the nuances of data breach notification laws, privacy laws like the CCPA, and data security laws like the SHIELD Act, lawyers can better protect client information and comply with their legal and ethical responsibilities.

3.1.3. *Industry Standards*

Once you understand the patchwork of federal and state laws that govern data security, you should consider the role of industry standards and frameworks. The standards can provide detailed, actionable guides for lawyers to strengthen their cybersecurity practices. Unlike often reactive laws and regulations, industry standards and frameworks help organizations proactively manage risks and improve resilience. For lawyers, adopting standards or using frameworks to guide security assessment and planning can enhance compliance with legal and ethical obligations while reducing vulnerability.

National Institute of Standards and Technology (NIST) Guidelines

The National Institute of Standards and Technology (NIST) develops widely respected guidelines for managing cybersecurity risks. In 2024, NIST released a revised Cybersecurity Risk Framework, which outlines six core functions: Govern, Identify, Protect, Detect, Respond, and Recover. (The Govern function was added in the 2024 revision.) Together, these functions provide a comprehensive approach to safeguarding sensitive information.[14]

By following NIST guidelines, lawyers can establish transparent processes for managing cybersecurity, identifying risks, implementing safeguards, monitoring threats, and responding to incidents. For example, the framework emphasizes the importance of access controls, data encryption, and regular employee training practices that align with a lawyer's ethical duties to maintain client confidentiality. NIST's flexible and scalable guidelines and accompanying materials make them a good choice for small practices.

ISO/IEC 27001 for Information Security Management

The ISO/IEC 27001 standard[15] provides a systematic approach to managing sensitive company and client information. It focuses on creating and maintaining an Information Security

14. NIST, *The NIST Cybersecurity Framework (CSF) 2.0*, (Feb. 26, 2024), https://nvlpubs.nist.gov/nistpubs/CSWP/NIST.CSWP.29.pdf.

NIST also publishes "crosswalks" developed by various contributors to map NIST frameworks to standards and other relevant guidance. For example, NIST's Privacy Framework material includes links for crosswalks to CCPA and GDPR regulations, the ISO/IEC 27701 standard for Privacy Information Management Systems security, and the NIST Cybersecurity Framework. *NIST Privacy Framework Crosswalks* webpage, https://www.nist.gov/privacy-framework/resource-repository/browse/crosswalks (visited Apr. 15, 2025).

15. Int'l Org. for Standardization, ISO/IEC 27001:2022, *Information Security, Cybersecurity and Privacy Protection—Information Security Management Systems—Requirements* (3d ed. 2022).

Management System (ISMS), a set of policies, procedures, and controls designed to manage risks effectively. While achieving ISO certification may have greater importance for larger organizations, the principles outlined in the standard have significant value for small firms.

ISO/IEC 27001 emphasizes risk assessment as the foundation of an effective security program. Lawyers can prioritize resources and implement appropriate safeguards by identifying vulnerabilities and evaluating potential impacts. The standard also highlights the importance of continuous improvement, ensuring that security measures evolve alongside emerging threats and technological changes.

Industry standards like ISO/IEC 27001 and frameworks like NIST's CRF 2.0 provide a roadmap for building a security culture within your practice. By using these tools in managing cybersecurity risk, you can go beyond compliance and set a standard of excellence that reinforces client trust and safeguards your professional reputation.

3.1.4. *Obligations Under ABA Model Rules*

After exploring federal, state, and industry standards, consider the ethical obligations guiding lawyers' professional conduct. The American Bar Association (ABA) Model Rules of Professional Conduct provide a foundational framework for the legal profession. These rules emphasize the ethical duties of competence, confidentiality, and oversight, which critically affect cybersecurity. For solo practitioners and small firm lawyers, understanding and adhering to these obligations is vital to protecting client information and maintaining professional integrity. Note, however, that while the Model Rules prevail in some states, others have adopted their own requirements. Know what controls are in each state where you practice, and make sure to comply with the applicable requirements. As you will find it easier to adhere to a single standard than many, you should abide by the most stringent standard applicable to your practice.

Model Rule 1.1: Competence

Model Rule 1.1 requires lawyers to provide competent representation, including the necessary knowledge and skill to handle legal matters effectively. Today, this duty extends to understanding technology basics, including cybersecurity. Lawyers must take reasonable steps to stay informed about emerging risks and implement measures to safeguard client information. This may include attending continuing legal education programs on emerging technology and cybersecurity, consulting with IT professionals, and staying current on best practices for data protection. Failure to adhere to this standard may result in ethical breaches and exposure of clients' sensitive information.

Model Rule 1.6: Confidentiality of Information

Model Rule 1.6[16] underscores a lawyer's duty to protect the confidentiality of client information. This rule obligates lawyers to take reasonable precautions to prevent unauthorized

16. Model Rules of Prof'l Conduct r. 1.6.

access to, or disclosure of, client data. The rise of cloud-based storage and digital communication has made complying with this duty even more complex.

Lawyers using third-party software and storage solutions or outsourced IT and security support must ensure that their service providers have implemented robust security measures. Conducting due diligence, reviewing contracts, and verifying compliance with industry standards are critical to safeguarding client data. The ethical obligation to protect confidentiality does not end with selecting a vendor; lawyers must also continually monitor these relationships to ensure ongoing compliance.

Model Rule 5.3: Responsibilities Regarding Nonlawyer Assistance

Model Rule 5.3[17] addresses lawyers' responsibility to oversee nonlawyers' work, including staff and third-party vendors. Oversight includes measures to ensure these individuals or entities adhere to cybersecurity practices that align with the lawyer's ethical obligations.

For solo practitioners and small firms, the oversight duty means training staff on data protection practices, implementing clear security policies, and vetting vendors to confirm cybersecurity compliance. A nonlawyer's failure to protect client information ultimately affects the lawyer, making this oversight a critical component of ethical practice.

3.1.5. *Commentary and Formal Opinions*

The ABA, through its Standing Committee on Ethics and Professional Responsibility, has issued formal opinions providing further guidance on cybersecurity obligations. ABA Formal Opinion 477R highlights the importance of securing electronic communications containing protected client information. It advises lawyers to evaluate the data's sensitivity, the likelihood of interception, and the availability of security measures such as encryption.[18]

ABA Formal Opinion 483[19] addresses lawyers' responsibilities following a data breach. It emphasizes the duty to notify affected clients, assess the scope of the breach, and take steps to prevent future incidents. These opinions reinforce the need for proactive and reactive measures to meet ethical and professional standards.

Together, the ABA Model Rules and related formal opinions establish clear ethical obligations for lawyers extending to cybersecurity. By understanding and adhering to these rules, lawyers can build practices that comply with professional standards and inspire trust and confidence in their clients. In an increasingly interconnected world, these obligations are essential to the survival and success of a legal practice.

17. Model Rules of Prof'l Conduct r. 5.3.
18. ABA Comm. on Ethics & Prof'l Responsibility, Formal Op. 477R (2017).
19. ABA Comm. on Ethics & Prof'l Resp., Formal Op. 483 (2018).

3.2. International Regulations

Having explored federal laws, state laws, industry standards, and the ethical obligations under the ABA Model Rules, it is time to turn to the global landscape.[20] For many lawyers, international regulations may seem far removed from their daily practice. However, globalization and the increasing mobility of clients mean that even solo practitioners and small firms may handle data subject to foreign laws.

3.2.1. *General Data Protection Regulation*

The GDPR is a comprehensive privacy law enacted in the European Union (EU). The GDPR establishes strict rules for collecting, processing, and storing personal data of individuals within the EU. Lawyers handling EU client data must understand and comply with its requirements, regardless of location.

The GDPR features key principles such as transparency, accountability, and data minimization. To comply, data controllers (which include lawyers collecting personal data) must process only data necessary for its intended purpose, inform clients about its usage, and ensure its protection.

Obligations under the GDPR include conducting Data Protection Impact Assessments (DPIAs) when processing activities pose a high risk to individual privacy. For example, a lawyer using advanced analytics or AI to manage potential risks might need a DPIA. Additionally, firms must designate a Data Protection Officer (DPO) in certain situations, such as when large-scale processing of sensitive data occurs.

Failure to comply with the GDPR can result in significant penalties. Lawyers can mitigate risk by understanding the GDPR requirements and implementing basic compliance measures, such as securing data storage and obtaining explicit client consent for data collection and use.

3.3. Other Global Regulations

Beyond the GDPR, other countries have enacted data protection laws that may impact lawyers handling international client data, including the following, non-exhaustive list offered for example:

Canada's Personal Information Protection and Electronic Documents Act (PIPEDA)[21] governs personal information collection, use, and disclosure in commercial activities. Lawyers must obtain consent to collect data, use collected data for its intended purpose, and store it securely.

Brazil's General Data Protection Law (LGPD)[22] mirrors the GDPR in many respects. It applies to any organization processing data about individuals in Brazil, regardless of

20. *See also* Handbook, Chapters 8, *What Cybersecurity Laws Govern? Applicability, Enforcement, and Compliance with International Cybersecurity Laws*, and 9, *Foreign and International Cybersecurity Laws*.

21. Personal Information Protection and Electronic Documents Act, S.C. 2000, c. 5 (Can.).

22. Lei No. 13.709, de 14 de Agosto de 2018, Diário Oficial da União [D.O.U.] de 15.8.2018 (Braz.).

the organization's location. Key requirements include obtaining consent, ensuring data accuracy, and providing individuals with access to their information.

3.4. Cross-Border Data Transfer Considerations

Handling client data that crosses international borders presents unique challenges. Many data protection laws, including the EU's GDPR, impose restrictions on transfers of personal data to countries that lack adequate privacy protections. Lawyers must use approved mechanisms to facilitate these transfers.

Standard Contractual Clauses (SCCs) and Binding Corporate Rules (BCRs) represent common solutions. SCCs are legal agreements that ensure data exported from the EU receives the same level of protection as it would under the GDPR. While more complex to implement, BCRs provide a framework for data transfers within multinational organizations. Understanding and incorporating these mechanisms into contracts and practices, giving them effect, can ensure compliance with international requirements.

International data protection laws no longer concern only multinational corporations. Solo practitioners and small firms (or their clients) may need to comply with GDPR, PIPEDA, and LGPD, for example, when handling client data from relevant foreign residents or jurisdictions. Lawyers can meet these challenges by understanding the key principles, specific obligations, and cross-border considerations. Adhering to these standards fulfills legal obligations and reinforces the professional commitment to safeguarding client information in a connected world.

Lawyers are bound by laws, ethical standards, and industry guidelines that require vigilance and care in handling sensitive information. Solo practitioners and small firms must rise to the challenge and adopt practices that ensure compliance while fostering client trust and confidence. Understanding these legal and ethical obligations is the first step in building a resilient and secure practice. By integrating the principles of technological competence, confidentiality, and oversight into daily operations, lawyers can safeguard their clients' data and professional reputations. As we move forward, the focus shifts from understanding obligations to leveraging the tools and technologies that make it possible to fulfill these responsibilities. With the right tools and strategies, even the smallest firm can protect its data and survive in a digital world.

4. Technology for Solo and Small Firm Lawyers: What Every Lawyer Needs to Know About the Cyber Network

Lawyers rely on technology, which evolves continuously and, at times, monumentally. Widespread internet use, beginning in the 1990s, and the public release of GenAI tools in 2022 are two monumental technological advances. Mastering the basics of the cyber network has evolved from an optional skill to an essential one that underpins the attorney's ability to protect client data, meet ethical obligations, and operate efficiently in an increasingly challenging, if not hostile, digital world. Indeed, the complexity of technology can often feel overwhelming, particularly for those without a technical background.

This section aims to demystify the technological concepts and systems that form the backbone of cybersecurity. We will examine the essential parts of the cyber network, help you better understand information transmission, identify potential vulnerabilities, and discuss measures to help you protect sensitive data.

4.1. Key Components of the Cyber Network

Understanding the essential components of the cyber network serves as the foundation of effective cybersecurity. Solo practitioners and small firm lawyers often personally manage their technology or rely on limited IT support. Those lawyers must understand the essential elements of the network and the factors that keep the network secure and protect them and their clients' data.

4.1.1. *Network Basics*

A network connects devices at its core, allowing them to share information and resources. Lawyers use local, cloud-based, and hybrid networks, combining local and cloud-based elements.

Local networks typically consist of computers, servers, and other devices connected within a physical office. These networks offer direct control over data storage and access but require strong internal safeguards to prevent breaches.

Cloud-based networks enable remote access to data and applications through the internet. These networks offer convenience and flexibility, particularly for lawyers working remotely or collaborating across locations. However, using cloud services requires careful vetting of providers and coordination to ensure robust security measures, such as data encryption and secure user authentication, to protect data and confidentiality.

All networks should have secure remote access. Virtual private networks (VPNs) provide a critical tool for solo and small firm lawyers. VPNs create, in effect, a tunnel through the internet, protecting the data as it traverses the network. A good VPN will encrypt data entering the network and decrypt it on arrival, ensuring that sensitive information remains private, notwithstanding travel over public WiFi (which we do not recommend, even with a VPN). Selecting a reliable VPN service and using it consistently provides a simple yet powerful step toward protecting your data.

4.1.2. *Firewalls*

Firewalls provide your network's first line of defense. They monitor and control incoming and outgoing traffic, blocking unauthorized access while allowing legitimate communication to flow through.

Affordable firewall options include both hardware and software solutions. Many modern routers have built-in firewalls, which provide essential protection. Consider standalone firewall devices or advanced software solutions offering customizable settings and detailed reporting for enhanced security. Regularly updating and configuring your firewall helps it remain effective against evolving threats.

4.1.3. *Endpoint Security*

Endpoint security protects the devices that connect to your network, such as laptops, smartphones, and tablets. These devices often represent the most vulnerable points in a network, making them prime targets for cybercriminals.

Basic endpoint security encompasses antivirus and anti-malware software, which identify and eliminate programs that can jeopardize data. Encryption tools add another layer of protection, limiting access to sensitive files and communications to authorized users.

Mobile device management (MDM) solutions can further enhance endpoint security by allowing you to enforce security policies, remotely wipe data from lost or stolen devices, and monitor device activity. These tools strengthen network security, particularly for devices used outside the office.

The network's components, including local and cloud-based connections, firewalls, and endpoints, form the backbone of a small practice's digital security. By understanding and implementing the tools and measures outlined in this subsection, you can create a secure foundation that protects your clients' data and upholds your practice's integrity.

4.2. Essential Cybersecurity Tools for Lawyers

While technology can seem complex, the right tools can simplify your approach to securing sensitive information. Adopting and using essential cybersecurity tools helps you protect yourself and meet your ethical obligations.

4.2.1. *Password Management*

Weak or reused passwords represent a leading cause of data breaches. Lawyers must enforce strong password policies and use tools designed to manage passwords securely. Password management solutions like LastPass and Dashlane store complex passwords in encrypted vaults, ensuring that users never rely on memory or insecure methods like written lists. Some password managers generate unique, strong passwords for each account, reducing the risk of unauthorized access. Be careful with using password management programs, however. They securely store all your passwords for you, but if someone obtains the password manager password, they can access the stored passwords. Pay particular attention to how you handle and store that password. Better yet, prefer password managers that use biometric access. That makes for a safer and more secure situation.

Policies should require passwords to be at least 12 characters long and include a mix of letters (upper and lower case), numbers, and symbols. The policy should also require regularly and frequently updating passwords and not reusing passwords within your system or across platforms. When it comes to passwords, longer equates with stronger, as longer passwords pose more difficulty for the bad guys trying to crack them and the tools at their disposal.

Many experts recommend eschewing passwords entirely and moving to passphrases. Properly constructed, a passphrase can give the bad guys and their software fits. An example of a good passphrase: "176bEWArE a*&^JabBERwocKSMIthson727+()@!" If you really want to make it tough, include the rest and make it longer: "176bEWArE the*&^J abBERwocKSMIthson727+()@! ThE jaWs so blite, the crows/S999 that HATcH! The fru-Mious 666BanDERsnatch[]." [**NOTE**: The misspellings and changed words did not occur inadvertently.] Ideally, the passphrase consists of a combination of random words with upper- and lower-case letters, numbers, and symbols. If you use a quote from literature, mix it up by changing a few words so it does not track directly, as we did in the foregoing example. The length and alterations to the phrase make it very hard to remember, so you will want (need) to employ a password manager if you move to passphrases.

4.2.2. *Data Encryption*

Encryption transforms sensitive information into unreadable code, ensuring only authorized individuals can access it. Email encryption tools like ProtonMail or Zix protect communications by ensuring only the intended recipient can read the message. File-level encryption solutions like VeraCrypt or Microsoft BitLocker secure sensitive documents stored on your devices or in the cloud. Encrypting your data significantly reduces the risk of exposure in the event of a breach or theft. If you password-protect (or passphrase-protect) encrypted files with strong passwords/passphrases, you increase your data protection.

Text messaging has assumed a significant place in today's universe of communication. In December 2024, CISA released the *Mobile Communications Best Practice Guidance*,[23] recommending:

- exclusive use of end-to-end encryption (E2EE) messaging apps, specifically highlighting Signal for its robust encryption;
- avoiding SMS and rich communication services (RCS) due to inconsistent or absent encryption;
- implementing phishing-resistant multi-factor authentication methods; and
- regular software updates and utilizing devices with strong security track records.

These recommendations were aimed at senior government officials but deemed applicable to all users. You should use them to protect your data and messages.

23. Cybersecurity & Infrastructure Sec. Agency, Mobile Communications Best Practice Guidance (Dec. 18, 2024), https://www.cisa.gov/sites/default/files/2024-12/guidance-mobile-communications-best-practices.pdf.

4.2.3. *Limitations of RCS and SMS*

RCS, intended as an upgrade to SMS, lacks consistent end-to-end encryption across different carriers and devices. Even with recent advancements, such as introducing the Messaging Layer Security (MLS) protocol in RCS Universal Profile 3.0, full implementation and adoption remain limited. Consequently, messages sent via RCS or SMS are vulnerable to interception and unauthorized access.

4.2.4. *Advantages of Signal and WhatsApp*

Signal and WhatsApp utilize the Signal Protocol to provide end-to-end encryption, ensuring that only the communicating users can access message content. Signal, in particular, is open-source and does not collect metadata, enhancing user privacy. WhatsApp, while also offering E2EE, is owned by Meta Platforms, Inc. (parent of Facebook) and collects certain metadata, which has raised privacy concerns among some users.

"Signalgate" refers to a political scandal involving a leak of sensitive U.S. government communications on the encrypted messaging app Signal. In March 2025, top administration officials, including the vice president, cabinet members, and intelligence agency heads, discussed a planned military strike against Yemen on a group chat, which included a journalist from The Atlantic. The press leak occurred when a White House staffer accidentally added the journalist to the Signal group. This incident raised concerns about the proper handling of sensitive information within the government. While the breakdown that led to Signalgate had nothing to do with the failure of Signal's security, it called into question the use of commercial applications for (at least government-level) security. You will need to determine your own reaction to Signalgate. We still trust the encryption currently afforded by the apps; but it is essential practice to double-check each transmittal to verify that nobody has been added to the communication who should not be there.

4.2.5. *Multi-Factor Authentication (MFA)*

Multi-factor authentication (MFA) requires two or more verification methods to protect your accounts. These could include something you know (like a password), something you have (like a smartphone or hardware token), or something that is a part of you (like a fingerprint or facial recognition).

Implementing multi-factor authentication (MFA) across systems and accounts provides an affordable and effective way to deter unauthorized access. Many platforms, such as Google Workspace and Microsoft 365, include built-in MFA options at no additional cost. Third-party solutions, like Authy or Duo Security, provide simple integrations with other applications. Utilizing MFA consistently improves the security of your accounts, even in the event of a compromised password. We like using biometric factors as one of our checkpoints. Biometric markers such as facial recognition or fingerprints can bolster your security profile. On the other hand, remember that the platforms using the biometric data for authentication must store that data. Before using biometric data on a platform, you should consider whether you trust that platform.

4.2.6. *Backup and Recovery Solutions*

Backing up your data represents one of the most critical steps in preparing for cyber incidents. Cloud-based backup services like Carbonite and Backblaze automatically store copies of your files in secure, off-site locations. These services increase the likelihood of recovering data following a ransomware attack, hardware failure, or accidental deletion.

Immutable backups offer an advanced layer of protection. You cannot alter, delete, or overwrite an immutable backup for a specified period. This prevents cybercriminals, rogue actors, or even accidental user errors from modifying or destroying critical data. Properly managed, immutable backups stored separately from the compromised system can make available a clean and uncorrupted version of your files, even in the face of sophisticated ransomware attacks.

Immutable backups work by creating write-once, read-many times (WORM) formats for stored data. Once written, the data remains unchanged. Many cloud-based backup solutions, such as Wasabi and Veeam, now include immutable storage options. These backups live apart from the active system. Robust access controls protect them from tampering.

Immutable backups let you restore operations without paying a ransom or facing significant downtime. Note, however, that if your backup includes the corrupting file, you will not be able to restore your operation from it safely. Additionally, as the immutable backup freezes your information at a fixed point in time, any restoration will take you back to that point in time. It will not include data entered after that point in time. Accordingly, you will want to create new immutable backups frequently.

Regularly testing your backup systems is just as important as creating them. Conduct routine checks to verify that you have complete, functional, and restorable backups. For small practices, combining standard and immutable backups as part of a comprehensive recovery plan improves the prospects for minimal disruption to operations in the face of unexpected events. By leveraging these tools, you can build resilience against even the most advanced cyber threats.

Whatever backup system(s) you employ, ensure you have multiple copies of your backups, properly secure each copy, and store them in various locations, both within and outside your physical office. You should maintain at least one copy in the cloud to protect it from loss due to physical theft or disasters, whether natural or man-made.

4.3. Unique Challenges for Solo and Small Firm Lawyers

Limited resources, dispersed work environments, and reliance on third-party services create obstacles that require tailored solutions. Solo and small firm attorneys must understand these challenges to overcome them and maintain a secure, efficient practice.

4.3.1. *Limited IT Budgets and Resources*

Solo practitioners and small firms typically operate on tight budgets with limited access to dedicated IT staff. Resource limitations make it harder to implement advanced cybersecurity measures or respond quickly to emerging threats. Many small firms rely on do-it-yourself solutions or affordable third-party services, which can leave gaps in their defenses if not carefully managed.

To address this challenge successfully, solo and small firm practices must prioritize cost-effective tools that provide maximum security with minimal complexity. Open-source software bundled with cybersecurity solutions and managed service providers can help reduce costs without sacrificing protection. Investing in regular cybersecurity training for all staff can also make a significant difference, helping the practice effectively use available resources.

4.3.2. *Managing Security Across Multiple Devices and Locations*

The flexibility of modern law practice often involves using multiple devices, such as laptops, smartphones, and tablets, across various locations. This environment creates vulnerabilities, as each device and location presents a potential entry point for cybercriminals. The rise of remote work further complicates securing your practice, especially when connecting to public or home networks.

To mitigate these risks, enforce strict security policies across all devices. Use MDM tools to monitor and control device activity, enable encryption, and update software regularly. Secure remote access through VPNs and educate staff about the dangers of connecting to unsecured networks. A consistent approach to device management helps protect your practice from vulnerabilities created by a dispersed workforce.

4.3.3. *Balancing Convenience and Security*

The tradeoff between convenience and security remains a constant concern. The pressure to streamline workflows to save time can sometimes lead to shortcuts, compromising cybersecurity. Examples include bypassing multi-factor authentication for quick access or using unsecured platforms for client communication.

Balancing convenience and security require a thoughtful approach. Identify tools and practices that improve efficiency without exposing your firm to unnecessary risks. For example, password management tools can simplify secure logins, while integrated communication platforms with built-in encryption can provide ease of use and data protection. Regularly reviewing your workflows can help you identify areas where convenience might outweigh security, allowing you to take corrective action.

4.3.4. *Dependence on Third-Party Services*

Small firms often depend on third-party vendors for legal technology solutions, such as document management systems, e-discovery tools, and billing software. While these services can enhance your practice, they also introduce potential vulnerabilities. A breach at a vendor's end could expose your clients' sensitive data, even if you have secured your internal systems. To manage this risk, vet vendors thoroughly before entering into agreements. Review their security policies, inquire about compliance with industry standards, and verify that contracts include data protection and breach notification provisions. Continuously monitor these relationships to confirm that vendors maintain their security practices.

The following section, The Solo and Small Firm Lawyers' Guide to Cybersecurity Risks, explores threats that target small practices and provides strategies for effectively identifying and mitigating them.

5. The Solo and Small Firm Lawyers' Guide to Cybersecurity Risks

While technology offers numerous benefits, it also introduces significant cybersecurity risks that can present particularly challenging situations for solo and small firm attorneys. Safeguarding client confidentiality and maintaining the integrity of legal practices requires understanding these risks and implementing effective security measures.

5.1. Cybersecurity Risks and Challenges

The plight of solo and small firm attorneys in the world of cybersecurity comes down to the fact that they face risks of the same nature and degree as those of larger firms but have fewer available resources to mitigate them. This means that solo and small firm attorneys must look to many of the same solutions available to larger firms and determine a reasonable and viable means for scaling them down to match available resources and address the firm's needs. Cybercriminals frequently target smaller practices, assuming (often correctly) that they lack advanced security measures. Sensitive client information, including personal injury claims, family law matters, and financial data, makes these attorneys prime targets.

The interconnected nature of digital communication and information storage means that a breach in a smaller firm can have a ripple effect, impacting other parties involved in a case. This includes clients, opposing counsel, and even the courts. The potential damage from a cyberattack is not necessarily proportional to the size of the firm or its caseload. That, incidentally, presents a two-way street. A data breach in another firm (larger or smaller) involved in the same case can reveal critical and confidential information from other firms and their clients that impacts every other firm involved in the case as well as the parties.

Blending personal and professional lives in the digital age means that an attorney's personal cyber vulnerabilities can spill over into and impact professional responsibilities. In our experience, such blending, while common to most attorneys, will more likely occur with solo and small firm practitioners, who do not generally have the protections provided by a larger firm with a dedicated IT staff. The results can prove devastating at the personal and professional levels. For instance, a cybercriminal can use a compromised personal email account to phish clients or colleagues, leading to broader security breaches and expanding the damage from personal connections to professional ones. If an attorney uses the same password for multiple accounts, breaching their personal account could also provide cybercriminals access to their professional accounts. Accordingly, an attorney's failure to utilize appropriate protective measures for personal accounts can open the door to professional accounts and systems for cybercriminals (who will follow paths to whatever information and assets they find valuable).

5.2. The Nature of Cybersecurity Threats

Solo and small firm lawyers face many cybersecurity threats, ranging from malware and ransomware attacks to phishing schemes and data breaches. All the threats we face as individuals are also present as professionals. The exposure of our personal also applies to our professional information, including firm data, client data, and confidential client information. Malware, including viruses and spyware, can infiltrate computer systems and mobile devices, compromise sensitive information, and disrupt operations.

5.2.1. *Common Cybersecurity Threats*

Solo and small firm lawyers must contend with various cyber threats, including:

- **Malware & Ransomware:** Malicious software can infiltrate systems, steal data, and disrupt operations. Bad actors use ransomware to encrypt files and then demand payment for decryption keys to release the hostage files. They may also attempt to extort payment in exchange for not releasing stolen data on the internet;
- **Phishing Attacks:** Deceptive emails trick attorneys into revealing sensitive information or downloading malware, potentially compromising client data. Phishing is a "social engineering" tactic; it exploits human behaviors; and
- **Data Breaches:** Unauthorized access to confidential information can occur through hacking, insider threats, and device theft.
  - Even if a firm implements best practices, breaches at third-party service providers, financial institutions, or opposing counsel can still impact the security of information in the hands of those parties.

5.2.2. *The Scope of Cybersecurity Risks for Solo and Small Firm Attorneys*

The cybersecurity risks solo and small firm attorneys face extend beyond their professional responsibilities and encompass personal and professional domains. These multifaceted risks can affect the integrity of legal practices, client relationships, and the personal lives of the attorneys themselves.

5.2.2.1. *Professional Risks*

Cyberattacks can jeopardize the confidentiality, integrity, and availability of client information. Clients entrust their attorneys with sensitive data, including personal identification numbers, financial details, and privileged communications. A breach of this data can have severe legal and ethical implications, potentially leading to disciplinary action regarding one's license to practice law, malpractice claims, loss of client trust, and damage to the attorney's reputation. Additionally, regulatory bodies impose strict data protection requirements; failure to comply can result in hefty fines and sanctions.

Phishing attacks, malware, ransomware, and data breaches present constant threats that solo and small firm attorneys must navigate. A sophisticated phishing attack might mimic an email from a trusted client requesting sensitive information that, once provided, can be used by cybercriminals to facilitate identity theft or fraudulent transactions.

Malware infections, which can occur by clicking on a malicious link or downloading a compromised file, can corrupt files and systems, leading to data loss and operational disruptions. Spyware can silently gather information from the attorney's computer, including keystrokes, passwords, and confidential client records, and send it to cybercriminals.

Ransomware attacks, where criminals encrypt the attorney's data and demand a ransom for its release, can render critical information inaccessible. An example includes the infamous WannaCry ransomware attack, which impacted organizations worldwide, locking users out of their systems and demanding payments in cryptocurrency. These incidents can halt legal proceedings, delay casework, and result in significant financial costs.

Additionally, solo and small firm lawyers often rely on cloud-based services and remote access solutions to manage their caseloads efficiently. While these technologies offer convenience, they also introduce potential vulnerabilities. Inadequate security configurations, weak passwords, and unencrypted data transmissions can expose these systems to unauthorized access and exploitation. For example, if an attorney uses an unsecured WiFi network at a coffee shop to access client files stored in the cloud, a hacker might intercept login information and gain access to that data.

5.2.2.2. *Personal Risks*

Cyber-attacks can target personal devices and accounts, compromising personal information such as social security numbers, bank account details, and private communications. Identity theft is a prevalent risk, where cybercriminals use stolen information to commit fraud, open credit accounts, and drain financial resources. For example, a cybercriminal might use social engineering techniques to gather personal information from social media profiles and then use that data to impersonate the attorney and conduct fraudulent activities.

The stress and anxiety resulting from cyber incidents can affect an attorney's mental health and overall well-being. The pressure to manage a cyberattack, restore compromised systems, and communicate with affected clients can prove overwhelming, particularly for solo practitioners who lack the support of a larger team. Dealing with the aftermath of a data breach could involve notifying clients, cooperating with law enforcement, and handling potentially massive legal and financial ramifications.

Solo and small firm attorneys must proactively address these risks by staying informed about emerging threats, implementing best practices for data protection, seeking professional cybersecurity assistance when needed, and implementing and maintaining robust cybersecurity systems. Doing so can reduce the risk to themselves and their practices.

5.2.3. *Unique Challenges for Solo and Small Firm Lawyers*

Unlike larger firms, solo and small firm attorneys rarely have a dedicated IT staff or the budget to invest in a robust cybersecurity infrastructure. Larger firms with dedicated IT departments and substantial budgets can implement advanced security protocols, conduct regular vulnerability assessments, and respond swiftly to cyber incidents. The lack of significant resources can make it difficult to implement comprehensive security measures, which would better enable solo and small firm practices to mitigate risk or respond effectively to cyber incidents.

Additionally, solo and small firm lawyers often handle many responsibilities beyond practicing law, including managing their business operations. This can lead to cybersecurity taking a backseat to more immediate concerns, increasing the risk of unaddressed vulnerabilities.

Larger firms benefit from economies of scale regarding cybersecurity. They can spread the cost of security measures across a more extensive client base and leverage their size to negotiate better deals with cybersecurity vendors. This advantage allows them to maintain a higher level of protection at a relatively lower cost per client. Larger firms can afford to invest in cutting-edge technology solutions, employee training programs, and comprehensive insurance policies to mitigate cyber risks at levels and in amounts that solo and small firm practices cannot.

Larger firms often have sophisticated document management systems and protocols to safeguard client data. They can also implement multi-layered security measures more efficiently, including encryption, secure access controls, and regular audits to protect data integrity. Solo and small firm lawyers may struggle to maintain rigorous data management practices, increasing the risk of unauthorized access or data breaches.

The increasing use of mobile devices and remote work practices exposes solo and small firm attorneys to additional cybersecurity risks. Mobile devices can be easily lost or stolen, and remote work environments may lack the same level of security as traditional office settings. The security of all devices and remote connections is crucial to mitigating these risks. While this risk applies to all attorneys, large firm IT departments often create better protections respecting the use of mobile devices and the handling of remote access than do solo and small firm practitioners, leaving the solo and small firm attorneys more exposed to risk.

Reliance on third-party service providers and cloud-based solutions also introduces exposure risks. While these solutions offer convenience and efficiency, they can become points of vulnerability if not properly handled. Attorneys must carefully vet their service providers and confirm that they adopt robust security measures to protect sensitive client information. Large firm IT departments and resources leave them better positioned than small firms or solo practices to address these issues.

Client relationships also vary between solo/small firms and larger firms. Solo and small firm lawyers often have closer, more personal relationships with their clients, which can lead to a greater reliance on digital communication and the sharing of sensitive information via email or other online platforms. This reliance on digital communication can more readily expose these lawyers to phishing attacks and other cyber threats to exploit those channels.

The workload and time constraints faced by solo and small firm lawyers can exacerbate their cybersecurity risks. Balancing legal practice with administrative tasks, including cybersecurity, can be overwhelming. This multitasking environment increases the likelihood of overlooked vulnerabilities and neglected cyber hygiene practices.

By prioritizing cybersecurity, seeking affordable yet practical solutions, and staying informed about emerging threats and best practices, solo and small firm lawyers can better protect their clients' confidential information and maintain the integrity of their practices.

5.2.4. *Legal and Ethical Considerations*

Beyond the practical aspects of cybersecurity, solo and small firm lawyers must also consider the legal and ethical implications of failing to protect client information adequately. The American Bar Association's Model Rules of Professional Conduct require lawyers to take reasonable steps to safeguard client data, including implementing measures to protect against unauthorized access and protect the confidentiality of communications.[24]

Failure to adhere to these ethical obligations can result in disciplinary action and damage the lawyer's reputation. Solo and small firm attorneys must stay informed about evolving cybersecurity standards and regulations and make sure that their practices comply. By staying informed about scammers' evolving tactics and adopting proactive measures to safeguard their practices, solo and small firm attorneys can better protect themselves and their clients from these malicious threats.

Attorneys can help protect their practices and the confidentiality of their clients' information by understanding the nature of cyber threats, implementing adequate security measures, and staying informed about legal and ethical obligations.

---

24. *See also* HANDBOOK, Chapter 10, *Lawyers' Professional Responsibility to Provide Data Security.*

6. Cybersecurity Risk Assessment

Start by understanding the risks to your practice. To take meaningful action, you need a process for evaluating and determining how to address those risks. We call this process a cybersecurity risk assessment.

A cybersecurity risk assessment systematically evaluates your systems, processes, and policies to identify vulnerabilities and gauge their potential impact. Proactively uncovering weaknesses helps protect your firm and your clients. Your practice handles sensitive client information, making it an attractive target for cybercriminals. A successful attack could disrupt your work, harm your reputation, and violate your ethical obligations to protect client data. A thorough assessment helps you prioritize your efforts and scale cybersecurity measures appropriately for your practice, focusing on the vulnerabilities most likely to cause harm.

You must conduct risk assessments regularly, with annual reviews as a baseline. You should also evaluate security when significantly changing your technology or operations. Examples include adopting new software, upgrading your network, or transitioning to remote work. By evaluating your security at these key moments, you allow your defenses to evolve with your practice.

This section will guide you through the essentials of cybersecurity risk assessment. Once you understand its purpose and value, you can take decisive steps to protect your practice and maintain your clients' trust.

6.1. Key Steps in Conducting a Cybersecurity Risk Assessment

The following steps outline the core components of conducting a cybersecurity risk assessment. This process lets you see your practice's security posture and create an improvement plan.

Step One: Identify Assets. Begin by taking stock of what you need to protect. Your assets include digital and physical components critical to your operations. Examples include client data, email systems, practice management software, laptops, smartphones, and your network infrastructure.

You will need a comprehensive inventory. Use spreadsheets or asset management software to document each asset's type, location, and importance. Free or low-cost solutions can simplify the process for smaller practices. The inventory should list each asset's purpose and user; it should also identify the security measures currently in place.

Step Two: Identify Threats. Examine the threats that might compromise your assets. Common threats for solo and small firms include phishing attacks, ransomware, unauthorized access, and malware. These threats exploit vulnerabilities and target your systems and data.

Emerging risks due to advancing technology add another layer of complexity. AI and GenAI technologies create new avenues for attacks, such as deepfake phishing schemes and maliciously altered AI-generated content.

Step Three: Identify Vulnerabilities. Vulnerabilities represent weaknesses that could allow a threat to succeed. Examples include outdated software, weak passwords, and the lack of data encryption.

Review your systems for gaps, such as unpatched software or poorly configured firewalls. Tools like Nessus Essentials and Qualys Community Edition can help scan for vulnerabilities without straining your budget. Regularly updating your software and enforcing strong password policies offer simple but effective measures to correct vulnerabilities and reduce exposure.

Step Four: Assess Risk. Assess the likelihood of each threat successfully exploiting a vulnerability and the potential impact if it does. Consider factors such as how often you handle sensitive client data, your reliance on mobile devices, your ability to access data remotely, and whether phishing attempts have frequently targeted your systems.

Risk assessment frameworks, such as NIST's Cybersecurity Framework and AI Risk Management Framework, provide structured methods for evaluating risk. These frameworks can help you quantify risk levels and prioritize actions based on your firm's circumstances.

Step Five: Prioritize Risks. Risks vary in significance. Prioritize based on severity and likelihood to focus on what matters most. High-priority vulnerabilities pose significant dangers to client data and your ability to continue to operate.

Use criteria such as the sensitivity of the asset involved, the potential harm to clients, and the cost of mitigation. By ranking risks, you can effectively allocate resources to address the most pressing concerns first.

6.2. Tools for Conducting a Cybersecurity Audit

After identifying risks and prioritizing vulnerabilities, you need to conduct a cybersecurity audit. The audit allows you to evaluate the current state of your defenses, measure their effectiveness, and uncover hidden weaknesses. Solo and small firm lawyers must carefully select and appropriately scale to size the right tools and methods to mitigate the risks faced by their practices. Choose tools that fit the size and needs of your practice.

6.2.1. *Overview of Affordable and User-Friendly Tools for Solo and Small Firms*

Several tools can work well for smaller practices, offering affordability, simplicity, and effectiveness. They can also provide critical insights into your security posture.

- **Network Vulnerability Scanners:** Tools like Nessus Essentials and OpenVAS allow you to scan your network for potential vulnerabilities. These applications identify weaknesses such as unpatched software or misconfigured settings and provide a roadmap for improvements. They are affordable, easy to use, and effective for small firms.
- **Endpoint Security Solutions:** Endpoint security protects devices like laptops, smartphones, and tablets. Programs such as Malwarebytes and Bitdefender offer strong

protection against malware, phishing attempts, and unauthorized access. Many of these tools are cost-effective and require minimal technical expertise.

- **Cloud-Based Cybersecurity Services:** Cloud services provide real-time protection and monitoring without extensive on-site infrastructure. Services like CrowdStrike and Microsoft Defender for Cloud offer scalable solutions accessible to smaller firms. These tools often include features such as threat detection, data encryption, and automated alerts.

6.2.2. *Manual Versus Automated Assessment Methods*

Choosing between manual and automated methods depends on your practice's complexity and resources. Manual assessments involve reviewing systems and processes by hand, which can work effectively for smaller setups but require substantial time. They work best on tasks such as reviewing password strength or updating software.

Automated tools streamline the process, scanning systems quickly and comprehensively. They can identify issues missed in manual reviews, such as network vulnerabilities or malware. Combining manual and automated methods may offer the best results for many small firms.

6.2.3. *Outsourcing Options and Their Cost Implications*

Outsourcing provides a practical solution if your firm lacks the time or expertise to conduct its own audit. Cybersecurity consultants and managed IT services specialize in auditing and implementing tailored solutions. While outsourcing can involve upfront costs, it often saves time and reduces the risk of missing critical vulnerabilities. As with everything else in this field for the solo and small firm attorney, you have tradeoffs to deal with in your analysis.

Costs vary based on the scope of services. For a basic audit, expect to pay a few hundred to several thousand dollars, depending upon the size of your operation. Comprehensive assessments or ongoing monitoring services will require a more significant investment. When evaluating whether your firm should engage outside assistance for monitoring, weigh the potential cost of a security breach against the cost of the service. With the right tools and approach, conducting a cybersecurity audit becomes manageable, even for the smallest practices.

6.2.4. *Documentation and Reporting*

You need to document the results of your cybersecurity audit so that you can convert your findings into actionable items. Proper documentation enables you to track progress, communicate risks, and create a roadmap for improvement. Maintaining organized records of your assessments also reinforces your firm's commitment to protecting client data. In the event of a cyber incident or regulatory inquiry, these records can demonstrate your diligence and preparedness.

6.2.4.1. *The Importance of Maintaining Detailed Records*

Records of your cybersecurity assessments provide a foundation for decision-making and risk management. They document the evaluation process, findings obtained, and methods selected to address identified risks. Over time, these records also help you identify trends, measure the impact of improvements, and evaluate compliance with ethical and legal obligations. Conversely, neglecting documentation can lead to repeated mistakes, overlooked vulnerabilities, and inefficiencies in addressing risks. Keeping detailed records enables you to allocate your efforts more effectively. As these risk assessments identify the firm's security weaknesses, they constitute high-value information to cybercriminals. Accordingly, you must handle that documentation as the firm's highly sensitive and confidential information.

6.2.4.2. *Suggested Format for Risk Assessment Reports*

A well-structured report makes your findings clear and actionable. You may want to use the following format or one similar to it:

- **Executive Summary:** Provide a concise assessment overview highlighting key findings, significant risks, and overall conclusions. This summary should give decision-makers a snapshot of the audit's results.
- **Identified Risks and Vulnerabilities:** Detail the risks discovered during the assessment. Include descriptions of each vulnerability, its location, and its potential impact. Organize these findings by priority to emphasize the most critical issues.
- **Recommendations for Mitigation:** Provide clear, practical steps to address each identified risk. Specify actions such as software updates, policy changes, or adopting new security tools. Assign timelines and responsibilities for accountability.

6.2.4.3. *Tools for Report Generation and Documentation*

Several tools can simplify the process of creating and maintaining risk assessment reports. These tools help organize data, standardize reporting formats, and track progress over time. Examples include:

- **Spreadsheets and Templates:** Programs like Microsoft Excel or Google Sheets allow you to create customizable templates for organizing findings and recommendations.
- **Cybersecurity Audit Software:** Tools such as Nessus or Qualys help scan for vulnerabilities and generate detailed reports, including prioritized recommendations.
- **Project Management Platforms:** Task management platforms like Trello or Asana can track the implementation of mitigation measures. These tools allow you to assign tasks, set deadlines, and monitor progress.

The following subsection illustrates these concepts through a case study of a cybersecurity audit for a small law firm.

6.2.4.4. *Case Study: Sample Cybersecurity Audit for a Small Law Firm*

Seeing a cybersecurity audit in action can help bring the process to life. This case study outlines the steps a hypothetical small law firm takes to conduct a cybersecurity audit, identify vulnerabilities, and develop an actionable mitigation plan. Studying this example can help you better understand how to apply these procedures to your own practice effectively.

Step-by-Step Example of an Audit

1. **Preparation and Asset Identification**
   The firm began preparing for the audit by completing an inventory of its assets. This included client data stored on-site and in a cloud-based practice management system, computers, a shared office network, and employee smartphones used for work. The audit documented each asset, noting its purpose, importance, and security measures in effect respecting that asset.
2. **Identifying Threats**
   The firm then identified potential threats, including common risks such as phishing, ransomware, and unauthorized access. The team also recognized emerging threats related to using artificial intelligence tools for document drafting and analysis. These tools require special attention due to the sensitive data they handle.
3. **Identifying Vulnerabilities**
   Using a combination of automated and manual methods, the firm uncovered several vulnerabilities:
   - Outdated antivirus software on two employee laptops.
   - Weak passwords used for cloud storage accounts.
   - Lack of multi-factor authentication on the firm's email system.
   - Poor network configuration, leaving the office WiFi open to unauthorized access.
4. **Assessing Risk**
   The firm evaluated the likelihood of an attack and the potential impact of each vulnerability. For example, it deemed weak passwords on cloud storage accounts high-risk due to the sensitive client data stored there. The outdated antivirus software posed a medium risk, as it could allow malware to spread to other systems.
5. **Prioritizing Risks**
   The team prioritized addressing high-risk vulnerabilities first. This included immediately strengthening password policies, requiring multi-factor authentication, and securing the office WiFi with a strong password. It deferred action on medium and low-risk vulnerabilities for correction in the near future.

Action Plan for Mitigation

The firm's action plan included the following steps:

- **Strengthening Passwords:** Implemented a firm-wide password manager to generate and store strong, unique passwords for all accounts.
- **Enabling Multi-Factor Authentication:** This feature adds a second layer of security for email and cloud storage accounts, reducing the risk of unauthorized access.
- **Updating Software:** Updated antivirus software across all devices and enabled automatic antivirus updates for all systems.
- **Securing the Network:** Reconfiguration of the office WiFi network to require a strong password and limit access to authorized devices. [**Note:** An even better approach would have included setting up a second WiFi guest network for the office for use by clients, opposing counsel, collaborating counsel, court reporters, etc., limiting access to the primary network to law firm employees.]
- **Employee Training:** The firm set up a short training session for attorneys and staff on recognizing phishing emails and maintaining good cybersecurity hygiene.

This example highlights how even a small firm with limited resources can conduct a comprehensive cybersecurity audit and create an effective mitigation plan. The following subsection explores the challenges solo and small firms may encounter during this process and provides strategies for overcoming them. Understanding these obstacles enables you to approach your cybersecurity efforts confidently.

6.2.4.5. *Challenges in Conducting Risk Assessments*

The case study illustrates how a cybersecurity audit can uncover vulnerabilities and lead to actionable solutions. However, conducting a risk assessment presents its own challenges. Solo and small firms often face obstacles that can make this process seem extremely difficult.

6.2.4.6. *Limited Technical Knowledge or Resources*

Many solo and small-firm lawyers lack specialized technical expertise. Unlike larger firms with dedicated IT departments, these practices often rely on basic tools and limited support, using the "do-it-yourself" approach to tech support. Understanding technical jargon, configuring systems securely, and interpreting assessment results can feel intimidating, particularly to those unfamiliar with technology.

To mitigate this effect, focus on user-friendly tools designed for non-technical users. Resources such as online tutorials, webinars, and guides from trusted cybersecurity organizations can help bridge the knowledge gap. If feasible, consider enlisting external support for complex tasks like vulnerability scanning and proper network configuration.

6.2.4.7. *Balancing Cost and Effectiveness*

Budget constraints present another common challenge. Cybersecurity tools and services can range from easily affordable to prohibitively expensive. You must determine which investments provide the best value for your firm with the least compromise to security.

Start by prioritizing the most critical risks and addressing them with cost-effective solutions. Free or low-cost tools, such as open-source vulnerability scanners and essential endpoint protection software, can deliver significant improvements. When outsourcing, compare quotes and seek providers who specialize in serving small businesses or law firms. The process of identifying the proper corrective action, the best tools to use to mitigate risk, and scaling risk mitigation to fit your firm properly requires considerable effort and benefits from substantial expertise. We do not suggest that you cannot do it all yourself, but you will benefit from getting some expert help, particularly the first time you do it.

6.2.4.8. *Overcoming Resistance to Change*

Change can prove challenging, particularly when it disrupts familiar workflows. Employees may resist adopting new practices, such as using a password manager or enabling multifactor authentication. This reaction can come from various sources, such as fear of change (intimidation) or inconvenience, both in learning the new requirements and applying them. Most of us do not want to take more time to do the same thing.

Resistance can hinder the implementation of necessary and important security measures. Education and communication provide the best approaches to overcoming this challenge. Explain the need for the changes and how they protect the firm and its clients. Include a discussion of the risks of not using cybersecurity risk mitigation. Require training so everyone understands how to use the new tools and follow the updated protocols. Use the training to build a case for using the new procedures. Reinforce the importance of cybersecurity as a shared responsibility within the practice.

By addressing these challenges, solo and small firms can navigate the complexities of cybersecurity risk assessments.

6.3. Best Practices for Solo and Small Firms

Following best practices can strengthen your defenses and help you manage risks effectively. A proactive climate and informed approach can help your firm build resilience against cyber threats.

6.3.1. *Regular Updates and Training for All Team Members*

Keeping everyone in your firm informed and prepared helps minimize cybersecurity risks. Regularly update your team on the latest threats and confirm that they understand their role in protecting sensitive data.

Periodic training sessions can focus on recognizing phishing attempts, using password managers, and following safe practices when working remotely. To address vulnerabilities promptly, make software and system updates routine tasks. Scheduling these updates and training sessions reduces the risk of lapses that could expose your firm to increased risk.

6.3.2. *Leveraging Third-Party Expertise Where Necessary*

When technical challenges exceed your in-house expertise, engage outside professionals to provide the support you need. Cybersecurity consultants and managed IT service providers can help with vulnerability assessments, network monitoring, and incident response planning.

When choosing a third-party provider, look for those specializing in small businesses, particularly those who work with small law firms. These providers often offer tailored services at a more accessible cost, allowing you to receive practical solutions without unnecessary complexity.

6.3.3. *Staying Informed About Emerging Cybersecurity Threats*

To protect your firm, you must stay informed about new threats and technological advancements. Subscribing to industry newsletters, attending webinars, and participating in professional associations can help keep you current. Focus on learning about risks specific to small firms and the legal industry. Understanding how emerging threats like AI-driven scams or sophisticated ransomware schemes might impact your practice helps you anticipate and address vulnerabilities proactively.

Key takeaways from this section include the importance of regularly conducting assessments, maintaining detailed records, and fostering a culture of vigilance. Do not think of risk assessment as a one-time task; it is an ongoing process that evolves with your technology, your practice, and the cybersecurity landscape.

6.3.4. *Risk Mitigation for Solo and Small Firm Lawyers*

While cybersecurity challenges can seem daunting, technology offers solutions to help solo and small firm lawyers protect their data. Cybersecurity software, such as antivirus programs, firewalls, and intrusion detection systems, help protect against threats. Additionally, secure cloud services offer a convenient and reliable way to store and back up data.

Legal-specific technology solutions, such as practice management software with built-in security features, can also enhance cybersecurity efforts. These tools often include encrypted communication channels, secure document storage, and audit trails to track access and changes to sensitive information.

6.4. Key Strategies for Mitigating Cybersecurity Risks

Understand that risk will continue no matter what you do. You can never escape risk; you can only mitigate it. This section helps you do that.

- o **Develop a Cybersecurity Policy**
  This section focuses on developing a cybersecurity policy that sets clear expectations, procedures, and best practices for protecting the firm's data. It should include:
  - Password management requirements,

- Data encryption protocols,
- Acceptable use policies for firm devices and software,
- Email and communication security measures,
- Incident response procedures.

To remain effective, cybersecurity policies must be consistently followed and regularly updated. Regular reviews help adapt to evolving threats, and every firm member must understand their role in maintaining security.

To illustrate best practices, the table below outlines key cybersecurity policy components and contrasts basic and comprehensive security measures:

Cybersecurity Policy Levels: Basic vs. Comprehensive Practices

Policy Component	Basic Policy	Comprehensive Practices
Password Management	Require strong passwords	Enforce password manager use & multi-factor authentication (MFA)
Data Encryption	Encrypt stored files	Use end-to-end encryption and secure cloud storage
Acceptable Use Policy	Limit access to sensitive data	Enforce role-based access and device monitoring
Email Security	Enable spam filtering	Use email encryption and phishing detection training
Incident Response	Assign a point of contact for security issues	Develop a formal incident response plan (IRP) with clear protocols

- **Education and Training**[25]

Education and training provide some of the most effective ways to combat cybersecurity threats. Regular training sessions can help everyone in the firm know the best practices for maintaining cybersecurity. As human error often causes cybersecurity breaches, regular training and awareness programs for all staff members help reduce risk.

Training should cover topics such as the following non-exhaustive list:

- **Phishing and Social Engineering:** Educate employees on recognizing phishing emails and other social engineering tactics cybercriminals use to access sensitive information.
- **Password Management:** Emphasize the importance of using strong, unique passwords/passphrases for all accounts and utilizing a password manager to store and manage them securely.
- **Device Security:** Instruct staff on securing their devices, including enabling auto-lock features, using strong passwords/passphrases, and regularly updating software to patch vulnerabilities.

25. *See infra* Section 7, Data Protection Training. *See also* HANDBOOK, Chapter 12, *Get SMART on Data Protection by Creating a Culture of Security Awareness.*

Simulated phishing exercises can help identify vulnerabilities and reinforce training. Creating a culture of cybersecurity awareness helps every team member understand their role in protecting the firm's data. Regular training sessions and updates on the latest cybersecurity threats can help employees remain vigilant and informed.

- **Implement Strong Password Requirements**

  Weak passwords offer a common entry point for cyber attackers. To mitigate this risk, implement a robust password policy. A strong password policy requires passwords at least 12 characters long, including upper and lower-case letters, numbers, and special characters. Longer passphrases provide more protection than passwords. Most password protocols allow passphrases. To create a strong passphrase, follow these rules (or let your password manager do the work):

  - Avoid choosing a popular phrase or saying unless you modify it significantly.
  - Stay away from song lyrics.
  - Include nonsense words.
  - Make the phrase at least 15 characters long.
  - Five words beat four; six words beat five. Longer is stronger.
  - Include symbols and numbers, along with upper- and lower-case letters.
  - Include random words.
  - Use a different phrase for each account.

  Regularly updating passwords at intervals, such as every 60 or 90 days, reduces the risk of unauthorized access. Password management software can help create, securely store, and manage complex passwords. Multi-factor authentication (MFA) adds an extra layer of security by requiring a password and a second factor, such as a smartphone app or biometric verification.

- **Utilize Encryption**

  Encryption provides an essential tool for protecting sensitive data. It converts data into a coded format that requires the correct decryption key to unlock. Encrypting sensitive data protects it from unauthorized access. Law firms should require encryption for data at rest (stored data) and in transit (data in the transmission process over networks). Key strategies include:

  - **Full Disk Encryption:** Encrypt the entire hard drive of computers and mobile devices to protect data in case of theft or loss.
  - **Email Encryption:** Use secure email encryption services to protect confidential communication with clients and colleagues.
  - **Secure File Sharing:** Implement secure file-sharing platforms that offer end-to-end encryption to protect the confidentiality of shared documents.

  Secure communication tools offering end-to-end encryption, for client interactions, such as encrypted messaging apps and secure video conferencing platforms, can further enhance data protection. Implementing these encryption practices can mean that even if intercepted, data remains unreadable and secure. You garner additional risk reduction by transmitting the decryption key for encrypted files to authorized users separately from the encrypted file or access to the encrypted file.

Lawyers should encrypt emails containing confidential information and stored data on computers, mobile devices, and the cloud.

- **Regular Software Updates**

  Cybercriminals often exploit vulnerabilities in software to gain unauthorized access to systems and data. To maintain security and reduce that exposure, keep all software, including operating systems, antivirus programs, browsers, and applications, up to date. Law firms should establish a patch management process that includes:

  - **Automated Updates:** Enable automatic updates for operating systems, applications, and security software to encourage the timely installation of patches.
  - **Vulnerability Scanning:** Regularly scan systems for vulnerabilities and promptly address any identified issues.
  - **Third-Party Software Management:** Monitor and update third-party software used by the firm to minimize security risks.

- **Backup Data**

  Regular data backups make it more likely that a firm can recover from cyber incidents such as ransomware attacks or system failures. An automated backup system that runs several times daily consistently backs up data. Make multiple backups, not just one. To maximize protection, keep some backups in the office and others stored in secure locations, such as off-site facilities or encrypted cloud services, to protect them from physical theft or damage. Periodically test backup procedures and restoration processes to verify that they work and can quickly and efficiently restore data if necessary.

- **Develop an Incident Response Plan**[26]

  While proactive measures can mitigate your risks, they cannot provide immunity to cyberattacks. Lawyers often function as disaster planners for their clients and should also do so concerning their own cyber risk. Assume the worst and prepare to deal with it!

  An incident response plan provides a structured approach to managing and mitigating the impact of cybersecurity ievents. A well-defined incident response plan enables the firm to respond quickly and effectively to cybersecurity incidents and data breaches. Key components of an incident response plan include:

  - **Incident Identification:** Establish procedures for detecting and reporting cybersecurity incidents.
  - **Notice to Insurers:** Document clear timelines and procedures for notifying insurance carriers, including malpractice and cyber (if the firm has purchased cyber coverage). The cyber insurer may provide incident response services.[27]

---

26. *See also* HANDBOOK, Chapter 13, *Achieving Preparedness through Standards and Planning & Best Practices for Incident Response.*

27. *See infra* Section 8, Cyber Insurance Primer for Solo and Small Firm Attorneys; *see also* HANDBOOK, Chapter 14, *Cyber Insurance for Law Firms and Legal Organizations.*

- **Containment and Mitigation:** Define steps to contain the breach, minimize damage, and prevent further unauthorized access.
- **Eradication and Recovery:** Outline processes for removing threats, restoring affected systems, and recovering lost data.
- **Communication Plan:** Develop a communication strategy for notifying clients, stakeholders, and regulatory authorities, if necessary.
- **Post-Incident Review:** Conduct a thorough review of the incident to identify weaknesses and implement improvements to prevent future breaches.

Establish relationships with cybersecurity professionals who can assist in investigating and resolving incidents (and have those professionals preapproved for payment under your insurance coverage). Review and update the incident response plan regularly to address evolving threats and lessons learned from past incidents suffered by your firm and others.

- **Employ Multi-Factor Authentication (MFA)**

  Multi-factor authentication (MFA) provides an additional layer of security by requiring users to verify their identity through multiple means before gaining access to accounts and systems. By implementing MFA, law firms can significantly reduce the risk of unauthorized access, even if login credentials are compromised. Typical forms of MFA include:

  - **SMS or Authenticator App Codes:** Users receive a one-time code via text message or an authenticator app, which is required in addition to their password.
  - **Biometric Verification:** Methods such as fingerprint or facial recognition add an extra layer of security for account access.
  - **Hardware Tokens:** Physical devices that generate time-sensitive codes provide additional security measures.

- **Secure Mobile Devices**

  With the increasing use of mobile devices for legal work, firms must establish and maintain the security of that technology. Implement policies requiring the use of strong passwords or biometrics to unlock devices. Enable remote wipe capabilities to erase data on a lost or stolen device. If available, turn on location services or the equivalent for each device. Verify that all mobile devices have up-to-date security software and encrypted storage. Ensure that all devices install system updates in a timely manner. Require the use of secure VPNs when accessing the firm's network remotely.

- **Eschew Public Networks**

  Although convenient, public WiFi networks pose significant risks to data and privacy. Often unsecured, these networks make it easier for cybercriminals to intercept data transmitted over them. Criminals frequently utilize a "man-in-the-middle" attack, where the attacker can eavesdrop on the connection between your device and the internet. This vulnerability can expose sensitive information, such as login credentials, personal data, and confidential communications, to unauthorized parties.

Using your own cellular hotspot instead of connecting to public WiFi limits that exposure. Cellular networks generally provide more security and encryption than public WiFi networks, reducing the risk of interception. Setting up a personal hotspot on your mobile device lets you create a private, secure connection for your laptop or tablet.

If you must use a public network, use it with a virtual private network (VPN). A VPN encrypts your internet traffic, creating a secure tunnel between your device and the VPN server. This encryption means your data should remain unreadable to an attacker, even if intercepted. VPNs can also mask your IP address, adding a layer of privacy by preventing websites and services from determining your location or tracking your online activities.

When selecting a VPN, choose a reputable provider with strong encryption standards and a "no-logs" policy to protect privacy respecting your browsing history. Additionally, enable multi-factor authentication (MFA) for your VPN account to add another layer of security.

- **Implement Robust Access Controls**

  Controlling access to sensitive data and systems helps minimize the risk of unauthorized access. Law firms should implement robust access control measures, including:

  - **Role-based Access Control (RBAC).** This control assigns access permission based on job roles and responsibilities, so that employees have only the data and systems necessary for their work.
  - **Least Privilege Principle:** This control limits user access rights to the minimum necessary to perform their job functions, reducing the potential impact of compromised accounts.
  - **Regular Access Reviews:** Periodically review access permissions to verify they remain appropriate, and revoke access for employees who no longer require it.

- **Conduct Regular Security Audits**

  Regular security audits help identify vulnerabilities and assess the effectiveness of existing cybersecurity measures. Internal and external audits allow for a comprehensive evaluation of the firm's defenses. Audits should include penetration testing to simulate attacks and uncover weaknesses. Based on audit findings, adjust your policies, procedures, and technical controls to enhance security.

- **Utilize Managed Security Services**

  Partnering with a managed security service provider (MSSP) can effectively enhance cybersecurity for solo and small firm law practices. MSSPs offer a range of services, including:

  - **24/7 Monitoring:** Continuous monitoring of networks and systems to detect and respond to threats in real-time.
  - **Threat Intelligence:** Access to up-to-date threat intelligence and expertise to stay ahead of emerging cyber threats.

- **Incident Response:** Professional incident response services handle security breaches and mitigate damage.
- **Compliance Assistance:** Support in maintaining compliance with industry regulations and standards.

By leveraging the expertise of MSSPs, law firms can strengthen their cybersecurity posture without requiring extensive in-house resources.

6.4.1. *SCENARIO*

Incident:

An attorney receives an email that appears to be from a trusted client. The email contains an attachment labeled "Updated Contract–Urgent." Without suspicion, the attorney downloads and opens the file. Immediately, the computer freezes, and a pop-up message appears:

"We have encrypted your files. Pay 5 Bitcoin within 48 hours to restore access."

Immediate Response Actions in Practice:

1. **Identify the Breach:**
    - The attorney recognizes the ransomware message and determines that the firm cannot access its files.
    - An inspection of additional devices reveals that the law firm cannot access its shared drive.
2. **Disconnect Affected Systems:**
    - The attorney unplugs the computer from the network to prevent further spread.
    - The firm contacts its IT consultant to assess the potential compromise of other systems.
3. **Change Passwords and Revoke Access:**
    - Using an uncompromised device, the firm immediately changes login credentials for cloud services and email accounts.
    - The firm revokes administrative access for potentially compromised accounts.
4. **Notify Necessary Parties:**
    - The attorney notifies the firm's insurance broker or carriers as required by the policies.
    - After assessing the situation with the assistance of a cybersecurity expert, the firm gives required notices such as:
        - Reporting the incident to the state bar ethics counsel to comply with applicable professional responsibility rules;
        - Notifying clients of potential delays in pending cases; and

5. **Engage Professional Support**
    - The firm hires a cybersecurity expert to investigate the attack and determine if it involved data exfiltration.
    - The expert confirms that the attack did not contaminate backups and that they do not contain the malware that encrypted the files, and then restores data from offline backups and reinforces security measures.
    - A forensic analysis identifies vulnerabilities and strengthens defenses against future threats.

Outcome:

Because the attorney acted quickly, the ransomware did not spread beyond the initially affected system. The firm recovered data from backups without paying the ransom, minimizing downtime. To prevent future incidents, the firm implemented a cybersecurity policy, including email filtering, staff training, and multi-factor authentication.

6.4.1.1. *Key Lesson: A rapid and strategic response can prevent a temporary disruption from becoming a catastrophic loss*

Post-Incident Recovery

Every incident provides an opportunity to improve security. After an attack:

- Conduct a post-mortem analysis: What went wrong? How did the breach occur?
- Update security protocols to address vulnerabilities.
- Review staff training to prevent similar incidents.
- If necessary, notify clients and regulators transparently and ethically.

A firm that learns from an incident becomes stronger, more resilient, and better prepared for future threats.

Note: Don't wait for it to happen to you! Learn from the mistakes of others. Keep current with information about cyberattacks and anticipate the one targeting your firm.

Summary of Key Takeaways

1. Solo and small firm lawyers must engage in cybersecurity preparedness.
2. A strong cybersecurity policy provides clear guidance and expectations.
3. Essential security measures reduce risks and protect client data.
4. Incident response planning enables quick and effective action during a breach.
5. Post-incident reviews strengthen defenses and prevent future attacks.

Cybersecurity requires continuous effort; one-and-done will not cut it. Proactive measures help prevent most threats and minimize damage when incidents occur. As technology evolves, so do cyber threats. Regularly update cybersecurity policies, train staff, and stay informed about emerging risks. Preparedness provides protection. Stay vigilant and remain secure.

7. Data Protection Training: Building a Culture of Awareness

Law firms, especially solo and small practices, face a high risk of cyberattacks. According to the 2023 ABA Cybersecurity TechReport, over 25% of law firms reported a cybersecurity breach.[28] A single mistake, such as clicking a malicious link or using a weak password, can jeopardize the entire firm. Technology cannot provide complete protection; in fact, complete protection, like perfection, does not exist. The best defense comes from fostering a culture of cybersecurity awareness, where every lawyer and staff member takes responsibility for safeguarding sensitive information.

Protecting client data and maintaining a firm's integrity requires creating a cybersecurity-aware culture. Human error remains a leading cause of cybersecurity failures. To build a secure environment, firms must instill a mindset where every employee understands the risks and actively works to mitigate them.

Leadership plays a critical role in establishing cybersecurity awareness. When firm leaders prioritize security, employees follow their example. Security-conscious behavior should become routine. Protecting client confidentiality goes beyond best practices; as an ethical obligation, it requires constant vigilance.

Awareness alone does not suffice. Cybersecurity must become second nature. To reduce risk, employees should develop proactive habits, such as verifying email senders and locking screens. Security practices should integrate seamlessly into daily workflows, reinforcing safe behavior at every level. A firm committed to a security-first mindset transforms cybersecurity from an obligation into a routine practice.

7.1. Data Protection and Training Topics

To translate awareness into action, firms must implement structured cybersecurity training programs that equip employees with practical skills. Training should be practical, relevant, and ongoing to help lawyers and staff recognize and prevent cyber threats. A well-structured program helps employees develop habits that reduce risk and strengthen the firm's defenses.

Successful cybersecurity training begins with understanding key threats. Employees must recognize phishing and social engineering tactics, including fraudulent emails, fake websites, and impersonation attempts. Training programs should provide them with the information and skills to do that. Secure password management remains critical. Employees must employ strong, unique passwords. Firms should require multi-factor authentication

28. John Simek, *2023 Cybersecurity TechReport*, Am. Bar Ass'n (Dec. 18, 2023), https://www.americanbar.org/groups/law_practice/resources/tech-report/2023/2023-cybersecurity-techreport/?login.

for added protection. Sensitive client data requires encryption, password protection, secure storage, and controlled access. Safe communication practices, such as encrypted messaging and verifying client identities, help prevent breaches. Remote work security also demands attention. Employees must understand the risks of public WiFi, unencrypted connections, and using personal devices for client-related work. Training sessions should address all of these topics. A well-trained team bolsters the firm's defense against cyber threats.

Make training frequent and engaging. A single session does not provide sufficient preparation. Regular training helps make cybersecurity a priority and impresses your staff with its importance. Hands-on exercises like simulated phishing attacks help employees recognize real threats. Interactive formats, including videos, workshops, and gamification, make training more effective and memorable. Cybersecurity training should feel like a natural part of daily work, not an obligation.

Cybersecurity awareness begins on day one. New hires must immediately understand the firm's policies and security expectations. Regular training refreshers prevent complacency and prepare employees for evolving threats. A well-maintained cybersecurity knowledge base gives employees quick access to critical information.

7.2. Implementing Practical Data Protection Measures

Training equips employees with knowledge, but firms must also adopt and enforce strong security measures to protect client data. Cybersecurity extends beyond technology. It requires clear policies, restricted access, proper training, and ongoing education. By implementing practical security practices, firms can reduce risk and respond effectively to potential threats.

Firms need to control access to sensitive data. Employees should follow the "least privilege" principle, accessing only the information necessary for their work. Password managers and multi-factor authentication add security layers, helping to prevent unauthorized access. Role-based permissions limit employees to viewing documents relevant to their tasks, minimizing risk and reducing the impact of a potential breach.

Beyond access controls, firms must establish clear and enforceable document and data security policies. All sensitive documents require encryption; firms should never store or transmit unprotected client data. Secure file-sharing tools must replace email attachments, which pose unnecessary risks. Firms should also implement strict data retention and disposal policies, keeping only necessary records and securely discarding outdated files. Protecting client data requires continuous diligence during representation and throughout the entire data lifecycle.

You cannot overlook mobile device security. Most lawyers work from mobile devices, making them prime targets for cyberattacks. Firms should enforce mobile security policies that require encrypted storage, remote wipe capabilities, and strong authentication for accessing client data. If employees use their own devices for work, they must conform to the firm's mobile device policy.

Even with strong security measures, breaches can still occur. Employees must know how to respond when they suspect a security incident. Encouraging prompt reporting and assuring employees that reporting suspicious activity will not lead to harsh consequences fosters a proactive security culture. Firms should establish clear escalation procedures, outlining whom to contact first and what immediate actions to take. Role-playing exercises and simulated attacks help employees prepare for actual incidents. A firm that responds swiftly minimizes damage, while hesitation risks everything.

Lawyers do not have to manage cybersecurity alone. Many resources can help firms stay informed and proactive. The ABA Cybersecurity Legal Task Force provides guidance tailored to legal professionals. Many state bar associations offer best practices and ethics guidance on cybersecurity. Free and paid training tools can supplement firm programs and update employees on evolving threats. Staying informed has never been easier, and taking advantage of these resources strengthens a firm's security posture.

7.2.1. *Steps to Maintain a Long-Term Culture of Awareness*

i. **Train consistently.** Regular training sessions make cybersecurity a priority and help employees stay aware of emerging threats.
ii. **Lead by example.** Leadership must prioritize cybersecurity and demonstrate best practices in daily work. When leaders take security seriously, employees follow.
iii. **Make cybersecurity part of daily routines.** Secure behaviors—such as locking screens, verifying email senders, and using strong passwords—should become second nature.

A firm that prioritizes cybersecurity thrives. Stay informed. Stay secure.

8. Cyber Insurance Primer for Solo and Small Firm Attorneys

8.1. Understanding the Importance of Protecting Your Practice

Cyber threats present an ever-growing concern for solo and small firm attorneys who handle sensitive client data daily. While large law firms may have dedicated IT departments and cybersecurity policies, smaller practices often operate with limited resources, making them prime targets for cyberattacks. That makes cyber insurance a necessary consideration for legal professionals seeking to mitigate the financial risks associated with data breaches, ransomware, and other cyber incidents.

8.2. What Does Cyber Insurance Do?

Cyber insurance refers to a specialized insurance policy designed to protect businesses from the financial costs and risks associated with cyberattacks, data breaches, and other cyber-related incidents. It can help cover the costs of cyber incidents, including legal fees, notification expenses, and even ransom payments in ransomware attacks. While general liability insurance policies often exclude cyber-related losses, cyber insurance specifically addresses risks tied to data security, regulatory compliance, and digital operations.

8.3. What Does Cyber Insurance Cover?

Cyber insurance policies can vary widely, but generally, they provide coverage for the areas listed below. Cyber insurance coverage should be coordinated closely with other insurance policies, such as malpractice coverage, to avoid gaps and overlaps contributing to coverage disputes.

8.3.1. *Cyber Insurance First-Party Coverage*

First-party coverage protects the law firm directly from losses incurred due to a cyber event. Key areas include:

- **Data Breach Response:** Costs associated with responding to a data breach, including notification expenses, credit monitoring services for affected clients, forensic investigation expenses, and public relations efforts to manage reputational damage.
- **Business Interruption:** Compensation for lost income and additional expenses incurred due to a cyber incident that disrupts normal business operations. This can include losses from downtime, data recovery, and the costs of implementing interim solutions to maintain operations.
- **Cyber Extortion (Ransomware):** Coverage for ransom payments and associated costs in the event of a ransomware attack. This can also include expenses related to negotiating with cyber extortionists and implementing measures to prevent future attacks.
- **Data Restoration:** Expenses related to restoring or recovering lost or damaged data due to a cyber incident. This might cover the costs of data recovery services, hardware replacement, and software reinstallation.
- **Reputation Management:** The costs of crisis management services to help restore the firm's reputation after a cyber incident. These can include media relations, advertising, and communication strategies to reassure clients and stakeholders.

8.3.2. *Cyber Insurance Third-Party Coverage*

Third-party coverage protects against claims made by clients or regulatory agencies due to a cyber incident affecting the firm. This includes:

- **Legal Defense:** This covers the costs of legal representation and defense in case of lawsuits or regulatory actions arising from a cyber incident. It can also cover attorney fees, court costs, and settlements or judgments related to the breach.
- **Liability Coverage:** Compensation for damages or settlements resulting from lawsuits filed by clients, partners, or third parties affected by a data breach or cyber-attack. This can include claims of negligence, breach of contract, and violations of privacy laws.

- **Network Security Liability:** Covers lawsuits related to unauthorized access, transmission of malware, or failure to secure confidential data.
- **Regulatory Actions:** Insurance does not generally cover fines or penalties imposed by regulatory bodies due to noncompliance with data protection laws and regulations. However, it may include the cost of responding to regulatory investigations.

8.3.3. *How Much Coverage Do You Need*

Choosing the right amount of cyber insurance coverage involves assessing several factors specific to your practice:

- **Data Sensitivity and Volume:** Evaluate the types and volumes of data you handle. The more sensitive and extensive the data, the higher the potential impact of a breach, necessitating more comprehensive coverage. Consider the types of client information, legal documents, and financial records stored digitally by your firm.
- **Risk Exposure:** Consider your firm's exposure to cyber risks. Factors such as technology use, the number of employees, and the nature of your practice can influence your risk profile. For example, a firm specializing in intellectual property law may have different risk considerations than a firm focusing on family law. Your firm will have a higher risk level if you handle personally identifiable information (PII), protected health information (PHI), or financial data; the more sensitive the data, the greater the potential liability.
- **Size of Your Practice:** Solo practitioners and small firms typically have fewer resources for cybersecurity defenses, increasing their vulnerability. However, they may also have a lower overall exposure than large firms managing thousands of client records.
- **Regulatory Compliance Requirements:** Certain areas of law, such as healthcare or finance, are subject to strict data protection regulations.
- **Potential Business Interruption Costs:** A cyberattack can halt business operations for days or weeks. Consider how much income you'd lose due to cybercriminals compromising your firm's systems. Also, consider how long the incident might impact them.
- **Contractual Obligations:** Some clients require law firms to carry a minimum level of cyber insurance as part of their engagement agreements. Check client contracts for compliance.
- **Financial Impact:** Estimate the potential economic impact of a cyber incident on your practice. This includes direct costs like data recovery and legal fees, and indirect costs such as lost billable hours, client attrition, and reputational damage.

8.4. Availability of and General Requirements to Qualify for Coverage

8.4.1. *Availability*

Many companies offer tailored cyber insurance policies specifically designed for small businesses, including law offices. You should work with an insurance broker specializing in cyber insurance that works with solo and small firm legal practices to find a policy that best meets your practice's unique needs.

8.4.2. *General Requirements*

Insurers typically require businesses to implement specific cybersecurity measures to qualify for cyber insurance coverage. These may include:

- **Risk Assessments:** Conduct regular risk assessments to identify and address potential vulnerabilities in your IT infrastructure.
- **Data Encryption:** Encrypt sensitive data to protect it in transit and at rest.
- **Firewalls and Antivirus Software:** Employ up-to-date firewalls and antivirus software to protect against malware and unauthorized access.
- **Employee Training:** Provide ongoing cybersecurity training to employees to help them know best practices and potential threats, such as phishing and social engineering attacks.
- **Incident Response Plan:** Have a documented incident response plan to quickly and effectively respond to cyber incidents.
- **Regular Updates and Patching:** Regularly update all software and operating systems with the latest security patches.

Meeting these requirements not only helps you qualify for coverage but can also reduce the risk of a cyber incident occurring. Additionally, demonstrating a strong cybersecurity posture may result in lower insurance premiums.

8.5. Key Considerations When Purchasing Cyber Insurance

When evaluating cyber insurance policies, keep these critical factors in mind:

8.5.1. *Exclusions and Limitations*

Not all cyber insurance policies cover the same risks. Typical exclusions may include:

- acts of war or nation-state cyberattacks;
- claims arising from employee negligence or unencrypted devices; and
- prior knowledge of a security vulnerability that wasn't remedied.

8.5.2. *Retroactive Coverage*

Cyber policies generally work prospectively, covering incidents occurring after the policy's effective date. However, some insurers offer retroactive coverage, which protects against later discovered breaches that may have happened before policy inception. Expect a policy with retroactive and prospective coverage to cost more than one with only prospective coverage.

8.5.3. *Legal and Forensic Support*

A good policy should include access to legal counsel and cybersecurity forensic experts to help manage the response to an attack.

8.5.4. *Cost of Premiums*

Premiums for cyber insurance vary based on various factors, including the firm's revenue, data exposure, and existing cybersecurity measures. Insurers may offer discounts for firms that implement strong security practices, such as:

- multi-factor authentication (MFA);
- regular cybersecurity training for staff; and
- encrypted data storage and secure file-sharing platforms.

8.5.5. *Is Cyber Insurance Worth It for Solo and Small Firms?*

While cyber insurance is not legally required for attorneys, the cost of a single cyberattack can far exceed the price of a policy. A 2023 IBM study found that the average cost of a data breach was $4.45 million, with legal and regulatory costs making up a significant portion.[29] IBM's 2025 Cost of Data Breach study reported an increase in the average data breach cost to $5 million.[30]Although smaller firms may not experience losses on that scale, even a minor incident can result in substantial expenses.

When to Consider Buying Cyber Insurance (or acquiring a greater amount of coverage):

- Your firm handles sensitive or regulated client data.
- You rely heavily on cloud-based storage or email communication.
- You lack a dedicated IT security team.
- Your clients require you to have cyber coverage.
- You want financial protection against ransomware attacks and lawsuits.

8.5.6. *When Cyber Insurance May Not Be as Necessary (acquiring a lesser amount of coverage):*

- You have robust cybersecurity measures and minimal online exposure.
- Your firm does not collect or store confidential client data digitally.
- Your existing errors and omissions (E&O) policy already includes adequate cyber liability coverage.

---

29. *IBM Report: Half of Breached Organizations Unwilling to Increase Security Spend Despite Soaring Breach Costs*, Int'l Bus. Machines Corp. (July 24, 2023), https://newsroom.ibm.com/2023-07-24-IBM-Report-Half-of-Breached-Organizations-Unwilling-to-Increase-Security-Spend-Despite-Soaring-Breach-Costs.

30. *Cost of a Data Breach Report 2025*, IBM, https://www.ibm.com/reports/data-breach (last visited Sept. 23, 2025).

8.5.7. *Final Thoughts about Cyber Insurance*

Cyber insurance can provide a critical financial safety net against cyberattacks and data breaches for solo and small firm attorneys. While not every firm may need extensive coverage, it's essential to evaluate risk exposure and consider whether the cost of a policy outweighs the potential financial and reputational damage of an incident. We recommend that all firms acquire a cyber insurance policy and that you focus not on whether to get it but rather on how much protection to acquire.

Before purchasing a policy, carefully review the coverage options, exclusions, and policy limits to confirm that they align with your firm's needs. Investing in proactive cybersecurity measures can reduce your risks and insurance premiums.

By taking a strategic approach, attorneys can protect their practice, clients, and professional reputation in an increasingly digital world.

9. When, Why, and How to Initiate the Cybersecurity Conversation with Your Client

9.1. When an Attorney Should Talk to a Client About Cybersecurity

Because lawyers have an ethical duty to protect client confidentiality, they must make cybersecurity a key part of their discussions with clients from the outset of representation and throughout the attorney-client relationship. We strongly recommend that you include in your written representation agreements with all clients an acknowledgment of these discussions and risk acceptance related to the firm's and the client's use of certain communication technologies.

When discussing cybersecurity issues with a client, you should address several key areas so that the client knows the potential risks and necessary precautions. This discussion should begin with preliminary conversations about the technology you use in your practice and the associated risks.

Cybersecurity discussions should include:

- Conversations introducing the topic of the firm's technology and the associated risk.
- Client responsibilities in securing communications and data.
- Shared understanding of what constitutes a breach and when it requires disclosure.
- How and when you will disclose a cybersecurity incident to a client.

9.1.1. *Preliminary Conversations About Cybersecurity Risks*

When meeting with a new client, include cybersecurity in the discussion of the terms of the engagement, especially if the matter involves highly sensitive information, such as intellectual property, trade secrets, financial records, sensitive personal information, or privileged legal strategy.

Approach the topic with sensitivity and clarity. Ideally, you will reassure clients and prospective clients that you and your firm will handle their information carefully, noting the kinds of proactive measures you take to protect it and keep it secure. The discussion might commence with language like:

> *We understand the security of your information is paramount. To protect your information, we have implemented robust cybersecurity measures, including encryption of all client confidential information stored and transmitted by the firm, regular security training, and monitoring of our systems.*

9.1.2. *Key Topics to Cover in Initial Conversations*

9.1.2.1. *The Technology the Law Firm Uses*

Clients should understand how the firm stores, transmits, and protects their information. You should explain (accurately and consistently):

- **Email Encryption:** Whether the firm uses end-to-end email encryption and whether and how clients should use encryption when sending sensitive materials.
- **Secure Portals for Document Sharing:** Many firms use platforms like Clio, NetDocuments, or iManage to share files securely instead of using standard email attachments.
- **Video Conferencing Security:** If using Zoom, Microsoft Teams, Google Meet, or similar platforms, attorneys should employ password protection for meetings and explain to clients the importance of avoiding public WiFi networks when joining.
- **Cloud-Based Case Management:** If the firm stores client files in the cloud, you should disclose the security measures in place (e.g., multi-factor authentication and encrypted storage).

Example Attorney Statement:

> *"Our firm uses encrypted email and a secure client portal to share documents safely. This helps protect your sensitive information as we exchange information with you. You should use these tools when you send confidential information to us. These tools lessen the risk of someone intercepting the information. We also encourage you to avoid using public WiFi when you send us confidential information and when you video conference with us."*

9.1.2.2. *Potential Risks of Using Certain Communication Methods*

Clients may not realize that their communication practices can introduce vulnerabilities and risks of a data breach. You should discuss:

- **Email:** Email carries many risks inherent to its operation. Email accounts can be hacked. Most email is not secure. If a client uses email to communicate with their lawyer, they should try to use a secure email system. Consider recommending clients use encrypted emails for sensitive information (check out Proton Mail) or your firm's client portal (highly recommended).

   - **Dangers of Business Clients Using Personal Email Accounts:** Business clients should avoid using personal email accounts (particularly those with weak security) for legal matters. They should ensure that their work email has robust security protections.
   - **Dangers of Personal (Non-Business) Clients Using Work or Public Email Accounts:** When lawyers are engaged for personal matters, clients should avoid using work-related email, as their employer may have access to the account. Providers can generally access free public email accounts such as Yahoo, Gmail, Apple, etc. While such accounts work well for regular communications, such as to friends and family, you should avoid them when sending confidential communications. Use our client portal or a secure form of email, like Proton, to communicate with our office.
- **Risks of Text Messaging:** While convenient, standard text messages often travel unencrypted, making them vulnerable to interception. Secure messaging apps (e.g., Signal or WhatsApp with encryption enabled) offer safer alternatives.
- **Social Engineering and Phishing Attacks:** You should warn the client about emails or phone calls requesting sensitive legal information, even if they appear to come from the firm.

Example Attorney Statement:

"We recommend you not send confidential information over free, open text, or personal email. Instead, use our secure portal or encrypted email. If you want to send a text message, use Signal or WhatsApp as they offer end-to-end encryption. Also, if you ever receive an email asking for confidential details, call our office to verify its legitimacy before responding."

9.1.3. *Client Responsibilities in Protecting Confidentiality*

Clients have a role in protecting the security of their legal information. You should guide clients to best practices, including:

- **Using Strong, Unique Passwords:** Encourage clients to create strong passwords or passphrases and use a password manager.
- **Enabling Multi-Factor Authentication (MFA):** Strongly encourage the use of MFA for all accounts, especially financial, medical, and client-related accounts.
- **Securing Physical Records:** Clients should always store legal documents and other physical records securely (locked, preferably in a fire- and water-resistant container).

- **Avoiding Public WiFi for Legal Communications:** To the extent possible, clients should avoid using public WiFi for legal communications and use a VPN for any remote access due to the susceptibility of public networks to hacking.

Example Attorney Statement:

"It's always good practice to take steps to secure your confidential business and personal information, including information about your legal case. You should use strong passwords or a passphrase and enable multi-factor authentication when that's an option. If you need help with our client portal, we can guide you through the process. A strong password contains at least 12 characters, consisting of a mix of upper-case and lower-case letters, numerals, and symbols. Passphrases are similar to passwords. They tend to be longer and more complex than passwords and have grown more popular as a result. Like passwords, passphrases should include a mix of upper-case and lower-case letters, numbers and symbols. The more randomized the words or characters in the phrase, the more secure the passphrase. Do not use the same password that you use for another account. Be careful about the personal information you share on social media."

9.1.4. *What Constitutes a Cybersecurity Breach*

You should explain what constitutes a cybersecurity breach. Any unauthorized access to sensitive information through hacking, phishing, or accidental disclosure constitutes a data breach. You should distinguish between minor security incidents where information is not compromised (like unsuccessful phishing attempts) and breaches requiring client notification.

For example:

A cybersecurity breach occurs when someone gains unauthorized access to our systems and potentially your confidential information. Breaches can happen through various means, such as a hacker breaking into our network or an employee accidentally sending an email to the wrong recipient.

Not all breaches require disclosure, but those resulting in a compromise of confidential client information do. You should explain the criteria for disclosure.

For example:

If a breach involves your confidential information, we must inform you. We will tell you what information was compromised, how the breach occurred, and what steps we are taking to address it. It takes time to investigate breaches so early notices may be incomplete.

9.1.4.1. *Examples of a Data Breach Requiring Disclosure*

- **Unauthorized Access to Client Files:** A hacker gains access to the firm's document management system.
- **Ransomware Attack:** A law firm's systems are locked down, and an attacker encrypts client files.
- **Phishing Attack on an Attorney:** A lawyer unknowingly provides login credentials to a scammer who accesses sensitive client information.
- **Loss or Theft of Devices:** A lawyer's laptop containing confidential files is stolen.

Example Attorney Statement:

> *"We recently experienced a security breach where unauthorized access to some client files occurred. We are actively investigating and have taken steps to contain the issue. We will provide details on what data was affected and what actions you should take to protect yourself."*

9.1.4.2. *Situations That May Not Require Disclosure*

- **Failed Cyberattack:** An attempted intrusion successfully blocked by security systems with no data exposure.
- **Accidental Internal Data Sharing:** If a paralegal mistakenly sends a file to the wrong firm employee but no external party accesses it.
- **Technical Issues with No Security Impact:** A firm's email system briefly goes down, but it shows no evidence of compromise on restoration.

9.1.5. *What Attorneys Should Disclose in the Event of a Breach*

When notifying clients about a breach, you must provide clear and accurate information. While certain breaches trigger specific disclosure requirements, absent specific requirements imposed by law, you should inform your clients about the nature of the breach, the information compromised, and the steps taken to mitigate the damage. Incident response experts may be available from your cyber insurance carrier to assist with required breach notices. The disclosure should include:

- **What Happened:** Explain the nature of the breach in non-technical terms.
- **What Information Was Affected:** Specify whether exposure included names, addresses, financial data, or legal case details.
- **What the Firm is Doing to Address the Issue:** Explain containment efforts, forensic investigations, and reporting to authorities if reporting is required.
- **What the Client Should Do:** If necessary, recommend steps such as changing passwords, monitoring credit reports, or filing a fraud alert.

Example Attorney Statement:

> *"Our law firm recently experienced a data security incident involving unauthorized access to some client records. We have already taken measures to secure our systems and have employed a cybersecurity expert to investigate. Based on our review, the incident may have affected your personal and case-related information. We recommend resetting your passwords and monitoring your financial accounts for any unusual activity. Please contact us with any concerns. We will keep you updated."*

9.1.6. *Best Practices in Approaching Cybersecurity Discussions with Clients*

Attorneys must have open and honest discussions with clients about the technology used in their practice and the associated risks. Handle cybersecurity conversations with transparency, professionalism, and reassurance. Consider these recommended practices:

- **Be Proactive:** Don't wait for a breach; educate clients on cybersecurity early in the relationship.
- **Use Plain Language:** Avoid technical jargon that may confuse or overwhelm clients.
- **Reassure Without Downplaying Risks:** Clients need to know their information is protected, but they also need to take precautions.
- **Encourage Two-Way Communication:** Invite clients to ask cybersecurity-related questions anytime.

Example Attorney Statement:

> *"Our firm treats cybersecurity as a priority. We take measures to keep your information secure. If you ever have concerns about how we handle your information or suspect a potential security issue, please reach out immediately. We prioritize your privacy and trust."*

Attorneys provide clients a valuable added service when educating clients about safe communication practices, mitigating risks, and responding transparently if a breach occurs. By prioritizing cybersecurity conversations early and reinforcing best practices, you can protect your clients while strengthening trust and professionalism.

9.1.7. *When an Attorney Should Discuss a Client's Need to Act on Cybersecurity Risks*

Failing to secure digital communications and sensitive legal information can jeopardize a client's case, expose privileged materials, or result in financial losses for the client. You should proactively discuss cybersecurity risks with your clients and advise them to act when necessary, particularly in the following scenarios:

9.1.7.1. *When the Client's Industry or Case Involves High Cybersecurity Risks*

Certain industries and legal matters are at greater risk of cyber threats. You should advise clients to implement strong cybersecurity measures when their legal situation involves:

- **High-profile or sensitive cases:** Cyberattacks commonly target lawsuits involving high-profile matters, high net-worth clients, or intellectual property.
- **Business transactions:** Mergers, acquisitions, and financial negotiations can attract cybercriminals seeking insider information.
- **Regulated industries:** Clients in healthcare, finance, or defense must comply with specific cybersecurity regulations (e.g., HIPAA, SEC cybersecurity rules).
- **Personal safety concerns:** Victims of stalking, harassment, or domestic violence may need enhanced cybersecurity to protect themselves.

Example Attorney Statement:

> *"Given the nature of your case, you may be a target for cyber threats. We advise you to use strong passwords or passphrases (preferred), enable multi-factor authentication on all sensitive accounts, and avoid discussing legal matters over unsecured channels."*

9.1.7.2. *If a Cyber Threat Has Already Targeted the Client*

If a client has been the victim of a phishing scam, ransomware attack, or unauthorized access to their accounts, an attorney should immediately discuss risk mitigation strategies.

9.1.7.2.1. Client Actions to Take after a Cyber Incident

- Change passwords for all legal, financial, and personal accounts.
- Enable multi-factor authentication (MFA) on all critical accounts.
- Monitor financial transactions for fraudulent activity and consider implementing credit locks or freezes with credit reporting agencies.
- Consider identity theft protection services if personal information is stolen.
- Report breaches to the relevant authorities.

Example Attorney Statement:

> *"Since your email account was compromised, we strongly recommend resetting all passwords and enabling multi-factor authentication immediately. Additionally, you should monitor your financial statements for any unusual activity and consider alerting your bank and other financial service providers to potential fraud."*

9.1.7.3. *If the Client's Actions or Negligence Could Compromise the Case*

Sometimes, a client's careless cybersecurity practices can endanger their legal position. You should intervene if you become aware of the client engaging in risky behaviors such as:

- Sending sensitive legal documents via an unencrypted personal email.
- Using unencrypted text messaging applications for the transmittal of confidential information.
- Sharing confidential case details on social media.
- Using the same password across multiple accounts.
- Falling for phishing attempts or failing to recognize social engineering scams.

Example Attorney Statement:

> *"I noticed that you sent case-sensitive documents through your personal email. This increases the risk of exposure. Please use our secure document-sharing portal to help protect confidentiality."*

9.1.7.4. *If the Client's Business or Personal Data is a Legal Liability*

Some clients, particularly business owners, executives, or professionals handling sensitive customer data, may be legally required to maintain strong cybersecurity measures. If your clients fit these profiles, you should discuss:

- **Compliance obligations:** Laws such as the General Data Protection Regulation (GDPR), the California Consumer Privacy Act (CCPA), and privacy provisions in Gramm-Leach-Bliley, and the HIPAA require businesses to safeguard customer data.
- **Contractual cybersecurity obligations:** Businesses often sign contracts requiring them to protect third-party data and notify stakeholders of breaches.
- **Potential liability risks:** A cyberattack exposing customer or employee information could result in lawsuits, regulatory fines, and reputational damage.

Example Attorney Statement:

> *"As a financial services provider, the law requires you to implement cybersecurity measures to protect customer data. A breach of your systems may impose liability under data protection laws. We recommend implementing stronger security protocols and conducting a cybersecurity audit for compliance with applicable laws and requirements."*

9.1.7.5. *When the Client Needs to Preserve Digital Evidence*

For some cases, such as those involving digital fraud, cyber harassment, employment disputes, or intellectual property theft, key evidence may exist in digital (electronic) form.

Attorneys should advise clients about properly preserving electronic evidence so that it will withstand challenges.

In all cases, it is important to advise clients about preserving records relevant to potential litigation matters, including records kept in electronic formats. A "litigation hold," also known as a "legal hold," is a process by which a person or organization preserves all forms of relevant information when litigation is reasonably anticipated. Implementing a litigation hold includes suspending routine data destruction policies and practices to ensure that emails, documents, and other records potentially related to the case are retained and not altered or deleted. Implementing a litigation hold is a critical step in complying with legal obligations during the discovery phase of a lawsuit or investigation. Therefore, you should explain that a litigation hold is a legal obligation to preserve relevant information once litigation is reasonably anticipated, ongoing, or threatened, and that failing to comply can lead to sanctions, adverse inferences, or loss of the case. You should make sure that the client understands that the duty to preserve continues throughout the litigation and includes data stored for the client by third parties, such as IT vendors and cloud services. The use of third parties to store data requires contacting them and informing them of the litigation hold as well.

The litigation hold applies to all potentially relevant documents, data, and communications, regardless of format or location, including (without limitation):

- Emails and attachments,
- Text messages and messaging apps (e.g., Slack, WhatsApp),
- Paper files and notes, and
- Digital files on personal devices, cloud storage, and backup systems.

Best Practices for Clients to Preserve Digital Evidence:

- Do not delete emails, text messages, or documents related to the case.
- Take screenshots and save copies of any relevant digital communications.
- Use secure storage to back up important legal files.
- In cases of cyber harassment, document all instances with timestamps and report them to the authorities.
- Make an immutable backup of each of your devices and store it securely for the duration of the litigation.

Example Attorney Statement in Focusing on Digital Evidence:

> *"Since this case involves potential cyber fraud, do not delete any related emails or text messages. We may need them as evidence. We recommend that you make an*

immutable backup of each of your devices and store it securely for the duration of the litigation. If you have data stored in the cloud or by service vendors, you will need to notify them as well."

9.1.7.6. *If the Client Will Travel to, or Work from, High-Risk Locations*

Clients traveling internationally, working remotely, or accessing legal documents from unsecured locations (e.g., coffee shops, hotels, airports) face heightened cybersecurity risks. You should provide guidance on securing data while on the move.

9.1.7.6.1. Client Cybersecurity Precautions When Traveling

- Limit devices taken out of the country; they could be subject to search at the border.
- Use a VPN to encrypt internet connections.
- Avoid logging into legal or financial accounts over public WiFi. In some countries, all internet traffic may be subject to government surveillance.
- Enable remote-wipe capabilities on mobile devices in case of loss or theft.
- Carry only necessary documents and store them securely.

Example Attorney Statement:

> *"Since you will be traveling abroad, we advise that you take only the devices you absolutely need and limit the files you take stored on those devices. When you use any device abroad, we advise using a VPN at all times, but at least whenever you access case-related documents. Also, avoid using hotel or airport WiFi to log into your legal accounts."*

9.1.8. *In Summary*

Attorneys must openly and honestly discuss the technology used in their practice and the associated risks with clients. They should clearly define what constitutes a breach and what requires disclosure, informing and reassuring clients about the measures in place to protect their information.

Attorneys should go beyond securing their own systems and proactively advise clients about cybersecurity risks, particularly as they relate to legal matters that are the subject of the representation. By addressing cybersecurity concerns at the right moments, whether at the start of representation, after a security incident, or when a client's actions put their case at risk, lawyers help clients protect their legal interests. Educating clients on cybersecurity has become essential to proper legal representation in the digital age.

10. A Scams Primer for Solo and Small Firm Attorneys

Scammers have increasingly targeted solo and small firm attorneys, recognizing that these legal practitioners may have fewer cybersecurity resources than large firms and access to a considerable amount of confidential information. Scammers employ various tactics to exploit vulnerabilities and gain access to sensitive information and financial assets. Attorneys must adopt proactive security measures to protect themselves and their clients from scams.

10.1. Scams Targeting Solo and Small Firm Attorneys

It is impossible to catalog scams in a short section of a book chapter, but we highlight a few common scams. These scams persist because, unfortunately, they work for scammers.

One common scam involves phishing emails that appear to come from a trusted source, such as a client or a colleague. These emails often contain malicious links or attachments that, when clicked, can install malware or ransomware on the attorney's computer or other device (cell phone, tablet, etc.). Scammers sometimes use social engineering techniques to manipulate attorneys into divulging confidential information or transferring funds to fraudulent accounts.

In another tactic, the impersonation scam, fraudsters pose as prospective clients with lucrative cases only to later request sensitive information or advance payments for supposed expenses. Once they obtain the desired information and/or payment, they vanish, leaving attorneys financially exposed and at risk of a data breach. Often, scammers attempt to get attorneys to write trust checks, distributing funds by convincing the attorney that funds were deposited in the attorney's trust account. Again, once the scammer receives the distribution, they disappear. The attorney later discovers the fraudulent nature of the so-called deposit and must repay the money to the trust account.

Scammers also target attorneys through phone calls, posing as representatives of reputable organizations such as banks or government agencies. They may claim that an urgent issue requires the attorney's immediate attention and press them to provide personal information or make payments to resolve it. Many scams work precisely because bad actors create a false sense of urgency or risk.

10.2. Prevention Strategies

To mitigate these risks, attorneys should:

- Be skeptical of unsolicited communications.
- Verify the sender's identity through independent means before responding to sensitive requests.
- Implement robust email filtering systems that flag potential spam.
- Educate staff on common scam tactics to enhance awareness and response.

- No matter what the client says, do not write a trust check until you have first verified with your bank that the funds deposited and to be distributed have cleared and posted to your trust account.
- Implement security procedures that include reliable verification of payment requests and wire instructions, including account details.

10.3. Risks and Examples

10.3.1. *Deepfake Technology*[31]

The rise of deepfake technology (digital replicas) poses a unique threat. Deepfakes are hyper-realistic manipulated videos or audio recordings. Deepfakes can be used maliciously to convincingly impersonate clients or colleagues. Fraudsters can readily access deepfake technology and image and voice samples from internet posts. For example, an attorney might receive a deepfake video call from someone they accept as a trusted contact, deceiving them into sharing sensitive information or authorizing financial transactions.

While deepfake technology presents a growing concern, cases of attorneys scammed through deepfake video calls remain relatively rare. Cybersecurity experts warn of this risk, but most reported scams still rely on voice phishing (vishing), pre-recorded deepfake audio, or AI-generated emails. Pay attention to the warnings as the technique continues to evolve. You should anticipate that evolution and prepare to avoid getting deceived by it.

10.3.2. *Ransomware and Data Encryption*

The claim that ransomware can encrypt "all client files" might overstate the case, unless the firm lacks proper backup and security measures. Many ransomware variants only encrypt files accessible from a compromised account. Nevertheless, clicking a malicious link that installs ransomware and encrypts vital files can disrupt operations until the victim firm satisfies a ransom demand.

10.3.3. *Social Media and Professional Networking Sites*

Scammers can create fake profiles, posing as potential clients or colleagues to establish trust and gather personal information. These interactions can ultimately lead to identity theft or the compromise of confidential information.

10.3.4. *LinkedIn and Social Engineering Scams*

While LinkedIn scams exist, they often involve investment fraud or business email compromise (BEC) rather than immediate identity theft. The profile-building process typically takes time, and attackers usually target larger firms or individuals with high-value contacts. Scammers may use LinkedIn (or other social media platforms) to build trust before

31. The next section of this chapter, Section 11, Disinformation and Deepfakes, discusses deepfakes in more detail. *See also* HANDBOOK, Chapter 6, *Dealing with Deepfakes: The Role for Lawyers and Law Firms*.

soliciting confidential information or proposing fraudulent business deals, often as part of a broader social engineering scheme.

10.3.5. *Spear Phishing Attacks*

Legal professionals should also guard against spear phishing attacks. Unlike general phishing attempts, spear phishing is a highly targeted scheme that leverages publicly available information to craft convincing, personalized messages. These attacks often involve thorough research on the victim, utilizing publicly available information to create convincing and tailored messages. The customized nature of spear phishing makes it more challenging to detect and can result in higher success rates for scammers.

Examples

- A managing partner at a small firm received an email, apparently from a close colleague, requesting the transfer of confidential case documents to a "secure server." The email was part of a spear phishing scheme, and resulted in a data breach.
- An attorney received an email from a large multinational corporate client with a link to a shared document for urgent review. Clicking the link installed ransomware, which encrypted all client files, leading to significant downtime and a ransom demand.
- A solo practitioner received a call from someone impersonating a bank fraud department representative. Believing the call was legitimate, the attorney provided banking details, leading to unauthorized withdrawals and financial loss.
- A small firm attorney built a professional relationship with a seemingly reputable individual on LinkedIn. After weeks of interaction, the scammer proposed a lucrative business deal that required sharing sensitive information, which was later misused.
- An attorney received a deep-fake video call from someone presenting as a long-time client, urgently requesting a funds transfer. The attorney complied, only later discovering that the client knew nothing about the request.

Solo and small firm attorneys must also guard against more traditional scams that have evolved with technology. For example, scammers may send fake invoices for services never rendered, relying on the busy nature of legal work to slip through unnoticed. In one instance, a small firm almost paid a substantial sum to a scammer posing as an IT service provider, fraudulently claiming to have performed essential maintenance work.

10.3.6. *Personal Exposure to Scams—Professional Impacts Can Follow*

Like all individuals, solo and small firm attorneys are vulnerable to scams seeking their personal information. Attorneys' personal exposure to scams can have profound professional implications. Identity theft poses one of the most severe consequences. Acquiring an attorney's personal information can lead to unauthorized access to personal and professional accounts, compromising client data and confidential information. This kind of breach can cause significant legal and financial repercussions, including lawsuits and loss of client confidence. Financial fraud can deplete a firm's resources, hindering operations and damaging its reputation. Ransomware attacks can delay work and legal proceedings, leading to client dissatisfaction and potential malpractice claims.

Scams that result in financial loss may also affect the professional stability and economic viability of small firms and solo practices. Unauthorized transactions and financial theft can deplete the firm's resources, impairing its ability to operate effectively. Additionally, recovering from financial scams requires time and effort, diverting attention from critical legal work and impacting overall productivity.

10.3.7. *Mitigation Strategies*

To mitigate risks, attorneys should adopt a multi-layered cybersecurity approach, including:

- Regular software updates and security patches,
- Strong, unique passwords with multi-factor authentication,
- Regular cybersecurity training for attorneys and staff,
- Verification of any financial transactions through independent means,
- Scrutiny of unsolicited communications, and
- Regular training to keep themselves and staff attuned to scammers' tactics.

11. Disinformation and Deepfakes

Although not a new methodology for fraudsters, the use, reach, and impact of false information have grown exponentially in the digital age. Disinformation, intentionally misleading content designed to deceive, has evolved into a powerful tool for manipulation. Deepfakes, synthetic media generated with AI-enabled applications, add an even more dangerous disinformation layer by creating hyper-realistic, yet entirely fabricated, videos, audio clips, and images. A 2019 Pew Research study[32] found that nearly two-thirds of Americans believe manipulated media creates "a great deal of confusion" about facts and current events. Disinformation threatens democratic processes, public trust, and even the legal system itself. It also facilitates a vast panoply of cybercrimes and scams.

The legal world faces particularly alarming risks. Deepfake videos can allow the presentation of fake evidence in court, impersonate attorneys to deceive clients, damage a lawyer's professional reputation, and more. For example, in one case, cybercriminals used AI-generated audio to impersonate a CEO, convincing an employee to transfer €220,000

32. Jeffrey Gottfried, *About Three-Quarters of Americans Favor Steps to Restrict Altered Videos and Images*, Pew Res. Ctr. (Jun. 14, 2019), https://www.pewresearch.org/short-reads/2019/06/14/about-three-quarters-of-americans-favor-steps-to-restrict-altered-videos-and-images/.

to a fraudulent account.[33] When cybercriminals target law firms with these tactics, they can generate financially and ethically serious consequences.

11.1. Real-World Reports of Disinformation

Several examples of disinformation and deepfakes have made the news in the last few years:

- In the lead-up to the 2024 U.S. presidential election, deepfake videos emerged targeting political figures. Someone shared a fabricated video that falsely depicted Vice President Kamala Harris at a communist rally to mislead voters.[34]
- The same article reported that then former President Donald Trump posted an image of Taylor Swift and "accepted her endorsement for his campaign, which she had never given."
- The Russian group Storm-1516 produced false narratives about political candidates to sway public opinion and influence U.S. elections.[35]
- During the COVID-19 pandemic, a significant amount of disinformation circulated, with 47% of surveyed U.S. adults reporting exposure to made-up news about the virus.[36]

These digital deceptions pose an even more significant threat to lawyers. Attorneys must proactively recognize, prevent, and respond to disinformation and deepfake-related attacks.

11.2. Legal Risks for Solo and Small Firm Lawyers

Disinformation and deepfake technology pose a growing threat to solo and small firm lawyers. The most serious risks include attorney impersonation, where AI-generated media convincingly replicates a lawyer's voice, face, and mannerisms in real-time. A client receiving a deepfake video call may believe they have their attorney online and unknowingly disclose confidential information to a scammer. Malicious actors can use a deepfake to orchestrate fraudulent financial transactions, leading to significant economic losses. Exposing confidential client information breaches attorney-client privilege. Misinformation (false information spread negligently) or disinformation introduced through impersonation could manipulate case strategies, influencing legal decisions based on false premises.

---

33. Catherine Stupp, *Fraudsters Use AI to Mimic CEO's Voice in Unusual Cybercrime Case*, Wall St. J. (Aug. 30, 2019, 12:52 PM ET), https://www.wsj.com/articles/fraudsters-use-ai-to-mimic-ceos-voice-in-unusual-cybercrime-case-11567157402.

34. Dan Merica & Ali Swenson, *Trump's Post of Fake Taylor Swift Endorsement Is His Latest Embrace of AI-Generated Images*, AP News (Aug. 20, 2024, 4:48 PM EDT), https://apnews.com/article/trump-taylor-swift-fake-endorsement-ai-fec99c412d960932839e3eab8d49fd5f.

35. David Gilbert, *Russian Propaganda Unit Appears to Be behind Spread of False Tim Walz Sexual Abuse Claims*, WIRED (Oct. 21, 2024, 2:16 PM), https://www.wired.com/story/russian-propaganda-unit-storm-1516-false-tim-walz-sexual-abuse-claims/.

36. Anton Konopliov, *Key Statistics on Fake News & Misinformation in Media in 2024*, Redline (Jun. 26, 2024), https://redline.digital/fake-news-statistics/.

To mitigate these risks, lawyers must take proactive security measures. Those security measures may be designed to end or interrupt a suspect interaction, providing an opportunity to verify the participants. For example, questions seeking information not widely known can help confirm identities. Asking a client to recall details from a previous discussion or using a pre-established verification phrase can prevent a scammer from successfully impersonating an attorney. Lawyers must educate firm employees and clients on the risks of deepfake fraud. Lawyers should advise clients to verify all legal instructions through a secondary, trusted method before acting. Additionally, implementing basic cybersecurity hygiene, such as multi-factor authentication for all client communication channels, can make it more challenging for malicious actors to access systems and impersonate real individuals with whom attorneys and their clients anticipate interacting. By integrating these precautions into daily practice, lawyers can better protect their clients from the growing dangers of AI-driven deception.

11.3. Reputational Damage and Defamation

Deepfake technology poses a serious risk to attorneys' reputations. Malicious actors can use manipulated videos or audio recordings to spread untrue and defamatory content, creating the false impression that an attorney has engaged in unethical or unprofessional conduct. Unlike traditional defamation, deepfakes develop a level of realism that makes them more difficult to disprove immediately. A convincing but fake video could spread rapidly online, damaging professional credibility before the truth comes to light.

False allegations may lead to a loss of client trust and a decline in referrals. If the deepfake contains fabricated, unethical statements or actions, it could trigger an ethics investigation, forcing the lawyer to defend against baseless claims. Negative media coverage could damage a lawyer's career prospects, causing lasting damage, even after the truth comes to light.

To protect against reputational harm, lawyers should monitor and manage their online presence. Setting up Google Alerts for their name and firm can help detect false or misleading content early. Maintaining an active digital presence through a professional website and verified social media accounts allows attorneys to establish a trusted source of information that can counter misinformation. If targeted by a deepfake attack, engaging public relations or legal professionals can help with issuing timely corrections to mitigate the damage. By staying vigilant and prepared, lawyers can better protect their reputations from the risks posed by AI-generated disinformation.

11.4. Financial and Cybersecurity Risks

Deepfake technology has become a powerful tool for cybercriminals, particularly in phishing attacks targeting law firms. Scammers can now use AI-generated voice and video impersonation to pose as attorneys, tricking clients or staff into authorizing fraudulent fund transfers. Similarly, a scammer can pose as a client, tricking the attorney into making a fraudulent fund transfer or taking other action, supposedly per the client's instructions. Deepfake phishing attacks often create a sense of urgency (common to traditional email scams) with a degree of authenticity that makes them harder to detect.

A convincing deepfake call or video message could lead to unauthorized funds transfers, resulting in significant financial losses for the firm or its clients. An attacker who successfully impersonates an attorney in a conversation with a client or staff member may access sensitive case information. These breaches can erode client trust and expose the firm to malpractice claims, damaging its reputation and financial stability.

Protecting against deepfake technology requires a multi-layered approach combining technological safeguards, user awareness, and proactive responses.

Individual Level:

- **Be skeptical and critical of online content:** Question the authenticity of videos, images, and audio, especially any that seem sensational or unbelievable.
- **Limit your digital footprint:** Be careful about what personal information you share online, especially high-quality photos and videos.
- **Enable strong privacy settings:** Use privacy settings on social media platforms and online services to control who can access your content.
- **Use digital watermarks:** Watermark photos and videos you share online to deter misuse and make deepfakes more traceable.
- **Stay informed:** Keep up to date on deepfake technology and detection methods.
- **Implement strong password/passphrase practices and multi-factor authentication (MFA):** Use long, strong, and unique passwords (passphrases preferred) for all accounts, and enable MFA whenever possible to add an extra layer of security.
- **Remain aware of phishing attempts:** Do not click suspicious links or download attachments from unknown sources and be wary of messages that prompt urgent action.
- **Report suspicious content:** If you encounter suspected deepfake content, report it to the platform where you found it.

Organizational Level:

- **Educate employees:** Conduct regular training and awareness programs to help employees identify deepfakes and understand the associated risks.
- **Invest in deepfake detection tools:** Implement AI-powered software and other technologies that can help analyze video and audio content for inconsistencies indicative of deepfakes.
- **Develop a crisis communication plan:** Prepare for the possibility of deepfake attacks by developing a detailed plan to respond to and mitigate potential damage.
- **Conduct regular monitoring and audits:** Continuously monitor your firm's online presence and assess the effectiveness of implemented security protocols.

- **Implement strong authentication methods:** Enforce MFA and other strong authentication methods for critical systems and accounts.
- **Adopt a zero-trust security model:** Verify all access requests and replace implicit trust with continuous validation.
- **Embrace research and development:** Support the development of new technologies and approaches to address the constantly evolving deepfake threat landscape.

Important Note: Deepfake technology is constantly evolving; it is crucial to continuously adapt and update security measures and detection methods.

Deepfake Threat	Potential Impact	Preventative Measure
Attorney Impersonation	Client leaks confidential information	Multi-factor authentication, identity verification questions
Deepfake Evidence in Court	False evidence affects case outcomes	Use forensic AI tools, request metadata, engage digital forensic experts
Financial Fraud	Scammers steal funds via deepfake video calls	Voice authentication codes, encrypted communication platforms
Reputational Damage	Fake videos damage lawyer's credibility	Google Alerts, professional online presence, PR response

11.5. Detecting and Responding to Deepfakes and Disinformation

As deepfake technology evolves, so must the lawyer's ability to recognize and respond to AI-generated deception. Detecting deepfakes requires both technological tools and critical analysis. Visual clues such as blurred edges, unnatural blinking, and mismatched lip movements may indicate manipulation. Audio inconsistencies, including robotic tones or irregular speech pacing, can also provide signs of AI-generated content. Beyond visual and audio cues, examining metadata can reveal suspicious edits that suggest tampering.

You can get tools that can help identify deepfakes. Deepware Scanner (https://deepware.ai/), for example, offers a free and accessible way to detect deepfakes. For broader monitoring and detection, Sensity AI (https://sensity.ai/) provides ongoing analysis of digital content. Lawyers should incorporate tools like these into their cybersecurity practices to verify the authenticity of videos and recordings.

If a deepfake fraudster targets a lawyer or law firm, the firm should take immediate action to protect itself. Start by documenting the attack, saving copies of the false content, and tracking where and how it spreads. Reporting the incident to relevant authorities, such as the state bar association or law enforcement, can help establish a formal record and potentially trigger an investigation. To prevent reputational harm, consider issuing a public correction through the firm's website or a press release to clarify misinformation. (Calling attention to false information can sometimes extend its reach, however, so pause to consider your public response strategy.) The firm may want to initiate legal action if the deepfake is defamatory. Consulting an attorney with expertise in this area to explore potential remedies can help protect professional integrity and mitigate damages. By staying vigilant and responding quickly, solo and small firm lawyers can reduce the impact of deepfake attacks on their practice and reputation.

11.6. Deepfake Evidence in Court

Deepfake technology presents a significant risk to the integrity of legal proceedings. Bad actors can manipulate AI-generated videos and audio recordings to create false evidence, depicting a client, witness, or attorney saying things they never actually said. For example, fraudsters might fabricate recordings of contract negotiations to support false claims or manipulate client statements to distort case facts. If admitted into court, such fabricated evidence could alter the outcome of a case, leading to wrongful judgments and undermining the credibility of legitimate testimony and the legal system itself.

There is also a risk that genuine audio and video recordings could be challenged as fake; the specter of deepfakes can cast doubt among judges and jurors.

Countering these risks requires that lawyers exercise vigilance in verifying the authenticity of digital evidence.

Note: Forensic AI tools, such as Deepware Scanner, can help detect signs of manipulation in videos and recordings. When presented with digital evidence, attorneys should request the original metadata containing crucial details about when and how the file was created. If you suspect a deepfake, work with digital forensic experts for additional analysis to confirm or challenge its validity. By adopting these protective measures, firm lawyers can help safeguard the integrity of the legal system against the growing threat of AI-generated deception.

Deepfake Digital Forensic Service Providers[37]	
Sensei Enterprises, Inc.	https://senseient.com/
Maryman	https://www.maryman.com
Powerhouse Forensics	https://powerhouseforensics.com/
Cyber Centaurs	https://cybercentaurs.com/

11.7. Legal and Ethical Responsibilities for Lawyers

Lawyers have a fundamental duty to uphold truthfulness in their practice. The ABA Model Rules of Professional Conduct, particularly Rule 3.3,[38] and Rule 4.1,[39] emphasize the obligations of honesty and transparency in representations to courts and clients. As deepfake technology becomes more sophisticated, attorneys must take steps to verify the authenticity of the evidence they present and ensure that their clients understand the risks posed by manipulated digital content.

37. Each website listed in this table was visited June 15, 2025.
38. Model Rules of Prof'l Conduct r. 3.3 (Candor Toward the Tribunal).
39. Model Rules of Prof'l Conduct r. 4.1 (Truthfulness in Statements to Others).

Lawyers should use forensic tools and expert analysis for digital media cases. Educating clients about the dangers of deepfakes can help prevent them from being deceived by fraudulent content or unknowingly relying on manipulated materials. Additionally, lawyers should advocate for stronger evidentiary standards to address the growing threat of AI-generated misinformation in legal proceedings.

Neglecting these responsibilities can have serious consequences. If an attorney unknowingly presents false evidence, they may face professional discipline, ethical sanctions, or malpractice claims. By remaining vigilant and adopting rigorous verification practices, solo and small firm lawyers can satisfy their ethical obligations while protecting their clients and the integrity of the legal system.

11.8. Evolving Legal Frameworks to Address Deepfake-related Fraud and Evidence Manipulation

Courts and lawmakers also recognize the need for stronger protections against the misuse of deepfakes. Some jurisdictions have enacted laws criminalizing the creation or distribution of deepfakes used for fraud, defamation, or election interference.[40] Others have expanded existing fraud and identity theft statutes to include synthetic media.

Expect courts to require stricter verification processes to determine the genuineness of a video or audio recording. Lawyers must properly vet any digital evidence they intend to offer to the court. They must also be prepared to challenge evidence presented by opposing counsel if there is reason to believe that it has been altered. As the law evolves, lawyers should monitor legislative changes, understand emerging case law, and educate their clients about the risks of deepfake-related fraud.

11.8.1. *A Proactive Approach to Digital Deception*

The rapid advancement of AI-powered disinformation has created new challenges for the legal profession. These threats are not theoretical. Deepfake scams, manipulated evidence, and reputational attacks have already occurred. More will occur. Staying ahead of these risks requires awareness, preparation, and strong security practices.

Lawyers must stay informed by following cybersecurity trends and attending legal technology continuing education programs. AI-based verification tools that assess the authenticity of digital media can help identify manipulated content before it causes harm. Implementing security measures, such as multi-factor authentication and encrypted communication platforms, adds additional protection against cyber threats. Finally, having a response plan enables quick action to mitigate damage if a deepfake attack occurs.

40. N. David Bleisch, *Deepfakes and American Elections*, ABA Task Force for Am. Dem. (May 6, 2024), https://www.americanbar.org/groups/public_interest/election_law/american-democracy/our-work/deepfakes-american-elections/.

12. External Resources and Internal References

12.1. Internal References

The entire Handbook has relevance to attorneys seeking knowledge and understanding of cybersecurity issues and the risks associated with technology, in general, and artificial intelligence, in particular. Accordingly, we recommend that you review the Handbook in its entirety. We recognize that many of you may not have the time to do that immediately. To help you move forward quickly, we have identified the most critical chapters for solo and small firm attorneys below and in several footnotes in this chapter.

Chapter 2: An Introduction to Artificial Intelligence
Chapter 3: Understanding Technology—What Every Lawyer Needs to Know About the Cyber Network and Artificial Intelligence
Chapter 4: Understanding Cybersecurity Risks
Chapter 5: Cybercrime
Chapter 6: Dealing with Deepfakes: The Role for Lawyers and Law Firms
Chapter 7: Legal Obligations to Provide Data Security
Chapter 10: Lawyers' Professional Responsibility to Provide Data Security
Chapter 11: Foundation of Risk Management in Cybersecurity
Chapter 14: Cyber Insurance for Law Firms and Legal Organizations

12.2. External Resources

The following list of vendors, service providers, and programs should give you a starting point in your quest for the right match for your firm. Inclusion in the list does not constitute a recommendation by the authors, the editors, or the American Bar Association.

DISCLAIMER: The listed companies and programs represent examples of what is available. Before opting for any vendor, you should do your own due diligence to confirm that the vendor provides a suitable structure for your firm. As we have no information about your operation, we have no way to evaluate suitability for use by your firm, and we do not intend the inclusion to suggest that we have determined it matches any firm's needs.

Security Tools for Solo & Small Firms[41]		
Password Management & Multi-Factor Authentication (MFA)		
1Password	https://1password.com/	Securely store and manage passwords
Dashlane	https://www.dashlane.com/	Encrypted password management
NordPass	https://nordpass.com/	Offers essential features like password sharing and data breach scanning.

41. Each website listed in this table was visited June 15, 2025.

Enpass	https://www.enpass.io	A secure password manager that stores credentials locally, offering cross-platform support and convenient auto-fill features.
Email & Document Security		
ProtonMail	https://proton.me/mail	End-to-end encrypted email
Virtru	https://www.virtru.com/	Email and file encryption for law firms
Secure Client Communication & File Sharing		
NetDocuments	https://www.netdocuments.com/	Secure legal document management
Tresorit	https://tresorit.com/	Encrypted file-sharing for law firms
Virtual Private Network (VPN)		
ExpressVPN	https://www.expressvpn.com	A high-speed VPN service that provides secure, private online browsing with a global network of servers.
NordVPN	https://nordvpn.com/	A feature-rich VPN known for its robust encryption, privacy features, and extensive worldwide server network.
CyberGhost	https://www.cyberghostvpn.com	A user-friendly VPN offering strong privacy protection, easy-to-use apps, and a wide selection of servers for enhanced online security.
Antivirus / Anti-Malware		
Norton 360	https://us.norton.com/	A comprehensive security suite that integrates antivirus, VPN, identity protection, and performance optimization to safeguard your devices.
Malware Bytes	https://www.malwarebytes.com	An anti-malware solution designed to detect and remove malware, ransomware, and other advanced threats, to provide a clean and secure system environment.
Bitdefender	https://www.bitdefender.com	A top-tier cybersecurity firm providing advanced antivirus, multi-layered threat protection, and comprehensive security solutions for various devices and networks.
Firewalls		
Fortinet FortiGate	https://www.fortinet.com/	Advanced threat protection, intrusion prevention, and VPN support
Check Point CloudGuard	https://www.checkpoint.com	A cloud security solution that provides automated threat prevention and posture management to secure cloud environments and applications.
Multi-Factor Authentication		
Authy	https://authy.com/	Two-factor authentication for law firm logins
Microsoft Authenticator	https://www.microsoft.com/en-us/account/authenticator	Integrates seamlessly with Microsoft's ecosystem and a range of third-party services to provide secure, convenient authentication.
Duo Security	https://duo.com/	While it is popular among larger organizations, Duo also offers scalable plans that can fit small practices, providing flexible authentication methods.

Cybersecurity Threat Monitoring		
Dark Web & Data Breach Monitoring		
Have I Been Pwned?	https://haveibeenpwned.com/	Check if your email address is in a data breach
SpyCloud	https://spycloud.com/	Monitor firm credentials for breaches
Ransomware & Incident Response		
No More Ransom	https://www.nomoreransom.org/	Ransomware recovery tools
CISA (Cybersecurity & Infrastructure Security Agency)	https://www.cisa.gov/	Government cybersecurity alerts and resources
Forensic Investigation & Deepfake Detection		
Deepware Scanner	https://deepware.ai/	Detect manipulated audio/video evidence
Sensity AI	https://sensity.ai/	Tracking and detection of AI generated synthetic media
Sensei Enterprises	https://senseient.com/	Digital forensic services for law firms

Additional Reading Material
Jeffrey M. Allen & Ashley Hallene, Unlocking the Future: Leveraging Technology for Personal and Professional Success (Am. Bar Ass'n 2025).
Jeffrey M. Allen & Ashley Hallene, Scams & Cybercrime Survival Guide: Recognizing, Avoiding, and Recovering from Online Scams and Cybercrime (Am. Bar Ass'n forthcoming 2026).

Artificial Intelligence Attribution:

We not only write about artificial intelligence, but we also use it in our writing. We want to acknowledge that fact and the programs we employed to assist us in creating this chapter. We used OpenAI's ChatGPT and Microsoft's CoPilot applications to assist with portions of the text and Microsoft Word's Editor, Grammarly, and WordRake in editing this chapter. We personally generated each prompt used with CoPilot and ChatGPT, including a requirement for an originally generated product in each prompt.

Chapter 16

In-House Counsel

Angeline G. Chen

1. The Cyber Threat Landscape for In-House Counsel

> *"Nothing in life is to be feared, it is only to be understood. Now is the time to understand more, so that we may fear less."*—Marie Curie

The role of in-house counsel, particularly that of the chief legal officer and the general counsel, is expanding rapidly both domestically and abroad.[1] In addition to being formal stewards of legal and compliance matters for their respective companies, in-house counsel are regularly now called upon to serve in a much broader role as executive leaders, fully integrated business partners, risk managers and advisors, critical participants in shaping company and business strategies, and "key members of the corporate decision-making team."[2]

At the same time, broader macro-level developments, technological advancements, and accelerating societal changes are transforming the corporate environments and industries in which lawyers operate.[3] Author and columnist Thomas Friedman noted a decade ago in his book *Thank You For Being Late*,[4] that the "Age of Acceleration" was already upon us

---

1. *See, e.g.*, Mark A. Cohen, *Chief Legal Officers: The Expanded Purview of a Trusted Advisor*, FORBES (Mar. 24, 2025), at https://www.forbes.com/sites/markcohen1/2025/03/24/chief-legal-officers-the-expanded-purview-of-a-trusted-advisor/; Jennifer Pettigrew & Katherine Jackson, *Rewriting the General Counsel Rulebook: From Misunderstood Asset to Strategic Powerhouse,* PAGEEXECUTIVE, https://www.pageexecutive.com/advice/insights/conscious-leadership/rewriting-general-counsel-rulebook (last visited July 1, 2025); Angus Haig, *The Evolving Role of In-House Counsel,* CTR. FOR LEGAL LEADERSHIP (undated), https://www.legalleadership.co.uk/knowledge/progressing-my-career/enhancing-your-role/the-evolving-role-of-in-house-counsel/ (last visited July 1, 2025); Elaine McArdle, *In the Driver's Seat: The Changing Role of the General Counsel*, HARV. L. TODAY (July 1, 2012), at https://today.law.harvard.edu/feature/in-the-drivers-seat-the-changing-role-of-the-general-counsel/; Juan Rivera & Jose M. Pineiro, *Beyond Legal: The Expanding Role of General Counsel*, FTI CONSULTING (Jan. 10, 2025), https://www.fticonsulting.com/insights/articles/beyond-legal-expanding-role-general-counsel.

For purposes of this chapter, we do not address the distinctions between a chief legal officer and a general counsel, as we are focused on whomever within the legal department bears the greatest responsibility for both running the legal function and advising the company's board and senior leadership. For those interested in the difference between the two roles, see Michael Sachs & Lee Udelsman, *GC or CLO—Or both? When The Two Titles Can Co-Exist* (Feb. 8, 2022), https://www.mlaglobal.com/en/insights/articles/gc-or-clo-or-both-when-the-two-titles-can-co-exist?byconsultantorauthor=michael-sachs.

2. McArdle, *supra* note 1.

3. Cohen, *supra* note 1.

4. THOMAS L. FRIEDMAN, THANK YOU FOR BEING LATE: AN OPTIMIST'S GUIDE TO THRIVING IN THE AGE OF ACCELERATIONS (2016).

as a result of the convergence of several global and interdependent trends in the economic, environmental, and societal domains. As the corporate world is swept into, and competes in, this Age of Acceleration, digitalizing[5] and transforming at an accelerated rate of organizational convergence and expansion, the legal profession must likewise adapt.

The inexorable advent and extended reach and embedment of artificial intelligence (AI) serves to layer even more complexity on the in-house counsel role. AI presents both ample risks and opportunities for the legal practitioner and for how the company conducts its business and how individuals do their jobs and live their lives.[6]

Meanwhile, global drivers ranging from the market and regulatory focus (and changes) on environmental, social, and governance (ESG), corporate social responsibility (CSR), and diversity, equity, and inclusion (DEI) principles over the last decade, shifting political philosophies, social unrest and often polarized views on issues of social justice and racial inequality, and global phenomena such as the COVID-19 pandemic and regional conflicts around the world highlight the imperative for general counsel and CLOs also to be positioned to provide insights and guidance on how companies traverse increasingly complex environments.[7] Recent events have also shown that administration change, even in the United States, can bring about material and rapid regulatory shifts, creating even more uncertainty.[8] As the environments in which an entity operates change and evolve, in-house

5. It is important to recognize the difference between "digitization," which refers to the act of converting physical or analog things such as paper documents, photographs, sounds, etc., into digital form (i.e. bits and bytes) and "digitalization," which refers to a transformation of the workplace through the integration of digital technologies and *digitized* information in order to create revenue, increase business optimization and efficiencies, transform processes, and otherwise create a work environment that leverages full and deliberate engagement of business systems and processes.

6. William Josten, *For In-House Counsel, Today's AI is a Study in Contrasts*, Thomson Reuters (Aug. 9, 2024), https://www.thomsonreuters.com/en-us/posts/legal/ai-in-house-counsel/. *See also* Thomson Reuters, Future of Professionals Report: How AI is the Catalyst for Transforming Every Aspect of Work 14 (Aug. 2023), https://www.thomsonreuters.com/content/dam/ewp-m/documents/thomsonreuters/en/pdf/reports/future-of-professionals-august-2023.pdf (noting that "60% of respondents indicated that a greater proportion of work will be carried out in-house over the next five years").

7. *See, e.g.*, Miriam Wrobel, *The Modern General Counsel: Managing in Times of Polarization*, (Apr. 3, 2025) (discussing the influence of growing social and political polarization on corporations), https://www.fticonsulting.com/insights/articles/modern-general-counsel-managing-times-polarization; Matthew K. Fawcett, *Insight: GCs Must Balance ESG in an Age of Activism*, Bloomberg L. (Mar. 4, 2020), https://news.bloomberglaw.com/us-law-week/insight-gcs-must-balance-esg-in-an-age-of-activism; Michael W. Peregrine, *The General Counsel as Key Corporate Social Responsibility Advisor*, Harv. L. Sch. F. on Corp. Governance Blog (Jun. 24, 2018), https://corpgov.law.harvard.edu/2018/06/24/the-general-counsel-as-key-corporate-social-responsibility-advisor/; John Amer & Teraesa Vinson, More than "just a lawyer": General counsel as senior leaders, Korn Ferry Inst. (2015), https://www.kornferry.com/content/dam/kornferry/docs/article-migration/General%20Counsel%20as%20Senior%20Leaders_V2.pdf; Lauren Boehmke & Matt Hurd, *How Covid-19 is changing the general counsel's leadership role* (Jan. 5, 2021), https://www.governance-intelligence.com/regulatory-compliance/how-covid-19-changing-general-counsels-leadership-role.

8. Jackson Dunn, *Wait and See Is Not a Viable Option: How General Counsel Can Take Action in Uncertain Times*, FTI Consulting (Mar. 21, 2025), https://www.fticonsulting.com/insights/articles/wait-see-not-viable-option-how-general-counsel-can-take-action-uncertain-times (noting general counsel are best suited to influence company responses through risk identification and assessment as well as development of strategies to respond and protect future growth of the company).

counsel must adapt, learn, and gather sufficient information, skills, and resources to advise effectively and influence the entity for the optimal outcome.

It is against this backdrop that in-house counsel, whose core responsibility remains advising and counseling their companies on how to navigate the legal parameters of their organizational existence, must be prepared to understand and advise their clients on the legal aspects of cybersecurity requirements and threats.

1.1. Role Differentiation

The role of in-house counsel is materially distinct from that of outside counsel in several ways. While it is beyond the scope of this chapter to discuss all such differences in depth, it is worth noting some of the core aspects of being in-house that make addressing cybersecurity issues, in particular, all the more challenging.

Chapters 14 and 15 of this Handbook discuss cybersecurity in the context of cyber insurance for law firms and in small law firm settings, and Chapter 10 addresses cybersecurity and professional responsibility. The examination of cyber issues presented in those chapters is largely applicable to corporate law departments, and we, therefore, encourage you to review those chapters closely. Law firms, however, independent of size or practice area(s), share certain core characteristics. They predominantly adopt a hierarchical model for operations, focusing on the singular purpose of providing legal services as a business. Firms take on clients whose needs align with the firm's specific areas of expertise, but law firm services offered are fundamentally the same: external legal advice provided to an entity or an individual as the client. Both law firm and client understand the scope and parameters of the work product to be provided by the law firm, *viz.*, professionally sound legal advice addressing the specific issue or question articulated by the client(s) and/or legal services focused on accomplishing a specific task (e.g., litigation or negotiations).

In contrast, in-house attorneys work for the sole benefit of a single client: the company.[9] Companies have different DNA than law firms. They typically have: (a) a broader, more complex charter addressing the full scope of needs arising from a wider and often varied scope and nature of products, services, or solutions offered to the marketplace; and (b) operations encompassing the interdependencies of the functions and entire workforce devoted to the company charter and organizational operations. In-house attorneys are integrated into the business on a sustained basis, not just for specific projects bounded by time or on a negotiated retainer, or even for designated topical areas. And because in-house counsel have one, and only one, client—the company[10]—this client relationship carries

9. For purposes of this work, "corporation," "organization" and other entity references are used interchangeably. In addition, the discussion and analysis are relevant not just to commercial organizations, but also to nonprofit organizations and associations. The key focus here being that the general counsel's client is the entity by which he or she is employed. For a more specifically focused discussion of nonprofit organizations, see HANDBOOK, Chapter 17, *Why Public Interest Attorneys Should Care about Cybersecurity*.

10. *See* MODEL RULES OF PROF'L CONDUCT r. 1.13(a) (AM. BAR ASS'N 2025) [hereinafter MRPC] ("A lawyer employed or retained by an organization represents the organization acting through its duly authorized constituents.")

with it the affirmative obligation to advance the needs of the organization over that of any individual employee (even officers and directors) if the latter conflicts with the organization's best interests, even though in-house lawyers must interact with multiple stakeholders who form and act on behalf of the entity.[11]

Thus, in addition to being required to act in a professional capacity as an attorney, in-house counsel's fiduciary duty is to serve and advance the needs of the business above all else.[12] This deceptively simple statement may seem to bear no distinction from the role of a law firm until one considers the fact that a corporation—as a juridical entity—is more than the sum of its parts. Those parts include the industry in which the company operates, the full breadth of its business and operational activity, its management, its workforce, its governance structure, its shareholders, the geographical locations in which it does business, and the like. All are relevant and must be taken into consideration by the in-house attorney, who must serve as a constant legal counselor and business partner attuned to these dynamics. By definition, the most effective in-house attorneys are familiar with, and strive to be aware of changes to, the relevant aspects and operations of the company, even if only to the extent such attributes are associated with the attorney's role and responsibilities.[13] Outside counsel, no matter how skilled or client-focused, are by definition always outsiders to the business; outside counsel can only see what is parceled to them and, therefore, can understand and advise solely on selected windows into the corporate organism.[14]

Today's in-house attorney must develop a broad range of competencies extending beyond expertise in specific areas of the law, and they must maintain situational awareness. In particular, in-house attorneys must learn to think and act operationally and strategically.[15] Successful in-house attorneys develop a broader business understanding, deeper expertise in compliance and risk management, and skills for managing the legal function and executing legal tasks independently yet collaboratively as a critical part of the company. Effective in-house counsel serve as leaders and influential advisors, and they are fully engaged in

---

11. *Id.* r. 1.13(b).

12. Ass'n of Corp. Counsel, ACC InfoPAK: Becoming In-house Counsel: A Guide for Law Students and Recent Graduates 1 (Dec. 2013) [hereinafter Becoming In-house Counsel], https://www.acc.com/sites/default/files/resources/vl/membersonly/InfoPAK/19654_2.pdf.

13. For example, it is not enough for a company's dedicated labor and employment counsel to know the substantive employment law and regulations. They must also work productively with the human resources function and understand at least the basics of the company's business and growth strategy to be optimally positioned to provide sound and current legal guidance. In-house counsel must also work within the company's legal function and broader company structure. Becoming In-house Counsel, *supra* note 12, is a useful reference for in-house counsel, too.

14. This is not to discount the effectiveness and value of outside counsel who establish committed relationships with their clients to better understand the company's needs or who ably serve smaller companies that do not have in-house attorneys. Indeed, the past decade has seen a rise in what are called "fractional general counsel" who often offer an effective strategic and economic option for companies that can neither afford nor desire to employ a dedicated senior level in-house counsel. *See The Growing Shift Toward Fractional General Counsel*, Priori Legal, Inc. (Mar. 5, 2025), https://www.priorilegal.com/blog/growing-shift-fractional-general-counsel.

15. *See* McArdle, *supra* note 1; Dunn, *supra* note 8; Harish Suryavanshi, *Today's In-house Counsel: Evolving Roles as Business Enablers,* Ass'n Corp. Counsel (Jan. 1, 2014), https://www.acc.com/resource-library/todays-house-counsel-evolving-roles-business-enablers.

the company's strategic activities.[16] In today's accelerated business environment, in-house counsel cannot wait for others to seek their advice; they must be on the frontlines with the business and, sometimes, get ahead to see around corners.[17] These skills are precisely aligned with how the in-house attorney must prepare to tackle the unique and distinctive legal challenges presented by cybersecurity.

1.2. The In-House Perspective

Legal analysis of cybersecurity issues in the corporate environment must take into account corporate strategy and enterprise risk management plans, environmental variables, workforce and system considerations, actual and potential interdependencies, and operational impacts.

The challenges and opportunities discussed in this Handbook become amplified and more complicated for in-house counsel. In-house counsel is tasked with maintaining awareness and a serviceable level (and at times, mastery) of legal subject matter, including understanding laws, regulations, and policies (such as those relevant to cybersecurity) –a task that is ongoing, emergent, and proactive. In-house counsel is also charged with determining the applicability and implementation of legal requirements to the company's operations, business activities, and strategies. The in-house attorney must execute this task in a manner that appropriately balances adherence to the law and attendant risks, while still facilitating the company's business objectives and positioning the company to achieve the same in a compliant and sustainable manner. The in-house attorney's role can only be accomplished by internal engagement supporting or relying upon, and coordinating closely with, other interdependent functions and personnel, many of whom may be outside or independent of the decision-making chain involved in executing any legal advice given. While some of these responsibilities can be supplemented by, or outsourced to, external resources such as law firms or consultants, in-house counsel ultimately bear the responsibility for identifying the legal issues and determining resources needed, including budget allocation and competent management of those funds, if and where external resources are deemed appropriate (and can be funded).

Outside counsel and other external resources cannot replicate these internal day-to-day relationships integral to the effective execution of legal guidance on a corporation's operational activities. There is a reason why so many in-house counsel tout variety and constant intellectual challenge as one of the most significant reasons they love their jobs, and why general counsel must become a Jack or Jill of all trades while a master of some.[18]

---

16. *See* Elizabeth Benegas, *Be Proactive: 5 Ways for In-house Legal Teams to Build a Better Relationship with the Business*, ACC DOCKET (Dec. 23, 2020); LexisNexis, Practice Notes: Identifying and nurturing value (2025) https://www.lexisnexis.co.uk/legal/guidance/identifying-nurturing-value.

17. David M. Love, III, Mark Roellig, & Tom Spelt, *So You Want to Be a General Counsel? How to Maximize Your Chances*, SPENCERSTUART (May 2023), https://www.spencerstuart.com/research-and-insight/so-you-want-to-be-a-general-counsel-how-to-maximize-your-chances.

18. McArdle, *supra* note 1.

With all this being said, where should in-house counsel begin in addressing cybersecurity? Key aspects of the cyber threat are clear: (1) the cyber threat is real—every company is a target;[19] (2) the types and avenues for attack continue to grow and become more sophisticated; (3) the attackers come from different sources—both external and internal—and have different motivations; (4) each attack or cyber incident creates a myriad of situation-specific issues potentially requiring legal review and advice; (5) while certain risks can be articulated, the distinction between legal and business risks is likely to be blurred or more inherently interdependent in the cyber domain than in other areas; (6) there is less certainty about the outcomes from the trade-offs among the interdependent risks; and (7) it is often not intuitive what laws and regulations may be implicated (or may be in potential conflict or interdependent with each other) for any given issue or situation, or even if such laws and regulations exist.

It is indisputable that companies ignore the threat at their peril, and stakeholders (including shareholders) are increasingly holding corporations accountable for their cybersecurity postures.[20] As then FBI Director Robert S. Mueller III quipped in 2012:

> [T]here are only two types of companies: those that have been hacked and those that will be hacked. And even they are converging into one category: companies that have been hacked and will be hacked again.[21]

In-house lawyers are uniquely positioned to provide critical insights and recommendations on the development of mitigation and defensive steps that work for their companies and stay within the parameters of the evolving legal and regulatory landscape. The influence and role of in-house counsel in supporting, and sometimes leading, the entity's corporate governance efforts with respect to cybersecurity is increasing, especially when there are conflicts of interest amongst stakeholders that carry legal ramifications, and because new laws and regulations, both domestic and international, must be taken into account. The company's legal department must speak up and weigh in when this occurs and, ultimately,

---

19. *See* Press Release, Gartner, *Gartner Identifies the Top Cybersecurity Trends for 2025* (Mar. 3, 2025), https://www.gartner.com/en/newsroom/press-releases/2025-03-03-gartner-identifiesthe-top-cybersecurity-trends-for-2025; *see also* Jason Remilard, *50 Things You Need to Know to Optimize Your Company's Approach to Data Privacy and Cybersecurity*, ENTREPRENEUR (June 22, 2021) https://www.entrepreneur.com/slideshow/365902; Steve Ursillo, Jr. & Christopher Arnold, Cybersecurity is Critical for all Organizations—Large and Small, INTERNAT'L FED. OF ACCT. (Oct. 23, 2023), https://www.ifac.org/knowledge-gateway/preparing-future-ready-professionals/discussion/cybersecurity-critical-all-organizations-large-and-small; Andrew Martins, *Cyberattacks and Your Small Business: A Primer for Cybersecurity*, BUS. NEWS DAILY (Oct. 24, 2023), https://www.businessnewsdaily.com/15295-cyberthreats-biggest-business-concern.html.

20. *See* Randi Zimmer, *After a Data Breach: Navigating Long-Tail Legal and Financial Risks*, JD SUPRA (Jan. 29, 2025), https://www.jdsupra.com/legalnews/after-a-data-breach-navigating-long-7783215/.

21. Robert S. Mueller, III, Remarks at RSA Cyber Security Conference, San Francisco, CA (Ma. 1, 2012), https://archives.fbi.gov/archives/news/speeches/combating-threats-in-the-cyber-world-outsmarting-terrorists-hackers-and-spies. *See* Richard Bejtlich, *The Origin of the Quote "There Are Two Types of Companies,"* TAOSECURITY BLOG (Dec. 18, 2018), https://taosecurity.blogspot.com/2018/12/the-origin-of-quote-there-are-two-types.html (exploring the history and variations of the commonly used phrase "There are two types of companies").

arbitrate if conflicts cannot be resolved or the impact of legal risks on operations must be understood, articulated, and mitigated.[22]

1.3. Duties and Responsibilities

The in-house attorney's specific duties and responsibilities will influence (and be influenced by) the level and scope of cybersecurity law competencies required. A quick assessment of what these might look like can be divided generally into two categories: those pertinent to the specific attorney's role and those pertinent to the corporation as an organization.

Any attorney presumptively understands the basic aspects of their role and perhaps the associated technical responsibilities. For example, an in-house M&A attorney will know the steps that must be taken to protect proprietary information regarding deals. An employment attorney will know that personally identifiable information needs to be properly identified, managed, and secured. Positionally, a chief legal officer or general counsel has a broader range of competencies, they interface with executive and upper management as peers, and they may interface with the board of directors. In addition, being in charge of managing the legal function and activities of the corporation places the CLO or GC in the ultimate position of responsibility for, at a minimum, addressing the legal aspects of cyber threats and cyber incidents, either directly or through staff and/or additional resources. Next-tier attorneys leading business units or groups of specialists may have a similar scope as the GC, whereas specialists need to focus on cybersecurity developments pertinent to their areas and internal client base. In-house counsel also often play a key role in drafting or reviewing company policies and procedures.

All attorneys have a duty to have and maintain a basic level of technological competence.[23] As a matter of common sense, technology is undeniably a facet of every form of legal practice. Recognizing the rising and ubiquitous use of computers, the internet, voice over IP (VOIP) technologies, mobile devices and more, in 2012, the American Bar Association (ABA) amended Comment 8 to its Model Rule 1.1, which requires lawyers to provide competent representation to their clients. The amended Comment expressly reflects a technology-focused duty: "a lawyer should keep abreast of changes in the law and its practice, *including the benefits and risks associated with relevant technology....*"[24] With the rapid advancement of technology in the subsequent decade (highlighted during the COVID-19 pandemic with remote meeting technologies and now with the easy access to AI tools such as ChatGPT and CoPilot), Comment 8 is now is commonly understood to mean that lawyers are not expected to become technological experts, but they must stay

---

22. *See, e.g.,* Opinion, Camilo Artiga-Purcell, *Cybersecurity Planning: A Critical Responsibility for In-House Counsel.* Legal Dive (Apr. 1, 2024), https://www.legaldive.com/news/cybersecurity-planning-a-critical-responsibility-for-in-house-counsel/711897/; H. Jeff Smith, The Shareholders vs. Stakeholders Debate, MITSloan Mgmt. Rev. (July 15, 2003) (noting such conflicts are addressed through legal application of the existing duties of care and loyalty), https://sloanreview.mit.edu/article/the-shareholders-vs-stakeholders-debate/.

23. *See* MRPC r. 1.1 cmt. 8.

24. *Id.*

informed about, and proficient in, relevant technology so that they remain technologically competent to perform their jobs.[25]

This expectation of technology competence raises the question "what level of proficiency is demanded of lawyers as an ethical and professional obligation to be 'reasonably competent' in addressing the legal risks associated with cybersecurity"? To what degree are we to hold lawyers accountable for their "failure to keep pace with the rapid evolution of technologies with which they may have had no special training or expertise"?[26]

While the answers to these questions lie outside the bounds of this chapter, the fact remains that the ingrained dependency of the legal profession on the use of technology demands that any lawyer, including in-house counsel, have at least an awareness of the fundamental issues and competencies that give rise to cyber-related legal risks posed to the company. Thus, having the ability to *recognize* and discuss basic aspects and elements of organizational cybersecurity, such as data breaches, insider threats, phishing, business email compromises, and incident response can be posited as fundamental and necessary skills. While every lawyer is not expected to be able to code or conduct pen testing personally, other competencies will extend beyond having a command of the lawyer's area of legal expertise alone.

Other key competencies of relevance in the cyber domain include emotional intelligence and the ability to collaborate on a 360-degree basis. The ability to interact with others in an effective and empathetic manner is important for any in-house attorney. Effective interactions draw directly on the capabilities to recognize, understand, and manage one's own emotions while also recognizing, understanding, and influencing the emotions of others.[27] In the cybersecurity context, understanding workforce motivations and behaviors is critical. People are at the center of efforts to secure data and establish a culture of cybersecurity awareness and vigilance: human error remains one of the highest risk factors for cyber incidents.[28] Understanding the different motivations of hackers also assists in identifying potential attack vectors and designing optimized mitigations against phishing attacks and

25. *See* Lisa Z. Rosenof, *The Fate of Comment 8: Analyzing a Lawyer's Ethical Obligation of Technological Competence*, 90 U. CIN. L. REV. 1320 (2022), https://scholarship.law.uc.edu/uclr/vol90/iss4/9/.

26. *Id.* 1333 (recognizing the challenges of requiring lawyers to develop the necessary competence in a subject matter they have not been professionally trained or equipped to do due to the "fast-paced nature of technology").

27. Ronda Muir, *Emotional Intelligence for Lawyers*, AM. BAR ASS'N (Sept. 30, 2015), https://www.americanbar.org/careercenter/blog/emotional-intelligence-for-lawyers/; *see also* DANIEL GOLEMAN, EMOTIONAL INTELLIGENCE: WHY IT CAN MATTER MORE THAN IQ. (2006) (25th anniversary ed.). For the importance of emotional intelligence in business leaders, see Jeff Moss, *Emotional Intelligence in Business and Leadership*, FORBES (Nov. 13, 2018, updated Apr. 14, 2022), https://www.forbes.com/sites/forbesnycouncil/2018/11/13/emotional-intelligence-in-business-and-leadership/?sh=603cfc2459eb; Joel Makhluf, *The Importance of Emotional Intelligence in Business*, BUS. J. (Aug. 11, 2017), https://www.bizjournals.com/bizjournals/how-to/human-resources/2017/08/the-importance-of-emotional-intelligence-in.html.

28. Nadja Fertasi, *Three Ways to Leverage Emotional Intelligence and Minimize Cyber Risk through Human Vulnerability*, GLOBAL CYBER ALLIANCE (Nov. 10, 2020), https://www.globalalliance.org/three-ways-to-leverage-emotional-intelligence-and-minimize-cyber-risk-through-human-vulnerability/.

other types of social engineering.[29] These soft-skill competencies are thus critical in enabling the company to successfully prepare and execute a sound strategy and plan for responding to cyber incidents in a manner that is legally compliant and navigates the company through competitive business environments to the most optimal outcome.

2. Fundamentals of What In-House Counsel Needs to Know

2.1. The Basics

In-house counsel may be tempted to defer tackling the challenges of cybersecurity, electing instead to operate under the assumption that the responsibility lies with some other part of the company; to wait until they are directed to review cybersecurity issues; or perhaps to decide that the easier path would be to take the chance they will not be confronted with a cyber incident. They do so at their (and their company's) peril. Statistical data regarding the vulnerability of companies to cyber threats are readily available, and examples of breached companies are covered in the news almost daily. The trend of high-visibility cyber incidents and their impacts continues—consider incidents such as the SolarWinds breach in 2020, the Colonial Pipeline, JBS, and Microsoft cyber breaches along with the Log4J vulnerability in 2021, the Real Estate Wealth Network breach in 2023, and the UnitedHealth Group breach in 2024[30]—as well as cases such as the 2014 Yahoo breach (and the subsequent departure of Yahoo's executive management, including the general counsel). These examples illustrate that the consequences of such a choice to defer attention to cybersecurity can be detrimental, and the company, its employees, shareholders, and customer base, all of whom may suffer the misfortune of insufficient attention.[31]

From a more positive perspective, engaging in cybersecurity also provides in-house counsel with an opportunity to develop new expertise and key competencies, and it may also position in-house counsel to gain visibility for recognition or advancement. As noted above, having at least a rudimentary understanding of cybersecurity issues is arguably now

---

29. Phishing remains one of the top attack vectors in cybersecurity breaches. *See* Verizon, 2025 Data Breach Investigations Report 10 (2025) [hereinafter 2025 DBIR], https://www.verizon.com/business/resources/Tbe6/reports/2025-dbir-data-breach-investigations-report.pdf.

30. For a list of significant cyber incidents, see the Ctr. for Strategic & Internat'l Stud. Significant Cyber Incidents website, which "records significant cyber incidents since 2006, focusing on cyber attacks on government agencies, defense and high tech companies, or economic crimes with losses of more than a million dollars." *Significant Cyber Incidents*, Ctr. for Strategic & Internat'l Stud., https://www.csis.org/programs/strategic-technologies-program/significant-cyber-incidents (last visited July 1, 2025) [hereinafter Significant Cyber Incidents].

31. *See, e.g.*, Daniel B. Garrie & Richard A. Kramer, *Navigating Personal Liability: Post-Data Breach Recommendations for Officers*, Corporate Compliance Insights (Apr. 16, 2024) https://www.corporatecomplianceinsights.com/personal-liability-data-breach/; Jennifer Williams-Alvarez, *After Yahoo, Are In-House Counsel Jobs at Risk Over Cybersecurity?*, Law.com (Mar. 2, 2017), https://www.law.com/article/almID/1202780379239/?slreturn=20250727192401; William Vogeler, *Why Your In-House Job Is at Risk Over Cybersecurity*, FindLaw (Mar. 7, 2017, updated Mar. 21, 2019), http://blogs.findlaw.com/in_house/2017/03/why-your-in-house-job-is-at-risk-over-cybersecurity.html.

a requirement for all in-house counsel; it certainly is for the general counsel or CLO, executive management and directors.[32]

In-house counsel may wonder where to start. As with other legal risks, the legal risks of cyber must be articulated in a manner relevant to the context of the business. This is necessary to establish a common understanding with other company functions and to garner necessary resources (internal and external talent and budget). To initiate this discussion *in advance* of a risk being realized, the attorney should be well-informed about key facts, prepared with useful questions, and speak from a viewpoint of risk management. There are ample resources available to assist in this endeavor. One example is the February 2024 update issued by the National Institute of Standards and Technology (NIST) to its comprehensive Cybersecurity Framework, which utilizes a risk management approach to lay out processes that can help enable companies to become informed about cybersecurity and better prioritize decisions.[33]

2.2. The Amorphous and Unusual Nature of the Threat Compared to Traditional Risks

Cyber threats are equal opportunity with many low barrier entry points. Size truly does not matter, nor does industry sector. No one is safe. Large corporations are obvious targets, especially in certain industry sectors such as healthcare, defense, and financial services, due to the core nature of the data in which those industries traffic. Small companies may be easier targets and should also be aware and vigilant. Verizon's 2021 Data Breach Investigations Report provided sobering confirmation that 46% of cyber breaches resulting in data loss occurred in small companies (defined as having fewer than 1,000 employees).[34] Verizon's 2025 Data Breach Report conveys an even more alarming statistic, noting that there "are almost four times the number of [small to medium-sized] businesses" that fall victim to cyber breaches than larger organizations.[35] Cyberattacks continue their upward trajectory, as does the number of attacks on smaller businesses.[36] The percentage of small businesses attacked does not convey the disproportionate impact and consequences a breach can have for small businesses, which have fewer resources and capabilities to rebound. For them, cyber breaches can be catastrophic.[37]

---

32. *See* Todd Renner & Evan Roberts, *The Role of General Counsel in Managing a Cybersecurity Crisis*, Ass'n of Corp. Counsel (Nov. 19, 2024), https://www.acc.com/resource-library/role-general-counsel-managing-cybersecurity-crisis; Sean Steele, *Cyber Risk Preparedness: The General Counsel's Responsibility*, Forbes (Oct. 6, 2023), https://www.forbes.com/councils/forbestechcouncil/2023/10/06/cyber-risk-preparedness-the-general-counsels-responsibility/; *see also* Conal Gallagher, *Who Is Responsible for Cybersecurity? You*, Forbes (Dec. 12, 2023), https://www.forbes.com/councils/forbestechcouncil/2023/12/12/who-is-responsible-for-cybersecurity-you/.

33. Nat'l Inst. of Standards & Tech., The NIST Cybersecurity Framework (CSF) 2.0 (Feb. 26, 2024), https://doi.org/10.6028/NIST.CSWP.29.

34. Verizon, 2021 Data Breach Investigations Report 89–90 (2021), https://www.verizon.com/business/resources/reports/2021-data-breach-investigations-report.pdf.

35. 2025 DBIR, *supra* note 29, at 86.

36. Eddie Lamb, Introduction, Hiscox Cyber Readiness Report 2023 3, https://www.hiscoxgroup.com/sites/group/files/documents/2023-10/Hiscox-Cyber-Readiness-Report-2023.pdf.

37. *Id.* at 9.

Threats emanate from many sources, both external and internal, from various actors with different motivations ranging from nation-states to organized crime syndicates, cyber-savvy criminals, hacktivists, and employees with malicious intent or who are simply careless.[38] Any one or more of these threats could be directed at any or all facets of the business: from the systems (to disrupt or halt operations), to the data (corporate espionage, corruption of information), to the personnel (identity theft, access, blackmail), to the end customer or end use (counterfeit parts). Attacks do not need to be sequential or coordinated. The price and barriers to entry are low with hacking tools and code easily available on the internet and darknets, often for free. Last, the cyber domain is literally "on" 24/7/365, and attacks can be launched from anywhere in the world regardless of borders.

2.3. Accelerated Global and Macro-Environmental Technology and Workforce Shifts

The accelerated adoption and integration of emergent technologies, such as artificial intelligence (AI), quantum computing, blockchain, and advanced communications such as 5G and 6G, concurrently enhance cybersecurity capabilities and introduce a host of new cybersecurity challenges and risks for in-house counsel to navigate.[39] In addition, shifts in how companies structure and manage data through third-party systems and service providers, most notably the increasing use of cloud-based services and data lakes, impact the legal risks associated with cybersecurity. Last, as illustrated most notably during the COVID-19 pandemic, the increasing mobility and hybrid/remote nature of the workforce influences every organization's cybersecurity considerations. We touch briefly on some of the more notable macro-environmental shifts below.

2.3.1. *Artificial Intelligence*

AI systems and applications provide organizations with powerful tools and enablers that can streamline and strengthen data analysis, risk management, and threat detection. AI capabilities also exponentially increase the organization's attack surface and can create a culture of complacency or inattentiveness.[40] Regardless of how they are used, AI technologies rely upon vast quantities of data, including potentially sensitive customer and employee data (including personally identifiable information) and proprietary corporate

38. FBI, FBI Director Addresses Cyber Security Gathering: Varied Group of Cyber Experts Exchange Ideas, FBI News (Mar. 8, 2017) ("Comey discussed the 'stack of bad actors' committing cyber crimes"), https://www.fbi.gov/news/stories/fbi-director-addresses-cyber-security-gathering.

39. Khalid Khan, Adnan Khurshid & Javier Cifuentes-Faura, *Is Artificial Intelligence a New Battleground for Cybersecurity?*, 28 Internet of Things (Dec. 2024), https://doi.org/10.1016/j.iot.2024.101428; Joe Patrice, *AI Delivers Fresh Nightmares for In-house Counsel*, Thomson Reuters (Feb. 19, 2025, 12:58 PM), https://abovethelaw.com/2025/02/ai-delivers-fresh-nightmares-for-in-house-counsel/; Lizzy Lim, *How N-House Lawyers Can (and Should) Use AI and ChatGPT*, Law Soc'y (June 8, 2023), https://www.lawsociety.org.uk/topics/in-house/how-in-house-lawyers-can-and-should-use-ai-and-chatgpt.

40. Interview by Tom Field, Information Media Security Group, with Andres Andreu, COO and CISO, Constella Intelligence, RSAC Conference 2025, *Agentic AI Expands the Corporate Attack Surface,* (May 4, 2025), https://www.govinfosecurity.com/agentic-ai-expands-corporate-attack-surface-a-28256.

information (including trade secrets).[41] These types of confidential information must be protected under evolving domestic and international regulatory frameworks (alongside often outdated existing laws that require interpretation about how they apply to emergent and shifting technological capabilities). Accordingly, in-house counsel must work closely with IT, risk management, and compliance teams to assess the specific risks associated with deploying AI technologies. Core considerations in this complicated domain include, but are not limited to:

- ***Data Governance and Data Assurance (Integrity)***: Data fed into a company's AI systems must be properly identified, protected, and managed in a manner that complies with privacy requirements under laws such as the European Union's General Data Protection Regulation (GDPR), state laws like the California Consumer Privacy Act (CCPA), and emerging international, federal, and state AI guidelines.[42]
- ***Security Parameters of AI Infrastructure***: The company's AI infrastructure and framework must be configured in a manner that protects it from adversarial attacks, data poisoning, and unauthorized access.[43]
- ***Transparency and Accessibility***: As with much of cybersecurity, humans tend to be the weakest link. Safe and effective adoption and use of AI tools requires training and well-crafted policies that enable the workforce to understand how the organization's AI tools are to be, and must be, used.[44]
- ***Threat Monitoring and Incident Response***: As AI tools and systems are deployed, new and enhanced AI capabilities should be leveraged and integrated with the company's broader cybersecurity processes and incident response plan. AI-generated insights should be vetted and incorporated into the organization's ongoing threat monitoring

41. N. Nivedhaa, *A Comprehensive Review of AI's Dependence on Data*, 1 INTERNAT'L J. OF ARTIFICIAL INTEL. AND DATA SCI. 1 (Jan.-June 2024).

42. Regulation (EU) 2016/679 of the European Parliament and of the Council of 27 April 2016 on the protection of natural persons with regard to the processing of personal data and on the free movement of such data, and repealing Directive 95/46/EC (General Data Protection Regulation); California Consumer Privacy Act of 2018 (CCPA), Cal. Civ. Code §§ 1798.100–1798.199.100 (West 2024). *See* Mike Green, *Overcoming Data Governance Challenges in AI Deployment*, RSA CONF. BLOG (Feb. 15, 2024), https://www.rsaconference.com/library/blog/overcoming-data-governance-challenges-in-ai-deployment. *See also*, Lior Gavish, *Data Lakes vs. Data Warehouses: The Truth Revealed*, MONTE CARLO BLOG (July 25, 2022), https://www.montecarlodata.com/blog-data-lake-vs-data-warehouse; Rihan Hai et al., *Data Lakes: A Survey of Functions and Systems*, 99 IEEE TRANSACTIONS ON KNOWLEDGE & DATA ENG'G 1 (Dec. 2023), https://www.researchgate.net/publication/370278973_Data_Lakes_A_Survey_of_Functions_and_Systems.

43. *See* Calvin Nobles, *The Weaponization of Artificial Intelligence in Cybersecurity: A Systematic Review*, 239 PROCEDIA COMPUTER SCI.547 (2024) https://doi.org/10.1016/j.procs.2024.06.206; Marcus Comiter, *Attacking Artificial Intelligence: AI's Security Vulnerability and What Policymakers Can Do About It*, BELFER CTR. FOR SCI.& INTERNAT'L AFF., HARV. KENNEDY SCH. (Aug. 2019), https://live-hksbelfer.pantheonsite.io/publication/AttackingAI.

44. *See* Legal Advisory, Portia S. Keady, *Developing Skills in AI: The Importance of AI Training for Employees*, NUTTER (June 13, 2024) https://www.nutter.com/printpilot-publication-developing-skills-in-ai.pdf?1747334183.

and incident response processes, including parameters for when legal review of incidents involving AI is warranted.[45]

- ***AI Supplier/Service Provider Oversight***: In-house counsel should review vendor agreements (including those for law firm engagements) to ensure they include appropriate terms and conditions addressing their use of AI and clearly identifying the supplier's cybersecurity, indemnification, and incident response obligations.

Governmental authorities are increasingly focused on AI governance.[46] In-house counsel must anticipate continuing and rapidly evolving federal, state, and international regulatory obligations, consider how deployment of AI tools and systems impacts the organization's cybersecurity posture, and provide input into how their companies can optimally adapt AI governance frameworks while managing legal compliance and cyber risks.

2.3.2. *Increased Reliance and Dependency on Cloud Services*

Organizations are increasingly relying upon cloud-based services to manage their data, facilitate workflows and business processes, and operationalize greater flexibility and workforce integration.[47] Examples of cloud-based services include software-as-a-service (SaaS), infrastructure-as-a-service (IaaS), platforms-as-a-service (PaaS), and function-as-a-service (FaaS).[48] The use of interdependent clouds to accommodate business needs creates an even more complex internet-based environment.[49] The ubiquitousness of mobile device usage by employees and suppliers makes the risks and challenges of internet-of-things (IoT) and wireless connectivity more complex than ever before. The resilience of adapting cloud-based capabilities for business operations was demonstrated during the COVID-19 pandemic as organizations and entire industry sectors that had adopted those capabilities were quicker to adjust to remote work when large swathes, if not entire, workforces and entity populations were suddenly forced out of the office to work from home.[50]

---

45. *See* Ron Dutta, *How to integrate AI into Your Cybersecurity (and Why You Should)*, TTEC Blog https://www.ttec.com/blog/how-integrate-ai-your-cybersecurity-and-why-you-should (last visited July 1, 2025); *Building Smarter Security Systems with AI Integration*, Cyber Mgmt. Alliance (Jan. 17, 2025) https://www.cm-alliance.com/cybersecurity-blog/building-smarter-security-systems-with-ai-integration.

46. *See, e.g.*, Mark Esposito, *Around the Globe, Governments Lean into AI,* 2 Atl. Dialogues 120 (2024), https://www.theatlantic.com/sponsored/google/governments-ai/3969/; Michael L. Littman et al., Gathering Strength, Gathering Storms: The One Hundred Year Study on Artificial Intelligence (AI100) 2021 Study Panel Report, Stan. U. (Sept. 2021), http://ai100.stanford.edu/2021-report; Sanam Hooshidary, Chelsea Canada & William Clark, *Artificial Intelligence in Government: The Federal and State Landscape,* Nat'l Conf. of St. Legis. (Nov. 22, 2024), https://www.ncsl.org/technology-and-communication/artificial-intelligence-in-government-the-federal-and-state-landscape.

47. *See What Is the Future of Cloud Computing?*, CompTIA Blog (Dec. 18, 2024), https://www.comptia.org/blog/what-is-the-future-of-cloud-computing; *What Are Cloud Services?* Red Hat (Mar. 14, 2022), https://www.redhat.com/en/topics/cloud-computing/what-are-cloud-services.

48. Red Hat, *supra* note 47.

49. CISO Advisory, *Cloud Security Essentials—Protecting Multi-Cloud Environments*, Cybersecurity News (May 17, 2025) [hereinafter CISO Advisory], https://cybersecuritynews.com/cloud-security/.

50. *Gartner Says More Than Half of Enterprise IT Spending in Key Market Segments Will Shift to the Cloud by 2025*, Gartner (Feb. 9, 2022) https://www.gartner.com/en/newsroom/press-releases/2022-02-09-gartner-

Along with the benefits, however, the increasing use of, unification, and dependency on cloud-based services exponentially increases cyber-related risks for organizations.[51] According to one security consultant, reportedly over 40% of security incidents originate from cloud environments.[52] Another noted that cloud intrusions experienced a significant surge in 2023.[53] Recognized security risks associated with cloud-based services include an expanded attack surface, complexities in managing a shared responsibility model and interdependent regulatory compliance, heightened insider threats (including employee usage of unauthorized cloud applications), and third-party / supplier risks.[54]

Legal departments should endeavor to be aware of relevant developments in the cloud-based services space and stay informed regarding changes in data protection laws and best practices in negotiating cloud service agreements, ensuring that such documents address key issues such as data protection, liability, incident reporting, and audit rights with terms acceptable to the company.[55] This guidance applies to law firms as well; studies done by the American Bar Association in 2023 indicate that 70% of law firms utilize cloud-based services in practicing law, and this percentage continues to increase.[56] In-house counsel should take steps to confirm that their outside firms are sufficiently technically competent to explain their firm's awareness and risk mitigation practices with respect to the firm's use of cloud-based services and obtain provisions documenting these practices and appropriate assurances protecting the company in retainer letters.

2.3.3. *Workplace and Workforce Environmental Changes*

Workplace and workforce environments continue to significantly evolve and transform in response to technological advances, changing demographics, cultural considerations, and shifts to hybrid and remote work arrangements.[57] In-house counsel should endeavor to

---

says-more-than-half-of-enterprise-it-spending; Gaurav Aggarwal, *How the Pandemic Has Accelerated Cloud Adoption*, FORBES (Jan. 15, 2021), https://www.forbes.com/councils/forbestechcouncil/2021/01/15/how-the-pandemic-has-accelerated-cloud-adoption/.

51. CISO Advisory, supra note 49.

52. *See 17 Security Risks of Cloud Computing in 2025*, SENTINELONE (Apr. 3, 2025), https://www.sentinelone.com/cybersecurity-101/cloud-security/security-risks-of-cloud-computing/.

53. Matt Kapko, *Cloud Intrusions Spiked 75% in 2023, CrowdStrike Says*, Cybersecurity Dive (Feb. 23, 2024), https://www.cybersecuritydive.com/news/cloud-intrusions-spike-crowdstrike/708315/.

54. *Id.*

55. Bhavna B. Sehgal, *A Starter Guide to Cloud Compliance*, CrowdStrike (July 9, 2024), https://www.crowdstrike.com/en-us/cybersecurity-101/cloud-security/cloud-compliance/; John C. Eustice, *Understanding Cloud Data Protection and Data Privacy*, THOMSON REUTERS, https://legal.thomsonreuters.com/en/insights/articles/understanding-data-privacy-and-cloud-computing (last visited July 1, 2025); Brandon Vogel, *What Lawyers Must Understand about Cloud Computing and Ethics While Working Remotely*, N.Y. ST. BAR ASS'N(Jan. 25, 2022) https://nysba.org/what-lawyers-must-understand-about-cloud-computing-and-ethics-while-working-remotely.

56. Michael D.J. Eisenberg, *2023 Cloud Computing TechReport*, ABA Law Practice Div. (Jan. 29, 2024), https://www.americanbar.org/groups/law_practice/resources/tech-report/2023/2023-cloud-computing-techreport.

57. THE CHANGING LANDSCAPE OF WORKPLACE AND WORKFORCE (HADI EL-FARR ED. 2024); THE CHANGING NATURE OF WORK (ANN HOWARD ED. 1995); Martin Krajcik, Dusana Alshatti Schmidt & Matus Barath, *Hybrid Work Model: An Approach to Work-Life Flexibility in a Changing Environment*, 13 Admin. Sci. 150 (Jun. 6, 2023), https://doi.org/10.3390/admsci13060150.

keep their finger on the pulse of these changes. AI tools build on the vast digitization of companies' records, increased reliance on the internet and digital collaboration tools, and remote and hybrid work models that have developed over the past decade. Generational changes have made workforces more adept at exploiting technology while arguably being more in need of cybersecurity awareness and training.

Such changes have direct and adaptive implications for cybersecurity risk management. For in-house counsel, such shifts can raise complex issues concerning wage and hour compliance, reasonable accommodations, workplace safety, employee privacy, and employee classifications in response to an increasingly decentralized and technology-dependent environment. Today's workforce relies heavily on personal devices and home or public networks, and employees (and some contractors) have direct access to the company's systems while utilizing cloud services (both corporate and personal), typically while using the same device. In-house counsel should work closely with both IT and human resources to ensure that cybersecurity policies and practices are adequate in addressing the cybersecurity risks attendant to such evolving workforce dynamics.

2.3.4. *Identification of Interdependencies and Essential Relationships*

Cybersecurity is a team sport, reliant upon generalists and specialists spanning the entire organization, including legal.[58] In-house counsel must work with other departments that form the organizational framework of the company in a manner that mitigates the risks created by the threat. Cyber risks include a combination of external attacks, insider threats, company information system and device vulnerabilities, and operational risks. Consideration should be given to how each of these threats might manifests itself in the corporate environment, and appropriate mitigation options should be identified and analyzed for effectiveness in addressing each of the risks. An established relationship between the legal and IT teams is essential, especially in preparing for a breach and reacting to a cyber incident.[59] Of equal importance is a strong working relationship with human resources, as a critical element of being able to educate the workforce and build a cyber-savvy culture. In addition to ensuring clear communication and strong relationships are built with other key functions, relationships with senior management and shareholders must also be considered essential to implementing effective cybersecurity practices and corresponding legal advice.

Relationships should also be established with certain governmental agencies, such as the FBI, that have cybersecurity resources and knowledge. Establishing an open dialogue of cooperation is valuable. The government is playing an increasing role in notifying companies of cyber breaches, often when the companies themselves are unaware of the ongoing

58. *See, e.g., Cybersecurity Is a Team Sport*, Ctr. for Internet Security Blog (undated), https://www.cisecurity.org/insights/blog/cybersecurity-is-a-team-sport.

59. *See* Report, Modern Counsel, The General Counsel's Guide to Digital Defense, (Sept. 20, 2016) [hereinafter Guide to Digital Defense], https://modern-counsel.com/download-the-gcs-guide-to-digital-defense/.

attack.[60] Companies are better served if they can draw upon an existing communication channel and relationship, particularly in the event the government must be notified of a breach or the company needs assistance in responding to a breach. Traditional views that argue against sharing information regarding a cyber breach with the government, especially law enforcement, typically arise out of fear of retributive enforcement actions or loss of competitive data. The more persuasive view in the face of increasing cyber threats, however, is that the private sector is far better served by sharing information and drawing upon the considerable expertise and knowledge of the U.S. government to the greatest extent possible.[61]

Governmental agencies and relationships are likewise goldmines for information useful to the company, enabling companies to have a more global view and understanding of how the cyber threat landscape is evolving. As the government itself is constantly under cyberattack, industry benefits from the government's "lessons learned" and a more informed understanding of where to focus limited resources, such as on the "insider threat."[62] Other data available from the government provides insight into the types of attacks (e.g., nation-state versus organized crime) and new threat vectors.[63] Such data is helpful in tailoring

---

60. While exact numbers are not available, a report released by the Office of the Inspector General (OIG) of the U.S. Department of Justice (DoJ) indicated that as of 2017, over 20,000 notifications had been issued by the Federal Bureau of Investigation (FBI) to companies impacted by cyberbreaches through the FBI's Cyber Guardian program. DoJ OIG, Audit of the Federal Bureau of Investigation's Cyber Victim Notification Process, (Mar. 2019), https://oig.justice.gov/reports/2019/a1923.pdf. The U.S. Cybersecurity & Infrastructure Security Agency (CISA) also maintains a website where it publishes Official Alerts & Statements issued by the FBI. *Official Alerts & Statements—FBI*, CISA, https://www.cisa.gov/stopransomware/official-alerts-statements-fbi (last visited July 2, 2025).

61. *See* James B. Comey, Director, FBI, Privacy, Public Safety, and Security: How We Can Confront the Cyber Threat Together, Remarks at the International Conference on Cyber Engagement at Georgetown University, Washington, D.C. (Apr. 26, 2016), https://www.fbi.gov/news/speeches-and-testimony/privacy-public-safety-and-security-how-we-can-confront-the-cyber-threat-together; *see also* Chris Johnson et al., Guide to Cyber Threat Information Sharing, NIST Special Pub. 800-150 (Oct. 2016), http://dx.doi.org/10.6028/NIST.SP.800-150; World Econ. F., Guidance on Public-Private Information Sharing against Cybercrime (Jan. 2017), https://www3.weforum.org/docs/WEF_Guidance_Cybercrime_report_2017.pdf.

62. A survey conducted by Mimecast found that 95% of the data breaches reported by respondents for 2024 were caused by human error. *The State of Human Risk 2025*, Mimecast https://www.mimecast.com/resources/ebooks/state-of-human-risk-2025/ (last visited Sept. 15, 2025). Mimecast concluded "that despite having spent billions to strengthen technology stacks, breaches continue unabated, mostly due to human error," and noted as another key point that AI tools "are successfully combating threats, but Generative AI is also still helping threat actors launch attacks." *Id.* Compare the findings in Verizon's 2025 DBIR, *supra* note 29, at 11, which found "the involvement of the human element in breaches remained roughly the same as last year, hovering around 60%." *See also* Jennifer Gregory, *CISOs List Human Error as Their Top Cybersecurity Risk*, IBM (Aug. 15, 2024), https://www.ibm.com/think/insights/cisos-list-human-error-top-cybersecurity-risk; *Insider Threat Mitigation*, CISA, https://www.cisa.gov/topics/physical-security/insider-threat-mitigation (last visited Sept. 23, 2025).

63. New technologies introduce new vulnerabilities, especially when combined with increased dependence on Internet-of-Things (IOT) devices and cloud-based content management systems. Attacks are increasing in number. For example, ransomware attacks increased by nearly 500% in 2020 according to the Bitdefender 2020 Consumer Threat Landscape Report, Macintosh HD:Users:Shared:dd:4work:Bitdefender-PR-Report-Mid2020-creat4740-en_EN:Bitdefender-PR-Report-Mid2020-creat4740-en_EN.indd). In 2024, Bitdefender reported that "[c]onsumers manage on average between 5 and 9 accounts online[, a] quarter of netizens have experienced at least one security event in the past year[, and] SMS scams are the most abundant threat consumers faced in the past 12 months." Bitdefender, 2024 Consumer Cybersecurity Assessment Report 3 (Apr. 2024) (surveying 7,335 general consumers across the UK, US, Germany, Spain, France, Italy, and Australia), https://www.bitdefender.com/

company policies and practices and developing more effective mitigation measures and controls.

Legal should also develop a strong and open relationship with the company's Communications department. In the aftermath of a cyber incident, Communications should be briefed and prepared as early as possible to respond to questions from the media and customers, following an appropriately crafted cyber incident / cyber response plan. (Ideally, the response plan will incorporate a documented communication management approach.)[64] This is a key element of effectively mitigating the potential for extensive reputational damage, or at least avoiding exacerbation of a bad situation by making an ill-advised or poorly timed remark or (in today's news and rumor-hungry climate) failing to make a public statement when one is needed. The communication strategy should leverage the benefits of sharing the company's perspective openly where appropriate.

Other key relationships should be tended in a manner prioritized in accordance with the company's business and internal infrastructure. Those constituencies reasonably would include human resources, finance, supply chain, key business partners, and operations. In addition, special care and tending must be paid to C-Suite engagement and communications with the board of sirectors.[65]

2.3.5. *Distinguishing Among Compliance in Operational Matters, Market-based Considerations, and Legal and Regulatory Matters*

In-house attorney must keep in mind the differences in providing advice for operational business activities, such as how to ensure business data remains available in a manner that allows the business to continue operating, for litigation or matters in formal legal dispute for a, and for legal and regulatory purposes, such as appropriately defining and protecting

---

en-us/blog/hotforsecurity/bitdefender-releases-2024-consumer-cybersecurity-assessment-report. Attacks are also more sophisticated, as evidenced by the zero-day exploits. See 2025 DBIR, supra note 29, at 10 ("The exploitation of vulnerabilities has seen another year of growth as an initial access vector for breaches, reaching 20%.... This was an increase of 34% in relation to last year's report and was supported, in part, by zero-day exploits targeting edge devices and virtual private networks (VPNs). The percentage of edge devices and VPNs as a target on our exploitation of vulnerabilities action was 22%, and it grew almost eight-fold12 from the 3% found in last year's report.").

64. *See Guidance on Effective Communications in a Cyber Incident*, U.K. Nat'l Cyber Security Ctr. (Oct. 16, 2024). https://www.ncsc.gov.uk/guidance/effective-communications-in-a-cyber-incident; *Emphasizing Preparedness: The Role of Out-of-Band Communications in Cyber Incident Response*, Marsh (Nov. 11, 2024), https://www.marsh.com/en/services/cyber-risk/insights/the-role-of-out-of-band-communications-in-cyber-incident-response.html; see also Handbook, Chapter 13, *Achieving Preparedness through Standards and Planning & Best Practices for Incident Response.*

65. *See* Rosalyn Page, *How CISOs Can Forge the Best Relationships for Cybersecurity Investment*, CSO Online (Jan. 8, 2025), https://www.csoonline.com/article/3625745/how-cisos-can-forge-the-best-relationships-for-cybersecurity-investment.html; Zac Amos, *Why Collaboration Is Essential for Cybersecurity Teams*, ISA Global Cybersecurity Alliance Blog, https://gca.isa.org/blog/why-collaboration-is-essential-for-cybersecurity-teams (last visited July 2, 2025); Jeffrey G. Proudfoot et al., *The Importance of Board Member Actions for Cybersecurity Governance and Risk Management*, 22 MIS Q. Exec. 235 (Dec. 2023), https://aisel.aisnet.org/misqe/vol22/iss4/6. An excellent resource for directors is the U.K. National Cyber Security Centre's website. *See Cyber Security Toolkit for Boards*, U.K. Nat'l Cyber Security Ctr., https://www.ncsc.gov.uk/collection/board-toolkit (last visited Sept. 23, 2025).

specific categories of data (such as personally identifiable information or protected health information) and disclosures required by regulatory agencies like the Securities & Exchange Commission (SEC) or other governmental requirements.[66]

Operational compliance addresses identification and mitigation of the risk of loss or failure of controls that result from inadequate or failed internal processes, people, and systems, or are the result of external events.[67] Operational risks include legal risks but exclude strategic and reputational risks. Market-based considerations address customer relations and communications, industry coalitions, interactions with business partners or competitors, and public relations, all of which may implicate legal or regulatory considerations. In contrast, legal and regulatory compliance address the consequences of failure to comply with specific laws, regulations, rules, codes of conduct or duties, or other standards monitored or enforced by agencies or organizations that are applicable to the entity or industry.

Examples of operational compliance include ensuring that the company maintains an ISO certification, following a sound strategic sourcing process, or advising on the establishment of disciplined supply chain security. Market-based considerations may involve advising on a new branding campaign, working with a trade association on new provisions of the Federal Acquisition Regulations, or establishing new, or revising existing, standards. Keeping these distinctions in mind is not only necessary to best evaluate legal risks versus business risks, but is also essential for ascertaining if and where legal privilege and direct legal or regulatory compliance lines should be drawn.

3. Be Prepared

In-house counsel should be proactive in ensuring the company is positioned as best as possible, within the parameters of available resources and maturity of the entity's corporate governance framework, to handle a cyber incident. How to best prepare? Certain fundamentals can be identified and prioritized in a tailored manner, taking account of existing resources (e.g., if there is an IT group or if IT is outsourced), corporate structure, existing command media, etc., and starting with a basic plan that incorporates the following elements.

66. For publicly traded companies, the lawyer can be expected to play a key role in ascertaining what needs to be publicly disclosed under SEC regulations versus potentially disclosing excessive information. See FBI, FBI Guidance to Victims of Cyber Incidents on SEC Reporting Requirements, https://www.fbi.gov/investigate/cyber/fbi-guidance-to-victims-of-cyber-incidents-on-sec-reporting-requirements (last visited July 2, 2025).

67. *See, e.g.*, CISA, Fact Sheet, Primary Mitigations to Reduce Cyber Threats to Operational Technology (May 6, 2025) (guidance issues jointly with the FBI, Environmental Protection Agency and Dep't of Energy, https://www.cisa.gov/resources-tools/resources/primary-mitigations-reduce-cyber-threats-operational-technology (last visited July 21, 2025); U.K. Nat'l Cyber Security Ctr, Guidance, *The Fundamentals and Basics of Cyber Risk*, https://www.ncsc.gov.uk/collection/risk-management/the-fundamentals-and-basics-of-cyber-risk (last visited July 2, 2025).

3.1. Understand as much as you can about the risks

1. ***Read, absorb, translate, and stay current.*** Bad actors in the cyber domain are getting better, becoming increasingly more sophisticated and clever. Cyber-related issues are relevant to all aspects of in-house practice, ranging from handling electronically stored HIPAA-protected personal health information or other personally identifiable information, digitized trade secrets, or M&A documentation, to company-sensitive and market competitive information as well as embedded software being sold to end consumers. In-house counsel must do what attorneys always must do: seek and obtain as much information as they can about the risks associated with cybersecurity, focusing on their company's particular industry and their specific role (*e.g.*, a general counsel versus a specialty area such as ERISA or labor and employment) and the organizational infrastructure in which they sit.

   The dynamic and evolving nature of cybersecurity demands that in-house counsel stay abreast of new developments as much as possible. New methods of attack and compromise are developed every day and originate from multiple sources and means. As technology evolves, so does a company's attack surface area. Regularly refreshing what in-house counsel knows and reevaluating assumptions that may be relied on in establishing the company's cybersecurity posture are a sound practice.

   Determine the most efficient way to get to the information most relevant to you and your company. Sign up for alerts on proposed regulations, developments, and industry trends. Follow blogs and podcasts focused on legal issues associated with cybersecurity. Many law firms offer cybersecurity news feeds, webinars, and panel presentations that provide high-level overviews and preliminary analyses, as well as specific programs on developing case law or trends. This information can be distilled and communicated to stakeholders.
2. ***Don't reinvent the wheel.*** Given the incredibly amorphous nature of cybersecurity, no single attorney can know everything—which underscores the imperative for creating a team to address cyber threats and a network to stay current on developments and trends in the law concerning cybersecurity. The good news is that a significant number of experts, organizations, and institutions have been tackling the issue for decades. There is a wealth of information available through the internet and other channels, often at little or no cost, and offering different perspectives. Find credible information and facts from reputable sources such as this Handbook, the 2025 ACC Foundation Report on the State of Cybersecurity,[68] and government entities like the FBI, National Institute of Standards and Technology, and the Department of Commerce, which post significant amounts of information and practical tips regarding cybersecurity. In many instances, government entities issue guidance documents to educate

68. ACC Foundation, 2025 State of Cybersecurity Report: An In-house Perspective, Ass'n of Corp. Counsel (Mar. 24, 2025), https://www.acc.com/resource-library/2025-state-cybersecurity-report-house-perspective.

specific industries.[69] For certain sectors, such as aerospace and defense, the government has been driven by the national security imperative to develop cybersecurity frameworks (such as the Department of Defense's Cybersecurity Maturity Model[70]) and best practice guidance (such as those captured in standards, like NIST 800-171, *Protecting Controlled Unclassified Information in Nonfederal Systems and Organizations*[71]) which can be leveraged and used for benchmarking and gap assessments.

3. ***Know your client.*** In-house counsel must apply the knowledge gathered to a specific company. This requires understanding the company's industry, business model, products and services, workforce composition, governance framework, and other relevant characteristics. Does the company operate globally? Does the relevant industry carry specific regulations (such as healthcare, financial, or defense)? Is the company publicly traded? Does the company have represented employees or employees with diverse citizenships or locations? Is it in manufacturing? Does it engage in research and development? Are there certain products, services, or strategies that expose the company to specific types or greater levels of cyber threats than others? Are the laws most relevant to the company's industry or market sector being expanded to include specific cybersecurity or other relevant data management or recordkeeping requirements (which would apply to digitized information or to the company's systems and networks)?
4. ***Know what and where your crown jewels are.*** Any digitized data or physical facility (accessible through electronic controls such as badges, connected to a supervisory control and data acquisition (SCADA) system, stored in a data lake, etc.) of value is a target. Information about a company's customers and workforce is also an attractive target, sometimes for obtaining credentials or enabling a phishing attack as an entry point to compromise the company's systems. Effective policies and procedures, along with a sound incident response plan, require knowing where the company's most important information and data are stored. Being able to create data maps and data inventories is necessary for creating an effective breach response plan. Creating data maps and inventories can be labor-intensive and must take into account the constantly changing types, amounts, and states of data managed by the corporation.[72]

---

69. *See., e.g.*, U.S. Food & Drug Admin., Guidance Document, Cybersecurity in Medical Devices: Quality System Considerations and Content of Premarket Submissions (June 2025), https://www.fda.gov/regulatory-information/search-fda-guidance-documents/cybersecurity-medical-devices-quality-system-considerations-and-content-premarket-submissions.

70. *Cybersecurity Maturity Model Certification*, Chief Info. Officer, U.S. Dept. of Defense, https://dodcio.defense.gov/cmmc/ (last visited Sept. 23, 2025).

71. Ron Ross & Victoria Pillitteri, NIST Special Pub. 800, NIST SP 800-171r3, Protecting Controlled Unclassified Information in Nonfederal Systems and Organizations, Nat'l Inst. of Standards & Tech. (May 2024), https://doi.org/10.6028/NIST.SP.800-171r3.

72. For an excellent roadmap to setting up a data security plan, see David Zetoony, *Data Privacy and Security: A Practical Guide for In-house Counsel*, Wash. Legal Found., 77 Contemporary Legal Note Series 1, 1–2 (May 2016) [hereinafter Data Privacy and Security Guide], https://iapp.org/media/pdf/resource_center/WLFDataPrivacyandSecurityHandbook.pdf.

Without data maps and inventories, however, there is no practical way to determine what has been lost or compromised in the event of a cyber breach. Such a determination is a necessary step in assessing the extent and nature of a breach and determining what legal obligations may apply and what next steps must be taken.[73]

3.2. Ensure that the company's governance framework encompasses cybersecurity and develop cyber incident and cyber-breach plans that align with that framework

Cyber incidents and company response planning should be considered from an enterprise-wide level. This exercise should entail developing a cyber breach and cyber incident response plan that accounts for all functions and incorporates a communications plan. Incident response planning should also include periodic reassessments of the company's cyber response plan, command media (policies and procedures), and organizational resources to identify any potential competency gaps in personnel or functional responsibilities.

1. ***Cyber incident/Cyber breach response plan.*** Many companies have crisis management plans. Cyber incident response plans can leverage such plans but should also lay out steps to be taken in the event of a cyber incident specifically. A cyber response plan should address specific elements of responding to a cyber event. The plan must be actionable and *practical*; when drafting the plan, it is advisable to obtain input from the functions and key personnel who will be involved in the various roles during execution. It helps to follow the risk management process approach known as the RACI model, where the plan clearly identifies what departments or individuals are R***esponsible*** for the specific issue or action; to whom each such individual is A***ccountable*** and who must *Approve* decisions or actions to be taken; what department or individuals are in a *Supporting* role; who must be C***onsulted*** to complete the task(s); and who must be I***nformed*** of status or results, but may not necessarily need to be consulted.[74]

   The key elements of the response plan[75] should include:

   - Identification of the response team, including the team lead. All team members should also have identified back-ups;

73. Brad Brian & Grant Davis-Denny, *Data Breaches and the Role of the In-house Attorney*, U.S. News—Best Lawyers 36–37 (2016).

74. *See* Atul Sharma, *RACI*, ProjectManagement.com (Feb. 4, 2025), https://www.projectmanagement.com/wikis/234008/raci#.

75. Certain industries and types of information are subject to sector-specific requirements, such as the requirements for handling protected health information under the Security and Privacy regulations issued by the Department of Health and Human Services pursuant to the Health Insurance Portability and Accountability Act of 1996 (HIPAA), codified at 45 C.F.R. pt. 164 (including Standards for the Protection of Electronic Protected Health Information, 45 C.F.R. §§ 164.302-164.318). See Handbook, Chapter 7, *Legal Obligations to Provide Data Security*. Any such applicable industry-specific legal or regulatory requirements should be incorporated into the response plan and communication plans.

- Provision for training on execution of the plan, in addition to substantive training on relevant policies and procedures. Active drills should be held periodically as if the company were responding to an actual cyber event;
- Checklists identifying what should be done, by whom, and what needs to be documented during and throughout various stages of the cyber event;
- Provision for identifying and fixing the cause of the breach, while continuing to conduct forensics to determine the extent and cause of the damage;
- Identification of all legal obligations and conflicting requirements or initiatives;
- A communications plan that covers status reports to executive management and the board of directors as well as a public affairs and customer relations component to address external messaging;[76]
- Contact information for any third-party consultants and service providers, such as forensic investigation and identity theft and data breach resolution vendors.

Form notifications and responses to queries can be drafted in advance to save time and effort in the midst of responding to a cyber event. Templates can prove especially helpful for small companies with limited resources.

2. ***Policies and procedures.*** The company should review its policies and procedures to ensure they align with the incident response plan and vice versa, as well as to avoid gaps in the policies and procedures relating to cybersecurity concerns. For example, if employees are permitted to use personal devices for work, the company should have a well-crafted "bring your own device," or "BYOD," policy, in addition to password requirements and other standard information security policies. Due to the rapid cycle of technological upgrades and evolving law, the company should review its command media related to cyber issues on an annual or more frequent basis.
3. ***Checklist for assessing the company governance framework and response plan and evaluating the company's cybersecurity posture periodically.*** A general checklist can be useful in assessing the company's governance framework. The following questions can help identify potential gaps:
   - Are cybersecurity policies and procedures in place?
   - Are emergent technologies and capabilities such as AI identified and evaluated for their impact or relevance to the company's cybersecurity posture before they are implemented and as they are updated with new features and functionality?
   - Does the company conduct regular assessments of its cybersecurity risks?
   - Does the company have training and education programs in place to ensure cybersecurity protocols are understood and followed?

76. Consideration can also be given to engaging a public relations firm specializing in crisis management in the event of a significant or large enough breach.

- Have all legally binding agreements been reviewed, especially with respect to any indemnity or warranty provisions, to understand the company's rights, liabilities, and obligations with respect to cybersecurity?
- Have supplier and service provider agreements been reviewed to ensure third-party obligations to the company are clearly identified, enforceable, and acceptable considering the company's risk assessment and risk tolerance?
- Is there a cyber incident response plan in place? Does it include a communications plan?
- Has an insurance assessment for cyber incidents been conducted? Is coverage sufficient?
- Have potential disclosure duties been identified, as well as triggering events?

Given the speed and vectors by which cyber threats evolve, the framework and response plan should be re-evaluated regularly to keep them current and understood, particularly in terms of their implementation within the company. The evaluation should also identify and address proactively any new or previously overlooked gaps and vulnerabilities.

3.3. Identify and establish key internal and external relationships

1. ***Within the corporation.*** As discussed in Section 1.3 above, having in-house counsel be part of the internal cybersecurity team is critical for success. There are ample resources available for companies on how to build teams to manage cybersecurity.[77] All point to the need for companies to have appropriate cybersecurity talent and to recognize the inter-disciplinary nature of strong cybersecurity teams and the need for executive support.[78] Legal is uniquely positioned to help articulate the risk parameters in the legal and regulatory arenas and can also provide valuable and relevant input for operational and market-based domains because of its work supporting those domains. If a team has already been established and Legal is not a member, in-house counsel should reach out and get involved. Cybersecurity should also be regularly included in board meetings or board committee proceedings, as appropriate.
2. ***External third parties.*** In-house counsel are especially important when the company engages with external parties. Relationships with cyber-knowledgeable law firms and

77. *See, e.g.*, Pam Nigro, *Building a Robust Cybersecurity Team: Five Essential Roles and Key Certifications*, Security Magazine (Apr. 14, 2025), https://www.securitymagazine.com/articles/101536-building-a-robust-cybersecurity-team-five-essential-roles-and-key-certifications; Tim McIntyre, *Insider Tips for Building Your Cybersecurity Team*, Security Magazine (Mar. 1, 2017), http://www.securitymagazine.com/articles/87844-insider-tips-for-building-your- cybersecurity-team; Forbes Tech. Council, *14 Effective Tips for Creating and Sustaining Strong Cybersecurity Teams*, Forbes (Jan. 10, 2020), https://www.forbes.com/councils/forbestechcouncil/2020/01/10/14-effective-tips-for-creating-and-sustaining-a-strong-cybersecurity-team/.

78. *See* Alejandra Quevedo, *How Cybersecurity Teams Can Convince the C-Suite of Their Value*, Harv. Bus. Rev. (Sept. 21, 2016), https://hbr.org/2016/09/how-cybersecurity-teams-can-convince-the-c-suite-of-their-value; Amos, *supra* note 65.

consultants enable in-house attorneys to more quickly retain outside service providers with the requisite expertise in the event of a cyber incident. Having such relationships established *before* a breach occurs helps ensure selection of competent external partners who can get up to speed much more quickly, and who are more familiar with the company's culture and governance framework. The same principles apply to potential technical subject matter experts that may be needed depending on the type of cyber incident that occurs. Other external parties that might be considered could include public relations firms specializing in crisis communications, key business partners, and lobbyists.

3. ***Governmental entities and officials.*** Multiple government agencies at all levels (federal, state, and local) and with different missions are examining and devoting resources to cyber issues. These efforts range from reports, trends, and metrics to services for the general public or industry segments. Relationships should be formed with these governmental agencies. Many cyber-attacks originate from nation-states and international crime syndicates. Defending against such attacks requires close coordination and interaction with relevant U.S. law enforcement and government agencies.

3.4. Identify legal issues associated with a cyber incident

3.4.1. *Leverage existing knowledge, available resources and other functions*

Cyber threats are now sufficiently common that one can identify in advance what legal issues and risks might arise before a cyber incident occurs. For example, in-house counsel can readily find resources to assist them in proactively considering the impact on the company and the legal or regulatory risks that would arise if there is a:

- Distributed denial of service attack or other disruption of internet-based service;
- Theft or other compromise of personally identifiable information or other confidential data owned or entrusted to the company; and/or
- Interrupted or suspended processing of payments, customer transactions, etc.

In addition, in-house counsel can ask questions or work with other functions and find resources to help familiarize themselves with:

- Technology and services (including outside service providers) the company has in place that would be impacted by, or utilized during, a cyber incident or breach;
- The appropriate authorizations that legally should be in place to permit network monitoring;
- The cyber incident and breach plans, and other relevant company policies and procedures; and
- Any legal areas and questions that might arise in the cybersecurity area. In this respect, in-house counsel should become familiar with potentially relevant technology laws

such as the Computer Fraud and Abuse Act, laws relating to electronic surveillance in the workplace, and privacy laws, among others.

Legal requirements arising from a cyber event can also be identified in advance for different scenarios, such as:

- The need for an investigation, remediation measures, or incident notification;
- The need to identify and comply with specific domestic and foreign laws and regulations regarding data or information security, as well as laws governing breach notification;
- The need for SEC or foreign exchange disclosures and considerations for potential or actual impact to share prices in the event of a public disclosure of an incident;
- Governmental notifications or inquiries regarding cyber incidents or investigations into the company's security posture;
- Class actions, shareholder derivative lawsuits, or other legal action taken by parties with standing;
- Placement of (or claim placement against) a cyber insurance policy;
- The need or desire to place or flow down information security requirements to the company's suppliers or partners; and
- Contractual disputes relating to cybersecurity controls.

3.4.2. *Attorney-client privilege and attorney-work product considerations*

Throughout a cyber incident, in-house counsel will also need to consider the applicability, reach, and possible waiver of the attorney-client privilege and attorney work product doctrines to: (a) information that has been compromised; (b) information generated in preparation for, during, or after, a cyber incident or breach; (c) any related investigations; (d) any disclosure made to governmental agencies; (e) governmental inquiries; and (f) information that may be potentially relevant to actual or anticipated litigation associated with the cyber incident or breach.

The issues attendant to the attorney-client privilege are further complicated in light of an ongoing debate about the appropriate scope of the privilege as applied in the corporate context. Although *Upjohn Co. v. United States*[79] established that the privilege attaches to corporations, confusion persists within organizations regarding who exactly holds the privilege (the corporation), who speaks for the corporation with respect to the privilege, and who can waive the privilege. Logistical challenges arise in certain circumstances, most notably in internal investigations, where *Upjohn* warnings should be provided to employees being interviewed to ensure that the corporate privilege is retained and an attorney-client privilege is not inadvertently created with the employee.

79. 449 U.S. 383 (1981).

Decisions must be made in the context of governmental investigations and potential corporate misconduct, where federal sentencing guidelines and agency guidance can take a company's cooperation into account—especially cooperation in sharing investigative information. Further complications in this often-difficult analysis for in-house counsel arise from the issuance of a 2015 U.S. Department of Justice memorandum commonly referred to as the "Yates Memo."[80] The Yates Memo updated the Justice Department's Principles of Federal Prosecution of Business Organizations, intending to provide more insight into the government's treatment of the privilege in the corporate context. Numerous other memoranda issued by various prior Deputy Attorneys General had been subjected to convoluted analysis and considerably eroded.

The Justice Department updated the Yates Memo in November 2018 to scale back the level of disclosure demanded of companies that are the target of a criminal investigation. Specifically, pursuant to the 2018 revisions, eligibility to receive cooperation credit in resolving investigations would no longer require a corporation to provide the U.S. government with "*all* relevant facts about the individuals involved in corporate misconduct." Instead, eligibility for cooperation credit would require disclosing information regarding only those individuals who are "substantially involved in or responsible for the criminal conduct."[81] The Yates Memo was revised again in September 2022 to add a timing element; disclosures of *all* relevant facts about individual misconduct (including evidence gathered through internal investigations) would have to be made more quickly. The 2022 revision also underscored the Justice Department's focus on evaluating the entity's historical compliance record with stricter enforcement measures taken on misconduct involving the same personnel, root causes, and/or types of misconduct.[82]

Corporations and individuals having cybersecurity responsibilities should not, however, interpret the current status or revisions as diminishing their duties or exposure. The Justice

80. *Individual Accountability*, U.S. DEPT. OF JUSTICE, https://www.justice.gov/archives/dag/individual-accountability (last visited Jul. 2, 2025); Memorandum, Sally Quillian Yates, Deputy Atty. Gen., Individual Accountability for Corporate Wrongdoing, (Sept. 9, 2015), https://www.justice.gov/d9/pages/attachments/2015/09/10/individual_accountability_for_corporate_wrongdoing_dag_memo2.pdf.

81. *See* Rod J. Rosenstein, Deputy Atty. Gen., Remarks at the American Conference Institute's 35th International Conference on the Foreign Corrupt Practices Act (Nov. 29, 2018), https://www.justice.gov/archives/opa/speech/deputy-attorney-general-rod-j-rosenstein-delivers-remarks-american-conference-institute-0; *see also* Thomas F. Carlucci, Lisa M. Noller & David W. Simon, *DOJ Announces Changes to the Yates Memo Policy on Individual Accountability*, NAT'L L. REV., LEGAL NEWS ALERT, (Dec. 4, 2018), https://natlawreview.com/article/doj-announces-changes-to-yates-memo-policy-individual-accountability.

82. Memorandum, Lisa Monaco, Deputy Atty. Gen., *Further Revisions to Corporate Criminal Enforcement Policies Following Discussions with Corporate Crime Advisory Group*, (Sept. 15, 2022), https://www.justice.gov/d9/pages/attachments/2022/09/15/2022.09.15_ccag_memo.pdf.

For a discussion on treatment of the privilege in the context of a cyber breach, see Bart Huffman & C.M. Salmon, *Privilege Considerations in Cyber Incident Response*, LAW360.COM (Aug. 29, 2016, 4:47 PM), https://www.law360.com/articles/833807/privilege-considerations-in-cyber-incident-response, and HANDBOOK, Chapter 14, *Cyber Insurance for Law Firms and Legal Organizations* (§ .2.3). *But see* Daniel Schwarcz, Josephine Wolff & Daniel W. Woods, *How Privilege Undermines Cybersecurity*, 36 HARV. J. LAW & TECH. 421 (Spring 2023).

Department's guidelines still require that corporations "identify every individual who was substantially involved in or responsible for the criminal conduct," not just those who were substantially involved in or responsible for the conduct at issue. The guidelines also emphasize making disclosures early in the investigative process. The guidelines reflect a shift from the Justice Department's historical prioritization of pursuing corporate settlements over individual prosecutions. Combined with the requirement to disclose *all* relevant facts, the current application of the Yates Memo arguably and practically creates a narrower scope in which to assert the attorney-client privilege because companies may be compelled or expected to disclose information gathered during cybersecurity incident investigations (including communications with in-house counsel) that otherwise might be protected in seeking cooperation credit.

Given the complexities involved in conducting internal investigations while responding to a cyber incident, in-house counsel must be especially diligent. Particularly in the initial stages of investigating cyber incidents, the risk of compromising the attorney-client privilege is significantly heightened, and steps that might preserve the privilege can complicate the organization's exchanges with the Justice Department if the incident potentially involves criminal conduct by company insiders.

3.5. Cultivate a Cyber-aware Culture and Community

In-house counsel should initiate and support efforts to ensure that the company's workforce and business partners are at least aware of cyber issues. All employees should receive training in cybersecurity, proper cyber hygiene, and the company's policies and procedures relating to cyber matters. Such training can be incorporated into the company's regular training programs on managing proprietary information, utilizing company information assets and systems, and similar topics. Educational efforts should be combined with checks on employee understanding and absorption, through simulations such as periodic mock phishing emails.[83]

Executive leaders should model behavior and support opportunities to create a culture of awareness about the significant adverse impact posed by cyber incidents and how such events and their aftermath might impact not only the corporation, but also its employees.

4. Responding to a Cyber Incident

No attorney is ever as fully prepared as they would wish when confronted with the realization that the company is under active attack. When the call is received, however, and the in-house attorney has no plan in place (or plans that do not fit the situation), they should

83. Further discussion of organizational culture can be found in HANDBOOK, Chapter 12, *Get SMART on Data Protection by Creating a Culture of Security Awareness.*

fall back to guiding principles for what to do and how to prioritize.[84] Templates are also available, which can serve as a helpful starting point.[85]

4.1. Identify the Attack and Damage

First, attempt to assess the type of attack, how much and what kind of damage is being, or has been, done, who the attacker is, and the source of the vulnerability that was exploited. If you do not know where to start, reach out to your IT resources. As soon as a basic understanding can be reasonably articulated, notify executive management (and your insurers if you are carrying cyber insurance) and the board of directors. Ensure that appropriate steps are taken to maintain the confidentiality of the investigation. Depending on the situation, consider when and how you might reach out to law enforcement. Consult outside counsel if you are unsure of the legal implications or issues presented.

4.2. Limit the Damage

Next, utilize any available resources and those you can obtain to minimize further damage. At this step, IT is again a critical partner. IT should be able to monitor or filter traffic, take steps to insulate the affected systems, and begin gathering data and information regarding the cyber incident. Likewise, the sophistication and complexity of cyber attacks nowadays also warrant enlisting the assistance of external resources with expertise in managing and responding to cyber incidents.

4.3. Record and Document

Begin compiling records on the extent, scope, and impact of the cyber incident. As it is unlikely you will be able to rule out potential criminal or legal action, records should be kept in a disciplined and ordered manner that ensures evidence is maintained and can be accounted for.

The U.S. Justice Department recommends retention of: (a) a description of all events relating to the incident, including dates and times; (b) information relating to phone calls, emails, and other communications regarding the incident; (c) the identity of all individuals working on aspects of the cyber incident, including a description of their specific roles, tasks, or responsibilities, amount of time spent, and approximate hourly rates for each; (d) identification of the systems, accounts, networks, databases, etc., affected by the cyber

---

84. *See* Guide to Digital Defense, *supra* note 59.

85. *See, e.g.*, Joshua M Franklin ed., Incident Response Policy Template: Critical Security Controls, Ctr. for Internet Sec. (Mar. 2023), https://www.cisecurity.org/insights/white-papers/incident-response-policy-template-for-cis-control-17 (Mar. 22, 2023);, *Incident Response Policy Template for CIS Control 17*, Ctr. for Internet Sec., https://www.cisecurity.org/insights/white-papers/incident-response-policy-template-for-cis-control-17; *Security Policy Templates*, SANS, https://www.sans.org/information-security-policy/ (updated Apr. 15, 2025); and numerous resources developed by the National Institute of Standards and Technology and published online, *Computer Security Resource Center*, Nat'l Inst. of Standards & Tech., https://csrc.nist.gov/ (last visited July 2, 2025). See also Handbook, Chapter 13, *Achieving Preparedness through Standards and Planning and Best Practices for Incident Response*.

incident; (e) information relating to the type and amount of damage sustained; (f) information regarding the company's network topology; (g) identification of software and applications being run on affected networks and devices; and (h) any unique aspects of the company's network architecture.[86]

4.4. Engage and Notify

If necessary (and not already done), engage outside counsel to assist. As appropriate, inform law enforcement agencies (U.S. Department of Homeland Security, FBI, local district attorney), and other pertinent government agencies that require notification. Identify and notify affected parties if any. Engage relevant third-party service providers (e.g., identity theft protection services if PII has been compromised).

4.5 Correct and Close

Ensure that vulnerabilities have been identified and patched, documentation is complete, and necessary parties have been provided with ongoing status and closure reports. Develop and establish policies and other mitigation and control measures to avoid being caught by surprise again or repeating the same missteps that led to the cyber incident. Ensure that a lessons learned session is held and followed by additional self-assessments (and possibly external reviews) to ensure that a sustainable and "learning" framework is established for the company's cybersecurity posture.

4.6. Follow-up

When and as appropriate, but certainly after the incident has been dealt with and remedied, ensure any reporting and disclosure requirements, including those to relevant government agencies and customers, have been identified, and craft appropriate language reporting the incident satisfying the form and substance of the applicable legal or regulatory disclosure requirements.

5. In the Aftermath

There have already been numerous examples of highly publicized breaches of corporations in the past few years, and certainly more are to come. Companies should keep in mind the variety of methods of attack and motivations that underpin such attacks and prioritize

86. U.S. Dept. of Justice, Computer Crime & Intellectual Property Section, Criminal Division, Best Practices for Victim Response and Reporting of Cyber Incidents, Version 2.0 (Sept. 2018), https://www.justice.gov/criminal-ccips/file/1096971/download; see also, *What We Investigate: The Cyber Threat*, FBI, https://www.fbi.gov/investigate/cyber (last visited July 2, 2025); *Welcome to the Internet Crime Complaint Center*, Internet Crime Complaint Ctr. ("The Internet Crime Complaint Center (IC3) is the central hub for reporting cyber-enabled crime. It is run by the FBI, the lead federal agency for investigating crime."), https://www.ic3.gov/ (last visited Sept. 23, 2025).

preparations to avert attacks and defend themselves. While much remains unknown to the public at large regarding even the more publicized breaches, conclusions can still be drawn from what *is* known. For example, pleadings made in the lawsuit filed against Sony following its embarrassing breach in 2014 allege that the breach was caused by the company's failure to properly secure its computer systems in a manner that could have prevented its systems from being hacked.[87]

In 2018, Marriott International, Inc. joined the ranks of numerous other companies in having to notify its customers that a breach of its systems resulted in the loss of personal information of nearly 500 million of its guests globally—a notification made all the more painful for the company because it also had to confirm that encrypted payment card numbers had been stolen.[88] Marriott and its subsidiary, Starwood Hotels & Resorts Worldwide, reached a settlement with the Federal Trade Commission in October 2024, pursuant to which it was required to implement a robust cybersecurity program, provide its U.S. customers with a way to request deletion of personal information in the hotel chain's systems, and take or implement additional remedial actions.[89] Pursuant to a separate settlement, the hotel chain also paid a $52 million penalty to 49 states and the District of Columbia to resolve legal actions arising from the breaches.[90]

In January 2024, a ransomware attack on a major mortgage lender, LoanDepot, resulted in the compromise of the sensitive data of nearly 17 million customers, including social security numbers, account information, names, and addresses. It also cost the company nearly $30 million in response and recovery costs, as well as $86.6 million to settle the class action lawsuit that followed.[91]

In mid-2024, CrowdStrike, a premier cybersecurity service provider, experienced a global outage that impacted over 8.5 million customer devices, resulting in widespread disruptions across multiple industries. This cyber incident was caused not by a breach, but rather by a poorly executed software update.[92] The cost impact of the CrowdStrike outage

---

87. *See* Steven Rubin & Jonathan Trafimow, Opinion, *Cyber Wars and the Legal Lessons from the Sony Hack*, LiveScience.com (Jan. 5, 2015, 2:21 PM), https://www.yahoo.com/news/cyber-wars-legal-lessons-sony-hack-op-ed-192143521.html.

88. *See Marriott Announces Starwood Guest Reservation Database Security Incident*, Marriott Int'l (Nov. 30, 2018), https://news.marriott.com/news/2018/11/30/marriott-announces-starwood-guest-reservation-database-security-incident.

89. *See FTC Takes Action against Marriott and Starwood Over Multiple Data Breaches*, FTC (Oct. 9, 2024), https://www.ftc.gov/news-events/news/press-releases/2024/10/ftc-takes-action-against-marriott-starwood-over-multiple-data-breaches.

90. *Id.*

91. Eduard Kovacs, *Ransomware Attack Cost LoanDepot $27 Million*, SecurityWeek (Aug. 7, 2024), https://www.securityweek.com/ransomware-attack-cost-loandepot-27-million/; Dieter Holger, *LoanDepot Paying Data Breach Victims after $86.6 Million Settlement*, ConsumerAff. (Mar. 12, 2025), https://www.consumeraffairs.com/news/loandepot-paying-data-breach-victims-after-866-million-settlement-031225.html.

92. Raphael Yahalom, *What the 2024 CrowdStrike Glitch Can Teach Us About Cyber Risk*, Harv. Bus. Rev. website HBR.org (Jan. 10, 2025), https://hbr.org/2025/01/what-the-2024-crowdstrike-glitch-can-teach-us-about-cyber-risk.

is estimated to be over $5 billion.[93] In addition, while CrowdStrike's liability was determined to be limited due to the terms and conditions in the company's customer agreements, the cyber insurance claims filed by affected parties resulted in projected insured losses of between $400 million and $1.5 billion, and are believed to be potentially the "single worst loss in the cyber insurance sector over 20 years."[94]

The saga of the 2017 Equifax breach continues to serve as a sober reminder of the need for discipline and basic preparedness. The underlying breach resulted from a vulnerability that hackers exploited to gain access to the company's networks. Equifax had been aware of the vulnerability, but it failed to patch the specific system that was breached—a failure that was not discovered until months later and well after the threat actors had gained access and stolen sensitive information about more than 147 million consumers.[95] Equifax reported that it spent $1.4 billion on recovery and response costs, which included expenses related to the subsequent investigations and remediation efforts, as well as legal fees, penalties, and settlements.[96] The company also suffered significant reputational damage and a decline in its stock value. Any company deciding to "accept the risk" of not reviewing and addressing cybersecurity risks, or give direction to patch, but failing to confirm vulnerable systems have, in fact, been patched, or failing to timely and adequately inform and respond to affected parties, is now clearly on notice that the consequences are severe, including, legal action.

The in-house legal community can point to concrete examples of how to shape and develop standards and defensible cybersecurity practices, as outlined in this chapter.[97] In-house counsel must consider aspects specific to the company's business. For instance,

---

93. David Jones, *CrowdStrike Disruption Direct Losses to Reach $5.4B for Fortune 500, Study Finds*, CYBERSECURITYDIVE (July 25, 2024), https://www.cybersecuritydive.com/news/crowdstrike-cost-fortune-500-losses-cyber-insurance/722396 (noting that the $5.4 billion estimate of direct financial losses excludes financial losses incurred by Microsoft).

94. *Id.* (citing CyberCube).

95. *See* ELECTRONIC PRIV. INFO. CTR., EQUIFAX DATA BREACH, https://archive.epic.org/privacy/data-breach/equifax/ (last visited July 27, 2025) (providing summary, background, and timeline of the Equifax data breach, which Equifax disclosed publicly on September 7, 2017, and noting a series of missteps in Equifax's incident response).

96. *See* Josh Fruhlinger, *Equifax Data Breach FAQ: What Happened, Who Was Affected, What Was the Impact?*, CSO (Feb. 12, 2020), https://www.csoonline.com/article/567833/equifax-data-breach-faq-what-happened-who-was-affected-what-was-the-impact.html; Matthew J. Schwartz, *Equifax's Data Breach Costs Hit $1.4 Billion* (May 13, 2019), https://www.bankinfosecurity.com/equifaxs-data-breach-costs-hit-14-billion-a-12473. That number did not include a settlement reached by Equifax later in 2019 with the Federal Trade Commission, the Consumer Financial Protection Bureau, and fifty U.S. states and territories requiring Equifax to pay at least $575 million and potentially as much as $700 million. *See* FED. TRADE COMM'N, EQUIFAX DATA BREACH SETTLEMENT(Nov. 2024) https://www.ftc.gov/enforcement/refunds/equifax-data-breach-settlement; see also Press Release, Fed. Trade Comm'n, *Equifax to Pay $575 Million as Part of Settlement with FTC, CFPB, and States Related to 2017 Data Breach: Settlement Includes Fund to Help Consumers Recover from Data Breach* (Jul. 22, 2019), https://www.ftc.gov/news-events/news/press-releases/2019/07/equifax-pay-575-million-part-settlement-ftc-cfpb-states-related-2017-data-breach.

97. David Fontaine & John Reed Stark, *Guest Post: Three Cybersecurity Lessons from Yahoo's Legal Department Woes*, The D&O Diary (Mar. 30, 2017), http://www.dandodiary.com/2017/03/articles/cyber-liability/guest-post-three-cybersecurity-lessons-yahoos-legal-department-woes/.

the Yahoo and Target breaches illustrate the additional legal complications (and impact to reputation and brand) associated with consumer data, as the Anthem breach does for healthcare data, and the SolarWinds and the Colonial Pipeline breaches do for utility and critical infrastructure consumers and users.[98] These cases are likewise helpful in better highlighting the risks to a company's reputation and other tangible consequences, such as an effect on stock prices and the need to think holistically regarding the types of operational risks that can arise from a company's business activities in unforeseen ways.

In-house counsel in industries with specific regulatory requirements relating to cybersecurity should stay current on developments. For example, U.S. federal contractors can examine the outcome of two *qui tam* actions. The first was filed by a former employee of Raytheon alleging that Raytheon failed to comply with required cybersecurity controls, including controls set forth in the National Institute of Standards and Technology ("NIST") Special Publication (SP) 800-171, in its performance of numerous federal contracts and subcontracts.[99] The company settled the U.S. Justice Department's False Claims Act allegations—including Raytheon's failure to comply with basic cybersecurity controls required pursuant to the Federal Acquisition Regulations, among other requirements—by agreeing to pay $8.4 million.[100] The second, also filed by a former employee, resulted in biotechnology company Illumina Inc. reaching a $9.8 million settlement with the Justice Department.[101] The settlement resolved allegations that the company sold its genomic-sequencing systems to multiple federal Departments and agencies despite knowing cybersecurity had not been incorporated into those systems as required, and also nonetheless certifying under Section 524B of the Federal Food, Drug, and Cosmetic Act that the products *did* comply with applicable cybersecurity controls.[102]

---

98. *See* Kolawole Samuel Adebayo, *Nearly 3 Years Later, SolarWinds CISO Shares 3 Lessons from the Infamous Attack*, DarkReading (Aug. 24, 2022), https://www.darkreading.com/cyber-risk/3-years-later-solarwinds-ciso-shares-3-lessons-from-the-infamous-attack; William Turton & Kartikay Mehrota, *Hackers Breached Colonial Pipeline Using Compromised Password*, Bloomberg L. (June 4, 2021, 3:58 PM), https://news.bloomberglaw.com/privacy-and-data-security/hackers-breached-colonial-pipeline-using-compromised-password; Katie Canales & Isabella Jibilian, *The US Is Readying Sanctions against Russia over the SolarWinds Cyber Attack*, Bus. Insider (Apr. 15, 2021, 1:25 PM), https://www.businessinsider.com/solarwinds-hack-explained-government-agencies-cyber-security-2020-12; Marianne Kolbasuk McGee, *A New In-Depth Analysis of Anthem Breach: Insurance Commissioners Conclude Nation-State Involved, Reach Settlement with Insurer*, BankInfoSecurity, (Jan. 10, 2017), https://www.bankinfosecurity.com/new-in-depth-analysis-anthem-breach-a-9627.

99. *Raytheon Companies and Nightwing Group to Pay $8.4M to Resolve False Claims Act Allegations Relating to Non-Compliance with Cybersecurity Requirements in Federal Contracts*, U.S. Dep't of Justice (May 1, 2025), https://www.justice.gov/opa/pr/raytheon-companies-and-nightwing-group-pay-84m-resolve-false-claims-act-allegations-relating; *see also* Tirzah S. Lollar, *DOJ Settles Another Cyber FCA Suit Related to Implementation of NIST SP Controls*, Arnold & Porter Blog (May 8, 2025), https://www.arnoldporter.com/en/perspectives/blogs/fca-qui-notes/posts/2025/05/continued-focus-on-implementation-of-nist-sp-controls.

100. *Id.*

101. *Illumina Inc. to Pay $9.8M to Resolve False Claims Act Allegations Arising from Cybersecurity Vulnerabilities in Genomic Sequencing Systems*, U.S. Dep't of Justice (July 31, 2025), https://www.justice.gov/opa/pr/illumina-inc-pay-98m-resolve-false-claims-act-allegations-arising-cybersecurity.

102. *Id.*; Federal Food, Drug, and Cosmetic Act, 21 U.S.C. § 360i(c); *see also* Melissa Taylormoore, Tara Lee, Bethany J. Hills & F. Paul Pittman, *DOJ Secures First of its Kind Cybersecurity False Claims Act Settlement*,

More recently, the Justice Department intervened in a whistleblower suit brought against the Georgia Institute of Technology ("Georgia Tech") and Georgia Tech Research Corp. ("GTRC") relating to allegations that Georgia Tech and GTRC failed to comply with cybersecurity requirements set forth in their contracts with the U.S. Defense Department.[103] The Justice Department's move to assume responsibility for litigating the case furthers its Civil Cyber-Fraud Initiative, an effort launched in October 2021 specifically to ensure companies with federal contracts and grants comply with cybersecurity requirements (both regulatory and contractual) under the False Claims Act.[104] Notably, the referenced actions relied upon false representations or inadequate implementation of cybersecurity controls and proceeded absent allegations of an actual security breach occurring.[105]

Social media and non-traditional media outlets make recovery and crisis management of a cyber incident, including mitigation of reputational damage, even more difficult. Where once the so-called "front page test"[106] might have been used to caution against unwise behavior, today the admonition is to avoid becoming a viral meme on YouTube, Facebook, Instagram, Snapchat, or TikTok. In our hyper-digitized world, false information spreads rapidly, and companies may have to combat disinformation regarding the breach itself.[107]

Companies can and should learn from each other, both the good and the bad. Publicized breaches underscore the need to constantly reassess a company's fundamental cybersecurity posture. Companies often rally to address bad situations and exert Herculean efforts to fix the problem. But after implementing new policies and training, some may be tempted to believe those measures are sufficient to forestall a repeat event. This is a particularly unsound assumption in the cyber domain, where threats continue to evolve and actors continue to multiply. Companies must remain vigilant about cybersecurity fundamentals even

---

White & Case Blog (Aug. 5, 2025), https://www.whitecase.com/insight-alert/doj-secures-first-its-kind-cybersecurity-false-claims-act-settlement.

103. United States ex rel. Craig v. Georgia Tech Res. Corp., No. 22-cv-02698 (N.D. Ga. Aug. 22, 2024); *see United States Files Suit Against the Georgia Institute of Technology and Georgia Tech Research Corporation Alleging Cybersecurity Violations*, Dep't of Justice (Aug. 22, 2024), https://www.justice.gov/archives/opa/pr/united-states-files-suit-against-georgia-institute-technology-and-georgia-tech-research.

104. *Deputy Attorney General Lisa O. Monaco Announces New Civil Cyber-Fraud Initiative*, Dep't of Justice (Oct. 6, 2021), https://www.justice.gov/archives/opa/pr/deputy-attorney-general-lisa-o-monaco-announces-new-civil-cyber-fraud-initiative; *see also* James Coker, *Georgia Tech Sued Over Cybersecurity Violations*, InfoSecurity Mag. (Aug. 23, 2024), https://www.infosecurity-magazine.com/news/georgia-tech-sued-cybersecurity.

105. *See* Melissa Taylormoore et al., *supra* note 102 (noting trend of the Justice Department's use of the False Claims Act to pursue claims involving cybersecurity-related misrepresentations).

106. The "front page test," sometimes called the "New York Times Test," cautions people to consider how they would feel if actions they are about to take or the things they are about to say were splashed across the front page of a national newspaper. *See* Robert Tanner, *The New York Times Test, Goldman Sachs and Greg Smith*, Management is a Journey, Blog (Nov. 28, 2022), https://managementisajourney.com/the-new-york-times-test-goldman-sachs-and-greg-smith.

107. Public Relations Society of America Inc., Reality Check: Navigating Misinformation & Disinformation, https://www.prsa.org/professional-development/prsa-resources/misinformation (last visited July 2, 2025).

as they monitor and defend against new threats.[108] In-house counsel must be guardians against complacency. Through collaboration and roundtable discussions with colleagues, in-house counsel can learn and share best practices and policy approaches that can be tailored to their respective organizations.

6. Special Considerations

This chapter focuses primarily on cyber threats to corporate assets and organizational activities. This is not intended to ignore other areas of the law that carry significant cyber considerations, such as consumer protection laws, privacy, and e-discovery. In addition, larger macro-developments, such as AI evolution, geopolitical conflict, and regulatory shifts, carry their own considerations that impact cybersecurity.

With respect to legal areas with direct, indirect, and overlapping relevance to cybersecurity as discussed elsewhere in this Handbook, our suggestion to in-house counsel is to be sufficiently familiar with what the company must do to comply with these concurrent obligations or mitigate attendant risks. This way, the team addressing cybersecurity can align cyber threat mitigation strategies and planning with these other areas.

Mention should likewise be made of the impact of other economic, technological, and sociological trends affecting the workplace, such as the increasing percentage of the workforce reaching retirement age and increased multi-generational workforce considerations. These trends, and associated lessons learned or resulting new or adjusted modes of operations, must be considered when drafting social media policies and procedures, when assessing the impact of social engineering attacks on company personnel and representatives, and when evaluating other aspects of the company's cybersecurity posture. Other trends also include the aftermath of influential external events, such as natural disasters like the severe wildfires in California and Nebraska and multiple hurricanes and other severe weather events, and the COVID-19 pandemic, which forced companies to implement or otherwise accommodate wholesale work-from-home arrangements on short notice.

In sum, in-house counsel are uniquely positioned to assume a leadership role and use their influence to better prepare their companies to deal with cyber threats. In addition, they have the rare opportunity to provide input into the ongoing dialogue regarding the balance between market autonomy and governmental regulation of industry in this constantly evolving and complex area. Given the vast array of actors and threats in the cyber domain, and the continued substantial dependence of the world on internet-driven commerce and

108. Perhaps this explains why even though Heartland was the victim of one of the earlier high-profile instances of corporate cyber breaches in 2009, it found itself suffering through a hellish version of "Groundhog Day" five years later as it once again found itself in the cyber breach spotlight. Tony Martin-Vegue, Opinion, *Lessons from the Heartland Payment Systems Data Breach, Redux*, CSO (June 15, 2015); Ericka Chickowski, *3 Lessons from Heartland Breach the Second Time Around*, DarkReading (June 2, 2015), https://www.darkreading.com/cyberattacks-data-breaches/3-lessons-from-heartland-breach-the-second-time-around.

communication, managing the risks requires all-hands-on-deck and a steady legal hand on the wheel.

7. Summary and Tips

In closing, in-house counsel should apply the following common-sense steps:

- Be proactive;
- Stay current on cybersecurity law developments;
- Broaden your risk management measures—
  - Ensure the company has a cyber incident and breach response plan, including a communications plan;
  - Consider obtaining cybersecurity insurance;
- Build your partnerships (internal and external)—
  - Functional partners: Stay close with Human Resources, Finance, and particularly IT. The rapid evolution of technologies and complex task of maintaining information systems will continue changing your work environment. Having an IT partner willing to work with you is an absolute priority;
  - Identify third-party entities that can be engaged if and where needed;
  - Select law firms that are knowledgeable about cyber threats and practice sound cybersecurity measures;
- Stay informed of emergent technologies, such as AI and cloud technologies, as well as workplace and workforce shifts, and the potential implications for cybersecurity
- Manage and provide input to your company's policies and procedures;
- Build a credible case for budget and resources to support cybersecurity initiatives;
- Expand your network and list of resources and references, including other organizations and industries, and obtain different perspectives and best practices that will assist in keeping current on developments and trends; and
- Take to heart the warning that it is not a question of if a cyber incident will occur, but when. Be ready and prepared for a crisis so that your response will be measured and thoughtful.

In addition to being helpful to in-house counsel, we hope this chapter is helpful to outside counsel in better understanding the perspectives of their clients. Having a stronger sense of the environment in which in-house counsel must operate, beyond the specific issue or project brought to outside counsel, will help law firms better shape their advice in a manner that assists in-house counsel to support *their* client in a practical manner.

Chapter 17
Why Public Interest Attorneys Should Care About Cybersecurity

Edward Marchewka and Ozoda Usmanova

1. Abstract

This chapter appeared in the Third Edition of the Cybersecurity Handbook as Chapter 12. The Third Edition material is updated and supplemented with "Recent Developments" that proceed in two parts. Part I focuses on NIST 800-171r3, *Protecting Controlled Unclassified Information in Nonfederal Systems and Organizations*, the U.S. Department of Defense Cybersecurity Maturity Model Certification (CMMC) Program, and updates to the Telephone Consumer Protection Act (TCPA). Part II provides an overview of public interest attorneys' use of generative AI (GenAI) and its impact on the cybersecurity of public interest organizations (PIOs).[1] We also offer key considerations and provide recommendations to PIO legal teams.[2]

2. What Makes Public Interest Organizations Unique

PIOs, non-governmental organizations (NGO), and nonprofit organizations (NPO) are not necessarily different from other organizations in many respects relevant to cybersecurity. For example, these types of organizations are allowed to make a profit. There is a saying in this space: "No margin, no mission." The organizations must generate positive value if they are to continue their good work. The terms NGO or NPO are misnomers. They are used as tax designations, but the organizations they describe would be more accurately referred

1. This chapter does not examine the implications of traditional AI, sometimes called narrow AI, which are a subset of artificial intelligence designed to respond to particular inputs with predictions based on data and specific rules those tools have been trained to follow. Bernard Marr, *The Difference Between Generative AI And Traditional AI: An Easy Explanation for Anyone*. FORBES (July 24, 2023), https://www.forbes.com/sites/bernardmarr/2023/07/24/the-difference-between-generative-ai-and-traditional-ai-an-easy-explanation-for-anyone/. *See also* HANDBOOK, Chapter 2, *An Introduction to Artificial Intelligence*.

2. See HANDBOOK, Chapter 10, *Lawyers' Professional Responsibility to Provide Data Security*.

to as non-taxable entities. The successful ones generate a profit that allows their mission-driven work to continue.

For ease of reference, this chapter generally uses the term "organization" and "PIO" to refer to entities characterized as PIOs, NGOs, and NPOs.

Because PIOs are highly mission-driven, information security often takes a backseat to the good work they undertake even though failures in information security will inevitably affect revenue and, thus, the mission. The strong drive for mission can exacerbate tensions that sometimes arise between board members and management about information security. Those tensions can be the product of knowledge gaps, where one party may have more interest and knowledge about information security risks than the other. This gap is called information asymmetry.[3]

Information asymmetry between information security professionals and executive leadership or the board can be hard to overcome. This challenge may be due to the immediate negative feelings that most people experience at the mention of cybersecurity,[4] misunderstanding or perhaps a fear of technology, or a lack of a direct connection between cybersecurity and the organization's direct mission. Failure to close the information asymmetry gap leads to a poor understanding of true cyber risk, which may result in emotional decision making rather than data-driven decision making. The result can be a lack of focus on information security and an increased risk of a cyber incident or breach, which can have devastating consequences.

Board members and executives must be informed of cybersecurity risks and their impact on the organization so that the board and executive leadership can serve the organization effectively in advancing its mission. As counsel, being aware of cybersecurity threats and the potential impact on the organization and its mission is paramount for assisting the board and executives to give the necessary attention to the risk while staying mission-focused and directing the organization toward positive social impact.

3. Impact of Cyber Breaches

It's a widespread misconception that organizations engaged in social good are less likely to be targeted by cybercriminals than big business organizations. In 2024, the U.S. Cybersecurity and Infrastructure Security Agency (CISA) released cybersecurity guidance to high-risk

3. Donald D. Bergh, David J. Ketchen, Jr., Ilaria Orlandi, Pursey Heugens & Brian K. Boyd, *Information Asymmetry in Management Research: Past Accomplishments and Future Opportunities*, 45 J of Mgt. 122–158 (2019), https://doi.org/10.1177/0149206318798026.

4. Karen Renaud, Verena Zimmermann, Tim Schürmann, & Carlos Böhm, *Exploring Cybersecurity-related Emotions and Finding That They Are Challenging to Measure*, 8 Hum. & Soc. Sci. Comm. 75 (2021), https://doi.org/10.1057/s41599-021-00746-5 (reporting on "widespread, but not universal, negativity toward cybersecurity" and research undertaken "to assess the nature of this negativity and to get a sense of its roots").

community (HRC) entities, including civil society organizations and individuals.[5] The CISA Guidance described civil society organizations as being "at high threat of being targeted by malicious cyber actors," while at the same time having "low defense capacity."[6] CISA cited reports from the information technology service firm Cloudflare that cyberattacks against civil society organizations are "generally increasing." In the second quarter of 2023, Cloudflare detected NPOs being "targeted more than any other industry when looking at malicious traffic to NPO websites as a proportion of total traffic."[7]

The experience of small businesses may be similar to that of many PIOs. A 2023 report offered the following small business statistics: 43% of cyberattacks target small businesses, 60% of small businesses that are victims of a cyberattack go out of business within six months of the attack, and only 14% of small businesses rate their ability to mitigate cyber risk as highly effective while 47% say they do not understand how to protect themselves from cyberattack.[8]

A more local survey reinforces the broader findings. The Berkeley Center for Long-Term Cybersecurity published a 2024 white paper reporting results of a cybersecurity-focused survey of 68 San Francisco-based nonprofits. Of the organizations surveyed, 85% reported experiencing at least one cyberattack, and "46% ... ranked funding as the greatest obstacle to improving their organization's cybersecurity, followed closely by a lack of knowledge on what to improve and difficulty prioritizing cybersecurity over competing objectives."[9]

Ethical norms do not bind malicious perpetrators. An organization's size does not matter either; organizations of all sizes, regardless of their mission, possess something of value—personal information. Bad actors do not shy away from stealing data from PIOs just like they would exfiltrate data from for-profit businesses and major corporations.

For example, a small homeless shelter was targeted in April 2019. The nonprofit Father Bill's and Mainspring, which serves the unhoused in Massachusetts, announced that it was a target of a ransomware attack, but it didn't believe that anyone's personal information was accessed or stolen.[10] The CEO of Father Bill's stated at the time of the incident that an antivirus software used by the nonprofit was able to stop the ransomware attack without

5. U.S. Cybersecurity & Infrastructure Agency, Mitigating Cyber Threats with Limited Resources: Guidance for Civil Society (May 2024) [hereinafter, CISA Guidance], https://www.cisa.gov/sites/default/files/2024-05/joint-guide-mitigating-cyber-threats-with-limited-resources-guidance-for-civil-society-508c_3.pdf.

6. *Id.* at 4.

7. *Id.* at 5.

8. Maddie Shepherd, *30 Surprising Small Business Cyber Security Statistics,* Fundera by Nerdwallet, (Jan. 23, 2023), www.fundera.com/resources/small-business-cyber-security-statistics#:%7E:text=Overview%3A%2030%20Small%20Business%20Cyber,than%20%242.2%20million%20a%20year.

9. Sarah Powazek & Shannon Pierson, CyberCAN: Cybersecurity for Cities and Nonprofits, Strategic Recommendations for the City and County of San Francisco to Improve Nonprofit Cybersecurity 4 (Nov. 2024), https://cltc.berkeley.edu/wp-content/uploads/2024/11/CyberCAN_Cybersecurity-for-Cities-and-Nonprofits.pdf.

10. Marc Larocque, *Massachusetts Nonprofit Shelter Targeted by Ransomware*, GovTech, June 28, 2019, www.govtech.com/security/massachusetts-nonprofit-shelter-targeted-by-ransomware.html.

locking up any of the office computers, that it was able to restore files from back-up, and that it reported the incident to the state attorney general and public as required by state law.[11] Significant credit should be given to this organization which, despite its small size, was prepared and able to respond effectively to an attack.

In February 2021, Midwest Transplant Network (MTN), an organ procurement organization in Kansas City, suffered a ransomware attack that compromised the records of over 17,000 individuals. The stolen protected health information about deceased donors and transplant recipients included names, dates of birth, organs donated, and transplant procedures. MTN was also briefly locked out of its systems.[12]

The impact of these breaches extends not only the theft of sensitive and valuable information, as in the case of MTN, but also to the disruption of the organization's ability to serve its constituents. MTN and Father Bill's had to spend staff time and resources on investigations and remediation instead of focusing on their missions.

Attacks on service providers pose another significant source of risk to mission-driven organizations. In another 2019 example, a third-party provider of network services to several nonprofits was targeted by a ransomware attack, which resulted in one organization losing all of its data and another nonprofit canceling a performance.[13] In both cases, operations were impacted, which affected these organizations' ability to fulfill their mission. In early 2020, Blackbaud, a cloud services provider serving the social-good community,[14] also fell victim to cyber extortion. The circumstances of the Blackbaud breach are described in a complaint issued by the Federal Trade Commission against Blackbaud on May 17, 2024.[15]

In its complaint against Blackbaud, the FTC alleged the facts summarized in this paragraph. Names, addresses, bank account information, records of individual donations, usernames, passwords, and other sensitive data about millions of individuals were compromised by hackers, who remained undetected by Blackbaud for three months.[16] Blackbaud failed to encrypt stored data, which "magnified the severity of the data breach." It also failed to implement appropriate data retention practices.[17] When the hacker was discovered, the hacker threatened to disclose the stolen information unless Blackbaud paid a ransom.

11. *Id.*

12. Dan Margolies, *Ransomware Attack on Midwest Transplant Network Affects More Than 17,000*, Kan. Pub. Radio (May 3, 2021), kansaspublicradio.org/kpr-news/ransomware-attack-midwest-transplant-network-affects-more-17000.

13. Kevin Coughlin, *"It Was like a Tornado": Cyber Thieves Demand $500K Ransom in Attack Targeting Contractor Serving Greater Morristown Nonprofits*, MorristownGreen.Com (Dec. 9, 2019), morristowngreen.com/2019/12/09/it-was-like-a-tornado-cyber-thieves-demand-500k-ransom-in-attack-targeting-contractor-serving-greater-morristown-nonprofits.

14. Members of the social-good community promote practices that are better for the environment and overall society and include nonprofits, foundations, corporations, education institutions, healthcare organizations, religious organizations, and individual change agents.

15. Complaint, *In re Blackbaud, Inc.*, FTC Case No. C-4804 (May 17, 2024), https://www.ftc.gov/system/files/ftc_gov/pdf/2023181_blackbaud_final_consent_package.pdf.

16. Id. ¶ 9.

17. *Id.* ¶ 10.

Blackbaud agreed to pay the attacker 24 Bitcoin, then worth approximately $235,000, but Blackbaud had no assurance the stolen data was deleted.[18] Blackbaud also delayed notifying its customers and, when it did provide notice of the incident, Blackbaud made false statements about the nature and extent of data exfiltrated.[19] Blackbaud agreed with the FTC to implement an information security program, among other actions, and to be subject to FTC monitoring for a period of 20 years.[20] The FTC did not fine Blackbaud, but Blackbaud agreed to pay $6.75 million as part of a settlement with the State of California,[21] and $49.5 million to settle claims brought by 49 states and the District of Columbia.[22]

World Vision, Save the Children, and Human Rights Watch were among the large nonprofits impacted by the Blackbaud breach. Media reported at the time that at least 200 organizations were compromised.[23] Those organizations were hampered in their own notification compliance by Blackbaud's reporting delay and inaccuracies.

Despite the increase in ransomware and other cyber attacks in recent years, many (perhaps most) PIOs lack dedicated staff to address cybersecurity and cyber incidents. Microsoft published *Nonprofit Guidelines for Cybersecurity and Privacy* in 2017.[24] Microsoft observed that "nonprofits generally lag for-profit organizations in adopting the robust policies, practices, and tools needed to adequately secure their environments."[25]

Microsoft based this observation on two small studies. Those studies provide additional support for the proposition that many PIOs struggle to manage their IT infrastructure and data, which are critical tasks for ensuring organizational assets are secure and monitored.

One study assessed the cybersecurity maturity of ten well-respected organizations with dedicated IT staff. Each achieved low scores—well below the score indicating sufficient cybersecurity infrastructure to respond adequately to evolving cybersecurity threats—and the lowest scores were "in the areas of data retention and destruction, and of managing the lifecycle of hardware and software."[26] Microsoft undertook the second small study

18. *Id.* ¶ 11.

19. *Id.* ¶¶ 12–15.

20. Decision & Order, *In re Blackbaud, Inc.*, FTC Case No. C-4804 (May 17, 2024), https://www.ftc.gov/system/files/ftc_gov/pdf/2023181_blackbaud_final_consent_package.pdf.

21. Final Judgment & Permanent Injunction, *California v. Blackbaud, Inc.*, Case No. 37-2024-00027643-CU-BT-CTL, (Sup. Ct. San Diego Cty. June 12, 2024). *See also* Cal. Dept. of Justice, *Attorney General Bonta Secures $6.75 Million Settlement against Blackbaud Over 2020 Data Breach* (Jun. 13, 2024), https://oag.ca.gov/news/press-releases/attorney-general-bonta-secures-675-million-settlement-against-blackbaud-over.

22. Blackbaud, *Blackbaud Resolves Multi-State Attorneys General Investigation of 2020 Security Incident*, (Oct. 5, 2023), https://www.blackbaud.com/newsroom/article/blackbaud-resolves-multi-state-attorneys-general-investigation-of-2020-security-incident.

23. Ben Parker, *Dozens of NGOs Hit by Hack on US Fundraising Database,* New Humanitarian, (Aug. 4, 2020), www.thenewhumanitarian.org/news/2020/08/04/NGO-fundraising-database-hack.

24. Microsoft Philanthropies, *Nonprofit Guidelines for Cybersecurity and Privacy* (2017) [hereinafter, MS Nonprofit Guidelines], https://www.microsoftalumni.com/s/1769/images/gid2/editor_documents/giving/microsoft_nonprofit_cybersecurity_and_data_privacy_best_practices_white_paper.pdf?gid=2&pgid=61&sessionid=4e57db08-0f9f-47df-a502-f29e03b19036&cc=1.

25. *Id.* at 5.

26. *Id.* This first study cited by Microsoft was undertaken by "NetHope, an international member-based nonprofit that focuses on promoting and supporting technology for nonprofits...." *Id.*

of 50 nonprofits with its partners TechSoup and Nten. Respondents in that study reported having modern IT infrastructure, but most of them failed to utilize important cybersecurity controls.[27] Microsoft recommended that PIOs use the U.S. National Institute of Standards and Technology (NIST) Cybersecurity Framework to "align their cybersecurity activities with their business requirements, tolerance for risk, and available resources."[28]

Essential security controls Microsoft found lacking in its survey included:

- Inventory and control of enterprise assets;
- Inventory and control of software assets;
- Data protection;
- Secure configuration of enterprise assets and software;
- Account management;
- Access control management;
- Continuous vulnerability management;
- Audit log management;
- Email and web browser protections;
- Malware defenses;
- Data recovery;
- Network infrastructure management;
- Network monitoring and defense;
- Security awareness and skills training;
- Service provider management;
- Application software security;
- Incident response management; and
- Penetration testing.[29]

27. *Id.* at 6. In the midst of the COVID-19 pandemic, Microsoft issued its 2021 Digital Defense Report. Its "most targeted sectors" assessment that year showed:

that nearly 80% of those targeted were either in government, NGOs, or think tanks. Think tanks often serve as policy incubators and implementers, with strong ties to current and former government officials and programs. Threat actors can and do exploit the connections between the more traditional NGO community and government organizations to position themselves to gain insights into national policy plans and intentions. As noted, it's the think tanks with ideas relevant to current or future government policy or political objectives that put these organizations into the line of sight for intelligence operations. When traditional NGOs have similar information, we also see them as an objective for nation state actors.

Microsoft Corp., *Microsoft Digital Defense Report* 52 (Oct. 2021), https://cdn-dynmedia-1.microsoft.com/is/content/microsoftcorp/microsoft/final/en-us/microsoft-brand/documents/FY21-Microsoft-Digital-Defense-Report.pdf.

28. MS Nonprofit Guidelines, *supra* note 24, at 6. In 2021, Microsoft announced the launch of its Security Program for Nonprofits using a suite of tools provided by Microsoft to complement its other security products. Justin Spelhaug, *Strengthening Cyber Defenses for Nonprofits*, MICROSOFT ON THE ISSUES blog (Oct. 21, 2021), https://blogs.microsoft.com/on-the-issues/2021/10/21/cyber-defenses-security-program-nonprofits/.

29. Center for Internet Security (CIS), *The 18 CIS Critical Security Controls*, www.cisecurity.org/controls/cis-controls-list (visited Feb. 10, 2025). According to CIS, "[t]he NIST Framework for Improving Critical Infrastructure Cybersecurity calls out the CIS Controls as one of the "informative references"—a way to help users

With the speed and persistence of cyber events, it is imperative that PIO board members and executives understand and embrace their responsibility to be stewards of the information under their control. From an optics perspective, protecting sensitive information is essential for maintaining a positive image and receiving donor and grant funding. Failure to implement appropriate cybersecurity and data privacy protections could result in significantly adverse reputational and financial impacts.

Beyond optics, board members have fiduciary duties to the organizations they oversee. Those duties entail procedures for the board to oversee risk management and compliance. A series of influential Delaware corporate law decisions sets the bar for board oversight and compliance requirements:[30] *In re Caremark International, Inc. Derivative Litigation* (*Caremark*),[31] *Stone v. Ritter* (*Stone*),[32] and *Marchand v. Barnhill* (*Marchand*).[33]

Caremark stands for the proposition that directors can be liable for breach of fiduciary duty when they fail "to act in circumstances in which due attention would arguably have prevented [a] loss."[34] For "due attention" to be given, the board must have appropriate information timely delivered as an ordinary part of its activities. Reporting, in turn, requires information and reporting systems to be established and monitored. The logical corollary, then, is that failure to maintain an adequate information and reporting system "under some circumstances may, in theory at least, render a director liable for losses caused by non-compliance with applicable legal standards."[35]

The bar set in *Caremark* for imposing liability on directors is high. The court explicitly noted and justified a high bar as being important to recruit and retain qualified directors:

> [I]n my opinion only a sustained or systematic failure of the board to exercise oversight—such as an utter failure to attempt to assure a reasonable information and reporting system exists—will establish the lack of good faith that is a necessary condition to liability. Such a test of liability—lack of good faith as evidenced by sustained or systematic failure of a director to exercise reasonable oversight—is quite high. But a demanding test of liability in the oversight context is probably beneficial to corporate shareholders as a class, as it is in the board decision context, since it makes board service by qualified persons more likely, while continuing to act as a stimulus to good faith performance of duty by such directors.[36]

---

implement the Framework using an existing, supported methodology. *CIS Critical Security Controls FAQ*, https://www.cisecurity.org/controls/cis-controls-faq (visited Feb. 10, 2025).

30. *See* E. Norman Veasey & Randy J. Holland, Caremark *at the Quarter-Century Watershed: Modern-Day Compliance Realities Frame Corporate Directors' Duty of Good Faith Oversight, Providing New Dynamics for Respecting Chancellor Allen's 1996* Caremark *Landmark*, 76 Bus. Law. 1 (2020-21).

31. *In re Caremark International, Inc. Derivative Litigation*, 698 A.2d 959 (Del. Ch. 1996).

32. *Stone v. Ritter*, 911 A.2d 362 (Del. 2006).

33. *Marchand v. Barnhill*, 212 A.3d 805 (Del. 2019).

34. *Caremark*, 698 A.2d at 967.

35. *Id.* at 970.

36. *Id.* at 971.

Caremark was decided by the Delaware Chancery Court. In *Stone*, the Delaware Supreme Court adopted the *Caremark* standard. The court articulated the elements of a *Caremark* claim as follows, and it held that the fiduciary duty implicated is the duty of loyalty. The conditions to establish director oversight liability are:

> (1) the directors utterly failed to implement any reporting or information system or controls or (2) having implemented such a system or controls, the directors consciously failed to monitor or oversee its operations, thus disabling themselves from being informed of risks or problems requiring their attention[; and] "[i]n either case, the imposition of liability requires a showing that the directors knew that they were not discharging their fiduciary obligations."[37]

Bad outcomes are not sufficient to succeed on a claim under the *Caremark/Stone* standard. Directors must have acted in bad faith.[38]

For many years, plaintiffs tried but failed to state claims under the *Caremark* standard of director liability. Then came *Marchand*. *Marchand* concerned the directors of Blue Bell Creameries USA, Inc., an ice cream maker that experienced a listeria outbreak causing consumer injuries and death, regulatory fines, plant shutdowns, financial losses, and reputational damage.[39] The complaint alleged that Blue Bell's board never received or sought information about food safety issues even though ice cream was the company's only product, the company was subject to federal and state food regulation, and management had received reports of listeria in the company's plants.[40]

The Delaware Supreme Court reversed a Chancery Court decision to dismiss the complaint against Blue Bell's directors. The Supreme Court found that "the complaint supports an inference that no system of board-level compliance monitoring and reporting existed at Blue Bell. Although *Caremark* is a tough standard for plaintiffs to meet, the plaintiff has met it here."[41]

We live in a more connected world than ever with virtually all businesses online and dependent upon technology for information transfer through services ranging from complete e-commerce operations to simple email services. Cyberattacks can be devastating for organizations and harmful for their constituents, including donors and stakeholders serviced by the PIO. Thus, all organizations need mechanisms for the board to receive information regarding cybersecurity risks, a means to discuss the risks, and expectations and procedures for management reporting risks to the board. Board attention sets the tone and establishes organizational infrastructure that promotes good cybersecurity practices so that

---

37. Veasey & Holland, *supra* note 30, at 9 (citing *Stone*, 911 A.2d at 370).
38. See *id.* at 9–10.
39. *Marchand*, 212 A.3d at 807.
40. *Id.* at 807–08.
41. *Id.* at 820–21.

PIOs are better situated to manage cyber risks while remaining focused on their missions and individual directors satisfy their duties to the organization consistent with standards like those established by *Caremark* and *Stone.*

4. Common Challenges and Solutions

4.1. Sensitive vs. Protected Data

One of the challenges that PIOs have is the delineation between sensitive and protected data. A comprehensive understanding of data privacy laws and regulations that affect a PIO is essential. For example, take a child's immunization record. In the hands of a doctor, the record is protected health information (PHI) covered by the Privacy Rule implemented by the U.S. Department of Health & Human Services under the Health Insurance Portability and Accountability Act of 1996 (HIPAA).[42] When the doctor passes that same piece of paper to the child's parent, the information in the hands of the parent is not subject to the Privacy Rule. In fact, the parent could take out an ad in the paper and publish it (not advisable). If the parent passes the immunization record to the child's school, the document in the school's possession is covered by the Family Educational Rights and Privacy Act (FERPA),[43] a federal privacy law that gives students and parents certain protections regarding children's education records, such as report cards, transcripts, disciplinary records, contact, family information, and class schedules. FERPA does not include a defined term "PHI." FERPA simply defines information as student information broadly, making the immunization record protected as sensitive health information. Every PIO must understand its legal obligations under various laws applicable to the organization and the data in its possession or control. Failure to do so could result in significant penalties and legal challenges.

4.2. Budget Constraints

Budget is a concern of most PIOs, and funds available for security may be limited by donor or grant restrictions. Depending upon the funding source, funds can be restricted at the donor's direction, preventing the organization from spending on administrative services like information security. Cash flow for grant-funded PIOs can also be challenging. Grant-funded or donor-funded organizations tend to focus their funds on mission-related activities. On the other hand, operationally funded organizations, which actively increase revenue through operations versus donations or grants, tend to have more spending

42. Standards for Privacy of Individually Identifiable Health Information, 45 CFR Part 160 and Part 164, Subparts A and E; Health Insurance Portability & Accountability Act of 1996, §§ 261–264, Public Law 104–191 (Aug. 21, 1996), 110 Stat. 1936.

43. Family Educational & Privacy Rights Act, 20 U.S.C. § 1232g (a)(4)(A) (2025) ("For the purposes of [FERPA], the term 'education records' means, except as may be provided otherwise in subparagraph (B), those records, files, documents, and other materials which- (i) contain information directly related to a student; and (ii) are maintained by an educational agency or institution or by a person acting for such agency or institution.").

capacity or flexibility. Even operationally funded PIOs need to be mindful of their operating ratios, however.

Due to budget constraints, nonprofits often rely on outdated hardware and software, making them even more susceptible to cyberattacks. Nonprofits that cannot afford expensive IT subscriptions and services often work with free and open-source applications, which may not have the necessary protections or provide secure storage for confidential information, such as donor information, securely. In fact, in lieu of a charge, "free" software may be provided subject to terms granting permission for the vendor to access and use customer data for some purposes. (This kind of consent is regularly included in terms for free, public versions of generative artificial intelligence tools.)

Furthermore, small nonprofits often lack a designated security administrator. PIOs have to compete in a tight labor market for cybersecurity staff. In 2023, ISC2, a member association for cybersecurity professionals, surveyed 14,865 cybersecurity practitioners and decisionmakers located around the world for its 2023 workforce report.[44] The ISC2 reported that the cybersecurity workforce grew between 2022 and 2023, but the workforce demand increased faster. ISC2 estimated "that in 2023 there [were] roughly 4 million cybersecurity professionals needed."[45] One of ICS2's key findings: "staffing shortages and skills gaps are consistent challenges."[46] They found:

> 67% of respondents reported that their organization has a shortage of cybersecurity staff needed to prevent and troubleshoot security issues. And 92% report having skills gaps in their organization—the most common being cloud computing security, AI/ML and Zero Trust implementation. We will examine these skills gaps in depth this year as 67% of those whose organizations had both shortages in total staff and skills gaps say that skills gaps are often worse.[47]

Added to this workforce dynamic, many PIOs have budget constraints that cause them to struggle with staffing for their mission-focused positions. IT and cyber are farther down the list of staffing priorities.

4.3. Personnel: Interns, Volunteers, Temp Workers

Significant sources of "free" labor for many PIOs are volunteers and interns. When working with interns and volunteers, public interest attorneys need to ensure that onboarding processes for those individuals include cyber awareness training to educate them on basic

44. ISC2, Inc., *ISCE Cybersecurity Workforce Study: How the Economy, Skills Gap and Artificial Intelligence are Challenging the Global Cybersecurity Workforce* 4 (2023), https://edge.sitecorecloud.io/internationf173-xmc4e73-prodbc0f-9660/media/Project/ISC2/Main/Media/documents/research/ISC2_Cybersecurity_Workforce_Study_2023.pdf.

45. *Id.*

46. *Id.* at 5.

47. *Id.*

cyber practices.[48] Training should emphasize the need for information integrity and confidentiality of clients' and donors' information.

While training of all employees is critical, expectations of, and commitments from, volunteers and interns often differ from those of employees, which makes regular training even more important. The consequences of violating cybersecurity policies tend to be less impactful for volunteers and interns than for employees. Staff may also assess volunteer behavior more leniently than they would the same behavior by an employee. For example, an employee's failure to take simple precautions may be viewed as unreasonable and considered negligent while the same failure by volunteers is excused because the volunteers are acting with altruistic intentions or should be given some latitude for human error even when dealing with sensitive information. Ideally, volunteers would be treated equally to employees in this regard, but in any case, it is a good idea for volunteers to acknowledge their access or potential access to sensitive or protected information with confidentiality and non-disclosure agreements. Trusting individuals to do the right thing is not sufficient and will not be enough to rely on when explaining data loss or data leakage.

Ongoing cyber awareness training with a periodic phishing simulation component serves as one tool to keep employee cyber awareness up to date. A further step for interns, volunteers, and temporary workers is a review of all relevant cyber policies. Failing to train staff on cyber-related policies, procedures, standards, and guidelines can open an organization to liability if staff's duties are not clearly articulated.

In the New York case *Sackin v. TransPerfect Global*,[49] TransPerfect reached a settlement to pay $23 million in a class action settlement arising from the loss of current and former employees' personally identifiable information (PII) in a phishing campaign. The employees' complaint alleged that TransPerfect failed to implement several basic cyber hygiene practices, including employee data security training. Had TransPerfect conducted regular training, it might have reduced its liability.

Phishing campaigns persist because they work, and bad actors' use of artificial intelligence makes phishing increasingly difficult to recognize. Training must be a continuing effort, and simulations should keep up with changes in phishing tactics.

4.4. Available Resources

Most PIOs are eligible for discounts for cybersecurity products and services due to their nonprofit status. Following are some recommendations to help PIOs find this support. A

---

48. *See* Handbook, Chapter 12, *Get SMART on Data Protection by Creating a Culture of Security Awareness*.

49. Final Judgment & Order of Dismissal, Sackin v. TransPerfect Glob., Inc., Case No. 17-cv-1469(LGS) (S.D.N.Y. Dec. 14, 2018); *see also TransPerfect Employee Data Breach Class Action Settlement*, Top Class Actions (Aug. 20, 2018) ("The identity theft protection coverage is valued at $3.5 million, while the reimbursement coverage offers an estimated $19.5 million to Class Members."), https://topclassactions.com/lawsuit-settlements/closed-settlements/transperfect-employee-data-breach-class-action-settlement/. The settlement followed a decision of the court denying in part TransPerfect's motion to dismiss claims arising from the incident. Sackin v. TransPerfect Glob., Inc., 278 F. Supp. 3d 739 (S.D.N.Y. 2017).

first step to take advantage of these discounts would be to sign up for a service similar to that of Tech Soup.[50] Tech Soup is an organization that partners with technology and affiliated service providers to provide discounted services to PIOs. There are eligibility criteria that must be satisfied for all donations or discounts. The grants and discounts are not limited to hardware and software. There are managed IT and security services available through this platform. Other organizations such as Google[51] and Microsoft[52] offer steep discounts on their products, many of which include security features. Microsoft also provides setup assistance for nonprofits, either directly or through partners. For example, Microsoft offers nonprofit digital skills training and courses[53] covering topics such as security, compliance, and information protection.

Following is a non-exhaustive list of companies in the cyber industry that offer additional benefits for PIOs. The list is not an endorsement of products or services, but is included here to illustrate the range of security technology and services nonprofits should be aware of:

- Okta—https://www.okta.com/solutions/nonprofits/—identity and access management
- Cofense—https://cofense.com/—anti-phishing solution
- Qlik—https://www.qlik.com/us—data integration and analytics platform
- Mimecast Limited—https://www.mimecast.com/solutions/protect-people/—human risk management
- Pluralsight—https://www.pluralsight.com/—technology and security training
- Splunk, a CISCO company—https://www.splunk.com/en_us/about-us/splunk-pledge/nonprofit-license-application.html—security information and event management (SIEM) platform
- Cisco—https://www.cisco.com/—networking and security equipment
- Relativity—https://www.relativity.com/—eDiscovery and data breach solutions
- Lucid Security https://lucidcyber.io/non-profit-charity-program

---

50. For information about TechSoup, see *Nonprofit Software to Carry Out Your Mission*, TechSoup, https://www.techsoup.org/nonprofit-software (last visited Sept. 23, 2025).

51. For information about Google for nonprofits, see *Google for Nonprofits*, Google, https://www.google.com/nonprofits/ (last visited Sept. 23, 2025).

52. For information about Microsoft Nonprofit, see *Nonprofits*, Microsoft, https://www.microsoft.com/en-us/nonprofits (last visited Sept. 23, 2025). At the time the Handbook was being readied for publication in Fall 2025, Microsoft offered nonprofits a free security assessment. *See Free security assessment for nonprofits*, Microsoft, https://nonprofits.tsi.microsoft.com/EN-US/security-assessment/ (last visited Sept. 23, 2025).

53. For information on Microsoft's training for nonprofits, see *Nonprofits*, *supra* note 53.

5. Recent Developments—Part I

5.1. NIST 800-171 Rev. 3[54] and CMMC[55]

Since the initial publication of this chapter in 2021, there have been significant changes to requirements for federal contractors under NIST 800-171 Rev. 3 that may significantly impact PIOs.

> This [NIST] publication provides federal agencies with recommended security requirements for protecting the confidentiality of CUI [Controlled Unclassified Information] when the information is resident in nonfederal systems and organizations. The requirements apply to components of nonfederal systems that process, store, or transmit CUI or that provide protection for such components. The security requirements are intended for use by federal agencies in contractual vehicles or other agreements established between those agencies and nonfederal organizations.[56]

With a lot of nonprofit revenue coming from federal contracts,[57] staying compliant with federal information security requirements is imperative for the many PIOs receiving federal funding. The challenge with these requirements is that PIOs may not know they are subject to the federal security requirements because those requirements flow down through subcontracting arrangements to third-party contractors, which can be the structure under which the PIO is funded.

Let's review the timeline of the security requirements that are the subject of NIST 800-171 Rev. 3. In November 2010, President Barack Obama signed Executive Order 13556,[58]

---

54. National Institute of Standards & Technology, *Protecting Controlled Unclassified Information in Nonfederal Systems and Organizations Rev. 3* (May 2024), https://csrc.nist.gov/pubs/sp/800/171/r3/final.

55. The U.S. Department of Defense final rule establishing the Cybersecurity Maturity Model Certification Program is codified at 32 CFR pt 170, 89 Fed. Reg. 83092 (Oct. 15, 2024) [hereinafter, CMMC Program Final Rule]. The CMMC Program Final Rule became effective December 16, 2024. "The purpose of CMMC is to verify that defense contractors are compliant with existing protections for federal contract information (FCI) and controlled unclassified information (CUI) and are protecting that information at a level commensurate with the risk from cybersecurity threats, including advanced persistent threats." U.S. Dept. of Defense, *Release: Cybersecurity Maturity Model Certification Program Final Rule Published*, (Oct. 11, 2024), https://www.defense.gov/News/Releases/Release/Article/3932947/cybersecurity-maturity-model-certification-program-final-rule-published/.

On September 10, 2025, the Defense Department issued a final rule to incorporate in the Defense Federal Acquisition Regulation Supplement (DFARS) contractual requirements relating to the CMMC Certification Program. 48 CFR pts 204, 212, 217 & 252, 90 Fed. Reg. 43,560 (Sept. 10, 2025). "This final DFARS rule also partially implements a section of the National Defense Authorization Act for Fiscal Year 2020 that directed the Secretary of Defense to develop a consistent, comprehensive framework to enhance cybersecurity for the U.S. defense industrial base." *Id.*

56. NIST 800-171 Rev. 3, *supra* note 54, at i.

57. *See* Charity CFO, *Is Your Nonprofit Ready for Federal Grant Funding* (May 22, 2022) (citing a 2019 Nonprofit Times report that "almost 80% of all nonprofit revenue comes from the US government in the form of federal grant funding or fees for services"), https://thecharitycfo.com/is-my-nonprofit-ready-for-federal-grant-funding/.

58. Executive Order 13556—Controlled Unclassified Information (Nov. 4, 2010), https://obamawhitehouse.archives.gov/the-press-office/2010/11/04/executive-order-13556-controlled-unclassified-information.

establishing the Controlled Unclassified Information (CUI) Program for all federal agencies to manage and safeguard CUI. In February 2013, President Obama signed Executive Order 13636,[59] titled *Improving Critical Infrastructure Cybersecurity*, with a directive for enhancing the security and resilience of the country's critical infrastructure through public and private partnerships. In June 2015, the National Institute of Standards and Technology (NIST) released publication 800-171, and federal agencies began to publish security requirements leveraging this new standard. The NIST 800-171 standard is not limited to the Defense Department at this point; other agencies have begun adopting the new standard. In June 2019, the Defense Department released its Cybersecurity Maturity Model Certification program to help its contractors comply with security requirements based on NIST 800-171. In February 2020, NIST released revision 2 of publication 800-171. In November 2021, the Defense Department released CMMC 2.0, which simplified a tiering system prescribing security requirements based on the sensitivity of information in the contractor's possession. NIST 800-171 Rev. 3 was released in May 2024. Most recently, the Defense Department issued a final rule adding contractual clauses to the Defense Federal Acquisition Regulation Supplement (DFARS) to implement the CMMC Program and related Certification Program requirements.

For clarity, it is important to note that NIST 800-171 Rev. 3 does not recommend a certification process. Early implementations of the security requirements relied on organizations to simply attest that they are following the NIST 800-171 framework. The attestation process was fraught with issues. In response, the Defense Department developed the Cybersecurity Maturity Model Certification (CMMC).[60] The Defense Department certification provided a model that federal agencies could leverage and rely on to ensure they meet the requirements of the Executive Orders. The security requirements are embodied in federal acquisition regulations as noted in the CMMC Program Final Rule:

> Currently, Federal contracts (including defense contracts) involving the transfer of FCI [federal contract information] to a non-Government organization follow the requirements specified in 48 CFR 52.204–21 (Federal Acquisition Regulation (FAR) clause 52.204–21), Basic Safeguarding of Covered Contractor Information Systems.13 FAR clause 52.204–21 requires compliance with 15 security requirements, FAR clause 52.204–21(b)(1), items (i) through (xv). These requirements are the minimum necessary for any entity wishing to receive FCI from the US Government (USG).

59. Executive Order 13636—Improving Critical Infrastructure Cybersecurity (Feb. 12, 2013), https://obamawhitehouse.archives.gov/the-press-office/2013/02/12/executive-order-improving-critical-infrastructure-cybersecurity.

60. CMMC Program Final Rule, *supra* note 55, 89 Fed. Reg. at 83,092. ("In 2019, DoD announced the development of CMMC to move away from a 'self-attestation' model of security.")

> Defense contracts involving the development or transfer of CUI to a non-Government organization require applicable requirements of DFARS [Defense Federal Acquisition Regulation Supplement] clause 252.204–7012.14. This clause requires defense contractors to provide adequate security on all covered contractor information systems by implementing the 110 security requirements specified in NIST SP 800–171.[61]

Organizations that want to qualify to receive federal contract information or controlled unclassified information will, initially, be permitted to select the assessment level for which they will be certified. Contracting opportunities may be restricted to organizations by certification level. The CMMC Program Final Rule summarizes the source and number of security requirements and the assessment requirements for each certification level.[62]

Higher levels of CMMC certification are made through Certified Third-Party Assessment Organizations (C3PAO).[63] Furthermore, it is expected that those organizations requiring CMMC compliance will be regularly audited to ensure they maintain compliance. Legal risks around noncompliance stem from failure to meet contractual obligations with the respective federal agency, legal action that diverts resources from operations, significant financial liabilities, and reputation losses.

5.2. TCPA[64] and The Campaign Registry's 10DLC[65]

Another significant regulation that may significantly impact PIOs is the Telephone Consumer Protection Act (TCPA). The TCPA was enacted in 1991 as an amendment to the Communications Act of 1934 to address telephone marketing efforts and certain practices around telemarketing. The TCPA gave birth to the Do Not Call Registry in 2003, and the TCPA was updated in 2012 to address text messaging.

While the TCPA is over 30 years old, there has been an uptick in cases around text messaging over the past two years. In February 2024, the Federal Communications Commission (FCC) approved and released a Report and Order and Further Notice of Proposed Rulemaking (Order), *Strengthening the Ability of Consumers to Stop Robocalls.*[66] The FCC subsequently published in the *Federal Register* a summary of the Order and a final rule amending regulations under the TCPA for the purpose of "mak[ing] it simpler

61. *Id.* at 83,094.
62. *Id.* at 83,094-95.
63. *See id.* at 83,095-96.
64. Telephone Consumer Protection Act of 1991, Pub. L. 102–243, §2, Dec. 20, 1991, 105 Stat. 2394. The TCPA, as amended, is codified at 47 U.S.C. § 227.
65. Campaign Registry, https://www.campaignregistry.com/ (last visited Sept. 23, 2025).
66. Federal Communications Comm., CG Docket No. 02-278, FCC 24-24, Report & Order & Further Notice of Proposed Rulemaking, Feb. 15, 2024, https://docs.fcc.gov/public/attachments/FCC-24-24A1.pdf.

for consumers to revoke consent to unwanted robocalls and robotexts while requiring that callers and texters honor these requests in a timely manner."[67]

Building on the 2017 *Messaging Principles and Best Practices* (updated in 2023)[68] from the Cellular Telecommunications Industry Association (CTIA), the Mobile Network Operators formed The Campaign Registry (TCR) establishing the requirements for 10-digit long code (10DLC) texting. The 10DLC allows organizations to text without needing a special short code for texting. 10DLC requires registration with TCR by various organizations in the texting process.

The TCPA authorizes private rights of action and statutory damages of $500 per violation.[69] The TCPA also gives courts discretion to award treble damages if the court finds violations to have been willfully or knowingly committed.[70] Liability can be significant as technology makes it very easy to mistakenly send out hundreds of thousands of messages in just a few hours. To ensure compliance with the TCPA for text messaging, prior express consent is required to send the messages.

The U.S. Court of Appeals for the Eleventh Circuit maintains that one text message can constitute a violation of Article III of the TCPA.[71] This circumstance can and has resulted in several cases being permitted to move forward. American Eagle Outfitters made a notable text messaging class action settlement in 2016; it was alleged to have sent 600,000 noncompliant text messages and settled the claims for $14.5 million.[72] Smaller claims have been settled since the September2024 changes from TCR. Even small claims, however, take time and resources from production.

PIOs need to be mindful of the regulatory requirements for information security flowing through contracts with federal agencies and restrictions on marketing calls and text messages. Failure to meet the information security requirements can result in breach of contract claims, financial penalties, and reputation harm. TCPA violations can add up quickly. Obtaining consent and maintaining diligent records documenting it are key for protecting organizations.

67. 89 Fed. Reg. 15,756 (Mar. 5, 2024).

68. CTIA, *Messaging Principles and Best Practices* (Jan. 19, 2017), https://api.ctia.org/docs/default-source/default-document-library/170119-ctia-messaging-principles-and-best-practices.pdf; CTIA, *Messaging Principles and Best Practices* (May 2023), https://api.ctia.org/wp-content/uploads/2023/05/230523-CTIA-Messaging-Principles-and-Best-Practices-FINAL.pdf.

69. 47 U.S.C. § 227(b)(3) (2025).

70. *Id.*

71. *Drazen v. Pinto*, No. 21-10199, 2024 WL 2122466 (11th Cir. May 13, 2024).

72. *See* Paul Tassin, *American Eagle Outfitters Settles Text Message Class Action for $14.5M*, Top Class Actions (Dec. 26, 2016), https://topclassactions.com/lawsuit-settlements/lawsuit-news/american-eagle-outfitters-settles-text-message-class-action-14-5m/.

6. Recent Developments—Part II

6.1. Generative Artificial Intelligence[73]

Since 2022, generative AI (GenAI) tools have gained prominence as a legal practice tool. A number of legal technology vendors offer products that include GenAI features. Public interest lawyers, just like their counterparts in the private sector,[74] have been using technologies like ChatGPT[75] and Google Gemini[76] to maximize productivity and automate repetitive tasks. Public interest nonprofits, which often face limited funding and budget constraints, can channel saved time and resources into high-impact advocacy work.

Below are few examples of how GenAI tools can benefit public interest legal work when they are used with appropriate oversight and checking:

1. GenAI can streamline research, break down complex concepts, draft templates, and summarize legal documents and expert opinions. Traditional legal research engines now have GenAI-enabled versions, such as Lexis AI and Westlaw Precision, marketed as providing faster and more accurate legal research utilizing NLP (natural language processing).
2. While TAR (technology-assisted review) and predictive coding have been used since 2012, GenAI is now being used in document review automation, streamlining litigation preparation.[77]
3. Public interest attorneys can use GenAI tools like Open AI's DALL·E 2 and Google Gemini to generate visuals and pamphlets, which can enhance the impact of their work.
4. Pro-se litigants and case managers who work with vulnerable populations can use AI to fill out forms in immigration, consumer protection, and landlord-tenant cases.
5. Fundraisers use AI to help write donor thank-you notes, newsletters, grant proposals, and press releases.[78]

---

73. See HANDBOOK, Chapter 2, *An Introduction to Artificial Intelligence*, for additional background about generative artificial intelligence tools.

74. *See, e.g.*, *How Law Firms Can Use AI to Level up Their Business,* THOMSON REUTERS (Sept. 25, 2023) https://legal.thomsonreuters.com/blog/how-law-firms-can-use-ai-to-level-up-their-business/.

75. ChatGPT is a GenAI tool provided by OpenAI, L.L.C. OpenAI describes its most recent version of ChatGPT at https://chatgpt.com/overview (last visited Sept. 23, 2025).

76. *See An Overview of the Gemini App,* GOOGLE, https://gemini.google/overview/?hl=en (last visited Sept. 23, 2025).

77. Relativity, *Generative AI Primer, From Beginning to Breakthrough: Navigating Document Review's AI Evolution* at 3 (undated), https://resources.relativity.com/rs/447-YBT-249/images/from-beginning-to-breakthrough-navigating-document-review-ai-evolution.pdf. *See also* Clio, *How AI Enhances Legal Document Review*, L. TECH. TODAY (Feb. 13, 2025), https://www.americanbar.org/groups/law_practice/resources/law-technology-today/2025/how-ai-enhances-legal-document-review/.

78. Beth Kanter, Allison Fine & Philip Deng, *8 Steps Nonprofits Can Take to Adopt AI Responsibly*, STANFORD SOC. INNOVATION REV. (Sep. 7, 2023), https://ssir.org/articles/entry/8_steps_nonprofits_can_take_to_adopt_ai_responsibly.

As with any technology, there are risks associated with use of GenAI tools. Public interest attorneys, especially those who work for legal aid organizations, are frequently understaffed and under-resourced, usually don't have an assigned paralegal and have to perform all duties from legal research to trial work themselves. Naturally, it would make sense to utilize any tools at their disposal to save time. Unfortunately, time constraints often mean busy lawyers use these tools without adequate training or a full understanding of the associated risks and limitations. Lawyers who do not manage GenAI responsibly risk confidentiality, security, and ethical issues.

6.2. Key Considerations

In July 2024, the American Bar Association ethics committee published its first formal opinion on attorney use of generative artificial intelligence tools.[79] The opinion cautions attorneys about their ethical obligation to understand the benefits and risks of any generative AI tool they use in legal practice under Model Rule 1.1.[80]

6.2.1. *Attorneys should be wary of AI hallucinations*[81]

In 2023, two New York attorneys made headlines for submitting a brief citing ChatGPT-generated cases that turned out to be fictitious.[82] The judge found the lawyers acted in bad faith "based upon acts of conscious avoidance and false and misleading statements to the Court," and imposed Rule 11 sanctions on both attorneys.[83] The judge did not fault the attorneys for using artificial intelligence technology, but rather for failing to check its work and standing by the fake quotes and citations even after the court and opposing counsel called them into question. The author attorney cited judicial authorities without reading them, and the reviewing attorney did not inquire into the author attorney's legal research before signing the submission.

---

79. ABA Comm'n on Ethics & Prof'l Responsibility, Formal Op. 512 (2024), *Generative Artificial Intelligence Tools* [hereinafter, ABA Formal Op. 512], https://www.americanbar.org/content/dam/aba/administrative/professional_responsibility/ethics-opinions/aba-formal-opinion-512.pdf. For additional discussion of cybersecurity and lawyers' ethical obligations, see HANDBOOK, Chapter 10, *Lawyers' Professional Responsibility to Provide Data Security*.

80. ABA Formal Op. 512, *supra* note 79, at 2–3.

81. Int'l Bus. Machines Corp., *What are AI Hallucinations?* (Sept. 1, 2023), https://www.ibm.com/think/topics/ai-hallucinations.

82. *See, e.g.*, Sara Merken, *New York Lawyers Sanctioned for Using Fake ChatGPT Cases in Legal Brief*, REUTERS (Jun. 26, 2023), https://www.reuters.com/legal/new-york-lawyers-sanctioned-using-fake-chatgpt-cases-legal-brief-2023-06-22/; Benjamin Weiser, *Here's What Happens When Your Lawyer Uses ChatGPT*, NY TIMES (May 27, 2023), https://www.nytimes.com/2023/05/27/nyregion/avianca-airline-lawsuit-chatgpt.html; Justin Wise, *Lawyer's AI Blunder Shows Perils of ChatGPT in "Early Days,"* BLOOMBURG LAW (May 31, 2023), https://news.bloomberglaw.com/business-and-practice/lawyers-ai-blunder-shows-perils-of-chatgpt-in-early-days.

83. Op. & Order on Sanctions, *Mata v. Avianca, Inc.*, Case No. 22-cv-1461 at 2 (S.D.N.Y. Jun. 22, 2023) [hereinafter *Mata* Sanctions Order]. The docket with links to the Court's various orders and transcript of the hearing relating to the lawyers' citation of cases generate by ChatGPT is available on the CourtListener website at https://www.courtlistener.com/docket/63107798/mata-v-avianca-inc/ (visited Feb. 17, 2025).

In their defense, one of the attorneys testified at the sanctions hearing that "he was 'operating under the false perception that this website [i.e., ChatGPT] could not possibly be fabricating cases on its own.'"[84] Yet, even after the series of motions and orders requesting copies of the cited cases and his attempts to find the cases using traditional legal research tools, the attorney resorted to ChapGPT to "produce" the cases because ChatGPT told him the cases were real.[85] The attorney apparently made no effort to understand the new technology; he took the results at face value.

Despite the widespread reporting about AI hallucinations, lawyers continue to fall into the trap of relying on generative artificial intelligence tools without carefully reviewing and validating the output.[86]

6.2.2. *Attorneys should be aware of technology malfunction*

In 2022, the wellness nonprofit National Eating Disorders Association (NEDA) released an AI wellness chatbot called, Tessa, to replace its popular telephone hotline.[87] A year later, NEDA announced that the chatbot "may have given information that was harmful" and took down the program.[88] Eating disorder specialists and advocates testing the chatbot reported the program gave them dieting advice that promoted disordered eating behaviors.[89]

The *New York Times* coverage included two statements worth noting for risk management. First, the chatbot's developer "had a lot of guardrails, was restricted to specific topics and gave disclaimers of consulting a professional."[90] Yet, the chatbot veered off in ways NEDA agreed could be harmful. Second, the *Times* quoted a psychologist who helped create the chatbot as saying it was "never designed as a one-on-one replacement for the helpline."[91] Deployers and users of AI must consider the context in which the tool is developed and deployed and confirm, with continuing oversight, that the tool is fit for the purpose it is used.

---

84. *Mata* Sanctions Order, *supra* note 83, at 6.

85. Id. at 20.

86. *See, e.g.,* Ord. on Sanctions & Other Disciplinary Action, *Wadsworth v. Walmart, Inc.,* Case No. 2:23-CV-118-KHR (D. Wyo. Feb. 24, 2025); Debra Cassens Weiss, *No. 42 Law Firm by Head Count Sanctioned Over Fake Case Citations Generated by AI,* ABA J. (Feb. 10, 2025 10:30 AM CST), https://www.abajournal.com/news/article/no-42-law-firm-by-headcount-could-face-sanctions-over-fake-case-citations-generated-by-chatgpt#google_vignette.

87. Lauren McCarthy, *A Wellness Chatbot Is Offline after Its 'Harmful' Focus on Weight Loss,* NY Times (Jun. 9, 2023), https://www.nytimes.com/2023/06/08/us/ai-chatbot-tessa-eating-disorders-association.html.

88. NEDA Instagram post, May 30, 2023, https://www.instagram.com/p/Cs4BiC9AhDe/ (visited Jun. 6, 2025).

89. *Id.*; *see also* Daysia Tolentino, *National Eating Disorders Association Pulls Chatbot after Users Say it gave Harmful Dieting Tips,* NBC News (Jun. 1, 2023), https://www.nbcnews.com/tech/neda-pulls-chatbot-eating-advice-rcna87231.

90. McCarthy, *supra* note 87.

91. *Id.*

6.2.3. *Use of GenAI carries confidentiality and privacy risks*

Confidentiality is an ethical duty of an attorney and one of the pillars of the CIA (confidentiality, integrity, and availability) triad in cybersecurity. Understandably, a busy legal aid attorney with a large caseload of pro bono cases might not have additional time to review a lengthy privacy policy before using ChatGPT or similar tools, but they should.

Use of GenAI in legal practice raises confidentiality concerns under Model Rule 1.6 due to the risk of disclosure of, or unauthorized access to, client information.[92] Attorneys must evaluate the risks of information being disclosed or accessed by others before inputting client information into GenAI tools.[93] GenAI also poses potential data security threats; information is shared with a third-party (the tool provider and possibly downstream contractors), and the PIO has no practical ability to monitor the security or use of the information sent outside its own systems.[94]

Public interest attorneys should carefully read the terms of use and privacy policy for the technology they use for client work, including free tools. They should also adjust their privacy settings before using any GenAI tools to ensure compliance with data protection laws like HIPAA and FERPA. A quick look at the privacy policy of major GenAI tools shows that there is a huge risk in sharing any personally identifiable information. Also, all users of these tools should be aware that terms of use, privacy policies, and other policies change frequently. Review of terms needs to be repeated regularly.

An example: OpenAI, the company that developed ChatGPT, states in its Privacy Policy that the users should take special care in deciding what information they provide when using the services.[95] It further shifts responsibility to the user, essentially saying you should tread with caution and at your own risk: "*In addition, we are not responsible for circumvention of any privacy settings or security measures contained on the Service, or third-party websites.*"

Permission to use input data for training and other purposes must be assumed. For ChatGPT, while users can limit some use of information input as prompts, they must change a default setting to get this result. OpenAI's Privacy Policy includes (or leads users to) the following:

- **Personal data is "Content" when it is input as a prompt:** "*User Content*: We collect Personal Data that you provide in the input to our Services ("Content"), including your prompts and other content you upload, such as files, images, and audio, depending on the features you use."[96]

---

92. Model Rules of Prof'l Conduct, Rule 1.6: Confidentiality of Information (Am. Bar Ass'n 2025).

93. ABA Formal Op. 512, *supra* note 79.

94. *See* Handbook, Chapter 2, *An Introduction to Artificial Intelligence*, and Chapter 4, *Understanding Cybersecurity Risks*.

95. OpenAI OpCo, LLC, Privacy Policy § 7. Security (Nov. 4, 2024) (emphasis added) https://openai.com/policies/row-privacy-policy/ (visited Feb. 16, 2025).

96. *Id.* § 1.

- **Content may be used for product development:** "[W]e may use Content you provide us to improve our Services, for example to train the models that power ChatGPT. Read our instructions on how you can opt out of our use of your Content to train our models."[97]
- **The instructions disclose that Content is used for training and require another click-through for information about how to opt out:** "We don't use your content to market our services or create advertising profiles of you—we use it to make our models more helpful. ChatGPT, for instance, improves by further training on the conversations people have with it, unless you opt out."[98]
- **A "Data Controls FAQ" includes opt-out instructions:** "How do I stop my chats from training ChatGPT (ie. "Improve the model for everyone")?[99]
- **The Privacy Policy and Instructions page are not entirely consistent about the use of personal information:** As noted above, the Privacy Policy says Personal Data used in prompts is Content that OpenAI may use for various broadly described purposes. The "How Your Data is Used" page says: "We retain certain data from your interactions with us, but *we take steps to reduce the amount of personal information* in our training datasets before they are used to improve and train our models."[100]
- **Free of charge isn't free; by default, inputs from paid subscribers are not used for training:** The "How Your Data is Used" page says "By default, we do not train on any inputs or outputs from our products for business users, including ChatGPT Business, ChatGPT Enterprise, and the API."[101]

OpenAI is not alone in using input information for training. Meta AI's GenAI tool, offered by the parent company of Facebook, explains the sources of its training data, which includes the following:

> Since it takes such a large amount of data to teach effective models, a combination of sources are used for training. We use information that is publicly available online and licensed information. We also use information shared on Meta Products. This information could be things like posts or photos and their captions. We do not use the content of your private messages with friends and family to train our AIs unless you or someone in the chat chooses to share those messages with our AIs.[102]

---

97. Id. § 2.

98. *How Your Data Is Used to Improve Model Performance,* OpenAI OpCo [hereinafter, *How Your Data is Used*] https://help.openai.com/en/articles/5722486-how-your-data-is-used-to-improve-model-performance (last visited Sept. 23, 2025). The quoted text is included in the cited OpenAI webpage as it appeared on September 23, 2025.

99. *Data Controls FAQ,* OpenAI OpCo, https://help.openai.com/en/articles/7730893-data-controls-faq (last visited Sept. 23, 2025). The quoted text is the question posed in the OpenAI FAQ as it appeared on the cited OpenAI webpage on September 23, 2025.

100. *How Your Data is Used, supra* note 98 (emphasis added).

101. *Id.*

102. *How Meta Uses Information for Generative AI Models and Features,* Meta, https://www.facebook.com/privacy/genai/ (last visited Sept. 23, 2025). The quoted text appears in the FAQ "*Where does Meta get training information?*" as it appeared on the cited Meta webpage on September 23, 2025.

In addition to the training data concern, lawyers should also take care in communicating with clients or allied service providers using any private messaging technology that could be a source of training data. Even if the lawyer adjusts their privacy settings to avoid sharing for training, a person on the other side of the communication may not. Breaking a closed communication loop could waive client-attorney privilege and breach confidentiality obligations.

6.2.4. *Pay attention to data retention policies and practices*

Who doesn't use Google search tools or other services? Google has integrated "conversational" AI features in many of its applications. Google published a "Gemini Apps Privacy Notice" to supplement its Privacy Policy.[103] Consider this disclosure about human reviewers:

> **How human reviewers improve Google services**
>
> A subset of chats are reviewed by human reviewers (including Google's trained service providers) to help improve Google services. These include Gemini models, other generative AI models that power Gemini Apps, and technologies that help reduce unintended activations.
>
> Reviewers assess if Gemini Apps' responses were low-quality, inaccurate, or harmful. They also suggest better responses. We use their suggestions to help our models respond better in the future.
>
> **How we protect your privacy in this process**
>
> We take your privacy seriously, and we do not sell your personal information to anyone. Chats are disconnected from your account before being sent to service providers. Reviewed chats are retained for up to three years.
>
> **How you can control what's shared with reviewers**
>
> To stop your future chats from being reviewed to improve Google services, turn off your Keep Activity setting. If that setting is on, don't enter data that's confidential or that you wouldn't want a reviewer to see or Google to use to improve its services.[104]

"'Gemini Apps' refers to Google's AI assistant."[105] Note that "Gemini Apps" is a changing universe, and the human reviewer disclosure does not limit in any way the body of conservations subject to human review. Lawyers should not assume these kinds of training practices are unique to any particular provider of GenAI tools.

---

103. *Gemini Apps Privacy Notice*, Google (Sept. 23, 2025), https://support.google.com/gemini/answer/13594961?hl=en.

104. *Id.*

105. *Id.*

6.2.5. *Be aware when using transcription assistants*

Transcription assistants like Zoom AI Companion or Otter.ai are embedded in online meeting platforms or separately enabled to work in conjunction with online calendars, both of which are commonly used in business settings. Legal aid organizations frequently use online meeting platforms to conduct intakes and discuss important case developments. Given the sensitive nature of the conversations, those types of meetings should not be recorded.

Even when meetings are not recorded intentionally, however, there are still risks that transcription tools could be used inadvertently. In the past, some Zoom users reported incidents when the third-party transcription software, Otter.ai, automatically joined a Zoom meeting, bypassing the waiting room, recorded the meeting, then emailed every participant a transcript of the meeting. All was done despite the recording feature being turned off. Otter.ai apparently found the meeting information through a participant's calendar.[106]

The messages exchanged in the Zoom Community indicate this problem was addressed in later versions of Zoom, but participant settings in one or more applications may need to be adjusted to avoid unwanted recording and transcription.[107] This is a useful illustration of the risk of integrating online services without appreciating the details of how they work or testing them as they are integrated before using them in actual practice.

6.2.6. *Special data categories*

There are public interest organizations that deal with medical and student records. Attorneys should be aware that standard software versions may not be HIPAA or FERPA compliant and should advise their organizations about legal requirements that need to be included in purchasing decisions.

6.2.7. *Enforce strict access controls*

Organizations need to weigh the risks and benefits of GenAI and set clear rules covering who can use GenAI, for what purposes, with what data, and with what level of review and oversight. GenAI risk management may require limiting who can use GenAI tools and access generated outputs within the organization.

6.2.8. *Create a comprehensive AI policy*

Just like an incident response plan, policies that address AI use, whether standalone or as part of another policy, must be periodically reviewed and revised to reflect technology updates and the organization's needs.

---

106. Zoom Communications, Inc., *Issues with Participants Joining with Otter.ai*, ZOOM COMMUNITY (Dec. 19, 2023 8:16 AM), https://community.zoom.com/t5/Zoom-AI-Companion/Issues-with-Participants-Joining-with-Otter-ai/m-p/158176.

107. *Id.*

The American Bar Association published Standards for the Provision of Civil Legal Aid.[108] Standard 4.10 addresses the effective use of technology. It provides:

> A legal aid organization should utilize technology to support efficient operations and the provision of high-quality and responsive services. Organizations should remain informed and educated about technology tools and systems used by courts, administrative agencies, and others in ways that impact clients, or that clients are required to use when accessing courts or other services. Wherever possible, organizations should strive to participate in the creation of technology tools used by courts and agencies and work toward integration of technology systems with justice system partners to create efficiencies and seamless experiences for clients while also preserving confidentiality of information. Further, information security and data protection are of paramount importance to legal services organizations and organizations should maintain strong practices around information security, backup, and disaster recovery.[109]

Commentary accompanying Standard 4.10 noted that "too little attention is being paid to [AI] by the legal aid community."[110] Continuing, the Commentary encourages legal aid organizations to be educated about the risks and benefits of using AI in their practices and as tools used by others in relation to their client work.[111] Note that the Standards, which were published in 2021, address AI tools broadly. The Commentary is not limited to GenAI.

> Organizations are encouraged to work with others in their jurisdictions to develop standards around the use of AI in the legal system and to develop expertise in this field in order to be a resource for evaluating the ethics and legality of these systems and their impact on clients.
>
> Decisions on whether to use AI tools should not be made by technical teams or vendors alone. The assessment should include ethics and privacy experts to ascertain the risk or potential that client-provided data could be used to create indexes or other tools that could eventually harm the communities served.[112]

AI policies should clearly outline consent requirements, data management, retention, security protocols, and compliance measures. They should also address training expectations.

PIO attorneys and staff should receive training on the capabilities, risks, and ethical implications of AI, including both traditional AI and GenAI tools. Human oversight is crucial. Public interest attorneys should have a clear understanding of AI risks and limitations and use AI as a supplement, not a substitute, for their expertise.

---

108. Am. Bar Assn, Standing Comm. on Legal Aid & Indigent Defense, STANDARDS FOR THE PROVISION OF CIVIL LEGAL AID (Aug. 2021).

109. *Id.* at 154.

110. *Id.* at 155.

111. *Id.*

112. *Id.*

6.2.9. *GenAI Summary*

If used responsibly, GenAI technology offers valuable opportunities to streamline complex legal work and make the justice system more accessible. The Pioneer Public Interest Law Center conducted a demonstration on ChatGPT and what the future could look like.[113] Prompts from a participating judge requested a breach of contract complaint, which was created in 53 seconds. A legal intern moved on to discovery and asked ChatGPT to create a list of interrogatories for a fictitious defendant; a complete set was delivered in 46 seconds.[114] Finally, ChatGPT generated a motion to dismiss in less than 50 seconds, with accurate case citations.[115] "You can't just sign this and file it," Judge Bailey said, "but it's a quite credible job."[116]

7. Recommendations and Wrap-Up

Below are several steps that PIOs can take to begin bolstering their programs for protecting the sensitive data they house.

1. **Locate and understand your data**
   Take an inventory of all the data your nonprofit collects and identify where it is stored, including knowing how sensitive data travels around, and in and out of, the organization. The inventory should include hardware assets and the software used to store and process the data. Nonprofits store and transfer personally identifiable information such as medical information, employee records, drivers' licenses, addresses, social security numbers, and credit card information. Security for these data is especially critical when they are stored in conjunction with contact information, like phone numbers and email addresses. Additionally, PIOs collect and store personal preference information such as donation habits, areas of interest, and newsletter subscriptions. PIOs should know whether the data collected and maintained is covered by federal or state regulations as "personally identifiable information." Establish a document retention policy to reduce storage costs and minimize the risk of storing archived data no longer needed.
2. **Effectively Review and Communicate Risk**
   Risk communications need to be done regularly in terms the board of directors and executives understand, which include both financial metrics and security metrics.[117] Speaking in terms the board understands means avoiding jargon, overly technical terms, and acronyms. Aggregating risks into larger buckets is not uncommon and

---

113. Chris Villani, *Better, Faster, Stranger: What Attys Think of Our AI Future*, Law360 (Nov. 27, 2024 2:49 PM EST), https://www.morganlewis.com/-/media/files/news/2024/better-faster-stranger-what-attys-think-of-our-ai-future.pdf.
114. *Id.*
115. *Id.*
116. *Id.*
117. Randall S. Wright, *Should Accounting be the Language of Business?*, 62 Res. Tech. Mgmt, 53–55 (2019).

has been shown to be an effective means to assess risks, such as a credit score. Use aggregate scores in cybersecurity evaluation, such as confidentiality, integrity, availability, human resources (people), finance, and reputation, to connect information security risks to the organization.[118] In aggregated buckets, a non-technical person can assess how risk may impact their area of responsibility in relation to other risks. Receiving and acting on these risks will help ensure that board members and executives meet their duties of care and loyalty and their fiduciary responsibilities while serving their organization's missions. Boards and executives can partner with organizations that work with PIOs to meet these requirements to understand and address their risks.

Some particular risks for boards to consider, which are not necessarily unique to NGOs and PIOs, are employees working from home, use of personal devices to access the organization's databases or emails, and lack of awareness and education among staff and volunteers. NGOs need to review their third-party risks periodically as well: how likely is it that your vendor's vulnerability could compromise your nonprofit's data security? Many nonprofits don't have permanent staff on payroll and often utilize contractors such as accounting firms, IT tech support, and cloud storage services. If any of these third-party vendors do not employ adequate data security protection, the nonprofit's data security will be at risk.

3. **Website security**

Hackers can access a nonprofit's site through a security breach, deface a website, or transform it into something unrecognizable. Hackers may create and add content that can damage a nonprofit's reputation. To improve website security, nonprofits should utilize the Open Web Application Security Project's (OWASP) resources. OWASP is a nonprofit foundation that works to improve software security.[119] OWASP offers complimentary guidelines, standards, articles, tools, and methodologies and aims to raise awareness about application security by identifying some of the most critical risks facing organizations.[120]

OWASP Top 10 provides a ranking of, and remediation guidance for, the top 10 most critical web application security risks.[121] The report is based on a consensus among security experts from around the world.[122] The risks are ranked based on the frequency of discovered security defects, the severity of the vulnerabilities, and the magnitude of their potential impacts. PIOs can use the direction from the OWASP Top 10 regarding the most prevalent security risks and leverage the report's findings

118. Todd Fitzgerald, CISO COMPASS: Navigating Cybersecurity Leadership Challenges with Insights from Pioneers (2018).

119. OWASP Foundation, https://owasp.org/ (last visited Sept. 23, 2025).

120. *About the OWASP Foundation*, OWASP Found., https://owasp.org/about/ (last visited Sept. 23, 2025).

121. OWASP *Top Ten*, OWASP Found., https://owasp.org/www-project-top-ten/ (last visited Sept. 23, 2025). Refer to the "Data 2025" tab for information about how OWASP collects data for the Top Ten.

122. *Id.*

and recommendations into their security practices, thereby reducing known risks in their web applications.

4. **Treat Your Passwords Like a Toothbrush**
   - Like a toothbrush, change your password periodically.
   - Like a toothbrush, don't allow someone else to use your password; train users not to share their passwords.
   - Like a toothbrush that can be hard, soft, electric, etc., make sure your password meets security requirements such as having sufficient length for its lifespan.

   Individuals can use Password Managers (offline versions recommended) to remember passwords, which can make it easier for users to have different passwords for different applications and websites. Use passphrases, for example, Il0v3S@turdays!, or one that consists of five or more random words with separators such as cat.summer.bottle.jurist.bluebook.[123] Do not reuse old passwords, and do not use the same password to access different systems or databases. Lastly, remember that length trumps complexity.

5. **Policies, Procedures, and Guidelines**

   Every PIO should maintain a solid set of policies, procedures, and guidelines in compliance with the nonprofit sector's regulatory requirements.[124] The regulatory environment requires the PIO to understand their legal obligations regarding privacy and security and then transfer those into policy. The policies, procedures, and guidelines should be clear and comprehensive to provide users throughout the organization direction on handling data and responding to incidents. There are many recognized security frameworks such as ISO 27001 and the National Institute for Science and Technology (NIST) Cybersecurity Framework that a PIO/NGO might choose to leverage to build their program and policies. NIST offers extensive cybersecurity research that is freely available.

   Staff should be trained on the PIO's policies, procedures, and guidelines. Training staff on best security practices will help to reduce the likelihood of an incident. Some of the critical training priorities to consider include reminders: not to click on links without verifying source legitimacy, not to leave sensitive information visible on the desk or monitor, to lock the screen when away, to shred documents containing PII before recycling, and to never share sensitive information over the phone. Nonprofits should create and regularly update a cybersecurity awareness program designed to continually educate staff about evolving threats and tactics and steps staff can take to access and use PIO's systems securely.

---

123. Aranza Trevino, *How to Create a Strong Passphrase*, Keeper Sec. (Mar. 4, 2024), https://www.keepersecurity.com/blog/2024/03/04/how-to-create-a-strong-passphrase/.

124. *See, e.g., supra*, text at notes 42–43 & 54–63.

A well-written Incident Response Plan (IRP) must be readily available. It should cover all the essential details such as incident response team contact information and step-by-step incident response actions.[125]

6. **Patch Systems**

   If a dam has a hole in it, engineers work to fill it. This concept should not be different for computer systems. Too many holes in a system—vulnerabilities—allow threats to exploit these weaknesses. PIOs should understand their systems and determine how best to patch them regularly and in a timely manner to reduce the likelihood of vulnerabilities from being exploited. In addition, the designated IT person or IT solution partner (e.g., a managed service provider) should continually maintain technology to keep it updated. They must ensure that IT systems are routinely patched for firmware updates and ensure endpoint protection software is regularly updated and that updates are applied to all endpoints.

7. **Use Multi-Factor Authentication (MFA)**

   MFA adds an extra step to verify the user is, in fact, who they say they are by using a combination of something they know, like a password, something they have, like a token or SMS code, or something they are, like a fingerprint or face recognition. Many people use multi-factor authentication when logging onto their bank or even their Google or Facebook accounts. Multi-factor authentication adds an additional layer of protection and will help reduce the likelihood of compromised credentials from being used negatively against an organization. Multi-factor authentication is commonly employed today and considered a reasonable practice for any organization. It is also, required by many regulators and recommended by many more.

8. **Encryption and Identity Management**

   Encryption and identity management are needed to ensure the right people have access to organizational data. The reason these two topics are tied together is that encryption protects against physical theft and eavesdropping. However, if a malicious actor compromises credentials (the identity), they will be able to bypass the encryption and retrieve the data. Nonetheless, encryption is important because it is one way to reduce the adverse consequences of data theft; encrypting or scrambling data effectively makes it useless to the thief. Data should also be protected with encryption when at rest and when in transit. In both states, at rest or in transit, only those with the decryption methods can access the data. PIOs can implement encryption in transit by adding TLS certificates to their webpages, using secure file sharing links in OneDrive and Google Drive, and encrypting messages sent via email. There are many ways to provide encryption within an enterprise, and a managed service provider can assist with that if in-house IT cannot.

125. *See* HANDBOOK, Chapter 13, *Achieving Preparedness through Standards and Planning and Best Practices for Incident Response.*

In line with this is the need for strong access management. Access management is the process that ensures that only authorized people have access to the technology resources they are intended to have to perform their job functions. For example, setting permission on files and data for the right groups of people. Through solid access management, the right users with the correct access will be able to access the data at the right time.

9. **Cyber Insurance**
   Nonprofits should investigate adding cybersecurity coverages to their existing insurance policies. Attorneys need to review the amount of coverage to ensure it is adequate to mitigate the costs of potential cyber incidents. Many policies can include coverage for incident response, forensics, and ransom payments. Be careful of the exceptions to these policies, as some have exclusions for social engineering.[126] Damages arising from a security event may be covered by elements of different policies. Organizations should look holistically at their insurance coverage to understand where different risks are covered to avoid gaps and to give timely notices under relevant policies when a security event happens.
10. **Don't Do It Alone**
   Cybersecurity is a complicated space that is constantly evolving. Just as there are lawyers to provide legal advice about almost every topic under the sun, cybersecurity professionals can provide guidance in this space. Many are willing to give back and assist PIOs. These professionals can be found through various trade organizations such as the Information Systems Audit and Control Association (ISACA), AITP Association of Information Technology Professionals (AITP), and InfraGard.[127] Seeking the advice of experts can provide the needed background to allow attorneys to evaluate the legal risks and effectively execute their duties. Having experts weigh in on technical aspects and risks and how they impact the business is critical in helping attorneys provide advice to the PIOs they are intended to protect.

7.1. Wrap Up

PIOs are not that different from other businesses when it comes to cybersecurity. PIOs have computers, and they have data that is valued from either a content perspective, it can be sold on the black market, or it is valued by the PIO as it is critical to operations. Interference with access to that data can disrupt business operations. As in for-profit businesses, if operations are disrupted, so are the means to generate revenue and, as mentioned at the beginning of this chapter, "No margin, no mission." In the PIO sector, that lack of business

126. For more detailed information about cyber insurance, see HANDBOOK, Chapter 14, *Cyber Insurance for Law Firms and Legal Organizations*.

127. InfraGard is a partnership between the Federal Bureau of Investigation (FBI) and members of the private sector for the protection of U.S. Critical Infrastructure. *See About Us*, INFRAGARD, https://www.infragardnational.org/about-us/overview/ (last visited Sept. 23, 2025).

operations and generating revenue, either through grants or operations, means that the social good delivery does not occur.

Continuing the mission is the imperative of the PIO. Steps to ensure the continued operation are essential. This means determining and understanding the risks in the environment by working with internal resources or partner organizations. After identifying risk, they must be presented to executives and the board for decisions on appropriate action and taking steps to avoid, transfer, reduce, or accept the risks. Making these tasks an on-going process will enable the PIO's leaders to satisfy fiduciary obligations like those examined in *Caremark* and *Stone* and help to ensure the PIO can remain focused on their mission.

Chapter 18

Large Law Firms

Alan Charles Raul

1. Introduction to Cybersecurity for Large Law Firms

Attorneys at law firms understand that the transactions and litigation that drive their practices are of significant interest not only to their clients but also to their clients' competitors, government regulators, the press, criminals, and others in the outside world. Attorneys are attuned to the confidentiality needs of their clients and must be ready, able, and willing to adjust their practices to protect client confidentiality. Clients entrust law firms with their most important business and legal information, and firms must take appropriate steps to safeguard that data. Failure to do so risks a firm's reputation. If a firm loses its clients' trust, it will also likely lose its clients. Failure to protect clients' data also entails a risk to the firm's lawyers' ability to meet their professional responsibilities.

Safeguarding data has become increasingly critical and challenging. Cyberattacks and data breaches can cause significant costs to commercial enterprises. Today, companies get regularly reminded to keep cybersecurity risks top of mind. A recent surge in ransomware attacks has publicly incapacitated companies across various industries, from the energy sector[1] to meatpacking facilities.[2] Cybersecurity has become the most pressing concern for CEOs, as costs continue to rise for companies, particularly in light of recent substantial fines related to data breaches. In 2023, the Data Protection Commission of Ireland fined a major social media company more than one billion dollars under the GDPR, and in 2024, a global hotel company agreed to pay a $52 million penalty to 49 states and the District of Columbia for failing to implement reasonable data security practices, contributing to three breaches over six years.[3]

1. *See* Seher Dareen & Srivastava Vallari, *Cyberattacks on US Utilities Surged 70% This Year, Says Check Point,* Reuters (Sept. 11, 2024), https://www.reuters.com/technology/cybersecurity/cyberattacks-us-utilities-surged-70-this-year-says-check-point-2024-09-11/.

2. *See* Dee-Ann Durbin & Frank Bajak, *JBS, World's Biggest Meat Supplier, Says Its Systems Are Coming Back Online after Cyberattack Shut Down Plaints in U.S.*, Wash. Post (June 1, 2021), https://www.washington-post.com/business/2021/06/01/jbs-cyberattack-meat-supply-chain/.

3. *See* Christopher Beveridge, *Irish Data Protection Commissioner Imposes a €1.2 Billion Fine on Meta Ireland,* BDO (Oct. 24, 2023), https://www.bdo.co.uk/en-gb/insights/advisory/risk-and-advisory-services/irish-data-protection-commissioner-imposes-a-1-2-billion-fine-on-meta-ireland#; Press Release, Fed. Trade Comm'n, *FTC Takes Action against Marriott and Starwood Over Multiple Data Breaches* (Oct. 9, 2024), https://www.ftc.gov/news-events/news/press-releases/2024/10/ftc-takes-action-against-marriott-starwood-over-multiple-data-breaches.

Companies of all sizes are now targets—as are courts, government agencies,[4] celebrities, political organizations, and law firms; and costs are rising. Analysts estimate that, as of 2020, cybercrime costs exceeded $1 trillion globally.[5] The Federal Bureau of Investigation's Internet Crime Complaint Center reported that in 2023, it "received a record number of complaints from the American public: 880,418 complaints with potential losses exceeding $12.5 billion, which is nearly a 10% increase in complaints and a 22% increase in losses compared to 2022."[6]

While companies have increasingly and proactively taken protective measures to defend against cyberattacks,[7] not all attorneys who provide them with services and advice have implemented adequate cybersecurity measures.[8] According to the 2023 ABA TechReport, 29% of responding law firms reported experiencing a security breach.[9] Despite this reality, only 34% of firms have an incident response plan, a decrease from 42% that reported having an incident response plan the previous year. However, among the 34% of positive responses, 78% of large law firms have implemented incident response plans.[10] Unfortunately, failures by lawyers to take reasonable measures to secure their data and networks can put both law firms and law firm clients at risk from harmful cyberattacks and espionage.

The past decade has demonstrated that hackers have grown increasingly aware of the critical role large law firms play in business and have targeted these firms.[11] Attorneys routinely advise on regulatory matters, conduct due diligence, negotiate transactions, engage in discovery, and litigate disputes for the world's largest companies. These attorneys often have access to a diverse array of their clients' most sensitive information, including trade secrets, intellectual property, financial data, corporate strategies, evidence from internal investigations into possible malfeasance, and internal research. A large law firm's computer system may represent a honeypot of valuable data for hackers bent on industrial espionage,

---

4. *See* Debra Cassens Weiss, *Federal Court Documents and DOJ Emails Compromised in Cybersecurity Breach*, ABA Journal (Jan. 7, 2021), https://www.abajournal.com/news/article/hackers-accessed-at-least-80-of-emails-in-new-york-federal-prosecutors-offices-justice-department-says.

5. *See* Steve Morgan, *Cybercrime to Cost the World 10.5 Trillion Annually by 2025*, Cybercrime Magazine (Nov. 13, 2020), https://cybersecurityventures.com/cybercrime-damage-costs-10-trillion-by-2025/; Lily Hay Newman, *The Year's Biggest Hacks, from Yahoo to the DNC*, Wired (Dec. 31, 2016), https://www.wired.com/2016/12/years-biggest-hacks-yahoo-dnc/.

6. *See* Internet Crime Complaint Ctr., Fed. Bureau of Investigation, Internet Crime Report 2023 (Mar. 6, 2024), https://www.ic3.gov/AnnualReport/Reports/2023_IC3Report.pdf.

7. *See* PricewaterhouseCoopers, PwC's 26th Annual Global CEO Survey: Winning today's race while running tomorrow's 14 (2023), https://www.pwc.com/gx/en/ceo-survey/2023/main/download/26th_CEO_Survey_PDF_v1.pdf.

8. *See* John Simek, *2023 Cybersecurity TechReport*, Law Practice Div., Am. Bar Assoc. (Dec. 18, 2023), https://www.americanbar.org/groups/law_practice/resources/tech-report/2023/2023-cybersecurity-techreport/.

9. *Id.*

10. *Id.*

11. *See* Sharon D. Nelson et al., *Law Firm Data Breaches Surge in 2023*, Above the Law (Aug. 1, 2023), https://abovethelaw.com/2023/08/law-firm-data-breaches-surge-in-2023/; Victoria Hudgins, *Meet the Hacker Groups Snatching Law Firms' Client Data*, Law.com, https://www.law.com/legaltechnews/2020/05/21/meet-the-hacker-groups-snatching-law-firms-client-data/ (noting in a span of nearly six months, at least seven law firms have been infiltrated by ransomware).

trade secret or intellectual property theft, public embarrassment, or other activities targeting multiple firm clients. For the most part, criminals can easily open the law firm's "treasure chest."

Some of the biggest New York law firms have acknowledged direct attacks as part of an insider-trading scheme targeting merger information. A Panama-based law firm suffered 2.6 terabytes of leaked data that disclosed client names and their alleged efforts to evade taxes. Recently, a breached vendor's file transfer system exposed private data of several prominent law firms.[12] Breaches like these can persist undetected for weeks or even months.[13] Criminals may target the firm, or specific attorneys, because they believe that the attorney will have access to highly sensitive information. But criminals may forgo targeting specific information, instead deploying all-encompassing ransomware. Both scenarios may cause significant disruption or lead to a breach of a lawyer's high standards and obligations to protect clients' information.[14]

Large law firms form a target-rich environment with sometimes significantly less cybersecurity protection than their clients.[15] As more firms move to the cloud and adopt new technologies, they create a greater risk of experiencing a breach unless they conduct relevant diligence and implement proper safeguards.

Many large firms quickly transitioned to fully remote work during the COVID-19 pandemic, without advance planning. During the pandemic, law firms experienced a significant increase in ransomware attacks. Even after the pandemic, ransomware attacks have continued. In 2023, 45 law firm ransomware attacks occurred, affecting approximately 1.6 million records.[16] Although several attacks did not expose client data, others did, including an attack on one of Hollywood's top talent firms that led to leaked contracts and other documents containing information about famous clients.[17] The increased use of new technology also raises the risk that a firm will be collateral damage from attacks on service providers or potentially unintended collateral from nation-state activities (e.g., Stuxnet, SolarWinds).

---

12. *See* Chris Opfer, *Jones Day Hit by Data Breach as Vendor Accellion Hack Widens*, Bloomberg Law (Feb. 16, 2021), https://news.bloomberglaw.com/business-and-practice/jones-day-hit-by-data-breach-as-vendor-accellion-hacks-widen.

13. *See* Lee Ponder, *Ghost in the Machine: When Cyberattacks Go Undetected,* Acronis (Oct. 24, 2024), https://www.acronis.com/en-us/blog/posts/ghost-in-the-machine-when-cyberattacks-go-undetected/ (noting examples of ransomware attacks in 2024 against for-profit and nonprofit companies, such as Dell Technologies and MITRE, that went undetected for weeks or months at a time).

14. *See* Verizon, 2020 Data Breach Investigations Report (2020), https://www.verizon.com/business/en-gb/resources/reports/2020-data-breach-investigations-report.pdf [hereinafter Verizon 2020 Report].

15. *See* Xiumei Dong, *Law Firms' Reported Cyberattacks Are "Tip of the Iceberg"*, Law360 (Nov. 4, 2020), https://www.law360.com/articles/1326001; Rhys Dipshan, *Firms See Cyber Incidents as Inevitable. So Why Aren't They Better Prepared?*, Law.com (Oct. 3, 2022), https://www.law.com/legaltechnews/2022/10/03/firms-expect-breaches-so-why-arent-they-better-prepared-397-62869/.

16. *See* Rebecca Moody, *Law Firms Hit with Average Ransom Demand of $2.5 Million,* Comparitech (Aug. 1, 2024), https://www.comparitech.com/blog/information-security/ransomware-attacks-law-firms/.

17. *See* Dong, *supra* note 15; *cf.*, Ashley Cullins, *Why High-Profile Hacks Could Increase Amid Pandemic-Prompted Remote Work*, Hollywood Reporter (May 18, 2020), https://www.hollywoodreporter.com/business/business-news/how-pandemic-related-remote-work-could-lead-an-increase-high-profile-hacks-1294980/.

Like government agencies and companies, law firms must continue to enhance their efforts in combating the growing threat of cyberattacks and espionage.

Beyond a lawyer's professional responsibility to protect client data,[18] affected firms face immediate and long-term costs, including breach investigation and notification, potential lawsuits, and the risk of losing clients and public trust.[19] If a firm does not have sufficient data security measures in place, clients may leave. Additionally, clients may find themselves held responsible for the data security incidents of their law firms.[20] The Association of Corporate Counsel (ACC) released its first set of model cybersecurity practices in 2017, drafted as a contract between the company and its outside counsel, which requires measures such as encrypting all confidential information and notifying of a breach within 24 hours.[21] Although the ACC recommends that in-house counsel use the model as a guide to meet a company's needs, rather than as a one-size-fits-all industry standard, a firm that fails to implement such protections may likely lose opportunities to represent clients in significant matters. Cautious in-house counsel may choose firms they believe appear more secure as they worry their decisions may face greater scrutiny in the event of a breach.[22] Firms can reduce these risks by preparing to react quickly and appropriately in line with an incident response policy and having a strong cybersecurity framework in place.[23] Preventing as many incidents as possible and addressing the threats and challenges facing firms today, while being prepared to handle an incident when it occurs, remains the best defense.

Law enforcement is well aware of efforts by hackers to infiltrate the computers and networks of America's largest law firms. As early as November 17, 2009, the FBI issued an alert to law firms and other professional services organizations, warning about the proliferation of "spear phishing" attacks.[24] Two years later, in late 2011, the FBI met with

---

18. On May 22, 2017, the American Bar Association issued revised Formal Opinion 477R to address "how a lawyer should comply with the core duty of confidentiality in an ever-changing technological world." The opinion concludes that lawyers should, inter alia, take "reasonable efforts to prevent inadvertent or unauthorized access" when transmitting information over the Internet and stay "abreast of the benefits and risks associated with relevant technology." ABA Comm. on Ethics & Prof'l Responsibility, Formal Op. 477R, at 2–3 (2017).

19. *See* Ryan Boysen, *What to Watch for in Legal Ethics in 2024*, LAW360 (Jan. 1, 2024), https://www.law360.com/articles/1780350/what-to-watch-for-in-legal-ethics-in-2024; *see also* HANDBOOK, Chapter 10, *Lawyers' Professional Responsibility to Provide Data Security*.

20. *See* Maria Dinzeo, *When Law Firms Get Hacked, Are Their Corporate Clients on the Hook?*, LAW.COM (Oct. 15, 2024), https://www.law.com/corpcounsel/2024/10/15/when-law-firms-get-hacked-are-their-corporate-clients-on-the-hook.

21. *See* ASS'N OF CORP. COUNSEL, MODEL INFORMATION PROTECTION AND SECURITY CONTROLS FOR OUTSIDE COUNSEL POSSESSING COMPANY CONFIDENTIAL INFORMATION (Mar. 10, 2017), https://www.acc.com/sites/default/files/resources/advocacy/1454057_1.pdf [hereinafter ACC MODEL SECURITY GUIDELINES].

22. *See* Camillo Artiga-Purcell, *Cybersecurity Planning: A Critical Responsibility for In-House Counsel*, LEGAL DIVE (Apr. 1, 2024), https://www.legaldive.com/news/cybersecurity-planning-a-critical-responsibility-for-in-house-counsel/711897/.

23. *See, e.g.*, Debra Cassens Weiss, *Seyfarth Shaw Is in "Restoration Phase" after Malware Attack*, ABA JOURNAL (Oct 16, 2020), https://www.abajournal.com/news/article/seyfarth-shaw-is-in-restoration-phas-after-malware-attack.

24. In this type of attack, hackers send spoofed messages—which appear to be genuine e-mails from trusted sources—to employees of the target organization with the intention of having the employees click on links that

representatives from major law firms to discuss the rising number of cyberattacks on the firms and to warn them that hackers perceive large firms as a relatively unprotected backdoor into corporate America. The ABA Journal reported on the lawyers' meeting with the FBI in an article entitled "Some NY Law Firm Reps Said to Be Clueless as FBI Warned of Hackers Seeking Corporate Data."[25]

Over a decade later, law firms and the FBI continue to work together. The FBI publishes notifications when it becomes aware of various schemes[26] and can serve as an active partner during cyberattack investigations.[27] While law firms might not be as "clueless" about hackers anymore, many firms still have "less-than-optimal information security practices and procedures," and malicious actors target these cybersecurity vulnerabilities.[28] Ransomware and malware attacks, along with subsequent litigation and regulatory enforcement, continue to plague law firms such that some clients will pay premiums to law firms with enhanced cybersecurity measures.[29] The security vulnerabilities and high target status of law firms are commonly acknowledged in the press. In March 2025, the FBI warned that hackers continued to target international law firms, specifically as part of insider trading schemes, suggesting an increase in the number of breaches and the breadth of hackers' motivations.[30] The disparity in levels of protection between law firms and their clients will persist unless law firms take proactive measures to enhance their security programs.

2. Cybersecurity Issues and Challenges for Large Firms

Firms face many cybersecurity issues and challenges today. All companies face an increased cybersecurity risk, but law firms are prime, high-visibility targets with large amounts of sensitive information that present special risks. All large global companies face additional challenges from a dispersed network, which law firms must address in addition to

---

lead to the installation of malware, and hacker backdoors, onto the network. Given that lawyers typically maintain many historical messages in their e-mail, access to attorney in-boxes can have serious data security consequences.

25. *See* Debra Cassens Weiss, *Some NY Law Firm Reps Said to Be Clueless as FBI Warned of Hackers Seeking Corporate Data*, ABA Journal (Jan. 31, 2012), http://www.abajournal.com/news/article/some_ny_law_firm_reps_said_to_be_clueless_as_fbi_warned_of_hackers_seeking_/.

26. The FBI continues to issue alerts, but recent warnings have been less tailored to specific industries. An increase in attacks, particularly ransomware, that can be leveraged to attack a wide range of industries and agencies has led to warnings that all industries should consider. *See, e.g.*, Cyber Div., Fed. Bureau of Investigation, *Mamba Ransomware Weaponizing DiskCryptor* (Mar. 23, 2021), https://www.ic3.gov/Media/News/2021/210323.pdf.

27. *See* Xiumei Dong, *Seyfarth Shaw Hit by Ransomware Attack*, Law360 (Oct. 12, 2020), https://www.law360.com/articles/1319008/seyfarth-shaw-hit-by-ransomware-attack.

28. *See* Dong, *supra* note 15.

29. *See* Integris, *Breaches and Bots: Law Firms Face a Trust Crisis with Clients, New Integris Survey Reveals,* Bus. Wire (Nov. 12, 2024, 9:35 AM), https://www.businesswire.com/news/home/20241112433654/en/Breaches-and-Bots-Law-Firms-Face-a-Trust-Crisis-with-Clients-New-Integris-Survey-Reveals.

30. *See FBI Alert Warns of Criminals Seeking Access to Law Firm Networks*, Broward Cty. Bar Ass'n (Apr. 5, 2025), https://www.browardbar.org/fbi-alert-warns-criminals-seeking-access-law-firm-networks/.

considering the challenges of law firm security culture. A law firm must navigate the current threat landscape and a combination of internal considerations to help defend itself against cybersecurity threats.

2.1. Today's Threat Landscape

Hackers use an ever-evolving arsenal of techniques to exploit law firms' systems. Many attacks, such as distributed denial-of-service (DDoS) attacks, exploit well-known network and system vulnerabilities.[31] Hackers often take the path of least resistance and attack the human element. One report by SlashNext notes a 341% growth in phishing attempts over the six months ending March 2024.[32] The use of social engineering techniques to gain access to firms' data often serves as a hacker's weapon of choice. Many notorious hacking exploits in recent years have been attributed to spear phishing. The social engineering component of a spear phishing attack often leads an organization insider to unwittingly install malware that the network's security system might otherwise prevent the hacker from installing.

For instance, when an organized group of hackers targeted firms involved in pending major mergers and acquisitions to gain insider information for stock trades, the hackers sent lawyers at the firms emails purporting to be from a well-known British publication, announcing that it was honoring the attorneys for their achievements.[33] When the target opened the malware-laden links or email attachments, the hackers gained access to the firms' networks, enabling them to gather information relating to non-public transactions. The U.S. Attorney for the Southern District of New York noted that the case "should serve as a wake-up call for law firms around the world: you are and will be targets of cyber hacking, because you have information valuable to would-be criminals."[34] Consequently, states like New York are trying to strengthen the commonly targeted "human element." Since January 1, 2023, New York requires that all new attorneys participate in cybersecurity continuing legal education programs as a prerequisite to practicing law in the state.[35]

---

31. While distributed denial of service (DDoS) attacks are primarily used to cause system downtime, often to cause embarrassment or as a form of hacktivism, they may be used as a diversionary tactic for hackers seeking to exploit a system. For instance, a DDoS attack may force IT staff to pay attention to the attack on one system resource, rendering it more difficult for them to monitor exploits occurring elsewhere on a system. *See* Robert Lemos, *DDoS Attacks on Major Banks Causing Problems for Customers*, eWeek (Dec. 28, 2012), https://www.eweek.com/security/ddos-attacks-on-major-banks-causing-problems-for-customers/ ("Fraudsters also use DDoS attacks to distract...personnel and technical resources while they gain unauthorized remote access.").

32. *See* Alessandro Mascellino, *Report Reveals 341% Rise in Advanced Phishing Attacks*, Infosecurity Magazine (May 22, 2024), https://www.infosecurity-magazine.com/news/341-rise-advanced-phishing-attacks.

33. *See* Ed Beeson, *Anatomy of a Hack*, Law360 (Mar. 27, 2017), https://www.law360.com/privacy/articles/905062/how-cybercriminals-are-breaching-biglaw-s-defenses.

34. *Manhattan U.S. Attorney Announces Arrest of Macau Resident and Unsealing of Charges against Three Individuals for Insider Trading Based on Information Hacked from Prominent U.S. Law Firms*, S.D.N.Y., U.S. Attorney's Office (Dec. 27, 2016), https://www.justice.gov/usao-sdny/pr/manhattan-us-attorney-announces-arrest-macau-resident-and-unsealing-charges-against.

35. *See With Threats Rising, New York Mandates Cybersecurity Training for Lawyers*, Esquire Deposition Sols. (Nov. 21, 2022), https://www.esquiresolutions.com/with-threats-rising-new-york-mandates-cybersecurity-training-for-lawyers/.

Further complicating matters, fraudulent emails are becoming increasingly difficult to distinguish from legitimate ones. Law firms can implement technical controls to assist users, such as flagging external email addresses as suspicious. However, phishing emails and social engineering attacks succeed because they exploit human error.[36]

Phishing awareness training can drastically reduce the number of employees who fall victim to phishing attempts. A recent benchmarking survey suggests that the number of employees in the legal industry who click on a suspicious link or obey a fraudulent request drops from 33.2% to 5.4% after a year of ongoing awareness training.[37] Law firms should focus their training on phishing techniques and consider other key aspects, such as whether the request is unusual or timed oddly, requires urgent action (e.g., password expirations or security alerts), or contains unexpected DocuSign requests or shipping delivery notices. Firms should always pay careful attention to wiring instructions, including verbally providing passwords and ensuring that the body of transaction and settlement agreements does not include wiring information.

Law firms representing clients conducting business in markets where hacking is endemic—for example, China or Russia—or in market sectors of critical interest to those countries also face a significant risk of government-backed cyber espionage. FireEye and other cybersecurity firms continue to discover advanced persistent threats (APTs) that target both public and private entities in the United States.[38] The FBI has warned law firms representing companies involved in business dealings or litigation with Chinese state-owned enterprises about their increased likelihood of cyberattacks.[39]

The number of nation states increasing these APT capabilities continues to rise, and their reach correspondingly widens.[40] As far back as 2010, law firms reported experiencing significant cyberattacks originating abroad that could reasonably be tied to their representation of a party adverse to a foreign state.[41] Today, firms increasingly face both direct targeting and incidental breaches, particularly as nation-state actors like Russia and China

36. See, *e.g.*, Verizon 2020 Report, *supra* note 14.

37. *See* KnowBe4, Phishing by Industry Benchmarking Report 2023 Edition (June 20, 2023), https://www.knowbe4.com/hubfs/2020PhishingByIndustryBenchmarkingReport.pdf.

38. An advanced persistent threat is a prolonged, targeted attack that aims to compromise a specific system and gain information. *See Advanced Persistent Threat*, Nat'l Inst. of Standards & Tech., https://csrc.nist.gov/glossary/term/advanced_persistent_threat (last visited July 27, 2025).

39. *See* Seol Namgoong et al., *FBI and CISA Warn of Chinese Cyberattacks on U.S. Critical Infrastructure*, Alston & Bird (Feb. 21, 2024), https://www.alstonprivacy.com/fbi-and-cisa-warn-of-chinese-cyberattacks-on-u-s-critical-infrastructure/.

40. Dep't of Homeland Sec., Commodification of Cyber Capabilities: A Grand Cyber Arms Bazaar (2019), https://permanent.fdlp.gov/gpo150408/ia_geopolitical-impact-cyber-threats-nation-state-actors.pdf (noting increasingly sophisticated and persistent campaigns targeting various sectors originating from more countries, including North Korea, Vietnam, and Ukraine).

41. *See* Jennifer Smith, *Lawyers Get Vigilant on Cybersecurity*, Wall St. J. (June 26, 2012), https://www.wsj.com/articles/SB10001424052702304458604577486761101726748 (citing the 2010 experience of Los Angeles firm Gipson Hoffman & Pancione, which represented a software company in a suit against the Chinese government and other defendants, only to receive a significant number of e-mails containing malware immediately following the filing of the lawsuit); Thomas Claburn, *Law Firm Suing China Hit by Cyber Attack*, InformationWeek (Jan. 14, 2010) https://www.darkreading.com/attacks-breaches/law-firm-suing-china-hit-by-cyber-attack.

improve tradecraft and gain access to numerous industries with a single exploit via common upstream service providers. This trend is underscored by the increasing frequency of Cybersecurity and Infrastructure Security Agency (CISA) alerts for vulnerabilities.[42] Several of these vulnerabilities have been active for months, allowing malicious actors time and access not only to obtain information, but also to alter or destroy it.[43] The U.S. Department of Justice "underscores the value of early, proactive engagement and cooperation between the private sector and the government" to help it pursue charges against individuals supporting these nation-state efforts.[44] These types of attacks may target American law firms that have global clients.[45]

2.2. A Large Law Firm's Additional Challenges and Considerations

Firms with multiple offices, both domestic and abroad, face additional risks due to their numerous locations, which increase potential hacking targets, access points, cultural and communication challenges, and potentially expedited notification deadlines (such as 72 hours for personal data breaches in the European Union). The experience of dealing with local law enforcement and computer emergency readiness teams (or government agencies) will likely vary considerably by country and jurisdiction.

Firms with a distributed presence must establish a cohesive cybersecurity policy and program to mitigate network gaps while balancing local data protection and transfer requirements. Similarly, law firms should ensure that their vendors and cloud providers, including outsourced hosting sites and data rooms, also offer adequate cybersecurity. Regulators in many industries have increasingly focused on vendor management and oversight due to the significant risks these service providers pose. This risk also applies to firms. Large-scale hacks, such as those targeting SolarWinds' network monitoring software used by thousands of institutions, including Fortune 500 companies and federal agencies, succeed as supply chain attacks that grant access to a wide range of institutions.[46] Incidents stemming from vendor-based vulnerabilities, ranging from attacks on file-sharing systems to

---

42. *See, e.g.*, Dina Temple-Raston, *A "Worst Nightmare" Cyberattack: The Untold Story of the SolarWinds Hack*, NPR (Apr. 16, 2021) https://www.npr.org/2021/04/16/985439655/a-worst-nightmare-cyberattack-the-untold-story-of-the-solarwinds-hack. *See* also *2021 Top Routinely Exploited Vulnerabilities*, CYBERSECURITY & INFRASTRUCTURE SEC. AGENCY (Apr. 22, 2022), https://www.cisa.gov/news-events/cybersecurity-advisories/aa22-117a (noting "malicious cyber actors targeted internet-facing systems, such as email servers and virtual private network (VPN) servers, with exploits of newly disclosed vulnerabilities" and circulating alerts for various cloud and exchange server products, file transfer software and VPN products following the December 2020 SolarWinds alert).

43. *Id.*

44. *See, e.g.*, *Manhattan U.S. Attorney Announces Charges Against Seven Iranians for Conducting Coordinated Campaign of Cyber Attacks Against U.S. Financial Sector on Behalf of Islamic Revolutionary Guard Corp-Sponsored Entities*, S.D.N.Y., U.S. ATTORNEY'S OFFICE (Mar. 24, 2016), https://www.justice.gov/usao-sdny/pr/manhattan-us-attorney-announces-charges-against-seven-iranians-conducting-coordinated.

45. *See* Alan Charles Raul, *Cybersecurity—It's Not Just about "National Security" Anymore: "Directors Desk" and Other Incidents Sound Wake-Up Call for the Executive Suite and Board Room*, BUREAU OF NAT'L AFFAIRS PRIVACY & SEC. LAW, 10 PVLR 347 (Feb. 28, 2011).

46. *See* Temple-Raston, *supra* note 42.

the ransomware attack on a vendor that exposed information of some law firm employees (including Social Security numbers) have affected numerous law firms.[47]

As law firms leverage new technologies that make working easier and more efficient, the potential access points to firm data also increase correspondingly. Many firms adopted new technologies to enable the sudden and substantial increase in fully remote or hybrid work due to the COVID-19 pandemic (and continuing post-pandemic work arrangements). Providing firm devices to remote lawyers and staff with forced security settings can help address some concerns related to remote work. However, law firms of all sizes still face increased risks from potential vulnerabilities at employees' homes, such as poorly set up routers and printers.[48] Remote employees should also be aware of their surroundings to protect information and privacy. This includes disabling personal digital assistants, such as Amazon's Echo and Alexa, Google Home, and Apple devices with Siri, as these devices could potentially overhear calls containing confidential client information.

Data security risks are not limited to cyber and technological risks in the remote environment. For example, there is an increased risk of breaches resulting from improper document destruction for items printed at home.

Lawyers at law firms must acknowledge that the "bring your own device," or "BYOD," issues prevalent in other workplaces also apply within the context of a law firm. Many employers now face the growing question of how to treat employees' portable devices (e.g., personal laptops, iPads, and smartphones), which employees frequently use to transport data or supplement devices provided by their employers. A liberal BYOD policy may result in employees or attorneys unknowingly or unwittingly introducing malware or viruses into a firm's network using a compromised personal device. At the same time, law firms need to consider the benefits that many attorneys and staff derive from using such devices in a world where clients expect (demand) 24/7 availability. They make the remote conduct of business manageable and allow for the transfer of large volumes of data that could otherwise hinder network administration.

Law firms may routinely obtain data related to clients that are regulated entities subject to specific statutory data security requirements, even though the firms and attorneys may not themselves be covered entities. This means the law firms process legally protected information while perhaps lacking commensurate infrastructure and relationships with government and private sector resources to detect and report threats. For instance, during

47. *See* Opfer, *supra* note 12.

48. *See, e.g.*, Alaa Pasha, *Increasing Law Firm Security With Workplace Management Technology*, Legaltech News (Apr. 25, 2024), https://www.law.com/legaltechnews/2024/04/25/increasing-law-firm-security-with-workplace-management-technology/; Nitzan Daube, *One of the Greatest Threats Facing the IoT: Router Security*, Cyber Defense Magazine (Aug. 3, 2019), https://www.cyberdefensemagazine.com/router-security/ (noting a 2018 report found a 539% increase in attacks targeting routers since 2017 and that 83%, of WiFi routers in US homes and offices leave their users at risk of cyberattacks due to inadequately updated firmware for security vulnerabilities); *see also* Lee Mathews, *Nearly a Million Printers at Risk of Attack, Thousands Hacked to Prove It*, Wall St. J. (Aug. 31, 2020), https://www.forbes.com/sites/leemathews/2020/08/31/800000-printers-vulnerable-28000-hacked/.

transactions or litigation, law firms may handle sensitive data regulated under the Health Insurance Portability and Accountability Act (HIPAA),[49] the Gramm-Leach-Bliley Act (GLBA),[50] or other similar statutes that mandate significant—and potentially specific—safeguards and levels of data privacy and security. While the covered entities providing lawyer data to the law firms may have adopted security regimes, the law firms representing these entities may not yet have achieved these security levels. Although covered entities should validate a law firm's controls before sharing such data to ensure both parties maintain compliance, firms should proactively establish expected controls through engagement agreements or other documents or interactions with clients. Additionally, given President Barack Obama's February 2013 executive order on cybersecurity,[51] President Donald Trump's 2017 follow-on executive order,[52] and President Joseph Biden's 2021 and 2025 executive orders on cybersecurity,[53] law firms working with critical infrastructure entities or serving directly as government contractors or subcontractors, must also be mindful of the security obligations in these federally-regulated sector.

Lawyers may wrongly assume that they fly more under the hackers' radar screen than their more famous or well-resourced clients. Information security is a hindrance, as law firms have become accustomed to using "open architecture" systems, affording quick access relatively free of intrusion. Lawyers may view security systems that slow down or complicate their ability to work remotely, share or access documents, or use personal devices (such as personal computers, smartphones, or USB drives) as unwarranted and unwanted impositions. The common refrain seems to be that "security comes at the price of convenience."[54] Too often, there is a perception that attorneys and other professionals prioritize convenience over security because clients expect their lawyers to be available (and working) 24/7, regardless of their location.

The culture of confidentiality and privacy that exists at most law firms also complicates the ability of law firms to deploy cutting-edge cybersecurity strategies. For example, network and computer monitoring can detect the installation of malware or the exfiltration of data to an unknown server; however, many lawyers may chafe at the concept of having their data flows monitored continuously. A risk-benefit analysis, illustrating the potential damage to the firm's clients and reputation, accompanied by an explanation of how the data tools work, could change internal perceptions of these practices. For instance, if software causes only minor interference with the speed at which an attorney reboots their

49. Health Insurance Portability and Accountability Act, Pub. L. No. 104–191, 110 Stat. 1936 (1996). For example, law firms that are "business associates" of their "covered entity" clients may be obligated to conduct specific HIPAA risk assessments.

50. Gramm-Leach-Bliley Act, Pub. L. No. 106–102, 113 Stat. 1338 (1999).

51. Exec. Order No. 13636, 78 Fed. Reg. 11,739 (Feb. 12, 2013).

52. Exec. Order No. 13800, 82 Fed. Reg. 22,391 (May 11, 2017).

53. Exec. Order No. 14028, 86 Fed. Reg. 26,633 (May 12, 2021); Exec. Order No. 14144 (Jan. 16, 2025).

54. *See* Natalie Posgate, *Legal Experts: Cyber Security Growing Issue for Lawyers*, TEX. L. BOOK (June 29, 2012).

computer, this cost, even in the aggregate, may pale compared to the risk of liability or lost business resulting from a potentially preventable cyberattack that compromises client data. Articulating risk to the firm's business and reputation will play a crucial role in changing this culture. As a law firm's security posture matures, improved information risk management will allow the firm to manage and mitigate risks by balancing the probability of an incident against the magnitude of the resulting loss.

Finally, the dynamics of partnerships at law firms may also hinder a firm's efforts toward data security and protection. Law firms' partners are owners of the firms, and they often have expectations that they will enjoy broad access rights to systems and data. While it may be reasonable for a smaller firm with a handful of partners to grant system-administrator-level rights to each partner, large firms have too many partners for this approach to be prudent. Instead, large-firm partners must expect to relinquish total control over the management of the computer system to permit the firm's IT department and experts to provide adequate security, execution, employee training, data protection, and cybersecurity to protect client data. The partners should establish cybersecurity governance strategies and policies and conduct ongoing oversight.

3. How Large Law Firms May Address Cyber Risk

As discussed elsewhere in this Handbook (see Chapters 7 and 10 in particular), law firms have legal and ethical obligations relating to data protection.[55] Fortunately, among service firms, law firms are particularly well-equipped to address cybersecurity challenges. Law firm cultures foster confidentiality and are generally accustomed to the type of top-down procedures necessary to enhance and prioritize data security. These cultural norms make law firms well-suited to take appropriate measures to protect their systems and data. Firms can leverage the culture of confidentiality to encourage more robust data protection, safeguarding clients' interests.

Failing to safeguard clients' most sensitive business and privileged information risks a firm's reputation and the ability of the firm's lawyers to meet their professional responsibilities. To mitigate these risks, firms should know their obligations to their clients and take reasonable steps to identify and defend against their exposure to cyberattacks and data breaches. Aside from defining and implementing a standardized, auditable, risk-based information security program, law firms should monitor and address new and immediate threats. The following multifaceted, seven-part plan provides a practical approach for

55. For example, in May 2017, the American Bar Association issued Formal Opinion 477R, updating a 1999 ethics opinion regarding confidentiality obligations to account for "the 'technology amendments' made to the Model Rules in 2012, identify some of the technology risks lawyers' face, and discuss factors other than the Model Rules of Professional Conduct that lawyers should consider when using electronic means to communicate regarding client matters." *See* ABA Comm. on Ethics & Prof'l Responsibility, *supra* note 18.

covering the bases: (1) strong governance and strategy; (2) cyber preparedness, including training and education; (3) administrative, technical, and physical measures including insider threat preparedness; (4) vendor management; (5) incident response and threat intelligence; (6) recovery and continuity; and (7) ongoing process improvements and consideration of lessons learned from their own and others' mistakes.

3.1. Governance and Strategy

Law firms should enhance their overall information security programs by establishing systems that minimize the likelihood and impact of a breach and implementing security programs tailored to their specific risks. They should adopt programs created with "reasonable" security requirements in mind, based on the firm's size and maturity.[56] In evaluating potential safeguards, firms should consider (1) the sensitivity of information; (2) the likelihood of disclosure if they do not deploy additional safeguards; (3) the cost of deploying additional safeguards; (4) the difficulty of implementing the safeguards; and (5) the extent to which the safeguards may impair the lawyers' ability to represent clients efficiently and effectively.[57]

Law firms should evaluate and categorize the client information and data they store and develop additional controls to safeguard the most valuable and sensitive data.[58] A law firm's risk assessment should evaluate system and network vulnerabilities for "persistent" threats, review exposure of valuable information and communication assets, evaluate exposure to third parties and service providers (including cloud and fileshare hosting providers). It should also consider possible countermeasures to disrupt or divert attacks on the firm's systems and networks. This process will involve large firms engaging with IT and audit experts to evaluate and test the firms' systems. During this assessment, law firms should evaluate areas in which they can improve data hygiene. By applying principles, including data minimization (limiting data collection), purpose specification (specifying a purpose at collection and restricting use to the specified purpose), and retention limitations (deleting data regularly and limiting the time the firm maintains data), law firms can help further mitigate the potential damage from a successful attack and enhance the firm's cyber strategy.[59]

Strengthening an information security program can significantly reduce the elapsed time between a security breach and its discovery. Faster discovery and response can limit the

56. As a starting place, firms may consider reviewing New York's Stop Hacks and Improve Electronic Data Security Act ("SHIELD Act"), 2019 N.Y. Ch. 117, as a source for benchmarking possible administrative, technical, and physical safeguards. *See also The 18 CIS Critical Security Controls*, Ctr. for Internet Sec., https://www.cisecurity.org/controls/cis-controls-list/ (last visited Aug. 8, 2025).

57. *See* Model Code of Professional Conduct r. 1.6 cmt. 16 (Am. Bar Ass'n 1983).

58. To evaluate risk, law firms should obtain a basic understanding of the NIST Cybersecurity Framework, which approaches cyber risks through the following parameters: govern, identify, protect, detect, respond, and recover, as discussed in more detail in Handbook, Chapter 3, *Understanding Technology—What Every Lawyer Needs to Know About the Cyber Network and Artificial Intelligence.*

59. *See, e.g.*, Falon Fatemi, *Best Practices for Data Hygiene*, Forbes (Jan. 30, 2019), https://www.forbes.com/sites/falonfatemi/2019/01/30/best-practices-for-data-hygiene/. *See also Guidelines on the Protection of Privacy and Transborder Flows of Personal Data*, O.E.C.D. Doc. C(80)58 (Sept. 23, 1980).

damage to firm systems and the amount of data available to an attacker.[60] At a minimum, a firm's security program should include mandated software patch installation, robust use of antivirus and anti-malware programs, well-maintained spam filters, the installation and use of system intrusion detection systems, continuous network monitoring for threats (both internal and external), incident response plans, and information security awareness training.

Just as privacy and data security practitioners advise their clients to establish information governance systems that identify cyber risks and assign organizational accountability for managing and mitigating those risks, law firms should take similar steps. For a large firm, this will likely involve several components. As a first step, firms should review and refine their information governance structure and perform asset mapping. This could involve the creation of a committee within the firm responsible for cybersecurity, data protection, and information privacy. The committee would establish expectations for firm management, provide ongoing reporting on information risks and controls, and review top-level policies and procedures. This committee should have the power to develop and implement accountability and reporting obligations within the firm, and should have adequate resources available to fulfill its tasks. Each firm should also consider, if it has not already done so, appointing a Chief Information Security Officer and a Chief Privacy Officer to assist in managing and mitigating risks. Firms should also consider acquiring cybersecurity insurance and understand what the policy covers and what it does not. The committee should also actively monitor legislative, policy, industry, contractual, litigation, marketplace, consumer, and employee developments and expectations with implications for managing and mitigating cyber risk.

Law firms should also discuss clients' expectations regarding data security with their clients. As part of their own efforts to improve cybersecurity, many large companies have started to develop protocols for managing outside access to their data. For instance, companies engaging in high-stakes financial transactions or litigation may require lawyers or bankers to visit the company's offices on-site to review documents, thereby reducing the risk that files get hacked or otherwise accessed while in the care of third parties.[61] Clients are increasingly demanding specific data security measures and auditing the computer and network security policies of their law firms, making the potential business costs of inadequate data security real and tangible to law firms.[62] It is also increasingly common for sophisticated clients, particularly in the financial sector, to require their outside law firms to respond to detailed information security questionnaires and provide assurance that they have satisfactory safeguards in place to protect the clients' data. And as all lawyers know,

---

60. *See* Alex Nelson et al., Nat'l Inst. of Standards & Tech., Incident Response Recommendations and Considerations for Cybersecurity Risk Management 2 (Apr. 2025), https://nvlpubs.nist.gov/nistpubs/SpecialPublications/NIST.SP.800-61r3.pdf.

61. *See* Michael A. Riley & Sophia Pearson, *China-Based Hackers Target Law Firms to Get Secret Deal Data*, Bloomberg (Jan. 31, 2012), http://www.bloomberg.com/news/2012-01-31/china-based-hackers-target-law-firms.html.

62. *See, e.g.*, ACC Model Security Guidelines, supra note 21.

there is nothing like client expectations to get (or keep) more legal business and motivate law firm behavior. Once the firm has a risk-based compliance regime in place, it should ensure that it has robust, firm-wide compliance and training programs that disseminate this information to create a cyber-savvy workforce.

3.2. Cyber Preparedness

Law firms should increase their cyber preparedness. Firms should consider ways to protect shared information, including the use of encryption and other secure tools. Such considerations should encompass encryption for all internal emails, including sensitive or confidential emails and documents, as well as the storage of client files and other sensitive firm files. Law firms should also prioritize security management for video and audio conference calls, particularly as more audio calls are made using VoIP technologies. Management of such calls should cover both the calls and any recordings made during the actual calls.

As the discussion of phishing techniques highlights, personnel education is critical to any effort to ensure adequate network security.[63] Each professional at a law firm and every administrative staff member must know the personal responsibility they owe to the firm, its clients, and partners, as well as the importance of respecting information security.

Many aspects of employee education are relatively self-evident. Inform attorneys and staff of the common threats faced by law firms and how those threats will appear to them (e.g., an email from an unknown address—or even an unanticipated email from a known address—requesting that the attorney click a link to review a request for counsel).[64] The education should also inform attorneys and staff of the firm's policies, the rationale for those policies, and the availability of firm support staff to address questions regarding the implementation of those policies. Law firms can educate their staff using periodic security awareness alerts, implementing an annual CLE requirement that covers security and privacy issues, testing phishing awareness, and conducting data breach tabletop exercises for those at the firm who would be responsible for incident response. While a law firm may have a high-level cybersecurity plan, it also needs to develop and implement plans that cover business continuity, incident response, and recovery in the event of an incident. You can find more information on training elsewhere in this Handbook, particularly in Chapter 12. Incident response is also discussed elsewhere in this Handbook, particularly in Chapter 13.

3.3. Administrative, Technical, and Physical Measures

As an extra layer of protection to counterbalance human error, law firms should implement administrative, technical, and physical measures, in addition to insider threat programs. They should automatically deploy patches and upgrades to network computers to

63. *See* KnowBe4, *supra* note 37.

64. *See Lawyers Must Be Vigilant in the Fact of Rising Malware Threats*, N.J. LAW JOURNAL (Sept. 27, 2024), https://www.law.com/njlawjournal/2024/09/27/lawyers-must-be-vigilant-in-the-face-of-rising-malware-threats/.

prevent hackers from exploiting known system vulnerabilities. The importance of deploying vendor-provided patches promptly to maintain a secure and reliable environment cannot be overstated; some studies suggest that as many as one in three incidents result from an unpatched vulnerability.[65] One report found that three-quarters of newly discovered vulnerabilities are exploited within 19 days.[66] Although the downtime required to install patches can create friction with lawyers' work demands, prompt updates are a necessity.

Firms should also log and monitor network access and deploy data loss prevention tools to track where data is going and to flag or block unusual file transfers. Law firms should establish policies supported by technological restrictions that prohibit the use of specific technologies and require the use of encrypted connections or devices when conducting work on behalf of the firm. These policies could, for instance: (1) mandate strong password requirements; (2) address the risks of using public Wi-Fi with firm computers; (3) prohibit the use of unsanctioned cloud storage for client files; (4) block the download of executable files or certain forms of scripts from non-white-listed websites; and (5) block private email, instant messaging, unauthorized downloads, and unsanctioned file transfer mechanisms.[67] If these or similar policies have not already been implemented, they may cause initial irritation because of the limitations they impose on attorneys' use of computers. However, explaining the cost-benefit analysis of these policies and their ability to mitigate the risk of human error in cyberattacks can lead to greater acceptance. Firm-sanctioned policies lay the groundwork for a mature, enforceable information security program. These policies will enable a firm to assess its security posture and subsequently improve.[68]

3.4. Vendor Management

Proper vendor management can further support a law firm's cybersecurity. Merely including a contractual provision that the vendor will follow best practices and indemnify the firm for any failure to do so will not suffice. A firm should conduct its own due diligence, review prospective vendors' security plans, and ask service providers about their cybersecurity, as well as their recovery and continuity plans. Law firms should request third-party audits and certifications as part of ongoing due diligence and efforts to protect client and personnel data. Firms should not overlook their vendor's management of service providers as well (e.g., fourth-party providers). It is crucial to understand which vendors or sub-vendors possess specific types of information, whether they have access to it, what privacy

65. *See* Steve Ranger, *Cybersecurity: One in Three Breaches Are Caused by Unpatched Vulnerabilities*, ZDNet.com (June 4, 2019), https://www.zdnet.com/article/cybersecurity-one-in-three-breaches-are-caused-by-unpatched-vulnerabilities/.

66. *See 75% of New Vulnerabilities Exploited within 19 Days*, Help Net Sec. (June 27, 2024), https://www.helpnetsecurity.com/2024/06/27/nvd-vulnerabilities.

67. *See* Posgate, *supra* note 54, at 2.

68. *See* Dan Roe, *How to Note Get Hacked in 2024*, Am. Lawyer (Feb. 5, 2024), https://www.law.com/americanlawyer/2024/02/05/how-to-not-get-hacked-in-2024/.

and security measures they have in place, and how they monitor their service providers to ensure compliance with these measures.[69]

3.5. Incident Response and Threat Intelligence

Law firms should acknowledge reality: no security system is impenetrable. Because breaches in security will occur, it is essential not only to lessen their likelihood but also to mitigate their impact. Firms should plan for responding to data security incidents by drafting an incident response plan that details who has responsibility for key decisions and outlines the processes to follow in the event of an incident. The firm's incident response plan should include a ransomware protocol, as payment demands continue to increase and attacks increasingly involve exfiltration of data.[70] The record for the largest known ransom payment has recently been broken, now standing at $75 million (almost twice the highest previously recognized payment).[71] If a firm determines that it would consider making a payment, it should plan to ensure OFAC compliance and, for global firms, also confirm that such a payment does not violate applicable foreign law prohibitions.[72]

The firm should identify applicable notification and reporting standards or requirements, from state- or sector-specific data breach notification laws to contractual provisions. Firms should consider when to consult with law enforcement to investigate an incident proactively.[73] They should also prepare to inform, where necessary or appropriate, any potentially affected clients of what occurred. The last step may be a tough pill to swallow, particularly given the premium that law firms place on their brand reputation. Required notification timelines are becoming increasingly shorter, with a 72-hour notice required under the EU's General Data Protection Regulation, effective May 2018, and some U.S. jurisdictions requiring notification

---

69. *See* Brad Hibbert, *Shielding Law Practices: Mitigating Vendor Risks to Safeguard Client Confidentiality*, Am. Lawyer (June 17, 2024), https://www.law.com/2024/06/17/shielding-law-practices-mitigating-vendor-risks-to-safeguard-client-confidentiality/.

70. *See* Sophos, Sophos 2021 Threat Report (Nov. 2020), https://www.sophos.com/en-us/medialibrary/PDFs/technical-papers/sophos-2021-threat-report.pdf.

71. *See Zscaler's Annual Ransomware Report Uncovers Record-Breaking Ransom Payment of US$75 Million, Reinforcing the Need for Zero Trust*, Zscaler (July 29, 2024), https://www.zscaler.com/press/zscaler-s-annual-ransomware-report-uncovers-record-breaking-ransom-payment-us-75-million.

72. *Id.*

73. Another factor that OFAC will consider under the Enforcement Guidelines is the reporting of ransomware attacks to appropriate U.S. government agencies and the nature and extent of a subject person's cooperation with OFAC, law enforcement, and other relevant agencies, including whether an apparent violation of U.S. sanctions is voluntarily self-disclosed. In the case of ransomware payments that may have a sanctions nexus, OFAC will consider a company's self-initiated and complete report of a ransomware attack to law enforcement or other relevant U.S. government agencies, such as CISA or the U.S. Department of the Treasury's Office of Cybersecurity and Critical Infrastructure Protection (OCCIP), made as soon as possible after discovery of an attack, to be a voluntary self-disclosure and a significant mitigating factor in determining an appropriate enforcement response. OFAC will also consider a company's full and ongoing cooperation with law enforcement both during and after a ransomware attack—e.g., providing all relevant information such as technical details, ransom payment demand, and ransom payment instructions as soon as possible—to be a significant mitigating factor.

Dep't of the Treasury, Updated Advisory on Potential Sanctions Risks for Facilitating Ransomware Payments 5 (Sept. 21, 2021), https://ofac.treasury.gov/media/912981/download?inline.

to regulators within 10 to 14 days.[74] Firms should create template documents that include the necessary content in a workable framework and prompt the drafter to enter key information, thereby helping the firm meet regulatory requirements, such as notifying individuals and credit reporting agencies.[75] Developing critical contact points with law enforcement and regulators and retaining incident response vendors in advance will further help lawyers know whom to call when faced with a breach.[76] Tabletop simulation exercises enable key law firm actors, along with external contacts if desired, to practice responding to a breach and identify any potential issues in a response plan before the stakes are real.

Firms should also identify and remediate the data security shortfalls that lead to security breaches. Threat intelligence may prevent a violation, and firm leadership should discuss how to obtain and integrate threat intelligence into the firm's program. Will the firm hire a third-party vendor to monitor and analyze the dark web and social media, providing early detection alerts of potential data leaks, breaches, and the sale of data? Will the firm participate in threat sharing under the Cybersecurity Information Sharing Act of 2015 and share threat data with the government?[77] How will the firm receive and respond to threat information from sector-specific threat-sharing platforms, such as the Legal Information Sharing and Analysis Center (LISSAC) or the Information Sharing and Analysis Organization (ISAO)? These organizations can enhance threat intelligence awareness and potentially help prevent an incident from occurring.[78] Once aware of security shortfalls, especially if a firm learns of them due to an attack on its own system, it is crucial to swiftly and adequately remediate the issues to help mitigate further attacks and potential liability claims.

3.6. Data Recovery and Business Continuity

A firm must protect itself through contingency planning for recovery and continuity in the event of a breach or ransomware attack. It is key to establish business continuity and

---

74. Some clients may be subject to shorter reporting timelines, such as the 72-hour notification period for entities subject to regulation by the New York Department of Financial Services. N.Y. Dep't of Financial Serv., 23 NYCRR 500.17.

75. Templates might include communication with regulators (including U.S., state, and international), communication to law enforcement, "risk of harm" assessment framework, affected individual notification letter, state attorney general and other state regulator reporting letter(s), credit reporting agency reporting letter, information sharing letter for law enforcement/DHS, notification letter to business customers, demand letter to vendors, notification letter to insurance carrier(s), and HIPAA business associate model documents.

76. A list of external resources and points of contact may include law enforcement and national security points of contact, pre-vetted forensics and credit monitoring service providers, and pre-vetted public relations and communication firms skilled in handling cyber incident responses.

77. Cyber threat indicators can potentially be shared with the U.S. government without waiving privilege. 6 U.S.C §1504(d)(1); U.S. DEP'T OF HOMELAND SEC. & U.S. DEP'T OF JUST., GUIDANCE TO ASSIST NON-FEDERAL ENTITIES TO SHARE CYBER THREAT INDICATORS AND DEFENSIVE MEASURES WITH FEDERAL ENTITIES UNDER THE CYBERSECURITY INFORMATION SHARING ACT OF 2015 18 (Oct. 2020), https://www.cisa.gov/sites/default/files/publications/Non-Federal%20Entity%20Sharing%20Guidance%20under%20the%20Cybersecurity%20Information%20Sharing%20Act%20of%202015_1.pdf.

78. Organizations offering legal services-specific threat intelligence include the Legal Services Information Sharing and Analysis Organization (LS-ISAO), the Legal Vendor Network, and the International Legal Technology Association LegalSEC (ILTA LegalSEC).

resiliency plans in the event of material cyber risks or disruptions, including ransomware attacks. A law firm's reputation depends on its ability to meet court, regulator, and client deadlines despite an incident.[79]

3.7. Continual Process Improvements from Lessons Learned

Finally, law firms should continually monitor and improve the above processes as hackers' methods evolve and technology changes. Firms should also adjust their cybersecurity plans as they learn lessons from others' public breaches, at law firms and companies. A data security incident may reflect poorly on a firm if it has not taken reasonable steps to ensure the security of client data and maintain that security. Having an effective data security program will ultimately reduce the number and scope of data security incidents affecting the firm. It will also reduce the likelihood that a firm will find itself in a position where it must report breaches to government authorities and/or clients. Ultimately, "cybersecurity is a team sport that [all parties] need to play effectively together."[80]

4. Top Twelve Considerations for Large Law Firm Lawyers

As a starting point for addressing cybersecurity, lawyers practicing in a firm should take these twelve steps to evaluate and mitigate risk. In the event of a breach, lawyers should also consider crisis management, public relations, and relationships with forensics firms. If a firm does not have its own cyber practice, it should consider consulting with a firm that does!

1. Evaluate the firm's current cybersecurity risk profile, considering the current data and device controls in place, the nature of data and information accessed by the firm, ethical obligations, and other relevant factors.
2. Evaluate client-specific data security considerations (e.g., for covered entities under GLBA or HIPAA, or clients entrusting sensitive corporate or personal data) that may require additional steps by the firm's lawyers.
3. Establish an information security and data governance committee within the firm to gain a foundational understanding of the NIST Cybersecurity Framework, which outlines approaches to addressing cyber risks and managing information security and cybersecurity risks. It should report regularly to the firm's most senior management.

79. See HANDBOOK, Chapter 13, *Achieving Preparedness through Standards and Planning and Best Practices for Incident Response,* for further discussion. *See also* Margeaux Green, *How Law Firms Can Prepare for Disasters with a Business Continuity Plan,* NWSIDEBAR (Nov. 29, 2021), https://nwsidebar.wsba.org/2021/11/29/how-law-firms-can-prepare-for-disasters-with-a-business-continuity-plan/.

80. *See* Ed Finkel, *Cybersecurity under Siege*, ABA JOURNAL, (Nov. 1, 2010, 10:58 AM), https://www.abajournal.com/magazine/article/cyberspace_under_siege.

4. Appoint an individual within the firm (or hire an individual from outside the firm) to serve as a Chief Information Security Officer responsible for managing the firm's day-to-day cybersecurity risks and staying up to date on new technology and threats.
5. Define and implement a standardized, auditable, risk-based information security program addressing cybersecurity, including vendor management and insider threats. This program should include establishing business continuity and resiliency plans in the event of material cyber risks or disruptions, such as ransomware attacks.
6. Establish stringent requirements for data security in software installations, cloud services, and other data services, as well as cybersecurity hygiene practices such as up-to-date vulnerability patching. Review vendor contracts and practices to ensure their security practices support or enhance the firm's internal data security requirements. Focus on internet-facing services such as cloud and email providers, file or data transfer and storage services, VPNs, firewalls, routers, and other edge devices and services.
7. International firms should adopt network segmentation infrastructures to improve cross-border performance and disaggregate sensitive data storage.
8. Develop, as part of the information security program, a data security incident response protocol or playbook that addresses notification to clients, government authorities, or individuals affected by breaches. Expect administrative personnel to escalate significant cyber incidents involving, for example, data breaches that may require notice to individuals, regulators, or clients, or those with a significant impact on critical firm systems or confidential information. As part of this process, consider consulting with law enforcement, when appropriate, about cybersecurity risks.
9. Develop controls for network interface devices, internet access, and the use of personal devices by firm members and employees.
10. Conduct training sessions and educate lawyers and staff within the firm on their obligations relating to cybersecurity and on their roles within the firm's information security program. Warn about the risk of falling prey to phishing attacks!
11. As firms evolve and adopt new artificial intelligence (AI) technologies to conduct their business, they must consider the associated cybersecurity and confidentiality risks and clearly delineate firm and client restrictions to employees.
12. Conduct routine audits of the firm's information security risks and vulnerabilities.

About the Contributors

Jeffrey Allen (Editor; Chapter 1, Introduction; Chapter 2, An Introduction to Artificial Intelligence; and Chapter 15, Cybersecurity for Solo and Small Firm Lawyers) is a principal in the law firm of Graves & Allen, with a civil practice that since 1973 has emphasized negotiation, structuring, and documentation of real estate, loan, and other business transactions, receiverships, and civil litigation. He has represented banking institutions, title companies, institutional and private lenders, borrowers, developers, contractors, real estate brokers, buyers, sellers, landlords, tenants, receivers, hotel operators, and other business interests. He has enjoyed a Martindale-Hubbell AV Rating for over 30 years and is a N. California Super Lawyer for over 10 years. He does extensive work as an arbitrator and mediator. Mr. Allen has taught at the University of California, St. Mary's College of Moraga, University of Phoenix, Cal State University of the East Bay, and the Oakland College of Law. He served on editorial boards for Experience Magazine, Voice of Experience, GP|Solo Magazine, GP|Solo eReport, and the Technology eReport (Editor in Chief for the last three publications). He has also served on the editorial board of the ABA Journal and as a member of SCOTIS. Mr. Allen has authored and co-authored many articles and six books on technology and law practice. He frequently presents at programs on technology and the practice of law.

Bryson Bort (Chapter 3, Understanding Technology—What Every Lawyer Needs to Know About the Cyber Network and Artificial Intelligence) is the Founder of SCYTHE, a start-up building a next-generation threat emulation platform, and GRIMM, a cybersecurity consultancy, and Co-Founder of the ICS Village, a non-profit advancing awareness of industrial control system security. He is a Senior Fellow at the National Security Institute, USMA EECS Advisory Board member, and Adjunct Senior Technical Advisor for the Institute of Security and Technology. As a U.S. Army Officer, he served as a Battle Captain and Brigade Engineering Officer in support of Operation Iraqi Freedom before leaving the Army as a Captain. He is recognized as a "Top 50 in Cyber" by Business Insider, "Security Executive Finalist of the Year" by SC Media, was awarded "Tech Titan" twice and is the 2023 SANS Difference Maker Award Winner for Innovator of the Year. Mr. Bort received his Bachelor of Science in computer science with honors from the United States Military Academy at West Point. He holds a master's degree in telecommunications management from the University of Maryland, a master's degree in business administration from the University of

Florida, and completed graduate studies in electrical engineering and computer science at the University of Texas.

Ruth Hill Bro (Chapter 7, Legal Obligations to Provide Data Security; Chapter 12, Get SMART on Data Protection by Creating a Culture of Security Awareness) has focused her legal career on advising businesses on privacy and information management strategy, cybersecurity, global compliance, e-workplace, and e-business. She's spoken and written extensively on these subjects, including The E-Business Legal Arsenal: Practitioner Agreements and Checklists (Editor, ABA, 2004); chapters in various ABA technology and security handbooks; Internet in the Workplace (co-author, 1997), Online Law (5 chapters, Addison-Wesley, 1996), and a law review article on e-signature legislation (1999). A longstanding ABA leader, Ms. Bro has served on numerous ABA-wide commissions/committees, including Technology & Information Systems (Chair, 2012–15), and is a founding member of the Task Force on Law and Artificial Intelligence and a Special Advisor for the Cybersecurity Legal Task Force (2017–2020 Co-Chair). In the ABA Science & Technology Law Section, Ms. Bro served as Section Chair (2008–2009); E-Privacy Law Committee Founder/Chair (2000–2005); Senior Advisor for the Privacy, Security, and Emerging Technology Division (2016–); and Planning Committee member of the annual Artificial Intelligence and Robotics National Institute (2019–), Internet of Things (IoT) National Institute (2015–2023), and Privacy and Emerging Technology National Institute (Co-Chair, 2024–). She also co-chairs the annual PLI Privacy and Cybersecurity Law Institute in Chicago (2022–). Now a consultant after 15 years of law firm practice (founding North American partner of the firm's Global Privacy Steering Committee), she earned her BA from Northwestern University and JD from the University of Chicago.

Angeline G. Chen (Chapter 16, In-House Counsel) is a senior executive and corporate attorney with more than thirty years of legal and business experience spanning multiple industries including aerospace and defense, software, manufacturing, and industrials. Her areas of expertise include national security, cybersecurity, governance, compliance, and mergers and acquisitions. She currently serves as the General Counsel, Chief Administrative Officer, and Corporate Secretary of Progress Federal Solutions, Inc. She has previously held senior leadership roles with DLA Piper, Siemens Government Technologies, Fincantieri Marine Group, Lockheed Martin, the National Security Agency, and INTELSAT. Her legal career started in private practice specializing in complex litigation focused on high technology and manufacturing sectors. Ms. Chen is a Director on the boards of Stantec, Inc., a publicly-traded Canadian corporation, and Progress Federal Solutions, and previously on a number of private company boards. Her academic experience includes over fifteen years as an adjunct professor teaching national security and technology law at the Antonin Scalia Law School, as well as serving as Executive-in-Residence and a professor for UMUC's M.B.A. program. Ms. Chen holds a B.A. and J.D. from Villanova University, an LL.M from the Georgetown University Law Center, an M.B.A. from the University of Maryland, and a M.Sc. in Cybersecurity from Brown University.

Daniel A. Cotter (Chapter 11, Foundation of Risk Management in Cybersecurity) is Attorney and Counselor at Dickinson Wright PLLC. Mr. Cotter focuses his practice in a variety of areas of corporate law and litigation, including insurance law, complex business disputes and counseling, employment law, corporate transactions, corporate governance and compliance, and cybersecurity and privacy law. He served as President of The Chicago Bar Association for the 2014–2015 bar year and is former Chair of The Young Lawyers Section of the CBA. Mr. Cotter was an adjunct professor at The John Marshall Law School, and has taught Insurance Law, Accounting for Lawyers, and SCOTUS Judicial Biography. Mr. Cotter graduated summa cum laude from The John Marshall Law School and received his B.A. in Accounting from Monmouth College, magna cum laude. He is a frequent writer and presenter on various substantive topics, including technology and privacy and insurance, and in 2019, his book, "The Chief Justices," was published.

Lothar Determann (Chapter 8, What Cybersecurity Laws Govern? Applicability, Enforcement, and Compliance with Domestic and Foreign Cybersecurity Laws) practices and teaches international data privacy, technology, commercial, and intellectual property law. At Baker McKenzie in San Francisco and Palo Alto, he has been counseling companies since 1998 on data privacy law compliance and taking products and business models international. Admitted to practice in California and Germany, he has been recognized as one of the top 10 Copyright Attorneys and Top 25 Intellectual Property Attorneys in California by the San Francisco & Los Angeles Daily Journal and as a leading lawyer by Chambers, Legal 500, Thomson Reuters, IAM, and others. Prof. Dr. Determann teaches Data Privacy Law, Computer Law and Internet Law at Freie Universität Berlin (since 1994) and University of California, Berkeley School of Law (since 2004), and he's held past teaching posts at UC Law SF (2010–2021), Stanford Law School (2011), and USF Law (2000–2005). He has authored more than 180 articles and treatise contributions, as well as 6 books, including *Determann's* Field Guide to Data Privacy Law (6th Edition, 2025), California Privacy Law Practical Guide and Commentary on U.S. Federal and California Law (5th Ed. 2023), and *Determann's* Field Guide to Artificial Intelligence Law (2024).

John DiMaria (Chapter 13, Achieving Preparedness through Standards and Planning and Best Practices for Incident Response), holds the credentials CSSBB, HISP, MHISP, AMBCI, and CERP. He is the Director of Operations Excellence and Research Fellow with the Cloud Security Alliance. He has 40 years of experience in Standards and management System Development, including Information Systems, Business Continuity, and Quality. Mr. DiMaria was one of the innovators and co-founders of the CSA STAR programs Open Certification Framework for cloud providers, and he developed the first certification scheme and process related to the NIST Cybersecurity Framework. He is a contributing author of the last three editions of the American Bar Association's Cybersecurity Handbook, and a working group member and a key contributor to the NIST Cybersecurity Framework. Mr. DiMaria also serves as a leading expert as the BCI SIG Vice-Chair for Cyber Resilience, Working Group Chair for the IEEE P3454™, Standard for Cloud Computing—Operational Resilience—Framework, Member of the MSECB Impartiality, Ethics, and Appeals Committee, and Customer Experience Advisory Member with Lindenwood University, St. Louis, MO. At CSA, he currently oversees the strategic execution of core operational functions, liaising across departments to provide tactical support and guidance, promoting operational efficiency and interdepartmental collaboration. Prior to joining CSA, Mr. DiMaria spent 20 years at the British Standards Institution managing assessment schemes and accreditation.

Matthew F. Ferraro (Chapter 6, Dealing with Deepfakes: The Role for Lawyers and Law Firms) is a partner at the international law firm Crowell & Moring LLP, where he helps clients address complex regulatory matters at the intersection of advanced technology, national security, and crisis management. He advises leading organizations on high-impact matters related to artificial intelligence (AI), deepfakes, cyberattacks, domestic and international privacy compliance, and crisis investigations. Mr. Ferraro served from August 2023 to January 2025 as the Senior Counselor for Cybersecurity and Emerging Technology to the Secretary of Homeland Security and the Executive Director of the Artificial Intelligence (AI) Safety and Security Board. In this role, Mr. Ferraro helped to shape and execute the Department's work on cybersecurity, AI, and other emerging technologies. He also ran a public-private advisory committee focused on AI's use in critical infrastructure. Prior to his service at the U.S. Department of Homeland Security, Mr. Ferraro practiced law at the law firm Wilmer Cutler Pickering Hale and Dorr LLP. Earlier in his career, Mr. Ferraro was an intelligence officer with the Office of the Director of National Intelligence and the Central Intelligence Agency. A life member of the Council on Foreign Relations and an Adjunct Professor of Law at the National Security Institute at George Mason University, he writes and speaks widely on national security, technology, and legal issues. Educated at Yale, Cambridge, and Stanford, Mr. Ferraro lives and works in Washington, D.C.

Ashley Hallene (Chapter 15, Cybersecurity for Solo and Small Firm Lawyers) is a Land Acquisition Specialist with Demeter Land Development, a Michigan-based company focused on securing land for renewable energy projects, particularly community solar and battery storage developments. A prolific writer and legal technology expert, she has authored or co-authored hundreds of articles on technology and law practice management. Ms. Hallene is the co-author, alongside attorney Jeffrey Allen, of several books, including Technology Tips for Seniors Volume 2.0 (2018), Technology Tips for Lawyers and other Business Professionals (2016), Technology Solutions for Today's Lawyer (2013), and The iPad for Lawyers (2013). Their most recent works are Unlocking the Future (2025) and Scams & Cybercrime Survival Guide (forthcoming 2026). Ms. Hallene has published in leading publications such as GP|Solo Magazine, Experience Magazine, Attorney at Work, and TechnoLawyer. Active in the American Bar Association, Ms. Hallene is a leader in the General Practice Solo & Small Firm Division and the Senior Lawyers Division, serving as Editor-in-Chief of GP|Solo eReport. She earned her J.D. from the University of Houston Law Center and her B.S. from the University of Houston. She lives in Houston, Texas, with her husband, Jack, and family.

Logan Hamilton (Handbook Administrator; Chapter 5, Cybercrime) served as Administrator for this Fourth Edition of the Cybersecurity Handbook while working as the ABA Cybersecurity Legal Task Force staff attorney. Mr. Hamilton is now an Associate at Fredrikson & Bryon P.A. in Minneapolis. He is CIPP/US certified and has a Master's in International Science & Technology Policy from the George Washington University. Before working for the ABA, Mr. Hamilton was a summer fellow at the National Defense Industrial Association and clerked at the Minnesota Court of Appeals and Hennepin County District Court. He received a J.D. from the University of Wisconsin Law School.

Kathleen Hom (Chapter 5, Cybercrime) currently serves on the American Bar Association's (ABA) Cybersecurity Legal Task Force and previously was an Observer to the United Nations Economic and Social Council in Geneva for the ABA. Ms. Hom is Senior Counsel at Accenture Federal Services, where she is an expert on supply chain and cybersecurity matters. She has extensive substantive experience in the federal sector, particularly on cybersecurity and national security issues, having advised at the Federal Communications Commission, Universal Service Administrative Company, U.S. Department of State, and Transportation Security Administration. She started her post-law school career as a fellow for Congressman John Lewis and prior to law school, Ms. Hom produced, wrote, and edited for six years at The Washington Post. She received her undergraduate degree from the University of Virginia and law degree from Santa Clara University.

Candace M. Jones (Editor) retired in 2022 from the Federal Reserve Bank of New York, where she served as a Vice President in the Legal Group, managing legal support for technology, security, and procurement matters. Since retiring, Ms. Jones has undertaken consulting legal roles and writing projects focusing on artificial intelligence, information technology, and cybersecurity. Ms. Jones is active in the American Bar Association's Business Law Section, where she served as Chair of the Cyberspace Law Committee and has been a contributing author to The Business Lawyer's Cyber & Tech Annual Survey and recently released book, The Law of Digital Content (Chapter 5, Data: Building Blocks of Digital Assets). As a member of the ABA Cybersecurity Legal Task Force in 2016, she co-authored the Vendor Contracting Project: Cybersecurity Checklist. Prior to joining the New York Fed, Ms. Jones served as Chief Legal Counsel for the Ohio Department of Development, and she was a partner in the Cleveland, Ohio firm Hahn, Loeser & Parks LLP.

Kevin Kalinich (Chapter 14, Cyber Insurance for Law Firms and Legal Organizations) joined Aon in September 2000 from Altima Technologies, where he served as Chief Executive Officer and led the successful launch of an Internet of Things intelligent visualization of network equipment software product with respect to telecommunications, data, cables, and computers. Prior to Altima, Mr. Kalinich was a partner at Chapman and Cutler Law Firm, where he represented domestic and international technology-focused public and private entities in general corporate matters, intellectual property, mergers and acquisitions, venture capital and institutional investor transactions; and professional athletes. He also served as Chicago Bar Association Legislative Liaison (Corporations Committee). Mr. Kalinich coached inner-city baseball at Cabrini-Green public housing projects for eight years, which is featured in the book and movie, "Hardball." He is former Chairman of The Frank Thomas Charitable Foundation. While in law school, Mr. Kalinich was a Graduate Assistant Football Coach at The University of Michigan, working for Bo Schembechler, and he was Los Angeles Coliseum Venue Captain at the 1984 Olympics.

Dr. Edward Marchewka (Chapter 17, Why Public Interest Attorneys Should Care About Cybersecurity) is the Chief Administrative Officer at PryorHealth, where he leads Information and Technology Services, Risk Management, Quality, and Facilities Operations across a multi-state healthcare network. He previously served as Director of IT, Data, and Security Services at Gift of Hope Organ & Tissue Donor Network and built the information security program at Chicago Public Schools. Dr. Marchewka holds a Doctorate in Business Administration from California Southern University, where he focused his dissertation on communicating cybersecurity risk. He also holds master's degrees in business and mathematics from Northern Illinois University and a Certificate in Non-Profit Management from Northwestern University. Dr. Marchewka maintains numerous industry certifications, including CISSP, PMP, CDPSE, and Lean Six Sigma Master Black Belt. He is the author of A Cybersecurity Leader's Journey: Speaking the Language of the Board and serves as an adjunct faculty member in cybersecurity at multiple universities. He was a finalist for Association of IT Professionals's CIO of the Year (2022) and is a national speaker on risk, leadership, and cybersecurity communications. His work centers on helping cybersecurity leaders close the gap between technical detail and executive understanding through trust-building, clear communication, and business-aligned metrics.

Lucian T. Pera (Chapter 10, Lawyers' Professional Responsibility to Provide Data Security) is a partner with the Memphis office of Adams & Reese, LLP. His practice includes legal ethics, media law, and commercial litigation. He represents lawyers, law firms, and others on issues of legal ethics and lawyer professional responsibility. The ABA Center for

Professional Responsibility has bestowed on him the prestigious Michael Franck Award, their highest award for work in the field of ethics and professional responsibility over his career. He served for five years on the ABA "Ethics 2000" Commission, which rewrote the ABA Model Rules of Professional Conduct. He has chaired the editorial board of the ABA/BNA Lawyers' Manual on Professional Conduct and served as president of the Association of Professional Responsibility Lawyers.

Kimberly K. Peretti (Chapter 7, Legal Obligations to Provide Data Security) is a partner at Alston & Bird where she co-chairs the Privacy, Cyber & Data Strategy practice. She is nationally known for her expertise in cybersecurity, handling high-profile data breach response matters across a wide range of industries. She also advises companies on cyber regulatory investigations and board-level cyber risk oversight. With over 25 years of experience as both an information security professional and attorney, Ms. Peretti brings a unique perspective shaped by her roles as a former senior litigator in the U.S. Department of Justice's Computer Crime and Intellectual Property Section (CCIPS) and a director in PwC's forensic services practice. Her work included leading landmark cybercrime prosecutions and guiding forensic investigations of nation-state attacks on critical infrastructure. She is a Certified Information Systems Security Professional (CISSP) and holds the NACD Certificate in Cybersecurity Oversight. She co-founded Alston & Bird's Women in Cyber Network™ and served on the U.S. Secret Service's Cyber Investigation Board. In 2025, she launched the Ransomware Fusion Center to help organizations prepare for and respond to ransomware threats. Ms. Peretti is a graduate of the University of Wisconsin and received her J.D. from Georgetown University and LL.M. from the University of Munich, Germany.

Claudia Rast (Chapter 13, Achieving Preparedness through Standards and Planning and Best Practices for Incident Response) is a shareholder in Butzel Long's Ann Arbor office, where she chairs the firm's IP, Cybersecurity and Emerging Technology Group. Her areas of practice focus on domestic and international privacy and data protection, data breach response, and technology licensing and protection. In addition to her legal practice, she is a frequent author on issues of cybersecurity, privacy, and data protection. As a member of the American Bar Association, Rast was appointed in 2020 to co-chair the ABA's Cybersecurity Legal Task Force, a task force on which she has served both as a liaison member and member-at-large since 2013. Ms. Rast co-authored chapters in the ABA's Cybersecurity Handbook (2nd ed. 2018), (3rd ed. 2022), and (4th ed. 2025), writing on incident response, and she was a contributing author to the Vendor Cybersecurity Checklist, 2nd Edition, published by the ABA in 2021. Ms. Rast received her B.S. from the University of Michigan and her J.D. from University of Detroit School of Law, where she was the editor-in-chief of the law review. After graduating from law school, she clerked for the Chief Justice of the Michigan Supreme Court, G. Mennen "Soapy" Williams.

Alan Charles Raul (Chapter 18, Large Law Firms) is a Lecturer at Harvard Law School, Board Chair and President of the Future of Privacy Forum, and Board Secretary of the Society for the Rule of Law. Mr. Raul founded and led a global law firm's Privacy and Cybersecurity practice for over twenty-five years. In addition to his teaching and board service, Mr. Raul continues to represent clients on U.S. and international matters through Raul Consulting Company. He advises companies on regulatory enforcement, crisis management, compliance and due diligence regarding data practices, information technology, artificial intelligence, and cyber attacks. Mr. Raul also addresses issues involving constitutional, administrative, and national security law. At Harvard Law School, Mr. Raul teaches "Digital Governance: Privacy, Artificial Intelligence and Information Technology." He is an Affiliate of Harvard's Berkman Klein Center for Internet and Society. Mr. Raul has served in government as Vice Chairman of the Privacy and Civil Liberties Oversight Board. He also served as General Counsel of the Office of Management and Budget; General Counsel of the U.S. Department of Agriculture; and Associate Counsel to the President. Mr. Raul received his J.D. from Yale Law School, M.P.A. from Harvard Kennedy School, and A.B. magna cum laude from Harvard College.

Jill D. Rhodes (Chapter 12, Get SMART on Data Protection by Creating a Culture of Security Awareness) is Senior Vice President/CISO at Option Care Health and is responsible for securing the organization and its data through the integration of information security governance, education, process development, and technology in all facets of the enterprise. Prior to moving to the private sector, Ms. Rhodes spent 20 years working in and with the national security and intelligence communities of the federal government. She was also a Foreign Service Officer with the US Agency for International Development, stationed in Bolivia and Russia, and she worked extensively throughout Eastern and Southern Africa. In 2025, Ms. Rhodes was honored with the Chicagoland Orbie Leadership Award and in 2019, the Chicago-area CISO of the Year award. She speaks nationally on a variety of security topics, was the co-editor of the first, second, and third editions of the *ABA Cybersecurity Handbook: A Resource for Attorneys, Law Firms, and Business Professionals* (2013, 2018, 2023) and edited the book *National Security Law, Fifty Years of Transformation: An Anthology* (2012). Ms. Rhodes is an executive member of the Board of Directors of Adelante Healthcare, a Community Healthcare Center in Maricopa County. She is a graduate of the University of Illinois at Urbana-Champaign, the University of Cincinnati College of Law (JD), and the George Washington University College of Law (LL.M.).

Harvey Rishikof (Chapter 9, Foreign and International Cybersecurity Laws) is Director of Policy and Cyber Security Research of the Applied Research Laboratory for Intelligence and Security, a University-Affiliated Research Center of the United States at the University of Maryland. He is also a Visiting Professor of Law at Carnegie Mellon University and senior counsel to the American Bar Association Standing Committee on Law and National

Security, having also served as Chair of the Standing Committee and Chair of the ABA's Cybersecurity Legal Task Force. Mr. Rishikof has been involved in a number of legal-policy projects sponsored by MITRE, the MacArthur Foundation, the Center for Strategic International Studies, the Hewlett Foundation, the Congressional "Solarium" Project, the National Science Foundation, and the National Academy of Sciences. Before joining the government, he was at the National War College in Washington, D.C., where he served as dean, professor of law and national security studies, and also chaired the department of national security strategy. He specializes in national security law, cyber international law, media, civil liberties, civilian/military relations, governmental process, and the U.S. Constitution. Mr. Rishikof's career includes experiences in the private sector, academia, and public service, and he is a lifetime member of the Council on Foreign Relations and the American Law Institute. He also is on the Board of Visitors for the National Intelligence University.

Paul Rosenzweig (Chapter 3, Understanding Technology—What Every Lawyer Needs to Know About the Cyber Network and Artificial Intelligence) practices law in a solo practice in Washington, DC, specializing in legal issues relating to national security and homeland security, with an emphasis on cybersecurity and privacy law. He is also the founder of Red Branch Consulting PLLC, a homeland security and cybersecurity consulting company, and a Senior Advisor to The Chertoff Group. Mr. Rosenzweig formerly served as Deputy Assistant Secretary for Policy in the Department of Homeland Security.

Thomas J. Smedinghoff (Chapter 7, Legal Obligations to Provide Data Security) has practiced technology law for over four decades, including as a partner in two global law firms and now as a legal consultant. Internationally recognized for addressing emerging legal issues involving e-business, identity management, and data security, he has helped develop electronic legal policy in the U.S. and globally and assisted the federal government and private sector businesses in structuring and implementing first-of-their-kind e-business legal infrastructures. Since 1997, Mr. Smedinghoff has served as a member of the U.S. Delegation to the United Nations Commission on International Trade Law (UNCITRAL), where he participates in the Working Group on Electronic Commerce; he helped negotiate the UN Convention on the Use of Electronic Communications in International Contracts (2005), and international model laws on electronic signatures (2001), identity management (2022), and AI/automated contracting (2024). He serves on the ABA Cybersecurity Legal Task Force (2019–2020 Co-Chair) and chairs the ABA Business Law Section's Identity Management Legal Task Force. Prior leadership positions have included ABA Science & Technology Law Section Chair (1999–2000) and E-Commerce Division Chair (1995–2003) and ABA advisor to the Uniform Law Commission committee that drafted the Uniform Electronic Transactions Act (1999). His extensive publications on e-transactions, identity management, privacy, and cybersecurity law include the books Guide to Cybersecurity Due

Diligence in M&A Transactions (co-editor, ABA, 2017), and Online Law (editor/primary author, Addison-Wesley, 1996). He graduated cum laude from Knox College (BA) and University of Michigan (JD).

Lucy L. Thomson, CISSP, CIPP/US (Chapter 4, Understanding Cybersecurity Risks) is the founding principal of Livingston PLLC in Washington, D.C. Her work focuses on cybersecurity, artificial intelligence (AI), global data privacy, compliance, and risk management. A career white collar crime prosecutor at the Department of Justice, Ms. Thomson managed and conducted complex litigation in the Criminal and Civil Rights Divisions. She subsequently worked as a senior principal engineer and privacy advocate at CSC, a global technology company. She has been appointed the Consumer Privacy Ombudsman in 38 federal bankruptcy cases, including the Celsius Network cryptocurrency case (S.D.N.Y.), and has overseen the disposition of 350 million consumer records. Active in the American Bar Association, Ms. Thomson serves as co-chair of the Task Force on Law and AI and is an elected member of the House of Delegates (since 2004). She is a past chair of the Science & Technology Law Section and a founding member of the Cybersecurity Legal Task Force. She is co-editor of Artificial Intelligence: Legal Issues, Policy, and Practical Strategies, editor of the Data Breach and Encryption Handbook, and a contributing author of book chapters and articles on challenges with emerging technology. She received a master's degree from Rensselaer Polytechnic Institute and her JD from Georgetown University Law Center.

Ozoda Usmanova (Chapter 17, Why Public Interest Attorneys Should Care About Cybersecurity) is a multilingual legal and technology professional with over 20 years of experience across both government and private sectors. Originally from Tashkent, Uzbekistan, she earned her first law degree from Tashkent State Institute of Law. She later completed her Master of Laws at Georgetown University Law Center, specializing in national security law with a focus on cybersecurity law. She is an alumna of the Hacking for Defense program and the Atlantic Council's Digital Forensic Research Lab's scholar program, and a recipient of the Department of Defense and National Security Education Program-sponsored scholarship. Ms. Usmanova holds several industry certifications, including an advanced cybersecurity certificate from Stanford University's School of Engineering. Ms. Usmanova is a native speaker of Russian and Uzbek, and proficient in Turkish, Japanese, and Chinese Mandarin.

Tanner Wilburn (Handbook Assistant; Chapter 9, Foreign and International Cybersecurity Laws) is a 2025 graduate of Indiana University's Maurer School of Law and holds an M.S. in Cybersecurity from the Luddy School of Informatics, Computing, and Engineering. He previously interned with the National Security Cyber Section of the U.S. Department of Justice's National Security Division and joined Mayer Brown's Washington, D.C. in the Fall of 2025.

Index

T